NEW DIRECTIONS IN THE LAW OF THE SEA

Documents ~ Volume I

Compiled and Edited by
S. Houston Lay, B.A., J.D., LL.M.
Robin Churchill, LL.M.
Myron Nordquist, B.S., J.D.

1973
OCEANA PUBLICATIONS, INC.
DOBBS FERRY, NEW YORK

THE BRITISH INSTITUTE OF
INTERNATIONAL AND COMPARATIVE LAW
LONDON, ENGLAND

Library of Congress Cataloging in Publication Data

Lay, S Houston, 1912- comp.
New directions in the law of the sea.

CONTENTS: v. 1-2. Documents.
1. Maritime law—Sources. I. Churchill, Robin, joint comp. II. Nordquist, Myron, joint comp. III. Title.
JX4408.L43 343.09'6 72-12713
ISBN 0-379-00029-6

Manufactured in the United States of America

PREFACE

This two-volume collection of documents will be complemented by the publication, in 1973, of a volume of papers selected from the proceedings of an International Conference on "New Directions in the Law of the Sea" sponsored by the British Institute of International and Comparative Law in London on February 2, 3 and 4, 1973. The third volume will also contain tables and a reference index to the work as a whole.

ACKNOWLEDGMENTS

The editors wish to express their appreciation to the following organizations and persons for their assistance in compiling the documents contained in these volumes:

The British Institute of International and Comparative Law, London, for extensive translation, research and secretarial services.

The United States Department of State, particularly Mr. Bernard H. Oxman, Mr. Louis Brown, Mr. William Sullivan and Ms. Katherine J. Cobates, for numerous documents and valuable advice.

California Western Law School of United States International University, especially Ms. Barbara Costly, for generous administrative help.

The American Society of International Law for permission to reproduce certain documents contained in *International Legal Materials.*

The North-East Atlantic Fisheries Commission, the Inter-Governmental Maritime Consultative Organization, the Food and Agriculture Organization, the Norwegian Foreign Office, the United Kingdom Foreign and Commonwealth Office and the United Kingdom Ministry of Agriculture, Fisheries and Food, for texts and other useful information.

Professor R. R. Baxter, Law School of Harvard University, for helpful comments.

Finally, a special note of gratitude to Professor K. R. Simmonds, Director, British Institute of International and Comparative Law, who has thoughtfully reviewed and counseled the editors during the preparation of these volumes.

October, 1972.

S. Houston Lay
Robin Churchill
Myron Nordquist

TABLE OF ABBREVIATIONS USED IN CITATIONS

AJIL	*American Journal of International Law*
Bevans	*Treaties and other International Agreements of the United States of America 1776-1949,* compiled under the direction of Charles I. Bevans, United States Department of State.
CFR	*United States Code of Federal Regulations.*
Cmnd.	*Command Paper Series* (published by Her Majesty's Stationery Office, London).
EAS	*Executive Agreement Series,* issued singly in pamphlets by the United States Department of State until replaced by the TIAS Series.
ILM	*International Legal Materials.*
LNTS	*League of Nations Treaty Series.*
S.I.	*Statutory Instrument* (of the United Kingdom).
Stat.	*United States Statutes at Large.*
TIAS	*Treaties and other International Acts Series,* issued singly in pamphlets by the United States Department of State.
TS	*Treaty Series,* issued singly in pamphlets by the United States Department of State until replaced in 1945 by the TIAS Series.
UKTS	*United Kingdom Treaty Series.*
UN Collection	*United Nations Legislative Series. National Legislation and Treaties relating to the Territorial Sea, the Contiguous Zone, the Continental Shelf, the High Seas and to Fishing and the Conservation of the Living Resources of the Sea.* 1970. ST/LEG/SER.B/15
UNTS	*United Nations Treaty Series.*
USC	*United States Code.*
U.S.T.	*United States Treaties and other International Agreements.* (Volumes published on a calender year basis beginning January 1, 1950).
Whiteman	*Digest of International Law,* prepared by and under the direction of Marjorie M. Whiteman, United States Department of State.

TABLE OF CONTENTS

II. REGULATION OF MARINE ACTIVITIES

INTRODUCTION

The International Law of the Sea is at present in a state of upheaval. Developments in technology have led to the sea being used in new ways. At the same time there has been increased activity in many of the well-established uses of the sea. Conflicts between the different uses of the sea are increasing, due partly to the fact that traditional maritime freedoms are being challenged by rising coastal State demands for exclusive use of the high seas off their shores. The result is that many of the existing rules of the Law of the Sea are becoming obsolete or inadequate. A tremendous debate has emerged over how the Law of the Sea should be re-shaped. Perhaps for the first time the legal problems arising from the use of the sea will be considered as a whole, and not as unrelated issues. There is a growing awareness that the sea is a single and unique environment and that its natural resources constitute one of mankind's most valuable assets that should not be squandered.

A number of International Conferences have recently been held or are planned for the near future to consider new rules for the International Law of the Sea. The most important of these is the Conference called for by the United Nations General Assembly in Resolution 2750 (XXV) of December 17, 1970 and which is scheduled to begin in 1973. Among the other major conferences meriting mention, are the Stockholm Conference on the Environment, held in June 1972, and the Conference on Marine Pollution to be convened by IMCO.

Before the 1958 and 1960 Conferences on the Law of the Sea, the United Nations Secretariat published a number of volumes containing the texts of treaties and national legislation relating to the Law of the Sea.[1] A further volume[2] has recently been published for the 1973 Conference. Between them, these volumes provide an excellent and comprehensive collection of legislation relating to the Law of the Sea. The present volumes do not duplicate the United Nations collections. Their function is different and they have consequently drawn on a wider range of documents. They are not limited to national legislation and treaties, but include such items as United Nations General Assembly Resolutions, Recommendations of International Fisheries Commissions, State Declarations and other evidence of State practice. Some indication of why the various documents were selected will be given below.

The present volumes are intended to serve two purposes. First, it is hoped that they will form a convenient and useful handbook as they contain all of the basic documents relating to the Law of the Sea. Secondly, they are intended to provide documentary information relevant to the present debate on the Law of the Sea and its future development. Many of the selections illustrate current trends in the Law of the Sea or point up possible ways in which the law may evolve in the future.

---

[1] Laws and Regulations on the Regime of the High Seas. UN Legislative Series Vol 1, ST/LEG/SER.B/1. 1951. Vol II, ST/LEG/SER.B/2. 1951. Laws and Regulations on the Regime of the Territorial Sea. UN Legislative Series ST/LEG/SER.B/6. 1957. Supplement to Laws and Regulations on the Regime of the High Seas (Vols I and II) and Laws concerning the Nationality of Ships. UN Legislative Series ST/LEG/SER.B/8. 1959.

[2] National Legislation and Treaties relating to the Territorial Sea, the Contiguous Zone, the Continental Shelf, the High Seas and to Fishing and Conservation of the Living Resources of the Sea. UN Legislative Series ST/LEG/SER.B/15. 1970.

Perhaps the most striking feature of recent years has been the way in which States have claimed increasingly larger areas of the sea with the object of exercising exclusive national jurisdiction for an ever greater number of purposes. Indeed, one of the large question marks hanging over the future of the International Law of the Sea is the extent to which international law will regulate marine activities. This basic dichotomy between national control and international regulation is reflected in our table of contents divisions I and II.

Part I deals with national claims to various marine areas, both as concerns the physical extent of the area claimed and the legal nature of the claim. Included in this Part are not only various examples of national legislation, but also multilateral agreements regulating the extent and nature of national claims, e.g. the Convention on the Territorial Sea and the Contiguous Zone, the Convention on International Civil Aviation and the Convention on the Continental Shelf. Section A deals with claims to the Territorial Sea. The Argentinian and Brazilian legislation has been chosen as representing two recent Latin American claims to a 200 mile territorial or quasi territorial sea. It will be seen that the legal concept of the territorial sea in this legislation is rather different from that of the Convention on the Territorial Sea and the Contiguous Zone. The recent French legislation also departs from the concepts of the Convention, notably in its provisions on the regulation of navigation through the territorial sea. It is also significant in representing a claim to a 12 mile territorial sea by a State which for many years has been one of the most consistent champions of the three mile territorial sea limit. The Indian Proclamation is interesting in that it sets out a view of the territorial sea which is also found in the legislation of a number of other Afro-Asian States, e.g. Burma, Kenya, Pakistan and Tanzania. Island archipelagoes have always represented something of a problem when it comes to drawing the baselines from which the territorial sea is delimited. The Philippines legislation represents one of the more extreme claims made in that extensive areas are enclosed as internal waters. The legislation of the USSR and Yugoslavia shows how restrictions may be asserted over navigation through the territorial sea. In addition the Yugoslav legislation neatly illustrates a number of other points: the direct adoption of the Geneva Convention on the Territorial Sea and the Contiguous Zone (including the use of straight baselines and the claim to a contiguous zone beyond the territorial sea) and the Geneva Convention on the Continental Shelf.

Section B deals with claims to exclusive fishing zones beyond the territorial sea. The Fisheries Convention of 1964 and the various provisions concerning the European Communities show how this question may be regulated at a regional level. The Franco-Spanish Agreement is one of the several bilateral agreements concluded as a result of the Fisheries Convention. It is one of the few involving a non-EEC member State or prospective member, and is the only agreement making special provision for local fishermen under Article 9 (ii) of the Convention. The Canadian legislation extends the territorial sea to 12 miles and claims an exclusive fishing zone beyond that: straight baselines have been used to enclose large areas of the high seas within this zone. Taken together with the Arctic Waters Pollution Prevention Act (see below under Part I, Section E), it is significant that these wide claims have been made by a State which has in the past been notably scrupulous in acting in accordance with established international law. The USA and Mexican legislation and the

USA-Mexican Agreement illustrate a fairly straightforward extension of fishing limits, followed by the usual kind of bilateral agreement providing transitional arrangements for the fishermen of a nearby country fishing in the exclusive fishing zone. The Resolution of the Althing of Iceland and the Icelandic Regulations are the main documents relating to the current dispute between Iceland and the United Kingdom over Iceland's decision to extend its fishing limits to 50 miles in spite of the UK-Iceland Agreement of 1961. Section C is concerned with claims to a fishery conservation zone. Among the few such claims which have been made are the USA Proclamation of 1945 and the claims made by India, Pakistan and Sri Lanka. Of these latter three rather similar claims, that of Pakistan has been chosen because it is the most recent.

Section D is concerned with claims to the continental shelf and agreements relating to the delimitation of the continental shelf between opposite or adjacent States. The USA Proclamation of 1945 was the first claim by a State to exercise sovereign rights over its continental shelf and set one of the most important precedents for the development of the Law of the Sea. A number of claims by other States will be found elsewhere in this book; Yugoslavia in Section A of Part I, and France, Iran, Malaysia, United Kingdom and U.S.S.R. in Section C of Part II. The Saudi Arabian Decree is included here as it asserts jurisdiction over a seabed area beyond the physical continental shelf. As regards delimitation agreements, the North Sea Agreements illustrate delimitation of the Continental Shelf in accordance with the principle of equidistance, while the Italy-Yugoslavia Agreement illustrates delimitation by different principles. In the case of the North Sea, there was one part of the Continental Shelf where agreement on delimitation could not initially be reached: the continental shelf adjacent to the coasts of Denmark, the Federal Republic of Germany and the Netherlands. This dispute was submitted to the International Court of Justice, which in its judgment of February 20, 1969 said that delimitation should be effected in accordance with "equitable principles." The Denmark-Federal Republic of Germany-Netherlands Agreements are the result. All the Agreements given here contain provisions for the exploitation of geological structures which straddle the boundary line — a common feature of continental shelf delimitation agreements. In addition the Denmark-Federal Republic of Germany-Netherlands Agreements contain some interesting provisions relating to submarine pipelines.

A new type of claim has been the assertion of jurisdiction to take measures to control pollution outside the territorial sea. Two examples are given in Section E. Canada enacted the Arctic Waters Pollution Prevention Act in 1970 to deal with the problem of preserving the delicate ecological balance in the Arctic. Under this Act, Canada claims wide powers of pollution control up to 100 miles from land. Powers to control pollution from oil tankers were embodied in the International Convention relating to Intervention on the High Seas in Cases of Oil Pollution Casualties, 1969. The text of this Convention (which is not yet in force) can be found under Part II, Section G. The United Kingdom legislation included here goes a good deal further than the powers conferred in the Convention.

Section F contains the most important Latin American Declarations. Certain Latin American States have taken a markedly different view of high seas doctrine than have traditional maritime powers. The influence of this Latin American viewpoint is clearly seen in Section G of Part I which includes the 200-mile patrimonial sea concept unveiled at the Santo Domingo Conference. The Yaounde Conference also concluded in favor of broad coastal State jurisdiction. Both Conferences revealed a sophisticated understanding of the real problems of reconciling new and traditional uses of the oceans by also endorsing a 12-mile territorial sea.

Part II is concerned with the regulation of marine activities. Here the emphasis is on regulation by international law, rather than by national action. The Optional Protocol of Signature concerning the Compulsory Settlement of Disputes arising from the Law of the Sea Conventions has been placed with the Convention on the High Seas in Section A, although it will of course be realised that it applies equally to the other three Geneva Conventions of 1958: the Convention on the Territorial Sea and the Contiguous Zone, the Convention on Fishing and Conservation of the Living Resources of the High Seas and the Convention on the Continental Shelf. Although pirate broadcasting has almost ceased (in European waters at least), it raises interesting problems of control and jurisdiction over activities on the High Seas. These problems are bound to re-occur, particularly with the increasing use of off-shore installations, both with those that are fixed to the seabed and with those that float. The solutions adopted to deal with pirate broadcasting will be very relevant in this context. The European Agreement represents a multilateral approach to these problems. Contracting States are allowed a certain latitude in the way they implement the Agreement, and therefore an example of such national legislation, that of the United Kingdom, has been included. Section B contains three principal treaties of recent years which limit military activities above, on, in or under the sea.

Section C deals with activities on the seabed. Several examples of national legislation regulating seabed activities are given. They have been chosen from States of varying geographical location with differing economic and political systems. Some emphasis was placed on selecting continental shelf legislation governing regions where active exploration and exploitation is taking place. The Convention on the Continental Shelf, the text of which will be found under Part I, Section D, is also, of course, highly relevant.

One of the oldest and most economically significant uses of the sea is fishing. A considerable number of documents on this subject are to be found in section D. The Convention on Fishing and Conservation of the Living Resources of the High Seas is the product of the 1958 Geneva Conference. Unlike the other three Conventions produced at that Conference, this Convention appears to have had little practical impact. The Conventions on the Northwest and North-East Atlantic Fisheries set up two Commissions which are responsible for putting forward Recommendations for regulating fishing in the North Atlantic, one of the most important and overfished grounds in the world. The International Convention for the High Seas Fisheries of the North Pacific Ocean performs a somewhat similar function for the North Pacific. This Convention also introduced the principle of abstention into international fishery agreements — a principle which has subsequently received very little following but which may yet prove viable. The International Convention for the Conservation of Atlantic Tunas marks a more up-to-date approach by placing more emphasis on scientific findings and by concentrating on a single species. The Canada-Norway Agreement on Sealing has been included as a recent and fairly typical example of one of the small number of agreements concerned with seals. In spite of its lack of success, the International Convention for the Regulation of Whaling remains the only multilateral agreement in this field.

In the past, the conservation side of fisheries has been neglected. It is, in fact, one of the most essential aspects of the law of the Sea, and will doubtless come to be better appreciated as fish stocks continue to decline. The materials given here are intended to serve as examples of the main types of conservation measures; restrictions on the size of nets which may be used, restrictions on the size of fish which may be caught, the establishment of closed areas and closed seasons, and the fixing of quotas. It should be noted that the Recommendations of the North-East Atlantic Fisheries Commission are legally binding on these member States which have not objected to them.

It is important not only that conservation measures should be adopted, but also that they should be observed and enforced. In an effort to reach agreement on a system of mutual inspection to this end, a Conference took place in London in 1967 which produced the Convention on Conduct of Fishing Operations in the North Atlantic. This agreement has not yet entered into force. In the meantime, and as a partial substitute, the Northwest and North-East Atlantic Fisheries Commissions have adopted schemes of joint enforcement.

A further aspect of fisheries regulations has been the creation, on a bilateral level, of conservation zones on the High Seas. The USA-USSR Agreement given here replaces earlier agreements of 1967 and 1968. The Brazil interim shrimp agreements and the Japan-Korea Agreement are further illustrations of bilateral efforts to conserve fishery resources.

The traditional Freedom of the Seas has often been thought of primarily in terms of the freedom of navigation. The presence of drilling rigs attached to the seabed, the increased size of tankers and the congestion occuring in certain waterways have all led to the recognition that some control over navigation on the high seas is necessary in the common interest. Since 1967 the Assembly of IMCO has recommended a number of Traffic Separation Schemes; the latest such recommendation is included in Section E. These recommendations are not legally binding, but observance of these schemes will become mandatory if the 1971 Amendments to the International Convention for the Safety of Life at Sea enter into force. The US-Soviet agreement to prevent incidents at sea is a unique bilateral attempt at solving difficult political as well as legal problems of interference on the high seas. A further aspect of the freedom of navigation is the question of passage through international straits (Section F). The Convention on the Territorial Sea and the Contiguous Zone (text in Part I, Section A) contains some provisions relevant to this question. An example of an agreement dealing with a specific waterway is the Montreux Convention regulating navigation through the Dardanelles and Bosporus. The Chinese legislation given here is an assertion of control over shipping through the Chiung Chow Strait. The whole question of navigation through straits has been of particular concern to the United States and the Soviet Union whose draft Articles submitted to the Preparatory Committee for the 1973 Conference are included here.

Growing concern is being expressed over the increasing pollution of the seas. The international steps so far taken to deal with this have centered mainly around the problems of oil pollution. In Section G are included the International Convention for the Prevention of Pollution of the Sea by Oil 1954 (as amended in 1962), together with the amendments to the Convention adopted in 1969 and 1971. The 1969 and 1971 amendments are printed separately since they have not yet come into force. The three Conventions produced at the Conferences held in Brussels in 1969 and 1971 have, like the amendments, received very few ratifications and have not yet come into force. Of more immediate practical interest to the victims of oil pollution are the arrangements for the payment of compensation for oil pollution damage agreed on by the tanker and oil companies (the TOVALOP and CRISTAL schemes). One way of dealing with oil pollution in the short run may be through regional arrangements. The only two agreements at present of this type, between the North Seas States and the Nordic States respectively, are included.

Nuclear-powered vessels present unusual concerns about pollution and radiation, in spite of their remarkable safety record. When the US Nuclear Ship *Savannah* left US waters for a visit to a number of European countries, a series of bilateral agreements was entered into by USA with the countries concerned. These agreements dealt, *inter alia,* with the question of pollution and the payment of large compensation for any damage caused. The UK-USA Agreement is typical of these agreements. The Convention relating to Civil Liability in the Field of Maritime Carriage of Nuclear Material, 1971, is intended to simplify the rules relating to the payment of compensation for damage caused arising out of the carriage of nuclear material.

Over the last two years attention has increasingly been focused on the question of pollution caused by the dumping of waste from ships and aircraft. The Convention for the Prevention of Marine Pollution by Dumping from Ships and Aircraft, 1972, represents the first multilateral agreement in this field. This Convention has served as a model for the draft global convention on dumping which was discussed at the Stockholm Conference in June 1972 and which is expected to be finalised and signed at a conference to be held in London from October 30-November 10, 1972. The Norwegian legislation is the result of an informal agreement between the Nordic States whereby each undertook to introduce legislation banning the dumping of waste at sea before the end of 1971. This legislation anticipates the 1972 Ocean Dumping Convention. The Singapore and United States legislation represents attempts to control pollution of the sea originating from such sources as rivers and sewage outfalls. The Soviet statute on the Northern Sea Route is an interesting example of how a major maritime nation approaches pollution threats incidental to navigation. Provisions relating to pollution arising from activities on the seabed can, of course, be seen in some of the national legislation relating to seabed activities under Part II, Section C.

The Conference on the Human Environment held in Stockholm in mid-1972 was a landmark effort to achieve world-wide consensus on how to deal with the gargantuan problems of preserving the earth's environment. It is still too early to evaluate the concrete achievements of the Stockholm Conference. Nevertheless, the Declaration on the Human Environment and the Marine Pollution Recommendations will surely provide a starting point for the development of more detailed rules concerning pollution of the oceans.

Section H on scientific research, concerns a subject which may become an innocent victim of the trend toward greater regulation of the oceans uses and its resources. While marine scientists are just beginning to perceive the extent of the potential restrictions on their high seas activities, international lawyers are hardly in a position to criticize. The unrefined state of international law is seen in the I.O.C. Resolution VI-13 and in two recent Working Papers submitted respectively by several Eastern European States and Canada to the Preparatory Committee for the Law of the Sea Conference.

Part III deals with the forth-coming Law of the Sea Conference. The potential mineral wealth of the seabed areas beyond the limits of national jurisdiction was first brought to the attention of the United Nations General Assembly in 1967 in a now famous address by Ambassador Pardo of Malta. The General Assembly was sufficiently inspired to establish a Committee to investigate the subject. In 1969, the General Assembly passed a controversial resolution calling for a moratorium on exploitation of deep seabed minerals pending the establishment of an international regime. The relevant portions of that resolution are included herein as the issue is a lively one which could still disrupt the negotiations. The next General Assembly resolution of note conferred a broad mandate on the Seabed Committee and charged it with making preparations for a comprehensive Conference on the Law of the Sea to commence in 1973, if sufficient progress was made. A companion resolution also passed on December 17, 1970 contains "principles" governing the exploration and exploitation of deep seabed resources. The "principles" are expected to form the basis for treaty articles on the subject at the Conference. Next in Section A are detailed the States which are members of the Seabed Committee and which have been contributing to discussions about up-dating the law of the sea. Finally, the list of subjects and issues which emerged from the fourth preparatory session held in July/August, 1972 is included. This list provides a fairly firm idea of the agenda for the Conference which will probably reach most substantive issues in 1974.

Section B contains a landmark statement by the President of the United States on oceans policy. The May 23, 1970 statement marked a more far-reaching shift in United States law of the sea policy than the 1945 Truman Proclamations. The ramifications of these new policies in re-shaping this time-honored portion of international law will not be clearly seen until after the Law of the Sea Conference is held. However, one immediate result was an innovative but complicated United States draft Convention on the international seabed area which was submitted to the Seabed Committee on August 3, 1970. This working paper was a major force in moving the Seabed Committee from the giving of general speeches to the making of concrete proposals. A summary of the draft convention, prepared by the Legal Advisor of the United States Department of State, is included.

Part IV contains reference documents, most of which have never before been marshalled in this form. The various lists, tables, charts and other factual presentations are intended, in part, to compensate for the lack of a reliable and systematic method of exhausting source materials in international law. The sad truth is that scholars, government officials and others with limited library facilities simply have no way to ascertain accurately what State practice is. In this connection, the editors feel compelled to state that, while an earnest effort was made to keep errors to a minimum, there are certain to be some mistakes and omissions in this part of the volumes. We welcome the efforts of others to improve upon what we have started.

The organization and selection of documents in an undertaking such as the present two volumes is inevitably very much a matter of personal choice and judgment. The editors have had as their aim the gathering together of the most significant or most representative materials in the space available. The selections are certain to be too long for some needs and too short for others. Nevertheless it is hoped that there will be something of interest here for everyone who has an interest in following the rapidly moving developments in the law of the sea.

I. NATIONAL CLAIMS TO MARINE AREAS

No. 7477. CONVENTION[1] ON THE TERRITORIAL SEA AND THE CONTIGUOUS ZONE. DONE AT GENEVA, ON 29 APRIL 1958

The States Parties to this Convention

Have agreed as follows:

PART I

TERRITORIAL SEA

SECTION I. GENERAL

Article 1

1. The sovereignty of a State extends, beyond its land territory and its internal waters, to a belt of sea adjacent to its coast, described as the territorial sea.

[1] In accordance with paragraph 1 of article 29, the Convention came into force on 10 September 1964, the thirtieth day following the date of deposit of the twenty-second instrument of ratification or accession. Following is a list of States on behalf of which the instruments of ratification or accession (*a*) were deposited with the Secretary-General of the United Nations, showing the respective dates of deposit:

United Kingdom of Great Britain and Northern Ireland	14 March 1960
Cambodia	18 March 1960 (*a*)
Haiti	29 March 1960
Union of Soviet Socialist Republics	22 November 1960
Malaysia	21 December 1960 (*a*)
Ukrainian Soviet Socialist Republic	12 January 1961
Byelorussian Soviet Socialist Republic	27 February 1961
United States of America	12 April 1961
Senegal	25 April 1961 (*a*)
*Nigeria	26 June 1961
Venezuela	15 August 1961
Czechoslovakia	31 August 1961
Israel	6 September 1961
Hungary	6 December 1961
Romania	12 December 1961
*Sierra Leone	13 March 1962
Madagascar	31 July 1962 (*a*)
Bulgaria	31 August 1962
Portugal	8 January 1963
South Africa	9 April 1963 (*a*)
Australia	14 May 1963
Dominican Republic	11 August 1964
Uganda	14 September 1964 (*a*)

For declarations and reservations made upon signature, see list of signatures and for those made upon ratification, as well as for objections to certain declarations and reservations, see pp. 277 to 282 of this volume.

* By communications received on 26 June 1961 and 13 March 1962, respectively, the Governments of Nigeria and Sierra Leone informed the Secretary-General that they consider themselves bound by the ratification by the Government of the United Kingdom of Great Britain and Northern Ireland of the Convention on the Territorial Sea and the Contiguous Zone, done at Geneva on 29 April 1958, which was effective for their territories prior to the attainment of independence.

2. This sovereignty is exercised subject to the provisions of these articles and to other rules of international law.

Article 2

The sovereignty of a coastal State extends to the air space over the territorial sea as well as to its bed and subsoil.

SECTION II. LIMITS OF THE TERRITORIAL SEA

Article 3

Except where otherwise provided in these articles, the normal baseline for measuring the breadth of the territorial sea is the low-water line along the coast as marked on large-scale charts officially recognized by the coastal State.

Article 4

1. In localities where the coast line is deeply indented and cut into, or if there is a fringe of islands along the coast in its immediate vicinity, the method of straight baselines joining appropriate points may be employed in drawing the baseline from which the breadth of the territorial sea is measured.

2. The drawing of such baselines must not depart to any appreciable extent from the general direction of the coast, and the sea areas lying within the lines must be sufficiently closely linked to the land domain to be subject to the régime of internal waters.

3. Baselines shall not be drawn to and from low-tide elevations, unless lighthouses or similar installations which are permanently above sea level have been built on them.

4. Where the method of straight baselines is applicable under the provisions of paragraph 1, account may be taken, in determining particular baselines, of economic interests peculiar to the region concerned, the reality and the importance of which are clearly evidenced by a long usage.

5. The system of straight baselines may not be applied by a State in such a manner as to cut off from the high seas the territorial sea of another State.

6. The coastal State must clearly indicate straight baselines on charts, to which due publicity must be given.

Article 5

1. Waters on the landward side of the baseline of the territorial sea form part of the internal waters of the State.

2. Where the establishment of a straight baseline in accordance with article 4 has the effect of enclosing as internal waters areas which previously had been considered as part of the territorial sea or of the high seas, a right of innocent passage, as provided in articles 14 to 23, shall exist in those waters.

Article 6

The outer limit of the territorial sea is the line every point of which is at a distance from the nearest point of the baseline equal to the breadth of the territorial sea.

Article 7

1. This article relates only to bays the coasts of which belong to a single State.

2. For the purposes of these articles, a bay is a well-marked indentation whose penetration is in such proportion to the width of its mouth as to contain landlocked waters and constitute more than a mere curvature of the coast. An indentation shall not, however, be regarded as a bay unless its area is as large as, or larger than, that of the semi-circle whose diameter is a line drawn across the mouth of that indentation.

3. For the purpose of measurement, the area of an indentation is that lying between the low-water mark around the shore of the indentation and a line joining the low-water marks of its natural entrance points. Where, because of the presence of islands, an indentation has more than one mouth, the semi-circle shall be drawn on a line as long as the sum total of the lengths of the lines across the different mouths. Islands within an indentation shall be included as if they were part of the water areas of the indentation.

4. If the distance between the low-water marks of the natural entrance points of a bay does not exceed twenty-four miles, a closing line may be drawn between these two low-water marks, and the waters enclosed thereby shall be considered as internal waters.

5. Where the distance between the low-water marks of the natural entrance points of a bay exceeds twenty-four miles, a straight baseline of twenty-four miles shall be drawn within the bay in such a manner as to enclose the maximum area of water that is possible with a line of that length.

6. The foregoing provisions shall not apply to so-called " historic " bays, or in any case where the straight baseline system provided for in article 4 is applied.

Article 8

For the purpose of delimiting the territorial sea, the outermost permanent harbour works which form an integral part of the harbour system shall be regarded as forming part of the coast.

Article 9

Roadsteads which are normally used for the loading, unloading and anchoring of ships, and which would otherwise be situated wholly or partly outside the outer limit of the territorial sea, are included in the territorial sea. The coastal State must clearly demarcate such roadsteads and indicate them on charts together with their boundaries, to which due publicity must be given.

Article 10

1. An island is a naturally-formed area of land, surrounded by water, which is above water at high-tide.

2. The territorial sea of an island is measured in accordance with the provisions of these articles.

Article 11

1. A low-tide elevation is a naturally-formed area of land which is surrounded by and above water at low-tide but submerged at high-tide. Where a low-tide elevation is situated wholly or partly at a distance not exceeding the breadth of the territorial sea from the mainland or an island, the low-water line on that elevation may be used as the baseline for measuring the breadth of the territorial sea.

2. Where a low-tide elevation is wholly situated at a distance exceeding the breadth of the territorial sea from the mainland or an island, it has no territorial sea of its own.

Article 12

1. Where the coasts of two States are opposite or adjacent to each other, neither of the two States is entitled, failing agreement between them to the contrary, to extend its territorial sea beyond the median line every point of which is equidistant from the nearest points on the baselines from which the breadth of the territorial seas of each of the two States is measured. The provisions of this paragraph shall not apply, however, where it is necessary by reason of historic title or other special circumstances to delimit the territorial seas of the two States in a way which is at variance with this provision.

2. The line of delimitation between the territorial seas of two States lying opposite to each other or adjacent to each other shall be marked on large-scale charts officially recognized by the coastal States.

Article 13

If a river flows directly into the sea, the baseline shall be a straight line across the mouth of the river between points on the low-tide line of its banks.

SECTION III. RIGHT OF INNOCENT PASSAGE

SUB-SECTION A. RULES APPLICABLE TO ALL SHIPS

Article 14

1. Subject to the provisions of these articles, ships of all States, whether coastal or not, shall enjoy the right of innocent passage through the territorial sea.

2. Passage means navigation through the territorial sea for the purpose either of traversing that sea without entering internal waters, or of proceeding to internal waters, or of making for the high seas from internal waters.

3. Passage includes stopping and anchoring, but only in so far as the same are incidental to ordinary navigation or are rendered necessary by *force majeure* or by distress.

4. Passage is innocent so long as it is not prejudicial to the peace, good order or security of the coastal State. Such passage shall take place in conformity with these articles and with other rules of international law.

5. Passage of foreign fishing vessels shall not be considered innocent if they do not observe such laws and regulations as the coastal State may make and publish in order to prevent these vessels from fishing in the territorial sea.

6. Submarines are required to navigate on the surface and to show their flag.

Article 15

1. The coastal State must not hamper innocent passage through the territorial sea.

2. The coastal State is required to give appropriate publicity to any dangers to navigation, of which it has knowledge, within its territorial sea.

Article 16

1. The coastal State may take the necessary steps in its territorial sea to prevent passage which is not innocent.

2. In the case of ships proceeding to internal waters, the coastal State shall also have the right to take the necessary steps to prevent any breach of the conditions to which admission of those ships to those waters is subject.

3. Subject to the provisions of paragraph 4, the coastal State may, without discrimination amongst foreign ships, suspend temporarily in specified areas of its territorial sea the innocent passage of foreign ships if such suspension is essential for the protection of its security. Such suspension shall take effect only after having been duly published.

4. There shall be no suspension of the innocent passage of foreign ships through straits which are used for international navigation between one part of the high seas and another part of the high seas or the territorial sea of a foreign State.

Article 17

Foreign ships exercising the right of innocent passage shall comply with the laws and regulations enacted by the coastal State in conformity with these articles and other rules of international law and, in particular, with such laws and regulations relating to transport and navigation.

SUB-SECTION B. RULES APPLICABLE TO MERCHANT SHIPS

Article 18

1. No charge may be levied upon foreign ships by reason only of their passage through the territorial sea.

2. Charges may be levied upon a foreign ship passing through the territorial sea as payment only for specific services rendered to the ship. These charges shall be levied without discrimination.

Article 19

1. The criminal jurisdiction of the coastal State should not be exercised on board a foreign ship passing through the territorial sea to arrest any person or to conduct any investigation in connexion with any crime committed on board the ship during its passage, save only in the following cases :

(*a*) If the consequences of the crime extend to the coastal State; or (*b*) If the crime is of a kind to disturb the peace of the country or the good order of the territorial sea; or

(*c*) If the assistance of the local authorities has been requested by the captain of the ship or by the consul of the country whose flag the ship flies; or

(*d*) If it is necessary for the suppression of illicit traffic in narcotic drugs.

2. The above provisions do not affect the right of the coastal State to take any steps authorized by its laws for the purpose of an arrest or investigation on board a foreign ship passing through the territorial sea after leaving internal waters.

3. In the cases provided for in paragraphs 1 and 2 of this article, the coastal State shall, if the captain so requests, advise the consular authority of the flag State before taking any steps, and shall facilitate contact between such authority and the ship's crew. In cases of emergency this notification may be communicated while the measures are being taken.

4. In considering whether or how an arrest should be made, the local authorities shall pay due regard to the interests of navigation.

5. The coastal State may not take any steps on board a foreign ship passing through the territorial sea to arrest any person or to conduct any investigation in connexion with any crime committed before the ship entered the territorial sea, if the ship, proceeding from a foreign port, is only passing through the territorial sea without entering internal waters.

Article 20

1. The coastal State should not stop or divert a foreign ship passing through the territorial sea for the purpose of exercising civil jurisdiction in relation to a person on board the ship.

2. The coastal State may not levy execution against or arrest the ship for the purpose of any civil proceedings, save only in respect of obligations or liabilities assumed or incurred by the ship itself in the course or for the purpose of its voyage through the waters of the coastal State.

3. The provisions of the previous paragraph are without prejudice to the right of the coastal State, in accordance with its laws, to levy execution against or to arrest, for the purpose of any civil proceedings, a foreign ship lying in the territorial sea, or passing through the territorial sea after leaving internal waters.

SUB-SECTION C. RULES APPLICABLE TO GOVERNMENT SHIPS OTHER THAN WARSHIPS

Article 21

The rules contained in sub-sections A and B shall also apply to government ships operated for commercial purposes.

Article 22

1. The rules contained in sub-section A and in article 18 shall apply to government ships operated for non-commercial purposes.

2. With such exceptions as are contained in the provisions referred to in the preceding paragraph, nothing in these articles affects the immunities which such ships enjoy under these articles or other rules of international law.

SUB-SECTION D. RULE APPLICABLE TO WARSHIPS

Article 23

If any warship does not comply with the regulations of the coastal State concerning passage through the territorial sea and disregards any request for compliance which is made to it, the coastal State may require the warship to leave the territorial sea.

PART II

CONTIGUOUS ZONE

Article 24

1. In a zone of the high seas contiguous to its territorial sea, the coastal State may exercise the control necessary to :

(*a*) Prevent infringement of its customs, fiscal, immigration or sanitary regulations within its territory or territorial sea;

(*b*) Punish infringement of the above regulations committed within its territory or territorial sea.

2. The contiguous zone may not extend beyond twelve miles from the baseline from which the breadth of the territorial sea is measured.

3. Where the coasts of two States are opposite or adjacent to each other, neither of the two States is entitled, failing agreement between them to the

contrary, to extend its contiguous zone beyond the median line every point of which is equidistant from the nearest points on the baselines from which the breadth of the territorial seas of the two States is measured.

PART III

FINAL ARTICLES

Article 25

The provisions of this Convention shall not affect conventions or other international agreements already in force, as between States Parties to them.

Article 26

This Convention shall, until 31 October 1958, be open for signature by all States Members of the United Nations or of any of the specialized agencies, and by any other State invited by the General Assembly of the United Nations to become a Party to the Convention.

Article 27

This Convention is subject to ratification. The instruments of ratification shall be deposited with the Secretary-General of the United Nations.

Article 28

This Convention shall be open for accession by any States belonging to any of the categories mentioned in article 26. The instruments of accession shall be deposited with the Secretary-General of the United Nations.

Article 29

1. This Convention shall come into force on the thirtieth day following the date of deposit of the twenty-second instrument of ratification or accession with the Secretary-General of the United Nations.

2. For each State ratifying or acceding to the Convention after the deposit of the twenty-second instrument of ratification or accession, the Convention shall enter into force on the thirtieth day after deposit by such State of its instrument of ratification or accession.

Article 30

1. After the expiration of a period of five years from the date on which this Convention shall enter into force, a request for the revision of this Con-

vention may be made at any time by any Contracting Party by means of a notification in writing addressed to the Secretary-General of the United Nations.

2. The General Assembly of the United Nations shall decide upon the steps, if any, to be taken in respect of such request.

Article 31

The Secretary-General of the United Nations shall inform all States Members of the United Nations and the other States referred to in article 26 :

(*a*) Of signatures to this Convention and of the deposit of instruments of ratification or accession, in accordance with articles 26, 27 and 28;

(*b*) Of the date on which this Convention will come into force, in accordance with article 29 :

(*c*) Of requests for revision in accordance with article 30.

Article 32

The original of this Convention, of which the Chinese, English, French, Russian and Spanish texts are equally authentic, shall be deposited with the Secretary-General of the United Nations, who shall send certified copies thereof to all States referred to in article 26.

IN WITNESS WHEREOF the undersigned Plenipotentiaries, being duly authorized thereto by their respective Governments, have signed this Convention.

DONE at Geneva, this twenty-ninth day of April one thousand nine hundred and fifty-eight.

No. 102. CONVENTION[1] ON INTERNATIONAL CIVIL AVIATION. SIGNED AT CHICAGO, ON 7 DECEMBER 1944

Preamble

Whereas the future development of international civil aviation can greatly help to create and preserve friendship and understanding among the nations and peoples of the world, yet its abuse can become a threat to the general security; and

Whereas it is desirable to avoid friction and to promote that cooperation between nations and peoples upon which the peace of the world depends;

Therefore, the undersigned governments having agreed on certain principles and arrangements in order that international civil aviation may be developed in a safe and orderly manner and that international air transport services may be established on the basis of equality of opportunity and operated soundly and economically;

Have accordingly concluded this Convention to that end.

PART I. AIR NAVIGATION

CHAPTER I

General principles and application of the Convention

Article 1

Sovereignty

The contracting States recognize that every State has complete and exclusive sovereignty over the airspace above its territory.

[1] Came into force on 4 April 1947, the thirtieth day after deposit with the Government of the United States of America of the twenty-sixth instrument of ratification thereof or notification of adherence thereto, in accordance with article 91 (*b*). For the list of States Parties to the Convention, see page 372.

Article 2

Territory

For the purposes of this Convention the territory of a State shall be deemed to be the land areas and territorial waters adjacent thereto under the sovereignty, suzerainty, protection or mandate of such State.

Article 3

Civil and state aircraft

(*a*) This Convention shall be applicable only to civil aircraft, and shall not be applicable to state aircraft.

(*b*) Aircraft used in military, customs and police services shall be deemed to be state aircraft.

(*c*) No state aircraft of a contracting State shall fly over the territory of another State or land thereon without authorization by special agreement or otherwise, and in accordance with the terms thereof.

(*d*) The contracting States undertake, when issuing regulations for their state aircraft, that they will have due regard for the safety of navigation of civil aircraft.

ARGENTINA

(*a*) LAW NO. 17,094-M 24 OF 29 DECEMBER 1966**

Article 1. The sovereignty of the Argentine nation shall extend over the sea adjacent to its territory for a distance of 200 nautical miles measured from the line of the lowest tide, except in the cases of the San Matías, Nuevo and San Jorge gulfs, where it will be measured from the line joining the promontories which form their mouth.

Article 2. The sovereignty of the Argentine nation shall also extend over the seabed and the subsoil of the submarine zones adjacent to its territory up to a depth of 200 metres or, beyond this limit, up to that depth of the overlying waters which allows exploitation of the natural resources of those zones.

Article 3. The provisions of this law shall not affect freedom of navigation or of air traffic.

Article 4. Within ninety days from the date of promulgation of this law, the National Executive Power shall issue regulations establishing the terms under which foreign ships may conduct operations designed to explore and exploit the natural resources of the sea within the 200-nautical-mile zone referred to in this law.

(*b*) DECREE NO. 5106 OF 4 JANUARY 1967**

Article 1. Pending the issuance of the regulations referred to in article 4 of Law 17,094, the Naval Operations Command shall be authorized to issue to foreign fishing vessels which request them permits to carry out fishing operations in the Argentine territorial sea at a distance of no less than twelve miles from the coast.

Article 2. The Naval Operations Command shall ensure that vessels requesting such permits meet all the safety standards laid down in the International Convention for the Safety of Life at Sea.

(*c*) LAW NO. 17,500 OF 25 OCTOBER 1967 CONCERNING THE PROMOTION OF FISHERIES**

Article 1. The resources of the Argentine territorial sea are the property of the national State, which shall authorize their exploitation in accordance with the provisions of this Act and the rules governing its application.

Article 2. Resources up to a distance of twelve nautical miles from the coast may be exploited only by vessels flying the national flag. In addition, the Executive Power shall each year select, within the Argentine territorial sea, a specific zone whose exploitation shall be reserved for vessels flying the national flag.

...

(*d*) DECREE NO. 8,802 OF 22 NOVEMBER 1967. PROVISIONAL REGULATIONS GOVERNING THE ISSUE TO FOREIGN VESSELS OF PERMITS FOR THE EXPLOITATION OF THE LIVING RESOURCES OF THE ARGENTINE TERRITORIAL SEA**

I. PERMITS: APPLICATION AND FORMALITIES

Article 1. Foreign vessels may engage in activities involving the exploitation of the living resources of the Argentine territorial sea beyond a distance of twelve nautical miles from the coast only if they have in their possession, before the commencement of their activities, a local registration document (*matricula*) and a

---

[1] *Supra* DIVISION I, SUB-DIVISION A, Chapter I, 1 (*a*).

[2] *Ibid.*, (*b*).

permit. The registration document shall remain in force for one calendar year. The permit shall be valid for 120 days reckoned from the date of issue.

...

II. DUTIES AND RIGHTS OF THE APPLICANT

...

Article 6. Foreign vessels authorized to engage in the exploitation of the living resources of the sea in waters under Argentine jurisdiction shall operate within the legal limits and shall comply with the provisions already in force and those which may be established by the Fisheries Directorate of the Secretariat of Agriculture in respect of:

(*a*) Prohibited zones and periods;

(*b*) Characteristics of equipment and gear;

(*c*) Methods and techniques;

(*d*) Non-exploitable species;

(*e*) Conservation of species;

(*f*) Any other measures which in the judgement of the aforesaid authority may help to ensure the rational exploitation of the living resources of the sea.

Article 7. Activities carried out under the permits granted shall be performed in such a manner as not to interfere with navigation or obstruct similar operations by vessels of Argentine registration.

Article 8. It shall be forbidden:

(*a*) To use explosives, toxic substances or other agents harmful to the living resources of the sea;

(*b*) To carry on board devices for fishing, hunting or extracting which are prohibited by the competent authority, or to transport explosives or toxic substances;

(*c*) To kill, mutilate or in any manner disable species which may be caught in fishing devices but are unsuitable for the particular purpose envisaged or for feeding the crew; such species shall be returned to the sea;

Article 9. Resources obtained from the sea by foreign vessels under the exploitation permits referred to in these regulations shall not be sold on the Argentine market except with the express authorization of the competent authority.

BRAZIL: DECREE-LAW EXTENDING TERRITORIAL SEA TO 200 MILES* (March 25, 1970)

WHEREAS:

The special interest of coastal States in maintaining the productivity of the living resources of the sea areas adjacent to their coasts is recognized by international law,

Such interest can be effectively protected only by the exercise of the sovereignty inherent in the concept of territorial sea;

All States have the competence to fix their territorial seas within reasonable limits, taking into account geographical, geological, and biological factors,as well as the needs of their populations and their security and defense;

Article 1. The territorial sea of Brazil encompasses a belt 200 nautical miles in breadth, measured from the low-water line of the Brazilian continental and insular coast, adopted with reference to the Brazilian nautical charts.

Sole paragraph. In places where the coast line has deep indentations or projections, or where a chain of islands exists along the coast and in its immediate vicinity, the method of straight baselines shall be adopted, joining appropriate points for drawing the line from which the breadth of the territorial sea shall be measured.

Article 2. Brazil's sovereignty extends to the air space above the territorial sea and to the bed and subsoil of that sea.

Article 3. The right of innocent passage in the Brazilian territorial sea is recognized for ships of all nationalities.

Paragraph 1. Innocent passage is considered to be the simple traversing of the territorial sea, without the exercise of any activities other than those connected with navigation and without stops other than those incidental to navigation.

Paragraph 2. In the territorial sea all ships must comply with Brazilian regulations designed to guarantee peace, order, and security, and to prevent pollution of the waters and harm to the resources of the sea.

---

*(Reproduced from an English translation provided by the U. S. Department of State. The official Portuguese text appeard in <u>Diario Oficial</u> of the Federal Republic of Brazil, March 30, 1970.

(The Decree-Law of April 1, 1971, regulating fishing in the Brazilian territorial sea, appears at I.L.M. page 1226.)

Paragraph 3. The Brazilian Government shall establish the regulations which, for reasons of security, it deems necessary and which must be observed by warships and other ships of foreign States.

Article 4. The Brazilian Government will regulate fishing, keeping in mind the rational utilization and conservation of the living resources of the territorial sea, as well as research and exploration activities.

Paragraph 1. The regulations may establish zones in which fishing shall be reserved exclusively for Brazilian vessels.

Paragraph 2. In the zones of the territorial sea that remain open to fishing by foreign vessels, such vessels may engage in their activities only when they are duly registered and authorized to do so, and they shall be obligated to respect the Brazilian regulations.

Paragraph 3. Special regimes of fishing, research, and exploration in the territorial sea may be defined by international agreements, in principle on the basis of reciprocity.

Article 5. This decree-law shall enter into force on the date of its publication, Decree-Law 553 of April 25, 1969, and all other provisions to the contrary being revoked.

BRAZIL: DECREE-LAW REGULATING FISHING IN TERRITORIAL SEA* (April 1, 1971)

DECREE Nr 68,459 OF APRIL 1, 1971.

Regulates fishing, with a view to the rational use and conservation of the living resources of the Brazilian territorial sea.

The President of the Republic, by virtue of constitutional powers, as per article 81, item III, and considering the provisions of Decree-law nr. 221 of February 28, 1967 and article 4 of Decree nr 1,098 of March 25, 1970, hereby decrees:

CHAPTER I
On Fishing Zones

Art. 1. The following fishing zones are established in the Brazilian territorial sea:

I. A zone contained within 100 (one hundred) nautical miles, measured from the low water mark at the continental and island coast of Brazil, used as reference on Brazilian nautical charts.

II. Beyond the zone specified under item I, up to a limit of two hundred nautical miles.

§ 1. In the zone referred to in item I of this article, fishing activities shall be conducted by Brazilian fishing vessels.

§ 2. In the zone referred to in item II of this article, fishing activities may be conducted by Brazilian and foreign fishing vessels.

§ 3. The exploitation of crustacea and

---

*(Reproduced from an English translation provided to <u>International Legal Materials</u> by the Embassy of Brazil at Washington, D. C. The official Portuguese text appeared in <u>Diario Oficial</u> of the Federal Republic of Brazil, April 2, 1971.

and other living resources, which are closely dependent on the seabed under the Brazilian territorial sea, is reserved to Brazilian fishing vessels.

§4. Under the terms of this Decree, foreign fishing vessels leased by Brazilian legal entities headquartered in Brazil shall be considered equal to Brazilian fishing vessels, subject to the provisions of this Decree, of the Regulations on Maritime Traffic and of the Brazilian Maritime Legislation.

§5. Under special circumstances, the Ministry of Agriculture, through SUDEPE, after consulting with the Navy Ministry, may allow foreign vessels to conduct fishing activities in areas within the zone referred to in item I of this article, subject to compensation in all cases.

Art. 2. Fishing vessels will be considered those which, properly registered, enrolled and authorized in accordance with this Decree and further legislation in force, are exclusively and permanently involved in capture, processing or research of fauna and flora whose natural or most frequent habitat is the sea or the seabed.

Paragraph. When engaged in research activities, fishing vessels shall be subject to the requirements put forth in special legislation on such matters.

CHAPTER II
On Activities of Fishing Vessels

Art. 3. Brazilian or leased foreign vessels engaged in fishing shall:

I. In the case of Brazilian vessels over twenty (20) gross tons, have their ownership registry issued by the Maritime Court.

II. Be registered in the General Fishing Register of the Superintendency for Development of Fisheries, if they exceed two (2) gross tons.

III. Be registered with the Port Authority.

Paragraph. Ownership registration of Brazilian fishing vessels shall be granted by the Maritime Court exclusively to Brazilian citizens by birth or naturalization or to companies set up in Brazil, pursuant to article 8 of Decree-law 221 of February 28, 1967.

Art. 4. Authorizations for leasing foreign fishing vessels or renewing such leases shall be granted by the Ministry of Agriculture, after consulting with the Navy Ministry, once the interested parties have submitted proof to SUDEPE to the effect that:

I. Brazilian-born citizens hold most of the capital in the fishing industry holding the lease.

II. As regards crews, the proportion of Brazilian citizens set forth in the Brazilian Labour Legislation shall be observed.

III. The vessel has all up-to-date certificates required under International Conventions in force in Brazil.

IV. The vessel is in perfect operating conditions for the type of fishing intended, this fact to be established by means of the inspections foreseen in the Regulations on Maritime Traffic.

§ 1. Leasing may under no condition create a privileged situation for foreign vessels and shall be authorized only when there is evidence that the vessel operation brings about an actual and indispensable increase in exports or in supplies to regions of insufficient production, and shall be granted initially for a period up to one (1) year, renewable in each case for two (2) further periods of equal length.

§ 2. The Ministers of the Navy and Agriculture shall annually submit to the President of the Republic conditions for appraisal of applications for the extension of leasing contracts, in the light of prevailing circumstances and the needs of the Brazilian fishing vessel industry.

§ 3. At the end of the lease and unless it is renewed, the vessel may only continue in operation if nationalized; such nationalization shall be initiated during the life of the lease.

§ 4. Nationalization may not be requested in the case of vessels built more than 5 (five) years before the date of such application.

§ 5. Once leasing is authorized, the vessel shall be registered with the Port Authority in order to be entitled to engage in fishing operations.

Art. 5. Foreign fishing vessels, not leased by Brazilian legal entities, may engage in fishing operations in the Brazilian territorial sea, the zone set forth in item II of article 1 of this Decree, when authorized by the Minister of Agriculture after consultation with the Navy Ministry.

§ 1. Fishing authorizations shall be granted for a maximum period of one (1) year, and may be renewed subject to the provisions of articles 6 and 7 of this Decree.

§ 2. Authorizations granted shall specify fishing methods and gear to be employed.

§ 3. Authorizations shall be valid only after payment of the registration and operation fees set forth in article 7.

Art. 6. Applications for authorization referred to above shall be addressed to the Ministry of Agriculture and presented to SUDEPE through a Brazilian legal entity of established integrity which undertakes legal and financial responsibility for the activities to be carried out, and shall contain:

I. Name, nationality and other useful information on the foreign citizen or company requesting authorization.

II. Technical data on the vessels to be used and their respective equipment, including photographs, copies of the original registry documents, certified and with official translation attached, crew list and respective functions on board and proof that the vessel carries all up-to-date certificates required by International Conventions in force in Brazil.

III. Planned fishing routes, also mapped on a nautical chart of appropriate scale, indicating fishing plans and purposes as well as methods and techniques to be employed.

IV. Commitment to reserve room on board of each vessel so that representatives appointed by the Navy Ministry or the Ministry of Agriculture (SUDEPE) may observe fishing operations, partially or in full.

Paragraph. Applications received and examined by SUDEPE shall be sent by the Ministry of Agriculture to the Navy Ministry for evaluation, final decision to grant or deny the request being in the hands of the Ministry of Agriculture.

Art. 7. After the request for authorization under article 6 has been granted, foreign fishing vessels not under lease shall undertake the following:

I. In order to be included in the General Fishing Register, pay a registration fee, in Brazilian currency, equivalent to US$ 500.00 (five hundred dollars).

II. In order to conduct fishing operations, pay an operation fee, in Brazilian currency, equivalent to US$ 20 00 (twenty dollars) per net registered ton of vessel.

Art. 8. The captains of foreign vessels operating in Brazilian territorial waters under the terms of articles 4 and 5 and § 5 of article 1 of this Decree shall be bound to:

I. Use fishing logs adopted by SUDEPE and send them, duly filled out, to that agency at a time to be indicated.

II. Be familiar and comply with Brazilian laws and regulations, especially as regards fishing and prevention of sea pollution.

III. Use only methods and gear authorized by SUDEPE.

IV. Inform the Navy Ministry, for purposes of Maritime Traffic Control, Coast Patrol, Naval Police and Search and Rescue Service; of the day and hour of entry and exit of the vessel into and from waters of the Brazilian territorial sea, as well as of the position of the vessel in said waters, daily. Such information shall be transmitted, through SUDEPE radiotelephone stations or through the nearest Coast Station, to the Naval District Command of the fishing area.

Art. 9. Foreign fishing vessels not under lease shall only land their catch at Brazilian ports under special circumstances and if duly authorized by SUDEPE.

Art. 10. Transshipment of catch between any vessels in the territorial sea is subject to authorization and shall be made under the terms of said authorization, which shall be granted by the Ministry of Agriculture, after consulting with the Navy Ministry in each instance.

CHAPTER III
On Control

Art. 11. Control of fishing activities in the Brazilian territorial sea shall be exercised the the Navy Ministry and the Ministry of Agriculture, through SUDEPE.

§ 1. Control by the Navy Ministry shall normally be entrusted to the Coast Patrol Service, according to Law nr 2,419 of February 10, 1955, and its regulation, and may also be carried out by other ships or vessels of the Navy.

§ 2. Control by SUDEPE shall be exercised by duly accredited officials, under the terms of articles 53 and 54 of Decree-law 221 of February 28, 1967.

§ 3. The captains of Navy ships and vessels, who in the course of control operations specified in § 1 make arrests, shall deliver those arrested to the Port Authorities for the necessary steps.

§ 4. Infringements or irregularities observed or repressed by captains of Navy ships and vessels shall be reported to the Port Authorities for due recording and legal action.

§ 5. Any foreign vessel that engages in the exploitation of the living resources of the Brazilian territorial sea without government authorization or in infringement of restrictions set forth in said authorization, is acting in infringement of articles 4 and 5 of the Decree. Such infringement shall be considered as contraband pursuant to the sole paragraph of article 9 of Decree-law 221 of February 28, 1967. Under such conditions, Government authorities may order seizure of the vessel, its equipment and cargo and hold the captain liable under the terms of criminal legislation in force.

§ 6. Naval District Commandants may, in joint action with SUDEPE and its agencies and whenever deemed convenient, place on board of the vessels of the Coast Patrol Service, of the Port Authorities used by the Naval Police or of any other vessels used in control operations, specially accredited federal or civil servants, qualified to advise the captains of the vessels carrying out fishing control operations.

Art. 12. Notwithstanding other legal sanctions under the terms of Brazilian law, fishing vessels shall be subject to fines as set forth in chapters VI and VII of Decree-law 221 of February 28, 1967.

Art. 13. Authorizations referred to under articles 4 and 5 of this Decree shall be definitely cancelled in case of infringement of any one of articles 1, 2, 3, 4, 5, 6, 8, 10 and 16 of this Decree.

Art. 14. Captains of Brazilian fishing vessels and ships of the Brazilian merchant fleet, when sighting foreign fishing vessels in the Brazilian territorial sea, shall report them to the Naval Authorities, specifying quantity, name and nationality of said vessels as well as day, hour and geographic position of same when sighted.

Art. 15. The Navy Ministry will arrange with the Air Ministry as regards air assistance required for control of fishing in the Brazilian territorial sea.

CHAPTER IV
General Provisions

Art. 16. SUDEPE shall periodically set forth the maximum tonnage, per species and fishing zone, to be captured by Brazilian or foreign vessels.

Paragraph. On the basis of the maximum tonnages established, SUDEPE shall take all measures deemed necessary for conservation of the living resources of the sea and have them duly publicized.

Art. 17. SUDEPE shall periodically publish lists of fishing gear authorized for each type of fishing operation.

Art. 18. Funds resulting from payments of fees and fines related to fishing operation under the terms of this Decree shall be deposited in the Banco do Brasil S.A., to the order of SUDEPE, under the heading "Recursos da Pesca", pursuant to article 72 of Decree-law of February 28, 1967.

Art. 19. The Ministry of Agriculture, through SUDEPE, may enter into agreement with the Navy Ministry for the purpose of authorizing transfer to the Naval Fund of income resulting from payment of fines set forth in article 12 of this Decree.

Art. 20. The provisions of this Decree may be derogated by international fishing agreements signed by Brazil, pursuant to § 3 of article 4 of Decree-law, 1,098 of March 25, 1970.

Art. 21. This Decree shall enter into force on the date of its publication, and Decree nrs 58,696 of June 22, 1966 and 65,005 of August 18, 1969, as well as other provisions to the contrary, are hereby revoked.

FRANCE: LAW EXTENDING TERRITORIAL WATERS TO 12 MILES*
(December 24, 1971)

LAW No 71-1060 of December 24, 1971 relating to the delimitation of the French territorial sea.

The National Assembly and the Senate having adopted,
The President of the Republic promulgates the law whose text follows:

Article 1. The French territorial waters extend to a limit fixed at 12 nautical miles measured from the baselines. The baselines are the low-water line, the straight baselines and the closing lines of bays, which are determined by a decree.
Within the territorial sea the sovereignty of France extends to the airspace as well as to the bed and the subsoil of the sea.

Article 2. Unless otherwise provided in some particular convention, the breadth of the territorial waters does not extend beyond a median line every point of which is equidistant from the nearest point on the baselines of the French coasts and the baselines of the foreign coasts opposite or adjacent to the French coasts.

Article 3. Where the distance between the baselines of the French coasts and the baselines of the coasts of an opposite foreign State is equal to - or less than - 24 miles or does not allow any longer the existence of a zone of high sea sufficient for navigation, regulations may be issued in order to insure a free maritime and aerial navigation, subject to the provisions of international conventions and, if need be, after an agreement has been reached with the concerned States.

---

*(Reproduced from an English translation provided to International Legal Materials by Francois Bellanger, Professor of Law, University of Strasbourg. The official French text appears in the Journal Officiel de la Republique Francaise, December 30, 1971.

(The French Decree of October 19, 1967, determining the baselines for French territorial waters, appears at 7 I.L.M. 347 (1968.)

Article 4. The provisions of the present law do not affect the exercise of the fishing rights granted to some foreign vessels according to international agreements and French municipal law.

Article 5. The present law is applicable to overseas territories.

The present law will be carried out as a law of the State.

Done in Paris, on December 24, 1971.

Georges POMPIDOU

By the President of the Republic:
The Prime Minister,
Jacques CHABAN-DELMAS

The Minister of State in charge of the overseas departments and territories,
Pierre MESSMER

The Minister of Foreign Affairs,
Maurice SCHUMANN

INDIA

PROCLAMATION[2] OF 30 SEPTEMBER 1967 BY THE PRESIDENT

PROCLAMATION

Whereas international law has always recognised that the sovereignty of a State extends to a belt of sea adjacent to its coast;

And whereas international practice is not uniform as regards the extent of this sea-belt commonly known as the territorial waters of a State;

And whereas by the Proclamation[3] issued by the President of India on the 22nd March, 1956 and published with the notification of the Government of India in the Ministry of External Affairs, No. S.R.O. 669, dated the 22nd March, 1956, the territorial waters of India were declared to extend into the sea to a distance of six nautical miles measured from the appropriate base line and by the Proclamation issued by the President of India on the 3rd December, 1956, and published with the notification of the Government of India in the Ministry of External Affairs, No. S.R.O. 2920, dated the 3rd December, 1956, the limit of contiguous zone was fixed at twelve nautical miles from the base line from which the width of the territorial waters is measured;

And whereas under international law and customs, a State has the right to fix the limits of its territorial waters up to a distance of twelve nautical miles measured from the appropriate base line;

And whereas several States have fixed the limits of their territorial waters up to a distance of twelve nautical miles from the appropriate baseline and such fixation is in consonance with the requirements and legitimate interests of all countries and especially the developing countries;

And whereas the Republic of India has the obligation to ensure its effective control over as wide an area of the sea adjacent to its coast as is compatible with international law, in order to safeguard its territorial integrity and as a developing country to exploit and utilise the natural resources of the sea in an efficient manner;

Now, therefore, in the Eighteenth Year of the Republic of India, I, Zakir Husain, President of India, hereby proclaim, in supersession of the Proclamations aforesaid, that the territorial waters of India extend into the sea to a distance of twelve nautical miles measured from the appropriate baseline.

---

[2] Notification of the Ministry of External Affairs, published in the *Gazette of India* of 30 September 1967, Registered no. D. 221.

[3] For the text, see ST/LEG/SER.B/6, p. 23.

PHILIPPINES

(*a*) Republic Act No. 3046 of 17 June 1961. An act to define the baselines of the territorial sea of the Philippines

Whereas, the Constitution of the Philippines describes the national territory as comprising all the territory ceded to the United States by the Treaty of Paris concluded between the United States and Spain on December 10, 1898, the limits of which are set forth in Article III of said treaty together with all the islands embraced in the treaty concluded in Washington, between the United States and Spain on November 7, 1900, and in the treaty concluded between the United States and Great Britain on January 2, 1930, and all the territory over which the Government of the Philippine Islands exercised jurisidiction at the time of the adoption of the Constitution;

Whereas, all the waters within the limits set forth in the above-mentioned treaties have always been regarded as part of the territory of the Philippine Islands;

Whereas, all the waters around, between and connecting the various islands of the Philippine archipelago, irrespective of their width or dimension, have always been considered as necessary appurtenances of the land territory, forming part of the inland or internal waters of the Philippines;

Whereas, all the waters beyond the outermost islands of the archipelago but within the limits of the boundaries set forth in the aforementioned treaties comprise the territorial sea of the Philippines;

Whereas, the baselines from which the territorial sea of the Philippines is determined consist of straight lines joining appropriate points of the outermost islands of the archipelago; and

Whereas, the said baselines should be clarified and specifically defined and described for the information of all concerned;

...

Section 1

...

Section 2. All waters within the baselines provided for in section one hereof are considered inland or internal waters of the Philippines.

(*b*) REPUBLIC ACT NO. 5446 OF 18 SEPTEMBER 1968. AN ACT TO AMEND SECTION ONE OF THE REPUBLIC ACT NUMBERED THIRTY HUNDRED AND FORTY SIX, ENTITLED "AN ACT TO DEFINE THE BASELINES OF THE TERRITORIAL SEA OF THE PHILIPPINES"

Section 1. To correct typographical errors, Section One of Republic Act numbered thirty hundred and forty six is amended to read as follows:

"*Section 1.* The baselines for the territorial sea of the Philippines are hereby defined and described specifically as follows:

UNION OF SOVIET SOCIALIST REPUBLICS

(*a*) REGULATIONS[1] OF 5 AUGUST 1960 FOR THE DEFENCE OF THE STATE FRONTIER OF THE UNION OF SOVIET SOCIALIST REPUBLICS**

I. GENERAL PROVISIONS

Article 1. The State frontier of the USSR is the line delimiting the land and water territory of the USSR. The surface extending vertically along the said line constitutes the frontier of the air space and subsoil of the USSR.

...

Article 3. Coastal maritime waters to a distance of twelve nautical miles measured from the low-water line, both continental and insular, or from the outer limit of internal maritime waters of the USSR, shall constitute the territorial sea of the USSR. In particular cases provided for in agreements between the USSR and other States, the breadth of the territorial sea may differ from the foregoing.

[1] The text of the Regulations, published under No. 34 (1018) on 30 August 1960 in the *Bulletin of the Supreme Soviet of the Union of Soviet Socialist Republics*, was confirmed by the Decree of the Presidium of the Supreme Soviet of the Union of Soviet Socialist Republics, dated 5 August 1960, and by the Act of the Union of Soviet Socialist Republics, dated 22 December 1960. For the Regulations of 15 June 1927, see ST/LEG/SER.B/6, p. 255.

The outer limit of the territorial sea shall constitute the State maritime frontier of the USSR.

In sections where the territorial sea of the USSR is contiguous to the territorial sea of adjacent States, the State maritime frontier of the USSR shall be determined in accordance with agreements concluded between the USSR and the adjacent States, or, in the absence of such agreements, in accordance with the principles accepted in the international practice of states or by a straight line connecting the points at which the land frontier reaches the sea.

Article 4. The internal maritime waters of the USSR shall consist of:

(*a*) The waters of USSR ports bounded to seaward by a line passing through the outermost seaward points of the hydraulic and other port installations;

(*b*) The waters of gulfs, bays, inlets and estuaries, the shores of which belong in their entirety to the USSR, up to a straight line drawn from one shore to the other at the place where, on the seaward side, one or more passages begin to take form, provided that the width of each passage does not exceed twenty-four nautical miles;

(*c*) The waters of gulfs, bays, inlets, estuaries, seas and straits which have historically belonged to the USSR.

Article 5. On navigable frontier rivers, the State frontier of the USSR shall be established along the middle of the main fairway or thalweg of the river, and on non-navigable rivers along the middle of the river or the middle of the main branch; on frontier lakes it shall be established along the middle of the lake or along a straight line connecting the points at which the land frontier reaches the shores of the lake. Save as otherwise provided in agreements between the USSR and other States, the portions of the State frontier running along a river or through a lake shall not be altered by reason of a change in the configuration of the banks or shores or in the water level or by reason of the deviation of the river-bed in either direction.

Article 6. The State frontier of the USSR shall be marked by clearly visible frontier marks (frontier posts, pyramids, cairns, mounds, buoys, sighting marks and other marks).

In certain places, the outer limit of the territorial sea of the USSR may, for purposes of orientation, be marked by buoys and spar-buoys.

...

II. RÉGIME OF THE STATE FRONTIER

Article 9. Areas in which navigation, anchorage, fishing and similar activities shall be permanently or temporarily prohibited may be established in particular sections of the internal maritime and territorial waters of the USSR by decision of the competent authorities. The establishment of such areas shall be announced in the "Notices to Mariners".

...

Article 11. Persons wishing to cross the State frontier of the USSR may do so only if they are in possession of the prescribed documents in proper form entitling them to enter or leave the USSR and shall do so at the places where frontier-crossing points are situated.

The conveyance across the frontier of matter in manuscript or printed form shall likewise be subject to control at the frontier-crossing points.

...

Article 15. Foreign non-military vessels shall enjoy the right of innocent passage through the territorial waters of the USSR. Innocent passage shall be understood to mean navigation through the territorial waters for the purpose of traversing the same without entering internal maritime waters or for the purpose of entering internal maritime waters or leaving internal maritime waters for the open sea. Passage shall be considered to be innocent if vessels steer the customary navigational course or the course recommended by the competent authorities, comply with the established régime and avoid areas closed to navigation as announced in the "Notices to Mariners".

The list of ports, bays and roadsteads open to foreign vessels, the procedure for entry and stay therein, for the conduct of cargo and passenger operations, for ship-to-shore communication, for the setting ashore of crew members and for visits aboard the vessels by persons other than crew members, and other matters connected with the entry of foreign non-military vessels into the territorial and internal maritime waters of the USSR shall be prescribed by the laws of the USSR and of the Union Republics and by special regulations and instructions issued by the competent authorities and published in the "Notices to Mariners" and other official publications.

Article 16. Foreign warships shall pass through the territorial waters and enter the internal maritime waters of the USSR, subject to the prior authorization of the Government of the USSR and in accordance with the procedure laid down in the rules for visits by foreign warships in the territorial and internal maritime waters of the USSR published in the "Notices to Mariners".

Foreign submarines authorized to stay in territorial and internal maritime waters of the USSR shall remain on the surface at all times.

Article 17. While in territorial and internal maritime waters of the USSR, foreign military and non-military vessels shall comply with the navigation, radiotelegraph, port, customs, sanitary and other regulations prescribed for vessels navigating and staying in such waters.

Article 18. Where foreign non-military vessels in distress are unable to comply with the rules of innocent passage through the territorial waters of the USSR, they shall so inform the authorities of the nearest Soviet port without delay. The giving of a false distress signal for the purpose of entering or staying in the territorial waters of the USSR illegally shall be regarded as a violation of the State frontier of the USSR. Vessels giving such a signal shall be liable to arrest.

Article 19. The taking of fish or crabs, killing of marine animals or conduct of any similar activity by foreign vessels in territorial and internal maritime waters of the USSR shall be prohibited except where such activity is authorized under agreements between the USSR and the States concerned. Foreign vessels shall likewise be prohibited from engaging in hydrographic operations or research in the said waters.

Foreign vessels which violate the foregoing provisions, or, being authorized to engage in fishing or similar activities, violate the regulations in force while doing so, shall be liable to arrest, and the persons responsible for the violation shall be prosecuted in accordance with the laws of the USSR and of the Union Republics.

...

Article 26. The following shall be regarded as violators of the State frontier of the USSR:

(*a*) Persons who, by foot or by land transport, or aircraft, cross or attempt to cross the State frontier at points other than the established frontier-crossing points or who do so at the established points but in an illegal manner;

(*b*) Persons discovered in territorial and internal maritime waters of the USSR or in the Soviet portion of frontier rivers and lakes, whether on vessels or floating objects or swimming, if they have illegally entered such waters or are attempting to leave them illegally;

(*c*) Foreign military and non-military vessels which have entered territorial and internal maritime waters of the USSR or the Soviet portion of frontier rivers and lakes in violation of the regulations in force with regard to such entry;

(*d*) Aircraft which cross the air-space frontier of the USSR without the authorization of the competent Soviet authorities to fly across the frontier and over the land or water territory of the USSR, or, having received such authorization, fly across the frontier at an unauthorized place or at an unauthorized altitude.

Article 27. Persons who violate or attempt to violate the State frontier of the USSR, and persons and their accomplices who convey or attempt to convey across the State frontier of the USSR any objects, materials, currency or items having the value of currency the import or export of which is prohibited shall be liable to arrest and prosecution in accordance with the laws of the USSR and of the Union Republics.

(*b*) NOTICE[1] CONCERNING FORTIFIED ZONES AND RULES FOR NAVIGATION THEREIN**

It may sometimes be found necessary to lay down special conditions, of permanent rather than a temporary nature, for navigation in certain areas contiguous to the Union of Soviet Socialist Republics. Such areas shall hereinafter be referred to as "fortified zones".

All ships sailing in waters contiguous to the Union of Soviet Socialist Republics shall be required to conform strictly to the "Rules for navigation in fortified zones of the USSR" set forth below.

Information concerning the areas declared to be fortified zones shall be published in the Notices to Mariners issued by the Hydrographic Department of the Ministry of Defence.

[1] *Notices to Mariners* of 1 January 1967, issue 1, No. 3. Except article 7, there is no substantial change in the text as reproduced in ST/LEG/SER.B/6, p. 263. The translation was revised.

Rules for navigation in fortified zones of the USSR

1. These rules shall apply to all foreign-going merchant ships, whether of USSR or foreign nationality.

2. Fortified zones shall be announced in the Notices to Mariners issued by the Hydrographic Department of the Ministry of Defence, and alleged ignorance of the said notices shall not constitute grounds for evading responsibility for breaches thereof.

3. No foreign-going merchant ship, whether of USSR or foreign nationality, may enter or leave a fortified zone without previous authorization.

Where entry into a port open to foreign-going merchant ships necessitates passage through a fortified zone, the procedure for entry into the fortified zone shall be prescribed in each case by a special notice.

4. No merchant ship may in any circumstances proceed through a fortified zone without a pilot.

When a ship is proceeding through a fortified zone, the master shall promptly carry out all instructions of the pilot in matters pertaining to compliance with the conditions for navigation in the said zone (black-out, keeping crew off the upper deck and so on).

5. A merchant ship proceeding through a fortified zone by night shall show only the prescribed lights, unless special orders to darken ship have been issued or the pilot has given instructions in that regard.

By day, a ship shall be required to fly its national flag, house pennant and distinguishing pennant.

6. A ship proceeding through a fortified zone shall not come to anchor at a distance less than three cables from the centre of the restricted fairway and from the prescribed course.

7. Merchant ships, in all cases, shall give way to formations of warships and shall refrain from cutting through a line of warships or approaching warships engaged in special exercises or in firing.

The procedure to be followed when meeting single warships not engaged in special exercises shall be governed by the regulations for the prevention of collisions of ships at sea.

8. On the approach of fog, a fortified zone shall be closed to the passage of merchant ships.

Notification concerning prohibited navigation and anchorage areas

It is sometimes necessary to prohibit vessels from navigating or anchoring in certain coastal waters of the USSR. In such cases, the boundaries of the areas in which navigation and anchorage are prohibited for all ships without exception shall be announced in the Notices to Mariners issued by the Hydrographic Department of the Ministry of Defence.

Such areas shall be declared, as a rule temporarily, to be prohibited for a specified period of time and shall be designated as "temporarily prohibited navigation areas".

Areas in which anchorage alone is prohibited shall be permanent and shall be designated as "prohibited anchorage areas".

The boundaries of such prohibited areas as announced in the Notices to Mariners issued by the Hydrographic Department of the Ministry of Defence must be marked on navigational charts.

YUGOSLAVIA

LAW[4] OF 22 MAY 1965 ON YUGOSLAVIA'S MARGINAL SEAS, CONTIGUOUS ZONE AND CONTINENTAL SHELF

Article 1

The sovereignty of Yugoslavia extends to its marginal seas, including also the air space above them as well as the bed and the subsoil of those seas.

The marginal seas of Yugoslavia are composed of the internal waters and the territorial sea.

...

Article 2

The terms used in the present Law have the following meanings:

...

(1) A foreign merchant ship is a ship of foreign nationality used for commercial purposes and any other ship which is not comprised by paragraphs 2 and 5 of the present article;

(2) A foreign fishing vessel is a vessel of foreign nationality which is equipped for fishing;

...

(4) A foreign warship is a ship of foreign nationality which belongs to the naval forces, bears the external marks distinguishing warships of its nationality, is under the command of a military person and is manned by a military crew;

(5) A foreign government ship is a ship owned or used by a foreign State, being not a warship and operated exclusively for non-commercial purposes of the respective State;

...

Article 11

The territorial sea is a belt of the sea whose breadth is 10 nautical miles measured from the baseline towards the high seas.

The baseline is formed by:

(1) a low-water line along the shore of the mainland and the isles;

(2) straight lines closing the mouths of bays;

(3) straight lines connecting the following points on the shore of the mainland and on the shore of the islands:

(*a*) cape Zarubača—the south-eastern cape of the island Mrkan—the southern cape of the island Sv. Andrija—cape Gruj (on the island Mljet).

(*b*) cape Korizmeni (island Mljet)—islet Glavat—cape Struga (island Lastovo) —cape Veljeg Mora (island Lastovo)—the south-western cape of the island Kopište —cape Velo Danče (island Korčula)—cape Proizd—the south-western cape of the island Vodnjak—cape Rat (island Drvenik Mali)—rock Mulo—rock Blitvenica—island Purara—island Balun—island Mrtovac—island Garmenjak Veli—a point on the island Dugi otok whose coordinates are 43° 53′ 12″ N and 15° 10′ 0″ E;

(*c*) cape Veli Rat (Dugi otok)—rock Masarine—cape Margarina (island Susak)—rock Albanež—island Grunj—rock Sv. Ivan na Pučini—rock Mramori—island Alteiž—cape Kastanjija.

The straight lines referred to in sub-paragraph 3 of paragraph 2 of the present article must be marked on the maritime chart "Jadransko more" (Adriatic Sea), scale 1:1,000.000, published by the Hydrographic Institute of the Yugoslav navy. A reproduction of that chart is an integral part of the present Law.

In determining the baselines of the territorial sea, the outermost permanent harbour works which form an integral part of the harbour system shall be considered as a part of the coast.

The outer limit of the territorial sea is a line every point of which is 10 nautical miles distant from the nearest point of the baseline.

...

Article 12

Subject to the provisions of the present Law and other federal regulations, ships of all States shall enjoy the right of innocent passage through the territorial sea.

As innocent passage is considered navigation through the territorial sea without entering internal waters, or for the purpose of proceeding to internal waters, or for the purpose of making for the high seas from internal waters, provided this is not prejudicial to Yugoslavia's good order, peace, or security.

The innocent passage referred to in paragraph 2 of the present article includes also the ship's stopping and anchoring in the territorial sea if this is caused by the needs of regular navigation, force majeure, or distress.

Article 13

During the passage through the territorial sea, a foreign fishing vessel is obliged to keep its fishing gear and equipment in the ship's hold or sealed up. Such a vessel must traverse the territorial sea by the shortest way, with a speed which is not higher than the economic one, without stopping or anchoring, excepted when indispensable because of force majeure.

During its passage through the territorial sea, a foreign fishing vessel must show visible marks indicating that it is a fishing vessel.

The provisions of paragraph 1 of the present article do not apply to a fishing vessel which, by a permit issued on the basis of an international treaty, is authorized to fish in the territorial sea, as long as it stays in the zone where it is permitted to fish.

Article 14

More than three foreign warships of the same nationality may not traverse the Yugoslav territorial sea at the same time.

Article 15

During the passage through the territorial sea, foreign submarines shall navigate on the surface of the sea and show the flag of their State.

Article 16

The provisions of article 8 of the present Law shall apply also to the staying of a foreign warship or a group of warships in the Yugoslav territorial sea.

...

Article 17

The Secretary of State for National Defence, in agreement with the Federal Secretary for Internal Affairs and the Federal Secretary for Transport and Communications, may as a necessary measure for Yugoslavia's security, determine several zones in the territorial sea through which zones the passage of foreign ships is provisionally suspended or limited.

The Secretary of State for National Defence, in agreement with the Federal Secretary for Internal Affairs and the Federal Secretary for Transport and Communications, shall prescribe which national ships and under which conditions are allowed to navigate through the forbidden zones referred to in paragraph 1 of the present article.

The regulations concerning the limits of the zones, the suspension or limitation referred to in paragraph 1 of the present article, together with necessary informations, shall be published in the Notice to Mariners.

Article 18

The contiguous zone is a belt of 2 nautical miles, measured from the outer limit of the territorial sea towards the high seas.

Article 19

In the contiguous zone the competent organ shall exercise the control for the purpose of preventing violations of customs, fiscal and sanitary regulations and regulations relating to the passage of the frontier which could be committed on land and in the marginal seas, as well as for the purpose of punishing the violations of these regulations.

Article 20

The continental shelf comprises the sea-bed and subsoil of the submarine areas outside the outer limit of the territorial sea to a depth of 200 metres and also beyond that limit to the line where the depth of the superjacent waters admits of the exploitation of natural resources of the sea-bed and the subsoil.

Article 21

Yugoslavia exercises sovereign rights over the continental shelf relating to the exploration and exploitation of the natural resources of the shelf.

Are considered as natural resources within the meaning of paragraph 1 of the present article mineral and other non-living resources of the sea-bed and its subsoil, as well as living organisms which, at the harvesting stage, are immobile on or under the sea-bed or are able to move only in constant physical contact with the sea-bed or the subsoil.

Article 22

The rights referred to in article 21, paragraph 1, of the present Law do not affect the legal status of the superjacent waters as high seas, or the legal status of the air-space above them. The exercise of these rights must not injustifiably interfere with navigation, fishing, the protection of living resources of the sea and with fundamental oceanographic or other scientific research open to publication.

Article 23

The exploration and exploitation of the natural resources of the continental shelf as well as the construction, operation and maintenance of installations and devices which are necessary for such explorations and exploitations may be performed under conditions provided for by laws and by regulations based on law.

The installations and devices referred to in paragraph 1 of the present article must be permanently marked by lights and other signals. These installations and devices must be removed when they are abandoned or when they cease to be used for the purposes for which they were erected.

Article 24

The operator of works for the exploration and exploitation of the natural resources in the continental shelf must establish safety zones around the installations and devices referred to in article 23 of the present Law, which zones may extend to a maximal distance of 500 metres as measured from every outer point of the installation or device. It is prohibited for the ships to navigate through these safety zones, except when allowed by special regulations.

The operator of the works referred to in paragraph 1 of the present article must undertake adequate measures on the installations and devices as well as in the safety zones for the purpose of preserving living resources of the sea from harmful waste.

Article 25

The installations and devices referred to in article 23, paragraph 1, and the safety zones referred to in article 24, paragraph 1, of the present Law must not be erected and established on points where they could interfere with the use of usual sea lanes essential to international navigation.

Article 8

(1) Once a Contracting Party applies the régime described in Articles 2 to 6, any right to fish which it may thereafter grant to a State not a Contracting Party shall extend automatically to the other Contracting Parties, whether or not they could claim this right by virtue of habitual fishing, to the extent that the State not a Contracting Party avails itself effectively and habitually of that right.

(2) If a Contracting Party which has established the régime described in Articles 2 to 6 should grant to another Contracting Party any right to fish which the latter cannot claim under Articles 3 and 4, the same right shall extend automatically to all other Contracting Parties.

Article 9

(1) In order to allow fishermen of other Contracting Parties, who have habitually fished in the belt provided for in Article 2 to adapt themselves to their exclusion from that belt, a Contracting Party which establishes the régime provided for in Articles 2 to 6, shall grant to such fishermen the right to fish in that belt for a transitional period, to be determined by agreement between the Contracting Parties concerned.

(2) If a Contracting Party establishes the régime described in Articles 2 to 6, it may, notwithstanding the provisions of Article 2, continue to accord the right to fish in the whole or part of the belt provided for in Article 2 to other Contracting Parties of which the fishermen have habitually fished in the area by reason of voisinage arrangements.

Article 10

Nothing in the present Convention shall prevent the maintenance or establishment of a special régime in matters of fisheries :

(*a*) as between States Members and Associated States of the European Economic Community,

(*b*) as between States Members of the Benelux Economic Union,

(*c*) as between Denmark, Norway and Sweden,

(*d*) as between France and the United Kingdom of Great Britain and Northern Ireland in respect of Granville Bay and the Minquiers and the Ecrehos,

(*e*) as between Spain, Portugal and their respective neighbouring countries in Africa,

(*f*) in the Skagerrak and the Kattegat.

Article 11

Subject to the approval of the other Contracting Parties, a coastal State may exclude particular areas from the full application of Articles 3 and 4 in order to give preference to the local population if it is overwhelmingly dependent upon coastal fisheries.

Article 12

The present Convention applies to the waters adjacent to the coasts of the Contracting Parties listed in Annex I. This Annex may be amended with the consent of the Governments of the Contracting Parties. Any proposal for amendment shall be sent to the Government of the United Kingdom of Great Britain and Northern Ireland which shall notify it to all Contracting Parties, and inform them of the date on which it enters into force.

Article 13

Unless the parties agree to seek a solution by another method of peaceful settlement, any dispute which may arise between Contracting Parties concerning the interpretation or application of the present Convention shall at the request of any of the parties be submitted to arbitration in accordance with the provisions of Annex II to the present Convention.

Article 14

(1) The present Convention shall be open for signature from 9th March, 1964 to 10th April, 1964. It shall be subject to ratification or approval by the signatory Governments, in accordance with their respective constitutional procedures. The instruments of ratification or approval shall be deposited as soon as possible with the Government of the United Kingdom of Great Britain and Northern Ireland.

(2) The present Convention shall enter into force upon the deposit of instruments of ratification or approval by eight signatory Governments. If, however, on 1st January, 1966, this condition is not fulfilled, those Governments which have deposited their instruments of ratification or approval may agree by special protocol on the date on which the Convention shall enter into force. In either case the Convention shall enter into force with respect to any Government that ratifies or approves thereafter on the date of deposit of its instrument of ratification or approval.

(3) Any State may at any time after the Convention has come into force accede thereto upon such conditions as may be agreed by it with the Contracting Parties. Accession on the conditions agreed shall be effected by notice in writing addressed to the Government of the United Kingdom of Great Britain and Northern Ireland.

(4) The Government of the United Kingdom of Great Britain and Northern Ireland shall inform all signatory and acceding Governments of all instruments of ratification or approval deposited and accessions received and shall notify signatory and acceding Governments of the dates on which and the Governments in respect of which the present Convention enters into force.

Article 15

The present Convention shall be of unlimited duration. However at any time after the expiration of a period of twenty years from the initial entry into force of the present Convention, any Contracting Party may denounce the Convention by giving two years' notice in writing to the Government of the United Kingdom of Great Britain and Northern Ireland. The latter shall notify the denunciation to the Contracting Parties.

ANNEX I

The coasts of the Contracting Parties to which the Convention applies are the following:

Belgium
All coasts.

Denmark
The coasts of the North Sea, the Skagerrak and the Kattegat (i.e. the area lying to the north and west of lines drawn from Hasenore Head to Gniben Point, from Korshage to Spodsbierg, and from Gilbierg Head to the Kullen).

France
The North Sea and the English Channel coasts and the European Atlantic coasts.

Federal Republic of Germany
The North Sea coast.

Ireland
All coasts.

Netherlands
The North Sea coast.

Portugal
The Atlantic coast, north of the 36th Parallel, and the coast of Madeira.

Spain
The Atlantic coast, north of the 36th Parallel.

Sweden
The west coast, north of a line drawn from the Kullen to Gilbierg Head.

United Kingdom of Great Britain and Northern Ireland
All coasts, including those of the Isle of Man and The Channel Islands.

ANNEX II

Arbitration

Article 1

(1) Within three months of the signature of the Convention, or of accession thereto, each signatory or acceding Government shall nominate five persons prepared to undertake the duties of arbiters and being nationals of a Member State of the Organisation for Economic Co-operation and Development.

(2) The persons thus nominated shall be included in a list, which shall be notified by the Government of the United Kingdom of Great Britain and Northern Ireland to all signatory and acceding Governments.

(3) Any change in the list of arbiters shall be notified in the same manner.

(4) The same person may be nominated by more than one Government.

(5) The arbiters shall be nominated for a term of six years, which may be renewed.

(6) In the event of death or resignation of an arbiter he shall be replaced in the manner fixed for his nomination and for a new period of six years.

Article 2

(1) The party requesting arbitration in accordance with this Annex shall inform the other party of the claim which it intends to submit to arbitration, and give a summary statement of the grounds on which such claim is based.

(2) The Arbitral Tribunal shall consist of five members. The parties shall each nominate one member, who may be chosen from among their respective nationals. The other three arbiters, including the President, shall be chosen by agreement between the parties from among the nationals of third States whose names appear in the list mentioned in Article 1.

Article 3

If the nomination of the members of the Arbitral Tribunal is not made within a period of one month from the date on which arbitration was first requested, the task of making the necessary nominations shall be entrusted to the President of the International Court of Justice. Should the latter be a national of one of the parties to the dispute, this task shall be entrusted to the Vice-President of the Court or to the next senior judge of the Court who is not a national of the parties.

Article 4

The arbiters to be nominated by the President of the International Court of Justice shall be chosen from among the nationals of the States Members of the Organisation for Economic Co-operation and Development and preferably from the list provided for in Article 1. The President of the International Court of Justice shall consult beforehand the parties to the dispute, and may consult the Director General of the Food and Agriculture Organisation of the United Nations and the President of the International Council for the Exploration of the Sea. The arbiters shall be of different nationalities.

Article 5

The parties may draw up a special agreement determining the subject of the dispute and the details of procedure.

Article 6

In the absence of sufficient particulars in a special agreement or in the present Annex regarding the questions mentioned in Article 5 of the present Annex, the provisions of Articles 59-82 of the Hague Convention for the Pacific Settlement of International Disputes of 18th October, 1907 shall apply as far as possible.

Article 7

The parties shall facilitate the work of the Arbitral Tribunal, and in particular shall supply it to the greatest possible extent with all relevant documents and information. They shall use the means at their disposal to allow it to proceed in their territory, and in accordance with their law, to the summoning and hearing of witnesses or experts and to visit the localities in question.

Article 8

In the absence of agreement to the contrary between the parties, the decisions of the Arbitral Tribunal, shall be taken by majority vote and, except in relation to questions of procedure, decisions shall be valid only if all members are present. The voting shall not be disclosed, nor any dissenting or separate opinions.

Article 9

(1) During the proceedings, each member of the Arbitral Tribunal shall receive emoluments, the amount of which shall be fixed by agreement between the parties, each of which shall contribute an equal share.

(2) The expenses of the Arbitral Tribunal shall be divided in the same manner.

Article 10

The validity of legal measures which entered into force before the date on which the Convention was opened for signature shall not be questioned in proceedings before the Arbitral Tribunal.

Article 11

(1) In the case of a dispute based on an allegation of injury to private interests which, according to the municipal law of one of the parties, falls within the competence of its judicial administrative authorities, the party in question may object to the dispute being submitted for settlement by the procedure laid down in this Annex until a decision with final effect has been pronounced, within a reasonable time, by the competent authority.

(2) If a decision with final effect has been pronounced in the State concerned, it will no longer be possible to resort to the procedure laid down in this Annex after the expiration of a period of five years from the date of the aforementioned decision.

Article 12

If the execution of an award of the Arbitral Tribunal would conflict with a judgment or measure enjoined by a court of law or other authority of one of the parties to the dispute, and if the municipal law of that party does not permit, or only partially permits, the consequences of the judgment or measure in question to be annulled, the Arbitral Tribunal shall, if necessary, grant the injured party equitable satisfaction.

Article 13

(1) In all cases where a dispute forms the subject of arbitration, and particularly if the question on which the parties differ arises out of acts already committed or on the point of being committed, the Arbitral Tribunal shall lay down within the shortest possible time the provisional measures to be adopted. The parties to the dispute shall be bound to accept such measures.

(2) The parties shall abstain from all measures likely to react prejudicially upon the execution of the award of the Arbitral Tribunal and, in general, shall abstain from any sort of action whatsoever which may aggravate or extend the dispute.

Article 14

(1) As soon as the Arbitral Tribunal is constituted, the President shall inform the Contracting Parties of the dispute submitted to it.

(2) Any Contracting Party may intervene, within a month from the date of receipt of this notification if it establishes a legitimate interest in the settlement of the dispute. Intervention shall be with the sole object of supporting or contesting the contentions, or part of the contentions, of the original parties to the dispute. An intervention shall not lead to modification of the original composition of the Arbitral Tribunal.

Article 15

Each of the Contracting Parties shall comply with the award of the Arbitral Tribunal in any dispute to which it is a party.

IN WITNESS WHEREOF the undersigned, being duly authorised thereto, have signed the present Convention.

DONE at London this ninth day of March, 1964, in the English and French languages, each text being equally authoritative, in a single original which shall be deposited in the archives of the Government of the United Kingdom of Great Britain and Northern Ireland, which shall transmit a certified true copy thereof to each signatory and acceding Government.

EUROPEAN COMMUNITIES
REGULATION (EEC) No. 2141/70 OF THE COUNCIL
of 20 October 1970
on the establishment of a common structural policy
for the fishing industry

THE COUNCIL OF THE EUROPEAN COMMUNITIES,

HAVING REGARD to the Treaty establishing the European Economic Community, and in particular Articles 7, 42, 43 and 235 thereof;

HAVING REGARD to the proposal from the Commission;

HAVING REGARD to the Opinion of the Assembly [1];

HAVING REGARD to the Opinion of the Economic and Social Committee [2];

WHEREAS the establishment of a common organization of the market in products of the fishing industry must be complemented by the establishment of a common structural policy for the fishing industry;

WHEREAS maritime fisheries form the most important part of the fishing industry in general and enjoy a special social structure and conditions specifically appropriate to the exploitation of the sea;

WHEREAS, under certain specific conditions concerning the flat or the registration of their ships, Community fishermen must have equality of access to fishing grounds and to their exploitation in maritime waters coming under the sovereignty or within the jurisdiction of Member States; whereas, however, as a transitional measure an exception to this rule may be permitted for certain types of fishing carried on by local population whose employment is strictly dependent on inshore fishing;

WHEREAS it must be possible to take Community measures with a view to safeguarding the resources present in the waters in question;

1 OJ No. C 116 of 8. November 1968 p.3 & 5

2 OJ No. C 76 of 17. June 1969 p.11

WHEREAS it is important that the fishing industry should develop in a rational manner and that those who live by that industry should be assured of an equitable standard of living; whereas to that end, Member States should be authorized to grant financial aid with a view to allowing those objectives to be achieved according to Community rules to be determined; whereas, furthermore, any common action to be decided upon with a view to the achievement of those objectives may be the subject of Community financing, in so far as it relates to the objectives referred to in Article 39 (1) (a) of the Treaty;

WHEREAS the setting up of a Permanent Structural Committee for the Fishing Industry will facilitate the development and implementation of a common structural policy by coordinating the policies of Member States and by ensuring constant cooperation between those States and the Commission; whereas, moreover, a constant exchange of information between these latter is essential for the effective coordination of such policies and must serve as a basis for any measures which may be adopted to that end in the field of structural improvement; whereas in particular the Commission is qualified to express its opinion on the projects and programmes envisaged by Member States in this connection;

HAS ADOPTED THIS REGULATION:

Article 1

With a view to promoting harmonious and balanced development of the fishing industry within the general economy and to encouraging rational exploitation of the biological resources of the sea and of inland waters, a common system shall be adopted for fishing in maritime waters, together with specific measures with a view to appropriate action and the coordination of Member States' structural policies in this sector.

Article 2

1. The system applied by each Member State in respect of fishing in the maritime waters coming under its sovereignty or within its jurisdiction must not lead to differences in treatment with regard to other Member States.

In particular, Member States shall ensure equal conditions of access to and exploitation of the fishing grounds situated in the waters referred to in the preceding paragraph, for all fishing vessels flying the flag of a Member State and regisistered in Community territory.

2. They shall communicate to Member States and to the Commission the existing legislative provisions and administrative rules and regulations in the field referred to in the first sub-paragraph of paragraph 1 together with those arising out of application of the provisions referred to in the second sub-paragraph of that paragraph.

3. The maritime waters referred to in this Article shall be those which are so described by the laws in force in each Member State.

Article 3

Member States shall notify other Member States and the Commission of any alterations they intend to make to the fishing industry system determined in pursuance of Article 2.

Article 4

1. By way of derogation from the provisions of Article 2, access to certain fishing areas situated within a limit of 3 nautical miles calculated from the base lines of the Member State bordering on the areas concerned may be limited, for certain types of fishing and for a period not exceeding five years from the time of entry into force of this Regulation, to the local population of the coastal regions concerned if that population depends primarily on inshore fishing.

2. The fishing areas and types of fishing referred to in paragraph 1 shall be determined by the Council, acting by qualified majority on a proposal from the Commission.

Article 5

Where fishing in the Member States' maritime waters as referred to in Article 2 lays certain of their resources open to the risk of over intensive exploitation, the Council may, acting on a proposal from the Commission under the procedure provided for in Article 43 (2) of the Treaty, adopt the necessary conservation measures.

In particular, these measures may include restrictions relating to the catching of certain species, to zones, periods, methods and to fishing tackle.

Article 6

1. From the entry into force of this Regulation Member States shall undertake the coordination of their structural policy for the fishing industry.

To that end they shall communicate to the Commission each year information regarding:

- the structural situation, taking into account regional conditions and regional development policies;
- liaison between structure and market policy;
- the nature and extent of measures for structural improvement planned for the current year;
- annual and multi-annual programmes and projects for research and scientific and technical assistance adopted by the public authorities or financially assisted by the latter together with any other information enabling efforts made in this field and in particular financial outlay made by public authorities to be assessed.

2. After consulting the Committee referred to in Article 12, the Commission shall determine the form and date of submission of the documents to be supplied by Member States.

Article 7

1. Each year the Commission shall submit a report to the Assembly and the Council concerning structure in the fishing industry.

2. That report shall include:-

(a) a Table giving the situation regarding structure in the fishing industry and the structural policies followed by Member States, together with an inventory of the measures taken within the framework of those policies;

(b) a study on the nature, geographical distribution, volume and financing of those measures, together with their effectiveness in relation to the objectives of the common policy for the fishing industry and the long-term possibilities for outlets which may normally be expected for products of the fishing industry;

(c) information concerning coordination on a Community scale of structural policies in the fishing industry, covering:-

- measures taken to that end;
- Community financing;
- results of those measures and financing;

(d) a statement of the situation regarding research and scientific and technical assistance in each Member State.

Article 8

The measures necessary for the coordination of Member States' policies of research and scientific and technical assistance in the fishing industry shall be adopted according to the procedure provided for in Article 43 (2) of the Treaty.

Article 9

1. Member States may grant financial aid in so far as the operations to which they relate contribute to the achievement of the objectives referred to in Article 10.

2. The common rules fixing the conditions for granting the aid referred to in paragraph 1 shall be adopted before 1 June 1970, according to the procedure provided for in Article 43 (2) of the Treaty.

Article 10

1. In order to promote the rational development of the fishing industry within the framework of economic expansion and social progress and in order to ensure an equitable standard of living for the population which depends on fishing for its living, the specific measures with a view to appropriate action referred to in Article 1 must contribute to:-

- increased productivity through a restructuring of fleets and other means of production, adapted to the evolution of technical progress together with intensification of the search for new fishing grounds and new methods of fishing;

- adaptation of production and marketing conditions according to market requirements, particularly by development of canning and processing installations in order to render more effective the activities of producer organizations;

- the improvement, linked with rate of technical progress, of the standard and conditions of living of any population which depends on fishing for its livelihood.

2. The provisions of paragraph 1, in so far as they relate to the objectives referred to in Article 39 (1) (a) of the Treaty, may be the subject of common action within the meaning of Article 6 (1) of Council Regulation (EEC) No. 729/70 [3] of 21 April 1970 on the financing of the common agricultural policy.

[3] OJ No. L 94 of 28 April 1970 p. 13

Article 11

1. Without prejudice to the provisions laid down in Article 3, Member States shall communicate the following documents to the Commission in good time, in so far as they refer to measures for the improvement of structures in the fishing industry:

- as far as possible, drafts of legislative provisions and administrative rules and regulations or, failing this, a description of the general lines of the proposed provisions;

- the proposed multi-annual plans and regional programmes.

2. The Commission

- may express its opinion on the legislative provisions and administrative rules and regulations, multi-annual plans and regional programmes which are communicated to it in accordance with Article 6;

- must express its opinion on these when a Member State so requests.

Article 12

1. With a view to promoting coordination of structural policies for the fishing industry and to encouraging closer and more constant cooperation between Member States and the Commission, a Permanent Structural Committee for the Fishing Industry shall be set up within the Commission (hereinafter called the "Committee").

2. The Committee shall be composed of representatives of each Member State. It shall be under the chairmanship of a representative of the Commission.

3. The Commission shall be responsible for the secretariat of the Committee.

4. The Committee shall adopt its own rules of procedure.

Article 13

The Committee shall be required, for the whole of the fisheries sector:

- to ensure that Member States and the Commission are kept mutually informed in the field of structural policies and in particular with regard to the measures governing maritime fishing;

- to study Member States' structural policies together with the measures and programmes provided for by the latter with a view to improvement of structures in that sector;

- to assist the Commission in the preparation of parts (a) and (b) of the report concerning structures in the fishing industry provided for in Article 7;

- to deliver opinions at the request of the Commission on problems relating to structure in the fishing industry.

Article 14

Where Council Regulation No. 17/64/EEC [4] of 4 February 1964 on the conditions for obtaining aid from the European Agricultural Guidance and Guarantee Fund and provisions subsequent thereto, refer to the Permanent Committee on agricultural organization, the latter shall be replaced for all problems in the fisheries sector, by the Permanent Structural Committee for the Fishing Industry.

Article 15

This Regulation shall enter into force on the third day following that of its publication in the Official Journal of the European Communities.

The system provided for by this Regulation shall be applicable from 1 February 1971, save for the provisions laid down in Article 10, which may be applied from the entry into force of this Regulation.

This Regulation shall be binding in its entirety and directly applicable in all Member States.

Done at Luxembourg, 20 October 1970.

For the Council

The President

H. D. Griesau

[4] OJ No. 34 of 27 February 1964 p. 586/64

Note: "This instrument is subject to adaptation on the enlargement of the Community to provide that Member States shall be authorized to restrict fishing in certain specified coastal waters until 31 December 1982."

TREATY CONCERNING THE ACCESSION OF THE KINGDOM OF DENMARK, IRELAND, THE KINGDOM OF NORWAY AND THE UNITED KINGDOM OF GREAT BRITAIN AND NORTHERN IRELAND TO THE EUROPEAN ECONOMIC COMMUNITY (WITH FINAL ACT). UK MISCELLANEOUS NO. 3 (1972) - PART 1. CMND. 4862-1. ARTICLES 100-103 OF THE FINAL ACT

FISHING RIGHTS

ARTICLE 100

1. Notwithstanding the provisions of Article 2 of Regulation (EEC) No. 2141/70 on the establishment of a common structural policy for the fishing industry, the Member States of the Community are authorized, until 31 December 1982, to restrict fishing in waters under their sovereignty or jurisdiction, situated within a limit of six nautical miles, calculated from the base lines of the coastal Member State, to vessels which fish traditionally in those waters and which operate from ports in that geographical coastal area; however, vessels from other regions of Denmark may continue to fish in the waters of Greenland until 31 December 1977 at the latest.

Member States may not, insofar as they avail themselves of this derogation, adopt provisions dealing with conditions for fishing in those waters which are less restrictive than those applied in practice at the time of accession.

2. The provisions laid down in the preceding paragraph and in Article 101 shall not prejudice the special fishing rights which each of the original Member States and the new Member States might have enjoyed on 31 January 1971 in regard to one or more other Member States; the Member States may exercise these rights for such time as derogations continue to apply in the areas concerned. As regards the waters of Greenland, however the special rights shall expire on the dates laid down for these rights.

3. If a Member State extends its fishing limits in certain areas to twelve nautical miles, the existing fishing activities within twelve nautical miles must be so pursued that there is no retrogade change by comparison with the situation on 31 January 1971.

4. In order to permit a satisfactory overall balance of fishing operations to be established within the Community during the period referred to in the first paragraph, the Member States need not make full use of the opportunities presented by the provisions of the first subparagraph of paragraph 1 in certain areas of the maritime waters under their sovereignty or jurisdiction.

The Member States shall inform the Commission of the measures which they adopt for this purpose; on a report from the Commission, the Council shall examine the situation and, in the light thereof, shall, where necessary, address recommendations to the Member States.

ARTICLE 101

The limit of six nautical miles referred to in Article 100 shall be extended to twelve nautical miles for the following areas:

1. Denmark
   - the Faroe Islands
   - Greenland
   - the west coast, from Thyborøn to Blaavandshuk.

2. France
   The coasts of the départements of Manche, Ille-et Vilaine, Côtes du Nord, Finistère and Morbihan.

3. Ireland
   - the north and west coasts, from Lough Foyle to Carnsore Point, for crustaceans and molluscs (shellfish).

4. Norway
   The coast between Egersund and the frontier between Norway and the Union of Soviet Socialist Republics.

5. United Kingdom
   - the Shetlands and Orkneys
   - the north and east of Scotland, from Cape Wrath to Berwick.
   - the north-east of England, from the river Coquet to Flamborough Head.
   - the south-west from Lyme Regis to Hartland Point (including twelve nautical miles around Lundy Island)
   - County Down

ARTICLE 102

From the sixth year after Accession at the latest, the Council, acting on a proposal from the Commission, shall determine conditions for fishing with a view to ensuring protection of the fishing grounds and conservation of the biological resources of the sea.

ARTICLE 103

Before 31 December 1982, the Commission shall present a report to the Council on the economic and social development of the coastal areas of the Member States and the state of stocks. On the basis of that report, and of the objectives of the common fisheries policy, the Council, acting on a proposal from the Commission, shall examine the provisions which could follow the derogations in force until 31 December 1982.

EXCHANGE OF NOTES BETWEEN SPAIN AND FRANCE CONSTITUTING A GENERAL AGREEMENT ON FISHERIES, MARCH 20, 1967.

Ministry of Foreign Affairs

March 20, 1967.

International Agreements

To the Spanish Embassy, Paris.

The Ministry of Foreign Affairs presents its compliments to the Spanish Embassy and has the honour to refer to the Franco-Spanish meeting which was held in Paris from January 23-25, 1967 with the object of concluding a General Agreement on Fisheries between France and Spain.

The representatives of the two Governments who took part in that meeting reached agreement and set out the terms thereof in a minute which they signed on January 25, 1967 and which reads as follows:

"Considering the intention of the Governments of the two countries to extend the limit of their exclusive fishery zone to 12 miles, and taking into account the fact that the two Governments are parties to the Fisheries Convention signed at London on March 9, 1964, the two delegations have agreed as follows:-

1. <u>Outer Zone from 6 to 12 miles</u>.

(a) In the outer zone from 6 to 12 miles along the coasts of Spain, French nationals shall enjoy permanently the right to fish:

- on the Atlantic coast from the Mouth of the Bidassoa to the northern bank of the Rio Mino, all species;

- on the Mediterranean coast from the Franco-Spanish frontier to Cape Creus, all species:

(b) In the zone from 6 to 12 miles along the coasts of France, Spanish nationals shall enjoy permanently the right to fish:

- on the Atlantic coast from the Mouth of the Bidassoa to the line of latitude running through the northern point of Belle-Ile, all species;

- on the Mediterranean coast from the frontier to Cape Leucate, all species.

II. Inner Zone from 3 to 6 miles.

1. The nationals of each State Party may continue to fish in the inner zone of the other State Party until December 31, 1968, except for those parts of the coast where new straight baselines and closing lines for bays have been drawn and where the transitional period shall be extended to December 31, 1969.

2. With the object of protecting resources, it is understood that at the earliest possible date which shall be determined by common agreement between the two countries, trawling shall be prohibited to Spanish nationals in the inner zone of the French Atlantic coast, and to French nationals in the inner zone of the Spanish coast.

3. In the case of surface fishing, the nationals of each country fishing in the inner zone of the Atlantic coast of the other country shall enjoy a delay of two years on the conditions set out in paragraph 1 above, either to December 31, 1970 or to December 31, 1971, depending on whether new baselines have been drawn or not.

III. Zone from 0 to 3 miles.

The nationals of each country shall be prohibited from fishing in the innermost zone from 0 to 3 miles of the other country.

Nevertheless the authorities of the maritime frontier districts of the Province of Guipuzcoa and of the District of Bayonne may agree on mutual measures to allow fishing which is in accordance with the traditional relations of the coastal populations on both sides of the frontier.

IV. Baselines

The two delegations have informed each other of the intentions of their Governments to establish new straight baselines and closing lines for bays in accordance with the provisions of the Geneva Convention on the Territorial Sea. The information which they exchanged concerning the proposed lines of delimitation did not give rise to any observation on either side.

V.

The two delegations agreed that the provisions of Articles I, II and III came within the framework of the voisinage arrangements set out in Article 9 (2) of the London Convention. Moreover these provisions are generally based on the recognition of the fishing customs of the nationals of the two countries. It is agreed that in the application of these provisions the two Parties will act in accordance with the general provisions of the London Convention of 1964.

VI. Protection of Resources.

The two delegations take note of the agreement concluded in 1963 between the experts of the two countries on measures to be taken for the protection of resources, and particularly of stocks of *merlu*, in the Gulf of Gascony. In particular, they approve the proposals which are at present being studied by those experts with the object of establishing fishing sectors.

VII.

The conclusions reached by the two delegations shall be embodied as soon as possible in an exchange of notes between the French Ministry of Foreign Affairs and the Spanish Embassy in France."

The Ministry of Foreign Affairs has the honour to inform the Spanish Embassy that the French Government approves this document and is ready, for its part, to apply its provisions.

The Ministry suggests to the Embassy that the present note together with the Embassy's reply shall constitute an agreement between the French and Spanish Governments which shall enter into force on the date appearing on the Embassy's reply.

The Ministry of Foreign Affairs takes this opportunity to renew to the Spanish Embassy the assurances of its highest consideration.

G.C.

Spanish Embassy, Paris

Paris, March 20, 1967

No. 203.

To the Ministry of Foreign Affairs, Paris.

The Spanish Embassy presents its compliments to the Ministry of Foreign Affairs and has the honour to acknowledge receipt of its note verbale of today's date referring to the Franco-Spanish meeting which was held in Paris from January 23-25, 1967 with the object of concluding a General Agreement on Fisheries between France and Spain.

The representatives of the two Governments who took part in that meeting reached agreement and set out the terms thereof in a minute which they signed on January 25, 1967 and which reads as follows:

"Considering the intention of the Governments of the two countries..."

The Spanish Embassy has the honour to inform the Ministry of Foreign Affairs that the Spanish Government approves this document and is ready, for its part, to apply its provisions.

The Spanish Embassy gives its consent to the suggestion that the note of the Ministry together with the Embassy's reply shall constitute an Agreement between the French and Spanish Governments which shall enter into force today.

The Spanish Government takes this opportunity to renew to the Ministry of Foreign Affairs the assurances of its highest consideration.

P.C.

AN ACT RESPECTING THE TERRITORIAL SEA AND FISHING ZONES OF CANADA

[Assented to 16th July, 1964.]

Her Majesty, by and with the advice and consent of the Senate and House of Commons of Canada enacts as follows:

SHORT TITLE.

1. This Act may be cited as the Territorial Sea and Fishing Zones Act.

PART I.

2. Every provision of this Act extends and applies to every Act of the Parliament of Canada, now or hereafter passed, and to every order, rule or regulation thereunder, except in so far as any such provision is inconsistent with the intent or object of such Act, order, rule or regulation, or would give to any word, expression or clause thereof an interpretation repugnant to the subject matter or the context, or is, in any such Act, order, rule or regulation, declared not applicable thereto.

3. (1) Subject to any exceptions under section 5, the territorial sea of Canada, comprises those areas of the sea having, as their inner limits, the baselines described in section 5 and, as their outer limits, lines measured seaward and equidistant from such baselines so that each point of the outer limit line of the territorial sea is distant three nautical miles from the nearest point of the baseline.

(2) The internal waters of Canada include any areas of the sea that are on the landward side of the baselines of the territorial sea of Canada.

4. (1) Subject to any exceptions under section 5, the fishing zones of Canada comprise those areas of the sea contiguous to the territorial sea of Canada and having, as their inner limits, the outer limits of the territorial sea and, as their outer limits, lines measured seaward and equidistant from such inner limits so that each point of the outer limit line of a fishing zone is distant nine nautical miles from the nearest point of the inner limit line.

(2) Unless otherwise specified therein, the laws of Canada respecting fishing and the exploitation of the living

resources of the sea apply to the fishing zones of Canada in the same way and to the same extent as they apply to the territorial sea of Canada.

5. (1) The Governor in Council may, by order in council, issue one or more lists of geographical co-ordinates of points from which baselines may be determined and may, as he deems necessary, amend such lists.

(2) In respect of any area for which geographical co-ordinates of points have been listed in a list issued pursuant to subsection (1) and subject to any exceptions in the list for the use of the low water line along the coast as the baseline between given points, baselines are straight lines joining the consecutive geographical co-ordinates of points so listed.

(3) In respect of any other area and until such time as geographical co-ordinates of points have, for such other area, been listed in a list issued pursuant to sub-section (1), baselines remain those applicable immediately before the coming into force of this section.

(4) Where, in his opinion, a portion of the territorial sea of Canada or a portion of the fishing zones of Canada, determined, respectively, in accordance with subsection (1) of section 3 or subsection (1) of section 4, would conflict with the territorial sea of a country other than Canada or would be unreasonably close to the coast of a country other than Canada, the Governor in Council may, by order in council, issue a list of geographical coordinates of points from which,

(a) in respect of the portion of the territorial sea of Canada designated in the list, an outer limit line may be determined in substitution for the territorial sea outer limit line described in subsection (1) of section 3, and
(b) in respect of the portion of the fishing zones of Canada designated in the list, an outer limit line may be determined in substitution for the fishing zone outer limit line described in subsection (1) of section 4,

and the outer limit lines referred to in paragraphs (a) and (b) shall, thereupon, be substituted.

(5) Where an outer limit line of a portion of the territorial sea of Canada has been substituted pursuant to subsection (4) of this section, section 4 shall not apply to

create a contiguous fishing zone in respect of such portion.

6. The Minister of Mines and Technical Surveys may cause charts to be issued delineating the territorial sea of Canada and the fishing zones of Canada or of any portions thereof as may be delineated consistent with the nature and scale of the chart.

PART II.

CONSEQUENTIAL AMENDMENTS.

[omitted]

Canadian Government Notice Establishing Fishing Zones*
(December 26, 1970)

DEPARTMENT OF EXTERNAL AFFAIRS
TERRITORIAL SEA AND FISHING ZONES ACT

Notice is hereby given that, pursuant to section 5A of the Territorial Sea and Fishing Zones Act, it is proposed, after the expiration of sixty days following publication of this notice in the Canada Gazette, to make the annexed Order prescribing as fishing zones of Canada certain areas of the sea adjacent to the coast of Canada.

Given at Ottawa, this 15th day of December, 1970

MITCHELL SHARP
Secretary of State for External Affairs

TERRITORIAL SEA AND FISHING ZONES ACT

Fishing Zones of Canada
(Zones 1, 2 and 3) Order

AT THE GOVERNMENT HOUSE AT OTTAWA

present:

His Excellency the Governor General in Council

His Excellency the Governor General in Council, on the recommendation of the Secretary of State for External Affairs, pursuant to section 5A of the Territorial Sea and Fishing Zones act, is pleased hereby to make the annexed Order prescribing as fishing zones of Canada certain areas of the sea adjacent to the coast of Canada.

*(Reproduced from the Canada Gazette, Vol. 104, No. 52 (December 26, 1970).

ORDER PRESCRIBING AS FISHING ZONES OF CANADA CERTAIN AREAS OF THE SEA ADJACENT TO THE COAST OF CANADA

1. This Order may be cited as the Fishing Zones of Canada (Zones 1, 2 and 3) Order.

2. In this Order,

(a) "C.H.S. Chart" means Canadian Hydrographic Service Chart; and

(b) "geographical co-ordinates of points" means the latitude and longitude of points determined by reference to columns III and IV in the description of Zones set out in the Schedule.

3. The areas of the sea adjacent to the coast of Canada and described in the Schedule are hereby prescribed as fishing zones of Canada:

Schedule

ZONE 1

GULF OF ST. LAWRENCE

being those areas of the sea adjacent to the coast of Canada, bounded by straight lines joining the geographical co-ordinates of points set out below:

Column 1 Area	Column II Locality	Column III Latitude	Column IV Longitude	Column V C.H.S. Chart
Strait of Belle Isle	1 Eastern White Island	51°34'52"N	55°21'00"W	4731
	2. Northeast Ledge	52°02'07"N	55°16'04"W	4705
	3. Double Island	52°15'30"N	55°32'58"W	4701
Cabot Strait	1. Money Point	47°01'46"N	60°23'25"W	4363
	2. St. Paul Island	47°11'28"N	60°08'45"W	4450
	3. Cape Ray	47°37'15"N	59°18'20"W	4015

ZONE 2

BAY OF FUNDY

being that area of the sea adjacent to the coast of Canada, bounded by straight lines joining the geographical co-ordinates of points set out below:

Column 1 Area	Column II Locality	Column III Latitude	Column IV Longitude	Column V C.H.S. Chart
Bay of Fundy	1. Whipple Point	44°14'12"N	66°23'48"W	4011
	2. Gannet Rock	44°30'34"N	66°46'57"W	4340
	3. Yellow Ledge	44°29'01"N	66°51'05"W	4340
	4. Machinas Seal Island	44°29'58"N	67°06'05"W	4340
	5. Machinas Seal Island	44°30'00"N	67°06'10"W	4340
	6. Machinas Seal Island	44°30'06"N	67°06'16"W	4340
	7. North Rock	44°32'16"N	67°05'18"W	4340
	8. Pandora Head Grand Manan	44°39'27"N	66°53'32"W	4340
	9. Grand Manan	44°39'41"N	66°53'27"W	4340
	10. Grand Manan	44°43'11"N	66°51'52"W	4340
	11. Grand Manan	44°43'23"N	66°51'44"W	4340
	12. Grand Manan	44°44'10"N	66°51'11"W	4340
	13. Grand Manan	44°45'37"N	66°50'06"W	4340
	14. Grand Manan Channel	44°47'39.58"N	66°53'09.62"W	4340

SCHEDULE

ZONE 3

Queen Charlotte Sound, Hecate Straight and Dixon Entrance

being that area of the sea adjacent to the coast of Canada, bounded by straight lines joining the geographical co-ordinates of points set out below:

Column I Area	Column II Locality	Column III Latitude	Column IV Longitude	Column V C.H.S. Chart
Queen Charlotte Sound	1. Winifred Island	50° 39' 40"N	128° 22' 00"W	3625
	2. Beresford Islands	50° 47' 03"N	128° 46' 04"W	3625
	3. Sartine Islands	50° 49' 02"N	128° 56' 24"W	3625
	4. Triangle Island	50° 51' 09"N	129° 05' 24"W	3625
	5. Kerouard Islands	51° 54' 20"N	130° 58' 12"W	3825
	6. Kerouard Islands	51° 54' 38"N	130° 59' 04"W	3825
	7. Kerouard Islands	51° 55' 20"N	131° 00' 17"W	3825
	8. Kunglit Island	51° 56' 37"N	131° 01' 52"W	3825
Dixon Entrance	1. Langara Island	54° 14' 58"N	133° 04' 48"W	3868
	2. Point A of Line A-B	54° 39'45.16"N	132° 40'57.18"W	3002

CANADA-UNITED STATES: STATEMENTS ON THE ESTABLISHMENT OF CANADIAN FISHING ZONES (December 1970)

Statement of Canadian Minister of Fisheries and Forestry* (December 18, 1970)

PROMULGATION OF FISHERIES CLOSING LINES

With the adoption of the amendments to the Territorial Sea and Fishing Zones Act earlier this year Parliament laid the foundation for the establishment of exclusive Canadian fishing zones comprising certain areas of the sea adjacent to the coast of Canada. As explained to the House on April 17, these provisions were enabling only and the creation of the new zones required executive action by way of an Order in Council. The required action is now being taken to draw "fisheries closing lines" across the entrances to the Gulf of St. Lawrence, the Bay of Fundy, Queen Charlotte Sound and Dixon Entrance-Hecate Strait. A Government Notice to this effect will be published in the Canada Gazette on December 26. The fisheries closing lines will then be brought into force immediately upon the expiration of the mandatory 60-day waiting period imposed by the amended Territorial Sea and Fishing Zones Act.

There are special geographic and legal factors pertaining to the areas affected by the Government's action, and Canada has historic and other claims to these areas. The establishment of exclusive fishing zones in the bodies of water under reference, as has been made clear on previous occasions, can in no way be construed as an abandonment of those claims by Canada. It is also well known that the new fishing zones we are creating are of vital importance to Canadian fishing interests. The Gulf of St. Lawrence alone has had landings of up to 550 million pounds valued at some $31 million, the Bay of Fundy's landings of 300 million pounds are worth $12 million, while the Pacific coast area contained within Dixon Entrance and Queen Charlotte Sound has landings of 180 million pounds, worth $37 million a year.

These are, of course, important considerations, but the Government objectives in introducing this imaginative concept of fisheries closing lines go beyond the securing of immediate economic benefits, as was outlined by the Secretary of State for External Affairs in his statement to the House of April 17. On that occasion, he pointed out that:

---

*(Reproduced from the Canadian House of Common Debates, Vol. 115, No. 50 (December 18, 1970), pp. 2244-2245.

"Now that the world is becoming aware that living resources are not infinitely renewable and that they can indeed be exhausted or depleted by overexploitation or wiped out by means of pollution of the sea, it is vitally necessary to apply to the exploitation of these resources some of the techniques which have been developed for offshore mineral resources. The action now being taken by Canada is a step in this direction, a step toward a more logical and systematic approach to the management of living marine resources.

Exclusive rights to harvest may be necessary, but they are not an end in themselves. The end we have in mind is conservation and rational management, and for this purpose we require jurisdiction. That jurisdiction, however, does not rule out the possibility of sharing fisheries exploitation with other countries; it does, however, allow us to set rules for that exploitation, to impose licensing requirements if necessary and thus to share the financial burden of conservation as well as the financial rewards of expolitation."

The fisheries closing lines being promulgated by the Government represent a very important step forward in the conservation and protection of Canada's coastal fisheries. It must be recognized, however, that there is also a need for international as well as national action if we are to preserve the marine environment and its living resources for future generations. For this reason the Government has been consulting with other interested countries for more than two years with respect to the convening of a Law of the Sea conference which would deal effectively with these problems.

The possibility of convening such a conference has been under discussion in the current session of the United Nations General Assembly and the Assembly has now resolved that a conference should be held in 1973. It is Canada's hope that there will emerge from that conference a rational system of fisheries conservation, management and exploitation in the common interest of all countries, including a clear recognition of the special rights and responsibilities of coastal states with respect to the living resources of the sea, and particularly the protection of the Atlantic and Pacific salmon stocks which are being maintained at considerable cost by the efforts of coastal states such as Canada and the USA.

In addition, it is Canada's view that the United Nations Conference on the Human Environment to be convened in Stockholm in June of 1972 will offer an important and indeed crucial opportunity for the international community to adopt a bold and constructive approach to the preservation of the marine environment. The living resources of the sea are the greatest wealth of the sea, and it is those resources, of course, which are most directly threatened by marine pollution. The Stockholm Conference, we hope, will include among its achievements the laying of a foundation for a global attack on marine pollution, including the work on this problem which we hope will be undertaken at the proposed conference on the Law of the Sea.

Having established the new fishing zones, the Government intends to conclude negotiations for the phasing out of the fishing activities of certain countries which have traditionally fished in the areas concerned, namely the United Kingdom, Denmark, France, Italy, Norway, Portugal and Spain. Canada has recently entered into an agreement on reciprocal fishing privileges with the U.S.A. and the activities of United States fishermen in the areas concerned will not be affected by the promulgation of our fisheries closing lines. There are as well other treaty arrangements with the United States and also France off Canada's east coast, and similarly the rights accruing under these treaties will be respected.

There may be differences of views as to whether or not a phasing-out period should be granted for countries which have carried on traditional fishing practices in areas over which a coastal state has established fisheries jurisdiction, as we are now doing in Canada's special bodies of water. There can, however, be no such differences of views with respect to areas which have become part of Canada's 12-mile territorial sea.

The extension of Canada's territorial sea to 12 miles and the establishment of exclusive Canadian fishing zones in the special bodies of water will permit us to conclude expeditiously the negotiations begun in 1964 following the passage of the Territorial Seas and Fishing Zones Act.

DEPARTMENT OF STATE
FOR THE PRESS

DECEMBER 18, 1970 NO. 357

UNITED STATES STATEMENT ON
CANADIAN FISHERIES CLOSING LINES ANNOUNCEMENT

Today, the Government of Canada announced the establishment of fisheries closing lines which purport to extend unilaterally Canadian jurisdiction over areas which are traditionally regarded as the high seas. The areas affected are: Strait of Belle Isle, Cabot Strait, Bay of Fundy, Queen Charlotte Sound, and Dixon Entrance.

The United States deeply regrets this action. The United States regards this unilateral act as totally without foundation in international law. The United States firmly opposes such unilateral extensions of jurisdiction and believes that outstanding issues concerning the oceans can only be resolved by effective international action.

In this respect, on December 17 the United Nations General Assembly approved by an overwhelming majority a resolution which scheduled a Law of the Sea Conference for 1973 which will deal with a wide range of oceans issues. Among the matters proposed for international action in the resolution are the question of preferential fishing rights for coastal states, conservation of living resources of the sea, and the protection of the marine environment, including the prevention of pollution. Canada, together with the United States and a number of other countries, was a co-sponsor of that resolution. Moreover, Canada, perhaps more than any other country, played a very important lead role in achieving a commitment by the international community to resolve these issues multilaterally.

Therefore, the United States is deeply disappointed and profoundly regrets that Canada has chosen to assert a unilateral claim of jurisdiction over ocean space <u>only one day</u> after the United Nations, with the approval of nearly all member states, including Canada, determined to resolve these problems regarding the law of the sea by international action.

* * *

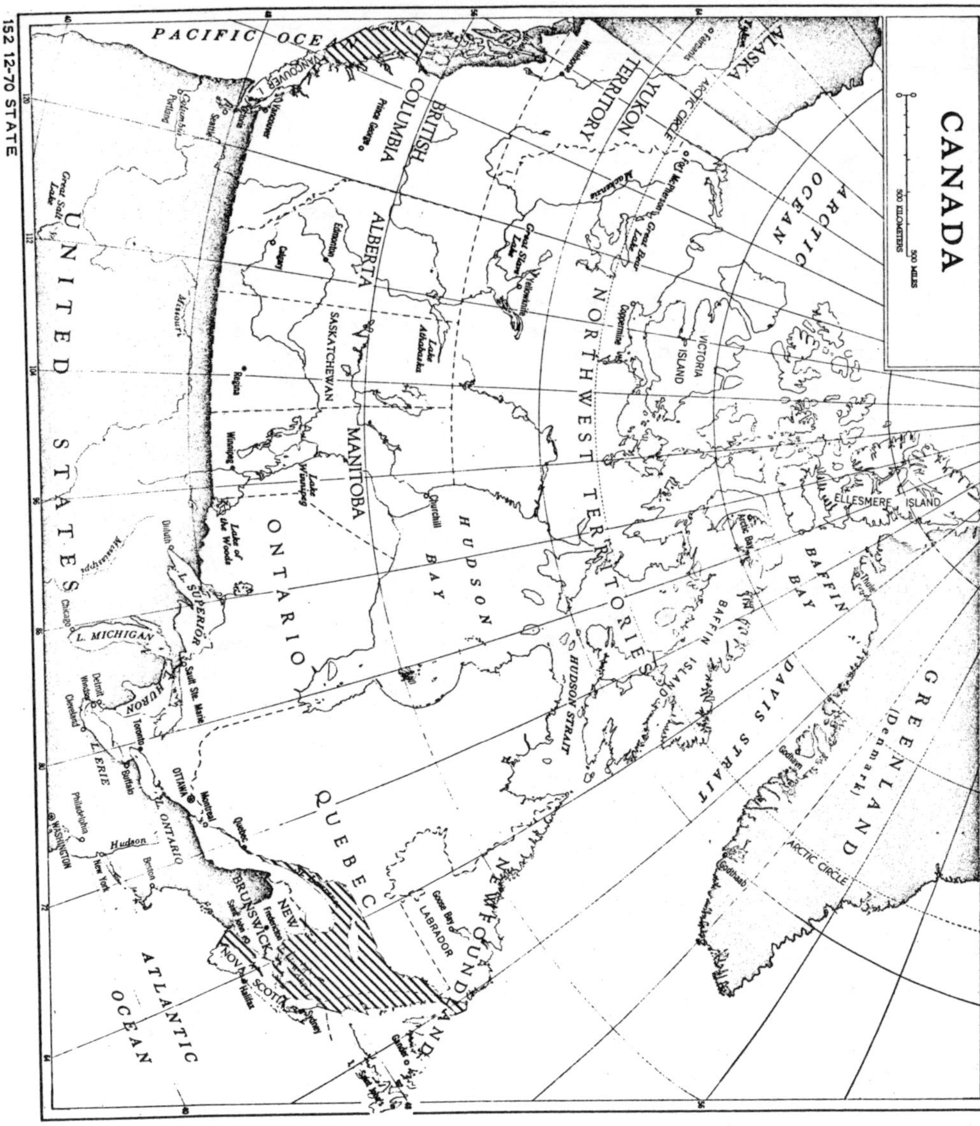

Areas Closed by Fisheries Lines

152 12-70 STATE

MEXICO

ACT[1] OF 13 DECEMBER 1966 ON THE EXCLUSIVE FISHING ZONE OF THE NATION

Article 1

The United Mexican States establish their exclusive jurisdiction for fishing purposes in a zone twelve nautical miles (22,224 metres) wide, measured from the base line from which the breadth of the territorial sea is measured.

Article 2

The legal régime on the exploitation of the living resources of the sea, within the territorial sea, shall be extended to the whole of the exclusive fishing zone of the nation mentioned in the preceding article.

Article 3

No provisions of this Act shall in any way modify the legal provisions[2] establishing the breadth of the territorial sea.

TRANSITIONAL ARTICLES: THREE

The Federal Executive shall establish the conditions and terms under which nationals of countries which have traditionally exploited the living resources of the sea in the zone three nautical miles outside the territorial sea may be authorized to continue their activities during a period which shall not exceed five years from 1 January 1968. In 1967, nationals of such countries may continue those activities without being subject to any special conditions.

(*f*) ACT[1] ESTABLISHING A FISHERIES ZONE CONTIGUOUS TO THE TERRITORIAL SEA OF THE UNITED STATES, 14 OCTOBER 1966

§ *1091. Establishment; fisheries rights*

There is established a fisheries zone contiguous to the territorial sea of the United States. The United States will exercise the same exclusive rights in respect to fisheries in the zone as it has in its territorial sea, subject to the continuation of traditional fishing by foreign states within this zone as may be recognized by the United States. (Pub. L. 89-658, § 1, Oct. 14, 1966, 80 Stat. 908.)

§ *1092. Description of boundaries*

The fisheries zone has as its inner boundary the outer limits of the territorial sea and as its seaward boundary a line drawn so that each point on the line is nine nautical miles from the nearest point in the inner boundary. (Pub. L. 89-658, § 2, Oct. 14, 1966, 80 Stat. 908.)

§ *1093. Substitution of description of boundaries where conflict of zones or waters*

Whenever the President determines that a portion of the fisheries zone conflicts with the territorial waters of fisheries zone of another country, he may establish a seaward boundary for such portion of the zone in substitution for the seaward boundary described in section 1092 of this title. (Pub. L. 89-658, § 3, Oct. 14, 1966, 80 Stat. 908.)

§ *1094. State jurisdiction over natural resources and waters*

Nothing in sections 1091—1094 of this title shall be construed as extending the jurisdiction of the States to the natural resources beneath and in the waters within the fisheries zone established by such sections or as diminishing their jurisdiction to such resources beneath and in the waters of the territorial seas of the United States. (Pub. L. 89-658, § 4, Oct. 14, 1966, 80 Stat. 908.)

---

[1] *United States Code* (Supplement II, 1965-1966), Title 16 (Conservation).

AGREEMENT BETWEEN THE UNITED STATES OF AMERICA AND THE UNITED MEXICAN STATES ON TRADITIONAL FISHING IN THE EXCLUSIVE FISHERY ZONES CONTIGUOUS TO THE TERRITORIAL SEAS OF BOTH COUNTRIES

Considering:

I. That the Government of the United States of America, pursuant to Public Law 89–658, approved October 14, 1966,[1] established an exclusive fishery zone contiguous to the territorial sea of the United States in which it will exercise the same exclusive rights in respect to fisheries as it has in its territorial sea, subject to the continuation of traditional fishing by the foreign states within this zone as may be recognized by the Government of the United States;

II. That the Government of Mexico, pursuant to the law of December 9, 1966, promulgated by the Mexican Congress, established the exclusive jurisdiction of Mexico, for fishing purposes, in a zone of 12 nautical miles (22,224 meters) in breadth, measured from the base line used to measure the breadth of the territorial sea, and provided that the legal regime for the exploitation of the living resources of the sea within the territorial sea extends to the entire exclusive fishery zone of the nation and that nothing contained in this law modifies in any way the legal provisions which determine the breadth of the territorial sea, and finally that Mexico's Federal Executive will determine the conditions and terms under which nationals of countries which traditionally have exploited the living resources of the sea within the 3 nautical mile zone beyond the territorial sea may be authorized to continue their activities for a period not to exceed five years, beginning on January 1, 1968;

III. That both Governments consider it necessary and convenient to establish the terms and conditions under which, without any modification of and in total accord with the laws cited in previous paragraphs I and II, fishing vessels of the United States and those of Mexico may, beginning January 1, 1968, continue their activities during five years in the waters within the exclusive fishery zone of the other country in which vessels of the same flag fished in a sustained manner during the five years immediately preceding January 1, 1968; and

IV. That both Governments state that the establishment of said terms and conditions does not imply a change of position or an abandonment of the positions maintained by each Government regarding the breadth of the territorial sea, this matter not being the object of this agreement, nor does it limit their freedom to continue

[1] 80 Stat. 908; 16 U.S.C. §§1091–1094.

defending them in the international forum or in any of the ways recognized by international law;

The Government of the United States of America and the Government of the United Mexican States

Agree to establish the following terms and conditions under which American and Mexican fishermen will continue to operate in the above-mentioned waters during the established period of five years:

1. Fishing vessels of the United States will be permitted to continue their activities in the exclusive fishery zone of the United Mexican States in the Gulf of Mexico:

(a) In the waters between 9 and 12 nautical miles off the coast of the mainland and around the islands of Mexico, measured from the baseline from which the breadth of the territorial sea is measured, bounded on the north by a line to be constructed by the International Boundary and Water Commission, United States and Mexico, as the maritime boundary between both countries, extended to the twelve nautical mile limit, and bounded on the south by a straight line connecting the geographic coordinates of 21°20′00″ north latitude, 86°38′00″ west longitude, and 21°20′00″ north latitude, 86°35′00″ west longitude (north-east of Isla Mujeres), where fishing vessels of the United States have traditionally carried on shrimp fishing, they will be permitted to continue to take shrimp and such species of fish as are taken incidentally;

(b) United States fishing vessels will be permitted to continue to fish for snappers (genera *Lutjanus*, *Rhomboplites*, *Ocyurus*, *Etelis*, *Holocentrus*, and *Pristipomoides*), groupers (genera *Epinephelus* and *Mycteroperca*), and other genera that are captured incidentally, such as *Seriola*, *Calamus*, *Stenotomus*, *Balistes*, *Paralichthys*, *Ancyclopsetta*, and *Cyclopsetta*, in waters between 9 and 12 nautical miles around Cayo Arcas, Arrecifes Triangulos, Cayo Arenas, and Arrecifes Alacran;

(c) The fishing referred to in subparagraphs (a) and (b) above will continue during the five years beginning January 1, 1968, at levels such that the total catch by U.S. vessels will not exceed the total in the five years immediately preceding that date.

2. In the maritime waters off the Mexican coast in the Pacific Ocean:

(a) In the waters between 9 and 12 nautical miles measured from the baseline from which the breadth of the territorial sea is measured, off the mainland and around the islands of Mexico, bounded on the north by a line to be constructed by the International Boundary and Water Commission, United

States and Mexico, as the maritime boundary between both countries, extended to the 12 nautical mile limit and bounded on the south by a straight line connecting the geographical coordinates of 14°32′42″ north latitude, 92°27′00″ west longitude, and 14°30′36″ north latitude, 92°29′18″ west longitude, where fishing vessels of the United States have traditionally carried on fishing, they will be permitted to fish for albacore (*Thunnus alalunga*), yellowfin tuna (*Thunnus albacares*), bluefin tuna (*Thunnus thynnus*), skipjack (*Euthynnus* (*Katsuwonus*) *pelamis*), bonito (*Sarda chiliensis*), thread herring (*Opisthonema* spp.), white sea bass (*Cynoscion nobilis*), giant sea bass (*Stereolepis gigas*), rockfishes (*Sebastodes* spp.), California halibut (*Paralichthys californicus*), yellowtail (*Seriola dorsalis*), barracuda (*Sphyraena argentea*), groupers (*Mycteroperca* spp.), and such other species as are commonly taken incidentally in fishing for the above-mentioned species, and for anchoveta (*Cetengraulis mysticetus*), northern anchovy (*Engraulis mordax*) and Pacific sardine (*Sardinops caerulea*) exclusively as tuna bait fish;

(b) The fishing referred to in subparagraph (a) above will continue during five years beginning on January 1, 1968, up to a total volume that will not exceed the total catch taken by U.S. vessels in the five years immediately preceding that date; and

(c) U.S. fishing vessels will be permitted, during the same term of five years, to continue sport or recreational fishing in the waters indicated.

3. Mexican fishermen will be permitted to continue their activities within the exclusive fishery zone of the United States, in regards to the Gulf of Mexico:

(a) In the waters between 9 and 12 nautical miles measured from the base line from which the breadth of the territorial sea is measured, off the mainland and around the islands of the United States, from the maritime boundary indicated in paragraph 1 (a) above to a line on the 26th parallel of north latitude connecting points 9 and 12 miles from the said baseline on the West Coast of Florida where fishing vessels of Mexico have carried on fishing traditionally and in a sustained manner, they will be permitted to fish for shrimp and other genera that are captured incidentally, as well as to fish for snappers (genera *Lutjanus*, *Rhomboplites*, *Ocyurus*, *Etelis*, *Holocentrus* and *Pristipomoides*); and

(b) The fishing referred to in subparagraph (a) above will continue during five years beginning on January 1, 1968, up to a total volume that will not exceed the total catch taken by Mexican vessels in the five years immediately preceding that date.

4. In the maritime waters off the United States coast on the Pacific Ocean:

(a) In the waters between 9 and 12 nautical miles measured from the baseline from which the breadth of the territorial sea is measured, off the mainland and around the islands of the United States, from the maritime boundary indicated in paragraph 2 (a) above, to a western extension of the California-Oregon border (42° north latitude) where fishing vessels of Mexico have carried on fishing traditionally and in a sustained manner, they will be permitted to fish for Pacific mackerel (*Pneumatophorus* spp.), yellowfin tuna (*Thunnus albacares*), bluefin tuna (*Thunnus thynnus*), albacore (*Thunnus alalunga*), yellowtail (*Seriola dorsalis*), hake (*Merluccius* spp.), giant sea bass (*Stereolepis gigas*), rockfishes (*Sebastodes* spp.), and such other species as are commonly taken incidentally in fishing for tuna, as well as anchoveta (*Cetengraulis mysticetus*), northern anchovy (*Engraulis mordax*) and Pacific sardine (*Sardinops caerulea*), these last ones exclusively as tuna bait fish; and

(b) The fishing referred to in subparagraph (a) above will continue during five years beginning on January 1, 1968, up to a total volume that will not exceed the total catch taken by Mexican vessels in the five years immediately preceding that date.

5. In the event that the International Boundary and Water Commission, United States and Mexico, is unable to complete the lines referred to in paragraphs 1(a), 2(a), 3(a) and 4(a) prior to January 1, 1968, it will, prior to that date, for the purposes of this agreement, prepare lines to be used as provisional boundaries until the two countries are able to agree on permanent boundaries of their exclusive fishery zones.

6. In view of the fact that the catch by United States vessels within the exclusive fishery zone of Mexico and the catch by Mexican vessels within the exclusive fishery zone of the United States have not substantially increased during recent years, both Governments agree that said catches should not increase, and because of this they do not consider it necessary to establish during the five years beginning January 1, 1968 specific control measures, other than the following:

(a) The Government of the United States of America will submit to the Government of Mexico, and the latter will submit to the former, before January 1, 1968, or, at the latest, 30 days after that date, a report designating the areas now included within the exclusive fishery zone of the other country where its fishermen have operated in a sustained manner during the years 1963 to 1966 inclusive, indicating the species caught and the volume of each species, and the two Governments will submit to each other similar reports for the year 1967 no later than June 30, 1968;

(b) The two Governments will report to each other before January 1, 1968, or, at the latest, 30 days after that date, the number of vessels and the types and net tonnage of said vessels as well as the types of fishing gear used during the previous years by their respective nationals;

(c) The two Governments will exchange, no later than January 31 of each year, and at such other times as it may become necessary owing to special circumstances, lists of vessels that will operate under the terms of the present agreement;

(d) Representatives of the two Governments will meet annually on mutually agreeable dates to review the operation of this agreement and to determine the need for any additional arrangements. To facilitate this review, the Government of the United States will submit to the Government of Mexico, and the latter will submit to the former, as soon as practicable after January 1, but not later than April 1, each year a report on the fishing activities of its nationals in the exclusive fishery zone of the other country, indicating the volume of catch of each species authorized to be taken and the areas in which such catches were made.

7. The United States and Mexican fishermen may continue to use, within the exclusive fishery zone of the other country, only vessels and fishing gear not prohibited by the laws of the respective country and of the same types as those employed during the five years prior to January 1, 1968, except that technological improvements to existing types of vessels and gear are not precluded, provided they are not inconsistent with the legislation of the respective country.

8. Notwithstanding the limitations on fishing indicated in paragraphs 1, 2, 3, 4, and 7 of this agreement, each Government may establish additional limitations when, in its judgment, they become indispensable in order to protect the living resources of the sea in the exclusive fishery zone under its jurisdiction, or when each Government or both Governments must establish extraordinary restrictions pursuant to resolutions or recommendations of international organizations of which they are members. In any of these eventualities, the interested Government will consult with the other Government before establishing the new limitations and will notify the other Government 60 days in advance of their application in order to reasonably allow the fishermen of the other country to adjust their activities accordingly.

9. The United States of America and the United Mexican States, in accordance with their respective laws on the exclusive fishery zone,

will exercise within their respective zones the same exclusive rights with respect to fisheries as they exercise in their territorial sea. Nevertheless, without renouncing their sovereign powers and in order to respect the traditional fisheries by their respective nationals in the zone of the other country during the period indicated in this agreement, both Governments state that it is their intention neither to impose duties or taxes nor to impose other fiscal obligations, nor to propose to their respective Congresses the establishment of financial burdens upon the fishermen of the other country, who, within the terms of this agreement, will continue to operate in the waters within their respective exclusive fishery zones during the five years beginning January 1, 1968.

10. Notwithstanding the provisions of the previous paragraph, if either of the two Governments, due to circumstances which may arise during the life of this agreement, should deem it necessary or convenient to establish and collect such taxes, duties or fiscal obligations from the fishermen of the other country, it will first grant the other Government the opportunity to express its point of view. If, finally, such taxes, duties or obligations are established, the other Government, in strict reciprocity, will have the right to impose identical or similar fiscal measures, within its exclusive fishery zone, upon the fishermen of the country that first applied them.

11. For purposes of this agreement, the Government of Mexico will permit only vessels flying the flag of the United States of America to continue to operate within its exclusive fishery zone. For purposes of this agreement, only vessels flying the Mexican flag will be permitted to operate within the exclusive fishery zone of the United States of America.

12. Any fishing vessel of either country operating under the present agreement which acts contrary to the provisions of the agreement will not have the protection of the agreement in the particular case and will be subject exclusively to the legal regime, penal and administrative, of the country having jurisdiction over the exclusive fisheries zone.

13. The Government of the United States understands that neither the enactment of the Mexican law on the exclusive fishery zone of the nation nor the provisions of the present agreement imply *ipso facto* and of themselves any change regarding the legal regime on the exploitation of the living resources of the Mexican territorial sea, including the provisions of Mexico's law relating to the imposition of fees and taxes on foreign fishermen who fish within Mexico's territorial sea, since the law on the fishery zone of the nation, in accordance with its Article 2 (transitory), only repeals previous provisions contrary to it, and this agreement, as was expressed in the points of initial consideration, is based on said law.

14. The Government of the United States of America will cooperate with the Government of Mexico in the formulation and execution of a program of scientific research and conservation of the stocks of shrimp and fish of common concern off the coast of Mexico,

consistent with the Convention on Fishing and Conservation of Living Resources of the High Seas, opened for signature at Geneva on April 29, 1958,[1] to which both Governments are parties. The two Governments at an appropriate time will meet to make the special arrangements necessary to formulate and execute such a program.

15. The provisions of this agreement will be enforced by the Government of the United States of America and by the Government of Mexico in their respective exclusive fishing zones.

16. This agreement shall be in effect for a period of five years beginning on January 1, 1968, provided that either Party may denounce the agreement at any time after one year from that date if in its judgment the agreement is not operating satisfactorily. Such denunciation shall have the effect of terminating the agreement six months from the date of the formal notice of denunciation.

If Your Excellency's Government agrees with the terms and conditions previously stated, that have been duly approved and accepted by my Government, I submit they be considered as a formal proposal, with the understanding that this note and the reply of Your Excellency stating the approval and acceptance of the note by the Government of Mexico, will constitute a formal agreement between our two Governments.

Accept, Excellency, the renewed assurances of my highest consideration.

DEAN RUSK

No. 5710. EXCHANGE OF NOTES CONSTITUTING AN AGREEMENT[1] BETWEEN ICELAND AND THE UNITED KINGDOM OF GREAT BRITAIN AND NORTHERN IRELAND SETTLING THE FISHERIES DISPUTE BETWEEN THE GOVERNMENT OF ICELAND AND THE GOVERNMENT OF THE UNITED KINGDOM OF GREAT BRITAIN AND NORTHERN IRELAND. REYKJAVIK, 11 MARCH 1961

March 11, 1961

I

Your Excellency,

I have the honour to refer to the discussions which have taken place in Reykjavik and London between our Governments concerning the fisheries dispute between our two countries. In view of these discussions my Government is willing to settle the dispute on the following basis:

1. The United Kingdom Government will no longer object to a twelve-mile fishery zone around Iceland measured from the base lines specified in paragraph 2 below which relate solely to the delimitation of that zone.

2. The base lines, which will be used for the purpose referred to in paragraph 1 above, will be those set out in the Icelandie Regulation No. 70 of June 30, 1958, as modified by the use of the base lines drawn between the following points:

A. Point 1 (Horn) to Point 5 (Asbuoarrif).
B. Point 12 (Langanes) to Point 16 (Glettinganes).
C. Point 51 (Geirfugladrangur) to Point 42 (Skalasnagi).
D. Point 35 (Geirfuglasker) to Point 39 (Eldeyjardrangur).

These modifications will enter into force immediately.

3. For a period of three years from the date of Your Excellency's reply to this Note, the Icelandic Government will not object to vessels registered in the United Kingdom fishing within the outer six miles of the fishery zone referred to in paragraphs 1 and 2 above within the following areas during the periods specified:

[1]Came into force on 11 March 1961 by the exchange of the said notes.

(i) Horn (Point 1) - Langanes (Point 12)(June to September).
(ii) Langanes (Point 12) - Glettinganes (Point 16) (May to December).
(iii) Glettinganes (Point 16) - Setusker (Point 20) (January to April and July to August).
(iv) Setusker (Point 20) - Meoallandssandur I (Point 30)(March to July)
(v) Meoallandssandur I (Point 30 - 20°west longitude (April to August).
(vi) 20°west longitude - Geirfugladrangur (Point 51) (March to May).
(vii) Geirfugladrangur (Point 51) - Bjargtangar (Point 43) (March to May).

4. There will, however, be no fishing by vessels registered in the United Kingdom in the outer six miles of the fishery zone referred to in paragraphs 1 and 2 during the aforesaid period of three years in the following areas:
(i) Between 63° 37' north latitude and 64° 13' north latitude (Faxafloi).
(ii) Between 64° 40' north latitude and 64° 52' north latitude (Snaefellsnes).
(iii) Between 65° north latitude and 65° 20' north latitude (Breioafjorour).
(iv) Between Bjargtangar (Point 43) and Horn (Point 1).
(v) Off the mainland in the area delimited by lines drawn from the southernmost point of Grimsey to base points 6 and 8.
(vi) Between 14° 58' west longitude and 15° 32' west longitude (Myrabugt).
(vii) Between 16° 12' west longitude and 16° 46' west longitude (Ingolfshofoi).

The Icelandic Government will continue to work for the implementation of the Althing Resolution of May 5, 1959, regarding the extension of fisheries jurisdiction around Iceland, but shall give to the United Kingdom Government six months' notice of such extension and, in case of a dispute in relation to such extension, the matter shall, at the request of either party, be referred to the International Court of Justice.

I have the honour to suggest that this Note and Your Excellency's reply thereto, confirming that its contents are acceptable to the United Kingdom Government, shall be registered with the Secretary General of the United Nations in accordance with Article 102 of the

United Nations Charter, and further to suggest that a settlement on this basis shall become effective forthwith.

I avail myself of this opportunity to renew to Your Excellency the assurances of my highest consideration.

(Signed)Guomundur I. GUOMUNDSSON

His Excellency Mr. Andrew C. Stewart
Ambassador Extraordinary and Plenipotentiary
British Embassy
Reykjavik

II

BRITISH EMBASSY
REYKJAVIK

March 11, 1961

Your Excellency,

I have the honour to acknowledge receipt of Your Excellency's Note of today's date reading as follows:

(See note I)

I have the honour to confirm that in view of the exceptional dependence of the Icelandic nation upon coastal fisheries for their livelihood and economic development, and without prejudice to the rights of the United Kingdom under international Law towards a third party, the contents of Your Excellency's Note are acceptable to the United Kingdom and the settlement of the dispute has been accomplished on the terms stated therein. I also confirm that the United Kingdom Government agrees that the settlement becomes effective forthwith and that the Notes exchanged today shall be registered with the Secretary-General of the United Nations in accordance with Article 102 of the United Nations Charter.

I avail myself of this opportunity to renew to Your Excellency the assurance of my highest consideration.

(Signed) Charles STEWART

His Excellency Mr. Guomundur I. Guomundsson
Minister for Foreign Affairs
Reykjavik

PERMANENT MISSION OF ICELAND
To The United Nations

The Permanent Mission of Iceland to the United Nations presents its compliments to the Permanent Missions and to the Offices of the Permanent Observers to the United Nations and has the honour to inform them that on February 15, 1972 the Althing of Iceland adopted unanimously the following resolution on the extension of the fisheries limits around Iceland:

"The Althing reiterates the fundamental policy of the Icelandic people that the continental shelf of Iceland and the superjacent waters are within the jurisdiction of Iceland and adopts the following resolution:

1. That the fishery limits will be extended to 50 miles from base-lines around the country, to become effective not later than September 1, 1972.

2. That the Governments of the United Kingdom and the Federal Republic of Germany be again informed that because of the vital interests of the nation and owing to changed circumstances the notes concerning fishery limits exchanged in 1961 are no longer applicable and that their provisions do not constitute an obligation for Iceland.

3. That efforts to reach a solution of the problems connected with the extension be continued through discussions with the Governments of the United Kingdom and the Federal Republic of Germany.

4. That effective supervision of the fishstocks in the Iceland area be continued in consultation with marine biologists and that the necessary measures be taken for the protection of the fishstocks and specified areas in order to prevent overfishing.

5. That cooperation with other nations be continued concerning the necessary measures to prevent marine pollution and authorizes the Government to declare unilaterally a special jurisdiction with regard to pollution in the seas surrounding Iceland."

The Permanent Mission of Iceland avails itself of this opportunity to renew to the Permanent Missions and the Offices of the Permanent Observers the assurances of its highest consideration.

New York, 17 February 1972

ICELAND

REGULATIONS*
Concerning the Fishery Limits off Iceland

ARTICLE I

The fishery limits off Iceland shall be drawn 50 nautical miles outside baselines drawn between the following points:

1.	Horn	66°27'4 N	22°24'3 W
2.	Asbudarrif	66°08'1 -	20°11'0 -
3.	Raudinupur	66°30'7 -	16°32'4 -
4.	Rifstangi	66°32'3 -	16°11'8 -
5.	Hraunhafnartangi	66°32'2 -	16°01'5 -
6.	Langanes	66°22'7 -	14°31'9 -
7.	Glettinganes	65°30'5 -	13°36'3 -
8.	Nordfjardarhorn	65°10'0 -	13°30'8 -
9.	Gerpir	65°04'7 -	13°29'6 -
10.	Holmur	64°58'9 -	13°30'6 -
11.	Hvitingar	64°23'9 -	14°28'0 -
12.	Stokksnes	64°14'1 -	14°58'4 -
13.	Hrollaugseyjar	64°01'7 -	15°58'7 -
14.	Tvisker	63°55'7 -	16°11'3-
15.	Ingolfshofdi	63°47'8 -	16°38'5 -
16.	Hvalsiki	63°44'1 -	17°33'5 -
17.	Medallandssandur 1	63°32'4 -	17°55'6 -
18.	Medallandssandur 11	63°30'6 -	17°59'9 -
19.	Myrnatangi	63°27'4 -	18°11'8 -
20.	Kotlutangi	63°23'4 -	18°42'8 -
21.	Lundadrangur	63°23'5 -	19°07'5 -
22.	Geirfuglasker	63°19'0 -	20°29'9 -
23.	Eldeyjardrangur	63°43'8 -	22°59'4 -
24.	Geirfugladrangur	63°40'7 -	23°17'1 -
25.	Skalasnagl	64°51'3 -	24°02'5 -
26.	Bjargtangar	65°30'2 -	24°32'1 -
27.	Kopanes	65°48'4 -	24°06'0 -
28.	Bardi	66°03'7 -	23°47'4 -
29.	Straumnes	66°25'7 -	23°08'4 -
30.	Kogur	66°28'3 -	22°55'5 -
31.	Horn	66°27'9 -	22°28'2 -

* Official English language text of the Icelandic Government regulations extending the fisheries limits to 50 miles effective September 1, 1972. The regulations were signed on July 14, 1972.

Limits shall also be drawn around the following points 50 nautical miles seaward:

32.	Kobeinsey	67°08'8 N 18°40'6 W
33.	Hvalbakur	64°35'8 - 13°16'6 -

Each nautical mile shall be equal to 1852 metres.

ARTICLE 2

Within the fishery limits all fishing activities by foreign vessels shall be prohibited in accordance with the provisions of Law No. 33 of 19 June 1922, concerning fishing inside the Fishery Limits.

ARTICLE 3

Icelandic vessels using bottom trawl, mid-water trawl or Danish seine-netting are prohibited from fishing inside the fishery limits in the following areas and periods:

1. Off the North-East Coast during the period 1 April to 1 June in an area which in the west is demarcated by a line drawn true North from Rifstangi (Basepoint 4) and in the east by a line which is drawn true North-East from Langanes (Basepoint 6).

2. Off the South-Coast during the period 20 March to 20 April in an area demarcated by lines drawn between the following points:

a) 63°32'0 N 21°25'0 W
b) 63°00'0 - 21°25'0 -
c) 63°00'0 - 22°00'0 -
d) 63°32'0 - 22°00'0 -

With these exceptions Icelandic vessels using bottom trawl, mid-water trawl or Danish seine-netting shall be allowed within the fishery limits in accordance with the provisions of Law No. 62 of 18 May 1967, concerning the Prohibition of Fishing with Trawl and Mid-water Trawl, cfr. Law No. 21 of 10 May 1969, or special provisions made before these regulations become effective.

ARTICLE 4

Trawlers shall have all their fishing gear properly stowed aboard while staying in areas where fishing is prohibited.

ARTICLE 5

Fisheries statistics shall be forwarded to the Fiskifelag Islands (Fisheries Association of Iceland) in the manner prescribed by Law No. 55 of 27 June 1941, concerning Catch and Fisheries Reports.

If the Ministry of Fisheries envisages the possibility of overfishing, the Ministry may limit the number of fishing vessels and the maximum catch of each vessel.

ARTICLE 6

Violations of the provisions of these Regulations shall be subject to the penalties provided for by Law No. 62 of 18 May 1967, concerning the Prohibition of Fishing with Trawl and Mid-water Trawl, as amended, Law No. 40 of 9 June 1960, concerning Limited Permissions for Trawling within the Fishery Limits off Iceland under Scientific Supervision, Law No. 33 of 19 June 1922, concerning Fishing inside the Fishery Limits, as amended, or if, the provisions of said Laws do not apply, to fines from kr. 1000.00 to kr. 100,000.00.

ARTICLE 7

These Regulations are promulgated in accordance with Law No. 44 of 5 April 1948, concerning the Scientific Conservation of the Continental Shelf Fisheries, cfr. Law No. 81 of 8 December 1952. When these Regulations become effective, Regulations No. 3 of 11 March 1961, concerning the Fishery Limits off Iceland shall cease to be effective.

ARTICLE 8

These regulations become effective on 1 September 1972.

Ministry of Fisheries, 14 July 1972

Ludvik Josepsson.

Jon L. Arnalds

RESOLUTION ON SPECIAL SITUATIONS RELATING TO COASTAL FISHERIES ADOPTED AT GENEVA ON 26 APRIL 1958

The United Nations Conference on the Law of the Sea,

Having considered the situation of countries or territories whose people are overwhelmingly dependent upon coastal fisheries for their livelihood or economic development,

Having considered also the situation of countries whose coastal population depends primarily on coastal fisheries for the animal protein of its diet and whose fishing methods are mainly limited to local fishing from small boats,

Recognizing that such situations call for exceptional measures befitting particular needs,

Considering that, because of the limited scope and exceptional nature of those situations, any measures adopted to meet them would be complementary to provisions incorporated in a universal system of international law,

Believing that States should collaborate to secure just treatment of such situations by regional agreements or by other means of international co-operation,

Recommends:

1. That where, for the purpose of conservation, it becomes necessary to limit the total catch of a stock or stocks of fish in an area of the high seas adjacent to the territorial sea of a coastal State, any other States fishing in that area should collaborate with the coastal State to secure just treatment of such situation, by establishing agreed measures which shall recognize and preferential requirements of the coastal State resulting from its dependence upon the fishery concerned while having regard to the interests of the other States;
2. That appropriate conciliation and arbitral procedures shall be established for the settlement of any disagreement.

"POLICY OF THE UNITED STATES WITH RESPECT TO COASTAL FISHERIES IN CERTAIN AREAS OF THE HIGH SEAS

"BY THE PRESIDENT OF THE UNITED STATES OF AMERICA

"A PROCLAMATION

"WHEREAS for some years the Government of the United States of America has viewed with concern the inadequacy of present arrangements for the protection and perpetuation of the fishery resources contiguous to its coasts, and in view of the potentially disturbing effect of this situation, has carefully studied the possibility of improving the jurisdictional basis for conservation measures and international cooperation in this field; and

"WHEREAS such fishery resources have a special importance to coastal communities as a source of livelihood and to the nation as a food and industrial resource; and

"WHEREAS the progressive development of new methods and techniques contributes to intensified fishing over wide sea areas and in certain cases seriously threatens fisheries with depletion; and

"WHEREAS there is an urgent need to protect coastal fishery resources from destructive exploitation, having due regard to conditions peculiar to each region and situation and to the special rights and equities of the coastal State and of any other State which may have established a legitimate interest therein;

"NOW, THEREFORE, I, HARRY S. TRUMAN, President of the United States of America, do hereby proclaim the following policy of the United States of America with respect to coastal fisheries in certain areas of the high seas:

"In view of the pressing need for conservation and protection of fishery resources, the Government of the United States regards it as proper to establish conservation zones in those areas of the high seas contiguous to the coasts of the United States wherein fishing activities have been or in the future may be developed and maintained on a substantial scale. Where such activities have been or shall hereafter be developed and maintained by its nationals alone, the United States regards it as proper to establish explicitly bounded conservation zones in which fishing activities shall be subject to the regulation and control of the United States. Where such activities have been or shall hereafter be legitimately developed and maintained jointly by nationals of the United States and nationals of other States, explicitly bounded conservation zones may be established under agreements between the United States and such other States; and all fishing activities in such zones shall be subject to regulation and control as provided in such agreements. The right of any State to establish conservation zones off its shores in accordance with the above principles is conceded, provided that corresponding recognition is given to any fishing interests of nationals of the United States which may exist in such areas. The character as high seas of the areas in which such conservation zones are established and the right to their free and unimpeded navigation are in no way thus affected.

"IN WITNESS WHEREOF, I have hereunto set my hand and caused the seal of the United States of America to be affixed.

"DONE at the City of Washington this twenty-eighth day of September, in the year of our Lord nineteen hundred and forty-five, and of the Independence of the United States of America the one hundred and seventieth.

[SEAL]

HARRY S. TRUMAN

By the President:
DEAN ACHESON
Acting Secretary of State."

Proclamation No. 2668, "Policy of the United States With Respect to Coastal Fisheries in Certain Areas of the High Seas", Sept. 28, 1945, 10 *Fed. Reg.* 12304; 3 CFR, 1943–1948 Comp., p. 68.

The companion Executive order contemplating the establishment of fishery conservation zones, issued by President Truman on September 28, 1945, read:

"EXECUTIVE ORDER

"PROVIDING FOR THE ESTABLISHMENT OF FISHERY CONSERVATION ZONES

"By virtue of and pursuant to the authority vested in me as President of the United States, it is hereby ordered that the Secretary of State and the Secretary of the Interior shall from time to time jointly recommend the establishment by Executive orders of fishery conservation zones in areas of the high seas contiguous to the coasts of the United States, pursuant to the proclamation entitled 'Policy of the United States With Respect to Coastal Fisheries in Certain Areas of the High Seas,' this day signed by me, and said Secretaries shall in each case recommend provisions to be incorporated in such orders relating to the administration, regulation and control of the fishery resources of and fishing activities in such zones, pursuant to authority of law heretofore or hereafter provided.

HARRY S. TRUMAN

THE WHITE HOUSE
September 28, 1945"

Executive Order No. 9634, Sept. 28, 1945, 10 *Fed. Reg.* 12305; 3 CFR, 1943–1948 Comp., p. 437.

A White House press release issued the same day—September 28, 1945—explained (so far as the Fisheries Proclamation and the companion Executive order were concerned):

"The President issued two proclamations on September 28 asserting the jurisdiction of the United States over the natural resources of the continental shelf under the high seas contiguous to the coasts of the United States and its territories, and providing for the establishment of conservation zones for the protection of fisheries in certain areas of the high seas contiguous to the United States. The action of the President in regard to both the resources of the continental shelf and the conservation of high-seas fisheries in which the United States has an interest was taken on the recommendation of the Secretary of State and the Secretary of the Interior.

"Two companion Executive orders were also issued by the President. One reserved and set aside the resources of the continental shelf under the high seas and placed them for administrative purposes, pending legislative action, under the jurisdiction and control of the Secretary of the Interior. The other provided for the establishment by Executive orders, on recommendation of the Secretary of State and the Secretary of the Interior, of fishery conservation zones in areas of the high seas contiguous to the coasts of the United States.

"Until the present the only high-seas fisheries in the regulation of which the United States has participated, under treaties or conventions, are those for whales, Pacific halibut, and fur seals.

"In areas where fisheries have been or shall hereafter be developed and maintained by nationals of the United States alone, explicitly bounded zones will be set up in which the United States may regulate and control all fishing activities.

"In other areas where the nationals of other countries as well as our own have developed or shall hereafter legitimately develop fisheries, zones may be established by agreements between the United States and such other states, and joint regulations and control will be put into effect.

"The United States will recognize the rights of other countries to establish conservation zones off their own coasts where the interests of nationals of the United States are recognized in the same manner that we recognize the interests of the nationals of the other countries.

"The assertion of this policy has long been advocated by conservationists, including a substantial section of the fishing industry of the United States, since regulation of a fishery resource within territorial waters cannot control the misuse or prevent the depletion of that resource through uncontrolled fishery activities conducted outside of the commonly accepted limits of territorial jurisdiction.

"As a result of the establishment of this new policy, the United States will be able to protect effectively, for instance, its most valuable fishery, that for the Alaska salmon. Through painstaking conservation efforts and scientific management the United States has made excellent progress in maintaining the salmon at high levels. However, since the salmon spends a considerable portion of its life in the open sea, uncontrolled fishery activities on the high seas, by nationals of either the United States or other countries, have constituted an ever present menace to the salmon fishery."

XIII *Bulletin*, Department of State, No. 327, Sept. 30, 1945, p. 484.

27. PAKISTAN

PROCLAMATION[1] BY THE PRESIDENT OF PAKISTAN DEALING WITH FISHING RIGHTS IN AREAS OF THE HIGH SEAS ADJACENT TO THE TERRITORIAL WATERS OF PAKISTAN, dated 19 February 1966

"*Whereas* the coastal communities of Pakistan have from time immemorial been engaged in fishing activities in the high seas adjacent to its territorial waters;

And whereas certain areas of these high seas provide fisheries, which contribute to the food and means of livelihood of large sections of the population;

And whereas Pakistan has a special interest in maintaining the productivity of the living resources in all such areas;

Now, therefore, I, Field Marshal Mohammad Ayub Khan, President of Pakistan, do hereby proclaim and declare as follows:—

(1) Pakistan shall have exclusive fishing rights in areas of the high seas adjacent to the territorial waters of Pakistan within a distance of twelve nautical miles from the coast-line;

(2) The Government of Pakistan may from time to time:

(i) establish conservation zones in areas of the high seas adjacent to the territorial waters of Pakistan, but within a distance of one hundred nautical miles from the outer limits of those waters;

(ii) take conservation measures in the zones so established in order to protect fisheries and other living resources of the sea from indiscriminate exploitation, depletion or destruction; and

(iii) subject to the provisions of any international agreement or convention to which Pakistan is, or may hereafter become a party, regulate all fishing activities in the said area of the high seas for the purpose aforesaid."

---

[1] *Notification* of the Ministry of Agriculture and Works, dated 19 February, 1966.

No. 7302. CONVENTION[1] ON THE CONTINENTAL SHELF. DONE AT GENEVA, ON 29 APRIL 1958

The States Parties to this Convention

Have agreed as follows :

Article 1

For the purpose of these articles, the term " continental shelf " is used as referring (*a*) to the seabed and subsoil of the submarine areas adjacent to the coast but outside the area of the territorial sea, to a depth of 200 metres or, beyond that limit, to where the depth of the superjacent waters admits of the exploitation of the natural resources of the said areas; (*b*) to the seabed and subsoil of similar submarine areas adjacent to the coasts of islands.

Article 2

1. The coastal State exercises over the continental shelf sovereign rights for the purpose of exploring it and exploiting its natural resources.

2. The rights referred to in paragraph 1 of this article are exclusive in the sense that if the coastal State does not explore the continental shelf or exploit its natural resources, no one may undertake these activities, or make a claim to the continental shelf, without the express consent of the coastal State.

[1] In accordance with article 11 (1), the Convention came into force on 10 June 1964, the thirtieth day following the date of deposit of the twenty-second instrument of ratification or accession. The following States have deposited their instruments of ratification or accession (*a*) on the dates indicated :

Australia	14 May	1963
Bulgaria	31 August	1962 (*a*)
Byelorussian Soviet Socialist Republic	27 February	1961
Cambodia	18 March	1960 (*a*)
Colombia	8 January	1962
Czechoslovakia	31 August	1961
Denmark	12 June	1963
Guatemala	27 November	1961
Haiti	29 March	1960
Israel	6 September	1961
Madagascar	31 July	1962 (*a*)
Malaysia	21 December	1960 (*a*)
Poland	29 June	1962
Portugal	8 January	1963
Romania	12 December	1961 (*a*)
Senegal	25 April	1961 (*a*)
South Africa	9 April	1963 (*a*)
Ukrainian Soviet Socialist Republic	12 January	1961
Union of Soviet Socialist Republics	22 November	1960
United Kingdom of Great Britain and Northern Ireland	11 May	1964
United States of America	12 April	1961
Venezuela (with express reservation in respect of article 6 of the Convention)	15 August	1961

3. The rights of the coastal State over the continental shelf do not depend on occupation, effective or notional, or on any express proclamation.

4. The natural resources referred to in these articles consist of the mineral and other non-living resources of the seabed and subsoil together with living organisms belonging to sedentary species, that is to say, organisms which, at the harvestable stage, either are immobile on or under the seabed or are unable to move except in constant physical contact with the seabed or the subsoil.

Article 3

The rights of the coastal State over the continental shelf do not affect the legal status of the superjacent waters as high seas, or that of the airspace above those waters.

Article 4

Subject to its right to take reasonable measures for the exploration of the continental shelf and the exploitation of its natural resources, the coastal State may not impede the laying or maintenance of submarine cables or pipe lines on the continental shelf.

Article 5

1. The exploration of the continental shelf and the exploitation of its natural resources must not result in any unjustifiable interference with navigation, fishing or the conservation of the living resources of the sea, nor result in any interference with fundamental oceanographic or other scientific research carried out with the intention of open publication.

2. Subject to the provisions of paragraphs 1 and 6 of this article, the coastal State is entitled to construct and maintain or operate on the continental shelf installations and other devices necessary for its exploration and the exploitation of its natural resources, and to establish safety zones around such installations and devices and to take in those zones measures necessary for their protection.

3. The safety zones referred to in paragraph 2 of this article may extend to a distance of 500 metres around the installations and other devices which have been erected, measured from each point of their outer edge. Ships of all nationalities must respect these safety zones.

4. Such installations and devices, though under the jurisdiction of the coastal State, do not possess the status of islands. They have no territorial sea of their own, and their presence does not affect the delimitation of the territorial sea of the coastal State.

5. Due notice must be given of the construction of any such installations, and permanent means for giving warning of their presence must be maintained. Any installations which are abandoned or disused must be entirely removed.

6. Neither the installations or devices, nor the safety zones around them, may be established where interference may be caused to the use of recognized sea lanes essential to international navigation.

7. The coastal State is obliged to undertake, in the safety zones, all appropriate measures for the protection of the living resources of the sea from harmful agents.

8. The consent of the coastal State shall be obtained in respect of any research concerning the continental shelf and undertaken there. Nevertheless the coastal State shall not normally withhold its consent if the request is submitted by a qualified institution with a view to purely scientific research into the physical or biological characteristics of the continental shelf, subject to the proviso that the coastal State shall have the right, if it so desires, to participate or to be represented in the research, and that in any event the results shall be published.

Article 6

1. Where the same continental shelf is adjacent to the territories of two or more States whose coasts are opposite each other, the boundary of the continental shelf appertaining to such States shall be determined by agreement between them. In the absence of agreement, and unless another boundary line is justified by special circumstances, the boundary is the median line, every point of which is equidistant from the nearest points of the baselines from which the breadth of the territorial sea of each State is measured.

2. Where the same continental shelf is adjacent to the territories of two adjacent States, the boundary of the continental shelf shall be determined by agreement between them. In the absence of agreement, and unless another boundary line is justified by special circumstances, the boundary shall be determined by application of the principle of equidistance from the nearest points of the baselines from which the breadth of the territorial sea of each State is measured.

3. In delimiting the boundaries of the continental shelf, any lines which are drawn in accordance with the principles set out in paragraphs 1 and 2 of this article should be defined with reference to charts and geographical features as they exist at a particular date, and reference should be made to fixed permanent identifiable points on the land.

Article 7

The provisions of these articles shall not prejudice the right of the coastal State to exploit the subsoil by means of tunnelling irrespective of the depth of water above the subsoil.

Article 8

This Convention shall, until 31 October 1958, be open for signature by all States Members of the United Nations or of any of the specialized agencies, and by any other State invited by the General Assembly of the United Nations to become a Party to the Convention.

Article 9

This Convention is subject to ratification. The instruments of ratification shall be deposited with the Secretary-General of the United Nations.

Article 10

This Convention shall be open for accession by any States belonging to any of the categories mentioned in article 8. The instruments of accession shall be deposited with the Secretary-General of the United Nations.

Article 11

1. This Convention shall come into force on the thirtieth day following the date of deposit of the twenty-second instrument of ratification or accession with the Secretary-General of the United Nations.

2. For each State ratifying or acceding to the Convention after the deposit of the twenty-second instrument of ratification or accession, the Convention shall enter into force on the thirtieth day after deposit by such State of its instrument of ratification or accession.

Article 12

1. At the time of signature, ratification or accession, any State may make reservations to articles of the Convention other than to articles 1 to 3 inclusive.

2. Any Contracting State making a reservation in accordance with the preceding paragraph may at any time withdraw the reservation by a communication to that effect addressed to the Secretary-General of the United Nations.

Article 13

1. After the expiration of a period of five years from the date on which this Convention shall enter into force, a request for the revision of this Convention

may be made at any time by any Contracting Party by means of a notification in writing addressed to the Secretary-General of the United Nations.

2. The General Assembly of the United Nations shall decide upon the steps, if any, to be taken in respect of such request.

Article 14

The Secretary-General of the United Nations shall inform all States Members of the United Nations and the other States referred to in article 8 :

(*a*) Of signatures to this Convention and of the deposit of instruments of ratification or accession, in accordance with articles 8, 9 and 10;

(*b*) Of the date on which this Convention will come into force, in accordance with article 11;

(*c*) Of requests for revision in accordance with article 13;

(*d*) Of reservations to this Convention, in accordance with article 12.

Article 15

The original of this Convention, of which the Chinese, English, French, Russian and Spanish texts are equally authentic, shall be deposited with the Secretary-General of the United Nations, who shall send certified copies thereof to all States referred to in article 8.

In witness whereof the undersigned Plenipotentiaries, being duly authorized thereto by their respective Governments, have signed this Convention.

Done at Geneva, this twenty-ninth day of April one thousand nine hundred and fifty-eight.

"BY THE PRESIDENT OF THE UNITED STATES OF AMERICA

"A PROCLAMATION

"WHEREAS the Government of the United States of America, aware of the long range world-wide need for new sources of petroleum and other minerals, holds the view that efforts to discover and make available new supplies of these resources should be encouraged; and

"WHEREAS its competent experts are of the opinion that such resources underlie many parts of the continental shelf off the coasts of the United States of America, and that with modern technological progress their utilization is already practicable or will become so at an early date; and

"WHEREAS recognized jurisdiction over these resources is required in the interest of their conservation and prudent utilization when and as development is undertaken; and

"WHEREAS it is the view of the Government of the United States that the exercise of jurisdiction over the natural resources of the subsoil and sea bed of the continental shelf by the contiguous nation is reasonable and just, since the effectiveness of measures to utilize or conserve these resources would be contingent upon cooperation and protection from the shore, since the continental shelf may be regarded as an extension of the land-mass of the coastal nation and thus naturally appurtenant to it, since these resources frequently form a seaward extension of a pool or deposit lying within the territory, and since self-protection compels the coastal nation to keep close watch over activities off its shores which are of the nature necessary for utilization of these resources;

"NOW, THEREFORE, I, HARRY S. TRUMAN, President of the United States of America, do hereby proclaim the following policy of the United States of America with respect to the natural resources of the subsoil and sea bed of the continental shelf.

"Having concern for the urgency of conserving and prudently utilizing its natural resources, the Government of the United States regards the natural resources of the subsoil and sea bed of the continental shelf beneath the high seas but contiguous to the coasts of the United States as appertaining to the United States, subject to its jurisdiction and control. In cases where the continental shelf extends to the shores of another State, or is shared with an adjacent State, the boundary shall be determined by the United States and the State concerned in accordance with equitable principles. The character as high seas of the waters above the continental shelf and the right to their free and unimpeded navigation are in no way thus affected.

"IN WITNESS WHEREOF, I have hereunto set my hand and caused the seal of the United States of America to be affixed.

"DONE at the City of Washington this twenty-eighth day of September, in the year of our Lord nineteen hundred and forty-five, and of the Independence of the United States of America the one hundred and seventieth.

[SEAL]

HARRY S. TRUMAN

By the President:
DEAN ACHESON
Acting Secretary of State"

Proclamation No. 2667, "Policy of the United States With Respect to the Natural Resources of the Subsoil and Sea Bed of the Continental Shelf", Sept. 28, 1945, 10 *Fed. Reg.* 12303; 3 CFR, 1943–1948 Comp., p. 67; XIII *Bulletin*, Department of State, No. 327, Sept. 30, 1945, p. 485.

A White House press release issued on the same day, September 28, 1945, contained the following commentary:

"The President issued two proclamations on September 28 asserting the jurisdiction of the United States over the natural resources of the continental shelf under the high seas contiguous to the coasts of the United States and its territories, and providing for the establishment of conservation zones for the protection of fisheries in certain areas of the high seas contiguous to the United States. The action of the President in regard to both the resources of the continental shelf and the conservation of high-seas fisheries in which the United States has an interest was taken on the recommendation of the Secretary of State and the Secretary of the Interior.

"Two companion Executive orders were also issued by the President. One reserved and set aside the resources of the continental shelf under the high seas and placed them for administrative purposes, pending legislative action, under the jurisdiction and control of the Secretary of the Interior. The other provided for the establishment by Executive orders, on recommendation of the Secretary of State and the Secretary of the Interior, of fishery conservation zones in areas of the high seas contiguous to the coasts of the United States.

[Commentary with reference to fisheries omitted.]

. . . .

"The policy proclaimed by the President in regard to the jurisdiction over the continental shelf does not touch upon the question of Federal versus State control. It is concerned solely with establishing the jurisdiction of the United States from an international standpoint. It will, however, make possible the orderly development of an underwater area 750,000 square miles in extent. Generally, submerged land which is contiguous to the continent and which is covered by no more than 100 fathoms (600 feet) of water is considered as the continental shelf.

"Petroleum geologists believe that portions of the continental shelf beyond the three-mile limit contain valuable oil deposits. The study of sub-surface structures associated with oil deposits which have been discovered along the Gulf coast of Texas, for instance, indicates that corresponding deposits may underlie the offshore or submerged land. The trend of oil-productive salt domes extends directly into the Gulf of Mexico off the Texas coast. Oil is also being taken at present from wells within the three-mile limit off the coast of California. It is quite possible, geologists say, that the oil deposits extend beyond this traditional limit of national jurisdiction.

"Valuable deposits of minerals other than oil may also be expected to be found in these submerged areas. Ore mines now extend under the sea from the coasts of England, Chile, and other countries.

"While asserting jurisdiction and control of the United States over the mineral resources of the continental shelf, the proclamation in no wise abridges the right of free and unimpeded navigation of waters of the character of high seas above the shelf, nor does it extend the present limits of the territorial waters of the United States.

"The advance of technology prior to the present war had already made possible the exploitation of a limited amount of minerals from submerged lands within the three-mile limit. The rapid development of technical knowledge and equipment occasioned by the war now makes possible the determination of the resources of the submerged lands outside of the three-mile limit. With the need for the discovery of additional resources of petroleum and other minerals, it became advisable for the United States to make possible orderly development of these resources. The proclamation of the President is designed to serve this purpose."

XIII *Bulletin*, Department of State, No. 327, Sept. 30, 1945, pp. 484–485.

The Executive Order, "Reserving and Placing Certain Resources of the Continental Shelf under the Control and Jurisdiction of the Secretary of the Interior", signed by President Truman on September 28, 1945, provided:

"By virtue of and pursuant to the authority vested in me as President of the United States, it is ordered that the natural resources of the subsoil and sea bed of the continental shelf beneath the high seas but contiguous to the coasts of the United States declared this day by proclamation to appertain to the United States and to be subject to its jurisdiction and control, be and they are hereby reserved, set aside, and placed under the jurisdiction and control of the Secretary of the Interior for administrative purposes, pending the enactment of legislation in regard thereto. Neither this Order nor the aforesaid proclamation shall be deemed to affect the determination by legislation or judicial decree of any issues between the United States and the several states, relating to the ownership or control of the subsoil and sea bed of the continental shelf within or outside of the three-mile limit." Executive Order No. 9633, Sept. 28, 1945, 10 *Fed. Reg.* 12305; 3 CFR, 1943–1948 Comp., p. 437; XIII *Bulletin*, Department of State, No. 327, Sept. 30, 1945, pp. 486–487.

3. DECLARATION OF 23 OCTOBER 1968 BY THE GERMAN DEMOCRATIC REPUBLIC, THE POLISH PEOPLE'S REPUBLIC AND THE UNION OF SOVIET SOCIALIST REPUBLICS ON THE CONTINENTAL SHELF OF THE BALTIC SEA**

The Governments of the German Democratic Republic, the Polish People's Republic and the Union of Soviet Socialist Republics,

Being guided by the desire to deepen and extend good-neighbourly and friendly relations between the Baltic States,

Desiring to confirm and further develop the provisions of the 1958 Geneva Convention on the Continental Shelf in conformity with the specific conditions of the Baltic Sea,

Proceeding from the fact that the solution of the questions of delimiting and using the continental shelf of the Baltic Sea is of interest to all Baltic States,

Considering it desirable that other Baltic States adhere to the present Declaration,

Declare that:

1. In accordance with the provisions of the 1958 Geneva Convention on the Continental Shelf and inasmuch as the Baltic Sea is a shallow sea, the surface and subsoil of the bed of that sea constitute a continuous continental shelf which is subject to delimitation among the respective Baltic States.

2. Each Baltic State, in conformity with article 2 of the 1958 Geneva Convention on the Continental Shelf, has sovereign rights over its continental shelf in the Baltic Sea for the purposes of exploring and exploiting the natural resources of the sea-bed and the subsoil thereof.

3. The continental shelf of the Baltic Sea must be used by all States exclusively for peaceful purposes.

4. Delimitation of the continental shelf of the Baltic Sea must be carried out in conformity with the principles set forth in the 1958 Geneva Convention on the Continental Shelf and, in particular, in article 6 of the said Convention.

5. The baselines for measuring the breadth of the territorial sea established by each of the parties to the Declaration in conformity with articles 3 and 4 of the 1958 Geneva Convention on the Territorial Sea and the Contiguous Zone shall be reciprocally recognized and considered to be the baselines for delimiting the continental shelf.

6. The exact co-ordinates of the boundaries of the continental shelf in the Baltic Sea shall be determined by bilateral or multilateral agreements concluded between the States concerned.

7. The rights of each coastal State over the continental shelf shall in no way affect the legal status of the superjacent waters as high seas or that of the airspace above those waters.

8. Exploration, exploitation and other uses of the continental shelf of the Baltic Sea must not result in any unjustifiable interference with navigation, fishing or the conservation of the living resources of the sea.

9. No portions of the continental shelf of the Baltic Sea may be given over for exploration, exploitation or any other use to non-Baltic States, their nationals or firms.

10. The parties to the Declaration shall consult with each other on questions of mutual interest in connexion with the use of the continental shelf of the Baltic Sea.

11. Every Baltic State may accede to the present Declaration. Each such State shall become a party to the Declaration as soon as written notification is given to the Government of the Union of Soviet Socialist Republics that it accepts the principles contained therein.

DONE in Moscow on 23 October 1968 in one copy in the Russian language.

For the German Democratic Republic

H. BITTNER

For the Polish People's Republic

J. PTASINSKI

For the Union of Soviet Socialist Republics

A. GROMYKO

CONTINENTAL SHELF BOUNDARY: ITALY - YUGOSLAVIA

On January 8, 1968, the Governments of Italy and Yugoslavia signed an Agreement establishing a continental shelf boundary in the Adriatic Sea. Ratifications were exchanged and the Agreement came into force on January 21, 1970. Yugoslavia is a party to the 1958 Geneva Convention on the Continental Shelf. Italy is not a party to the Convention, but has enacted legislation concerning jurisdiction over the continental shelf (Act No. 613 of July 21, 1967, Law for Exploration and Production of Liquid and Gaseous Hydrocarbons in the Territorial Sea and Continental Shelf).

The Italian - Yugoslav Agreement provides for the following:

> The Government of the Italian Republic and the Government of the Socialist Federative Republic of Yugoslavia desiring to stabilize the line of demarcation between their respective parts of the continental shelf, have agreed as follows:

Article 1

The line of demarcation of the continental shelf between the contracting parties is constituted by arcs of the great circle between the points defined in values of latitude and longitude set forth later in the present article.

These coordinates are graphically set forth on the Italian nautical map No. I.I. 170, scale of 1:750,000 (edition February 1964) found in the volume of Avviso ai Naviganti 1966 No. 20, and on Yugoslav nautical map H.I. of the JRM, scale 1:750,000 No. 101 (edition of February 1963) and No. 102 (edition December 1952) revised in June 1966.

The points in the line of demarcation are traced on maps identical to those above cited and are attached to the present agreement.

The contracting parties agree that for the moment the demarcation will not be made beyond point 43.

The coordinates are as follows: (See Italian text for coordinates of 43 points.)

Point	Italian Coordinates on Map No. 170	Yugoslav Coordinates on Map No. 101
01	45° 27'.2 N 13° 12'.7 E	45° 27'.2 N 13° 12'.9 E
02	45° 25'.9 13° 11'.4	45° 25'.5 13° 11'.1
03	45° 20'.1 13° 06'.1	45° 20'.1 13° 06'.0
04	45° 16'.8 13° 03'.8	45° 16'.8 13° 03'.8
05	45° 12'.3 13° 01'.2	45° 12'.3 13° 01'.1
06	45° 11'.1 13° 00'.5	45° 11'.0 13° 00'.1
07	44° 58'.5 13° 04'.7	44° 58'.4 13° 04'.3
08	44° 46'.1 13° 06'.4	44° 46'.3 13° 06'.1

Point	Italian Coordinates on Map No. 170	Yugoslav Coordinates on Map No. 101
09	44° 44'.3 N 13° 06'.8 E	44° 44'.1 N 13° 06'.6 E
10	44° 30'.0 13° 08'.1	44° 30'.3 13° 07'.7
11	44° 28'.6 13° 11'.0	44° 28'.5 13° 10'.7
12	44° 27'.9 13° 11'.7	44° 28'.1 13° 11'.7
13	44° 17'.8 13° 28'.3	44° 17'.7 13° 27'.8
14	44° 12'.5 13° 37'.9	44° 12'.7 13° 38'.1
15	44° 10'.8 13° 40'.0	44° 10'.7 13° 40'.3
16	44° 00'.5 14° 00'.9	44° 00'.7 14° 01'.2
17	43° 57'.5 14° 05'.0	43° 57'.7 14° 04'.9
18	43° 54'.0 14° 10'.3	43° 54'.3 14° 10'.2
19	43° 43'.0 14° 21'.4	43° 43'.0 14° 21'.4
20	43° 40'.3 14° 23'.5	43° 40'.2 14° 23'.8
21	43° 38'.4 14° 24'.5	43° 38'.6 14° 24'.9
22	43° 26'.4 14° 26'.4	43° 35'.9 14° 26'.4
23	43° 31'.6 14° 30'.4	43° 32'.2 14° 30'.1
24	43° 29'.7 14° 32'.0	43° 30'.1 14° 31'.9
25	43° 25'.2 14° 34'.9	43° 25'.4 14° 35'.6
26	43° 13'.0 14° 46'.0	43° 12'.7 14° 46'.3
27	43° 10'.6 14° 47'.9	43° 10'.3 14° 48'.1
28	43° 03'.8 14° 54'.5	43° 03'.7 14° 55'.1
29	43° 00'.8 14° 57'.9	43° 00'.9 14° 58'.0

Point	Italian Coordinates on Map No. 170	Yugoslav Coordinates on Map No. 101
30	42° 59'.2 N 15° 00'.7 E	42° 59'.3 N 15° 00'.8 E
31	42° 47'.9 15° 09'.5	42° 47'.7 15° 09'.7
32	42° 36'.8 15° 21'.8	42° 36'.7 15° 22'.0
33	42° 29'.5 15° 44'.8	42° 29'.6 15° 45'.0
34	34. Located 12 miles from the lighthouse of the Island of Pelagosa on the bearing of 103° from the lighthouse itself (true bearing) The line of delimitation from point 34 to 35 follows a circle with a radius of 12 miles from the lighthouse of the Island of Pelagosa.	
35	35. Located 12 miles from the lighthouse of the Island of Pelagosa on the bearing (alignment) from the lighthouse of the Island of Pelagosa to the lighthouse of Vieste. The line of delimitation from point 35 to 36 follows a circle with a radius of 12 miles from the islet of Caiola.	
36	36. Located 12 miles from the Islet of Caiola on the bearing (alignment) from the lighthouse of the Island of Pelagosa to point 37.	
37	42° 16'.0 16° 37'.1	42° 15'.9 N 16° 37'.3
38	42° 07'.0 16° 56'.8	42° 07'.0 16° 56'.7
39	41° 59'.5 17° 13'.0	41° 59'.4 17° 13'.1
40	41° 54'.8 17° 18'.7	41° 54'.6 N.B: These 17° 19'.0 coordinates are found on Map 102.
41	41° 50'.2 17° 37'.0	41° 49'.9 17° 37'.4
42	41° 38'.5 18° 00'.0	41° 38'.1 18° 00'.0
43	41° 30'.0 18° 13'.0	41° 30'.0 18° 12'.9

Article 2

In case it is ascertained that natural resources of the sea bottom or under the sea bottom extend on both sides of the demarcation line of the continental shelf with the consequence that the resources of the shelf belonging to one of the contracting parties can be in whole or in part exploited from the part of the shelf belonging to the other contracting party, the competent authorities of the contracting parties will themselves be in contact with one another with the intention of reaching an understanding of the manner in which the foresaid resources shall be exploited previous to consultations by the holders of any eventual concessions.

Article 3

In case of controversy concerning the position of any installation or equipment with reference to the line of demarcation set forth in Article 1 of present agreement, the competent authorities of the contracting parties shall determine by mutual agreement in which part of the continental shelf such installations or equipment may be actually situated.

Article 4

The present agreement does not influence the juridical state of the waters or air space over the continental shelf.

Article 5

The present agreement shall be ratified in conformation with the constitutional norms of the contracting parties and shall enter into force on the date of exchange of the instruments of ratification which shall take place in Belgrade at the earliest possible date. The accord is made in two original copies in Italian and Serbo-Croatian, both texts being of equal validity.

Done in Rome January 8, 1968.

ANALYSIS

The terminal and turning points of this continental shelf boundary (CSB) have been plotted on United States Naval Oceanographic Bottom Contour Chart No. BC 3919N. The Italian coordiante values from the Agreement were utilized in plotting the CSB.

There are two rather distinct geophysical regimes of the Adriatic Sea. The northern half, except for a small area of depths of from 100 to 147 fathoms, is less than 100 fathoms in depth and therefore considered to be all continental shelf. The depth of the southern half in contrast is predominantly over 100 fathoms.

Generally, the equidistance principle was employed in dividing the shelf area between the two countries, except from points 26 to 38. The deviation from the equidistance principle provided the Italians with a more equitable share of the continental shelf. The Italians were granted areal concessions to offset the dislocations in the CSB caused by the Yugoslav islands of Jabuka, Pelagruz and Kajola, which are located well out in the Adriatic Sea. To compensate the Italians for the locational influence exerted by the Yugoslav island of Jabuka, the two countries agreed to the eastward displacement of the CSB (points 26-31) from a line that would have existed had the equidistance principle been strictly employed. A second example involves the areal impact of the Yugoslav islands of Pelagruz and Kajola, which was controlled by restricting the Yugoslav claim to the shelf to the 12-mile area around the islands. A third eastward displacement of the CSB, which offsets the locational impact of Kajola similar to the Jabuka example above, was agreed upon concerning points 37 and 38. This areal control about the Yugoslav islands, relative to points 26-31 and 37-38, thus increased the Italian claim to the shelf to a line which is the median line between continental Italy and the major Yugoslav islands.

The CSB extends for a distance of 353 nautical miles and is comprised of 43 turning or terminal points which are separated by an average distance of 8.2 nautical miles. The minimum depth at any of the points is 14 fathoms in the Gulf of Venice. The maximum depth of 650 fathoms is in the southern reaches of the Adriatic. The average depth of the points is 110.4 fathoms. The CSB passes through areas of less than 100 fathoms in depth except for two segments. From point 29 to just short of point 31, the CSB, for a distance of 14 nautical miles, passes through an area of over 100 fathoms in depth. Also, from points 37 to 43, a distance of 75.5 nautical miles, the depths are over 100 fathoms.

Point 1 in the Gulf of Trieste was selected as the starting point for the CSB as the boundary through the former Free Territory of Trieste has not been definitively established between Italy and Yugoslavia.

The CSB terminates at point 43 which is the beginning of the area where Albanian claims to the shelf are asserted.

The table below presents the physical characteristics of the CSB. In many instances the land features are identified simply as the mainland or an island because the scale of the map is such that many of the mainland and island features are not identifiable.

PHYSICAL CHARACTERISTICS

Terminal or Turning Point	Distance between Points	Depth	Italian Territory	Distance from Terminal or Turning Points	Yugoslav Territory
	nautical miles	fathoms		nautical miles	
1		14	Pta. del Tagliamento	12	Rt. Savudrija
	1.5				
2		14	Pta. del Tagliamento	13	Rt. Savudrija
	7				
3		16	Mainland	18	Mainland
	4				
4		16	Mainland	20	Mainland
	5				
5		18	Mainland	23	Mainland
	1.5				
6		18	Mainland	23.5	Island
	13.5				
7		20	Pta della Maestra	23	Island
	12.5				
8		23	Island	26.5	Island
	2				
9		23	Mainland	27.5	Island
	14.5				
10		24	Mainland	34.5	Brionski O.
	2.5				
11		24	Mainland	34.5	Hrid Porer
	1				
12		24	Mainland	34	Hrid Porer
	15.5				
13		33	Mainland	32.5	Hrid Porer
	8.5				
14		36	Mainland	33	O. Susak
	3				
15		32	Mainland	33	O. Susak
	18				
16		36	Mainland	31	Island
	4.5				
17		37	Mainland	31.5	O. Premuda
	5				
18		38	Mainland	32	Rt. Veli Rat
	13.5				
19		37	Mainland	33	Island
	3				

PHYSICAL CHARACTERISTICS (Cont'd)

Terminal or Turning Points	Distance between Points	Depth	Italian Territory	Distance from Terminal or Turning Points	Yugoslav Territory
	nautical miles	fathoms		nautical miles	
20		39	Mainland	33.5	Island
	2.5				
21		40	Mainland	34	O. Dugi Otok
	2.5				
22		42	Mainland	35	O. Dugi Otok
	5				
23		40	Mainland	35.5	O. Dugi Otok
	2				
24		41	Mainland	36	O. Sestrice
	4.5				
25		48	Mainland	37	Island
	14.5				
26		53	Mainland (40.5)	X	(31) O. Jabuka
	3				
27		56	Mainland (41.5)	X	(29) O. Jabuka
	8.5				
28		64	Mainland (44.5)	X	(24) O. Jabuka
	3.5				
29		100	Mainland (46.5)	X	(22) O. Jabuka
	3.5				
30		100	Mainland (45)	X	(21) O. Jabuka
	12.5				
31		75	Mainland (41.5)	X	(22.5) O. Jabuka
	14				
32		71	Ia. Pianosa	29	O. Andrija
	18				
33		61	Ia. Pianosa (16)	X	(23.5) O. Pelagruz
	11				
34		61	Ia. Pianosa (16.5)	X	(12) O. Pelagruz
	18 (Straight line)				
35		66	Mainland (17)	X	(12) O. Pelagruz
	16 "				
36		97	Mainland (29)	X	(12) O. Kajola
	2.5				
37		100	Mainland (30)	X	(14.5) O. Kajola
38		210	Mainland (37)	X	(31) O. Kajola
	9				
39		500	Island	46	O. Kajola
	6.5				
40		515	Island	50	O. Ogiran
	9				
41		615	Mainland	51	O. Sveti Andrija
	21				
42		650	Mainland	51.5	Ostri Rt.
	13				
43		620	Mainland	50.0	Rt. Mendra

SUMMARY

The important feature of this Agreement is the method of jurisdictional delimitation of the shelf employed in view of the presence of small islands located many miles from the mainland near the middle of the sea. If the basic formula for delimiting the CSB set forth in the Geneva Convention on the Continental Shelf had been strictly followed, Italy would have been placed in a disadvantageous position vis-a-vis Yugoslavia in delimiting the continental shelf boundary. The Yugoslav islands of Jabuka, Kajola and Pelagruz would have dislocated the CSB had the equidistance principle been literally utilized. This potential inequity was offset by the two concessions made by the Yugoslavs to the Italians, the latter responding with a lesser concession to the Yugoslavs. The northernmost Yugoslav concession totalled 1,680 square kilometers, the southernmost 1,400 square kilometers. The islands used in determining the new boundary were those larger islands located closer to the Yugoslav coast. Around the islands of Kajola and Pelagruz, the Yugoslavs conceded to Italy the area that was outside the 12 nautical mile territorial sea of the respective islands. The Italian concession of 416 square kilometers negates the influence of the island of Pianosa and the mainland was used in determining the continental shelf boundary. The areal exchange was of the ratio of about 7.4 to 1 with the Yugoslavs contributing the larger amount.

This Agreement is an example of what has been achieved through negotiation when strict application of the equidistant principle results in a disproportionate division of the shelf between two countries as a consequence of the random location of small islands.

SAUDI ARABIAN DECREE RELATING TO OWNERSHIP OF RED SEA RESOURCES*
[September 7, 1968]

ROYAL DECREE NO. M-27 DATED 9/7/1388 HEGRIA

With the help of Almighty God, We, Feisal, Ibn Abdel Aziz Abl Saud, King of Saudi Arabia Kingdom,

Having persuaded Section 19 of the Council of Ministers Regulations issued by Royal Decree No. 28 dated 22nd Shawaal 1377 Hegria and in accordance with the resolution of the Council of Ministers Number 1006 dated 7/7/1388 Hegria and in accordance with what the Deputy Prime Minister has submitted to us, we order the following:

First We approve the regulations of owning the Red Sea resources in the form annexed to this decree.

Second The Deputy Prime Minister and the Minister of Petroleum and Mineral Resources shall execute this our decree.

(Sgd) Feisal

PROJECT REGULATIONS RELATING TO OWNERSHIP OF RED SEA RESOURCES

Section 1. The Saudi Arabia Kingdom owns all the hydrocarbon materials and minerals existing in the strata of the seabed and this is in respect to the zone extending in the Red Sea bed adjacent to the Saudi continental shelf, which materials and minerals are hereinafter referred to as "resources".

Section 2. These "resources" are deemed to be a part of the Saudi Territory and to be treated as the property of the state according to the first section of mining regulations in respect to which Royal Decree No. 90 dated 11/9/82 has been issued.

Section 3. The Government of the Saudi Arabia Kingdom alone shall have the individual right to explore and mine these "resources" and to exploit them, and nobody, public or private, national or foreign, can exercise any form of this right except with the express permit from the competent Saudi Authorities and in accordance with the regulations applicable in the Saudi Arabia Kingdom.

And the Government of the Saudi Arabia Kingdom may exercise its rights in exploring or mining these "resources" and exploiting them by way of sharing with the neighbouring governments which have similar rights recognised by the government of the Saudi Arabia Kingdom in common zones.

Section 4. These "resources" shall not be owned by possession or prescription and the rules of limitation by lapse of time shall not apply to the ownership of the state thereto.

Section 5. The Ministry of Petroleum and Mineral Resources shall be the competent authority to supervise these "resources" and to apply the Saudi rules and regulations relating thereto.

Section 6. The application of these regulations shall not affect the description of the high seas or obstruct navigation therein within the limits provided for by the established rules of public international law.

---

*[Reprinted from an unofficial English translation of Royal Decree No. M-27 issued by the King of Saudi Arabia.]

NORTH SEA CONTINENTAL SHELF BOUNDARIES

Of the countries bordering the North Sea, Denmark, Germany, the Netherlands, Norway and the United Kingdom have reached agreements on the division of the continental shelf. Belgium and France have not. The North Sea continental shelf thus has been subdivided except for the area in dispute between Germany and the Netherlands and Denmark which was recently the subject of a ruling by the International Court of Justice.

Only Denmark, the Netherlands and the United Kingdom, of the five countries entering into continental shelf agreements, are parties to the Geneva Convention on the Continental Shelf. Germany, although not a party to the Convention, adopted the Convention's definition of the continental shelf in issuing the German Proclamation on the Continental Shelf of January 20, 1964. Norway adopted the exploitability criterion of the Geneva Convention as reflected in the Norwegian Provisional Act of June 21, 1963, relating to the Exploitation and Exploration of Submarine Natural Resources. France and Belgium have not entered into any continental shelf boundary agreements. France has ratified the Geneva Convention on the Continental Shelf; Belgium has not.

The North Sea has an area of approximately 222,000 square miles. Water depths are less than 100 fathoms except for the Norwegian Trench and Devils Hole. The latter is a small area with depths up to 130 fathoms and it is located at about 57° N. Latitude and 1° E. Longitude.

The Norwegian Trench lies off the south and west coasts of Norway. Adjacent to the Norwegian Coast is a narrow band of water of less than 100 fathoms in depth. This narrow shelf, which separates the Norwegian Trench from the coast, ranges in width from 2 to 10 nautical miles. The shelf has an average width of about 3 nautical miles. The Norwegian Trench has depths up to 265 fathoms on the west coast and 371 fathoms on the southeast coast. The greatest width of the Trench related to the continental shelf boundary (CSB) is 81 nautical miles which is at Point 8 of the Norway-United Kingdom Agreement. The narrowest width of 20 nautical miles is located at Lindesness on the southern Norwegian coast.

The seven agreements concerning the CSB in the North Sea are all based on the equidistance principle. Bilateral negotiations were successful in resolving territorial issues in the North Sea, except for the continental shelf boundaries between Germany and Denmark and Germany and the Netherlands. Agreement was reached only on the coastal sections of the shelf. The February 20, 1969, decision of the International Court of Justice on division of the areas in dispute between the three countries rejected the argument that the equidistance principle had been adopted as a rule of customary international law. While the Court refrained from setting the precise boundaries to be drawn between the respective continental shelves, it did endorse the principle of the national prolongation or continuation of the land territory from the coast as the measure to be employed under the subject circumstances for determining an equitable delimitation of the area.

NORWAY AND UNITED KINGDOM CONTINENTAL SHELF BOUNDARY

The Governments of the Kingdom of Norway and the United Kingdom of Great Britain and Northern Ireland signed an Agreement delimiting the continental shelf boundary (CSB) between the two countries on March 10, 1965. The Agreement was ratified and came into force on June 29, 1965.

The Agreement set forth the following principles:

Article 1

The dividing line between that part of the Continental Shelf which appertains to the United Kingdom of Great Britain and Northern Ireland and that part which appertains to the Kingdom of Norway shall be based, with certain minor divergencies for administrative convenience, on a line, every point of which is equidistant from the nearest points of the baselines from which the territorial sea of each country is measured.

Article 2

(1) In implementation of the principle set forth in Article 1, the dividing line shall be arcs of Great Circles between the following points, in the sequence given below:

Point 1. 56° 05' 12" N., 3° 15' 00" E.
Point 2. 56° 35' 42" N., 2° 36' 48" E.
Point 3. 57° 54' 18" N., 1° 57' 54" E.
Point 4. 58° 25' 48" N., 1° 29' 00" E.
Point 5. 59° 17' 24" N., 1° 42' 42" E.
Point 6. 59° 53' 48" N., 2° 04' 36" E.
Point 7. 61° 21' 24" N., 1° 47' 24" E.
Point 8. 61° 44' 12" N., 1° 33' 36" E.

The positions of the points in this Article are defined by latitude and longitude on European Datum (1st Adjustment 1950).

(2) The dividing line has been drawn on the chart annexed to this Agreement.

Article 3

(1) In the south the termination point of the dividing line shall be point No. 1, which is the point of intersection of the dividing lines between the Continental Shelves of the United Kingdom of Great Britain and Northern Ireland, the Kingdom of Norway and the Kingdom of Denmark. The position of the above-mentioned point No. 1 shall be subject to acceptance by the Kingdom of Denmark.

(2) For the time being the Contracting Parties have not deemed it necessary to draw the dividing line further north than point No. 8.

Article 4

If any single geological petroleum structure or petroleum field, or any single geological structure or field of any other mineral deposit, including sand or gravel, extends across the dividing line and the part of such structure or field which is situated on one side of the dividing line is exploitable, wholly or in part, from the other side of the dividing line, the Contracting Parties shall, in consultation with the licensees, if any, seek to reach agreement as to the manner in which the structure or field shall be most effectively exploited and the manner in which the proceeds deriving therefrom shall be apportioned.

Article 5

This Agreement shall not affect the status of the superjacent waters or air space above.

Article 6

(1) This Agreement shall be ratified. Instruments of ratification shall be exchanged at Oslo as soon as possible

(2) The Agreement shall enter into force on the date of the exchange of instruments of ratification.

IN WITNESS WHEREOF the undersigned, being duly authorised thereto by their respective Governments, have signed the present Agreement.

DONE in duplicate at London the 10th day of March, 1965, in the English and Norwegian languages, both texts being equally authoritative.

ANALYSIS

The Norway-United Kingdom CSB has a length of 359 nautical miles. The equidistance principle was employed for the entire length of the CSB.

There are eight terminal or turning points on the CSB. These eight points are separated by an average distance of 44.9 nautical miles. The distances between points ranges from 24 to 88 nautical miles. The average water depth at the eight points is 63.1 fathoms with a depth range of 38 to 100 fathoms.

The eight terminal or turning points of the CSB are an average distance of 113.6 nautical miles from Norwegian and British territory. The distances range from 82 nautical miles at Point 7, to 160 nautical miles from land at Point 1.

Point 1, the southern terminus of the CSB, is coextensive with Point 8 of the Denmark-Norway CSB, and with Point 1 of the Denmark-United Kingdom CSB. The northern terminus of the CSB at Point 8 is located in the Norwegian Sea and it coincides with the 100 fathom contour.

TABLE I. PHYSICAL CHARACTERISTICS OF THE NORWAY-UNITED KINGDOM CONTINENTAL SHELF BOUNDARY

Continental Shelf Boundary Point	Distance between Points (nautical miles)	Water Depth (fathoms)	United Kingdom Territory	Distance Land to Continental Shelf Boundary Point (nautical miles)	Norway Territory
1		40	Mainland	(160)	Mainland
	37				
2		38	Farn Island	(151)	Island
	83				
3		42	Buchan Ness	(125)	Mainland
	36				
4		67	Rattray Head	(116)	Island
	53				
5		63	Sumburgh Head	(98)	Utsire I.
	38				
6		62	Out Skerries	(90)	Island
	88				
7		93	Island	(82)	Island
	24				
8		100	Island	(87)	Gunnarskjaen

The distinguishing feature of this Agreement between Norway and the United Kingdom is that the deep Norwegian Trench was ignored in the determination of the CSB. If the coastal 100 fathom contour had been used in delimiting the Norwegian claim to the continental shelf, their claim would have been virtually non-existent due to the narrow coastal zone of depths less than 100 fathoms in depth. Thus, the Trench was ignored as a limiting factor and the CSB was delimited based strictly on the equidistance principle without regard to the 100 fathom contour.

It is estimated that about 1/3 to 2/5 of the Norwegian shelf, as delimited by the Norway-United Kingdom CSB, is over 100 fathoms in depth.

DENMARK AND NORWAY CONTINENTAL SHELF BOUNDARY

The Government of the Kingdom of Norway and the Government of the Kingdom of Denmark signed an Agreement dividing the continental shelf between the two countries on December 8, 1965. The ratifications were exchanged and the Agreement came into force on June 22, 1966.

The Agreement set forth the following principles:

Article 1

The boundary between the areas of the continental shelf over which Denmark and Norway respectively exercise sovereignty shall be the median line, which shall be determined so that every point of the line shall be equidistant from the nearest points on the base lines from which the limits of the contracting parties' outer territorial waters are measured.

Article 2

With a view to an appropriate application of the principle expressed in Article 1, the boundary shall be drawn in straight lines (compass lines) through the following points and in the order given below:

Point 1	58°15,8'N	10°02,0'E
" 2	57°59,3'N	9°23,0'E
" 3	57°41,8'N	8°53,3'E
" 4	57°37,1'N	8°27,5'E
" 5	57°29,9'N	7°59,0'E
" 6	57°10,5'N	6°56,2'E
" 7	56°35,5'N	5°02,0'E
" 8	56°05,2'N	3°15,0'E

The geographical coordinates cited above refer to the appended Norwegian chart no. 301, 1941 edition, printed in November 1963, on which the demarcation line has been drawn. The chart shall constitute an integral part of this treaty.

Article 3

The terminal points of the Danish-Norwegian demarcation line are the points where the lines meet the demarcation lines of other states' areas of the continental shelf.

The contracting parties intend, if necessary, to fix these points definitely after consultation with the third country concerned.

Article 4

If it is found that natural resources on or below the seabed extend to both sides of the boundary between the contracting parties' continental shelf, so that resources which are found in one party's area could wholly or in part be extracted from the other party's area, agreement on the exploitation of these natural resources shall be concluded at the request of one of the contracting parties.

Article 5

This treaty has been drawn up in two original copies, one Norwegian and one Danish text, both to the same effect.

The treaty shall be ratified and exchange of ratification documents shall take place in Copenhagen.

The treaty shall enter into force on the day the ratification documents are exchanged.

Oslo, December 8, 1965.

ANALYSIS

The Denmark-Norway CSB has a length of 255 nautical miles and extends from the middle of the North Sea into the Skagerrak. There are eight terminal or turning points which have an average distance of 31.9 nautical miles between them. The distance between the points ranges from 14 to 71 nautical miles. The average water depth at the points is 83.5 fathoms, with a depth range of 30 to 254 fathoms.

The CSB is an average distance of 58.4 nautical miles from both Danish and Norwegian territory. The points on the CSB range from 30 to 160 nautical miles from the land. Point 1 of the Denmark-Norway CSB is coextensive with Point 5 of the Norway-Sweden CSB. Point 8 of the CSB corresponds to Point 1 of both the Norway-United Kingdom CSB, and the Denmark-United Kingdom CSB.

As was the case in the Norway-United Kingdom CSB Agreement, the deep Norwegian Trench was ignored as a factor limiting the Norwegian claim to the continental shelf. Similarily, as in the Norway-United Kingdom Agreement, 1/3 to 2/5 of the Norwegian claim to the shelf as delimited by the Denmark-Norway CSB is over 100 fathoms in depth. Only a small portion of the Danish shelf (around points 1 and 2) is over 100 fathoms, but depths do extend to as much as 250 fathoms.

TABLE II. PHYSICAL CHARACTERISTICS OF THE DENMARK-NORWAY CONTINENTAL SHELF BOUNDARY

Continental Shelf Boundary Point	Distance between Points (nautical miles)	Water Depth (fathoms)	Norway Territory	Distance Land to Continental Shelf Boundary Point (nautical miles)	Denmark Territory
1		254	Island	(35)	The Skaw
	25				
2		100	Torungen	(30)	Hirshals
	24				
3		50	Island	(32)	Mainland
	14				
4		87	Island	(30)	Manstholm
	17				
5		75	Island	(31)	Manstholm
	38				
6		30	Island	(47)	Mainland
	71				
7		32	Mainland	(102)	Mainland
	66				
8		40	Mainland	(160)	Mainland

DENMARK AND UNITED KINGDOM CONTINENTAL SHELF BOUNDARY

On March 3, 1966, the Government of the Kingdom of Denmark and the Government of the United Kingdom of Great Britain and Northern Ireland signed an Agreement delimiting the continental shelf between the two countries. Instruments of ratification were exchanged and the Agreement entered into force on February 6, 1967.

The Agreement set forth the following principles:

Article 1

The dividing line between that part of the Continental Shelf which appertains to the United Kingdom of Great Britain and Northern Ireland and that part which appertains to the Kingdom of Denmark is in principle a line which at every point is equidistant from the nearest points of the baselines from which the territorial sea of each country is measured.

Article 2

(1) In implementation of the principle set forth in Article 1, the dividing line shall be an arc of a Great Circle between the following points:

1. 56° 05' 12" N., 3° 15' 00" E.
2. 55° 50' 06" N., 3° 24' 00" E.

The positions of the two above-mentioned points are defined by latitude and longitude on European Datum (1st Adjustment 1950).

(2) The dividing line has been drawn on the chart annexed to this Agreement.

Article 3

(1) In the north the termination point of the dividing line is the point of intersection of the dividing lines between the Continental Shelves of the United Kingdom of Great Britain and Northern Ireland, the Kingdom of Denmark and the Kingdom of Norway.

(2) In the south the termination point of the dividing line is the point of intersection of the dividing lines between the Continental Shelves of the United Kingdom of Great Britain and Northern Ireland, the Kingdom of Denmark and the Kingdom of the Netherlands.

Article 4

If any single geological petroleum structure or petroleum field, or any single geological structure or field of any other mineral deposit, including sand or gravel, extends across the dividing line and the part of such structure or field which is situated on one side of the dividing line is exploitable, wholly or in part, from the other side of the dividing line, the Contracting Parties shall seek to reach agreement as to the exploitation of such structure or field.

Article 5

(1) This Agreement shall be ratified. Instruments of ratification shall be exchanged at Copenhagen as soon as possible.

(2) The Agreement shall enter into force on the date of the exchange of instruments of ratification.

Done in duplicate at London the 3rd day of March, 1966, in the English and Danish languages, both texts being equally authoritative.

ANALYSIS

The CSB consists of only two points and extends for a distance of 16 nautical miles. The CSB was delimited using the equidistance principle. The two points have an average depth of 35 fathoms and are an average of 158 nautical miles from Danish and British territory.

Point 1 of the CSB is contiguous with Point 1 of the Norway-United Kingdom CSB, as well as Point 8 of the Denmark-Norway CSB.

TABLE III. PHYSICAL CHARACTERISTICS OF THE DENMARK-UNITED KINGDOM CONTINENTAL SHELF BOUNDARY

Continental Shelf Boundary Point	Distance between Points (nautical miles)	Water Depth (fathoms)	United Kingdom Territory	Distance Land to Continental Shelf Boundary Point (nautical miles)	Denmark Territory
1		40	Mainland	(160)	Lyngvig
	16				
2		30	Flamborough Head	(156)	Blaavands Huk

NETHERLANDS-UNITED KINGDOM CONTINENTAL SHELF BOUNDARY

The Government of the Kingdom of the Netherlands and the Government of the United Kingdom of Great Britain and Northern Ireland signed an Agreement on October 6, 1965, delimiting the continental shelf under the North Sea between the two countries. Instruments of ratification were exchanged at The Hague and the Agreement came into force on December 26, 1966.

Article 1

(1) Subject to Article 2 of this Agreement the dividing line between that part of the Continental Shelf which appertains to the United Kingdom of Great Britain and Northern Ireland and that part which appertains to the Kingdom of the Netherlands shall be arcs of Great Circles between the following points in the sequence given below:

1.	51° 48' 18" N.,	2° 28' 54" E.
2.	51 59 00	2 37 36
3.	52 01 00	2 39 30
4.	52 05 18	2 42 12
5.	52 06 00	2 42 54
6.	52 12 24	2 50 24
7.	52 17 24	2 56 00
8.	52 25 00	3 03 30
9.	52 37 18	3 11 00
10.	52 47 00	3 12 18
11.	52 53 00	3 10 30
12.	53 18 06	3 03 24
13.	53 28 12	3 01 00
14.	53 35 06	2 59 18
15.	53 40 06	2 57 24
16.	53 57 48	2 52 00
17.	54 22 48	2 45 48
18.	54 37 18	2 53 54
19.	55 50 06	3 24 00

The positions of the points in this Article are defined by latitude and longitude on European Datum (1st Adjustment 1950).

(2) The dividing line has been drawn on the chart annexed to this Agreement.

Article 2

(1) In the south the termination point of the dividing line shall be point No. 1, which is the point of intersection of the dividing lines between the Continental Shelves of the United Kingdom of Great Britain and Northern Ireland, the Kingdom of the Netherlands and the Kingdom of Belgium.

(2) In the north the termination point of the dividing line shall be point No. 19, which is the point of intersection of the dividing lines between the Continental Shelves of the United Kingdom of Great Britain and Northern Ireland, the Kingdom of the Netherlands and the Kingdom of Denmark.

Article 3

Should any dispute arise concerning the position of any installation or other device or a well's intake in relation to the dividing line, the Contracting Parties shall in consultation determine on which side of the dividing line the installation or other device or the well's intake is situated.

Article 4

(1) This Agreement shall be ratified. Instrument of ratification shall be exchanged at The Hague as soon as possible.

(2) This Agreement shall enter into force on the date of the exchange of instruments of ratification.

IN WITNESS WHEREOF the undersigned being duly authorised thereto by their respective Governments have signed the present Agreement.

DONE in duplicate at London the 6th October, 1965 in the English and Netherlands languages, both texts being equally authoritative.

ANALYSIS

The CSB was delimited according to the equidistance principle and it extends for a distance of 255 nautical miles. There are 19 terminal or turning points on the CSB, with an average of 13.4 nautical miles between the points. The distance between the points range from 2 to 75 nautical miles. The water depth at the points ranges from 13 to 30 fathoms, with an average depth of 19.2 fathoms.

The 19 points of the CSB are an average distance of 63.3 nautical miles from Dutch and British territory. The distance from land of the points ranges from 39 to 156 nautical miles.

The southern terminus of the CSB, at Point 1, marks the point of intersection of British, Dutch and Belgian jurisdiction on the continental shelf. The northern terminus, at Point 19, corresponds to Point 2 of the Denmark-United Kingdom CSB and Point "D" of the Denmark-Netherlands CSB.

TABLE IV. PHYSICAL CHARACTERISTICS OF THE NETHERLANDS-UNITED KINGDOM CONTINENTAL SHELF BOUNDARY

Continental Shelf Boundary Point	Distance between Points (nautical miles)	Water Depth (fathoms)	United Kingdom Territory	Distance Land to Continental Shelf Boundary Point (nautical miles)	Netherlands Territory
1		19	Orfordness	(39)	Walcheran
	12				
2		18	Orfordness	(40)	Walcheran
	3				
3		21	Orfordness	(40)	Walcheran
	4				
4		22	Mainland	(41)	Walcheran
	2				
5		22	Mainland	(41)	Walcheran
	7				
6		21	Lowestoft	(42)	Schouwen
	6				
7		19	Mainland	(44)	Schouwen
	9				
8		19	Lowestoft	(47)	Hook of Holland
	14				
9		13	Lowestoft	(51)	Scheveningen
	10				
10		20	Caister	(53)	Egmond
	6				
11		19	Caister	(53)	Mainland
	26				
12		15	Mainland	(60)	Texel I.
	10				
13		16	Mainland	(66)	Texel I.
	7				
14		17	Mainland	(69)	Trexel I.
	4				
15		18	Mainland	(72)	Texel I.
	19				
16		20	Mainland	(83)	Vlieland
	26				
17		17	Flamborough Head	(100)	Vlieland
	15				
18		17	Flamborough Head	(106)	Vlieland
	75				
19		30	Flamborough Head	(156)	Vlieland

DENMARK-NETHERLANDS CONTINENTAL SHELF BOUNDARY

The Government of the Kingdom of Denmark and the Government of the Kingdom of the Netherlands signed an Agreement on March 31, 1966, delimiting the continental shelf underneath the North Sea between the two countries. The instruments of ratification were exchanged at Copenhagen and the Agreement came into force on August 1, 1967.

The Agreement set forth the following principles:

Article 1

1. In applying the principle of equidistance set forth in the preamble of the present Agreement, the boundary line between the portion of the continental shelf belonging to the Kingdom of Denmark, and the portion belonging to the Kingdom of the Netherlands, shall be the great circle arcs between the following points, in the order given:

A. 55° 02' 36" N -- 5° 29' 09" E
B. 55° 26' 11" N -- 4° 25' 34" E
C. 55° 46' 22" N -- 3° 36' 40" E
D. 55° 50' 06" N -- 3° 24' 00" E

The positions of the points given in this Article are expressed in the latitude and longitude in accordance with the European Datum (first Revision, 1950).

2. The boundary line has been entered on the chart annexed to this Agreement.

Article 2

1. Upon the request of one of the Contracting Parties, the other Contracting Party shall as promptly as possible make known its viewpoint as to the location of any existing or projected installation, other facility, or well-head in relation to the boundary line.

2. In the event of a dispute concerning the location of any installation, other facility, or well-head in relation to the boundary line, the Contracting Parties shall mutually determine on which side of the boundary line such installation, facility, or well-head is situated.

Article 3

1. This Agreement shall be ratified. The instruments of ratification shall be exchanged at Copenhagen at the earliest possible date.

2. The Agreement shall enter into force on the date of exchange of the instruments of ratification.

In Witness Whereof, the undersigned, duly authorized thereto by their respective Governments, have signed this Agreement.

Done at The Hague, on March 31, 1966, in duplicate, in the Danish and Netherlands languages, both texts being equally authentic.

ANALYSIS

The Denmark-Netherlands CSB has a length of 85 nautical miles. The CSB was delimited according to the equidistance principle. The four terminal or turning points are separated by an average distance of 21.2 nautical miles, with a distance range of from 8 to 43 nautical miles. The depth at the points ranges from 20 to 30 fathoms, with an average depth of 24.2 fathoms.

The average distance of the four points from Danish and Dutch territory is 131 nautical miles The distance from land of the points ranges from 94 to 156 nautical miles.

TABLE V. PHYSICAL CHARACTERISTICS OF THE DENMARK-NETHERLANDS CONTINENTAL SHELF BOUNDARY

Continental Shelf Boundary Point	Distance between Points (nautical miles)	Water Depth (fathoms)	Denmark Territory	Distance, Land to Continental Shelf Boundary Point (nautical miles)	Netherlands Territory
A		21	Blaavands Huk	(94)	Ameland
	43				
B		20	Blaavands Huk	(123)	Terschelling
	34				
C		26	Blaavands Huk	(152)	Terschelling
	8				
D		30	Blaavands Huk	(156)	Terschelling

Point "D" of the Denmark-Netherlands CSB is coextensive with Point 2 of the Denmark-United Kingdom CSB, and with Point 19 of the Netherlands-United Kingdom CSB. Point "A" of the Denmark-Netherlands CSB is the location of the point where German claims to the shelf become a factor. The acceptance of Point "A" as the site of the beginning of German jurisdiction on the continental shelf assumes that the various claims to the shelf were delimited according to the equidistance principle.

The German Government disputed the Denmark-Netherlands CSB and contended that the equidistance principle does not provide an equitable division of the North Sea continental shelf off the German coast. The Germans contended that their claim should extend to the middle of the North Sea, i.e., at Point 19 of the Netherlands-United Kingdom CSB and Point 2 of the Denmark-United Kingdom CSB.

The February 20, 1969, ICJ ruling stated that the equidistance method of dividing the continental shelf, as embodied in the 1958 Convention on the Continental Shelf (which has not been ratified by Germany), is not obligatory in all cases. The ruling contained guidelines for negotiations by the parties of a settlement "in accordance with equitable principles." Since the ICJ ruling there have been efforts on the part of the parties concerned to reach some form of agreement. However, no solution has been reached yet.

Since the Germans have contested the delimitation of the North Sea according to the Denmark-Netherlands Agreement, there are now two undivided areas of the continental shelf in the area of Danish, Dutch and German jurisdiction. From Point "A" of the Denmark-Netherlands CSB, the shelf has not been divided for a distance of 69 nautical miles, or to Point S' of the Denmark-Germany CSB. There is also 66 nautical miles of undelimited shelf between Point E_3 of the Germany-Netherlands CSB and Point "A" of the Denmark-Netherlands CSB.

DENMARK-GERMANY CONTINENTAL SHELF BOUNDARY

On June 9, 1965, the Government of the Kingdom of Denmark and the Government of the Federal Republic of Germany signed an Agreement delimiting, in the coastal regions, the continental shelf of the North Sea. Attached to the Agreement was a Protocol stating that because of differences in point-of-view the shelf would not be divided farther out in the North Sea. Ratifications were exchanged and the Agreement came into force on May 27, 1966.

The Agreement set forth the following principles:

Article 1

The boundary line between the Danish and German portions of the continental shelf of the North Sea shall run, in the coastal regions, in a straight line from the point indicated in the 1921 description of the frontier at which the prolongation of the line connecting the East List Beacon with the median point of the line connecting the two West List Beacons reaches the open sea to a point 55°10' 03.4" N, 7°33' 09.6" E by the

European Datum System (corresponding to the Danish geographical co-ordinates 55°10' 01.1" N, 7°33' 16.7" E and the German geographical co-ordinates 55°10' 07.1"N, 7°33' 07.7" E).

Article 3

(1) This Treaty requires ratification. Ratification instruments will be exchanged in Copenhagen as soon as possible.

(2) This Treaty enters into force on the day of exchange of the ratification instruments.

Executed in Bonn on June 9, 1965 in two original copies with one German and one Danish text, both to the same effect.

Protocol

The Danish-German negotiations conducted at the instance of Germany concerning the delimitation of the continental shelf adjacent to the Danish and German coast have disclosed that there are differences of views concerning the principles of delimitation of the continental shelf of the North Sea. Agreement could be reached only on the course of the boundary line of the continental shelf in the coastal regions; each Contracting Party reserves its legal position with respect to the further course of the boundary line.

With respect to the continental shelf adjacent to the coasts of the Baltic Sea opposite each other, it is agreed that the boundary shall be determined according to the median line. Each Contracting Party accordingly declares that it will raise no objections of principle if the other Contracting Party delimits its portion of the continental shelf of the Baltic Sea on the basis of the median line.

ANALYSIS

The coastal CSB of the Denmark-Germany Agreement is an extension of the international maritime boundary between the two countries. Point "S" of the CSB marks the seaward limit of the international maritime boundary. The water depth is 3 fathoms at Point "S".

The CSB extends 26 nautical miles into the North Sea and the terminus is Point "S'". The water depth at "S'" is 13 fathoms. Point "S'" is separated by a distance of 69 nautical miles from the Denmark-Netherlands CSB, and this area of the shelf is delimited.

TABLE VI. PHYSICAL CHARACTERISTICS OF THE DENMARK-GERMANY CONTINENTAL SHELF BOUNDARY

Continental Shelf Boundary Point	Distance between Points (nautical miles)	Water Depth (fathoms)	Denmark Territory	Distance, Land to Continental Shelf Boundary Point (nautical miles)	Germany Territory
S		3	Terminal point of the international maritime boundary.		
	26				
S'		13	Blaavands Huk	(30)	Sylt I.

The international maritime boundary between Denmark and Germany is discussed in the following publication: U.S. Department of State, Office of the Geographer. Denmark-Germany Boundary, International Boundary Study No. 81 of June 14, 1968.

GERMANY-NETHERLANDS CONTINENTAL SHELF BOUNDARY

On December 1, 1964, the Government of the Federal Republic of Germany and the Government of the Kingdom of the Netherlands signed an Agreement concerning the lateral delimitation of the continental shelf in the vicinity of the coast. Ratifications were exchanged and the Agreement came into force on September 18, 1965.

The Agreement set forth the following principles:

Article 1

(1) Up to fifty-fourth parallel of north latitude, the boundary between the Netherlands and German parts of the continental shelf of the North Sea shall run from the northern end of the line which was agreed upon in the Supplementary Agreement of 14 May 1962 to the Ems-Dollard Treaty of 8 April 1960, and which divides the frontier area of the Ems Estuary lengthwise, along the shortest line passing through points E_1 and E_2 to point E_3.

(2) The co-ordinates of the points (according to German marine charts No. 50, July 1956 edition, and No. 90, May 1964 edition) are the following:

Point E_1: 53°45'06" N, 6°19'56" E;
Point E_2: 53°48'56" N, 6°15'49" E;
Point E_3: 54°00'00" N, 6°06'26" E.

Article 2

(1) The determination of this treaty is not concerned with the question of the course of the State Boundary in the Ems Estuary. Both parties to the Treaty reserve their rights on this question.

(2) The Judgment of Article 46, Paragraph 2, of the Ems-Dollart Treaty remains unchanged.

Article 4

(1) This Treaty requires ratification. Ratification instruments will be exchanged in The Hague as soon as possible.

(2) This Treaty enters into force on the day of exchange of the ratification instruments.

Executed in Bonn on December 1, 1964 in two original copies with one German and one Dutch text, both to the same effect.

ANALYSIS

The Germany-Netherlands CSB extends for a distance of 26 nautical miles into the North Sea. The landward terminus of the CSB is Point "c"" which is the terminal point of the Germany-Netherlands international maritime boundary. The water depth at Point "c"" is 2 fathoms.

The average distance between the points of the CSB is 8.7 nautical miles, with a range of from 4 to 12 nautical miles. The water depth at the points ranges from 2 to 15 fathoms, with an average depth of 9.8 fathoms.

The distance from land of the points ranges from 12 to 29 nautical miles, with an average distance of 19.3 nautical miles. Point E_3 of the CSB is 66 nautical miles from Point "A" of the Denmark-Netherlands CSB and this area of the shelf is undelimited..

TABLE VII. PHYSICAL CHARACTERISTICS OF THE GERMANY-NETHERLANDS CONTINENTAL SHELF BOUNDARY

Continental Shelf Boundary Point	Distance between Points (nautical miles)	Water Depth (fathoms)	Germany Territory	Distance Land to Continental Shelf Boundary Point (nautical miles)	Netherlands Territory
C"		2	Terminal point of the international maritime boundary		
	10				
E_1		12	Borkum	12	Island
	4				
E_2		10	Borkum	17	Island
	12				
E_3		15	Borkum	29	

The international maritime boundary between Germany and the Netherlands is discussed in the following publication: U.S. Department of State, Office of the Geographer. Germany-Netherlands Boundary, International Boundary Study No. 31, of April 6, 1964.

JUDGMENT

Present: *President* Bustamante y Rivero; *Vice-President* Koretsky; *Judges* Sir Gerald Fitzmaurice, Tanaka, Jessup, Morelli, Sir Muhammad Zafrulla Khan, Padilla Nervo, Forster, Gros, Ammoun, Bengzon, Petrén, Lachs, Onyeama; *Judges* ad hoc Mosler, Sørensen; *Registrar* Aquarone.

In the North Sea Continental Shelf cases,

between

the Federal Republic of Germany,
represented by

Dr. G. Jaenicke, Professor of International Law in the University of Frankfurt am Main,

as Agent,

assisted by

Dr. S. Oda, Professor of International Law in the University of Sendai,

as Counsel,

Dr. U. Scheuner, Professor of International Law in the University of Bonn,
Dr. E. Menzel, Professor of International Law in the University of Kiel,
Dr. Henry Herrmann, of the Massachusetts Bar, associated with Messrs. Goodwin, Procter and Hoar, Counsellors-at-Law, Boston,
Dr. H. Blomeyer-Bartenstein, Counsellor 1st Class, Ministry of Foreign Affairs,
Dr. H. D. Treviranus, Counsellor, Ministry of Foreign Affairs,

as Advisers,

and by Mr. K. Witt, Ministry of Foreign Affairs,

as Expert,

and

the Kingdom of Denmark,
represented by

Mr. Bent Jacobsen, Barrister at the Supreme Court of Denmark,

as Agent and Advocate,

assisted by

Sir Humphrey Waldock, C.M.G., O.B.E., Q.C., Professor of International Law in the University of Oxford,

as Counsel and Advocate,

H.E. Mr. S. Sandager Jeppesen, Ambassador, Ministry of Foreign Affairs,

Mr. E. Krog-Meyer, Head of The Legal Department, Ministry of Foreign Affairs,
Dr. I. Foighel, Professor in the University of Copenhagen,
Mr. E. Lauterpacht, Member of the English Bar and Lecturer in the University of Cambridge,

Mr. M. Thamsborg, Head of Department, Hydrographic Institute,

as Advisers,

and by

Mr. P. Boeg, Head of Secretariat, Ministry of Foreign Affairs,
Mr. U. Engel, Head of Section, Ministry of Foreign Affairs,

as Secretaries,

and between

the Federal Republic of Germany,
represented as indicated above,

and

the Kingdom of the Netherlands,
represented by

Professor W. Riphagen, Legal Adviser to the Ministry of Foreign Affairs, Professor of International Law at the Rotterdam School of Economics,

as Agent,

assisted by

Sir Humphrey Waldock, C.M.G., O.B.E., Q.C., Professor of International Law in the University of Oxford,

as Counsel,

Rear-Admiral W. Langeraar, Chief of the Hydrographic Department, Royal Netherlands Navy,

Mr. G. W. Maas Geesteranus, Assistant Legal Adviser to the Ministry of Foreign Affairs,

Miss F. Y. van der Wal, Assistant Legal Adviser to the Ministry of Foreign Affairs,

as Advisers,

and by

Mr. H. Rombach, Divisional Head, Hydrographic Department, Royal Netherlands Navy,

as Deputy-Adviser,

THE COURT,

composed as above,

delivers the following Judgment:

By a letter of 16 February 1967, received in the Registry on 20 February 1967, the Minister for Foreign Affairs of the Netherlands transmitted to the Registrar:

(a) an original copy, signed at Bonn on 2 February 1967 for the Governments of Denmark and the Federal Republic of Germany, of a Special Agreement for the submission to the Court of a difference between those two States concerning the delimitation, as between them, of the continental shelf in the North Sea;

(b) an original copy, signed at Bonn on 2 February 1967 for the Governments of the Federal Republic of Germany and the Netherlands, of a Special Agreement for the submission to the Court of a difference between those

two States concerning the delimitation, as between them, of the continental shelf in the North Sea;

(c) an original copy, signed at Bonn on 2 February 1967 for the three Governments aforementioned, of a Protocol relating to certain procedural questions arising from the above-mentioned Special Agreements.

Articles 1 to 3 of the Special Agreement between the Governments of Denmark and the Federal Republic of Germany are as follows:

"*Article 1*

(1) The International Court of Justice is requested to decide the following question:

What principles and rules of international law are applicable to the delimitation as between the Parties of the areas of the continental shelf in the North Sea which appertain to each of them beyond the partial boundary determined by the above-mentioned Convention of 9 June 1965?

(2) The Governments of the Kingdom of Denmark and of the Federal Republic of Germany shall delimit the continental shelf in the North Sea as between their countries by agreement in pursuance of the decision requested from the International Court of Justice.

Article 2

(1) The Parties shall present their written pleadings to the Court in the order stated below:

1. a Memorial of the Federal Republic of Germany to be submitted within six months from the notification of the present Agreement to the Court;
2. a Counter-Memorial of the Kingdom of Denmark to be submitted within six months from the delivery of the German Memorial;
3. a German Reply followed by a Danish Rejoinder to be delivered within such time-limits as the Court may order.

(2) Additional written pleadings may be presented if this is jointly proposed by the Parties and considered by the Court to be appropriate to the case and the circumstances.

(3) The foregoing order of presentation is without prejudice to any question of burden of proof which might arise.

Article 3

The present Agreement shall enter into force on the day of signature thereof."

Articles 1 to 3 of the Special Agreement between the Governments of the Federal Republic of Germany and the Netherlands are as follows:

"*Article 1*

(1) The International Court of Justice is requested to decide the following question:

What principles and rules of international law are applicable to the delimitation as between the Parties of the areas of the continental shelf in the North Sea which appertain to each of them beyond the partial boundary determined by the above-mentioned Convention of 1 December 1964?

(2) The Governments of the Federal Republic of Germany and of the Kingdom of the Netherlands shall delimit the continental shelf of the North Sea as between their countries by agreement in pursuance of the decision requested from the International Court of Justice.

Article 2

(1) The Parties shall present their written pleadings to the Court in the order stated below:

1. a Memorial of the Federal Republic of Germany to be submitted within six months from the notification of the present Agreement to the Court;
2. a Counter-Memorial of the Kingdom of the Netherlands to be submitted within six months from the delivery of the German Memorial;
3. a German Reply followed by a Netherlands Rejoinder to be delivered within such time-limits as the Court may order.

(2) Additional written pleadings may be presented if this is jointly proposed by the Parties and considered by the Court to be appropriate to the case and the circumstances.

(3) The foregoing order of presentation is without prejudice to any question of burden of proof which might arise.

Article 3

The present Agreement shall enter into force on the day of signature thereof."

The Protocol between the three Governments reads as follows:

"Protocol

At the signature of the Special Agreement of today's date between the Government of the Federal Republic of Germany and the Governments of the Kingdom of Denmark and the Kingdom of the Netherlands respectively, on the submission to the International Court of Justice of the differences between the Parties concerning the delimitation of the continental shelf in the North Sea, the three Governments wish to state their agreement on the following:

1. The Government of the Kingdom of the Netherlands will, within a month from the signature, notify the two Special Agreements together with the present Protocol to the International Court of Justice in accordance with Article 40, paragraph 1, of the Statute of the Court.

2. After the notification in accordance with item 1 above the Parties will ask the Court to join the two cases.

3. The three Governments agree that, for the purpose of appointing a judge *ad hoc*, the Governments of the Kingdom of Denmark and the Kingdom of the Netherlands shall be considered parties in the same interest within the meaning of Article 31, paragraph 5, of the Statute of the Court."

Pursuant to Article 33, paragraph 2, of the Rules of Court, the Registrar at once informed the Governments of Denmark and the Federal Republic of Germany of the filing of the Special Agreements. In accordance with Article 34, paragraph 2, of the Rules of Court, copies of the Special Agreements were transmitted to the other Members of the United Nations and to other non-member States entitled to appear before the Court.

By Orders of 8 March 1967, taking into account the agreement reached between the Parties, 21 August 1967 and 20 February 1968 were fixed respectively as the time-limits for the filing of the Memorials and Counter-Memorials. These pleadings were filed within the time-limits prescribed. By Orders of 1 March 1968, 31 May and 30 August 1968 were fixed respectively as the time-limits for the filing of the Replies and Rejoinders.

Pursuant to Article 31, paragraph 3, of the Statute of the Court, the Government of the Federal Republic of Germany chose Dr. Hermann Mosler, Professor of International Law in the University of Heidelberg, to sit as Judge *ad hoc* in both cases. Referring to the agreement concluded between them according to which they should be considered parties in the same interest within the meaning of Article 31, paragraph 5, of the Statute, the Governments of Denmark and the Netherlands chose Dr. Max Sørensen, Professor of International Law in the University of Aarhus, to sit as Judge *ad hoc* in both cases.

By an Order of 26 April 1968, considering that the Governments of Denmark and the Netherlands were, so far as the choice of a Judge *ad hoc* was concerned, to be reckoned as one Party only, the Court found that those two Governments were in the same interest, joined the proceedings in the two cases and, in modification of the directions given in the Orders of 1 March 1968, fixed 30 August 1968 as the time-limit for the filing of a Common Rejoinder for Denmark and the Netherlands.

The Replies and the Common Rejoinder having been filed within the time-limits prescribed, the cases were ready for hearing on 30 August 1968.

Pursuant to Article 44, paragraph 2, of the Rules of Court, the pleadings and annexed documents were, after consultation of the Parties, made available to the Governments of Brazil, Canada, Chile, Colombia, Ecuador, Finland, France, Honduras, Iran, Norway, Sweden, United Kingdom of Great Britain and Northern Ireland, United States of America and Venezuela. Pursuant to paragraph 3 of the same Article, those pleadings and annexed documents were, with the consent of the Parties, made accessible to the public as from the date of the opening of the oral proceedings.

Hearings were held from 23 to 25 October, from 28 October to 1 November, and on 4, 5, 7, 8 and 11 November 1968, in the course of which the Court heard, in the order agreed between the Parties and accepted by the Court, the oral arguments and replies of Professor Jaenicke, Agent, and Professor Oda, Counsel, on behalf of the Government of the Federal Republic of Germany; and of Mr. Jacobsen and Professor Riphagen, Agents, and Sir Humphrey Waldock, Counsel, on behalf of the Governments of Denmark and the Netherlands.

In the course of the written proceedings, the following Submissions were presented by the Parties:

On behalf of the Government of the Federal Republic of Germany,

in the Memorials:

"May it please the Court to recognize and declare:

1. The delimitation of the continental shelf between the Parties in the North Sea is governed by the principle that each coastal State is entitled to a just and equitable share.

2. The method of determining boundaries of the continental shelf in such a way that every point of the boundary is equidistant from the nearest points of the baselines from which the breadth of the territorial sea of each State is measured (equidistance method), is not a rule of customary international law and is therefore not applicable as such between the Parties.

3. The equidistance method cannot be employed for the delimitation of the continental shelf unless it is established by agreement, arbitration, or otherwise, that it will achieve a just and equitable apportionment of the continental shelf among the States concerned.

4. As to the delimitation of the continental shelf between the Parties in the North Sea, the equidistance method cannot find application, since it would not apportion a just and equitable share to the Federal Republic of Germany";

in the Replies:

"May it please the Court to recognize and declare:

1. The delimitation of the continental shelf between the Parties in the North Sea is governed by the principle that each coastal State is entitled to a just and equitable share.

2. *(a)* The method of determining boundaries of the continental shelf in such a way that every point of the boundary is equidistant from the nearest points of the baselines from which the breadth of the territorial sea of each State is measured (equidistance method) is not a rule of customary international law.

(b) The rule contained in the second sentence of paragraph 2 of Article 6 of the Continental Shelf Convention, prescribing that in the absence of agreement, and unless another boundary is justified by special circumstances, the boundary shall be determined by application of the principle of equidistance, has not become customary international law.

(c) Even if the rule under *(b)* would be applicable between the Parties, special circumstances within the meaning of that rule would exclude the application of the equidistance method in the present case.

3. *(a)* The equidistance method cannot be used for the delimitation of the continental shelf unless it is established by agreement, arbitration, or otherwise, that it will achieve a just and equitable apportionment of the continental shelf among the States concerned.

(b) As to the delimitation of the continental shelf between the Parties in the North Sea, the Kingdom of Denmark and the Kingdom of the Netherlands cannot rely on the application of the equidistance method, since it would not lead to an equitable apportionment.

4. Consequently, the delimitation of the continental shelf in the North Sea between the Parties is a matter which has to be settled by agreement. This agreement should apportion a just and equitable share to each of the Parties in the light of all factors relevant in this respect."

On behalf of the Government of Denmark,

in its Counter-Memorial:

"Considering that, as noted in the Compromis, disagreement exists between the Parties which could not be settled by detailed negotiations, regarding the further course of the boundary beyond the partial boundary determined by the Convention of 9 June 1965;

Considering that under the terms of Article 1, paragraph 1, of the Compromis the task entrusted to the Court is not to formulate a basis for the delimitation of the continental shelf in the North Sea as between the Parties *ex aequo et bono*, but to decide what principles and rules of international law are applicable to the delimitation as between the Parties of the areas of the continental shelf in the North Sea which appertain to each of them beyond the partial boundary, determined by the above-mentioned Convention of 9 June 1965;

In view of the facts and arguments presented in Parts I and II of this Counter-Memorial,

May it please the Court to adjudge and declare:

1. The delimitation as between the Parties of the said areas of the continental shelf in the North Sea is governed by the principles and rules of international law which are expressed in Article 6, paragraph 2, of the Geneva Convention of 1958 on the Continental Shelf.

2. The Parties being in disagreement, unless another boundary is justified by special circumstances, the boundary between them is to be determined by application of the principle of equidistance from the nearest points of the baselines from which the breadth of the territorial sea of each State is measured.

3. Special circumstances which justify another boundary line not having been established, the boundary between the Parties is to be determined by application of the principle of equidistance indicated in the preceding Submission."

On behalf of the Government of the Netherlands,

in its Counter-Memorial:

"Considering that, as noted in the Compromis, disagreement exists between the Parties which could not be settled by detailed negotiations, regarding the further course of the boundary beyond the partial boundary determined by the Treaty of 1 December 1964;

Considering that under the terms of Article 1, paragraph 1, of the Compromis the task entrusted to the Court is not to formulate a basis for the delimitation of the continental shelf in the North Sea as between the Parties *ex aequo et bono*, but to decide what principles and rules of international law are applicable to the delimitation as between the Parties of the areas of the continental shelf in the North Sea which appertain to each of them beyond the partial boundary determined by the above-mentioned Treaty of 1 December 1964;

In view of the facts and arguments presented in Parts I and II of this Counter-Memorial,

May it please the Court to adjudge and declare:

1. The delimitation as between the Parties of the said areas of the continental shelf in the North Sea is governed by the principles and rules of international law which are expressed in Article 6, paragraph 2, of the Geneva Convention of 1958 on the Continental Shelf.

2. The Parties being in disagreement, unless another boundary is justified by special circumstances, the boundary between them is to be determined by application of the principle of equidistance from the nearest points of the baselines from which the breadth of the territorial sea of each State is measured.

3. Special circumstances which justify another boundary line not having been established, the boundary between the Parties is to be determined by application of the principle of equidistance indicated in the preceding Submission."

On behalf of the Governments of Denmark and the Netherlands,

in the Common Rejoinder:

"May it further please the Court to adjudge and declare:

4. If the principles and rules of international law mentioned in Submission 1 of the respective Counter-Memorials are not applicable as between the Parties, the boundary is to be determined between the Parties on the basis of the exclusive rights of each Party over the continental shelf adjacent to its coast and of the principle that the boundary is to leave to each Party every point of the continental shelf which lies nearer to its coast than to the coast of the other Party."

In the course of the oral proceedings, the following Submissions were presented by the Parties:

On behalf of the Government of the Federal Republic of Germany,

at the hearing on 5 November 1968:

"1. The delimitation of the continental shelf between the Parties in the North Sea is governed by the principle that each coastal State is entitled to a just and equitable share.

2. *(a)* The method of determining boundaries of the continental shelf in such a way that every point of the boundary is equidistant from the nearest points of the baselines from which the breadth of the territorial sea of each State is measured (equidistance method) is not a rule of customary international law.

(b) The rule contained in the second sentence of paragraph 2 of Article 6 of the Continental Shelf Convention, prescribing that in the absence of agreement, and unless another boundary is justified by special circumstances, the boundary shall be determined by application of the principle of equidistance, has not become customary international law.

(c) Even if the rule under *(b)* would be applicable between the Parties, special circumstances within the meaning of that rule would exclude the application of the equidistance method in the present case.

3. *(a)* The equidistance method cannot be used for the delimitation of the continental shelf unless it is established by agreement, arbitration, or otherwise, that it will achieve a just and equitable apportionment of the continental shelf among the States concerned.

(b) As to the delimitation of the continental shelf between the Parties in the North Sea, the Kingdom of Denmark and the Kingdom of the Netherlands cannot rely on the application of the equidistance method, since it would not lead to an equitable apportionment.

4. Consequently, the delimitation of the continental shelf, on which the Parties must agree pursuant to paragraph 2 of Article 1 of the Special Agreement, is determined by the principle of the just and equitable share, based on criteria relevant to the particular geographical situation in the North Sea."

On behalf of the Government of Denmark,

at the hearing on 11 November 1968, Counsel for that Government stated that it confirmed the Submissions presented in its Counter-Memorial and in the Common Rejoinder and that those Submissions were identical *mutatis mutandis* with those of the Government of the Netherlands.

On behalf of the Government of the Netherlands,

at the hearing on 11 November 1968:

"With regard to the delimitation as between the Federal Republic of Germany and the Kingdom of the Netherlands of the boundary of the areas of the continental shelf in the North Sea which appertain to each of them beyond the partial boundary determined by the Convention of 1 December 1964.

May it please the Court to adjudge and declare:

1. The delimitation as between the Parties of the said areas of the continental shelf in the North Sea is governed by the principles and rules of international law which are expressed in Article 6, paragraph 2, of the Geneva Convention of 1958 on the Continental Shelf.

2. The Parties being in disagreement, unless another boundary is justified by special circumstances, the boundary between them is to be determined by application of the principle of equidistance from the nearest points of the baselines from which the breadth of the territorial sea of each State is measured.

3. Special circumstances which justify another boundary line not having been established, the boundary between the Parties is to be determined by application of the principle of equidistance indicated in the preceding Submission.

4. If the principles and rules of international law mentioned in Submission 1 are not applicable as between the Parties, the boundary is to be determined between the Parties on the basis of the exclusive rights of each Party over the continental shelf adjacent to its coast and of the principle that the boundary is to leave to each Party every point of the continental shelf which lies nearer to its coast than to the coast of the other Party."

* * * * *

1. By the two Special Agreements respectively concluded between the Kingdom of Denmark and the Federal Republic of Germany, and between the Federal Republic and the Kingdom of the Netherlands, the Parties have submitted to the Court certain differences concerning "the delimita-

tion as between the Parties of the areas of the continental shelf in the North Sea which appertain to each of them"—with the exception of those areas, situated in the immediate vicinity of the coast, which have already been the subject of delimitation by two agreements dated 1 December 1964, and 9 June 1965, concluded in the one case between the Federal Republic and the Kingdom of the Netherlands, and in the other between the Federal Republic and the Kingdom of Denmark.

2. It is in respect of the delimitation of the continental shelf areas lying beyond and to seaward of those affected by the partial boundaries thus established, that the Court is requested by each of the two Special Agreements to decide what are the applicable "principles and rules of international law". The Court is not asked actually to delimit the further boundaries which will be involved, this task being reserved by the Special Agreements to the Parties, which undertake to effect such a delimitation "by agreement in pursuance of the decision requested from the . . . Court"—that is to say on the basis of, and in accordance with, the principles and rules of international law found by the Court to be applicable.

*

3. As described in Article 4 of the North Sea Policing of Fisheries Convention of 6 May 1882, the North Sea, which lies between continental Europe and Great Britain in the east-west direction, is roughly oval in shape and stretches from the straits of Dover northwards to a parallel drawn between a point immediately north of the Shetland Islands and the mouth of the Sogne Fiord in Norway, about 75 kilometres above Bergen, beyond which is the North Atlantic Ocean. In the extreme northwest, it is bounded by a line connecting the Orkney and Shetland island groups; while on its north-eastern side, the line separating it from the entrances to the Baltic Sea lies between Hanstholm at the north-west point of Denmark, and Lindesnes at the southern tip of Norway. Eastward of this line the Skagerrak begins. Thus, the North Sea has to some extent the general look of an enclosed sea without actually being one. Round its shores are situated, on its eastern side and starting from the north, Norway, Denmark, the Federal Republic of Germany, the Netherlands, Belgium and France; while the whole western side is taken up by Great Britain, together with the island groups of the Orkneys and Shetlands. From this it will be seen that the continental shelf of the Federal Republic is situated between those of Denmark and the Netherlands.

4. The waters of the North Sea are shallow, and the whole seabed consists of continental shelf at a depth of less than 200 metres, except for the formation known as the Norwegian Trough, a belt of water 200-650 metres deep, fringing the southern and south-western coasts of Norway to a width averaging about 80-100 kilometres. Much the greater part of this continental shelf has already been the subject of delimitation

by a series of agreements concluded between the United Kingdom (which, as stated, lies along the whole western side of it) and certain of the States on the eastern side, namely Norway, Denmark and the Netherlands. These three delimitations were carried out by the drawing of what are known as "median lines" which, for immediate present purposes, may be described as boundaries drawn between the continental shelf areas of "opposite" States, dividing the intervening spaces equally between them. These lines are shown on Map 1 on page 15, together with a similar line, also established by agreement, drawn between the shelf areas of Norway and Denmark. Theoretically it would be possible also to draw the following median lines in the North Sea, namely United Kingdom/Federal Republic (which would lie east of the present line United Kingdom/Norway-Denmark-Netherlands); Norway/Federal Republic (which would lie south of the present line Norway/Denmark); and Norway/Netherlands (which would lie north of whatever line is eventually determined to be the continental shelf boundary between the Federal Republic and the Netherlands). Even if these median lines were drawn however, the question would arise whether the United Kingdom, Norway and the Netherlands could take advantage of them as against the parties to the existing delimitations, since these lines would, it seems, in each case lie beyond (i.e., respectively to the east, south and north of) the boundaries already effective under the existing agreements at present in force. This is illustrated by Map 2 on page 15.

5. In addition to the partial boundary lines Federal Republic/Denmark and Federal Republic/Netherlands, which, as mentioned in paragraph 1 above, were respectively established by the agreements of 9 June 1965 and 1 December 1964, and which are shown as lines A-B and C-D on Map 3 on page 16, another line has been drawn in this area, namely that represented by the line E-F on that map. This line, which divides areas respectively claimed (to the north of it) by Denmark, and (to the south of it) by the Netherlands, is the outcome of an agreement between those two countries dated 31 March 1966, reflecting the view taken by them as to what are the correct boundary lines between their respective continental shelf areas and that of the Federal Republic, beyond the partial boundaries A-B and C-D already drawn. These further and unagreed boundaries to seaward, are shown on Map 3 by means of the dotted lines B-E and D-E. They are the lines, the correctness of which in law the Court is in effect, though indirectly, called upon to determine. Also shown on Map 3 are the two pecked lines B-F and D-F, representing approximately the boundaries which the Federal Republic would have wished to obtain in the course of the negotiations that took place between the Federal Republic and the other two Parties prior to the submission of the matter to the Court. The nature of these negotiations must now be described.

*

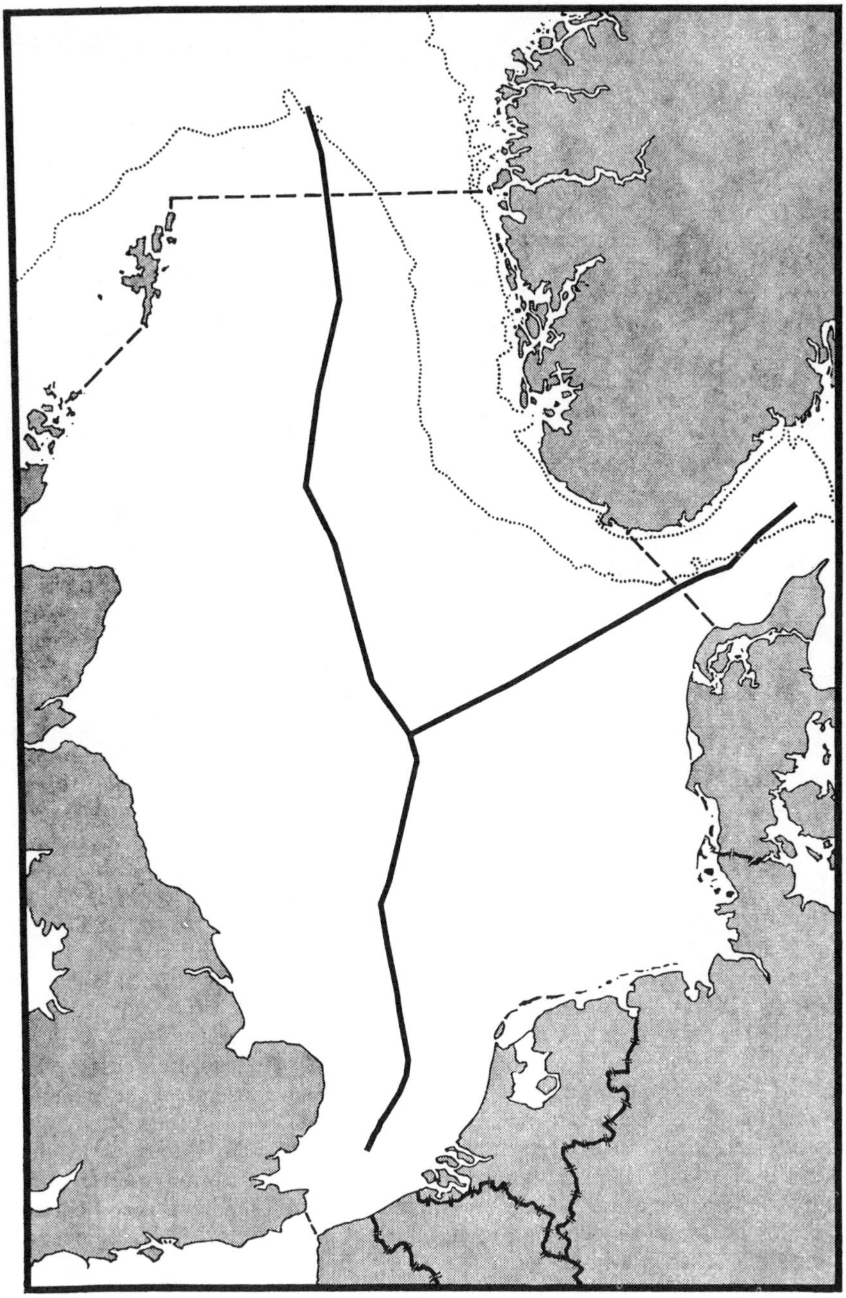

Map 1
(See paragraphs 3 and 4)

Carte 1
(Voir paragraphes 3 et 4)

200 metres line	....	Isobathe des 200 mètres
Limits fixed by the 1882 Convention	— — — — — —	Limites définies par la convention de 1882
Median lines	————————	Lignes médianes

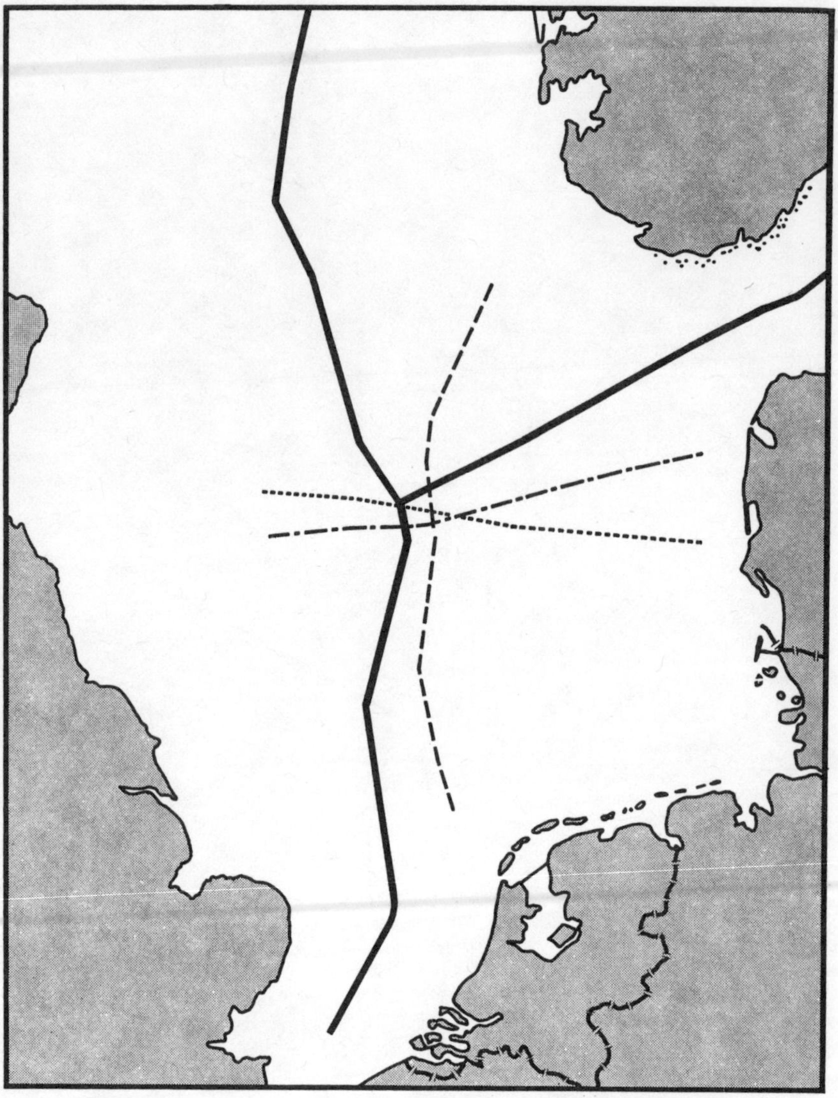

Map 2
(See paragraph 4)

Carte 2
(Voir paragraphe 4)

United Kingdom/Norway-Denmark-Netherlands and Norway/Denmark	———	Royaume-Uni/Norvège-Danemark-Pays-Bas et Norvège/Danemark
United Kingdom/Federal Republic	— — — — — —	Royaume-Uni/République fédérale
Norway/Federal Republic	-—-—-—-—-	Norvège/République fédérale
Norway/Netherlands	- - - - - - - - - - - -	Norvège/Pays-Bas

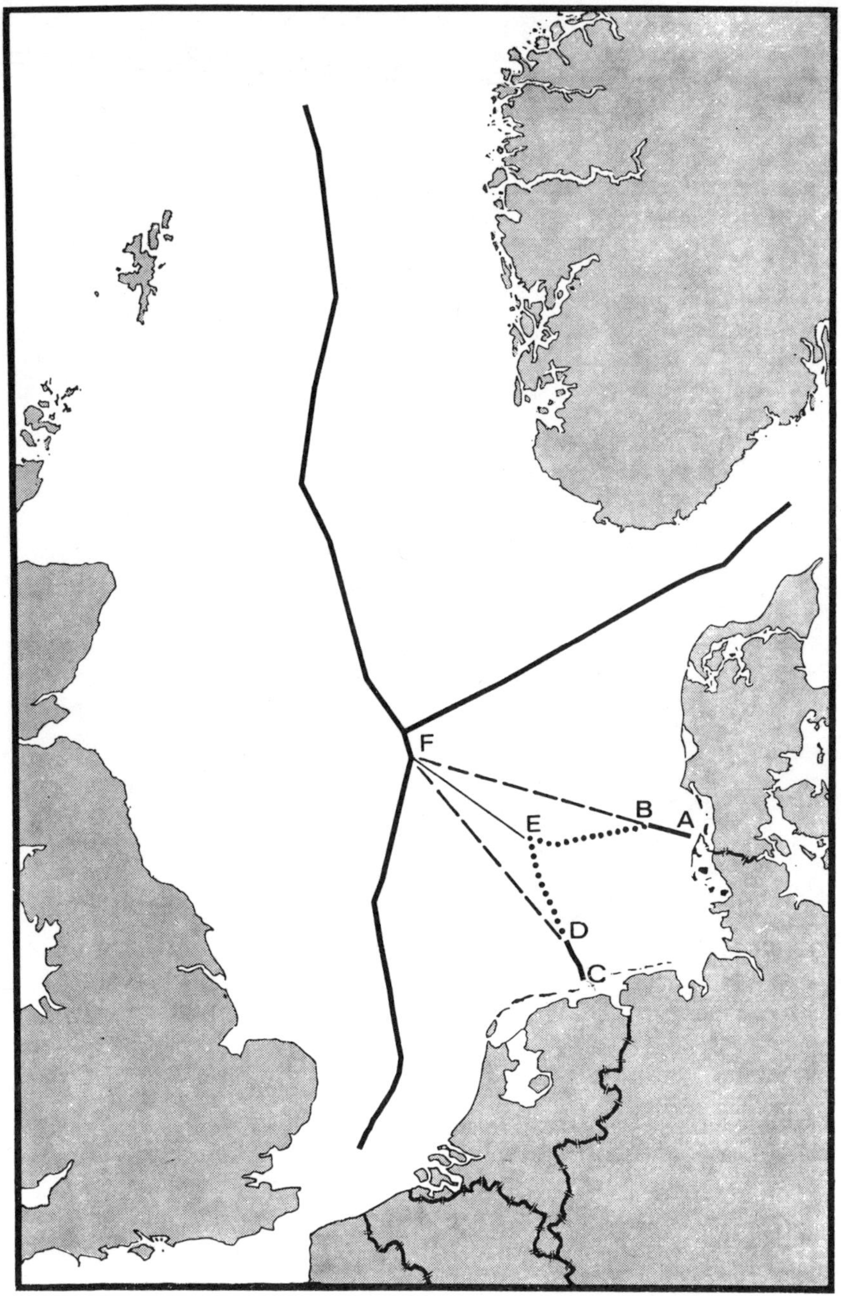

Map 3
(See paragraphs 5-9)

Carte 3
(Voir paragraphes 5-9)

The maps in the present Judgment were prepared on the basis of documents submitted to the Court by the Parties, and their sole purpose is to provide a visual illustration of the paragraphs of the Judgment which refer to them.

Les cartes jointes au présent arrêt ont été établies d'après les documents soumis à la Cour par les Parties et ont pour seul objet d'illustrer graphiquement les paragraphes de l'arrêt qui s'y réfèrent.

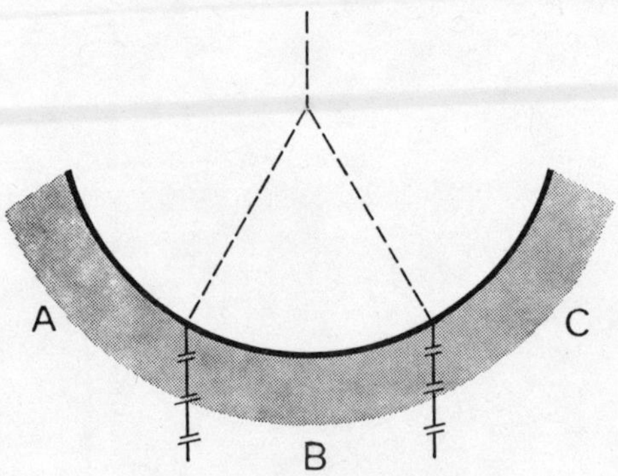

I

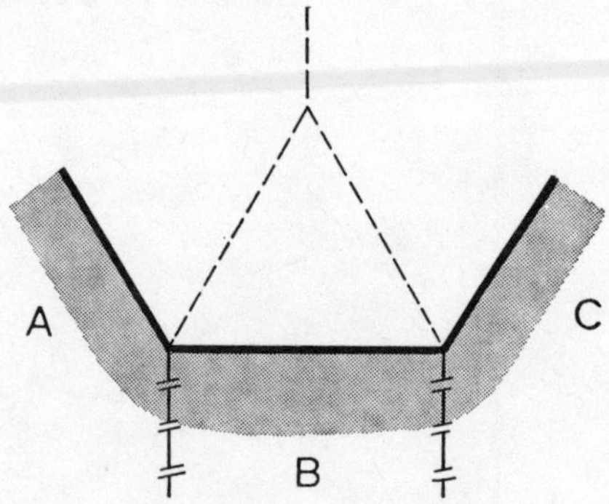

II

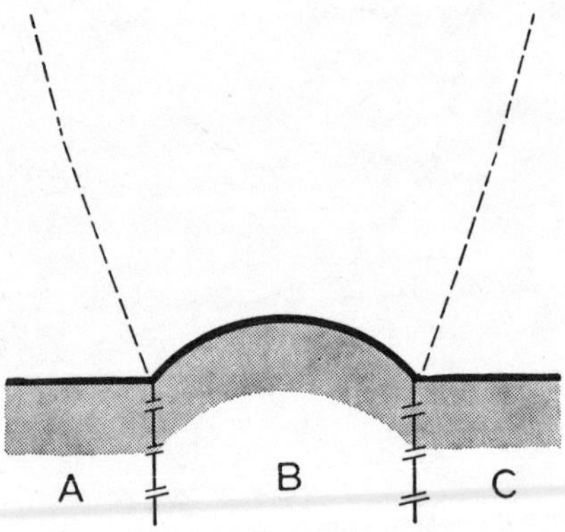

III

Sketches illustrating the geographical situations described in paragraph 8 of the Judgment

Croquis illustratifs des situations géographiques décrites au paragraphe 8 de l'arrêt

6. Under the agreements of December 1964 and June 1965, already mentioned, the partial boundaries represented by the map lines A-B and C-D had, according to the information furnished to the Court by the Parties, been drawn mainly by application of the principle of equidistance, using that term as denoting the abstract concept of equidistance. A line so drawn, known as an "equidistance line", may be described as one which leaves to each of the parties concerned all those portions of the continental shelf that are nearer to a point on its own coast than they are to any point on the coast of the other party. An equidistance line may consist either of a "median" line between "opposite" States, or of a "lateral" line between "adjacent" States. In certain geographical configurations of which the Parties furnished examples, a given equidistance line may partake in varying degree of the nature both of a median and of a lateral line. There exists nevertheless a distinction to be drawn between the two, which will be mentioned in its place.

7. The further negotiations between the Parties for the prolongation of the partial boundaries broke down mainly because Denmark and the Netherlands respectively wished this prolongation also to be effected on the basis of the equidistance principle,—and this would have resulted in the dotted lines B-E and D-E, shown on Map 3; whereas the Federal Republic considered that such an outcome would be inequitable because it would unduly curtail what the Republic believed should be its proper share of continental shelf area, on the basis of proportionality to the length of its North Sea coastline. It will be observed that neither of the lines in question, taken by itself, would produce this effect, but only both of them together—an element regarded by Denmark and the Netherlands as irrelevant to what they viewed as being two separate and self-contained delimitations, each of which should be carried out without reference to the other.

8. The reason for the result that would be produced by the two lines B-E and D-E, taken conjointly, is that in the case of a concave or recessing coast such as that of the Federal Republic on the North Sea, the effect of the use of the equidistance method is to pull the line of the boundary inwards, in the direction of the concavity. Consequently, where two such lines are drawn at different points on a concave coast, they will, if the curvature is pronounced, inevitably meet at a relatively short distance from the coast, thus causing the continental shelf area they enclose, to take the form approximately of a triangle with its apex to seaward and, as it was put on behalf of the Federal Republic, "cutting off" the coastal State from the further areas of the continental shelf outside of and beyond this triangle. The effect of concavity could of course equally be produced for a country with a straight coastline if the coasts of adjacent countries protruded immediately on either side of it. In contrast to this, the effect of coastal projections, or of convex or outwardly curving coasts such as are, to a moderate extent, those of Denmark and the Netherlands, is to cause boundary lines drawn on an equidistance basis to leave the

coast on divergent courses, thus having a widening tendency on the area of continental shelf off that coast. These two distinct effects, which are shown in sketches I-III to be found on page 16, are directly attributable to the use of the equidistance method of delimiting continental shelf boundaries off recessing or projecting coasts. It goes without saying that on these types of coasts the equidistance method produces exactly similar effects in the delimitation of the lateral boundaries of the territorial sea of the States concerned. However, owing to the very close proximity of such waters to the coasts concerned, these effects are much less marked and may be very slight,—and there are other aspects involved, which will be considered in their place. It will suffice to mention here that, for instance, a deviation from a line drawn perpendicular to the general direction of the coast, of only 5 kilometres, at a distance of about 5 kilometres from that coast, will grow into one of over 30 at a distance of over 100 kilometres.

9. After the negotiations, separately held between the Federal Republic and the other two Parties respectively, had in each case, for the reasons given in the two preceding paragraphs, failed to result in any agreement about the delimitation of the boundary extending beyond the partial one already agreed, tripartite talks between all the Parties took place in The Hague in February-March 1966, in Bonn in May and again in Copenhagen in August. These also proving fruitless, it was then decided to submit the matter to the Court. In the meantime the Governments of Denmark and the Netherlands had, by means of the agreement of 31 March 1966, already referred to (paragraph 5), proceeded to a delimitation as between themselves of the continental shelf areas lying between the apex of the triangle notionally ascribed by them to the Federal Republic (point E on Map 3) and the median line already drawn in the North Sea, by means of a boundary drawn on equidistance principles, meeting that line at the point marked F on Map 3. On 25 May 1966, the Government of the Federal Republic, taking the view that this delimitation was *res inter alios acta*, notified the Governments of Denmark and the Netherlands, by means of an aide-mémoire, that the agreement thus concluded could not "have any effect on the question of the delimitation of the German-Netherlands or the German-Danish parts of the continental shelf in the North Sea".

10. In pursuance of the tripartite arrangements that had been made at Bonn and Copenhagen, as described in the preceding paragraph, Special Agreements for the submission to the Court of the differences involved were initialled in August 1966 and signed on 2 February 1967. By a tripartite Protocol signed the same day it was provided *(a)* that the Government of the Kingdom of the Netherlands would notify the two Special Agreements to the Court, in accordance with Article 40, paragraph 1, of the Court's Statute, together with the text of the Protocol itself; *(b)* that after such notification, the Parties would ask the Court to join the two cases; and *(c)* that for the purpose of the appointment

of a judge *ad hoc*, the Kingdoms of Denmark and the Netherlands should be considered as being in the same interest within the meaning of Article 31, paragraph 5, of the Court's Statute. Following upon these communications, duly made to it in the implementation of the Protocol, the Court, by an Order dated 26 April 1968, declared Denmark and the Netherlands to be in the same interest, and joined the proceedings in the two cases.

11. Although the proceedings have thus been joined, the cases themselves remain separate, at least in the sense that they relate to different areas of the North Sea continental shelf, and that there is no *a priori* reason why the Court must reach identical conclusions in regard to them,—if for instance geographical features present in the one case were not present in the other. At the same time, the legal arguments presented on behalf of Denmark and the Netherlands, both before and since the joinder, have been substantially identical, apart from certain matters of detail, and have been presented either in common or in close co-operation. To this extent therefore, the two cases may be treated as one; and it must be noted that although two separate delimitations are in question, they involve—indeed actually give rise to—a single situation. The fact that the question of either of these delimitations might have arisen and called for settlement separately in point of time, does not alter the character of the problem with which the Court is actually faced, having regard to the manner in which the Parties themselves have brought the matter before it, as described in the two preceding paragraphs.

12. In conclusion as to the facts, it should be noted that the Federal Republic has formally reserved its position, not only in regard to the Danish-Netherlands delimitation of the line E-F (Map 3), as noted in paragraph 9, but also in regard to the delimitations United Kingdom/Denmark and United Kingdom/Netherlands mentioned in paragraph 4. In both the latter cases the Government of the Federal Republic pointed out to all the Governments concerned that the question of the lateral delimitation of the continental shelf in the North Sea between the Federal Republic and the Kingdoms of Denmark and the Netherlands was still outstanding and could not be prejudiced by the agreements concluded between those two countries and the United Kingdom.

* * *

13. Such are the events and geographical facts in the light of which the Court has to determine what principles and rules of international law are applicable to the delimitation of the areas of continental shelf involved. On this question the Parties have taken up fundamentally different positions. On behalf of the Kingdoms of Denmark and the Netherlands it is contended that the whole matter is governed by a

mandatory rule of law which, reflecting the language of Article 6 of the Convention on the Continental Shelf concluded at Geneva on 29 April 1958, was designated by them as the "equidistance-special circumstances" rule. According to this contention, "equidistance" is not merely a method of the cartographical construction of a boundary line, but the essential element in a rule of law which may be stated as follows,—namely that in the absence of agreement by the Parties to employ another method or to proceed to a delimitation on an *ad hoc* basis, all continental shelf boundaries must be drawn by means of an equidistance line, unless, or except to the extent to which, "special circumstances" are recognized to exist,—an equidistance line being, it will be recalled, a line every point on which is the same distance away from whatever point is nearest to it on the coast of each of the countries concerned—or rather, strictly, on the baseline of the territorial sea along that coast. As regards what constitutes "special circumstances", all that need be said at this stage is that according to the view put forward on behalf of Denmark and the Netherlands, the configuration of the German North Sea coast, its recessive character, and the fact that it makes nearly a right-angled bend in mid-course, would not of itself constitute, for either of the two boundary lines concerned, a special circumstance calling for or warranting a departure from the equidistance method of delimitation: only the presence of some special feature, minor in itself—such as an islet or small protuberance—but so placed as to produce a disproportionately distorting effect on an otherwise acceptable boundary line would, so it was claimed, possess this character.

14. These various contentions, together with the view that a rule of equidistance-special circumstances is binding on the Federal Republic, are founded by Denmark and the Netherlands partly on the 1958 Geneva Convention on the Continental Shelf already mentioned (preceding paragraph), and partly on general considerations of law relating to the continental shelf, lying outside this Convention. Similar considerations are equally put forward to found the contention that the delimitation on an equidistance basis of the line E-F (Map 3) by the Netherlands-Danish agreement of 31 March 1966 (paragraph 5 above) is valid *erga omnes*, and must be respected by the Federal Republic unless it can demonstrate the existence of juridically relevant "special circumstances".

15. The Federal Republic, for its part, while recognizing the utility of equidistance as a method of delimitation, and that this method can in many cases be employed appropriately and with advantage, denies its obligatory character for States not parties to the Geneva Convention, and contends that the correct rule to be applied, at any rate in such circumstances as those of the North Sea, is one according to which each of the States concerned should have a "just and equitable share" of the available continental shelf, in proportion to the length of its coastline or sea-frontage. It was also contended on behalf of the Federal Republic

that in a sea shaped as is the North Sea, the whole bed of which, except for the Norwegian Trough, consists of continental shelf at a depth of less than 200 metres, and where the situation of the circumjacent States causes a natural convergence of their respective continental shelf areas, towards a central point situated on the median line of the whole seabed —or at any rate in those localities where this is the case—each of the States concerned is entitled to a continental shelf area extending up to this central point (in effect a sector), or at least extending to the median line at some point or other. In this way the "cut-off" effect, of which the Federal Republic complains, caused, as explained in paragraph 8, by the drawing of equidistance lines at the two ends of an inward curving or recessed coast, would be avoided. As a means of giving effect to these ideas, the Federal Republic proposed the method of the "coastal front", or façade, constituted by a straight baseline joining these ends, upon which the necessary geometrical constructions would be erected.

16. Alternatively, the Federal Republic claimed that if, contrary to its main contention, the equidistance method was held to be applicable, then the configuration of the German North Sea coast constituted a "special circumstance" such as to justify a departure from that method of delimitation in this particular case.

17. In putting forward these contentions, it was stressed on behalf of the Federal Republic that the claim for a just and equitable share did not in any way involve asking the Court to give a decision *ex aequo et bono* (which, having regard to the terms of paragraph 2 of Article 38 of the Court's Statute, would not be possible without the consent of the Parties),—for the principle of the just and equitable share was one of the recognized general principles of law which, by virtue of paragraph 1 *(c)* of the same Article, the Court was entitled to apply as a matter of the *justitia distributiva* which entered into all legal systems. It appeared, moreover, that whatever its underlying motivation, the claim of the Federal Republic was, at least ostensibly, to a just and equitable share of the space involved, rather than to a share of the natural resources as such, mineral or other, to be found in it, the location of which could not in any case be fully ascertained at present. On the subject of location the Court has in fact received some, though not complete information, but has not thought it necessary to pursue the matter, since the question of natural resources is less one of delimitation than of eventual exploitation.

*

18. It will be convenient to consider first the contentions put forward on behalf of the Federal Republic. The Court does not feel able to accept them—at least in the particular form they have taken. It considers

that, having regard both to the language of the Special Agreements and to more general considerations of law relating to the régime of the continental shelf, its task in the present proceedings relates essentially to the delimitation and not the apportionment of the areas concerned, or their division into converging sectors. Delimitation is a process which involves establishing the boundaries of an area already, in principle, appertaining to the coastal State and not the determination *de novo* of such an area. Delimitation in an equitable manner is one thing, but not the same thing as awarding a just and equitable share of a previously undelimited area, even though in a number of cases the results may be comparable, or even identical.

19. More important is the fact that the doctrine of the just and equitable share appears to be wholly at variance with what the Court entertains no doubt is the most fundamental of all the rules of law relating to the continental shelf, enshrined in Article 2 of the 1958 Geneva Convention, though quite independent of it,—namely that the rights of the coastal State in respect of the area of continental shelf that constitutes a natural prolongation of its land territory into and under the sea exist *ipso facto* and *ab initio*, by virtue of its sovereignty over the land, and as an extension of it in an exercise of sovereign rights for the purpose of exploring the seabed and exploiting its natural resources. In short, there is here an inherent right. In order to exercise it, no special legal process has to be gone through, nor have any special legal acts to be performed. Its existence can be declared (and many States have done this) but does not need to be constituted. Furthermore, the right does not depend on its being exercised. To echo the language of the Geneva Convention, it is "exclusive" in the sense that if the coastal State does not choose to explore or exploit the areas of shelf appertaining to it, that is its own affair, but no one else may do so without its express consent.

20. It follows that even in such a situation as that of the North Sea, the notion of apportioning an as yet undelimited area, considered as a whole (which underlies the doctrine of the just and equitable share), is quite foreign to, and inconsistent with, the basic concept of continental shelf entitlement, according to which the process of delimitation is essentially one of drawing a boundary line between areas which already appertain to one or other of the States affected. The delimitation itself must indeed be equitably effected, but it cannot have as its object the awarding of an equitable share, or indeed of a share, as such, at all,—for the fundamental concept involved does not admit of there being anything undivided to share out. Evidently any dispute about boundaries must involve that there is a disputed marginal or fringe area, to which both parties are laying claim, so that any delimitation of it which does not leave it wholly to one of the parties will in practice divide it between them in certain shares, or operate as if such a division had been made.

But this does not mean that there has been an apportionment of something that previously consisted of an integral, still less an undivided whole.

* * *

21. The Court will now turn to the contentions advanced on behalf of Denmark and the Netherlands. Their general character has already been indicated in paragraphs 13 and 14: the most convenient way of dealing with them will be on the basis of the following question—namely, does the equidistance-special circumstances principle constitute a mandatory rule, either on a conventional or on a customary international law basis, in such a way as to govern any delimitation of the North Sea continental shelf areas between the Federal Republic and the Kingdoms of Denmark and the Netherlands respectively? Another and shorter way of formulating the question would be to ask whether, in any delimitation of these areas, the Federal Republic is under a legal obligation to accept the application of the equidistance-special circumstances principle.

22. Particular attention is directed to the use, in the foregoing formulations, of the terms "mandatory" and "obligation". It has never been doubted that the equidistance method of delimitation is a very convenient one, the use of which is indicated in a considerable number of cases. It constitutes a method capable of being employed in almost all circumstances, however singular the results might sometimes be, and has the virtue that if necessary,—if for instance, the Parties are unable to enter into negotiations,—any cartographer can *de facto* trace such a boundary on the appropriate maps and charts, and those traced by competent cartographers will for all practical purposes agree.

23. In short, it would probably be true to say that no other method of delimitation has the same combination of practical convenience and certainty of application. Yet these factors do not suffice of themselves to convert what is a method into a rule of law, making the acceptance of the results of using that method obligatory in all cases in which the parties do not agree otherwise, or in which "special circumstances" cannot be shown to exist. Juridically, if there is such a rule, it must draw its legal force from other factors than the existence of these advantages, important though they may be. It should also be noticed that the counterpart of this conclusion is no less valid, and that the practical advantages of the equidistance method would continue to exist whether its employment were obligatory or not.

24. It would however be ignoring realities if it were not noted at the same time that the use of this method, partly for the reasons given in paragraph 8 above and partly for reasons that are best appreciated by reference to the many maps and diagrams furnished by both sides in the course of the written and oral proceedings, can under certain circumstances produce results that appear on the face of them to be extraordinary, unnatural or unreasonable. It is basically this fact which un-

derlies the present proceedings. The plea that, however this may be, the results can never be inequitable, because the equidistance principle is by definition an equitable principle of delimitation, involves a postulate that clearly begs the whole question at issue.

* * *

25. The Court now turns to the legal position regarding the equidistance method. The first question to be considered is whether the 1958 Geneva Convention on the Continental Shelf is binding for all the Parties in this case—that is to say whether, as contended by Denmark and the Netherlands, the use of this method is rendered obligatory for the present delimitations by virtue of the delimitations provision (Article 6) of that instrument, according to the conditions laid down in it. Clearly, if this is so, then the provisions of the Convention will prevail in the relations between the Parties, and would take precedence of any rules having a more general character, or derived from another source. On that basis the Court's reply to the question put to it in the Special Agreements would necessarily be to the effect that as between the Parties the relevant provisions of the Convention represented the applicable rules of law—that is to say constituted the law for the Parties—and its sole remaining task would be to interpret those provisions, in so far as their meaning was disputed or appeared to be uncertain, and to apply them to the particular circumstances involved.

26. The relevant provisions of Article 6 of the Geneva Convention, paragraph 2 of which Denmark and the Netherlands contend not only to be applicable as a conventional rule, but also to represent the accepted rule of general international law on the subject of continental shelf delimitation, as it exists independently of the Convention, read as follows:

> "1. Where the same continental shelf is adjacent to the territories of two or more States whose coasts are opposite each other, the boundary of the continental shelf appertaining to such States shall be determined by agreement between them. In the absence of agreement, and unless another boundary line is justified by special circumstances, the boundary is the median line, every point of which is equidistant from the nearest point of the baselines from which the breadth of the territorial sea of each State is measured.
>
> 2. Where the same continental shelf is adjacent to the territories of two adjacent States, the boundary of the continental shelf shall be determined by agreement between them. In the absence of agreement, and unless another boundary line is justified by special circumstances, the boundary shall be determined by application of the principle of equidistance from the nearest points of the baselines from which the breadth of the territorial sea of each State is measured."

The Convention received 46 signatures and, up-to-date, there have been 39 ratifications or accessions. It came into force on 10 June 1964, having received the 22 ratifications or accessions required for that purpose (Article 11), and was therefore in force at the time when the various delimitations of continental shelf boundaries described earlier (paragraphs 1 and 5) took place between the Parties. But, under the formal provisions of the Convention, it is in force for any individual State only in so far as, having signed it within the time-limit provided for that purpose, that State has also subsequently ratified it; or, not having signed within that time-limit, has subsequently acceded to the Convention. Denmark and the Netherlands have both signed and ratified the Convention, and are parties to it, the former since 10 June 1964, the latter since 20 March 1966. The Federal Republic was one of the signatories of the Convention, but has never ratified it, and is consequently not a party.

27. It is admitted on behalf of Denmark and the Netherlands that in these circumstances the Convention cannot, as such, be binding on the Federal Republic, in the sense of the Republic being contractually bound by it. But it is contended that the Convention, or the régime of the Convention, and in particular of Article 6, has become binding on the Federal Republic in another way,—namely because, by conduct, by public statements and proclamations, and in other ways, the Republic has unilaterally assumed the obligations of the Convention; or has manifested its acceptance of the conventional régime; or has recognized it as being generally applicable to the delimitation of continental shelf areas. It has also been suggested that the Federal Republic had held itself out as so assuming, accepting or recognizing, in such a manner as to cause other States, and in particular Denmark and the Netherlands, to rely on the attitude thus taken up.

28. As regards these contentions, it is clear that only a very definite, very consistent course of conduct on the part of a State in the situation of the Federal Republic could justify the Court in upholding them; and, if this had existed—that is to say if there had been a real intention to manifest acceptance or recognition of the applicability of the conventional régime—then it must be asked why it was that the Federal Republic did not take the obvious step of giving expression to this readiness by simply ratifying the Convention. In principle, when a number of States, including the one whose conduct is invoked, and those invoking it, have drawn up a convention specifically providing for a particular method by which the intention to become bound by the régime of the convention is to be manifested—namely by the carrying out of certain prescribed formalities (ratification, accession), it is not lightly to be presumed that a State which has not carried out these formalities, though at all times fully able and entitled to do so, has nevertheless somehow become bound in another way. Indeed if it were a question not of obligation but of rights,—if, that is to say, a State which, though entitled

to do so, had not ratified or acceded, attempted to claim rights under the convention, on the basis of a declared willingness to be bound by it, or of conduct evincing acceptance of the conventional régime, it would simply be told that, not having become a party to the convention it could not claim any rights under it until the professed willingness and acceptance had been manifested in the prescribed form.

29. A further point, not in itself conclusive, but to be noted, is that if the Federal Republic had ratified the Geneva Convention, it could have entered—and could, if it ratified now, enter—a reservation to Article 6, by reason of the faculty to do so conferred by Article 12 of the Convention. This faculty would remain, whatever the previous conduct of the Federal Republic might have been—a fact which at least adds to the difficulties involved by the Danish-Netherlands contention.

30. Having regard to these considerations of principle, it appears to the Court that only the existence of a situation of estoppel could suffice to lend substance to this contention,—that is to say if the Federal Republic were now precluded from denying the applicability of the conventional régime, by reason of past conduct, declarations, etc., which not only clearly and consistently evinced acceptance of that régime, but also had caused Denmark or the Netherlands, in reliance on such conduct, detrimentally to change position or suffer some prejudice. Of this there is no evidence whatever in the present case.

31. In these circumstances it seems to the Court that little useful purpose would be served by passing in review and subjecting to detailed scrutiny the various acts relied on by Denmark and the Netherlands as being indicative of the Federal Republic's acceptance of the régime of Article 6;—for instance that at the Geneva Conference the Federal Republic did not take formal objection to Article 6 and eventually signed the Convention without entering any reservation in respect of that provision; that it at one time announced its intention to ratify the Convention; that in its public declarations concerning its continental shelf rights it appeared to rely on, or at least cited, certain provisions of the Geneva Convention. In this last connection a good deal has been made of the joint Minute signed in Bonn, on 4 August 1964, between the then-negotiating delegations of the Federal Republic and the Netherlands. But this minute made it clear that what the Federal Republic was seeking was an agreed division, rather than a delimitation of the central North Sea continental shelf areas, and the reference it made to Article 6 was specifically to the first sentence of paragraphs 1 and 2 of that Article, which speaks exclusively of delimitation by agreement and not at all of the use of the equidistance method.

32. In the result it appears to the Court that none of the elements invoked is decisive; each is ultimately negative or inconclusive; all are capable of varying interpretations or explanations. It would be one

thing to infer from the declarations of the Federal Republic an admission accepting the fundamental concept of coastal State rights in respect of the continental shelf: it would be quite another matter to see in this an acceptance of the rules of delimitation contained in the Convention. The declarations of the Federal Republic, taken in the aggregate, might at most justify the view that to begin with, and before becoming fully aware of what the probable effects in the North Sea would be, the Federal Republic was not specifically opposed to the equidistance principle as embodied in Article 6 of the Convention. But from a purely negative conclusion such as this, it would certainly not be possible to draw the positive inference that the Federal Republic, though not a party to the Convention, had accepted the régime of Article 6 in a manner binding upon itself.

33. The dangers of the doctrine here advanced by Denmark and the Netherlands, if it had to be given general application in the international law field, hardly need stressing. Moreover, in the present case, any such inference would immediately be nullified by the fact that, as soon as concrete delimitations of North Sea continental shelf areas began to be carried out, the Federal Republic, as described earlier (paragraphs 9 and 12), at once reserved its position with regard to those delimitations which (effected on an equidistance basis) might be prejudicial to the delimitation of its own continental shelf areas.

*

34. Since, accordingly, the foregoing considerations must lead the Court to hold that Article 6 of the Geneva Convention is not, as such, applicable to the delimitations involved in the present proceedings, it becomes unnecessary for it to go into certain questions relating to the interpretation or application of that provision which would otherwise arise. One should be mentioned however, namely what is the relationship between the requirement of Article 6 for delimitation by agreement, and the requirements relating to equidistance and special circumstances that are to be applied in "the absence of" such agreement,—i.e., in the absence of agreement on the matter, is there a presumption that the continental shelf boundary between any two adjacent States consists automatically of an equidistance line,—or must negotiations for an agreed boundary prove finally abortive before the acceptance of a boundary drawn on an equidistance basis becomes obligatory in terms of Article 6, if no special circumstances exist?

35. Without attempting to resolve this question, the determination of which is not necessary for the purposes of the present case, the Court draws attention to the fact that the delimitation of the line E-F, as shown on Map 3, which was effected by Denmark and the Netherlands under the agreement of 31 March 1966 already mentioned (paragraphs 5 and 9), to which the Federal Republic was not a party, must have been based on

the tacit assumption that, no agreement to the contrary having been reached in the negotiations between the Federal Republic and Denmark and the Netherlands respectively (paragraph 7), the boundary between the continental shelf areas of the Republic and those of the other two countries must be deemed to be an equidistance one;—or in other words the delimitation of the line E-F, and its validity *erga omnes* including the Federal Republic, as contended for by Denmark and the Netherlands, presupposes both the delimitation and the validity on an equidistance basis, of the lines B-E and D-E on Map 3, considered by Denmark and the Netherlands to represent the boundaries between their continental shelf areas and those of the Federal Republic.

36. Since, however, Article 6 of the Geneva Convention provides only for delimitation between "adjacent" States, which Denmark and the Netherlands clearly are not, or between "opposite" States which, despite suggestions to the contrary, the Court thinks they equally are not, the delimitation of the line E-F on Map 3 could not in any case find its validity in Article 6, even if that provision were opposable to the Federal Republic. The validity of this delimitation must therefore be sought in some other source of law. It is a main contention of Denmark and the Netherlands that there does in fact exist such another source, furnishing a rule that validates not only this particular delimitation, but all delimitations effected on an equidistance basis,—and indeed requiring delimitation on that basis unless the States concerned otherwise agree, and whether or not the Geneva Convention is applicable. This contention must now be examined.

* * *

37. It is maintained by Denmark and the Netherlands that the Federal Republic, whatever its position may be in relation to the Geneva Convention, considered as such, is in any event bound to accept delimitation on an equidistance-special circumstances basis, because the use of this method is not in the nature of a merely conventional obligation, but is, or must now be regarded as involving, a rule that is part of the *corpus* of general international law;—and, like other rules of general or customary international law, is binding on the Federal Republic automatically and independently of any specific assent, direct or indirect, given by the latter. This contention has both a positive law and a more fundamentalist aspect. As a matter of positive law, it is based on the work done in this field by international legal bodies, on State practice and on the influence attributed to the Geneva Convention itself,—the claim being that these various factors have cumulatively evidenced or been creative of the *opinio juris sive necessitatis*, requisite for the formation of new rules of customary international law. In its fundamentalist aspect, the view put forward derives from what might be called the natural law of the con-

tinental shelf, in the sense that the equidistance principle is seen as a necessary expression in the field of delimitation of the accepted doctrine of the exclusive appurtenance of the continental shelf to the nearby coastal State, and therefore as having an *a priori* character of so to speak juristic inevitability.

38. The Court will begin by examining this latter aspect, both because it is the more fundamental, and was so presented on behalf of Denmark and the Netherlands—i.e., as something governing the whole case; and because, if it is correct that the equidistance principle is, as the point was put in the course of the argument, to be regarded as inherent in the whole basic concept of continental shelf rights, then equidistance should constitute the rule according to positive law tests also. On the other hand, if equidistance should not possess any *a priori* character of necessity or inherency, this would not be any bar to its having become a rule of positive law through influences such as those of the Geneva Convention and State practice,—and that aspect of the matter would remain for later examination.

*

39. The *a priori* argument starts from the position described in paragraph 19, according to which the right of the coastal State to its continental shelf areas is based on its sovereignty over the land domain, of which the shelf area is the natural prolongation into and under the sea. From this notion of appurtenance is derived the view which, as has already been indicated, the Court accepts, that the coastal State's rights exist *ipso facto* and *ab initio* without there being any question of having to make good a claim to the areas concerned, or of any apportionment of the continental shelf between different States. This was one reason why the Court felt bound to reject the claim of the Federal Republic (in the particular form which it took) to be awarded a "just and equitable share" of the shelf areas involved in the present proceedings. Denmark and the Netherlands, for their part, claim that the test of appurtenance must be "proximity", or more accurately "closer proximity": all those parts of the shelf being considered as appurtenant to a particular coastal State which are (but only if they are) closer to it than they are to any point on the coast of another State. Hence delimitation must be effected by a method which will leave to each one of the States concerned all those areas that are nearest to its own coast. Only a line drawn on equidistance principles will do this. Therefore, it is contended, only such a line can be valid (unless the Parties, for reasons of their own, agree on another), because only such a line can be thus consistent with basic continental shelf doctrine.

40. This view clearly has much force; for there can be no doubt that as a matter of normal topography, the greater part of a State's continental

shelf areas will in fact, and without the necessity for any delimitation at all, be nearer to its coasts than to any other. It could not well be otherwise; but *post hoc* is not *propter hoc*, and this situation may only serve to obscure the real issue, which is whether it follows that every part of the area concerned must be placed in this way, and that it should be as it were prohibited that any part should not be so placed. The Court does not consider that it does follow, either from the notion of proximity itself, or from the more fundamental concept of the continental shelf as being the natural prolongation of the land domain—a concept repeatedly appealed to by both sides throughout the case, although quite differently interpreted by them.

41. As regards the notion of proximity, the idea of absolute proximity is certainly not implied by the rather vague and general terminology employed in the literature of the subject, and in most State proclamations and international conventions and other instruments—terms such as "near", "close to its shores", "off its coast", "opposite", "in front of the coast", "in the vicinity of", "neighbouring the coast", "adjacent to", "contiguous", etc.,—all of them terms of a somewhat imprecise character which, although they convey a reasonably clear general idea, are capable of a considerable fluidity of meaning. To take what is perhaps the most frequently employed of these terms, namely "adjacent to", it is evident that by no stretch of imagination can a point on the continental shelf situated say a hundred miles, or even much less, from a given coast, be regarded as "adjacent" to it, or to any coast at all, in the normal sense of adjacency, even if the point concerned is nearer to some one coast than to any other. This would be even truer of localities where, physically, the continental shelf begins to merge with the ocean depths. Equally, a point inshore situated near the meeting place of the coasts of two States can often properly be said to be adjacent to both coasts, even though it may be fractionally closer to the one than the other. Indeed, local geographical configuration may sometimes cause it to have a closer physical connection with the coast to which it is not in fact closest.

42. There seems in consequence to be no necessary, and certainly no complete, identity between the notions of adjacency and proximity; and therefore the question of which parts of the continental shelf "adjacent to" a coastline bordering more than one State fall within the appurtenance of which of them, remains to this extent an open one, not to be determined on a basis exclusively of proximity. Even if proximity may afford one of the tests to be applied and an important one in the right conditions, it may not necessarily be the only, nor in all circumstances, the most appropriate one. Hence it would seem that the notion of adjacency, so constantly employed in continental shelf doctrine from the start, only implies proximity in a general sense, and does not imply any fundamental or inherent rule the ultimate effect of which would be to

prohibit any State (otherwise than by agreement) from exercising continental shelf rights in respect of areas closer to the coast of another State.

43. More fundamental than the notion of proximity appears to be the principle—constantly relied upon by all the Parties—of the natural prolongation or continuation of the land territory or domain, or land sovereignty of the coastal State, into and under the high seas, via the bed of its territorial sea which is under the full sovereignty of that State. There are various ways of formulating this principle, but the underlying idea, namely of an extension of something already possessed, is the same, and it is this idea of extension which is, in the Court's opinion, determinant. Submarine areas do not really appertain to the coastal State because—or not only because—they are near it. They are near it of course; but this would not suffice to confer title, any more than, according to a well-established principle of law recognized by both sides in the present case, mere proximity confers *per se* title to land territory. What confers the *ipso jure* title which international law attributes to the coastal State in respect of its continental shelf, is the fact that the submarine areas concerned may be deemed to be actually part of the territory over which the coastal State already has dominion,—in the sense that, although covered with water, they are a prolongation or continuation of that territory, an extension of it under the sea. From this it would follow that whenever a given submarine area does not constitute a natural—or the most natural—extension of the land territory of a coastal State, even though that area may be closer to it than it is to the territory of any other State, it cannot be regarded as appertaining to that State;—or at least it cannot be so regarded in the face of a competing claim by a State of whose land territory the submarine area concerned is to be regarded as a natural extension, even if it is less close to it.

44. In the present case, although both sides relied on the prolongation principle and regarded it as fundamental, they interpreted it quite differently. Both interpretations appear to the Court to be incorrect. Denmark and the Netherlands identified natural prolongation with closest proximity and therefrom argued that it called for an equidistance line: the Federal Republic seemed to think it implied the notion of the just and equitable share, although the connection is distinctly remote. (The Federal Republic did however invoke another idea, namely that of the proportionality of a State's continental shelf area to the length of its coastline, which obviously does have an intimate connection with the prolongation principle, and will be considered in its place.) As regards equidistance, it clearly cannot be identified with the notion of natural prolongation or extension, since, as has already been stated (paragraph 8), the use of the equidistance method would frequently cause areas which are the natural prolongation or extension of the territory of one State to be attributed to another, when the configuration of the latter's coast makes the equidistance line swing out laterally across the former's

coastal front, cutting it off from areas situated directly before that front.

45. The fluidity of all these notions is well illustrated by the case of the Norwegian Trough (paragraph 4 above). Without attempting to pronounce on the status of that feature, the Court notes that the shelf areas in the North Sea separated from the Norwegian coast by the 80-100 kilometres of the Trough cannot in any physical sense be said to be adjacent to it, nor to be its natural prolongation. They are nevertheless considered by the States parties to the relevant delimitations, as described in paragraph 4, to appertain to Norway up to the median lines shown on Map 1. True these median lines are themselves drawn on equidistance principles; but it was only by first ignoring the existence of the Trough that these median lines fell to be drawn at all.

*

46. The conclusion drawn by the Court from the foregoing analysis is that the notion of equidistance as being logically necessary, in the sense of being an inescapable *a priori* accompaniment of basic continental shelf doctrine, is incorrect. It is said not to be possible to maintain that there is a rule of law ascribing certain areas to a State as a matter of inherent and original right (see paragraphs 19 and 20), without also admitting the existence of some rule by which those areas can be obligatorily delimited. The Court cannot accept the logic of this view. The problem arises only where there is a dispute and only in respect of the marginal areas involved. The appurtenance of a given area, considered as an entity, in no way governs the precise delimitation of its boundaries, any more than uncertainty as to boundaries can affect territorial rights. There is for instance no rule that the land frontiers of a State must be fully delimited and defined, and often in various places and for long periods they are not, as is shown by the case of the entry of Albania into the League of Nations (*Monastery of Saint Naoum*, *Advisory Opinion, 1924*, *P.C.I.J.*, *Series B*, *No. 9*, at p. 10).

* * *

47. A review of the genesis and development of the equidistance method of delimitation can only serve to confirm the foregoing conclusion. Such a review may appropriately start with the instrument, generally known as the "Truman Proclamation", issued by the Government of the United States on 28 September 1945. Although this instrument was not the first or only one to have appeared, it has in the opinion of the Court a special status. Previously, various theories as to the nature and extent of the rights relative to or exercisable over the continental shelf had been advanced by jurists, publicists and technicians. The Truman Proclamation however, soon came to be regarded as the starting point of the posi-

tive law on the subject, and the chief doctrine it enunciated, namely that of the coastal State as having an original, natural, and exclusive (in short a vested) right to the continental shelf off its shores, came to prevail over all others, being now reflected in Article 2 of the 1958 Geneva Convention on the Continental Shelf. With regard to the delimitation of lateral boundaries between the continental shelves of adjacent States, a matter which had given rise to some consideration on the technical, but very little on the juristic level, the Truman Proclamation stated that such boundaries "shall be determined by the United States and the State concerned in accordance with equitable principles". These two concepts, of delimitation by mutual agreement and delimitation in accordance with equitable principles, have underlain all the subsequent history of the subject. They were reflected in various other State proclamations of the period, and after, and in the later work on the subject.

48. It was in the International Law Commission of the United Nations that the question of delimitation as between adjacent States was first taken up seriously as part of a general juridical project; for outside the ranks of the hydrographers and cartographers, questions of delimitation were not much thought about in earlier continental shelf doctrine. Juridical interest and speculation was focussed mainly on such questions as what was the legal basis on which any rights at all in respect of the continental shelf could be claimed, and what was the nature of those rights. As regards boundaries, the main issue was not that of boundaries between States but of the seaward limit of the area in respect of which the coastal State could claim exclusive rights of exploitation. As was pointed out in the course of the written proceedings, States in most cases had not found it necessary to conclude treaties or legislate about their lateral sea boundaries with adjacent States before the question of exploiting the natural resources of the seabed and subsoil arose;—practice was therefore sparse.

49. In the records of the International Law Commission, which had the matter under consideration from 1950 to 1956, there is no indication at all that any of its members supposed that it was incumbent on the Commission to adopt a rule of equidistance because this gave expression to, and translated into linear terms, a principle of proximity inherent in the basic concept of the continental shelf, causing every part of the shelf to appertain to the nearest coastal State and to no other, and because such a rule must therefore be mandatory as a matter of customary international law. Such an idea does not seem ever to have been propounded. Had it been, and had it had the self-evident character contended for by Denmark and the Netherlands, the Commission would have had no alternative but to adopt it, and its long continued hesitations over this matter would be incomprehensible.

50. It is moreover, in the present context, a striking feature of the Commission's discussions that during the early and middle stages, not only was the notion of equidistance never considered from the standpoint of its having *a priori* a character of inherent necessity: it was never given any special prominence at all, and certainly no priority. The Commission discussed various other possibilities as having equal if not superior status such as delimitation by agreement, by reference to arbitration, by drawing lines perpendicular to the coast, by prolonging the dividing line of adjacent territorial waters (the principle of which was itself not as yet settled), and on occasion the Commission seriously considered adopting one or other of these solutions. It was not in fact until after the matter had been referred to a committee of hydrographical experts, which reported in 1953, that the equidistance principle began to take precedence over other possibilities: the Report of the Commission for that year (its principal report on the topic of delimitation as such) makes it clear that before this reference to the experts the Commission had felt unable to formulate any definite rule at all, the previous trend of opinion having been mainly in favour of delimitation by agreement or by reference to arbitration.

51. It was largely because of these difficulties that it was decided to consult the Committee of Experts. It is therefore instructive in the context (i.e., of an alleged inherent necessity for the equidistance principle) to see on what basis the matter was put to the experts, and how they dealt with it. Equidistance was in fact only one of four methods suggested to them, the other three being the continuation in the seaward direction of the land frontier between the two adjacent States concerned; the drawing of a perpendicular to the coast at the point of its intersection with this land frontier; and the drawing of a line perpendicular to the line of the "general direction" of the coast. Furthermore the matter was not even put to the experts directly as a question of continental shelf delimitation, but in the context of the delimitation of the lateral boundary between adjacent territorial waters, no account being taken of the possibility that the situation respecting territorial waters might be different.

52. The Committee of Experts simply reported that after a thorough discussion of the different methods—(there are no official records of this discussion)—they had decided that "the (lateral) boundary through the territorial sea—if not already fixed otherwise—should be drawn according to the principle of equidistance from the respective coastlines". They added, however, significantly, that in "a number of cases this may not lead to an equitable solution, which should be then arrived at by negotiation". Only after that did they add, as a rider to this conclusion, that they had considered it "important to find a formula for drawing the international boundaries in the territorial waters of States, which could also be used for the delimitation of the respective continental shelves of two States bordering the same continental shelf".

53. In this almost impromptu, and certainly contingent manner was the principle of equidistance for the delimitation of continental shelf boundaries propounded. It is clear from the Report of the Commission for 1953 already referred to (paragraph 50) that the latter adopted it largely on the basis of the recommendation of the Committee of Experts, and even so in a text that gave priority to delimitation by agreement and also introduced an exception in favour of "special circumstances" which the Committee had not formally proposed. The Court moreover thinks it to be a legitimate supposition that the experts were actuated by considerations not of legal theory but of practical convenience and cartography of the kind mentioned in paragraph 22 above. Although there are no official records of their discussions, there is warrant for this view in correspondence passing between certain of them and the Commission's Special Rapporteur on the subject, which was deposited by one of the Parties during the oral hearing at the request of the Court. Nor, even after this, when a decision in principle had been taken in favour of an equidistance rule, was there an end to the Commission's hesitations, for as late as three years after the adoption of the report of the Committee of Experts, when the Commission was finalizing the whole complex of drafts comprised under the topic of the Law of the Sea, various doubts about the equidistance principle were still being voiced in the Commission, on such grounds for instance as that its strict application would be open, in certain cases, to the objection that the geographical configuration of the coast would render a boundary drawn on this basis inequitable.

54. A further point of some significance is that neither in the Committee of Experts, nor in the Commission itself, nor subsequently at the Geneva Conference, does there appear to have been any discussion of delimitation in the context, not merely of two adjacent States, but of three or more States on the same coast, or in the same vicinity,—from which it can reasonably be inferred that the possible resulting situations, some of which have been described in paragraph 8 above, were never really envisaged or taken into account. This view finds some confirmation in the fact that the relevant part of paragraph 2 of Article 6 of the Geneva Convention speaks of delimiting the continental shelf of "two" adjacent States (although a reference simply to "adjacent States" would have sufficed), whereas in respect of median lines the reference in paragraph 1 of that Article is to "two or more" opposite States.

55. In the light of this history, and of the record generally, it is clear that at no time was the notion of equidistance as an inherent necessity of continental shelf doctrine entertained. Quite a different outlook was indeed manifested from the start in current legal thinking. It was, and

it really remained to the end, governed by two beliefs;—namely, first, that no one single method of delimitation was likely to prove satisfactory in all circumstances, and that delimitation should, therefore, be carried out by agreement (or by reference to arbitration); and secondly, that it should be effected on equitable principles. It was in pursuance of the first of these beliefs that in the draft that emerged as Article 6 of the Geneva Convention, the Commission gave priority to delimitation by agreement,—and in pursuance of the second that it introduced the exception in favour of "special circumstances". Yet the record shows that, even with these mitigations, doubts persisted, particularly as to whether the equidistance principle would in all cases prove equitable.

56. In these circumstances, it seems to the Court that the inherency contention as now put forward by Denmark and the Netherlands inverts the true order of things in point of time and that, so far from an equidistance rule having been generated by an antecedent principle of proximity inherent in the whole concept of continental shelf appurtenance, the latter is rather a rationalization of the former—an *ex post facto* construct directed to providing a logical juristic basis for a method of delimitation propounded largely for different reasons, cartographical and other. Given also that for the reasons already set out (paragraphs 40-46) the theory cannot be said to be endowed with any quality of logical necessity either, the Court is unable to accept it.

*

57. Before going further it will be convenient to deal briefly with two subsidiary matters. Most of the difficulties felt in the International Law Commission related, as here, to the case of the lateral boundary between adjacent States. Less difficulty was felt over that of the median line boundary between opposite States, although it too is an equidistance line. For this there seems to the Court to be good reason. The continental shelf area off, and dividing, opposite States, can be claimed by each of them to be a natural prolongation of its territory. These prolongations meet and overlap, and can therefore only be delimited by means of a median line; and, ignoring the presence of islets, rocks and minor coastal projections, the disproportionally distorting effect of which can be eliminated by other means, such a line must effect an equal division of the particular area involved. If there is a third State on one of the coasts concerned, the area of mutual natural prolongation with that of the same or another opposite State will be a separate and distinct one, to be treated in the same way. This type of case is therefore different from that of laterally adjacent States on the same coast with no immediately opposite coast in front of it, and does not give rise to the same kind of problem—a conclusion which also finds some confirmation in the dif-

ference of language to be observed in the two paragraphs of Article 6 of the Geneva Convention (reproduced in paragraph 26 above) as respects recourse in the one case to median lines and in the other to lateral equidistance lines, in the event of absence of agreement.

58. If on the other hand, contrary to the view expressed in the preceding paragraph, it were correct to say that there is no essential difference in the process of delimiting the continental shelf areas between opposite States and that of delimitations between adjacent States, then the results ought in principle to be the same or at least comparable. But in fact, whereas a median line divides equally between the two opposite countries areas that can be regarded as being the natural prolongation of the territory of each of them, a lateral equidistance line often leaves to one of the States concerned areas that are a natural prolongation of the territory of the other.

59. Equally distinct in the opinion of the Court is the case of the lateral boundary between adjacent territorial waters to be drawn on an equidistance basis. As was convincingly demonstrated in the maps and diagrams furnished by the Parties, and as has been noted in paragraph 8, the distorting effects of lateral equidistance lines under certain conditions of coastal configuration are nevertheless comparatively small within the limits of territorial waters, but produce their maximum effect in the localities where the main continental shelf areas lie further out. There is also a direct correlation between the notion of closest proximity to the coast and the sovereign jurisdiction which the coastal State is entitled to exercise and must exercise, not only over the seabed underneath the territorial waters but over the waters themselves, which does not exist in respect of continental shelf areas where there is no jurisdiction over the superjacent waters, and over the seabed only for purposes of exploration and exploitation.

* * *

60. The conclusions so far reached leave open, and still to be considered, the question whether on some basis other than that of an *a priori* logical necessity, i.e., through positive law processes, the equidistance principle has come to be regarded as a rule of customary international law, so that it would be obligatory for the Federal Republic in that way, even though Article 6 of the Geneva Convention is not, as such, opposable to it. For this purpose it is necessary to examine the status of the principle as it stood when the Convention was drawn up, as it resulted from the effect of the Convention, and in the light of State practice subsequent to the Convention; but it should be clearly understood that in the pronouncements the Court makes on these matters it has in view solely the delimitation provisions (Article 6) of the Convention, not other parts of it, nor the Convention as such.

61. The first of these questions can conveniently be considered in the form suggested on behalf of Denmark and the Netherlands themselves in the course of the oral hearing, when it was stated that they had not in fact contended that the delimitation article (Article 6) of the Convention "embodied already received rules of customary law in the sense that the Convention was merely declaratory of existing rules". Their contention was, rather, that although prior to the Conference, continental shelf law was only in the formative stage, and State practice lacked uniformity, yet "the process of the definition and consolidation of the emerging customary law took place through the work of the International Law Commission, the reaction of governments to that work and the proceedings of the Geneva Conference"; and this emerging customary law became "crystallized in the adoption of the Continental Shelf Convention by the Conference".

62. Whatever validity this contention may have in respect of at least certain parts of the Convention, the Court cannot accept it as regards the delimitation provision (Article 6), the relevant parts of which were adopted almost unchanged from the draft of the International Law Commission that formed the basis of discussion at the Conference. The status of the rule in the Convention therefore depends mainly on the processes that led the Commission to propose it. These processes have already been reviewed in connection with the Danish-Netherlands contention of an *a priori* necessity for equidistance, and the Court considers this review sufficient for present purposes also, in order to show that the principle of equidistance, as it now figures in Article 6 of the Convention, was proposed by the Commission with considerable hesitation, somewhat on an experimental basis, at most *de lege ferenda*, and not at all *de lege lata* or as an emerging rule of customary international law. This is clearly not the sort of foundation on which Article 6 of the Convention could be said to have reflected or crystallized such a rule.

*

63. The foregoing conclusion receives significant confirmation from the fact that Article 6 is one of those in respect of which, under the reservations article of the Convention (Article 12) reservations may be made by any State on signing, ratifying or acceding,—for, speaking generally, it is a characteristic of purely conventional rules and obligations that, in regard to them, some faculty of making unilateral reservations may, within certain limits, be admitted;—whereas this cannot be so in the case of general or customary law rules and obligations which, by their very nature, must have equal force for all members of the international community, and cannot therefore be the subject of any right of unilateral exclusion exercisable at will by any one of them in its own

favour. Consequently, it is to be expected that when, for whatever reason, rules or obligations of this order are embodied, or are intended to be reflected in certain provisions of a convention, such provisions will figure amongst those in respect of which a right of unilateral reservation is not conferred, or is excluded. This expectation is, in principle, fulfilled by Article 12 of the Geneva Continental Shelf Convention, which permits reservations to be made to all the articles of the Convention "other than to Articles 1 to 3 inclusive"—these three Articles being the ones which, it is clear, were then regarded as reflecting, or as crystallizing, received or at least emergent rules of customary international law relative to the continental shelf, amongst them the question of the seaward extent of the shelf; the juridical character of the coastal State's entitlement; the nature of the rights exercisable; the kind of natural resources to which these relate; and the preservation intact of the legal status as high seas of the waters over the shelf, and the legal status of the superjacent air-space.

64. The normal inference would therefore be that any articles that do not figure among those excluded from the faculty of reservation under Article 12, were not regarded as declaratory of previously existing or emergent rules of law; and this is the inference the Court in fact draws in respect of Article 6 (delimitation), having regard also to the attitude of the International Law Commission to this provision, as already described in general terms. Naturally this would not of itself prevent this provision from eventually passing into the general *corpus* of customary international law by one of the processes considered in paragraphs 70-81 below. But that is not here the issue. What is now under consideration is whether it originally figured in the Convention as such a rule.

65. It has however been suggested that the inference drawn at the beginning of the preceding paragraph is not necessarily warranted, seeing that there are certain other provisions of the Convention, also not excluded from the faculty of reservation, but which do undoubtedly in principle relate to matters that lie within the field of received customary law, such as the obligation not to impede the laying or maintenance of submarine cables or pipelines on the continental shelf seabed (Article 4), and the general obligation not unjustifiably to interfere with freedom of navigation, fishing, and so on (Article 5, paragraphs 1 and 6). These matters however, all relate to or are consequential upon principles or rules of general maritime law, very considerably ante-dating the Convention, and not directly connected with but only incidental to continental shelf rights as such. They were mentioned in the Convention, not in order to declare or confirm their existence, which was not necessary, but simply to ensure that they were not prejudiced by the exercise of continental shelf rights as provided for in the Convention. Another method of

drafting might have clarified the point, but this cannot alter the fact that no reservation could release the reserving party from obligations of general maritime law existing outside and independently of the Convention, and especially obligations formalized in Article 2 of the contemporaneous Convention on the High Seas, expressed by its preamble to be declaratory of established principles of international law.

66. Article 6 (delimitation) appears to the Court to be in a different position. It does directly relate to continental shelf rights as such, rather than to matters incidental to these; and since it was not, as were Articles 1 to 3, excluded from the faculty of reservation, it is a legitimate inference that it was considered to have a different and less fundamental status and not, like those Articles, to reflect pre-existing or emergent customary law. It was however contended on behalf of Denmark and the Netherlands that the right of reservation given in respect of Article 6 was not intended to be an unfettered right, and that in particular it does not extend to effecting a total exclusion of the equidistance principle of delimitation,—for, so it was claimed, delimitation on the basis of that principle is implicit in Articles 1 and 2 of the Convention, in respect of which no reservations are permitted. Hence the right of reservation under Article 6 could only be exercised in a manner consistent with the preservation of at least the basic principle of equidistance. In this connection it was pointed out that, of the no more than four reservations so far entered in respect of Article 6, one at least of which was somewhat far-reaching, none has purported to effect such a total exclusion or denial.

67. The Court finds this argument unconvincing for a number of reasons. In the first place, Articles 1 and 2 of the Geneva Convention do not appear to have any direct connection with inter-State delimitation as such. Article 1 is concerned only with the outer, seaward, limit of the shelf generally, not with boundaries between the shelf areas of opposite or adjacent States. Article 2 is equally not concerned with such boundaries. The suggestion seems to be that the notion of equidistance is implicit in the reference in paragraph 2 of Article 2 to the rights of the coastal State over its continental shelf being "exclusive". So far as actual language is concerned this interpretation is clearly incorrect. The true sense of the passage is that in whatever areas of the continental shelf a coastal State has rights, those rights are exclusive rights, not exercisable by any other State. But this says nothing as to what in fact are the precise areas in respect of which each coastal State possesses these exclusive rights. This question, which can arise only as regards the fringes of a coastal State's shelf area is, as explained at the end of paragraph 20 above, exactly what falls to be settled through the process of delimitation, and this is the sphere of Article 6, not Article 2.

68. Secondly, it must be observed that no valid conclusions can be drawn from the fact that the faculty of entering reservations to Article 6 has been exercised only sparingly and within certain limits. This is the affair exclusively of those States which have not wished to exercise the faculty, or which have been content to do so only to a limited extent. Their action or inaction cannot affect the right of other States to enter reservations to whatever is the legitimate extent of the right.

*

69. In the light of these various considerations, the Court reaches the conclusion that the Geneva Convention did not embody or crystallize any pre-existing or emergent rule of customary law, according to which the delimitation of continental shelf areas between adjacent States must, unless the Parties otherwise agree, be carried out on an equidistance-special circumstances basis. A rule was of course embodied in Article 6 of the Convention, but as a purely conventional rule. Whether it has since acquired a broader basis remains to be seen: *qua* conventional rule however, as has already been concluded, it is not opposable to the Federal Republic.

* * *

70. The Court must now proceed to the last stage in the argument put forward on behalf of Denmark and the Netherlands. This is to the effect that even if there was at the date of the Geneva Convention no rule of customary international law in favour of the equidistance principle, and no such rule was crystallized in Article 6 of the Convention, nevertheless such a rule has come into being since the Convention, partly because of its own impact, partly on the basis of subsequent State practice,—and that this rule, being now a rule of customary international law binding on all States, including therefore the Federal Republic, should be declared applicable to the delimitation of the boundaries between the Parties' respective continental shelf areas in the North Sea.

71. In so far as this contention is based on the view that Article 6 of the Convention has had the influence, and has produced the effect, described, it clearly involves treating that Article as a norm-creating provision which has constituted the foundation of, or has generated a rule which, while only conventional or contractual in its origin, has since passed into the general *corpus* of international law, and is now accepted as such by the *opinio juris*, so as to have become binding even for countries which have never, and do not, become parties to the Convention. There is no doubt that this process is a perfectly possible one and does from time to time occur: it constitutes indeed one of the recognized methods by which new rules of customary international law may be formed. At the same time this result is not lightly to be regarded as having been attained.

72. It would in the first place be necessary that the provision con-

cerned should, at all events potentially, be of a fundamentally norm-creating character such as could be regarded as forming the basis of a general rule of law. Considered *in abstracto* the equidistance principle might be said to fulfil this requirement. Yet in the particular form in which it is embodied in Article 6 of the Geneva Convention, and having regard to the relationship of that Article to other provisions of the Convention, this must be open to some doubt. In the first place, Article 6 is so framed as to put second the obligation to make use of the equidistance method, causing it to come after a primary obligation to effect delimitation by agreement. Such a primary obligation constitutes an unusual preface to what is claimed to be a potential general rule of law. Without attempting to enter into, still less pronounce upon any question of *jus cogens*, it is well understood that, in practice, rules of international law can, by agreement, be derogated from in particular cases, or as between particular parties,—but this is not normally the subject of any express provision, as it is in Article 6 of the Geneva Convention. Secondly the part played by the notion of special circumstances relative to the principle of equidistance as embodied in Article 6, and the very considerable, still unresolved controversies as to the exact meaning and scope of this notion, must raise further doubts as to the potentially norm-creating character of the rule. Finally, the faculty of making reservations to Article 6, while it might not of itself prevent the equidistance principle being eventually received as general law, does add considerably to the difficulty of regarding this result as having been brought about (or being potentially possible) on the basis of the Convention: for so long as this faculty continues to exist, and is not the subject of any revision brought about in consequence of a request made under Article 13 of the Convention—of which there is at present no official indication—it is the Convention itself which would, for the reasons already indicated, seem to deny to the provisions of Article 6 the same norm-creating character as, for instance, Articles 1 and 2 possess.

73. With respect to the other elements usually regarded as necessary before a conventional rule can be considered to have become a general rule of international law, it might be that, even without the passage of any considerable period of time, a very widespread and representative participation in the convention might suffice of itself, provided it included that of States whose interests were specially affected. In the present case however, the Court notes that, even if allowance is made for the existence of a number of States to whom participation in the Geneva Convention is not open, or which, by reason for instance of being land-locked States, would have no interest in becoming parties to it, the number of ratifications and accessions so far secured is, though respectable, hardly sufficient. That non-ratification may sometimes be due to factors other than active disapproval of the convention concerned can hardly constitute a basis on which positive acceptance of its principles can be implied: the reasons are speculative, but the facts remain.

74. As regards the time element, the Court notes that it is over ten years since the Convention was signed, but that it is even now less than five since it came into force in June 1964, and that when the present proceedings were brought it was less than three years, while less than one had elapsed at the time when the respective negotiations between the Federal Republic and the other two Parties for a complete delimitation broke down on the question of the application of the equidistance principle. Although the passage of only a short period of time is not necessarily, or of itself, a bar to the formation of a new rule of customary international law on the basis of what was originally a purely conventional rule, an indispensable requirement would be that within the period in question, short though it might be, State practice, including that of States whose interests are specially affected, should have been both extensive and virtually uniform in the sense of the provision invoked;—and should moreover have occurred in such a way as to show a general recognition that a rule of law or legal obligation is involved.

*

75. The Court must now consider whether State practice in the matter of continental shelf delimitation has, subsequent to the Geneva Convention, been of such a kind as to satisfy this requirement. Leaving aside cases which, for various reasons, the Court does not consider to be reliable guides as precedents, such as delimitations effected between the present Parties themselves, or not relating to international boundaries, some fifteen cases have been cited in the course of the present proceedings, occurring mostly since the signature of the 1958 Geneva Convention, in which continental shelf boundaries have been delimited according to the equidistance principle—in the majority of the cases by agreement, in a few others unilaterally—or else the delimitation was foreshadowed but has not yet been carried out. Amongst these fifteen are the four North Sea delimitations United Kingdom/Norway-Denmark-Netherlands, and Norway/Denmark already mentioned in paragraph 4 of this Judgment. But even if these various cases constituted more than a very small proportion of those potentially calling for delimitation in the world as a whole, the Court would not think it necessary to enumerate or evaluate them separately, since there are, *a priori*, several grounds which deprive them of weight as precedents in the present context.

76. To begin with, over half the States concerned, whether acting unilaterally or conjointly, were or shortly became parties to the Geneva Convention, and were therefore presumably, so far as they were concerned, acting actually or potentially in the application of the Convention. From their action no inference could legitimately be drawn as to the existence of a rule of customary international law in favour of the equidistance principle. As regards those States, on the other hand, which were not, and have not become parties to the Convention, the basis of

their action can only be problematical and must remain entirely speculative. Clearly, they were not applying the Convention. But from that no inference could justifiably be drawn that they believed themselves to be applying a mandatory rule of customary international law. There is not a shred of evidence that they did and, as has been seen (paragraphs 22 and 23), there is no lack of other reasons for using the equidistance method, so that acting, or agreeing to act in a certain way, does not of itself demonstrate anything of a juridical nature.

77. The essential point in this connection—and it seems necessary to stress it—is that even if these instances of action by non-parties to the Convention were much more numerous than they in fact are, they would not, even in the aggregate, suffice in themselves to constitute the *opinio juris*;—for, in order to achieve this result, two conditions must be fulfilled. Not only must the acts concerned amount to a settled practice, but they must also be such, or be carried out in such a way, as to be evidence of a belief that this practice is rendered obligatory by the existence of a rule of law requiring it. The need for such a belief, i.e., the existence of a subjective element, is implicit in the very notion of the *opinio juris sive necessitatis*. The States concerned must therefore feel that they are conforming to what amounts to a legal obligation. The frequency, or even habitual character of the acts is not in itself enough. There are many international acts, e.g., in the field of ceremonial and protocol, which are performed almost invariably, but which are motivated only by considerations of courtesy, convenience or tradition, and not by any sense of legal duty.

78. In this respect the Court follows the view adopted by the Permanent Court of International Justice in the *Lotus* case, as stated in the following passage, the principle of which is, by analogy, applicable almost word for word, *mutatis mutandis*, to the present case (*P.C.I.J., Series A, No. 10*, 1927, at p. 28):

> "Even if the rarity of the judicial decisions to be found . . . were sufficient to prove . . . the circumstance alleged . . ., it would merely show that States had often, in practice, abstained from instituting criminal proceedings, and not that they recognized themselves as being obliged to do so; for only if such abstention were based on their being conscious of having a duty to abstain would it be possible to speak of an international custom. The alleged fact does not allow one to infer that States have been conscious of having such a duty; on the other hand, . . . there are other circumstances calculated to show that the contrary is true."

Applying this dictum to the present case, the position is simply that in certain cases—not a great number—the States concerned agreed to draw or did draw the boundaries concerned according to the principle of equidistance. There is no evidence that they so acted because they felt legally compelled to draw them in this way by reason of a rule of customary law obliging them to do so—especially considering that they might have been motivated by other obvious factors.

79. Finally, it appears that in almost all of the cases cited, the delimitations concerned were median-line delimitations between opposite States, not lateral delimitations between adjacent States. For reasons which have already been given (paragraph 57) the Court regards the case of median-line delimitations between opposite States as different in various respects, and as being sufficiently distinct not to constitute a precedent for the delimitation of lateral boundaries. In only one situation discussed by the Parties does there appear to have been a geographical configuration which to some extent resembles the present one, in the sense that a number of States on the same coastline are grouped around a sharp curve or bend of it. No complete delimitation in this area has however yet been carried out. But the Court is not concerned to deny to this case, or any other of those cited, all evidential value in favour of the thesis of Denmark and the Netherlands. It simply considers that they are inconclusive, and insufficient to bear the weight sought to be put upon them as evidence of such a settled practice, manifested in such circumstances, as would justify the inference that delimitation according to the principle of equidistance amounts to a mandatory rule of customary international law,—more particularly where lateral delimitations are concerned.

80. There are of course plenty of cases (and a considerable number were cited) of delimitations of waters, as opposed to seabed, being carried out on the basis of equidistance—mostly of internal waters (lakes, rivers, etc.), and mostly median-line cases. The nearest analogy is that of adjacent territorial waters, but as already explained (paragraph 59) the Court does not consider this case to be analogous to that of the continental shelf.

*

81. The Court accordingly concludes that if the Geneva Convention was not in its origins or inception declaratory of a mandatory rule of customary international law enjoining the use of the equidistance principle for the delimitation of continental shelf areas between adjacent States, neither has its subsequent effect been constitutive of such a rule; and that State practice up-to-date has equally been insufficient for the purpose.

*

82. The immediately foregoing conclusion, coupled with that reached earlier (paragraph 56) to the effect that the equidistance principle could not be regarded as being a rule of law on any *a priori* basis of logical

necessity deriving from the fundamental theory of the continental shelf, leads to the final conclusion on this part of the case that the use of the equidistance method is not obligatory for the delimitation of the areas concerned in the present proceedings. In these circumstances, it becomes unnecessary for the Court to determine whether or not the configuration of the German North Sea coast constitutes a "special circumstance" for the purposes either of Article 6 of the Geneva Convention or of any rule of customary international law,—since once the use of the equidistance method of delimitation is determined not to be obligatory in any event, it ceases to be legally necessary to prove the existence of special circumstances in order to justify not using that method.

* * * * *

83. The legal situation therefore is that the Parties are under no obligation to apply either the 1958 Convention, which is not opposable to the Federal Republic, or the equidistance method as a mandatory rule of customary law, which it is not. But as between States faced with an issue concerning the lateral delimitation of adjacent continental shelves, there are still rules and principles of law to be applied; and in the present case it is not the fact either that rules are lacking, or that the situation is one for the unfettered appreciation of the Parties. Equally, it is not the case that if the equidistance principle is not a rule of law, there has to be as an alternative some other single equivalent rule.

84. As already indicated, the Court is not called upon itself to delimit the areas of continental shelf appertaining respectively to each Party, and in consequence is not bound to prescribe the methods to be employed for the purposes of such a delimitation. The Court has to indicate to the Parties the principles and rules of law in the light of which the methods for eventually effecting the delimitation will have to be chosen. The Court will discharge this task in such a way as to provide the Parties with the requisite directions, without substituting itself for them by means of a detailed indication of the methods to be followed and the factors to be taken into account for the purposes of a delimitation the carrying out of which the Parties have expressly reserved to themselves.

85. It emerges from the history of the development of the legal régime of the continental shelf, which has been reviewed earlier, that the essential reason why the equidistance method is not to be regarded as a rule of law is that, if it were to be compulsorily applied in all situations, this would not be consonant with certain basic legal notions which, as has been observed in paragraphs 48 and 55, have from the beginning reflected the *opinio juris* in the matter of delimitation; those principles being that delimitation must be the object of agreement between the States concerned, and that such agreement must be arrived at in accordance with equitable principles. On a foundation of very general precepts of justice and good faith, actual rules of law are here involved which govern the

delimitation of adjacent continental shelves—that is to say, rules binding upon States for all delimitations;—in short, it is not a question of applying equity simply as a matter of abstract justice, but of applying a rule of law which itself requires the application of equitable principles, in accordance with the ideas which have always underlain the development of the legal régime of the continental shelf in this field, namely:

(a) the parties are under an obligation to enter into negotiations with a view to arriving at an agreement, and not merely to go through a formal process of negotiation as a sort of prior condition for the automatic application of a certain method of delimitation in the absence of agreement; they are under an obligation so to conduct themselves that the negotiations are meaningful, which will not be the case when either of them insists upon its own position without contemplating any modification of it;

(b) the parties are under an obligation to act in such a way that, in the particular case, and taking all the circumstances into account, equitable principles are applied,—for this purpose the equidistance method can be used, but other methods exist and may be employed, alone or in combination, according to the areas involved;

(c) for the reasons given in paragraphs 43 and 44, the continental shelf of any State must be the natural prolongation of its land territory and must not encroach upon what is the natural prolongation of the territory of another State.

* * *

86. It is now necessary to examine these rules more closely, as also certain problems relative to their application. So far as the first rule is concerned, the Court would recall not only that the obligation to negotiate which the Parties assumed by Article 1, paragraph 2, of the Special Agreements arises out of the Truman Proclamation, which, for the reasons given in paragraph 47, must be considered as having propounded the rules of law in this field, but also that this obligation merely constitutes a special application of a principle which underlies all international relations, and which is moreover recognized in Article 33 of the Charter of the United Nations as one of the methods for the peaceful settlement of international disputes. There is no need to insist upon the fundamental character of this method of settlement, except to point out that it is emphasized by the observable fact that judicial or arbitral settlement is not universally accepted.

87. As the Permanent Court of International Justice said in its Order of 19 August 1929 in the case of the *Free Zones of Upper Savoy and the District of Gex*, the judicial settlement of international disputes "is simply an alternative to the direct and friendly settlement of such disputes between the parties" (*P.C.I.J., Series A, No. 22*, at p. 13). Defining the content of the obligation to negotiate, the Permanent Court, in its

Advisory Opinion in the case of *Railway Traffic between Lithuania and Poland*, said that the obligation was "not only to enter into negotiations but also to pursue them as far as possible with a view to concluding agreements", even if an obligation to negotiate did not imply an obligation to reach agreement (*P.C.I.J., Series A/B, No. 42*, 1931, at p. 116). In the present case, it needs to be observed that whatever the details of the negotiations carried on in 1965 and 1966, they failed of their purpose because the Kingdoms of Denmark and the Netherlands, convinced that the equidistance principle alone was applicable, in consequence of a rule binding upon the Federal Republic, saw no reason to depart from that rule; and equally, given the geographical considerations stated in the last sentence of paragraph 7 above, the Federal Republic could not accept the situation resulting from the application of that rule. So far therefore the negotiations have not satisfied the conditions indicated in paragraph 85 *(a)*, but fresh negotiations are to take place on the basis of the present Judgment.

* * *

88. The Court comes next to the rule of equity. The legal basis of that rule in the particular case of the delimitation of the continental shelf as between adjoining States has already been stated. It must however be noted that the rule rests also on a broader basis. Whatever the legal reasoning of a court of justice, its decisions must by definition be just, and therefore in that sense equitable. Nevertheless, when mention is made of a court dispensing justice or declaring the law, what is meant is that the decision finds its objective justification in considerations lying not outside but within the rules, and in this field it is precisely a rule of law that calls for the application of equitable principles. There is consequently no question in this case of any decision *ex aequo et bono*, such as would only be possible under the conditions prescribed by Article 38, paragraph 2, of the Court's Statute. Nor would this be the first time that the Court has adopted such an attitude, as is shown by the following passage from the Advisory Opinion given in the case of *Judgments of the Administrative Tribunal of the I.L.O. upon Complaints Made against Unesco* (*I.C.J. Reports 1956*, at p. 100):

> "In view of this the Court need not examine the allegation that the validity of the judgments of the Tribunal is vitiated by excess of jurisdiction on the ground that it awarded compensation *ex aequo et bono*. It will confine itself to stating that, in the reasons given by the Tribunal in support of its decision on the merits, the Tribunal said: 'That redress will be ensured *ex aequo et bono* by the granting to the complainant of the sum set forth below.' It does not appear from the context of the judgment that the Tribunal thereby intended to depart from principles of law. The apparent intention was to say

that, as the precise determination of the actual amount to be awarded could not be based on any specific rule of law, the Tribunal fixed what the Court, in other circumstances, has described as the true measure of compensation and the reasonable figure of such compensation (*Corfu Channel* case, Judgment of December 15th, 1949, *I.C.J. Reports 1949*, p. 249)."

89. It must next be observed that, in certain geographical circumstances which are quite frequently met with, the equidistance method, despite its known advantages, leads unquestionably to inequity, in the following sense:

(*a*) The slightest irregularity in a coastline is automatically magnified by the equidistance line as regards the consequences for the delimitation of the continental shelf. Thus it has been seen in the case of concave or convex coastlines that if the equidistance method is employed, then the greater the irregularity and the further from the coastline the area to be delimited, the more unreasonable are the results produced. So great an exaggeration of the consequences of a natural geographical feature must be remedied or compensated for as far as possible, being of itself creative of inequity.

(*b*) In the case of the North Sea in particular, where there is no outer boundary to the continental shelf, it happens that the claims of several States converge, meet and intercross in localities where, despite their distance from the coast, the bed of the sea still unquestionably consists of continental shelf. A study of these convergences, as revealed by the maps, shows how inequitable would be the apparent simplification brought about by a delimitation which, ignoring such geographical circumstances, was based solely on the equidistance method.

90. If for the above reasons equity excludes the use of the equidistance method in the present instance, as the sole method of delimitation, the question arises whether there is any necessity to employ only one method for the purposes of a given delimitation. There is no logical basis for this, and no objection need be felt to the idea of effecting a delimitation of adjoining continental shelf areas by the concurrent use of various methods. The Court has already stated why it considers that the international law of continental shelf delimitation does not involve any imperative rule and permits resort to various principles or methods, as may be appropriate, or a combination of them, provided that, by the application of equitable principles, a reasonable result is arrived at.

91. Equity does not necessarily imply equality. There can never be any question of completely refashioning nature, and equity does not require that a State without access to the sea should be allotted an area of continental shelf, any more than there could be a question of rendering the situation of a State with an extensive coastline similar to that of a

State with a restricted coastline. Equality is to be reckoned within the same plane, and it is not such natural inequalities as these that equity could remedy. But in the present case there are three States whose North Sea coastlines are in fact comparable in length and which, therefore, have been given broadly equal treatment by nature except that the configuration of one of the coastlines would, if the equidistance method is used, deny to one of these States treatment equal or comparable to that given the other two. Here indeed is a case where, in a theoretical situation of equality within the same order, an inequity is created. What is unacceptable in this instance is that a State should enjoy continental shelf rights considerably different from those of its neighbours merely because in the one case the coastline is roughly convex in form and in the other it is markedly concave, although those coastlines are comparable in length. It is therefore not a question of totally refashioning geography whatever the facts of the situation but, given a geographical situation of quasi-equality as between a number of States, of abating the effects of an incidental special feature from which an unjustifiable difference of treatment could result.

92. It has however been maintained that no one method of delimitation can prevent such results and that all can lead to relative injustices. This argument has in effect already been dealt with. It can only strengthen the view that it is necessary to seek not one method of delimitation but one goal. It is in this spirit that the Court must examine the question of how the continental shelf can be delimited when it is in fact the case that the equidistance principle does not provide an equitable solution. As the operation of delimiting is a matter of determining areas appertaining to different jurisdictions, it is a truism to say that the determination must be equitable; rather is the problem above all one of defining the means whereby the delimitation can be carried out in such a way as to be recognized as equitable. Although the Parties have made it known that they intend to reserve for themselves the application of the principles and rules laid down by the Court, it would, even so, be insufficient simply to rely on the rule of equity without giving some degree of indication as to the possible ways in which it might be applied in the present case, it being understood that the Parties will be free to agree upon one method rather than another, or different methods if they so prefer.

93. In fact, there is no legal limit to the considerations which States may take account of for the purpose of making sure that they apply equitable procedures, and more often than not it is the balancing-up of all such considerations that will produce this result rather than reliance on one to the exclusion of all others. The problem of the relative weight to be accorded to different considerations naturally varies with the circumstances of the case.

94. In balancing the factors in question it would appear that various aspects must be taken into account. Some are related to the geological, others to the geographical aspect of the situation, others again to the

idea of the unity of any deposits. These criteria, though not entirely precise, can provide adequate bases for decision adapted to the factual situation.

95. The institution of the continental shelf has arisen out of the recognition of a physical fact; and the link between this fact and the law, without which that institution would never have existed, remains an important element for the application of its legal régime. The continental shelf is, by definition, an area physically extending the territory of most coastal States into a species of platform which has attracted the attention first of geographers and hydrographers and then of jurists. The importance of the geological aspect is emphasized by the care which, at the beginning of its investigation, the International Law Commission took to acquire exact information as to its characteristics, as can be seen in particular from the definitions to be found on page 131 of Volume I of the *Yearbook of the International Law Commission* for 1956. The appurtenance of the shelf to the countries in front of whose coastlines it lies, is therefore a fact, and it can be useful to consider the geology of that shelf in order to find out whether the direction taken by certain configurational features should influence delimitation because, in certain localities, they point-up the whole notion of the appurtenance of the continental shelf to the State whose territory it does in fact prolong.

96. The doctrine of the continental shelf is a recent instance of encroachment on maritime expanses which, during the greater part of history, appertained to no-one. The contiguous zone and the continental shelf are in this respect concepts of the same kind. In both instances the principle is applied that the land dominates the sea; it is consequently necessary to examine closely the geographical configuration of the coastlines of the countries whose continental shelves are to be delimited. This is one of the reasons why the Court does not consider that markedly pronounced configurations can be ignored; for, since the land is the legal source of the power which a State may exercise over territorial extensions to seaward, it must first be clearly established what features do in fact constitute such extensions. Above all is this the case when what is involved is no longer areas of sea, such as the contiguous zone, but stretches of submerged land; for the legal régime of the continental shelf is that of a soil and a subsoil, two words evocative of the land and not of the sea.

97. Another factor to be taken into consideration in the delimitation of areas of continental shelf as between adjacent States is the unity of any deposits. The natural resources of the subsoil of the sea in those parts which consist of continental shelf are the very object of the legal régime established subsequent to the Truman Proclamation. Yet it frequently occurs that the same deposit lies on both sides of the line dividing a continental shelf between two States, and since it is possible to exploit such a deposit from either side, a problem immediately arises on account of the risk of prejudicial or wasteful exploitation by one or other of the States concerned. To look no farther than the North Sea, the practice

of States shows how this problem has been dealt with, and all that is needed is to refer to the undertakings entered into by the coastal States of that sea with a view to ensuring the most efficient exploitation or the apportionment of the products extracted—(see in particular the agreement of 10 March 1965 between the United Kingdom and Norway, Article 4; the agreement of 6 October 1965 between the Netherlands and the United Kingdom relating to "the exploitation of single geological structures extending across the dividing line on the continental shelf under the North Sea"; and the agreement of 14 May 1962 between the Federal Republic and the Netherlands concerning a joint plan for exploiting the natural resources underlying the area of the Ems Estuary where the frontier between the two States has not been finally delimited.) The Court does not consider that unity of deposit constitutes anything more than a factual element which it is reasonable to take into consideration in the course of the negotiations for a delimitation. The Parties are fully aware of the existence of the problem as also of the possible ways of solving it.

98. A final factor to be taken account of is the element of a reasonable degree of proportionality which a delimitation effected according to equitable principles ought to bring about between the extent of the continental shelf appertaining to the States concerned and the lengths of their respective coastlines,—these being measured according to their general direction in order to establish the necessary balance between States with straight, and those with markedly concave or convex coasts, or to reduce very irregular coastlines to their truer proportions. The choice and application of the appropriate technical methods would be a matter for the parties. One method discussed in the course of the proceedings, under the name of the principle of the coastal front, consists in drawing a straight baseline between the extreme points at either end of the coast concerned, or in some cases a series of such lines. Where the parties wish to employ in particular the equidistance method of delimitation, the establishment of one or more baselines of this kind can play a useful part in eliminating or diminishing the distortions that might result from the use of that method.

99. In a sea with the particular configuration of the North Sea, and in view of the particular geographical situation of the Parties' coastlines upon that sea, the methods chosen by them for the purpose of fixing the delimitation of their respective areas may happen in certain localities to lead to an overlapping of the areas appertaining to them. The Court considers that such a situation must be accepted as a given fact and resolved either by an agreed, or failing that by an equal division of the overlapping areas, or by agreements for joint exploitation, the latter solution appearing particularly appropriate when it is a question of preserving the unity of a deposit.

* * *

100. The Court has examined the problems raised by the present case in its own context, which is strictly that of delimitation. Other questions relating to the general legal régime of the continental shelf, have been examined for that purpose only. This régime furnishes an example of a legal theory derived from a particular source that has secured a general following. As the Court has recalled in the first part of its Judgment, it was the Truman Proclamation of 28 September 1945 which was at the origin of the theory, whose special features reflect that origin. It would therefore not be in harmony with this history to over-systematize a pragmatic construct the developments of which have occurred within a relatively short space of time.

* * * * *

101. For these reasons,

THE COURT,

by eleven votes to six,

finds that, in each case,

(A) the use of the equidistance method of delimitation not being obligatory as between the Parties; and

(B) there being no other single method of delimitation the use of which is in all circumstances obligatory;

(C) the principles and rules of international law applicable to the delimitation as between the Parties of the areas of the continental shelf in the North Sea which appertain to each of them beyond the partial boundary determined by the agreements of 1 December 1964 and 9 June 1965, respectively, are as follows:

(1) delimitation is to be effected by agreement in accordance with equitable principles, and taking account of all the relevant circumstances, in such a way as to leave as much as possible to each Party all those parts of the continental shelf that constitute a natural prolongation of its land territory into and under the sea, without encroachment on the natural prolongation of the land territory of the other;

(2) if, in the application of the preceding sub-paragraph, the delimitation leaves to the Parties areas that overlap, these are to be divided between them in agreed proportions or, failing agreement, equally, unless they decide on a régime of joint jurisdiction, user, or exploitation for the zones of overlap or any part of them;

(D) in the course of the negotiations, the factors to be taken into account are to include:

(1) the general configuration of the coasts of the Parties, as well as the presence of any special or unusual features;
(2) so far as known or readily ascertainable, the physical and geological structure, and natural resources, of the continental shelf areas involved;
(3) the element of a reasonable degree of proportionality, which a delimitation carried out in accordance with equitable principles ought to bring about between the extent of the continental shelf areas appertaining to the coastal State and the length of its coast measured in the general direction of the coastline, account being taken for this purpose of the effects, actual or prospective, of any other continental shelf delimitations between adjacent States in the same region.

Done in English and in French, the English text being authoritative at the Peace Palace, The Hague, this twentieth day of February, one thousand nine hundred and sixty-nine, in four copies, one of which will be placed in the archives of the Court and the others transmitted to the Government of the Federal Republic of Germany, to the Government of the Kingdom of Denmark and to the Government of the Kingdom of the Netherlands, respectively.

(Signed) J. L. BUSTAMANTE R.,
President.

(Signed) S. AQUARONE,
Registrar.

DENMARK-FEDERAL REPUBLIC OF GERMANY-NETHERLANDS: AGREEMENTS DELIMITING THE CONTINENTAL SHELF IN THE NORTH SEA*

[Done at Copenhagen, January 28, 1971]

Protocol**

I

1. The Federal Republic of Germany, the Kingdom of Denmark and the Kingdom of the Netherlands have, on the basis of the judgment of the International Court of Justice of 20 February 1969, conducted tripartite negotiations on the delimitation of the continental shelf under the North Sea. In those negotiations the two treaties signed today were drawn up, viz.:

   (a) the Treaty between the Federal Republic of Germany and the Kingdom of Denmark relating to the Delimitation of the Continental Shelf under the North Sea,

   (b) the Treaty between the Federal Republic of Germany and the Kingdom of the Netherlands relating to the Delimitation of the Continental Shelf under the North Sea.

   These treaties concur in so far as the actual conditions permit.

2. In appreciation of the fact that the two treaties together determine the configuration and size of the German part of the continental shelf under the North Sea and are consequently closely connected, the Governments of the three signatory States propose to exchange the instruments of ratification to the two treaties in Bonn on the same day in order that they may enter into force simultaneously.

II

The Government of the Kingdom of Denmark and the Government of the Kingdom of the Netherlands confirm that

> the Agreement between the Government of the Kindgom of Denmark and the Government of the Kingdom of the Netherlands concerning the Delimitation of the Continental Shelf under the North Sea between the Two Countries, dated 31 March 1966,

shall cease to have effect as soon as either of the treaties specified in Part I above enters into force.

---

*[In accordance with the Special Agreements of February 2, 1967, between the Governments of Denmark and the Federal Republic of Germany and the Federal Republic of Germany and the Netherlands [8 International Legal Materials 343 (1969)], the respective governments agreed to "delimit the continental shelf in the North Sea as between their countries by agreement in pursuance of the decision requested from the International Court of Justice". The International Court of Justice delivered its Judgment on February 20, 1969 [8 International Legal Materials 340 (1969)]. After extended tripartite negotiations, three agreements on the delimitation of the continental shelf in the North Sea were signed in Copenhagen on January 28, 1971: a protocol between the Federal Republic of Germany, Denmark and the Netherlands, a treaty between the Federal Republic of Germany and Denmark, and a treaty between the Federal Republic of Germany and the Netherlands. As of May 17, 1971, the agreements had not been ratified.]

**[Reprinted from an English translation provided to International Legal Materials by the Embassy of the Federal Republic of Germany at Washington, D.C.]

III

The German part of the continental shelf under the North Sea, which is delimitated by the treaties specified in Part I above on the basis of the judgment of the International Court of Justice, is contiguous to the British part of the continental shelf.

1. The Government of the Federal Republic of Germany therefore proposes to establish by treaty with the Government of the United Kingdom of Great Britain and Northern Ireland the Anglo-German boundary line on the continental shelf as the line which runs from the termination point of the German-Danish boundary line on the continental shelf to the termination point of the German-Netherlands boundary line on the continental shelf.

2. The Government of the Kingdom of Denmark proposes to amend, in agreement with the Government of the United Kingdom,

   the Agreement between the Government of the Kingdom of Denmark and the Government of the United Kingdom of Great Britain and Northern Ireland relating to the Delimitation of the Continental Shelf between the Two Countries, dated 3 March 1966,

   in so far as such amendment has become necessary by virtue of the treaty specified in Part I, 1 (a) above.

3. The Government of the Kingdom of the Netherlands proposes to amend, in agreement with the Government of the United Kingdom,

   the Agreement between the Government of the Kingdom of the Netherlands and the Government of the United Kingdom of Great Britain and Northern Ireland relating to the Delimitation of the Continental Shelf under the North Sea between the Two Countries, dated 6 October 1965,

   in so far as such amendment has become necessary by virtue of the treaty specified in Part I, 1 (b) above.

DONE at Copenhagen on January 28, 1971 in three originals in the German, Danish and Dutch languages, all three texts being equally authentic.

For the Government of the Federal Republic of Germany:

For the Government of the Kingdom of Denmark:

For the Government of the Kingdom of the Netherlands:

Treaty

between

The Federal Republic of Germany

and

the Kingdom of Denmark

relating to

the Delimitation of the Continental Shelf under the North Sea*

The Federal Republic of Germany

and

the Kingdom of Denmark,

intending to establish the common boundary of their respective parts of the continental shelf under the North Sea in so far as this has not already been done by means of the Treaty of 9 June 1965 concerning the Delimitation of the Continental Shelf of the North Sea near the Coast,

anxious to regulate the economic exploitation of the continental shelf in so far as this is in their common interest,

on the basis of the judgment of the International Court of Justice of 20 February 1969 in the disputes over the delimitation of the continental shelf under the North Sea between the Federal Republic of Germany on the one hand and the Kingdom of the Netherlands on the other,

taking into account the boundary lines of the continental shelf that are not affected by the judgment of the International Court of Justice,

have agreed as follows:

Article 1

(1) The dividing line between the German and the Danish part of the continental shelf under the North Sea shall, in extension of the partial boundary determined by the Treaty of 9 June 1965, be arcs of Great Circles between the following points:

S_1	55°10'03,4"	N	07°33'09,6"	E
S_2	55°30'40,3"	N	05°45'00,0"	E
S_3	55°15'00,0"	N	05°24'12,0"	E
S_4	55°15'00,0"	N	05°09'00,0"	E
S_5	55°24'15,0"	N	04°45'00,0"	E
S_6	55°46'21,8"	N	04°15'00,0"	E
S_7	55°55'09,4"	N	03°21'00,0"	E

*[Reprinted from an English translation provided to International Legal Materials by the Embassy of the Federal Republic of Germany at Washington, D.C. The translation of Annex 2 of the treaty was provided by the Embassy of Denmark at Washington, D.C.]

The positions of the points are defined by latitude and longitude on European Datum System (1st Adjustment 1950).

(2) The termination point S_7 of the dividing line shall be the point of intersection of the dividing lines between the German, Danish and British parts of the continental shelf under the North Sea.

(3) The dividing line and the partial boundary established by the Treaty of 9 June 1965 have been drawn on the chart attached to this Treaty as Annex 1.

Article 2

(1) Should any mineral resources be discovered on the continental shelf of either Contracting Party and should the other Contracting Party consider that the deposit thus discovered extend to its own continental shelf, it may put forward its view to the other Contracting Party, together with the supporting data. If that other Contracting Party does not share this view, the arbitral tribunal provided for under Article 5 of the present Treaty shall find on this question at the request of either Contracting Party.

(2) Should the Contracting Parties agree or should the arbitral tribunal have found that the deposit is located on the continental shelf of both Contracting Parties, the Governments of the Contracting Parties shall reach agreement as to its exploitation, taking into account the interests of both Contracting Parties on the principle that each Contracting Party is entitled to the mineral resources located on its continental shelf. In the event that mineral resources have already been extracted from the field which crosses the dividing line, the agreement should also contain provisions regarding adequate compensation.

(3) With the approval of the Governments of the Contracting Parties an agreement pursuant to paragraph 2 of this Article may also be concluded wholly or in part between the beneficiaries. A beneficiary shall be any person or persons who has a right to extract mineral resources.

(4) Should an agreement pursuant to paragraph 2 or 3 of this Article not be reached, either Contracting Party may appeal to the arbitral tribunal in accordance with the provisions of Article 5 of this Treaty. The arbitral tribunal may in such cases also decide ex aequo et bono. The arbitral tribunal shall be authorized to make an interim order after hearing the Contracting Parties.

Article 3

Notwithstanding international regulations concerning the laying of pipelines on the continental shelf, pipelines that are laid on the continental shelf in connexion with the exploitation of mineral resources shall in order to prevent the pollution of the sea and to avert any other hazards be subject to the legal provisions relating to the installation and operation of pipelines that are applicable in the territory of the Contracting Party upon whose continental shelf such pipelines are laid.

Article 4

(1) The enterprises designated in Annex 2 to this Treaty shall upon application be granted permission in accordance with German law to explore and extract in the area designated in the said Annex oil and gas and any other substances yielded during such extraction.

(2) The application for the permission required in accordance with paragraph 1 of this Article must be made within twelve months of the entry into force of this Treaty.

Article 5

(1) Disputes between the Contracting Parties concerning the interpretation or application of the present Treaty or of any arrangement made pursuant to paragraph 2 of Article 2 of the Treaty should, if possible, be settled by negotiation.

(2) If a dispute has not been settled in this manner within a reasonable period of time it shall upon the request of either Contracting Party be submitted to an arbitral tribunal for decision.

(3) Such arbitral tribunal shall be constituted for each individual case. In so far as the Contracting Parties do not agree on the facilitated procedure of appointing one judge to decide in the dispute, an arbitral tribunal consisting of three members shall be constituted as follows: Each Contracting Party shall appoint one member, and these two members shall agree upon a national of a third State as their chairman to be appointed by the two Contracting Parties. Such members shall be appointed within two months, and such chairman within a further two months, from the date on which either Contracting Party has decided to apply to have the dispute settled by an arbitral tribunal.

(3) If the periods specified in paragraph 3 above have not been observed, either Contracting Party may invite the President of the International Court of Justice to make the necessary appointments. If the President is a national of either Contracting Party or if he is otherwise prevented from discharging the said function, the Vice-President should make the necessary appointments. If the Vice-President, too, is a national of either Contracting Party or is likewise prevented from discharging the said function, the member of the Court of Justice next in seniority who is not a national of either Contracting Party and is not prevented from doing so should make the appointments.

(5) The arbitral tribunal shall decide by a majority vote. Each Contracting Party shall bear the cost of its own member and of its representatives in the arbitral proceedings; the cost of the chairman and the remaining costs shall be borne in equal parts by both Contracting Parties.

(6) The arbitral tribunal or the single judge shall decide on the basis of the rules of international law applicable between the Contracting Parties. The decision shall be binding.

(7) The arbitral tribunal or the single judge shall determine its or his own procedure in so far as no other arrangement is made under the present Treaty or by the Contracting Parties upon the appointment of the arbitral tribunal or the single judge.

Article 6

Articles 2 and 3, as well as Article 5 in so far as it concerns the settlement of disputes over the interpretation or application of Articles 2 and 3, shall apply mutatis mutandis to the areas of the continental shelf near the coast delimitated by the Treaty of 9 June 1965.

Article 7

This Treaty shall also apply to Land Berlin provided that the Government of the Federal Republic of Germany does not make a contrary declaration to the Government of the Kingdom of Denmark within three months of the entry into force of the present Treaty.

Article 8

(1) The present Treaty is subject to ratification. The instruments of ratification shall be exchanged in Bonn.

(2) The present Treaty shall enter into force one month after the exchange of instruments of ratification.

DONE at Copenhagen on January 28, 1971 in duplicate in the German and Danish languages, both texts being equally authentic.

For the Federal Republic of Germany: For the Kingdom of Denmark:

ANNEX 1

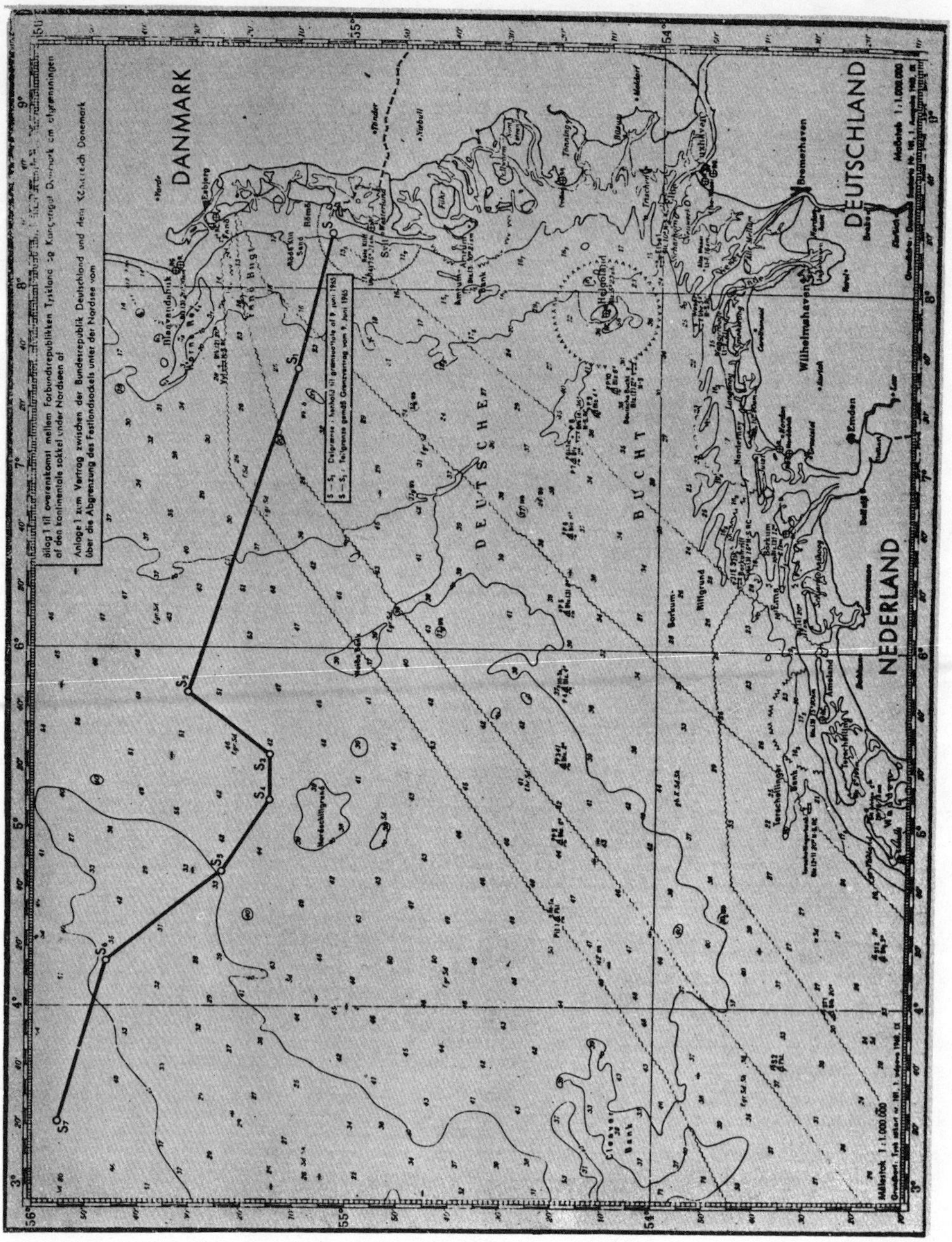

ANNEX 2

(to Article 4)

(1) Enterprises: Dansk Boreselskab Aktieselskab, Aktieselskabet Dampskibsselskabet Svendborg and Dampskibsselskabet af 1912 Aktieselskab, individually or jointly, or an affiliated company established under Danish or German law, by one or several of the above-mentioned enterprises at the time when an application is filed.

(2) License area: The area circumscribed by arcs of great circles between the following points:

55°15'00,0" N	05°24'12,0" E
55°15'00,0" N	05°09'00,0" E
55°24'15,0" N	04°45'00,0" E
55°20'55,1" N	04°40'00,0" E
55°07'56,2" N	05°15'00,0" E

The positions of these points are defined by latitude and longitude on the European Datum System (1st Adjustment 1950).

Treaty between the Kingdom of the Netherlands and the Federal Republic of Germany on the delimitation of the Continental Shelf under the North Sea*

The Kingdom of the Netherlands and the Federal Republic of Germany,

In order to fix the boundaries between the parts of the continental shelf under the North Sea to which each party is entitled, in so far as this was not already done under the Treaty of December 1, 1964 concerning the boundary delimitation of the continental shelf close to the coast,

Also wishing to regulate the economic use of the continental shelf in so far as their joint interests demand such regulation,

On the basis of the judgment of the International Court of Justice of February 20, 1969 on the disputes between the Federal Republic of Germany on one hand and the Kingdom of Denmark and the Kingdom of the Netherlands on the other, on the delimitation of the continental shelf under the North Sea,

With due observance of the boundaries of the continental shelf which have not been fixed by the judgment of the International Court of Justice,

Have agreed as follows:

Article 1

(1) In addition to that part of the boundary fixed under the Treaty of December 1, 1964, the boundary between the Dutch and German parts of the continental shelf under the North Sea is formed by great circles arcs between the points given below, in the same order:

---

*[Reprinted fron an English translation provided to International Legal Materials by the U.S. Department of State.]

E3 as fixed in the Treaty of December 1, 1964

E4:	54°	11'	12"	N,	06°	00'	00"	E
E5:	54°	37'	12"	N,	05°	00'	00"	E
E6:	55°	00'	00"	N,	05°	00'	00"	E
E7:	55°	20'	00"	N,	04°	20'	00"	E
E8:	55°	45'	54"	N,	03°	22'	13"	E

The location of points E4 to E8 inclusive is expressed in latitude and longitude according to European co-ordinates (1st Settlement 1950).

(2) The boundary's terminal point E8 is the point of intersection of the boundaries between the Dutch, German, and English parts of the continental shelf under the North Sea.

(3) By way of illustration, this boundary, as well as the part of the boundary fixed by the Treaty of December 1, 1964, are drawn on the map of Annex 1 of this Treaty.

Article 2

(1) If one of the Contracting Parties proves the presence of minerals in or on the continental shelf and the other Contracting Party is of the opinion that this definite presence extends to its part of the continental shelf, the latter may then inform the former of this, accompanied by data on which the latter bases its judgment. If the first-mentioned party does not share the other party's opinion, the arbitration court will, on request of one of the parties, make a decision in accordance with Article 5.

(2) If the Contracting Parties agree, or if the arbitration court decides upon the existence of minerals extending to both parties' parts in or on the continental shelf, the Governments of the Contracting Parties will then issue regulations for exploitation, which, with due observance of the parties' interests, will be based on the principle that each party is entitled to minerals in or on its part of the continental shelf. In case minerals have already been obtained from those parts claimed by the other party, the regulation will also provide for an appropriate settlement.

(3) A regulation as envisaged in (2) can also be made, wholly or partly by the persons entitled thereto, with the permission of the Contracting Parties' Governments. The person who has an exploitation right for the respective minerals is the one who is so entitled.

(4) If a regulation, in conformity with (2) or (3), cannot be effected within a reasonable period of time, each Contracting Party may appeal to the arbitration court in accordance with Article 5. In such cases the arbitration court may also pronounce judgment EX AEQUO ET BONO. After hearing the Contracting Parties, the court is authorized to make preliminary provisions.

Article 3

Without prejudice to the rules of international law concerning the construction of pipelines on the continental shelf, pipelines which are constructed on the continental shelf in connection with the exploitation of minerals with a view to stopping sea pollution and other dangers are subject to stipulations, concerning the construction and use of pipelines, of the Contracting Party on whose part of the continental shelf such pipelines are constructed.

Article 4

(1) Upon application, exploration and exploitation licenses for petroleum and natural gas in accordance with German law, as well as for other

materials obtained through this exploitation, shall be granted to enterprises mentioned in Annex 2 of this Treaty for the areas indicated in the same Annex which are part of the German continental shelf according to Article 1 of this Treaty.

(2) Within one year after this Treaty becomes effective, the license envisaged in the preceding paragraph must be obtained from the proper German authority.

Article 5

(1) Disputes between the Contracting Parties on the interpretation or application of this Treaty or of the regulation made as a result of paragraph 2 of Article 2 will be settled by negotiation as far as possible.

(2) If a dispute cannot be settled in this way within a reasonable period of time, one of the Contracting Parties may apply to an arbitration court in order to come to a decision.

(3) The arbitration court is appointed AD HOC. If the Contracting Parties, by means of a simplified procedure in joint consultation, do not appoint one single arbiter to settle the dispute, an arbitration court of three persons will be composed in this manner:

Each Contracting Party appoints one member and those two members reach agreement on a citizen of a third State, who will be elected chairman.

The members must be elected within two months and the chairman within another two months after one of the parties has requested settlement of the dispute by an arbitration court.

(4) If the periods mentioned in the third paragraph cannot be met, either of the Contracting Parties may request the President of the International Court of Justice to make the required appointment. If the President has the same nationality as one of the Contracting Parties or if he is unable to carry out his duties, the appointment will be carried out by the Vice President. If the Vice President is also of the same nationality as one of the Contracting Parties, or also engaged in other duties, the appointment will be made by one of the Court of Justice's members, next in rank, who has not the same nationality nor is engaged.

(5) The arbitration court shall decide by majority. Each of the Contracting Parties shall bear the cost of its member and of its representation at the arbitral procedure; the chairman's charges as well as other expenses are shared by the two parties.

(6) The arbitration court or the single arbiter shall decide on the basis of international law which is applicable between the Contracting Parties. The decision shall be binding.

(7) The arbitration court or the single arbiter shall determine the procedure, in so far as this is not determined by this Treaty or by the Contracting Parties with the establishment of the arbitration court or the appointment of the single arbiter.

Article 6

Articles 2 and 3, as well as Article 5 as far as this concerns the settlement of disputes over the interpretation or application of Articles 2 and 3, shall be applied in the same way with respect to that area of the continental shelf near the coast on which a boundary has been established by the Treaty of December 1, 1964.

Article 7

This Treaty also applies to Land Berlin, unless the Government of the Federal Republic of Germany informs the Government of the Kingdom of the Netherlands to the contrary within three months after the Treaty becomes effective.

Article 8

(1) This Treaty shall be ratified. The instruments of ratification shall be exchanged in Bonn.

(2) This Treaty becomes effective one month after the exchange of the instruments of ratification takes place.

In witness whereof the Plenipotentiaries thereto have signed the present Treaty.

Done at Copenhagen, January 28, 1971, in duplicate, in the Dutch and German languages, both texts being equally authoritative.

On behalf of the Kingdom of the Netherlands:

On behalf of the Federal Republic of Germany:

- - - - - - - - - - - -

ANNEX 1

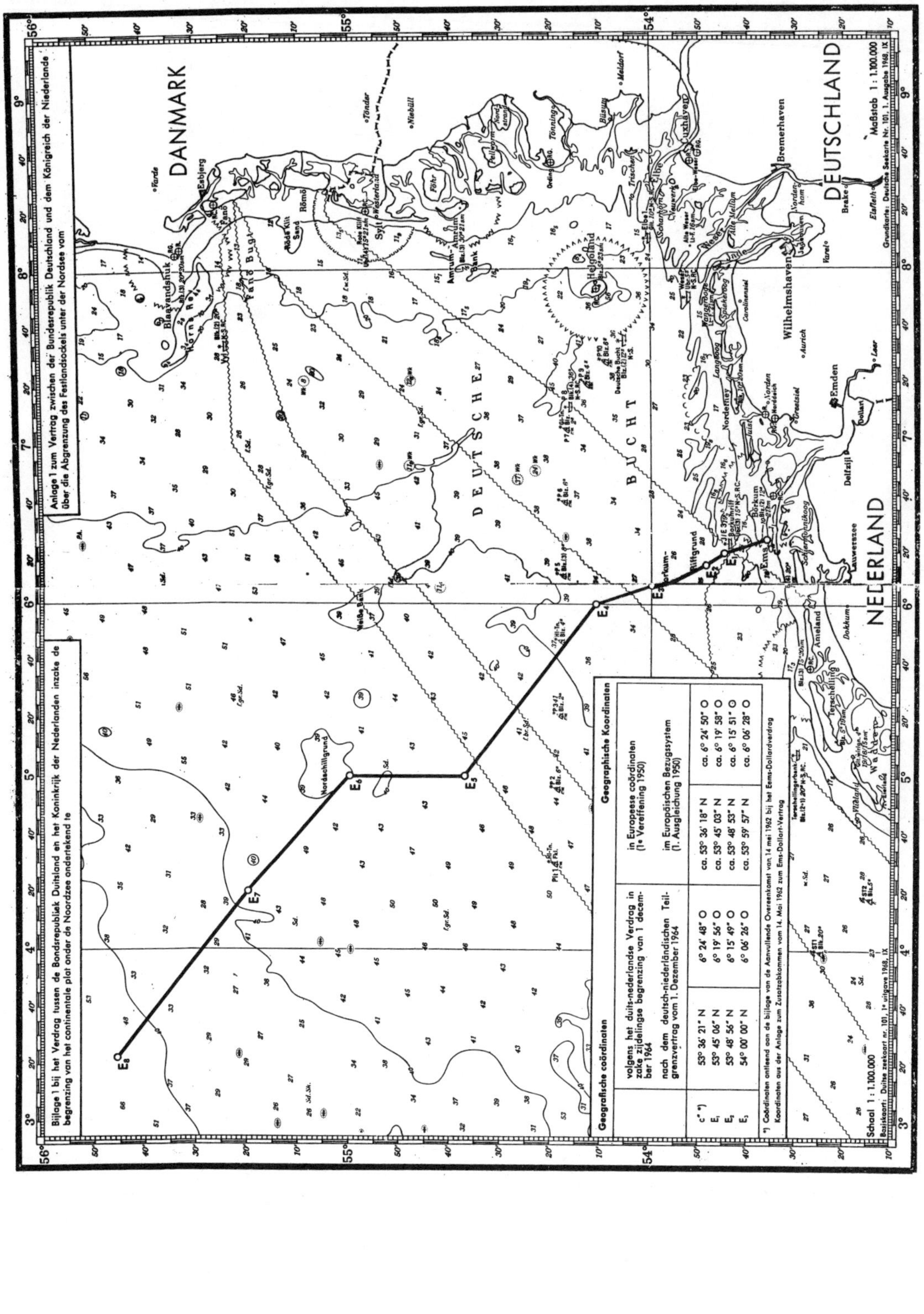
Bijlage 1 bij het Verdrag tussen de Bondsrepubliek Duitsland en het Koninkrijk der Nederlanden inzake de begrenzing van het continentale plat onder de Noordzee ondertekend te
Anlage 1 zum Vertrag zwischen der Bundesrepublik Deutschland und dem Königreich der Niederlande über die Abgrenzung des Festlandsockels unter der Nordsee vom
DANMARK
DEUTSCHE BUCHT
DEUTSCHLAND
NEDERLAND
Geografische coördinaten
Geographische Koordinaten
volgens het duits-nederlandse Verdrag in zake zijdelingse begrenzing van 1 december 1964
nach dem deutsch-niederländischen Teilgrenzvertrag vom 1. Dezember 1964
in Europeese coördinaten (1e Vereffening 1950)
im Europäischen Bezugssystem (1. Ausgleichung 1950)
c* *) 53° 36' 21" N 6° 24' 48" O ca. 53° 36' 18" N ca. 6° 24' 50" O
E1 53° 45' 06" N 6° 19' 56" O ca. 53° 45' 03" N ca. 6° 19' 58" O
E2 53° 48' 56" N 6° 15' 49" O ca. 53° 48' 53" N ca. 6° 15' 51" O
E3 54° 00' 00" N 6° 06' 26" O ca. 53° 59' 57" N ca. 6° 06' 28" O
*) Coördinaten ontleend aan de bijlage van de Aanvullende Overeenkomst van 14 mei 1962 bij het Eems-Dollardverdrag
Koordinaten aus der Anlage zum Zusatzabkommen vom 14. Mai 1962 zum Ems-Dollart-Vertrag
Schaal 1 : 1.100.000
Basiskaart: Duitse zeekaart nr. 101, 1e uitgave 1968, IX
Maßstab 1 : 1.100.000
Grundkarte: Deutsche Seekarte Nr. 101, 1. Ausgabe 1968, IX

ANNEX 2
(to Article 4)

Enterprises holding concessions	Areas[1] for which licenses can be requested
1. Amoco Hanseatic Petroleum Company 2. Exploratie- en Produktie-maatschappij Dyas N.V. 3. Gelsenberg AG	B/7, B/10
1. Gewerkschaft Norddeutschland 2. German Gulf Oil Production Company	B/15, C/16
Gewerkschaft Brigitta	B/14, B/18, G/10
1. Entreprise de Recherches et d'Activités Pétrolières 2. Société Nationale des Pétroles d'Aquitaine 3. Compagnie Française des Pétroles 4. Eurafrep N.V. 5. Corexland N.V. 6. Cofraland N.V.	G/4, G/7
Placid International Oil Ltd.	G/11, G/14
1. Deutsche Tenneco Oil Company 2. Monsanto Oil Company of Germany 3. Ethyl Germany Inc. 4. N.V. Laura & Vereeniging	A/6, A/9, A/12

[1]Specification of the licensed areas according to the map attached to the Royal Decree of January 27, 1967 for the execution of Article 12 of the Mining Law, Continental Shelf (Dutch Government Gazette 1967, 24).

2nd Session, 28th Parliament, 18-19 Elizabeth II, 1969-70

THE HOUSE OF COMMONS OF CANADA

Preamble

An Act to prevent pollution of areas of the arctic waters adjacent to the mainland and islands of the Canadian arctic

Whereas Parliament recognizes that recent developments in relation to the exploitation of the natural resources of arctic areas, including the natural resources of the Canadian arctic, and the transportation of those resources to the markets of the world are of potentially great significance to international trade and commerce and to the economy of Canada in particular;

And whereas Parliament at the same time recognizes and is determined to fulfil its obligation to see that the natural resources of the Canadian arctic are developed and exploited and the arctic waters adjacent to the mainland and islands of the Canadian arctic are navigated only in a manner that takes cognizance of Canada's responsibility for the welfare of the Eskimo and other inhabitants of the Canadian arctic and the preservation of the peculiar ecological balance that now exists in the water, ice and land areas of the Canadian arctic;

Now therefore, Her Majesty, by and with the advice and consent of the Senate and House of Commons of Canada, enacts as follows:

SHORT TITLE

1. This Act may be cited as the *Arctic Waters Pollution Prevention Act.*

INTERPRETATION

2. In this Act,

(*a*) "analyst" means a person designated as an analyst pursuant to the *Canada Water Act* or the *Northern Inland Waters Act*;

(*b*) "icebreaker" means a ship specially designed and constructed for the purpose of assisting the passage of other ships through ice;

(*c*) "owner" in relation to a ship, includes any person having for the time being, either by law or by contract, the same rights as the owner of the ship as regards the possession and use thereof;

(*d*) "pilot" means a person licensed as a pilot pursuant to the *Canada Shipping Act*;

(*e*) "pollution prevention officer" means a person designated as a pollution prevention officer pursuant to section 14;

(*f*) "ship" includes any description of vessel or boat used or designed for use in navigation without regard to method or lack of propulsion;

(*g*) "shipping safety control zone" means an area of the arctic waters prescribed as a shipping safety control zone by order of the Governor in Council made under section 11; and

(*h*) "waste" means

(i) any substance that, if added to any waters, would degrade or alter or form part of a process of degradation or alteration of the quality of those waters to an extent that is detrimental to their use by man or by any animal, fish or plant that is useful to man, and

(ii) any water that contains a substance in such a quantity or concentration, or that has been so treated, processed or changed, by heat or other means, from a natural state that it would, if added to any waters, degrade or alter or form part of a process of degradation or alteration of the quality of those waters to an extent that is detrimental to their use by man or by any animal, fish or plant that is useful to man,

and without limiting the generality of the foregoing, includes anything that, for the purposes of the *Canada Water Act,* is deemed to be waste.

APPLICATION OF ACT

3. (1) Except where otherwise provided, this Act applies to the waters (in this Act referred to as the "arctic waters") adjacent to the mainland and islands of the Canadian arctic within the area enclosed by the sixtieth parallel of north latitude, the one hundred and forty-first meridian of longitude and a line measured seaward from the nearest Canadian land a distance of one hundred nautical miles; except that in the area between the islands of the Canadian arctic and Greenland, where the line of equidistance between the islands of the Canadian arctic and Greenland is less than one hundred nautical miles from the nearest Canadian land, there shall be substituted for the line measured seaward one hundred nautical miles from the nearest Canadian land such line of equidistance.

(2) For greater certainty, the expression "arctic waters" in this Act includes all waters described in subsection (1) and, as this Act applies to or in respect of any person described in paragraph (*a*) of subsection (1) of section 6, all waters adjacent thereto lying north of the sixtieth parallel of north latitude, the natural resources of whose subjacent submarine areas Her Majesty in right of Canada has the right to dispose of or exploit, whether the waters so described or such adjacent waters are in a frozen or a liquid state, but does not include inland waters.

DEPOSIT OF WASTE

4. (1) Except as authorized by regulations made under this section, no person or ship shall deposit or permit the deposit of waste of any type in the arctic waters or in any place on the mainland or islands of the Canadian arctic under any conditions where such waste or any other waste that results from the deposit of such waste may enter the arctic waters.

(2) Subsection (1) does not apply to the deposit of waste in waters that form part of a water quality management area designated pursuant to the *Canada Water Act* if the waste so deposited is of a type and quantity and is deposited under conditions authorized by regulations made by the Governor in Council under paragraph (*a*) of subsection (2) of section 16 of that Act with respect to that water quality management area.

(3) The Governor in Council may make regulations for the purposes of this section prescribing the type and quantity of waste, if any, that may be deposited by any person or ship in the arctic waters or in any place on the mainland or islands of the Canadian arctic under any conditions where such waste or any other waste that results from the deposit of such waste may enter the arctic waters, and prescribing the conditions under which any such waste may be so deposited.

5. (1) Any person who

(*a*) has deposited waste in violation of subsection (1) of section 4, or

(*b*) carries on any undertaking on the mainland or islands of the Canadian arctic or in the arctic waters that, by reason of any accident or other occurrence, is in danger of causing any deposit of waste described in that subsection otherwise than of a type, in a quantity and under conditions prescribed by regulations made under that section,

shall forthwith report the deposit of waste or the accident or other occurrence to a pollution prevention officer at such location and in such manner as may be prescribed by the Governor in Council.

(2) The master of any ship that has deposited waste in violation of subsection (1) of section 4, or that is in distress and for that reason is in danger of causing any deposit of waste described in that subsection otherwise than of a type, in a quantity and under conditions prescribed by regulations made under that section, shall forthwith report the deposit of waste or the condition of distress to a pollution prevention officer at such location and in such manner as may be prescribed by the Governor in Council.

6. (1) The following persons, namely:

(*a*) any person who is engaged in exploring for, developing or exploiting any natural resource on any land adjacent to the arctic waters or in any submarine area subjacent to the arctic waters,

(*b*) any person who carries on any undertaking on the mainland or islands of the Canadian arctic or in the arctic waters, and

(*c*) the owner of any ship that navigates within the arctic waters and the owner or owners of the cargo of any such ship,

are respectively liable and, in the case of the owner of a ship and the owner or owners of the cargo thereof, are jointly and severally liable, up to the amount determined in the manner provided by regulations made under section 9 in respect of the activity or undertaking so engaged in or carried on or in respect of that ship, as the case may be,

(*d*) for all costs and expenses of and incidental to the taking of action described in subsection (2) on the direction of the Governor in Council, and

(*e*) for all actual loss or damage incurred by other persons

resulting from any deposit of waste described in subsection (1) of section 4 that is caused by or is otherwise attributable to that activity or undertaking or that ship, as the case may be.

(2) Where the Governor in Council directs any action to be taken by or on behalf of Her Majesty in right of Canada to repair or remedy any condition that results from a deposit of waste described in subsection (1), or to reduce or mitigate any damage to or destruction of life or property that results or may reasonably be expected to result from such deposit of waste, the costs and expenses of and incidental to the taking of such action, to the extent that such costs and expenses can be established to have been reasonably incurred in the circumstances, are, subject to this section, recoverable by Her Majesty in right of Canada from the person or persons described in paragraph (*a*), (*b*) or (*c*) of that subsection, with costs, in proceedings brought or taken therefor in the name of Her Majesty.

(3) All claims pursuant to this section against a person or persons described in paragraph (*a*), (*b*) or (*c*) of subsection (1) may be sued for and recovered in any court of competent jurisdiction in Canada, and all such claims shall rank *pari passu* up to the limit of the amount determined in the manner provided by regulations made under section 9 in respect of the activity or undertaking engaged in or carried on by the person or persons against whom the claims are made, or in respect of the ship of which any such person is the owner or of all or part of whose cargo any such person is the owner.

(4) No proceedings in respect of a claim pursuant to this section shall be commenced after two years from the time when the deposit of waste in respect of which the proceedings are brought or taken occurred or first occurred, as the case may be, or could reasonably be expected to have become known to those affected thereby.

7. (1) The liability of any person pursuant to section 6 is absolute and does not depend upon proof of fault or negligence, except that no person is liable pursuant to that section for any costs, expenses or actual loss or damage incurred by another person whose conduct caused any deposit of waste described in subsection (1) of that section, or whose conduct contributed to any such deposit of waste, to the degree to which his conduct contributed thereto, and nothing in this Act shall be construed as limiting or restricting any right of recourse or indemnity that a person liable pursuant to section 6 may have against any other person.

(2) For the purposes of subsection (1), a reference to any conduct of "another person" includes any wrongful act or omission by that other person or by any person for whose wrongful act or omission that other person is by law responsible.

(3) Notwithstanding anything in this Act, no person is liable pursuant to section 6, either alone or jointly and severally with any other person or persons, by reason only of his being the owner of all or any part of the cargo of a ship if he can establish that the cargo or part thereof of which he is the owner is of such a nature, or is of such a nature and is carried in such a quantity that, if it and any other cargo of the same nature that is carried by that ship were deposited by that ship in the arctic waters, the deposit thereof would not constitute a violation of subsection (1) of section 4.

8. (1) The Governor in Council may require

(*a*) any person who engages in exploring for, developing or exploiting any natural resource on any land adjacent to the arctic waters or in any submarine area subjacent to the arctic waters,

(*b*) any person who carries on any undertaking on the mainland or islands of the Canadian arctic or in the arctic waters that will or is likely to result in the deposit of waste in the arctic waters or in any place under any conditions where such waste or any other waste that results from the deposit of such waste may enter the arctic waters,

(*c*) any person, other than a person described in paragraph (*a*), who proposes to construct, alter or extend any work or works on the mainland or islands of the Canadian arctic or in the arctic waters that, upon completion thereof, will form all or part of an undertaking described in paragraph (*b*), or

(*d*) the owner of any ship that proposes to navigate or that navigates within any shipping safety control zone specified by the Governor in Council and, subject to subsection (3) of section 7, the owner or owners of the cargo of any such ship,

to provide evidence of financial responsibility, in the form of insurance or an indemnity bond satisfactory to the Governor in Council, or in any other form satisfactory to him, in an amount determined in the manner provided by regulations made under section 9.

(2) Evidence of financial responsibility in the form of insurance or an indemnity bond shall be in a form that will enable any person entitled pursuant to section 6 to claim against the person or persons giving such evidence of financial responsibility

to recover directly from the proceeds of such insurance or bond.

9. The Governor in Council may make regulations for the purposes of section 6 prescribing, in respect of any activity or undertaking engaged in or carried on by any person or persons described in paragraph (*a*), (*b*) or (*c*) of subsection (1) of section 6, or in respect of any ship of which any such person is the owner or of all or part of whose cargo any such person is the owner, the manner of determining the limit of liability of any such person or persons pursuant to that section, which prescribed manner shall, in the case of the owner of any ship and the owner or owners of the cargo thereof, take into account the size of such ship and the nature and quantity of the cargo carried or to be carried by it.

PLANS AND SPECIFICATIONS OF WORKS

10. (1) The Governor in Council may require any person who proposes to construct, alter or extend any work or works on the mainland or islands of the Canadian arctic or in the arctic waters that, upon completion thereof, will form all or part of an undertaking the operation of which will or is likely to result in the deposit of waste of any type in the arctic waters or in any place under any conditions where such waste or any other waste that results from the deposit of such waste may enter the arctic waters, to provide him with a copy of such plans and specifications relating to the work or works as will enable him to determine whether the deposit of waste that will or is likely to occur if the construction, alteration or extension is carried out in accordance therewith would constitute a violation of subsection (1) of section 4.

(2) If, after reviewing any plans and specifications provided to him under subsection (1) and affording to the person who provided those plans and specifications a reasonable opportunity to be heard, the Governor in Council is of the opinion that the deposit of waste that will or is likely to occur if the construction, alteration or extension is carried out in accordance with such plans and specifications would constitute a violation of subsection (1) of section 4, he may, by order, either

(*a*) require such modifications in those plans and specifications as he considers to be necessary, or

(*b*) prohibit the carrying out of the construction, alteration or extension.

SHIPPING SAFETY CONTROL ZONES

11. (1) Subject to subsection (2), the Governor in Council may, by order, prescribe as a shipping safety control zone any area of the arctic waters specified in the order, and may, as he deems necessary, amend any such area.

(2) A copy of each order that the Governor in Council proposes to make under subsection (1) shall be published in the *Canada Gazette;* and no order may be made by the Governor in Council under subsection (1) based upon any such proposal except after the expiration of sixty days following publication of the proposal in the *Canada Gazette.*

12. (1) The Governor in Council may make regulations applicable to ships of any class or classes specified therein, prohibiting any ship of that class or of any of those classes from navigating within any shipping safety control zone specified therein

(*a*) unless the ship complies with standards prescribed by the regulations relating to

(i) hull and fuel tank construction, including the strength of materials used therein, the use of double hulls and the subdivision thereof into watertight compartments,

(ii) the construction of machinery and equipment and the electronic and other navigational aids and equipment and telecommunications equipment to be carried and the manner and frequency of maintenance thereof,

(iii) the nature and construction of propelling power and appliances and fittings for steering and stabilizing,

(iv) the manning of the ship, including the number of navigating and look-out personnel to be carried who are qualified in a manner prescribed by the regulations,

(v) with respect to any type of cargo to be carried, the maximum quantity thereof that may be carried, the method of stowage thereof and the nature or type and quantity of supplies and equipment to be carried for use in repairing or remedying any condition that may result from the deposit of any such cargo in the arctic waters,

(vi) the freeboard to be allowed and the marking of load lines,

(vii) quantities of fuel, water and other supplies to be carried, and

(viii) the maps, charts, tide tables and any other documents or publications relating to navigation in the arctic waters to be carried;

(*b*) without the aid of a pilot, or of an ice navigator who is qualified in a manner prescribed by the regulations, at any time or during any period or periods of the year, if any, specified in the regulations, or without icebreaker assistance of a kind prescribed by the regulations; and

(*c*) during any period or periods of the year, if any, specified in the regulations or when ice conditions of a kind specified in the regulations exist in that zone.

(2) The Governor in Council may by order exempt from the application of any regulations made under subsection (1) any ship or class of ship that is owned or operated by a sovereign power other than Canada where the Governor in Council is satisfied that appropriate measures have been taken by or under the authority of that sovereign power to ensure the compliance of such ship with, or with standards substantially equivalent to, standards prescribed by regulations made under paragraph (*a*) of subsection (1) that would otherwise be applicable to it within any shipping safety control zone, and that in all other respects all reasonable precautions have been or will be taken to reduce the danger of any deposit of waste resulting from the navigation of such ship within that shipping safety control zone.

(3) The Governor in Council may make regulations providing for the issue to the owner or master of any ship that proposes to navigate within any shipping safety control zone specified therein, of a certificate evidencing, in the absence of any evidence to the contrary, the compliance of such ship with standards prescribed by regulations made under paragraph (*a*) of subsection (1) that are or would be applicable to it within that shipping safety control zone, and governing the use that may be made of any such certificate and the effect that may be given thereto for the purposes of any provision of this Act.

13. (1) Where the Governor in Council has reasonable cause to believe that a ship that is within the arctic waters and is in distress, stranded, wrecked, sunk or abandoned, is depositing waste or is likely to deposit waste in the arctic waters, he may cause the ship or any cargo or other material on board the ship to be destroyed, if necessary, or to be removed if possible to such place and sold in such manner as he may direct.

(2) The proceeds from the sale of a ship or any cargo or other material pursuant to subsection (1) shall be applied towards meeting the expenses incurred by the Government of Canada in removing and selling the ship, cargo or other material, and any surplus shall be paid to the owner of that ship, cargo or other material.

POLLUTION PREVENTION OFFICERS

14. (1) The Governor in Council may designate any person as a pollution prevention officer with such of the powers set out in sections 15 and 23 as are specified in the certificate of designation of such person.

(2) A pollution prevention officer shall be furnished with a certificate of his designation specifying the powers set out in sections 15 and 23 that are vested in him, and a pollution prevention officer, on exercising any such power shall, if so required, produce the certificate to any person in authority who is affected thereby and who requires him to do so.

15. (1) A pollution prevention officer may, at any reasonable time,

(*a*) enter any area, place or premises (other than a ship, a private dwelling place or any part of any area, place or premises other than a ship that is designed to be used and is being used as a permanent or temporary private dwelling place) occupied by any person described in paragraph (*a*) or (*b*) of subsection (1) of section 8, in which he reasonably believes

(i) there is being or has been carried on any activity that may result in or has resulted in waste, or

(ii) there is any waste

that may be or has been deposited in the arctic waters or on the mainland or islands of the Canadian arctic under any conditions where such waste or any other waste that results from the deposit of such waste may enter the arctic waters in violation of subsection (1) of section 4;

(*b*) examine any waste found therein in bulk or open any container found therein that he has reason to believe contains any waste and take samples thereof; and

(*c*) require any person in such area, place or premises to produce for inspection or for the purpose of obtaining copies thereof or extracts therefrom, any books or other documents or papers concerning any matter relevant to the administration of this Act or the regulations.

(2) A pollution prevention officer may, at any reasonable time,

(*a*) enter any area, place or premises (other than a ship, a private dwelling place or any part of any area, place or premises other than a ship that is designed to be used and is being used as a permanent or temporary private dwelling place) in which any construction, alteration or extension of a work or works described in section 10 is being carried on; and

(*b*) conduct such inspections of the work or works being constructed, altered or extended as he deems necessary in order to determine whether any plans and specifications provided to the Governor in Council, and any modifications required by the Governor in Council, are being complied with.

(3) A pollution prevention officer may

(*a*) go on board any ship that is within a shipping safety control zone and conduct such inspections thereof as will enable him to determine whether the ship complies with standards prescribed by any regulations made under section 12 that are applicable to it within that shipping safety control zone;

(*b*) order any ship that is in or near a shipping safety control zone to proceed outside such zone in such manner as he may direct, to remain outside such zone or to anchor in a place selected by him,

(i) if he suspects, on reasonable grounds, that the ship fails to comply with standards prescribed by any regulations made under section 12 that are or would be applicable to it within that shipping safety control zone,

(ii) if such ship is within the shipping safety control zone or is about to enter the zone in contravention of a regulation made under paragraph (*b*) or (*c*) of subsection (1) of section 12, or

(iii) if, by reason of weather, visibility, ice or sea conditions, the condition of the ship or its equipment or the nature or condition of its cargo, he is satisfied that such an order is justified in the interests of safety; and

(*c*) where he is informed that a substantial quantity of waste has been deposited in the arctic waters or has entered the arctic waters, or where on reasonable grounds, he is satisfied that a grave and imminent danger of a substantial deposit of waste in the arctic waters exists,

(i) order all ships within a specified area of the arctic waters to report their positions to him, and

(ii) order any ship to take part in the clean-up of such waste or in any action to control or contain the waste.

16. The owner or person in charge of any area, place or premises entered pursuant to subsection (1) or (2) of section 15, the master of any ship boarded pursuant to paragraph (*a*) of subsection (3) of that section and every person found in the area, place or premises or on board the ship shall give a pollution prevention officer all reasonable assistance in his power to enable the pollution prevention officer to carry out his duties and functions under this Act and shall furnish the pollution prevention officer with such information as he may reasonably require.

17. (1) No person shall obstruct or hinder a pollution prevention officer in the carrying out of his duties or functions under this Act.

(2) No person shall knowingly make a false or misleading statement, either verbally or in writing, to a pollution prevention officer engaged in carrying out his duties or functions under this Act.

OFFENCES

18. (1) Any person who violates subsection (1) of section 4 and any ship that violates that subsection is guilty of an offence and liable on summary conviction to a fine not exceeding, in the case of a person, five thousand dollars, and in the case of a ship, one hundred thousand dollars.

(2) Where an offence is committed by a person under subsection (1) on more than one day or is continued by him for more than one day, it shall be deemed to be a separate offence for each day on which the offence is committed or continued.

19. (1) Any person who

(*a*) fails to make a report to a pollution prevention officer as and when required under subsection (1) of section 5, (*b*) fails to provide the Governor in Council with evidence of financial responsibility as and when required under subsection (1) of section 8,

(*c*) fails to provide the Governor in Council with any plans and specifications required of him under subsection (1) of section 10, or

(*d*) constructs, alters or extends any work described in subsection (1) of section 10

(i) otherwise than in accordance with any plans and specifications provided to the Governor in Council in accordance with a requirement made under that subsection, or with any such plans and specifications as required to be modified by any order made under subsection (2) of that section, or

(ii) contrary to any order made under subsection (2) of that section prohibiting the carrying out of such construction, alteration or extension,

is guilty of an offence and is liable on summary conviction to a fine not exceeding twenty-five thousand dollars.

(2) Any ship

(*a*) that navigates within a shipping safety control zone while not complying with standards prescribed by any regulations made under section 12 that are applicable to it within that shipping safety control zone,

(*b*) that navigates within a shipping safety control zone in contravention of a regulation made under paragraph (*b*) or (*c*) of subsection (1) of section 12,

(*c*) that, having taken on board a pilot in order to comply with a regulation made under paragraph (*b*) of subsection (1) of section 12, fails to comply with any reasonable direction given to it by the pilot in carrying out his duties,

(*d*) that fails to comply with any order of a pollution prevention officer under paragraph (*b*) or (*c*) of subsection (3) of section 15 that is applicable to it,

(*e*) the master of which fails to make a report to a pollution prevention officer as and when required under subsection (2) of section 5, or

(*f*) the master of which or any person on board which violates section 17,

is guilty of an offence and is liable on summary conviction to a fine not exceeding twenty-five thousand dollars.

(3) Any person, other than the master of a ship or any person on board a ship, who violates section 17 is guilty of an offence punishable on summary conviction.

20. (1) In a prosecution of a person for an offence under subsection (1) of section 18, it is sufficient proof of the offence to establish that it was committed by an employee or agent of the accused whether or not the employee or agent is identified or has been prosecuted for the offence, unless the accused establishes that the offence was committed without his knowledge or consent and that he exercised all due diligence to prevent its commission.

(2) In a prosecution of a ship for an offence under this Act, it is sufficient proof that the ship has committed the offence to establish that the act or neglect that constitutes the offence was committed by the master of or any person on board the ship, other than a pollution prevention officer or a pilot taken on board in compliance with a regulation made under paragraph (*b*) of subsection (1) of section 12, whether or not the person on board the ship

has been identified; and for the purposes of any prosecution of a ship for failing to comply with any order or direction of a pollution prevention officer or a pilot, any order given by such pollution prevention officer or any direction given by such pilot to the master or any person on board the ship shall be deemed to have been given to the ship.

21. (1) Subject to this section, a certificate of an analyst stating that he has analysed or examined a sample submitted to him by a pollution prevention officer and stating the result of his analysis or examination is admissible in evidence in any prosecution for a violation of subsection (1) of section 4 and in the absence of evidence to the contrary is proof of the statements contained in the certificate without proof of the signature or the official character of the person appearing to have signed the certificate.

(2) The party against whom a certificate of an analyst is produced pursuant to subsection (1) may, with leave of the court, require the attendance of the analyst for the purposes of cross-examination.

(3) No certificate shall be received in evidence pursuant to subsection (1) unless the party intending to produce it has given to the party against whom it is intended to be produced reasonable notice of such intention together with a copy of the certificate.

22. (1) Where any person or ship is charged with having committed an offence under this Act, any court in Canada that would have had cognizance of the offence if it had been committed by a person within the limits of its ordinary jurisdiction has jurisdiction to try the offence as if it had been so committed.

(2) Where a ship is charged with having committed an offence under this Act, the summons may be served by leaving the same with the master or any officer of the ship or by posting the summons on some conspicuous part of the ship, and the ship may appear by counsel or agent, but if it does not appear, a summary conviction court may, upon proof of service of the summons, proceed *ex parte* to hold the trial.

SEIZURE AND FORFEITURE

23. (1) Whenever a pollution prevention officer suspects on reasonable grounds that

(*a*) any provision of this Act or the regulations has been contravened by a ship, or

(*b*) the owner of a ship or the owner or owners of all or part of the cargo thereof has or have committed an offence under paragraph (*b*) of subsection (1) of section 19,

he may, with the consent of the Governor in Council, seize the ship and its cargo anywhere in the arctic waters or elsewhere in the territorial sea or internal or inland waters of Canada.

(2) Subject to subsection (3) and section 24, a ship and cargo seized under subsection (1) shall be retained in the custody of the pollution prevention officer making the seizure or shall be delivered into the custody of such person as the Governor in Council directs.

(3) Where all or any part of a cargo seized under subsection (1) is perishable, the pollution prevention officer or other person having custody thereof may sell the cargo or the portion thereof that is perishable, as the case may be, and the proceeds of the sale shall be paid to the Receiver General or shall be deposited in a chartered bank to the credit of the Receiver General.

24. (1) Where a ship is convicted of an offence under this Act, or where the owner of a ship or an owner of all or part of the cargo thereof has been convicted of an offence under paragraph (*b*) of subsection (1) of section 19, the convicting court may, if the ship and its cargo were seized under subsection (1) of section 23, in addition to any other penalty imposed, order that the ship and cargo or the ship or its cargo or any part thereof be forfeited, and upon the making of such order the ship and cargo or the ship or its cargo or part thereof is or are forfeited to Her Majesty in right of Canada.

(2) Where any cargo or part thereof that is ordered to be forfeited under subsection (1) has been sold under subsection (3) of section 23, the proceeds of such sale are, upon the making of such order, forfeited to Her Majesty in right of Canada.

(3) Where a ship and cargo have been seized under subsection (1) of section 23 and proceedings that could result in an order that the ship and cargo be forfeited have been instituted, the court in or before which the proceedings have been instituted may, with the consent of the Governor in Council, order redelivery thereof to the person from whom they were seized upon security by bond, with two sureties, in an amount and form satisfactory to the Governor in Council, being given to Her Majesty in right of Canada.

(4) Any ship and cargo seized under subsection (1) of section 23 or the proceeds realized from a sale of any perishable cargo under subsection (3) of that section shall be returned or paid to the person from whom the ship and cargo were seized within thirty days from the seizure thereof unless, prior to the expiration of the thirty days, proceedings are instituted in respect of an offence alleged to have been committed by the ship against this Act or in respect of an offence under paragraph (*b*) of subsection (1) of section 19 alleged to have been committed by the owner of the ship or an owner of all or part of the cargo thereof.

(5) Where proceedings referred to in subsection (4) are instituted and, at the final conclusion of those proceedings, a ship and cargo or ship or cargo or part thereof is or are ordered to be forfeited, they or it may, subject to section 25, be disposed of as the Governor in Council directs.

(6) Where a ship and cargo have been seized under subsection (1) of section 23 and proceedings referred to in subsection (4) have been instituted, but the ship and cargo or ship or cargo or part thereof or any proceeds realized from the sale of any part of the cargo are not at the final conclusion of the proceedings ordered to be forfeited, they or it shall be returned or the proceeds shall be paid to the person from whom the ship and cargo were seized, unless there has been a conviction and a fine imposed in which case the ship and cargo or proceeds may be detained until the fine is paid, or the ship and cargo may be sold under execution in satisfaction of the fine, or the proceeds realized from a sale of the cargo or any part thereof may be applied in payment of the fine.

25. (1) The provisions of section 64A of the *Fisheries Act* apply, with such modifications as the circumstances require, in respect of any ship and cargo forfeited under this Act as though the ship and cargo were, respectively, a vessel and goods forfeited under subsection (5) of section 64 of that Act.

(2) References to "the Minister" in section 64A of the *Fisheries Act* shall, in applying that section for the purposes of this Act, be read as references to the Governor in Council and the phrase "other than a person convicted of the offence

that resulted in the forfeiture or a person in whose possession the vessel, vehicle, article, goods or fish were when seized" shall be deemed to include a reference to the owner of the ship where it is the ship that is convicted of the offence that results in the forfeiture.

DELEGATION

26. (1) The Governor in Council may, by order, delegate to any member of the Queen's Privy Council for Canada designated in the order the power and authority to do any act or thing that the Governor in Council is directed or empowered to do under this Act; and upon the making of such an order, the provision or provisions of this Act that direct or empower the Governor in Council and to which the order relates shall be read as if the title of the member of the Queen's Privy Council for Canada designated in the order were substituted therein for the expression "the Governor in Council".

(2) This section does not apply to authorize the Governor in Council to delegate any power vested in him under this Act to make regulations, to prescribe shipping safety control zones or to designate pollution prevention officers and their powers, other than pollution prevention officers with only those powers set out in subsection (1) or (2) of section 15.

DISPOSITION OF FINES

27. All fines imposed pursuant to this Act belong to Her Majesty in right of Canada and shall be paid to the Receiver General.

COMING INTO FORCE

* **28.** This Act shall come into force on a day to be fixed by proclamation.

*Proclamation of this Act and Accompanying Regulations made on August 2, 1972.

U.S. Statement on Canada's Proposed Legislation*

DEPARTMENT OF STATE STATEMENT ON GOVERNMENT OF CANADA'S BILLS ON LIMITS OF THE TERRITORIAL SEA, FISHERIES AND POLLUTION

Last week the Canadian Government introduced in the House of Commons two bills dealing with pollution in the Arctic, fisheries and the limits of the territorial sea. The enactment and implementation of these measures would affect the exercise by the United States and other countries of the right to freedom of the seas in large areas of the high seas and would adversely affect our efforts to reach international agreement on the use of the seas.

The bills seek to establish pollution zones in Arctic waters up to 100 miles from every point of Canadian coastal territory above the 60th parallel. Within these zones, Canada would assert the right to control all shipping, to prescribe standards of vessel construction, navigation and operation, and to prohibit, if Canada deemed it necessary, the free passage of vessels in those waters. Additionally, the legislation seeks to authorize the establishment of exclusive Canadian fisheries in areas of the high seas beyond 12 miles, such as the Gulf of St. Lawrence and the Bay of Fundy, and of a 12-mile territorial sea off Canada's coasts.

International law provides no basis for these proposed unilateral extensions of jurisdictions on the high seas, and the United States can neither accept nor acquiesce in the assertion of such jurisdiction.

We are concerned that this action by Canada if not opposed by us, would be taken as precedent in other parts of the world for other unilateral infringements of the freedom of the seas. If Canada had the right to claim and exercise exclusive pollution and resources jurisdiction on the high seas, other countries could assert the right to exercise jurisdiction for other purposes, some reasonable and some not, but all equally invalid according to international law. Merchant shipping would be severely restricted, and naval mobility would be seriously jeopardized. The potential for serious international dispute and conflict is obvious.

The United States has long sought international solutions rather than national approaches to problems involving the high seas. We are working for appropriate action within the United Nations framework looking toward the conclusion of a new international treaty dealing with the limit of the territorial sea, freedom of transit through and over international straits and defining preferential fishing rights for coastal states on the high seas.

We are also seeking new international means for controlling pollution on the high seas. Last fall 47 countries, including the United States and Canada, participated in the preparation of two international conventions establishing the right of a coastal state to take certain limited anti-pollution measures against vessels on the high seas, and also imposing strict liability upon the owners of vessels responsible for pollution.

---

*[Reproduced from U.S. Department of State Press Release No. 121 of April 15, 1970.

[The proposed legislation on Arctic pollution and territorial sea and fishing zones appears at page 543. The Canadian declaration concerning the compulsory jurisdiction of the International Court of Justice appears at page 598. A summary of the Canadian note of April 16, 1970, in reply to the U.S. Government, appears at page 607.]

These conventions which the United States has recently signed were concluded under U.N. auspices at Brussels. Other international approaches to control of pollution are underway at NATO and the U.N. Moreover, the United States is acutely aware of the peculiar ecological nature of the Arctic region, and the potential dangers of oil pollution in that area. The Arctic is a region important to all nations in its unique environment, its increasing significance as a world trade route and as a source of natural resources. We believe the Arctic beyond national jurisdiction should be subject to internationally agreed rules protecting its assets, both living and non-living, and have noted with pleasure the Canadian Prime Minister's public statement that Canada would be prepared to enter into multilateral efforts to develop agreed rules of environmental protection. To this end, we intend shortly to ask other interested states to join in an international conference designed to establish rules for the Arctic beyond national jurisdiction by international agreement. We would be pleased if Canada were to join us in organizing such a conference.

We regret that the Canadian Government, while not excluding these cooperative international approaches to our mutual problems involving the oceans, now proposes to take unilateral action to assert its own jurisdiction and establish its own rules pending the conclusion of international agreements satisfactory to it. For the reasons indicated earlier the United States can not accept these unilateral jurisdictional assertions and we have urged the Canadian Government to defer making them effective while cooperating in efforts promptly to reach internationally agreed solutions.

If, however, the Canadian Government is unwilling to await international agreement, we have urged that in the interest of avoiding a continuing dispute and undermining our efforts to achieve international agreement, that we submit our differences regarding pollution and exclusive fisheries jurisdiction beyond 12 miles to the International Court of Justice, the forum where disputes of this nature should rightfully be settled. Canada's action last week excluded such disputes from its acceptance of the International Court's compulsory jurisdiction. However, such action only prevents Canada from being forced into the Court. It does not preclude Canada voluntarily joining with us in submitting these disputes to the Court or an appropriate chamber of the Court.

With respect to the 12-mile limit on the territorial sea, we have publicly indicated our willingness to accept such limit, but only as part of an agreed international treaty also providing for freedom of passage through and over international straits.

The history of U.S.-Canadian relations is unique in world affairs for its closeness and cooperation. We are confident that, in this spirit, our two countries will continue to resolve our differences amicably and with mutual understanding.

* * *

Canadian Reply to the U.S. Government*

SUMMARY OF CANADIAN NOTE OF APRIL 16
TABLED BY THE SECRETARY OF STATE FOR EXTERNAL AFFAIRS
IN THE HOUSE APRIL 17

The Canadian Government is unable to accept the views of the United States Government concerning the Arctic Waters Pollution Prevention Bill and the amendments to the Territorial Sea and Fishing Zones Act, and regrets that the United States is not prepared to accept or acquiesce in them. The Canadian Government cannot accept in particular the view that international law provides no basis for the proposed measures. For many years, large numbers of states have asserted various forms of limited jurisdiction beyond their territorial sea over marine areas adjacent to their coasts. The position of the United States Government is that the waters beyond a three-mile limit are high seas and that no state has a right to exercise exclusive pollution or resources jurisdiction on the high seas beyond a three-mile territorial sea. The Canadian Government does not accept this view which indeed the United States itself does not adhere to in practice. For example, as early as 1790, at a time when the international norm for the breadth of the territorial sea was without question three miles, the United States claimed jurisdiction up to twelve miles for customs purposes and enacted appropriate enforcement legislation, which is still in force. Since 1935 the United States has claimed the

*[Reproduced from a text provided by the Canadian Embassy at Washington, D.C.

[The U.S. statement on Canada's proposed legislation appears at page 605. The proposed legislation on Arctic pollution and territorial sea and fishing zones appears at page 543. The Canadian Prime Minister's remarks concerning the legislation appear at page 600. The Canadian declaration concerning the compulsory jurisdiction of the International Court of Justice appears at page 598.]

authority to extend customs enforcement activities as far out to sea as 62 miles, in clear contradiction of applicable international law. In 1966, the United States established exclusive fisheries jurisdiction beyond its three-mile territorial sea extending out to twelve miles from shore, and the United States has just passed analogous legislation asserting exclusive pollution control jurisdiction beyond its three-mile territorial sea and up to twelve miles. Canada reserves to itself the same rights as the United States has asserted to determine for itself how best to protect its vital interests, including in particular its national security. It is the further view of the Canadian Government that a danger to the environment of a state constitutes a threat to its security. Thus the proposed Canadian Arctic Waters Pollution Prevention Legislation constitutes a lawful extension of a limited form of jurisdiction to meet particular dangers, and is of a different order from unilateral interferences with the freedom of the high seas such as, for example, the atomic tests carried out by the United States and other states which, however necessary they may be, have appropriated to their own use vast areas of the high seas and constituted grave perils to those who would wish to utilize such areas during the period of the test blast. The most recent example of such a test by the United States and its consequences for the freedom of the high seas, as was pointed out by some governments at that time, occurred in October 1969 when the United States warned away shipping within a 50-mile radius of the test it was conducting at Amchitka Island. The proposed anti-pollution legislation, proposed fisheries protection legislation and the proposed 12-mile territorial sea consititute a threat to no state and a peril to no one.

It is a well-established principle of international law that customary international law is developed by state practice. Recent and important instances of such state practice on the law of the sea are, for example, the Truman Proclamation of 1945 proclaiming United States jurisdiction over the continental shelf and the unilateral establishment in 1966 by the United States of exclusive fishing zones. Overwhelming evidence that international law can be and is developed by state practice lies in the fact that in 1958, at the time of the first of recent failures of the international community to reach agreement on the breadth of the territorial sea, some 14 states claimed a 12-mile territorial sea, whereas by 1970 some 45 states have established a 12-mile territorial sea and 57 states have established a territorial sea of 12 miles or more. Indeed, the three-mile territorial sea, now claimed by only 24 countries, was itself established by state practice.

The United States Government is aware of the major efforts made by Canada at the 1958 and 1960 Geneva Law of the Sea Conferences to bring about an agreed rule of law on the breadth of the territorial sea and on the breadth of contiguous zones for the exercise of various other types of limited jurisdiction. Subsequent to the failure of the 1958 and 1960 conferences Canada joined with other countries in a further extensive and vigorous multilateral campaign to bring about agreement on these questions, but these efforts failed because the United States ultimately declined to participate in them. In 1964, when Canada passed legislation establishing a nine-mile contiguous fishing zone, the United States objected to it, only to follow suit two years later, thereby confirming its acquiescence in both the substance and the manner of Canada's action. In discussions between Canada and the United States from time to time over the last ten years, Canada has made clear its serious concern over the unresolved questions of the breadth of the territorial sea and the rights of coastal states to assert limited forms of jurisdiction beyond the territorial sea for the purpose of protecting their vital interests. With respect to the Arctic Waters Pollution Prevention Bill, the Canadian Delegation at the November 1969 Brussels I.M.C.O. Conference made strenuous efforts to bring about international agreement on effective pollution prevention measures, but the results of that conference fell short of effective protection for coastal states and the world's marine environment.

It is well known that Canada takes second place to no nation in pressing for multilateral solutions to problems of international law, and that Canada has repeatedly and consistently shown its good faith by its continuous efforts to produce agreed rules of law. The Canadian Government is, however, determined to fulfil its fundamental responsibilities to the Canadian people and to the international community for the protection of Canada's offshore marine environment and its living resources, and the proposed legislation is directed to these ends.

The Canadian Government has long been concerned about the inadequacies of international law in failing to give the necessary protection to the marine environment and to ensure the conservation of fisheries resources. The proposed anti-pollution legislation is based on the overriding right of self-defence of coastal states to protect themselves against grave threats to their environment. Traditional principles of international law concerning pollution of the sea are based in the main on ensuring freedom of navigation to shipping states, which are now engaged in the large scale carriage of oil and other potential pollutants. Such traditional concepts are of little or no relevance anywhere in the world if they can be cited as precluding action by a coastal state to protect this environment. Such concepts are particularly irrelevant, however, to an area having the unique characteristics of the Arctic, where there is an intimate relationship between the sea, the ice and the land, and where the permanent defilement of the environment could occur and result in the destruction of whole species. It is idle, moreover, to talk of freedom of the high seas with respect to an area, large parts of which are covered with ice throughout the year, other parts of which are covered with ice most of each year, and where the local inhabitants use the frozen sea as an extension of the land to travel over it by dogsled and snowmobile far more than they can use it as water. While the Canadian Government is determined to open up the Northwest Passage to safe navigation, it cannot accept the suggestion that the Northwest Passage constitutes high seas.

In these circumstances the Canadian Government is not prepared to await the gradual development of international law, either by other states through their practice nor through the possible development of rules of law through multilateral treaties. The Canadian Government has repeatedly made clear that it is fully prepared to participate actively in multilateral action aimed at producing agreed safety and anti-pollution standards and protection of the living resources of the sea but is not prepared to abdicate in the meantime its own primary responsibilities concerning these questions.

With respect to the Bill which would authorize the establishment of a 12-mile territorial sea off Canada's coasts, the large number of coastal states now claiming a territorial sea of 12 miles or more, and the recent efforts of the United States directed towards a rule of law on the territorial sea, rights of passage and fisheries jurisdiction, provide the best evidence of the validity of the Canadian position on this question. The Canadian Government is aware of United States interest in ensuring freedom of transit through international straits, but rejects any suggestion that the Northwest Passage is such an international strait. The widespread interest in opening up the Northwest Passage to commercial shipping and the well-known commitment of the Canadian Government to this end are themselves ample proof that it has not heretofore been possible to utilize the Northwest Passage as a route for shipping. The Northwest Passage has not attained the status of an international strait by customary usage nor has it been defined as such by conventional international law. The Canadian Government reiterates its determination to open up the Northwest Passage to safe navigation for the shipping of all nations subject, however, to necessary conditions required to protect the delicate ecological balance of the Canadian Arctic.

Canada's new reservation to its acceptance of the compulsory jurisdiction of the international court does not in any way reflect lack of confidence in the court but takes into account the limitations within which the court must operate and the deficiencies of the law which it must interpret and apply. Canada's readiness to submit to the international judicial process remains general in scope and is subject only to certain limited and clearly defined exceptions rather than to a general exception which can be defined at will so as to include any particular matter

It is the earnest hope of the Canadian Government that it will be possible to achieve internationally accepted rules for Arctic navigation within the framework of Canada's proposed legislation. It is recognized that the interests of other states are inevitably affected in any exercise of jurisdiction over areas of the sea. These interests have been taken into account in drafting this legislation; Canada has, for instance, provided that naval vessels and other ships owned by foreign governments may be exempted from the application of Canadian anti-pollution regulations if the ships in question substantially meet Canadian standards. Canada will give the interests of other states, including the United States, further consideration in entering into consultations with them before promulgating safety regulations under the Arctic Waters Bill.

The Canadian Government is pleased to note that the United States confirms that it is acutely aware of the peculiar ecological nature of the Arctic region and the potential dangers of oil pollution in that area. The Canadian Government agrees that the Arctic is a "region important to all nations in its unique environment, its increasing significance as a world trade route, and as a source of natural resources". The Canadian Government does not, however, agree that the Arctic as a whole should be subjected to an international regime protecting its assets both living and non-living, if that is what is proposed by the United States. Canada's sovereignty over the islands of the Arctic Archipelago is not of course, in issue, nor are Canada's sovereign rights over its northern continental shelf and the Canadian Government assumes that the United States Government is not suggesting an international regime to cover these environments (nor the land mass and adjacent submarine resources of Alaska). With respect to the waters of the Arctic Archipelago, the position of Canada has always been that these waters are regarded as Canadian. While Canada would be pleased to discuss with other stated international standards of navigation safety and environmental protection to be applicable to the waters of the Arctic, the Canadian Government cannot accept any suggestion that Canadian waters should be internationalized. The Canadian Government notes that the United States intends shortly to ask other interested states to join in an international conference designed to establish internationally agreed rules protecting the living and non-living assets of the Arctic beyond national jurisdiction, and notes that the United States Government would be pleased to join the Canadian Government in such a conference. Before the Canadian Government can express a definitive view on this question, further information will be required as to the scope, nature and territorial application of the rules the United States proposes, since the Canadian Government obviously cannot participate in any international conference called for the purpose of discussing questions falling wholly within Canadian domestic jurisdiction. With regard to matters properly of an international character, the Prime Minister took the lead in his statement to Canadian Parliament on October 24 last, in inviting the international community to join Canada in promoting a new concept, an international legal regime to ensure to human beings the right to live in a wholesome natural environment.

With respect to the proposed legislation permitting the establishment of exclusive fishing zones, it is the considered view of the Canadian Government that neither existing customary international law nor contemporary conventional international law are adequate to prevent the continuing and increasingly rapid depletion of the living resources of the sea. The Canadian Government is aware of the proposals of the United States and other states concerning possible solutions to this problem through a multilateral approach, and intends to participate actively and constructively in any conferences to be held to consider such questions. The Government in the meantime proposes to take all measures necessary for the protection and conservation of the living resources of the sea adjacent to Canada's coast. It is Canada's expectation that other states will take similar action since it is becoming increasingly apparent that there is no other effective way of preventing the rapid depletion of the living resources of the marine environment.

The Canadian Government is pledged to the development of the use of Canada's Arctic waters for the encouragement and expansion of Canada's northern economy and has adopted a functional and constructive approach to these questions which does not interfere with and indeed can facilitate the legitimate activities of others. The two bills reflect the determination of the Canadian Government to fulfil its responsibilities to its own people and to the international community to preserve the ecological balance of Canada and to protect and conserve the living resources of its marine environment.

The Canadian Government reaffirms its faith in the spirit of co-operation which Canada and the United States have shown throughout so much of the history of their relations and is confident that it will be possible to resolve their differences amicably and with mutual understanding.

UNITED KINGDOM: OIL IN NAVIGABLE WATERS ACT 1971*

ELIZABETH II

1971 CHAPTER 21

An Act to amend the Oil in Navigable Waters Acts 1955 and 1963 and section 5 of the Continental Shelf Act 1964; to make further provision for preventing pollution of the sea by oil; and for purposes connected therewith. [8th April 1971]

BE IT ENACTED by the Queen's most Excellent Majesty, by and with the advice and consent of the Lords Spiritual and Temporal, and Commons, in this present Parliament assembled, and by the authority of the same, as follows:—

1. For subsection (1) of section 1 of the Oil in Navigable Waters Act 1955 (which prohibits the discharge of certain oils into certain sea areas) there shall be substituted the following subsection:— **Discharge of certain oils into the sea. 1955 c. 25.**

" (1) If any oil to which this section applies or any mixture containing such oil is discharged from a ship registered in the United Kingdom into any part of the sea outside the territorial waters of the United Kingdom, the owner or master of the ship shall, subject to the provisions of this Act, be guilty of an offence under this section."

2. In section 3 of the Oil in Navigable Waters Act 1955 (discharge of oil into United Kingdom waters) the following shall be substituted for subsection (1):— **Discharge of oil into United Kingdom waters.**

" (1) If any oil or mixture containing oil is discharged as mentioned in the following paragraphs into waters to which this section applies, then, subject to the provisions of this Act, the following shall be guilty of an offence under this section, that is to say—

(*a*) if the discharge is from a vessel, the owner or master of the vessel, unless he proves that the discharge took place and was caused as mentioned in paragraph (*b*) of this subsection;

(*b*) if the discharge is from a vessel but takes place in the course of a transfer of oil to or from another vessel or a place on land and is caused by the act or omission of a person in charge of any apparatus in that other vessel or that place, the owner or master of that other vessel or, as the case may be, the occupier of that place;

(*c*) if the discharge is from a place on land, the occupier of that place unless he proves that the discharge was caused as mentioned in paragraph (*d*) of this subsection;

(*d*) if the discharge is from a place on land and is caused by the act of a person who is in that place without the permission (express or implied) of the occupier, that person;

(*e*) if the discharge takes place otherwise than as mentioned in the preceding paragraphs and is the result of any operations for the exploration of the sea-bed and subsoil or the exploitation of their natural resources, the person carrying on the operations ".

Special defences. 1955 c. 25.

3.—(1) In section 4(2)(*b*) of the Oil in Navigable Waters Act 1955 (defence of leakage not due to want of care) for the words " that the leakage was not due " there shall be substituted the words " that neither the leakage nor any delay in discovering it was due ".

(2) In section 4(3) of that Act (defence of escape not due to want of care) for the words " that the escape of the oil or mixture was not due " there shall be substituted the words " that neither the escape of the oil or mixture nor any delay in discovering it was due ".

(3) For section 4(4) of that Act there shall be substituted the following subsection:—

" (4) Where any oil or a mixture containing oil is alleged to have escaped and a person is charged with an offence under the last preceding section as a person carrying on operations for the exploration of the sea bed and subsoil or the exploitation of their natural resources, it shall be a defence to prove that neither the escape nor any delay in discovering it was due to any want of reasonable care and that as soon as practicable after it was discovered all reasonable steps were taken for stopping or reducing it ".

Oil records. 1955 c. 25.

4. For section 7 of the Oil in Navigable Waters Act 1955 (which provides for the keeping of records of matters relating to oil) there shall be substituted the following section:—

" 7.—(1) The Board of Trade may make regulations requiring oil record books to be carried in ships registered in the United Kingdom and requiring the master of any such ship to record in the oil record book carried by it—

(*a*) the carrying out, on board or in connection with the ship, of such of the following operations as may be prescribed, that is to say, operations relating to—

(i) the loading of oil cargo, or

(ii) the transfer of oil cargo during a voyage, or

(iii) the discharge of oil cargo, or

(iv) the ballasting of oil tanks (whether cargo or bunker fuel tanks) and the discharge of ballast from, and cleaning of, such tanks, or

(v) the separation of oil from water, or from other substances, in any mixture containing oil, or

(vi) the disposal of any oil or water, or any other substance, arising from operations relating to any of the matters specified in the preceding sub-paragraphs, or

(vii) the disposal of any other oil residues;

(*b*) any occasion on which oil or a mixture containing oil is discharged from the ship for the purpose of securing the safety of any vessel, or of preventing damage to any vessel or cargo, or of saving life;

(*c*) any occasion on which oil or a mixture containing oil is found to be escaping, or to have escaped, from the ship in consequence of damage to the ship, or by reason of leakage.

(2) The Board of Trade may make regulations requiring the keeping of records relating to the transfer of oil to and from vessels while they are within the seaward limits of the territorial waters of the United Kingdom; and the requirements of any regulations made under this subsection shall be in addition to the requirements of any regulations made under subsection (1) of this section.

(3) Any records required to be kept by regulations made under subsection (2) of this section shall, unless the vessel is a barge, be kept by the master of the vessel, and shall, if the vessel is a barge, be kept, in so far as they relate to the transfer of oil to the barge, by the person supplying the oil and, in so far as they relate to the transfer of oil from the barge, by the person to whom the oil is delivered.

(4) Regulations under this section requiring the carrying of oil record books or the keeping of records may—

(*a*) prescribe the form of the oil record books or records and the nature of the entries to be made in them;

(*b*) require the person providing or keeping the books or records to retain them for a prescribed period;

(*c*) require that person, at the end of the prescribed period, to transmit the books or records to a place or person determined by or under the regulations;

(*d*) provide for the custody or disposal of the books or records after their transmission to such a place or person.

(5) If any ship fails to carry such an oil record book as it is required to carry under this section the owner or master shall be liable on summary conviction to a fine not exceeding £500; if any person fails to comply with any requirements imposed on him by or under this section, he shall be liable on summary conviction to a fine not exceeding £500; and if any person makes an entry in any oil record book carried or record kept under this section which is to his knowledge false or misleading in any material particular, he shall be liable on summary conviction to a fine not exceeding £500, or imprisonment for a term not exceeding six months, or both, or on conviction on indictment to a fine or to imprisonment for a term not exceeding two years or both.

(6) In any proceedings under this Act—

(*a*) any oil record book carried or record kept in pursuance of regulations made under this section shall be admissible as evidence, and in Scotland shall be sufficient evidence, of the facts stated in it;

(*b*) any copy of an entry in such an oil record book or record which is certified by the master of the ship in which the book is carried or by the person by whom the record is required to be kept to be a true copy of the entry shall be admissible as evidence, and in Scotland shall be sufficient evidence, of the facts stated in the entry;

(*c*) any document purporting to be an oil record book carried or record kept in pursuance of regulations made under this section, or purporting to be such a certified copy as is mentioned in the preceding paragraph, shall, unless the contrary is proved, be presumed to be such a book, record or copy, as the case may be.

(7) Any functions conferred on the Board of Trade by subsection (1) or subsection (2) of this section shall be exercisable concurrently with the Board by the Secretary of State."

Duty to report discharges of oil into waters of harbour. 1955 c. 25.

5. In section 10(1) of the Oil in Navigable Waters Act 1955 (duty to report discharges) the following shall be substituted for paragraphs (*a*) and (*b*)—

" (*a*) is discharged from a vessel into the waters of a harbour in the United Kingdom; or

(*b*) is found to be escaping or to have escaped, from a vessel into any such waters; or ".

Discharge of oil from pipe-lines or as a result of certain operations. 1964 c. 29.

6. In section 5(1) of the Continental Shelf Act 1964 (discharge of oil from pipe-lines or as a result of operations for the exploration of the sea bed and subsoil or the exploitation of their natural resources)—

(*a*) for the words " any mixture containing not less than one hundred parts of such oil in a million parts of the mixture " there shall be substituted the words " any mixture containing such oil "; and (*b*) for the words " that he took all reasonable care to prevent it " there shall be substituted the words " that neither the escape nor any delay in discovering it was due to any want of reasonable care ".

Increase of maximum fine for certain offences.

7. The limit of the fine that may be imposed on summary conviction in respect of offences committed after the coming into force of this section under section 1 or section 3 of the Oil in Navigable Waters Act 1955 or section 5 of the Continental Shelf Act 1964, shall, instead of the sum of one thousand pounds specified in section 6 of the Oil in Navigable Waters Act 1955 and section 5(2) of the Continental Shelf Act 1964 be the sum of fifty thousand pounds.

Shipping casualties.

8.—(1) The powers conferred by this section shall be exercisable where—

(*a*) an accident has occurred to or in a ship, and

(*b*) in the opinion of the Secretary of State oil from the ship will or may cause pollution on a large scale in the United Kingdom or in the waters in or adjacent to the United Kingdom up to the seaward limits of territorial waters, and

(*c*) in the opinion of the Secretary of State the use of the powers conferred by this section is urgently needed.

(2) For the purpose of preventing or reducing oil pollution, or the risk of oil pollution, the Secretary of State may give directions as respects the ship or its cargo—

(*a*) to the owner of the ship, or to any person in possession of the ship, or

(*b*) to the master of the ship, or

(*c*) to any salvor in possession of the ship, or to any person who is the servant or agent of any salvor in possession of the ship, and who is in charge of the salvage cperation.

(3) Directions under subsection (2) above may require the person to whom they are given to take, or refrain from taking, any action of any kind whatsoever, and without prejudice to the generality of the preceding provisions of this subsection the directions may require—

(*a*) that the ship is to be, or is not to be, moved, or is to be moved to a specified place, or is to be removed from a specified area or locality, or

(*b*) that the ship is not to be moved to a specified place or area, or over a specified route, or

(*c*) that any oil or other cargo is to be, or is not to be, unloaded or discharged, or

(*d*) that specified salvage measures are to be, or are not to be, taken.

(4) If in the opinion of the Secretary of State the powers conferred by subsection (2) above are, or have proved to be, inadequate for the purpose, the Secretary of State may, for the purpose of preventing or reducing oil pollution, or the risk of oil pollution, take, as respects the ship or its cargo, any action of any kind whatsoever, and without prejudice to the generality of the preceding provisions of this subsection the Secretary of State may—

(*a*) take any such action as he has power to require to be taken by a direction under this section,

(*b*) undertake operations for the sinking or destruction of the ship, or any part of it, of a kind which is not within the means of any person to whom he can give directions,

(*c*) undertake operations which involve the taking over of control of the ship.

(5) The powers of the Secretary of State under subsection (4) above shall also be exercisable by such persons as may be authorised in that behalf by the Secretary of State.

(6) Every person concerned with compliance with directions given, or with action taken, under this section shall use his best endeavours to avoid any risk to human life.

(7) If the person to whom a direction is duly given under this section contravenes, or fails to comply with, any requirement of the direction, he shall be guilty of an offence under this section.

(8) In proceedings for an offence under subsection (7) above, it shall be a defence for the accused to prove that he has used all due diligence to ensure compliance with the direction, or that he had reasonable cause for believing that compliance with the direction would have involved a serious risk to human life.

(9) If a person wilfully obstructs any person who is acting in compliance with a direction under this section, or who is acting under subsection (4) or (5) of this section, the first mentioned person shall be guilty of an offence under this section.

(10) Her Majesty may by Order in Council provide that this section and Schedule 2 to this Act, together with any other provisions of this Act, shall apply to a ship—

(*a*) which is not a ship registered in the United Kingdom, and

(*b*) which is for the time being outside the territorial waters of the United Kingdom,

in such cases and circumstances as may be specified in the Order, and subject to such exceptions, adaptations and modifications, if any, as may be so specified.

An Order in Council under this subsection may contain such transitional and other consequential provisions as appear to Her Majesty to be expedient.

(11) Except as provided by an Order in Council under subsection (10) above, no direction under this section shall apply to a ship which is not registered in the United Kingdom and which is for the time being outside the territorial waters of the United Kingdom, and no action shall be taken under subsection (4) or (5) above as respects any such ship.

(12) No direction under this section shall apply to any vessel of Her Majesty's Navy, or to any Government ship, and no action shall be taken under subsection (4) or (5) above as respects any such vessel or ship.

In this subsection " Government ship " has the same meaning as in section 80 of the Merchant Shipping Act 1906. **1906 c. 48.**

(13) A person guilty of an offence under this section shall be liable—

(*a*) on summary conviction to a fine not exceeding £50,0C0,

(*b*) on conviction on indictment to a fine.

(14) The provisions of this section are without prejudice to any rights or powers of Her Majesty's Government in the United Kingdom exercisable apart from this section whether under international law or otherwise.

(15) Schedule 2 to this Act shall have effect for supplementing this section and this section is in that Schedule referred to as " the principal section ".

(16) In this section, unless the context otherwise requires—

" accident " includes the loss, stranding, abandonment of or damage to a ship,

" specified ", in relation to a direction under this section, means specified by the direction.

Application to hovercraft. 1968 c. 59.

9. The enactments and instruments with respect to which provision may be made by an Order in Council under section 1(1)(*h*) of the Hovercraft Act 1968 shall include this Act and any instrument made under it.

Provisions as to Northern Ireland.

10.—(1) This Act extends to Northern Ireland.

(2) The provisions of the Oil in Navigable Waters Acts 1955 and 1963 and of this Act, so far as they relate to matters with respect to which the Parliament of Northern Ireland has power to make laws, shall not be taken to restrict that power, and any laws made by that Parliament in the exercise of that power shall have effect notwithstanding anything in those provisions.

Amendments and repeals. 1955 c. 25.

11.—(1) The Oil in Navigable Waters Act 1955 shall have effect subject to the minor and consequential amendments specified in Schedule 1 to this Act.

(2) The enactments mentioned in Schedule 3 to this Act are hereby repealed to the extent specified in the third column of that Schedule.

Citation, construction and commencement.

12.—(1) This Act may be cited as the Oil in Navigable Waters Act 1971.

(2) This Act shall be construed as one with the Oil in Navigable Waters Acts 1955 and 1963 and those Acts and this Act may be cited together as the Oil in Navigable Waters Acts 1955 to 1971.

(3) This Act shall come into force on such day as the Secretary of State may by order appoint, and different days may be so appointed for different provisions of this Act.

SCHEDULES

SCHEDULE 1

Section 11(1).

MINOR AND CONSEQUENTIAL AMENDMENTS OF OIL IN NAVIGABLE WATERS ACT 1955

1955 c. 25.

1. In section 1(2) for the words " a prohibited sea area " there shall be substituted the words " any part of the sea outside the territorial waters of the United Kingdom ".

2. In section 11(5) for the words from " of any records " to " are to be kept " there shall be substituted the words " of any oil record book required to be carried or records required to be kept in pursuance of regulations made under section 7 of this Act shall include power to copy any entry therein and require the master ".

3. In section 11(6) the following shall be substituted for paragraphs (*b*) and (*c*):—

" (*b*) to require the production of any oil record book required to be carried or records required to be kept in pursuance of regulations made under section 7 of this Act;

(*c*) to copy any entry in any such book or record and require the master to certify the copy as a true copy of the entry ".

4. In section 18(1) for the words " records required to be kept " there shall be substituted the words " oil record books required to be carried ".

5. In section 18(2) for the word " records " in both places where it occurs there shall be substituted the words " oil record books ".

6. In section 22(3) for the words " this Act " there shall be substituted the words " the provisions of this Act other than section 10 ".

SCHEDULE 2

Section 8.

SHIPPING CASUALTIES

Right to recover in respect of unreasonable loss or damage

1.—(1) If any action duly taken by a person in pursuance of a direction given to him under the principal section, or any action taken under subsection (4) or (5) of the principal section—

(*a*) was not reasonably necessary to prevent or reduce oil pollution, or risk of oil pollution, or

(*b*) was such that the good it did or was likely to do was disproportionately less than the expense incurred, or damage suffered, as a result of the action,

a person incurring expense or suffering damage as a result of, or by himself taking, the action shall be entitled to recover compensation from the Secretary of State.

Sch. 2

(2) In considering whether sub-paragraph (1) above applies, account shall be taken of—

(a) the extent and risk of oil pollution if the action had not been taken,

(b) the likelihood of the action being effective, and

(c) the extent of the damage which has been caused by the action.

(3) Any reference in this paragraph to the taking of any action includes a reference to a compliance with a direction not to take some specified action.

(4) The Admiralty jurisdiction of the High Court of the Court of Session and of the Supreme Court of Northern Ireland shall include jurisdiction to hear and determine any claim arising under this paragraph.

Directions

2.—(1) If the Secretary of State is satisfied that a company or other body is not one to whom section 412 or section 437 of the Companies Act 1948 (service of notices) applies so as to authorise the service of a direction on that body under either of those sections, he may give a direction under the principal section—

1948 c. 38.

(a) to that body, as the owner of, or the person in possession of, a ship, by serving the direction on the master of the ship,

(b) to that body, as a salvor, by serving the direction on the person in charge of the salvage operations.

(2) For the purpose of giving or serving a direction under the principal section to or on any person on a ship, a person acting on behalf of the Secretary of State shall have the right to go on board the ship.

(3) If a person wilfully obstructs any person acting on behalf of the Secretary of State in connection with the giving or service of a direction under the principal section, the first-mentioned person shall be guilty of an offence under the principal section.

(4) In the application of sub-paragraph (1) above to Northern Ireland for references to sections 412 and 437 of the Companies Act 1948 there shall be substituted references to sections 361 and 385 of the Companies Act (Northern Ireland) 1960.

1960 c. 22. (N.I.)

Ship under arrest

3.—(1) It is hereby declared that any action taken as respects a ship which is under arrest or as respects the cargo of such a ship, being action duly taken in pursuance of a direction given under the principal section, or being any action taken under subsection (4) or (5) of the principal section—

(a) does not constitute contempt of court, and

(b) does not in any circumstances make the Admiralty Marshal liable in any civil proceedings.

Sch. 2

(2) The reference in this paragraph to the Admiralty Marshal includes a reference to the Admiralty Marshal of the Supreme Court of Northern Ireland.

SCHEDULE 3

Section 11(2).

ENACTMENTS REPEALED

Chapter	Short Title	Extent of Repeal
3 & 4 Eliz. 2. c. 25.	The Oil in Navigable Waters Act 1955.	Section 2. In section 4, in subsection (3) the words "or as the person in charge of any apparatus". In section 22(1) the definition of "mile". Section 23(7). The Schedule.
1963 c. 28.	The Oil in Navigable Waters Act 1963.	Sections 1 and 2. In Schedule 1, paragraphs 1 and 2(2).

The Oil in Navigable Waters (Shipping Casualties) Order 1971

Made - - -	*27th October* 1971
Laid before Parliament	*2nd November* 1971
Coming into Operation	*22nd November* 1971

At the Court at Buckingham Palace, the 27th day of October 1971

Present,

The Queen's Most Excellent Majesty in Council

Her Majesty in exercise of the powers conferred upon her by section 8(10) of the Oil in Navigable Waters Act 1971(**a**) and of all other powers enabling Her in that behalf, is pleased by and with the advice of Her Privy Council to order, and it is hereby ordered, as follows:—

1.—(1) This Order may be cited as the Oil in Navigable Waters (Shipping Casualties) Order 1971 and shall come into operation on 22nd November 1971.

(2) The Interpretation Act 1889(**b**) shall apply to the interpretation of this Order as it applies to the interpretation of an Act of Parliament.

2. Subject to the exceptions and modifications in Article 3 of this Order, section 8 of and Schedule 2 to the Oil in Navigable Waters Act 1971 shall apply to a ship—

(*a*) which is not registered in the United Kingdom; and

(*b*) which is for the time being outside the territorial waters of the United Kingdom

in any case in which the Secretary of State is satisfied that there is a need to protect the coast of the United Kingdom or the waters in or adjacent to the United Kingdom up to the seaward limits of territorial waters against grave and imminent danger of oil pollution.

3. In respect of a ship to which the said section 8 and Schedule 2 are applied by Article 2 of this Order the power conferred on the Secretary of State by subsection (2) of section 8 to give directions shall only be exercisable in relation to—

(*a*) an individual who is a citizen of the United Kingdom and Colonies, or

(*b*) a body corporate which is established under the laws of a part of the United Kingdom

and subsection (9) of section 8 (offence of obstruction) shall only apply to such an individual or body corporate.

W. G. Agnew.

(**a**) 1971 c. 21. (**b**) 1889 c. 63.

AGREEMENTS [3] BETWEEN CHILE, ECUADOR AND PERU, SIGNED AT THE FIRST CONFERENCE ON THE EXPLOITATION AND CONSERVATION OF THE MARITIME RESOURCES OF THE SOUTH PACIFIC, SANTIAGO, 18 AUGUST 1952

(*a*) DECLARATION ON THE MARITIME ZONE [4]

1. Governments are bound to ensure for their peoples access to necessary food supplies and to furnish them with the means of developing their economy.

2. It is therefore the duty of each Government to ensure the conservation and protection of its natural resources and to regulate the use thereof to the greatest possible advantage of its country.

[3] Ratified by all the signatory States. Costa-Rica has acceded.

[4] *Revista Peruana de Derecho Internacional*, tomo XIV, No. 45, 1954, pp. 104 *et seq*. Translation by the Secretariat of the United Nations.

3. Hence it is likewise the duty of each Government to prevent the said resources from being used outside the area of its jurisdiction so as to endanger their existence, integrity and conservation to the prejudice of peoples so situated geographically that their seas are irreplaceable sources of essential food and economic materials.

For the foregoing reasons the Government of Chile, Ecuador and Peru, being resolved to preserve for and make available to their respective peoples the natural resources of the areas of sea adjacent to their coasts, hereby declare as follows:

(I) Owing to the geological and biological factors affecting the existence, conservation and development of the marine fauna and flora of the waters adjacent to the coasts of the declarant countries, the former extent of the territorial sea and contiguous zone is insufficient to permit of the conservation, development and use of those resources, to which the coastal countries are entitled.

(II) The Governments of Chile, Ecuador and Peru therefore proclaim as a principle of their international maritime policy that each of them possesses sole sovereignty and jurisdiction over the area of sea adjacent to the coast of its own country and extending not less than 200 nautical miles from the said coast.

(III) Their sole jurisdiction and sovereignty over the zone thus described includes sole sovereignty and jurisdiction over the sea floor and subsoil thereof.

(IV) The zone of 200 nautical miles shall extend in every direction from any island or group of islands forming part of the territory of a declarant country. The maritime zone of an island or group of islands belonging to one declarant country and situated less than 200 nautical miles from the general maritime zone of another declarant country shall be bounded by the parallel of latitude drawn from the point at which the land frontier between the two countries reaches the sea.

(V) This Declaration shall not be construed as disregarding the necessary restrictions on the exercise of sovereignty and jurisdiction imposed by international law to permit the innocent and inoffensive passage of vessels of all nations through the zone aforesaid.

(VI) The Governments of Chile, Ecuador and Peru state that they intend to sign agreements or conventions to put into effect the principles set forth in this Declaration and to establish general regulations for the control and protection of hunting and fishing in their respective maritime zones and the control and co-ordination of the use and working of all other natural products or resources of common interest present in the said waters.

AGREEMENTS [1] BETWEEN CHILE, ECUADOR AND PERU, SIGNED AT THE SECOND CONFERENCE ON THE EXPLOITATION AND CONSERVATION OF THE MARITIME RESOURCES OF THE SOUTH PACIFIC, LIMA, 4 DECEMBER 1954

(*a*) AGREEMENT SUPPLEMENTARY TO THE DECLARATION OF SOVEREIGNTY OVER THE MARITIME ZONE OF TWO HUNDRED MILES [2]

The Governments of the Republics of Chile, Ecuador and Peru, in conformity with the provisions of resolution X of 8 October 1954, signed at Santiago de Chile by the Standing Committee of the Conference on the Exploitation and Conservation of the Maritime Resources of the South Pacific,

Having noted the proposals and recommendations approved in October of this year by the said Standing Committee,

Have appointed the following plenipotentiaries:

. . .

AND WHEREAS

Chile, Ecuador and Peru have proclaimed their sovereignty over the sea adjacent to the coasts of their respective countries to a distance of not less than two hundred nautical miles from the said coasts, the sea-bed and the subsoil of this maritime zone being included;

The Governments of Chile, Ecuador and Peru, at the First Conference on the Exploitation and Conservation of the Maritime Resources of the South Pacific, held at Santiago de Chile in 1952, expressed their intention of entering into agreements or conventions relating to the application of the principles governing that sovereignty, for the purpose in particular of regulating and protecting hunting and fisheries within their several maritime zones:

[1] Ratified (up to June 1955) by: Peru.

[2] *Ibid.*, No. 46, 1954, pp. 276 *et seq.* Translation by the Secretariat of the United Nations.

NOW THEREFORE THE SAID PLENIPOTENTIARIES HEREBY AGREE AS FOLLOWS:

1. Chile, Ecuador and Peru shall consult with one another for the purpose of upholding, in law, the principle of their sovereignty over the maritime zone to a distance of not less than two hundred nautical miles, including the sea-bed and the subsoil corresponding thereto. The term " nautical mile " means the equivalent of one minute of the arc measured on the Equator, or a distance of 1,852.8 metres.

2. If any complaints or protests should be addressed to any of the Parties, or if proceedings should be instituted against a Party in a court of law or in an arbitral tribunal, whether possessing general or special jurisdiction, the contracting countries undertake to consult with one another concerning the case to be presented for the defence and furthermore bind themselves to co-operate fully with one another in the joint defence.

3. In the event of a violation of the said maritime zone by force, the State affected shall report the event immediately to the other Contracting Parties, for the purpose of determining what action should be taken to safeguard the sovereignty which has been violated.

4. Each of the Contracting Parties undertakes not to enter into any agreements, arrangements or conventions which imply a diminution of the sovereignty over the said zone, though this provision shall not prejudice their rights to enter into agreements or to conclude contracts which do not conflict with the common rules laid down by the contracting countries.

5. All the provisions of this Agreement shall be deemed to be an integral and supplementary part of, and not in any way to abrogate, the resolutions and decisions adopted at the Conference on the Exploitation and Conservation of the Maritime Resources of the South Pacific, held at Santiago de Chile in August 1952.

MONTEVIDEO DECLARATION ON THE LAW OF THE SEA

Adopted May 8, 1970

The States represented at the Montevideo Meeting on the Law of the Sea,

RECOGNIZING that there exists a geographic, economic and social link between the sea, the land, and its inhabitants, Man, which confers on the coastal peoples legitimate priority in the utilization of the natural resources provided by their marine environment,

RECOGNIZING likewise that any norms governing the limits of national sovereignty and jurisdiction over the sea, its soil and its subsoil, and the conditions for the exploitation of their resources, must take account of the geographical realities of the coastal States and the special needs and economic and social responsibilities of developing States,

CONSIDERING: that scientific and technological advances in the exploitation of the natural wealth of the sea have brought in their train the danger of plundering its living resources through injudicious or abusive harvesting practices or through the disturbance of ecological conditions, a fact which supports the right of coastal States to take the necessary measures to protect those resources within areas of jurisdiction more extensive than has traditionally been the case and to regulate within such areas any fishing or aquatic hunting, carried out by vessels operating under the national or a foreign flag, subject to national legislation and to agreements concluded with other States,

that a number of declarations, resolutions and treaties, many of them inter-American, and multilateral declarations and agreements concluded between Latin American States, embody legal principles which justify the right of States to extend their sovereignty and jurisdiction to the extent necessary to conserve, develop and exploit the natural resources of the maritime area adjacent to their coasts, its soil and its subsoil,

that, in accordance with those legal principles the signatory States have, by reason of conditions peculiar to them, extended their sovereignty or exclusive rights of jurisdiction over the maritime area adjacent to their coasts, its soil and its subsoil to a distance of 200 nautical miles from the baseline of the territorial sea,

that the implementation of measures to conserve the resources of the sea, its soil and its subsoil by coastal States in the areas of maritime jurisdiction adjacent to their coasts ultimately benefits mankind, which possesses in the oceans a major source of means for its subsistence and development,

that the sovereign right of States to their natural resources has been recognized and reaffirmed by many resolutions of the General Assembly and other United Nations bodies,

that it is advisable to embody in a joint declaration the principles emanating from the recent movement towards the progressive development of international law, which is receiving ever-increasing support from the international community,

DECLARE the following to be Basic Principles of the Law of the Sea:

1. the right of coastal States to avail themselves of the natural resources of the sea adjacent to their coasts and of the soil and subsoil thereof in order to promote the maximum development of their economies and to raise the levels of living of their peoples;

2. the right to establish the limits of their maritime sovereignty and jurisdiction in accordance with their geographical and geological characteristics and with the factors governing the existence of marine resources and the need for their rational utilization;

3. the right to explore, to conserve the living resources of the sea adjacent to their territories, and to establish regulations for fishing and aquatic hunting;

4. the right to explore, conserve and exploit the natural resources of their continental shelves to where the depth of the superjacent waters admits of the exploitation of such resources;

5. the right to explore, conserve and exploit the natural resources of the soil and subsoil of the sea-bed and ocean floor up to the limit within which the State exercises its jurisdiction over the sea;

6. the right to adopt, for the aforementioned purposes, regulatory measures applicable in areas under their maritime sovereignty and jurisdiction, without prejudice to freedom of navigation by ships and overflying by aircraft of any flag.

Furthermore, the signatory States, encouraged by the results of this Meeting, express their intention to co-ordinate their future action with a view to defending effectively the principles embodied in this Declaration.

This Declaration shall be known as the "Montevideo Declaration on the Law of the Sea."

[LIMA DECLARATION]

COMMITTEE ON THE PEACEFUL USES OF THE
SEA-BED AND THE OCEAN FLOOR BEYOND THE
LIMITS OF NATIONAL JURISDICTION

Letter dated 14 August 1970 from the Chairman of the delegation of Peru addressed to the Chairman of the Committee on the Peaceful Uses of the Sea-Bed and the Ocean Floor beyond the Limits of National Jurisdiction

I have the honour to send you herewith the texts of the Latin American Declaration on the Law of the Sea and the Pertinent resolutions adopted at the Latin American Meeting on Aspects of the Law of the Sea, held at Lima from 4 to 8 August 1970.

As I consider their content to be of interest for our work, I should be glad if you would kindly arrange for these documents to be circulated in the official languages of the Committee on the Peaceful Uses of the Sea-bed and the Ocean Floor beyond the Limits of National Jurisdiction, of which you are Chairman.

Accept Sir, etc.

Alfonso Arias-Schreiber
Ambassador, Chairman of the delegation

DECLARATION OF THE LATIN AMERICAN STATES ON THE LAW OF THE SEA*

The Latin American Meeting on Aspects of the Law of the Sea,

Considering:

That there is a geographical, economic and social link be-

---

* Editor's Note: The Declaration was approved 14 to 3, with one abstention. For: Argentina, Brazil, Chile, Colombia, Dominican Republic, Ecuador, El Salvador, Guatemala, Honduras, Mexico, Nicaragua, Panama, Peru, Uruguay; Against: Bolivia, Paraguay, and Venezuela; Abstained: Trinidad and Tobago.

Barbados and Jamaica were absent when the vote was taken. Costa Rica was represented by an observer.

tween the sea, the land, and man who inhabits it, which confers on coastal populations a legitimate priority right to utilize the natural resources of their maritime environment;

That in consequence of that priority relationship, the right has been recognized of coastal States to establish the extent of their maritime sovereignty or jurisdiction in accordance with reasonable criteria, having regard to their geographical, geological and biological situation and their socio-economic needs and responsibilities;

That the dangers and damage resulting from indiscriminate and abusive practices in the extraction of marine resources, among other reasons, have led an important group of coastal States to extend the limits of their sovereignty or jurisdiction over the sea, with due respect for freedom of navigation and flight in transit for ships and aircraft, without distinction as to flag;

That certain forms of utilization of the marine environment have likewise been giving rise to grave dangers of contamination of the waters and disturbance of the ecological balance, to combat which it is necessary that the coastal States should take steps to protect the health and interests of their populations;

That the development of scientific research in the marine environment requires the widest possible co-operation among States, so that all may contribute and share in its benefits, without prejudice to the authorization, supervision and participation of the coastal State when such research is carried out within the limits of its sovereignty or jurisdiction;

That in declarations, resolutions and treaties, especially inter-American instruments, and also in unilateral declarations and in agreements signed between Latin American States legal principles are embodied which justify the aforementioned rights;

That the sovereign right of States over their natural resources has been recognized and reaffirmed in numerous resolutions of the General Assembly and other United Nations bodies;

That in the exercise of these rights the respective rights of other neighbouring coastal States on the same sea must be mutually respected; and

That it is desirable to assemble and reaffirm the foregoing concepts in a joint declaration which will take into account the plurality of existing legal regimes on maritime sovereignty or jurisdiction in Latin American countries.

DECLARES as common principles of the Law of the Sea:

1. The inherent right of the coastal State to explore, conserve and exploit the natural resources of the sea adjacent to its coasts and the soil and subsoil thereof, likewise of the Continental Shelf and its subsoil, in order to promote the maximum development of its economy and to raise the level of living of its people;

2. The right of the coastal State to establish the limits of its maritime sovereignty or jurisdiction in accordance with reasonable criteria, having regard to its geographical, geological and biological characteristics, and the need to make rational use of its resources;

3. The right of the coastal State to take regulatory measures for the aforementioned purposes, applicable in the areas of its maritime sovereignty or jurisdiction, without prejudice to freedom of navigation and flight in transit of ships and aircraft, without distinction as to flag;

4. The right of the coastal State to prevent contamination of the waters and other dangerous and harmful effects that may result from the use, exploration or exploitation of the area adjacent to its coasts;

5. The right of the coastal State to authorize, supervise and participate in all scientific research activities which may be carried out in the maritime zones subject to its sovereignty or jurisdiction, and to be informed of the findings and the results of such research.

This declaration shall be known as the "Declaration of the Latin American States on the Law of the Sea".

Lima, 8 August 1970.

RESOLUTION 1
ON THE SEA-BED AND OCEAN FLOOR
BEYOND THE LIMITS OF NATIONAL JURISDICTION

The Latin American Meeting on Aspects of the Law of the Sea

Considering:

That the Latin American States have declared on various occasions that the sea-bed and ocean floor and the subsoil thereof beyond the limits of national jurisdiction, including the resources of that zone, should be the common heritage of mankind;

That, in order to ensure that the exploration, conservation and exploitation of the sea-bed and ocean floor, and the subsoil thereof, beyond the limits of national jurisdiction, shall be carried out for the benefit of all mankind, irrespective of the geographical location of States and taking into consideration the special interests of the developing States, whether coastal or land-locked, it is essential that these activities be carried out under an international regime which shall include suitable machinery for ensuring joint participation in the administration of the zone and in the benefits derived therefrom;

That the United Nations Committee on the Peaceful Uses of the Sea-bed and the Ocean Floor beyond the Limits of National Jurisdiction is at present engaged on the task of drawing up a declaration of principles which should establish the broad lines of the future regime;

That a group of fifteen States, with the participation of Latin American countries, has submitted to the said Committee, in document A/AC.138/SC.1/L.2, dated 23 March 1970, a draft General Assembly resolution containing general principles relating to the sea-bed and ocean floor and the subsoil thereof beyond the limits of national jurisdiction;

That, to succeed in its task, the said Committee must observe in its work a suitable order of priority corresponding to rational criteria for the formulation of rules of international law; and

That the introduction of proposals for the establishment of an interim regime for the international zone might not only delay the completion of the first essential stage, which is to draw up a declaration of principle and the broad lines of a permanent regime, but might also hamper the said Committee in the proper discharge of its mandate;

Decides to recommend to Governments participating in this Meeting that they take account of the following objectives;

(1) that the United Nations Committee on the Sea-Bed and Ocean Floor should continue to give priority to the task of preparing a declaration of principles which would establish the broad lines of the future permanent regime to be established for that zone;

(2) that the said declaration of principles should serve merely as the basis for the Committee's subsequent work, under the mandate conferred on it by General Assembly resolutions 2467 (XXIII) and 2574 (XXIV);

(3) that it would be premature to establish an interim regime for the international zone and to establish the extra-jurisdictional limits of the sea-bed and ocean floor until the above-mentioned stages have been completed;

(4) that in the light of the reports prepared by the Secretary-General of the United Nations on the various possible types of international machinery for the exploration, conservation and exploitation of the sea-bed and ocean floor and the sub-soil thereof beyond the limits of national jurisdiction, the Latin American Governments shall agree on a common position with regard to determination of the most suitable arrangement for organizing the said machinery and on the question of the desirability of including in it regional or sub-regional systems;

(5) that, without prejudice to any suggestions which they may see fit to make concerning the declaration of principles mentioned under (1), they should at the appropriate time support the broad lines contained in document A/AC.138/SC.1/L.2 of 23 March 1970.

RESOLUTION 2
(OMITTED)

RESOLUTION 3
ON THE PROBLEM OF THE CONTAMINATION OF THE MARINE ENVIRONMENT

The Latin American Meeting on Aspects of the Law of the Sea:

Recognizing that the exploration, exploitation and use of the oceans and the soil and subsoil thereof and other activities carried out in non-marine environments have recently been creating a serious danger of contamination of waters and disturbance of the ecological balance of the marine environment;

Considering, consequently, the urgent need to take appropriate measures to prevent, control, reduce or eliminate contamination and any other dangerous and harmful effects that may result from the said activities;

Considering further that such measures must include not only rules to govern the exploration, exploitation and utilization of the oceans and the soil and subsoil thereof, and other activities which may affect the marine environment, but also rules relating to the system of liability for the resulting damages;

Recalling the progress made in these matters by various governmental bodies and by the Food and Agriculture Organization of the United Nations, the United Nations Educational, Scientific and Cultural Organization and its Intergovernmental Oceanographic Commission, the Inter-Governmental Maritime Consultative Organization and the International Atomic Energy Agency.

Recalling also resolution 2467 B (XXIII) of the United Nations General Assembly of the United Nations;

Noting with concern that, notwithstanding the repeated protests of many States, nuclear weapons tests continue to be carried out in the marine environment, destroying important living resources, contaminating the waters by their radioactive effects and disturbing the existing biological, chemical and physical processes and balances;

Considering that, for all these reasons, and without prejudice to any international agreements that have been concluded or which may be concluded on these matters, it is necessary to reaffirm the right of coastal States to take any steps and measures that they may deem necessary for the proper protection of the interests of their peoples against the dangers of contamination and other harmful effects that may result from the use, exploration and exploitation of the seas contiguous to their territories, or from other activities carried out in non-marine environments that may affect the said interests;

Recommends to the Governments participating in this Meeting;

(a) That they reaffirm their decision to take such steps and measures as they may deem appropriate to prevent, control and reduce or eliminate contamination and other dangerous and harmful effects resulting from the exploration, exploitation and use of the sea adjacent to their coasts and of the soil and subsoil thereof, and from any other activities carried out in non-marine environments that may affect the interests of their people, in exercise of the right of coastal States to protect its maritime heritage;

(b) That they reaffirm their opposition to the continuance of those nuclear weapons tests, mainly in the marine environment, which produce effects harmful to the resources of the sea, contamination of waters and disturbance of their existing biological, chemical and physical processes and balances;

(c) That they exchange views and information on appropriate measures for the above-mentioned purposes and on draft international agreements relating to these matters;

(d) That they agree on common positions so that when these matters are discussed in international organizations and at international conferences, their respective representatives may take due account of the rights and interests of coastal States.

RESOLUTION 4

(OMITTED)

RESOLUTION 5
ON THE LEGAL ASPECTS OF SCIENTIFIC OCEANOGRAPHIC RESEARCH

The Latin American Meeting on Aspects of the Law of the Sea:

Recalling the resolutions adopted by the General Assembly of the United Nations at its twenty-fourth session on the legal aspects of scientific oceanographic research;

Considering the desirability of a careful study of resolution VI-13 of the Intergovernmental Oceanographic Commission on the promotion of basic scientific research;

Bearing in mind, in particular, the action at present being taken by the said Intergovernmental Oceanographic Commission with a view to the preparation of a draft Convention on the legal status of systems for the acquisition of oceanographic data (SADO);

Considering the importance from the standpoint of basic legal issues such as the sovereignty and jurisdiction of the coastal States, of any criteria that are adopted on this matter.

DECIDES:

(1) To recommend that the Governments participating in this Meeting undertake a continuing exchange of views with a view to co-ordinating and harmonizing their positions in the various forums dealing with the legal problems of scientific oceanographic research;

(2) To recommend also that these Governments adopt a common stand on the question of the desirability of those matters being considered jointly in the United Nations, so that the developing States, and particularly the Latin American countries, may participate actively in the formulation of any rules it is desired to adopt.

(3) To reaffirm:

(a) That any scientific research carried out within the maritime jurisdiction of a State shall be subject to prior authorization by that State and shall comply with the conditions laid down by that authority;

(b) That the coastal State has the right to participate in any research that may be carried out within its jurisdiction and to benefit from the results of that research;

(c) That all the samples obtained in research of this kind shall be the property of the State in whose jurisdiction the research is carried out and that they may be appropriated by those conducting the research only with the express consent of that State;

(d) That any scientific research which is authorized as such shall continue to be of a strictly and exclusively scientific character.

TEXT OF THE DECLARATION OF SANTO DOMINGO APPROVED BY THE MEETING OF MINISTERS ON JUNE 7, 1972

TERRITORIAL SEA

1. The sovereignty of a State extends, beyond its land territory and its internal waters, to an area of the sea adjacent to its coast, designated as the territorial sea, including the superjacent air space as well as the subjacent seabed and subsoil.

2. The breadth of the territorial sea and the manner of its delimitation should be the subject of an international agreement, preferably of a worldwide scope. In the meantime, each State has the right to establish the breadth of its territorial sea up to a limit of 12 nautical miles to be measured from the applicable baseline.

3. Ships of all States, whether coastal or not, should enjoy the right of innocent passage through the territorial sea, in accordance with International Law.

PATRIMONIAL SEA

1. The coastal State has sovereign rights over the renewable and non renewable natural resources, which are found in the waters, in the seabed and in the subsoil of an area adjacent to the territorial sea called the patrimonial sea.

2. The coastal State has the duty to promote and the right to regulate the conduct of scientific research within the patrimonial sea, as well as the right to adopt the necessary measures to prevent marine pollution and to ensure its sovereignty over the resources of the area.

3. The breadth of this zone should be the subject of an international agreement, preferably of a worldwide scope. The whole of the area of both the territorial sea and the patrimonial sea, taking into account geographic circumstances, should not exceed a maximum of 200 nautical miles.

4. The delimitation of this zone between two or more States, should be carried out in accordance with the peaceful procedures stipulated in the Charter of the United Nations.

5. In this zone ships and aircraft of all States, whether coastal or not, should enjoy the right of freedom of navigation and overflight with no restrictions other than those resulting from the exercise by the Coastal State of its rights within the area. Subject only to these limitations, there will also be freedom for the laying of submarine cables and pipelines.

CONTINENTAL SHELF

1. The coastal State exercises over the continental shelf sovereign rights for the purpose of exploring it and exploiting its natural resources.

2. The continental shelf includes the seabed and subsoil of the submarine areas adjacent to the coast, but outside the area of the territorial sea, to a depth of 200 metres or, beyond that limit, to where the depth of the super-jacent waters admits the exploitation of the natural resources of the said areas.

3. In addition, the States participating in this Conference consider that the Latin American Delegations in the Committee on the Seabed and Ocean Floor of the United Nations should promote a study concerning the advisability and timing for the establishment of precise outer limits of the continental shelf taking into account the outer limits of the continental rise.

4. In that part of the continental shelf covered by the patrimonial sea the legal regime provided for this area shall apply. With respect to the part beyond the patrimonial sea, the régime established for the continental shelf by International Law shall apply.

INTERNATIONAL SEABED

1. The seabed and its resources, beyond the patrimonial sea and beyond the continental shelf not covered by the former, are the common heritage of mankind, in accordance with the Declaration adopted by the General Assembly of the United Nations in Resolution 2749 (XXV) of December 17, 1970.

2. This area shall be subject to the régime to be established by international agreement, which should create an international authority empowered to undertake all activities in the area, particularly the exploration, exploitation, protection of the marine environment and scientific research, either on its own, or through third parties, in the manner and under the conditions that may be established by common agreement.

HIGH SEAS

The waters situated beyond the outer limits of the patrimonial sea constitute an international area designated as high seas, in which there exists freedom of navigation, of overflight and of laying submarine cables and pipelines. Fishing in this zone should be neither unrestricted nor indiscriminate and should be the subject of adequate international regulation, preferably of worldwide scope and general acceptance.

MARINE POLLUTION

1. It is the duty of every State to refrain from performing acts which may pollute the sea and its seabed, either inside or outside its respective jurisdictions.

2. The international responsibility of physical or juridical persons damaging the marine environment is recognized. With regard to this matter the drawing up of an international agreement, preferably of a worldwide scope, is desirable.

REGIONAL COOPERATION

1. Recognizing the need for the countries in the area to unite their efforts and adopt a common policy vis a vis the problems peculiar to the Caribbean Sea relating mainly to scientific research, pollution of the marine environment, conservation, safeguarding and exploitation of the resources of the sea;

2. Decide to hold periodic meetings, if possible once a year, of senior governmental officials, for the purpose of coordinating and harmonizing national efforts and policies in all aspects of oceanic space with a view of ensuring maximum utilization of resources by all the peoples of the region.

The first meeting may be convoked by any of the States participating in this Conference.

* * * * * * *

Finally, the feelings of peace and respect for international law which have always inspired the Latin American countries are hereby reaffirmed. It is within this spirit of harmony and solidarity, and for the strengthening of the norms of the inter-American system, that the principles of this document shall be realized.

The present Declaration shall be called "Declaration of Santo Domingo".

Done in Santo Domingo de Guzmon, Dominican Repùblic this ninth day of June one thousand nine hundred and seventy-two (1972), in a single copy in the English, French and Spanish languages, each text being equally authentic.

Conclusions in the General Report of the African States Regional Seminar on the Law of the Sea, held in Yaoundé, from 20-30 June 1972.

After examining the reports, conclusions and recommendations of the various working groups, which were discussed and amended, the seminar adopted the following recommendations:

I. (a) On the territorial sea, the contiguous zone and the high seas:

(1) The African States have the right to determine the limits of their jurisdiction over the Seas adjacent to their coasts in accordance with reasonable criteria which particularly take into account their own geographical, geological, biological and national security factors.

(2) The Territorial Sea should not extend beyond a limit of 12 nautical miles.

(3) The African States have equally the right to establish beyond the Territorial Sea an Economic Zone over which they will have an exclusive jurisdiction for the purpose of control regulation and national exploitation of the living resources of the Sea and their reservation for the primary benefit of their peoples and their respective economies, and for the purpose of the prevention and control of pollution

The establishment of such a zone shall be without prejudice to the following freedoms: Freedom of navigation, freedom of over-flight, freedom to lay submarine cables and pipelines.

(4) The exploitation of the living resources within the economic zone should be open to all African States both land-locked and near land-locked, provided that the enterprises of these States desiring to exploit these resources are effectively controlled by African capital and personnel.

To be effective, the rights of land-locked States, shall be complemented by the right of transit.

These rights shall be embodied in multilateral or regional or bilateral agreements.

(5) The limit of the Economic Zone shall be fixed in nautical miles in accordance with regional considerations taking duly into account the resources

of the region and the rights and interests of the land-locked and near land-locked States, without prejudice to limits already adopted by some States within the region.

(6) The limits between two or more States shall be fixed in conformity with the United Nations Charter and that of the Organization of African Unity.
(7) The African States shall mutually recognize their existing historic rights.

However certain participants expressed reservations as to a 12 miles limit for the territorial sea and as to fixing a precise limit.

On recommendation No. 5 others thought that the general principles of International Law should be referred to in order to fix maritime limits.

(b) On "Historic Rights" and "Historic Bays":
(1) That the "historic rights" acquired by certain neighbouring African States in a part of the Sea which may fall within the exclusive jurisdiction of another State should be recognized and safeguarded.
(2) The impossibility for an African State to provide evidence of an uninterrupted claim over a historic bay should not constitute an obstacle to the recognition of the rights of that State over such a bay.

Adopted without reservation.

II. On the biological resources of the sea, fishing and maritime pollution,

Recommendations

The Participants:

Recommend to African States to extend their sovereignty over all the resources of the high sea adjacent to their Territorial Sea within an economic zone to be established and which will include at least the continental shelf.

Call upon all African States to uphold the principle of this extension at the next International Conference on the Law of the Sea.

Suggest that African States should promote a new policy of co-operation for the development of fisheries so as to increase their participation in the exploitation of marine resources.

Recommend to African States to take all measures to fight pollution and in particular:

- by establishing national laws to protect their countries from pollution;
- by advocating in International Organizations the conclusion of appropriate agreements on control measures against pollution.

Adopted without reservation.

III. On the continental shelf and the Sea-bed:

<u>Recommendations</u>

(1) The Economic Zone embodies all economic resources comprising both living and non-living resources such as oil, natural gas and other mineral resources.
(2) Political and strategic aspects of the sea-bed were considered. The need to use the sea-bed exclusively for peaceful purposes presupposes the definition of a legal régime to ensure greater security of the sea while guaranteeing the respect of the rights of coastal states.
(3) The participants considered that natural resources outside the Economic Zone should be managed by the International authority.
(4) The participants stressed the necessity for the Agency to function democratically and the need for adequate continental representation therein. Representation should not be based on the sole criterion of maritime strength and account should be taken of the existing imbalance between developed and developing countries.
(5) The Seminar categorically rejected the veto system and considered the system of weighted voting undemocratic.

IV. Concerning settlement to the conflicts which may arise between coastal States and the International Community.

Recommendations

In the light of their discussions the Seminar approves the principle of setting up an international governing body to manage the common heritage outside the limits of national jurisdiction. It considers that this body conform with the spirit of the resolution which provided for its creation, and for this reason must be structured and operate in such a way that the developing countries should be the primary controllers and beneficiaries.

The Seminar recommends that the international body should carry out its wishes on the Sea-bed and sub-soil for the benefit of the International Community.

Therefore, it considers that its action will depend on the desire of States to extend their limits of jurisdiction. The Seminar noted that it was important for this body to avoid being a simple administrative apparatus issuing licenses and distributing royalties.

It considers that to be efficient the International body must seek the best ways and means to involve the business concerns of developing countries in exploiting the resources available in its zone of using these resources to promote the progress of mankind in the developing countries so as to correct the grave imbalance between the nations.

The Seminar considers that all these objectives can be achieved if the participation of developing countries in the planning, setting up, and operation of this body is assured without restriction.

Adopted unanimously:

The participants expressed the unanimous wish that these recommendations should be notified to all African States and to the OAU.

II. REGULATION OF MARINE ACTIVITIES

CONVENTION[1] ON THE HIGH SEAS. DONE AT GENEVA, ON 29 APRIL 1958

The States Parties to this Convention,

Desiring to codify the rules of international law relating to the high seas,

Recognizing that the United Nations Conference on the Law of the Sea, held at Geneva from 24 February to 27 April 1958, adopted the following provisions as generally declaratory of established principles of international law,

Have agreed as follows :

Article 1

The term " high seas " means all parts of the sea that are not included in the territorial sea or in the internal waters of a State.

Article 2

The high seas being open to all nations, no State may validly purport to subject any part of them to its sovereignty. Freedom of the high seas is ex-

[1] In accordance with article 34, the Convention came into force on 30 September 1962, the thirtieth day following the date of deposit of the twenty-second instrument of ratification or accession. Following is a list of States on behalf of which the instruments of ratification or accession (*a*) were deposited with the Secretary-General of the United Nations, showing the respective dates of deposit :

Afghanistan	28 April	1959	*Nigeria	26 June	1961
United Kingdom of Great Britain and Northern Ireland	14 March	1960	Indonesia	10 August	1961
Cambodia	18 March	1960 (*a*)	Venezuela	15 August	1961
Haiti	29 March	1960	Czechoslovakia	31 August	1961
Union of Soviet Socialist Republics	22 November	1960	Israel	6 September	1961
Federation of Malaya	21 December	1960 (*a*)	Guatemala	27 November	1961
Ukrainian Soviet Socialist Republic	12 January	1961	Hungary	6 December	1961
Byelorussian Soviet Socialist Republic	27 February	1961	Romania	12 December	1961
United States of America	12 April	1961	*Sierra Leone	13 March	1962
Senegal	25 April	1961 (*a*)	Poland	29 June	1962
			Madagascar	31 July	1962 (*a*)
			Bulgaria	31 August	1962
			Central African Republic	15 October	1962 (*a*)
			Nepal	28 December	1962
			Portugal	8 January	1963

For declarations and reservations made upon signature, see list of signatures and for those made upon ratification, as well as for objections to certain declarations and reservations, see pp. 162 to 167.

* By communications received on 26 June 1961 and 13 March 1962, respectively, the Governments of Nigeria and Sierra Leone have informed the Secretary-General that they consider themselves bound by the ratification by the Government of the United Kingdom of Great Britain and Northern Ireland of the Convention of the High Seas, done at Geneva on 29 April 1958, which was effective for their territories prior to the attainment of independence.

ercised under the conditions laid down by these articles and by the other rules of international law. It comprises, *inter alia*, both for coastal and non-coastal States :

(1) Freedom of navigation;
(2) Freedom of fishing;
(3) Freedom to lay submarine cables and pipelines;
(4) Freedom to fly over the high seas.

These freedoms, and others which are recognized by the general principles of international law, shall be exercised by all States with reasonable regard to the interests of other States in their exercise of the freedom of the high seas.

Article 3

1. In order to enjoy the freedom of the seas on equal terms with coastal States, States having no sea-coast should have free access to the sea. To this end States situated between the sea and a State having no sea-coast shall by common agreement with the latter, and in conformity with existing international conventions, accord :

(*a*) To the State having no sea-coast, on a basis of reciprocity, free transit through their territory; and

(*b*) To ships flying the flag of that State treatment equal to that accorded to their own ships, or to the ships of any other States, as regards access to sea-ports and the use of such ports.

2. States situated between the sea and a State having no sea-coast shall settle, by mutual agreement with the latter, and taking into account the rights of the coastal State or State of transit and the special conditions of the State having no sea-coast, all matters relating to freedom of transit and equal treatment in ports, in case such States are not already parties to existing international conventions.

Article 4

Every State, whether coastal or not, has the right to sail ships under its flag on the high seas.

Article 5

1. Each State shall fix the conditions for the grant of its nationality to ships, for the registration of ships in its territory, and for the right to fly its flag. Ships have the nationality of the State whose flag they are entitled to fly. There must exist a genuine link between the State and the ship; in particular, the State must effectively exercise its jurisdiction and control in administrative, technical and social matters over ships flying its flag.

2. Each State shall issue to ships to which it has granted the right to fly its flag documents to that effect.

Article 6

1. Ships shall sail under the flag of one State only and, save in exceptional cases expressly provided for in international treaties or in these articles, shall be subject to its exclusive jurisdiction on the high seas. A ship may not change its flag during a voyage or while in a port of call, save in the case of a real transfer of ownership or change of registry.

2. A ship which sails under the flags of two or more States, using them according to convenience, may not claim any of the nationalities in question with respect to any other State, and may be assimilated to a ship without nationality.

Article 7

The provisions of the preceding articles do not prejudice the question of ships employed on the official service of an inter-governmental organization flying the flag of the organization.

Article 8

1. Warships on the high seas have complete immunity from the jurisdiction of any State other than the flag State.

2. For the purposes of these articles, the term " warship " means a ship belonging to the naval forces of a State and bearing the external marks distinguishing warships of its nationality, under the command of an officer duly commissioned by the government and whose name appears in the Navy List, and manned by a crew who are under regular naval discipline.

Article 9

Ships owned or operated by a State and used only on government non-commercial service shall, on the high seas, have complete immunity from the jurisdiction of any State other than the flag State.

Article 10

1. Every State shall take such measures for ships under its flag as are necessary to ensure safety at sea with regard *inter alia* to :

(*a*) The use of signals, the maintenance of communications and the prevention of collisions;

(*b*) The manning of ships and labour conditions for crews taking into account the applicable international labour instruments;

(*c*) The construction, equipment and seaworthiness of ships.

2. In taking such measures each State is required to conform to generally accepted international standards and to take any steps which may be necessary to ensure their observance.

Article 11

1. In the event of a collision or of any other incident of navigation concerning a ship on the high seas, involving the penal or disciplinary responsibility of the master or of any other person in the service of the ship, no penal or disciplinary proceedings may be instituted against such persons except before the judicial or administrative authorities either of the flag State or of the State of which such person is a national.

2. In disciplinary matters, the State which has issued a master's certificate or a certificate of competence or licence shall alone be competent, after due legal process, to pronounce the withdrawal of such certificates, even if the holder is not a national of the State which issued them.

3. No arrest or detention of the ship, even as a measure of investigation, shall be ordered by any authorities other than those of the flag State.

Article 12

1. Every State shall require the master of a ship sailing under its flag, in so far as he can do so without serious danger to the ship, the crew or the passengers,

(*a*) To render assistance to any person found at sea in danger of being lost;

(*b*) To proceed with all possible speed to the rescue of persons in distress if informed of their need of assistance, in so far as such action may reasonably be expected of him;

(*c*) After a collision, to render assistance to the other ship, her crew and her passengers and, where possible, to inform the other ship of the name of his own ship, her port of registry and the nearest port at which she will call.

2. Every coastal State shall promote the establishment and maintenance of an adequate and effective search and rescue service regarding safety on and over the sea and—where circumstances so require—by way of mutual regional arrangements co-operate with neighbouring States for this purpose.

Article 13

Every State shall adopt effective measures to prevent and punish the transport of slaves in ships authorized to fly its flag, and to prevent the unlawful use of its flag for that purpose. Any slave taking refuge on board any ship, whatever its flag, shall *ipso facto* be free.

Article 14

All States shall co-operate to the fullest possible extent in the repression of piracy on the high seas or in any other place outside the jurisdiction of any State.

Article 15

Piracy consists of any of the following acts :

(1) Any illegal acts of violence, detention or any act of depredation, committed for private ends by the crew or the passengers of a private ship or a private aircraft, and directed :

(*a*) On the high seas, against another ship or aircraft, or against persons or property on board such ship or aircraft;

(*b*) Against a ship, aircraft, persons or property in a place outside the jurisdiction of any State;

(2) Any act of voluntary participation in the operation of a ship or of an aircraft with knowledge of facts making it a pirate ship or aircraft;

(3) Any act of inciting or of intentionally facilitating an act described in sub-paragraph 1 or sub-paragraph 2 of this article.

Article 16

The acts of piracy, as defined in article 15, committed by a warship, government ship or government aircraft whose crew has mutinied and taken control of the ship or aircraft are assimilated to acts committed by a private ship.

Article 17

A ship or aircraft is considered a pirate ship or aircraft if it is intended by the persons in dominant control to be used for the purpose of committing one of the acts referred to in article 15. The same applies if the ship or aircraft has been used to commit any such act, so long as it remains under the control of the persons guilty of that act.

Article 18

A ship or aircraft may retain its nationality although it has become a pirate ship or aircraft. The retention or loss of nationality is determined by the law of the State from which such nationality was derived.

Article 19

On the high seas, or in any other place outside the jurisdiction of any State, every State may seize a pirate ship or aircraft, or a ship taken by piracy and under the control of pirates, and arrest the persons and seize the property on board. The courts of the State which carried out the seizure may decide upon the penalties to be imposed, and may also determine the action to be taken with regard to the ships, aircraft or property, subject to the rights of third parties acting in good faith.

Article 20

Where the seizure of a ship or aircraft on suspicion of piracy has been effected without adequate grounds, the State making the seizure shall be liable to the State the nationality of which is possessed by the ship or aircraft, for any loss or damage caused by the seizure.

Article 21

A seizure on account of piracy may only be carried out by warships or military aircraft, or other ships or aircraft on government service authorized to that effect.

Article 22

1. Except where acts of interference derive from powers conferred by treaty, a warship which encounters a foreign merchant ship on the high seas is not justified in boarding her unless there is reasonable ground for suspecting :

(*a*) That the ship is engaged in piracy; or

(*b*) That the ship is engaged in the slave trade; or

(*c*) That though flying a foreign flag or refusing to show its flag, the ship is, in reality, of the same nationality as the warship.

2. In the cases provided for in sub-paragraphs (*a*), (*b*) and (*c*) above, the warship may proceed to verify the ship's right to fly its flag. To this end, it may send a boat under the command of an officer to the suspected ship. If suspicion remains after the documents have been checked, it may proceed to a further examination on board the ship, which must be carried out with all possible consideration.

3. If the suspicions prove to be unfounded, and provided that the ship boarded has not committed any act justifying them, it shall be compensated for any loss or damage that may have been sustained.

Article 23

1. The hot pursuit of a foreign ship may be undertaken when the competent authorities of the coastal State have good reason to believe that the ship has violated the laws and regulations of that State. Such pursuit must be commenced when the foreign ship or one of its boats is within the internal waters or the territorial sea or the contiguous zone of the pursuing State, and may only be continued outside the territorial sea or the contiguous zone if the pursuit has not been interrupted. It is not necessary that, at the time when the foreign ship within the territorial sea or the contiguous zone receives the order to stop, the ship giving the order should likewise be within the territorial sea or the contiguous zone. If the foreign ship is within a contiguous zone, as defined in article 24 of the Convention on the Territorial Sea and the Contiguous Zone, the pursuit may only be undertaken if there has been a violation of the rights for the protection of which the zone was established.

2. The right of hot pursuit ceases as soon as the ship pursued enters the territorial sea of its own country or of a third State.

3. Hot pursuit is not deemed to have begun unless the pursuing ship has satisfied itself by such practicable means as may be available that the ship pursued or one of its boats or other craft working as a team and using the ship pursued as a mother ship are within the limits of the territorial sea, or as the case may be within the contiguous zone. The pursuit may only be commenced after a visual or auditory signal to stop has been given at a distance which enables it to be seen or heard by the foreign ship.

4. The right of hot pursuit may be exercised only by warships or military aircraft, or other ships or aircraft on government service specially authorized to that effect.

5. Where hot pursuit is effected by an aircraft :

(*a*) The provisions of paragraph 1 to 3 of this article shall apply *mutatis mutandis*;

(*b*) The aircraft giving the order to stop must itself actively pursue the ship until a ship or aircraft of the coastal State, summoned by the aircraft, arrives to take over the pursuit, unless the aircraft is itself able to arrest the ship. It does not suffice to justify an arrest on the high seas that the ship was merely sighted by the aircraft as an offender or suspected offender, if it was not both ordered to stop and pursued by the aircraft itself or other aircraft or ships which continue the pursuit without interruption.

6. The release of a ship arrested within the jurisdiction of a State and escorted to a port of that State for the purposes of an enquiry before the competent authorities may not be claimed solely on the ground that the ship, in the course of its voyage, was escorted across a portion of the high seas, if the circumstances rendered this necessary.

7. Where a ship has been stopped or arrested on the high seas in circumstances which do not justify the exercise of the right of hot pursuit, it shall be compensated for any loss or damage that may have been thereby sustained.

Article 24

Every State shall draw up regulations to prevent pollution of the seas by the discharge of oil from ships or pipelines or resulting from the exploitation and exploration of the seabed and its subsoil, taking account of existing treaty provisions on the subject.

Article 25

1. Every State shall take measures to prevent pollution of the seas from the dumping of radio-active waste, taking into account any standards and regulations which may be formulated by the competent international organizations.

2. All States shall co-operate with the competent international organizations in taking measures for the prevention of pollution of the seas or air space above, resulting from any activities with radio-active materials or other harmful agents.

Article 26

1. All States shall be entitled to lay submarine cables and pipelines on the bed of the high seas.

2. Subject to its right to take reasonable measures for the exploration of the continental shelf and the exploitation of its natural resources, the coastal State may not impede the laying or maintenance of such cables or pipelines.

3. When laying such cables or pipelines the State in question shall pay due regard to cables or pipelines already in position on the seabed. In particular, possibilities of repairing existing cables or pipelines shall not be prejudiced.

Article 27

Every State shall take the necessary legislative measures to provide that the breaking or injury by a ship flying its flag or by a person subject to its jurisdiction of a submarine cable beneath the high seas done wilfully or through culpable negligence, in such a manner as to be liable to interrupt or obstruct telegraphic or telephonic communications, and similarly the breaking or injury of a submarine pipeline or high-voltage power cable shall be a punishable offence. This provision shall not apply to any break or injury caused by persons who acted merely with the legitimate object of saving their lives or their ships, after having taken all necessary precautions to avoid such break or injury.

Article 28

Every State shall take the necessary legislative measures to provide that, if persons subject to its jurisdiction who are the owners of a cable or pipeline beneath the high seas, in laying or repairing that cable or pipeline, cause a break in or injury to another cable or pipeline, they shall bear the cost of the repairs.

Article 29

Every State shall take the necessary legislative measures to ensure that the owners of ships who can prove that they have sacrificed an anchor, a net or any other fishing gear, in order to avoid injuring a submarine cable or pipeline, shall be indemnified by the owner of the cable or pipeline, provided that the owner of the ship has taken all reasonable precautionary measures beforehand.

Article 30

The provisions of this Convention shall not affect conventions or other international agreements already in force, as between States Parties to them.

Article 31

This Convention shall, until 31 October 1958, be open for signature by all States Members of the United Nations or of any of the specialized agencies, and by any other State invited by the General Assembly of the United Nations to become a Party to the Convention.

Article 32

This Convention is subject to ratification. The instruments of ratification shall be deposited with the Secretary-General of the United Nations.

Article 33

This Convention shall be open for accession by any States belonging to any of the categories mentioned in article 31. The instruments of accession shall be deposited with the Secretary-General of the United Nations.

Article 34

1. This Convention shall come into force on the thirtieth day following the date of deposit of the twenty-second instrument of ratification or accession with the Secretary-General of the United Nations.

2. For each State ratifying or acceding to the Convention after the deposit of the twenty-second instrument of ratification or accession, the Convention shall enter into force on the thirtieth day after deposit by such State of its instrument of ratification or accession.

Article 35

1. After the expiration of a period of five years from the date on which this Convention shall enter into force, a request for the revision of this Convention may be made at any time by any Contracting Party by means of a notification in writing addressed to the Secretary-General of the United Nations.

2. The General Assembly of the United Nations shall decide upon the steps, if any, to be taken in respect of such request.

Article 36

The Secretary-General of the United Nations shall inform all States Members of the United Nations and the other States referred to in article 31 :

(*a*) Of signatures to this Convention and of the deposit of instruments of ratification or accession, in accordance with articles 31, 32 and 33;

(*b*) Of the date on which this Convention will come into force, in accordance with article 34;

(*c*) Of requests for revision in accordance with article 35.

Article 37

The original of this Convention, of which the Chinese, English, French, Russian and Spanish texts are equally authentic, shall be deposited with the

Secretary-General of the United Nations, who shall send certified copies thereof to all States referred to in article 31.

In witness whereof the undersigned Plenipotentiaries, being duly authorized thereto by their respective Governments, have signed this Convention.

Done at Geneva, this twenty-ninth day of April one thousand nine hundred and fifty-eight.

No. 6466. OPTIONAL PROTOCOL OF SIGNATURE[1] CONCERNING THE COMPULSORY SETTLEMENT OF DISPUTES. ADOPTED BY THE UNITED NATIONS CONFERENCE ON THE LAW OF THE SEA, HELD AT GENEVA FROM 24 FEBRUARY TO 27 APRIL 1958, AND OPENED FOR SIGNATURE ON 29 APRIL 1958

The States Parties to this Protocol and to any one or more of the Conventions on the Law of the Sea adopted by the United Nations Conference on the Law of the Sea held at Geneva from 24 February to 27 April 1958,

Expressing their wish to resort, in all matters concerning them in respect of any dispute arising out of the interpretation or application of any article of any Convention on the Law of the Sea of 29 April 1958, to the compulsory jurisdiction of the International Court of Justice, unless some other form of settlement is provided in the Convention or has been agreed upon by the Parties within a reasonable period,

Have agreed as follows :

Article I

Disputes arising out of the interpretation or application of any Convention on the Law of the Sea shall lie within the compulsory jurisdiction of the International Court of Justice, and may accordingly be brought before the Court by an application made by any party to the dispute being a Party to this Protocol.

Article II

This undertaking relates to all the provisions of any Convention on the Law of the Sea except, in the Convention on Fishing and Conservation of the Living Resources of the High Seas, articles 4, 5, 6, 7 and 8, to which articles 9, 10, 11 and 12 of that Convention remain applicable.

---

[1] Came into force on 30 September 1962, the date of entry into force of the Convention on the High Seas (see p. 11 of this volume), between the following States parties to the said Convention which have signed the Protocol without reservation as to ratification or have deposited an instrument of ratification (*r*) thereof on the dates indicated :

Federation of Malaya	1 May	1961
Haiti	29 March	1960 (*r*)
Madagascar	10 August	1962
United Kingdom of Great Britain and Northern Ireland	9 September	1958

and on 27 January 1963 as between those States and Nepal for which the Convention on the High Seas came into force on that date and on behalf of which the Optional Protocol was signed without reservation as to ratification on 29 April 1958.

Furthermore, the instruments of ratification of the said Convention and Protocol by Portugal were deposited on 8 January 1963, to take effect on 7 February 1963.

Article III

The Parties may agree, within a period of two months after one party has notified its opinion to the other that a dispute exists, to resort not to the International Court of Justice but to an arbitral tribunal. After the expiry of the said period, either Party to this Protocol may bring the dispute before the Court by an application.

Article IV

1. Within the same period of two months, the Parties to this Protocol may agree to adopt a conciliation procedure before resorting to the International Court of Justice.

2. The conciliation commission shall make its recommendations within five months after its appointment. If its recommendations are not accepted by the parties to the dispute within two months after they have been delivered, either party may bring the dispute before the Court by an application.

Article V

This Protocol shall remain open for signature by all States who become Parties to any Convention on the Law of the Sea adopted by the United Nations Conference on the Law of the Sea and is subject to ratification, where necessary, according to the constitutional requirements of the signatory States.

Article VI

The Secretary-General of the United Nations shall inform all States who become Parties to any Convention on the Law of the Sea of signatures to this Protocol and of the deposit of instruments of ratification in accordance with article V.

Article VII

The original of this Protocol, of which the Chinese, English, French, Russian and Spanish texts are equally authentic, shall be deposited with the Secretary-General of the United Nations, who shall send certified copies thereof to all States referred to in article V.

IN WITNESS WHEREOF the undersigned Plenipotentiaries, being duly authorized thereto by their respective Governments, have signed this Protocol.

DONE at Geneva, this twenty-ninth day of April one thousand nine hundred and fifty-eight.

No. 9066. EUROPEAN AGREEMENT [1] FOR THE PREVENTION OF BROADCASTS TRANSMITTED FROM STATIONS OUTSIDE NATIONAL TERRITORIES. DONE AT STRASBOURG, ON 22 JANUARY 1965

The member States of the Council of Europe signatory hereto,

Considering that the aim of the Council of Europe is to achieve a greater unity between its Members ;

Considering that the Radio Regulations annexed to the International Telecommunication Convention [2] prohibit the establishment and use of broadcasting stations on board ships, aircraft or any other floating or airborne objects outside national territories ;

Considering also the desirability of providing for the possibility of preventing the establishment and use of broadcasting stations on objects affixed to or supported by the bed of the sea outside national territories ;

Considering the desirability of European collaboration in this matter,

Have agreed as follows :

Article 1

This Agreement is concerned with broadcasting stations which are installed or maintained on board ships, aircraft, or any other floating or

[1] Came into force on 19 October 1967, i.e., one month after the date of deposit of the third instrument of ratification, in accordance with article 9 (1), with respect to the following States, on whose behalf instruments of ratification were deposited with the Secretary-General of the Council of Europe on the dates indicated below :

State	*Date of deposit*
Denmark	22 September 1965
Sweden	15 June 1966
Belgium	18 September 1967

The Agreement subsequently came into force with respect to the following States one month after the date of deposit of their instruments of ratification as indicated below :

State	*Date of deposit*	*Date of entry into force*
United Kingdom of Great Britain and Northern Ireland (also applicable to Channel Islands and the Isle of Man)*	2 November 1967	3 December 1967
France	5 March 1968	6 April 1968

* For the text of the declaration made at the time of signature, see p. 253 of this volume.

[2] United Kingdom, *Treaty Series, No. 74 (1961)*, Cmnd. 1484.

airborne objects and which, outside national territories, transmit broadcasts intended for reception or capable of being received, wholly or in part, within the territory of any Contracting Party, or which cause harmful interference to any radio-communication service operating under the authority of a Contracting Party in accordance with the Radio Regulations.

Article 2

1. Each Contracting Party undertakes to take appropriate steps to make punishable as offences, in accordance with its domestic law, the establishment or operation of broadcasting stations referred to in Article 1, as well as acts of collaboration knowingly performed.

2. The following shall, in relation to broadcasting stations referred to in Article 1, be acts of collaboration :

(*a*) the provision, maintenance or repairing of equipment ;

(*b*) the provision of supplies ;

(*c*) the provision of transport for, or the transporting of, persons, equipment or supplies ;

(*d*) the ordering or production of material of any kind, including advertisements, to be broadcast ;

(*e*) the provision of services concerning advertising for the benefit of the stations.

Article 3

Each Contracting Party shall, in accordance with its domestic law, apply the provisions of this Agreement in regard to :

(*a*) its nationals who have committed any act referred to in Article 2 on its territory, ships or aircraft, or outside national territories on any ships, aircraft or any other floating or airborne object ;

(*b*) non-nationals who, on its territory, ships or aircraft, or on board any floating or airborne object under its jurisdiction have committed any act referred to in Article 2.

Article 4

Nothing in this Agreement shall be deemed to prevent a Contracting Party :

(*a*) from also treating as punishable offences acts other than those referred to in Article 2 and also applying the provisions concerned to persons other than those referred to in Article 3 ;

(*b*) from also applying the provisions of this Agreement to broadcasting stations installed or maintained on objects affixed to or supported by the bed of the sea.

Article 5

The Contracting Parties may elect not to apply the provisions of this Agreement in respect of the services of performers which have been provided elsewhere than on the stations referred to in Article 1.

Article 6

The provisions of Article 2 shall not apply to any acts performed for the purpose of giving assistance to a ship or aircraft or any other floating or airborne object in distress or of protecting human life.

Article 7

No reservation may be made to the provisions of this Agreement.

Article 8

1. This Agreement shall be open to signature by the member States of the Council of Europe, which may become Parties to it either by :

(*a*) signature without reservation in respect of ratification or acceptance, or

(*b*) signature with reservation in respect of ratification or acceptance followed by ratification or acceptance.

2. Instruments of ratification or acceptance shall be deposited with the Secretary-General of the Council of Europe.

Article 9

1. This Agreement shall enter into force one month after the date on which three member States of the Council shall, in accordance with the provisions of Article 8, have signed the Agreement without reservation in respect of ratification or acceptance, or shall have deposited their instrument of ratification or acceptance.

2. As regards any member State which shall subsequently sign the Agreement without reservation in respect of ratification or acceptance or which shall ratify or accept it, the Agreement shall enter into force one month after the date of such signature or the date of deposit of the instrument of ratification or acceptance.

Article 10

1. After this Agreement has entered into force, any Member or Associate Member of the International Telecommunication Union which is not a Member of the Council of Europe may accede to it subject to the prior agreement of the Committee of Ministers.

2. Such accession shall be effected by depositing with the Secretary-General of the Council of Europe an instrument of accession which shall take effect one month after the date of its deposit.

Article 11

1. Any Contracting Party may, at the time of signature or when depositing its instrument of ratification, acceptance or accession, specify the territory or territories to which this Agreement shall apply.

2. Any Contracting Party may, when depositing its instrument of ratification, acceptance or accession or at any later date, by declaration addressed to the Secretary-General of the Council of Europe, extend this Agreement to any other territory or territories specified in the declaration and for whose international relations it is responsible or on whose behalf it is authorised to give undertakings.

3. Any declaration made in pursuance of the preceding paragraph may, in respect of any territory mentioned in such declaration, be withdrawn according to the procedure laid down in Article 12 of this Agreement.

Article 12

1. This Agreement shall remain in force indefinitely.

2. Any Contracting Party may, in so far as it is concerned, denounce this Agreement by means of a notification addressed to the Secretary-General of the Council of Europe.

3. Such denunciation shall take effect six months after the date of receipt by the Secretary-General of such notification.

Article 13

The Secretary-General of the Council of Europe shall notify the member States of the Council and the Government of any State which has acceded to this Agreement of :

(*a*) any signature without reservation in respect of ratification or acceptance ;

(*b*) any signature with reservation in respect of ratification or acceptance ;

(*c*) any deposit of an instrument of ratification, acceptance or accession ;

(*d*) any date of entry into force of this Agreement in accordance with Articles 9 and 10 thereof ;

(*e*) any declaration received in pursuance of paragraphs 2 and 3 of Article 11 ;

(*f*) any notification received in pursuance of the provisions of Article 12 and the date on which denunciation takes effect.

In witness whereof the undersigned, being duly authorised thereto, have signed this Agreement.

Done at Strasbourg, this 22nd day of January 1965 in English and French, both texts being equally authoritative, in a single copy which shall remain deposited in the archives of the Council of Europe. The Secretary-General of the Council of Europe shall transmit certified copies to each of the signatory and acceding States.

Marine, &c., Broadcasting (Offences) Act 1967

CHAPTER 41

An Act to suppress broadcasting from ships, aircraft and certain marine structures. [14th July 1967]

BE IT ENACTED by the Queen's most Excellent Majesty, by and with the advice and consent of the Lords Spiritual and Temporal, and Commons, in this present Parliament assembled, and by the authority of the same, as follows:—

Prohibition of broadcasting from ships and aircraft.

1.—(1) It shall not be lawful for a broadcast to be made from a ship or aircraft while it is in or over the United Kingdom or external waters, nor shall it be lawful for a broadcast to be made from a ship registered in the United Kingdom, the Isle of Man or any of the Channel Islands or an aircraft so registered while the ship or aircraft is elsewhere than in or over the United Kingdom or external waters.

(2) If a broadcast is made from a ship in contravention of the foregoing subsection, the owner of the ship, the master of the ship and every person who operates, or participates in the operation of, the apparatus by means of which the broadcast is made shall be guilty of an offence; and if a broadcast is made from an aircraft in contravention of that subsection, the operator of the aircraft, the commander of the aircraft and every person who operates, or participates in the operation of, the apparatus by means of which the broadcast is made shall be guilty of an offence.

(3) A person who procures the making of a broadcast in contravention of subsection (1) above shall be guilty of an offence.

(4) In subsection (2) above—

(*a*) "master", in relation to a ship, includes any other person (except a pilot) having command or charge of the ship;

(*b*) " operator ", in relation to an aircraft, means the person for the time being having the management of the aircraft.

Prohibition of broadcasting from marine structures.

2.—(1) It shall not be lawful for a broadcast to be made from—

(*a*) a structure in external waters or in tidal waters in the United Kingdom, being a structure affixed to, or supported by, the bed of those waters and not being a ship ; or

(*b*) any other object in such waters, being neither a structure affixed or supported as aforesaid nor a ship or aircraft ;

and if a broadcast is made in contravention of the foregoing provision, every person who operates, or participates in the operation of, the apparatus by means of which the broadcast is made shall be guilty of an offence.

(2) A person who procures the making of a broadcast in contravention of the foregoing subsection shall be guilty of an offence.

Prohibition of acts connected with broadcasting from certain ships and aircraft, and from marine structures outside United Kingdom.

3.—(1) If a broadcast is made—

(*a*) from a ship other than one registered in the United Kingdom, the Isle of Man or any of the Channel Islands while the ship is on the high seas ; or

(*b*) from an aircraft other than one so registered while the aircraft is on or over the high seas ; or

(*c*) from a structure on the high seas, being a structure affixed to, or supported by, the bed of those seas and not being a ship ; or

(*d*) from any other object on those seas, being neither a structure affixed or supported as aforesaid nor a ship or aircraft ;

any of the persons mentioned in subsection (3) below who operates, or participates in the operation of, the apparatus by means of which the broadcast is made shall be guilty of an offence.

(2) A person who procures a broadcast to be made as mentioned in the foregoing subsection shall be guilty of an offence.

(3) The persons referred to in subsection (1) above are the following, namely:—

(*a*) a citizen of the United Kingdom and colonies ;

1948 c. 56.

(*b*) a British subject by virtue of section 2 of the British Nationality Act 1948 (continuance of certain citizens of the Republic of Ireland, therein referred to as Eire, as British subjects) ;

(c) a British subject without citizenship by virtue of section 13 or section 16 of that Act (which relate respectively to British subjects whose citizenship has not been ascertained at the commencement of that Act and to persons who had ceased to be British on loss of British nationality by a parent);

(d) a British subject by virtue of the British Nationality Act 1965; and 1965 c. 34.

(e) a British protected person (within the meaning of the British Nationality Act 1948). 1948 c. 56.

Prohibition of acts facilitating broadcasting from ships, aircraft, &c.

4.—(1) A person who does any of the acts mentioned in subsection (3) below, while satisfying the condition as to knowledge or belief mentioned in the case of that act, shall be guilty of an offence if—

(a) he does the act in the United Kingdom or external waters or in a ship registered in the United Kingdom, the Isle of Man or any of the Channel Islands or an aircraft so registered while the ship or aircraft is elsewhere than in or over the United Kingdom or external waters; or

(b) being a person mentioned in section 3(3) of this Act, he does the act on or over the high seas.

(2) A person who, in the United Kingdom, procures another person to do, outside the United Kingdom, anything which, if it had been done in the United Kingdom by the last-mentioned person, would have constituted an offence under the foregoing subsection, shall be guilty of an offence.

(3) The acts, and conditions as to knowledge or belief, referred to in subsection (1) above are the following, namely:—

(a) furnishing or agreeing to furnish to another a ship or aircraft knowing, or having reasonable cause to believe, that broadcasts are to be made from it in contravention of section 1(1) of this Act or while it is on or over the high seas;

(b) carrying or agreeing to carry in a ship or aircraft wireless telegraphy apparatus knowing, or having reasonable cause to believe, that by means thereof broadcasts are to be made from the ship or aircraft as aforesaid;

(c) supplying to, or installing in, a ship or aircraft wireless telegraphy apparatus knowing, or having reasonable cause to believe, that by means thereof broadcasts are to be made from the ship or aircraft as aforesaid;

(d) supplying any wireless telegraphy apparatus for installation on or in, or installing any such apparatus on or in, any structure or other object (not being, in either case, a ship or aircraft) knowing, or having reasonable cause to believe, that by means of that apparatus broadcasts are to be made from the object in contravention of section 2(1) of this Act or while the object is on the high seas ;

(*e*) repairing or maintaining any wireless telegraphy apparatus knowing, or having reasonable cause to believe, that, by means thereof, broadcasts are made, or are to be made, in contravention of section 1(1) or 2(1) of this Act or as mentioned in section 3(1) of this Act ;

(*f*) knowing, or having reasonable cause to believe, in the case of a ship or aircraft, that broadcasts are made, or are to be made, from it in contravention of section 1(1) of this Act or while it is on or over the high seas—

(i) supplying any goods or materials for its operation or maintenance, for the operation or maintenance of wireless telegraphy apparatus installed therein or for the sustentation or comfort of the persons on board of it ;

(ii) carrying by water or air goods or persons to or from it ;

(iii) engaging a person as an officer or one of the crew of it ;

(*g*) knowing, or having reasonable cause to believe, in the case of a structure or other object (not being, in either case, a ship or aircraft), that broadcasts are made, or are to be made, from it in contravention of section 2(1) of this Act or while it is on the high seas—

(i) supplying any goods or materials for its maintenance, for the operation or maintenance of wireless telegraphy apparatus installed therein or thereon or for the sustentation or comfort of the persons therein or thereon ;

(ii) carrying by water or air goods or persons thereto or therefrom ;

(iii) engaging a person to render services therein or thereon.

Prohibition of acts relating to matter broadcast from ships, aircraft, &c.

5.—(1) A person who does any of the acts mentioned in subsection (3) below, and, if any intent or circumstances is or are specified in relation to the act, does it with that intent or in those circumstances, shall be guilty of an offence if—

(*a*) he does the act in the United Kingdom or external waters or in a ship registered in the United Kingdom, the Isle of Man or any of the Channel Islands or an aircraft so registered while the ship or aircraft is elsewhere than in or over the United Kingdom or external waters; or

(*b*) being a person mentioned in section 3(3) of this Act, he does the act on or over the high seas.

(2) A person who, in the United Kingdom, procures another person to do, outside the United Kingdom, anything which, if it had been done in the United Kingdom by the last-mentioned person, would have constituted an offence under the foregoing subsection, shall be guilty of an offence.

(3) The acts, and, where relevant, the intent and circumstances, referred to in subsection (1) above are the following namely:—

(*a*) supplying a cinematograph film or a record with intent that a broadcast of the film or, as the case may be, the recording embodied in the record may be made in contravention of section 1(1) or 2(1) of this Act or as mentioned in section 3(1) thereof;

(*b*) making a literary, dramatic or musical work with intent that a broadcast of the work may be made as aforesaid;

(*c*) making an artistic work with intent that the work may be included in a television broadcast made as aforesaid;

(*d*) participating in a broadcast made as aforesaid, being actually present as an announcer, as a performer or one of the performers concerned in an entertainment given, or as the deliverer of a speech;

(*e*) advertising by means of a broadcast made as aforesaid or inviting another to advertise by means of a broadcast to be so made;

(*f*) publishing the times or other details of any broadcasts which are to be so made, or (otherwise than by publishing such details) publishing an advertisement of matter calculated to promote, directly or indirectly, the interests of a business whose activities consist in or include the operation of a station from which broadcasts are or are to be so made.

(4) For the purposes of this section if, by means of a broadcast made in contravention of section 1(1) or 2(1) of this Act or as mentioned in section 3(1) thereof, it is stated, suggested or implied that any entertainment of which a broadcast is so made has been supplied by, or given at the expense of, a person, he shall, unless he proves that it was not so supplied or given, be deemed thereby to have advertised.

(5) For the purposes of this section advertising by means of a broadcast shall be deemed to take place as well wherever the broadcast is received as where it is made.

(6) In this section " speech " includes lecture, address and sermon, and references in this section to a cinematograph film, a record and a literary, dramatic, musical or artistic work shall be construed in like manner as references thereto in the Copyright Act 1956.

1956 c. 74.

Penalties and legal proceedings.

6.—(1) A person guilty of an offence under this Act shall be liable—

(*a*) on summary conviction, to imprisonment for a term not exceeding three months or to a fine not exceeding £400, or to both ;

(*b*) on conviction on indictment, to imprisonment for a term not exceeding two years or to a fine, or to both.

(2) Where an offence under this Act which has been committed by a body corporate is proved to have been committed with the consent or connivance of, or to be attributable to any neglect on the part of, a director, manager, secretary or other similar officer of the body corporate, or any person who was purporting to act in any such capacity, he, as well as the body corporate, shall be guilty of that offence and shall be liable to be proceeded against accordingly.

(3) Proceedings for an offence under this Act may be taken, and the offence may for all incidental purposes be treated as having been committed, in any place in the United Kingdom.

(4) Notwithstanding anything in any enactment relating to courts of summary jurisdiction, summary proceedings for an offence under this Act may be instituted at any time within two years from the time when the offence was committed.

(5) Proceedings for an offence under this Act shall not, in England or Wales, be instituted otherwise than by or on behalf of the Director of Public Prosecutions and shall not, in Northern Ireland, be instituted otherwise than by or on behalf of the Attorney General for Northern Ireland ; but this shall not prevent the issue or execution of a warrant for the arrest of any person in respect of such an offence or the remanding in custody or on bail of any person charged with such an offence.

(6) A member of a police force shall, for the purpose of the enforcement of this Act, have in external waters all the powers, protection and privileges which he has in the area for which he acts as constable.

(7) In this section " director " in relation to a body corporate established by or under an enactment for the purpose of carrying on under national ownership an industry or part of an industry or undertaking, being a body corporate whose affairs are managed by the members thereof, means a member of that body corporate.

(8) In the application of this section to Northern Ireland, the following subsection shall be substituted for subsection (6):—

" (6) A member of the Royal Ulster Constabulary shall, for the purpose of the enforcement of this Act, have in external waters all the powers, protection and privileges which he has in Northern Ireland ".

Special defence available in proceedings for carrying goods or persons in contravention of section 4.

7.—(1) In any proceedings against a person for an offence under section 4 of this Act consisting in the carriage of goods or persons to or from a ship or aircraft it shall be a defence for him to prove—

(*a*) that the ship or aircraft was, or was believed to be, wrecked, stranded or in distress, and that the goods or persons carried were carried for the purpose of preserving the ship or aircraft, or its cargo or apparel, or saving the lives of persons on board of it; or

(*b*) that a person on board of the ship or aircraft was, or was believed to be, suffering from hurt, injury or illness, and that the goods or persons were carried for the purpose of securing that the necessary surgical or medical advice and attendance were rendered to him.

(2) In any proceedings against a person for an offence under section 4 of this Act consisting in the carriage of goods or persons to or from an object other than a ship or aircraft it shall be a defence for him to prove—

(*a*) that the object was, or was believed to be, unsafe, and that the goods or persons carried were carried for the purpose of saving the lives of persons therein or thereon; or

(*b*) that a person therein or thereon was, or was believed to be, suffering from hurt, injury or illness, and that the goods or persons were carried for the purpose of securing that the necessary surgical or medical advice and attendance were rendered to him.

(3) In any proceedings against a person for an offence under section 4 of this Act consisting in the carriage of a person to or from a ship or aircraft or to or from an object other than a ship or aircraft, it shall be a defence for him to prove that the person carried was visiting the ship, aircraft or object, as the case may be, for the purpose of exercising or performing any power or duty conferred or imposed on him by law.

(4) The references in subsections (1)(*a*) and (2)(*a*) above to persons' having been carried for the purpose of saving lives shall not be construed so as to exclude the persons whose lives it was the purpose to save and the references in subsections (1)(*b*) and (2)(*b*) above to persons' having been carried as therein mentioned shall not be construed so as to exclude the person who was, or was believed to be, suffering as so mentioned.

Saving for things done under wireless telegraphy licence.

8. Nothing in this Act shall render it unlawful to do anything under and in accordance with a wireless telegraphy licence, or to procure anything to be so done.

Interpretation.

9.—(1) In this Act—

"broadcast" means a broadcast by wireless telegraphy of sounds or visual images intended for general reception (whether the sounds or images are actually received by any person or not), but does not include a broadcast consisting in a message or signal sent in connection with navigation or for the purpose of securing safety;

"external waters" means the whole of the sea adjacent to the United Kingdom which is within the seaward limits of the territorial waters adjacent thereto;

"the high seas" means the seas outside the seaward limits of the territorial waters adjacent to the United Kingdom or to any country or territory outside the United Kingdom;

"ship" includes every description of vessel used in navigation;

"wireless telegraphy", "wireless telegraphy apparatus" and "wireless telegraphy licence" have the same meanings respectively as in the Wireless Telegraphy Act 1949.

1949 c. 54.

(2) For the purposes of this section, the seaward limits of the territorial waters adjacent to the United Kingdom shall be determined by reference to the baseline established by the Territorial Waters Order in Council 1964 or by any subsequent Order of Her Majesty made in Council under Her royal prerogative for establishing the baseline from which the breadth of the territorial sea adjacent to the United Kingdom, the Channel Islands and the Isle of Man is measured.

Power to extend Act to Isle of Man and Channel Islands.

10.—(1) Her Majesty may by Order in Council direct that this Act shall extend to the Isle of Man or any of the Channel Islands, with such exceptions, adaptations and modifications as may be specified in the Order.

(2) An Order in Council under this section may be varied or revoked by a subsequent Order of Her Majesty in Council.

11.—(1) This Act may be cited as the Marine, &c., Broadcasting (Offences) Act 1967.

Short title and commencement.

(2) This Act shall not come into operation before the expiry of one month beginning with the day on which it is passed, but subject thereto it shall come into operation on a day to be appointed by Her Majesty in Council.

TREATY BANNING NUCLEAR WEAPON TESTS IN THE ATMOSPHERE, IN OUTER SPACE AND UNDER WATER

The Governments of the United States of America, the United Kingdom of Great Britain and Northern Ireland, and the Union of Soviet Socialist Republics, hereinafter referred to as the "Original Parties",

Proclaiming as their principal aim the speediest possible achievement of an agreement on general and complete disarmament under strict international control in accordance with the objectives of the United Nations which would put an end to the armaments race and eliminate the incentive to the production and testing of all kinds of weapons, including nuclear weapons,

Seeking to achieve the discontinuance of all test explosions of nuclear weapons for all time, determined to continue negotiations to this end, and desiring to put an end to the contamination of man's environment by radioactive substances,

Have agreed as follows:

ARTICLE I

1. Each of the Parties to this Treaty undertakes to prohibit, to prevent, and not to carry out any nuclear weapon test explosion, or any other nuclear explosion, at any place under its jurisdiction or control:

(a) in the atmosphere; beyond its limits, including outer space; or underwater, including territorial waters or high seas; or

(b) in any other environment if such explosion causes radioactive debris to be present outside the territorial limits of the State under whose jurisdiction or control such explosion is conducted. It is understood in this connection that the provisions of this subparagraph are without prejudice to the conclusion of a treaty resulting in the permanent banning of all nuclear test explosions, including all such explosions underground, the conclusion of which, as the Parties have stated in the Preamble to this Treaty, they seek to achieve.

2. Each of the Parties to this Treaty undertakes furthermore to refrain from causing, encouraging, or in any way participating in, the carrying out of any nuclear weapon test explosion, or any other nuclear explosion, anywhere which would take place in any of the environments described, or have the effect referred to, in paragraph 1 of this Article.

ARTICLE II

1. Any Party may propose amendments to this Treaty. The text of any proposed amendment shall be submitted to the Depositary Governments which shall circulate it to all Parties to this Treaty. Thereafter, if requested to do so by one-third or more of the Parties, the Depositary Governments shall convene a conference, to which they shall invite all the Parties, to consider such amendment.

2. Any amendment to this Treaty must be approved by a majority of the votes of all the Parties to this Treaty, including the votes of all of the Original Parties. The amendment shall enter into force for all Parties upon the deposit of instruments of ratification by a majority of all the Parties, including the instruments of ratification of all of the Original Parties.

ARTICLE III

1. This Treaty shall be open to all States for signature. Any State which does not sign this Treaty before its entry into force in accordance with paragraph 3 of this Article may accede to it at any time.

2. This Treaty shall be subject to ratification by signatory States. Instruments of ratification and instruments of accession shall be deposited with the Governments of the Original Parties—the United States of America, the United Kingdom of Great Britain and Northern Ireland, and the Union of Soviet Socialist Republics—which are hereby designated the Depositary Governments.

3. This Treaty shall enter into force after its ratification by all the Original Parties and the deposit of their instruments of ratification.

4. For States whose instruments of ratification or accession are deposited subsequent to the entry into force of this Treaty, it shall enter into force on the date of the deposit of their instruments of ratification or accession.

5. The Depositary Governments shall promptly inform all signatory and acceding States of the date of each signature, the date of deposit of each instrument of ratification of and accession to this Treaty, the date of its entry into force, and the date of receipt of any requests for conferences or other notices.

6. This Treaty shall be registered by the Depositary Governments pursuant to Article 102 of the Charter of the United Nations.

ARTICLE IV

This Treaty shall be of unlimited duration.

Each Party shall in exercising its national sovereignty have the right to withdraw from the Treaty if it decides that extraordinary events, related to the subject matter of this Treaty, have jeopardized the supreme interests of its country. It shall give notice of such withdrawal to all other Parties to the Treaty three months in advance.

ARTICLE V

This Treaty, of which the English and Russian texts are equally authentic, shall be deposited in the archives of the Depositary Governments. Duly certified copies of this Treaty shall be transmitted by the Depositary Governments to the Governments of the signatory and acceding States.

In witness whereof the undersigned, duly authorized, have signed this Treaty.

Done in triplicate at the city of Moscow the fifth day of August, one thousand nine hundred and sixty-three.

For the Government of the United States of America:

Dean Rusk
WAH

For the Government of the United Kingdom of Great Britain and Northern Ireland:

Home
H

For the Government of the Union of Soviet Socialist Republics:

A. Gromyko
A.G.

I certify that the foregoing is a true copy of the Treaty banning nuclear weapon tests in the atmosphere in outer space and under water, signed at Moscow on August 5, 1963 in the English and Russian languages, a signed original of which is deposited in the archives of the Government of the United States of America.

IN TESTIMONY WHEREOF, I, George W. Ball, Acting Secretary of State of the United States of America, have hereunto caused the seal of the Department of State to be affixed and my name subscribed by the Authentication Officer of the said Department, at the city of Washington, in the District of Columbia, this eighth day of August, 1963.

[SEAL]

GEORGE W. BALL
Acting Secretary of State
By BARBARA HARTMAN
Authentication Officer
Department of State

8/8/63

TREATY ON THE PROHIBITION OF THE EMPLACEMENT OF NUCLEAR WEAPONS AND OTHER WEAPONS OF MASS DESTRUCTION ON THE SEABED AND THE OCEAN FLOOR AND IN THE SUBSOIL THEREOF

The States Parties to this Treaty,

Recognizing the common interest of mankind in the progress of the exploration and use of the seabed and the ocean floor for peaceful purposes,

Considering that the prevention of a nuclear arms race on the seabed and the ocean floor serves the interests of maintaining world peace, reduces international tensions and strengthens friendly relations among States,

Convinced that this Treaty constitutes a step towards the exclusion of the seabed, the ocean floor and the subsoil thereof from the arms race,

Convinced that this Treaty constitutes a step towards a treaty on general and complete disarmament under strict and effective international control, and determined to continue negotiations to this end,

Convinced that this Treaty will further the purposes and principles of the Charter of the United Nations, in a manner consistent with the principles of international law and without infringing the freedoms of the high seas,

Have agreed as follows:

ARTICLE I

1. The States Parties to this Treaty undertake not to emplant or emplace on the seabed and the ocean floor and in the subsoil thereof beyond the outer limit of a seabed zone, as defined in article II, any nuclear weapons or any other types of weapons of mass destruction as well as structures, launching installations or any other facilities specifically designed for storing, testing or using such weapons.

2. The undertakings of paragraph 1 of this article shall also apply to the seabed zone referred to in the same paragraph, except that within such seabed zone, they shall not apply either to the coastal State or to the seabed beneath its territorial waters.

3. The States Parties to this Treaty undertake not to assist, encourage or induce any State to carry out activities referred to in paragraph 1 of this article and not to participate in any other way in such actions.

ARTICLE II

For the purpose of this Treaty, the outer limit of the seabed zone referred to in article I shall be coterminous with the twelve-mile outer limit of the zone referred to in part II of the Convention on the Territorial Sea and the Contiguous Zone, signed at Geneva on April 29, 1958, and shall be measured in accordance with the provisions of part I, section II, of that Convention and in accordance with international law.

Article III

1. In order to promote the objectives of and insure compliance with the provisions of this Treaty, each State Party to the Treaty shall have the right to verify through observation the activities of other States Parties to the Treaty on the seabed and the ocean floor and in the subsoil thereof beyond the zone referred to in article I, provided that observation does not interfere with such activities.

2. If after such observation reasonable doubts remain concerning the fulfillment of the obligations assumed under the Treaty, the State Party having such doubts and the State Party that is responsible for the activities giving rise to the doubts shall consult with a view to removing the doubts. If the doubts persist, the State Party having such doubts shall notify the other States Parties, and the Parties concerned shall cooperate on such further procedures for verification as may be agreed, including appropriate inspection of objects, structures, installations or other facilities that reasonably may be expected to be of a kind described in article I. The Parties in the region of the activities, including any coastal State, and any other Party so requesting, shall be entitled to participate in such consultation and cooperation. After completion of the further procedures for verification, an appropriate report shall be circulated to other Parties by the Party that initiated such procedures.

3. If the State responsible for the activities giving rise to the reasonable doubts is not identifiable by observation of the object, structure, installation or other facility, the State Party having such doubts shall notify and make appropriate inquiries of States Parties in the region of the activities and of any other State Party. If it is ascertained through these inquiries that a particular State Party is responsible for the activities, that State Party shall consult and cooperate with other Parties as provided in paragraph 2 of this article. If the identity of the State responsible for the activities cannot be ascertained through these inquiries, then further verification procedures, including inspection, may be undertaken by the inquiring State Party, which shall invite the participation of the Parties in the region of the activities, including any coastal State, and of any other Party desiring to cooperate.

4. If consultation and cooperation pursuant to paragraphs 2 and 3 of this article have not removed the doubts concerning the activities and there remains a serious question concerning fulfillment of the obligations assumed under this Treaty, a State Party may, in accordance with the provisions of the Charter of the United Nations, refer the matter to the Security Council, which may take action in accordance with the Charter.

5. Verification pursuant to this article may be undertaken by any State Party using its own means, or with the full or partial assistance of any other State Party, or through appropriate international procedures within the framework of the United Nations and in accordance with its Charter.

6. Verification activities pursuant to this Treaty shall not interfere with activities of other States Parties and shall be conducted with due regard for rights recognized under international law, including the freedoms of the high seas and the rights of coastal States with respect to the exploration and exploitation of their continental shelves.

ARTICLE IV

Nothing in this Treaty shall be interpreted as supporting or prejudicing the position of any State Party with respect to existing international conventions, including the 1958 Convention on the Territorial Sea and the Contiguous Zone, or with respect to rights or claims which such State Party may assert, or with respect to recognition or non-recognition of rights or claims asserted by any other State, related to waters off its coasts, including, *inter alia*, territorial seas and contiguous zones, or to the seabed and the ocean floor, including continental shelves.

ARTICLE V

The Parties to this Treaty undertake to continue negotiations in good faith concerning further measures in the field of disarmament for the prevention of an arms race on the seabed, the ocean floor and the subsoil thereof.

ARTICLE VI

Any State Party may propose amendments to this Treaty. Amendments shall enter into force for each State Party accepting the amendments upon their acceptance by a majority of the States Parties to the Treaty and, thereafter, for each remaining State Party on the date of acceptance by it.

ARTICLE VII

Five years after the entry into force of this Treaty, a conference of Parties to the Treaty shall be held at Geneva, Switzerland, in order to review the operation of this Treaty with a view to assuring that the purposes of the preamble and the provisions of the Treaty are being realized. Such review shall take into account any relevant technological developments. The review conference shall determine, in accordance with the views of a majority of those Parties attending, whether and when an additional review conference shall be convened.

ARTICLE VIII

Each State Party to this Treaty shall in exercising its national sovereignty have the right to withdraw from this Treaty if it decides that extraordinary events related to the subject matter of this Treaty have jeopardized the supreme interests of its country. It shall give notice of such withdrawal to all other States Parties to the Treaty and to the United Nations Security Council three months in advance. Such notice shall include a statement of the extraordinary events it considers to have jeopardized its supreme interests.

ARTICLE IX

The provisions of this Treaty shall in no way affect the obligations assumed by States Parties to the Treaty under international instruments establishing zones free from nuclear weapons.

ARTICLE X

1. This Treaty shall be open for signature to all States. Any State which does not sign the Treaty before its entry into force in accordance with paragraph 3 of this article may accede to it at any time.

2. This Treaty shall be subject to ratification by signatory States. Instruments of ratification and of accession shall be deposited with the Governments of the United States of America, the United Kingdom of Great Britain and Northern Ireland, and the Union of Soviet Socialist Republics, which are hereby designated the Depositary Governments.

3. This Treaty shall enter into force after the deposit of instruments of ratification by twenty-two Governments, including the Governments designated as Depositary Governments of this Treaty.

4. For States whose instruments of ratification or accession are deposited after the entry into force of this Treaty, it shall enter into force on the date of the deposit of their instruments of ratification or accession.

5. The Depositary Governments shall promptly inform the Governments of all signatory and acceding States of the date of each signature, of the date of deposit of each instrument of ratification or of accession, of the date of the entry into force of this Treaty, and of the receipt of other notices.

6. This Treaty shall be registered by the Depositary Governments pursuant to Article 102 of the Charter of the United Nations.

ARTICLE XI

This Treaty, the English, Russian, French, Spanish and Chinese texts of which are equally authentic, shall be deposited in the archives of the Depositary Governments. Duly certified copies of this Treaty shall be transmitted by the Depositary Governments to the Governments of the States signatory and acceding thereto.

IN WITNESS WHEREOF the undersigned, being duly authorized thereto, have signed this Treaty.

DONE in triplicate, at the cities of Washington, London and Moscow, this eleventh day of February, one thousand nine hundred seventy-one.

TREATY BETWEEN THE UNITED STATES OF AMERICA AND THE UNION OF SOVIET SOCIALIST REPUBLICS ON THE LIMITATION OF ANTI-BALLISTIC MISSILE SYSTEMS

The United States of America and the Union of Soviet Socialist Republics, hereinafter referred to as the Parties,

Proceeding from the premise that nuclear war would have devastating consequences for all mankind,

Considering that effective measures to limit anti-ballistic missile systems would be a substantial factor in curbing the race in strategic offensive arms and would lead to a decrease in the risk of outbreak of war involving nuclear weapons,

Proceeding from the premise that the limitation of anti-ballistic missile systems, as well as certain agreed measures with respect to the limitation of strategic offensive arms, would contribute to the creation of more favorable conditions for further negotiations on limiting strategic arms,

Mindful of their obligations under Article VI of the Treaty on the Non-Proliferation of Nuclear Weapons,

Declaring their intention to achieve at the earliest possible date the cessation of the nuclear arms race and to take effective measures toward reductions in strategic arms, nuclear disarmament, and general and complete disarmament,

Desiring to contribute to the relaxation of international tension and the strengthening of trust between States,

Have agreed as follows:

Article I

1. Each Party undertakes to limit anti-ballistic missile (ABM) systems and to adopt other measures in accordance with the provisions of this Treaty.

2. Each Party undertakes not to deploy ABM systems for a defense of the territory of its country and not to provide a base for such a defense, and not to deploy ABM systems for defense of an individual region except as provided for in Article III of this Treaty.

Article II

1. For the purposes of this Treaty an ABM system is a system to counter strategic ballistic missiles or their elements in flight trajectory, currently consisting of:

(*a*) ABM interceptor missiles, which are interceptor missiles constructed and deployed for an ABM role, or of a type tested in an ABM mode;

(*b*) ABM launchers, which are launchers constructed and deployed for launching ABM interceptor missiles; and

(*c*) ABM radars, which are radars constructed and deployed for an ABM role, or of a type tested in an ABM mode.

2. The ABM system components listed in paragraph 1 of this Article include those which are:

(*a*) operational;

(*b*) under construction;

(*c*) undergoing testing;

(*d*) undergoing overhaul, repair or conversion; or

(*e*) mothballed.

ARTICLE III

Each Party undertakes not to deploy ABM systems or their components except that:

(*a*) within one ABM system deployment area having a radius of one hundred and fifty kilometers and centered on the Party's national capital, a Party may deploy: (1) no more than one hundred ABM launchers and no more than one hundred ABM interceptor missiles at launch sites, and (2) ABM radars within no more than six ABM radar complexes, the area of each complex being circular and have a diameter of no more than three kilometers; and

(*b*) within one ABM system deployment area having a radius of one hundred and fifty kilometers and containing ICBM silo launchers, a Party may deploy: (1) no more than one hundred ABM launchers and no more than one hundred ABM interceptor missiles at launch sites, (2) two large phased-array ABM radars comparable in potential to corresponding ABM radars operational or under construction on the date of signature of the Treaty in an ABM system deployment area containing ICBM silo launchers, and (3) no more than eighteen ABM radars each having a potential less than the potential of the smaller of the above-mentioned two large phased-array ABM radars.

ARTICLE IV

The limitations provided for in Article III shall not apply to ABM systems or their components used for development or testing, and located within current or additionally agreed test ranges. Each Party may have no more than a total of fifteen ABM launchers at test ranges.

ARTICLE V

1. Each Party undertakes not to develop, test, or deploy ABM systems or components which are sea-based, air-based, space-based, or mobile land-based.

2. Each Party undertakes not to develop, test, or deploy ABM launchers for launching more than one ABM interceptor missile at a time from each launcher, nor to modify deployed launchers to provide them with such a capability, nor to develop, test, or deploy automatic or semi-automatic or other similar systems for rapid reload or ABM launchers.

ARTICLE VI

To enhance assurance of the effectiveness of the limitations on ABM systems and their components provided by this Treaty, each Party undertakes:

(*a*) not to give missiles, launchers, or radars, other than ABM interceptor missiles, ABM launchers, or ABM radars, capabilities to counter strategic ballistic missiles or their elements in flight trajectory, and not to test them in an ABM mode; and

(*b*) not to deploy in the future radars for early warning of strategic ballistic missile attack except at locations along the periphery of its national territory and oriented outward.

ARTICLE VII

Subject to the provisions of this Treaty, modernization and replacement of ABM systems or their components may be carried out.

ARTICLE VIII

ABM systems or their components in excess of the numbers or outside the areas specified in this Treaty, as well as ABM systems or their components prohibited by this Treaty, shall be destroyed or dismantled under agreed procedures within the shortest possible agreed period of time.

ARTICLE IX

To assure the viability and effectiveness of this Treaty, each Party undertakes not to transfer to other States, and not to deploy outside its national territory, ABM systems or their components limited by this Treaty.

ARTICLE X

Each Party undertakes not to assume any international obligations which would conflict with this Treaty.

ARTICLE XI

The Parties undertake to continue active negotiations for limitations on strategic offensive arms.

ARTICLE XII

1. For the purpose of providing assurance of compliance with the provisions of this Treaty, each Party shall use national technical means of verification at its disposal in a manner consistent with generally recognized principles of international law.

2. Each Party undertakes not to interfere with the national technical means of verification of the other Party operating in accordance with paragraph 1 of this Article.

3. Each Party undertakes not to use deliberate concealment measures which impede verification by national technical means of compliance with the provisions of this Treaty. This obligation shall not require changes in current construction, assembly, conversion, or overhaul practices.

ARTICLE XIII

1. To promote the objectives and implementation of the provisions of this Treaty, the Parties shall establish promptly a Standing Consultative Commission, within the framework of which they will:

(*a*) consider questions concerning compliance with the obligations assumed and related situations which may be considered ambiguous;

(*b*) provide on a voluntary basis such information as either Party considers necessary to assure confidence in compliance with the obligations assumed;

(*c*) consider questions involving unintended interference with national technical means of verification;

(*d*) consider possible changes in the strategic situation which have a bearing on the provisions of this Treaty;

(*e*) agree upon procedures and dates for destruction or dismantling of ABM systems or their components in cases provided for by the provisions of this Treaty;

(*f*) consider, as appropriate, possible proposals for further increasing the viability of this Treaty, including proposals for amendments in accordance with the provisions of this Treaty;

(*g*) consider, as appropriate, proposals for further measures aimed at limiting strategic arms.

2. The Parties through consultation shall establish, and may amend as appropriate, Regulations for the Standing Consultative Commission governing procedures, composition and other relevant matters.

Article XIV

1. Each Party may propose amendments to this Treaty. Agreed amendments shall enter into force in accordance with the procedures governing the entry into force of this Treaty.

2. Five years after entry into force of this Treaty, and at five year intervals thereafter, the Parties shall together conduct a review of this Treaty.

Article XV

1. This Treaty shall be of unlimited duration.

2. Each Party shall, in exercising its national sovereignty, have the right to withdraw from this Treaty if it decides that extraordinary events related to the subject matter of this Treaty have jeopardized its supreme interests. It shall give notice of its decision to the other Party six months prior to withdrawal from the Treaty. Such notice shall include a statement of the extraordinary events the notifying Party regards as having jeopardized its supreme interests.

Article XVI

1. This Treaty shall be subject to ratification in accordance with the constitutional procedures of each Party. The Treaty shall enter into force on the day of the exchange of instruments of ratification.

2. This Treaty shall be registered pursuant to Article 102 of the Charter of the United Nations.

Done at Moscow on May 26, 1972, in two copies, each in the English and Russian languages, both texts being equally authentic.

For the United States of America:

Richard Nixon,
President of the United States of America.

For the Union of Soviet Socialist Republics:

L. I. Brezhnev,
General Secretary of the Central Committee of the CPSU.

INTERIM AGREEMENT BETWEEN THE UNITED STATES OF AMERICA AND THE UNION OF SOVIET SOCIALIST REPUBLICS ON CERTAIN MEASURES WITH RESPECT TO THE LIMITATION OF STRATEGIC OFFENSIVE ARMS

The United States of America and the Union of Soviet Socialist Republics, hereinafter referred to as the Parties,

Convinced that the Treaty on the Limitation of Anti-Ballistic Missile Systems and this Interim Agreement on Certain Measures with Respect to the Limitation of Strategic Offensive Arms will contribute to the creation of more favorable conditions for active negotiations on limiting strategic arms as well as to the relaxation of international tension and the strengthening of trust between States,

Taking into account the relationship between strategic offensive and defensive arms,

Mindful of their obligations under Article VI of the Treaty on the Non-Proliferation of Nuclear Weapons,

Have agreed as follows:

Article I

The Parties undertake not to start construction of additional fixed land-based intercontinental ballistic missile (ICBM) launchers after July 1, 1972.

Article II

The Parties undertake not to convert land-based launchers for light ICBMs, or for ICBMs of older types deployed prior to 1964, into land-based launchers for heavy ICBMs of types deployed after that time.

Article III

The Parties undertake to limit submarine-launched ballistic missile (SLBM) launchers and modern ballistic missile submarines to the numbers operational and under construction on the date of signature of this Interim Agreement, and in addition to launchers and submarines constructed under procedures established by the Parties as replacements for an equal number of ICBM launchers of older types deployed prior to 1964 or for launchers on older submarines.

Article IV

Subject to the provisions of this Interim Agreement, modernization and replacement of strategic offensive ballistic missiles and launchers covered by this Interim Agreement may be undertaken.

Article V

1. For the purpose of providing assurance of compliance with the provisions of this Interim Agreement, each Party shall use national

technical means of verification at its disposal in a manner consistent with generally recognized principles of international law.

2. Each Party undertakes not to interfere with the national technical means of verification of the other Party operating in accordance with paragraph 1 of this Article.

3. Each Party undertakes not to use deliberate concealment measures which impede verification by national technical means of compliance with the provisions of this Interim Agreement. This obligation shall not require changes in current construction, assembly, conversion, or overhaul practices.

Article VI

To promote the objectives and implementation of the provisions of this Interim Agreement, the Parties shall use the Standing Consultative Commission established under Article XIII of the Treaty on the Limitation of Anti-Ballistic Missile Systems in accordance with the provisions of that Article.

Article VII

The Parties undertake to continue active negotiations for limitations on strategic offensive arms. The obligations provided for in this Interim Agreement shall not prejudice the scope or terms of the limitations on strategic offensive arms which may be worked out in the course of further negotiations.

Article VIII

1. This Interim Agreement shall enter into force upon exchange of written notices of acceptance by each Party, which exchange shall take place simultaneously with the exchange of instruments of ratification of the Treaty on the Limitation of Anti-Ballistic Missile Systems.

2. This Interim Agreement shall remain in force for a period of five years unless replaced earlier by an agreement on more complete measures limiting strategic offensive arms. It is the objective of the Parties to conduct active follow-on negotiations with the aim of concluding such an agreement as soon as possible.

3. Each Party shall, in exercising its national sovereignty, have the right to withdraw from this Interim Agreement if it decides that extraordinary events related to the subject matter of this Interim Agreement have jeopardized its supreme interests. It shall give notice of its decision to the other Party six months prior to withdrawal from this Interim Agreement. Such notice shall include a statement of the extraordinary events the notifying Party regards as having jeopardized its supreme interests.

Done at Moscow on May 26, 1972, in two copies, each in the English and Russian languages, both texts being equally authentic.

For the United States of America:

Richard Nixon,
President of the United States of America.

For the Union of Soviet Socialist Republics:

L. I. Brezhnev,
General Secretary of the Central Committee of the CPSU.

PROTOCOL TO THE INTERIM AGREEMENT BETWEEN THE UNITED STATES OF AMERICA AND THE UNION OF SOVIET SOCIALIST REPUBLICS ON CERTAIN MEASURES WITH RESPECT TO THE LIMITATION OF STRATEGIC OFFENSIVE ARMS

The United States of America and the Union of Soviet Socialist Republics, hereinafter referred to as the Parties,

Having agreed on certain limitations relating to submarine-launched ballistic missile launchers and modern ballistic missile submarines, and to replacement procedures, in the Interim Agreement,

Have agreed as follows:

The Parties understand that, under Article III of the Interim Agreement, for the period during which that Agreement remains in force:

The U.S. may have no more than 710 ballistic missile launchers on submarines (SLBMs) and no more than 44 modern ballistic missile submarines. The Soviet Union may have no more than 950 ballistic missile launchers on submarines and no more than 62 modern ballistic missile submarines.

Additional ballistic missile launchers on submarines up to the above-mentioned levels, in the U.S.—over 656 ballistic missile launchers on nuclear-powered submarines, and in the U.S.S.R.—over 740 ballistic missile launchers on nuclear-powered submarines, operational and under construction, may become operational as replacements for equal numbers of ballistic missile launchers of older types deployed prior to 1964 or of ballistic missile launchers on older submarines.

The deployment of modern SLBMs on any submarine, regardless of type, will be counted against the total level of SLBMs permitted for the U.S. and the U.S.S.R.

This Protocol shall be considered an integral part of the Interim Agreement.

DONE at Moscow this 26th day of May, 1972.

For the United States of America:

RICHARD NIXON,
President of the United States of America.

For the Union of Soviet Socialist Republics:

L. I. BREZHNEV,
General Secretary of the Central Committee of the CPSU.

ENCLOSURE 3

1. Agreed Interpretations

(*a*) *Initialed Statements.*—The texts of the statements set out below were agreed upon and initialed by the Heads of the Delegations on May 26, 1972.

ABM TREATY

[A]

The Parties understand that, in addition to the ABM radars which may be deployed in accordance with subparagraph (a) of Article III of the Treaty, those non-phased-array ABM radars operational on the date of signature of the Treaty within the ABM system deployment area for defense of the national capital may be retained.

[B]

The Parties understand that the potential (the product of mean emitted power in watts and antenna area in square meters) of the smaller of the two large phased-array ABM radars referred to in subparagraph (b) of Article III of the Treaty is considered for purposes of the Treaty to be three million.

[C]

The Parties understand that the center of the ABM system deployment area centered on the national capital and the center of the ABM system deployment area containing ICBM silo launchers for each Party shall be separated by no less than thirteen hundred kilometers.

[D]

The Parties agree not to deploy phased-array radars having a potential (the product of mean emitted power in watts and antenna area in square meters) exceeding three million, except as provided for in Articles III, IV and VI of the Treaty, or except for the purposes of tracking objects in outer space or for use as national technical means of verification.

[E]

In order to insure fulfillment of the obligation not to deploy ABM systems and their components except as provided in Article III of the Treaty, the Parties agree that in the event ABM systems based on other physical principles and including components capable of substituting for ABM interceptor missiles, ABM launchers, or ABM radars are created in the future, specific limitations on such systems and their components would be subject to discussion in accordance with Article XIII and agreement in accordance with Article XIV of the Treaty.

[F]

The Parties understand that Article V of the Treaty includes obligations not to develop, test or deploy ABM interceptor missiles for the delivery by each ABM interceptor missile of more than one independently guided warhead.

[G]

The Parties understand that Article IX of the Treaty includes the obligation of the US and the USSR not to provide to other States technical descriptions or blueprints specially worked out for the construction of ABM systems and their components limited by the Treaty.

INTERIM AGREEMENT

[H]

The Parties understand that land-based ICBM launchers referred to in the Interim Agreement are understood to be launchers for strategic ballistic missiles capable of ranges in excess of the shortest distance between the northeastern border of the continental U.S. and the northwestern border of the continental USSR.

[I]

The Parties understand that fixed land-based ICBM launchers under active construction as of the date of signature of the Interim Agreement may be completed.

[J]

The Parties understand that in the process of modernization and replacement the dimensions of land-based ICBM silo launchers will not be significantly increased.

[K]

The Parties understand that dismantling or destruction of ICBM launchers of older types deployed prior to 1964 and ballistic missile launchers on older submarines being replaced by new SLBM launchers on modern submarines will be initiated at the time of the beginning of sea trials of a replacement submarine, and will be completed in the shortest possible agreed period of time. Such dismantling or destruction, and timely notification thereof, will be accomplished under procedures to be agreed in the Standing Consultative Commission.

[L]

The Parties understand that during the period of the Interim Agreement there shall be no significant increase in the number of ICBM or SLBM test and training launchers, or in the number of such launchers for modern land-based heavy ICBMs. The Parties further understand that construction or conversion of ICBM launchers at test ranges shall be undertaken only for purposes of testing and training.

(b) *Common Understandings.*—Common understanding of the Parties on the following matters was reached during the negotiations:

A. INCREASE IN ICBM SILO DIMENSIONS

Ambassador Smith made the following statement on May 26, 1972:

> The Parties agree that the term "significantly increased" means that an increase will not be greater than 10–15 percent of the present dimensions of land-based ICBM silo launchers.

Minister Semenov replied that this statement corresponded to the Soviet understanding.

B. LOCATION OF ICBM DEFENSES

The U.S. Delegation made the following statement on May 26, 1972:

> Article III of the ABM Treaty provides for each side one ABM system deployment area centered on its national capital and one ABM system deployment area containing ICBM silo launchers. The two sides have registered agreement on the following statement: "The Parties understand that the center of the ABM system deployment area centered on the national capital and the center of the ABM system deployment area containing ICBM silo launchers for each Party shall be separated by no less than thirteen hundred kilometers." In this connection, the U.S. side notes that its ABM system deployment area for defense of ICBM silo launchers, located west of the Mississippi River, will be centered in the Grand Forks ICBM silo launcher deployment area. (See Initialed Statement [C].)

C. ABM TEST RANGES

The U.S. Delegation made the following statement on April 26, 1972:

> Article IV of the ABM Treaty provides that "the limitations provided for in Article III shall not apply to ABM systems or their components used for development or testing, and located within current or additionally agreed test ranges." We believe it would be useful to assure that there is no misunderstanding as to current ABM test ranges. It is our understanding that ABM test ranges encompass the area within which ABM components are located for test purposes. The current U.S. ABM test ranges are at White Sands, New Mexico, and at Kwajalein Atoll, and the current Soviet ABM test range is near Sary Shagan in Kazakhstan. We consider that non-phased array radars of types used for range safety or instrumentation purposes may be located outside of ABM test ranges. We interpret the reference in Article IV to "additionally agreed test ranges" to mean that ABM components will not be located at any other test ranges without prior agreement between our Governments that there will be such additional ABM test ranges.

On May 5, 1972, the Soviet Delegation stated that there was a common understanding on what ABM test ranges were, that the use of the types of non-ABM radars for range safety or instrumentation was not limited under the Treaty, that the reference in Article IV to "additionally agreed" test ranges was sufficiently clear, and that national means permitted identifying current test ranges.

D. MOBILE ABM SYSTEMS

On January 28, 1972, the U.S. Delegation made the following statement:

> Article V(1) of the Joint Draft Text of the ABM Treaty includes an undertaking not to develop, test, or deploy mobile land-based ABM systems and their components. On May 5, 1971, the U.S. side indicated that, in its view, a prohibition on deployment of mobile ABM systems and components would rule out the deployment of ABM launchers and radars which were not permanent fixed types. At that time, we asked for the Soviet view of this interpretation. Does the Soviet side agree with the U.S. side's interpretation put forward on May 5, 1971?

On April 13, 1972, the Soviet Delegation said there is a general common understanding on this matter.

E. STANDING CONSULTATIVE COMMISSION

Ambassador Smith made the following statement on May 22, 1972:

> The United States proposes that the sides agree that, with regard to initial implementation of the ABM Treaty's Article XIII on the Standing Consultative Commission (SCC) and of the consultation Articles to the Interim Agreement on offensive arms and the Accidents Agreement,* agreement establishing the SCC will be worked out early in the follow-on SALT negotiations; until that is completed, the following arrangements will prevail: when SALT is in session, any consultation desired by either side under these Articles can be carried out by the two SALT Delegations; when SALT is not in session, *ad hoc* arrangements for any desired consultations under these Articles may be made through diplomatic channels.

Minister Semenov replied that, on an *ad referendum* basis, he could agree that the U.S. statement corresponded to the Soviet understanding.

F. STANDSTILL

On May 6, 1972, Minister Semenov made the following statement:

> In an effort to accommodate the wishes of the U.S. side, the Soviet Delegation is prepared to proceed on the basis that the two sides will in fact observe the obligations of both the

*See Article 7 of Agreement to Reduce the Risk of Outbreak of Nuclear War Between the United States of America and the Union of Soviet Socialist Republics, signed Sept. 30, 1971.

Interim Agreement and the ABM Treaty beginning from the date of signature of these two documents.

In reply, the U.S. Delegation made the following statement on May 20, 1972:

The U.S. agrees in principle with the Soviet statement made on May 6 concerning observance of obligations beginning from date of signature but we would like to make clear our understanding that this means that, pending ratification and acceptance, neither side would take any action prohibited by the agreements after they had entered into force. This understanding would continue to apply in the absence of notification by either signatory of its intention not to proceed with ratification or approval.

The Soviet Delegation indicated agreement with the U.S. statement.

2. Unilateral Statements

(a) The following noteworthy unilateral statements were made during the negotiations by the United States Delegation:

A. WITHDRAWAL FROM THE ABM TREATY

On May 9, 1972, Ambassador Smith made the following statement:

The U.S. Delegation has stressed the importance the U.S. Government attaches to achieving agreement on more complete limitations on strategic offensive arms, following agreement on an ABM Treaty and on an Interim Agreement on certain measures with respect to the limitation of strategic offensive arms. The U.S. Delegation believes that an objective of the follow-on negotiations should be to constrain and reduce on a long-term basis threats to the survivability of our respective strategic retaliatory forces. The USSR Delegation has also indicated that the objectives of SALT would remain unfulfilled without the achievement of an agreement providing for more complete limitations on strategic offensive arms. Both sides recognize that the initial agreements would be steps toward the achievement of more complete limitations on strategic arms. If an agreement providing for more complete strategic offensive arms limitations were not achieved within five years, U.S. supreme interests could be jeopardized. Should that occur, it would constitute a basis for withdrawal from the ABM Treaty. The U.S. does not wish to see such a situation occur, nor do we believe that the USSR does. It is because we wish to prevent such a situation that we emphasize the importance the U.S. Government attaches to achievement of more complete limitations on strategic offensive arms. The U.S. Executive will inform the Congress, in connection with Congressional consideration of the ABM Treaty and the Interim Agreement, of this statement of the U.S. position.

B. LAND-MOBILE ICBM LAUNCHERS

The U.S. Delegation made the following statement on May 20, 1972:

In connection with the important subject of land-mobile ICBM launchers, in the interest of concluding the Interim Agreement the U.S. Delegation now withdraws its proposal that Article I or an agreed statement explicitly prohibit the deployment of mobile land-based ICBM launchers. I have been instructed to inform you that, while agreeing to defer the question of limitation of operational land-mobile ICBM launchers to the subsequent negotiations on more complete limitations on strategic offensive arms, the U.S. would consider the deployment of operational land-mobile ICBM launchers during the period of the Interim Agreement as inconsistent with the objectives of that Agreement.

C. COVERED FACILITIES

The U.S. Delegation made the following statement on May 20, 1972:

I wish to emphasize the importance that the United States attaches to the provisions of Article V, including in particular their application to fitting out or berthing submarines.

D. "HEAVY" ICBM'S

The U.S. Delegation made the following statement on May 26, 1972:

The U.S. Delegation regrets that the Soviet Delegation has not been willing to agree on a common definition of a heavy missile. Under these circumstances, the U.S. Delegation believes it necessary to state the following: The United States would consider any ICBM having a volume significantly greater than that of the largest light ICBM now operational on either side to be a heavy ICBM. The U.S. proceeds on the premise that the Soviet side will give due account to this consideration.

E. TESTED IN ABM MODE

On April 7, 1972, the U.S. Delegation made the following statement:

Article II of the Joint Text Draft uses the term "tested in an ABM mode," in defining ABM components, and Article VI includes certain obligations concerning such testing. We believe that the sides should have a common understanding of this phrase. First, we would note that the testing provisions of the ABM Treaty are intended to apply to testing which occurs after the date of signature of the Treaty, and not to any testing which may have occurred in the past. Next, we would amplify the remarks we have made on this subject during the previous Helsinki phase by setting forth the objectives which govern the U.S. view on the subject, namely, while prohibiting testing of non-ABM components for ABM purposes: not to precent testing of ABM components, and not to prevent testing of non-ABM components for non-ABM purposes. To clarify our interpretation of "tested in an ABM mode," we note that we would consider a launcher, missile or radar to be "tested in an ABM mode" if, for example, any of the following events occur: (1) a launcher is used to launch an ABM interceptor missile, (2) an interceptor missile is flight tested against a target vehicle which has a flight trajectory with characteristics of a strategic ballistic missile flight trajectory, or is flight tested in conjunction with the test of an ABM interceptor missile or an ABM radar at the same test range, or is flight tested to an altitude inconsistent with interception of targets against which air defenses are deployed, (3) a radar makes measurements on a cooperative target vehicle of the kind referred to in item (2) above during the reentry portion of its trajectory or makes measurements in conjunction with the test of an ABM interceptor missile or an ABM radar at the same test range. Radars used for purposes such as range safety or instrumentation would be exempt from application of these criteria.

F. NO-TRANSFER ARTICLE OF ABM TREATY

On April 18, 1972, the U.S. Delegation made the following statement:

In regard to this Article [IX], I have a brief and I believe self-explanatory statement to make. The U.S. side wishes to make clear that the provisions of this Article do not set a precedent for whatever provision may be considered for a Treaty on Limiting Strategic Offensive Arms. The question of transfer of strategic offensive arms is a far more complex issue, which may require a different solution.

G. NO INCREASE IN DEFENSE OF EARLY WARNING RADARS

On July 28, 1970, the U.S. Delegation made the following statement:

Since Hen House radars [Soviet ballistic missile early warning radars] can detect and track ballistic missile warheads at great distances, they have a significant ABM potential. Accordingly, the U.S. would regard any increase in the defenses of such radars by surface-to-air missiles as inconsistent with an agreement.

* * * * * * *

(b) The following noteworthy unilateral statement was made by the Delegation of the U.S.S.R. and is shown here with the U.S. reply:

On May 17, 1972, Minister Semenov made the following unilateral "Statement of the Soviet Side":

Taking into account that modern ballistic missile submarines are presently in the possession of not only the U.S., but also of its NATO allies, the Soviet Union agrees that for the period of effectiveness of the Interim 'Freeze' Agreement

> the U.S. and its NATO allies have up to 50 such submarines with a total of up to 800 ballistic missile launchers thereon (including 41 U.S. submarines with 656 ballistic missile launchers). However, if during the period of effectiveness of the Agreement U.S. allies in NATO should increase the number of their modern submarines to exceed the numbers of submarines they would have operational or under construction on the date of signature of the Agreement, the Soviet Union will have the right to a corresponding increase in the number of its submarines. In the opinion of the Soviet side, the solution of the question of modern ballistic missile submarines provided for in the Interim Agreement only partially compensates for the strategic imbalance in the deployment of the nuclear-powered missile submarines of the USSR and the U.S. Therefore, the Soviet side believes that this whole question, and above all the question of liquidating the American missile submarine bases outside the U.S., will be appropriately resolved in the course of follow-on negotiations.

On May 24, Ambassador Smith made the following reply to Minister Semenov:

> The United States side has studied the "statement made by the Soviet side" of May 17 concerning compensation for submarine basing and SLBM submarines belonging to third countries. The United States does not accept the validity of the considerations in that statement.

On May 26 Minister Semenov repeated the unilateral statement made on May 24. Ambassador Smith also repeated the U.S. rejection on May 26.

○

IRAN: LAW OF JUNE 19, 1955 CONCERNING THE CONTINENTAL SHELF

Article 1

The term "Continental Shelf" as used in this Law shall have the same meaning as the English term "Continental Shelf" and the French term "Plateau Continental".

Article 2

The area and the natural resources of the seabed and the subsoil thereof to the limits of the continental shelf extend from the coasts of Iran and the coasts of the Iranian islands in the Persian Gulf and Gulf of Oman, belong to the Iranian Government and are under the sovereignty of the Government of Iran.

Note: The rules of international law in respect of inland seas shall apply to the Caspian Sea.

Article 3

Where the continental shelf as referred to in the foregoing article extends to the coast of another country or coincides with that of a neighboring country, and if disputes arise concerning the limits of Iran's continental shelf, such disputes shall be settled in conformity with the rules of equity, and the Government shall take the necessary steps for the settlement of any disputes through the diplomatic channels.

Article 4

This Law shall in no way affect the provisions of the

Law of 24 Tir 1313 concerning the delimitation of Iran's territorial sea and zone of maritime control, and the said Law shall remain in force.

Article 5

This Law shall in no way affect the regime of the waters of the continental shelf with respect to the right of freedom of navigation and arrangements concerning submarine cables. The Government may establish the facilities required for the exploration and exploitation of the natural resources of the continental shelf and it shall take the necessary steps to guarantee the safety of these facilities.

IRAN

(*b*) ACT OF 31 JULY 1957 ON SURVEY, EXPLORATION AND EXPLOITATION OF THE OIL RESOURCES IN THE IRANIAN TERRITORY AND ITS CONTINENTAL SHELF[1]

Article 1. With a view to extending as rapidly as possible the operations of research, exploration and extraction of petroleum throughout the country and the continental shelf, excluding that part of Iranian territory which has been defined as the area of operations of the Consortium in accordance with the Agreement for the Sale of Oil dated 29th October, 1954, and also with a view to extending promptly the operations of refining, transportation and sale, throughout the territory as well as abroad, of all petroleum to be obtained from outside the Consortium area, the National Iranian Oil Company is authorised to proceed in accordance with the rules and provisions of this Act.

Note 1. Petroleum, as used in this Act, means crude oil, natural gas, asphalt, all liquid hydrocarbons whether found in a natural state or obtained through separation from crude or natural gas by means of different processes, and any finished or semi-finished product derived from such substances by condensation, refining, chemical treatment, or other method or process, whether now known or not.

. . .

Article 2. In execution of the provisions of this Act, the National Iranian Oil Company may negotiate with any person, whether Iranian or foreign, whose technical and financial competence shall have been established, and may conclude with such person any agreement[2] which it deems appropriate, on the basis of the terms and stipulations of this Act and other conditions not inconsistent with the laws of the country. The agreement thus drawn up shall be signed by the National Iranian Oil Company and submitted to the Council of Ministers, which if it confirms the same, shall place it before the Legislature for approval. Agreements thus signed shall be enforceable after approval by the Legislature and with effect from the date of such approval.

---

[1] *Official Gazette* No. 3642. English text provided by the Permanent Mission of Iran to the United Nations.

[2] In accordance with the explanatory remarks made in the note of 20 June 1968 from the Permanent Representative of Iran to the United Nations, those agreements together with the relevant laws and regulations provide the body of rules which govern Iran's actions and policies with respect to matters related to the law of the sea. The following agreements between the Iranian National Oil Company and a number of foreign entities for exploitation of the Iranian off-shore resources are in force:

1. Agreement between National Iranian Oil Company and Pan American Petroleum Corporation, dated 24 April 1958.
2. Agreement between National Iranian Oil Company and Farsi Petroleum Company (F.P.C.) dated 19 January 1965.
3. Joint Structure Agreement between National Iranian Oil Company and Iranian Marine International Oil Company, dated 17 January 1965.
4. Joint Structure Agreement between National Iranian Oil Company and Bataafse Petroleum Maatschappij N.V., dated 16 January 1965.

FRANCE: Law No. 68-1181 of December 30, 1968 relating to the Exploration of the Continental Shelf and to the Exploitation of its Natural Resources.

Chapter 1. General Provisions

Article 1

In conformity with the Geneva Convention on the Continental Shelf of April 29, 1958, published by Decree No. 65-1049 of November 29, 1965, the French Republic exercises sovereign rights for the purpose of exploring the continental shelf adjacent to its territory and of exploiting its natural resources.

The continental shelf over which the French Republic exercises the rights defined above shall be, in its entirety and whatever its geographical location and the status of the territories to which it is adjacent, subject to a single legal regime laid down by the present Law, subject to the provisions of Articles 35 and 36.

Article 2

Every activity undertaken by a public or private person on the continental shelf, with the object of its exploration or of exploiting its natural resources, shall require the prior obtaining of a permit.

As regards the exploitation of vegetable and animal resources belonging to sedentary species, French nationals shall be exempted from the need to have the permit referred to in the first paragraph except in cases where such exploitation entails placing fishing equipment or equipment for marine cultivation on the continental shelf.

Article 3

For the purposes of the present Law, the expression "installations and devices" means:

(i) Drillings rigs and other structures for exploration including their attachments;

(ii) Ships taking part directly in exploration and exploitation activities.

Article 4

A safety zone may be established around the installations and devices defined in Article 3. This zone may be extended to a distance of 500 metres measured from each point of the outer edge of these installations and devices. Access without permission to this zone, by whatever means, for reasons unconnected with the exploration or exploitation operations is prohibited.

Restrictions may be imposed on the overflight of installations and devices and safety zones to the extent necessary for the protection of these installations and devices and for the safety of aerial navigation.

Article 5

Subject to the provisions of this Law and the measures taken for its implementation, French laws and regulations shall apply during the period when the activities referred to in Article 2 are being carried out on the installations and devices defined in Article 3, as if they were on the territory of metropolitan France. They shall apply in the same manner and under the same conditions to the installations and devices themselves.

These laws and regulations shall apply under the same

conditions to the safety zones, for the purpose of controlling operations being carried out there as well as for the maintenance of public order.

Article 6

Research, exploitation and transportation by pipeline of all mineral or fossil substances of the subsoil of the continental shelf or lying in its seabed shall be subject to the regime applicable in the metropolitan territory to geological deposits falling within the category of mines. In all cases the length of the concession, whatever the substance, is not to exceed 50 years.

Article 7

Unless exceptional derogation is made by the competent Minister, all maritime or aerial transport between French territory and the installations and devices placed on the adjacent continental shelf shall be reserved for French ships and aircraft.

Article 8

The installation and devices defined in Article 3 (i) above shall be considered as being moveable property and shall be mortgageable under the conditions set out in Articles 43-57 of Law No. 67-5 of January 3, 1967 concerning the Status of Ships and Other Vessels.

Article 9

Seamen who are engaged on board the installation and devices defined in Article 3 (i) above in activities concerning the exploration and exploitation of the resources of the continental shelf may, if they so request, remain subject to the social security regime for seamen and continue to benefit from the provisions of the Maritime Labour Code as regards sickness and injury as well as repatriation; in this case the employer shall assume, with respect to them, the obligations of the shipowner.

Chapter II. Provisions relating to Safety Measures.

Article 10

The installations and devices defined in Article 3 (i) above shall be subject to the laws and regulations concerning the safety of life at sea.

In addition, where they are capable of floating, they shall be subject to the laws and regulations concerning registration and seaworthiness, as well as the regulations concerning the prevention of collisions of sea, during the time when they are afloat.

In the application of these laws and regulations, the person on these installations and devices in charge of the work of exploration or exploitation shall be considered to be the captain for the purpose of these laws and regulations. In all cases he shall be subject to the jurisdiction of the common law.

Article 11

The owner or operator of an installation or device defined in Article 3 (i) above resting on the seabed, or the person on board assuming command of the work of exploration, shall be responsible, to the extent he is concerned, for the installation and functioning of a system of maritime signalling and for seeing that it is kept in good working order. In all cases the expenses of signalling shall be borne by the owner or operator. These provisions shall apply, if necessary, to signalling in the safety zones established by Article 4.

Where the persons referred to in the preceeding paragraph fail to comply with the directions given to them by the competent authorities in pursuance of this Article and without prejudice to the institution of legal proceedings, the said authorities may, after an injunction has proved ineffective, take, <u>propio motu</u> and at the expense of the owner or operator, the necessary measures.

In order to ensure that these persons comply with the obligations imposed on them by this Article, the competent authorities shall have access to the installations and devices, as well as to the signalling apparatus.

Article 12

Nautical information concerning exploration or exploitation activities on the continental shelf should be given to the competent authorities.

This obligation, according to the circumstances, shall rest on the owner or operator of an installation or device defined in Article 3 above or the person on board in charge of the work.

Article 13

Articles 70-74 of the Maritime Ports Code shall apply to the system of signalling on the installations or devices defined in Article 3 (i) of this Law as well as to that of the safety zones established by Article 4 of this Law.

For the purpose of Articles 70-72 of the Maritime Ports Code, the person on the installation or device in charge of the work of exploration or exploitation shall be considered as the captain or master. In all cases common law jurisdiction shall be applicable.

Article 14

The owner or operator is under an obligation to remove entirely installations or devices which are no longer in use. If circumstances so demand, they may be compelled to respect this obligation and they must begin and complete the work within the time provided.

If they refuse or neglect to carry out this work, it may be carried out as of right and at their expense and risk.

In this case the owner or operator may forfeit their rights over the installations or devices.

Chapter III. Customs and Tax Provisions.

Article 15

In customs matters, products coming from the continental shelf shall be regarded as coming from a new part of the customs territory laid down in Article 1 of the Customs Code.

For the application of fiscal legislation, these products should be regarded as coming from the territory of metropolitan France.

Article 16

Industrial materials, as well as the products necessary for their functioning and upkeep, which are used on the continental shelf for the exploration or exploitation of hydrocarbons and other mineral and organic substances of which a list is to be fixed by Decree, shall be exempt from import duties.

Article 17

Customs officials may examine installations and devices at any time. They may also carry out examinations on the means of transport used for the exploration of the continental shelf or the exploitation of its natural resources, inside the safety zones established by Article 4 above and in the maritime customs zone.

Article 18

The installations and devices which are being used at the place of the exploration or exploitation of the continental shelf on the date of entry into force of this Law, as well as the materials and other goods which are on these installations and devices on that date, shall be deemed to have been imported on that date.

Article 19

The taxes referred to in Part II of Book I of the General Tax Code and levied on behalf of local authorities and various other bodies, shall not be applicable to the continental shelf, except for the indirect taxation provided for in Chapter II of Section III.

Chapter IV. Provisions relating to Royalties.

Article 20

Holders of licenses for liquid hydrocarbons or gas on the continental shelf shall be liable to pay the annual royalty provided for in Article 31 of the Mining Code.

Article 21

Holders of licenses for the exploitation of liquid hydrocarbons or gas, as well as the holders of licenses and permits for the exploitation of all other mineral substances coming under the mining regulations by virtue of Article 6 above, shall be liable to pay a fixed royalty per metric ton, whose rate shall be determined taking into account the value of the substance in question.

A finance Law shall determine, before January 1, 1970, the conditions under which the proceeds of this royalty shall be divided between the State and local authorities.

Article 22

The exploitation of vegetable or animal resources which entails placing fishing equipment or equipment for marine cultivation on the continental shelf, shall be subject to the payment of an annual royalty to the State.

Article 23

The rate of the royalties laid down by this Chapter, as well as the basis of the royalty laid down by the preceding Article, shall be fixed by Finance Laws.

Chapter V. Penal Provisions.

Article 24

Anyone who undertakes on the continental shelf an activity with the object of its exploration or of exploiting its natural resources without the permit provided for in Article 2 above or without observing the conditions laid down in that permit, shall be punished with imprisonment of between 11 days and three months and a fine of between 1,000 and 5,000 francs or only one of these two penalties. In cases of repetition of the offense, the fine shall range from 2,000 francs to 10,000 francs and in addition, a sentence of imprisonment not exceeding five years may also be imposed.

In addition the court may order, if circumstances so demand, either the removal of the installations and devices placed in position for exploration or exploitation without the permit referred to in the preceeding paragraph, or that they be brought into conformity with the conditions laid down in that permit. The court may grant the defendant a period in which to remove the installations or devices or to bring them into conformity.

The penalties provided for in the first paragraph shall apply likewise to cases of failure to remove installations or to alter them within the prescribed period referred to in the second paragraph.

If after the expiry of the period fixed by the court, the installations and devices have not been removed or brought into conformity, the administrative authority designated by a decree of the Conseil d'Etat may proceed with the necessary measures to carry out the judicial decision, proprio motu and with the costs and risks to be borne by the defendant.

Article 25

Unless they have already been covered and dealt with under Article 24 above, and provided that they have been committed on the continental shelf, breaches of the provisions of the Mining Code referred to in Articles 141 and 142 of that Code shall be punished in accordance with the penalties laid down by these Articles. However, fines shall be between 1,000 and 5,000 francs in the case of offenses set out in Article 141 and between 1,000 and 2,500 francs in the case of offenses set out in Article 142. In cases of repetition of the offense, these amounts shall be doubled.

Article 26

Where an offense referred to in Article 24 of this Law has been the subject of a report, cessation of the work of exploration or exploitation may be ordered until the final decision of the judicial authority, either on the demand of the Public Prosecutor acting at the request of the administrative authority designated in accordance with Article 24, or proprio motu, by the examining magistrate seized of the case or the court of summary jurisdiction.

The judicial authority shall decide after having heard

the owner or operator or after having duly summoned him to appear within 48 hours.

The judicial decision is immediately enforceable notwithstanding any right of appeal.

From the moment a report referred to in the first paragraph of this Article has been drawn up, the administrative authority may likewise order the cessation of the work by a reasoned decision, if the judicial authority has not yet given its decision. A copy of this decision shall be transmitted without delay to the Public Prosecutor.

The administrative authority shall take all measures of coercion necessary to ensure that its decision is immediately complied with.

The judicial authority may at any moment, acting *proprio motu* or at the request of either the administrative authority or the owner or the operator, decide that the measures taken to ensure discontinuance of the work should cease or should be continued. In any case the decision of the administrative authority shall cease to have effect where a case has been dismissed.

The administrative authority shall be informed of the judicial decision and shall, if necessary, ensure its execution.

Where proceedings have not been instituted, the Public Prosecutor shall inform the administrative authority thereof, which, either *proprio motu* or at the request of the owner or operator, shall discontinue the measures which it had taken.

Article 27

Continuing to explore or exploit, notwithstanding a judicial or administrative decision ordering the cessation of such operations, shall be punishable with imprisonment of between 11 days and three months and a fine of between 1,000 and 5,000 francs or only one of these two penalties.

Article 28

Without prejudice to the application of the laws and regulations concerning the prevention of pollution of the sea by oil to the installations and devices referred to in Article 3 (ii) of this Law, it shall be an offense, punishable with a fine of between 2,000 and 20,000 francs and, in cases of repetition, with imprisonment of between six days and six months and with a fine of between 5,000 and 50,000 francs or only one of these two penalties, to discharge or allow to escape into the sea from an installation or device referred to in Article 3 (i) while exploring or exploiting the natural resources of the continental shelf, any of the substances listed in Article 3 (i) of the International Convention for the Prevention of Pollution of the Sea by Oil, signed at London, May 12, 1954, as defined by Article 1 (i) of the Convention.

The owner or operator of the installations or devices referred to in Article 3 of this Law or the person on board these installations and devices assuming command of the work of exploration or exploitation shall be punished with imprisonment of between 10 days and six months and a fine of between 5,000 and 50,000 francs when the offense has been committed on his express orders.

Any owner or operator of these installations or devices who has not given the person on board these installations and devices assuming command of the work of exploration or exploitation express orders to comply with the provisions, failure to observe which is punishable under paragraph 1 of this Article, shall be considered to be an accessory to an offense under that paragraph.

It shall not be an offense under paragraph 1 of this Article when:

(a) the discharge occurs in order to ensure the safety of the installation or device referred to in Article 3 (i) of this Law or to avoid serious damage being done to them or to save life at sea;

(b) the escape results from unforeseeable and inevitable damage or leaks, provided that all the necessary measures have been taken after the damage occured or after the leak was discovered to prevent, stop or reduce the escape.

Articles 5, 6 and 7 of Law No. 64-1331 of December 26, 1964 for the Prevention of Pollution of the Sea by Oil shall apply to breaches of this Article.

Article 29

The owner or operator who has failed or neglected to comply with the provisions of paragraph 1 of Article 14 above, after having received notice of his obligation under that paragraph, shall be punished by imprisonment between 11 days and three months and a fine between 1,000 and 5,000 francs or only one of these two penalties.

Article 30

Any breach of the provisions of paragraph 1 of Article 11 above shall be punished by the penalties provided for in Articles 80 and 81 of the Disciplinary and Penal Code of the Merchant Marine.

Article 31

Any breach of the provisions of Article 12 above shall be punished by the penalties laid down in Articles 5 and 6 (iii) of Law No. 67-405 of May 20, 1967 on the Safety of Life at Sea and Habitability on Board Ships.

Article 32

Except in the case of force majeure, anyone who unlawfully enters a safety zone as defined in Article 4 above or who unlawfully flies over such a safety zone, after the competent authorities have taken the appropriate measures to inform the navigator of the position of this zone, shall be punished with imprisonment between 11 days and three months and with a fine of between 1,000 and 5,000 francs or only one of these two penalties. In cases of repetition of the offense, the fine may be doubled and in addition a sentence of imprisonment not exceeding two years may also be imposed.

Article 33

The following are competent to examine breaches of Articles 13, 24, 27, 29, 30, 31 and 32 of this Law: -

Officers and members of the police;
Administrators of Maritime Affairs;
Mining Engineers or engineers under their orders;
Government Civil Engineers in Maritime Service;
Officers and Petty Officers commanding State Ships;
Commanders of State Aircraft;
Customs Officers;
Members of the Marine Police and Fishery Protection Service.

The reports setting out these breaches shall be transmitted to the Public Prosecutor.

Chapter VII. Miscellaneous Provisions

Article 34

The National Centre for the Exploitation of the Oceans (C.N.E.X.O.) shall have access to documents and information of a geological, hydrological or mining nature and which are referred to in Article 132 of the Mining Code; in addition it may ask for any documents or information of a biological nature.

The employees of C.N.E.X.O who have access to these documents or this information shall be compelled to observe professional secrecy under conditions which shall be laid down by Decree.

Article 35

The installations and devices defined in Article 3 above and the safety zones established by Article 4 shall be subject to the criminal legislation and criminal procedure in force at the seat of the tribunal de grande instance or tribunal de première instance under whose jurisdiction they fall.

Article 36

The conditions for the adaptation of this Law to operations being carried out on the continental shelf adjacent to Overseas Territories shall be fixed by Decree of the Conseil d'Etat.

Article 37

The holders of licenses for research on the continental shelf which were obtained before this Law came into force shall continue to benefit from the provisions in the Decrees granting those licenses.

They shall bring the installations and devices, as well as the rules governing their operation, into conformity with the provisions of this Law within a period of one year from the date of its promulgation.

Article 38

The way in which this Law shall be applied, particularly as regards Articles 2, 5, 8, 11, 12, 14 and 35, shall be fixed by Decree of the Conseil d'Etat.

MALAYSIA

(*a*) CONTINENTAL SHELF ACT, 1966 (ACT OF PARLIAMENT NO. 57 OF 1966, 28 JULY 1966)

...

Interpretation

2. In this Act, unless the context otherwise requires—

"continental shelf"means the sea-bed and subsoil of those submarine areas adjacent to the coast of the States of Malaya but beyond the limits of the territorial waters adjacent to those States, the surface of which lies at a depth no greater than 200 metres below the surface of the sea, or, where depth of the superadjacent waters admits of the exploitation of the natural resources of the said areas, at any greater depth:

Provided that in the case of the west coast of the States of Malaya the extent of the continental shelf shall be determined in accordance with Article 6 of the Geneva Convention on the Continental Shelf (1958) set out in the Schedule to this Act;

"Minister" means the Minister charged with the responsibility for lands and mines;

"natural resources" means—

(*a*) the mineral and other natural non-living resources of the sea-bed and subsoil; and

(*b*) living organisms belonging to sedentary species, that is to say, organisms which, at the harvestable stage, either are immobile on or under the sea-bed or are unable to move except in constant physical contact with the sea-bed or the subsoil;

"petroleum" includes any mineral oil or relative hydrocarbon and natural gas existing in its natural condition in strata, but does not include coal or bituminous shales or other stratified deposits from which oils can be extracted by destructive distillation.

Rights with respect to continental shelf

3. All rights with respect to the continental shelf and its natural resources for the purpose of exploring the shelf and exploiting those resources are hereby vested in the Federation and exercisable by the Government of the Federation.

Exploration, prospecting and mining for petroleum and other minerals on continental shelf

4. (1) No person shall explore, prospect or bore for or carry on any operations for the getting of petroleum in the sea-bed or subsoil of the continental shelf except in pursuance of a licence issued, or by virtue of a petroleum agreement entered into, under the provisions of the Petroleum Mining Act, 1966;[1] and the provisions of this Act shall apply in all respects to the exploration, prospecting and mining for petroleum in the sea-bed or subsoil of the continental shelf.

(2) For the purpose of the following subsections, the expression "minerals" shall be construed as to mean minerals other than petroleum.

(3) No person shall explore, prospect or bore for or carry on any operations for the getting of minerals in the sea-bed or subsoil of the continental shelf except in pursuance of a licence issued under the provisions of the following subsections.

...

(6) The grant of a licence under subsection (4) shall in every case be in the absolute discretion of the Minister and any number of such licences may be granted to the same person; and every licence may be so granted as to be enjoyed by the licensee thereof in common with other licensees to whom licences under subsection (4) may have been granted or may hereafter be granted.

(7) Any person who explores, prospects, bores or mines for, or carries on operations for the recovery of any minerals in the sea-bed or subsoil of the continental shelf otherwise than pursuant to a licence under subsection (4) and in accordance with the conditions of the licence (not being a condition relating to the payment of royalties to the Government of the Federation) commits an offence, and shall on conviction be liable to a term of imprisonment not exceeding two years or to a fine not exceeding twenty thousand dollars or to both such imprisonment and fine; and all machinery, tools, plant, buildings and other property together with any minerals or other products which may be found upon or proved to have been obtained from the area of the continental shelf so unlawfully explored, prospected or mined shall be liable to forfeiture.

Application of criminal and civil law

5. (1) Subject to the provisions of this Act, for the purposes of this Act and of every other written law (whether passed before or after the passing of this Act) for the time being in force in the Federation—

(*a*) every act or omission which takes place on or under or above, or any waters within five hundred metres of, any installation or device (whether temporary or permanent) constructed, erected, placed, or used in, on, or above the continental

---

[1] No. 58 of 1966. See *infra*. (*b*).

shelf in connection with the exploration of the continental shelf or the exploitation of its natural resources shall be deemed to take place in the Federation; and

(*b*) every such installation or device or any waters within five hundred metres of such installation or device shall be deemed to be situated in the Federation, and for the purposes of jurisdiction shall be deemed to be situated in that part of the Federation above high-water mark at ordinary spring tides which is nearest to that installation or device; and

(*c*) every Court in the Federation which would have jurisdiction (whether civil or criminal) in respect of that act or omission if it had taken place in the Federation shall have jurisdiction accordingly; and

(*d*) every power of arrest or of entry or search or seizure or other power that could be exercised under any written law (whether passed before or after the passing of this Act) in respect of any such act or omission or suspected act or omission if it had taken place or was suspected to have taken place in the Federation may be exercised on or in respect of any such installation or device or any waters within five hundred metres thereof as if the installation or device or such waters were in the Federation; and

(*e*) without limiting the provisions of the Customs Ordinance, 1952,[1] every installation or device, and any materials or parts used in the construction of an installation or device, which are brought into the waters above the continental shelf from parts beyond the seas shall be deemed to have been imported into the Federation at the time when the installation or device is constructed, erected, or placed in, on, or above the continental shelf in connection with the exploration of the continental shelf or the exploitation of its natural resources.

...

Power to make regulations

6. (1) The Yang di-Pertuan Agong may from time to time make regulations for all or any of the following purposes—

(*a*) regulating the construction, erection, or use of installations or devices in, on, or above the continental shelf, or any specified part thereof, in connection with the exploration of the shelf or that part thereof or the exploitation of its natural resources;

(*b*) prohibiting the construction, erection, placing, or use of installations or devices in, on, or above the continental shelf in places where they could cause interference with the use of recognised sea lanes essential to coastwise or international navigation;

(*c*) establishing safety zones, extending to a distance not exceeding five hundred metres measured from each point of the outer edge of the installation or device, around any such installations or devices in, on, or above the continental shelf;

(*d*) prescribing such measures as he considers necessary in any such safety zone for the protection of the installation or device with respect to which the safety zone is established;

(*e*) regulating or prohibiting the entry of ships into any such safety zone;

(*f*) prescribing measures to be taken in any such safety zone for the protection

[1] No. 42 of 1952.

of the living resources of the sea and the natural resources of the continental shelf from harmful agents;

(*g*) prescribing the notice to be given of the construction, erection, or placing of installations or devices in, on, or above the continental shelf;

(*h*) prescribing the permanent means to be installed for the purpose of giving warning to shipping and aircraft of the presence of installations or devices in, on, or above the continental shelf;

(*i*) providing for the removal of installations or devices constructed, erected, or placed in, on or above the continental shelf which have been abandoned or become disused;

(*j*) prohibiting or restricting any exploration of the continental shelf or any specified part thereof or any exploitation of its natural resources which in the opinion of the Yang di-Pertuan Agong could result in an unjustifiable interference with navigation, fishing, or the conservation of the living resources of the sea, or could interfere with national defence or with oceanographic or other scientific research or with submarine cables or pipelines;

(*k*) providing for such matters as are necessary for giving full effect to the provisions of this Act and for the due administration thereof;

(*l*) prescribing penalties for breaches of the regulations, not exceeding five thousand dollars.

(2) In this section the term "continental shelf" includes the sea-bed and subsoil of the submarine areas within the limits of the territorial waters adjacent to the States of Malaya:

Provided that nothing in this section shall affect the rights and powers of the State Authority under the National Land Code[1] or any other written law in respect of areas within the limits of the territorial waters of the State.

(*b*) PETROLEUM MINING ACT, 1966 (ACT OF PARLIAMENT NO. 58 OF 1966)

...

2. *Interpretation*

"continental shelf" has the meaning ascribed to it under section 2 of the Continental Shelf Act, 1966;[2]

...

"land" means any area of on-shore land within the States of Malaya and includes off-shore land adjacent to and contiguous with such on-shore land;

...

"off-shore land" means the area of the continental shelf;

"on-shore land" includes the foreshores and submarine areas beneath the territorial waters of the States of Malaya;

...

"petroleum" includes any mineral oil or relative hydrocarbon and natural gas existing in its natural condition in strata but does not include coal or bitu-

[1] No. 56 of 1965.

[2] No. 57 of 1966: *supra* under (*a*).

minous shales or other stratified deposits from which oil can be extracted by destructive distillation;

...

Restriction on petroleum exploring, prospecting or mining

3. (1) No person shall explore, prospect or mine for petroleum or do any act with a view to such exploring, prospecting or mining upon any land except by virtue of an exploration licence or a petroleum agreement issued or entered into under the provisions of this Act.

(2) Any person who acts in contravention of this section or of any of the conditions of the said exploration licence or a petroleum agreement which has been issued or entered into by him shall be guilty of an offence and shall on conviction be liable to a term of imprisonment not exceeding two years, or to a fine not exceeding twenty thousand dollars, or to both such imprisonment and fine; and all machinery, tools, plant, buildings and other property together with any minerals or other products which may be found upon or proved to have been obtained from the land so unlawfully explored, prospected or mined shall be liable to forfeiture.

Continental Shelf Act 1964

CHAPTER 29

An Act to make provision as to the exploration and exploitation of the continental shelf; to enable effect to be given to certain provisions of the Convention on the High Seas done in Geneva on 29th April 1958; and for matters connected with those purposes.

[15th April 1964]

BE IT ENACTED by the Queen's most Excellent Majesty, by and with the advice and consent of the Lords Spiritual and Temporal, and Commons, in this present Parliament assembled, and by the authority of the same, as follows:—

Exploration and exploitation of continental shelf.

1.—(1) Any rights exercisable by the United Kingdom outside territorial waters with respect to the sea bed and subsoil and their natural resources, except so far as they are exercisable in relation to coal, are hereby vested in Her Majesty.

(2) In relation to any coal with respect to which those rights are exercisable the Coal Industry Nationalisation Act 1946 shall apply as it applies in relation to coal in Great Britain, but with the modification that the National Coal Board shall not engage in any operations for the purpose of working or getting the coal without the consent of the Minister of Power, which may be given on such terms and subject to such conditions as he thinks fit.

(3) In relation to any petroleum with respect to which those rights are exercisable sections 2 and 6 of the Petroleum (Production) Act 1934 (which relate to the granting of licences to search and bore for, and get, petroleum) shall apply as they apply in relation to petroleum in Great Britain, and section 3 of that Act (which enables persons holding licences under that Act to acquire

ancillary rights) and section 5 of that Act (which makes provision as to receipts and expenditure under that Act) shall have effect as if this subsection were part of that Act.

(4) Model clauses prescribed under section 6 of the Petroleum (Production) Act 1934 as applied by the preceding subsection shall include provision for the safety, health and welfare of persons employed on operations undertaken under the authority of any licence granted under that Act as so applied.

(5) The Minister of Power shall for each financial year prepare and lay before Parliament a report stating—

(*a*) the licences under the said Act of 1934 granted in that year in respect of areas beyond low-water mark and the persons to whom and the areas in respect of which they were granted, and the like information as respects such licences held at the end of that year;

(*b*) the total amount of natural gas and of other petroleum gotten in that year in pursuance of licences held in respect of such areas; and

(*c*) the method used for arriving at the amounts payable by way of consideration for such licences.

(6) The general duty of the Minister of Power of securing the effective and co-ordinated development of such resources in Great Britain as are mentioned in section 1(1) of the Ministry of Fuel and Power Act 1945 shall extend to any such resources outside Great Britain with respect to which the said rights are exercisable.

(7) Her Majesty may from time to time by Order in Council designate any area as an area within which the rights mentioned in subsection (1) of this section are exercisable, and any area so designated is in this Act referred to as a designated area.

(8) In this section " coal " has the same meaning as in the Coal Industry Nationalisation Act 1946 and " petroleum " has the same meaning as in the Petroleum (Production) Act 1934.

Protection of installations in designated areas.

2.—(1) The Minister of Power may for the purpose of protecting any installation in a designated area by order made by statutory instrument prohibit ships, subject to any exceptions provided by the order, from entering without his consent such part of that area as may be specified in the order.

(2) If any ship enters any part of a designated area in contravention of an order under this section its owner or master shall be liable—

(*a*) on summary conviction, to a fine not exceeding one hundred pounds or to imprisonment for a term not exceeding three months, or to both;

(*b*) on conviction on indictment, to a fine, or to imprisonment for a term not exceeding one year, or to both;

unless he proves that the prohibition imposed by the order was not, and would not on reasonable inquiry have become, known to the master.

(3) Any order under this section may be varied or revoked by a subsequent order, and any statutory instrument containing such an order shall be subject to annulment in pursuance of a resolution of either House of Parliament.

Application of criminal and civil law.

3.—(1) Any act or omission which—

(*a*) takes place on, under or above an installation in a designated area or any waters within five hundred metres of such an installation; and

(*b*) would, if taking place in any part of the United Kingdom, constitute an offence under the law in force in that part,

shall be treated for the purposes of that law as taking place in that part.

(2) Her Majesty may by Order in Council make provision for the determination, in accordance with the law in force in such part of the United Kingdom as may be specified in the Order, of questions arising out of acts or omissions taking place in a designated area, or in any part of such an area, in connection with the exploration of the sea bed or subsoil or the exploitation of their natural resources, and for conferring jurisdiction with respect to such questions on courts in any part of the United Kingdom so specified.

(3) Any jurisdiction conferred on any court under this section shall be without prejudice to any jurisdiction exercisable apart from this section by that or any other court.

(4) Any Order in Council under this section may be varied or revoked by a subsequent Order in Council and any statutory instrument containing such an Order shall be subject to annulment in pursuance of a resolution of either House of Parliament.

Safety of navigation.

4.—(1) Part II of the Coast Protection Act 1949 (which requires the consent of the Minister of Transport to the carrying out of certain works on the sea shore if obstruction or danger to navigation is likely to result) except section 34(1)(*b*) (which restricts the deposit of materials) shall apply in relation to any part of the sea bed in a designated area as it applies in relation to the sea shore; and section 46 of that Act (local inquiries) shall extend to any matter arising under this section.

(2) Any person guilty of an offence under the said Part II as applied by this section shall be liable, on summary conviction to a fine not exceeding one hundred pounds, and on conviction on indictment to a fine.

Discharge of oil.

5.—(1) If any oil to which section 1 of the Oil in Navigable Waters Act 1955 applies or any mixture containing not less than one hundred parts of such oil in a million parts of the mixture is discharged or escapes into any part of the sea—

(*a*) from a pipe-line; or

(*b*) (otherwise than from a ship) as the result of any operations for the exploration of the sea bed and subsoil or the exploitation of their natural resources in a designated area,

the owner of the pipe-line or, as the case may be, the person carrying on the operations shall be guilty of an offence unless he proves, in the case of a discharge from a place in his occupation, that it was due to the act of a person who was there without his permission (express or implied) or, in the case of an escape, that he took all reasonable care to prevent it and that as soon as practicable after it was discovered all reasonable steps were taken for stopping or reducing it.

(2) A person guilty of an offence under this section shall be liable, on summary conviction to a fine not exceeding one thousand pounds, and on conviction on indictment to a fine.

Wireless telegraphy.

6. An Order in Council under section 3 of this Act may make provision for treating for the purposes of the Wireless Telegraphy Act 1949 and any regulations made thereunder any installation in an area or part with respect to which provision is made under that section and any waters within five hundred metres of such an installation as if they were situated in such part of the United Kingdom as may be specified in the Order.

Radioactive substances.

7. An Order in Council under section 3 of this Act may make provision for treating for the purposes of the Radioactive Substances Act 1960 and any orders and regulations made thereunder any installation in an area or part with respect to which provision is made under that section and any waters within five hundred metres of such an installation as if they were situated in such part of the United Kingdom as may be specified in the Order, and for modifying the provisions of that Act in their application to such an installation or waters.

Submarine cables and pipe-lines.

8.—(1) Section 3 (punishment for damaging cables) of the Submarine Telegraph Act 1885 and Article IV and paragraph 1 of Article VII (liability to pay compensation for damage to cables and for loss of gear sacrificed to avoid such damage) of the Convention set out in the Schedule to that Act (which by virtue of section 2 thereof has the force of law) shall apply in relation to all submarine cables under the high seas (and not only to those to which that Convention applies) and to pipe-lines under the high seas; and the said section 3 shall be construed as referring to telephonic as well as telegraphic communication, and, in relation to high-voltage power cables and to pipe-lines, as if the words from " in such manner " to the end of subsection (1) were omitted.

(2) Sections 6(3) (limitation of proceedings) and 13 (cesser of Act on cesser of Convention) of that Act are hereby repealed.

Use and supply of natural gas.

9.—(1) The following provisions of this section shall have effect with respect to the use and supply of any natural gas gotten in pursuance of a licence under the Petroleum (Production) Act 1934 as applied by section 1(3) of this Act, and section 52 of the Gas Act 1948 shall not apply to any such gas.

(2) The holder of the licence shall not without the consent of the Minister of Power use the gas in Great Britain and no person shall without that consent supply the gas to any other person at premises in Great Britain.

(3) The Minister of Power shall not give his consent under this section to the supply of gas at any premises unless satisfied—

(*a*) that the supply is for industrial purposes and that the Area Board in whose area the premises are situated has been given an opportunity of purchasing the gas at a reasonable price; or

(*b*) that the supply is for such purposes as are mentioned in subsection (4) of this section;

but shall give his consent under this section to the supply or use of any gas if satisfied that it is for the purposes mentioned in that subsection.

(4) The said purposes are industrial purposes which do not consist of or include the use of the gas as a fuel except in so far as the gas is used to provide heat or other energy required—

(*a*) for a process in which the gas is used otherwise than as a fuel; or

(*b*) where such a process is one of a series, for any further process in the same series, not being a process in which a bulk product is converted into manufactured articles;

and in determining whether any industrial purposes are as mentioned in this subsection the use of any gas derived, otherwise than as a by-product, from any natural gas shall be treated as the use of that natural gas.

(5) For the purposes of this section gas provided by a company for the use of any subsidiary or holding company thereof, or of any subsidiary of such a holding company shall be deemed to be used by that company.

(6) This section shall not affect the supply of gas by any person otherwise than through pipes or the supply of gas by or to an Area Board.

(7) In this section " Area Board " has the same meaning as in the Gas Act 1948 and " holding company " and " subsidiary " have the same meanings as in the Companies Act 1948.

Modification of National Insurance Acts.

10.—(1) The Minister of Pensions and National Insurance may by regulations make provision—

(*a*) for treating as insurable employment for the purposes of the National Insurance (Industrial Injuries) Acts 1946 to 1963 any prescribed employment which is employment in connection with the exploitation of the resources mentioned in section 1(1) of this Act or with the exploration of the sea bed and subsoil in any designated area; and

(*b*) for modifying the provisions of those Acts in their application in relation to persons who are insured persons by virtue of this subsection and in particular, but without prejudice to the generality of this paragraph, for treating accidents arising out of and in the course of any such employment as happening while those persons are in Great Britain and for treating as accidents so arising accidents happening while those persons are proceeding to or from their work or in any other prescribed circumstances.

(2) The Minister of Pensions and National Insurance may by regulations make provision for modifying the provisions of the National Insurance Acts 1946 to 1963 in their application in relation to persons in any prescribed employment (whether under a contract of service or not) in connection with the exploitation or exploration mentioned in subsection (1) of this section, and in particular, but without prejudice to the generality of this subsection, for the insurance under those Acts of persons in such employment notwithstanding that they do not fulfil the conditions of section 1 of the National Insurance Act 1946.

(3) Subsection (1) of this section shall be construed as one with the National Insurance (Industrial Injuries) Act 1946 and subsection (2) of this section as one with the National Insurance Act 1946.

Prosecution of offences, etc.

11.—(1) Proceedings for any offence under this Act (including an offence under another Act as applied by or under this Act and anything that is an offence by virtue of section 3(1) of this Act) may be taken, and the offence may for all incidental purposes be treated as having been committed, in any place in the United Kingdom.

(2) Where a body corporate is guilty of such an offence and the offence is proved to have been committed with the consent or connivance of, or to be attributable to any neglect on the part of, any director, manager, secretary or other similar officer of the

body corporate or any person who was purporting to act in any such capacity he, as well as the body corporate, shall be guilty of the offence and shall be liable to be proceeded against and punished accordingly.

In this subsection, " director " in relation to a body corporate established for the purpose of carrying on under national ownership any industry or part of an industry or undertaking, being a body corporate whose affairs are managed by its members, means a member of that body corporate.

(3) A constable shall on any installation in a designated area have all the powers, protection and privileges which he has in the area for which he acts as constable.

12. Nothing in this Act shall be taken to restrict the powers of the Parliament of Northern Ireland to make laws; and any laws made by that Parliament with respect to any matter with respect to which it has that power shall have effect notwithstanding anything in this Act. **Northern Ireland.**

13. This Act may be cited as the Continental Shelf Act 1964. **Short title.**

Submerged Lands Act

To confirm and establish the titles of the States to lands beneath navigable waters within State boundaries and to the natural resources within such lands and waters, to provide for the use and control of said lands and resources, and to confirm the jurisdiction and control of the United States over the natural resources of the seabed of the Continental Shelf seaward of State boundaries.

Be it enacted by the Senate and House of Representatives of the United States of America in Congress assembled, That this Act may be cited as the "Submerged Lands Act".

TITLE I

DEFINITION

Sec. 2. When used in this Act —

(a) The term "lands beneath navigable waters" means —

(1) all lands within the boundaries of each of the respective States which are covered by nontidal waters that were navigable under the laws of the United States at the time such State became a member of the Union, or acquired sovereignty over such lands and waters thereafter, up to the ordinary high water mark as heretofore or hereafter modified by accretion, erosion, and reliction;

(2) all lands permanently or periodically covered by tidal waters up to but not above the line of mean high tide and seaward to a line three geographical miles distant from the coast line of each such State and to the boundary line of each such State where in any case such boundary as it existed at the time such State became a member of the Union, or as heretofore approved by Congress, extends seaward (or into the Gulf of Mexico) beyond three geographical miles, and

(3) all filled in, made, or reclaimed lands which formerly were lands beneath navigable waters, as hereinabove defined;

(b) The term "boundaries" includes the seaward boundaries of a State or its boundaries in the Gulf of Mexico or any of the Great Lakes as they existed at the time such State became a member of the Union, or as heretofore approved by the Congress, or as extended or confirmed pursuant to section 4 hereof but in no event shall the term "boundaries" or the term "lands beneath navigable waters" be interpreted as extending from the coast line more than three geographical miles into the Atlantic Ocean or the Pacific Ocean, or more than three marine leagues into the Gulf of Mexico;

(c) The term "coast line" means the line of ordinary low water along that portion of the coast which is in direct contact with the open sea and the line marking the seaward limit of inland waters;

(d) The terms "grantees" and "lessees" include (without limiting the generality thereof) all political subdivisions, municipalities, public and private corporations, and other persons holding grants or leases from a State, or from its predecessor sovereign if legally validated, to lands beneath navigable waters if such grants or leases were issued in accordance with the constitution, statutes, and decisions of the courts of the State in which such lands are situated, or of its predecessor sovereign; *Provided, however,* That nothing herein shall be construed as conferring upon said grantees or lessees any greater rights or interests other than are described herein and in their respective grants from the State, or its predecessor sovereign;

(e) The term "natural resources" includes, without limiting the generality thereof, oil, gas, and all other minerals, and fish, shrimp, oysters, clams, crabs, lobsters, sponges, kelp, and other marine animal and plant life but does not include water power, or the use of water for the production of power;

(f) The term "lands beneath navigable waters" does not include the beds of streams in lands now or heretofore constituting a part of the public lands of the United States if such streams were not meandered in connection with the public survey of such lands under the laws of the United States and if the title to the beds of such streams was lawfully patented or conveyed by the United States or any State to any person;

(g) The term "State" means any State of the Union;

(h) The term "person" includes, in addition to a natural person, an association, a State, a political subdivision of a State, or a private, public, or municipal corporation.

TITLE II

LANDS BENEATH NAVIGABLE WATERS WITHIN STATE BOUNDARIES

Sec. 3. Rights of the States. —

(a) It is hereby determined and declared to be in the public interest that (1) title to and ownership of the lands beneath navigable waters within the boundaries of the respective States, and the natural resources within such lands and waters, and (2) the right and power to manage, administer, lease, develop, and use the said lands and natural resources all in accordance with applicable State law be, and they are hereby, subject to the provisions hereof, recognized, confirmed, established, and vested in and assigned to the respective States or the persons who were on June 5, 1950, entitled thereto under the law of the respective States in which the land is located, and the respective grantees, lessees, or successors in interest thereof;

(b)(1) The United States hereby releases and relinquishes unto said States and persons aforesaid, except as otherwise reserved herein, all right, title, and interest of the United States, if any it has, in and to all said lands, improvements, and natural resources; (2) the United States hereby releases and relinquishes all claims of the United States, if any it has, for money or damages arising out of any operations of said States or persons pursuant to State authority upon or within said lands and navigable waters; and (3) the Secretary of the Interior or the Secretary of the Navy or the Treasurer of the United States shall pay to the respective States or their grantees issuing leases covering such lands or natural resources all moneys paid thereunder to the Secretary of the Interior or to the Secretary of the Navy or to the Treasurer of the United States and subject to the control of any of them or to the control of the United States on the effective date of this Act, except that portion of such moneys which (1) is required to be returned to a lessee; or (2) is deductible as provided by stipulation or agreement between the United States and any of said States;

(c) The rights, powers, and titles hereby recognized, confirmed, established, and vested in and assigned to the respective States and their grantees are subject to each lease executed by a State, or its grantee, which was in force and effect on June 5, 1950, in accordance with its terms and provisions and the laws of the State issuing, or whose grantee issued, such lease, and such rights, powers, and titles are further subject to the rights herein now granted to any person holding any such lease to continue to maintain the lease, and to conduct operations thereunder, in accordance with its provisions, for the full term thereof, and any extensions, renewals, or replacements authorized therein, or heretofore authorized by the laws of the State issuing, or whose grantee issued such lease: *Provided, however,* That, if oil or gas was not being produced from such lease on and before December 11, 1950, or if the primary term of such lease has expired since December 11, 1950, then for a term from the effective date hereof equal to the term remaining unexpired on December 11, 1950, under the provisions of such lease or any extensions, renewals, or replacements authorized therein, or heretofore authorized by the laws of the State issuing, or whose grantee issued, such lease: *Provided, however,* That within ninety days from the effective date hereof (i) the lessee shall pay to the State or its grantee issuing such lease all rents, royalties, and other sums payable between June 5, 1950, and the effective date hereof, under such lease and the laws of the State issuing or whose grantee issued such lease, except such rents, royalties, and other sums as have been paid to the State, its grantee, the Secretary of the Interior or the Secretary of the Navy or the Treasurer of the United States and not refunded to the lessee; and (ii) the lessee shall file with the Secretary of the Interior or the Secretary of the Navy and with the State issuing or whose grantee issued such lease, instruments consenting to the payment by the Secretary of the Interior or the Secretary of the Navy or the Treasurer of the United States to the State or its grantee issuing the lease, of all rents, royalties, and other payments under the control of the Secretary of the Interior or the Secretary of the Navy or the Treasurer of the United States or the United States which have been paid, under the lease, except such rentals, royalties, and other payments as have also been paid by the lessee to the State or its grantee;

(d) Nothing in this Act shall affect the use, development, improvement, or control by or under the constitutional authority of the United States of said lands and waters for the purposes of navigation or flood control or the production of power, or be construed as the release or relinquishment of any rights of the United States arising under the constitutional authority of Congress to regulate or improve navigation, or to provide for flood control, or the production of power;

(e) Nothing in this Act shall be construed as affecting or intended to affect or in any way interfere with or modify the laws of the States which lie wholly or in part westward of the ninety-eighth meridian, relating to the ownership and control of ground and surface waters; and the control, appropriation, use, and distribution of such waters shall continue to be in accordance with the laws of such States.

Sec. 4. Seaward Boundaries. —

The seaward boundary of each original coastal State is hereby approved and confirmed as a line three geographical miles distant from its coast line or, in the case of the Great Lakes, to the international boundary. Any State admitted subsequent to the formation of the Union which has not already done so may extend its seaward boundaries to a line three geographical miles distant from its coast line, or to the international boundaries of the United States in the Great Lakes or any other body of water traversed by such boundaries. Any claim heretofore or hereafter asserted either by constitutional provision, statute, or otherwise, indicating the intent of a State so to extend its boundaries is hereby approved and confirmed, without prejudice to its claim, if any it has, that its boundaries extend beyond that line. Nothing in this section is to be construed as questioning or in any manner prejudicing the existence of any State's seaward boundary beyond three geographical miles if it was so provided by its constitution or laws prior to or at the time such State became a member of the Union, or if it has been heretofore approved by Congress.

Sec. 5. Exceptions From Operation of Section 3 of This Act. —

There is excepted from the operation of section 3 of this Act —

(a) all tracts or parcels of land together with all accretions thereto, resources therein, or improvements thereon, title to which has been lawfully and expressly acquired by the United States from any State or from any person in whom title had vested under the law of the State or of the United States, and all lands which the United States lawfully holds under the law of the State; all lands expressly retained by or ceded to the United States when the State entered the Union (otherwise than by a general retention or cession of lands underlying the marginal sea); all lands acquired by the United States by eminent domain proceedings, purchase, cession, gift, or otherwise in a proprietary capacity; all lands filled in, built up, or otherwise reclaimed by the United States for its own use; and any rights the United States has in lands presently and actually occupied by the United States under claim of right;

(b) such lands beneath navigable waters held, or any interest in which is held by the United States for the benefit of any tribe, band, or group of Indians or for individual Indians; and

(c) all structures and improvements constructed by the United States in the exercise of its navigational servitude.

Sec. 6. Powers Retained by the United States. —

(a) The United States retains all its navigational servitude and rights in and powers of regulation and control of said lands and navigable waters for the constitutional purposes of commerce, navigation, national defense, and international affairs, all of which shall be paramount to, but shall not be deemed to include, proprietary rights of ownership, or the rights of management, administration, leasing, use, and development of the lands and natural resources which are specifically recognized, confirmed, established, and vested in and assigned to the respective States and others by section 3 of this Act.

(b) In time of war or when necessary for national defense, and the Congress or the President shall so prescribe, the United States shall have the right of first refusal to purchase at the prevailing market price, all or any portion of the said natural resources, or to acquire and use any portion of said lands by proceeding in accordance with due process of law and paying just compensation therefore.

Sec. 7. Nothing in this Act shall be deemed to amend, modify, or repeal the Acts of July 26, 1866 (14 Stat. 251), July 9, 1870 (16 Stat. 217), March 3, 1877 (19 Stat. 377), June 17, 1902 (32 Stat. 388), and December 22, 1944 (58 Stat. 887), and Acts amendatory thereof or supplementary thereto.

Sec. 8. Nothing contained in this Act shall affect such rights, if any, as may have been acquired under any law of the United States by any person in lands subject to this Act and such rights, if any, shall be governed by the law in effect at the time they may have been acquired: *Provided, however,* That nothing contained in this Act is intended or shall be construed as a finding, interpretation, or construction by the Congress that the law under which such rights may be claimed in fact or in law applies to the lands subject to this Act, or authorizes or compels the granting of such rights in such lands, and that the determination of the applicability or effect of such law shall be unaffected by anything contained in this Act.

Sec. 9. Nothing in this Act shall be deemed to affect in any wise the rights of the United States to the natural resources of that portion of the subsoil and seabed of the Continental Shelf lying seaward and outside of the area of lands beneath navigable waters, as defined in section 2 hereof, all of which natural resources appertain to the United States, and the jurisdiction and control of which by the United States is hereby confirmed.

Sec. 10. Executive Order Numbered 10426, dated January 16, 1953, entitled "Setting Aside Submerged Lands of the Continental Shelf as a Naval Petroleum Reserve", is hereby revoked insofar as it applies to any lands beneath navigable waters as defined in section 2 hereof.

Sec. 11. Separability. —

If any provision of this Act, or any section, subsection, sentence, clause, phrase or individual word, or the application thereof to any person or circumstance is held invalid, the validity of the remainder of the Act and of the application of any such provision, section, subsection, sentence, clause, phrase or individual word to other persons and circumstances shall not be affected thereby; without limiting the generality of the foregoing, if subsection 3(a)1, 3(a)2, 3(b)1, 3(b)2, 3(b)3, or 3(c) or any provision of any of those subsections is held invalid, such subsection or provision shall be held separable and the remaining subsections and provisions shall not be affected thereby.

Approved May 22, 1953.

OUTER CONTINENTAL SHELF LANDS ACT

To provide for the jurisdiction of the United States over the submerged lands of the outer Continental Shelf, and to authorize the Secretary of the Interior to lease such lands for certain purposes.

Be it enacted by the Senate and House of Representatives of the United States of America in Congress assembled, That this Act may be cited as the "Outer Continental Shelf Lands Act."

Sec. 2. Definitions. — When used in this Act—

(a) The term "outer Continental Shelf" means all submerged lands lying seaward and outside of the area of lands beneath navigable waters as defined in section 2 of the Submerged Lands Act (Public Law 31, Eighty-third Congress, first session), and of which the subsoil and seabed appertain to the United States and are subject to its jurisdiction and control;

(b) The term "Secretary" means the Secretary of the Interior;

(c) The term "mineral lease" means any form of authorization for the exploration for, or development or removal of deposits of, oil, gas, or other minerals; and

(d) The term "person" includes, in addition to a natural person, an association, a State, a political subdivision of a State, or a private, public, or municipal corporation.

Sec. 3. Jurisdiction Over Outer Continental Shelf. —

(a) It is hereby declared to be the policy of the United States that the subsoil and seabed of the outer Continental Shelf appertain to the United States and are subject to its jurisdiction, control, and power of dispostion as provided in this Act.

(b) This Act shall be construed in such manner that the character as high seas of the waters above the outer Continental Shelf and the right to navigation and fishing therein shall not be affected.

Sec. 4. Laws Applicable to Outer Continental Shelf. —

(a)(1) The Constitution and laws and civil and political jurisdiction of the United States are hereby extended to the subsoil and seabed of the outer Continental Shelf and to all artificial islands and fixed structures which may be erected thereon for the purpose of exploring for, developing, removing, and transporting resources therefrom, to the same extent as if the outer Continental Shelf were an area of exclusive Federal jurisdiction located within a State; *Provided, however,* That mineral leases on the outer Continental Shelf shall be maintained or issued only under the provisions of this Act.

(2) To the extent that they are applicable and not inconsistent with this Act or with other Federal laws and regulations of the Secretary now in effect or hereafter adopted, the civil and criminal laws of each adjacent State as of the effective date of this Act are hereby declared to be the law of the United States for that portion of the subsoil and seabed of the outer Continental Shelf, and artificial islands and fixed structures erected thereon, which would be within the area of the State if its boundaries were extended seaward to the outer margin of the outer Continental Shelf, and the President shall determine and publish in the Federal Register such projected lines extending seaward and defining each such area. All of such applicable laws shall be administered and enforced by the appropriate officers and courts of the United States. State taxation laws shall not apply to the outer Continental Shelf.

(3) The provisions of this section for adoption of State law as the law of the United States shall never be interpreted as a basis for claiming any interest in or jurisdiction on behalf of any State for any purpose over the seabed and subsoil of the outer Continental Shelf, or the property and natural resources thereof or the revenues therefrom.

(b) The United States district courts shall have original jurisdiction of cases and controversies arising out of or in connection with any operations conducted on the outer Continental Shelf for the purpose of exploring for, developing, removing or transporting by pipeline the natural resources, or involving rights to the natural resources of the subsoil and seabed of the outer Continental Shelf, and proceedings with respect to any such case or controversy may be instituted in the judicial district in which any defendant resides or may be found, or in the judicial district of the adjacent State nearest the place where the cause of action arose.

(c) With respect to disability or death of an employee resulting from any injury occurring as the result of operations described in subsection (b), compensation shall be payable under the provisions of the Longshoremen's and Harbor Workers' Compensation Act. For the purposes of the extension of the provisions of the Longshoremen's and Harbor Workers' Compensation Act under this section —

(1) the term "employee" does not include a master or member of a crew of any vessel, or an officer or employee of the United States or any agency thereof or of any State or foreign government, or of any political subdivision thereof;

(2) the term "employer" means an employer any of whose employees are employed in such operations; and

(3) the term "United States" when used in a geographical sense includes the outer Continental Shelf and artificial islands and fixed structures thereon.

(d) For the purposes of the National Labor Relations Act, as amended, any unfair labor practice, as defined in such Act, occurring upon any artificial island or fixed structure referred to in subsection (a) shall be deemed to have occurred within the judicial district of the adjacent State nearest the place of location of such island or structure.

(e)(1) The head of the Department in which the Coast Guard is operating shall have authority to promulgate and enforce such reasonable regulations with respect to lights and other warning devices, safety equipment, and other matters relating to the promotion of safety of life and property on the islands and structures referred to in subsection (a) or on the waters adjacent thereto, as he may deem necessary.

(2) The head of the Department in which the Coast Guard is operating may mark for the protection of navigation any such island or structure whenever the owner has failed suitably to mark the same in accordance with regulations issued hereunder, and the owner shall pay the cost thereof. Any person, firm, company, or corporation who shall fail or refuse to obey any of the lawful rules and regulations issued hereunder shall be guilty of a misdemeanor and shall be fined not more than $100 for each offense. Each day during which such violation shall continue shall be considered a new offense.

(f) The authority of the Secretary of the Army to prevent obstruction to navigation in the navigable waters of the United States is hereby extended to artificial islands and fixed structures located on the outer Continental Shelf.

(g) The specific application by this section of certain provisions of law to the subsoil and seabed of the outer Continental Shelf and the artificial islands and fixed structures referred to in subsection (a) or to acts or offenses occurring or committed thereon shall not give rise to any inference that the application to such islands and structures, acts, or offenses of any other provision of law is not intended.

Sec. 5. Administration of Leasing of the Outer Continental Shelf. —

(a)(1) The Secretary shall administer the provisions of this Act relating to the leasing of the outer Continental Shelf, and shall prescribe such rules and regulations as may be necessary to carry out such provisions. The Secretary may at any time prescribe and amend such rules and regulations as he determines to be necessary and proper in order to provide for the prevention of waste and conservation of the natural resources of the outer Continental Shelf, and the protection of correlative rights therein, and, notwithstanding any other provisions herein, such rules and regulations shall apply to all operations conducted under a lease issued or maintained under the provisions of this Act. In the enforcement of conservation laws, rules, and regulations the Secretary is authorized to cooperate with the conservation agencies of the adjacent States. Without limiting the generality of the foregoing provisions of this section, the rules and regulations prescribed by the Secretary thereunder may provide for the assignment or relinquishment of leases, for the sale of royalty oil and gas accruing or reserved to the United States at not less than market value, and, in the interest of conservation, for unitization, pooling, drilling agreements, suspension of operations or production, reduction of rentals or royalties, compensatory royalty agreements, subsurface storage of oil or gas in any of said submerged lands, and drilling or other easements necessary for operations or production.

(2) Any person who knowingly and willfully violates any rule or regulation prescribed by the Secretary for the prevention of waste, the conservation of the natural resources, or the protection of correlative rights shall be deemed guilty of a misdemeanor and punishable by a fine of not more than $2,000 or by imprisonment for not more than six months, or by both such fine and imprisonment, and each day of violation shall be deemed to be a separate offense. The issuance and continuance in effect of any lease, or of any extension, renewal, or replacement of any lease under the provisions of this Act shall be conditioned upon compliance with the regulations issued under this Act and in force and effect on the date of the issuance of the lease if the lease is issued under the provisions of section 8 hereof, or with the regulations issued under the provisions of section 6(b), clause (2), hereof if the lease is maintained under the provisions of section 6 hereof.

(b)(1) Whenever the owner of a nonproducing lease fails to comply with any of the provisions of this Act, or of the lease, or of the regulations issued under this Act and in force and effect on the date of the issuance of the lease if the lease is issued under the provisions of section 8 hereof, or of the regulations issued under the provisions of section 6(b), clause (2), hereof, if the lease is maintained under the provisions of section 6 hereof, such lease may be cancelled by the Secretary, subject to the right of judicial review as provided in section 8 (j), if such default continues for the period of thirty days after mailing of notice by registered letter to the lease owner at his record post office address.

(2) Whenever the owner of any producing lease fails to comply with any of the provisions of this Act, or of the lease, or of the regulations issued under this Act and in force and effect on the date of the issuance of the lease if the lease is issued under the provisions of section 8 hereof, or of the regulations issued under the provisions of section 6(b), clause (2), hereof, if the lease is maintained under the provisions of section 6 hereof, such lease may be forfeited and cancelled by an appropriate proceeding in any United States district court having jurisdiction under the provisions of section 4(b) of this Act.

(c) Rights-of-way through the submerged lands of the outer Continental Shelf, whether or not such lands are included in a lease maintained or issued pursuant to this Act, may be granted by the Secretary for pipeline purposes for the transportation of oil, natural gas, sulphur, or other mineral under such regulations and upon such conditions as to the application therefor and the survey, location and width thereof as may be prescribed by the Secretary, and upon the express condition that such oil or gas pipelines shall transport or purchase without discrimination, oil or natural gas produced from said submerged lands in the vicinity of the pipeline in such proportionate amounts as the Federal Power Commission, in the case of gas, and the Interstate Commerce Commission, in the case of oil, may, after a full hearing with due notice thereof to the interested parties, determine to be reasonable, taking into account, among other things, conservation and the prevention of waste. Failure to comply with the provisions of this section or the regulations and conditions prescribed thereunder shall be ground for forfeiture of the grant in an appropriate judicial proceeding instituted by the United States in any United States district court having jurisdiction under the provisions of section 4(b) of this Act.

Sec. 6. Maintenance of Leases on Outer Continental Shelf. —

(a) The provisions of this section shall apply to any mineral lease covering submerged lands of the outer Continental Shelf issued by any State (including any extension, renewal, or replacement thereof heretofore granted pursuant to such lease or under the laws of such State) if —

(1) such lease, or a true copy thereof, is filed with the Secretary by the lessee or his duly authorized agent within ninety days from the effective date of this Act, or within such further period or periods as provided in section 7 hereof or as may be fixed from time to time by the Secretary.

(2) such lease, was issued prior to December 21, 1948, and would have been on June 5, 1950, in force and effect in accordance with its terms and provisions and the law of the State issuing it had the State had authority to issue such lease;

(3) there is filed with the Secretary, within the period or periods specified in paragraph (1) of this subsection, (A) a certificate issued by the State official or agency having jurisdiction over such lease stating that it would have been in force and effect as required by the provisions of paragraph (2) of this subsection, or (B) in the absence of such certificate, evidence in the form of affidavits, receipts, cancelled checks, or other documents that may be required by the Secretary, sufficient to prove that such lease would have been so in force and effect;

(4) except as otherwise provided in section 7 hereof, all rents, royalties, and other sums payable under such lease between June 5, 1950, and the effective date of this Act, which have not been paid in accordance with the provisions thereof, or to the Secretary or to the Secretary of the Navy, are paid to the Secretary within the period or periods specified in paragraph (1) of this subsection, and all rents, royalties, and other sums payable under such lease after the effective date of this Act, are paid to the Secretary, who shall deposit such payments in the Treasury in accordance with section 9 of this Act;

(5) the holder of such lease certifies that such lease shall continue to be subject to the overriding royalty obligations existing on the effective date of this Act.

(6) such lease was not obtained by fraud or misrepresentation;

(7) such lease, if issued on or after June 23, 1947, was issued upon the basis of competitive bidding;

(8) such lease provides for a royalty to the lessor on oil and gas of not less than 12½ per centum and on sulphur of not less than 5 per centum in amount or value of the production saved, removed, or sold from the lease, or, in any case in which the lease provides for a lesser royalty, the holder thereof consents in writing, filed with the Secretary, to the increase of the royalty to the minimum herein specified;

(9) the holder thereof pays to the Secretary within the period or periods specified in paragraph (1) of this subsection an amount equivalent to any severance, gross production, or occupation taxes imposed by the State issuing the lease on the production from the lease, less the State's royalty interest in such production, between June 5, 1950, and the effective date of this Act and not heretofore paid to the State, and thereafter pays to the Secretary as an additional royalty on the production from the lease, less the United States' royalty interest in such production, a sum of money equal to the amount of the severance, gross production, or occupation taxes which would have been payable on such production to the State issuing the lease under its laws as they existed on the effective date of this Act;

(10) such lease will terminate within a period of not more than five years from the effective date of this Act in the absence of production or operations for drilling, or, in any case in which the lease provides for a longer period, the holder thereof consents in writing, filed with the Secretary, to the reduction of such period so that it will not exceed the maximum period herein specified; and

(11) the holder of such lease furnishes such surety bond, if any, as the Secretary may require and complies with such other reasonable requirements as the Secretary may deem necessary to protect the interests of the United States.

(b) Any person holding a mineral lease, which as determined by the Secretary meets the requirements of subsection (a) of this section, may continue to maintain such lease, and may conduct operations thereunder, in accordance with (1) its provisions as to the area, the minerals covered, rentals and, subject to the provisions of paragraphs (8), (9) and (10) of subsection (a) of this section, as to royalties and as to the term thereof and of any extensions, renewals, or replacements authorized therein or heretofore authorized by the laws of the State issuing such lease, or, if oil or gas was not being produced in paying quantities from such lease on or before December 11, 1950, or if production in paying quantities has ceased since June 5, 1950, or if the primary term of such lease has expired since December 11, 1950, then for a term from the effective date hereof equal to the term remaining unexpired on December 11, 1950, under the provisions of such lease or any extensions, renewals, or replacements authorized therein, or heretofore authorized by the laws of such State, and (2) such regulations as the Secretary may under section 5 of this Act prescribe within ninety days after making his determination that such lease meets the requirements of subsection (a) of this section: *Provided, however,* That any rights to sulphur under any lease maintained under the provisions of this subsection shall not extend beyond the primary term of such lease or any extension thereof under the provisions of such subsection (b) unless sulphur is being produced in paying quantities or drilling, well reworking, plant construction, or other operations for the production of sulphur, as approved by the Secretary, are being conducted on the area covered by such lease on the date of expiration of such primary term or extension: *Provided further,* That if sulphur is being produced in paying quantities on such date, then such rights shall continue to be maintained in accordance with such lease and the provisions of this Act: *Provided further,* That, if the primary term of a lease being maintained under subsection (b) hereof has expired prior to the effective date of this Act and oil or gas is being produced in paying quantities on such date, then such rights to sulphur as the lessee may have under such lease shall continue for twenty-four months from the effective date of this Act and as long thereafter as sulphur is produced in paying quantities, or drilling, well working, plant construction, or other operations for the production of sulphur, as approved by the Secretary, are being conducted on the area covered by the lease.

(c) The permission granted in subsection (b) of this section shall not be construed to be a waiver of such claims, if any, as the United States may have against the lessor or the lessee or any other person respecting sums payable or paid for or under the lease, or respecting activities conducted under the lease, prior to the effective date of this Act.

(d) Any person complaining of a negative determination by the Secretary of the Interior under this section may have such determination reviewed by the United States District Court for the District of Columbia by filing a petition for review within sixty days after receiving notice of such action by the Secretary.

(e) In the event any lease maintained under this section covers lands beneath navigable waters, as that term is used in the Submerged Lands Act, as well as lands of the outer Continental Shelf, the provisions of this section shall apply to such lease only insofar as it covers lands of the outer Continental Shelf.

Sec. 7. Controversy Over Jurisdiction. —

In the event of a controversy between the United States and a State as to whether or not lands are subject to the provisions of this Act, the Secretary is authorized, notwithstanding the provisions of subsections (a) and (b) of section 6 of this Act, and with the concurrence of the Attorney General of the United States, to negotiate and enter into agreements with the State, its political subdivision or grantee or a lessee thereof, respecting operations under existing mineral leases and payment and impounding of rents, royalties, and other sums payable thereunder, or with the State, its political subdivision or grantee, respecting the issuance or nonissuance of new mineral leases pending the settlement or adjudication of the controversy. The authorization contained in the preceding sentence of this section shall not be construed to be a limitation upon the authority conferred on the Secretary in other sections of this Act. Payments made pursuant to such agreement, or pursuant to any stipulation between the United States and a State, shall be considered as compliance with section 6(a)(4) hereof. Upon the termination of such agreement or stipulation by reason of the final settlement or adjudication of such controversy, if the lands subject to any mineral lease are determined to be in whole or in part lands subject to the provisions of this Act, the lessee, if he has not already done so, shall comply with the requirements of section 6(a), and thereupon the provisions of section 6(b) shall govern such lease. The notice concerning "Oil and Gas Operations in the Submerged Coastal Lands of the Gulf of Mexico" issued by the Secretary on December 11, 1950 (15 F. R. 8835), as amended by the notice dated January 26, 1951 (16 F. R. 953), and as supplemented by the notices dated February 2, 1951 (16 F. R. 1203), March 5, 1951 (16 F. R. 2195), April 23, 1951 (16 F. R. 3623), June 25, 1951 (16 F. R. 6404), August 22, 1951 (16 F. R. 8720), October 24, 1951 (16 F. R. 10998), December 21, 1951 (17 F. R. 43), March 25, 1952 (17 F. R. 2821), June 26, 1952 (17 F. R. 5833), and December 24, 1952 (18 F. R. 48), respectively, is hereby approved and confirmed.

Sec. 8. Leasing of Outer Continental Shelf. —

(a) In order to meet the urgent need for further exploration and development of the oil and gas deposits of the submerged lands of the outer Continental Shelf, the Secretary is authorized to grant to the highest responsible qualified bidder by competitive bidding under regulations promulgated in advance, oil and gas leases on submerged lands of the outer Continental Shelf which are not covered by leases meeting the requirements of subsection (a) of section 6 of this Act. The bidding shall be (1) by sealed bids, and (2) at the discretion of the Secretary, on the basis of a cash bonus with a royalty fixed by the Secretary at not less than 12½ per centum in amount or value of the production saved, removed or sold, or on the basis of royalty, but at not less than the per centum above mentioned, with a cash bonus fixed by the Secretary.

(b) An oil and gas lease issued by the Secretary pursuant to this section shall (1) cover a compact area not exceeding five thousand seven hundred and sixty acres, as the Secretary may determine, (2) be for a period of five years and as long thereafter as oil or gas may be produced from the area in paying quantitites, or drilling or well reworking operations as approved by the Secretary are conducted thereon, (3) require the payment of a royalty of not less than 12½ per centum, in the amount or value of the production saved, removed, or sold from the lease, and (4) contain such rental provisions and such other terms and provisions as the Secretary may prescribe at the time of offering the area for lease.

(c) In order to meet the urgent need for further exploration and development of the sulphur deposits in the submerged lands of the outer Continental Shelf, the Secretary is authorized to grant to the qualified persons offering the highest cash bonuses on a basis of competitive bidding sulphur leases on submerged lands of the outer Continental Shelf, which are not covered by leases which include sulphur and meet the requirements of subsection (a) of section 6 of this Act, and which sulphur leases shall be offered for bid by sealed bids and granted on separate leases from oil and gas leases, and for a separate consideration, and without priority or preference accorded to oil and gas lessees on the same area.

(d) A sulphur lease issued by the Secretary pursuant to this section shall (1) cover an area of such size and dimensions as the Secretary may determine, (2) be for a period of not more than ten years and so long thereafter as sulphur may be produced from the area in paying quantities or drilling, well reworking, plant construction, or other operations for the production of sulphur, as approved by the Secretary, are conducted thereon, (3) require the payment to the United States of such royalty as may be specified in the lease but not less than 5 per centum of the gross production or value of the sulphur at the wellhead, and (4) contain such rental provisions and such other terms and provisions as the Secretary may by regulation prescribe at the time of offering the area for lease.

(e) The Secretary is authorized to grant to the qualified persons offering the highest cash bonuses on a basis of competitive bidding leases of any mineral other than oil, gas, and sulphur in any area of the outer Continental Shelf not then under lease for such mineral upon such royalty, rental, and other terms and conditions as the Secretary may prescribe at the time of offering the area for lease.

(f) Notice of sale of leases, and the terms of bidding, authorized by this section shall be published at least thirty days before the date of sale in accordance with rules and regulations promulgated by the Secretary.

(g) All moneys paid to the Secretary for or under leases granted pursuant to this section shall be deposited in the Treasury in accordance with section 9 of this Act.

(h) The issuance of any lease by the Secretary pursuant to this Act, or the making of any interim arrangements by the Secretary pursuant to section 7 of this Act shall not prejudice the ultimate settlement or adjudication of the question as to whether or not the area involved is in the outer Continental Shelf.

(i) The Secretary may cancel any lease obtained by fraud or misrepresentation.

(j) Any person complaining of a cancellation of a lease by the Secretary may have the Secretary's action reviewed in the United States District Court for the District of Columbia by filing a petition for review within sixty days after the Secretary takes such action.

Sec. 9. Disposition of Revenues. —

All rentals, royalties, and other sums paid to the Secretary or the Secretary of the Navy under any lease on the outer Continental Shelf for the period from June 5, 1950, to date, and thereafter shall be deposited in the Treasury of the United States and credited to miscellaneous receipts.

Sec. 10. Refunds. —

(a) Subject to the provisions of subsection (b) hereof, when it appears to the satisfaction of the Secretary that any person has made a payment to the United States in connection with any lease under this Act in excess of the amount he was lawfully required to pay, such excess shall be repaid without interest to such person or his legal representative, if a request for repayment of such excess is filed with the Secretary within two years after the making of the payment, or within ninety days after the effective date of this Act. The Secretary shall certify the amounts of all such repayments to the Secretary of the Treasury, who is authorized and directed to make such repayments out of any moneys in the special account established under section 9 of this Act and to issue his warrant in settlement thereof.

(b) No refund of or credit for such excess payment shall be made until after the expiration of thirty days from the date upon which a report giving the name of the person to whom the refund or credit is to be made, the amount of such refund or credit, and a summary of the facts upon which the determination of the Secretary was made is submitted to the President of the Senate and the Speaker of the House of Representatives for transmittal to the appropriate legislative committee of each body, respectively: *Provided*, That if the Congress shall not be in session on the date of such submission or shall adjourn prior to the expiration of thirty days from the date of such submission, then such payment or credit shall not be made until thirty days after the opening day of the next succeeding session of Congress.

Sec. 11. Geological and Geophysical Explorations. —

Any agency of the United States and any person authorized by the Secretary may conduct geological and geophysical explorations in the outer Continental Shelf, which do not interfere with or endanger actual operations under any lease maintained or granted pursuant to this Act, and which are not unduly harmful to aquatic life in such area.

Sec. 12. Reservations. —

(a) The President of the United States may, from time to time, withdraw from disposition any of the unleased lands of the outer Continental Shelf.

(b) In time of war, or when the President shall so prescribe, the United States shall have the right of first refusal to purchase at the market price all or any portion of any mineral produced from the outer Continental Shelf.

(c) All leases issued under this Act, and leases, the maintenance and operation of which are authorized under this Act, shall contain or be construed to contain a provision whereby authority is vested in the Secretary, upon a recommendation of the Secretary of Defense, during a state of war or national emergency declared by the Congress or the President of the United States after the effective date of this Act, to suspend operations under any lease; and all such leases shall contain or be construed to contain provisions for the payment of just compensation to the lessee whose operations are thus suspended.

(d) The United States reserves and retains the right to designate by and through the Secretary of Defense, with the approval of the President, as areas restricted from exploration and operation that part of the outer Continental Shelf needed for national defense; and so long as such designation remains in effect no exploration or operations may be conducted on any part of the surface of such area except with the concurrence of the Secretary of Defense; and if operations or production under any lease theretofore issued on lands within any such restricted area shall be suspended, any payment of rentals, minimum royalty, and royalty prescribed by such lease likewise shall be suspended during such period of suspension of operation and production, and the term of such lease shall be extended by adding thereto any such suspension period, and the United States shall be liable to the lessee for such compensation as is required to be paid under the Constitution of the United States.

(e) All uranium, thorium, and all other materials determined pursuant to paragraph (1) of subsection (b) of section 5 of the Atomic Energy Act of 1946, as amended, to be peculiarly essential to the production of fissionable material, contained, in whatever concentration, in deposits in the subsoil or seabed of the outer Continental Shelf are hereby reserved for the use of the United States.

(f) The United States reserves and retains the ownership of and the right to extract all helium, under such rules and regulations as shall be prescribed by the Secretary, contained in gas produced from any portion of the outer Continental Shelf which may be subject to any lease maintained or granted pursuant to this Act, but the helium shall be extracted from such gas so as to cause no substantial delay in the delivery of gas produced to the purchaser of such gas.

Sec. 13. Naval Petroleum Reserve Executive Order Repealed. —

Executive Order Numbered 10426, dated January 16, 1953, entitled "Setting Aside Submerged Lands of the Continental Shelf as a Naval Petroleum Reserve," is hereby revoked.

Sec. 14. Prior Claims Not Affected. —

Nothing herein contained shall affect such rights, if any, as may have been acquired under any law of the United States by any person in lands subject to this Act and such rights, if any, shall be governed by the law in effect at the time they may have been acquired: *Provided, however,* That nothing herein contained is intended or shall be construed as a finding, interpretation, or construction by the Congress that the law under which such rights may be claimed in fact applies to the lands subject to this Act or authorizes or compels the granting of such rights in such lands, and that the determination of the applicability or effect of such law shall be unaffected by anything herein contained.

Sec. 15. Report by Secretary. —

As soon as practicable after the end of each fiscal year, the Secretary shall submit to the President of the Senate and the Speaker of the House of Representatives a report detailing the amounts of all moneys received and expended in connection with the administration of this Act during the preceding fiscal year.

Sec. 16. Appropriations. —

There is hereby authorized to be appropriated such sums as may be necessary to carry out the provisions of this Act.

Sec. 17. Separability. —

If any provision of this Act, or any section, subsection, sentence, clause, phrase or individual word, or the application thereof to any person or circumstance is held invalid, the validity of the remainder of the Act and of the application of any such provision, section, subsection, sentence, clause, phrase or individual word to other persons and circumstances shall not be affected thereby.

Approved August 7, 1953.

UNION OF SOVIET SOCIALIST REPUBLICS

(*a*) DECREE[3] OF THE PRESIDIUM OF THE SUPREME SOVIET OF THE UNION OF SOVIET SOCIALIST REPUBLICS DATED 6 FEBRUARY 1968 ENTITLED "ON THE CONTINENTAL SHELF OF THE USSR"**

1. The USSR exercises sovereign rights over the continental shelf adjacent to the outer limit of the territorial sea of the USSR, for the purpose of exploring it and exploiting its natural resources.

---

[3] *Bulletin of the Supreme Soviet of the Union of Soviet Socialist Republics* No. 6 (1404) of 6 February 1968.

The continental shelf of the USSR consists of the sea-bed and the subsoil of the submarine areas adjacent to the coast or to the islands of the USSR but outside the area of the territorial sea, to a depth of 200 metres or, beyond that limit, to where the depth of the superjacent waters admits of the exploitation of the natural resources of the said areas.

The sea-bed and the subsoil of depressions entirely surrounded by the continental shelf of the USSR, irrespective of their depth, are part of the continental shelf of the USSR.

2. Where the boundary of the continental shelf of the USSR is adjacent to those of other States, that boundary shall be determined by agreements with those States. In the absence of such agreements, and unless another boundary line is justified by special circumstances:

(*a*) The boundary of the continental shelf of the USSR with a State whose coasts are opposite those of the USSR shall be the median line, every point of which is equidistant from the nearest points of the baselines from which the breadth of the territorial sea of the USSR and of the other State is measured;

(*b*) The boundary of the continental shelf of the USSR with a State whose shelf is contiguous to that of the USSR shall be determined by application of the principle of equidistance from the nearest points of the baselines from which the breadth of the territorial sea of the USSR and of the other State is measured.

3. The natural resources of the continental shelf are the State property of the USSR. The exploration and exploitation of those resources and any research on the continental shelf shall be carried out in accordance with the current legislation of the Union of Soviet Socialist Republics and the union republics.

The natural resources of the continental shelf mean the mineral and other non-living resources of the sea-bed and the subsoil, together with living organisms belonging to sedentary species, that is to say, organisms which, at the harvestable stage, either are immobile on or under the sea-bed or are unable to move except in constant physical contact with the sea-bed or the subsoil. A list of the species of living organisms which are natural resources of the continental shelf of the USSR shall be drawn up by the Ministry of Fishing of the USSR and published for purposes of general information.

4. For the purpose of the exploration and exploitation of the natural resources of the continental shelf, the competent authorities of the USSR shall authorize the construction of installations and other devices and the establishment around such installations and devices of safety zones which may extend to a distance of 500 metres from the installations and devices, measured from any point on their outer edge. The construction of any such installations and devices and of the establishment of safety zones shall be announced in the "Notices to Navigators" of the Hydrographic Department of the Ministry of Defence of the USSR.

These installations or devices and the safety zones around them shall not be established where interference may be caused to the use of recognized sea lanes essential to international navigation.

Such installations and devices and the safety zones around them shall be under the jurisdiction of the Union of Soviet Socialist Republics.

Foreign ships may enter the safety zones only with the special permission of the competent Soviet authorities.

The organization responsible for the maintenance and operation of such installations and devices shall be obliged to protect them, to maintain permanent means for giving warning of their presence and to undertake, in the safety zones, measures for the protection of the living resources of the sea from harmful agents. Any installations or devices which are permanently disused must be entirely removed.

5. Foreign physical and juridical persons shall be prohibited from surveying, exploring or exploiting the natural resources or carrying on any other activity on the continental shelf of the USSR unless such activity is specifically provided for by an agreement between the USSR and the foreign State concerned or by special permission granted by the competent authorities of the USSR.

6. Persons guilty of violating this Decree may be sentenced by a court to a fine of up to 10,000 roubles or imprisonment for up to one year or both, unless the legislation of the Union of Soviet Socialist Republics and the union republics provides a stricter punishment for the violation in question.

7. If article 5 of this Decree is violated, the vessel and all the instruments and tools used by the person committing the violation and anything which has been obtained illegally shall be liable to confiscation.

8. The task of protecting the natural resources of the continental shelf of the USSR shall be the responsibility of the fisheries supervision bodies which, in performing their duties, shall be guided by the current legislation of the Union of Soviet Socialist Republics and the union republics, and by agreements of the Union of Soviet Socialist Republics and the union republics with other States.

Where necessary, border guards shall assist the above-mentioned bodies in taking action to protect the natural resources of the continental shelf of the USSR.

9. The task of checking that the mineral and other non-living resources of the continental shelf of the USSR are being properly exploited shall be the responsibility of the organs of the State Inspectorate of Mine Engineering of the USSR, which shall be guided by the current regulations, instructions and other regulatory enactments designed to protect the country's mineral wealth.

(*b*) Resolution No. 564 of 18 July 1969 of the Council of Ministers of the USSR concerning the procedure for carrying out work on the continental shelf and the protection of its natural resources**

In accordance with the Decree of the Presidium of the Supreme Soviet of the Union of Soviet Socialist Republics dated 6 February 1968, entitled "On the continental shelf of the USSR", and with a view to ensuring the rational utilization of the natural resources of the continental shelf of the USSR, the Council of Ministers of the Union of Soviet Socialist Republics has resolved that:

1. The study, exploration and exploitation of the natural resources of the continental shelf of the USSR shall be permitted after registration according to the procedure prescribed by the present Resolution.

Registration shall be required in the case of operations concerned with the study, exploration and exploitation of natural resources of the continental shelf of the USSR if such operations are to be carried out on the sea-bed or in the subsoil of the submarine areas adjacent to the outer limit of the territorial sea of the USSR to a depth of 200 metres or, beyond that limit, to where the depth of the superjacent waters admits of the aforementioned operations being carried out, and also on the sea-bed or in the subsoil of depressions entirely surrounded by the continental shelf of the USSR, irrespective of their depth, save as otherwise provided in an international agreement to which the USSR is a party.

2. The registration of operations concerned with the study, exploration and exploitation of natural resources of the continental shelf of the USSR shall be effected:

(*a*) By the authorities of the Ministry of Geology of the USSR, in the case of study and exploration of mineral and other non-living resources of the continental shelf;

(*b*) By those authorities of the State Mining Inspectorate of the USSR responsible for issuing mining concessions, in the case of exploitation of mineral and other non-living resources of the continental shelf;

(*c*) By the fishery conservation authorities of the Ministry of Fisheries of the USSR in the case of study, exploration and the taking, on the continental shelf, of living organisms belonging to sedentary species.

The procedure for the registration of operations carried out on the continental shelf of the USSR shall be established by the Ministries and departments effecting such registration, in consultation with the Ministry of Defence of the USSR, the State Security Committee of the Council of Ministers of the USSR, and the Ministry of Fisheries of the USSR.

Compliance with the requirements of the present section shall not dispense foreign bodies corporate and individuals or Soviet organizations from the obligation to obtain the appropriate permit for the execution of work in cases where the obtaining of such a permit is prescribed by the legislation in force.

3. Permits for the construction of installations and other devices on the continental shelf of the USSR for the purposes of study, exploration and exploitation of its natural resources and permits for the establishment of safety zones around such installations and devices shall be issued by the Ministry of Defence of the USSR in accordance with regulations established by the said Ministry in consultation with the State Security Committee of the Council of Ministers of the USSR, the Ministry of Foreign Affairs of the USSR, the Ministry of the Merchant Marine, the Ministry of Fisheries of the USSR, the Ministry of Geology of the USSR, the State Mining Inspectorate of the USSR and the Ministry of Reclamation and Water Resources Management of the USSR.

Permits for foreign vessels to enter the safety zones shall be issued by the Ministries and departments engaged in operations on the continental shelf of the USSR, in consultation with the Ministry of Defence of the USSR and the State Security Committee of the Council of Ministers of the USSR.

4. The construction of installations and other devices on the continental shelf of the USSR, and the maintenance, operation, protection and dismantling thereof, shall be carried out in accordance with regulations established by the Ministries and departments engaged in the exploration and exploitation of the natural resources of the continental shelf, in consultation with the Ministry of Defence of the USSR, the State Security Committee of the Council of Ministers of the USSR, the Ministry of Fisheries of the USSR, the State Mining Inspectorate

of the USSR and the Ministry of Reclamation and Water Resources Management of the USSR.

Regulations governing the establishment of safety zones and navigation procedures within such zones shall be established by the Ministry of Defence of the USSR.

5. Organizations and persons carrying out work on the continental shelf of the USSR shall be required to utilize the natural resources of the continental shelf in a rational manner, prevent the continental shelf and the superjacent waters from being polluted by industrial or other commercial refuse, sewage, radioactive substances or industrial waste, and take measures for protecting plant and animal life.

6. Operations on the continental shelf of the USSR must be carried out in compliance with:

(*a*) The regulations governing the study and exploration of the mineral and other non-living resources of the continental shelf, established by the Ministry of Geology of the USSR in consultation with the Ministry of Fisheries of the USSR;

(*b*) The safety regulations governing the execution of work on the continental shelf and the regulations governing the exploitation and protection of the mineral and other non-living resources of the continental shelf, established by the State Mining Inspectorate of the USSR in consultation with the Ministry of Fisheries of the USSR and the other Ministries and departments concerned;

(*c*) The regulations governing the study and exploration, and the taking and protection, on the continental shelf, of living organisms belonging to sedentary species, established by the Ministry of Fisheries of the USSR.

...

No. 8164. CONVENTION[1] ON FISHING AND CONSERVATION OF THE LIVING RESOURCES OF THE HIGH SEAS. DONE AT GENEVA, ON 29 APRIL 1958

The States Parties to this Convention,

Considering that the development of modern techniques for the exploitation of the living resources of the sea, increasing man's ability to meet the need of the world's expanding population for food, has exposed some of these resources to the danger of being over-exploited,

Considering also that the nature of the problems involved in the conservation of the living resources of the high seas is such that there is a clear necessity that they be solved, whenever possible, on the basis of international co-operation through the concerted action of all the States concerned,

Have agreed as follows :

Article 1

1. All States have the right for their nationals to engage in fishing on the high seas, subject (*a*) to their treaty obligations, (*b*) to the interests and rights of

[1] In accordance with article 18, paragraph 1, the Convention came into force on 20 March 1966, that is to say, on the thirtieth day following the date of deposit of the twenty-second instrument of ratification or accession. The following States have deposited their instruments of ratification or accession (*a*) on the dates indicated :

United Kingdom of Great Britain and Northern Ireland*	14 March	1960
Cambodia	18 March	1960 (*a*)
Haiti	29 March	1960
Malaysia	21 December	1960 (*a*)
United States of America**	12 April	1961
Senegal	25 April	1961 (*a*)
Nigeria	26 June	1961
Sierra Leone	13 March	1962
Madagascar	31 July	1962 (*a*)
Colombia	3 January	1963
Portugal	8 January	1963
South Africa	9 April	1963 (*a*)
Australia	14 May	1963
Venezuela	10 July	1963
Jamaica	16 April	1964
Dominican Republic	11 August	1964
Uganda	14 September	1964 (*a*)
Finland	16 February	1965
Upper Volta	4 October	1965 (*a*)
Malawi	3 November	1965 (*a*)
Yugoslavia	28 January	1966
Netherlands	18 February	1966

* With the following declaration :

" In depositing their instrument of ratification... Her Majesty's Government in the United Kingdom of Great Britain and Northern Ireland declare that, save as may be stated in any further and separate notices that may hereafter be given, ratification of this Convention on behalf of the United Kingdom does not extend to the States in the Persian Gulf enjoying British protection. Multilateral conventions to which the United Kingdom becomes a party are not extended to these States until such time as an extension is requested by the Ruler of the State concerned. "

** The instrument of ratification of the Government of the United States of America specifies that the ratification is subject to the following understanding : " that such ratification shall not be construed to impair the applicability of the principle of ' abstention ', as defined in paragraph A.1 of the documents of record in the proceedings of the Conference above referred to [United Nations Conference on the Law of the Sea, held at Geneva from 24 February to 27 April 1958], identified as A/CONF. 13/C.3/L.69, 8 April 1958 ".

coastal States as provided for in this Convention, and (*c*) to the provisions contained in the following articles concerning conservation of the living resources of the high seas.

2. All States have the duty to adopt, or to co-operate with other States in adopting, such measures for their respective nationals as may be necessary for the conservation of the living resources of the high seas.

Article 2

As employed in this Convention, the expression " conservation of the living resources of the high seas " means the aggregate of the measures rendering possible the optimum sustainable yield from those resources so as to secure a maximum supply to food and other marine products. Conservation programmes should be formulated with a view to securing in the first place a supply of food for human consumption.

Article 3

A State whose nationals are engaged in fishing any stock or stocks of fish or other living marine resources in any area of the high seas where the nationals of other States are not thus engaged shall adopt, for its own nationals, measures in that area when necessary for the purpose of the conservation of the living resources affected.

Article 4

1. If the nationals of two or more States are engaged in fishing the same stock or stocks of fish or other living marine resources in any area or areas of the high seas, these States shall, at the request of any of them, enter into negotiations with a view to prescribing by agreement for their nationals the necessary measures for the conservation of the living resources affected.

2. If the States concerned do not reach agreement within twelve months, any of the parties may initiate the procedure contemplated by article 9.

Article 5

1. If, subsequent to the adoption of the measures referred to in articles 3 and 4, nationals of other States engage in fishing the same stock or stocks of fish or other living marine resources in any area or areas of the high seas, the other States shall apply the measures, which shall not be discriminatory in form or in fact, to their own nationals not later than seven months after the date on which the measures shall have been notified to the Director-General of the Food and Agriculture Organization of the United Nations. The Director-General shall

notify such measures to any State which so requests and, in any case, to any State specified by the State initiating the measure.

2. If these other States do not accept the measures so adopted and if no agreement can be reached within twelve months, any of the interested parties may initiate the procedure contemplated by article 9. Subject to paragraph 2 of article 10, the measures adopted shall remain obligatory pending the decision of the special commission.

Article 6

1. A coastal State has a special interest in the maintenance of the productivity of the living resources in any area of the high seas adjacent to its territorial sea.

2. A coastal State is entitled to take part on an equal footing in any system of research and regulation for purposes of conservation of the living resources of the high seas in that area, even though its nationals do not carry on fishing there.

3. A state whose nationals are engaged in fishing in any area of the high seas adjacent to the territorial sea of a State shall, at the request of that coastal State, enter into negotiations with a view to prescribing by agreement the measures necessary for the conservation of the living resources of the high seas in that area.

4. A State whose nationals are engaged in fishing in any area of the high seas adjacent to the territorial sea of a coastal State shall not enforce conservation measures in that area which are opposed to those which have been adopted by the coastal State, but may enter into negotiations with the coastal State with a view to prescribing by agreement the measures necessary for the conservation of the living resources of the high seas in that area.

5. If the States concerned do not reach agreement with respect to conservation measures within twelve months, any of the parties may initiate the procedure contemplated by article 9.

Article 7

1. Having regard to the provisions of paragraph 1 of article 6, any coastal State may, with a view to the maintenance of the productivity of the living resources of the sea, adopt unilateral measures of conservation appropriate to any stock of fish or other marine resources in any area of the high seas adjacent to its territorial sea, provided that negotiations to that effect with the other States concerned have not led to an agreement within six months.

2. The measures which the coastal State adopts under the previous paragraph shall be valid as to other States only if the following requirements are fulfilled:

(*a*) That there is a need for urgent application of conservation measures in the light of the existing knowledge of the fishery;

(*b*) That the measures adopted are based on appropriate scientific findings;

(*c*) That such measures do not discriminate in form or in fact against foreign fishermen.

3. These measures shall remain in force pending the settlement, in accordance with the relevant provisions of this Convention, of any disagreement as to their validity.

4. If the measures are not accepted by the other States concerned, any of the parties may initiate the procedure contemplated by article 9. Subject to paragraph 2 of article 10, the measures adopted shall remain obligatory pending the decision of the special commission.

5. The principles of geographical demarcation as defined in article 12 of the Convention on the Territorial Sea and the Contiguous Zone[1] shall be adopted when coasts of different States are involved.

Article 8

1. Any State which, even if its nationals are not engaged in fishing in an area of the high seas not adjacent to its coast, has a special interest in the conservation of the living resources of the high seas in that area, may request the State or States whose nationals are engaged in fishing there to take the necessary measures of conservation under articles 3 and 4 respectively, at the same time mentioning the scientific reasons which in its opinion make such measures necessary, and indicating its special interest.

2. If no agreement is reached within twelve months, such State may initiate the procedure contemplated by article 9.

Article 9

1. Any dispute which may arise between States under articles 4, 5, 6, 7 and 8 shall, at the request of any of the parties, be submitted for settlement to a special commission of five members, unless the parties agree to seek a solution by another method of peaceful settlement, as provided for in Article 33 of the Charter of the United Nations.

2. The members of the commission, one of whom shall be designated as chairman, shall be named by agreement between the States in dispute within three months of the request for settlement in accordance with the provisions of this article. Failing agreement they shall, upon the request of any State party,

[1] United Nations, *Treaty Series*, Vol. 516, p. 205.

be named by the Secretary-General of the United Nations, within a further three-month period, in consultation with the States in dispute and with the President of the International Court of Justice and the Director-General of the Food and Agriculture Organization of the United Nations, from amongst well-qualified persons being nationals of States not involved in the dispute and specializing in legal, administrative or scientific questions relating to fisheries, depending upon the nature of the dispute to be settled. Any vacancy arising after the original appointment shall be filled in the same manner as provided for the initial selection.

3. Any State party to proceedings under these articles shall have the right to name one of its nationals to the special commission, with the right to participate fully in the proceedings on the same footing as a member of the commission, but without the right to vote or to take part in the writing of the commission's decision.

4. The commission shall determine its own procedure, assuring each party to the proceedings a full opportunity to be heard and to present its case. It shall also determine how the costs and expenses shall be divided between the parties to the dispute, failing agreement by the parties on this matter.

5. The special commission shall render its decision within a period of five months from the time it is appointed unless it decides, in case of necessity, to extend the time limit for a period not exceeding three months.

6. The special commission shall, in reaching its decisions, adhere to these articles and to any special agreements between the disputing parties regarding settlement of the dispute.

7. Decisions of the commission shall be by majority vote.

Article 10

1. The special commission shall, in disputes arising under article 7, apply the criteria listed in paragraph 2 of that article. In disputes under articles 4, 5, 6 and 8, the commission shall apply the following criteria, according to the issues involved in the dispute :

(*a*) Common to the determination of disputes arising under articles 4, 5 and 6 are the requirements :

(i) That scientific findings demonstrate the necessity of conservation measures;

(ii) That the specific measures are based on scientific findings and are practicable; and

(iii) That the measures do not discriminate, in form or in fact, against fishermen of other States;

(*b*) Applicable to the determination of disputes arising under article 8 is the requirement that scientific findings demonstrate the necessity for conservation measures, or that the conservation programme is adequate, as the case may be.

2. The special commission may decide that pending its award the measures in dispute shall not be applied, provided that, in the case of disputes under article 7, the measures shall only be suspended when it is apparent to the commission on the basis of *prima facie* evidence that the need for the urgent application of such measures does not exist.

Article 11

The decisions of the special commission shall be binding on the States concerned and the provisions of paragraph 2 of Article 94 of the Charter of the United Nations shall be applicable to those decisions. If the decisions are accompanied by any recommendations, they shall receive the greatest possible consideration.

Article 12

1. If the factual basis of the award of the special commission is altered by substantial changes in the conditions of the stock or stocks of fish or other living marine resources or in methods of fishing, any of the States concerned may request the other States to enter into negotiations with a view to prescribing by agreement the necessary modifications in the measures of conservation.

2. If no agreement is reached within a reasonable period of time, any of the States concerned may again resort to the procedure contemplated by article 9 provided that at least two years have elapsed from the original award.

Article 13

1. The regulation of fisheries conducted by means of equipment embedded in the floor of the sea in areas of the high seas adjacent to the territorial sea of a State may be undertaken by that State where such fisheries have long been maintained and conducted by its nationals, provided that non-nationals are permitted to participate in such activities on an equal footing with nationals except in areas where such fisheries have by long usage been exclusively enjoyed by such nationals. Such regulations will not, however, affect the general status of the areas as high seas.

2. In this article, the expression " fisheries conducted by means of equipment embedded in the floor of the sea " means those fisheries using gear with supporting members embedded in the sea floor, constructed on a site and left there to operate permanently or, if removed, restored each season on the same site.

Article 14

In articles 1, 3, 4, 5, 6 and 8, the term " nationals " means fishing boats or craft of any size having the nationality of the State concerned, according to the law of that State, irrespective of the nationality of the members of their crews.

Article 15

This Convention shall, until 31 October 1958, be open for signature by all States Members of the United Nations or of any of the specialized agencies, and by any other State invited by the General Assembly of the United Nations to become a Party to the Convention.

Article 16

This Convention is subject to ratification. The instruments of ratification shall be deposited with the Secretary-General of the United Nations.

Article 17

This Convention shall be open for accession by any States belonging to any of the categories mentioned in article 15. The instruments of accession shall be deposited with the Secretary-General of the United Nations.

Article 18

1. This Convention shall come into force on the thirtieth day following the date of deposit of the twenty-second instrument of ratification or accession with the Secretary-General of the United Nations.

2. For each State ratifying or acceding to the Convention after the deposit of the twenty-second instrument of ratification or accession, the Convention shall enter into force on the thirtieth day after deposit by such State of its instrument of ratification or accession.

Article 19

1. At the time of signature, ratification or accession, any State may make reservations to articles of the Convention other than to articles 6, 7, 9, 10, 11 and 12.

2. Any contracting State making a reservation in accordance with the preceding paragraph may at any time withdraw the reservation by a communication to that effect addressed to the Secretary-General of the United Nations.

Article 20

1. After the expiration of a period of five years from the date on which this Convention shall enter into force, a request for the revision of this Convention may be made at any time by any contracting party by means of a notification in writing addressed to the Secretary-General of the United Nations.

2. The General Assembly of the United Nations shall decide upon the steps, if any, to be taken in respect of such request.

Article 21

The Secretary-General of the United Nations shall inform all States Members of the United Nations and the other States referred to in article 15 :

(*a*) Of signatures to this Convention and of the deposit of instruments of ratification or accession, in accordance with articles 15, 16 and 17;
(*b*) Of the date on which this Convention will come into force, in accordance with article 18;
(*c*) Of requests for revision in accordance with article 20;
(*d*) Of reservations to this Convention, in accordance with article 19.

Article 22

The original of this Convention, of which the Chinese, English, French, Russian and Spanish texts are equally authentic, shall be deposited with the Secretary-General of the United Nations, who shall send certified copies thereof to all States referred to in article 15.

IN WITNESS WHEREOF the undersigned plenipotentiaries, being duly authorized thereto by their respective governments, have signed this Convention.

DONE at Geneva, this twenty-ninth day of April one thousand nine hundred and fifty-eight.

No. 2053. INTERNATIONAL CONVENTION[1] FOR THE NORTHWEST ATLANTIC FISHERIES. DONE AT WASHINGTON, ON 8 FEBRUARY 1949 [2]

The Governments whose duly authorized representatives have subscribed hereto, sharing a substantial interest in the conservation of the fishery resources of the Northwest Atlantic Ocean, have resolved to conclude a convention for the investigation, protection and conservation of the fisheries of the Northwest Atlantic Ocean, in order to make possible the maintenance of a maximum sustained catch from those fisheries and to that end have, through their duly authorized representatives, agreed as follows :

Article I

1. The area to which this Convention applies, hereinafter referred to as " the Convention area ", shall be all waters, except territorial waters, bounded by a line beginning at a point on the coast of Rhode Island in 71° 40′ west longitude; thence due south to 39° 00′ north latitude; thence due east to 42° 00′ west longitude; thence due north to 59° 00′ north latitude; thence due west to 44° 00′ west longitude; thence due north to the coast of Greenland; thence along the west coast of Greenland to 78° 10′ north latitude; thence southward to a point in 75° 00′ north latitude and 73° 30′ west longitude; thence along a rhumb line to a point in 69° 00′ north latitude and 59° 00′ west longitude; thence due south to 61° 00′ north latitude; thence due west to 64° 30′ west longitude; thence due south to the coast of Labrador; thence in a southerly direction along the coast

[1] In accordance with article XV the convention came into force on 3 July 1950, upon the deposit with the Government of the United States of America of the fourth instrument of ratification, with respect to the following Governments which deposited their instruments of ratification on the dates indicated :

United States of America	1 September 1949	Iceland	13 February 1950
United Kingdom of Great Britain and Northern Ireland	15 December 1949	Canada	3 July 1950
		(The ratification by Canada of the Convention extends to Newfoundland with a reservation)*	

and thereafter with respect to each of the following Governments on the date of deposit of its instrument of ratification, as indicated below :

Denmark	14 December 1950	Norway	2 July 1952
Spain (with a reservation)**	17 January 1952	Portugal	19 July 1952
		Italy	19 August 1952

* " Any claims Canada may have in regard to the limits of territorial waters or to the jurisdiction over fisheries, particularly as a result of the entry of Newfoundland into Confederation, will not be prejudiced."

** " Reserving paragraph 2 of Article I."

[2] Amendments to Articles II(5), IV(2), VII(2), VIII(1), (5), (7) and (8) can be found at the end of the Convention.

of Labrador to the southern terminus of its boundary with Quebec; thence in a westerly direction along the coast of Quebec, and in an easterly and southerly direction along the coasts of New Brunswick, Nova Scotia, and Cape Breton Island to Cabot Strait; thence along the coasts of Cape Breton Island, Nova Scotia, New Brunswick, Maine, New Hampshire, Massachusetts, and Rhode Island to the point of the beginning.

2. Nothing in this Convention shall be deemed to affect adversely (prejudice) the claims of any Contracting Government in regard to the limits of territorial waters or to the jurisdiction of a coastal state over fisheries.

3. The Convention area shall be divided into five sub-areas, the boundaries of which shall be those defined in the Annex to this Convention, subject to such alterations as may be made in accordance with the provisions of paragraph 2 of Article VI.

Article II

1. The Contracting Governments shall establish and maintain a Commission for the purposes of this Convention. The Commission shall be known as the International Commission for the Northwest Atlantic Fisheries, hereinafter referred to as " the Commission ".

2. Each of the Contracting Governments may appoint not more than three Commissioners and one or more experts or advisers to assist its Commissioner or Commissioners.

3. The Commission shall elect from its members a Chairman and a Vice Chairman, each of whom shall serve for a term of two years and shall be eligible for re-election but not to a succeeding term. The Chairman and Vice Chairman must be Commissioners from different Contracting Governments.

4. The seat of the Commission shall be in North America at a place to be chosen by the Commission.

5. The Commission shall hold a regular annual meeting at its seat or at such place in North America as may be agreed upon by the Commission.

6. Any other meeting of the Commission may be called by the Chairman at such time and place as he may determine, upon the request of the Commissioner of a Contracting Government and subject to the concurrence of the Commissioners of two other Contracting Governments, including the Commissioner of a Government in North America.

7. Each Contracting Government shall have one vote which may be cast by any Commissioner from that Government. Decisions of the Commission shall be taken by a two-thirds majority of the votes of all the Contracting Governments.

8. The Commission shall adopt, and amend as occasion may require, financial regulations and rules and by-laws for the conduct of its meetings and for the exercise of its functions and duties.

Article III

1. The Commission shall appoint an Executive Secretary according to such procedure and on such terms as it may determine.

2. The staff of the Commission shall be appointed by the Executive Secretary in accordance with such rules and procedures as may be determined and authorized by the Commission.

3. The Executive Secretary shall, subject to the general supervision of the Commission, have full power and authority over the staff and shall perform such other functions as the Commission shall prescribe.

Article IV

1. The Contracting Governments shall establish and maintain a Panel for each of the sub-areas provided for by Article I, in order to carry out the objectives of this Convention. Each Contracting Government participating in any Panel shall be represented on such Panel by its Commissioner or Commissioners, who may be assisted by experts or advisers. Each Panel shall elect from its members a Chairman who shall serve for a period of two years and shall be eligible for re-election but not to a succeeding term.

2. After this Convention has been in force for two years, but not before that time, Panel representation shall be reviewed annually by the Commission, which shall have the power, subject to consultation with the Panel concerned, to determine representation on each Panel on the basis of current substantial exploitation in the sub-area concerned of fishes of the cod group (*Gadiformes*), of flat-fishes (*Pleuronectiformes*), and of rosefish (*genus Sebastes*), except that each Contracting Government with coastline adjacent to a sub-area shall have the right of representation on the Panel for the sub-area.

3. Each Panel may adopt, and amend as occasion may require, rules of procedure and by-laws for the conduct of its meetings and for the exercise of its functions and duties.

4. Each Government participating in a Panel shall have one vote, which shall be cast by a Commissioner representing that Government. Decisions of the Panel shall be taken by a two-thirds majority of the votes of all the Governments participating in that Panel.

5. Commissioners of Contracting Governments not participating in a particular Panel shall have the right to attend the meetings of such Panel as observers, and may be accompanied by experts and advisers.

6. The Panels shall, in the exercise of their functions and duties, use the services of the Executive Secretary and the staff of the Commission.

Article V

1. Each Contracting Government may set up an Advisory Committee composed of persons, including fishermen, vessel owners and others, well informed concerning the problems of the fisheries of the Northwest Atlantic Ocean. With the assent of the Contracting Government concerned, a representative or representatives of an Advisory Committee may attend as observers all non-executive meetings of the Commission or of any Panel in which their Government participates.

2. The Commissioners of each Contracting Government may hold public hearings within the territories they represent.

Article VI

1. The Commission shall be responsible in the field of scientific investigation for obtaining and collating the information necessary for maintaining those stocks of fish which support international fisheries in the Convention area and the Commission may, through or in collaboration with agencies of the Contracting Governments or other public or private agencies and organizations or, when necessary, independently:

(*a*) make such investigations as it finds necessary into the abundance, life history and ecology of any species of aquatic life in any part of the Northwest Atlantic Ocean;

(*b*) collect and analyze statistical information relating to the current conditions and trends of the fishery resources of the Northwest Atlantic Ocean;

(*c*) study and appraise information concerning the methods for maintaining and increasing stocks of fish in the Northwest Atlantic Ocean;

(*d*) hold or arrange such hearings as may be useful or essential in connection with the development of complete factual information necessary to carry out the provisions of this Convention;

(*e*) conduct fishing operations in the Convention area at any time for purposes of scientific investigation;

(*f*) publish and otherwise disseminate reports of its findings and statistical, scientific and other information relating to the fisheries of the Northwest Atlantic Ocean as well as such other reports as fall within the scope of this Convention.

2. Upon the unanimous recommendation of each Panel affected, the Commission may alter the boundaries of the sub-areas set out in the Annex. Any such alteration shall forthwith be reported to the Depositary Government which shall inform the Contracting Governments, and the sub-areas defined in the Annex shall be altered accordingly.

3. The Contracting Governments shall furnish to the Commission, at such time and in such form as may be required by the Commission, the statistical information referred to in paragraph 1 (*b*) of this Article.

Article VII

1. Each Panel established under Article IV shall be responsible for keeping under review the fisheries of its sub-area and the scientific and other information relating thereto.

2. Each Panel, upon the basis of scientific investigations, may make recommendations to the Commission for joint action by the Contracting Governments on the matters specified in paragraph 1 of Article VIII.

3. Each Panel may recommend to the Commission studies and investigations within the scope of this Convention which are deemed necessary in the development of factual information relating to its particular sub-area.

4. Any Panel may make recommendations to the Commission for the alteration of the boundaries of the sub-areas defined in the Annex.

5. Each Panel shall investigate and report to the Commission upon any matter referred to it by the Commission.

6. A Panel shall not incur any expenditure except in accordance with directions given by the Commission.

Article VIII

1. The Commission may, on the recommendations of one or more Panels, and on the basis of scientific investigations, transmit to the Depositary Government proposals, for joint action by the Contracting Governments, designed to keep the stocks of those species of fish which support international fisheries in the Convention area at a level permitting the maximum sustained catch by the application, with respect to such species of fish, of one or more of the following measures :

(*a*) establishing open and closed seasons;

(*b*) closing to fishing such portions of a sub-area as the Panel concerned finds to be a spawning area or to be populated by small or immature fish;

(*c*) establishing size limits for any species;

(*d*) prescribing the fishing gear and appliances the use of which is prohibited;

(*e*) prescribing an over-all catch limit for any species of fish.

2. Each recommendation shall be studied by the Commission and thereafter the Commission shall either

(*a*) transmit the recommendation as a proposal to the Depositary Government with such modifications or suggestions as the Commission may consider desirable, or

(*b*) refer the recommendation back to the Panel with comments for its reconsideration.

3. The Panel may, after reconsidering the recommendation returned to it by the Commission, reaffirm that recommendation, with or without modification.

4. If, after a recommendation is reaffirmed, the Commission is unable to adopt the recommendation as a proposal, it shall send a copy of the recommendation to the Depositary Government with a report of the Commission's decision. The Depositary Government shall transmit copies of the recommendation and of the Commission's report to the Contracting Governments.

5. The Commission may, after consultation with all the Panels, transmit proposals to the Depositary Government within the scope of paragraph 1 of this Article affecting the Convention area as a whole.

6. The Depositary Government shall transmit any proposal received by it to the Contracting Governments for their consideration and may make such suggestions as will facilitate acceptance of the proposal.

7. The Contracting Governments shall notify the Depositary Government of their acceptance of the proposal, and the Depositary Government shall notify the Contracting Governments of each acceptance communicated to it, including the date of receipt thereof.

8. The proposal shall become effective for all Contracting Governments four months after the date on which notifications of acceptance shall have been received by the Depositary Government from all the Contracting Governments participating in the Panel or Panels for the sub-area or sub-areas to which the proposal applies.

9. At any time after the expiration of one year from the date on which a proposal becomes effective, any Panel Government for the sub-area to which the proposal applies may give to the Depositary Government notice of the termination of its acceptance of the proposal and, if that notice is not withdrawn, the proposal shall cease to be effective for that Panel Government at the end of one year from the date of receipt of the notice by the Depositary Government. At any time after a proposal has ceased to be effective for a Panel Government under this paragraph, the proposal shall cease to be effective for any other Contracting Government upon the date a notice of withdrawal by such Government is received by the Depositary Government. The Depositary Government shall notify all Contracting Governments of every notice under this paragraph immediately upon the receipt thereof.

Article IX

The Commission may invite the attention of any or all Contracting Governments to any matters which relate to the objectives and purposes of this Convention.

Article X

1. The Commission shall seek to establish and maintain working arrangements with other public international organizations which have related objectives, particularly the Food and Agriculture Organization of the United Nations and the International Council for the Exploration of the Sea, to ensure effective collaboration and coordination with respect to their work and, in the case of the International Council for the Exploration of the Sea, the avoidance of duplication of scientific investigations.

2. The Commission shall consider, at the expiration of two years from the date of entry into force of this Convention, whether or not it should recommend to the Contracting Governments that the Commission be brought within the framework of a specialized agency of the United Nations.

Article XI

1. Each Contracting Government shall pay the expenses of the Commissioners, experts and advisers appointed by it.

2. The Commission shall prepare an annual administrative budget of the proposed necessary administrative expenditures of the Commission and an annual special projects budget of proposed expenditures on special studies and investigations to be undertaken by or on behalf of the Commission pursuant to Article VI or by or on behalf of any Panel pursuant to Article VII.

3. The Commission shall calculate the payments due from each Contracting Governemnt under the annual administrative budget according to the following formula:

(*a*) from the administrative budget there shall be deducted a sum of 500 United States dollars for each Contracting Government;

(*b*) the remainder shall be divided into such number of equal shares as corresponds to the total number of Panel memberships;

(*c*) the payment due form any Contracting Government shall be the equivalent of 500 United States dollars plus the number of shares equal to the number of Panels in which that Government participates.

4. The Commission shall notify each Contracting Government the sum due from that Government as calculated under paragraph 3 of this Article and as soon as possible thereafter each Contracting Government shall pay to the Commission the sum so notified.

5. The annual special projects budget shall be allocated to the Contracting Governments according to a scale to be determined by agreement among the Contracting Governments, and the sums so allocated to any Contracting Government shall be paid to the Commission by that Government.

6. Contributions shall be payable in the currency of the country in which the seat of the Commission is located, except that the Commission may accept payment in the currencies in which it may be anticipated that expenditures of the Commission will be made from time to time, up to an amount established each year by the Commission in connection with the preparation of the annual budgets.

7. At its first meeting the Commission shall approve an administrative budget for the balance of the first financial year in which the Commission functions and shall transmit to the Contracting Governments copies of that budget together with notices of their respective allocations.

8. In subsequent financial years, the Commission shall submit to each Contracting Government drafts of the annual budgets together with a schedule of allocations, not less than six weeks before the annual meeting of the Commission at which the budgets are to be considered.

Article XII

The Contracting Governments agree to take such action as may be necessary to make effective the provisions of this Convention and to implement any proposals which become effective under paragraph 8 of Article VIII. Each Contracting Government shall transmit to the Commission a statement of the action taken by it for these purposes.

Article XIII

The Contracting Governments agree to invite the attention of any Government not a party to this Convention to any matter relating to the fishing activities in the Convention area of the national or vessels of that Government which appear to affect adversely the operations of the Commission or the carrying out of the objectives of this Convention.

Article XIV

The Annex, as attached to this Convention and as modified from time to time, forms an integral part of this Convention.

Article XV

1. This Convention shall be ratified by the signatory Governments and the instruments of ratification shall be deposited with the Government of the United States of America, referred to in this Convention as the " Depositary Government ".

2. This Convention shall enter into force upon the deposit of instruments of ratification by four signatory Governments, and shall enter into force with respect to each Government which subsequently ratifies on the date of the deposit of its instrument of ratification.

3. Any Government which has not signed this Convention may adhere thereto by a notification in writing to the Depositary Government. Adherences received by the Depositary Government prior to the date of entry into force of this Convention shall become effective on the date this Convention enters into force. Adherences received by the Depositary Government after the date of entry into force of this Convention shall become effective on the date of receipt by the Depositary Government.

4. The Depositary Government shall inform all signatory Governments and all adhering Governments of all ratifications deposited and adherences received.

5. The Depositary Government shall inform all Governments concerned of the date this Convention enters into force.

Article XVI

1. At any time after the expiration of ten years from the date of entry into force of this Convention, any Contracting Government may withdraw from the Convention on December thirty-first of any year by giving notice on or before the preceding June thirtieth to the Depositary Government which shall communicate copies of such notice to the other Contracting Governments.

2. Any other Contracting Government may thereupon withdraw from this Convention on the same December thirty-first by giving notice to the Depositary Government within one month of the receipt of a copy of a notice of withdrawal given pursuant to paragraph 1 of this Article.

Article XVII

1. The original of this Convention shall be deposited with the Government of the United States of America, which Government shall communicate certified copies thereof to all the signatory Governments and all the adhering Governments.

2. The Depositary Government shall register this Convention with the Secretariat of the United Nations.

3. This Convention shall bear the date on which it is opened for signature and shall remain open for signature for a period of fourteen days thereafter.

IN WITNESS WHEREOF the undersigned, having deposited their respective full powers, have signed this Convention.

DONE in Washington this eighth day of February 1949 in the English language.

ANNEX

1. The sub-areas provided for by Article I of this Convention shall be as follows :

Sub-area 1—That portion of the Convention area which lies to the north and east of a rhumb line from a point in 75° 00' north latitude and 73° 30' west longitude to a doint in 69° 00' north latitude and 59° 00' west longitude; east of 59° 00' west longitude; and to the north and east of a rhumb line from a point in 61° 00' north latitude and 59° 00' west longitude to a point in 52° 15' north latitude and 42° 00' west longitude.

Sub-area 2—That portion of the Convention area lying to the south and west of sub-area 1 defined above and to the north of the parallel of 52° 15' north latitude.

Sub-area 3—That portion of the Convention area lying south of the parallel of 52° 15' north latitude; and to the east of a line extending due north from Cape Bauld on the north coast of Newfoundland to 52° 15' north latitude; to the north of the parallel of 39° 00' north latitude; and to the east and north of a rhumb line extending in a northwesterly direction which passes through a point in 43° 30' north latitude, 55° 00' west longitude, in the direction of a point in 47° 50' north latitude, 60° 00' west longitude, until it intersects a straight line connecting Cape Ray, on the coast of Newfoundland, with Cape North on Cape Breton Island; thence in a northeasterly direction along said line to Cape Ray.

Sub-area 4—That portion of the Convention area lying to the west of sub-area 3 defined above, and to the east of a line described as follows : beginning at the terminus of the international boundary between the United States of America and Canada in Grand Manan Channel, at a point in 44° 46' 35.34" north latitude, 66° 54' 11.23" west longitude; thence due south to the parallel of 43° 50' north latitude; thence due west to the meridian of 67° 40' west longitude; thence due south to the parallel of 42° 20' north latitude; thence due east to a point in 66° 00' west longitude; thence along a rhumb line in a southeasterly direction to a point in 42° 00' north latitude, 65° 40' west longitude; thence due south to the parallel of 39° 00' north latitude.

Sub-area 5—That portion of the Convention area lying west of the western boundary of sub-area 4 defined above.

2. For a period of two years from the date of entry into force of this Convention, Panel representation for each sub-area shall be as follows :

(*a*) *Sub-area 1*—Denmark, France, Italy, Norway, Portugal, Spain, United Kingdom;
(*b*) *Sub-area 2*—Denmark, France, Italy, Newfoundland;
(*c*) *Sub-area 3*—Canada, Denmark, France, Italy, Newfoundland, Portugal, Spain, United Kingdom;
(*d*) *Sub-area 4*—Canada, France, Italy, Newfoundland, Portugal, Spain, United States;
(*e*) *Sub-area 5*—Canada, United States;

it being understood that during the period between the signing of this Convention and the date of its entry into force, any signatory or adhering Government may, by notification to the Depositary Government, withdraw from the list of members of a Panel for any sub-area or be added to the list of members of the Panel for any sub-area on which it is not named. The Depositary Government shall inform all the other Governments concerned of all such notifications received and the memberships of the Panels shall be altered accordingly.

The text of the Convention given here is the text as it has been amended by: (i) Protocol relating to the Holding of Annual Meetings, Washington, June 25, 1956; (ii) Protocol relating to Entry into Force of Proposals adopted by the Commission, Washington, November 29, 1965; (iii) Protocol relating to Measures of Control, Washington, November 29, 1965; (iv) Protocol relating to Panel Membership and to Regulatory Measures, Washington, October 1, 1969.

The Articles of the Convention which have been amended are: Articles II (5), IV (2), VII (2), VIII (1), (5), (7) and (8).

5. The Commission shall hold a regular annual meeting at its seat or at such other place in North America or elsewhere as may be agreed upon by the Commission.

2. Panel representation shall be reviewed annually by the Commission, which shall have the power, subject to consultation with the Panel conceneded, to determine representation on each Panel on the basis of current substantial exploitation of the stocks of fish in the subarea concerned or on the basis of current substantial exploitation of harp and hood seals in the Convention Area, except that each Contracting Government with coastline adjacent to a subarea shall have the right of representation on the Panel for the subarea.

2. Each Panel, upon the basis of scientific investigations, and economical and technical considerations, may make recommendations to the Commission for joint action by the Contracting Governments within the scope of paragraph 1 of Article VIII.

1. The Commission may, on the recommendations of one or more Panels, and on the basis of scientific investigations, and economic and technical considerations, transmit to the Depositary Government appropriate proposals, for joint action by the Contracting Governments, designed to achieve the optimum utilization of the stocks of those species of fish which support international fisheries in the Convention Area.

5. The Commission may, after consultation with all the Panels, transmit proposals to the Depositary Government within the scope of paragraph 1 of this Article affecting the Convention area as a whole and may also , on its own initiative, make proposals for national and international measures of control on the high seas for the purposes of ensuring the application of the Convention and the measures in force thereunder.

7. (a) Each proposal made by the Commission under paragraphs 1 or 5 of this Article shall become effective for all Contracting Governments six months after the date on the notification from the Depositary Government transmitting the proposal to the Contracting Governments, except as otherwise provided herein.

(b) If any Contracting Government participating in the Panel or Panels for the sub-area or sub-areas to which a proposal applies, or any Contracting Government in the case of a proposal made under paragraph 5 above, presents to the Depositary Government objection to any proposal within six months of the date on the notification of the proposal by the Depositary Government, the proposal shall not become effective for any Government for an additional sixty days. Thereupon any other Contracting Government participating in the Panel or Panels concerned, or any other Contracting Government in the case of a proposal made under paragraph 5 above, may similarly object prior to the expiration of the additional sixty-day period, or within thirty days after receiving notice of an objection by another Contracting Government made within such additional sixty days, whichever date shall be the later. The proposal shall become effective for all Contracting Governments except those Governments which have presented objections, at the end of the extended period or periods for objecting. If, however, objections have been presented by a majority of Contracting Governments participating in the Panel or Panels concerned, or by a majority of all Contracting Governments in the case of a proposal made under paragraph 5, the proposal shall not become effective unless any or all of the Contracting Governments nevertheless agree as among themselves to give effect to it on an agreed date.

(c) Any Contracting Government which has objected to a proposal may at any time withdraw that objection and the proposal shall become effective with respect to such Government, immediately if the proposal is already in effect, or at such time as it becomes effective under the terms of this Article.

8. The Depositary Government shall notify each Contracting Government immediately upon receipt of each objection and of each withdrawal of objection, and of the entry into force of any proposal.

No. 2053. INTERNATIONAL CONVENTION FOR THE NORTHWEST ATLANTIC FISHERIES. DONE AT WASHINGTON, ON 8 FEBRUARY 1949[1]

DECLARATION OF UNDERSTANDING[2] REGARDING THE ABOVE-MENTIONED CONVENTION. SIGNED AT WASHINGTON, ON 24 APRIL 1961

Official text: English.

Registered by the United States of America on 16 October 1963.

1. The Governments parties to the International Convention for the Northwest Atlantic Fisheries signed at Washington under date of February 8, 1949,[1] which Convention is hereinafter referred to as the Convention, hereby declare their understanding that the words " fish ", " fishes ", " fishery ", " fisheries ", and " fishing " as they appear in the Convention include and apply to mollusks, as well as finny fish.

2. Governments parties to the Convention may become parties to the present Declaration by:

(*a*) Signature without reservation as to acceptance;

(*b*) Signature with reservation as to acceptance, followed by acceptance; or

(*c*) Acceptance.

3. Acceptance shall be effected by written notification to the Government of the United States of America.

---

[1] United Nations, *Treaty Series*, Vol. 157, p. 157; Vol. 174, p. 338; Vol. 200, p. 317; Vol. 308, p. 312; Vol. 331, p. 388; Vol. 458, p. 296, and Vol. 478.

[2] In accordance with article 4, the Declaration came into force on 5 June 1963, the date upon which all the Governments parties to the Convention had become parties to the said Declaration, as indicated below:

By signature without reservation as to acceptance	*Date of signature*
Denmark	2 May 1961
United Kingdom of Great Britain and Northern Ireland	2 May 1961
France	5 May 1961
Spain	5 May 1961
Federal Republic of Germany	8 May 1961
Iceland	8 May 1961
Norway	8 May 1961
Portugal	8 May 1961
Union of Soviet Socialist Republics	8 May 1961

By signature with reservation as to acceptance, followed by acceptance:	*Date of signature*	*Date of acceptance*
United States of America	24 April 1961	9 February 1962

By acceptance	*Date of acceptance*
Italy	14 September 1961
Canada	15 September 1961
Poland	5 June 1963

4. This Declaration shall enter into force on the date upon which all the Governments parties to the Convention have become parties to this Declaration. Any Government becoming a party to the Convention after this Declaration enters into force shall accept this Declaration, such acceptance to be effective on the same date that such Government becomes a party to the Convention.

5. The Government of the United States of America shall inform all Governments signatory or adhering to the Convention of all signatures and acceptances of this Declaration and of the date upon which this Declaration enters into force.

6. The original of this Declaration shall be deposited with the Government of the United States of America, which Government shall communicate certified copies thereof to all the Governments signatory or adhering to the Convention.

7. This Declaration shall bear the date on which it is opened for signature and shall remain open for signature or acceptance for a period of fourteen days thereafter, following which period it shall remain open for acceptance.

In witness whereof the undersigned, being duly authorized thereto by their respective Governments, have signed this Declaration.

Done at Washington this twenty-fourth day of April 1961 in the English language.

PROTOCOL TO THE INTERNATIONAL CONVENTION FOR THE NORTHWEST ATLANTIC FISHERIES

The Governments parties to the International Convention for the Northwest Atlantic Fisheries signed at Washington under date of February 8, 1949, which Convention, as amended,[1] is hereinafter referred to as the Convention, desiring to extend the provisions of the Convention to harp and hood seals, agree as follows:

Article I

The provisions of the Convention shall be applicable with respect to harp and hood seals in conformity with Articles II and III of this Protocol.

Article II

1. The Contracting Governments shall establish and maintain a Panel with jurisdiction respecting harp and hood seals in the Convention area. Initial representation on the Panel shall be determined by the International Commission for the Northwest Atlantic Fisheries on the basis of current substantial exploitation of harp and hood seals in the Convention area, except that each Contracting Government with coastline adjacent to the Convention area shall have the right to representation on the Panel.

2. Panel representation shall be reviewed annually by the Commission, which shall have the power, subject to consultation with the Panel, to determine representation on the Panel on the same basis as provided in paragraph 1 of this Article for initial representation.

Article III

Proposals in accordance with Article VIII of the Convention for joint action by Contracting Governments with respect to harp and hood seals shall become effective for all Contracting Governments four months after the date on which notifications of acceptance have been received by the Depositary Government from all the Contracting Governments participating in the Panel for harp and hood seals.

Article IV

1. This Protocol shall be open for signature and ratification or for adherence on behalf of any Government party to the Convention.

---

[1] TIAS 2089, 4170, 5380; 1 UST 477; 10 UST 59; 14 UST 924.

2. This Protocol shall enter into force on the date on which instruments of ratification have been deposited with, or written notifications of adherence have been received by, the Government of the United States of America, on behalf of all the Governments parties to the Convention.

3. Any Government becoming a party to the Convention after this Protocol enters into force shall adhere to this Protocol, such adherence to be effective on the same date that such Government becomes a party to the Convention.

4. The Government of the United States of America shall inform all Governments signatory or adhering to the Convention of all ratifications deposited and adherences received and of the date this Protocol enters into force.

ARTICLE V

1. The original of this Protocol shall be deposited with the Government of the United States of America, which Government shall communicate certified copies thereof to all the Governments signatory or adhering to the Convention.

2. This Protocol shall bear the date on which it is opened for signature and shall remain open for signature for a period of fourteen days thereafter, following which period it shall be open for adherence.

IN WITNESS WHEREOF the undersigned, having deposited their respective full powers, have signed this Protocol.

DONE at Washington this fifteenth day of July, 1963 in the English language.

PROTOCOL
TO THE INTERNATIONAL CONVENTION FOR THE NORTHWEST ATLANTIC FISHERIES RELATING TO AMENDMENTS TO THE CONVENTION

The Governments parties to the International Convention for the Northwest Atlantic Fisheries signed at Washington under date of February 8, 1949,(1) which Convention, as amended,(2) is hereinafter referred to as the Convention, desiring to facilitate the entry into force of amendments to the Convention, agree as follows:

ARTICLE I

Article XVII of the Convention is renumbered " Article XVIII " and a new Article XVII is inserted to read as follows:

" *Article XVII*

" 1. Any Contracting Government or the Commission may propose amendments to this Convention to be considered and acted upon by a regular meeting of the Commission or by a special meeting of the Commission called in accordance with the provisions of paragraph 6 of Article II of the Convention. Any such proposed amendment shall be sent to the Executive Secretary at least ninety days prior to the meeting at which it is proposed to be acted upon, and he shall immediately transmit the proposal to all Contracting Governments and to all Commissioners.

" 2. A proposed amendment to the Convention shall be adopted by the Commission by a three-fourths majority of the votes of all Contracting Governments. The text of any proposed amendment so adopted shall be transmitted by the Depositary Government to all Contracting Governments.

" 3. Any amendment shall take effect for all Contracting Governments one hundred and twenty days following the date on the notification by the Depositary Government of receipt of written notification of approval by three-fourths of all Contracting Governments unless any other Contracting Government notifies the Depositary Government that it objects to the amendment, within ninety days of the date on the notification by the Depositary Government of such receipt, in which case the amendment shall not take effect for any Contracting Government. Any Contracting Government which has objected to an amendment may

(1) Treaty Series No. 62 (1950), Cmd. 8071.
(2) Treaty Series No. 22 (1959), Cmnd. 687.
Treaty Series No. 40 (1966), Cmnd. 3044.
Treaty Series No. 73 (1970), Cmnd. 4435.
Treaty Series No. 74 (1970), Cmnd. 4436.

at any time withdraw that objection. If all objections to an amendment are withdrawn, the amendment shall take effect for all Contracting Governments one hundred and twenty days following the date on the notification by the Depositary Government of receipt of the last withdrawal.

"4. Any Government which becomes a party to the Convention after an amendment has been adopted in accordance with paragraph 2 of this Article shall be deemed to have approved the said amendment.

"5. The Depositary Government shall promptly notify all Contracting Governments of the receipts of notifications of approval of amendments, the receipt of notifications of objection or withdrawal of objections, and the entry into force of amendments."

Article II

1. This Protocol shall be open for signature and ratification or approval or for adherence on behalf of any Government party to the Convention.

2. This Protocol shall enter into force on the date on which instruments of ratification or approval have been deposited with, or written notices of adherence have been received by, the Government of the United States of America, on behalf of all Governments parties to the Convention.

3. Any Government which becomes a party to the Convention after this Protocol has been opened for signature shall at the same time adhere to this Protocol.

4. The Government of the United States of America shall inform all Governments signatory or adhering to the Convention of all ratifications and approvals deposited and adherences received and of the date this Protocol enters into force.

5. Any Protocol amending the Convention which has been signed but which has not entered into force at the date of entry into force of the present Protocol shall thereafter enter into force in accordance with the provisions of the present Protocol; provided, however, that, if instruments of ratification or approval or notices of adherence with respect to such Protocol have been received by the Depositary Government from three-fourths of all Contracting Governments at the time of entry into force of the present Protocol, the date on which the ninety, and one hundred and twenty, day periods specified in the first sentence of paragraph 3 of Article XVII shall commence with regard to such amendment shall be the date of entry into force of the present Protocol.

Article III

1. The original of this Protocol shall be deposited with the Government of the United States of America, which Government shall communicate certified copies thereof to all the Governments signatory or adhering to the Convention.

2. This Protocol shall bear the date on which it is opened for signature and shall remain open for signature for a period of fourteen days thereafter, following which period it shall be open for adherence.

IN WITNESS WHEREOF the undersigned, having deposited their respective full powers, have signed this Protocol.

DONE at Washington this sixth day of October 1970, in the English language.

INTERNATIONAL CONVENTION FOR THE HIGH SEAS FISHERIES OF THE NORTH PACIFIC OCEAN

The Governments of the United States of America, Canada and Japan, whose respective duly accredited representatives have subscribed hereto,

Acting as sovereign nations in the light of their rights under the principles of international law and custom to exploit the fishery resources of the high seas, and

Believing that it will best serve the common interest of mankind, as well as the interests of the Contracting Parties, to ensure the maximum sustained productivity of the fishery resources of the North Pacific Ocean, and that each of the Parties should assume an obligation, on a free and equal footing, to encourage the conservation of such resources, and

Recognizing that in view of these considerations it is highly desirable (1) to establish an International Commission, representing the three Parties hereto, to promote and coordinate the scientific studies necessary to ascertain the conservation measures required to secure the maximum sustained productivity of fisheries of joint interest to the Contracting Parties and to recommend such measures to such Parties and (2) that each Party carry out such conservation recommendations, and provide for necessary restraints on its own nationals and fishing vessels,

Therefore agree as follows:

Article I

1. The area to which this Convention applies, hereinafter referred to as "the Convention area", shall be all waters, other than territorial waters, of the North Pacific Ocean which for the purposes hereof shall include the adjacent seas.

2. Nothing in this Convention shall be deemed to affect adversely (prejudice) the claims of any Contracting Party in regard to the limits of territorial waters or to the jurisdiction of a coastal state over fisheries.

3. For the purposes of this Convention the term "fishing vessel" shall mean any vessel engaged in catching fish or processing or transporting fish loaded on the high seas, or any vessel outfitted for such activities.

Article II

1. In order to realize the objectives of this Convention, the Contracting Parties shall establish and maintain the International North Pacific Fisheries Commission, hereinafter referred to as "the Commission."

2. The Commission shall be composed of three national sections, each consisting of not more than four members appointed by the governments of the respective Contracting Parties.

3. Each national section shall have one vote. All resolutions, recommendations and other decisions of the Commission shall be made only by a unanimous vote of the three national sections except when under the provisions of Article III, Section 1 (c) (ii) only two participate.

4. The Commission may decide upon and amend, as occasion may require, by-laws or rules for the conduct of its meetings.

5. The Commission shall meet at least once each year and at such other times as may be requested by a majority of the national sections. The date and place of the first meeting shall be determined by agreement between the Contracting Parties.

6. At its first meeting the Commission shall select a Chairman, Vice-Chairman and Secretary from different national sections. The Chairman, Vice-Chairman and Secretary shall hold office for a period of one year. During succeeding years selection of a Chairman, Vice-Chairman and Secretary from the national sections shall be made in such a manner as will provide each Contracting Party in turn with representation in those offices.

7. The Commission shall decide on a convenient place for the establishment of the Commission's headquarters.

8. Each Contracting Party may establish an Advisory Committee for its national section, to be composed of persons who shall be well informed concerning North Pacific fishery problems of common concern. Each such Advisory Committee shall be invited to attend all sessions of the Commission except those which the Commission decides to be *in camera*.

9. The Commission may hold public hearings. Each national section may also hold public hearings within its own country.

10. The official languages of the Commission shall be Japanese and English. Proposals and data may be submitted to the Commission in either language.

11. Each Contracting Party shall determine and pay the expenses incurred by its national section. Joint expenses incurred by the Commission shall be paid by the Commission through contributions made by the Contracting Parties in the form and proportion recommended by the Commission and approved by the Contracting Parties.

12. An annual budget of joint expenses shall be recommended by the Commission and submitted to the Contracting Parties for approval.

13. The Commission shall authorize the disbursement of funds for the joint expenses of the Commission and may employ personnel and acquire facilities necessary for the performance of its functions.

ARTICLE III

1 The Commission shall perform the following functions:

(a) In regard to any stock of fish specified in the Annex, study for the purpose of determining annually whether such stock continues to qualify for abstention under the provisions of Article IV. If the Commission determines that such stock no longer meets the conditions of Article IV, the Commission shall recommend that it be removed from the Annex. Provided, however, that with respect to the stocks of fish originally specified in the Annex, no determination or recommendation as to whether such stock continues to qualify for abstention shall be made for five years after the entry into force of this Convention.

(b) To permit later additions to the Annex, study, on request of a Contracting Party, any stock of fish of the Convention area, the greater part of which is harvested by one or more of the Contracting Parties, for the purpose of determining whether such stock qualifies for abstention under the provisions of Article IV. If the Commission decides that the particular stock fulfills the conditions of Article IV it shall recommend, (1) that such stock be added to the Annex, (2) that the appropriate Party or Parties abstain from fishing such stock and (3) that the Party or Parties participating in the fishing of such stock continue to carry out necessary conservation measures.

(c) In regard to any stock of fish in the Convention area;

(i) Study, on request of any Contracting Party concerned, any stock of fish which is under substantial exploitation by two or more of the Contracting Parties, and which is not covered by a conservation agreement between such Parties existing at the time of the conclusion of this Convention, for the purpose of determining need for joint conservation measures;

(ii) Decide and recommend necessary joint conservation measures including any relaxation thereof to be taken as a result of such study. Provided, however, that only the national sections of the Contracting Parties engaged in substantial exploitation of such stock of fish may participate in such decision and recommendation. The decisions and recommendations shall be reported regularly to all the Contracting Parties, but shall apply only to the Contracting Parties the national sections of which participated in the decisions and recommendations.

(iii) Request the Contracting Party or Parties concerned to report regularly the conservation measures adopted from time to time with regard to the stocks of fish specified in the Annex, whether or not covered by conservation agreements between the Contracting Parties, and transmit such information to the other Contracting Party or Parties.

(d) Consider and make recommendations to the Contracting Parties concerning the enactment of schedules of equivalent penalties for violations of this Convention.

(e) Compile and study the records provided by the Contracting Parties pursuant to Article VIII.

(f) Submit annually to each Contracting Party a report on the Commission's operations, investigations and findings, with appropriate recommendations, and inform each Contracting Party, whenever it is deemed advisable, on any matter relating to the objectives of this Convention.

2. The Commission may take such steps, in agreement with the Parties concerned, as will enable it to determine the extent to which the undertakings agreed to by the Parties under the provisions of Article V, Section 2 and the measures recommended by the Commission under the provisions of this Article and accepted by the Parties concerned have been effective.

3. In the performance of its functions, the Commission shall, insofar as feasible, utilize the technical and scientific services of, and information from, official agencies of the Contracting Parties and their political sub-divisions and may, when desirable and if available, utilize the services of, and information from, any public or private institution or organization or any private individual.

Article IV

1. In making its recommendations the Commission shall be guided by the spirit and intent of this Convention and by the considerations below mentioned.

(a) Any conservation measures for any stock of fish decided upon under the provisions of this Convention shall be recommended for equal application to all Parties engaged in substantial exploitation of such stock.

(b) With regard to any stock of fish which the Commission determines reasonably satisfies all the following conditions, a recommendation shall be made as provided for in Article III, Section 1, (b).

(i) Evidence based upon scientific research indicates that more intensive exploitation of the stock will not provide a substantial increase in yield which can be sustained year after year,

(ii) The exploitation of the stock is limited or otherwise regulated through legal measures by each Party which is substantially engaged in its exploitation, for the purpose of maintaining or increasing its maximum sustained productivity; such limitations and regulations being in accordance with conservation programs based upon scientific research, and

(iii) The stock is the subject of extensive scientific study designed to discover whether the stock is being fully utilized and the conditions necessary for maintaining its maximum sustained productivity.

Provided, however, that no recommendation shall be made for abstention by a Contracting Party concerned with regard to: (1) any stock of fish which at any time during the twenty-five years next preceding the entry into force of this Convention has been under substantial exploitation by that Party having regard to the conditions referred to in Section 2 of this Article; (2) any stock of fish which is harvested in greater part by a country or countries not party to this Convention; (3) waters in which there is historic intermingling of fishing operations of the Parties concerned, intermingling of the stocks of fish exploited by these operations, and a long-established history of joint conservation and regulation among the Parties concerned so that there is consequent impracticability of segregating the operations and administering control. It is recognized that the conditions specified in subdivision (3) of this proviso apply to Canada and the United States of America in the waters off the Pacific Coasts of the United States of America and Canada from and including the waters of the Gulf of Alaska southward and, therefore, no recommendation shall be made for abstention by either the United States of America or Canada in such waters.

2. In any decision or recommendation allowances shall be made for the effect of strikes, wars, or exceptional economic or biological conditions which may have introduced temporary declines in or suspension of productivity, exploitation, or management of the stock of fish concerned.

Article V

1. The Annex attached hereto forms an integral part of this Convention. All references to "Convention" shall be understood as

39328 O—54——2

including the said Annex either in its present terms or as amended in accordance with the provisions of Article VII.

2. The Contracting Parties recognize that any stock of fish originally specified in the Annex to this Convention fulfills the conditions prescribed in Article IV and accordingly agree that the appropriate Party or Parties shall abstain from fishing such stock and the Party or Parties participating in the fishing of such stock shall continue to carry out necessary conservation measures.

Article VI

In the event that it shall come to the attention of any of the Contracting Parties that the nationals or fishing vessels of any country which is not a Party to this Convention appear to affect adversely the operations of the Commission or the carrying out of the objectives of this Convention, such Party shall call the matter to the attention of other Contracting Parties. All the Contracting Parties agree upon the request of such Party to confer upon the steps to be taken towards obviating such adverse effects or relieving any Contracting Party from such adverse effects.

Article VII

1. The Annex to this Convention shall be considered amended from the date upon which the Commission receives notification from all the Contracting Parties of acceptance of a recommendation to amend the Annex made by the Commission in accordance with the provisions of Article III, Section 1 or of the Protocol to this Convention.

2. The Commission shall notify all the Contracting Parties of the date of receipt of each notification of acceptance of an amendment to the Annex.

Article VIII

The Contracting Parties agree to keep as far as practicable all records requested by the Commission and to furnish compilations of such records and other information upon request of the Commission. No Contracting Party shall be required hereunder to provide the records of individual operations.

Article IX

1. The Contracting Parties agree as follows:

(a) With regard to a stock of fish from the exploitation of which any Contracting Party has agreed to abstain, the nationals and fishing vessels of such Contracting Party are prohibited from engaging in the exploitation of such stock of fish in waters specified in the Annex, and from loading, processing, possessing, or transporting such fish in such waters.

(b) With regard to a stock of fish for which a Contracting Party has agreed to continue to carry out conservation measures, the nationals and fishing vessels of such Party are prohibited from engaging in fishing activities in waters specified in the Annex in violation of regulations established under such conservation measures.

2. Each Contracting Party agrees, for the purpose of rendering effective the provisions of this Convention, to enact and enforce necessary laws and regulations, with regard to its nationals and fishing vessels, with appropriate penalties against violations thereof and to transmit to the Commission a report on any action taken by it with regard thereto.

ARTICLE X

1. The Contracting Parties agree, in order to carry out faithfully the provisions of this Convention, to cooperate with each other in taking appropriate and effective measures and accordingly agree as follows:

(a) When a fishing vessel of a Contracting Party has been found in waters in which that Party has agreed to abstain from exploitation in accordance with the provisions of this Convention, the duly authorized officials of any Contracting Party may board such vessel to inspect its equipment, books, documents, and other articles and question the persons on board.

Such officials shall present credentials issued by their respective Governments if requested by the master of the vessel.

(b) When any such person or fishing vessel is actually engaged in operations in violation of the provisions of this Convention, or there is reasonable ground to believe was obviously so engaged immediately prior to boarding of such vessel by any such official, the latter may arrest or seize such person or vessel. In that case, the Contracting Party to which the official belongs shall notify the Contracting Party to which such person or vessel belongs of such arrest or seizure, and shall deliver such vessel or persons as promptly as practicable to the authorized officials of the Contracting Party to which such vessel or person belongs at a place to be agreed upon by both Parties. Provided, however, that when the Contracting Party which receives such notification cannot immediately accept delivery and makes request, the Contracting Party which gives such notification may keep such person or vessel under surveillance within its own territory, under the conditions agreed upon by both of the Contracting Parties.

(c) Only the authorities of the Party to which the above-mentioned person or fishing vessel belongs may try the offense and impose penalties therefor. The witnesses and evidence necessary for establishing the offense, so far as they are under the control of any of the Parties to this Convention, shall be furnished as promptly as possible to the Contracting Party having jurisdiction to try the offense.

2. With regard to the nationals or fishing vessels of one or more Contracting Parties in waters with respect to which they have agreed to continue to carry out conservation measures for certain stocks of fish in accordance with the provisions of this Convention, the Contracting Parties concerned shall carry out enforcement severally or jointly. In that case, the Contracting Parties concerned agree to report periodically through the Commission to the Contracting Party which has agreed to abstain from the exploitation of such stocks of fish on the enforcement conditions, and also, if requested, to provide opportunity for observation of the conduct of enforcement.

3. The Contracting Parties agree to meet, during the sixth year of the operation of this Convention, to review the effectiveness of the enforcement provisions of this Article and, if desirable, to consider means by which they may more effectively be carried out.

Article XI

1. This Convention shall be ratified by the Contracting Parties in accordance with their respective constitutional processes and the instruments of ratification shall be exchanged as soon as possible at Tokyo.

2. This Convention shall enter into force on the date of the exchange of ratifications.[1] It shall continue in force for a period of ten years and thereafter until one year from the day on which a Contracting Party shall give notice to the other Contracting Parties of an intention of terminating the Convention, whereupon it shall terminate as to all Contracting Parties.

In witness whereof, the respective Plenipotentiaries, duly authorized, have signed the present Convention.

---

[1] June 12, 1953.

DONE in triplicate, in the English and Japanese languages, both equally authentic, at Tokyo this ninth day of May, one thousand nine hundred fifty-two.

UNITED STATES OF AMERICA:

ROBERT MURPHY

CANADA:

A R MENZIES

JAPAN:

K. OKAZAKI

K HIROKAWA.

[SEAL] [SEAL] [SEAL]

Annex

1. With regard to the stocks of fish in the respective waters named below, Japan agrees to abstain from fishing, and Canada and the United States of America agree to continue to carry out necessary conservation measures, in accordance with the provisions of Article V, Section 2 of this Convention:

(a) Halibut (*Hippoglossus stenolepis*)

The Convention area off the coasts of Canada and the United States of America in which commercial fishing for halibut is being or can be prosecuted. Halibut referred to herein shall be those originating along the coast of North America.

(b) Herring (*Clupea pallasii*)

The Convention area off the coasts of Canada and the United States of America, exclusive of the Bering Sea and of the waters of the North Pacific Ocean west of the meridian passing through the extremity of the Alaskan Peninsula, in which commercial fishing for herring of North America origin is being or can be prosecuted.

(c) Salmon (*Oncorhynchus gorbuscha*, *Oncorhynchus keta*, *Oncorhynchus kisutch*, *Oncorhynchus nerka*, *Oncorhynchus tschawytscha*)

The Convention area off the coasts of Canada and the United States of America, exclusive of the Bering Sea and of the waters of the North Pacific Ocean west of a provisional line following the meridian passing through the western extremity of Atka Island; in which commercial fishing for salmon originating in the rivers of Canada and the United States of America is being or can be prosecuted.

2. With regard to the stocks of fish in the waters named below, Canada and Japan agree to abstain from fishing, and the United States of America agrees to continue to carry out necessary conservation measures, in accordance with the provisions of Article V, Section 2 of this Convention:

Salmon (*Oncorhynchus gorbuscha*, *Oncorhynchus keta*, *Oncorhynchus kisutch*, *Oncorhynchus nerka and Oncorhynchus tschawytscha*)

The Convention area of the Bering Sea east of the line starting from Cape Prince of Wales on the west coast of Alaska, running westward to 168°58′22.59″ West Longitude; thence due south to a point 65°15′00″ North Latitude; thence along the great circle course which passes through 51° North Latitude and 167° East Longitude, to its intersection with meridian 175° West Longitude; thence south along a provisional line which follows this meridian to the territorial waters limit of Atka Island; in which commercial fishing for salmon originating in the rivers of the United States of America is being or can be prosecuted.

PROTOCOL TO THE INTERNATIONAL CONVENTION FOR THE HIGH SEAS FISHERIES OF THE NORTH PACIFIC OCEAN

The Governments of the United States of America, Canada and Japan, through their respective Plenipotentiaries, agree upon the following stipulation in regard to the International Convention for the High Seas Fisheries of the North Pacific Ocean, signed at Tokyo on this ninth day of May, nineteen hundred fifty-two.

The Governments of the United States of America, Canada and Japan agree that the line of meridian 175° West Longitude and the line following the meridian passing through the western extremity of Atka Island, which have been adopted for determining the areas in which the exploitation of salmon is abstained or the conservation measures for salmon continue to be enforced in accordance with the provisions of the Annex to this Convention, shall be considered as provisional lines which shall continue in effect subject to confirmation or readjustment in accordance with the procedure mentioned below.

The Commission to be established under the Convention shall, as expeditiously as practicable, investigate the waters of the Convention area to determine if there are areas in which salmon originating in the rivers of Canada and of the United States of America intermingle with salmon originating in the rivers of Asia. If such areas are found the Commission shall conduct suitable studies to determine a line or lines which best divide salmon of Asiatic origin and salmon of Canadian and United States of America origin, from which certain Contracting Parties have agreed to abstain in accordance with the provisions of Article V, Section 2, and whether it can be shown beyond a reasonable doubt that this line or lines more equitably divide such salmon than the provisional lines specified in sections 1(c) and 2 of the Annex. In accordance with these determinations the Commission shall recommend that such provisional lines be confirmed or that they be changed in accordance with these results, giving due consideration to adjustments required to simplify administration.

In the event, however, the Commission fails within a reasonable period of time to recommend unanimously such line or lines, it is agreed that the matter shall be referred to a special committee of scientists consisting of three competent and disinterested persons, no one of whom shall be a national of a Contracting Party, selected by mutual agreement of all Parties for the determination of this matter.

It is further agreed that when a determination has been made by a majority of such special committee, the Commission shall make a recommendation in accordance therewith.

The Governments of the United States of America, Canada and Japan, in signing this Protocol, desire to make it clear that the procedure set forth herein is designed to cover a special situation. It is not, therefore, to be considered a precedent for the final resolution of any matters which may, in the future, come before the Commission.

This Protocol shall become effective from the date of entry into force of the said Convention. [1]

IN WITNESS WHEREOF, the respective Plenipotentiaries have signed this Protocol.

DONE in triplicate at Tokyo this ninth day of May, one thousand nine hundred fifty-two.

UNITED STATES OF AMERICA:
ROBERT MURPHY

CANADA:
A R MENZIES

JAPAN:
K. OKAZAKI
K. HIROKAWA.

[1] June 12, 1953.

No. 7078. NORTH-EAST ATLANTIC FISHERIES CONVENTION.[1] SIGNED AT LONDON, ON 24 JANUARY 1959

The States Parties to this Convention

Desiring to ensure the conservation of the fish stocks and the rational exploitation of the fisheries of the North-East Atlantic Ocean and adjacent waters, which are of common concern to them;

Have agreed as follows :

Article 1

(1) The area to which this Convention applies (hereinafter referred to as " the Convention area ") shall be all waters which are situated

(*a*) within those parts of the Atlantic and Arctic Oceans and their dependent seas which lie north of 36° north latitude and between 42° west longitude and 51° east longitude, but excluding

(i) the Baltic Sea and Belts lying to the south and east of lines drawn from Hasenore Head to Gniben Point, from Korshage to Spodsbierg and from Gilbierg Head to the Kullen, and

---

[1] In accordance with article 15 (2), the Convention came into force on 27 June 1963, upon the deposit of instruments of ratification by all signatory States to the Convention. The instruments of ratification were deposited with the Government of the United Kingdom of Great Britain and Northern Ireland on the dates indicated :

United Kingdom of Great Britain and Northern Ireland	27 August 1959	Spain	7 November 1960
Norway	12 January 1960	Poland	22 February 1961
Sweden	31 March 1960	Belgium (with a declaration)**	15 September 1961
Iceland	12 April 1960	France	20 March 1962
Netherlands (with a statement)*	21 April 1960	Ireland	2 October 1962
Denmark	14 July 1960	Portugal	13 December 1962
Union of Soviet Socialist Republics	25 August 1960	Federal Republic of Germany	27 June 1963

* In depositing their instrument of ratification the Government of the Netherlands stated that the measures mentioned in Article 7, paragraph 1 (*c*) to (*f*) inclusive will only be acceptable to the Netherlands if an international control system is introduced at the same time, in such a manner that acceptance of a recommendation ex-Article 13, paragraph 3, should precede the acceptance of a recommendation ex-Article 7, paragraph 1 (*c*) to (*f*) inclusive.

** [*Translation by the Government of the United Kingdom — Traduction du Gouvernement du Royaume-Uni*] In depositing their instrument of ratification the Government of Belgium declared that they could only accept the measures mentioned in Article 7, paragraph 1 (*c*) to (*f*) inclusive on the condition that a system of international control is introduced at the same time; the acceptance of a recommendation provided for in Article 13, paragraph 3, should therefore precede the acceptance of a recommendation provided for in Article 7, paragraph 1 (*c*) to (*f*) inclusive.

(ii) the Mediterranean Sea and its dependent seas as far as the point of intersection of the parallel of 36° latitude and the meridian of 5° 36′ west longitude.

(*b*) within that part of the Atlantic Ocean north of 59° north latitude and between 44° west longitude and 42° west longitude.

(2) The Convention area shall be divided into regions, the boundaries of which shall be those defined in the Annex to this Convention. The regions shall be subject to such alterations as may be made in accordance with the provisions of paragraph (4) of Article 5 of this Convention.

(3) For the purposes of this Convention

(*a*) the expression " vessel " means any vessel or boat employed in fishing for sea fish or in the treatment of sea fish which is registered or owned in the territories of, or which flies the flag of, any Contracting State; and

(*b*) the expression " territories ", in relation to any Contracting State, extends to

(i) any territory within or adjacent to the Convention area for whose international relations the Contracting State is responsible;

(ii) any other territory, not situated within the Convention area or adjacent to it, for whose international relations the Contracting State is responsible and for which such State shall have made known, by written declaration to the Government of the United Kingdom of Great Britain and Northern Ireland (hereinafter referred to as the Government of the United Kingdom), either at the time of signature, of ratification, or of adherence, or subsequently, that this Convention shall apply to it;

(iii) the waters within the Convention area where the Contracting State has exclusive jurisdiction over fisheries.

Article 2

Nothing in this Convention shall be deemed to affect the rights, claims, or views of any Contracting State in regard to the extent of jurisdiction over fisheries.

Article 3

(1) A North-East Atlantic Fisheries Commission (hereinafter referred to as the Commission) is hereby established and shall be maintained for the purposes of this Convention.

(2) Each Contracting State may appoint as its Delegation to the Commission not more than two Commissioners and such experts and advisers to assist them as that State may determine.

(3) The Commission shall elect its own President and not more than two Vice-Presidents who need not be chosen from the Commissioners or their experts or advisers. If a member of a Delegation has been elected President he shall forthwith cease to act as a member of that Delegation, and if a Commissioner has been elected the State concerned shall have the right to appoint another person to serve in his place.

(4) The Office of the Commission shall be in London.

(5) Except where the Commission determines otherwise, it shall meet once a year in London at such time as it shall decide : provided, however, that upon the request of a Commissioner of a Contracting State and subject to the concurrence of a Commissioner of each of three other Contracting States, the President shall, as soon as practicable, summon a meeting at such time and place as he may determine.

(6) The Commission shall appoint its own Secretary and may from time to time appoint such other staff as it may require.

(7) The Commission may set up such Committees as it considers desirable to perform such functions as it may determine.

(8) Each Delegation shall have one vote in the Commission which may be cast only by a Commissioner of the State concerned. Decisions shall be taken by a simple majority except where otherwise specifically provided. If there is an even division of votes on any matter which is subject to a simple majority decision, the proposal shall be regarded as rejected.

(9) Subject to the provisions of this Article, the Commission shall draw up its own Rules of Procedure, including provisions for the election of the President and Vice-Presidents and their terms of office.

(10) The Government of the United Kingdom shall call the first meeting of the Commission as soon as practicable after the coming into force of this Convention, and shall communicate the provisional agenda to each of the other Contracting States not less than two months before the date of the meeting.

(11) Reports of the proceedings of the Commission shall be transmitted and proposals and recommendations shall be notified as soon as possible to all Contracting States in English and in French.

Article 4

(1) Each Contracting State shall pay the expenses of the Commissioners, experts and advisers appointed by it.

(2) The Commission shall prepare an annual budget of the proposed expenditures of the Commission.

(3) In any year in which the annual budget amounts to £200 or less for each Contracting State, the total sum shall be shared equally between Contracting States.

(4) In any year in which the annual budget exceeds £200 for each Contracting State, the Commission shall calculate the payments due from each Contracting State according to the following formula :

(*a*) from the budget there shall be deducted a sum of £200 for each Contracting State;

(*b*) the remainder shall be divided into such number of equal shares as correspond to the total number of Regional Committee memberships;

(*c*) the payment due from any Contracting State shall be the equivalent of £200 plus the number of shares equal to the number of Regional Committees in which that State participates.

(5) The Commission shall notify to each Contracting State the sum due from that State as calculated under paragraph (3) or (4) of this Article and as soon as possible thereafter each Contracting State shall pay to the Commission the sum so notified.

(6) Contributions shall be payable in the currency of the country in which the Office of the Commission is located, except that the Commission may accept payment in the currencies in which it may be expected that expenditures of the Commission will be made from time to time, up to an amount established each year by the Commission when preparing the annual budget.

(7) At its first meeting the Commission shall approve a budget for the balance of the first financial year in which the Commission functions and shall transmit to the Contracting States copies of that budget together with notices of their respective contributions as assessed under paragraph (3) or (4) of this Article.

(8) In subsequent financial years, the Commission shall submit to each Contracting State drafts of annual budgets, together with a schedule of allocations, not less than six weeks before the annual meeting of the Commission at which the budgets are to be considered.

Article 5

(1) The Commission shall establish a Regional Committee, with the powers and duties described in Article 6 of this Convention, for each of the regions into which the Convention area is divided.

(2) The representation on any Regional Committee so established shall be determined by the Commission, provided, however, that any Contracting State with a coastline adjacent to that region, or exploiting the fisheries of the region, has automatically the right of representation on the Regional Committee.

Contracting States exploiting elsewhere a stock which is also fished in that region shall have the opportunity of being represented on the Regional Committee.

(3) Subject to the provisions of Article 6 of this Convention, the Commission shall determine the terms of reference of, and the procedure to be followed by, each Regional Committee.

(4) The Commission may at any time alter the boundaries and vary the number of the regions defined in the Annex to this Convention, provided this is by the unanimous decision of the Delegations present and voting and no objection is made within three months thereafter by any Contracting State not represented, or not voting, at the meeting.

Article 6

(1) It shall be the duty of the Commission :

(*a*) to keep under review the fisheries in the Convention area;

(*b*) to consider, in the light of the technical information available, what measures may be required for the conservation of the fish stocks and for the rational exploitation of the fisheries in the area;

(*c*) to consider, at the request of any Contracting State, representations made to it by a State which is not a party to this Convention for the opening of negotiations on the conservation of fish stocks in the Convention area or any part thereof; and

(*d*) to make to Contracting States recommendations, based as far as praticable on the results of scientific research and investigation, with regard to any of the measures set out in Article 7 of this Convention.

(2) It shall be the duty of a Regional Committee to perform, in relation to its Region, functions of review and consideration similar to those described in paragraph (1) of this Article in relation to the Commission and the Convention area. A Regional Committee may initiate proposals for measures in relation to its region and shall consider any such proposals as may be remitted to it by the Commission.

(3) A Regional Committee may prepare draft recommendations for consideration by the Commission, which may adopt any such draft recommendations, with any modifications it may consider desirable, as recommendations for the purpose of Article 7 of this Convention.

(4) A Regional Committee may at any time apoint sub-committees to study specific problems affecting parts of the Region and to report thereon to the Regional Committee.

Article 7

(1) The measures relating to the objectives and purposes of this Convention which the Commission and Regional Committees may consider, and on which the Commission may make recommendations to the Contracting States, are

(*a*) any measures for the regulation of the size of mesh of fishing nets;

(*b*) any measures for the regulation of the size limits of fish that may be retained on board vessels, or landed, or exposed or offered for sale;

(*c*) any measures for the establishment of closed seasons;

(*d*) any measures for the establishment of closed areas;

(*e*) any measures for the regulation of fishing gear and appliances, other than regulation of the size of mesh of fishing nets;

(*f*) any measures for the improvement and the increase of marine resources, which may include artificial propagation, the transplantation of organisms and the transplantation of young.

(2) Measures for regulating the amount of total catch, or the amount of fishing effort in any period, or any other kinds of measures for the purpose of the conservation of the fish stocks in the Convention area, may be added to the measures listed in paragraph (1) of this Article on a proposal adopted by not less than a two-thirds majority of the Delegations present and voting and subsequently accepted by all Contracting States in accordance with their respective constitutional procedures.

(3) The measures provided for in paragraph (1) and (2) of this Article may relate to any or all species of sea fish and shell fish, but not to sea mammals; to any or all methods of fishing; and to any or all parts of the Convention area.

Article 8

(1) Subject to the provisions of this Article, the Contracting States undertake to give effect to any recommandation made by the Commission under Article 7 of this Convention and adopted by not less than a two-thirds majority of the Delegations present and voting.

(2) Any Contracting State may, within ninety days of the date of notice of a recommendation to which paragraph (1) of this Article applies, object to it and in that event shall not be under obligation to give effect to the recommendation.

(3) In the event of an objection being made within the ninety-day period, any other Contracting State may similarly object at any time within a further

period of sixty days, or within thirty days after receiving notice of an objection by another Contracting State made within the further period of sixty days.

(4) If objections to a recommendation are made by three or more of the Contracting States, all the other Contracting States shall be relieved forthwith of any obligation to give effect to that recommendation but any or all of them may nevertheless agree among themselves to give effect to it.

(5) Any Contracting State which has objected to a recommendation may at any time withdraw that objection and shall then, subject to the provisions of paragraph (4) of this Article, give effect to the recommendation within ninety days, or as from the date determined by the Commission under Article 9 of this Convention, whichever is the later.

(6) The Commission shall notify each Contracting State immediately upon receipt of each objection and withdrawal.

Article 9

Any recommendation to which paragraph (1) of Article 8 of this Convention applies shall, subject to the provisions of that Article, become binding on the Contracting States from the date determined by the Commission, which shall not be before the period for objection provided in Article 8 has elapsed.

Article 10

(1) At any time after two years from the date on which it has been required to give effect to any recommendation to which paragraph (1) of Article 8 of this Convention applies, any Contracting State may give the Commission notice of the termination of its acceptance of the recommendation and, if that notice is not withdrawn, the recommendation shall cease to be binding on that Contracting State at the end of twelve months from the date of the notice.

(2) At any time after a recommendation has ceased to be binding on a Contracting State under paragraph (1) of this Article, the recommendation shall cease to be binding on any other Contracting State which so desires upon the date of notice to the Commission of withdrawal of acceptance of that recommention by such other State.

(3) The Commission shall notify all Contracting States of every notice under this Article immediately upon the receipt thereof.

Article 11

(1) In order that the recommendations made by the Commission for the conservation of the stocks of fish within the Convention area shall be based so far as practicable upon the results of scientific research and investigation, the Commission shall when possible seek the advice of the International Council for the Exploration of the Sea and the co-operation of the Council in carrying out any necessary investigations and, for this purpose, may make such joint arrangements as may be agreed with the International Council for the Exploration of the Sea or may make such other arrangements as it may think fit.

(2) The Commission may seek to establish and maintain working arrangements with any other international organisation which has related objectives.

Article 12

(1) The Contracting States undertake to furnish on the request of the Commission any available statistical and biological information the Commission may need for the purposes of this Convention.

(2) The Commission may publish or otherwise disseminate reports of its activities and such other information relating to the fisheries in the Convention area or any part of that area as it may deem appropriate.

Article 13

(1) Without prejudice to the sovereign rights of States in regard to their territorial and internal waters, each Contracting State shall take in its territories and in regard to its own nationals and its own vessels appropriate measures to ensure the application of the provisions of this Convention and of the recommendations of the Commission which have become binding on that Contracting State and the punishment of infractions of the said provisions and recommendations.

(2) Each Contracting State shall transmit annually to the Commission a statement of the action taken by it for these purposes.

(3) The Commission may by a two-thirds majority make recommendations for, on the one hand, measures of national control in the territories of the Contracting States and, on the other hand, national and international measures of control on the high seas, for the purpose of ensuring the application of the Convention and the measures in force thereunder. Such recommendations shall be subject to the provisions of Articles 8, 9 and 10.

Article 14

The provisions of this Convention shall not apply to fishing operations conducted solely for the purpose of scientific investigations by vessels authorised by a Contracting State for that purpose, or to fish taken in the course of such operations, but in any of the territories of any Contracting State bound by a recommendation to which paragraph (1) of Article 8 applies, fish so taken shall not be sold or exposed or offered for sale in contravention of any such recommendation.

Article 15

(1) This Convention shall be open for signature until 31st March, 1959. It shall be ratified as soon as possible and the instruments of ratification shall be deposited with the Government of the United Kingdom.

(2) This Convention shall enter into force upon the deposit of instruments of ratification by all signatory States. If, however, after the lapse of one year from 31st March, 1959, all the signatory States have not ratified this Convention, but not less than seven of them have deposited instruments of ratification, these latter States may agree among themselves by special protocol on the date on which this Convention shall enter into force; and in that case this Convention shall enter into force with respect to any State that ratifies thereafter on the date of deposit of its instrument of ratification.

(3) Any State which has not signed this Convention may accede thereto at any time after it has come into force in accordance with paragraph (2) of this Article. Accession shall be effected by means of a notice in writing addressed to the Government of the United Kingdom and shall take effect on the date of its receipt. Any State which accedes to this Convention shall simultaneously undertake to give effect to those recommendations which are, at the time of its accession, binding on all the other Contracting States as well as to any other recommendations which are, at that time, binding on one or more of the Contracting States and are not specifically excluded by the acceding State in its notice of accession.

(4) The Government of the United Kingdom shall inform all signatory and acceding States of all ratifications deposited and accessions received and shall notify signatory States of the date and the States in respect of which this Convention enters into force.

Article 16

(1) In respect of each State Party to this Convention, the provisions of Articles 5, 6, 7, 8 and 9 and Annexes I, II and III of the Convention for the Regulation of the Meshes of Fishing Nets and the Size Limits of Fish, signed at London, on 5th April, 1946, as amended[1] by decisions made under paragraph

[1] United Nations, *Treaty Series*, Vol. 231, p. 199; Vol. 354, p. 408; Vol. 431, p. 304; Vol. 456, p. 496, and Vol. 482.

(10) of Article 12 of that Convention, shall remain in force but shall be deemed for the purposes of the present Convention to be a recommendation made and given effect without objection under this Convention as from the date of its entry into force in respect of that State within the area covered by the 1946 Convention; provided that in the period of two years after the coming into force of this Convention, any Contracting State may, on giving twelve month's written notice to the Government of the United Kingdom, withdraw from the whole or any part of the said recommendation. If a Contracting State has, in accordance with the provisions of this Article, given notice of its witdrawal from a part of the said recommendation, any other Contracting State may, with effect from the same date, give notice of its withdrawal from the same or any other part of the said recommendation, or from the recommendation as a whole.

(2) The provisions of the Convention for the Regulation of the Meshes of Fishing Nets and the Size Limits of Fish signed at London on 5th April, 1946, shall, save as provided in paragraph (1) of this Article, cease to apply to each Contracting State to this Convention as from the date of the entry into force of this Convention in respect of that State.

Article 17

At any time after two years from the date on which this Convention has come into force with respect to a Contracting State, that State may denounce the Convention by means of a notice in writing addressed to the Government of the United Kingdom. Any such denunciation shall take effect twelve months after the date of its receipt, and shall be notified to the Contracting States by the Government of the United Kingdom.

IN WITNESS WHEREOF the undersigned, being duly authorised thereto, have signed this Convention.

DONE in London this twenty fourth day of January nineteen hundred and fifty nine in two copies, one in the English language, the other in the French language. Both texts shall be deposited in the archives of the Government of the United Kingdom and shall be regarded as equally authentic.

The Government of the United Kingdom shall transmit certified copies of both texts of this Convention in the two languages to all the signatory and acceding States.

ANNEX

The regions provided for by Article 1 of this Convention shall be as follows :

Region 1—The part of the Convention area bounded on the south by a line running from a point 59° north latitude 44° west longitude due east to the meridian of 42° west longitude; thence due south to the parallel of 48° north latitude; thence due east do the meridian of 18° west longitude; thence due north to the parallel of 60° north latitude; thence due east to the meridian of 5° west longitude; thence due north to the parallel of 60° 30′ north latitude; thence due east to the meridian of 4° west longitude; thence due north to the parallel of 62° north latitude; thence due east to the coast of Norway; thence north and east along the coast of Norway and along the coast of the Union of Soviet Socialist Republics as far as the meridian of 51° east longitude.

Region 2—The part of the Convention area not covered by Region 1 and north of 48° north latitude.

Region 3—The part of the Convention area between 36° and 48° north latitude.

F.A.O.: INTERNATIONAL CONVENTION FOR CONSERVATION OF ATLANTIC TUNAS*

[Done at Rio de Janeiro, May 14, 1966]

INTERNATIONAL CONVENTION FOR THE CONSERVATION OF ATLANTIC TUNAS

PREAMBLE

The Governments whose duly authorised representatives have subscribed hereto, considering their mutual interest in the populations of tuna and tuna-like fishes found in the Atlantic Ocean, and desiring to co-operate in maintaining the populations of these fishes at levels which will permit the maximum sustainable catch for food and other purposes, resolve to conclude a Convention for the conservation of the resources of tuna and tuna-like fishes of the Atlantic Ocean, and to that end agree as follows:

Article I

The area to which this Convention shall apply, hereinafter referred to as the "Convention area", shall be all waters of the Atlantic Ocean, including the adjacent Seas.

Article II

Nothing in this Convention shall be considered as affecting the rights, claims or views of any Contracting Party in regard to the limits of territorial waters or the extent of jurisdiction over fisheries under international law.

Article III

1. The Contracting Parties hereby agree to establish and maintain a Commission to be known as the International Commission for the Conservation of Atlantic Tunas, hereinafter referred to as "the Commission", which shall carry out the objectives set forth in this Convention.

2. Each of the Contracting Parties shall be represented on the Commission by not more than three Delegates. Such Delegates may be assisted by experts and advisors.

3. Except as may otherwise be provided in this Convention, decisions of the Commission shall be taken by a majority of the Contracting Parties, each Contracting Party having one vote. Two-thirds of the Contracting Parties shall constitute a quorum.

4. The Commission shall hold a regular meeting once every two years. A special meeting may be called at any time at the request of a majority of the Contracting Parties or by decision of the Council as constituted in Article V.

5. At its first meeting, and thereafter at each regular meeting, the Commission shall elect from among its Members a Chairman, a first Vice-Chairman and a second Vice-Chairman who shall not be re-elected for more than one term.

6. The meetings of the Commission and its subsidiary bodies shall be public unless the Commission otherwise decides.

---

*[Reproduced from Message from the President of the United States Transmitting the International Convention for the Conservation of Atlantic Tunas, Signed at Rio de Janeiro under Date of May 14, 1966, Executive Document U, 89th Cong., 2d Sess. (October 18, 1966), pp. 5-15.

7. The official languages of the Commission shall be English, French and Spanish.

8. The Commission shall have authority to adopt such rules of procedure and financial regulations as are necessary to carry out its functions.

9. The Commission shall submit a report to the Contracting Parties every two years on its work and findings and shall also inform any Contracting Party, whenever requested, on any matter relating to the objectives of the Convention.

ARTICLE IV

1. In order to carry out the objectives of this Convention the Commission shall be responsible for the study of the populations of tuna and tuna-like fishes (the Scombriformes with the exception of the families Trichiuridae and Gempylidae and the genus Scomber) and such other species of fishes exploited in tuna fishing in the Convention area as are not under investigation by another international fishery organization. Such study shall include research on the abundance, biometry and ecology of the fishes; the oceanography of their environment; and the effects of natural and human factors upon their abundance. The Commission, in carrying out these responsibilities shall, insofar as feasible, utilise the technical and scientific services of, and information from, official agencies of the Contracting Parties and their political sub-divisions and may, when desirable, utilise the available services and information of any public or private institution, organization or individual, and may undertake within the limits of its budget independent research to supplement the research work being done by governments, national institutions or other international organizations.

2. The carrying out of the provisions in paragraph 1 of this Article shall include:

(a) collecting and analysing statistical information relating to the current conditions and trends of the tuna fishery resources of the Convention area;

(b) studying and appraising information concerning measures and methods to ensure maintenance of the populations of tuna and tuna-like fishes in the Convention area at levels which will permit the maximum sustainable catch and which will ensure the effective exploitation of these fishes in a manner consistent with this catch;

(c) recommending studies and investigations to the Contracting Parties;

(d) publishing and otherwise disseminating reports of its findings and statistical, biological and other scientific information relative to the tuna fisheries of the Convention area.

ARTICLE V

1. There is established within the Commission a Council which shall consist of the Chairman and the Vice-Chairmen of the Commission together with the representatives of not less than four and not more than eight Contracting Parties. The Contracting Parties represented on the Council shall be elected at each regular meeting of the Commission. However, if at any time the number of the Contracting

Parties exceeds forty, the Commission may elect an additional two Contracting Parties to be represented on the Council. The Contracting Parties of which the Chairman and Vice-Chairmen are nationals shall not be elected to the Council. In elections to the Council the Commission shall give due consideration to the geographic, tuna fishing and tuna processing interests of the Contracting Parties, as well as to the equal right of the Contracting Parties to be represented on the Council.

2. The Council shall perform such functions as are assigned to it by this Convention or are designated by the Commission, and shall meet at least once in the interim between regular meetings of the Commission. Between meetings of the Commission the Council shall make necessary decisions on the duties to be carried out by the staff and shall issue necessary instructions to the Executive Secretary. Decisions of the Council shall be made in accordance with rules to be established by the Commission.

ARTICLE VI

To carry out the objectives of this Convention the Commission may establish Panels on the basis of species, group of species, or of geographic areas. Each Panel in such case:

(a) shall be responsible for keeping under review the species, group of species, or geographic area under its purview, and for collecting scientific and other information relating thereto;

(b) may propose to the Commission, upon the basis of scientific investigations, recommendations for joint action by the Contracting Parties;

(c) may recommend to the Commission studies and investigations necessary for obtaining information relating to its species, group of species, or geographic area, as well as the co-ordination of programmes of investigations by the Contracting Parties.

ARTICLE VII

The Commission shall appoint an Executive Secretary who shall serve at the pleasure of the Commission. The Executive Secretary, subject to such rules and procedures as may be determined by the Commission, shall have authority with respect to the selection and administration of the staff of the Commission. He shall also perform, *inter alia*, the following functions as the Commission may prescribe:

(a) co-ordinating the programmes of investigation by the Contracting Parties;

(b) preparing budget estimates for review by the Commission;

(c) authorizing the disbursement of funds in accordance with the Commission's budget;

(d) accounting for the funds of the Commission;

(e) arranging for co-operation with the organizations referred to in Article XI of this Convention;

(f) preparing the collection and analysis of data necessary to accomplish the purposes of the Convention particularly those data relating to the current and maximum sustainable catch of tuna stocks;

(g) preparing for approval by the Commission scientific, administrative and other reports of the Commission and its subsidiary bodies.

Article VIII

1. (a) The Commission may, on the basis of scientific evidence make recommendations designed to maintain the populations of tuna and tuna-like fishes that may be taken in the Convention area at levels which will permit the maximum sustainable catch. These recommendations shall be applicable to the Contracting Parties under the conditions laid down in paragraphs 2 and 3 of this Article.

(b) The recommendations referred to above shall be made:

(i) at the initiative of the Commission if an appropriate Panel has not been established or with the approval of at least two-thirds of all the Contracting Parties if an appropriate Panel has been established;

(ii) on the proposal of an appropriate Panel if such a Panel has been established;

(iii) on the proposal of the appropriate Panels if the recommendation in question relates to more than one geographic area, species or group of species.

2. Each recommendation made under paragraph 1 of this Article shall become effective for all Contracting Parties six months after the date of the notification from the Commission transmitting the recommendation to the Contracting Parties, except as provided in paragraph 3 of this Article.

3. (a) If any Contracting Party in the case of a recommendation made under paragraph 1(b)(i) above, or any Contracting Party member of a Panel concerned in the case of a recommendation made under paragraph 1(b) (ii) or (iii) above, presents to the Commission an objection to such recommendation within the six months period provided for in paragraph 2 above, the recommendation shall not become effective for an additional sixty days.

(b) Thereupon any other Contracting Party may present an objection prior to the expiration of the additional sixty days period, or within forty-five days of the date of the notification of an objection made by another Contracting Party within such additional sixty days, whichever date shall be the later.

(c) The recommendation shall become effective at the end of the extended period or periods for objection, except for those Contracting Parties that have presented an objection.

(d) However, if a recommendation has met with an objection presented by only one or less than one-fourth of the Contracting Parties, in accordance with sub-paragraphs (a) and (b) above, the Commission shall immediately notify the Contracting Party or Parties having presented such objection that it is to be considered as having no effect.

(e) In the case referred to in sub-paragraph (d) above the Contracting Party or Parties concerned shall have an additional period of sixty days from the date of said notification in which to reaffirm their objection. On the expiry of this period the recommendation shall become effective, except with respect to any Contracting Party having presented an objection and reaffirmed it within the delay provided for.

(f) If a recommendation has met with objection from more than one-fourth but less than the majority of the Contracting Parties, in accordance with sub-paragraphs (a) and (b) above, the recommendation shall become effective for the Contracting Parties that have not presented an objection thereto.

(g) If objections have been presented by a majority of the Contracting Parties the recommendation shall not become effective.

4. Any Contracting Party objecting to a recommendation may at any time withdraw that objection, and the recommendation shall become effective with respect to such Contracting Party immediately if the recommendation is already in effect, or at such time as it may become effective under the terms of this Article.

5. The Commission shall notify each Contracting Party immediately upon receipt of each objection and of each withdrawal of an objection, and of the entry into force of any recommendation.

Article IX

1. The Contracting Parties agree to take all action necessary to ensure the enforcement of this Convention. Each Contracting Party shall transmit to the Commission, biennially or at such other times as may be required by the Commission, a statement of the action taken by it for these purposes.

2. The Contracting Parties agree:

(a) to furnish, on the request of the Commission, any available statistical, biological and other scientific information the Commission may need for the purposes of this Convention;

(b) when their official agencies are unable to obtain and furnish the said information, to allow the Commission, through the Contracting Parties, to obtain it on a voluntary basis direct from companies and individual fishermen.

3. The Contracting Parties undertake to collaborate with each other with a view to the adoption of suitable effective measures to ensure the application of the provisions of this Convention and in particular to set up a system of international enforcement to be applied to the Convention area except the territorial sea and other waters, if any, in which a state is entitled under international law to exercise jurisdiction over fisheries.

Article X

1. The Commission shall adopt a budget for the joint expenses of the Commission for the biennium following each regular meeting.

2. Each Contracting Party shall contribute annually to the budget of the Commission an amount equal to:

(a) U.S.$1,000 (one thousand United States dollars) for Commission membership.

(b) U.S.$1,000 (one thousand United States dollars) for each Panel membership.

(c) If the proposed budget for joint expenses for any biennium should exceed the whole amount of contributions to be made by the Contracting Parties under (a) and (b) of this paragraph, one-third of the amount of such excess shall be contributed by the Contracting Parties in proportion to their contributions made under (a) and (b) of this paragraph. For the remaining two-thirds the Commission shall determine on the basis of the latest available information:

(i) the total of the round weight of catch of Atlantic tuna and tuna-like fishes and the net weight of canned products of such fishes for each Contracting Party;

(ii) the total of (i) for all Contracting Parties.

Each Contracting Party shall contribute its share of the remaining two thirds in the same ratio that its total in (i) bears to the total in (ii). That part of the budget referred to in this sub-paragraph shall be set by agreement of all the Contracting Parties present and voting.

3. The Council shall review the second half of the biennial budget at its regular meeting between Commission meetings and, on the basis of current and anticipated developments, may authorise re-apportionment of amounts in the Commission budget for the second year within the total budget approved by the Commission.

4. The Executive Secretary of the Commission shall notify each Contracting Party of its yearly assessment. The contributions shall be payable on January first of the year for which the assessment was levied. Contributions not received before January first of the succeeding year shall be considered as in arrears.

5. Contributions to the biennial budget shall be payable in such currencies as the Commission may decide.

6. At its first meeting the Commission shall approve a budget for the balance of the first year the Commission functions and for the following biennium. It shall immediately transmit to the Contracting Parties copies of these budgets together with notices of the respective assessments for the first annual contribution.

7. Thereafter, within a period not less than sixty days before the regular meeting of the Commission which precedes the biennium, the Executive Secretary shall submit to each Contracting Party a draft biennial budget together with a schedule of proposed assessments.

8. The Commission may suspend the voting rights of any Contracting Party when its arrears of contributions equal or exceed the amount due from it for the two preceding years.

9. The Commission shall establish a Working Capital Fund to finance operations of the Commission prior to receiving annual contributions, and for such other purposes as the Commission may determine. The Commission shall determine the level of the Fund, assess advances necessary for its establishment, and adopt regulations governing the use of the Fund.

10. The Commission shall arrange an annual independent audit of the Commission's accounts. The reports of such audits shall be reviewed and approved by the Commission, or by the Council in years when there is no regular Commission meeting.

11. The Commission may accept contributions, other than provided for in paragraph 2 of this Article, for the prosecution of its work.

Article XI

1. The Contracting Parties agree that there should be a working relationship between the Commission and the Food and Agriculture Organization of the United Nations. To this end the Commission shall enter into negotiations with the Food and Agriculture Organization of the United Nations with a view to concluding an agreement pursuant to Article XIII of the Organization's Constitution. Such agreement should provide, inter alia, for the Director-General of the Food and Agriculture Organization of the United Nations to appoint

a Representative who would participate in all meetings of the Commission and its subsidiary bodies, but without the right to vote.

2. The Contracting Parties agree that there should be co-operation between the Commission and other international fisheries commissions and scientific organizations which might contribute to the work of the Commission. The Commission may enter into agreements with such commissions and organizations.

3. The Commission may invite any appropriate international organization and any Government which is a member of the United Nations or of any Specialized Agency of the United Nations and which is not a member of the Commission, to send observers to meetings of the Commission and its subsidiary bodies.

Article XII

1. This Convention shall remain in force for ten years and thereafter until a majority of Contracting Parties agree to terminate it.

2. At any time after ten years from the date of entry into force of this Convention, any Contracting Party may withdraw from the Convention on December thirty-first of any year including the tenth year by written notification of withdrawal given on or before December thirty-first of the preceding year to the Director-General of the Food and Agriculture Organization of the United Nations.

3. Any other Contracting Party may thereupon withdraw from this Convention with effect from the same December thirty-first by giving written notification of withdrawal to the Director-General of the Food and Agriculture Organization of the United Nations not later than one month from the date of receipt of information from the Director-General of the Food and Agriculture Organization of the United Nations concerning any withdrawal, but not later than April first of that year.

Article XIII

1. Any Contracting Party or the Commission may propose amendments to this Convention. The Director-General of the Food and Agriculture Organization of the United Nations shall transmit a certified copy of the text of any proposed amendment to all the Contracting Parties. Any amendment not involving new obligations shall take effect for all Contracting Parties on the thirtieth day after its acceptance by three-fourths of the Contracting Parties. Any amendment involving new obligations shall take effect for each Contracting Party accepting the amendment on the ninetieth day after its acceptance by three-fourths of the Contracting Parties and thereafter for each remaining Contracting Party upon acceptance by it. Any amendment considered by one or more Contracting Parties to involve new obligations shall be deemed to involve new obligations and shall take effect accordingly. A government which becomes a Contracting Party after an amendment to this Convention has been opened for acceptance pursuant to the provisions of this Article shall be bound by the Convention as amended when the said amendment comes into force.

2. Proposed amendments shall be deposited with the Director-General of the Food and Agriculture Organization of the United Nations. Notifications of acceptance of amendments shall be

deposited with the Director-General of the Food and Agriculture Organization of the United Nations.

ARTICLE XIV

1. This Convention shall be open for signature by any Government which is a member of the United Nations or of any Specialized Agency of the United Nations. Any such Government which does not sign this Convention may adhere to it at any time.

2. This Convention shall be subject to ratification or approval by signatory countries in accordance with their constitutions. Instruments of ratification, approval, or adherence shall be deposited with the Director-General of the Food and Agriculture Organization of the United Nations.

3. This Convention shall enter into force upon the deposit of instruments of ratification, approval, or adherence by seven Governments and shall enter into force with respect to each Government which subsequently deposits an instrument of ratification, approval or adherence on the date of such deposit.

ARTICLE XV

The Director-General of the Food and Agriculture Organization of the United Nations shall inform all Governments referred to in paragraph 1 of Article XIV of deposits of instruments of ratification, approval or adherence, the entry into force of this Convention, proposals for amendments, notifications of acceptance of amendments, entry into force of amendments, and notifications of withdrawal.

ARTICLE XVI

The original of this Convention shall be deposited with the Director-General of the Food and Agriculture Organization of the United Nations who shall send certified copies to the Governments referred to in paragraph 1 of Article XIV.

IN WITNESS WHEREOF the representatives duly authorized by their respective Governments have signed the present Convention. Done at Rio de Janeiro this fourteenth day of May 1966 in a single copy in the English, French and Spanish languages, each version being equally authoritative.

Certified true copy of the International Convention for the Conservation of Atlantic Tunas.

ROME, *29 July 1966*.

ORIS V. WELLS
(For B. R. Sen, Director-General,
Food and Agriculture Organization
of the United Nations).

Agreement between the Government of Norway and the Government of Canada on Sealing and the Conservation of the Seal Stocks in the Northwest Atlantic.

The Government of Norway and the Government of Canada:

desirous of continuing and further developing the close co-operation in solving common problems concerning sealing and the conservation of the seal stocks in the Northwest Atlantic;

desirous of developing and maintaining the most effective conservation measures in order to secure the best possible protection of the seal stocks in this area and a rational utilization of these resources;

desirous of extending and co-ordinating their scientific research concerning the seal stocks in this area;

desirous of ensuring that humane catching methods are used in sealing; and,

desirous of taking effective steps jointly and separately in attaining these aims;

have agreed as follows:

Article I

The area to which this agreement applies shall, subject to Article XII, include all waters of the Northwest Atlantic North of 45° North latitude and West of 45° West longitude.

Article II

This agreement applies to harp seal (Phoca groenlandica).

On a proposal by the commission established under Article III the application of this agreement may be extended to hooded seal (Cystophora cristata), bearded seal (Erignatus barbatus) and walrus (Odobenus rosmarus).

Article III

The contracting parties shall establish a commission consisting of three representatives appointed by each country.

The commission shall hold at least one regular annual meeting at such time and place as may be agreed upon. The Chairman of the meeting shall be provided alternatively by Canada and Norway.

The representatives of the contracting parties attending meetings of the commission may be assisted by experts or advisers.

Each contracting party shall have one vote in the commission. Decisions shall be taken by unanimous vote.

Article IV

The commission is entrusted with the following functions:

(a) on the basis of scientific and practical research to submit proposals to the contracting parties with regard to, inter alia, sealing and the conservation of the seal stocks, national quotas, opening and closing dates, humane hunting methods and the prevention of cruelty or suffering to the animals,

(b) to submit proposals to the contracting parties with regard to the establishment of inspection and control procedures required to ensure the implementation and enforcement of the provisions of this agreement,

(c) to submit proposals to the contracting parties concerning scientific research to be undertaken jointly or separately with respect to sealing and the conservation of the seal stocks, or concerning of the co-ordination of such research.

Article V

The contracting parties undertake as far as possible to supply the commission with such information of a statistical, practical and scientific nature as the commission deems necessary for its work.

Article VI

Each contracting party shall bear the costs of its participation in the commission and of its scientific research.

Expenditures incurred in joint research projects and other joint expenditures shall be shared between the parties, as may be agreed in accordance with Article VII, following upon proposals of the commission.

Article VII

The proposals of the commission concerning conservation measures, other measures to regulate sealing activities, scientific research, the sharing of the expenses of joint research or other joint expenditures, and the extension of this agreement to other species, shall be submitted to the contracting parties for their approval and shall be binding upon them following such approval.

Approved proposals of the commission with regard to conservation measures and other measures to regulate sealing shall be put into effect by the parties not later than two months following approval, unless the parties agree otherwise.

Article VIII

Each contracting party undertakes to put into effect and enforce such measures as may be necessary to implement this agreement.

Article IX

Each contracting party shall be entitled, subject to this agreement, notwithstanding national quotas agreed by the contracting parties, to issue permits to its nationals for the taking of the species covered by this agreement on the high seas or in its own territorial sea, for the following purposes:

(a) for scientific research

(b) for the local population

(c) for expeditions, provided that the catch is used for food, animal feed or similar needs.

The contracting parties shall inform the commission of such permits issued.

Article X

Either contracting party may terminate this agreement by three years' notice in writing. No such notice shall be given by either party before December 31st, 1975.

Upon such notice the contracting parties shall as soon as possible enter into negotiations in good faith on future arrangements concerning conservation and sealing.

Article XI

By agreement of the contracting parties, other states interested in the conservation of the species referred to in this agreement may be invited to accede to Articles I to X of this agreement.

Article XII

Subject to the provisions of this agreement, in view of the fact that the movements of the seal herds are governed by unpredictable weather conditions and consequently that, in certain years, the ice on which the seals are concentrated drifts inside the Canadian territorial sea, Norwegian vessels engaged in sealing operations are allowed, notwithstanding the provisions of the Exchange of Notes between the Government of Canada and the Government of Norway of July 15th, 1971, to take seals

(a) within the outer nine miles of the territorial sea on the Atlantic coast of Canada between 48°00' North latitude

(b) up to but not closer than three miles from the nearest land in all the waters of Notre Dame Bay and of the Strait of Belle Isle northeast of a straight line drawn from the lighthouse at Amour Point to the lighthouse on Flowers Island in Flowers Cove, Newfoundland.

Norwegian sealing is not otherwise allowed in the Gulf of St. Lawrence.

Article XIII

This agreement is subject to ratification and shall enter into force on the date of the exchange of the instruments of ratification, which shall take place at Oslo as soon as possible.

IN WITNESS WHEREOF, THE UNDERSIGNED, being duly authorized thereto by their respective Governments, have signed this Agreement.

DONE in two copies at Ottawa this fifteenth day of July 1971, in the Norwegian, English and French languages, each version being equally authentic.

For the Government of Norway: For the Government of Canada:

Torfinn Oftedal (u.) J. Alan Beesley (u.)

INTERNATIONAL CONVENTION FOR THE REGULATION OF WHALING

The Governments whose duly authorized representatives have subscribed hereto,

Recognizing the interest of the nations of the world in safeguarding for future generations the great natural resources represented by the whale stocks;

Considering that the history of whaling has seen overfishing of one area after another and of one species of whale after another to such a degree that it is essential to protect all species of whales from further overfishing;

Recognizing that the whale stocks are susceptible of natural increases if whaling is properly regulated, and that increases in the size of whale stocks will permit increases in the numbers of whales which may be captured without endangering these natural resources;

Recognizing that it is in the common interest to achieve the optimum level of whale stocks as rapidly as possible without causing widespread economic and nutritional distress;

Recognizing that in the course of achieving these objectives, whaling operations should be confined to those species best able to sustain exploitation in order to give an interval for recovery to certain species of whales now depleted in numbers;

Desiring to establish a system of international regulation for the whale fisheries to ensure proper and effective conservation and development of whale stocks on the basis of the principles embodied in the provisions of the International Agreement for the Regulation of Whaling signed in London on June 8, 1937 [1] and the protocols to that Agreement signed in London on June 24, 1938 [2] and November 26, 1945; [3] and

Having decided to conclude a convention to provide for the proper conservation of whale stocks and thus make possible the orderly development of the whaling industry;

Have agreed as follows:

---

1 Treaty Series 933; 52 Stat. 1460.

2 Treaty Series 944; 53 Stat. 1794.

3 Treaties and Other International Acts Series 1597.

Article I

1. This Convention includes the Schedule attached thereto which forms an integral part thereof. All references to "Convention" shall be understood as including the said Schedule either in its present terms or as amended in accordance with the provisions of Article V.

2. This Convention applies to factory ships, land stations, and whale catchers under the jurisdiction of the Contracting Governments, and to all waters in which whaling is prosecuted by such factory ships, land stations, and whale catchers.

Article II

As used in this Convention

1. "factory ship" means a ship in which or on which whales are treated whether wholly or in part;

2. "land station" means a factory on the land at which whales are treated whether wholly or in part;

3. "whale catcher" means a ship used for the purpose of hunting, taking, towing, holding on to, or scouting for whales;

4. "Contracting Government" means any Government which has deposited an instrument of ratification or has given notice of adherence to this Convention.

Article III

1. The Contracting Governments agree to establish an International Whaling Commission, hereinafter referred to as the Commission, to be composed of one member from each Contracting Government. Each member shall have one vote and may be accompanied by one or more experts and advisers.

2. The Commission shall elect from its own members a Chairman and Vice Chairman and shall determine its own Rules of Procedure. Decisions of the Commission shall be taken by a simple majority of those members voting except that a three-fourths majority of those members voting shall be required for action in pursuance of Article V. The Rules of Procedure may provide for decisions otherwise than at meetings of the Commission.

3. The Commission may appoint its own Secretary and staff.

4. The Commission may set up, from among its own members and experts or advisers, such committees as it considers desirable to perform such functions as it may authorize.

5. The expenses of each member of the Commission and of his experts and advisers shall be determined and paid by his own Government.

6. Recognizing that specialized agencies related to the United Nations will be concerned with the conservation and development of

whale fisheries and the products arising therefrom and desiring to avoid duplication of functions, the Contracting Governments will consult among themselves within two years after the coming into force of this Convention to decide whether the Commission shall be brought within the framework of a specialized agency related to the United Nations.

7. In the meantime the Government of the United Kingdom of Great Britain and Northern Ireland shall arrange, in consultation with the other Contracting Governments, to convene the first meeting of the Commission, and shall initiate the consultation referred to in paragraph 6 above.

8. Subsequent meetings of the Commission shall be convened as the Commission may determine.

Article IV

1. The Commission may either in collaboration with or through independent agencies of the Contracting Governments or other public or private agencies, establishments, or organizations, or independently

(a) encourage, recommend, or if necessary, organize studies and investigations relating to whales and whaling;

(b) collect and analyze statistical information concerning the current condition and trend of the whale stocks and the effects of whaling activities thereon;

(c) study, appraise, and disseminate information concerning methods of maintaining and increasing the populations of whale stocks.

2. The Commission shall arrange for the publication of reports of its activities, and it may publish independently or in collaboration with the International Bureau for Whaling Statistics at Sandefjord in Norway and other organizations and agencies such reports as it deems appropriate, as well as statistical, scientific, and other pertinent information relating to whales and whaling.

Article V

1. The Commission may amend from time to time the provisions of the Schedule by adopting regulations with respect to the conservation and utilization of whale resources, fixing (a) protected and unprotected species; (b) open and closed seasons; (c) open and closed waters, including the designation of sanctuary areas; (d) size limits for each species; (e) time, methods, and intensity of whaling (including the maximum catch of whales to be taken in any one season); (f) types and specifications of gear and apparatus and appliances which may be

used; (g) methods of measurement; and (h) catch returns and other statistical and biological records.

2. These amendments of the Schedule (a) shall be such as are necessary to carry out the objectives and purposes of this Convention and to provide for the conservation, development, and optimum utilization of the whale resources; (b) shall be based on scientific findings; (c) shall not involve restrictions on the number or nationality of factory ships or land stations, nor allocate specific quotas to any factory ship or land station or to any group of factory ships or land stations; and (d) shall take into consideration the interests of the consumers of whale products and the whaling industry.

3. Each of such amendments shall become effective with respect to the Contracting Governments ninety days following notification of the amendment by the Commission to each of the Contracting Governments, except that (a) if any Government presents to the Commission objection to any amendment prior to the expiration of this ninety-day period, the amendment shall not become effective with respect to any of the Governments for an additional ninety days; (b) thereupon, any other Contracting Government may present objection to the amendment at any time prior to the expiration of the additional ninety-day period, or before the expiration of thirty days from the date of receipt of the last objection received during such additional ninety-day period, whichever date shall be the later; and (c) thereafter, the amendment shall become effective with respect to all Contracting Governments which have not presented objection but shall not become effective with respect to any Government which has so objected until such date as the objection is withdrawn. The Commission shall notify each Contracting Government immediately upon receipt of each objection and withdrawal and each Contracting Government shall acknowledge receipt of all notifications of amendments, objections, and withdrawals.

4. No amendments shall become effective before July 1, 1949.

Article VI

The Commission may from time to time make recommendations to any or all Contracting Governments on any matters which relate to whales or whaling and to the objectives and purposes of this Convention.

Article VII

The Contracting Governments shall ensure prompt transmission to the International Bureau for Whaling Statistics at Sandefjord in Norway, or to such other body as the Commission may designate, of notifications and statistical and other information required by this

Convention in such form and manner as may be prescribed by the Commission.

Article VIII

1. Notwithstanding anything contained in this Convention, any Contracting Government may grant to any of its nationals a special permit authorizing that national to kill, take, and treat whales for purposes of scientific research subject to such restrictions as to number and subject to such other conditions as the Contracting Government thinks fit, and the killing, taking, and treating of whales in accordance with the provisions of this Article shall be exempt from the operation of this Convention. Each Contracting Government shall report at once to the Commission all such authorizations which it has granted. Each Contracting Government may at any time revoke any such special permit which it has granted.

2. Any whales taken under these special permits shall so far as practicable be processed and the proceeds shall be dealt with in accordance with directions issued by the Government by which the permit was granted.

3. Each Contracting Government shall transmit to such body as may be designated by the Commission, insofar as practicable, and at intervals of not more than one year, scientific information available to that Government with respect to whales and whaling, including the results of research conducted pursuant to paragraph 1 of this Article and to Article IV.

4. Recognizing that continuous collection and analysis of biological data in connection with the operations of factory ships and land stations are indispensable to sound and constructive management of the whale fisheries, the Contracting Governments will take all practicable measures to obtain such data.

Article IX

1. Each Contracting Government shall take appropriate measures to ensure the application of the provisions of this Convention and the punishment of infractions against the said provisions in operations carried out by persons or by vessels under its jurisdiction.

2. No bonus or other remuneration calculated with relation to the results of their work shall be paid to the gunners and crews of whale catchers in respect of any whales the taking of which is forbidden by this Convention.

3. Prosecution for infractions against or contraventions of this Convention shall be instituted by the Government having jurisdiction over the offense.

4. Each Contracting Government shall transmit to the Commission full details of each infraction of the provisions of this Convention by

persons or vessels under the jurisdiction of that Government as reported by its inspectors. This information shall include a statement of measures taken for dealing with the infraction and of penalties imposed.

Article X

1. This Convention shall be ratified and the instruments of ratification shall be deposited with the Government of the United States of America.

2. Any Government which has not signed this Convention may adhere thereto after it enters into force by a notification in writing to the Government of the United States of America.

3. The Government of the United States of America shall inform all other signatory Governments and all adhering Governments of all ratifications deposited and adherences received.

4. This Convention shall, when instruments of ratification have been deposited by at least six signatory Governments, which shall include the Governments of the Netherlands, Norway, the Union of Soviet Socialist Republics, the United Kingdom of Great Britain and Northern Ireland, and the United States of America, enter into force [1] with respect to those Governments and shall enter into force with respect to each Government which subsequently ratifies or adheres on the date of the deposit of its instrument of ratification or the receipt of its notification of adherence.

5. The provisions of the Schedule shall not apply prior to July 1, 1948. Amendments to the Schedule adopted pursuant to Article V shall not apply prior to July 1, 1949.

Article XI

Any Contracting Government may withdraw from this Convention on June thirtieth of any year by giving notice on or before January first of the same year to the depositary Government, which upon receipt of such a notice shall at once communicate it to the other Contracting Governments. Any other Contracting Government may, in like manner, within one month of the receipt of a copy of such a notice from the depositary Government, give notice of withdrawal, so that the Convention shall cease to be in force on June thirtieth of the same year with respect to the Government giving such notice of withdrawal.

This Convention shall bear the date on which it is opened for signature and shall remain open for signature for a period of fourteen days thereafter.

[1] Nov. 10, 1948, *post*, p. 16.

IN WITNESS WHEREOF the undersigned, being duly authorized, have signed this Convention.

DONE in Washington this second day of December 1946, in the English language, the original of which shall be deposited in the archives of the Government of the United States of America. The Government of the United States of America shall transmit certified copies thereof to all the other signatory and adhering Governments.

SCHEDULE TO THE INTERNATIONAL WHALING CONVENTION, 1946

The Schedule printed on the following pages contains the amendments made by the International Whaling Commission at its Twenty-third Meeting in Washington from 21 to 25 June, 1971.

The 1971 amendments, including deletions, occur in paragraphs 1 (*a*), 1 (*b*), 1 (*c*), 8 (*a*), 8 (*f*), 8 (*g*), 8 (*h*), 8 (*i*) and 8 (*j*). Changes and additions are shown in bold type.

No objections were received to the amendments to paragraphs 1 (*a*), 1 (*b*), 1 (*c*), 8 (*a*), 8 (*f*), 8 (*h*) and 8 (*i*) of the Schedule and these amendments became binding on all Contracting Governments from 5 October, 1971. The amendment concerning paragraph 8 (*j*) did not come into operation until 3 January, 1972, owing to objections by the Governments of Japan and the Soviet Union which were received within the prescribed period.

SCHEDULE TO THE INTERNATIONAL WHALING CONVENTION, 1946(1)

(Revised to include the Amendments adopted at the Twenty-third Meeting of the International Whaling Commission)

1.—(*a*) There shall be maintained on each factory ship at least two inspectors of whaling for the purpose of maintaining twenty-four hour inspection **provided that at least one such inspector shall be maintained on each catcher functioning as a factory ship.** These inspectors shall be appointed and paid by the Government having jurisdiction over the factory ship; provided that inspectors need not be appointed to ships which, apart from the storage of products, are used during the season solely for freezing or salting the meat and entrails of whales intended for human food or feeding animals.

(*b*) Adequate inspection shall be maintained at each land station. The inspectors serving at each land station shall be appointed and paid by the Government having jurisdiction over the land station.

(*c*) **There shall be received such observers as the member countries may arrange to place on factory ships and land stations or groups of land stations of other member countries. The observers shall be appointed by the Commission and paid by the Government nominating them.**

2. It is forbidden to take or kill gray whales or right whales, except by aborigines or a Contracting Government on behalf of aborigines and only when the meat and products of such whales are to be used exclusively for local consumption by the aborigines.

3. It is forbidden to take or kill calves or suckling whales or female whales which are accompanied by calves or suckling whales.

4.—(1) (*a*) It is forbidden to kill blue whales in the North Atlantic Ocean for three years ending on 24th February, 1973.

(*b*) It is forbidden to kill or attempt to kill blue whales in the North Pacific Ocean and its dependent waters north of the Equator for five years beginning with the 1971 season.

(2) It is forbidden to use a factory ship or whale catcher attached thereto for the purpose of taking or treating baleen whales except minke whales in any of the following areas:

(*a*) in the waters north of 66° North Latitude except that from 150° East Longitude eastwards as far as 140° West Longitude the taking or killing of baleen whales by a factory ship or whale catcher shall be permitted between 66° North Latitude and 72° North Latitude;

(*b*) in the Atlantic Ocean and its dependent waters north of 40° South Latitude;

---

(1) Treaty Series No. 5 (1949), Cmd. 7604.

(*c*) in the Pacific Ocean and its dependent waters east of 150° West Longitude between 40° South Latitude and 35° North Latitude;

(*d*) in the Pacific Ocean and its dependent waters west of 150° West Longitude between 40° South Latitude and 20° North Latitude;

(*e*) in the Indian Ocean and its dependent waters north of 40° South Latitude.

5. It is forbidden to use a factory ship or whale catcher attached thereto for the purpose of taking or treating baleen whales in the waters south of 40° South Latitude from 70° West Longitude westward as far as 160° West Longitude. [This paragraph as a result of a decision of the fourteenth meeting was rendered inoperative until the Commission otherwise decides.]

6.—(1) It is forbidden to kill or attempt to kill humpback whales in the North Atlantic Ocean for a period ending on 8th November, 1972. Notwithstanding this close season the taking of 10 humpback whales per year is permitted in Greenland waters provided that whale catchers of less than 50 gross register tonnage are used for this purpose.

(2) It is forbidden to kill or attempt to kill humpback whales in the waters south of the Equator.

(3) It is forbidden to kill or attempt to kill blue whales in the waters south of the Equator.

(4) It is forbidden to kill or attempt to kill humpback whales in the North Pacific Ocean and its dependent waters north of the Equator for three years beginning with the 1971 season.

(5) It is forbidden to use a factory ship or whale catcher attached thereto for the purpose of taking or treating sperm whales in the waters between 40° South Latitude and 40° North Latitude.*

7.—(*a*) It is forbidden to use a factory ship or whale catcher attached thereto for the purpose of taking or treating baleen whales (excluding minke whales) in any waters south of 40° South Latitude, except during the period from 12th December to 7th April following, both days inclusive.

(*b*) It is forbidden to use a factory ship or whale catcher attached thereto for the purpose of taking or treating sperm or minke whales, except as permitted by the Contracting Governments in accordance with sub-paragraphs (*c*), (*d*) and (*e*) of this paragraph.

(*c*) Each Contracting Government shall declare for all factory ships and whale catchers attached thereto under its jurisdiction, one continuous open season not to exceed eight months out of any period of twelve months during which the taking or killing of sperm whales by whale catchers may be permitted; provided that a separate open season may be declared for each factory ship and the whale catchers attached thereto.

* Paragraph 6 (5) came into force on 4th January, 1966, but is not binding on Japan, Norway and the Union of Soviet Socialist Republics, all of whom objected within the prescribed period.

(*d*) Each Contracting Government shall declare for all factory ships and whale catchers attached thereto under its jurisdiction one continuous open season not to exceed six months out of any period of twelve months during which the taking or killing of minke whales by the whale catchers may be permitted.

Provided that:

(i) a separate open season may be declared for each factory ship and the whale catchers attached thereto;

(ii) the open season need not necessarily include the whole or any part of the period declared for other baleen whales pursuant to sub-paragraph (*a*) of this paragraph.

(*e*) Each Contracting Government shall declare for all whale catchers under its jurisdiction not operating in conjunction with a factory ship or land station one continuous open season not to exceed six months out of any period of twelve months during which the taking or killing of minke whales by such whale catchers may be permitted. Notwithstanding this paragraph one continuous open season not to exceed eight months may be implemented so far as Greenland is concerned.

8.—(*a*) The number of baleen whales taken during the open season in waters south of 40° South Latitude by factory ships or whale catchers attached thereto under the jurisdiction of the Contracting Governments shall not exceed **2,300** blue whale units in **1971/72.**

(*b*) For the purposes of sub-paragraph (*a*) of this paragraph, blue whale units shall be calculated on the basis that one blue whale equals:

(1) Two fin whales or

(2) Two and a half humpback whales or

(3) Six sei or Bryde's whales.

(*c*) Notification shall be given in accordance with the provisions of Article VII of the Convention, within two days after the end of each calendar week, of data on the number of blue whale units taken in any waters south of 40° South Latitude by all factory ships or whale catchers attached thereto under the jurisdiction of each Contracting Government, provided that when the number of blue whale units is deemed by the Bureau of International Whaling Statistics to have reached 85 per cent of whatever total catch limit is imposed by the Commission notification shall be given as aforesaid at the end of each day of data on the number of blue whale units taken.

(*d*) If it appears that the maximum catch of whales permitted by sub-paragraph (*a*) of this paragraph may be reached before 7th April of any year, the Bureau of International Whaling Statistics shall determine, on the basis of the data provided, the date on which the maximum catch of whales shall be deemed to have been reached and shall notify the master of each factory ship and each Contracting Government of that date not less than four days in advance thereof. The taking or attempting to take baleen whales by factory ships or whale catchers attached thereto shall be illegal in any waters south of 40° South Latitude after midnight of the date so determined.

(*e*) Notification shall be given in accordance with the provisions of Article VII of the Convention of each factory ship intending to engage in whaling operations in any waters south of 40° South Latitude.

(*f*) Subject to sub-paragraph (*h*), the number of fin whales taken in the North Pacific Ocean and dependent waters excluding the catch in the East China Sea shall not exceed **1,046** whales in **1972.**

(*g*) Subject to sub-paragraph (*h*), the number of sei and Bryde's whales combined taken in the North Pacific Ocean and dependent waters shall not exceed **3,768** whales in **1972.** The numbers taken in **1973** shall be further adjusted on the basis of the latest scientific assessment so that the catch shall be less than the estimate of the sustainable yield.

(*h*) **Until the end of 1972** the catch specified in either sub-paragraph (*f*) or (*g*) may be exceeded by not more than 10% provided that an appropriate reduction is made in the catch specified in the other sub-paragraph.

(*i*) **The number of sperm whales taken in the North Pacific Ocean and dependent waters shall not exceed 10,841 whales in 1972.**

(*j*) ***The number of sperm whales taken in the area south of the Equator and between 20° East Longitude and 70° East Longitude in the 1971/72 pelagic season shall not exceed 923 whales and in the 1972 coastal season shall not exceed 1,824 whales. These figures in subsequent seasons to be further adjusted on the basis of the latest scientific assessment.**

9.—(*a*) It is forbidden to take or kill any blue, sei, Bryde's or humpback whales below the following lengths:

Blue whales 70 feet (21·3 metres)

Sei and Bryde's whales 40 feet (12·2 metres)

Humpback whales 35 feet (10·7 metres)

except that blue whales of not less than 65 feet (19·8 metres) and sei and Bryde's whales of not less than 35 feet (10·7 metres) in length may be taken for delivery to land stations, provided that, except in the North-east Pacific area for a period of three years starting 1st April, 1971, the meat of such whales is to be used for local consumption as human or animal food.

(*b*) It is forbidden to take or kill any fin whales below 57 feet (17·4 metres) in length in the Southern Hemisphere, and it is forbidden to take or kill fin whales below 55 feet (16·8 metres) in the Northern Hemisphere; except that fin whales of not less than 55 feet (16·8 metres) may be taken for delivery to land stations in the Southern Hemisphere and fin whales of not less than 50 feet (15·2 metres) may be taken for delivery to land stations in the Northern Hemisphere, provided that, except in the North-east Pacific area for a period of three years starting 1st April, 1971, in each case the meat of such whales is to be used for local consumption as human or animal food.

(*c*) It is forbidden to take or kill any sperm whales below 38 feet (11·6 metres) in length, except that sperm whales of not less than 35 feet (10·7 metres) in length may be taken for delivery to land stations.

(*d*) Whales must be measured when at rest on deck or platform, as accurately as possible by means of a steel tape measure fitted at the zero end with a spiked handle which can be stuck into the deck planking abreast of

* Paragraph 8 (*j*) came into force on 3rd January, 1972, but is not binding on Japan and the Union of Soviet Socialist Republics, both of whom objected within the prescribed period.

one end of the whale. The tape measure shall be stretched in a straight line parallel with the whale's body and read abreast the other end of the whale. The ends of the whale, for measurement purposes, shall be the point of the upper jaw and the notch between the tail flukes. Measurements, after being accurately read on the tape measure, shall be logged to the nearest foot, that is to say, any whale between 75 feet 6 inches and 76 feet 6 inches shall be logged as 76 feet, and any whale between 76 feet 6 inches and 77 feet 6 inches shall be logged as 77 feet. The measurement of any whale which falls on an exact half foot shall be logged at the next half foot, *e.g.* 76 feet 6 inches precisely shall be logged as 77 feet.

10.—(*a*) It is forbidden to use a whale catcher attached to a land station for the purpose of killing or attempting to kill baleen and sperm whales except as permitted by the Contracting Government in accordance with sub-paragraphs (*b*), (*c*) and (*d*) of this paragraph.

(*b*) Each Contracting Government shall declare for all land stations under its jurisdiction, and whale catchers attached to such land stations, one open season during which the taking or killing of baleen (excluding minke) whales by the whale catchers shall be permitted. Such open season shall be for a period of not more than six consecutive months in any period of twelve months and shall apply to all land stations under the jurisdiction of the Contracting Government; provided that a separate open season may be declared for any land station used for the taking or treating of baleen (excluding minke) whales which is more than 1,000 miles from the nearest land station used for the taking or treating of baleen (excluding minke) whales under the jurisdiction of the same Contracting Government.

(*c*) *Each Contracting Government shall declare for all land stations under its jurisdiction and for whale catchers attached to such land stations, one open season not to exceed eight continuous months in any one period of twelve months, during which the taking or killing of sperm whales by the whale catchers shall be permitted, such period of eight months to include the whole of the period of six months declared for baleen whales (excluding minke whales) as provided for in sub-paragraph (*b*) of this paragraph; provided that a separate open season may be declared for any land station used for the taking or treating of sperm whales which is more than 1,000 miles from the nearest land station used for the taking or treating of sperm whales under the jurisdiction of the same Contracting Government.

(*d*) Each Contracting Government shall declare for all land stations under its jurisdiction and for whale catchers attached to such land stations one open season not to exceed six continuous months in any period of twelve months during which the taking or killing of minke whales by the whale catchers shall be permitted (such period not being necessarily concurrent with the period declared for other baleen whales, as provided for in sub-paragraph (*b*) of this paragraph); provided that a separate open season may be declared for any land station used for the taking or treating of minke

* *Note.*—This sub-paragraph 10 (*c*) came into force as from 21st February, 1952, in respect of all Contracting Governments, except the Commonwealth of Australia, who lodged an objection to it within the prescribed period, and this objection was not withdrawn. The provisions of this sub-paragraph are not therefore binding on the Commonwealth of Australia.

whales which is more than 1,000 miles from the nearest land station used for the taking or treating of minke whales under the jurisdiction of the same Contracting Government.

Except that a separate open season may be declared for any land station used for the taking or treating of minke whales which is located in an area having oceanographic conditions clearly distinguishable from those of the area in which are located the other land stations used for the taking or treating of minke whales under the jurisdiction of the same Contracting Government; but the declaration of a separate open season by virtue of the provisions of this sub-paragraph shall not cause thereby the period of time covering the open seasons declared by the same Contracting Government to exceed nine continuous months of any twelve months.

(*e*) The prohibitions contained in this paragraph shall apply to all land stations as defined in Article II of the Whaling Convention of 1946 and to all factory ships which are subject to the regulations govering the operation of land stations under the provisions of paragraph 17 of this Schedule.

11. It is forbidden to use a factory ship which has been used during a season in any waters south of 40° South Latitude for the purpose of treating baleen whales, apart from minke whales in any other area except the North Pacific Ocean and its dependent waters north of the Equator for the same purpose within a period of one year from the termination of that season; provided that catch limits in the North Pacific Ocean and dependent waters are established as provided in paragraph 8 (*f*), (*g*) and (*h*) and provided that this paragraph shall not apply to a ship which has been used during the season solely for freezing or salting the meat and entrails of whales intended for human food or feeding animals.

12.—(*a*) It is forbidden to use a factory ship or a land station for the purpose of treating any whales (whether or not killed by whale catchers under the jurisdiction of a Contracting Government) the killing of which by whale catchers under the jurisdiction of a Contracting Government is prohibited by the provisions of paragraphs 2, 4, 5, 6, 7, 8 or 10 of this Schedule.

(*b*) All other whales (except minke whales) taken shall be delivered to the factory ship or land station and all parts of such whales shall be processed by boiling or otherwise, except the internal organs, whale bone and flippers of all whales, the meat of sperm whales and of parts of whales intended for human food or feeding animals. A Contracting Government may in less developed regions exceptionally permit treating of whales without use of land stations, provided that such whales are fully utilised in accordance with this paragraph.

(*c*) Complete treatment of the carcases of "dauhval" and of whales used as fenders will not be required in cases where the meat or bone of such whales is in bad condition.

13.—(*a*) The taking of whales for treatment by a factory ship shall be so regulated or restricted by the master or person in charge of the factory ship that no whale carcase (except of a whale used as a fender, which shall be processed as soon as is reasonably practicable) shall remain in the sea for a longer period than thirty-three hours from the time of killing to the time when it is hauled up for treatment.

(*b*) Whales taken by all whale catchers, whether for factory ships or land stations, shall be clearly marked so as to identify the catcher and to indicate the order of catching.

(*c*) All whale catchers operating in conjunction with a factory ship shall report by radio to the factory ship:

(1) The time when each whale is taken

(2) Its species, and

(3) Its marking effected pursuant to sub-paragraph (*b*) of this paragraph.

(*d*) The information specified in sub-paragraph (*c*) of this paragraph shall be entered immediately by a factory ship in a permanent record which shall be available at all times for examination by the whaling inspectors; and in addition there shall be entered in such permanent record the following information as soon as it becomes available:

(1) Time of hauling up for treatment

(2) Length, measured pursuant to sub-paragraph (*d*) of paragraph 9

(3) Sex

(4) If female, whether milk-filled or lactating

(5) Length and sex of foetus, if present, and

(6) A full explanation of each infraction.

(*e*) A record similar to that described in sub-paragraph (*d*) of this paragraph shall be maintained by land stations, and all of the information mentioned in the said sub-paragraph shall be entered therein as soon as available.

14. Gunners and crews of factory ships, land stations, and whale catchers, shall be engaged on such terms that their remuneration shall depend to a considerable extent upon such factors as the species, size and yield of whales taken and not merely upon the number of the whales taken. No bonus or other remuneration shall be paid to the gunners or crews of whale catchers in respect of the taking of milk-filled or lactating whales.

15. Copies of all official laws and regulations relating to whales and whaling and changes in such laws and regulations shall be transmitted to the Commission.

16. Notification shall be given in accordance with the provisions of Article VII of the Convention with regard to all factory ships and land stations of statistical information (*a*) concerning the number of whales of each species taken, the number thereof lost, and the number treated at each factory ship or land station, and (*b*) as to the aggregate amounts of oil of each grade and quantities of meal, fertiliser (guano), and other products derived from them, together with (*c*) particulars with respect to each whale treated in the factory ship or land station as to the date and approximate latitude and longitude of taking, the species and sex of the whale, its length and, if it contains a foetus, the length and sex, if ascertainable, of the foetus.

The data referred to in (*a*) and (*c*) above shall be verified at the time of the tally and there shall also be notification to the Commission of any information which may be collected or obtained concerning the calving grounds and migration routes of whales.

In communicating this information there shall be specified:

(*a*) The name and gross tonnage of each factory ship

(*b*) The number of whale catchers, including separate totals for surface vessels and aircraft and specifying, in the case of surface vessels, the average length and horse power of whale catchers

(*c*) A list of the land stations which were in operation during the period concerned.

17.—(*a*) A factory ship which operates solely within territorial waters in one of the areas specified in sub-paragraph (*c*) of this paragraph, by permission of the Government having jurisdiction over those waters, and which flies the flag of that Government shall, while so operating, be subject to the regulations governing the operation of land stations and not to the regulations governing the operation of factory ships.

(*b*) Such factory ship shall not, within a period of one year from the termination of the season in which she so operated, be used for the purpose of treating baleen whales in any of the other areas specified in sub-paragraph (*c*) of this paragraph or south of 40° South Latitude.

(*c*) The areas referred to in sub-paragraphs (*a*) and (*b*) are:

(1) On the coast of Madagascar and its dependencies

(2) On the west coasts of French Africa

(3) On the coasts of Australia, namely on the whole east coast and on the west coast in the area known as Shark Bay and northward to North-west Cape and including Exmouth Gulf and King George's Sound, including the Port of Albany*

(4) On the Pacific coast of the United States of America between 35° North Latitude and 49° North Latitude.

18.—(1) The following expressions have the meanings respectively assigned to them, that is to say:

" baleen whale " means any whale which has baleen or whale bone in the mouth, *i.e.* any whale other than a toothed whale

" blue whale " (*Balaenoptera* or *Sibbaldus musculus*) means any whale known by the name of blue whale, Sibbald's rorqual, or sulphur bottom

" Bryde's whale " (*Balaenoptera edeni* or *brydei*) means any whale known by the name of " Bryde's whale "

" dauhval " means any unclaimed dead whale found floating

" fin whale " (*Balaenoptera physalus*) means any whale known by the name of common finback, common rorqual, finback, finner, fin whale, herring whale, razorback, or true fin whale

" gray whale " (*Rhachianectes glaucus*) means any whale known by the name of gray whale, California gray, devil fish, hard head, mussel digger, gray back or rip sack

" humpback whale " (*Megaptera nodosa* or *novaeangliae*) means any whale known by the name of bunch, humpback, humpback whale, humpbacked whale, hump whale or hunchbacked whale

" minke whale " (*Balaenoptera acutorostrata, B. Davidsoni, B. huttoni*) means any whale known by the name of lesser rorqual, little piked whale, minke whale, pike-headed whale or sharp headed finner

" right whale " (*Balaena mysticetus, Eubalaena glacialis, E. australis,* etc.; *Neobalaena marginata*) means any whale known by the name of Atlantic right whale, Arctic right whale, Biscayan right whale, bowhead, great polar whale, Greenland right whale, Greenland whale, Nordkaper, North Atlantic right whale, North Cape whale, Pacific right whale, pygmy right whale, Southern pygmy right whale, or Southern right whale

" sei whale " (*Balaenoptera borealis*) means any whale known by the name of sei whale, Rudolphi's rorqual, pollack whale, or coalfish whale

" sperm whale " (*Physeter catodon*) means any whale known by the name of sperm whale, spermacet whale, cachalot or pot whale

" toothed whale " means any whale which has teeth in the jaws.

(2) " Whales taken " means whales that have been killed and either flagged or made fast to catchers.

---

* *Note.*—Paragraph 17 (*a*), (*b*) and (*c*) (1) to (3) was inserted by the Commission at its first meeting in 1949, and came into force on 11th January, 1950, as regards all Contracting Governments except France, who therefore remain bound by the provisions of the original paragraph 17, which reads as follows:

17. Notwithstanding the definition of land station contained in Article II of the Convention, a factory ship operating under the jurisdiction of a Contracting Government, and the movements of which are confined solely to the territorial waters of that Government, shall be subject to the regulations governing the operation of land stations, within the following areas:

(*a*) on the coast of Madagascar and its dependencies, and on the west coasts of French Africa;

(*b*) on the west coast of Australia in the area known as Shark Bay and northward to North-west Cape and including Exmouth Gulf and King George's Sound, including the port of Albany; and on the east coast of Australia, in Twofold Bay and Jervis Bay.

Paragraph 17 (*c*) (4) was inserted by the Commission at its eleventh meeting in 1959 and came into force on 5th October, 1959, as regards all Contracting Governments.

NORTH-EAST ATLANTIC FISHERIES CONVENTION

List of Recommendations

(This list includes all current Recommendations agreed by the Commission up to and including the Ninth Meeting, and shows the period of validity of each of them.)

Recommendation 1

Mesh of Nets

(This Recommendation is in effect at the time of going to press, and is of indefinite duration.)

No vessel shall carry on board or use any trawl, Danish seine or similar net towed or hauled through the sea which has in any part meshes of dimensions smaller than the minimum size specified in this recommendation. The minimum sizes shall be such that when the mesh is stretched diagonally lengthwise of the net a flat gauge 2 mm. thick of the appropriate width shall pass through it easily when the net is wet. The appropriate width of gauge in relation to any type of net in any part of the Convention area shall be as follows:-

Part of Convention Area	Type of Net	Appropriate Width
(a) (i) Waters in Region 1 with the exception of the area described in (a) (ii) below.	Seine net	110 mm.
	Such part of any trawl net as is made of cotton, hemp, polyamide fibres or polyester fibres.	120 mm.
	Such part of any trawl net as is made of any other material	130 mm.

Part of Convention Area	Type of Net	Appropriate Width
(a) (ii) The area contained by a line drawn eastwards from 10°W longitude along the parallel of 63° N latitude to 4°W longitude, thence south to 60°30'N latitude thence west to 5°W longitude, thence south to 60°N latitude, thence west to 15° W longitude, thence north to 62° N latitude, thence east to 10°W longitude, thence north to 63° latitude.	Seine net	105 mm.
	Such part of any trawl net as is made of manila or sisal.	110 mm.
	Such part of any trawl net as is made of any other material.	105 mm.
(b) Other waters north of 48° north.	Seine net, or such part of any trawl net as is made of single twine and contains no manila or sisal.	70 mm.
	Such part of any trawl net as is made of double twine and contains no manila or sisal.	75 mm.
	Such part of any trawl net as is made of manila or sisal.	80 mm.
(c) Waters south of 48° north.	Seine net, or such part of any trawl net as is made of single twine and contains no manila or sisal.	60 mm.

Part of Convention Area	Type of Net	Appropriate Width
	Such part of any trawl net as is made of double twine and contains no manila or sisal.	65 mm.
	Such part of any trawl net as is made of manila or sisal.	70 mm.

Recommendation 2

Mixed Fisheries

(This Recommendation is in effect at the time of going to press, and is of indefinite duration.)

Notwithstanding Recommendation 1 vessels fishing for Mackerel, clupeoid fishes, sand eels (Ammodytes), Norway pout (Gadus esmarkii), smelts, ells, great weevers (Trachinus draco,), capelin (Mallotus villosus), blue whiting (Gadus poutassou), horse mackerel (Trachurus trachurus), Polar cod (Boreogadus saida), shrimps, prawns, nephrops or molluscs, saury (Scombresox saurus)

or

for Dicologlossa (or Dicologoglossa) cuneata in the area contained within a line joining the following points: -

(i) 46°16'N - 01°36'W whaling lighthouse
(ii) 46°05'N - 01°44'W
(iii) 45°40'N - 01°34'W
(iv) 44°40'N - 01°34'W
and then due east to the coast,

may carry on board and use nets having meshes of dimensions

smaller than those therein specified; except that this recommendation shall not apply to vessels fishing for horse mackerel and blue whiting in Region 3 or for blue whiting in that part of Region 2 south of 52° 30' N and west of 7°W; provided that

(a) any fishing instrument used by such vessels for the capture of any of the descriptions of fish specified in this recommendation shall not be used for the purpose of catching other descriptions of fish;

(b) no vessel shall carry on board or use any net having in the cod-end meshes of dimensions between 50 mm. (irrespective of the material used) and those specified in Recommendation 1 in the area defined in paragraph (b) of that recommendation except those waters east of a line drawn from Hanstholm to Lindesnes and in the area specified in Recommendation 2 (A).

Recommendation 2 (A)

(This Recommendation is in effect at the time of going to press, and expires on 31st December, 1973.)

Until 31st December, 1973, vessels based on and landing their catches in ports in the area in the Irish Sea between parallels 54° 30' and 53° north latitude, and west of 5°15' west longitude may carry on board and use for the purpose of catching whiting nets not having in any part meshes of less than 60 mm. notwithstanding Recommendations 1 and 2 (b).

Recommendation 3

Attachments to Nets

(This Recommendation is in effect at the time of going to press, and paragraph (a) is of indefinite duration. Paragraph (b) expires on 31st December, 1972.)

(a) No vessel shall use any device by means of which the mesh in any part of a fishing net to which Recommendation 1 applies is obstructed or otherwise in effect diminished, provided that it shall not be unlawful to attach to the underside of the cod-end of a trawl net any canvas, netting, or other material, for the purpose of preventing or reducing wear or tear.

(b) Until 31st December, 1972, the Governments of Contracting States may, notwithstanding sub-paragraph (a) above authorize for trawl nets to which paragraph (a) of Recommendation 1 applies the attachment of chafers or covers to the upper side of the cod-ends of trawl nets for the purpose of preventing wear or tear, subject to such chafers or covers complying with one of the following specifications:-

1. A piece of netting having in all its parts meshes the dimensions of which when measured wet are not less than those of the meshes of the net to which it is attached and provided that

(i) it is fastened to the cod-end only along its forward and lateral edges

(ii) its width is at least one and a half times the width of the part of the cod-end which is covered by it (such width being measured at right angles to the long axis of the cod-end) and

(iii) if there is a splitting strop, it extends no more than four meshes forward of the splitting strop and ends not less than four meshes forward of the cod-line mesh, or

if there is no splitting strop, it extends no more than one third of the length of the cod-end measured from not less than four meshes in front of the cod-line mesh.

2. Pieces of netting, having in all their parts, meshes the dimensions of which when measured wet are not less than those of the meshes of the net to which they are attached and provided that each piece of netting is:-

(i) fastened by its forward edge only across the cod-end at right angles to its long axis

(ii) of a width of at least the width of the cod-end (such width being measured at right angles to the long axis of the cod-end at the point of attachment) and,

(iii) is not more than 10 meshes long; and the aggregate length of all the pieces of netting so attached does not exceed two thirds of the length of the cod-end.

3. A piece of netting, made of the same material as the cod-end, having in all its parts a mesh twice the mesh size of the cod-end when measured wet and fastened to the cod-end along the forward, lateral and rear edges only of the netting in such a way that each mesh of the netting coincides with four meshes of the cod-end.

Recommendation 4

Undersized Fish

(This Recommendation is in effect at the time of going to press, and is of indefinite duration.)

Sea fish of the descriptions specified in this recommendation which are caught in any area defined in Recommendation 1 and which are of a size, measured from the tip of the snout to the end of the tail fin, smaller than the minimum size specified for each description in relation to that area shall be treated as undersized; such undersized fish shall not be retained on board any vessel except for the purpose of transplantation to other fishing grounds, but shall be returned immediately to the sea; and shall not be landed, and if below the minimum sizes specified in relation to the area defined in paragraph (b) of that recommendation shall not be sold, exposed or offered for sale in the territory of a contracting state, whether they are whole or have had their heads or any other parts removed;

	Minimum Size (cm) for areas described in Recommendation 1		
	Area (a) (i) and (ii)	Area (b)	Area (c)
Cod (Gadus morhua)	34	30	
Haddock (Melanogrammus aeglefinus)	31	27	

Hake (Merluccius merluccius)........	30	30	30
Plaice (Pleuronectes platessa)........	25	25	
Witch (Glyptocephalus cynoglossus) ..	28	28	
Lemon Sole (Microstomus kitt)	25	25	
Sole (solea solea)	24	24	24
Turbot (Scophthalmus maximum)	30	30	
Brill (Scophthalmus rhombus)	30	30	
Megrim (Lepidorhombus whiff)	25	25	
Whiting (Merlangius merlangus)	23	23	
Dab (Limanda limanda)	15	15	

Recommendation 5

Industrial Landings

(This Recommendation is in effect at the time of going to press, and expires on 1st January, 1974.)

Notwithstanding Recommendation 4 and until 1st January, 1974, 10 per cent by weight of each total landing or part thereof from the fisheries specified in Recommendation 2 which is not intended for human consumption in the form of fish may consist of undersized fish of the descriptions specified in Recommendation 4; and whiting between 20 cm. and 23 cm. in length shall not be treated as undersized for this purpose.

Recommendation 6

Skagerak and Kattegat

(This Recommendation is in effect at the time of going to press, and expires on 1st January, 1980.)

Notwithstanding Recommendations 1 and 4, and until 1st January, 1980, vessels of bhp not exceeding 150 fishing for whiting east of a line drawn from Hanstholm to Lindesnes may use nets having meshes of dimensions smaller than those specified in Recommendation 1, and may land undersized whiting without restriction as to quantity, provided that such landings shall not include fish of the other descriptions specified in Recommendation 4.

Recommendation 7

High Seas Fishery for Salmon

(This Recommendation is in effect at the time of going to press, and is subject to review as shown in the final paragraph.)

Fishing for salmon shall be regulated by the following measures:—

1. Closed Season

In Regions 1 and 2 of the Convention area, outside national fishery limits, fishing for salmon shall be prohibited from July 1st to May 5th, both dates inclusive.

Where salmon occurs within the national fishery limits of Contracting States, those States shall prescribe annual closed seasons during which fishing for salmon shall be prohibited.

2. Minimum size

No salmon of a size less than 60 cm., measured from the tip of the snout to the end of the tail fin shall be retained on board, but shall be returned immediately to the sea.

3. Mesh of Nets

Drift nets, anchored nets and seines used for fishing of salmon shall have a minimum mesh size of 160 mm. The mesh size is to be measured in accordance with the mesh regulations already in force under Recommendation 1.

4. Other Measures for the Regulation of Fishing Gear

In the fishery for salmon

a) any hooks used shall have a gape of not less than 1.9 cm;

b) the leader attaching the hook to the line shall have a minimum strength comparable to 0.6 monofil nylon;

c) the use of any trawl net, any monofilament net, or any troll shall be prohibited.

5. Closed areas

Fishing for salmon in the Convention area, outside national fishery limits, shall be prohibited

a) between latitudes 63° and 68°N and east of longitude 0°

b) east of longitude 22°.

The regulations under 2, 3 and 4 shall apply within the whole Convention area, but outside national fishery limits.

This regulation for salmon fisheries shall be subject to review by the Commission after 31st December, 1972 or in any case if substantial changes occur in the catches of salmon on the high seas or in home waters, or in the fish stocks.

Recommendation 7 (A)

(This Recommendation was agreed at the Ninth Meeting, and will become effective on 1st January, 1972. In common with Recommendation 7, it is subject to review after 31st December, 1972.)

Fishing for Atlantic Salmon shall be prohibited from 1st January 1972 in the waters of Region 2 outside national fishery limits south of 62°N latitude and between longitude 2°E and longitude 11° W. This prohibition shall be subject to review after one year.

Proposed Recommendations 8 and 8A

NORTH EAST ATLANTIC FISHERIES COMMISSION

NORTH SEA HERRING

The Commission met in Moscow on 9th to 11th December, 1971.

To replace Recommendations 8 and 8A, which expire on 28th February, 1972, the Commission made a Recommendation as follows:-

"Considering

the information given by the Liaison Committee on the state of the North Sea herring stocks and on the necessity to reduce fishing effort both on juveniles and adults in order to achieve a recovery of the stock to a satisfactory level:

Considering

that a majority have expressed themselves in favour of measures for the protection of juvenile herring, such as the introduction of a minimum size and an extended close season during the first half of the year to allow an increase in weight and quality and preference for human consumption, but that the situation of certain countries which have important industries based on fishing for juvenile herring does not enable them to associate themselves with the majority view, and that in these circumstances such a measure would have little effect:

The Commission has agreed the following Recommendation: -

1. In the period begining on 1st April 1972 and ending on 15th June 1972 and in the period begining on 1st February 1973 and ending on 15th June 1973 fishing for herring (Clupea harengus) shall be prohibited in the North Sea and Skagerrak.

2. If, before 1st March 1972 and 1st January 1973 respectively, the competent authority of a Contracting State notifies the Commission that in order to avoid special difficulties a quantity of herring not exceeding 1,250 tons in 1972 and 2,500 tons in 1973 and used for human consumption or bait should be exempted from the provisions of the Recommendation, then

(a) those provisions shall be modified to the extent of the quantity so notified in their application to nationals of that Contracting State.

(b) the competent authority of the Contracting State shall report to the Commission on the steps it has taken or proposes to take to ensure that the exemption granted in this paragraph is not abused.

(c) the Commission shall inform all Contracting States of the exemptions, notified on behalf of any Contracting State.

3. For the purposes of this Recommendation the North Sea and Skagerrak means all Convention waters in the area bounded on the north by 62°N latitude, on the west by longitude 4°W from its junction with 62°N latitude to the Scottish coast and in the English Channel 1^{O}W and on the East by the line drawn from Skagen to Pater Noster Lighthouse.

4. Notwithstanding paragraph 1 above, 10% by weight of each landing of fish may consist of herring.

5. Notwithstanding the above, and taking account of the special constitutional status of the Faroe Island, Faroese fishermen shall have the right to catch 1,250 tons in 1972 and 2,500 tons in 1973 in the North Sea and Skagerrak for human consumption or bait in the closed periods, additional to the quantities allowed to Denmark under this Recommendation.

6. Being aware that the above regulation does not amount to the reduction of fishing mortality which seems necessary for the recovery of the stocks within a reasonable time, the Commission resolves to consider the introduction of further reductions of fishing intensity in the following years. In such further discussions it shall also seek to achieve the best possible equality of sacrifice for each country. The Commission requests member countries to consider restrictions they would be willing to introduce and to inform the Commission in this respect not later than one month before the Tenth Meeting."

Office of the Commission

Moscow

14th December, 1971

AGREEMENT OF 20 DECEMBER 1962 BETWEEN DENMARK, THE FEDERAL REPUBLIC OF GERMANY AND SWEDEN CONCERNING THE PROTECTION OF THE SALMON POPULATION IN THE BALTIC SEA **

The Kingdom of Denmark, the Federal Republic of Germany and the Kingdom of Sweden, desiring to conclude an agreement concerning the protection of the salmon population (*Salmo salar*) in the Baltic Sea, have agreed as follows:

Article 1

The area to which this Agreement applies shall comprise the Baltic Sea, including the Gulf of Bothnia and the Gulf of Finland. This area shall be delimited with respect to the Öresund, the Store Baelt and the Lille Baelt by the following lines:

(*a*) Falsterbo lighthouse – Stevn lighthouse
(*b*) Jungshoved – Bøgenaessand
(*c*) Hestehoved lighthouse – Maddes Klint
(*d*) Skelby church – Flinthorne Odde
(*e*) Kappel church – Gulstav
(*f*) Ristingehale – Ærøhale
(*g*) Skjoldnaes – Pøls Huk
(*h*) Christian X bridge at Sønderborg.

Article 2

Nothing in this Agreement may be construed as restricting the exclusive right of vessels of a Contracting Party to fish in waters over which, as regards fisheries, that Contracting Party has exclusive jurisdiction.

Article 3

Nothing in this Agreement may be construed as restricting the claims of any Contracting Party in regard to the limits of its territorial sea.

Article 4

The provisions of this Agreement shall apply to all vessels of the Contracting Parties which are within or outside the waters over which, as regards fisheries, one of the Contracting Parties has exclusive jurisdiction.

Article 5

The Contracting Parties shall not, for the purposes of salmon fishing with nets or hooks, permit the use of tackle having measurements other than those prescribed below:

Seine nets for catching salmon must be so constructed that when the mesh is stretched diagonally lengthwise of the net a flat gauge two millimetres thick shall pass through it easily when the net is wet. The breadth of this gauge shall be 165 millimetres for seine nets made of natural fibres and 157 millimetres for seine nets made of synthetic fibres.

Seine nets already in use which have a mesh size less than 170 millimetres in the case of nets made of natural fibres or less than 160 millimetres in the use of nets made of synthetic fibres may continue to be used until they are worn out but not beyond five years from the date on which this Agreement comes into force.

The gap width of fish-hooks (the shortest distance between the tip of the hook and the shank) on travel-lines and fixed lines used for catching salmon shall be at least 19 millimetres. Fish-hooks already in use which have a gap width less than 19 millimetres may continue to be used but not beyond three years from the date on which this Agreement comes into force.

Article 6

No ship may retain on board any salmon caught in the water area specified in article 1 which do not measure at least 60 centimetres (measured from the tip of the snout to the end of the longest portion of the caudal fin). Such salmon must be returned immediately to the sea.

Article 7

Each of the Contracting Parties shall make regulations under which it shall be unlawful to land, offer, keep in stock for sale, put up for sale, sell, otherwise deal in or purchase for resale salmon which are not of the minimum length specified in article 6. This prohibition shall apply only to salmon which have been caught in the water area specified in article 1 of this Agreement.

Article 8

The provisions of this Agreement shall not apply to fishing which is carried out with a view to the preservation of fish stocks or for scientific purposes nor to the salmon caught in this connexion. Such salmon may be landed for scientific purposes; in all other respects, the provisions of article 7 shall apply.

Article 9

Each of the Contracting Parties shall make such regulations as are necessary to give effect to this Agreement. These regulations shall also apply to salmon fishing in waters over which, as regards fisheries, the Contracting Party has exclusive jurisdiction.

The Contracting Parties shall communicate to each other the texts of the regulations which are made to give effect to this Agreement.

Article 10

A Standing Committee shall be set up in which each Contracting Party shall be represented by one voting member. Each of the Contracting Parties may, in addition, appoint experts and advisers. The decisions of the Committee shall be taken by unanimous vote.

It shall be the function of the Committee to establish and co-ordinate technical contacts with international organizations, research institutions of the Contracting Parties and scientists with a view to fostering the development of salmon stocks in the Baltic Sea, fish-breeding methods and the rational exploitation of the salmon population. The Committee shall also, on the basis of available information, consider whether there are grounds for modifying or amending this Agreement and, if necessary, shall make appropriate recommendations to the Contracting Parties.

The Committee shall establish its own rules of procedure.

The Committee shall meet at the request of one of the Contracting Parties but in any case not less than once every three years.

The Government of the Kingdom of Sweden, as soon as possible after the entry into force of this Agreement, shall call the first meeting of the Committee.

Each Contracting Party shall bear the expenses of its representative, experts and advisers.

AGREEMENT BETWEEN THE GOVERNMENTS OF ICELAND, NORWAY AND THE SOVIET UNION ON THE REGULATION OF THE FISHING OF ATLANTO-SCANDIAN HERRING

The Governments of Iceland, Norway and the Soviet Union,

Who with the object of protecting stocks have found it necessary to regulate the fishing of Atlanto-Scandian Herring,

Have agreed on the following: -

Article I

Fishing for sexually mature herring of the Norwegian spring spawning type shall be prohibited in Statistics Areas I, II and Vb of the International Council for the Exploration of the Sea from the date that this Agreement enters into force.

This prohibition does not apply to fishing in connection with scientific research carried out by Fisheries Authorities with the object of obtaining information on the state of stocks and the movement of fish.

Article II

Each State Party undertakes to limit its fishing for small and fat herring in Statistics Areas I and II of the International Council for the Exploration of the Sea to 45% of the amount caught in 1969 according to the said statistics.

Article III

The States Parties shall draw up regulations for the implementation of the provisions contained in Articles I and II, and shall inform each other of the steps that they have taken.

Article IV

The competent organs of the States Parties shall send each other monthly figures of catches if the total catch exceeds 100 metric tons.

Article V

This Agreement shall enter into force on the day when it has been signed by all three Parties and shall remain in force until December 31, 1972.

In witness whereof the undersigned being duly authorized by their respective governments have signed this Agreement.

Done at Moscow on February 25, 1972 in three copies in the Icelandic, Norwegian and Russian languages, all texts being equally authentic.

May 9, 1972

UNITED STATES AND BRAZIL
SIGN SHRIMPING AGREEMENT

The Government of the United States of America and the Government of the Federative Republic of Brazil today signed an agreement establishing a shrimp conservation zone off the coast of Brazil within which the activities of shrimp vessels of the two countries will be regulated. The agreement was signed by Ambassador William Rountree for the United States and Foreign Minister Mario Gibson Barbosa for Brazil. It will be submitted promptly to the Senate for its advise and consent to ratification. The ratified agreement would remain in effect at least until January 1, 1974.

The agreement reflects the mutual concern of the two countries for conservation of the shrimp resources. The two parties expressly reserve their juridical positions on the question of territorial seas and fisheries jurisdiction under international law.

The United States Government considers the signature of this agreement to be a constructive resolution of a complicated and difficult problem. The two nations have once again affirmed the value of negotiated solutions and the traditional spirit of friendship and cooperation which has characterized their relations over almost 150 years.

* * * * *

AGREEMENT BETWEEN THE GOVERNMENT OF THE FEDERATIVE REPUBLIC OF BRAZIL AND THE GOVERNMENT OF THE UNITED STATES OF AMERICA CONCERNING SHRIMP

The Parties to this Agreement,

Note the position of the Government of the Federative Republic of Brazil,

that it considers its territorial sea to extend to a distance of 200 nautical miles from Brazil's coast,

that the exploitation of crustaceans and other living resources, which are closely dependent on the seabed under the Brazilian territorial sea, is reserved to Brazilian fishing vessels, and

that exceptions to this provision can only be granted through international agreements,

Note also the position of the Government of the United States of America that it does not consider itself obligated under international law to recognize territorial sea claims of more than 3 nautical miles nor fisheries jurisdiction of more than 12 nautical miles, beyond which zone of jurisdiction all nations have the right to fish freely, and that it does not consider that all crustaceans are living organisms belonging to sedentary species as defined in the 1958 Geneva Convention on the Continental Shelf, and further

Recognizing that the difference in the respective juridical positions of the Parties has given rise to certain problems relating to the conduct of shrimp fisheries,

Considering the tradition of both Parties for resolving international differences by having recourse to negotiation,

Believing it is desirable to arrive at an interim solution for the conduct of shrimp fisheries without prejudice to either Party's juridical position concerning the extent of territorial seas or fisheries jurisdiction under international law,

Concluding that, while general international solutions to issues of maritime jurisdiction are being sought and until more adequate information regarding the shrimp fisheries is available, it is desirable to conclude an interim agreement which takes into account their mutual interest in the conservation of the shrimp resources of the area of this Agreement,

Have Agreed as Follows:

Article I

This Agreement shall apply to the fishery for shrimp (Penaeus (M.) duorarum notialis, Penaeus braziliensis and Penaeus (M.) aztecus subtilis) in an area of the broader region in which the shrimp fisheries of the Parties are conducted, hereinafter referred to as the "area of agreement" and defined as follows: the waters off the coast of Brazil having the isobath of thirty (30) meters as the south-west limit and the latitude 1° north as the southern limit and 47° 30' west longitude as the eastern limit.

Article II

1. Taking into account their common concern with preventing the depletion of the shrimp stocks in the area of agreement and the substantial difference in the stages of development of their respective fishing fleets, which results correspondingly in different kinds of impact on the resources, the two Parties agree that, during the term of this Agreement, the Government of the Federative Republic of Brazil is to apply the measures set forth in Annex I to this Agreement and the Government of the United States of America is to apply the measures set forth in Annex II to this Agreement.

2. The measures set forth in Annexes may be changed by agreement of the Parties through consultation pursuant to Article X.

Article III

1. Information on catch and effort and biological data relating to shrimp fisheries in the area of agreement shall be collected and exchanged, as appropriate, by the Parties. Unless the Parties decide otherwise, such exchange of information shall be made in accordance with the procedure described in this Article.

2. Each vessel fishing under this Agreement shall maintain a fishing log, according to a commonly agreed model. Such fishing logs shall be delivered quarterly to the appropriate Party which shall use the data therein contained, and other information it obtains about the area of agreement, to prepare reports on the fishing conditions in that area, which shall be transmitted periodically to the other Party as appropriate.

3. Duly appointed organizations from both Parties shall meet in due time to exchange scientific data, publications and knowledge acquired on the shrimp fisheries in the area of agreement.

Article IV

1. The Party which under Article V has the responsibility for enforcing observance of the terms of the Agreement by vessels of the other Party's flag shall receive from the latter Party the information necessary for identification and other enforcement functions, including name, port of registry, port where operations are usually based, general description with photograph in profile, radio-frequencies by which communications may be established, main engine horsepower and speed, length, and fishing method and gear employed.

2. Such information shall be assembled and organized by the flag Government and communications relating to such information shall be carried out each year between the appropriate authorities of the Parties.

3. The Party which receives such information shall verify whether it is complete and in good order, and shall inform the other Party about the vessels found to comply with the requirements of paragraph 1 of this Article, as well as about those which would, for some reason, require further consultation among the Parties.

4. Each of those vessels found in order shall receive and display an identification sign, agreed between the Parties.

Article V

1. In view of the fact that Brazilian authorities can carry out an effective enforcement presence in the area of Agreement, it shall be incumbent on the Government of Brazil to ensure that the conduct of shrimp fisheries conforms with the provisions of this Agreement.

2. A duly authorized official of Brazil, in exercising the responsibility described in paragraph 1 of this Article may, if he has reasonable cause to believe that any provision of this Agreement has been violated, board and search a shrimp fishing vessel. Such action shall not unduly hinder fishing operations. When, after boarding or boarding and searching a vessel, the official continues to have reasonable cause to believe that any provision of this Agreement has been violated,

he may seize and detain such vessel. In the case of a boarding or seizure and detention of a United States vessel, the Government of Brazil shall promptly inform the Government of the United States of its action.

3. After satisfaction of the terms of Article VI as referred to in paragraph 4 of this Article, a United States vessel seized and detained under the terms of this Agreement shall, as soon as practicable, be delivered to an authorized official of the United States at the nearest port to the place of seizure, or any other place which is mutually acceptable to the competent authorities of both Parties. The Government of Brazil shall, after delivering such vessel to an authorized official of the United States, provide a certified copy of the full report of the violation and the circumstances of the seizure and detention.

4. If the reason for seizure and detention falls within the terms of Article II or Article IV, paragraph 4 of this Agreement, a United States vessel seized and detained shall be delivered to an authorized official of the United States, after satisfaction of the terms of Article VI relating to unusual expenses.

5. If the nature of the violation warrants it, and after carrying out the provision of Article X, vessels may also suffer forfeiture of that part of the catch determined to be taken illegally and forfeiture of the fishing gear.

6. In the case of vessels delivered to an authorized official of the United States under paragraphs 3 or 4 of this Article, the Government of Brazil will be informed of the institution and disposition of any case by the United States.

Article VI

In connection with the enforcement arrangements specified in Article V, including in particular any unusual expenses incurred in carrying out the seizure and detention of a United States vessel under the terms of paragraph 4 of Article V, and taking into account Brazil's regulation of its flag vessels in the area of agreement, the Government of Brazil will be compensated in an amount determined and confirmed in an exchange of notes between the Parties. The amount of compensation shall be related to the level of fishing by United States nationals in the area of agreement and to the total enforcement activities to be undertaken by the Government of Brazil pursuant to the terms of this Agreement.

Article VII

The implementation of this Agreement may be reviewed at the request of either Party six months after the date on which this Agreement becomes effective, in order to deal with administrative issues arising in connection with this Agreement.

Article VIII

The Parties shall examine the possibilities of cooperating in the development of their fishing industries; the expansion of the international trade of fishery products; the improvement of storage, transportation and marketing of fishery products; and the encouragement of joint ventures between the fishing industries of the two Parties.

Article IX

Nothing contained in this Agreement shall be interpreted as prejudicing the position of either Party regarding the matter of territorial seas or fisheries jurisdiction under international law.

Article X

Problems concerning the interpretation and implementation of this Agreement shall be resolved through diplomatic channels.

Article XI

This Agreement shall enter into force on a date to be mutually agreed by exchange of notes, upon completion of the internal procedures of both parties and shall remain in force until January 1, 1974, unless the Parties agree to extend it.

In witness whereof the undersigned representatives have signed the present agreement and affixed thereto their seals.

Done in duplicate this 9th day of May, 1972, in the English and Portuguese languages both texts being equally authoritative.

ANNEX I

a) Prohibition of shrimp fishing activities, for conservation purposes, in spawning and breeding areas;
b) Prohibition of the use of chemical, toxic or explosive substances in or near fishing areas;
c) Registry of all fishing vessels with the Maritime Port Authority (Capitania dos Portos) and with SUDEPE;
d) Payment of fees and taxes for periodical inspections;
e) Use of the SUDEPE fishing logs to be returned after each trip or weekly;
f) Prohibition of the use of fishing gear and of other equipment considered by SUDEPE to have destructive effects on the stocks;
g) Prohibition of discharging oil and organic waste.

ANNEX II

a) Not more than 325 vessels flying the United States flag shall fish for shrimp in the area of agreement and the United States Government undertakes to maintain a presence of no more than 160 of those vessels in the area at any one time. Such vessels shall be of the same type and have the same gear as those commonly employed in this fishery in the past, noting that electric equipment for fishing purposes has not been commonly employed by boats in this fishery in the past.
b) Shrimp fishing in the area of agreement shall be limited to the period from March 1 to November 30.
c) Shrimp fishing in that part of the area of agreement southeast of a bearing of 240° from Ponta do Ceu radio-beacon shall be limited to the period March 1 to July 1.
d) Transshipment of catch may be made only between vessels authorized under this Agreement to fish in the area of agreement.

AGREED MINUTE RELATING TO THE AGREEMENT BETWEEN THE GOVERNMENT OF THE FEDERATIVE REPUBLIC OF BRAZIL AND THE GOVERNMENT OF THE UNITED STATES OF AMERICA CONCERNING SHRIMP

The Delegations of the Government of Brazil and the Government of the United States of America consider it desirable to record the points set out below relating to the Agreement between the two Governments concerning shrimp signed on the 9th day of May, 1972:

The Brazilian Delegation informed the United States Delegation that the portion of the area of Agreement between the true bearing of 240° and 225°, drawn from the Ponta do Ceu radio-beacon, has a special interest to the Brazilian shrimp vessels, in view of its vicinity to both the port and the industries existing in Belem, State of Para. Under these circumstances, the Brazilian Delegation informed the United States Delegation that it was not the intention of the Brazilian Government to re-include such region in agreements it might conclude after 1973.

The United States Delegation stated its view to the Brazilian Delegation that the area of the Agreement between the true bearing of 240° and 225°, drawn from the Ponta do Ceu radio-beacon, lies on the high seas and is thus open to fishing by all nations.

Both the Brazilian and the United States Delegations agreed that, based on the available information, the expression "of the same type", included in item A of Annex II in relation to United States vessels that have in the past fished in the area of the Agreement, means vessels having a length up to approximately eighty five feet.

With respect to item A of Annex II, both Delegations agreed that an excess of up to 15 vessels in the area of agreement over the figure of 160 shall constitute, during the first fishing season of the Agreement, a situation requiring consultations between the Parties within the scope of Article X with a view toward arriving at as promptly as possible the agreed figure. In view of the special nature of the arrangements contained in item A of Annex II, both Delegations understand that consultations referred to in paragraph 2, Article II will be held as soon after the close of the current fishing season as possible, to examine the operation of this provision with a view toward revising, if necessary, the measures outlined in item A of Annex II or revising the procedures necessary to achieve better compliance with them.

Note

The Embassy of the United States of America presents its compliments to the Ministry of External Relations of the Federative Republic of Brazil, and with reference to the Agreement Concerning Shrimp signed on this date, as well as the accompanying exchange of Notes related to Article VI of that Agreement, has the honor to inform the Ministry of the following:

Pending the entering into force of the agreement as provided for in article eleven, the Government of the United States of America is prepared to make every effort to encourage the voluntary compliance by its industry of the provisions of the Agreement so as to ensure that events in the interim period do not prejudice the successful implementation of those provisions. It is the understanding of the Government of the United States of America that the Government of the Federative Republic of Brazil intends also to abide by the spirit of the proposed interim Agreement.

Following the exchange of instruments of ratification, but prior to the passage of enabling legislation, the Government of the United States of America proposes to continue its efforts to encourage voluntary compliance.

In the period between the completion of internal procedures as noted in article eleven and the entering into force of the Agreement, the Government of the United States of America will seek, *inter alia*, with the voluntary cooperation of U. S. flag vessel owners,

1. To achieve the objectives of Article II
2. To institute appropriate Article III procedures
3. To achieve the intent of Articles IV and V.

In stating its willingness to encourage the voluntary compliance with appropriate provisions of the Agreement so that the intent of the accord may be achieved while awaiting its entering into force, it is the understanding of the Government of the United States of America that the Government of the Federative Republic of Brazil agrees that in this same interim period both Parties should have as their objective the achievement of the intent of the Agreement.

With specific reference to Article III, paragraph 2, the Government of the United States of America shall treat the information obtained from individual fishing logs as confidential.

Reply to the Note from the American Embassy:

The Ministry of External Relations of the Federative Republic of Brazil presents its compliments to the Embassy of the United States of America and has the honor to acknowledge receipt of the Embassy's note of today's date, which reads as following:

(Note of the USA)

2. In reply, the Ministry of External Relations wishes to confirm that the understanding referred to in the penultimate paragraph of the Embassy's note is shared by the Brazilian Government.

3. Furthermore, the Ministry of External Relations wishes to state that, pending the entry into force of the Agreement, it is the intent of the Brazilian Government to apply its provisions in so far as possible from today and in a manner which will ensure that events in the interim will not prejudice the successful implementation of those provisions.

4. With specific reference to Article III, paragraph 2, the Government of the Federative Republic of Brazil shall treat the information obtained from individual fishing logs as confidential.

Brasilia, May 9, 1972

Excellency:

I have the honor to refer to the Agreement on Shrimp signed today by the Governments of the Federative Republic of Brazil and the United States of America and to confirm, on behalf of my Government, the following:

a) The Government of the United States of America shall, after the appropriation of funds by Congress, compensate the Government of Brazil in an annual amount of U.S. $200,000 (two hundred thousand dollars) pursuant to the terms of Article VI;

b) The Government of the United States of America shall, after the appropriation of funds by Congress, further compensate the Government of Brazil in the amount of U.S. $100.00 (one hundred dollars) for each day a United States flag shrimp fishing vessel is under the control of Brazilian enforcement authorities pursuant to the terms of paragraph 2 of Article V.

I have the honor to propose that this Note and Your Excellency's reply confirming the above points of understanding on behalf of your Government shall be regarded as constituting satisfaction of the terms of Article VI of the aforementioned Agreement between the two Governments.

Accept, Excellency, the renewed assurances of my highest consideration.

His Excellency

Mario Gibson Barboza

Minister of Foreign Affairs

Brasilia

Brasilia, May 9, 1972

Excellency,

I have the honor to acknowledge receipt of Your Excellency's note, of today's date, which reads as follows:

(Note of the USA)

2. In reply, I wish to confirm, on behalf of the Brazilian Government, that the above points of understanding shall be regarded as constituting satisfaction of the terms of Article VI of the Agreement on Shrimp, signed today by the two Governments.

I avail myself . . . .

Embassy of Trinidad and Tobago
Rio de Janeiro

MAY 19, 1972

Excellency,

I have the honour to refer to recent conversations in which representatives of the Government of Trinidad and Tobago and the Government of the Federative Republic of Brazil having considered, in a spirit of mutual understanding, the situation relating to shrimping in the waters adjacent to the coast of Brazil, and motivated by the friendly relations existing between the two Governments and peoples have agreed to the following:

1) Nothing contained in this Agreement, the text of which appears hereunder, would necessarily constitute a precedent.

2) This Agreement shall govern the operation of shrimp catch by Trinidad and Tobago flag vessels in the waters adjacent to the coast of Brazil during the period from May 1st, 1972, to November 30, 1973.

3) Nothing in this Agreement shall be deemed to prejudice, in any way, the legal position of either Government in regard to the limits of territorial seas and fisheries jurisdiction.

4) The species to be fished are the following: *Penaeus* (M.) *duorarum notialis*, *Penaeus brasiliensis* and *Penaeus* (M.) *aztecus subtilis*. The simultaneous and inevitable catch of other marine species in quantities and conditions which characterize them as incident fauna of the shrimp species authorized under the

Agreement shall not be considered as a violation of the Agreement. The shrimping activities shall be conducted exclusively within a zone having the isobath of thirty (30) meters as the southwest limit and the latitude 1° north as the southern limit and 47°30' west longitude as the eastern limit. Shrimp fishing, however, in the part of the above-mentioned zone which lies southeast of a bearing of 240° drawn from the Ponta do Ceu radio-beacon shall be limited to the period March 1st to July 1st.

5) Twenty shrimp trawlers flying the Trinidad and Tobago flag shall be admitted to catch shrimp in the zone described in Article 4 of this Agreement. These trawlers shall not exceed eighty-five feet in length, except for two trawlers that shall not exceed ninety feet, and shall not employ electric equipment for fishing purposes.

6) The season during which the shrimping activities referred to in this Agreement are to be conducted shall be between March 1st and November 30th of each year.

7) The Government of Trinidad and Tobago will furnish the Government of the Federative Republic of Brazil, through the diplomatic channel, with a list of the vessels to be covered by this Agreement as well as with the basic data relating to these vessels. Such data shall include the name, length, radio-frequency, maximum speed, gross and net tonnage of each vessel, a description of its navigation

and fishing equipment, the communications equipment, and the identification signal to be used. In addition, the port registry, the name of the vessel's captain, the name and legal address of its registered office in Trinidad and Tobago shall also be provided.

8) To complete the registration procedure, the Government of the Federative Republic of Brazil will inform the Government of Trinidad and Tobago of the vessels authorized to fish under the terms of this Agreement.

9) Before the beginning of the shrimping activities of the authorized vessels, the Government of Trinidad and Tobago shall

a) produce to the Brazilian Embassy in Port of Spain the documents of the vessel (registry certification, crew list, up-to-date seaworthiness certificates, insurance certificate);

b) hand in photographs of the vessel and an indication of its methods and gear;

c) pay for each vessel a fee of US $100.00 (one hundred dollars) for each month of operation in the 1972 season, this fee being calculated from a date one month following the date of authorization of the vessel to November 30th, 1972, and pay a fee of US$ 900.00 (nine hundred dollars) for the 1973 season.

10) Each of the authorized vessels shall display an identification sign, agreed between the Parties, and shall

carry the appropriate documents of identification, to be produced, on request of the Brazilian authorities.

11) While conducting fishing activities according to the provisions of this Agreement the captains of the trawlers shall:

a) proceed directly to the authorized fishing zone defined in Article 4;

b) fill out fishing logs furnished by the Brazilian Embassy in Port of Spain and return them to the Embassy within 14 days of their return to Port of Spain;

c) be familiar with and respect Brazilian laws and regulations, particularly those regarding fishing and prevention of sea pollution;

d) land the catch in Trinidad and Tobago, transshipment being permitted only between vessels registered under this Agreement.

12) The Government of Trinidad and Tobago will supply the Government of the Federative Republic of Brazil periodically with statistical data relating to the size and species of the catches captured by Trinidad and Tobago vessels in the waters adjacent to the coast of Brazil.

13) a) While in Brazilian territorial waters the Trinidad and Tobago shrimp trawlers shall be subject to Brazilian surveillance. Duly appointed officials may board the trawlers for inspection.

b) The Brazilian Embassy in Port of Spain shall be informed of the estimated dates of arrival at the fishing zones and of the dates of departure from and return to ports of Trinidad and Tobago.

14) Infringements of Brazilian law occurring in Brazilian territorial waters shall be dealt with according to Brazilian law.

15) Problems concerning the interpretation and implementation of the present agreement shall be solved through diplomatic channels.

16) At the request of either Party, both Parties shall, within one month, conduct consultations for a review of the operation of this Agreement or of its provisions.

I have the honour to propose that if the above terms are acceptable to the Government of the Federative Republic of Brazil, the present Note together with Your Excellency's Note in reply indicating your Government's concurrence therewith shall constitute an agreement between the two Governments, to come into force on the date of Your Excellency's Note in reply.

Please accept, Excellency, the assurances of my highest consideration.

Gerard Montano
Ambassador

His Excellency

Dr. Mario Gibson Barboza
Minister of External Affairs
Brazil

CONVENTION ON CONDUCT OF FISHING OPERATIONS IN THE NORTH ATLANTIC*

[Opened for signature at London, June 1, 1967]

The Governments of Belgium, Canada, Denmark, the French Republic, the Federal Republic of Germany, Iceland, Ireland, Italy, Luxembourg, the Netherlands, Norway, the Polish People's Republic, Portugal, Spain, Sweden, the United States of America, the Union of Soviet Socialist Republics, and the United Kingdom of Great Britain and Northern Ireland,

Desiring to ensure good order and conduct on the fishing grounds in the North Atlantic area;

Have agreed as follows:

ARTICLE 1

(1) The present Convention applies to the waters of the Atlantic and Arctic Oceans and their dependent seas which are more specifically defined in Annex I to this Convention.

(2) In this Convention

"fishing vessel" means any vessel engaged in the business of catching fish;

"vessel" means any fishing vessel and any vessel engaged in the business of processing fish or providing supplies or services to fishing vessels.

ARTICLE 2

Nothing in this Convention shall be deemed to affect the rights, claims or views of any Contracting Party in regard to the limits of territorial waters or national fishery limits, or of the jurisdiction of a coastal State over fisheries.

ARTICLE 3

(1) The fishing vessels of each Contracting Party shall be registered and marked in accordance with the regulations of that Party in order to ensure their identification at sea.

(2) The competent authority of each Contracting Party shall specify one or more letters and a series of numbers for each port or district.

(3) Each Contracting Party shall draw up a list showing these letters.

(4) This list, and all modifications which may subsequently be made in it, shall be notified to the other Contracting Parties.

(5) The provisions of Annex II to this Convention shall apply to fishing vessels and their small boats and fishing implements.

*[Reproduced from the Annex to the Final Act of the Fisheries Policing Conference, done at London, March 17, 1967.]

Article 4

(1) In addition to complying with the rules relating to signals as prescribed in the International Regulations for Preventing Collisions at Sea, the fishing vessels of each Contracting Party shall comply with the provisions of Annex III to this Convention.

(2) No other additional light and sound signals than those provided in the Annex shall be used.

Article 5

Nets, lines and other gear anchored in the sea and nets or lines which drift in the sea shall be marked in order to indicate their position and extent. The marking shall be in accordance with the provisions of Annex IV to this Convention.

Article 6

(1) Subject to compliance with the International Regulations for Preventing Collisions at Sea all vessels shall conduct their operations so as not to interfere with the operations of fishing vessels or fishing gear and shall conform to the provisions of Annex V to this Convention.

(2) For the better implementation of these provisions the competent authorities of Contracting Parties may at their discretion notify the competent authorities of other Contracting Parties likely to be concerned of concentrations or probable concentrations known to them of fishing vessels or fishing gear, and Contracting Parties receiving such notification shall take such steps as are practicable to inform their vessels thereof. The authorised officers appointed in accordance with Article 9 of this Convention may also draw the attention of vessels to fishing gear placed in the sea.

Article 7

(1) In any dispute that arises between the nationals of different Contracting Parties concerning damaged gear or damage to vessels resulting from entanglement of gear, the following procedure will apply in the absence of agreement among the Contracting Parties concerning the resolution of such disputes:

> At the request of the Contracting Party of a complainant each Contracting Party concerned will appoint a review board or other appropriate authority for handling the claim. These boards or other authorities will examine the facts and endeavour to bring about a settlement.

(2) These arrangements are without prejudice to the rights of complainants to prosecute their claims by way of ordinary legal procedure.

ARTICLE 8

(1) Each Contracting Party undertakes to take such measures as may be appropriate to implement and enforce the provisions of this Convention with respect to its vessels and gear.

(2) Within the area where a coastal State has jurisdiction over fisheries, the implementation and enforcement of the provisions of this Convention shall be the responsibility of the coastal State.

(3) Within that area the coastal State may make special rules and exemptions from any of the Rules in Annexes II to V to this Convention for vessels or gear which by reason of their size or type operate or are set only in coastal waters, provided that there shall be no discrimination in form or in fact against vessels of other Contracting Parties entitled to fish in those waters. Before making special rules and exemptions under this paragraph in respect of areas in which foreign fishing vessels operate a Contracting Party shall inform the Contracting Parties concerned of their intentions and consult them if they so wish.

ARTICLE 9

(1) To facilitate the implementation of the provisions of the Convention the arrangements set out in this Article and in Annex VI to this Convention shall apply outside national fishery limits.

(2) Authorised officers means officers who may be appointed by the Contracting Parties for the purpose of these arrangements.

(3) Any Contracting Party shall, upon the request of another Contracting Party, notify the latter of the names of the authorised officers who have been appointed or of the ships in which such officers are carried.

(4) Authorised officers shall observe whether the provisions of the Convention are being carried out, enquire and report on infringements of the provisions of the Convention, seek information in cases of damage, where desirable draw the attention of vessels of Contracting Parties to the provisions of the Convention, and shall co-operate for these purposes with the authorised officers of other Contracting Parties.

(5) If an authorised officer has reason to believe that a vessel of any Contracting Party is not complying with the provisions of the Convention, he may identify the vessel, seek to obtain the necessary information from the vessel and report. If the matter is sufficiently serious, he may order the vessel to stop and, if it is necessary in order to verify the facts of the case, he may board the vessel for enquiry and report.

(6) If an authorised officer has reason to believe that a vessel or its gear has caused damage to a vessel or fishing gear and that this may be due to a breach of the Convention, he may, under the same conditions as in the preceding paragraph, order any vessel concerned to stop and board it for enquiry and report.

(4) Notwithstanding the provisions of paragraph (3), the parties may agree to submit the dispute to arbitration in accordance with another arrangement operating between the parties.

(5) If within six months from the date of the request for arbitration the parties are unable to agree on the organisation of the arbitration, any one of those parties may refer the dispute (as referred to in paragraph (1)) to the International Court of Justice by request in conformity with the Statute of the Court.

(6) Notwithstanding the provision of paragraph (1), the parties may agree to submit the dispute to the International Court of Justice.

Article 14

(1) Except as provided in paragraphs (2) and (3) below and paragraph (3) of Article 17, no reservations may be made to the present Convention without the agreement of the Contracting Parties and signatory Governments. When one year has elapsed after the entry into force of the Convention, the agreement of the Contracting Parties only shall be required.

(2) At the time of signature, ratification, approval or accession any State may make a reservation to Article 13 of the present Convention.

(3) Any State may, at the time of signature, ratification, approval or accession, make a reservation to paragraphs (5) and (6) of Article 9 with respect to one or more of the other Contracting Parties or signatory Governments.

(4) Any State which has made a reservation in accordance with the preceding paragraphs or paragraph (3) of Article 17 may at any time withdraw the reservation by a communication to that effect addressed to the depositary Government.

Article 15

The present Convention shall be open for signature at London from 1st June to 30th November, 1967. It is subject to ratification or approval. The instruments of ratification or approval shall be deposited as soon as possible with the Government of the United Kingdom of Great Britain and Northern Ireland.

Article 16

(1) The present Convention shall enter into force on the ninetieth day following the date of deposit of the tenth instrument of ratification or approval.

(2) Thereafter the Convention shall enter into force for each State on the ninetieth day after deposit of its instrument of ratification or approval.

ARTICLE 17

(1) Any State which has not signed the Convention may accede thereto at any time after the Convention has entered into force, provided that three-fourths of the Contracting Parties and signatory Governments agree to the proposed accession. When one year has elapsed after the entry into force of the Convention, the agreement of three-fourths of the Contracting Parties only shall be required.

(2) Accession shall be effected by the deposit of an instrument of accession with the Government of the United Kingdom of Great Britain and Northern Ireland. The Convention shall enter into force for each acceding State on the ninetieth day after the deposit of its instrument of accession.

(3) At any time up to the entry into force of the Convention for a State which accedes under this Article, a Contracting Party may make a reservation to paragraphs (5) and (6) of Article 9 with respect to that State.

ARTICLE 18

(1) Any Contracting Party may, when depositing its instrument of ratification, approval or accession, or at any later date, by declaration addressed to the depositary Government, extend this Convention to any territory or territories for whose international relations it is responsible. The provisions of this Convention shall enter into force for such territory or territories on the ninetieth day after receipt of such declaration, or on the date on which the Convention enters into force in accordance with paragraph (1) of Article 16, whichever is the later.

(2) Any declaration made in pursuance of the preceding paragraph may, in respect of any territory mentioned in such declaration, be withdrawn according to the procedure laid down in Article 19.

ARTICLE 19

At any time after four years from the date on which this Convention has entered into force in accordance with paragraph (1) of Article 16, any Contracting Party may denounce the Convention by means of a notice in writing addressed to the depositary Government. Any such notice shall take effect twelve months after the date of its receipt. The Convention shall remain in force as between the other Parties.

ARTICLE 20

When the present Convention has entered into force, it shall be registered by the depositary Government with the Secretariat of the United Nations in accordance with Article 102 of its Charter.

IN WITNESS WHEREOF the undersigned, being duly authorised thereto, have signed the present Convention.

DONE at London this first day of June, 1967, in the English and French languages, each text being equally authentic, in a single original which shall be deposited in the archives of the Government of the United Kingdom of Great Britain and Northern Ireland, which shall transmit a certified true copy thereof to each signatory and acceding Government.

Annex I

AREA OF APPLICATION OF CONVENTION

The waters of the Atlantic and Arctic Oceans and dependent seas to which this Convention applies are the waters seaward of the baselines of the territorial sea within the area bounded:

(*a*) in the south by a line drawn due west along 36° north latitude to 42° west longitude, thence due south to 35° north latitude, thence due west along 35° north latitude;

(*b*) in the west by a line drawn southward from a point on the coast of Greenland at 78° 10′ north latitude to a point in 75° north latitude and 73° 30′ west longitude, thence along a rhumb line to a point in 69° north latitude and 59° west longitude, thence due south to 61° north latitude, thence due west to 64° 30′ west longitude, thence due south to the coast of Labrador, and thence south along the coast of North America;

(*c*) in the east by 51° east longitude, but excluding—

(i) the Baltic Sea and Belts lying to the south and east of lines drawn from Hasenore Head to Gniben Point and from Gilbierg Head to the Kullen; and

(ii) the Mediterranean Sea and its dependent seas as far as the meridian of 5° 36′ west longitude.

Annex II

IDENTIFICATION AND MARKING OF FISHING VESSELS AND GEAR

Rule 1

(1) The letter or letters of the port or district in which each fishing vessel is registered and the number under which it is registered shall be painted on the bow of the fishing vessel at both sides, and may also be painted on the upper part of the fishing vessel so as to be clearly visible from the air.

(2) The name of the fishing vessel, if any, and the name of the port or district in which it is registered shall be painted on the fishing vessel so as to be clearly visible.

(3) The names, letters and numbers placed on a fishing vessel shall be large enough to be easily recognised and shall not be effaced, altered, made illegible, covered or concealed.

(4) Small boats and, where practicable, all fishing implements shall be marked with the letter or letters and number of the fishing vessel to which they belong. The ownership of nets or other fishing implements may be distinguished by private marks.

Rule 2

(1) Each fishing vessel shall carry on board an official document, issued by the competent authority of its country, showing the name, if any, and description of the vessel, its nationality, its registration letter or letters and number, and the name of the owner or of the firm or association to which it belongs.

(2) Each fishing vessel shall carry a national flag in good condition to be shown at the request of the competent authorities.

(3) The nationality of a fishing vessel shall not be concealed in any manner whatsoever.

ANNEX III

ADDITIONAL SIGNALS TO BE USED BY FISHING VESSELS

Rule 1

General

(1) Subject to compliance with the International Regulations for Preventing Collisions at Sea, the Rules herein are intended to prevent damage to fishing gear or accidents in the course of fishing operations.

(2) The Rules herein concerning lights shall apply in all weathers from sunset to sunrise when fishing vessels are engaged in fishing as a fleet and during such times no other lights shall be exhibited, except the lights prescribed in the International Regulations for Preventing Collisions at Sea and such lights as cannot be mistaken for the prescribed lights or do not impair their visibility or distinctive character, or interfere with the keeping of a proper look-out. These lights may also be exhibited from sunrise to sunset in restricted visibility and in all other circumstances when it is deemed necessary.

(3) For the purpose of these Rules the words employed shall have the meaning set down in the International Regulations for Preventing Collisions at Sea except that the term " fishing vessel " shall have the meaning assigned to it in Article 1 (2) of this Convention.

(4) The lights mentioned herein shall be placed where they can best be seen. They should be at least 3 feet (0·92 m.) apart but at a lower level than the lights prescribed in Rule 9 (*c*) (i) and (*d*) of the International Regulations for Preventing Collisions at Sea 1960. They shall be visible

at a distance of at least 1 mile, all round the horizon as nearly as possible and their visibility shall be less than the visibility of lights exhibited in accordance with Rule 9 (*b*) of the above Regulations.

Rule 2

Signals for Trawling and Drift netting

(1) Fishing vessels, when engaged in trawling, whether using demersal or pelagic gear shall exhibit:

(i) when shooting their nets:
two white lights in a vertical line one over the other;

(ii) when hauling their nets:
one white light over one red light in a vertical line one over the other;

(iii) when the net has come fast upon an obstruction:
two red lights in a vertical line one over the other.

(2) Fishing vessels engaged in drift netting may exhibit the lights prescribed in (1) above.

(3) Each fishing vessel engaged in pair trawling shall exhibit:

(i) by day: the "T" flag—"Keep clear of me. I am engaged in pair trawling", hoisted at the foremast;

(ii) by night: a searchlight shone forward and in the direction of the other fishing vessel of the pair;

(iii) when shooting or hauling the net or when the net has come fast upon an obstruction: the lights prescribed in (1) above.

(4) This rule need not be applied to fishing vessels of less than 65 feet (19·80 m.) in length. Any such exception and the areas in which fishing vessels so excepted are likely to be numerous shall be notified to the competent authorities of the other Contracting Parties likely to be concerned.

Rule 3

Light signals for Purse Seining

(1) Fishing vessels engaged in fishing with purse seines shall show two amber coloured lights, in a vertical line one over the other. These lights shall be flashing intermittently about once a second in such a way that when the lower is out the upper is on and vice versa. These lights shall only be shown while the fishing vessel's free movement is hampered by its fishing gear, warning other vessels to keep clear of it.

(2) This rule need not be applied to fishing vessels of less than 85 feet (25·90 m.) in length. Any such exception and areas in which fishing vessels so excepted are likely to be numerous shall be notified to the competent authorities of the other Contracting Parties likely to be concerned.

Rule 4

Sound signals

No sound signals shall be used other than those prescribed by the International Regulations for Preventing Collisions at Sea and the International Code of Signals.

ANNEX IV

MARKING OF NETS, LINES AND OTHER GEAR

Rule 1

Anchored gear

(1) The ends of nets, lines and other gear anchored in the sea shall be fitted with flag or radar reflector buoys by day and light buoys by night sufficient to indicate their position and extent. Such lights should be visible at a distance of at least 2 miles in good visibility.

(2) By day the westernmost (meaning the half compass circle from south through west to and including north) end buoy of such gear extending horizontally in the sea shall be fitted with two flags one above the other or one flag and a radar reflector, and the easternmost (meaning the half compass circle from north through east to and including south) end buoy shall be fitted with one flag or a radar reflector. By night the westernmost end buoy shall be fitted with two white lights and the easternmost end buoy with one white light. In addition a buoy fitted with one flag or a radar reflector by day and one white light by night may be set 70–100 metres from each end buoy to indicate the direction of the gear.

(3) On such gear extending more than 1 mile additional buoys shall be placed at distances of not more than 1 mile so that no part of the gear extending 1 mile or more shall be left unmarked. By day every buoy shall be fitted with a flag or a radar reflector and by night as many buoys as possible with one white light. In no case shall the distance between two lights on the same gear exceed 2 miles.

(4) On such gear which is attached to a fishing vessel a buoy shall not be required at the end attached to the fishing vessel.

(5) The flagpole of each buoy shall have a height of at least 2 metres above the buoy.

Rule 2

Drift gear

(1) Nets or lines which drift in the sea shall be marked at each end and at distances of not more than 2 miles by a buoy with a pole not less than 2 metres above the buoy. The pole shall carry a flag or a radar reflector by day and a white light by night visible at a distance of at least 2 miles in good visibility.

(2) On gear which is attached to a fishing vessel a buoy shall not be required at the end attached to the fishing vessel.

ANNEX V

RULES GOVERNING THE OPERATIONS OF VESSELS

Rule 1

Subject to compliance with the International Regulations for Preventing Collisions at Sea all vessels shall conduct their operations so as not to interfere with the operations of fishing vessels, or fishing gear.

Rule 2

Vessels arriving on fishing grounds where fishing vessels are already fishing or have set their gear for that purpose shall inform themselves of the position and extent of gear already placed in the sea and shall not place themselves or their fishing gear so as to interfere with or obstruct fishing operations already in progress.

Rule 3

No vessel shall anchor or remain on a fishing ground where fishing is in progress if it would interfere with such fishing unless required for the purpose of its own fishing operations or in consequence of accident or other circumstances beyond its control.

Rule 4

Except in cases of *force majeure* no vessel shall dump in the sea any article or substance which may interfere with fishing or obstruct or cause damage to fish, fishing gear or fishing vessels.

Rule 5

No vessel shall use or have on board explosives intended for the catching of fish.

Rule 6

In order to prevent damage, fishing vessels engaged in trawling and other fishing vessels with gear in motion shall take all practicable steps to avoid nets and lines or other gear which is not being towed.

Rule 7

(1) When nets belonging to different fishing vessels get foul of each other, they shall not be severed without the consent of the parties concerned unless it is impossible to disengage them by other means.

(2) When fishing vessels fishing with lines entangle their lines, the fishing vessel which hauls up the lines shall not sever them unless they cannot be disengaged in any other way, in which case any lines which may be severed shall where possible be immediately joined together again.

(3) Except in cases of salvage and the cases to which the two preceding paragraphs relate, nets, lines or other gear shall not under any pretext whatever, be cut, hooked, held on to or lifted up except by the fishing vessel to which they belong.

(4) When a vessel fouls or otherwise interferes with gear not belonging to it, it shall take all necessary measures for reducing to a minimum the injury which may result to such gear. The fishing vessel to which the gear belongs shall, at the same time, avoid any action tending to aggravate such damage.

ANNEX VI

RULES APPLYING TO AUTHORISED OFFICERS

(1) An authorised officer shall carry a document of identity written in English, French and the language of the authorised officer (if different) in a form agreed by the Contracting Parties on the request of the depositary Government.

(2) Any orders to stop given by an authorised officer shall be given by the appropriate signal in the International Code of Signals.

(3) On boarding a vessel an authorised officer shall exhibit his document of identity.

(4) On boarding a vessel an authorised officer may require the master of the vessel to exhibit the document specified in Annex II Rule 2 (1) and the fact of such document having been exhibited shall immediately be endorsed upon it by the authorised officer or on some other official document of the vessel.

(5) On each occasion on which an authorised officer boards a vessel, he shall draw up a report in the form set out in the Appendix indicating the circumstances of the boarding and the information he secures.

(6) This report shall be drawn up in the language of the authorised officer and shown to the master of the vessel boarded, who shall be given an opportunity of adding in his own language any remarks he or any member of his crew may wish to make. The authorised officer shall sign the report in the presence of the master and give him a copy. A copy of the report shall be sent to the competent authority of the country of the vessel boarded. In cases of damage copies of the report shall also be sent to the competent authorities in the countries to which the other parties concerned belong.

(7) Whenever an authorised officer observes a vessel infringing the provisions of the Convention, he may report the occurrence to the competent authority of the country of the vessel, having first made every effort to communicate to the vessel in question by signal or otherwise his intention to report the infringement. If he orders the vessel to stop but does not board it, he shall report the circumstances to the competent authority of the country of the vessel.

(8) Ships carrying authorised officers, which may be vessels as defined in Article 1 (2), shall fly a special flag or pennant. The special flag or pennant shall be in a form agreed by the Contracting Parties on the request of the depositary Government. Authorised officers shall exercise their powers under paragraphs (5) or (6) of Article 9, and communicate with vessels, only from surface craft.

Appendix

REPORT IN ACCORDANCE WITH PARAGRAPH (5) OF ANNEX VI TO THE CONVENTION

(*Strike out what does not apply*)

Authorised Officer

(*To be filled in block letters*)

1. Name and nationality.
2. Name of ship carrying him.

Position, Date and Time of Occurrence

3.

Provisions of the Convention in Question

4.

INFORMATION ON EACH VESSEL INVOLVED

General

5. Nationality.
6. Vessel's name and registration.
7. Skipper's name.
8. Owner's name and address.

(Items 5–8: *To be filled in block letters*)

9. Position, date and time of boarding.

At the Time of Occurrence

10. Fishing gear in use.
11. Stopped, anchored or estimated course and speed.
12. Signals or lights displayed and sound signals made.
13. Warnings given to other vessel(s).
14. Direction in which gear was shot or lying.
15. The horizontal distance gear extended from the vessel.

CONDITIONS AT THE TIME OF OCCURRENCE

16. Visibility.
17. Wind force and direction.
18. State of sea and tide and direction and strength of currents.
19. Other relevant conditions.
20. Describe, with the help of diagrams if necessary, the relative positions of vessels and gear.
21. Marking of any anchored or drifting gear involved.

ADDITIONAL INFORMATION

22. Full particulars of loss or damage, giving condition of any gear involved.
23. Narrative description of occurrence.
24. Comments by Authorised Officer.
25. Statements by Witnesses.
26. Statements by Skippers of vessels involved.
27. Statements of photographs taken, with description of subjects (photographs to be attached to copy of report submitted to flag State).

Signature of Authorised Officer ....

The above report was prepared and signed by the Authorised Officer in our presence.

Signatures of Skippers ....

Signatures of Witnesses ....

NORTH-EAST ATLANTIC FISHERIES COMMISSION

Scheme of Joint Enforcement, 1969

SCHEDULE 1

Part I

Scheme of Joint Enforcement

Recommendation

Pursuant to Article 13(3) of the Convention the Commission recommends the establishment of the following arrangements for international control outside territorial waters and fishery limits for the purpose of ensuring the application of the Convention and the measures in force thereunder:—

(1) Control shall be carried out by inspectors of the fishery control services of Contracting States. The names of the inspectors appointed for that purpose by their respective governments shall be notified to the Commission.

(2) Ships carrying inspectors shall fly a special flag or pennant approved by the Commission to indicate that the inspector is carrying out international inspection duties. The names of the ships so used for the time being, which may be either special inspection vessels or fishing vessels, shall be notified to the Commission.

(3) Each inspector shall carry a document of identity supplied by the authorities of the flag state in a form approved by the Commission and given him on appointment stating that he has authority to act under the arrangements approved by the Commission.

(4) Subject to the arrangements agreed under paragraph (9), a vessel of any Contracting State employed for the time being in fishing for sea fish or in the treatment of sea fish in the Convention area shall stop when given the appropriate signal in the International Code of Signals by a ship carrying an inspector unless actually fishing, shooting or hauling, in which case it shall stop immediately it has finished hauling. The master of the vessel shall permit the inspector, who may be accompanied by a witness, to board it. The master shall enable the inspector to make such examination of catch, nets or other gear and any relevant documents as the inspector deems necessary to verify the observance of the Commission's recommendations in force in relation to the flag state of the vessel concerned and the inspector may ask for any explanations that he deems necessary.

(5) On boarding the vessel an inspector shall produce the document described in (3) above. Inspections shall be made so that the vessel suffers the minimum interference and inconvenience. An inspector shall limit his enquiries to the ascertainment of the facts in relation to the observance of the Commission's recommendations in force in relation to the flag state of the vessel concerned. In making his examination an inspector may ask the master for any assistance he may require. He shall draw up a report of his inspection in a form approved by the Commission. He shall sign the report in the presence of the master of the vessel who shall be entitled to add or have added to the report any observations which he may think suitable and must sign such observations. Copies of the report shall be given to the master of the vessel and to the Inspector's Government who shall transmit copies to the appropriate authorities of the flag state of the vessel and to the Commission. Where any infringement of the recommendations is discovered the inspector should where possible also inform the competent authorities of the flag state, as notified to the Commission, and any inspection ship of the flag state known to be in the vicinity.

(6) Resistance to an inspector or failure to comply with his directions shall be treated by the flag state of the vessel as if the inspector were an inspector of that state.

(7) Inspectors shall carry out their duties under these arrangments in accordance with the rules set out in this recommendation but they shall remain under the operational control of their national authorities and shall be responsible to them.

(8) Contracting States shall consider and act on reports of foreign inspectors under these arrangements on the same basis as reports of national inspectors. The provisions of this paragraph shall not impose any obligation on a Contracting State to give the report of a foreign inspector a higher evidential value than it would possess in the inspector's own country. Contracting States shall collaborate in order to facilitate judicial or other proceedings arising from a report of an inspector under these arrangements.

(9) (i) Contracting States shall inform the Commission by 1st March each year of their provisional plans for participation in these arrangements in the following year and the Commission may make suggestions to Contracting States for the co-ordination of national operations in this field including the number of inspectors and ships carrying inspectors.

(ii) The arrangements set out in this Recommendation and the plans for participation shall apply between Contracting States unless otherwise agreed between them; and such agreement shall be notified to the Commission:

Provided, however, that implementation of the scheme shall be suspended between any two Contracting States, if either of them has notified the Commission to that effect, pending completion of an agreement.

(10) (i) When nets are inspected the meshes of the cod-end are to be examined with a flat gauge with parallel sides, a thickness of 2 mm. and the appropriate width made of any durable material that will retain its shape and constructed with a wedge shaped section or sections have a taper of 2 cm. in 8 cm. calibrated to measure the width of the meshes in which the section or sections are inserted. An illustration of such a gauge is appended.

(ii) The appropriate width is the appropriate width prescribed in the Commission's recommendations for the type of net inspected and the area on which the inspection takes place which are in force in relation to the flag state of the vessel concerned.

(iii) At least 20 consecutive meshes of the cod-end running parallel to its long axis, starting at least ten meshes from the lacings, are to be examined, or the maximum number if less than 20.

(iv) The gauge should be inserted into the meshes when wet so as to measure the long axis of the mesh when stretched diagonally lengthwise. If the section of the gauge with parallel sides passes easily through a mesh it is not undersized. If the inspector has any doubt as to whether the gauge passes easily through, he shall insert the gauge in the mesh held horizontally and attach a weight of 5 kilogrammes to the gauge and if the section in the gauge with parallel sides passes through the mesh the mesh is not undersized.

(v) The number of undersized meshes and the width of each mesh examined shall be entered in the inspector's report, together with the average width of the meshes examined.

(vi) Inspectors shall have authority to inspect all nets other than those which are dry and stowed away below deck.

(11) The inspector shall affix an identification mark approved by the Commission, to any net which appears to have been used in contravention of the Commission's recommendations in force in relation to the flag state of the vessel concerned and shall record this fact in his report.

(12) The inspector may photograph the net in such a way that the identification mark and the measurement of the net is visible, in which case the subjects photographed should be listed in the report and copies of the photographs should be attached to the copy of the report to the flag state.

(13) The inspector shall so far as reasonably practicable examine the catch and may take such measurements as he deems necessary to establish whether and to what extent undersized fish of protected species are present in the part of the catch inspected. He shall report his findings including the number of fish measured and the size of any fish which are undersized to the authorities of the flag state of the inspected vessel as soon as possible.

RESERVATIONS

(*a*) As between the Union of Soviet Socialist Republics and other Contracting States the provisions of the Scheme relating to inspection of gear below deck and of catch do not apply.

(*b*) As between Poland and other Contracting States the provisions of the Scheme relating to inspection of gear or catch below deck do not apply.

(*c*) As between Sweden and other Contracting States the provisions of the Scheme relating to inspection of gear or catch below deck do not apply.

PART II

Convention Area

All waters which are situated

(*a*) within those parts of the Atlantic and Arctic Oceans and their dependent seas which lie north of 36° north latitude and between 42° west longitude and 51° east longitude, but excluding

(i) the Baltic Sea and Belts lying to the south and east of lines drawn from Hasenore Head to Gniben Point, from Korshage to Spodsbierg and from Gilbierg Head to the Kullen, and

(ii) the Mediterranean Sea and its dependent seas as far as the point of intersection of the parallel of 36° north latitude and the meridian of 5° 36′ west longitude.

(*b*) within that part of the Atlantic Ocean north of 59° north latitude and between 44° west longitude and 42° west longitude.

SCHEDULE 2

Foreign Countries which are parties to the Scheme

1. Belgium
2. Denmark
3. France
4. Iceland
5. Norway
6. Poland
7. Portugal
8. Spain
9. Sweden
10. Union of Soviet Socialist Republics
11. The Federal Republic of Germany (as from 1972)
12. The Netherlands (as from 1972)

INTERNATIONAL COMMISSION FOR THE NORTHWEST ATLANTIC FISHERIES

Scheme of Joint Enforcement, 1971

SCHEDULE 1

PART I

SCHEME OF JOINT ENFORCEMENT

Recommendation

That, pursuant to paragraph 5 of Article VIII of the Convention, the following arrangements be established, as from 1st July 1971, for international control outside national fishery limits for the purpose of ensuring the application of the Convention and the measures in force thereunder:—

(1) Control shall be carried out by inspectors of the fishery control services of Contracting Governments. The names of the inspectors appointed for that purpose by their respective governments shall be notified to the Commission.

(2) Ships carrying inspectors shall fly a special flag or pennant approved by the Commission to indicate that the inspector is carrying out international inspection duties. The names of the ships so used for the time being, which may be either special inspection vessels or fishing vessels, shall be notified to the Commission.

(3) Each inspector shall carry a document of identity supplied by the authorities of the flag state in a form approved by the Commission and given him on appointment stating that he has authority to act under the arrangements approved by the Commission.

(4) Subject to the arrangements agreed under paragraph (9), a vessel employed for the time being in fishing for sea fish or in the treatment of sea fish in the Convention area shall stop when given the appropriate signal in the International Code of Signals by a ship carrying an inspector unless actually fishing, shooting or hauling, in which case it shall stop immediately it has finished hauling. The master of the vessel shall permit the inspector, who may be accompanied by a witness, to board it. The master shall enable the inspector to make such examination of catch, nets or other gear and any relevant documents as the inspector deems necessary to verify the observance of the Commission's recommendations in force in relation to the flag state of the vessel concerned and the inspector may ask for any explanations that he deems necessary.

(5) On boarding the vessel an inspector shall produce the document described in (3) above. Inspections shall be made so that the vessel suffers the minimum interference and inconvenience. An inspector shall limit his enquiries to the ascertainment of the facts in relation to the observance of the Commission's recommendations in force in relation to the flag state of the vessel concerned. In making his examination an inspector may ask the master for any assistance he may require. He shall draw up a report of his inspection in a form approved by the Commission. He shall sign the report in the presence of the master of the vessel who shall be entitled to add or have added to the report any observations which he may think suitable and must sign such observations. Copies of the report shall be given to the master of the vessel and to the Inspector's Government who shall transmit copies to the appropriate authorities of the flag state of the vessel and to the Commission. Where any infringement of the recommendations is discovered the inspector should where possible also inform the competent authorities of the flag state, as notified to the Commission, and any inspection ship of the flag state known to be in the vicinity.

(6) Resistance to an inspector or failure to comply with his directions shall be treated by the flag state of the vessel as if the inspector were an inspector of that state.

(7) Inspectors shall carry out their duties under these arrangements in accordance with the rules set out in this recommendation but they shall remain under the operational control of their national authorities and shall be responsible to them.

(8) Contracting Governments shall consider and act on reports of foreign inspectors under these arrangements on the same basis as reports of national inspectors. The provisions of this paragraph shall not impose any obligation on a Contracting Government to give the report of a foreign inspector a higher evidential value than it would possess in the inspector's own country. Contracting Governments shall collaborate in order to facilitate judicial or other proceedings arising from a report of an inspector under these arrangements.

(9) (i) Contracting Governments shall inform the Commission by 1st March each year of their provisional plans for participation in these arrangements in the following year and the Commission may make suggestions to Contracting Governments for the co-ordination of national operations in this field including the number of inspectors and ships carrying inspectors.

(ii) The arrangements set out in this Recommendation and the plans for participation shall apply between Contracting Goverments unless otherwise agreed between them; and such agreement shall be notified to the Commission.

Provided, however, that implementation of the scheme shall be suspended between any two Contracting Governments if either of them has notified the Commission to that effect, pending completion of an agreement.

(10) (i) Nets shall be inspected in accordance with the regulations in force for the subarea in which the inspection takes place. The number of undersized meshes and the width of each mesh examined shall be entered in the inspector's report, together with the average width of the meshes examined.

(ii) Inspectors shall have authority to inspect all nets.

(11) The inspector shall affix an identification mark approved by the Commission, to any net which appears to have been used in contravention of the Commission's recommendations in force in relation to the flag state of the vessel concerned and shall record this fact in his report.

(12) The inspector may photograph the net in such a way that the identification mark and the measurement of the net is visible, in which case the subjects photographed should be listed in the report and copies of the photographs should be attached to the copy of the report to the flag state.

(13) The inspector shall have authority, subject to any limitations imposed by the Commission, to carry out such examination and measurement of the catch as he deems necessary to establish whether the Commission's recommendations are being complied with. He shall report his findings to the authorities of the flag state of the inspected vessel as soon as possible.

Reservations

(*a*) as between the Union of Soviet Socialist Republics and other Contracting Governments the provisions of the Scheme relating to inspection of gear below deck and of catch do not apply;

(*b*) as between Poland and other Contracting Governments the provisions of the Scheme relating to inspection of gear or catch below deck do not apply; and

(*c*) as between Romania and other Contracting Governments the provisions of the Scheme relating to inspection of gear below deck and of catch do not apply.

Part II

Convention Area

All waters, except territorial waters, bounded by a line beginning at a point on the coast of Rhode Island in 71° 40′ west longitude; thence due south to 39° north latitude; thence due east to 42° west longitude; thence due north to 59° north latitude; thence due west to 44° west longitude; thence due north to the coast of Greenland; thence along the west coast of Greenland to 78° 10′ north latitude; thence southwards to a point in 75° north latitude and 73° 30′ west longitude; thence along a rhumb line to a point in 69° north latitude and 59° west longitude; thence due south to 61° north latitude; thence due west to 64° 30′ west longitude; thence due south to the coast of Labrador; thence in a southerly direction along the coast of Labrador to the southern terminus of its boundary with Quebec; thence in a westerly direction along the coast of Quebec, and in an easterly and southerly direction along the coasts of New Brunswick, Nova Scotia, and Cape Breton Island to Cabot Strait, thence along the coasts of Cape Breton Island, Nova Scotia, New Brunswick, Maine, New Hampshire, Massachusetts, and Rhode Island to the point of beginning.

SCHEDULE 2

Foreign Countries which are parties to the Scheme

1. Denmark
2. France
3. Iceland
4. Italy

5. Japan
6. Norway
7. Poland
8. Portugal
9. Romania
10. Spain
11. Union of Soviet Socialist Republics
12. United States of America
13. Federal Republic of Germany (as from 1972)

AGREEMENT BETWEEN JAPAN AND THE REPUBLIC OF KOREA CONCERNING FISHERIES*

[Signed at Tokyo, June 22, 1965]

Japan and the Republic of Korea

Desiring that the maximum sustained productivity of the fishery resources in waters of mutual interest be maintained;

Firmly believing that the conservation of such resources and their rational exploitation and development will serve the interests of both countries;

Confirming that the principle of freedom of the high seas shall be respected unless otherwise prescribed by special provisions in the present Agreement;

Recognizing the desirability of eliminating the causes of disputes which may arise from their geographical proximity and the intermingling of their respective fisheries; and

Desiring mutual cooperation for the development of their fisheries,

Have agreed as follows:

Article I

1. The High Contracting Parties mutually recognize that each High Contracting Party has the right to establish a sea zone (hereinafter "fishery zone"), extending not more than 12 nautical miles from its respective coastal base line, over which it will have exclusive jurisdiction with respect to fisheries. However, in case either High Contracting Party uses the straight base line for the establishment of its fishery zone, the straight base line shall be determined through consultation with the other High Contracting Party.

2. The High Contracting Parties shall not present objections when one Party excludes the fishing vessels of the other Party from engaging in fishing operations in its fishery zone.

3. Areas where the fishery zones of the High Contracting Parties overlap shall be divided in two by straight lines joining the ends of the overlapping areas with the midpoints of straight lines drawn across the areas at their widest points.

Article II

1. The High Contracting Parties shall establish a joint control zone encircled by the lines described below (excluding territorial waters and the Republic of Korea's fishery zone).

(a) A line north on the 124th E meridian north of 37°30' N.

(b) Thence, a line joining the following coordinates in order:

(I) 37° 30' N, 124° E
(II) 36° 45' N, 124° 30' E
(III) 33° 30' N, 124° 30' E
(IV) 32° 30' N, 126° E
(V) 32° 30' N, 127° E
(VI) 34° 34' 30" N, 129° 2' 50" E
(VII) 34° 44' 10" N, 129° 8' E
(VIII) 34° 50' N, 129° 14' E
(IX) 35° 30' N, 130° E
(X) 37° 30' N, 131° 10' E
(XI) High peak of Uamnyong

*[Translated for International Legal Materials by Dr. Sung Yoon Cho, Legal Specialist, Far Eastern Law Division, Library of Congress. As of October 1, 1965, ratifications had not yet been exchanged. The Treaty on Basic Relations between Japan and Korea, signed June 22, 1965, appears at 4 International Legal Materials 924 (1965).]

Article III

Until conservation measures necessary for maintaining the maximum sustained productivity of fishery resources are implemented on the basis of exhaustive scientific research, the provisional fishery control measures listed in the Annex, which forms an integral part of this Agreement, shall be enforced in the joint control zones with respect to dragnet fishing and surrounding net fishing, and mackerel fishing by fishing vessels of not less than 60 tons. (Ton represents gross ton. The tonnage shall be indicated by deducting the tonnage permitted for improving living quarters on the vessels.)

Article IV

1. The right of control (including the right to halt and inspect vessels) and jurisdiction in waters outside the exclusive fishery zone shall be exercised only by the High Contracting Party to which the ship belongs.

2. The High Contracting Parties shall exercise appropriate guidance and supervision in order to guarantee the faithful observance of the provisional fishery control measures by their own nationals and fishing vessels, and shall carry out domestic measures, including appropriate penalties against violations thereof.

Article V

Joint resources survey zones shall be established outside of the joint control zones. The scope of the said zones and the surveys to be conducted within these zones shall be determined through consultation between the two High Contracting Parties, on the basis of recommendations made by the Joint Fisheries Commission provided for in Article VI.

Article VI

1. The High Contracting Parties shall establish and maintain the Japan-Republic of Korea Joint Fisheries Commission (hereinafter referred to as the "Commission") in order to realize the purposes of this Agreement.

2. The Commission shall be composed of two national sections, each consisting of three members appointed by the Governments of the respective High Contracting Parties.

3. All resolutions, recommendations, and other decisions of the Commission shall be made only with the concurrence of the national sections.

4. The Commission may decide upon and revise, as occasion may require, rules for the conduct of its meetings.

5. The Commission shall meet at least once each year and, in addition, it may meet as requested by one of the national sections. The date and place of the first meeting shall be determined by agreement between the High Contracting Parties.

6. At its first meeting, the Commission shall select a Chairman and Vice-Chairman, one from each national section. The Chairman and Vice-Chairman shall hold office for a period of one year. During the succeeding years selection of a Chairman and a Vice-Chairman from the national sections shall be made in such a manner as will provide each High Contracting Party in turn with representation in those offices.

7. A standing secretariat shall be established under the Commission to carry out the business of the Commission.

8. The official languages of the Commission shall be Japanese and Korean. Proposals and data may be presented in either official language, or, if necessary, they may be presented in English.

9. In the event that the Commission concludes that joint expenses are necessary, such expenses shall be paid by the Commission through contributions made by the High Contracting Parties in the form and proportion recommended by the

Commission and approved by the High Contracting Parties.

10. The Commission may delegate the disbursement of funds for the joint expenses of the Commission.

Article VII

1. The Commission shall perform the following functions:

(a) The Commission shall make recommendations to the High Contracting Parties concerning scientific research for the purpose of studying the fishery resources in the sea areas of mutual interest and concerning control measures within the joint control zones to be carried out on the basis of the results of such research and study;

(b) The Commission shall make recommendations to the High Contracting Parties on the scope of the joint resources survey zones;

(c) When it is deemed necessary, the Commission shall review matters concerning provisional fishery control measures and make recommendations to the High Contracting Parties concerning measures to be taken as a result of such review (including the revision of the provisionsl control measures);

(d) The Commission shall review necessary matters concerning safe operations and order among the fishing vessels of the High Contracting Parties and general policies for settling accidents occurring at sea between the fishing vessels of the High Contracting Parties, and shall make recommendations to the High Contracting Parties concerning measures to be taken as a result of such review;

(e) The Commission shall compile and study data, statistics, and records which the High Contracting Parties submit at the request of the Commission;

(f) The Commission shall consider and make recommendations to the High Contracting Parties concerning the enactment of schedules of equivalent penalties for violations of this Agreement;

(g) The Commission shall submit annually its business report to the High Contracting Parties; and

(h) The Commission shall study the various technical questions arising in connection with the implementation of this Agreement, and shall, when it is deemed necessary, make recommendations to the High Contracting Parties on the steps to be taken.

2. The Commission may establish such subsidiary organs as it deems necessary for the performance of its functions.

3. The Governments of the High Contracting Parties shall respect to the extent possible the recommendations made by the Commission in accordance with the provisions of paragraph 1.

Article VIII

1. The High Contracting Parties shall take measures as may be appropriate to guarantee the observance of international practices concerning navigation by their nationals and fishing vessels, to promote safe operations between the fishing vessels of the High Contracting Parties, to maintain proper order among them, and to achieve smooth and speedy settlements of accidents arising at sea between the fishing vessels of the High Contracting Parties.

2. In order to achieve the objective of paragraph 1, the authorities concerned of the two High Contracting Parties shall maintain as closely as possible mutual contact and cooperation.

Article IX

1. Any dispute between the High Contracting Parties concerning the

interpretation or implementation of this Agreement shall be settled primarily through diplomatic channels.

2. Any dispute which cannot be settled under the provision of paragraph 1 shall be submitted for decision to an arbitration commission of three arbitrators; one to be appointed by the Government of each High Contracting Party within a period of thirty days from the date of receipt by the Government of either High Contracting Party from that of the other High Contracting Party of a note requesting arbitration of the dispute; and the third to be agreed upon by the two arbitrators so chosen or to be nominated by the Government of a third power as agreed upon by the two arbitrators within a further period of thirty days. However, the third arbitrator must not be a national of either High Contracting Party.

3. If, within the periods respectively referred to, the Government of either High Contracting Party fails to appoint an arbitrator, or the third arbitrator of the third nation is not agreed upon, the arbitration commission shall be composed of one arbitrator to be nominated by the Government of each of two nations respectively chosen by the Government of each High Contracting Party within a period of thirty days, and the third arbitrator to be nominated by the Government of a third power decided upon by agreement between the Governments so chosen.

4. The Governments of the High Contracting Parties shall accept decisions rendered by the arbitration commission established in accordance with the provisions of this Article.

Article X

1. The present Agreement shall be ratified. The instruments of ratification shall be exchanged at Seoul as soon as possible. This Agreement shall enter into force as from the date on which the instruments of ratification are exchanged.

2. The present Agreement shall continue in force for a period of five years and thereafter until one year from the day on which a High Contracting Party shall give notice to the other High Contracting Party of an intention to terminate the Agreement.

In witness whereof, the undersigned, duly authorized by the respective Governments, have signed the present Agreement.

Done in duplicate at Tokyo, this twenty-second day of June of the year one thousand nine hundred and sixty-five in the Japanese and Korean languages, each text being equally authentic.

For Japan

Etsusaburo Shiina
Shinichi Takasugi

For the Republic of Korea

Tong Won Lee
Dong Jo Kim

UNION OF SOVIET SOCIALIST REPUBLICS

Fisheries: Certain Fishery Problems on the High Seas in the Western Areas of the Middle Atlantic Ocean

Agreement signed at Washington December 11, 1970; Entered into force January 1, 1971.

AGREEMENT BETWEEN
THE GOVERNMENT OF THE UNITED STATES OF AMERICA AND
THE GOVERNMENT OF THE UNION OF SOVIET SOCIALIST REPUBLICS
ON CERTAIN FISHERY PROBLEMS ON THE HIGH SEAS
IN THE WESTERN AREAS OF THE MIDDLE ATLANTIC OCEAN

The Government of the United States of America and the Government of the Union of Soviet Socialist Republics,

Considering it desirable that the fisheries in the Western areas of the high seas in the Middle Atlantic Ocean be conducted on a rational basis with due attention to their mutual interests, proceeding from generally recognized principles of international law,

Considering it necessary to conduct the fisheries in the said areas with due consideration of the state of fish stocks, based on the results of scientific investigations, for the purpose of ensuring the maintenance of maximum sustainable yields and the maintenance of the said fisheries,

Taking into account the need for expanding and coordinating scientific research in the field of fisheries and the exchange of scientific data,

Have agreed on the following:

1. The Government of the United States of America and the Government of the Union of Soviet Socialist Republics consider it desirable to expand research pertaining to the species of fish of interest to both parties, on a national basis as well as in the form of coordinated research according to agreed programs. The competent agencies of both Governments shall ensure the following, at least on an annual basis:

a. An exchange of scientific and statistical data, published works and the results of fishery research;

b. Meetings of scientists and, in appropriate cases, the participation of the scientists of each Government in fishery research conducted on the research vessels of the other Government.

Each Government will take the necessary steps to ensure that its competent agencies conduct the corresponding fishery research and develop the most rational fishing technology in accordance with a coordinated program, which has been developed by the scientists of both countries.

2. The Government of the United States of America and the Government of the Union of Soviet Socialist Republics, for the purpose of reproduction and maintenance of fish stocks, will take appropriate measures to ensure that their citizens and vessels will:

a. Refrain from fishing during the period from January 1 through April 15, to ensure access of red hake and silver hake to the spawning grounds and to protect certain winter concentrations of scup and flounders; said abstention will apply to an area of the Mid-Atlantic bounded by straight lines connecting the following coordinates in the order listed:

North Latitude	West Longitude
40°05'	71°40'
39°50'	71°40'
37°50'	74°00'
37°50'	74°25'
38°24'	73°44'
39°40'	72°32'

b. Refrain from increasing the catch of red hake, silver hake, scup, flounders, and black sea bass above the 1967 levels in the waters situated west and south of Sub-area 5 of the Convention area of the 1949 International Convention for the Northwest Atlantic Fisheries and north of 34° North Latitude;

c. Refrain, in the waters specified in sub-paragraph b of this paragraph, from conducting specialized fisheries for scup and flounders in all instances, and from increasing their incidental catch of these species, that is, the catch taken unintentionally when conducting specialized fisheries for other species;

d. Refrain, in the waters specified in sub-paragraph b of this paragraph, from fishing menhaden during the period from January 1 through April 30;

e. The provisions of sub-paragraphs a, b, and c of this paragraph shall not apply to vessels under 110 feet in length, nor to vessels fishing for crustacea or molluscs.

3. Both Governments will take appropriate measures to ensure that their citizens and vessels will, in the waters covered by this Agreement, conduct their fishing with due regard for the conservation of the stocks of fish.

4. Fishing vessels of the Union of Soviet Socialist Republics may conduct loading operations in the waters of the nine-mile fishery zone contiguous to the territorial sea of the United States of America in the following areas bounded by straight lines connecting the coordinates in the order listed:

a. during the period from November 15 through May 15

North Latitude	West Longitude
40°44'00"	72°27'00"
40°38'00"	72°27'00"
40°34'31"	72°40'00"
40°32'41"	72°46'26"
40°32'32"	72°53'26"
40°36'54"	72°53'26"
40°40'55"	72°40'00"

b. during the period from September 15 through May 15

North Latitude	West Longitude
39°38'05"	74°02'06"
39°35'06"	73°55'24"
39°32'30"	73°57'18"
39°35'30"	74°04'00"

5. Fishing vessels of the Union of Soviet Socialist Republics may fish during the period from January 1 through March 31, within the nine-mile fishery zone contiguous to the territorial sea of the United States of America, in the waters bounded by straight lines connecting the following coordinates in the order listed:

North Latitude	West Longitude
40°40'55"	72°40'00"
40°34'31"	72°40'00"
40°32'41"	72°46'26"
40°32'32"	72°53'26"
40°36'54"	72°53'26"

6. Each Government will, within the scope of its domestic laws and regulations, facilitate entry into appropriate ports for fishing and fishery research vessels of the other Government. This shall apply with respect to the procedure for presenting crew lists for the above-mentioned vessels and to the providing of fresh water, fuel and provisions.

7. Under conditions of force majeure, each Government will, within the scope of its domestic laws and regulations, facilitate entry of fishing and fishery research vessels into its respective open ports after appropriate notification has been given.

8. Both Governments consider it useful to arrange, when appropriate, for visits of representatives of fishermen's organizations of the two countries to each other's fishing vessels operating in the western part of the Middle Atlantic. Such visits may be arranged on mutually agreeable terms determined in each particular case by the Regional Director of the National Marine Fisheries Service in Gloucester, Massachusetts and the chiefs of the joint fleet expeditions of the Main Administrations "ZAPRYBA" or "SEVRYBA" as appropriate.

9. Nothing in this Agreement shall be interpreted as prejudicing the views of either Government with regard to freedom of fishing on the high seas or to traditional fisheries.

10. This Agreement constitutes an extension and modification of the provisions of the Agreement between the Government of the United States of America and the Government of the Union of Soviet Socialist Republics signed in Washington on December 13, 1968.[1] The present Agreement shall enter into force on January 1, 1971 and shall remain in force through December 31, 1972. At the request of either Government, representatives of the two Governments will

[1] TIAS 6603; 19 UST 7661.

meet at a mutually convenient time with a view to modifying the present Agreement. In any event, representatives of the two Governments will meet at a mutually convenient time prior to the expiration of the period of validity of this Agreement to review the operation of this Agreement and to decide on future arrangements.

IN WITNESS WHEREOF the undersigned, being duly authorized for this purpose, have signed this Agreement.

DONE in Washington, December 11, 1970, in duplicate, in English and Russian, both texts being equally authentic.

FOR THE GOVERNMENT OF THE UNITED STATES OF AMERICA:

Donald L. McKernan [1]

FOR THE GOVERNMENT OF THE UNION OF SOVIET SOCIALIST REPUBLICS: [2]

[signature]

---

[1] Donald L. McKernan

[2] Vladimir M. Kamentsev

UNION OF SOVIET SOCIALIST REPUBLICS

Fisheries: Certain Fishery Problems on the High Seas in the Western Areas of the Middle Atlantic Ocean

Protocol to the agreement of December 11, 1970.
Signed at Washington February 2, 1971;
Entered into force February 7, 1971.

PROTOCOL TO THE AGREEMENT BETWEEN
THE GOVERNMENT OF THE UNITED STATES OF AMERICA AND
THE GOVERNMENT OF THE UNION OF SOVIET SOCIALIST REPUBLICS
ON CERTAIN FISHERY PROBLEMS ON THE HIGH SEAS
IN THE WESTERN AREAS OF THE MIDDLE ATLANTIC OCEAN

The Government of the United States of America and the Government of the Union of Soviet Socialist Republics,

Considering that interim measures are necessary for the conservation and protection of the stocks of river herring,

Considering that a common understanding is desirable on implementation of paragraph 6 of the Agreement Between the Government of the United States of America and the Government of the Union of Soviet Socialist Republics on Certain Fishery Problems on the High Seas in the Western Areas of the Middle Atlantic Ocean, hereinafter referred to as the Agreement,

Noting the discussions on these matters during the meeting of the two Governments in Washington in December 1970, and

Taking into account the provisions of paragraph 10 of the Agreement,

Have agreed to the following:

---

1. The Government of the Union of Soviet Socialist Republics will take appropriate measures to ensure that its citizens and vessels will limit their catch of river herring so that it will not exceed 4,000 metric tons in each year in the waters specified in sub-paragraph b of paragraph 2 of the Agreement.

2. The Government of the United States of America, in implementation of paragraph 6 of the Agreement, will take appropriate measures to ensure the following:

a. The provisions of paragraph 6 shall apply to the entry of not more than four Soviet fishing vessels or fishery support vessels each month into each of the Ports of Baltimore and Philadelphia. In addition, and without regard to the foregoing, special provisions shall be made as necessary in furtherance of paragraph 6 regarding the entry of Soviet research vessels which are engaged in a mutually agreed research program in accordance with the terms of paragraph 1 of the Agreement.

b. The Government of the United States will accept applications for entry into the Ports of Baltimore and Philadelphia pursuant to paragraph 6 either at the American Embassy in Moscow or at the Department of State in Washington at least 7 days prior to entry. Applications may be made in Washington either by the Soviet Embassy or by a commercial shipping agent designated by the appropriate Soviet authorities.

c. The Government of the United States at its Embassy in Moscow will accept crew lists in application for visas valid for a period of six months and for multiple entries into United States ports pursuant to the provisions of paragraph 6. Such a crew list shall be submitted at least 21 days prior to the first entry of a vessel into a port of the United States. Submission of an amended (supplemental) crew list subsequent to departure of a vessel from Soviet ports will also be subject to the provisions of this sub-paragraph, provided that visas issued thereunder shall only be valid for six months from the date of issuance of the original crew list visa. An application for port entry under sub-paragraph b of this paragraph shall specify if shore leave is requested under such a multiple entry visa.

d. Subject to the provisions of the Agreement and this Protocol, it is understood that the entry of Soviet vessels into any United States port is subject to the applicable laws and regulations of the United States.

e. Each of the above understandings may be modified by mutual consent at any time.

3. The above provisions shall form an integral part of the Agreement. This Protocol shall enter into force on February 7, 1971, and shall remain in force during the period of validity of the Agreement, subject to the provisions of paragraph 10 thereof.

IN WITNESS WHEREOF the undersigned, being duly authorized for this purpose, have signed this Protocol.

DONE in Washington, February 2, 1971, in duplicate, in English and Russian, both texts being equally authentic.

FOR THE GOVERNMENT OF THE UNITED STATES OF AMERICA:

Donald L. McKernan [1]

FOR THE GOVERNMENT OF THE UNION OF SOVIET SOCIALIST REPUBLICS:

[signature] [2]

[1] Donald L. McKernan
[2] Vladimir M. Kamentsev

NEW DIRECTIONS IN THE LAW OF THE SEA

Documents ~ Volume II

Compiled and Edited by
S. Houston Lay, B.A., J.D., LL.M.
Robin Churchill, LL.M.
Myron Nordquist, B.S., J.D.

1973
OCEANA PUBLICATIONS, INC.
DOBBS FERRY, NEW YORK

THE BRITISH INSTITUTE OF
INTERNATIONAL AND COMPARATIVE LAW
LONDON, ENGLAND

Library of Congress Cataloging in Publication Data

Lay, S Houston, 1912- comp.
New directions in the law of the sea.

CONTENTS: v. 1-2. Documents.
1. Maritime law—Sources. I. Churchill, Robin, joint comp. II. Nordquist, Myron, joint comp. III. Title.
JX4408.L43 343.09'6 72-12713
ISBN 0-379-00029-6

Manufactured in the United States of America

TABLE OF CONTENTS

II. REGULATION OF MARINE ACTIVITIES (continued)

II. REGULATION OF MARINE ACTIVITIES
(continued)

ANNEX VI

NEW REGULATION 8, CHAPTER V OF THE INTERNATIONAL CONVENTION FOR THE SAFETY OF LIFE AT SEA, 1960

Chapter V

Regulation 8

Routeing

(a) The practice of following, particularly in converging areas, routes adopted for the purpose of separation of traffic including avoidance of passage through areas designated as areas to be avoided by ships or certain classes of ships, or for the purpose of avoiding unsafe conditions, has contributed to the safety of navigation and is recommended for use by all ships concerned.

(b) The Organization is recognized as the only international body for establishing and adopting measures on an international level concerning routeing and areas to be avoided by ships or certain classes of ships. It will collate and disseminate to Contracting Governments all relevant information.

(c) The selection of the routes and the initiation of action with regard to them, and the delineation of what constitutes converging areas, will be primarily the responsibility of the Governments concerned. In the development of routeing schemes which impinge upon international waters, or such other schemes they may wish adopted by the Organizations, they will give due consideration to relevant information published by the Organization.

(d) Contracting Governments will use their influence to secure the appropriate use of adopted routes and will do everything in their power to ensure adherence to the measures adopted by the Organization in connection with routeing of ships.

(e) Where the Organization has adopted traffic separation schemes which specify one-way traffic lanes, ships using these lanes shall proceed in the specified direction of traffic flow. Ships crossing the lanes shall do so as far as practicable at right angles.

(f) Contracting Governments will also induce all ships proceeding on voyages in the vicinity of the Grand Banks of Newfoundland to avoid, as far as practicable, the fishing banks of Newfoundland north of latitude 43°N and to pass outside regions known or believed to be endangered by ice.

INTER-GOVERNMENTAL MARITIME
CONSULTATIVE ORGANIZATION

ASSEMBLY - 6th session
Agenda item 11

RECOMMENDATION ON ESTABLISHMENT OF FAIRWAYS THROUGH OFF-SHORE EXPLORATION AREAS

RESOLUTION A. 179 (VI)
adopted on 28 October 1969

THE ASSEMBLY,

NOTING Article 16 (i) of the IMCO Convention concerning the functions of the Assembly,

RECOGNIZING the need for ensuring unencumbered exploitation of sea-bed resources as well as safety at sea,

HAVING CONSIDERED difficulties which would result from the congestion of navigable waters by off-shore platforms or other structures,

HAVING ALSO CONSIDERED the Recommendation adopted by the Maritime Safety Committee at its eighteenth session,

RECOMMENDS that Governments:

(i) ensure that the exploitation of sea-bed resources does not seriously obstruct sea approaches and shipping routes;

(ii) consider the establishment of fairways or shipping routes through off-shore resource exploration areas at an early stage so as to ensure the unencumbered passage of marine traffic through the areas at all stages of exploitation;

(iii) take into account the principles adopted by IMCO with respect to routeing when considering the establishment of such fairways or shipping routes.

INTER-GOVERNMENTAL MARITIME
CONSULTATIVE ORGANIZATION

ASSEMBLY - 7th session
Agenda item 8

OBSERVANCE OF TRAFFIC SEPARATION SCHEMES

RESOLUTION A. 228 (VII)
adopted on 12 October 1971

THE ASSEMBLY,

NOTING Article 16 (i) of the Convention in the Inter-Governmental Maritime Consultative Organization concerning the function of the Assembly,

HAVING EXAMINED the Recommendation on Observance of Traffic Separation Schemes adopted by the Maritime Safety Commit at its twenty-third session,

NOTING that in a recent survey of the recommended Dover Strait Traffic Separation Scheme about 5 per cent of ships were proceeding in the wrong lane,

NOTING FURTHER that collisions continue to occur in this area through which some 600 ships pass daily, a high proportion involving ships proceeding in the wrong lane,

ENDORSES the action taken by the Maritime Safety Committe

RECOMMENDS that Member Governments of the Organizatic should make it an offence for ships of their flag which use any traf separation scheme adopted by the Organization to proceed against the established direction of traffic flow.

Proclamation 3632

REGULATIONS FOR PREVENTING COLLISIONS AT SEA

By the President of the United States of America

A PROCLAMATION

Whereas certain regulations designated as Regulations for Preventing Collisions at Sea, 1960, were approved by the International Conference on Safety of Life at Sea, 1960, held at London from May 17 to June 17, 1960; and

Whereas the Act of September 24, 1963 (Public Law 88–131, 77 Stat. 194),[1] hereinafter referred to as the Act, authorizes the President of the United States of America to proclaim those regulations, which are set forth in Section 4 of the Act, and to specify the effective date thereof, the regulations to have effect (after the effective date thus specified), as if enacted by statute; and

Whereas on March 12, 1964, the Government of the United States of America communicated to the Inter-Governmental Maritime Consultative Organization, as depository agency, its acceptance of the regulations; and

Whereas the Government of the United States of America has been notified by the Inter-Governmental Maritime Consultative Organization, as depository agency, that substantial unanimity has been reached as to the acceptance by interested countries, and that it has fixed September 1, 1965, as the date on and after which the regulations shall be applied by the governments which have accepted them; and

Whereas the Act provides that the Regulations for Preventing Collisions at Sea, 1948 (65 Stat. 406),[2] as proclaimed and made effective as of January 1, 1954, by Proclamation No. 3030 of August 15, 1953,[3] shall be of no further force or effect after the effective date proclaimed for the Regulations for Preventing Collisions at Sea, 1960.

Now, therefore, I, Lyndon B. Johnson, President of the United States of America, under and by virtue of the authority vested in me by the Act, do hereby proclaim the Regulations for Preventing Collisions at Sea, 1960, as set forth in Section 4 of the Act, which regulations are attached hereto and made a part hereof, and do hereby specify that the effective date thereof shall be September 1, 1965.

[1] 33 U.S.C. § 1051.

[2] 33 U.S.C. § 143.

[3] 68 Stat. (pt. 2) c4.

Proclamation No. 3030 is superseded effective as of September 1, 1965.

IN WITNESS WHEREOF, I have hereunto set my hand and caused the Seal of the United States of America to be affixed.

DONE at the City of Washington this twenty-ninth day of December in the year of our Lord nineteen hundred and sixty-four, [SEAL] and of the Independence of the United States of America the one hundred and eighty-ninth.

LYNDON B. JOHNSON

By the President:
DEAN RUSK
Secretary of State

"Regulations for Preventing Collisions at Sea

"Part A.—Preliminary and Definitions

"Rule 1

"(a) These Rules shall be followed by all vessels and seaplanes upon the high seas and in all waters connected therewith navigable by seagoing vessels, except as provided in Rule 30. Where, as a result of their special construction, it is not possible for seaplanes to comply fully with the provisions of Rules specifying the carrying of lights and shapes, these provisions shall be followed as closely as circumstances permit.

"(b) The Rules concerning lights shall be complied with in all weathers from sunset to sunrise, and during such times no other lights shall be exhibited, except such lights as cannot be mistaken for the prescribed lights or do not impair their visibility or distinctive character, or interfere with the keeping of a proper look-out. The lights prescribed by these Rules may also be exhibited from sunrise to sunset in restricted visibility and in all other circumstances when it is deemed necessary.

"(c) In the following Rules, except where the context otherwise requires—

"(i) the word 'vessel' includes every description of water craft, other than a seaplane on the water, used or capable of being used as a means of transportation on water;

"(ii) the word 'seaplane' includes a flying boat and any other aircraft designed to manoeuvre on the water;

"(iii) the term 'power-driven vessel' means any vessel propelled by machinery;

"(iv) every power-driven vessel which is under sail and not under power is to be considered a sailing vessel, and every vessel under power, whether under sail or not, is to be considered a power-driven vessel;

"(v) a vessel or seaplane on the water is 'under way' when she is not at anchor, or made fast to the shore, or aground;

"(vi) the term 'height above the hull' means height above the uppermost continuous deck;

"(vii) the length and breadth of a vessel shall be her length overall and largest breadth;

"(viii) the length and span of a seaplane shall be its maximum length and span as shown in its certificate of airworthiness, or as determined by measurement in the absence of such certificate;

"(ix) vessels shall be deemed to be in sight of one another only when one can be observed visually from the other;

"(x) the word 'visible', when applied to lights, means visible on a dark night with a clear atmosphere;

"(xi) the term 'short blast' means a blast of about one second's duration;

"(xii) the term 'prolonged blast' means a blast of from four to six seconds' duration;

"(xiii) the word 'whistle' means any appliance capable of producing the prescribed short and prolonged blasts;

"(xiv) the term 'engaged in fishing' means fishing with nets, lines or trawls but does not including fishing with trolling lines.

"PART B.—LIGHTS AND SHAPES

"Rule 2

"(a) A power-driven vessel when under way shall carry—

"(i) On or in front of the foremast, or if a vessel without a foremast then in the forepart of the vessel, a white light so constructed as to show an unbroken light over an arc of the horizon of 225 degrees (20 points of the compass), so fixed as to show the light 112½ degrees (10 points) on each side of the vessel, that is, from right ahead to 22½ degrees (2 points) abaft the beam on either side, and of such a character as to be visible at a distance of at least 5 miles.

"(ii) Either forward or abaft the white light prescribed in sub-section (i) a second white light similar in construction and character to that light. Vessels of less than 150 feet in length shall not be required to carry this second white light but may do so.

"(iii) These two white lights shall be so placed in a line with and over the keel that one shall be at least 15 feet higher than the other and in such a position that the forward light shall always be shown lower than the after one. The horizontal distance between the two white lights shall be at least three times the vertical distance. The lower of these two white lights or, if only one is carried, then that light, shall be placed at a height above the hull of not less than 20 feet, and, if the breadth of the vessel exceeds 20 feet, then at a height above the hull not less than such breadth, so however that the light need not be placed at a greater height above the hull than 40 feet. In all circumstances the light or lights, as the case may be, shall be so placed as to be clear of and above all other lights and obstructing superstructures.

"(iv) On the starboard side a green light so constructed as to show an unbroken light over an arc of the horizon of 112½ degrees (10 points of the compass), so fixed as to show the light from right ahead to 22½ degrees (2 points) abaft the beam on the starboard side, and of such a character as to be visible at a distance of at least 2 miles.

"(v) On the port side a red light so constructed as to show an unbroken light over an arc of the horizon of 112½ degrees (10 points of the compass), so fixed as to show the light from right ahead to 22½ degrees (2 points) abaft the beam on the port side, and of such a character as to be visible at a distance of at least 2 miles.

"(vi) The said green and red sidelights shall be fitted with inboard screens projecting at least 3 feet forward from the light, so as to prevent these lights from being seen across the bows.

"(b) A seaplane under way on the water shall carry—

"(i) In the forepart amidships where it can best be seen a white light, so constructed as to show an unbroken light over an arc of the horizon of 220 degrees of the compass, so fixed as to show the light 110 degrees on each side of the seaplane, namely, from right ahead to 20 degrees abaft the beam on either side, and of such a character as to be visible at a distance of at least 3 miles.

"(ii) On the right or starboard wing tip a green light, so constructed as to show an unbroken light over an arc of the horizon of 110 degrees of the compass, so fixed as to show the light from right ahead to 20 degrees abaft the beam on the starboard side, and of such a character as to be visible at a distance of at least 2 miles.

"(iii) On the left or port wing tip a red light, so constructed as to show an unbroken light over an arc of the horizon of 110 degrees of the compass, so fixed as to show the light from right ahead to 20 degrees abaft the beam on the port side, and of such a character as to be visible at a distance of at least 2 miles.

"Rule 3

"(a) A power-driven vessel when towing or pushing another vessel or seaplane shall, in addition to her sidelights, carry two white lights in a vertical line one over the other, not less than 6 feet apart, and when towing and the length of the tow, measuring from the stern of the towing vessel to the stern of the last vessel towed, exceeds 600 feet, shall carry three white lights in a vertical line one over the other, so that the upper and lower lights shall be the same distance from, and not less than 6 feet above or below, the middle light. Each of these lights shall be of the same construction and character and one of them shall be carried in the same position as the white light prescribed in Rule 2(a)(i). None of these lights shall be carried at a height of less than 14 feet above the hull. In a vessel with a single mast, such lights may be carried on the mast.

"(b) The towing vessel shall also show either the stern light prescribed in Rule 10 or in lieu of that light a small white light abaft the funnel or aftermast for the tow to steer by, but such light shall not be visible forward of the beam.

"(c) Between sunrise and sunset a power-driven vessel engaged in towing, if the length of tow exceeds 600 feet, shall carry, where it can best be seen, a black diamond shape at least 2 feet in diameter.

"(d) A seaplane on the water, when towing one or more seaplanes or vessels, shall carry the lights prescribed in Rule 2(b) (i), (ii) and (iii); and, in addition, she shall carry a second white light of the same construction and character as the white light prescribed in Rule 2(b) (i), and in a vertical line at least 6 feet above or below such light.

"Rule 4

"(a) A vessel which is not under command shall carry, where they can best be seen, and, if a power-driven vessel, in lieu of the lights prescribed in Rule 2(a) (i) and (ii), two red lights in a vertical line one over the other not less than 6 feet apart, and of such a character as to be visible all round the horizon at a distance of at least 2 miles. By day, she shall carry in a vertical line one over the other not less than 6 feet apart, where they can best be seen, two black balls or shapes each not less than 2 feet in diameter.

"(b) A seaplane on the water which is not under command may carry, where they can best be seen, and in lieu of the light prescribed in Rule 2(b)(i), two red lights in a vertical line, one over the other, not less than 3 feet apart, and of such a character as to be visible all round the horizon at a distance of at least 2 miles, and may by day carry in a vertical line one over the other not less than 3 feet apart, where they can best be seen, two black balls or shapes, each not less than 2 feet in diameter.

"(c) A vessel engaged in laying or in picking up a submarine cable or navigation mark, or a vessel engaged in surveying or underwater operations, or a vessel engaged in replenishment at sea, or in the launching or recovery of aircraft when from the nature of her work she is unable to get out of the way of approaching vessels, shall carry, in lieu of the lights prescribed in Rule 2(a) (i) and (ii), or Rule 7(a)(i), three lights in a vertical line one over the other so that the upper and lower lights shall be the same distance from, and not less than 6 feet above or below, the middle light. The highest and lowest of these lights shall be red, and the middle light shall be white, and they shall be of such a character as to be visible all round the horizon at a distance of at least 2 miles. By day, she shall carry in a vertical line one over the other not less than 6 feet apart, where they can best be seen, three shapes each not less than 2 feet in diameter, of which the highest and lowest shall be globular in shape and red in colour, and the middle one diamond in shape and white.

"(d) (i) A vessel engaged in minesweeping operations shall carry at the fore truck a green light, and at the end or ends of the fore yard on the side or sides on which danger exists, another such light or lights. These lights shall be carried in addition to the light prescribed in Rule 2(a) (i) or Rule 7(a) (i), as appropriate, and shall be of such a character as to be visible all round the horizon at a distance of at least 2 miles. By day she shall carry black balls, not less than 2 feet in diameter, in the same position as the green lights.

"(ii) the showing of these lights or balls indicates that it is dangerous for other vessels to approach closer than 3,000 feet astern of the minesweeper or 1,500 feet on the side or sides on which danger exists.

"(e) The vessels and seaplanes referred to in this Rule, when not making way through the water, shall show neither the coloured sidelights nor the stern light, but when making way they shall show them.

"(f) The lights and shapes prescribed in this Rule are to be taken by other vessels and seaplanes as signals that the vessel or seaplane showing them is not under command and cannot therefore get out of the way.

"(g) These signals are not signals of vessels in distress and requiring assistance. Such signals are contained in Rule 31.

"Rule 5

"(a) A sailing vessel under way and any vessel or seaplane being towed shall carry the same lights as are prescribed in Rule 2 for a power-driven vessel or a seaplane under way, respectively, with the exception of the white lights prescribed therein, which they shall never carry. They shall also carry stern lights as prescribed in Rule 10, provided that vessels towed, except the last vessel of a tow, may carry, in lieu of such stern light, a small white light as prescribed in Rule 3(b).

"(b) In addition to the lights prescribed in section (a), a sailing vessel may carry on the top of the foremast two lights in a vertical line one over the other, sufficiently separated so as to be clearly distinguished. The upper light shall be red and the lower light shall be green. Both lights shall be constructed and fixed as prescribed in Rule 2(a) (i) and shall be visible at a distance of at least 2 miles.

"(c) A vessel being pushed ahead shall carry, at the forward end, on the starboard side a green light and on the port side a red light, which shall have the same characteristics as the lights prescribed in Rule 2(a) (iv) and (v) and shall be screened as provided in Rule 2(a) (vi), provided that any number of vessels pushed ahead in a group shall be lighted as one vessel.

"(d) Between sunrise and sunset a vessel being towed, if the length of the tow exceeds 600 feet, shall carry where it can best be seen a black diamond shape at least 2 feet in diameter.

"Rule 6

"(a) When it is not possible on account of bad weather or other sufficient cause to fix the green and red sidelights, these lights shall be kept at hand lighted and ready for immediate use, and shall, on the approach of or to other vessels, be exhibited on their respective sides in sufficient time to prevent collision, in such manner as to make them most visible, and so that the green light shall not be seen on the port side nor the red light on the starboard side, nor, if practicable, more than 22½ degrees (2 points) abaft the beam on their respective sides.

"(b) To make the use of these portable lights more certain and easy, the lanterns containing them shall each be painted outside with the colour of the lights they respectively contain, and shall be provided with proper screens.

"Rule 7

"Power-driven vessels of less than 65 feet in length, vessels under oars or sails of less than 40 feet in length, and rowing boats, when under way shall not be required to carry the lights prescribed in Rules 2, 3 and 5, but if they do not carry them they shall be provided with the following lights—

"(a) Power-driven vessels of less than 65 feet in length, except as provided in sections (b) and (c), shall carry—

"(i) In the forepart of the vessel, where it can best be seen, and at a height above the gunwale of not less than 9 feet, a white light constructed and fixed as prescribed in Rule 2(a)(i) and of such a character as to be visible at a distance of at least 3 miles.

"(ii) Green and red sidelights constructed and fixed as prescribed in Rule 2(a)(iv) and (v), and of such a character as to be visible at a distance of at least 1 mile, or a combined lantern showing a green light and a red light from right ahead to 22½ degrees (2 points) abaft the beam on their respective sides. Such lantern shall be carried not less than 3 feet below the white light.

"(b) Power-driven vessels of less than 65 feet in length when towing or pushing another vessel shall carry—

"(i) In addition to the sidelights or the combined lantern prescribed in section (a)(ii) two white lights in a vertical line, one over the other not less than 4 feet apart. Each of these lights shall be of the same construction and character as the white light prescribed in section (a)(i) and one of them shall be carried in the same position. In a vessel with a single mast such lights may be carried on the mast.

"(ii) Either a stern light as prescribed in Rule 10 or in lieu of that light a small white light abaft the funnel or aftermast for the tow to steer by, but such light shall not be visible forward of the beam.

"(c) Power-driven vessels of less than 40 feet in length may carry the white light at a less height than 9 feet above the gunwale but it shall be carried not less than 3 feet above the sidelights or the combined lantern prescribed in section (a)(ii).

"(d) Vessels of less than 40 feet in length, under oars or sails, except as provided in section (f), shall, if they do not carry the sidelights, carry, where it can best be seen, a lantern showing a green light on one side and a red light on the other, of such a character as to be visible at a distance of at least 1 mile, and so fixed that the green light shall not be seen on the port side, nor the red light on the starboard side. Where it is not possible to fix this light, it shall be kept ready for immediate use and shall be exhibited in sufficient time to prevent collision and so that the green light shall not be seen on the port side nor the red light on the starboard side.

"(e) The vessels referred to in this Rule when being towed shall carry the sidelights or the combined lantern prescribed in sections (a) or (d) of this Rule, as appropriate, and a stern light as prescribed in Rule 10, or, except the last vessel of the tow, a small white light as prescribed in section (b)(ii). When being pushed ahead they shall carry at the forward end the sidelights or combined lantern prescribed in sections (a) or (d) of this Rule, as appropriate, provided that any number of vessels referred to in this Rule when pushed ahead in a group shall be lighted as one vessel under this Rule unless the overall length of the group exceeds 65 feet when the provisions of Rule 5(c) shall apply.

"(f) Small rowing boats, whether under oars or sail, shall only be required to have ready at hand an electric torch or a lighted lantern, showing a white light, which shall be exhibited in sufficient time to prevent collision.

"(g) The vessels and boats referred to in this Rule shall not be required to carry the lights or shapes prescribed in Rules 4(a) and 11(e) and the size of their day signals may be less than is prescribed in Rules 4(c) and 11(c).

"Rule 8

"(a) A power-driven pilot-vessel when engaged on pilotage duty and under way—

"(i) Shall carry a white light at the masthead at a height of not less than 20 feet above the hull, visible all round the horizon at a distance of at least 3 miles and at a distance of 8 feet below it a red light similar in construction and character. If such a vessel is of less than 65 feet in length she may carry the white light at a height of not less than 9 feet above the gunwale and the red light at a distance of 4 feet below the white light.

"(ii) Shall carry the sidelights or lanterns prescribed in Rule 2(a) (iv) and (v) or Rule 7(a) (ii) or (d), as appropriate, and the stern light prescribed in Rule 10.

"(iii) Shall show one or more flare-up lights at intervals not exceeding 10 minutes. An intermittent white light visible all round the horizon may be used in lieu of flare-up lights.

"(b) A sailing pilot-vessel when engaged on pilotage duty and under way—

"(i) Shall carry a white light at the masthead visible all round the horizon at a distance of at least 3 miles.

"(ii) Shall be provided with the sidelights or lantern prescribed in Rules 5(a) or 7(d), as appropriate, and shall, on the near approach of or to other vessels, have such lights ready for use, and shall show them at short intervals to indicate the direction in which she is heading, but the green light shall not be shown on the port side nor the red light on the starboard side. She shall also carry the stern light prescribed in Rule 10.

"(iii) Shall show one or more flare-up lights at intervals not exceeding ten minutes.

"(c) A pilot-vessel when engaged on pilotage duty and not under way shall carry the lights and show the flares prescribed in sections (a) (i) and (iii) or (b) (i) and (iii), as appropriate, and if at anchor shall also carry the anchor lights prescribed in Rule 11.

"(d) A pilot-vessel when not engaged on pilotage duty shall show the lights or shapes for a similar vessel of her length.

"Rule 9

"(a) Fishing vessels when not engaged in fishing shall show the lights or shapes for similar vessels of their length.

"(b) Vessels engaged in fishing, when under way or at anchor, shall show only the lights and shapes prescribed in this Rule, which lights and shapes shall be visible at a distance of at least 2 miles.

"(c) (i) Vessels when engaged in trawling, by which is meant the dragging of a dredge net or other apparatus through the water, shall carry two lights in a vertical line, one over the other, not less than 4 feet nor more than 12 feet apart. The upper of these lights shall be green and the lower light white and each shall be visible all round the horizon. The lower of these two lights shall be carried at a height above the sidelights not less than twice the distance between the two vertical lights.

"(ii) Such vessels may in addition carry a white light similar in construction to the white light prescribed in Rule 2(a) (i) but such light shall be carried lower than and abaft the all-round green and white lights.

"(d) Vessels when engaged in fishing, except vessels engaged in trawling, shall carry the lights prescribed in section (c) (i) except that the upper of the two vertical lights shall be red. Such vessels if of less than 40 feet in length may carry the red light at a height of not less than 9 feet above the gunwale and the white light not less than 3 feet below the red light.

"(e) Vessels referred to in sections (c) and (d), when making way through the water, shall carry the sidelights or lanterns prescribed in Rule 2(a) (iv) and (v) or Rule 7 (a) (ii) or (d), as appropriate, and the stern light prescribed in Rule 10. When not making way through the water they shall show neither the sidelights nor the stern light.

"(f) Vessels referred to in section (d) with outlying gear extending more than 500 feet horizontally into the seaway shall carry an additional all-round white light at a horizontal distance of not less than 6 feet nor more than 20 feet away from the vertical lights in the direction of the outlying gear. This additional white light shall be placed at a height not exceeding that of the white light prescribed in section (c) (i) and not lower than the sidelights.

"(g) In addition to the lights which they are required by this Rule to carry, vessels engaged in fishing may, if necessary in order to attract the attention of an approaching vessel, use a flare-up light, or may direct the beam of their searchlight in the direction of a danger threatening the approaching vessel, in such a way as not to embarrass other vessels. They may also use working lights but fishermen shall take into account that specially bright or insufficiently screened working lights may impair the visibility and distinctive character of the lights prescribed in this Rule.

"(h) By day vessels when engaged in fishing shall indicate their occupation by displaying where it can best be seen a black shape consisting of two cones each not less than 2 feet in diameter with their points together one above the other. Such vessels if of less than 65 feet in length may substitute a basket for such black shape. If their outlying gear extends more than 500 feet horizontally into the seaway vessels engaged in fishing shall display in addition one black conical shape, point upwards, in the direction of the outlying gear.

"Note.—Vessels fishing with trolling lines are not 'engaged in fishing' as defined in Rule 1(c) (xiv).

"Rule 10

"(a) Except where otherwise provided in these Rules, a vessel when under way shall carry at her stern a white light, so constructed that it shall show an unbroken light over an arc of the horizon of 135 degrees (12 Points of the compass), so fixed as to show the light 67½ degrees (6 points) from right aft on each side of the vessel, and of such a character as to be visible at a distance of at least 2 miles.

"(b) In a small vessel, if it is not possible on account of bad weather or other sufficient cause for this light to be fixed, an electric torch or a lighted lantern showing a white light shall be kept at hand ready for use and shall, on the approach of an overtaking vessel, be shown in sufficient time to prevent collision.

"(c) A seaplane on the water when under way shall carry on her tail a white light, so constructed as to show an unbroken light over an arc of the horizon of 140 degrees of the compass, so fixed as to show the light 70 degrees from right aft on each side of the seaplane, and of such a character as to be visible at a distance of at least 2 miles.

"Rule 11

"(a) A vessel of less than 150 feet in length, when at anchor, shall carry in the forepart of the vessel, where it can best be seen, a white light visible all round the horizon at a distance of at least 2 miles. Such a vessel may also carry a second white light in the position prescribed in section (b) of this Rule but shall not be required to do so. The second white light, if carried, shall be visible at a distance of at least 2 miles and so placed as to be as far as possible visible all round the horizon.

"(b) A vessel of 150 feet or more in length, when at anchor, shall carry near the stem of the vessel, at a height of not less than 20 feet above the hull, one such light, and at or near the stern of the vessel and at such a height that it shall be not less than 15 feet lower than the forward light, another such light. Both these lights shall be visible at a distance of at least 3 miles and so placed as to be as far as possible visible all round the horizon.

"(c) Between sunrise and sunset every vessel when at anchor shall carry in the forepart of the vessel, where it can best be seen, one black ball not less than 2 feet in diameter.

"(d) A vessel engaged in laying or in picking up a submarine cable or navigation mark, or a vessel engaged in surveying or underwater operations, when at anchor, shall carry the lights or shapes prescribed in Rule 4(c) in addition to those prescribed in the appropriate preceding sections of this Rule.

"(e) A vessel aground shall carry the light or lights prescribed in sections (a) or (b) and the two red lights prescribed in Rule 4(a). By day she shall carry, where they can best be seen, three black balls, each not less than 2 feet in diameter, placed in a vertical line one over the other, not less than 6 feet apart.

"(f) A seaplane on the water under 150 feet in length, when at anchor, shall carry, where it can best be seen, a white light, visible all round the horizon at a distance of at least 2 miles.

"(g) A seaplane on the water 150 feet or upwards in length, when at anchor, shall carry, where they can best be seen, a white light forward and a white light aft, both lights visible all round the horizon at a distance of at least 3 miles; and, in addition, if the seaplane is more than 150 feet in span, a white light on each side to indicate the maximum span, and visible, so far as practicable, all round the horizon at a distance of 1 mile.

"(h) A seaplane aground shall carry on anchor light or lights as prescribed in sections (f) and (g), and in addition may carry two red lights in a vertical line, at least 3 feet apart, so placed as to be visible all round the horizon.

"Rule 12

"Every vessel or seaplane on the water may, if necessary in order to attract attention, in addition to the lights which she is by these Rules required to carry, show a flare-up light or use a detonating or other efficient sound signal that cannot be mistaken for any signal authorised elsewhere under these Rules.

"Rule 13

"(a) Nothing in these Rules shall interfere with the operation of any special rules made by the Government of any nation with respect to additional station and signal lights for ships of war, for vessels sailing under convoy, for fishing vessels engaged in fishing as a fleet or for seaplanes on the water.

"(b) Whenever the Government concerned shall have determined that a naval or other military vessel or waterborne seaplane of special construction or purpose cannot comply fully with the provisions of any of these Rules with respect to the number, position, range or arc of visibility of lights or shapes, without interfering with the military function of the vessel or seaplane, such vessel or seaplane shall comply with such other provisions in regard to the number, position, range or arc of visibility of lights or shapes as her Government shall have determined to be the closest possible compliance with these Rules in respect of that vessel or seaplane.

"Rule 14

"A vessel proceeding under sail, when also being propelled by machinery, shall carry in the daytime forward, where it can best be seen, one black conical shape, point downwards, not less than 2 feet in diameter at its base.

"PART C.—SOUND SIGNALS AND CONDUCT IN RESTRICTED VISIBILITY

"PRELIMINARY

"1. The possession of information obtained from radar does not relieve any vessel of the obligation of conforming strictly with the Rules and, in particular, the obligations contained in Rules 15 and 16.

"2. The Annex to the Rules contains recommendations intended to assist in the use of radar as an aid to avoiding collision in restricted visibility.

"Rule 15

"(a) A power-driven vessel of 40 feet or more in length shall be provided with an efficient whistle, sounded by steam or by some substitute for steam, so placed that the sound may not be intercepted by any obstruction, and with an efficient fog horn to be sounded by mechanical means, and also with an efficient bell. A sailing vessel of 40 feet or more in length shall be provided with a similar fog horn and bell.

"(b) All signals prescribed in this Rule for vessels under way shall be given—

"(i) by power-driven vessels on the whistle;

"(ii) by sailing vessels on the fog horn;

"(iii) by vessels towed on the whistle or fog horn.

"(c) In fog, mist, falling snow, heavy rainstorms, or any other condition similarly restricting visibility, whether by day or night, the signals prescribed in this Rule shall be used as follows—

"(i) A power-driven vessel making way through the water shall sound at intervals of not more than 2 minutes a prolonged blast.

"(ii) A power-driven vessel under way, but stopped and making no way through the water, shall sound at intervals of not more than 2 minutes two prolonged blasts, with an interval of about 1 second between them.

"(iii) A sailing vessel under way shall sound, at intervals of not more than 1 minute, when on the starboard tack one blast, when on the port tack two blasts in succession, and when with the wind abaft the beam three blasts in succession.

"(iv) A vessel when at anchor shall at intervals of not more than 1 minute ring the bell rapidly for about 5 seconds. In vessels of more than 350 feet in length the bell shall be sounded in the forepart of the vessel, and in addition there shall be sounded in the after part of the vessel, at intervals of not more than 1 minute for about 5 seconds, a gong or other instrument, the tone and sounding of which cannot be confused with that of the bell. Every vessel at anchor may in addition, in accordance with Rule 12, sound three blasts in succession, namely, one short, one prolonged, and one short blast, to give warning of her position and of the possibility of collision to an approaching vessel.

"(v) A vessel when towing, a vessel engaged in laying or in picking up a submarine cable or navigation mark, and a vessel under way which is unable to get out of the way of an approaching vessel through being not under command or unable to manoeuvre as required by these Rules shall, instead of the signals prescribed in subsections (i), (ii) and (iii) sound, at intervals of not more than 1 minute, three blasts in succession, namely, one prolonged blast followed by two short blasts.

"(vi) A vessel towed, or, if more than one vessel is towed, only the last vessel of the tow, if manned, shall, at intervals of not more than 1 minute, sound four blasts in succession, namely, one prolonged blast followed by three short blasts. When practicable, this signal shall be made immediately after the signal made by the towing vessel.

"(vii) A vessel aground shall give the bell signal and, if required, the gong signal, prescribed in sub-section (iv) and shall, in addition, give 3 separate and distinct strokes on the bell immediately before and after such rapid ringing of the bell.

"(viii) A vessel engaged in fishing when under way or at anchor shall at intervals of not more than 1 minute sound the signal prescribed in sub-section (v). A vessel when fishing with trolling lines and under way shall sound the signals prescribed in sub-sections (i), (ii) or (iii) as may be appropriate.

"(ix) A vessel of less than 40 feet in length, a rowing boat, or a seaplane on the water, shall not be obliged to give the above-mentioned signals but if she does not, she shall make some other efficient sound signal at intervals of not more than 1 minute.

"(x) A power-driven pilot-vessel when engaged on pilotage duty may, in addition to the signals prescribed in sub-sections (i), (ii) and (iv), sound an identity signal consisting of 4 short blasts.

"Rule 16

"(a) Every vessel, or seaplane when taxi-ing on the water, shall, in fog, mist, falling snow, heavy rainstorms or any other condition similarly restricting visibility, go at a moderate speed, having careful regard to the existing circumstances and conditions.

"(b) A power-driven vessel hearing, apparently forward of her beam, the fog-signal of a vessel the position of which is not ascertained, shall, so far as the circumstances of the case admit, stop her engines, and then navigate with caution until danger of collision is over.

"(c) A power-driven vessel which detects the presence of another vessel forward of her beam before hearing her fog signal or sighting her visually may take early and substantial action to avoid a close quarters situation but, if this cannot be avoided, she shall, so far as the circumstances of the case admit, stop her engines in proper time to avoid collision and then navigate with caution until danger of collision is over.

"PART D.—STEERING AND SAILING RULES

"PRELIMINARY

"1. In obeying and construing these Rules, any action taken should be positive, in ample time, and with due regard to the observance of good seamanship.

"2. Risk of collision can, when circumstances permit, be ascertained by carefully watching the compass bearing of an approaching vessel. If the bearing does not appreciably change, such risk should be deemed to exist.

"3. Mariners should bear in mind that seaplanes in the act of landing or taking off, or operating under adverse weather conditions, may be unable to change their intended action at the last moment.

"4. Rules 17 to 24 apply only to vessels in sight of one another.

"Rule 17

"(a) When two sailing vessels are approaching one another, so as to involve risk of collision, one of them shall keep out of the way of the other as follows—

"(i) When each has the wind on a different side, the vessel which has the wind on the port side shall keep out of the way of the other.

"(ii) When both have the wind on the same side, the vessel which is to windward shall keep out of the way of the vessel which is to leeward.

"(b) For the purposes of this Rule the windward side shall be deemed to be the side opposite to that on which the mainsail is carried or, in the case of a square-rigged vessel, the side opposite to that on which the largest fore-and-aft sail is carried.

"Rule 18

"(a) When two power-driven vessels are meeting end on, or nearly end on, so as to involve risk of collision, each shall alter her course to starboard, so that each may pass on the port side of the other. This Rule only applies to cases where vessels are meeting end on, or nearly end on, in such a manner as to involve risk of collision, and does not apply to two vessels which must, if both keep on their respective course, pass clear of each other. The only cases to which it does apply are when each of two vessels is end on, or nearly end on, to the other; in other words, to cases in which, by day, each vessel sees the masts of the other in a line, or nearly in a line, with her own; and by night, to cases in which each vessel is in such a position as to see both the sidelights of the other. It does not apply, by day, to cases in which a vessel sees another ahead crossing her own course; or, by night, to cases where the red light of one vessel is opposed to the red light of the other or where the green light of one vessel is opposed to the green light of the other or where a red light without a green light or a green light without a red light is seen ahead, or where both green and red lights are seen anywhere but ahead.

"(b) For the purposes of this Rule and Rules 19 to 29 inclusive, except Rule 20(c) and Rule 28, a seaplane on the water shall be deemed to be a vessel, and the expression 'power-driven vessel' shall be construed accordingly.

"Rule 19

"When two power-driven vessels are crossing, so as to involve risk of collision, the vessel which has the other on her own starboard side shall keep out of the way of the other.

"Rule 20

"(a) When a power-driven vessel and a sailing vessel are proceeding in such directions as to involve risk of collision, except as provided for in Rules 24 and 26, the power-driven vessel shall keep out of the way of the sailing vessel.

"(b) This Rule shall not give to a sailing vessel the right to hamper, in a narrow channel, the safe passage of a power-driven vessel which can navigate only inside such channel.

"(c) A seaplane on the water shall, in general, keep well clear of all vessels and avoid impeding their navigation. In circumstances, however, where risk of collision exists, she shall comply with these Rules.

"Rule 21

"Where by any of these Rules one of two vessels is to keep out of the way, the other shall keep her course and speed. When, from any cause, the latter vessel finds herself so close that collision cannot be avoided by the action of the giving-way vessel alone, she also shall take such action as will best aid to avert collision (see Rules 27 and 29).

"Rule 22

"Every vessel which is directed by these Rules to keep out of the way of another vessel shall, so far as possible, take positive early action to comply with this obligation, and shall, if the circumstances of the case admit, avoid crossing ahead of the other.

"Rule 23

"Every power-driven vessel which is directed by these Rules to keep out of the way of another vessel shall, on approaching her, if necessary, slacken her speed or stop or reverse.

"Rule 24

"(a) Notwithstanding anything contained in these Rules, every vessel overtaking any other shall keep out of the way of the overtaken vessel.

"(b) Every vessel coming up with another vessel from any direction more than 22½ degrees (2 points) abaft her beam, i.e., in such a position, with reference to the vessel which she is overtaking, that at night she would be unable to see either of that vessel's sidelights, shall be deemed to be an overtaking vessel; and no subsequent alteration of the bearing between the two vessels shall make the overtaking vessel a crossing vessel within the meaning of these Rules, or relieve her of the duty of keeping clear of the overtaken vessel until she is finally past and clear.

"(c) If the overtaking vessel cannot determine with certainty whether she is forward of or abaft this direction from the other vessel, she shall assume that she is an overtaking vessel and keep out of the way.

"Rule 25

"(a) In a narrow channel every power-driven vessel when proceeding along the course of the channel shall, when it is safe and practicable, keep to that side of the fairway or mid-channel which lies on the starboard side of such vessel.

"(b) Whenever a power-driven vessel is nearing a bend in a channel where a vessel approaching from the other direction cannot be seen, such power-driven vessel, when she shall have arrived within one-half (½) mile of the bend, shall give a signal by one prolonged blast on her whistle which signal shall be answered by a similar blast given by any approaching power-driven vessel that may be within hearing around the bend. Regardless of whether an approaching vessel on the farther side of the bend is heard, such bend shall be rounded with alertness and caution.

"(c) In a narrow channel a power-driven vessel of less than 65 feet in length shall not hamper the safe passage of a vessel which can navigate only inside such channel.

"Rule 26

"All vessels not engaged in fishing, except vessels to which the provisions of Rule 4 apply, shall, when under way, keep out of the way of vessels engaged in fishing. This Rule shall not give to any vessel engaged in fishing the right of obstructing a fairway used by vessels other than fishing vessels.

"Rule 27

"In obeying and construing these Rules due regard shall be had to all dangers of navigation and collision, and to any special circumstances, including the limitations of the craft involved, which may render a departure from the above Rules necessary in order to avoid immediate danger.

"Part E.—Sound Signals for Vessels in Sight of One Another

"Rule 28

"(a) When vessels are in sight of one another, a power-driven vessel under way, in taking any course authorised or required by these Rules, shall indicate that course by the following signals on her whistle, namely—

"One short blast to mean 'I am altering my course to starboard'.

"Two short blasts to mean 'I am altering my course to port'.

"Three short blasts to mean 'My engines are going astern'.

"(b) Whenever a power-driven vessel which, under these Rules, is to keep her course and speed, is in sight of another vessel and is in doubt whether sufficient action is being taken by the other vessel to avert collision, she may indicate such doubt by giving at least five short and rapid blasts on the whistle. The giving of such a signal shall not relieve a vessel of her obligations under Rules 27 and 29 or any other Rule, or of her duty to indicate any action taken under these Rules by giving the appropriate sound signals laid down in this Rule.

"(c) Any whistle signal mentioned in this Rule may be further indicated by a visual signal consisting of a white light visible all round the horizon at a distance of at least 5 miles, and so devised that it will operate simultaneously and in conjunction with the whistle-sounding mechanism and remain lighted and visible during the same period as the sound signal.

"(d) Nothing in these Rules shall interfere with the operation of any special rules made by the Government of any nation with respect to the use of additional whistle signals between ships of war or vessels sailing under convoy.

"PART F.—MISCELLANEOUS

"Rule 29

"Nothing in these Rules shall exonerate any vessel, or the owner, master or crew thereof, from the consequences of any neglect to carry lights or signals, or of any neglect to keep a proper look-out, or of the neglect of any precaution which may be required by the ordinary practice of seamen, or by the special circumstances of the case.

"Rule 30

"Reservation of Rules for Harbours and Inland Navigation

"Nothing in these Rules shall interfere with the operation of a special rule duly made by local authority relative to the navigation of any harbour, river, lake, or inland water, including a reserved seaplane area.

"Rule 31

"Distress Signals

"(a) When a vessel or seaplane on the water is in distress and requires assistance from other vessels or from the shore, the following shall be the signals to be used or displayed by her, either together or separately, namely—

"(i) A gun or other explosive signal fired at intervals of about a minute.

"(ii) A continuous sounding with any fog-signalling apparatus.

"(iii) Rockets or shells, throwing red stars fired one at a time at short intervals.

"(iv) A signal made by radiotelegraphy or by any other signalling method consisting of the group . . . — — — . . . in the Morse Code.

"(v) A signal sent by radiotelephony consisting of the spoken word 'Mayday'.

"(vi) The International Code Signal of distress indicated by N.C.

"(vii) A signal consisting of a square flag having above or below it a ball or anything resembling a ball.

"(viii) Flames on the vessel (as from a burning tar barrel, oil barrel, &c.).

"(ix) A rocket parachute flare or a hand flare showing a red light.

"(x) A smoke signal giving off a volume of orange-coloured smoke.

"(xi) Slowly and repeatedly raising and lowering arms outstretched to each side.

"NOTE.—Vessels in distress may use the radiotelegraph alarm signal or the radiotelephone alarm signal to secure attention to distress calls and messages. The radiotelegraph alarm signal, which is designed to actuate the radiotelegraph auto alarms of vessels so fitted, consists of a series of twelve dashes, sent in 1 minute, the duration of each dash being 4 seconds, and the duration of the interval between 2 consecutive dashes being 1 second. The radiotelephone alarm signal consists of 2 tones transmitted alternately over periods of from 30 seconds to 1 minute.

"(b) The use of any of the foregoing signals, except for the purpose of indicating that a vessel or seaplane is in distress, and the use of any signals which may be confused with any of the above signals, is prohibited.

"ANNEX TO THE RULES

"RECOMMENDATIONS ON THE USE OF RADAR INFORMATION AS AN AID TO AVOIDING COLLISIONS AT SEA

"(1) Assumptions made on scanty information may be dangerous and should be avoided.

"(2) A vessel navigating with the aid of radar in restricted visibility must, in compliance with Rule 16(a), go at a moderate speed. Information obtained from the use of radar is one of the circumstances to be taken into account when determining moderate speed. In this regard it must be recognised that small vessels, small icebergs and similar floating objects may not be detected by radar. Radar indications of one or more vessels in the vicinity may mean that "moderate speed" should be slower than a mariner without radar might consider moderate in the circumstances.

"(3) When navigating in restricted visibility the radar range and bearing alone do not constitute ascertainment of the position of the other vessel under Rule 16(b) sufficiently to relieve a vessel of the duty to stop her engines and navigate with caution when a fog signal is heard forward of the beam.

"(4) When action has been taken under Rule 16(c) to avoid a close quarters situation, it is essential to make sure that such action is having the desired effect. Alterations of course or speed or both are matters as to which the mariner must be guided by the circumstances of the case.

"(5) Alteration of course alone may be the most effective action to avoid close quarters provided that—

"(a) There is sufficient sea room.

"(b) It is made in good time.

"(c) It is substantial. A succession of small alterations of course should be avoided.

"(d) It does not result in a close quarters situation with other vessels.

"(6) The direction of an alteration of course is a matter in which the mariner must be guided by the circumstances of the case. An alteration to starboard, particularly when vessels are approaching apparently on opposite or nearly opposite courses, is generally preferable to an alteration to port.

"(7) An alteration of speed, either alone or in conjunction with an alteration of course, should be substantial. A number of small alterations of speed should be avoided.

"(8) If a close quarters situation is imminent, the most prudent action may be to take all way off the vessel."

INTER-GOVERNMENTAL MARITIME CONSULTATIVE ORGANIZATION

ORGANISATION INTERGOUVERNEMENTALE CONSULTATIVE DE LA NAVIGATION MARITIME

Telegrams: INMARCOR LONDON W.C.2
Telephone: CHANCERY 2156

CHANCERY HOUSE,
CHANCERY LANE,
LONDON, W.C.2

A1/C/4.01 (NV.13)

IMCO

The Secretary-General of the Inter-Governmental Maritime Consultative Organization presents his compliments and has the honour to state that the Government of Japan deposited, on 7 August 1964, an Instrument of Acceptance of the International Regulations for Preventing Collisions at Sea, 1960.

An up-to-date list of countries which have accepted the Regulations, together with the number and gross tonnage of merchant ships registered in each of the countries, is attached.

Since the merchant ships of 100 gross tons and over belonging to the countries which have accepted the Regulations now amounts to more than 75 per cent by number of the world total, the Secretary-General concludes that in accordance with the Recommendation of the Maritime Safety Committee at its eighth session as reported to the eleventh session of the Council substantial unanimity as to the acceptance of the Regulations should be considered to have been reached.

In accordance with the relevant provisions in the Final Act of the International Conference on Safety of Life at Sea, the Secretary-General therefore has pleasure in fixing *1 September 1965* as the date on and after which the 1960 Collision Regulations shall be applied by the Governments which have agreed to accept them. He has no doubt that those Governments which have not so far accepted the Regulations will now wish to do so as soon as possible.

Further acceptances of the Regulations will be notified on 1 January 1965, and thence quarterly, indicating the acceptances received up to the end of each previous quarter.

The Secretary-General avails himself of this opportunity to renew the assurance of his highest consideration.

11 AUGUST 1964

J R

[SEAL]

THE SECRETARY OF STATE OF THE
UNITED STATES OF AMERICA

COUNTRIES WHICH HAVE ACCEPTED THE INTERNATIONAL REGULATIONS FOR PREVENTING COLLISIONS AT SEA, 1960 AND THEIR MERCHANT FLEETS

As at 7 August 1964

Country	Number*	Gross Tonnage*
World total	39, 571	145, 863, 463
Belgium	200	718, 313
Burma	29	47, 247
Cameroun	1	108
Canada	1, 087	1, 796, 440
Denmark	879	2, 418, 207
Finland	395	926, 047
France	1, 498	5, 216, 098
Ghana	25	72, 805
Greece	1, 256	7, 093, 974
India	309	1, 211, 139
Ireland	83	176, 838
Israel	78	426, 180
Japan	4, 819	9, 976, 668
Liberia	893	11, 391, 210
Madagascar	11	13, 983
Netherlands	1, 904	5, 226, 815
Norway	2, 764	13, 668, 815
Pakistan	90	298, 653
Paraguay	21	16, 520
Peru	55	116, 623
Philippines	162	406, 311
Poland	365	925, 428
Portugal	335	673, 757
Roumania	26	90, 436
Spain	1, 633	2, 007, 340
Sweden	1, 208	4, 176, 326
Union of Soviet Socialist Republics	1, 432	5, 433, 765
United Arab Republic	117	242, 040
United Kingdom	4, 751	21, 565, 150
United States of America	3, 706	23, 132, 781
Viet-Nam	23	14, 210
Yugoslavia	273	965, 449
Total	30, 428	120, 445, 676
Percentage of world total	76. 9%	82. 6%

*Source: Lloyd's Register of Shipping Statistical Tables 1963

AGREEMENT BETWEEN THE GOVERNMENT OF THE UNITED STATES OF AMERICA AND THE GOVERNMENT OF THE UNION OF SOVIET SOCIALIST REPUBLICS ON THE PREVENTION OF INCIDENTS ON AND OVER THE SEA

The Government of the United States of America and the Government of the Union of Soviet Socialist Republics,

Desiring to assure the safety of navigation of the ships of their respective Armed Forces on the high seas and flight of their military aircraft over the high seas, and

Guided by the principles and rules of international law,

Have decided to conclude this Agreement and have agreed as follows:

ARTICLE I

For the purposes of this Agreement, the following definitions shall apply:

1. "Ship" means:

(A) A warship belonging to the naval forces of the Parties bearing the external marks distinguishing warships of its nationality, under the command of an officer duly commissioned by the government and whose name appears in the navy list, and manned by a crew who are under regular naval discipline;

(B) Naval auxiliaries of the Parties, which include all naval ships authorized to fly the naval auxiliary flag where such a flag has been established by either party.

2. "Aircraft" means all military manned heavier-than-air and lighter-than-air craft, excluding space craft.

3. "Formation" means an ordered arrangement of two or more ships proceeding together and normally maneuvered together.

ARTICLE II

The Parties shall take measures to instruct the commanding officers of their respective ships to observe strictly the letter and spirit of the International Regulations for Preventing Collisions at Sea, hereinafter referred to as the Rules of the

Road. The Parties recognize that their freedom to conduct operations on the high seas is based on the principles established under recognized international law and codified in the 1958 Geneva Convention on the High Seas.

ARTICLE III

1. In all cases ships operating in proximity to each other, except when required to maintain course and speed under the Rules of the Road, shall remain well clear to avoid risk of collision.

2. Ships meeting or operating in the vicinity of a formation of the other Party shall, while conforming to the Rules of the Road, avoid maneuvering in a manner which would hinder the evolutions of the formation.

3. Formations shall not conduct maneuvers through areas of heavy traffic where internationally recognized traffic separation schemes are in effect.

4. Ships engaged in surveillance of other ships shall stay at a distance which avoids the risk of collision and also shall avoid executing maneuvers embarrassing or endangering the ships under surveillance. Except when required to maintain course and speed under the Rules of the Road, a surveillant shall take positive early action so as, in the exercise of good seamanship, not to embarrass or endanger ships under surveillance.

5. When ships of both parties maneuver in sight of one another, such signals (flag, sound, and light) as are prescribed by the Rules of the Road, the International Code of Signals, or other mutually agreed signals, shall be adhered to for signaling operations and intentions.

6. Ships of the Parties shall not simulate attacks by aiming guns, missile launchers, torpedo tubes, and other weapons in the direction of a passing ship of the other Party, not launch any object in the direction of passing ships of the other Party, and not use searchlights or other power illumination devices to illuminate the navigation bridges of passing ships of the other Party.

7. When conducting exercises with submerged submarines, exercising ships shall show the appropriate signals prescribed by the International Code of Signals to warn ships of the presence of submarines in the area.

8. Ships of one Party when approaching ships of the other Party conducting operations as set forth in rule 4 (C) of the Rules of the Road, and particularly ships engaged in launching or landing aircraft as well as ships engaged in replenishment underway, shall take appropriate measures not to hinder maneuvers of such ships and shall remain well clear.

ARTICLE IV

Commanders of aircraft of the Parties shall use the greatest caution and prudence in approaching aircraft and ships of the other Party operating on and over the high seas, in particular, ships engaged in launching or landing aircraft, and in the interest of mutual safety shall not permit: simulated attacks by the simulated use of weapons against aircraft and ships, or performance of various aerobatics over ships, or dropping various objects near them in such a manner as to be hazardous to ships or to constitute a hazard to navigation.

ARTICLE V

1. Ships of the Parties operating in sight of one another shall raise proper signals concerning their intent to begin launching or landing aircraft.

2. Aircraft of the Parties flying over the high seas in darkness or under instrument conditions shall, whenever feasible, display navigation lights.

ARTICLE VI

Both Parties shall:

1. Provide through the established system of radio broadcasts of information and warning to mariners, not less than 3 to 5 days in advance as a rule, notification of actions on the high seas which represent a danger to navigation or to aircraft in flight.

2. Make increased use of the informative signals contained in the International Code of Signals to signify the intentions of their respective ships when maneuvering in proximity to one another. At night or in conditions of reduced visability, or under conditions of lighting and such distances when signal flags are not distinct, flashing light should be used to inform ships of maneuvers which may hinder the movements of others or involve a risk of collision.

3. Utilize on a trial basis signals additional to those in the International Code of Signals, submitting such signals to the Intergovernmental Maritime Consultative Organization for its consideration and for the information of other States.

ARTICLE VII

The Parties shall exchange appropriate information concerning instances of collisions, incidents which result in damage, or other incidents at sea between ships and aircraft of the Parties. The United States Navy shall provide such information through the Soviet Naval Attache in Washington and the Soviet Navy shall provide such information through the United States Naval Attache in Moscow.

ARTICLE VIII

This Agreement shall enter into force on the date of its signature and shall remain in force for a period of three years. It will thereafter be renewed without further action by the Parties for successive periods of three years each.

This agreement may be terminated by either Party upon six months written notice to the other Party.

ARTICLE IX

The Parties shall meet within one year after the date of the signing of this Agreement to review the implementation of its terms. Similar consultations shall be held thereafter annually, or more frequently as the Parties may decide.

ARTICLE X

The Parties shall designate members to form a committee which will consider specific measures in conformity with this Agreement. The committee will, as a particular part of its work, consider the practical workability of concrete fixed distances to be observed in encounters between ships, aircraft, and ships and aircraft. The committee will meet within six months of the date of signature of this Agreement and submit its recommendations for decision by the Parties during the consultations prescribed in Article IX.

Done in duplicate on the 25th day of May, 1972 in Moscow in the English and Russian languages each being equally authentic.

FOR THE GOVERNMENT OF THE UNITED STATES OF AMERICA:

Secretary of the Navy

FOR THE GOVERNMENT OF THE UNION OF SOVIET SOCIALIST REPUBLICS:

Commander-in-Chief of the Soviet Navy and Deputy Minister of Defense

# # # # #

[1] TRADUCTION. — TRANSLATION.

No. 4015. — CONVENTION [2] REGARDING THE RÉGIME OF THE STRAITS. SIGNED AT MONTREUX, JULY 20TH, 1936.

French official text communicated by the Permanent Delegate of Turkey to the League of Nations. The registration of this Convention took place December 11th, 1936.

HIS MAJESTY THE KING OF THE BULGARIANS, THE PRESIDENT OF THE FRENCH REPUBLIC, HIS MAJESTY THE KING OF GREAT BRITAIN, IRELAND AND THE BRITISH DOMINIONS BEYOND THE SEAS, EMPEROR OF INDIA, HIS MAJESTY THE KING OF THE HELLENES, HIS MAJESTY THE EMPEROR OF JAPAN, HIS MAJESTY THE KING OF ROUMANIA, THE PRESIDENT OF THE TURKISH REPUBLIC, THE CENTRAL EXECUTIVE COMMITTEE OF THE UNION OF SOVIET SOCIALIST REPUBLICS, AND HIS MAJESTY THE KING OF YUGOSLAVIA ;

Desiring to regulate transit and navigation in the Straits of the Dardanelles, the Sea of Marmora and the Bosphorus comprised under the general term " Straits " in such manner as to safeguard, within the framework of Turkish security and of the security, in the Black Sea, of the riparian States, the principle enshrined in Article 23 of the Treaty [3] of Peace signed at Lausanne on the 24th July, 1923 ;

Have resolved to replace by the present Convention the Convention [4] signed at Lausanne on the 24th July, 1923, and have appointed as their Plenipotentiaries :

HIS MAJESTY THE KING OF THE BULGARIANS :

Dr. Nicolas P. NICOLAEV, Minister Plenipotentiary, Secretary-General of the Ministry of Foreign Affairs and of Cults ;

M. Pierre NEÏCOV, Minister Plenipotentiary, Director of Political Affairs at the Ministry of Foreign Affairs and of Cults ;

---

[1] Traduction du Foreign Office de Sa Majesté britannique.

[1] Translation of His Britannic Majesty's Foreign Office.

[2] *Ratifications deposited at Paris :*

GREAT BRITAIN AND NORTHERN IRELAND AND ALL PARTS OF THE BRITISH EMPIRE WHICH ARE NOT SEPARATE MEMBERS OF THE LEAGUE OF NATIONS	November 9th, 1936.
AUSTRALIA	November 9th, 1936.
BULGARIA	November 9th, 1936.
FRANCE	November 9th, 1936.
GREECE	November 9th, 1936.
ROUMANIA	November 9th, 1936.
TURKEY	November 9th, 1936.
UNION OF SOVIET SOCIALIST REPUBLICS	November 9th, 1936.
YUGOSLAVIA	November 9th, 1936.
JAPAN	April 19th, 1937.

The *procès-verbal* of deposit of the first six ratifications, including that of Turkey, provided for in Article 26 of the Convention, was drawn up on November 9th, 1936.

The present Convention, the provisions of which were provisionally applied as from August 15th, 1936, came finally into force on November 9th, 1936.

[3] Vol. XXVIII, page 11, of this Series.

[4] Vol. XXVIII, page 115, of this Series.

The President of the French Republic :

M. Paul-Boncour, Senator, Permanent Delegate of France to the League of Nations, former President of the Council, former Minister for Foreign Affairs, Chevalier of the Legion of Honour, Croix de Guerre ;

M. Henri Ponsot, Ambassador Extraordinary and Plenipotentiary of the French Republic at Angora, Grand Officer of the Legion of Honour ;

His Majesty the King of Great Britain, Ireland and the British Dominions beyond the Seas, Emperor of India :

For Great Britain and Northern Ireland and all Parts of the British Empire which are not Separate Members of the League of Nations :

The Right Honourable Lord Stanley, P.C., M.C., M.P., Parliamentary Secretary to the Admiralty ;

For the Commonwealth of Australia :

The Right Honourable Stanley Melbourne Bruce, C.H., M.C., High Commissioner for the Commonwealth of Australia in London ;

His Majesty the King of the Hellenes :

M. Nicolas Politis, Envoy Extraordinary and Minister Plenipotentiary of Greece in Paris, former Minister for Foreign Affairs ;

M. Raoul Bibica Rosetti, Permanent Delegate of Greece to the League of Nations ;

His Majesty the Emperor of Japan :

M. Naotake Sato, Jusammi, Grand-Cordon of the Order of the Rising Sun, Ambassador Extraordinary and Plenipotentiary in Paris ;

M. Massa-aki Hotta, Jushii, Second Class of the Order of the Rising Sun, Envoy Extraordinary and Minister Plenipotentiary at Berne ;

His Majesty the King of Roumania :

M. Nicolas Titulesco, Minister Secretary of State for the Department of Foreign Affairs ;

M. Constantin Contzesco, Minister Plenipotentiary, Delegate of Roumania to the European and International Commissions of the Danube ;

M. Vespasien Pella, Envoy Extraordinary and Minister Plenipotentiary at The Hague ;

The President of the Turkish Republic :

Dr. Rüştü Aras, Minister for Foreign Affairs, Deputy for Smyrna ;

M. Suad Davaz, Ambassador Extraordinary and Plenipotentiary of the Turkish Republic in Paris ;

M. Numan Menemençioğlu, Ambassador of Turkey, Secretary-General of the Ministry for Foreign Affairs ;

M. Asim Gündüz, General Commanding an Army Corps, Deputy Chief of the General Staff ;

M. Necmeddin Sadak, Permanent Delegate of Turkey to the League of Nations, Deputy for Sivas, *Rapporteur* for the Committee of Foreign Affairs ;

The Central Executive Committee of the Union of Soviet Socialist Republics :

M. Maxime Litvinoff, Member of the Central Executive Committee of the Union of Soviet Socialist Republics, People's Commissar for Foreign Affairs ;

His Majesty the King of Yugoslavia :

M. Ivan Soubbotitch, Permanent Delegate of the Kingdom of Yugoslavia to the League of Nations ;

Who, after having exhibited their full powers, found in good and due form, have agreed on the following provisions :

Article 1.

The High Contracting Parties recognise and affirm the principle of freedom of transit and navigation by sea in the Straits.

The exercise of this freedom shall henceforth be regulated by the provisions of the present Convention.

SECTION I.

MERCHANT VESSELS.

Article 2.

In time of peace, merchant vessels shall enjoy complete freedom of transit and navigation in the Straits, by day and by night, under any flag and with any kind of cargo, without any formalities, except as provided in Article 3 below. No taxes or charges other than those authorised by Annex I to the present Convention shall be levied by the Turkish authorities on these vessels when passing in transit without calling at a port in the Straits.

In order to facilitate the collection of these taxes or charges merchant vessels passing through the Straits shall communicate to the officials at the stations referred to in Article 3 their name, nationality, tonnage, destination and last port of call (provenance).

Pilotage and towage remain optional.

Article 3.

All ships entering the Straits by the Ægean Sea or by the Black Sea shall stop at a sanitary station near the entrance to the Straits for the purposes of the sanitary control prescribed by Turkish law within the framework of international sanitary regulations. This control, in the case of ships possessing a clean bill of health or presenting a declaration of health testifying that they do not fall within the scope of the provisions of the second paragraph of the present Article, shall be carried out by day and by night with all possible speed, and the vessels in question shall not be required to make any other stop during their passage through the Straits.

Vessels which have on board cases of plague, cholera, yellow fever, exanthematic typhus or smallpox, or which have had such cases on board during the previous seven days, and vessels which have left an infected port within less than five times twenty-four hours shall stop at the sanitary stations indicated in the preceding paragraph in order to embark such sanitary guards as the Turkish authorities may direct. No tax or charge shall be levied in respect of these sanitary guards and they shall be disembarked at a sanitary station on departure from the Straits.

Article 4.

In time of war, Turkey not being belligerent, merchant vessels, under any flag or with any kind of cargo, shall enjoy freedom of transit and navigation in the Straits subject to the provisions of Articles 2 and 3.

Pilotage and towage remain optional.

Article 5.

In time of war, Turkey being belligerent, merchant vessels not belonging to a country at war with Turkey shall enjoy freedom of transit and navigation in the Straits on condition that they do not in any way assist the enemy.

Such vessels shall enter the Straits by day and their transit shall be effected by the route which shall in each case be indicated by the Turkish authorities.

Article 6.

Should Turkey consider herself to be threatened with imminent danger of war, the provisions of Article 2 shall nevertheless continue to be applied except that vessels must enter the Straits by day and that their transit must be effected by the route which shall, in each case, be indicated by the Turkish authorities.

Pilotage may, in this case, be made obligatory, but no charge shall be levied.

Article 7.

The term " merchant vessels " applies to all vessels which are not covered by Section II of the present Convention.

SECTION II.

VESSELS OF WAR.

Article 8.

For the purposes of the present Convention, the definitions of vessels of war and of their specification together with those relating to the calculation of tonnage shall be as set forth in Annex II to the present Convention.

Article 9.

Naval auxiliary vessels specifically designed for the carriage of fuel, liquid or non-liquid, shall not be subject to the provisions of Article 13 regarding notification, nor shall they be counted for the purpose of calculating the tonnage which is subject to limitation under Articles 14 and 18, on condition that they shall pass through the Straits singly. They shall, however, continue to be on the same footing as vessels of war for the purpose of the remaining provisions governing transit.

The auxiliary vessels specified in the preceding paragraph shall only be entitled to benefit by the exceptional status therein contemplated if their armament does not include : for use against floating targets, more than two guns of a maximum calibre of 105 millimetres ; for use against aerial targets, more than two guns of a maximum calibre of 75 millimetres.

Article 10.

In time of peace, light surface vessels, minor war vessels and auxiliary vessels, whether belonging to Black Sea or non-Black Sea Powers, and whatever their flag, shall enjoy freedom of transit through the Straits without any taxes or charges whatever, provided that such transit is begun during daylight and subject to the conditions laid down in Article 13 and the Articles following thereafter.

Vessels of war other than those which fall within the categories specified in the preceding paragraph shall only enjoy a right of transit under the special conditions provided by Articles 11 and 12.

Article 11.

Black Sea Powers may send through the Straits capital ships of a tonnage greater than that laid down in the first paragraph of Article 14, on condition that these vessels pass through the Straits singly, escorted by not more than two destroyers.

Article 12.

Black Sea Powers shall have the right to send through the Straits, for the purpose of rejoining their base, submarines constructed or purchased outside the Black Sea, provided that adequate notice of the laying down or purchase of such submarines shall have been given to Turkey.

Submarines belonging to the said Powers shall also be entitled to pass through the Straits to be repaired in dockyards outside the Black Sea on condition that detailed information on the matter is given to Turkey.

In either case, the said submarines must travel by day and on the surface, and must pass through the Straits singly.

Article 13.

The transit of vessels of war through the Straits shall be preceded by a notification given to the Turkish Government through the diplomatic channel. The normal period of notice shall be eight days ; but it is desirable that in the case of non-Black Sea Powers this period should be increased to fifteen days. The notification shall specify the destination, name, type and number of the vessels, as also the date of entry for the outward passage and, if necessary, for the return journey. Any change of date shall be subject to three days' notice.

Entry into the Straits for the outward passage shall take place within a period of five days from the date given in the original notification. After the expiry of this period, a new notification shall be given under the same conditions as for the original notification.

When effecting transit, the commander of the naval force shall, without being under any obligation to stop, communicate to a signal station at the entrance to the Dardanelles or the Bosphorus the exact composition of the force under his orders.

Article 14.

The maximum aggregate tonnage of all foreign naval forces which may be in course of transit through the Straits shall not exceed 15,000 tons, except in the cases provided for in Article 11 and in Annex III to the present Convention.

The forces specified in the preceding paragraph shall not, however, comprise more than nine vessels.

Vessels, whether belonging to Black Sea or non-Black Sea Powers, paying visits to a port in the Straits, in accordance with the provisions of Article 17, shall not be included in this tonnage.

Neither shall vessels of war which have suffered damage during their passage through the Straits be included in this tonnage ; such vessels, while undergoing repair, shall be subject to any special provisions relating to security laid down by Turkey.

Article 15.

Vessels of war in transit through the Straits shall in no circumstances make use of any aircraft which they may be carrying.

Article 16.

Vessels of war in transit through the Straits shall not, except in the event of damage or peril of the sea, remain therein longer than is necessary for them to effect the passage.

Article 17.

Nothing in the provisions of the preceding Articles shall prevent a naval force of any tonnage or composition from paying a courtesy visit of limited duration to a port in the Straits, at the invitation of the Turkish Government. Any such force must leave the Straits by the same route as that by which it entered, unless it fulfils the conditions required for passage in transit through the Straits as laid down by Articles 10, 14 and 18.

Article 18.

(1) The aggregate tonnage which non-Black Sea Powers may have in that sea in time of peace shall be limited as follows :

(a) Except as provided in paragraph *(b)* below, the aggregate tonnage of the said Powers shall not exceed 30,000 tons ;

(b) If at any time the tonnage of the strongest fleet in the Black Sea shall exceed by at least 10,000 tons the tonnage of the strongest fleet in that sea at the date of the

signature of the present Convention, the aggregate tonnage of 30,000 tons mentioned in paragraph *(a)* shall be increased by the same amount, up to a maximum of 45,000 tons. For this purpose, each Black Sea Power shall, in conformity with Annex IV to the present Convention, inform the Turkish Government, on the 1st January and the 1st July of each year, of the total tonnage of its fleet in the Black Sea ; and the Turkish Government shall transmit this information to the other High Contracting Parties and to the Secretary-General of the League of Nations ;

(c) The tonnage which any one non-Black Sea Power may have in the Black Sea shall be limited to two-thirds of the aggregate tonnage provided for in paragraphs *(a)* and *(b)* above ;

(d) In the event, however, of one or more non-Black Sea Powers desiring to send naval forces into the Black Sea, for a humanitarian purpose, the said forces, which shall in no case exceed 8,000 tons altogether, shall be allowed to enter the Black Sea without having to give the notification provided for in Article 13 of the present Convention, provided an authorisation is obtained from the Turkish Government in the following circumstances : if the figure of the aggregate tonnage specified in paragraphs *(a)* and *(b)* above has not been reached and will not be exceeded by the despatch of the forces which it is desired to send, the Turkish Government shall grant the said authorisation within the shortest possible time after receiving the request which has been addressed to it ; if the said figure has already been reached or if the despatch of the forces which it is desired to send will cause it to be exceeded, the Turkish Government will immediately inform the other Black Sea Powers of the request for authorisation, and if the said Powers make no objection within twenty-four hours of having received this information, the Turkish Government shall, within forty-eight hours at the latest, inform the interested Powers of the reply which it has decided to make to their request.

Any further entry into the Black Sea of naval forces of non-Black Sea Powers shall only be effected within the available limits of the aggregate tonnage provided for in paragraphs *(a)* and *(b)* above.

(2) Vessels of war belonging to non-Black Sea Powers shall not remain in the Black Sea more than twenty-one days, whatever be the object of their presence there.

Article 19.

In time of war, Turkey not being belligerent, warships shall enjoy complete freedom of transit and navigation through the Straits under the same conditions as those laid down in Articles 10 to 18.

Vessels of war belonging to belligerent Powers shall not, however, pass through the Straits except in cases arising out of the application of Article 25 of the present Convention, and in cases of assistance rendered to a State victim of aggression in virtue of a treaty of mutual assistance binding Turkey, concluded within the framework of the Covenant of the League of Nations, and registered and published in accordance with the provisions of Article 18 of the Covenant.

In the exceptional cases provided for in the preceding paragraph, the limitations laid down in Articles 10 to 18 of the present Convention shall not be applicable.

Notwithstanding the prohibition of passage laid down in paragraph 2 above, vessels of war belonging to belligerent Powers, whether they are Black Sea Powers or not, which have become separated from their bases, may return thereto.

Vessels of war belonging to belligerent Powers shall not make any capture, exercise the right of visit and search, or carry out any hostile act in the Straits.

Article 20.

In time of war, Turkey being belligerent, the provisions of Articles 10 to 18 shall not be applicable ; the passage of warships shall be left entirely to the discretion of the Turkish Government.

Article 21.

Should Turkey consider herself to be threatened with imminent danger of war she shall have the right to apply the provisions of Article 20 of the present Convention.

Vessels which have passed through the Straits before Turkey has made use of the powers conferred upon her by the preceding paragraph, and which thus find themselves separated from their bases, may return thereto. It is, however, understood that Turkey may deny this right to vessels of war belonging to the State whose attitude has given rise to the application of the present Article.

Should the Turkish Government make use of the powers conferred by the first paragraph of the present Article, a notification to that effect shall be addressed to the High Contracting Parties and to the Secretary-General of the League of Nations.

If the Council of the League of Nations decide by a majority of two-thirds that the measures thus taken by Turkey are not justified, and if such should also be the opinion of the majority of the High Contracting Parties signatories to the present Convention, the Turkish Government undertakes to discontinue the measures in question as also any measures which may have been taken under Article 6 of the present Convention.

Article 22.

Vessels of war which have on board cases of plague, cholera, yellow fever, exanthematic typhus or smallpox or which have had such cases on board within the last seven days and vessels of war which have left an infected port within less than five times twenty-four hours must pass through the Straits in quarantine and apply by the means on board such prophylactic measures as are necessary in order to prevent any possibility of the Straits being infected.

SECTION III.

Aircraft.

Article 23.

In order to assure the passage of civil aircraft between the Mediterranean and the Black Sea, the Turkish Government will indicate the air routes available for this purpose, outside the forbidden zones which may be established in the Straits. Civil aircraft may use these routes provided that they give the Turkish Government, as regards occasional flights, a notification of three days, and as regards flights on regular services, a general notification of the dates of passage.

The Turkish Government moreover undertake, notwithstanding any remilitarisation of the Straits, to furnish the necessary facilities for the safe passage of civil aircraft authorised under the air regulations in force in Turkey to fly across Turkish territory between Europe and Asia. The route which is to be followed in the Straits zone by aircraft which have obtained an authorisation shall be indicated from time to time.

SECTION IV.

General Provisions.

Article 24.

The functions of the International Commission set up under the Convention relating to the régime of the Straits of the 24th July, 1923, are hereby transferred to the Turkish Government.

The Turkish Government undertake to collect statistics and to furnish information concerning the application of Articles 11, 12, 14 and 18 of the present Convention.

They will supervise the execution of all the provisions of the present Convention relating to the passage of vessels of war through the Straits.

As soon as they have been notified of the intended passage through the Straits of a foreign naval force the Turkish Government shall inform the representatives at Angora of the High Contracting Parties of the composition of that force, its tonnage, the date fixed for its entry into the Straits, and, if necessary, the probable date of its return.

The Turkish Government shall address to the Secretary-General of the League of Nations and to the High Contracting Parties an annual report giving details regarding the movements of foreign vessels of war through the Straits and furnishing all information which may be of service to commerce and navigation, both by sea and by air, for which provision is made in the present Convention.

Article 25.

Nothing in the present Convention shall prejudice the rights and obligations of Turkey, or of any of the other High Contracting Parties members of the League of Nations, arising out of the Covenant of the League of Nations.

SECTION V.

Final Provisions.

Article 26.

The present Convention shall be ratified as soon as possible.

The ratifications shall be deposited in the archives of the Government of the French Republic in Paris.

The Japanese Government shall be entitled to inform the Government of the French Republic through their diplomatic representative in Paris that the ratification has been given, and in that case they shall transmit the instrument of ratification as soon as possible.

A *procès-verbal* of the deposit of ratifications shall be drawn up as soon as six instruments of ratification, including that of Turkey, shall have been deposited. For this purpose the notification provided for in the preceding paragraph shall be taken as the equivalent of the deposit of an instrument of ratification.

The present Convention shall come into force on the date of the said *procès-verbal*.

The French Government will transmit to all the High Contracting Parties an authentic copy of the *procès-verbal* provided for in the preceding paragraph and of the *procès-verbaux* of the deposit of any subsequent ratifications.

Article 27.

The present Convention shall, as from the date of its entry into force, be open to accession by any Power signatory to the Treaty of Peace at Lausanne signed on the 24th July, 1923.

Each accession shall be notified, through the diplomatic channel, to the Government of the French Republic, and by the latter to all the High Contracting Parties.

Accessions shall come into force as from the date of notification to the French Government.

Article 28.

The present Convention shall remain in force for twenty years from the date of its entry into force.

The principle of freedom of transit and navigation affirmed in Article 1 of the present Convention shall however continue without limit of time.

If, two years prior to the expiry of the said period of twenty years, no High Contracting Party shall have given notice of denunciation to the French Government the present Convention shall continue in force until two years after such notice shall have been given. Any such notice shall be communicated by the French Government to the High Contracting Parties.

In the event of the present Convention being denounced in accordance with the provisions of the present Article, the High Contracting Parties agree to be represented at a conference for the purpose of concluding a new Convention.

Article 29.

At the expiry of each period of five years from the date of the entry into force of the present Convention each of the High Contracting Parties shall be entitled to initiate a proposal for amending one or more of the provisions of the present Convention.

To be valid, any request for revision formulated by one of the High Contracting Parties must be supported, in the case of modifications to Articles 14 or 18, by one other High Contracting Party, and, in the case of modifications to any other Article, by two other High Contracting Parties.

Any request for revision thus supported must be notified to all the High Contracting Parties three months prior to the expiry of the current period of five years. This notification shall contain details of the proposed amendments and the reasons which have given rise to them.

Should it be found impossible to reach an agreement on these proposals through the diplomatic channel, the High Contracting Parties agree to be represented at a conference to be summoned for this purpose.

Such a conference may only take decisions by a unanimous vote, except as regards cases of revision involving Articles 14 and 18, for which a majority of three-quarters of the High Contracting Parties shall be sufficient.

The said majority shall include three-quarters of the High Contracting Parties which are Black Sea Powers, including Turkey.

In witness whereof, the above-mentioned Plenipotentiaries have signed the present Convention.

Done at Montreux the 20th July, 1936, in eleven copies, of which the first copy, to which the seals of the Plenipotentiaries have been affixed, will be deposited in the archives of the Government of the French Republic and of which the remaining copies have been transmitted to the signatory Powers.

(L. S.) N. P. Nicolaev.
(L. S.) Pierre Neĭcov.
(L. S.) J. Paul-Boncour.
(L. S.) H. Ponsot.
(L. S.) Stanley.
(L. S.) S. M. Bruce.
(L. S.) N. Politis.
(L. S.) Raoul Bibica Rosetti.

The undersigned, Plenipotentiaries of Japan, declare, in the name of their Government, that the provisions of the present Convention do not in any sense modify the position of Japan as a State not a member of the League of Nations, whether in relation to the Covenant of the League of Nations or in regard to treaties of mutual assistance concluded within the framework of the said Covenant, and that in particular Japan reserves full liberty of interpretation as regards the provisions of Articles 19 and 25 so far as they concern that Covenant and those treaties.

(L. S.) N. SATO.
(L. S.) Massa-aki HOTTA.

(L. S.) N. TITULESCO.
(L. S.) Cons. CONTZESCO.
(L. S.) V. V. PELLA.
(L. S.) Dr. R. ARAS.
(L. S.) Suad DAVAZ.
(L. S.) N. MENEMENCIOGLU.
(L. S.) Asim GÜNDÜZ.
(L. S.) N. SADAK.
(L. S.) Maxime LITVINOFF.
(L. S.) Dr. I. V. SOUBBOTITCH.

ANNEX I.

The taxes and charges which may be levied in accordance with Article 2 of the present Convention shall be those set forth in the following table. Any reductions in these taxes or charges which the Turkish Government may grant shall be applied without any distinction based on the flag of the vessel :

Nature of service rendered	Amount of tax or charge to be levied on each ton of net register tonnage *Francs gold* [1]
(a) Sanitary Control Stations.	0.075
(b) Lighthouses, Light and Channel Buoys :	
Up to 800 tons	0.42
Above 800 tons	0.21
(c) Life Saving Services, including Life-boats, Rocket Stations, Fog Sirens, Direction-finding Stations, and any Light Buoys not comprised in *(b)* above, or other similar installations .	0.10

2. The taxes and charges set forth in the table attached to paragraph 1 of the present Annex shall apply in respect of a return voyage through the Straits (that is to say, a voyage from the Ægean Sea to the Black Sea and return back to the Ægean Sea or else a voyage through the Straits from the Black Sea to the Ægean Sea followed by a return voyage into the Black Sea) ; if, however, a merchant vessel re-enters the Straits with the object of returning into the Ægean Sea or to the Black Sea, as the case may be, more than six months after the date of entry into the Straits for the outward voyage, such vessel may be called upon to pay these taxes and charges a second time, provided no distinction is made based on the flag of the vessel.

[1] 100 piastres at present equals 2.5 francs gold (approx.).

3. If, on the outward voyage, a merchant vessel declares an intention of not returning, it shall only be obliged as regards the taxes and charges provided for in paragraphs *(b)* and *(c)* of the first paragraph of the present Annex, to pay half the tariff indicated.

4. The taxes and charges set forth in the table attached to the first paragraph of the present Annex, which are not to be greater than is necessary to cover the cost of maintaining the services concerned and of allowing for the creation of a reasonable reserve fund or working balance, shall not be increased or added to except in accordance with the provisions of Article 29 of the present Convention. They shall be payable in gold francs or in Turkish currency at the rate of exchange prevailing on the date of payment.

5. Merchant vessels may be required to pay taxes and charges for optional services, such as pilotage and towage, when any such service shall have been duly rendered by the Turkish authorities at the request of the agent or master of any such vessel. The Turkish Government will publish from time to time the tariff of the taxes and charges to be levied for such optional services.

6. These tariffs shall not be increased in cases in the event of the said services being made obligatory by reason of the application of Article 5.

ANNEX II.[1]

A. Standard Displacement.

(1) The standard displacement of a surface vessel is the displacement of the vessel, complete, fully manned, engined, and equipped ready for sea, including all armament and ammunition, equipment, outfit, provisions and fresh water for crew, miscellaneous stores and implements of every description that are intended to be carried in war, but without fuel or reserve feed water on board.

(2) The standard displacement of a submarine is the surface displacement of the vessel complete (exclusive of the water in non-watertight structure), fully manned, engined and equipped ready for sea, including all armament and ammunition, equipment, outfit, provisions for crew, miscellaneous stores and implements of every description that are intended to be carried in war, but without fuel, lubricating oil, fresh water or ballast water of any kind on board.

(3) The word " ton " except in the expression " metric tons " denotes the ton of 2,240 lb (1,016 kilos).

B. Categories.

(1) *Capital Ships* are surface vessels of war belonging to one of the two following sub-categories:

(a) Surface vessels of war, other than aircraft-carriers, auxiliary vessels, or capital ships of sub-category *(b)*, the standard displacement of which exceeds 10,000 tons (10,160 metric tons) or which carry a gun with a calibre exceeding 8 in. (203 mm.) ;

(b) Surface vessels of war, other than aircraft-carriers, the standard displacement of which does not esceed 8,000 tons (8,128 metric tons) and which carry a gun with a calibre exceeding 8 in. (203 mm.).

(2) *Aircraft-Carriers* are surface vessels of war, whatever their displacement, designed or adapted primarily for the purpose of carrying and operating aircraft at sea. The fitting of a landing-on or flying-off deck on any vessel of war, provided such vessel has not been designed or adapted primarily for the purpose of carrying and operating aircraft at sea, shall not cause any vessel so fitted to be classified in the category of aircraft-carriers.

[1] The wording of the present Annex is taken from the London Naval Treaty of March 25th, 1936.

The category of aircraft-carriers is divided into two sub-categories as follows :

(a) Vessels fitted with a flight deck, from which aircraft can take off, or on which aircraft can land from the air ;

(b) Vessels not fitted with a flight deck as described in *(a)* above.

(3) *Light Surface Vessels* are surface vessels of war other than aircraft-carriers, minor war vessels or auxiliary vessels, the standard displacement of which exceeds 100 tons (102 metric tons) and does not exceed 10,000 tons (10,160 metric tons), and which do not carry a gun with a calibre exceeding 8 in. (203 mm.).

The category of light surface vessels is divided into three sub-categories as follows :

(a) Vessels which carry a gun with a calibre exceeding 6.1 in. (155 mm.) ;

(b) Vessels which do not carry a gun with a calibre exceeding 6.1 in. (155 mm.) and the standard displacement of which exceeds 3,000 tons (3,048 metric tons) ;

(c) Vessels which do not carry a gun with a calibre exceeding 6.1 in. (155 mm.) and the standard displacement of which does not exceed 3,000 tons (3,048 metric tons).

(4) *Submarines* are all vessels designed to operate below the surface of the sea.

(5) *Minor War Vessels* are surface vessels of war, other than auxiliary vessels, the standard displacement of which exceeds 100 tons (102 metric tons) and does not exceed 2,000 tons (2,032 metric tons), provided they have none of the following characteristics :

(a) Mount a gun with a calibre exceeding 6.1 in. (155 mm.) ;
(b) Are designed or fitted to launch torpedoes ;
(c) Are designed for a speed greater than twenty knots.

(6) *Auxiliary Vessels* are naval surface vessels the standard displacement of which exceeds 100 tons (102 metric tons), which are normally employed on fleet duties or as troop transports, or in some other way than as fighting ships, and which are not specifically built as fighting ships, provided they have none of the following characteristics :

(a) Mount a gun with a calibre exceeding 6.1 in. (155 mm.) ;
(b) Mount more than eight guns with a calibre exceeding 3 in. (76 mm.) ;
(c) Are designed or fitted to launch torpedoes ;
(d) Are designed for protection by armour plate ;
(e) Are designed for a speed greater than twenty-eight knots ;
(f) Are designed or adapted primarily for operating aircraft at sea ;

(g) Mount more than two aircraft-launching apparatus.

C. OVER-AGE.

Vessels of the following categories and sub-categories shall be deemed to be " over-age " when the undermentioned number of years have elapsed since completion :

(a) Capital ships . . . . 26 years ;
(b) Aircraft-carriers . . . . 20 years ;
(c) Light surface vessels, sub-categories *(a)* and *(b)* :

(i) If laid down before 1st January, 1920 . . . . 16 years ;
(ii) If laid down after 31st December, 1919 . . . . 20 years ;

(d) Light surface vessels, sub-category *(c)* . . . . 16 years ;
(e) Submarines . . . . 13 years ;

ANNEX III.

It is agreed that, of the three over-age training ships, as indicated below, belonging to the Japanese Fleet, two units may be allowed to visit ports in the Straits at the same time.

The aggregate tonnage of these two vessels shall in this case be considered as being equivalent to 15,000 tons.

	Date when laid down	Date of entry into service	Standard displacement (tons)	Armaments
Asama	20–X–1896	18–III–1899	9,240	IV × 200 mm. XII × 150 mm.
Yakumo	1–IX–1898	20–VI–1900	9,010	IV × 200 mm. XII × 150 mm.
Iwate.	11–XI–1898	18–III–1901	9,180	IV × 200 mm. XIV × 150 mm.

ANNEX IV.

1. The categories and sub-categories of vessels to be included in the calculation of the total tonnage of the Black Sea Powers provided for in Article 18 of the present Convention are the following :

Capital Ships :
- Sub-category *(a)* ;
- Sub-category *(b)*.

Aircraft-Carriers :
- Sub-category *(a)* ;
- Sub-category *(b)*.

Light Surface Vessels :
- Sub-category *(a)* ;
- Sub-category *(b)* ;
- Sub-category *(c)*.

Submarines :
- As defined in Annex II to the present Convention.

The displacement which is to be taken into consideration in the calculation of the total tonnage is the standard displacement as defined in Annex II. Only those vessels shall be taken into consideration which are not over-age according to the definition contained in the said Annex.

2. The notification provided for in Article 18, paragraph *(b)*, shall also include the total tonnage of vessels belonging to the categories and sub-categories mentioned in paragraph 1 of the present Annex.

PROTOCOL.

At the moment of signing the Convention bearing this day's date, the undersigned Plenipotentiaries declare for their respective Governments that they accept the following provisions:

(1) Turkey may immediately remilitarise the zone of the Straits as defined in the Preamble to the said Convention.

(2) As from the 15th August, 1936, the Turkish Government shall provisionally apply the régime specified in the said Convention.

(3) The present Protocol shall enter into force as from this day's date.

Done at Montreux, the 20th July, 1936.

N. P. NICOLAEV.
Pierre NEÏCOV.
J. PAUL-BONCOUR.
H. PONSOT.
STANLEY.
S. M. BRUCE.
N. POLITIS.
Raoul BIBICA ROSETTI.
N. SATO. *(ad referendum).*
Massa-aki HOTTA *(ad referendum).*
N. TITULESCO.
Cons. CONTZESCO.
V. V. PELLA.
Dr. R. ARAS.
Suad DAVAZ.
N. MENEMENCIOGLU.
Asim GÜNDÜZ.
N. SADAK.
Maxime LITVINOFF.
Dr. I. V. SOUBBOTITCH.

COMMUNIST CHINESE REGULATIONS ON SHIPPING IN CHIUNGCHOW STRAIT*

Order of the State Council of the Chinese People's Republic
(adopted at the 145th plenary session June 5, 1964;
promulgated and put into effect by the
Premier of the State Council, Chou En-lai, June 28, 1964.)

Regulations governing foreign nonmilitary vessels passing through the Chiungchow Strait:

Article 1--According to the "CPR Government statement on territorial waters" Chiungchow Strait is China's inner sea. All foreign military vessels are not allowed to pass through it and all foreign nonmilitary vessels must request permission to pass through it in accordance with the regulations.

Article 2--For the convenience of exercising control over the Chiungchow Strait, the "Chiungchow Strait Administration of the CPR" is established. (A simplified name to be used henceforth will be Chiungchow Strait Administration).**

Article 3--The district under the control of the Chiungchow Strait Administration (a simplified name to be used henceforth will be administrative district) comprises waters west of the east line drawn between the Mulantao (2651 2936 7333) light post (about 20 degrees, 9 minutes, 37 seconds north latitude and 110 degrees, 41 minutes east longitude) and Shengkouhousha (3932 3699 0709 3097) light post (about 20 degrees, 26 minutes, north latitude and 110 degrees 30 minutes 22 seconds east longitude), and east of the west line drawn between the Chiaoweichiao (3330 1442 6037) light post (about 20 degrees, 13 minutes, 30 seconds north latitude and 109 degrees, 55 minutes, 30 seconds east longitude) and the Linkaochiao (5259 7559 6037) light post (about 20 degrees zero minutes, 22 seconds north latitude and 109 degrees, 42 minutes, 6 seconds east longitude).

*(Reprinted from a translation of a Peking radio broadcast. Chiungchow Strait is the passage between the Luichow Peninsula on the mainland of China and Hainan Island, leading from the South China Sea to the Gulf of Tonkin.)

**(All parenthetical phrases are in the original text.)

Article 4--The following procedures must be followed by any foreign nonmilitary vessel that wishes to pass through the Chiungchow Strait:

1--Forty-eight hours prior to the vessel's entry into the administrative district or prior to the vessel's departure from a port, it must cable the Chiungchow Strait Administration informing the latter in detail about its name, nationality, tonnage, speed, color, and smokestack marks as well as the date and the name of the place of embarkation and disembarkation, and requesting permission to pass through the strait.
2--After receiving approval to pass through the strait, the vessel should report to the Chiungchow Strait Administration, 24 hours before it enters the administrative district or two hours after it sails from a port, the estimated time of entry into the administrative district. All cables requesting and granting permission for passing through the strait will be relayed by the Haikou Branch of the China Foreign Shipping Agency Company.

Article 5--The Chiungchow Strait Administration reserves the right to revoke its approval granted to a foreign nonmilitary vessel to pass through the strait and can forbid it to pass through any time it deems necessary.

Article 6--All foreign nonmilitary vessels can only pass through the administrative district in daytime. They must enter the administrative district after sunrise and leave the district before sunset. The Chiungchow Strait Administration will make concrete time allotments for the vessels' entry into and departure from the strait in accordance with the speed of the vessels that request permission to pass through the strait.

Article 7--All foreign nonmilitary vessels must use the middle waterway while passing through the Chiungchow Strait unless specially permitted by the Chiungchow Strait Administration.

Article 8--When passing through the administrative district, all foreign nonmilitary vessels can only cruise in the following designated area which comprises waters north of the line drawn from a point four nautical miles from the Mulantao light post on the east line to a point four nautical miles from the Linkaochiao light post on the west line, and south of the line drawn from a point six nautical miles from the Mulantao light post on the east line through a point four nautical miles due south of the Chiaoweichiao light post to a point 14 nautical miles from the Linkaochiao light post on the west line.

Article 9--All foreign nonmilitary vessels must pass through the Chiungchow Strait according to the time and area designated. Whenever signals from the shore or other vessels are noticed, the vessels that are entering or passing through the strait should answer immediately and unconditionally comply with directions given by the signals. The vessels will bear all the consequences themselves if they do not comply with the above-mentioned regulation.

Article 10--When passing through the Chiungchow Strait, nonmilitary vessels are not allowed to use radar. If unfavorable navigational conditions such as fog, storm, or poor visibility call for the use of radar the vessels must report to the Chiungchow Strait Administration, stating the reason as well as position, speed, and so on. Radar can only be used when permission is granted. In case of emergency and if the safety of the vessels is jeopardized, the vessels should request approval from the administration while using radar and submit a detail report afterwards to the administration on the situation and the total time during which radar is used.

Article 11--When passing through the Chiungchow Strait, foreign nonmilitary vessels are not allowed to take pictures, to make surveys, or to carry out activities against the laws of the CPR.

Article 12--The following actions will be taken if foreign nonmilitary vessels violate the regulations:

1--If the vessels have not yet entered the administrative district they will be ordered to stop entering the district, to turn back, or to make a detour around Hainan Island, or they can just wait until all procedures are followed and an approval is given to pass the strait.

2--If they have already entered the administrative district, they will be ordered to stop navigation and be subject to inspection at Haikou Port. Proper disciplinary actions will be taken, depending upon the results of the inspection. According to the actual situation, the vessels will then either be allowed to pass through the administrative district or to turn back from it until they are out of the strait under escort.

UNITED NATIONS
GENERAL ASSEMBLY

Distr.
LIMITED
A/AC.138/SC.II/L.4
30 July 1971
ORIGINAL: ENGLISH

COMMITTEE ON THE PEACEFUL USES OF THE SEA-BED AND THE OCEAN FLOOR BEYOND THE LIMITS OF NATIONAL JURISDICTION

Sub-Committee II

Draft Articles on the Breadth of the Territorial Sea, Straits, and Fisheries Submitted by the United States *

ARTICLE I

1. Each State shall have the right, subject to the provisions of Article II, to establish the breadth of its territorial sea within limits of no more than 12 nautical miles, measured in accordance with the provisions of the 1958 Geneva Convention on the Territorial Sea and Contiguous Zone.

2. In instances where the breadth of the territorial sea of a State is less than 12 nautical miles, such State may establish a fisheries zone contiguous to its territorial sea provided, however, that the total breadth of the territorial sea and fisheries zone shall not exceed 12 nautical miles. Such State may exercise within such a zone the same rights in respect to fisheries as it has in its territorial sea.

ARTICLE II

1. In straits used for international navigation between one part of the high seas and another part of the high seas or the territorial sea of a foreign State, all ships and aircraft in transit shall enjoy the same freedom of navigation and overflight, for the purpose of transit through and over such straits, as they have on the high seas.

---

* Draft Article III on Fisheries is omitted.

Coastal States may designate corridors suitable for transit by all ships and aircraft through and over such straits. In the case of straits where particular channels of navigation are customarily employed by ships in transit, the corridors, so far as ships are concerned, shall include such channels.

2. The provisions of this Article shall not affect conventions or other international agreements already in force specifically relating to particular straits.

UNITED NATIONS
GENERAL ASSEMBLY

A/AC.138/SC.II/L.7
25 July 1972

COMMITTEE ON THE PEACEFUL USES OF THE SEA-BED AND THE OCEAN FLOOR BEYOND THE LIMITS OF NATIONAL JURISDICTION
SUB-COMMITTEE II

UNION OF SOVIET SOCIALIST REPUBLICS:
Draft articles on straits used for international navigation

Article . . .

1. In straits used for international navigation between one part of the high seas and another part of the high seas, all ships in transit shall enjoy the same freedom of navigation, for the purpose of transit through such straits, as they have on the high seas. Coastal States may, in the case of narrow straits, designate corridors suitable for transit by all ships through such straits. In the case of straits where particular channels of navigation are customarily employed by ships in transit, the corridors shall include such channels.

2. The freedom of navigation provided for in this article, for the purpose of transit through the straits, shall be exercised in accordance with the following rules:

(a) Ships in transit through the straits shall take all necessary steps to avoid causing any threat to the security of the coastal States of the straits, and in particular warships in transit through such straits shall not in the area of the straits engage in any exercises or gunfire, use weapons of any kind, launch their aircraft, undertake hydrographical work or engage in other acts of a nature unrelated to the transit;

(b) Ships in transit through the straits shall strictly comply with the international rules concerning the prevention of collisions between ships or other accidents and, in straits where separate lanes are designated for the passage of ships in each direction, shall not cross the dividing line between the lanes. They shall also avoid making unnecessary manoeuvres;

(c) Ships in transit through the straits shall take precautionary measures to avoid causing pollution of the waters and coasts of the straits, or any other kind of damage to the coastal States of the straits;

(d) Liability for any damage which may be caused to the coastal States of the straits as a result of the transit of ships shall rest with the flag-State of the ship which has caused the damage or with juridical persons under its jurisdiction or acting on its behalf;

(e) No State shall be entitled to interrupt or stop the transit of ships through the straits, or engage therein in any acts which interfere with the transit of ships, or require ships in transit to stop or communicate information of any kind.

3. The provisions of this article:

(a) shall apply to straits lying within the territorial waters of one or more coastal States;

(b) shall not affect the sovereign rights of the coastal States with respect to the surface, the sea-bed and the living and mineral resources of the straits;

(c) shall not affect the legal régime of straits through which transit is regulated by international agreements specifically relating to such straits.

<u>Article</u> . . .

1. In the case of straits over which the airspace is used for flights by foreign aircraft between one part of the high seas and another part of the high seas, all aircraft shall enjoy the same freedom of overflight over such straits as they have in the airspace over the high seas. Coastal states may designate special air corridors suitable for overflight by aircraft, and special altitudes for aircraft flying in different directions, and may establish particulars for radio-communication with them.

2. The freedom of overflight by aircraft over the straits, as provided for in this article, shall be exercised in accordance with the following rules:

(a) Overflying aircraft shall take the necessary steps to keep within the boundaries of the corridors and at the altitudes designated by the coastal States for flights over the straits, and to avoid overflying the territory of a coastal State, unless such overflight is provided for by the delimitation of the corridor designated by the coastal State;

(b) Overflying aircraft shall take all necessary steps to avoid causing any threat to the security of the coastal States, and in particular military aircraft shall not in the area of the straits engage in any exercises or gunfire, use weapons of any kind, take aerial photographs, circle or dive down towards ships, take on fuel or engage in other acts of a nature unrelated to the overflight;

(c) Liability for any damage which may be caused to the coastal States as a result of the overflight of aircraft over the straits shall rest with the State to which the aircraft that has caused the damage belongs, or with Juridical persons under its jurisdiction or acting on its behalf;

(d) No State shall be entitled to interrupt or stop the overflight of foreign aircraft, in accordance with this article, in the airspace over the straits.

3. The provisions of this article:

(a) shall apply to flights by aircraft over straits lying within the territorial waters of one or more coastal States;

(b) shall not affect the legal régime of straits over which overflight is regulated by international agreements specifically relating to such straits.

MULTILATERAL

International Convention for the Prevention of Pollution of the Sea by Oil, 1954

Opened for signature at London May 12, 1954;
Ratification advised by the Senate of the United States of America, subject to an understanding, reservations, and a recommendation, May 16, 1961;
Ratified, and acceptance declared, by the President of the United States of America, subject to the said understanding, reservations, and recommendation, May 29, 1961;
Acceptance deposited with the Intergovernmental Maritime Consultative Organization, subject to the said understanding, reservations, and recommendation, September 8, 1961;
Proclaimed by the President of the United States of America December 8, 1961;
Entered into force for the United States of America December 8, 1961.

THE INTERNATIONAL CONVENTION FOR THE PREVENTION OF POLLUTION OF THE SEA BY OIL, 1954

The Governments represented at the International Conference on Pollution of the Sea by Oil held in London from 26th April, 1954, to 12th May, 1954,

Desiring to take action by common agreement to prevent pollution of the sea by oil discharged from ships, and considering that this end may best be achieved by the conclusion of a Convention,

Have accordingly appointed the undersigned plenipotentiaries, who, having communicated their full powers, found in good and due form, have agreed as follows:-

Article I

(1) For the purposes of the present Convention, the following expressions shall (unless the context otherwise requires) have the meanings hereby respectively assigned to them, that is to say:-

"The Bureau" has the meaning assigned to it by Article XXI:
"Discharge" in relation to oil or to an oily mixture means any discharge or escape howsoever caused;

"Heavy diesel oil" means marine diesel oil, other than those distillates of which more than 50 per cent. by volume distils at a temperature not exceeding 340° C. when tested by A.S.T.M. Standard Method D.158/53;
"Mile" means a nautical mile of 6080 feet or 1852 metres;
"Oil" means crude oil, fuel oil, heavy diesel oil and lubricating oil, and "oily" shall be construed accordingly.

(2) For the purposes of the present Convention the territories of a Contracting Government mean the territory of the country of which it is the Government and any other territory for the international relations of which the Government is responsible and to which the Convention shall have been extended under Article XVIII.

Article II

The present Convention shall apply to sea-going ships registered in any of the territories of a Contracting Government, except

(i) ships for the time being used as naval auxiliaries;

(ii) ships of under 500 tons gross tonnage;

(iii) ships for the time being engaged in the whaling industry;

(iv) ships for the time being navigating the Great Lakes of North America and their connecting and tributary waters as far east as the lower exit of the Lachine Canal at Montreal in the Province of Quebec, Canada.

Article III

(1) Subject to the provisions of Articles IV and V, the discharge from any tanker, being a ship to which the Convention applies, within any of the prohibited zones referred to in Annex A to the Convention in relation to tankers of-

(a) oil;

(b) any oily mixture the oil in which fouls the surface of the sea, shall be prohibited.

For the purposes of this paragraph the oil in an oily mixture of less than 100 parts of oil in 1,000,000 parts of the mixture shall not be deemed to foul the surface of the sea.

(2) Subject to the provisions of Articles IV and V, any discharge into the sea from a ship, being a ship to which the Convention applies and not being a tanker, of oily ballast water or tank washings shall be made as far as practicable from land. As from a date three years after the date on which the Convention comes into force, paragraph (1) of this Article shall apply to ships other than tankers as it applies to tankers, except that:-

(a) the prohibited zones in relation to ships other than tankers shall be those referred to as such in Annex A to the Convention; and

(b) the discharge of oil or of an oily mixture from such a ship shall not be prohibited when the ship is proceeding to a port not provided with such reception facilities as are referred to in Article VIII.

(3) Any contravention of paragraphs (1) and (2) of this Article shall be an offence punishable under the laws of the territory in which the ship is registered.

Article IV

(1) Article III shall not apply to:-

(a) the discharge of oil or of an oily mixture from a ship for the purpose of securing the safety of the ship, preventing damage to the ship or cargo, or saving life at sea; or

(b) the escape of oil, or of an oily mixture, resulting from damage to the ship or unavoidable leakage, if all reasonable precautions have been taken after the occurrence of the damage or discovery of the leakage for the puspose of preventing or minimising the escape;

(c) the discharge of sediment:-

(i) which cannot be pumped from the cargo tanks of tankers by reason of its solidity; or

(ii) which is residue arising from the purification or clarification of oil fuel or lubricating oil, provided that such discharge is made as far from land as is practicable.

(2) In the event of such discharge or escape as is referred to in this Article a statement shall be made in the oil record book required by Article IX of the circumstances of and reason for the discharge.

Article V

Article III shall not apply to the discharge from the bilges of a ship:-

(a) of any oily mixture during the period of twelve months following the date on which the Convention comes into force in respect of the territory in which the ship is registered;

(b) after the expiration of such period, of an oily mixture containing no oil other than lubricating oil.

Article VI

The penalties which may be imposed in pursuance of Article III under the law of any of the territories of a Contracting Government in respect of the unlawful discharge from a ship of oil or of an oily mixture into waters outside the territorial waters of that territory shall not be less than the penalties which may be imposed under the law of that territory in respect of the unlawful discharge of oil or of an oily mixture from a ship into such territorial waters.

Article VII

As from a date twelve months after the present Convention comes into force in respect of any of the territories of a Contracting Government all ships registered in that territory shall be required to be so fitted as to prevent the escape of fuel oil or heavy diesel oil into bilges the contents of which are discharged into the sea without being passed through an oily-water separator.

Article VIII

As from a date three years after the present Convention comes into force in respect of any of the territories of a Contracting Government, that Government shall ensure the provision in each main port in that territory of facilities adequate for the reception, without causing undue delay to ships, of such residues from oily ballast water and tank washings as would remain for disposal by ships, other than tankers, using the port, if the water had been separated by the use of an oily-water separator, a settling tank or otherwise. Each Contracting Government shall from time to time determine which ports are the main ports in its territories for the purposes of this Article, and shall notify the Bureau in writing accordingly indicating whether adequate reception facilities have been installed.

Article IX

(1) There shall be carried in every ship to which the Convention applies an oil record book (whether as part of the ship's official logbook or otherwise) in the form specified in Annex B to the present Convention. The appropriate entries shall be made in that book, and each page of the book, including any statement under paragraph (2) of Article IV, shall be signed by the officer or officers in charge of the operations concerned and by the master of the ship. The written entries in the oil record book shall be in an official language of the territory in which the ship is registered, or in English or French.

(2) The competent authorities of any of the territories of a Contracting Government may inspect on board any such ship while within a port in that territory the oil record book required to be carried in the ship in compliance with the provisions of the Convention, and may make a true copy of any entry in that book and may require the master of the ship to certify that the copy is a true copy of such entry. Any copy so made which purports to have been certified by the master of the ship as a true copy of an entry in the ship's oil record book shall be made admissible in any judicial proceedings as evidence of the facts stated in the entry. Any action by the competent authorities under this paragraphy shall be taken as expeditiously as possible and the ship shall not be delayed.

Article X

(1) Any Contracting Government may furnish to the Contracting Government in the territory of which a ship is registered particulars in writing of evidence that any provision of the Convention has been contravened in respect of that ship, wheresoever the alleged contravention may have taken place. If it is practicable to do so, the competent authorities of the former Government shall notify the master of the ship of the alleged contravention.

(2) Upon receiving such particulars the latter Government shall investigate the matter, and may request the former Government to furnish further or better particulars of the alleged contravention. If the Government in the territory of

which the ship is registered is satisfied that sufficient evidence is available in the form required by law to enable proceedings against the owner or master of the ship to be taken in respect of the alleged contravention, it shall cause such proceedings to be taken as soon as possible, and shall inform the other Contracting Government and the Bureau of the result of such proceedings.

Article XI

Nothing in the present Convention shall be construed as derogating from the powers of any Contracting Government to take measures within its jurisdiction in respect of any matter to which the Convention relates or as extending the jurisdiction of any Contracting Government.

Article XII

Each Contracting Government shall send to the Bureau and to the appropriate organ of the United Nations:-

(a) the text of laws, decrees, orders and regulations in force in its territories which give effect to the present Convention;

(b) all official reports or summaries of official reports in so far as they show the results of the application of the provisions of the Convention, provided always that such reports or summaries are not, in the opinion of that Government, of a confidential nature.

Article XIII

Any dispute between Contracting Governments relating to the interpretation or application of the present Convention which cannot be settled by negotiation shall be referred at the request of either party to the International Court of Justice for decision unless the parties in dispute agree to submit it to arbitration.

Article XIV

(1) The present Convention shall remain open for signature for three months from this day's date and shall thereafter remain open for acceptance.

(2) Governments may become parties to the Convention by-

(i) signature without reservation as to acceptance;

(ii) signature subject to acceptance followed by acceptance; or

(iii) acceptance.

(3) Acceptance shall be effected by the deposit of an instrument of acceptance with the Bureau, which shall inform all Governments that have already signed or accepted the Convention of each signature and deposit of an acceptance and of the date of such signature or deposit.

Article XV

(1) The present Convention shall come into force twelve months after the date on which not less than ten Governments have become parties to the Convention, including five Governments of countries each with not less than 500,000 gross tons of tanker tonnage.

(2)--(a) For each Government which signs the Convention without reservation as to acceptance or accepts the Convention before the date on which the Convention comes into force in accordance with paragraph (1) of this Article it shall come into force on that date. For each Government which accepts the Convention on or after that date, it shall come into force three months after the date of the deposit of that Government's acceptance.

(b) The Bureau shall, as soon as possible, inform all Governments which have signed or accepted the Convention of the date on which it will come into force.

Article XVI

(1) Upon the request of any Contracting Government a proposed amendment of the present Convention shall be communicated by the Bureau to all Contracting Governments for consideration.

(2) Any amendment communicated to Contracting Governments for consideration under paragraph (1) of this Article shall be deemed to have been accepted by all Contracting Governments and shall come into force on the expiration of a period of six months after it has been so communicated, unless any one of the Contracting Governments shall have made a declaration not less than two months before the expiration of that period that it does not accept the amendment.

(3)-- (a) A conference of Contracting Governments to consider amendments of the Convention proposed by any Contracting Government shall be convened by the Bureau upon the request of one-third of the Contracting Governments.

(b) Every amendment adopted by such a conference by a two-thirds majority vote of the Contracting Governments represented shall be communicated by the Bureau to all Contracting Governments for their acceptance.

(4) Any amendment communicated to Contracting Governments for their acceptance under paragraph (3) of this Article shall come into force for all Contracting Governments, except those which before it comes into force make a declaration that they do not accept the amendment, twelve months after the date on which the amendment is accepted by two-thirds of the Contracting Governments.

(5) Any declaration under this Article shall be made by a notification in writing to the Bureau which shall notify all Contracting Governments of the receipt of the declaration.

(6) The Bureau shall inform all signatory and Contracting Governments of any amendments which come into force under this Article, together with the date on which such amendments shall come into force.

Article XVII

(1) The present Convention may be denounced by any Contracting Government at any time after the expiration of a period of five years from the date on which the Convention comes into force for that Government.

(2) Denunciation shall be effected by a notification in writing addressed to the Bureau, which shall notify all the Contracting Governments of any denunciation received and of the date of its receipt.

(3) A denunciation shall take effect twelve months, or such longer period as may be specified in the notification, after its receipt by the Bureau.

Article XVIII

(1) -- (a) Any Government may, at the time of signature or acceptance of the present Convention, or at any time thereafter, declare by notification in writing given to the Bureau that the Convention shall extend to any of the territories for whose international relations it is responsible.

(b) The Convention shall, from the date of the receipt of the notificaiton, or from such other date as may be specified in the notification, extend to the territories named therein.

(2) -- (a) Any Contracting Government which has made a declaration under paragraph (1) of this Article may, at any time after the expiration of a period of five years from the date on which the Convention has been so extended to any territory, give notification in writing to the Bureau, declaring that the Convention shall cease to extend to any such territory named in the notification.

(b) The Convention shall cease to extend to any territory mentioned in such notification twelve months, or such longer period as may be specified therein, after the date of receipt of the notification by the Bureau.

(3) The Bureau shall inform all Contracting Governments of the extension of the Convention to any territories under paragraph (1) of this Article, and of the termination of any such extension under paragraph (2) of this Article, stating in each case the date from which the Convention has been, or will cease to be, so extended.

Article XIX

(1) In case of war or other hostilities, a Contracting Government which considers that it is affected, whether as a belligerent or as a neutral, may suspend the operation of the whole or any part of the present Convention in respect of all or any of its territories. The suspending Government shall immediately give notice of any such suspension to the Bureau.

(2) The suspending Government may at any time terminate such suspension and shall in any event terminate it as soon as it ceases to be justified under paragraph (1) of this Article. Notice of such termination shall be given immediately to the Bureau by the Government concerned.

(3) The Bureau shall notify all Contracting Governments of any suspension or termination of suspension under this Article.

Article XX

As soon as the present Convention comes into force it shall be registered by the Bureau with the Secretary-General of the United Nations.

Article XXI

The duties of the Bureau shall be carried out by the Government of the United Kingdom of Great Britain and Northern Ireland unless and until the Inter-Governmental Maritime Consultive Organisation comes into being and takes over the duties assigned to it under the Convention signed at Geneva on the 6th day of March, 1948, (1) and thereafter the duties of the Bureau shall be carried out by the said Organisation.

[1] TIAS 4044; 9 UST 621.

In witness whereof the undersigned plenipotentiaries have signed the present Convention.

Done in London this twelfth day of May, 1954, in English and French, both texts being equally authoritative, in a single copy, which shall be deposited with the Bureau and of which the Bureau shall transmit certified copies to all signatory and Contracting Governments.

ANNEX [1]

The following are the amendments to the International Convention for the Prevention of Pollution of the Sea by Oil, 1954:

1. The existing text of Article I of the Convention is replaced by the following:

Article I

(1) For the purposes of the present Convention, the following expressions shall (unless the context otherwise requires) have the meanings hereby respectively assigned to them, that is to say:

'The Bureau' has the meaning assigned to it by Article XXI;

'Discharge' in relation to oil or to oily mixture means any discharge or escape howsoever caused;

'Heavy diesel oil' means marine diesel oil, other than those distillates of which more than 50 per cent by volume distils at a temperature not exceeding 340° C. when tested by A.S.T.M. Standard Method D.86/59;

'Mile' means a nautical mile of 6,080 feet or 1,852 metres;

'Oil' means crude oil, fuel oil, heavy diesel oil and lubricating oil, and 'oily' shall be construed accordingly;

'Oily mixture' means a mixture with an oil content of 100 parts or more in 1,000,000 parts of the mixture;

'Organization' means the Inter-Governmental Maritime Consultative Organization;

'Ship' means any sea-going vessel of any type whatsoever, including floating craft, whether self-propelled or towed by another vessel, making a sea voyage; and 'tanker' means a ship in which the greater part of the cargo space is constructed or adapted for the carriage of liquid cargoes in bulk and which is not, for the time being, carrying a cargo other than oil in that part of its cargo space.

(2) For the purposes of the present Convention, the territories of a Contracting Government mean the territory of the country of which it is the Government and any other territory for the international relations of which it is responsible and to which the Convention shall have been extended under Article XVIII.

---

1 The text of the amendments constituted the Annex to the Final Act of the Conference of Contracting Governments.

2. The existing text of Article II of the Convention is replaced by the following:

Article II

(1) The present Convention shall apply to ships registered in any of the territories of a Contracting Government and to unregistered ships having the nationality of a Contracting Party, except:

(*a*) tankers of under 150 tons gross tonnage and other ships of under 500 tons gross tonnage, provided that each Contracting Government will take the necessary steps, so far as is reasonable and practicable, to apply the requirements of the Convention to such ships also, having regard to their size, service and the type of fuel used for their propulsion;

(*b*) ships for the time being engaged in the whaling industry when actually employed on whaling operations;

(*c*) ships for the time being navigating the Great Lakes of North America and their connecting and tributary waters as far east as the lower exit of St. Lambert Lock at Montreal in the Province of Quebec, Canada;

(*d*) naval ships and ships for the time being used as naval auxiliaries.

(2) Each Contracting Government undertakes to adopt appropriate measures ensuring that requirements equivalent to those of the present Convention are, so far as is reasonable and practicable, applied to the ships referred to in subparagraph (*d*) of paragraph (1) of this Article.

3. The existing text of Article III of the Convention is replaced by the following:

Article III

Subject to the provisions of Articles IV and V:

(*a*) the discharge from a tanker to which the present Convention applies, within any of the prohibited zones referred to in Annex A to the Convention, of oil or oily mixture shall be prohibited;

(*b*) the discharge from a ship to which the present Convention applies, other than a tanker, of oil or oily mixture shall be made as far as practicable from land. As from a date three years after that on which the Convention comes into force for the relevant territory in respect of the ship in accordance with paragraph (1) of Article II, sub-paragraph (*a*) of this Article shall apply to a ship other than a tanker, except that the discharge of oil or of oily mixture from such a ship shall not be prohibited when the ship is proceeding to a port not provided with such facilities for ships other than tankers as are referred to in Article VIII;

(c) the discharge from a ship of 20,000 tons gross tonnage or more, to which the present Convention applies and for which the building contract is placed on or after the date on which this provision comes into force, of oil or oily mixture shall be prohibited. However, if, in the opinion of the master, special circumstances make it neither reasonable nor practicable to retain the oil or oily mixture on board, it may be discharged outside the prohibited zones referred to in Annex A to the Convention. The reasons for such discharge shall be reported to the Contracting Government of the relevant territory in respect of the ship in accordance with paragraph (1) of Article II. Full details of such discharges shall be reported to the Organization at least every twelve months by Contracting Governments.

4. The existing text of Article IV of the Convention is replaced by the following:

Article IV

Article III shall not apply to:

(a) the discharge of oil or of oily mixture from a ship for the purpose of securing the safety of a ship, preventing damage to a ship or cargo, or saving life at sea;

(b) the escape of oil or of oily mixture resulting from damage to a ship or unavoidable leakage, if all reasonable precautions have been taken after the occurrence of the damage or discovery of the leakage for the purpose of preventing or minimizing the escape;

(c) the discharge of residue arising from the purification or clarification of fuel oil or lubricating oil, provided that such discharge is made as far from land as is practicable.

5. The existing text of Article V of the Convention is replaced by the following:

Article V

Article III shall not apply to the discharge from the bilges of a ship:

(a) during the period of twelve months following the date on which the present Convention comes into force for the relevant territory in respect of the ship in accordance with paragraph (1) of Article II, of oily mixture;

(*b*) after the expiration of such period, of oily mixture containing no oil other than lubricating oil which has drained or leaked from machinery spaces.

6. The existing text of Article VI of the Convention is replaced by the following:

Article VI

(1) Any contravention of Articles III and IX shall be an offence punishable under the law of the relevant territory in respect of the ship in accordance with paragraph (1) of Article II.

(2) The penalties which may be imposed under the law of any of the territories of a Contracting Government in respect of the unlawful discharge from a ship of oil or oily mixture outside the territorial sea of that territory shall be adequate in severity to discourage any such unlawful discharge and shall not be less than the penalties which may be imposed under the law of that territory in respect of the same infringements within the territorial sea.

(3) Each Contracting Government shall report to the Organization the penalties actually imposed for each infringement.

7. The existing text of Article VII of the Convention is replaced by the following:

Article VII

(1) As from a date twelve months after the present Convention comes into force for the relevant territory in respect of a ship in accordance with paragraph (1) of Article II, such a ship shall be required to be so fitted as to prevent, so far as reasonable and practicable, the escape of fuel oil or heavy diesel oil into bilges, unless effective means are provided to ensure that the oil in the bilges is not discharged in contravention of this Convention.

(2) Carrying water ballast in oil fuel tanks shall be avoided if possible.

8. The existing text of Article VIII of the Convention is replaced by the following:

Article VIII

(1) Each Contracting Government shall take all appropriate steps to promote the provision of facilities as follows:

(*a*) according to the needs of ships using them, ports shall be provided with facilities adequate for the reception, without causing undue delay to ships, of such residues and oily mixtures as would remain for disposal from ships other than tankers if the bulk of the water had been separated from the mixture;

(*b*) oil loading terminals shall be provided with facilities adequate for the reception of such residues and oily mixtures as would similarly remain for disposal by tankers;

(*c*) ship repair ports shall be provided with facilities adequate for the reception of such residues and oily mixtures as would similarly remain for disposal by all ships entering for repairs.

(2) Each Contracting Government shall determine which are the ports and oil loading terminals in its territories suitable for the purposes of sub-paragraphs (a), (b) and (c) of paragraph (1) of this Article.

(3) As regards paragraph (1) of this Article, each Contracting Government shall report to the Organization, for transmission to the Contracting Government concerned, all cases where the facilities are alleged to be inadequate.

9. The existing text of Article IX of the Convention is replaced by the following:

Article IX

(1) Of the ships to which the present Convention applies, every ship which uses oil fuel and every tanker shall be provided with an oil record book, whether as part of the ship's official log book or otherwise, in the form specified in Annex B to the Convention.

(2) The oil record book shall be completed on each occasion, whenever any of the following operations takes place in the ship:

(*a*) ballasting of and discharge of ballast from cargo tanks of tankers;

(*b*) cleaning of cargo tanks of tankers;

(*c*) settling in slop tanks and discharge of water from tankers;

(*d*) disposal from tankers of oily residues from slop tanks or other sources;

(*e*) ballasting, or cleaning during voyage, of bunker fuel tanks of ships other than tankers;

(*f*) disposal from ships other than tankers of oily residues from bunker fuel tanks or other sources;

(*g*) accidental or other exceptional discharges or escapes of oil from tankers or ships other than tankers.

In the event of such discharge or escape of oil or oily mixture as is referred to in sub-paragraph (*c*) of Article III or in Article IV, a statement shall be made in the oil record book of the circumstances of, and reason for, the discharge or escape.

(3) Each operation described in paragraph (2) of this Article shall be fully recorded without delay in the oil record book so that all the entries in the book appropriate to that operation are completed. Each page of the book shall be signed by the officer or officers in charge of the operations concerned and, when the ship is manned, by the master of the ship. The written entries in the oil record book shall be in an official language of the relevant territory in respect of the ship in accordance with paragraph (1) of Article II, or in English or French.

(4) Oil record books shall be kept in such a place as to be readily available for inspection at all reasonable times, and, except in the case of unmanned ships under tow, shall be kept on board the ship. They shall be preserved for a period of two years after the last entry has been made.

(5) The competent authorities of any of the territories of a Contracting Government may inspect on board any ship to which the present Convention applies, while within a port in that territory, the oil record book required to be carried in the ship in compliance with the provisions of this Article, and may make a true copy of any entry in that book and may require the master of the ship to certify that the copy is a true copy of such entry. Any copy so made which purports to have been certified by the master of the ship as a true copy of an entry in the ship's oil record book shall be made admissible in any judicial proceedings as evidence of the facts stated in the entry. Any action by the competent authorities under this paragraph shall be taken as expeditiously as possible and the ship shall not be delayed.

10. The existing text of Article X of the Convention is replaced by the following:

Article X

(1) Any Contracting Government may furnish to the Government of the relevant territory in respect of the ship in accordance with paragraph (1) of Article II particulars in writing of evidence that any provision of the present Convention has been contravened in respect of that ship, wheresoever the alleged contravention may have taken place. If it is practicable to do so, the competent authorities of the former Government shall notify the master of the ship of the alleged contravention.

(2) Upon receiving such particulars, the Government so informed shall investigate the matter, and may request the other Government

to furnish further or better particulars of the alleged contravention. If the Government so informed is satisfied that sufficient evidence is available in the form required by its law to enable proceedings against the owner or master of the ship to be taken in respect of the alleged contravention, it shall cause such proceedings to be taken as soon as possible, and shall inform the other Government and the Organization of the result of such proceedings.

11. The existing text of Article XIV of the Convention is replaced by the following:

Article XIV

(1) The present Convention shall remain open for signature for three months from this day's date and shall thereafter remain open for acceptance.

(2) Subject to Article XV, the Governments of States Members of the United Nations or of any of the Specialized Agencies or parties to the Statute of the International Court of Justice may become parties to the present Convention by:

(*a*) signature without reservation as to acceptance;
(*b*) signature subject to acceptance followed by acceptance, or
(*c*) acceptance.

(3) Acceptance shall be effected by the deposit of an instrument of acceptance with the Bureau, which shall inform all Governments that have already signed or accepted the present Convention of each signature and deposit of an acceptance and of the date of such signature or deposit.

12. The existing text of Article XVI of the Convention is replaced by the following:

Article XVI

(1) (*a*) The present Convention may be amended by unanimous agreement between the Contracting Governments.

(*b*) Upon request of any Contracting Government a proposed amendment shall be communicated by the Organization to all Contracting Governments for consideration and acceptance under this paragraph.

(2) (*a*) An amendment to the present Convention may be proposed to the Organization at any time by any Contracting Government, and such proposal if adopted by a two-thirds majority of the Assembly of the Organization upon recommendation adopted by a two-thirds majority of the Maritime Safety Committee of the Organization shall be communicated by the Organization to all Contracting Governments for their acceptance.

(*b*) Any such recommendation by the Maritime Safety Committee shall be communicated by the Organization to all

Contracting Governments for their consideration at least six months before it is considered by the Assembly.

(3) (*a*) A conference of Governments to consider amendments to the present Convention proposed by any Contracting Government shall at any time be convened by the Organization upon the request of one-third of the Contracting Governments.

(*b*) Every amendment adopted by such conference by a two-thirds majority of the Contracting Governments shall be communicated by the Organization to all Contracting Governments for their acceptance.

(4) Any amendment communicated to Contracting Governments for their acceptance under paragraph (2) or (3) of this Article shall come into force for all Contracting Governments, except those which before it comes into force make a declaration that they do not accept the amendment, twelve months after the date on which the amendment is accepted by two-thirds of the Contracting Governments.

(5) The Assembly, by a two-thirds majority vote, including two-thirds of the Governments represented on the Maritime Safety Committee, and subject to the concurrence of two-thirds of the Contracting Governments to the present Convention, or a conference convened under paragraph (3) of this Article by a two-thirds majority vote, may determine at the time of its adoption that the amendment is of such an important nature that any Contracting Government which makes a declaration under paragraph (4) of this Article and which does not accept the amendment within a period of twelve months after the amendment comes into force, shall, upon the expiry of this period, cease to be a party to the present Convention.

(6) The Organization shall inform all Contracting Governments of any amendments which come into force under this Article, together with the date on which such amendments shall come into force.

(7) Any acceptance or declaration under this Article shall be made by a notification in writing to the Organization which shall notify all Contracting Governments of the receipt of the acceptance or declaration.

13. The existing text of Article XVIII of the Convention is replaced by the following:

Article XVIII

(1) (*a*) The United Nations in cases where they are the administering authority for a territory or any Contracting Government responsible for the international relations of a territory shall as soon as possible consult with such territory in an endeavour to extend the present Convention to that territory and may at any time by notification in writing

given to the Bureau declare that the Convention shall extend to such territory.

(b) The present Convention shall from the date of the receipt of the notification or from such other date as may be specified in the notification extend to the territory named therein.

(2) (a) The United Nations in cases where they are the administering authority for a territory or any Contracting Government which has made a declaration under paragraph (1) of this Article, at any time after the expiry of a period of five years from the date on which the present Convention has been so extended to any territory, may by a notification in writing given to the Bureau after consultation with such territory declare that the Convention shall cease to extend to any such territory named in the notification.

(b) The present Convention shall cease to extend to any territory mentioned in such notification one year, or such longer period as may be specified therein, after the date of receipt of the notification by the Bureau.

(3) The Bureau shall inform all the Contracting Governments of the extension of the present Convention to any territory under paragraph (1) of this Article, and of the termination of any such extension under the provisions of paragraph (2) stating in each case the date from which the Convention has been or will cease to be so extended.

14. The existing text of Annex A to the Convention is replaced by the following:

ANNEX A

PROHIBITED ZONES

(1) All sea areas within 50 miles from the nearest land shall be prohibited zones.

For the purposes of this Annex, the term 'from the nearest land' means 'from the base-line from which the territorial sea of the territory in question is established in accordance with the Geneva Convention on the Territorial Sea and the Contiguous Zone, 1958'. [1]

(2) The following sea areas, insofar as they extend more than 50 miles from the nearest land, shall also be prohibited zones:

(a) *Pacific Ocean*

The Canadian Western Zone

The Canadian Western Zone shall extend for a distance of 100 miles from the nearest land along the west coast of Canada.

[1] TIAS 5639; 15 UST 1606.

(*b*) *North Atlantic Ocean, North Sea and Baltic Sea*

(i) *The North-West Atlantic Zone*
The North-West Atlantic Zone shall comprise the sea areas within a line drawn from latitude 38° 47′ north, longitude 73° 43′ west to latitude 39° 58′ north, longitude 68° 34′ west thence to latitude 42° 05′ north, longitude 64° 37′ west thence along the east coast of Canada at a distance of 100 miles from the nearest land.

(ii) *The Icelandic Zone*
The Icelandic Zone shall extend for a distance of 100 miles from the nearest land along the coast of Iceland.

(iii) *The Norwegian, North Sea and Baltic Sea Zone*
The Norwegian, North Sea and Baltic Sea Zone shall extend for a distance of 100 miles from the nearest land along the coast of Norway and shall include the whole of the North Sea and of the Baltic Sea and its Gulfs.

(iv) *The North-East Atlantic Zone*
The North-East Atlantic Zone shall include the sea areas within a line drawn between the following positions:

Latitude	*Longitude*
62° north	2° east,
64° north	00°
64° north	10° west,
60° north	14° west;
54° 30′ north	30° west,
53° north	40° west;
44° 20′ north	40° west,
44° 20′ north	30° west;
46° north	20° west, thence towards Cape

Finisterre at the intersection of the 50-mile limit.

(v) *The Spanish Zone*
The Spanish Zone shall comprise the areas of the Atlantic Ocean within a distance of 100 miles from the nearest land along the coast of Spain and shall come into operation on the date on which the present Convention shall have come into force in respect of Spain.

(vi) *The Portuguèse Zone*
The Portuguese Zone shall comprise the area of the Atlantic Ocean within a distance of 100 miles from

the nearest land along the coast of Portugal and shall come into operation on the date on which the present Convention shall have come into force in respect of Portugal.

(c) *Mediterranean and Adriatic Seas*

The Mediterranean and Adriatic Zone

The Mediterranean and Adriatic Zone shall comprise the sea areas within a distance of 100 miles from the nearest land along the coasts of each of the territories bordering the Mediterranean and Adriatic Seas and shall come into operation in respect of each territory on the date on which the present Convention shall have come into force in respect of that territory.

(d) *Black Sea and Sea of Azov*

The Black Sea and Sea of Azov Zone

The Black Sea and Sea of Azov Zone shall comprise the sea areas within a distance of 100 miles from the nearest land along the coasts of each of the territories bordering the Black Sea and Sea of Azov and shall come into operation in respect of each territory on the date on which the present Convention shall have come into force in respect of that territory.

Provided that the whole of the Black Sea and the Sea of Azov shall become a prohibited zone on the date on which the present Convention shall have come into force in respect of Roumania and the Union of Soviet Socialist Republics.

(e) *Red Sea*

The Red Sea Zone

The Red Sea Zone shall comprise the sea areas within a distance of 100 miles from the nearest land along the coasts of each of the territories bordering the Red Sea and shall come into operation in respect of each territory on the date on which the present Convention shall have come into force in respect of that territory.

(f) *Persian Gulf*

(i) *The Kuwait Zone*

The Kuwait Zone shall comprise the sea area within a distance of 100 miles from the nearest land along the coast of Kuwait.

(ii) *The Saudi Arabian Zone*

The Saudi Arabian Zone shall comprise the sea area within a distance of 100 miles from the nearest land along the coast of Saudi Arabia and shall come into operation on the date on which the present Convention shall have come into force in respect of Saudi Arabia.

(*g*) *Arabian Sea, Bay of Bengal and Indian Ocean*

(i) *The Arabian Sea Zone*

The Arabian Sea Zone shall comprise the sea areas within a line drawn between the following positions:

Latitude	*Longitude*
23° 33′ north	68° 20′ east,
23° 33′ north	67° 30′ east;
22° north	68° east,
20° north	70° east;
18° 55′ north	72° east,
15° 40′ north	72° 42′ east;
8° 30′ north	75° 48′ east,
7° 10′ north	76° 50′ east;
7° 10′ north	78° 14′ east,
9° 06′ north	79° 32′ east,

and shall come into operation on the date on which the present Convention shall have come into force in respect of India.

(ii) *The Bay of Bengal Coastal Zone*

The Bay of Bengal Coastal Zone shall comprise the sea areas between the nearest land and a line drawn between the following positions:

Latitude	*Longitude*
10° 15′ north	80° 50′ east,
14° 30′ north	81° 38′ east;
20° 20′ north	88° 10′ east,
20° 20′ north	89° east,

and shall come into operation on the date on which the present Convention shall have come into force in respect of India.

(iii) *The Malagasy Zone*

The Malagasy Zone shall comprise the sea area within a distance of 100 miles from the nearest land along the coast of Madagascar west of the meridians of Cape d'Ambre in the north and of Cape Ste. Marie in the south and within a distance of 150 miles from the nearest land along the coast of Madagascar east of these meridians, and shall come into operation when the present Convention shall have come into force in respect of Madagascar.

(*h*) *Australia*

The Australian Zone

The Australian Zone shall comprise the sea area within a distance of 150 miles from the nearest land along the coasts of Australia, except off the north and west coasts of the

Australian mainland between the point opposite Thursday Island and the point on the west coast at 20° south latitude.

(3) (*a*) Any Contracting Government may propose:

(i) the reduction of any zone off the coast of any of its territories;

(ii) the extension of any such zone to a maximum of 100 miles from the nearest land along any such coast,

by making a declaration to that effect and the reduction or extension shall come into force after the expiration of a period of six months after the declaration has been made, unless any one of the Contracting Governments shall have made a declaration not less than two months before the expiration of that period to the effect that it considers that the destruction of birds and adverse effects on fish and the marine organisms on which they feed would be likely to occur or that its interests are affected either by reason of the proximity of its coasts or by reason of its ships trading in the area, and that it does not accept the reduction or extension, as the case may be.

(*b*) Any declaration under this paragraph shall be made by a notification in writing to the Organization which shall notify all Contracting Governments of the receipt of the declaration.

(4) The Organization shall prepare a set of charts indicating the extent of the prohibited zones in force in accordance with paragraph (2) of this Annex and shall issue amendments thereto as may be necessary.

15. The following changes to be made in Annex B to the Convention:

1. Throughout the Annex replace the words 'Identity numbers of tank(s)' by 'Identity numbers of tank(s) concerned'.

2. In Form I(*a*) replace the words 'Place or position of ship' by 'Place or position of ship at time of discharge'.

3. In Form I(*d*) and Form II(*a*) and (*b*) replace the words 'Place or position of ship' by 'Place or position of ship at time of disposal'.

4. In Form I(*c*) add a new line 17 as follows: '17. Approximate quantities of water discharged' and re-number lines in (*d*) 18 to 20.

5. Delete the words 'from ship' in the headings of Forms I(*d*) and II(*b*).

6. In Form III replace the words 'Place or position of ship' by 'Place or position of ship at time of occurrence'.

AMENDMENTS TO THE INTERNATIONAL CONVENTION FOR THE PREVENTION OF THE POLLUTION OF THE SEA BY OIL

Inter-Governmental Maritime Consultative Organization
Assembly - 6th session, Agenda item 10.

Resolution A.175(VI) Adopted on 21 October 1969

The Assembly,

Recalling its Resolution A.142(V) adopted on 26 October 1967 by which it approved the work programme of the Organization in particular with respect to the possible need for amending the International Convention for the Prevention of Pollution of the Sea by Oil, 1954 in accordance with the conclusions of the third extraordinary session of the Council,

Recalling further its Resolution A.151 (ES.IV) concerning proposals for amending Article X, Resolution A.153 (ES.IV) concerning proposals for amending Article IX and X, and Resolution A.155 (ES.IV) concerning proposals for amending Article III of the Convention in sufficient time to permit their consideration by the Assembly at its next regular session,

Noting Article 16 (i) of the Convention on the Inter-Governmental Maritime Consultative Organization, concerning the functions of the Assembly,

IMCO: A VI/Res. 175, October 23, 1969

Noting further that Article XVI of the International Convention for the Prevention of Pollution of the Sea by Oil, 1954, provides for procedures of amendment involving participation by the Organization,

Having considered certain amendments to the International Convention for the Prevention of Pollution of the Sea by Oil, 1954, and the Annexes thereto, forming the subject of a recommendation adopted by the Maritime Safety Committee at its nineteenth session in accordance with Article XVI of that Convention with a view to preventing and controlling deliberate pollution of the sea by oil,

Recalling Resolution 1 of the International Conference on Prevention of Pollution of the Sea by Oil, 1962, concerning the complete avoidance, as soon as practicable, of the discharge of persistent oils into the sea and considering that the amendments to the Convention, as recommended by the Maritime Safety Committee, will enable significant progress to be made towards the ultimate achievement of complete avoidance of discharge,

Adopts the following Amendments to the Articles and the Annexes to the Convention the texts of which are attached to this Resolution:

(a) The replacement of paragraph 1 of Article I by a new paragraph;
(b) the replacement of Article III, by a new Article;
(c) the deletion of paragraph (c) of Article IV;
(d) the replacement of Article V by a new Article;
(e) the replacement of Article VII by a new Article;
(f) the replacement of paragraphs (1) and (2) of Article IX by new paragraphs;
(g) the replacement of paragraph (2) of Article X by a new paragraph;
(h) the deletion of Annex A;
(i) the replacement of Annex B by a new Annex;

Requests the Secretary-General of the Organization, in conformity with Article XVI (1) (b), to communicate, for consideration and acceptance, certified copies of this Resolution and its attachment, to all Contracting Governments to the International Convention for the Prevention of Pollution of the Sea by Oil, 1954, together with copies to all Members of the Organization, and

Invites all Governments concerned to accept the Amendments at the earliest possible date.

AMENDMENTS TO THE INTERNATIONAL CONVENTION FOR THE PREVENTION OF POLLUTION OF THE SEA BY OIL, 1954, AND ITS ANNEXES

Article I

The existing text of paragraph (1) is replaced by the following:

(1) For the purposes of the present Convention, the following expressions shall (unless the context otherwise requires) have the meanings hereby respectively assigned to them that is to say:

"The Bureau" has the meaning assigned to it by Article XXI;

"Discharge" in relation to oil or to oily mixture means any discharge or escape howsoever caused;

"Heavy diesel oil" means diesel oil, other than those distillates of which more than 50 per cent by volume distils at a temperature not exceeding 340°C. when tested by A.S.T.M. Standard Method D.86/59;

"Instantaneous rate of discharge of oil eontent" means the rate of discharge of oil in litres per hour at any instant divided by the speed of the ship in knots at the same instant;

"Mile" means a nautical mile of 6,080 feet or 1,852 metres;

"Nearest land." The term "from the nearest land" means "from the base-line from which the territorial sea of the territory in question is established in accordance with the Geneva Convention on the Territorial Sea and the Contiguous Zone, 1958";

"Oil" means crude oil, fuel oil, heavy diesel oil and lubricating oil, and "oily" shall be construed accordingly;

"Oily mixture" means a mixture with any oil content;

"Organization" means the Inter-Governmental Maritime Consultative Organization;

"Ship" means any sea-going vessel of any type whatsoever, including floating craft, whether self-propelled or towed by another vessel, making a sea voyage; and "tanker" means a ship in which the greater part of the cargo space is constructed or adapted for the carriage of liquid cargoes in bulk and which is not, for the time being, carrying a cargo other than oil in that part of its cargo space.

Article III

The existing text of Article III is replaced by the following: Subject to provisions of Articles IV and V -

(a) the discharge from a ship to which the present Convention applies, other than a tanker, of oil or oily mixture shall be prohibited except when the following conditions are all satisfied:

(i) the ship is proceeding en route;

(ii) the instantaneous rate of discharge of oil content does not exceed 60 litres per mile;

(iii) the oil content of the discharge is less than 100 parts per 1,000,000 parts of the mixture;

(iv) the discharge is made as far as practicable from land;

(b) the discharge from a tanker to which the present Convention applies of oil or oily mixture shall be prohibited except when the following conditions are all satisfied:

(i) the tanker is proceeding en route;
(ii) the instantaneous rate of discharge of oil content does not exceed 60 litres per mile;
(iii) the total quantity of oil discharged on a ballast voyage does not exceed 1/15,000 of the total cargo-carrying capacity;
(iv) the tanker is more than 50 miles from the nearest land;

(c) the provisions of sub-paragraph (b) of this Article shall not apply to:

(i) the discharge of ballast from a cargo tank which, since the cargo was last carried therein, has been so cleaned that any effluent therefrom, if it were discharged from a stationary tanker into clean calm water on a clear day, would produce no visible traces of oil on the surface of the water; or
(ii) the discharge of oil or oily mixture from machinery space bilges, which shall be governed by the provisions of sub-paragraph (a) of this article

Article IV

Paragraph (c) is deleted.

Article V

The existing text of Article V is replaced by the following:

Article III shall not apply to the discharge of oil mixture from the bilges of a ship during the period of twelve months following the date on which the present Convention comes into force for the relevant territory in accordance with paragraph (1) of Article II.

Article VII

The existing text of Article VII is replaced by the following:

(1) As from a date twelve months after the present Convention comes into force for the relevant territory in respect of a ship in accordance with paragraph (1) of Article II, such a ship shall be required to be so fitted as to prevent, as far as reasonable and practicable, the escape of oil into bilges, unless effective means are provided to ensure that the oil in the bilges is not discharged in contravention of this Convention.

(2) Carrying water ballast in oil fuel tanks shall be avoided if possible.

Article IX

The existing texts of paragraphs (1) and (2) are replaced by the following:

(1) Of the ships to which the present Convention applies, every ship which uses oil fuel and every tanker shall be provided with an oil record book, whether as part of the ship's official log book or otherwise, in the form specified in the Annex to this Convention.

(2) The oil record book shall be completed on each occasion, on a tank-to-tank basis, whenever any of the following operations take place in the ship:

(a) For tankers:

(i) loading of oil cargo;
(ii) transfer of oil cargo during voyage;
(iii) discharge of oil cargo;
(iv) ballasting of cargo tanks;
(v) cleaning of cargo tanks;
(vi) discharge of dirty ballast;
(vii) discharge of water from slop-tanks;
(viii) disposal of residues;
(ix) discharge overboard of bilge water containing oil which has accumulated in machinery spaces whilst in port, and the routine discharge at sea of bilge water containing oil unless the latter has been entered in the appropriate log book;

(b) For ships other than tankers:

(i) ballasting or cleaning of bunker fuel tanks;
(ii) discharge of dirty ballast or cleaning water from tanks referred to under (i) of this sub-paragraph;
(iii) disposal of residues;
(iv) discharge overboard of bilge water containing oil which has accumulated in machinery spaces whilst in port, and the routine discharge at sea of bilge water containing oil unless the latter has been entered in the appropriate log book.

In the event of such discharge or escape of oil or oily mixture as is referred to in Article IV, a statement shall be made in the oil record book of the circumstances of, and the reason for, the discharge or escape.

Article X

The existing text of paragraph (2) is replaced by the following:

(2) Upon receiving such particulars, the Government so informed shall investigate the matter, and may request the other Government to furnish further or better particulars of the alleged contravention. If the Government so informed is satisfied that sufficient evidence is available in the form required by its law to enable proceedings against the owner or master of the ship to be taken in respect of the alleged contravention, it shall cause such proceedings to be taken as soon as possible. That Government shall promptly inform the Government whose official has reported the alleged contravention, as well as the Organization, of the action taken as a consequence of the information communicated.

Annex A

Annex A is deleted.

Annex B

Annex B is deleted and replaced by the following:

ANNEX-FORM OF OIL RECORD BOOK
I-FOR TANKERS

Name of ship --
Total cargo carrying capacity of ship in cubic metres ------
(a) Loading of oil cargo
1. Date and place of Loading ------ ----- ------
2. Types of oil loaded -------- ------- -------
3. Identity of tank(s) loaded ----- ----- -----
(b) Transfer of oil cargo during voyage
4. Date of transfer -------------- ---- -----
5. Identity of tank(s)
i From ------------------------------ --------- ------
ii To -------------------------------- --------- ------
6. Was (were) tank(s) in 5 (i) emptied? --- ---
(c) Discharge of oil cargo
7. Date and place of discharge ----- ----- ----
8. Identity of tank(s) discharged ---- ---- ---
9. Was (were) tank(s) emptied? ------ ---- ----
(d) Ballasting of cargo tanks
10. Identity of tank(s) ballasted ----- ---- ---
11. Date and position of ship at start of ballasting ---------------- ------ ---
(e) Cleaning of cargo tanks
12. Identity of tank(s) cleaned ------ ---- ----

13. Date and duration of cleaning ----- ----- --
14. Methods of cleaning* -------- ------ ------

(f) Discharge of dirty ballast

15. Identity of tank(s) ------- ------- -------
16. Date and position of ship at start of discharge to sea ----------- -------- ------
17. Date and position of ship at finish of discharge to sea ------------- ------- -----
18. Ship's speed (s) during discharge --- --- ---
19. Quantity discharged to sea ----- ----- -----
20. Quantity of polluted water transferred to slop tank(s) (identify slop tank(s)) ------- ------
21. Date and port of discharge into shore reception facilities (if applicable) ---- ----

(g) Discharge of water from slop tanks

22. Identity of slop tank(s) -------- ----- ----
23. Time of settling from last entry of residues, or ------------------- --------- --------
24. Time of settling from last discharge ---- --
25. Date, time and position of ship at start of discharge ----------- ------- --------
26. Sounding of total contents at start of discharge ------------------- ------- ------
27. Sounding of interface at start of discharge ------------------ ------- ------
28. Bulk quantity discharged and rate of discharge ------------------ -------- ------
29. Final quantity discharged and rate of discharge ------------------- -------- -----
30. Date, time and position of ship at end of discharge ----------------- ------- ------
31. Ship's speed(s) during discharge ---- -----
32. Sounding of interface at end of discharge ------------ -------- -------

(h) Disposal of residues

33. Identity of tank(s) --------- ------- -----
34. Quantity disposed from each tank --- --- ---
35. Method of disposal of residue:
    (a) Reception facilities ----- ----- ----
    (b) Mixed with cargo ----- ----- --------
    (c) Transferred to another (other) tank(s) (identify tank(s)) --- ----- -----
    (d) Other method --------- ------- -----
36. Date and port of disposal of residue

* Hand hosing, machine washing or chemical cleaning. Where chemically cleaned, the chemical concerned and the amount used should be stated.

(i) Discharge overboard of bilge water containing oil which has accumulated in machinery spaces (including pump rooms) while in port.*
   37. Port ---------------- ---------- -------
   38. Duration of stay ------------- ------ ----
   39. Quantity disposed ------------ ------ ----
   40. Date and place of disposal ----- ------ ----
   41. Method of disposal (state whether a separator was used) ------------- -------- -------

(j) Accidental or other exceptional discharges of oil
   42. Date and time of occurrence ----- ----- ----
   43. Place or position of ship at time of occurrence -------------------- ------- -----
   44. Approximate quantity and type of oil --- ---
   45. Circumstances of discharge or escape and general remarks ----------- ----- ------

----------------(Signature of Officer or Officers in charge of operation concerned).

----------------(Signature of Master).

II-FOR SHIPS OTHER THAN TANKERS

Name of ship --

(a) Ballasting or cleaning of bunker fuel tanks
   1. Identity of tank(s) ballasted ---- ---- ----
   2. Whether cleaned since they last contained oil and, if not, type of oil previously carried ---------------- -------- -----
   3. Date and position of ship at start of cleaning -------------- -------- --------
   4. Date and position of ship at start of ballasting ------------- --------- -----

(b) Discharge of dirty ballast or cleaning water from tanks referred to under (a).
   5. Identity of tank(s) ---------- ------- -----
   6. Date and position of ship at start of discharge -------------- --------- --------
   7. Date and position of ship at finish of discharge ------------------- ------- ----

* The routine discharge at sea of bilge water containing any oil from machinery spaces including pump room bilges need not be entered in the oil record book but, if not, it must be entered in the appropriate log book, stating whether or not the discharge was made through a separator. Where the pump starts automatically and discharges through a separator at all times it will be sufficient to enter each day "Automatic discharge from bilges through separator".

8. Ship's speed(s) during discharge ---- --- ---
9. Method of discharge (state whether separator used) ------------------ --------- ------
10. Quantity discharged ------------ ----- ----

(c) Disposal of residues

11. Quantity of residue retained on board ------ ----------- -------- --------- ----------
12. Methods of disposal of residue:
    (a) reception facilities ------ ----- ----
    (b) mixed with next bunkering ---- ---- --
    (c) transferred to another (other) tank(s) ------------- ------ -----
13. Date and port of disposal of residue --- ---

(d) Discharge overboard of bilge water containing oil which has accumulated in machinery spaces whilst in port*

14. Port ----------------- ----------- -------
15. Duration of stay ------- ----------- -------
16. Quality disposed ------ ------------ -------
17. Date and place of disposal --------- -------
18. Method of disposal (state whether separator was used) ---------------- ------- -----

(e) Accidental or other exceptional discharges of oil

19. Date and time of occurrence ------ ------ ----
20. Place or position of ship at time of occurrence --------------- -------- -------
21. Approximate quantity and type of oil --- ----
22. Circumstances of discharge or escape and general remarks ----------- -------- -------

--------------------(Signature of Officer or Officers in charge of operations concerned).

--------------------(Signature of Master).

* The routine discharge at sea of bilge water containing any oil from machinery spaces need not be entered in the oil record book but if not, it must be entered in the appropriate log book, stating whether or not the discharge was made through a separator. Where the pump starts automatically and discharges through a separator at all times it will be sufficient to enter each day "Automatic discharge from bilges through a separator".

AMENDMENTS TO THE INTERNATIONAL CONVENTION FOR THE PREVENTION OF POLLUTION OF THE SEA BY OIL, 1954 CONCERNING TANK ARRANGEMENTS AND LIMITATION OF TANK SIZE
(Resolution A.246(VII) adopted on 15 October 1971)

The Assembly,

Noting Article 16 (i) of the Convention on the Inter-Governmental Maritime Consultative Organization concerning the functions of the Assembly,

Being conscious of the responsibility of the Organization for taking effective measures for the prevention and control of pollution of the marine environment which may arise from maritime activities,

Realizing that notwithstanding the adoption by the Organization of various measures for preventing collisions and strandings of ships, it is not possible to eliminate entirely accidents which may lead to release of oil, but desiring to minimize ensuing damage to the environment.

Recognizing that construction of oil tankers of large size without accompanying control of size of internal arrangement of cargo tanks leads to the possibility, in the event of a single accident, of serious environmental pollution,

Having examined the Recommendations relating to tank arrangements and to the limitation of tank size prepared by the Maritime Safety Committee at its twenty-third session,

Considering that the universal implementation of such requirements can best be achieved by amending the International Convention for the Prevention of Pollution of the Sea by Oil, 1954,

Noting that Article XVI of the International Convention for the Prevention of Pollution of the Sea by Oil, 1954 provides for procedures of amendment involving participation by the Organization,

Adopts the following amendments to the Articles and Annexes to that Convention, the texts of which are attached to this Resolution:

(a) the addition of a new Article VI bis, and
(b) the addition of a new Annex C,

Requests the Secretary-General of the Organization, in conformity with sub-paragraph (2) (a) of Article XVI to communicate for consideration and acceptance, certified copies of this Resolution and its Annexes, to all Contracting Governments to the International Convention for the Prevention of Pollution of the Sea by Oil, 1954, together with copies to all Members of the Organization,

Invites all governments concerned to accept the amendments at the earliest possible date, and

Determines in accordance with paragraph (5) of Article XVI that these amendments are of such an important nature that any Contracting Government which makes a declaration under paragraph (4) of Article XVI and which does not accept the amendments within a period of 12 months after the amendments come into force, shall, upon the expiry of this period, cease to be a Party to the present Convention.

ANNEX I

Add new Article VI bis as follows:

Article VI bis

(1) Every tanker to which the present Convention applies and for which the building contract is placed on or after the date of coming into force of this Article shall be constructed in accordance with the provisions of Annex C. In addition, every tanker to which the present Convention applies and for which the building contract is placed, or in the absence of a building contract the keel of which is laid or which is at a similar stage of construction, before the date of coming into force of this Article shall be required, within two years after that date, to comply with the provisions of Annex C, where such a tanker falls into either of the following categories:

(a) a tanker, the delivery of which is after 1 January 1977; or

(b) a tanker to which both the following conditions apply:

(i) delivery is not later than 1 January 1977; and

(ii) the building contract is placed after 1 January 1972, or in cases where no building contract has previously been placed, the keel is laid or the tanker is at a similar stage of construction, after 30 June 1972.

(2) A tanker required under paragraph (1) of this Article to be constructed in accordance with Annex C and so constructed shall carry on board a certificate issued or authorized by the responsible Contracting Government attesting such compliance. A tanker which under paragraph (1) of this Article is not required to be constructed in accordance with Annex C shall carry on board a certificate to that effect issued or authorized by the responsible Contracting Government, or if the tanker does comply with Annex C although not required to do so, it may carry on board a certificate issued or authorized by the responsible Contracting Government attesting such compliance. A Contracting Government shall not permit such tankers under its flag to trade unless the appropriate certificate has been issued.

(3) Certificates issued under the authority of a Contracting Government shall be accepted by the other Contracting Governments for all purposes covered by the present Convention. They shall be regarded by the other Contracting Governments as having the same force as certificates issued by them.

(4) If a Contracting Government has clear grounds for believing that a tanker required under paragraph (1) of this Article to be constructed in accordance with Annex C entering ports in its territory or using off-shore terminals under its control does not in fact comply with Annex C, such Contracting Government may request consultation with the Government with which the tanker is registered. If, after such consultation or otherwise, the Contracting Government is satisfied that the tanker does not comply with Annex C, such Contracting Government may for this reason deny such a tanker access to ports in its territorial waters or to off-shore terminals under its control until such time as the Contracting Government is satisfied that the tanker does comply.

ANNEX II

ANNEX C
(not included)

INTERNATIONAL CONVENTION RELATING TO INTERVENTION ON THE HIGH SEAS IN CASES OF OIL POLLUTION CASUALTIES

The States Parties to the present Convention,

Conscious of the need to protect the interests of their peoples against the grave consequences of a maritime casualty resulting in danger of oil pollution of sea and coastlines,

Convinced that under these circumstances measures of an exceptional character to protect such interests might be necessary on the high seas and that these measures do not affect the principle of freedom of the high seas,

Have agreed as follows:

Article I

1. Parties to the present Convention may take such measures on the high seas as may be necessary to prevent, mitigate or eliminate grave and imminent danger to their coastline or related interests from pollution or threat of pollution of the sea by oil, following upon a maritime casualty or acts related to such a casualty, which may reasonably be expected to result in major harmful consequences.

2. However, no measures shall be taken under the present Convention against any warship or other ship owned or operated by a State and used, for the time being, only on government non-commercial service.

Article II

For the purposes of the present Convention:

1. "maritime casualty" means a collision of ships, stranding or other incident of navigation, or other occurrence on board a ship or external to it resulting in material damage or imminent threat of material damage to a ship or cargo;

2. "ship" means:

(*a*) any sea-going vessel of any type whatsoever, and

(*b*) any floating craft, with the exception of an installation or device engaged in the exploration and exploitation of the resources of the sea-bed and the ocean floor and the subsoil thereof;

3. "oil" means crude oil, fuel oil, diesel oil and lubricating oil;

4. "related interests" means the interests of a coastal State directly affected or threatened by the maritime casualty, such as:

(*a*) maritime coastal, port or estuarine activities, including fisheries activities, constituting an essential means of livelihood of the persons concerned;

(*b*) tourist attractions of the area concerned;

(*c*) the health of the coastal population and the well-being of the area concerned, including conservation of living marine resources and of wildlife;

5. "Organization" means the Inter-Governmental Maritime Consultative Organization.

Article III

When a coastal State is exercising the right to take measures in accordance with Article I, the following provisions shall apply:

(*a*) before taking any measures, a coastal State shall proceed to consultations with other States affected by the maritime casualty, particularly with the flag State or States;

(*b*) the coastal State shall notify without delay the proposed measures to any persons physical or corporate known to the coastal State, or made known to it during the consultations, to have interests which can reasonably be expected to be affected by those measures. The coastal State shall take into account any views they may submit;

(*c*) before any measure is taken, the coastal State may proceed to a consultation with independent experts, whose names shall be chosen from a list maintained by the Organization;

(*d*) in cases of extreme urgency requiring measures to be taken immediately, the coastal State may take measures rendered necessary by the urgency of the situation, without prior notification or consultation or without continuing consultations already begun;

(*e*) a coastal State shall, before taking such measures and during their course, use its best endeavours to avoid any risk to human life, and to afford persons in distress any assistance of which they may stand in need, and in appropriate cases to facilitate the repatriation of ships' crews, and to raise no obstacle thereto;

(*f*) measures which have been taken in application of Article I shall be notified without delay to the States and to the known physical or corporate persons concerned, as well as to the Secretary-General of the Organization.

Article IV

1. Under the supervision of the Organization, there shall be set up and maintained the list of experts contemplated by Article III of the present Convention, and the Organization shall make necessary and appropriate regulations in connexion therewith, including the determination of the required qualifications.

2. Nominations to the list may be made by Member States of the Organization and by Parties to this Convention. The experts shall be paid on the basis of services rendered by the States utilizing those services.

Article V

1. Measures taken by the coastal State in accordance with Article I shall be proportionate to the damage actual or threatened to it.

2. Such measures shall not go beyond what is reasonably necessary to achieve the end mentioned in Article I and shall cease as soon as that end has been achieved; they shall not unnecessarily interfere with the rights and interests of the flag State, third States and of any persons, physical or corporate, concerned.

3. In considering whether the measures are proportionate to the damage, account shall be taken of:

(*a*) the extent and probability of imminent damage if those measures are not taken; and

(*b*) the likelihood of those measures being effective; and

(*c*) the extent of the damage which may be caused by such measures.

ARTICLE VI

Any Party which has taken measures in contravention of the provisions of the present Convention causing damage to others, shall be obliged to pay compensation to the extent of the damage caused by measures which exceed those reasonably necessary to achieve the end mentioned in Article I.

ARTICLE VII

Except as specifically provided, nothing in the present Convention shall prejudice any otherwise applicable right, duty, privilege or immunity or deprive any of the Parties or any interested physical or corporate person of any remedy otherwise applicable.

ARTICLE VIII

1. Any controversy between the Parties as to whether measures taken under Article I were in contravention of the provisions of the present Convention, to whether compensation is obliged to be paid under Article VI, and to the amount of such compensation shall, if settlement by negotiation between the Parties involved or between the Party which took the measures and the physical or corporate claimants has not been possible, and if the Parties do not otherwise agree, be submitted upon request of any of the Parties concerned to conciliation or, if conciliation does not succeed, to arbitration, as set out in the Annex to the present Convention.

2. The Party which took the measures shall not be entitled to refuse a request for conciliation or arbitration under provisions of the preceding paragraph solely on the grounds that any remedies under municipal law in its own court have not been exhausted.

ARTICLE IX

1. The present Convention shall remain open for signature until 31 December 1970 and shall thereafter remain open for accession.

2. States Members of the United Nations or any of the Specialized Agencies or of the International Atomic Energy Agency or Parties to the Statute of the International Court of Justice may become Parties to this Convention by:

(*a*) signature without reservation as to ratification, acceptance or approval;

(*b*) signature subject to ratification, acceptance or approval followed by ratification, acceptance or approval; or

(*c*) accession.

ARTICLE X

1. Ratification, acceptance, approval or accession shall be effected by the deposit of a formal instrument to that effect with the Secretary-General of the Organization.

2. Any instrument of ratification, acceptance, approval or accession deposited after the entry into force of an amendment to the present Convention with respect to all existing Parties or after the completion of all measures required for the entry into force of the amendment with respect to those Parties shall be deemed to apply to the Convention as modified by the amendment.

ARTICLE XI

1. The present Convention shall enter into force on the ninetieth day following the date on which Governments of fifteen States have either signed it without reservation as to ratification, acceptance or approval or have deposited instruments of ratification, acceptance, approval or accession with the Secretary-General of the Organization.

2. For each State which subsequently ratifies, accepts, approves or accedes to it the present Convention shall come into force on the ninetieth day after deposit by such State of the appropriate instrument.

ARTICLE XII

1. The present Convention may be denounced by any Party at any time after the date on which the Convention comes into force for that State.

2. Denunciation shall be effected by the deposit of an instrument with the Secretary-General of the Organization.

3. A denunciation shall take effect one year, or such longer period as may be specified in the instrument of denunciation, after its deposit with the Secretary-General of the Organization.

ARTICLE XIII

1. The United Nations where it is the administering authority for a territory, or any State Party to the present Convention responsible for the international relations of a territory, shall as soon as possible consult with the appropriate authorities of such territories or take such other measures as may be appropriate, in order to extend the present Convention to that territory and may at any time by notification in writing to the Secretary-General of the Organization declare that the present Convention shall extend to such territory.

2. The present Convention shall, from the date of receipt of the notification or from such other date as may be specified in the notification, extend to the territory named therein.

3. The United Nations, or any Party which has made a declaration under paragraph 1 of this Article may at any time after the date on which the Convention has been so extended to any territory declare by notification in writing to the Secretary-General of the Organization that the present Convention shall cease to extend to any such territory named in the notification.

4. The present Convention shall cease to extend to any territory mentioned in such notification one year, or such longer period as may be specified therein, after the date of receipt of the notification by the Secretary-General of the Organization.

Article XIV

1. A Conference for the purpose of revising or amending the present Convention may be convened by the Organization.

2. The Organization shall convene a Conference of the States Parties to the present Convention for revising or amending the present Convention at the request of not less than one-third of the Parties.

Article XV

1. The present Convention shall be deposited with the Secretary-General of the Organization.

2. The Secretary-General of the Organization shall:

(*a*) inform all States which have signed or acceded to the Convention of:

(i) each new signature or deposit of instrument together with the date thereof;

(ii) the deposit of any instrument of denunciation of this Convention together with the date of the deposit;

(iii) the extension of the present Convention to any territory under paragraph 1 of Article XIII and of the termination of any such extension under the provisions of paragraph 4 of that Article stating in each case the date on which the present Convention has been or will cease to be so extended;

(*b*) transmit certified true copies of the present Convention to all Signatory States and to all States which accede to the present Convention.

Article XVI

As soon as the present Convention comes into force, the text shall be transmitted by the Secretary-General of the Organization to the Secretariat of the United Nations for registration and publication in accordance with Article 102 of the Charter of the United Nations.

Article XVII

The present Convention is established in a single copy in the English and French languages, both texts being equally authentic. Official translations in the Russian and Spanish languages shall be prepared and deposited with the signed original.

In witness whereof the undersigned being duly authorized by their respective Governments for that purpose have signed the present Convention.

Done at Brussels this twenty-ninth day of November 1969.

ANNEX

Chapter I.—Conciliation

ARTICLE 1

Provided the Parties concerned do not decide otherwise, the procedure for conciliation shall be in accordance with the rules set out in this Chapter.

ARTICLE 2

1. A Conciliation Commission shall be established upon the request of one Party addressed to another in application of Article VIII of the Convention.

2. The request for conciliation submitted by a Party shall consist of a statement of the case together with any supporting documents.

3. If a procedure has been initiated between two Parties, any other Party the nationals or property of which have been affected by the same measures, or which is a coastal State having taken similar measures, may join in the conciliation procedure by giving written notice to the Parties which have originally initiated the procedure unless either of the latter Parties object to such joinder.

ARTICLE 3

1. The Conciliation Commission shall be composed of three members: one nominated by the coastal State which took the measures, one nominated by the State the nationals or property of which have been affected by those measures and a third, who shall preside over the Commission and shall be nominated by agreement between the two original members.

2. The Conciliators shall be selected from a list previously drawn up in accordance with the procedure set out in Article 4 below.

3. If within a period of 60 days from the date of receipt of the request for conciliation, the Party to which such request is made has not given notice to the other Party to the controversy of the nomination of the Conciliator for whose selection it is responsible, or if, within a period of 30 days from the date of nomination of the second of the members of the Commission to be designated by the Parties, the first two Conciliators have not been able to designate by common agreement the Chairmen of the Commission, the Secretary-General of the Organization shall upon request of either Party and within a period of 30 days, proceed to the required nomination. The members of the Commission thus nominated shall be selected from the list prescribed in the preceding paragraph.

4. In no case shall the Chairman of the Commission be or have been a national of one of the original Parties to the procedure, whatever the method of his nomination.

ARTICLE 4

1. The list prescribed in Article 3 above shall consist of qualified persons designated by the Parties and shall be kept up to date by the Organization. Each Party may designate for inclusion on the list four

persons, who shall not necessarily be its nationals. The nominations shall be for periods of six years each and shall be renewable.

2. In the case of the decease or resignation of a person whose name appears on the list, the Party which nominated such person shall be permitted to nominate a replacement for the remainder of the term of office.

ARTICLE 5

1. Provided the Parties do not agree otherwise, the Conciliation Commission shall establish its own procedures, which shall in all cases permit a fair hearing. As regards examination, the Commission, unless it unanimously decides otherwise, shall conform with the provisions of Chapter III of The Hague Convention for the Peaceful Settlement of International Disputes of 18 October 1907.

2. The Parties shall be represented before the Conciliation Commission by agents whose duty shall be to act as intermediaries between the Parties and the Commission. Each of the Parties may seek also the assistance of advisers and experts nominated by it for this purpose and may request the hearing of all persons whose evidence the Party considers useful.

3. The Commission shall have the right to request explanations from agents, advisers and experts of the Parties as well as from any persons whom, with the consent of their Governments, it may deem useful to call.

ARTICLE 6

Provided the Parties do not agree otherwise, decisions of the Conciliation Commission shall be taken by a majority vote and the Commission shall not pronounce on the substance of the controversy unless all its members are present.

ARTICLE 7

The Parties shall facilitate the work of the Conciliation Commission and in particular, in accordance with their legislation, and using all means at their disposal:

(*a*) provide the Commission with the necessary documents and information;

(*b*) enable the Commission to enter their territory, to hear witnesses or experts, and to visit the scene.

ARTICLE 8

The task of the Conciliation Commission will be to clarify the matters under dispute, to assemble for this purpose all relevant information by means of examination or other means, and to endeavour to reconcile the Parties. After examining the case, the Commission shall communicate to the Parties a recommendation which appears to the Commission to be appropriate to the matter and shall fix a period of not more than 90 days within which the Parties are called upon to state whether or not they accept the recommendation.

ARTICLE 9

The recommendation shall be accompanied by a statement of reasons. If the recommendation does not represent in whole or in part the unanimous opinion of the Commission, any Conciliator shall be entitled to deliver a separate opinion.

ARTICLE 10

A conciliation shall be deemed unsuccessful if, 90 days after the Parties have been notified of the recommendation, either Party shall not have notified the other Party of its acceptance of the recommendation. Conciliation shall likewise be deemed unsuccessful if the Commission shall not have been established within the period prescribed in the third paragraph of Article 3 above, or provided the Parties have not agreed otherwise, if the Commission shall not have issued its recommendation within one year from the date on which the Chairman of the Commission was nominated.

ARTICLE 11

1. Each member of the Commission shall receive remuneration for his work, such remuneration to be fixed by agreement between the Parties which shall each contribute an equal proportion.

2. Contributions for miscellaneous expenditure incurred by the work of the Commission shall be apportioned in the same manner.

ARTICLE 12

The parties to the controversy may at any time during the conciliation procedure decide in agreement to have recourse to a different procedure for settlement of disputes.

Chapter II.—Arbitration

Article 13

1. Arbitration procedure, unless the Parties decide otherwise, shall be in accordance with the rules set out in this Chapter.

2. Where conciliation is unsuccessful, a request for arbitration may only be made within a period of 180 days following the failure of conciliation.

Article 14

The Arbitration Tribunal shall consist of three members: one Arbitrator nominated by the coastal State which took the measures, one Arbitrator nominated by the State the nationals or property of which have been affected by those measures, and another Arbitrator who shall be nominated by agreement between the two first-named, and shall act as its Chairman.

Article 15

1. If, at the end of a period of 60 days from the nomination of the second Arbitrator, the Chairman of the Tribunal shall not have been nominated, the Secretary-General of the Organization upon request of either Party shall within a further period of 60 days proceed to such nomination, selecting from a list of qualified persons previously drawn up in accordance with the provisions of Article 4 above. This list shall be separate from the list of experts prescribed in Article IV of the Convention and from the list of Conciliators prescribed in Article 4 of the present Annex; the name of the same person may, however, appear both on the list of Conciliators and on the list of Arbitrators. A person who has acted as Conciliator in a dispute may not, however, be chosen to act as Arbitrator in the same matter.

2. If, within a period of 60 days from the date of the receipt of the request, one of the Parties shall not have nominated the member of the Tribunal for whose designation it is responsible, the other Party may directly inform the Secretary-General of the Organization who shall nominate the Chairman of the Tribunal within a period of 60 days, selecting him from the list prescribed in paragraph 1 of the present Article.

3. The Chairman of the Tribunal shall, upon nomination, request the Party which has not provided an Arbitrator, to do so in the same manner and under the same conditions. If the Party does not make the required nomination, the Chairman of the Tribunal shall request the Secretary-General of the Organization to make the nomination in the form and conditions prescribed in the preceding paragraph.

4. The Chairman of the Tribunal, if nominated under the provisions of the present Article, shall not be or have been a national of one of the Parties concerned, except with the consent of the other Party or Parties.

5. In the case of the decease or default of an Arbitrator for whose nomination one of the Parties is responsible, the said Party shall nominate a replacement within a period of 60 days from the date of

decease or default. Should the said Party not make the nomination, the arbitration shall proceed under the remaining Arbitrators. In the case of decease or default of the Chairman of the Tribunal, a replacement shall be nominated in accordance with the provisions of Article 14 above, or in the absence of agreement between the members of the Tribunal within a period of 60 days of the decease or default, according to the provisions of the present Article.

ARTICLE 16

If a procedure has been initiated between two Parties, any other Party, the nationals or property of which have been affected by the same measures or which is a coastal State having taken similar measures, may join in the arbitration procedure by giving written notice to the Parties which have originally initiated the procedure unless either of the latter Parties object to such joinder.

ARTICLE 17

Any Arbitration Tribunal established under the provisions of the present Annex shall decide its own rules of procedure.

ARTICLE 18

1. Decisions of the Tribunal both as to its procedure and its place of meeting and as to any controversy laid before it, shall be taken by majority vote of its members; the absence or abstention of one of the members of the Tribunal for whose nomination the Parties were responsible shall not constitute an impediment to the Tribunal reaching a decision. In cases of equal voting, the Chairman shall cast the deciding vote.

2. The Parties shall facilitate the work of the Tribunal and in particular, in accordance with their legislation, and using all means at their disposal:

(*a*) provide the Tribunal with the necessary documents and information;

(*b*) enable the Tribunal to enter their territory, to hear witnesses or experts, and to visit the scene.

3. Absence or default of one Party shall not constitute an impediment to the procedure.

ARTICLE 19

1. The award of the Tribunal shall be accompanied by a statement of reasons. It shall be final and without appeal. The Parties shall immediately comply with the award.

2. Any controversy which may arise between the Parties as regards interpretation and execution of the award may be submitted by either Party for judgment to the Tribunal which made the award, or, if it is not available, to another Tribunal constituted for this purpose in the same manner as the original Tribunal.

INTERNATIONAL CONVENTION ON CIVIL LIABILITY FOR OIL POLLUTION DAMAGE

The States Parties to the present Convention,

Conscious of the dangers of pollution posed by the worldwide maritime carriage of oil in bulk,

Convinced of the need to ensure that adequate compensation is available to persons who suffer damage caused by pollution resulting from the escape or discharge of oil from ships,

Desiring to adopt uniform international rules and procedures for determining questions of liability and providing adequate compensation in such cases,

Have agreed as follows:

Article I

For the purposes of this Convention:

1. "Ship" means any sea-going vessel and any seaborne craft of any type whatsoever, actually carrying oil in bulk as cargo.
2. "Person" means any individual or partnership or any public or private body, whether corporate or not, including a State or any of its constituent subdivisions.
3. "Owner" means the person or persons registered as the owner of the ship or, in the absence of registration, the person or persons owning the ship. However in the case of a ship owned by a State and operated by a company which in that State is registered as the ship's operator, "owner" shall mean such company.
4. "State of the ship's registry" means in relation to registered ships the State of registration of the ship, and in relation to unregistered ships the State whose flag the ship is flying.
5. "Oil" means any persistent oil such as crude oil, fuel oil, heavy diesel oil, lubricating oil and whale oil, whether carried on board a ship as cargo or in the bunkers of such a ship.
6. "Pollution damage" means loss or damage caused outside the ship carrying oil by contamination resulting from the escape or discharge of oil from the ship, wherever such escape or discharge may occur, and includes the costs of preventive measures and further loss or damage caused by preventive measures.
7. "Preventive measures" means any reasonable measures taken by any person after an incident has occurred to prevent or minimize pollution damage.
8. "Incident" means any occurrence, or series of occurrences having the same origin, which causes pollution damage.
9. "Organization" means the Inter-Governmental Maritime Consultative Organization.

Article II

This Convention shall apply exclusively to pollution damage caused on the territory including the territorial sea of a Contracting State and to preventive measures taken to prevent or minimize such damage.

Article III

1. Except as provided in paragraphs 2 and 3 of this Article, the owner of a ship at the time of an incident, or where the incident consists of a series of occurrences at the time of the first such occurrence, shall be liable for any pollution damage caused by oil which has escaped or been discharged from the ship as a result of the incident.

2. No liability for pollution damage shall attach to the owner if he proves that the damage:

(*a*) resulted from an act of war, hostilities, civil war, insurrection or a natural phenomenon of an exceptional, inevitable and irresistible character, or

(*b*) was wholly caused by an act or omission done with intent to cause damage by a third party, or

(*c*) was wholly caused by the negligence or other wrongful act of any Government or other authority responsible for the maintenance of lights or other navigational aids in the exercise of that function.

3. If the owner proves that the pollution damage resulted wholly or partially either from an act or omission done with intent to cause damage by the person who suffered the damage or from the negligence of that person, the owner may be exonerated wholly or partially from his liability to such person.

4. No claim for compensation for pollution damage shall be made against the owner otherwise than in accordance with this Convention. No claim for pollution damage under this Convention or otherwise may be made against the servants or agents of the owner.

5. Nothing in this Convention shall prejudice any right of recourse of the owner against third parties.

Article IV

When oil has escaped or has been discharged from two or more ships, and pollution damage results therefrom, the owners of all the ships concerned, unless exonerated under Article III, shall be jointly and severally liable for all such damage which is not reasonably separable.

Article V

1. The owner of a ship shall be entitled to limit his liability under this Convention in respect of any one incident to an aggregate amount of 2,000 francs for each ton of the ship's tonnage. However, this aggregate amount shall not in any event exceed 210 million francs.

2. If the incident occurred as a result of the actual fault or privity of the owner, he shall not be entitled to avail himself of the limitation provided in paragraph 1 of this Article.

3. For the purpose of availing himself of the benefit of limitation provided for in paragraph 1 of this Article the owner shall constitute a fund for the total sum representing the limit of his liability with the Court or other competent authority of any one of the Contracting States in which action is brought under Article IX. The fund can be constituted either by depositing the sum or by producing a bank guarantee or other guarantee, acceptable under the legislation of the Contracting State where the fund is constituted, and considered to be adequate by the Court or another competent authority.

4. The fund shall be distributed among the claimants in proportion to the amounts of their established claims.

5. If before the fund is distributed the owner or any of his servants or agents or any person providing him insurance or other financial security has as a result of the incident in question, paid compensation for pollution damage, such person shall, up to the amount he has paid, acquire by subrogation the rights which the person so compensated would have enjoyed under this Convention.

6. The right of subrogation provided for in paragraph 5 of this Article may also be exercised by a person other than those mentioned therein in respect of any amount of compensation for pollution damage which he may have paid but only to the extent that such subrogation is permitted under the applicable national law.

7. Where the owner or any other person establishes that he may be compelled to pay at a later date in whole or in part any such amount of compensation, with regard to which such person would have enjoyed a right of subrogation under paragraphs 5 or 6 of this Article, had the compensation been paid before the fund was distributed, the Court or other competent authority of the State where the fund has been constituted may order that a sufficient sum shall be provisionally set aside to enable such person at such later date to enforce his claim against the fund.

8. Claims in respect of expenses reasonably incurred or sacrifices reasonably made by the owner voluntarily to prevent or minimize pollution damage shall rank equally with other claims against the fund.

9. The franc mentioned in this Article shall be a unit consisting of sixty-five and a half milligrams of gold of millesimal fineness nine hundred. The amount mentioned in paragraph 1 of this Article shall be converted into the national currency of the State in which the fund is being constituted on the basis of the value of that currency by reference to the unit defined above on the date of the constitution of the fund.

10. For the purpose of this Article the ship's tonnage shall be the net tonnage of the ship with the addition of the amount deducted from the gross tonnage on account of engine room space for the purpose of ascertaining the net tonnage. In the case of a ship which cannot be measured in accordance with the normal rules of tonnage measurement, the ship's tonnage shall be deemed to be 40 per cent of the weight in tons (of 2240 lbs) of oil which the ship is capable of carrying.

11. The insurer or other person providing financial security shall be entitled to constitute a fund in accordance with this Article on the same conditions and having the same effect as if it were constituted

by the owner. Such a fund may be constituted even in the event of the actual fault or privity of the owner but its constitution shall in that case not prejudice the rights of any claimant against the owner.

Article VI

1. Where the owner, after an incident, has constituted a fund in accordance with Article V, and is entitled to limit his liability,

(*a*) no person having a claim for pollution damage arising out of that incident shall be entitled to exercise any right against any other assets of the owner in respect of such claim;

(*b*) the Court or other competent authority of any Contracting State shall order the release of any ship or other property belonging to the owner which has been arrested in respect of a claim for pollution damage arising out of that incident, and shall similarly release any bail or other security furnished to avoid such arrest.

2. The foregoing shall, however, only apply if the claimant has access to the Court administering the fund and the fund is actually available in respect of his claim.

Article VII

1. The owner of a ship registered in a Contracting State and carrying more than 2,000 tons of oil in bulk as cargo shall be required to maintain insurance or other financial security, such as the guarantee of a bank or a certificate delivered by an international compensation fund, in the sums fixed by applying the limits of liability prescribed in Article V, paragraph 1 to cover his liability for pollution damage under this Convention.

2. A certificate attesting that insurance or other financial security is in force in accordance with the provisions of this Convention shall be issued to each ship. It shall be issued or certified by the appropriate authority of the State of the ship's registry after determining that the requirements of paragraph 1 of this Article have been complied with. This certificate shall be in the form of the annexed model and shall contain the following particulars:

(*a*) name of ship and port of registration;

(*b*) name and principal place of business of owner;

(*c*) type of security;

(*d*) name and principal place of business of insurer or other person giving security and, where appropriate, place of business where the insurance or security is established;

(*e*) period of validity of certificate which shall not be longer than the period of validity of the insurance or other security.

3. The certificate shall be in the official language or languages of the issuing State. If the language used is neither English nor French, the text shall include a translation into one of these languages.

4. The certificate shall be carried on board the ship and a copy shall be deposited with the authorities who keep the record of the ship's registry.

5. An insurance or other financial security shall not satisfy the requirements of this Article if it can cease, for reasons other than the expiry of the period of validity of the insurance or security specified

in the certificate under paragraph 2 of this Article, before three months have elapsed from the date on which notice of its termination is given to the authorities referred to in paragraph 4 of this Article, unless the certificate has been surrendered to these authorities or a new certificate has been issued within the said period. The foregoing provisions shall similarly apply to any modification which results in the insurance or security no longer satisfying the requirements of this Article.

6. The State of registry shall, subject to the provisions of this Article, determine the conditions of issue and validity of the certificate.

7. Certificates issued or certified under the authority of a Contracting State shall be accepted by other Contracting States for the purposes of this Convention and shall be regarded by other Contracting States as having the same force as certificates issued or certified by them. A Contracting State may at any time request consultation with the State of a ship's registry should it believe that the insurer or guarantor named in the certificate is not financially capable of meeting the obligations imposed by this Convention.

8. Any claim for compensation for pollution damage may be brought directly against the insurer or other person providing financial security for the owner's liability for pollution damage. In such case the defendant may, irrespective of the actual fault or privity of the owner, avail himself of the limits of liability prescribed in Article V, paragraph 1. He may further avail himself of the defenses (other than the bankruptcy or winding up of the owner) which the owner himself would have been entitled to invoke. Furthermore, the defendant may avail himself of the defense that the pollution damage resulted from the wilful misconduct of the owner himself, but the defendant shall not avail himself of any other defense which he might have been entitled to invoke in proceedings brought by the owner against him. The defendant shall in any event have the right to require the owner to be joined in the proceedings.

9. Any sums provided by insurance or by other financial security maintained in accordance with paragraph 1 of this Article shall be available exclusively for the satisfaction of claims under this Convention.

10. A Contracting State shall not permit a ship under its flag to which this Article applies to trade unless a certificate has been issued under paragpaph 2 or 12 of this Article.

11. Subject to the provisions of this Article, each Contracting State shall ensure, under its national legislation, that insurance or other security to the extent specified in paragraph 1 of this Article is in force in respect of any ship, wherever registered, entering or leaving a port in its territory, or arriving at or leaving an off-shore terminal in its territorial sea, if the ship actually carries more than 2,000 tons of oil in bulk as cargo.

12. Insurance or other financial security is not maintained in respect of a ship owned by a Contracting State, the provisions of this Article relating thereto shall not be applicable to such ship, but the ship shall carry a certificate issued by the appropriate authorities of the State of the ship's registry stating that the ship is owned by that State and that the ship's liability is covered within the limits pre-

scribed by Article V, paragraph 1. Such a certificate shall follow as closely as practicable the model prescribed by paragraph 2 of this Article.

Article VIII

Rights of compensation under this Convention shall be extinguished unless an action is brought thereunder within three years from the date when the damage occurred. However, in no case shall an action be brought after six years from the date of the incident which caused the damage. Where this incident consists of a series of occurrences, the six years' period shall run from the date of the first such occurrence.

Article IX

1. Where an incident has caused pollution damage in the territory including the territorial sea of one or more Contracting States, or preventive measures have been taken to prevent or minimize pollution damage in such territory including the territorial sea, actions for compensation may only be brought in the Courts of any such Contracting State or States. Reasonable notice of any such action shall be given to the defendant.

2. Each Contracting State shall ensure that its Courts possess the necessary jurisdiction to entertain such actions for compensation.

3. After the fund has been constituted in accordance with Article V the Courts of the State in which the fund is constituted shall be exclusively competent to determine all matters relating to the apportionment and distribution of the fund.

Article X

1. Any judgment given by a Court with jurisdiction in accordance with Article IX which is enforceable in the State of origin where it is no longer subject to ordinary forms of review, shall be recognized in any Contracting State, except:

(*a*) where the judgment was obtained by fraud; or

(*b*) where the defendant was not given reasonable notice and a fair opportunity to present his case.

2. A judgment recognized under paragraph 1 of this Article shall be enforceable in each Contracting State as soon as the formalities required in that State have been complied with. The formalities shall not permit the merits of the case to be re-opened.

Article XI

1. The provisions of this Convention shall not apply to warships or other ships owned or operated by a State and used, for the time being, only on Government non-commercial service.

2. With respect to ships owned by a Contracting State and used for commercial purposes, each State shall be subject to suit in the jurisdictions set forth in Article IX and shall waive all defences based on its status as a sovereign State.

Article XII

This Convention shall supersede any International Conventions in force or open for signature, ratification or accession at the date on which the Convention is opened for signature, but only to the extent that such Conventions would be in conflict with it; however, nothing in this Article shall affect the obligations of Contracting States to non-Contracting States arising under such International Conventions.

Article XIII

1. The present Convention shall remain open for signature until 31 December 1970 and shall thereafter remain open for accession.

2. States Members of the United Nations or any of the Specialized Agencies or of the International Atomic Energy Agency or Parties to the Statute of the International Court of Justice may become Parties to this Convention by:

(*a*) signature without reservation as to ratification, acceptance or approval;

(*b*) signature subject to ratification, acceptance or approval followed by ratification, acceptance or approval; or

(*c*) accession.

Article XIV

1. Ratification, acceptance, approval or accession shall be effected by the deposit of a formal instrument to that effect with the Secretary-General of the Organization.

2. Any instrument of ratification, acceptance, approval or accession deposited after the entry into force of an amendment to the present Convention with respect to all existing Contracting States, or after the completion of all measures required for the entry into force of the amendment with respect to those Contracting States shall be deemed to apply to the Convention as modified by the amendment.

Article XV

1. The present Convention shall enter into force on the ninetieth day following the date on which Governments of eight States including five States each with not less than 1,000,000 gross tons of tanker tonnage have either signed it without reservation as to ratification, acceptance or approval or have deposited instruments of ratification, acceptance, approval or accession with the Secretary-General of the Organization.

2. For each State which subsequently ratifies, accepts, approves or accedes to it the present Convention shall come into force on the ninetieth day after deposit by such State of the appropriate instrument.

Article XVI

1. The present Convention may be denounced by any Contracting State at any time after the date on which the Convention comes into force for that State.

2. Denunciation shall be effected by the deposit of an instrument with the Secretary-General of the Organization.

3. A denunciation shall take effect one year, or such longer period as may be specified in the instrument of denunciation, after its deposit with the Secretary-General of the Organization.

Article XVII

1. The United Nations, where it is the administering authority for a territory, or any Contracting State responsible for the international relations of a territory, shall as soon as possible consult with the appropriate authorities of such territory or take such other measures as may be appropriate, in order to extend the present Convention to that territory and may at any time by notification in writing to the Secretary-General of the Organization declare that the present Convention shall extend to such territory.

2. The present Convention shall, from the date of receipt of the notification or from such other date as may be specified in the notification, extend to the territory named therein.

3. The United Nations, or any Contracting State which has made a declaration under paragraph 1 of this Article may at any time after the date on which the Convention has been so extended to any territory declare by notification in writing to the Secretary-General of the Organization that the present Convention shall cease to extend to any such territory named in the notification.

4. The present Convention shall cease to extend to any territory mentioned in such notification one year, or such longer period as may be specified therein, after the date of receipt of the notification by the Secretary-General of the Organization.

Article XVIII

1. A Conference for the purpose of revising or amending the present Convention may be convened by the Organization.

2. The Organization shall convene a Conference of the Contracting States for revising or amending the present Convention at the request of not less than one-third of the Contracting States.

Article XIX

1. The present Convention shall be deposited with the Secretary-General of the Organization.

2. The Secretary-General of the Organization shall:

(*a*) inform all States which have signed or acceded to the Convention of

(*i*) each new signature or deposit of instrument together with the date thereof;

(*ii*) the deposit of any instrument of denunciation of this Convention together with the date of the deposit;

(*iii*) the extension of the present Convention to any territory under paragraph 1 of Article XVII and of the termination of any such extension under the provisions of paragraph 4 of that Article stating in each case the date on which the present Convention has been or will cease to be so extended;

(b) transmit certified true copies of the present Convention to all Signatory States and to all States which accede to the present Convention.

ARTICLE XX

As soon as the present Convention comes into force, the text shall be transmitted by the Secretary-General of the Organization to the Secretariat of the United Nations for registration and publication in accordance with Article 102 of the Charter of the United Nations.

ARTICLE XXI

The present Convention is established in a single copy in the English and French languages, both texts being equally authentic. Official translations in the Russian and Spanish languages shall be prepared and deposited with the signed original.

IN WITNESS WHEREOF the undersigned being duly authorized by their respective Governments for that purpose have signed the present Convention.

DONE at Brussels this twenty-ninth day of November 1969.

INTERNATIONAL CONVENTION ON THE ESTABLISHMENT OF AN INTERNATIONAL FUND FOR COMPENSATION FOR OIL POLLUTION DAMAGE

(Supplementary to the International Convention on Civil Liability for Oil Pollution Damage, 1969)

The States Parties to the present Convention,

BEING PARTIES to the International Convention on Civil Liability for Oil Pollution Damage, adopted at Brussels on 29 November 1969,

CONSCIOUS of the dangers of pollution posed by the world-wide maritime carriage of oil in bulk,

CONVINCED of the need to ensure that adequate compensation is available to persons who suffer damage caused by pollution resulting from the escape or discharge of oil from ships,

CONSIDERING that the International Convention of 29 November 1969, on Civil Liability for Oil Pollution Damage, by providing a régime for compensation for pollution damage in Contracting States and for the costs of measures, wherever taken, to prevent or minimize such damage, represents a considerable progress towards the achievement of this aim,

CONSIDERING HOWEVER that this régime does not afford full compensation for victims of oil pollution damage in all cases while it imposes an additional financial burden on shipowners,

CONSIDERING FURTHER that the economic consequences of oil pollution damage resulting from the escape or discharge of oil carried in bulk at sea by ships should not exclusively be borne by the shipping industry but should in part be borne by the oil cargo interests,

CONVINCED of the need to elaborate a compensation and indemnification system supplementary to the International Convention on Civil Liability for Oil Pollution Damage with a view to ensuring that full compensation will be available to victims of oil pollution incidents and that the shipowners are at the same time given relief in respect of the additional financial burdens imposed on them by the said Convention,

TAKING NOTE of the Resolution on the Establishment of an International Compensation Fund for Oil Pollution Damage which was adopted on 29 November 1969 by the International Legal Conference on Marine Pollution Damage,

HAVE AGREED as follows:

General Provisions

Article 1

For the purposes of this Convention—

1. "Liability Convention" means the International Convention on Civil Liability for Oil Pollution Damage, adopted at Brussels on 29 November 1969.

2. "Ship", "Person", "Owner", "Oil," "Pollution Damage", "Preventive Measures", "Incident" and "Organization", have the same meaning as in Article I of the Liability Convention, provided however that, for the purposes of these terms, "oil" shall be confined to persistent hydrocarbon mineral oils.

3. "Contributing Oil" means crude oil and fuel oil as defined in sub-paragraphs (a) and (b) below:

(a) "Crude Oil" means any liquid hydrocarbon mixture occurring naturally in the earth whether or not treated to render it suitable for transportation. It also includes crude oils from which certain distillate fractions have been removed (sometimes referred to as "Topped Crudes") or to which certain distillate fractions have been added (sometimes referred to as "spiked" or "reconstituted" crudes).

(b) "Fuel Oil" means heavy distillates or residues from crude oil or blends of such materials intended for use as a fuel for the production of heat or power of a quality equivalent to the "American Society for Testing and Materials' Specification or Number Four Fuel Oil (Designation D 396–69)", or heavier.

4. "Franc" means the unit referred to in Article V, paragraph 9 of the Liability Convention.

5. "Ship's tonnage" has the same meaning as in Article V, paragraph 10, of the Liability Convention.

6. "Ton", in relation to oil, means a metric ton.

7. "Guarantor" means any person providing insurance or other financial security to cover an owner's liability in pursuance of Article VII, paragraph 1, of the Liability Convention.

8. "Terminal installation" means any site for the storage of oil in bulk which is capable of receiving oil from waterborne transportation, including any facility situated off-shore and linked to such site.

9. Where an incident consists of a series of occurrences, it shall be treated as having occurred on the date of the first such occurrence.

Article 2

1. An International Fund for compensation for pollution damage, to be named "The International Oil Pollution Compensation Fund" and hereinafter referred to as "The Fund", is hereby established with the following aims:

(a) to provide compensation for pollution damage to the extent that the protection afforded by the Liability Convention is inadequate;

(b) to give relief to shipowners in respect of the additional financial burden imposed on them by the Liability Convention, such relief being subject to conditions designed to ensure compliance with safety at sea and other conventions;

(c) to give effect to the related purposes set out in this Convention.

2. The Fund shall in each Contracting State be recognized as a legal person capable under the laws of that State of assuming rights and obligations and of being a party in legal proceedings before the courts of that State. Each Contracting State shall recognize the Director of the Fund (hereinafter referred to as "The Director") as the legal representative of the Fund.

Article 3

This Convention shall apply:

1. With regard to compensation according to Article 4, exclusively to pollution damage caused on the territory including the territorial sea of a Contracting State, and to preventive measures taken to prevent or minimize such damage;

2. With regard to indemnification of shipowners and their guarantors according to Article 5, exclusively in respect of pollution damage caused on the territory, including the territorial sea, of a State party to the Liability Convention by a ship registered in or flying the flag of a Contracting State and in respect of preventive measures taken to prevent or minimize such damage.

Compensation and indemnification

Article 4

1. For the purpose of fulfilling its function under Article 2, paragraph 1(a), the Fund shall pay compensation to any person suffering pollution damage if such person has been unable to obtain full and adequate compensation for the damage under the terms of the Liability Convention,

(a) because no liability for the damage arises under the Liability Convention;

(b) because the owner liable for the damage under the Liability Convention is financially incapable of meeting his obligations in full and any financial security that may be provided under Article VII of that Convention does not cover or is insufficient to satisfy the claims for compensation for the damage; an owner being treated as financially incapable of meeting his obligations and a financial security being treated as insufficient if the person suffering the damage has been unable to obtain full satisfaction of the amount of compensation due under the Liability Convention after having taken all reasonable steps to pursue the legal remedies available to him;

(c) because the damage exceeds the owner's liability under the Liability Convention as limited pursuant to Article V, paragraph 1, of that Convention or under the terms of any other international Convention in force or open for signature, ratification or accession at the date of this Convention.

Expenses reasonably incurred or sacrifices reasonably made by the owner voluntarily to prevent or minimize pollution damage shall be treated as pollution damage for the purposes of this Article.

2. The Fund shall incur no obligation under the preceding paragraph if:

(a) it proves that the pollution damage resulted from an act of war, hostilities, civil war or insurrection or was caused by oil which has escaped or been discharged from a warship or other ship owned or operated by a State and used, at the time of the incident, only on Government noncommercial service; or

(b) the claimant cannot prove that the damage resulted from an incident involving one or more ships.

3. If the Fund proves that the pollution damage resulted wholly or partially either from an act or omission done with intent to cause

damage by the person who suffered the damage or from the negligence of that person, the Fund may be exonerated wholly or partially from its obligation to pay compensation to such person provided, however, that there shall be no such exoneration with regard to such preventive measures which are compensated under paragraph 1. The Fund shall in any event be exonerated to the extent that the shipowner may have been exonerated under Article III, paragraph 3, of the Liability Convention.

4. (a) Except as otherwise provided in subparagraph (b) of this paragraph, the aggregate amount of compensation payable by the Fund under this Article shall in respect of any one incident be limited, so that the total sum of that amount and the amount of compensation actually paid under the Liability Convention for pollution damage caused in the territory of the Contracting States, including any sums in respect of which the Fund is under an obligation to indemnify the owner pursuant to Article 5, paragraph 1, of this Convention, shall not exceed 450 million francs.

(b) The aggregate amount of compensation payable by the Fund under this Article for pollution damage resulting from a natural phenomenon of an exceptional, inevitable and irresistible character shall not exceed 450 million francs.

5. Where the amount of established claims against the Fund exceeds the aggregate amount of compensation payable under paragraph 4, the amount available shall be distributed in such a manner that the proportion between any established claim and the amount of compensation actually recovered by the claimant under the Liability Convention and this Convention shall be the same for all claimants.

6. The Assembly of the Fund (hereinafter referred to as "the Assembly") may, having regard to the experience of incidents which have occurred and in particular the amount of damage resulting therefrom and to changes in the monetary values, decide that the amount of 450 million frances referred to in paragraph 4, sub-paragraphs (a) and (b), shall be changed; provided, however, that this amount shall in no case exceed 900 million francs or be lower than 450 million francs. The changed amount shall apply to incidents which occur after the date of the decision effecting the change.

7. The Fund shall, at the request of a Contracting State, use its good offices as necessary to assist that State to secure promptly such personnel, material and services as are necessary to enable the State to take measures to prevent or mitigate pollution damage arising from an incident in respect of which the Fund may be called upon to pay compensation under this Convention.

8. The Fund may on conditions to be laid down in the Internal Regulations provide credit facilities with a view to the taking of preventive measures against pollution damage arising from a particular incident in respect of which the Fund may be called upon to pay compensation under this Convention.

Article 5

1. For the purpose of fulfilling its function under Article 2, paragraph 1(b), the Fund shall indemnify the owner and his guarantor for that portion of the aggregate amount of liability under the Liability Convention which:

(a) is in excess of an amount equivalent to 1,500 francs for each ton of the ship's tonnage or of an amount of 125 million francs, whichever is the less, and

(b) is not in excess of an amount equivalent to 2,000 francs for each ton of the said tonnage or an amount of 210 million francs, whichever is the less,

provided, however, that the Fund shall incur no obligation under this paragraph where the pollution damage resulted from the willful misconduct of the owner himself.

2. The Assembly may decide that the Fund shall, on conditions to be laid down in the Internal Regulations, assume the obligations of a guarantor in respect of ships referred to in Article 3, paragraph 2, with regard to the portion of liability referred to in paragraph 1 of this Article. However, the Fund shall assume such obligations only if the owner so requests and if he maintains adequate insurance or other financial security covering the owner's liability under the Liability Convention up to an amount equivalent to 1,500 francs for each ton of the ship's tonnage or an amount of 125 million francs, whichever is the less. If the Fund assumes such obligations, the owner shall in each Contracting State be considered to have complied with Article VII of the Liability Convention in respect of the portion of his liability mentioned above.

3. The Fund may be exonerated wholly or partially from its obligations under paragraph 1 towards the owner and his guarantor if the Fund proves that as a result of the actual fault or privity of the owner:

(a) the ship from which the oil causing the pollution damage escaped did not comply with the requirements laid down in:

(i) the International Convention for the Prevention of Pollution of the Sea by Oil, 1954, as amended in 1962; or

(ii) the International Convention for the Safety of Life at Sea, 1960; or

(iii) the International Convention on Load Lines, 1966; or

(iv) the International Regulations for Preventing Collisions at Sea, 1960; or

(v) any amendments to the above-mentioned Conventions which have been determined as being of an important nature in accordance with Article XVI(5) of the Convention mentioned under (i), Article IX(e) of the Convention mentioned under (ii) or Article 29 (3)(d) or (4)(d) of the Convention mentioned under (iii), provided, however, that such amendments had been in force for at least twelve months at the time of the incident;

and

(b) the incident or damage was caused wholly or partially by such non-compliance.

The provisions of this paragraph shall apply irrespective of whether the Contracting State in which the ship was registered or whose flag it was flying is a Party to the relevant Instrument.

4. Upon the entry into force of a new Convention designed to replace, in whole or in part, any of the Instruments specified in paragraph 3, the Assembly may decide at least six months in advance a date on which the new Convention will replace such Instrument or part thereof for the purpose of paragraph 3. However, any State Party to this Convention may declare to the Director before that date

that it does not accept such replacement; in which case the decision of the Assembly shall have no effect in respect of a ship registered in, or flying the flag of, that State at the time of the incident. Such a declaration may be withdrawn at any later date and shall in any event cease to have effect when the State in question becomes a party to such new Convention.

5. A ship complying with the requirements in an amendment to an Instrument specified in paragraph 3 or with requirements in a new Convention, where the amendment or Convention is designed to replace in whole or in part such Instrument, shall be considered as complying with the requirements in the said Instrument for the purposes of paragraph 3.

6. Where the Fund, acting as a guarantor by virtue of paragraph 2, has paid compensation for pollution damage in accordance with the Liability Convention, it shall have a right of recovery from the owner if and to the extent that the Fund would have been exonerated pursuant to paragraph 3 from its obligations under paragraph 1 to indemnify the owner.

7. Expenses reasonably incurred and sacrifices reasonably made by the owner voluntarily to prevent or minimize pollution damage shall be treated as included in the owner's liability for the purposes of this Article.

Article 6

1. Rights to compensation under Article 4 or indemnification under Article 5 shall be extinguished unless an action is brought thereunder or a notification has been made pursuant to Article 7, paragraph 6, within three years from the date when the damage occurred. However, in no case shall an action be brought after six years from the date of the incident which caused the damage.

2. Notwithstanding paragraph 1, the right of the owner or his guarantor to seek indemnification from the Fund pursuant to Article 5, paragraph 1, shall in no case be extinguished before the expiry of a period of six months as from the date on which the owner or his guarantor acquired knowledge of the bringing of an action against him under the Liability Convention.

Article 7

1. Subject to the subsequent provisions of this Article, any action against the Fund for compensation under Article 4 or indemnification under Article 5 of this Convention shall be brought only before a court competent under Article IX of the Liability Convention in respect of actions against the owner who is or who would, but for the provisions of Article III, paragraph 2, of that Convention, have been liable for pollution damage caused by the relevant incident.

2. Each Contracting State shall ensure that its courts possess the necessary jurisdiction to entertain such actions against the Fund as are referred to in paragraph 1.

3. Where an action for compensation for pollution damage has been brought before a court competent under Article IX of the Liability Convention against the owner of a ship or his guarantor, such court shall have exclusive jurisdictional competence over any action against the Fund for compensation or indemnification under the provisions of Article 4 or 5 of this Convention in respect of the same damage.

However, where an action for compensation for pollution damage under the Liability Convention has been brought before a court in a State Party to the Liability Convention but not to this Convention, any action against the Fund under Article 4 or under Article 5, paragraph 1, of this Convention shall at the option of the claimant be brought either before a court of the State where the Fund has its headquarters or before any court of a State Party to this Convention competent under Article IX of the Liability Convention.

4. Each Contracting State shall ensure that the Fund shall have the right to intervene as a party to any legal proceedings instituted in accordance with Article IX of the Liability Convention before a competent court of that State against the owner of a ship or his guarantor.

5. Except as otherwise provided in paragraph 6, the Fund shall not be bound by any judgment or decision in proceedings to which it has not been a party or by any settlement to which it is not a party.

6. Without prejudice to the provisions of paragraph 4, where an action under the Liability Convention for compensation for pollution damage has been brought against an owner or his guarantor before a competent court in a Contracting State, each party to the proceedings shall be entitled under the national law of that State to notify the Fund of the proceedings. Where such notification has been made in accordance with the formalities required by the law of the court seized and in such time and in such a manner that the Fund has in fact been in a position effectively to intervene as a party to the proceedings, any judgment rendered by the court in such proceedings shall, after it has become final and enforceable in the State where the judgment was given, become binding upon the Fund in the sense that the facts and findings in that judgment may not be disputed by the Fund even if the Fund has not actually intervened in the proceedings.

Article 8

Subject to any decision concerning the distribution referred to in Article 4, paragraph 5, any judgment given against the Fund by a court having jurisdiction in accordance with Article 7, paragraphs 1 and 3, shall, when it has become enforceable in the State of origin and is in that State no longer subject to ordinary forms of review, be recognized and enforceable in each Contracting State on the same conditions as are prescribed in Article X of the Liability Convention.

Article 9

1. Subject to the provisions of Article 5, the Fund shall, in respect of any amount of compensation for pollution damage paid by the Fund in accordance with Article 4, paragraph 1, of this Convention, acquire by subrogation the rights that the person so compensated may enjoy under the Liability Convention against the owner or his guarantor.

2. Nothing in this Convention shall prejudice any right of recourse or subrogation of the Fund against persons other than those referred to in the preceding paragraph. In any event the right of the Fund to subrogation against such person shall not be less favourable than that of an insurer of the person to whom compensation or indemnification has been paid.

3. Without prejudice to any other rights of subrogation or recourse against the Fund which may exist, a Contracting State or agency thereof which has paid compensation for pollution damage in accordance with provisions of national law shall acquire by subrogation the rights which the person so compensated would have enjoyed under this Convention.

Contributions

Article 10

1. Contributions to the Fund shall be made in respect of each Contracting State by any person who, in the calendar year referred to in Article 11, paragraph 1, as regards initial contributions and in Article 12, paragraphs 2 (a) or (b), as regards annual contributions, has received in total quantities exceeding 150,000 tons:

(a) in the ports or terminal installations in the territory of that State contributing oil carried by sea to such ports or terminal installations; and

(b) in any installations situated in the territory of that Contracting State contributing oil which has been carried by sea and discharged in a port or terminal installation of a non-Contracting State, provided that contributing oil shall only be taken into account by virtue of this sub-paragraph on first receipt in a Contracting State after its discharge in that non-Contracting State.

2. (a) For the purposes of paragraph 1, where the quantity of contributing oil received in the territory of a Contracting State by any person in a calendar year when aggregated with the quantity of contributing oil received in the same Contracting State in that year by any associated person or persons exceeds 150,000 tons, such person shall pay contributions in respect of the actual quantity received by him notwithstanding that that quantity did not exceed 150,000 tons.

(b) "Associated person" means any subsidiary or commonly controlled entity. The question whether a person comes within this definition shall be determined by the national law of the State concerned.

Article 11

1. In respect of each Contracting State initial contributions shall be made of an amount which shall for each person referred to in Article 10 be calculated on the basis of a fixed sum for each ton of contributing oil received by him during the calendar year preceding that in which this Convention entered into force for that State.

2. The sum referred to in paragraph 1 shall be determined by the Assembly within two months after the entry into force of this Convention. In performing this function the Assembly shall, to the extent possible, fix the sum in such a way that the total amount of initial contributions would, if contributions were to be made in respect of 90 per cent of the quantities of contributing oil carried by sea in the world, equal 75 million francs.

3. The initial contributions shall in respect of each Contracting State be paid within three months following the date at which the Convention entered into force for that State.

Article 12

1. With a view to assessing for each person referred to in Article 10 the amount of annual contributions due, if any, and taking account of the necessity to maintain sufficient liquid funds, the Assembly shall for each calendar year make an estimate in the form of a budget of:

(i) *Expenditure*

(a) costs and expenses of the administration of the Fund in the relevant year and any deficit from operations in preceding years;

(b) payments to be made by the Fund in the relevant year for the satisfaction of claims against the Fund due under Article 4 or 5, including repayment on loans previously taken by the Fund for the satisfaction of such claims, to the extent that the aggregate amount of such claims in respect of any one incident does not exceed 15 million francs;

(c) payments to be made by the Fund in the relevant year for the satisfaction of claims against the Fund due under Article 4 or 5, including repayments on loans previously taken by the Fund for the satisfaction of such claims, to the extent that the aggregate amount of such claims in respect of any one incident is in excess of 15 million francs;

(ii) *Income*

(a) surplus funds from operations in preceding years, including any interest;

(b) initial contributions to be paid in the course of the year;

(c) annual contributions, if required to balance the budget;

(d) any other income.

2. For each person referred to in Article 10 the amount of his annual contribution shall be determined by the Assembly and shall be calculated in respect of each Contracting State:

(a) in so far as the contribution is for the satisfaction of payments referred to in paragraph 1(i) (a) and (b) on the basis of a fixed sum for each ton of contributing oil received in the relevant State by such persons during the preceding calendar year; and

(b) in so far as the contribution is for the satisfaction of payments referred to in paragraph 1(i) (c) of this Article on the basis of a fixed sum for each ton of contributing oil received by such person during the calendar year preceding that in which the incident in question occurred, provided that State was a party to this Convention at the date of the incident.

3. The sums referred to in paragraph 2 above shall be arrived at by dividing the relevant total amount of contributions required by the total amount of contributing oil received in all Contracting States in the relevant year.

4. The Assembly shall decide the portion of the annual contribution which shall be immediately paid in cash and decide on the date of payment. The remaining part of each annual contribution shall be paid upon notification by the Director.

5. The Director may, in cases and in accordance with conditions to be laid down in the Internal Regulations of the Fund, require a contributor to provide financial security for the sums due from him.

6. Any demand for payments made under paragraph 4 shall be called rateably from all individual contributors.

Article 13

1. The amount of any contribution due under Article 12 and which is in arrear shall bear interest at a rate which shall be determined by the Assembly for each calendar year provided that different rates may be fixed for different circumstances.

2. Each Contracting State shall ensure that any obligation to contribute to the Fund arising under this Convention in respect of oil received within the territory of that State is fulfilled and shall take any appropriate measures under its law, including the imposing of such sanctions as it may deem necessary, with a view to the effective execution of any such obligation; provided, however, that such measures shall only be directed against those persons who are under an obligation to contribute to the Fund.

3. Where a person who is liable in accordance with the provisions of Articles 10 and 11 to make contributions to the Fund does not fulfil his obligations in respect of any such contribution or any part thereof and is in arrear for a period exceeding three months, the Director shall take all appropriate action against such person on behalf of the Fund with a view to the recovery of the amount due. However, where the defaulting contributor is manifestly insolvent or the circumstances otherwise so warrant, the Assembly may, upon recommendation of the Director, decide that no action shall be taken or continued against the contributor.

Article 14

1. Each Contracting State may at the time when it deposits its instrument of ratification or accession or at any time thereafter declare that it assumes itself obligations that are incumbent under this Convention on any person who is liable to contribute to the Fund in accordance with Article 10, paragraph 1, in respect of oil received within the territory of that State. Such declaration shall be made in writing and shall specify which obligations are assumed.

2. Where a declaration under paragraph 1 is made prior to the entry into force of this Convention in accordance with Article 40, it shall be deposited with the Secretary-General of the Organization who shall after the entry into force of the Convention communicate the declaration to the Director.

3. A declaration under paragraph 1 which is made after the entry into force of this Convention shall be deposited with the Director.

4. A declaration made in accordance with this Article may be withdrawn by the relevant State giving notice thereof in writing to the Director. Such notification shall take effect three months after the Director's receipt thereof.

5. Any State which is bound by a declaration made under this Article shall, in any proceedings brought against it before a competent court in respect of any obligation specified in the declaration, waive any immunity that it would otherwise be entitled to invoke.

Article 15

1. Each Contracting State shall ensure that any person who receives contributing oil within its territory in such quantities that he is

liable to contribute to the Fund appears on a list to be established and kept up to date by the Director in accordance with the subsequent provisions of this Article.

2. For the purposes set out in paragraph 1, each Contracting State shall communicate, at a time and in the manner to be prescribed in the Internal Regulations, to the Director the name and address of any person who in respect of that State is liable to contribute to the Fund pursuant to Article 10, as well as data on the relevant quantities of contributing oil received by any such person during the preceding calendar year.

3. For the purposes of ascertaining who are, at any given time, the persons liable to contribute to the Fund in accordance with Article 10, paragraph 1, and of establishing, where applicable, the quantities of oil to be taken into account for any such person when determining the amount of his contribution, the list shall be *prima facie* evidence of the facts stated therein.

Organization and Administration

Article 16

The Fund shall have an Assembly, a Secretariat headed by a Director and, in accordance with the provisions of Article 21, an Executive Committee.

Assembly

Article 17

The Assembly shall consist of all Contracting States to this Convention.

Article 18

The functions of the Assembly shall, subject to the provisions of Article 26, be:

1. to elect at each regular session its Chairman and two Vice-Chairman who shall hold office until the next regular session;
2. to determine its own rules of procedure, subject to the provisions of this Convention;
3. to adopt Internal Regulations necessary for the proper functioning of the Fund;
4. to appoint the Director and make provisions for the appointment of such other personnel as may be necessary and determine the terms and conditions of service of the Director and other personnel;
5. to adopt the annual budget and fix the annual contributions;
6. to appoint auditors and approve the accounts of the Fund;
7. to approve settlements of claims against the Fund, to make decisions in respect of the distribution among claimants of the available amount of compensation in accordance with Article 4, paragraph 5, and to determine the terms and conditions according to which provisional payments in respect of claims shall be made with a view to ensuring that victims of pollution damage are compensated as promptly as possible;
8. to elect the members of the Assembly to be represented on the Executive Committee, as provided in Articles 21, 22 and 23;
9. to establish any temporary or permanent subsidiary body it may consider to be necessary;

10. to determine which non-Contracting States and which intergovernmental and international non-governmental organizations shall be admitted to take part, without voting rights, in meetings of the Assembly, the Executive Committee, and subsidiary bodies;

11. to give instructions concerning the administration of the Fund to the Director, the Executive Committee and subsidiary bodies;

12. to review and approve the reports and activities of the Executive Committee;

13. to supervise the proper execution of the Convention and of its own decisions;

14. to perform such other functions as are allocated to it under the Convention or are otherwise necessary for the proper operation of the Fund.

Article 19

1. Regular sessions of the Assembly shall take place once every calendar year upon convocation by the Director; provided, however, that if the Assembly allocates to the Executive Committee the functions specified in Article 18, paragraph 5, regular sessions of the Assembly shall be held once every two years.

2. Extraordinary sessions of the Assembly shall be convened by the Director at the request of the Executive Committee or of at least one-third of the members of the Assembly and may be convened on the Director's own initiative after consultation with the Chairman of the Assembly. The Director shall give members at least thirty days' notice of such sessions.

Article 20

A majority of the members of the Assembly shall constitute a quorum for its meetings.

Executive Committee

Article 21

The Executive Committee shall be established at the first regular session of the Assembly after the date on which the number of Contracting States reaches fifteen.

Article 22

1. The Executive Committee shall consist of one-third of the members of the Assembly but of not less than seven or more than fifteen members. Where the number of members of the Assembly is not divisible by three, the one-third referred to shall be calculated on the next higher number which is divisible by three.

2. When electing the members of the Executive Committee the Assembly shall:

(a) secure an equit able geographical distribution of the seats on the Committee on the basis of an adequate representation of Contracting States particularly exposed to the risks of oil pollution and of Contracting States having large tanker fleets; and

(b) elect one half of the members of the Committee, or in case the total number of members to be elected is uneven, such number of the members as is equivalent to one half of the total number less one, among those Contracting States in the territory of which the largest quantities of oil to be taken into account under Article 10 were received during the preceding calendar year, provided that the number of States eligible under this sub-paragraph shall be limited as shown in the table below:

Total number of members on the committee	Number of States eligible under subparagraph (b)	Number of States to be elected under subparagraph (b)
7	5	3
8	6	4
9	6	4
10	8	5
11	8	5
12	9	6
13	9	6
14	11	7
15	11	7

3. A member of the Assembly which was eligible but was not elected under sub-paragraph (b) shall not be eligible to be elected for any remaining seat on the Executive Committee.

Article 23

1. Members of the Executive Committee shall hold office until the end of the next regular session of the Assembly.
2. Except to the extent that may be necessary for complying with the requirements of Article 22, no State Member of the Assembly may serve on the Executive Committee for more than two consecutive terms.

Article 24

The Executive Committee shall meet at least once every calendar year at thirty days' notice upon convocation by the Director, either on his own initiative or at the request of its Chairman or of at least one-third of its members. It shall meet at such places as may be convenient.

Article 25

At least two-thirds of the members of the Executive Committee shall constitute a quorum for its meetings.

Article 26

1. The functions of the Executive Committee shall be:

(a) to elect its Chairman and adopt its own rules of procedure, except as otherwise provided in this Convention;

(b) to assume and exercise in place of the Assembly the following functions:

(i) making provision for the appointment of such personnel, other than the Director, as may be necessary and determining the terms and conditions of service of such personnel;

(ii) approving settlements of claims against the Fund and taking all other steps envisaged in relation to such claims in Article 18, paragraph 7;

(iii) giving instructions to the Director concerning the administration of the Fund and supervising the proper execution, by him of the Convention, of the decisions of the Assembly and of the Committee's own decisions; and

(c) to perform such other functions as are allocated to it by the Assembly.

2. The Executive Committee shall each year prepare and publish a report of the activities of the Fund during the previous calendar year.

Article 27

Members of the Assembly who are not members of the Executive Committee shall have the right to attend its meetings as observers.

Secretariat

Article 28

1. The Secretariat shall comprise the Director and such staff as the administration of the Fund may require.

2. The Director shall be the legal representative of the Fund.

Article 29

1. The Director shall be the chief administrative officer of the Fund and shall, subject to the instructions given to him by the Assembly and by the Executive Committee, perform those functions which are assigned to him by this Convention, the Internal Regulations, the Assembly and the Executive Committee.

2. The Director shall in particular:

(a) appoint the personnel required for the administration of the Fund;

(b) take all appropriate measures with a view to the proper administration of the Fund's assets;

(c) collect the contributions due under this Convention while observing in particular the provisions of Article 13, paragraph 3;

(d) to the extent necessary to deal with claims against the Fund and carry out the other functions of the Fund, employ the services of legal, financial and other experts;

(e) take all appropriate measures for dealing with claims against the Fund within the limits and on conditions to be laid down in the International Regulations, including the final settlement of claims without the prior approval of the Assembly or the Executive Committee where these Regulations so provide;

(f) prepare and submit to the Assembly or to the Executive Committee, as the case may be, the financial statements and budget estimates for each calendar year;

(g) assist the Executive Committee in the preparation of the report referred to in Article 26, paragraph 2;

(h) prepare, collect and circulate the papers, documents, agenda, minutes and information that may be required for the work of the Assembly, the Executive Committee and subsidiary bodies.

Article 30

In the performance of their duties the Director and the staff and experts appointed by him shall not seek or receive instructions from any Government or from any authority external to the Fund. They shall refrain from any action which might reflect on their position as international officials. Each Contracting State on its part undertakes to respect the exclusively international character of the responsibilities of the Director and the staff and experts appointed by him, and not to seek to influence them in the discharge of their duties.

Finances

Article 31

1. Each Contracting State shall bear the salary, travel and other expenses of its own delegation to the Assembly and of its representatives on the Executive Committee and on subsidiary bodies.
2. Any other expenses incurred in the operation of the Fund shall be borne by the Fund.

Voting

Article 32

The following provisions shall apply to voting in the Assembly and the Executive Committee:

(a) each member shall have one vote;

(b) except as otherwise provided in Article 33, decisions of the Assembly and the Executive Committee shall be by a majority vote of the members present and voting;

(c) decisions where a three-fourths or a two-thirds majority is required shall be by a three-fourths or two-thirds majority vote, as the case may be, of those present;

(d) for the purpose of this Article the phrase "members present" means "members present at the meeting at the time of the vote", and the phrase "members present and voting" means "members present and casting an affirmative or negative vote". Members who abstain from voting shall be considered as not voting.

Article 33

1. The following decisions of the Assembly shall require a three-fourths majority:

(a) an increase in accordance with Article 4, paragraph 6, in the maximum amount of compensation payable by the Fund;

(b) a determination, under Article 5, paragraph 4, relating to the replacement of the Instruments referred to in that paragraph;

(c) the allocation to the Executive Committee of the functions specified in Article 18, paragraph 5.

2. The following decisions of the Assembly shall require a two-thirds majority:

(a) a decision under Article 13, paragraph 3, not to take or continue action against a contributor;

(b) the appointment of the Director under Article 18, paragraph 4;

(c) the establishment of subsidiary bodies, under Article 18, paragraph 9.

Article 34

1. The Fund, its assets, income, including contributions, and other property shall enjoy in all Contracting States exemption from all direct taxation.

2. When the Fund makes substantial purchases of movable or immovable property, or has important work carried out which is necessary for the exercise of its official activities and the cost of which includes indirect taxes or sales taxes, the Governments of Member States shall take, whenever possible, appropriate measures for the remission or refund of the amount of such duties and taxes.

3. No exemption shall be accorded in the case of duties, taxes or dues which merely constitute payment for public utility services.

4. The Fund shall enjoy exemption from all customs duties, taxes and other related taxes on articles imported or exported by it or on its behalf for its official use. Articles thus imported shall not be transferred either for consideration or gratis on the territory of the country into which they have been imported except on conditions agreed by the government of that country.

5. Persons contributing to the Fund and victims and owners of ships receiving compensation from the Fund shall be subject to the fiscal legislation of the State where they are taxable, no special exemption or other benefit being conferred on them in this respect.

6. Information relating to individual contributors supplied for the purpose of this Convention shall not be divulged outside the Fund except in so far as it may be strictly necessary to enable the Fund to carry out its functions including the bringing and defending of legal proceedings.

7. Independently of existing or future regulations concerning currency or transfers, Contracting States shall authorize the transfer and payment of any contribution to the Fund and of any compensation paid by the Fund without any restriction.

Transitional Provisions

Article 35

1. The Fund shall incur no obligation whatsoever under Article 4 or 5 in respect of incidents occurring within a period of one hundred and twenty days after the entry into force of this Convention.

2. Claims for compensation under Article 4 and claims for indemnification under Article 5, arising from incidents occurring later than one hundred and twenty days but not later than two hundred and forty days after the entry into force of this Convention may not be brought against the Fund prior to the elapse of the two hundred and fortieth day after the entry into force of this Convention.

Article 36

The Secretary-General of the Organization shall convene the first session of the Assembly. This session shall take place as soon as possible after entry into force of this Convention and, in any case, not more than thirty days after such entry into force.

Final Clauses

Article 37

1. This Convention shall be open for signature by the States which have signed or which accede to the Liability Convention, and by any State represented at the Conference on the Establishment of an International Fund for Compensation for Oil Pollution Damage, 1971. The Convention shall remain open for signature until 31 December 1972.

2. Subject to paragraph 4, this Convention shall be ratified, accepted or approved by the States which have signed it.

3. Subject to paragraph 4, this Convention is open for accession by States which did not sign it.

4. This Convention may be ratified, accepted, approved or acceded to, only by States which have ratified, accepted, approved or acceded to the Liability Convention.

Article 38

1. Ratification, acceptance, approval or accession shall be effected by the deposit of a formal instrument to that effect with the Secretary-General of the Organization.

2. Any instrument of ratification, acceptance, approval or accession deposited after the entry into force of an amendment to this Convention with respect to all existing Contracting States or after the completion of all measures required for the entry into force of the amendment with respect to those Parties shall be deemed to apply to the Convention as modified by the amendment.

Article 39

Before this Convention comes into force a State shall, when depositing an instrument referred to in Article 38, paragraph 1, and annually thereafter at a date to be determined by the Secretary-General of the Organization, communicate to him the name and address of any person who in respect of that State would be liable to contribute to the Fund pursuant to Article 10 as well as data on the relevant quantities of contributing oil received by any such person in the territory of that State during the preceding calendar year.

Article 40

1. This Convention shall enter into force on the ninetieth day following the date on which the following requirements are fulfilled:

(a) at least eight States have deposited instruments of ratification, acceptance, approval or accession with the Secretary-General of the Organization, and

(b) the Secretary-General of the Organization has received information in accordance with Article 39 that those persons in such States who would be liable to contribute pursuant to Article 10 have received during the preceding calendar year a total quantity of at least 750 million tons of contributing oil.

2. However, this Convention shall not enter into force before the Liability Convention has entered into force.

3. For each State which subsequently ratifies, accepts, approves or accedes to it, this Convention shall enter into force on the ninetieth day after deposit by such State of the appropriate instrument.

Article 41

1. This Convention may be denounced by any Contracting State at any time after the date on which the Convention comes into force for that State.

2. Denunciation shall be effected by the deposit of an instrument with the Secretary-General of the Organization.

3. A denunciation shall take effect one year, or such longer period as may be specified in the instrument of denunciation, after its deposit with the Secretary-General of the Organization.

4. Denunciation of the Liability Convention shall be deemed to be a denunciation of this Convention. Such denunciation shall take effect on the same date as the denunciation of the Liability Convention takes effect according to paragraph 3 of Article XVI of that Convention.

5. Notwithstanding a denunciation by a Contracting State pursuant to this Article, any provisions of this Convention relating to the obligations to make contributions under Article 10 with respect to an incident referred to in Article 12, paragraph 2(b), and occurring before the denunciation takes effect shall continue to apply.

Article 42

1. Any Contracting State may, within ninety days after the deposit of an instrument of denunciation the result of which it considers will significantly increase the level of contributions for remaining Contracting States, request the Director to convene an extraordinary session of the Assembly. The Director shall convene the Assembly to meet not later than sixty days after recepit of the request.

2. The Director may convene, on his own initiative, an extraordinary session of the Assembly to meet within sixty days after the deposit of any instrument of denunication, if he considers that such denunciation will result in a significant increase in the level of contributions for the remaining Contracting States.

3. If the Assembly at an extraordinary session convened in accordance with paragraph 1 or 2 decides that the denunciation will result in a significant increase in the level of contributions for the remaining Contracting States, any such State may, not later than one hundred and twenty days before the date on which that denunciation takes effect, denounce this Convention with effect from the same date.

Article 43

1. This Convention shall cease to be in force on the date when the number of Contracting States falls below three.

2. Contracting States which are bound by this Convention on the date before the day it ceases to be in force shall enable the Fund to exercise its functions as described under Article 44 and shall, for that purpose only, remain bound by this Convention.

Article 44

1. If this Convention ceases to be in force, the Fund shall nevertheless

(a) meet its obligations in respect of any incident occurring before the Convention ceased to be in force;

(b) be entitled to exercise its rights to contributions to the extent that these contributions are necessary to meet the obligations under sub-paragraph (a), including expenses for the administration of the Fund necessary for this purpose.

2. The Assembly shall take all appropriate measures to complete the winding up of the Fund, including the distribution in an equitable manner of any remaining assets among those persons who have contributed to the Fund.

3. For the purposes of this Article the Fund shall remain a legal person.

Article 45

1. A Conference for the purpose of revising or amending this Convention may be convened by the Organization.

2. The Organization shall convene a Conference of the Contracting States for the purpose of revising or amending this Convention at the request of not less than one-third of all Contracting States.

Article 46

1. This Convention shall be deposited with the Secretary-General of the Organization.

2. The Secretary-General of the Organization shall:

(a) inform all States which have signed or acceded to this Convention of:

(i) each new signature or deposit of instrument and the date thereof;

(ii) the date of entry into force of the Convention;

(iii) any denunciation of the Convention and the date on which it takes effect;

(b) transmit certified true copies of this Convention to all Signatory States and to all States which accede to the Convention.

Article 47

As soon as this Convention enters into force, a certified true copy thereof shall be transmitted by the Secretary-General of the Organization to the Secretariat of the United Nations for registration and publication in accordance with Article 102 of the Charter of the United Nations.

Article 48

This Convention is established in a single original in the English and French languages, both texts being equally authentic. Official translations in the Russian and Spanish languages shall be prepared by the Secretariat of the Organization and deposited with the signed original.

IN WITNESS WHEREOF the undersigned plenipotentiaries being duly authorized for that purpose have signed the present Convention.

DONE at Brussels this eighteenth day of December one thousand nine hundred and seventy-one.

Certified true copy of the International Convention on the Establishment of an International Fund for Compensation for Oil Pollution Damage, 1971, done at Brussels on 18 December 1971, the original of which is deposited with the Inter-Governmental Maritime Consultative Organization.

THOMAS S. FISHER,
(For the Secretary-General of the Inter-Governmental
Maritime Consultative Organization.)

London, 14 March 1972.

RESOLUTION OF THE CONFERENCE

The States represented at the Conference on the Establishment of an International Fund for Compensation for Oil Pollution Damage,

HAVING adopted the International Convention on the establishment of the said Fund,

CONSCIOUS of the necessity that, before the Convention enters into force, and for some time thereafter some administrative and organizational measures have to be prepared in order to ensure that the Fund, as from the dates of entry into force of the Convention, can operate properly, without prejudice as to the location of the headquarters of the Fund,

REQUEST the Inter-Governmental Maritime Consultative Organization, on the basis that all expenses incurred would be repaid by the Fund:

1. To ask the Secretary-General of IMCO to convene, in accordance with Article 36 of the said Convention, and make the necessary preparations for, the first session of the Assembly of the Fund;

2. To give all necessary assistance for the setting-up of the Fund;

3. To provide accommodation and supporting services as appropriate;

4. To provide the necessary staff on a temporary basis.

AGREEMENT FOR CO-OPERATION IN DEALING WITH POLLUTION OF THE NORTH SEA BY OIL

The Governments of
the Kingdom of Belgium
the Kingdom of Denmark
the French Republic
the Federal Republic of Germany
the Kingdom of the Netherlands
the Kingdom of Norway
the Kingdom of Sweden
the United Kingdom of Great Britain and Northern Ireland

Recognizing that grave pollution of the sea by oil in the North Sea area involves a danger to the coastal states,

Noting that the Council of the Inter-Governmental Maritime Consultative Organization at its third extraordinary session in May, 1967, decided to include among the matters requiring study as a matter of urgency, *inter alia,*

> " procedures whereby States, regionally or inter-regionally where applicable, can co-operate at short notice to provide manpower, supplies, equipment and scientific advice to deal with discharge of oil or other noxious or hazardous substances including consideration of the possibility of patrols to ascertain the extent of the discharge and the manner of treating it both on sea and land ",

Have agreed on the following:

ARTICLE 1

This Agreement shall apply whenever the presence or the prospective presence of oil polluting the sea within the North Sea area, as defined in Article 2 of this Agreement, presents a grave and imminent danger to the coast or related interests of one or more Contracting Parties.

ARTICLE 2

For the purposes of this Agreement the North Sea area means the North Sea proper southwards of latitude 61° N together with

(*a*) the Skagerrak, the southern limit of which is determined by a line joining Skagen and Pater Noster Skären;

(*b*) the English Channel and its approaches eastwards of a line drawn fifty nautical miles to the west of a line joining the Scilly Isles and Ushant.

ARTICLE 3

The Contracting Parties consider that protection against pollution of the kind referred to in Article 1 of this Agreement is a matter which calls for active co-operation between the Contracting Parties.

ARTICLE 4

Contracting Parties undertake to inform the other Contracting Parties about

(*a*) their national organization for dealing with oil pollution;

(*b*) the competent authority responsible for receiving reports of oil pollution and for dealing with questions concerning measures of mutual assistance between Contracting Parties;

(*c*) new ways in which oil pollution may be avoided and about new effective measures to deal with oil pollution.

ARTICLE 5

(1) Whenever a Contracting Party is aware of a casualty or the presence of oil slicks in the North Sea area likely to constitute a serious threat to the coast or related interests of any other Contracting Party, it shall inform that other Party without delay through its competent authority.

(2) The Contracting Parties undertake to request the masters of all ships flying their flags and pilots of aircraft registered in their countries to report without delay through the channels which may be most practicable and adequate in the circumstances:

(*a*) all casualties causing or likely to cause oil pollution of the sea;

(*b*) the presence, nature and extent of oil slicks on the sea likely to constitute a serious threat to the coast or related interests of one or more Contracting Parties.

ARTICLE 6

(1) For the sole purposes of this Agreement the North Sea area is divided into the zones described in the Annex to this Agreement.

(2) The Contracting Party within whose zone a situation of the kind described in Article 1 occurs, shall make the necessary assessments of the nature and extent of any casualty or, as the case may be, of the type and approximate quantity of oil floating on the sea, and the direction and speed of movement of the oil.

(3) The Contracting Party concerned shall immediately inform all the other Contracting Parties through their competent authorities of its assessments and of any action which it has taken to deal with the floating oil and shall keep the oil under observation as long as it is drifting in its zone.

(4) The obligations of the Contracting Parties under the provisions of this Article with respect to the zones of joint responsibility shall be the subject of special technical arrangements to be concluded between the Parties concerned. These arrangements shall be communicated to the other Contracting Parties.

(5) In no case shall the division into zones referred to in this Article be invoked as a precedent or argument in any matter concerning sovereignty or jurisdiction.

Article 7

A Contracting Party requiring assistance to dispose of oil floating on the sea or polluting its coast may call on the help of the the other Contracting Parties, starting with those which also seem likely to be affected by the floating oil. Contracting Parties called upon for help in accordance with this Article shall use their best endeavours to bring such assistance as is within their power.

Article 8

Any Contracting Party which has taken action in accordance with Article 7 of this Agreement shall submit a report thereon to the other Contracting Parties and to the Inter-Governmental Maritime Consultative Organisation.

Article 9

(1) This Agreement shall be open for signature by the Governments mentioned in the preamble from 9 June 1969.

(2) These Governments may become parties to this Agreement either by signature without reservation as to ratification or approval or by signature subject to ratification or approval followed by ratification or approval.

(3) Instruments of ratification or approval shall be deposited with the Government of the Federal Republic of Germany.

(4) This Agreement shall enter into force two months after the date on which six Governments have signed the Agreement without reservation as to ratification or approval[1] or have deposited an instrument of ratification or approval.

(5) For each Government which subsequently signs the Agreement without reservation as to ratification or approval, or ratifies or approves it, it shall enter into force two months after the date of its signature or of the deposit of its instrument of ratification or approval.

Article 10

(1) After this Agreement has been in force for five years it may be denounced by any Contracting Party.

(2) Denunciation shall be effected by a notification in writing addressed to the Government of the Federal Republic of Germany which shall notify all the other Contracting Parties of any denunciation received and of the date of its receipt.

(3) A denunciation shall take effect one year after its receipt by the Government of the Federal Republic of Germany.

---

(1) The Agreement entered into force on 9 August, 1969.

In witness whereof the undersigned, being duly authorized by their respective Governments, have signed this Agreement.

Done at Bonn on this ninth day of June, 1969, in the English and French languages, both texts being equally authoritative, in a single copy which shall be deposited in the archives of the Government of the Federal Republic of Germany which shall transmit a duly certified copy to each of the other signatory Governments. This Agreement shall be registered with the United Nations in conformity with Article 102 of the Charter of the United Nations.[2]

En foi de quoi, les soussignés, dûment autorisés par leurs Gouvernements respectifs, ont signé le présent Accord.

Fait à Bonn le neuvième jour du mois de juin 1969 en langues française et anglaise, les deux textes faisant également foi, en un exemplaire unique qui sera déposé dans les archives du Gouvernement de la République fédérale d'Allemagne et dont une copie certifiée conforme sera transmise par ce Gouvernement à tous les autres Gouvernements signataires. Le présent Accord sera déposé pour enregistrement auprès de l'Organisation des Nations Unies conformément à l'Article 102 de la Charte des Nations Unies.

For the Government of the Kingdom of Belgium:

Pour le Gouvernement du Royaume de Belgique :

WALTER LORIDAN

For the Government of the Kingdom of Denmark:

Pour le Gouvernement du Royaume de Danemark :

K. KNUTH-WINTERFELT

For the Government of the French Republic:

Pour le Gouvernement de la République française :

FRANÇOIS SEYDOUX

For the Government of the Federal Republic of Germany:

Pour le Gouvernement de la République fédérale d'Allemagne :

WILLY BRANDT

---

(2) Treaty Series No. 67 (1946), Cmd. 7015.

ANNEX

Description of the zones referred to in Article 6 of this Agreement

The zones with the exception of the zones of joint responsibility are limited by lines joining the following points:

Denmark

55° 03′ N	8° 22′ E
55° 10′ N	7° 30′ E
55° 10′ N	2° 15′ E
57° 00′ N	1° 30′ E
57° 00′ N	6° 40′ E
58° 10′ N	10° 00′ E
57° 48′ N	10° 57′ E
57° 44′ N	10° 38′ E (Skagen)

Germany

53° 34′ N	6° 38′ E
54° 00′ N	5° 30′ E
54° 00′ N	2° 40′ E
55° 10′ N	2° 15′ E
55° 10′ N	7° 30′ E
55° 03′ N	8° 22′ E

Netherlands

51° 32′ N	3° 18′ E
51° 32′ N	2° 06′ E
52° 30′ N	3° 10′ E
54° 00′ N	2° 40′ E
54° 00′ N	5° 30′ E
53° 34′ N	6° 38′ E

Norway

61° 00′ N	4° 30′ E
61° 00′ N	2° 00′ E
57° 00′ N	1° 30′ E
57° 00′ N	6° 40′ E
58° 10′ N	10° 00′ E
58° 54·5′ N	10° 43′ E

To be continued along the Norwegian-Swedish border.

Sweden

57° 54′ N (Pater Noster lighthouse)	11° 28′ E
57° 48′ N	10° 57′ E
58° 10′ N	10° 00′ E
58° 54·5′ N	10° 43′ E

To be continued along the Norwegian-Swedish border.

United Kingdom

61° 00′ N	0° 50′ W
61° 00′ N	2° 00′ E
57° 00′ N	1° 30′ E
52° 30′ N	3° 10′ E
51° 32′ N	2° 06′ E

The zones of joint responsibility are as follows:

(1) *Belgium, France and United Kingdom*
Sea area between parallels 51° 32′ N and 51° 06′ N.

(2) *France and United Kingdom*
The English Channel south-west of parallel 51° 06′ N to a line drawn between the points 49° 52′ N 07° 44′ W and 48° 27′ N 06° 25′ W.

AGREEMENT BETWEEN NORWAY, DENMARK, FINLAND, AND SWEDEN CONCERNING CO-OPERATION IN TAKING MEASURES AGAINST POLLUTION OF THE SEA BY OIL.

The Governments of Norway, Denmark, Finland and Sweden,

Desiring to co-operate in dealing with any significant pollution of the sea by oil which threatens the coasts or related interests of one of the Contracting States, and to co-operate in furthering supervision of compliance with the International Convention for the Prevention of Pollution of the Sea by Oil and the national regulations based on that Convention, and

Taking into account the Agreement of June 9, 1969 for Co-operation in Dealing with Pollution of the North Sea by Oil,

Have agreed as follows:

Article 1

A Contracting State shall without delay inform the competent authority of another Contracting State of the sighting of any significant oil slick which it is feared will drift towards the territory of the latter State.

Article 2

A Contracting State threatened by any significant oil pollution which it is feared may affect another Contracting State, shall investigate the situation, including the state of the oil, its approximate quantity or extent, position, direction of movement and speed; the result of this investigation shall be communicated without delay to the other State, together with information on the measures which have been taken or which it is intended to take.

Article 3

A Contracting State requiring assistance to deal with oil which is threatening its coast or related interests, may request help from the other Contracting States. Such a request shall be addressed first to those States which can also be expected to be affected by the oil. A Contracting State which pursuant to this Article has been asked for assistance, shall do what is possible to render such assistance.

Article 4

(a) The Contracting States undertake to provide themselves with equipment for dealing with any significant oil slicks at sea.

(b) In order to achieve the greatest possible efficacy in the use of this equipment, stocks of anti-oil material should be built up and positioned following discussion with the other Contracting States to the extent which is thought necessary.

(c) A Contracting State shall inform the other Contracting States of the equipment it has for dealing with oil pollution.

(d) A Contracting State shall inform the other Contracting States of its experience in the materials and methods of dealing with oil pollution.

Article 5.

A Contracting State shall inform the other contracting States of any significant oil slick which has led it to take action, of the measures taken and their result.

Article 6.

A Contracting State shall inform the competent authority of another Contracting State of any case where a vessel registered in the latter State has been observed committing an offense within the territorial or adjacent waters of the Contracting States against the regulations concerning pollution by oil.

Article 7.

The Contracting States shall render assistance to each other in the investigation of offenses against the regulations concerning pollution by oil which are presumed to have been committed within the territorial or adjacent waters of the contracting States.

Such assistance may include inspection of the oil record book, the ship's official log-book and the engine-room log, the taking of oil samples and so on.

Article 8.

The Contracting States shall exchange information concerning:

(a) existing facilities and facilities under construction for the reception of oily residues from ships;

(b) national regulations and other conditions which are relevant to the avoidance of oil pollution;

(c) the authorities in the respective Contracting States to which information shall be given in accordance with the present Agreement.

Article 9.

The competent authorities shall co-operate directly in planning and the other measures required of them for implementing this Agreement.

Article 10.

If one of the Contracting States desires to denounce the Agreement, written notice to that effect shall be given to the Danish Government, which shall forthwith inform the other Contracting States of the denunciation and of the date of receipt of the notice.

A denunciation shall take effect twelve months after its receipt by the Danish Government or at such later date as may be specified in the notice.

Article 11.

The Agreement shall be deposited with the Danish Ministry of Foreign Affairs, and certified copies thereof shall be transmitted by the said Ministry to the Government of each of the Contracting States.

Article 12.

The Agreement is open for signature from September 16, 1971 and comes into force one month after it has been signed by Denmark, Finland, Norway and Sweden. At the same time the Agreement of December 8, 1967 between Denmark, Finland, Norway and Sweden concerning Co-operation to

Ensure Compliance with the Regulations for Preventing Pollution of the Sea by Oil shall cease to have effect.

In witness whereof the respective plenipotentiaries have signed this Agreement.

Done at Copenhagen on September 16, 1971 in a single copy in the Danish, Finnish, Norwegian and Swedish languages, all texts being equally authentic.

TANKER OWNERS VOLUNTARY AGREEMENT CONCERNING LIABILITY FOR OIL POLLUTION*

[Signed January 7, 1969]

EXPLANATION OF THE TANKER OWNERS VOLUNTARY AGREEMENT CONCERNING LIABILITY FOR OIL POLLUTION ("TOVALOP")

This memorandum is designed to serve as a brief summary of the principal points of the Tanker Owners Voluntary Agreement Concerning Liability for Oil Pollution, which, for the sake of convenience, is called "TOVALOP". As a word of caution, this explanation should not be considered as a substitute for the TOVALOP and its related documents and nothing contained herein should be construed as modifying or amending them.

TOVALOP originated from the determination of certain tanker owners to take constructive action with respect to oil pollution. These owners recognized that marine casualties may, on occasion, lead to pollution of coast lines, at least when crude oil, fuel oil, heavy diesel oil or lubricating oil is discharged. (For convenience these materials will be referred to simply as "oil"). These owners were aware of the fact that traditional maritime laws and practice do not always provide an adequate means for reimbursing national governments who incur expenditures to avoid or mitigate damage from such pollution, as well as tanker owners who, on their own initiative incur this kind of expenditure. They recognized also that traditional maritime law and practice do not encourage voluntary action by tanker owners, or joint measures by governments and tanker owners, against such pollution.

In an effort to establish responsibility to national governments with respect to these matters, to assure that there will be financial capability to fulfil this responsibility and otherwise to alleviate this situation, these tanker owners have developed an Agreement called "TOVALOP" which is available to all tanker owners throughout the world.

TOVALOP provides that a Participating Tanker Owner will reimburse national governments for expenses reasonably incurred by them to prevent or clean up pollution of coast lines as the result of the negligent discharge of oil from one of his tankers. The tanker causing the discharge is presumed to be negligent unless the owner can establish that discharge occurred without the tanker's fault. The Participating Owner would not, under TOVALOP, reimburse prevention or clean-up costs incurred by private parties. However, if a national government spends monies to remove oil from privately owned coast lines, it could, in the case of negligence of the discharging tanker, recover these expenses from the tanker owner.

In the event of a negligent discharge of oil, where the oil pollutes or causes grave and imminent danger of pollution to coast lines within the jurisdiction of a national government, the tanker owner involved is obligated to reimburse the national government concerned for oil removal costs reasonably incurred by it up to a maximum of $100.00 (U.S.) per gross registered ton of the tanker discharging the oil, or $10,000,000 (U.S.), whichever is lesser. If the owner himself also helps remove the oil, his costs in effect result in prorating the government's claim where the combined costs exceed these limits.

TOVALOP also contains provisions for reimbursing a tanker owner for any expenses reasonably incurred by him to prevent or clean up pollution from a discharge of oil. These provisions are designed to encourage a tanker owner to take prompt action to remove or mitigate pollution damage.

TOVALOP applies only to physical contamination to land adjoining waters navigated by tankers including structures built on this land. It doesn't cover fire or explosion damage, consequential damage, or ecological damage.

TOVALOP will be administered by a limited company registered in England, and headquartered in London, which will be called The International Tanker Owners Pollution Federation Limited and each tanker owner who becomes a party to TOVALOP would be a member of this Federation. TOVALOP requires each tanker owner who becomes a party to establish and maintain financial capability to fulfil his contractual obligations described above. The parties to TOVALOP have made provision to establish their financial capability by forming another limited company registered in Bermuda called International Tanker

*[Reproduced from TOVALOP, a booklet published by The International Tanker Owners Pollution Federation Limited in London.

[The original signatories to the agreement are B.P. Tanker Company Limited, Esso Transport Company, Inc., Gulf Oil Corporation, Mobil Oil Corporation, Shell International Petroleum Company Limited, Standard Oil Company of California, and Texaco Inc.

Indemnity Association Limited. This Association will provide insurance coverage for all tankers owned by the Parties to TOVALOP, and thus assure that they would be capable of fulfilling their financial commitments. Alternative coverage may be provided should the Association consider this necessary.

TAVALOP is structured so that all tanker owners of the world can at any time become participants. Tanker owners owning at least 50 per cent. of the tankers of the world (excluding tankers owned by a government or government agency and tankers of under 5,000 d.w.t.) as measured by deadweight tonnage must become parties before the principal obligations of an owner under TOVALOP come into existence and TOVALOP itself becomes fully effective, and TOVALOP will lapse if 80 per cent. (with the same exclusions just mentioned) do not become parties at the end of two years after its effective date.

In the case of any disputes, a national government can enforce the liability of a tanker owner who is a party to TOVALOP through arbitarion under the Rules of the International Chamber of Commerce. This latter feature should avoid the problems of establishing jurisdiction and effecting collection which exist at present in maritime law and practice.

When a tanker owner becomes a party to TOVALOP he continues in the Agreement for an initial period of five years from its effective date and for successive two-year periods, unless he elects to withdraw at the end of one of these periods. All tanker tonnage (including barges capable of seagoing service) owned or bareboat chartered by a party to the Agreement will be covered, excluding LNG and LPG carriers.

In summary, TOVALOP does the following:—

(1) Encourages immediate remedial action by Participating Tanker Owners in the event of a discharge of oil.

(2) Assures financial capability of Participating Tanker Owners to fulfil their obligations under TOVALOP through insurance coverage.

(3) Avoids jurisdictional problems under existing maritime law and practice.

(4) Places on tanker owner the burden of disproving negligence.

(5) Provides a national government with machinery for making valid claims notwithstanding the fact that such government might not, under international or local law, have a legal obligation to remove oil discharged from a tanker or a legal right to recover removal expenses.

TANKER OWNERS VOLUNTARY AGREEMENT CONCERNING LIABILITY FOR OIL POLLUTION

Preamble

The Parties to this Agreement are Tanker Owners whose vessels are engaged in the transportation of Oil in bulk by sea, and who recognize that Coast Lines may on occasion sustain Damage by Pollution as a result of Oil discharged when marine casualties occur. They are furthermore aware of the fact that traditional maritime laws and practice do not always provide an adequate means for re-imbursing Governments which incur expenditures to avoid or mitigate such damage, as well as Tanker Owners who, on their own initiative, incur such expenditures. They recognize also that traditional legal regimes do not encourage joint measures by Governments and Tanker Owners against such damage.

In a voluntary effort to establish their responsibility to Governments with respect to these matters, to assure that they will be capable of fulfilling this responsibility, and otherwise to alleviate this situation, the Parties who as of this Seventh day of January, 1969, have executed this Agreement and such other parties who may, as is herein provided, subsequently become Parties to this Agreement, in consideration of their mutual promises herein, have agreed with one another, and do hereby agree as follows:

I. Definitions

Whenever the following words and phrases appear in the Preamble and other Clauses hereof, they shall have the meaning indicated below:

(*a*) "Tanker" means any tank vessel (whether or not self-propelled) designed and constructed for the carriage by sea in bulk of crude petroleum and hydrocarbon fuels and oils derived therefrom (excluding however, liquefied petroleum gas and liquefied natural gas), whether or not such vessel is operated in sea-going service.

(*b*) To "own" a Tanker means to hold title thereto, except that in the case of a Tanker under bareboat charter (that is, a Tanker chartered upon terms providing that the Charterer shall man, victual, and navigate the Tanker at his own expense or by his own procurement) to "own" a Tanker means to be such Charterer, to the exclusion of the holder of title to said Tanker. The term "Tanker Owner" means any individual, partnership, corporate body, or Government who so owns a Tanker.

(*c*) "Participating Owner" means a Tanker Owner who has become a Party to this Agreement.

(*d*) "Participating Tankers" means all Tankers owned by a Participating Owner.

(*e*) "Oil" means crude oil, fuel oil, heavy diesel oil, and lubricating oil, whether or not carried as cargo.

(*f*) "Discharge of Oil" means any discharge of Oil from a Tanker, including any spilling, leaking, pumping, emitting, emptying or dumping of Oil.

(*g*) "Coast Lines" means land (including structural improvements thereon) adjoining the sea, inland waterways, lakes, bays, harbours, and estuaries.

(*h*) "Damage by Pollution" means physical contamination damage to Coast Lines resulting directly from a Discharge of Oil, and does not include damage from fire or explosion, consequential damage, or ecological impairment.

(*i*) "Government" means a National Government recognized as such under international law or custom.

(*j*) "Incident" means any occurrence or series of occurrences having the same origin which causes, or creates a grave and imminent danger of causing Damage by Pollution to Coast Lines from a Discharge of Oil.

(*k*) "Remove" means to take all reasonable measures to prevent potential Damage by Pollution and to mitigate Damage by Pollution from a Discharge of Oil, and "Removal" means the taking of such measures.

II. General Conditions

(A) Any Tanker Owner in the world may become a Party to this Agreement.

(B) The Parties to this Agreement will form, or cause to be formed, under and pursuant to the laws of England, a company limited by guarantee to be named "The International Tanker Owners Pollution Federation Limited" (hereinafter called the "Federation"), which will administer this Agreement.

(C) Each Party to the Agreement will (i) from and after the date of this Agreement or as of the later date on which he becomes a Party hereto, as the case may be, abide by the Memorandum and Articles of Association of the Federation and all rules or directives of the Federation, and (ii) upon the "Effective Date" hereof as provided in Clause III, or as soon thereafter as he becomes a Party to this Agreement, establish and maintain his financial capability to fulfil his obligations under this Agreement as prescribed in said Memorandum, Articles, Rules and directives.

(D) A Tanker Owner who is not one of the original signatories to this Agreement will become a Party to this Agreement upon acceptance by the Federation of an application in the form annexed hereto as Exhibit "A", wherein the applicant shall indicate his commitment to be bound by this Agreement and to become a member of the Federation.

(E) The rights and obligations of each Party to this Agreement under this Clause II, except as otherwise stated herein, shall come into effect upon the date said Party becomes a Party hereto.

III. Duration and Coverage

(A) This Agreement shall come into effect (except as otherwise specified in Clause II) upon a date selected and announced by the Federation which shall be as early as is practicable after a determination by the Federation that fifty per cent. of the Tankers of the world (excluding Tankers owned by a Government or Government agency and Tankers of under 5,000 deadweight tonnage) as measured by deadweight tonnage have become Participating Tankers. The date so selected and announced shall be known as "Effective Date".

(B) Each Participating Owner shall be a Party to this Agreement for the interval indicated below:—

(i) A Participating Owner who becomes a Party prior to the expiration of five years from the Effective Date shall be a Party until the expiration of said five year interval and for successive intervals of two years each, unless he gives written notice of withdrawal to the Federation prior to the commencement of the last year of said five year interval or prior to the last year of any subsequent two-year interval, said withdrawal being effective at the end of the interval during which notice has been so given. Notwithstanding the foregoing, however, this Agreement shall terminate earlier if the deadweight tonnage of Participating Tankers, as determined by the Federation, fails to include at least 80 per cent. of the Tankers of the world, (with the exclusions mentioned in the preceding paragraph), as measured by deadweight tonnage at the end of two years from the Effective Date.

(ii) A Participating Owner who becomes a Party during any successive two year interval as referred to in sub-paragraph (B) (i) above, shall be a Party until the expiration of the two year successive interval during the first year of which he gives written notice of withdrawal to the Federation.

(C) The rights and obligations of each Party to this Agreement shall apply with respect to all Tankers at any time owned by him while he is a Party to this Agreement.

(D) Termination of this Agreement or withdrawal therefrom under this Clause III, or otherwise, shall not terminate the rights and obligations of any Participating Owner then accrued hereunder. Upon termination of this Agreement the Federation shall continue in existence for such reasonable period as is necessary to wind up its affairs.

IV. Liability and Responsibility to Governments

(A) If a discharge of Oil occurs from a Participating Tanker through the negligence of that Tanker (and regardless of the decree of its fault), and if the Oil causes Damage by Pollution to Coast Lines within the jurisdiction of a Government, or creates a grave and imminent danger of Damage by Pollution thereto, then the Participating Owner of that Tanker shall Remove the Oil so discharged, or pay the costs reasonably incurred by the Government concerned to Remove the said Oil, subject to the maximum liability set forth in Clause VI.

(B) The Participating Owner shall be liable under Paragraph (A) hereof unless he can prove that the Discharge of Oil from his Participating Tanker occurred without fault on the part of said Tanker.

V. Removal by Participating Owner

The Federation, in connection with prescribing steps whereby each Participating Owner shall establish financial capability as provided in Clause II (C) (ii),and to encourage Participating Owners to take prompt Removal action (such Removal not constituting an admission of negligence), shall make arrangements whereby a Participating Owner who incurs reasonable expenditures for Removal of Oil discharged from a Participating Tanker owned by him shall be entitled to reimbursement therefor, without regard to negligence, subject to the terms of such arrangements.

VI. Maximum Liability

(A) The liability of a Participating Owner, pursuant to Clause IV, shall, with respect to each of his Participating Tankers involved in any one Incident, in no event exceed U.S. $100.00 per gross registered ton of each such Participating Tanker, subject to a maximum of US. $10,000,000.00 in respect of each such Participating Tanker.

(B) In the event that a Participating Owner incurs liability hereunder to several Governments with respect to any one Incident and that the amounts reasonably spent by these Governments for Removal of Oil exceeds the limit referred to in Paragraph (A) hereof, then the Participating Owner's maximum liability to a particular Government shall be that portion of said limit that such Government's Removal expenses bear to the aggregate of the several Governments' Removal expenses.

(C) If, however, a Participating Owner and a Government (or Governments) incur Removal expenses as a result of the same Incident, then the Participating Owner's liability shall in no event exceed that part of the limit prescribed in Paragraph (A) hereof which the Government's (or Governments') Removal expenses bear to the aggregate of the Government's (or Governments') Removal expenses and the Participating Owner's Removal expenses.

VII. Procedure and Miscellaneous

(A) In the event of a Discharge of Oil from a Participating Tanker, the Participating Owner of said Tanker shall notify the Federation of such Discharge and the action (if any) taken and intended to be taken by him to Remove the Oil, and whether a claim has been filed against said Owner by any Government (or Governments).

(B) The Federation shall, on behalf of the Participating Owner concerned, send the Government or Governments concerned a copy of this Agreement and a confirmation that the owner of the Participating Tanker is, or was, at the time of such Discharge, a Participating Owner.

(C) The Government or Governments concerned should then, if they believe they have a valid claim hereunder and if they have not already done so, file notice of claim on the Participating Owner, sending a copy to the Federation.

(D) A Participating Owner shall have no liability hereunder to a Government unless that Government's claim hereunder, including the amount thereof and supporting data, is filed with said Owner, with a copy to the Federation, within one year of the date of the commencement of the alleged Discharge of Oil involved.

(E) The Government or Governments concerned may, in the event of a dispute under this Agreement with a Participating Owner, commence arbitration proceedings, in accordance with Paragraph (K) hereof, within two years from the date of the commencement of the alleged Discharge of Oil involving said Owner and said proceedings shall be the exclusive means for enforcing a Participating Owner's liability hereunder. Each Participating Owner by becoming a Party to this Agreement, and for so long as he remains bound thereby, shall be deemed irrevocably to have offered to any such Government to submit all such disputes to arbitration as provided in said Paragraph (K).

(F) Any payment hereunder to a Government by or on behalf of a Participating Owner shall be in full settlement of all said Government's claims against said Owner, the Participating Tanker involved, their officers, agents, employees and underwriters, which arise out of or are connected with the Discharge of Oil involved.

(G) With the exception of Governments who take advantage of this Agreement, this Agreement shall not affect any other rights of claim or suit which may be legally available to other claimants. This Agreement does not create any rights in persons, partnerships, corporations, or other entities other than Governments.

(H) This Agreement does not create any rights against the Federation and the Federation shall have no liability hereunder or otherwise to any Government, person, partnership, corporation or other entity.

(I) No rights or obligations created hereunder or connected herewith may be assigned or transferred.

(J) No Party to this Agreement shall be subject to any liability to a Government hereunder with respect to a Discharge of Oil from a Participating Tanker owned by another Participating Owner.

(K) All claims by a Government or Governments against a Participating Owner under this Agreement shall, if not otherwise disposed of, be finally settled under the rules of conciliation and arbitration of the International Chamber of Commerce by one or more arbitrators appointed in accordance with the rules. In any such proceeding, the Government or Governments shall have the burden of proving the Oil was discharged from the Participating Tanker.

(L) No Removal by a Participating Owner, or making of a settlement payment with respect to any claim under this Agreement, shall be deemed (i) an admission of, or evidence of, liability on the part of the Participating Owner involved to any Government or any other claimant in any proceeding, or (ii) submission to any jurisdiction on the part of said Participating Owner for any purpose whatsoever.

(M) No arbitration award against a Participating Owner under this Agreement shall be deemed (i) an admission of, or evidence of, liability on the part of said Participating Owner in any other proceeding or to any other claimant, or (ii) submission to any jurisdiction on the part of said Participating Owner for any purpose whatsoever other than as provided in this Clause VII.

VIII. Amendments

This Agreement may be amended by Special Resolution adopted at an Extraordinary General Meeting of the members of the Federation upon a poll vote in which at least 75 per cent. of the votes cast are in favour of said Resolution. A Participating Owner who votes against such Resolution shall thereupon have the option to withdraw from this Agreement within 60 days of the date of said Special Resolution by written notice to the Federation, without, however affecting his rights and liabilities accrued at the time of his withdrawal.

IX. Law Governing

This Agreement shall be governed by the laws of England. However, anything herein to the contrary notwithstanding, a Participating Owner shall not be required:—

(*a*) To incur any obligation or take any action, with respect to any Incident in which a Participating Tanker owned by him is involved, which would violate the laws or government regulations of the flag of said Participating Tanker, or

(*b*) To incure any obligation or take any action which would violate any other laws or government regulations as may apply to said Participating Owner, or

(*c*) To incur any obligation or take any action which would, if a majority of the stock of said Participating Owner is owned, directly or indirectly by another corporation, partnership or individual, violate any laws or government regulations which may apply to said other corporation, partnership or individual.

IN WITNESS WHEREOF, the parties have caused this Agreement to be executed as of the date indicated in the Preamble hereto, or upon the date on which their application is accepted by the Federation as provided in Clause II (D).

OIL COMPANIES: CONTRACT REGARDING AN INTERIM SUPPLEMENT TO TANKER LIABILITY FOR OIL POLLUTION*
[Signed January 14, 1971

"CRISTAL"

CONTRACT REGARDING AN INTERIM SUPPLEMENT TO TANKER LIABILITY FOR OIL POLLUTION

PREAMBLE

The Parties to this Contract are various Oil Companies and the Oil Companies Institute For Marine Pollution Compensation Limited, an entity organised and existing under the Laws of Bermuda (hereinafter referred to as the "Institute").

The Parties recognise that marine casualties involving tankers carrying bulk oil cargoes can, on occasion, cause extensive pollution damage on the escape or discharge of oil into the sea. They believe that by increasing the responsibility of tanker owners with respect to pollution damage, the occurrence of such incidents can be reduced, and therefore they strongly favour ratification by the nations of the world of the International Convention on Civil Liability for Oil Pollution Damage adopted at Brussels on November 29, 1969 (hereinafter referred to as "CLC").

The Parties further recognise that in some instances persons sustaining pollution damage may be unable, even after ratification of CLC, (as under current legal regimes), to recover adequate compensation for pollution damage.

The Parties accordingly advocate, in addition to ratification of CLC, the adoption and ratification by the nations of the world of a Convention creating an International Compensation Fund or its equivalent whereby persons who sustain pollution damage for which a tanker owner is liable under CLC would have available supplemental compensation beyond the limits established in CLC. Moreover, the Parties have decided, pending the enactment of such a Convention, to establish by contract a means for providing supplemental compensation for pollution damage beyond the limits of liability presently available under existing legal regimes, including Tanker Owners Voluntary Agreement Concerning Liability for Oil Pollution ("TOVALOP"), and beyond the limits of liability that will be applicable under CLC, once it enters into force.

In view of the above considerations, the Parties who, as of this 14th day of January, 1971, have executed this Contract and those Oil Companies who later become Parties, have agreed, and do hereby agree, that the Institute will pay such supplemental compensation and that the Oil Company Parties will assure the availability of funds to permit payment thereof, upon the following terms and conditions:

---

*[Reproduced from the text provided by Standard Oil Company of New Jersey.

[The Tanker Owners Voluntary Agreement Concerning Liability for Oil Pollution of January 7, 1969, appears at 8 International Legal Materials 497 (1969). The International Convention on Civil Liability for Oil Pollution Damage of November 29, 1969, appears at 9 International Legal Materials 45 (1970).]

I. *Definitions.*

For the purpose of this Contract, including the Preamble:

(A)—"Tanker" or "Ship" means any sea-going vessel and anv sea-borne craft of any type whatsoever, actually carrying oil in bulk as cargo.

(B)—"Person" means any individual or partnership or any public or private body, whether corporate or not, including a State or any of its constituent subdivisions.

(C)—"Owner" means the person or persons registered as the owner of the ship or, in the absence of registration, the person or persons owning the ship. However, in the case of a ship owned by a State and operated by a company which in that State is registered as the ship's operator, "Owner" shall mean such company.

(D)—"Oil" means any persistent oil such as crude oil, fuel oil, heavy diesel oil and lubricating oil whether carried on board a ship as cargo or in the bunkers of a ship.

(E)—"Pollution Damage" means loss or damage caused outside the ship carrying oil by contamination resulting from the escape or discharge of oil from the ship, wherever such escape or discharge may occur, provided that said loss or damage is caused on the territory including the territorial sea, of any nation, and includes the costs of preventive measures and further loss or damage directly resulting from such preventive measures but shall exclude any loss or damage which is remote, or speculative, or which does not result directly from the escape or discharge.

(F)—"Preventive Measures" means any reasonable measures taken by any person after an incident has occurred to prevent or minimise pollution damage.

(G)—"Incident" means any occurrence, or series of occurrences having the same origin, which causes pollution damage.

(H)—"Oil Company" means any person engaged in the production, refining or marketing of oil, or whose affiliates are so engaged.

(I)—"Crude/Fuel Oil Receipts" means crude oil received by an Oil Company at refineries for processing which was transported all or part of the way from point of origin to said refineries by ship, and fuel oil received by it at an installation for storage and terminalling which was transported all or part of the way from point of manufacture to said installation by ship.

(J)—"Contract Year" means any twelve month period commencing upon the Effective Date [as referred to in Clause III (A) hereof] or any anniversary thereof.

(K)—"Oil Company Party" means (i) any Oil Company which is an initial signatory to this Contract, including an Oil Company which is affiliated with such Company and which, prior to the Effective Date, is designated by such Company as desiring to become a Party, and (ii) any Oil Company which becomes a Party upon acceptance of an application signed by it pursuant to Clause II (B) hereof, including any Oil Company which is affiliated with such Company and which, at the time of such application, is designated by such Company as desiring to become a Party.

II. *General Conditions.*

(A)—Any Oil Company in the world which is willing to be bound by this Contract and to become a shareholder in the Institute and to abide by its By-Laws, Rules and Directives, may become an Oil Company Party to this Contract.

(B)—An Oil Company which is not one of the initial signatories to this Contract or was not designated by an initial signatory as desiring to become a Party, will become an Oil Company Party to this Contract upon acceptance by the Institute of an application in the form attached hereto as "Exhibit A".

(C)—The obligations of an Oil Company under this Contract shall extend solely to the Institute.

Effective Date and Duration.

(A)—This Contract shall come in effect upon a date selected and announced by the Institute to its shareholders (herein referred to as the "Effective Date") which shall be as early as is practicable after the Institute determines that the total of all Crude/Fuel Oil Receipts, during the calendar year first preceding the calendar year in which such determination is made, of all Oil Companies which are Parties to this Contract as of the time of said determination, constitute at least 50% of the Crude/Fuel Oil Receipts of all Oil Companies during such preceding year.

(B)—(i) Each Oil Company which becomes a Party hereto prior to October 6, 1974 shall be bound by the provisions hereof from the date it becomes a Party until October 6, 1974 and thereafter for successive periods of one year from said October 6, 1974 unless it gives written notice of withdrawal to the Institute prior to April 1, 1974 or prior to April 1 in any such successive yearly period, said withdrawal being effective as of October 6th following the date on which notice has been so given.

(ii) Each Oil Company which becomes a Party hereto after October 6, 1974 shall be bound by the provisions hereof from the date it becomes a Party until October 6 next following the date it becomes a Party and thereafter for successive periods of one year commencing on said October 6, 1974 and each anniversary thereof unless it gives written notice of withdrawal to the Institute prior to April 1 of any such yearly period, said withdrawal being effective as of October 6 following the date upon which notice has been so given.

(C)—Notwithstanding the provisions of Clause III (B) hereof—

(1) This Contract shall terminate (i) at the end of two Contract Years from the Effective Date unless at any time within that two Contract Year period the Institute determines and announces to its shareholders that the total of all Crude/Fuel Oil Receipts, during the calendar year first preceding the calendar year in which the determination is made, of Oil Companies which are Parties to this Contract as of the time of such determination, constitute at least 80% of the total Crude/Fuel Oil Receipts of all Oil Companies during such preceding calendar year, or (ii) upon the termination of TOVALOP before CLC comes into force, or (iii) at the time a Convention comes into force creating an International Compensation Fund or its equivalent.

(2) This Contract may be terminated, at the discretion of the Institute at the end of five Contract Years from the Effective Date if CLC has not come into force prior to that time.

(D)—Termination of this Contract under this Clause III or otherwise shall not terminate the rights and obligations of any Party already accrued hereunder.

IV. *Functions of the Institute.*

(A)—After the Effective Date, the Institute shall compensate persons for pollution damage sustained by them as the result of an incident when at the time of the incident the oil was owned by an Oil Company Party as follows:

(1) Prior to the time CLC enters into force, whenever (i) the Owner or Bareboat Charterer of the ship from which the oil escaped or was discharged was a Party to TOVALOP at the time of the incident and (ii) the Owner of said ship would have been liable to said persons sustaining pollution damage under the provisions of CLC for the damage if CLC had been in force at the time of the incident and had been applicable to the incident.

(2) After the time CLC comes into force whenever the provisions of CLC apply to the incident, and by reason thereof the Owner of the ship from which the oil escaped or was discharged was, in fact, liable to said persons sustaining pollution damage for said damage.

(B)—The compensation to be paid by the Institute under Clause IV (A) to all persons sustaining pollution damage as a result of said incident (regardless of the number of ships from which oil has escaped or been discharged) shall in no event exceed Thirty Million U. S. Dollars (U. S. $30,000,000.00) less the sum of the following:

(1) The Owner's or Bareboat Charterer's maximum liability for said pollution damage under TOVALOP, *plus*

(2) The amount of expenditures that the Owner or Bareboat Charterer was entitled to make for "Removal of Oil" (as defined in TOVALOP) and to receive reimbursement for as provided in TOVALOP, *plus*

(3) The maximum liability of Owner or Bareboat Charterer with respect to such damage under applicable law, statutes, regulations or conventions, *plus*

(4) The maximum amount to which such persons sustaining pollution damage were entitled from any other person or from the ship or from any other vessel under applicable law, statutes, regulations or conventions providing for compensation for all or part of said damage.

(C)—If the total pollution damage resulting from an incident exceeds the net amount referred to in Clause IV (B), then said net amount shall be prorated by the Institute among the persons sustaining said damage.

(D) —Notwithstanding the foregoing, if a person sustaining pollution damage fails to exercise due diligence to recover compensation for such damage from (i) the Owner or Bareboat Charterer of the ship from which the escape or discharge of oil occurred, or (ii) any other person, or (iii) the ship or any other vessel, then to the extent that said Owner, Bareboat Charterer, person, ship or other vessel are liable for part or all of said damage, the Institute shall not compensate said person sustaining pollution damage under this Clause IV.

(E) —The net amount provided for in Clause IV (B) shall be reduced by any amounts paid, or agreed to be paid, by the Institute in settlement of claims made under this Contract.

V. *The Fund.*

The Institute, in order to assure its financial capability to pay compensation under Clause IV hereof, shall maintain and administer a Fund created as follows:

(1) The Fund shall initially be constituted in the amount of Five Million U. S. Dollars (U. S. $5,000,000.00) (hereinafter referred to as the "Initial Call").

(2) As soon as practicable after the Effective Date the Institute shall assess each Oil Company Party to this Contract as of the Effective Date and each such Party shall pay to the Institute that portion of the Initial Call calculated by dividing its total Crude/Fuel Oil Receipts for the calendar year immediately preceding the Effective Date by the total Crude/Fuel Oil Receipts during such preceding calendar year of all Oil Companies who were Parties to this Contract at the Effective Date and by multiplying this percentage by said Initial Call.

(3) Any Oil Company becoming a Party to this Contract subsequent to the Effective Date shall be assessed by the Institute and shall pay to the Institute that portion of the Initial Call calculated in the same manner as under Clause V (2). At such time appropriate adjustment shall be made in the portion of the Initial Call of all Oil Companies then Parties to this Contract and, at the discretion of the Institute, such Oil Companies shall receive an appropriate refund or a credit against future assessments.

(4) The Institute shall, from time to time during each Contract Year estimate the amount reasonably required by it to pay compensation in accordance with Clause IV and shall determine what portion of any such amount ("such amount" being hereinafter referred to as a "Periodic Call"), shall be in cash and what portion shall be in other forms.

(5) The Institute shall, at such times as are appropriate during each Contract Year, assess each Oil Company Party and each such Party shall pay to the Institute that portion of any Periodic Call made during said Contract Year calculated by dividing its total Crude/Fuel Oil Receipts for the calendar year first preceding the commencement of said Contract Year by the total of the Crude/Fuel Oil Receipts during such preceding calendar year of all Oil Companies who were Parties to this Contract at the date of such assessment and by multiplying this percentage by the amount of said Periodic Call, provided however, that notwithstanding the foregoing, (i) each such Oil Company Party (whether or not it had any Crude/Fuel Oil Receipts in such preceding calendar year) shall pay a minimum charge determined by the Institute for each Contract Year, which minimum charge may be offset against any portions of an assessment otherwise payable hereunder, and (ii) no Oil Company Party shall be liable for that portion of an assessment which relates to payment of compensation by the Institute in excess of Five Hundred Thousand U. S. Dollars (U. S. $500,000.00) with respect to any one incident which occurred prior to the date upon which it becomes a Party to this Contract.

(6) Except as provided in Clause V (3) hereof, in the case of any Oil Company which becomes a Party hereto during a Contract Year after the commencement thereof, the Institute shall assess such Company in the manner provided in Clause V (5) hereof, but only in respect of that portion of said Contract Year during which it has been an Oil Company Party to this Contract.

(7) Upon termination of this Contract, any amounts remaining in the Fund shall be equitably distributed among the Oil Companies then Parties hereto.

VI. *Notice of Claim.*

The Institute shall not entertain any claim by any person allegedly sustaining pollution damage unless such person gives notice of claim to the Institute within one year of the date of the alleged incident giving rise to such a claim.

VII. *Rules and Directives.*

The Institute shall have the right to make rules and directives from time to time with respect to the interpretation and administration of this Contract.

VIII. *Amendment.*

This Contract may be amended by Special Resolution adopted at an Extraordinary General Meeting of the Institute upon a vote in which at least 75% of the votes cast are in favour of said Resolution. However, and notwithstanding the provisions of Clause III (B), an Oil Company Party which votes against said Resolution shall have the option to withdraw herefrom on giving sixty days written notice to the Institute without, however, affecting its rights and obligations accrued at the time of withdrawal.

IX. *Law Governing.*

(A) This Contract shall be construed and shall take effect in accordance with the laws of England and the Courts of England shall have exclusive jurisdiction over any matter arising therefrom.

(B) This Contract shall not be construed as creating a trust.

(C) Anything to the contrary herein notwithstanding, a Party hereto shall not be required to incur any obligation or take any action which would violate any laws or government regulations which apply to it or, in the event its stock or shares are owned by another person, which would violate any laws or government regulations which apply to said person.

IN WITNESS WHEREOF, the Parties have entered into this Contract as of the date indicated in the Preamble hereto, or upon the date on which their application is accepted by the Institute as provided in Clause II (B).

AGIP SPA

By: ....
Giancarlo Gini

AMOCO TRADING INTERNATIONAL LIMITED

By: ....

BRITISH PETROLEUM COMPANY LIMITED

By: ....
P. A. Medcraft, Attorney-in-Fact

CITIES SERVICE TANKERS CORPORATION

By: ....
G. H. Blohm, President

COMPAGNIE FRANCAISE DES PETROLES

By: ....
B. A. Dubais, Attorney-in-Fact

ELF UNION

By: ....
B. A. Dubais, Attorney-in-Fact

ESSO PETROLEUM COMPANY, LIMITED

By: ....
R. E. Howe, Attorney-in-Fact

GULF OIL CORPORATION

By: ....
W. C. Brodhead, Vice President

ASIA OIL COMPANY, LIMITED
DAIKYO OIL COMPANY, LIMITED
FUJI KOSAN COMPANY, LIMITED
FUJI OIL COMPANY, LIMITED
GENERAL SEKIYU SEISEI K.K.
IDEMITSU KOSAN COMPANY LIMITED
KASHIMA OIL COMPANY LIMITED
KOA OIL COMPANY LIMITED
KYOKUTO PETROLEUM INDUSTRIES LIMITED
KYUSHU OIL COMPANY LIMITED
MARUZEN OIL COMPANY LIMITED
MITSUBISHI OIL COMPANY LIMITED
MITSUBISHI SHOJI KAISHA LIMITED
NIPPON MINING COMPANY LIMITED
NIPPON OIL COMPANY LIMITED
NIPPON PETROLEUM REFINING COMPANY LIMITED
SEIBU SEKIYU K.K.
SHELL SEKIYU K.K.
SHOWA OIL COMPANY LIMITED
TAIYO OIL COMPANY LIMITED
TOA NENRYO KOGYO K.K.
TOA OIL COMPANY LIMITED
TOHO OIL COMPANY LIMITED

By: ....
Masashi Kato, Attorney-in-Fact

MOBIL OIL CORPORATION

By: ....
E. S. Checket, Vice President

PETROFINA S.A.

By: ....
John Mackenzie, Attorney-in-Fact

SHELL INTERNATIONAL PETROLEUM COMPANY LIMITED

By: ....
A. S. M. Hetherington, Duly Authorized Attorney

SOCIEDADE PORTEGUESO DE NAVIOS TANQUES LIMITADA

By: ....

TEXACO INC.

By: ....
John I. Mingay, Senior Vice President

STANDARD OIL COMPANY OF CALIFORNIA

By: ....
L. C. Ford, Attorney-in-Fact

SUN OIL COMPANY

By: ....

"EXHIBIT A"

TO: Oil Companies Institute For Marine Pollution Compensation Limited

The undersigned, and such of its affiliates as it may designate in an attachment hereto, hereby applies (apply) to become an Oil Company Party (Parties) to the Contract Regarding an Interim Supplement to Tanker Liability for Oil Pollution ("CRISTAL"), dated as of 14 January, 1971, and agrees (agree), if this application is accepted, to fulfil all the obligations of an Oil Company Party, to become a shareholder in the Oil Companies Institute For Marine Pollution Compensation Limited, and to abide by its By-Laws, Rules and Directives.

....

Accepted upon this

..................day of..................

Oil Companies Institute For Marine Pollution Compensation Limited

UNITED KINGDOM OF GREAT BRITAIN AND NORTHERN IRELAND

Maritime Matters: Use of United Kingdom Ports and Territorial Waters by the N.S. *Savannah*

Agreement effected by exchange of notes
Signed at London June 19, 1964;
Entered into force June 19, 1964.

The British Secretary of State for Foreign Affairs to the American Ambassador

FOREIGN OFFICE, S.W.1.
No. GN 1018/67 *June 19, 1964*

YOUR EXCELLENCY

I have the honour to refer to discussions which have taken place between the Government of the United Kingdom of Great Britain and Northern Ireland and the Government of the United States of America in anticipation of visits of N.S. *Savannah* to ports in United Kingdom territory. I now have the honour to propose an Agreement between the Government of the United Kingdom of Great Britain and Northern Ireland and the Government of the United States of America in the following terms:

(1) The operation of N.S. *Savannah* shall be subject to the provisions of the present Agreement including, in respect of conditions for the use of waters and ports, those of Annex 1 which is an integral part hereof, and, in respect of legal liability, the provisions of Annex 2, which is also an integral part hereof.

(2) For the purposes of this Agreement, the term "United Kingdom territory" means, except where otherwise expressly provided, the United Kingdom of Great Britain and Northern Ireland and any territory to which the Agreement has been extended in accordance with paragraph (3) of this Agreement.

(3) (a) The Government of the United Kingdom may at any time declare by notification in writing to the Government of the United States that this Agreement shall extend to all or any of the territories for the international relations of which the Government of the United Kingdom are responsible.

(b) This Agreement shall, from the date of receipt of such notification, or from such other date as may be stated in the notification, extend to the territories specified therein.

(c) The application of this Agreement to any territory in respect of which a notification of extension has been made may be terminated by a notification addressed to the Government of the United States by the Government of the United Kingdom. Such notification shall take effect from the date of its receipt, or from such other later date as may be stated therein.

(4) Either Government may terminate this Agreement by notification addressed to the other, such termination to take effect six months after the date of such notification.

(5) A copy of this Agreement shall be transmitted to the Inter-Governmental Maritime Consultative Organisation by the Government of the United Kingdom.

2. If the above proposal is acceptable to the Government of the United States of America, I have the honour to suggest that this Note, together with Your Excellency's reply to that effect, shall be regarded as constituting an Agreement between the Government of the United Kingdom of Great Britain and Northern Ireland and the Government of the United States of America on the above terms which shall enter into force on the date of Your Excellency's reply.

I have the honour to be, with the highest consideration,

Your Excellency's obedient Servant,

(For the Secretary of State)

DENYS BROWN

His Excellency
The Honourable
DAVID K. E. BRUCE, C.B.E.,
etc., etc., etc.,
24/32 Grosvenor Square,
W.1.

ANNEX 1

1. Entry of N.S. *Savannah* into any port in United Kingdom territory shall be subject to the prior approval of the Government of the United Kingdom and also, in the case of entry into any port of a territory outside the United Kingdom to which this Annex has been extended in accordance with paragraph (3) of the Agreement, the Government of that territory.

2. To enable the Government of the United Kingdom to consider the grant of the approval referred to in Article 1 of this Annex, the Gov-

ernment of the United States shall provide sufficient information to enable the Government of the United Kingdom to satisfy themselves as to the safety of N.S. *Savannah*. This information shall be supplied in a form and at a time to be agreed and shall include detailed technical information concerning her design, construction, operation and the safeguards incorporated into the ship's nuclear plant and an analysis of hypothetical accidents. This information shall be supplemented from time to time by the Government of the United States to reflect significant design, construction and operation modifications which would necessitate a reappraisal of the Safety Assessment.

3. The Government of the United States shall advise the Government of the United Kingdom that N.S. *Savannah* is constructed and equipped to comply with the requirements of the International Regulations for Preventing Collisions at Sea [[1]] and with the requirements applicable to comparable ships propelled by conventional means of the International Conventions for the Safety of Life at Sea [[2]] and respecting Load Lines [[3]] for the time being in force as between the two Governments. If N.S. *Savannah* does not comply in all respects with the requirements of the aforesaid Regulations and Conventions, a schedule of the differences shall be furnished to the Government of the United Kingdom.

4. The Government of the United States shall assure the Government of the United Kingdom that the Master, officers and crew members of N.S. *Savannah* possess qualifications and experience appropriate to their responsibility and duties.

5. (a) As soon as practicable after receipt of the information referred to in Articles 2 and 3 of this Annex, the Government of the United Kingdom shall notify the Government of the United States whether this information is acceptable as a basis for arrangements to be made for N.S. *Savannah* to enter such ports in United Kingdom territory as may be specified from time to time by the Government of the United Kingdom.

(b) The Government of the United Kingdom shall ensure that arrangements are made for the acceptance of N.S. *Savannah* in such specified ports in United Kingdom territory. The arrangements shall include arrangements with the appropriate port authorities and the provision of such services as may be required for the safety of N.S. *Savannah*.

6. The Government of the United States shall ensure that timely information of the intended arrival of N.S. *Savannah* in any specified port in United Kingdom territory and of the route proposed to be followed after entry into the territorial waters of United Kingdom

---

[1] TIAS 2899; 4 UST 2956.

[2] TIAS 2495; 3 UST (pt. 3) 3450.

[3] TS 858; 47 Stat. 2228.

territory shall be given by the Operators or Master to the Port Authority concerned and to the Government of the United Kingdom.

7. Authorities designated by the Government of the United Kingdom in accordance with arrangements to be made, shall have reasonable access to N.S. *Savannah* for the purpose of inspecting and monitoring her and her records and programme data while she is within the territorial waters of United Kingdom territory and determining whether she is in a safe condition and is being operated in accordance with the Ship's Operating Manual.

8. The Government of the United States shall ensure that no disposal of radioactive materials, including radioactive waste, shall take place from N.S. *Savannah* while she is within the territorial waters of United Kingdom territory without the prior approval of the Government of the United Kingdom.

9. The Government of the United Kingdom shall accept radioactive waste removed from N.S. *Savannah* provided a specific request for removal has been made to and approved by the appropriate United Kingdom authorities and such waste is packaged in a manner satisfactory to those authorities.

10. The Government of the United States shall ensure that the Master of N.S. *Savannah* shall maintain all safety precautions in any port in United Kingdom territory in accordance with the requirements of the Ship's Operating Manual and the requirements of the Government of the United Kingdom. During the stay of N.S. *Savannah* in port the Master shall co-operate as may be necessary with the Port Authority concerned in measures to ensure safety.

11. (a) Radiological control in N.S. *Savannah* and environmental monitoring shall be the responsibility of the Master of N.S. *Savannah* and shall be carried out in accordance with the requirements of the Ship's Operating Manual.

(b) The Government of the United Kingdom and the Port Authority concerned shall have the right to undertake such radiological monitoring in N.S. *Savannah* as they may consider necessary during her stay in any port in United Kingdom territory.

12. Arrangements relating to the control of public access to N.S. *Savannah* shall be the responsibility of the Master and shall be made in conjunction with authorities designated by the Government of the United Kingdom.

13. Authorities designated by the Government of the United Kingdom or by the Port Authority concerned shall have the right at any time to require the Master of N.S. *Savannah* to remove the ship from any port and/or to close down her reactor provided that due consideration shall be given to the safety of the ship and to the view of the Master.

14. The Government of the United States shall instruct the Master of N.S. *Savannah* that except as may be laid down in the Operating Manual and agreed by the Government of the United Kingdom, no work or operations which might give rise to a nuclear incident (including fuelling or defuelling operations) shall be undertaken within any port in United Kingdom territory.

15. The Government of the United States shall instruct the Master of N.S. *Savannah* to inform immediately the Government of the United Kingdom and any Port Authority concerned in the event of any accident to N.S. *Savannah* or other incident which might affect the safety of persons in United Kingdom territory and in such an event to consult with the Government of the United Kingdom and the Port Authority on the action to be taken.

16. In the event of the entry into force of any general multilateral convention relating to the safety and operating procedure of nuclear-powered merchant ships by which either the Government of the United States or the Government of the United Kingdom or both become bound, this Annex shall be amended by agreement between the two Governments so as to conform with the provisions of such convention or shall be terminated by either Government giving to the other not less than six months' notice of termination.

ANNEX 2

1. In this Annex, the expression "Indemnification Agreement" means the Agreement of Indemnification between the United States Atomic Energy Commission and the United States Maritime Administration whereunder the Atomic Energy Commission acting under the authority of the United States Atomic Energy Act of 1954,[1] as amended, has agreed to indemnify the United States Maritime Administration and other persons indemnified against claims for public liability arising from a nuclear incident in connexion with the design, development, construction, operation, repair, maintenance or use of the N.S. *Savannah* to the amount of U.S. $500 million including the reasonable costs of investigating and settling claims and defending suits for damage (the terms "person indemnified", "public liability" and "nuclear incident" being defined in Section 11 of the United States Atomic Energy Act of 1954, [2] as amended, are used in this Annex with the meanings there assigned to them).

2. The Government of the United States shall provide compensation for all loss, damage, death or injury in United Kingdom territory (including territorial waters) arising out of a nuclear incident involving N.S. *Savannah* to the extent that the Government of the United

[1] 68 Stat. 919; 42 U.S.C. § 2011 note.

[2] 71 Stat. 576; 42 U.S.C. § 2014.

States, the United States Maritime Administration or a person indemnified under the Indemnification Agreement is liable for public liability in respect of such loss, damage, death or injury.

3. The aggregate liability of the Government of the United States in accordance with Article 2 of this Annex shall not exceed $500 million for any single incident regardless of where damage may be incurred.

4. In respect of the loss, damage, death or injury referred to in Article 2 above, and subject to the provisions of this Annex the Government of the United States and the United States Maritime Administration –

(a) shall not, in proceedings brought *in personam*, plead sovereign immunity but shall submit to the jurisdiction of courts in United Kingdom territory having jurisdiction;

(b) shall not seek to invoke the provisions of the law of any part of United Kingdom territory or any other law relating to limitation of liability;

(c) shall not pursue any right of recourse against any person who may have caused or contributed to such loss, damage, death or injury.

5. The Government of the United States shall ensure that prompt payment is made in respect of the liability referred to in Article 2 of this Annex.

6. If the Indemnification Agreement should for any reason be terminated or revised the Government of the United States shall not cause or permit the entry of N.S. *Savannah* into the internal or territorial waters of United Kingdom territory unless there is in effect either

(a) an agreement of indemnification entered into by the United States Atomic Energy Commission under the authority of Section 170 of the United States Atomic Energy Act of 1954, [1] as amended, and affording an equivalent measure of indemnification to that provided by the Indemnification Agreement; or

(b) an agreement of indemnification in some other form acceptable to the Government of the United Kingdom.

7. The Maritime Transportation and Litigation Agreement of December 4, 1942 [2] shall not apply to any nuclear incident involving N.S. *Savannah*.

---

[1] 71 Stat. 576; 72 Stat. 525; 42 U.S.C. § 2210.

[2] EAS 282; 56 Stat. 1780.

The American Ambassador to the British Secretary of State for Foreign Affairs

No. 62 LONDON, *June 19, 1964*

EXCELLENCY:

I have the honor to acknowledge receipt of Your Excellency's note No. GN 1018/67 of this same date proposing an Agreement between the Government of the United Kingdom of Great Britain and Northern Ireland and the Government of the United States of America, which Note read as follows:

[as above]

The foregoing proposals are acceptable to the Government of the United States of America and I have the honor to confirm that your Note, together with this reply, shall be regarded as constituting an Agreement between the Government of the United Kingdom of Great Britain and Northern Ireland and the Government of the United States of America which shall enter into force on today's date.

Accept, Excellency, the renewed assurances of my highest consideration.

DAVID BRUCE

His Excellency
Rt. Hon. R. A. BUTLER, C.H., M.P.,
Secretary of State for Foreign Affairs,
London.

UNITED KINGDOM OF GREAT BRITAIN AND NORTHERN IRELAND

Maritime Matters: Visit of N.S. *Savannah* to Hong Kong

Agreement modifying the agreement of June 19, 1964.
Effected by exchange of notes
Signed at London June 12, 1967;
Entered into force June 12, 1967.

The British Secretary of State for Foreign Affairs to the American Ambassador

FOREIGN OFFICE,
LONDON, S.W.1.
12 June, 1967.

(SRN 1/4/1)

YOUR EXCELLENCY,

I have the honour to refer to the Exchange of Notes of the 19th of June, 1964[1] constituting an Agreement between the Government of the United Kingdom of Great Britain and Northern Ireland and the Government of the United States of America in anticipation of visits of N.S. "Savannah" to ports in United Kingdom territory, and to the proposed visit of N.S. "Savannah" to Hong Kong.

2. I have the honour to inform you that, pursuant to paragraph 3(a) thereof, the Agreement is hereby extended to Hong Kong.

3. In consideration of the fact that N.S. "Savannah" is now operated not directly by the Government of the United States but is under bare-boat charter to a private operator, First Atomic Ship Transport Incorporated, and that the United States Atomic Energy Commission has entered into an agreement of indemnification with First Atomic Ship Transport Incorporated under the authority of Section 170 of the United States Atomic Energy Act of 1954, as amended,[2] and that similar arrangements may in future be made with other private operators, I have the honour to propose the follow-

---

[1] TIAS 5633; 15 UST 1511.
[2] 71 Stat. 576; 42 USC 2210.

ing modifications to the Agreement for the purposes of its extension to Hong Kong.

4. The Government of the United Kingdom are prepared while such arrangements are in effect to release the Government of the United States from their obligations under Annex 1 to the Agreement with the exception of paragraph 16 thereof, on condition that First Atomic Ship Transport Incorporated or other private operator undertakes in writing to fulfil the same obligations, and on condition that the Government of the United Kingdom retain their rights under paragraphs 1, 7, 11(b), and 13 of that Annex.

5. With respect to Annex 2 to the Agreement, I have the honour to propose that, unless the context otherwise requires, the expression "United States Maritime Administration" wherever it occurs shall be construed to mean the United States Maritime Administration or a private operator, as referred to in the third paragraph above, with whom an agreement of indemnification is in effect as described in paragraph 6(a) of that Annex.

6. I have the honour to propose that these modifications should enter into force on the date of Your Excellency's reply confirming that they are acceptable to the Government of the United States, and should remain in force unless terminated by either Party upon two months notice in writing to the other Party.

I have the honour to be, with the highest consideration,

Your Excellency's obedient Servant

E. G. WILLAN

(For the Secretary of State)

His Excellency, the Honourable
DAVID K. E. BRUCE, C.B.E.,
Embassy of the United States,
Grosvenor Square.
London, W.1.

The American Ambassador to the British Secretary of State for Foreign Affairs

No. 9 LONDON, *June 12, 1967*

EXCELLENCY:

I have the honor to acknowledge receipt of Your Excellency's note No. SRN 1/4/1 of this same date referring to the Agreement constituted by the Exchange of Notes of June 19, 1964, and proposing modifications to the Agreement for the purposes of its extension to Hong Kong, which Note read as follows:

[as above]

The foregoing proposals are acceptable to the Government of the United States of America and I have the honor to confirm that your Note, together with this reply, shall be regarded as effecting, in accordance with the terms of the Note, modification of the Agreement of June 19, 1964 between the Government of the United Kingdom of Great Britain and Northern Ireland and the Government of the United States of America, which shall enter into force on today's date.

Accept, Excellency, the renewed assurances of my highest consideration.

DAVID BRUCE

His Excellency
Rt. Hon. GEORGE BROWN, M.P.,
Secretary of State for Foreign Affairs,
London.

CONVENTION RELATING TO CIVIL LIABILITY IN THE FIELD OF MARITIME CARRIAGE OF NUCLEAR MATERIAL

The High Contracting Parties,

CONSIDERING that the Paris Convention of July 29th, 1960, on Third Party Liability in the Field of Nuclear Energy and its Additional Protocol of January 28th, 1964, (hereinafter referred to as "the Paris Convention") and the Vienna Convention of May 21st, 1963, on Civil Liability for Nuclear Damage (hereinafter referred to as "the Vienna Convention") provide that, in the case of damage caused by a nuclear incident occurring in the course of maritime carriage of nuclear material covered by such Conventions, the operator of a nuclear installation is the person liable for such damage,

CONSIDERING that similar provisions exist in the national law in force in certain States,

CONSIDERING that the application of any preceding international Convention in the field of maritime transport is however maintained,

DESIROUS of ensuring that the operator of a nuclear installation will be exclusively liable for damage caused by a nuclear incident occurring in the course of maritime carriage of nuclear material,

HAVE AGREED as follows:

ARTICLE 1

Any person who by virtue of an international convention or national law applicable in the field of maritime transport might be held liable for damage caused by a nuclear incident shall be exonerated from such liability:

(a) if the operator of a nuclear installation is liable for such damage under either the Paris or the Vienna Convention, or

(b) if the operator of a nuclear installation is liable for

such damage by virtue of a national law governing the liability for such damage, provided that such law is in all respects as favourable to persons who may suffer damage as either the Paris or the Vienna Convention.

ARTICLE 2

1. The exoneration provided for in Article 1 shall also apply in respect of damage caused by a nuclear incident:

(a) to the nuclear installation itself or to any property on the site of that installation which is used or to be used in connexion with that installation, or

(b) to the means of transport upon which the nuclear material involved was at the time of the nuclear incident,

for which the operator of the nuclear installation is not liable because his liability for such damage has been excluded pursuant to the provisions of either the Paris or the Vienna Convention, or, in cases referred to in Article 1 (b), by equivalent provisions of the national law referred to therein.

2. The provisions of paragraph 1 shall not, however, affect the liability of any individual who has caused the damage by an act or omission done with intent to cause damage.

ARTICLE 3

No provision of the present Convention shall affect the liability of the operator of a nuclear ship in respect of damage caused by a nuclear incident involving the nuclear fuel of or radioactive products or waste produced in such ship.

ARTICLE 4

The present Convention shall supersede any international Conventions in the field of maritime transport which, at the date on which the present Convention is opened for signature, are in force or open for signature, ratification or accession but only to the extent that such Conventions would be in conflict with it; however, nothing in this Article shall affect the obligations of the Contracting

Parties to the present Convention to non-Contracting States arising under such international Conventions.

ARTICLE 5

1. The present Convention shall be opened for signature in Brussels and shall remain open for signature in London at the Headquarters of the Inter-Governmental Maritime Consultative Organization (hereinafter referred to as "the Organization") until December 31st, 1972, and shall thereafter remain open for accession.

2. States Members of the United Nations or any of the Specialized Agencies or of the International Atomic Energy Agency or Parties to the Statute of the International Court of Justice may become Parties to the present Convention by:

(a) signature without reservation as to ratification, acceptance or approval;

(b) signature subject to ratification, acceptance or approval followed by ratification, acceptance or approval; or

(c) accession.

3. Ratification, acceptance, approval or accession shall be effected by the deposit of a formal instrument to that effect with the Secretary-General of the Organization.

ARTICLE 6

1. The present Convention shall enter into force on the ninetieth day following the date on which five States have either signed it without reservation as to ratification, acceptance or approval or have deposited instruments of ratification, acceptance, approval or accession with the Secretary-General of the Organization.

2. For any State which subsequently signs the present Convention without reservation as to ratification, acceptance or approval, or deposits its instrument of ratification, acceptance, approval or accession, the Convention shall come into force on the ninetieth day after the date of such signature or deposit.

ARTICLE 7

1. The present Convention may be denounced by any Contracting Party to it at any time after the date on which the Convention comes into force for that State.

2. Denunciation shall be effected by a notification in writing delivered to the Secretary-General of the Organization.

3. A denunciation shall take effect one year, or such longer period as may be specified in the notification, after its receipt by the Secretary-General of the Organization.

4. Notwithstanding a denunciation by a Contracting Party pursuant to this Article the provisions of the present Convention shall continue to apply to any damage caused by a nuclear incident occurring before the denunciation takes effect.

ARTICLE 8

1. The United Nations where it is the administering authority for a territory, or any Contracting Party to the present Convention responsible for the international relations of a territory, may at any time by notification in writing to the Secretary-General of the Organization declare that the present Convention shall extend to such territory.

2. The present Convention shall, from the date of receipt of the notification or from such other date as may be specified in the notification, extend to the territory named therein.

3. The United Nations, or any Contracting Party which had made a declaration under paragraph 1 of this Article may at any time after the date on which the Convention has been so extended to any territory declare by notification in writing to the Secretary-General of the Organization that the present Convention shall cease to extend to any such territory named in the notification.

4. The present Convention shall cease to extend to any territory mentioned in such notification one year, or such longer period as

may be specified therein, after the date of receipt of the notification by the Secretary-General of the Organization.

ARTICLE 9

1. A Conference for the purpose of revising or amending the present Convention may be convened by the Organization.

2. The Organization shall convene a Conference of the Contracting Parties to the present Convention for revising or amending it at the request of not less than one-third of the Contracting Parties.

ARTICLE 10

A Contracting Party may make reservations corresponding to those which it has validly made to the Paris or Vienna Convention. A reservation may be made at the time of signature, ratification, acceptance, approval or accession.

ARTICLE 11

1. The present Convention shall be deposited with the Secretary-General of the Organization.

2. The Secretary-General of the Organization shall:

(a) inform all States which have signed or acceded to the present Convention of:

(i) each new signature and each deposit of an instrument together with the date thereof;

(ii) any reservation made in conformity with the present Convention;

(iii) the date of entry into force of the present Convention;

(iv) any denunciation of the present Convention and the date on which it takes effect;

(v) the extension of the present Convention to any territory under paragraph 1 of Article 8 and of the termination of any such extension under the provisions of paragraph 4 of that Article stating in each case the date on which the present Convention has been or will cease to be so extended;

(b) transmit certified true copies of the present Convention to all Signatory States and to all States which have acceded to the present Convention.

3. As soon as the present Convention comes into force, a certified true copy thereof shall be transmitted by the Secretary-General of the Organization to the Secretariat of the United Nations for registration and publication in accordance with Article 102 of the Charter of the United Nations.

ARTICLE 12

The present Convention is established in a single original in the English and French languages, both texts being equally authentic. Official translations in the Russian and Spanish languages shall be prepared by the Secretariat of the Organization and deposited with the signed original.

In witness whereof the undersigned being duly authorized by their respective Governments for that purpose have signed the present Convention.

Done at Brussels this seventeenth day of December 1971.

CONVENTION FOR THE PREVENTION OF MARINE POLLUTION BY DUMPING FROM SHIPS AND AIRCRAFT

Signed at Oslo, Norway, on 15 February 1972

Circulated in accordance with the request made at the 16th meeting of Sub-Committee III

The Contracting Parties

RECOGNIZING that the marine environment and the living resources which it supports are of vital importance to all nations;

MINDFUL that the ecological equilibrium and the legitimate uses of the sea are increasingly threatened by pollution;

RECOGNIZING that concerted action by Governments at national, regional and global levels is essential to prevent and combat marine pollution;

NOTING that this pollution has many sources, including dumping from ships and aircraft and discharges through rivers, estuaries, outfalls and pipelines within national jurisdiction, that it is important that states use the best practicable means to prevent such pollution, and that products and processes which will minimize the amount of harmful waste requiring disposal should be developed;

BEING CONVINCED that international action to control the pollution of the sea by the dumping of harmful substances from ships and aircraft can and should be taken without delay, but that this action should not preclude discussion of measures to control other sources of marine pollution as soon as possible;

CONSIDERING that the states bordering the North-East Atlantic have a particular responsibility to protect the waters of this region;

HAVE AGREED as follows:

Article 1.

The Contracting Parties pledge themselves to take all possible steps to prevent the pollution of the sea by substances that are liable to create hazards to human health, to harm living resources and marine life, to damage amenities or to interfere with other legitimate uses of the sea.

Article 2.

The area to which this Convention applies shall be the high seas and the territorial sea which are situated

a) within those parts of the Atlantic and Arctic Oceans and their dependent seas which lie north of 36° north latitude and between 42° west longitude and 51° east longitude, but excluding

(i) the Baltic Sea and Belts lying to the south and east of lines drawn from Hasenore Head to Gniben Point, from Korshage to Spodsbierg and from Gilbierg Head to the Kullen, and

(ii) the Mediterranean Sea and its dependent seas as far as the point of intersection of the parallel of 36° north latitude and the meridian of 5°36' west longitude.

b) within that part of the Atlantic Ocean north of 59° north latitude and between 44° west longitude and 42° west longitude.

Article 3.

The Contracting Parties agree to apply the measures which they adopt in such a way as to prevent the diversion of dumping of harmful substances into seas outside the area to which this Convention applies.

Article 4.

The Contracting Parties shall harmonize their policies and introduce, individually and in common, measures to prevent the pollution of the sea by dumping by or from ships and aircraft.

Article 5.

The dumping of the substances listed in Annex I to this Convention is prohibited.

Article 6.

No waste containing such quantities of the substances and materials listed in Annex II to this Convention as the Commission established under the provisions of Article 16, hereinafter referred to as «the Commission», shall define as significant, shall be dumped without a specific permit in each case from the appropriate national authority or authorities. When such permits are issued, the provisions of Annexes II and III to this Convention shall be applied.

Article 7.

No substance or material shall be dumped without the approval of the appropriate national authority or authorities. When such approval is granted, the provisions of Annex III to this Convention shall be applied.

Article 8.

1) The provisions of Articles 5, 6 and 7 shall not apply in case of force majeure due to stress of weather or any other cause when the safety of human life or of a ship or aircraft is threatened. Such dumping shall immediately be reported to the Commission, together with full details of the circumstances and of the nature and quantities of the substances and materials dumped.

2) The provisions of Article 5 shall not apply where these substances occur as trace contaminants in waste to which they have not been added for the purpose of being dumped. However, such dumping shall remain subject to Articles 6 and 7.

Article 9.

If a Contracting Party in an emergency considers that a substance listed in Annex I to this Convention cannot be disposed of on land without unacceptable danger or damage, the Contracting Party concerned shall forthwith consult the Commission. The Commission shall recommend methods of storage or the most satisfactory means of destruction or disposal under the prevailing circumstances. The Contracting Party shall inform the Commission of the steps adopted in pursuance of its recommendation. The Contracting Parties pledge themselves to assist one another in such situations.

Article 10.

The composition of the waste shall be ascertained by the appropriate national authority or authorities in accordance with the provisions of Annex III to this Convention before any permit or approval for the dumping of waste at sea is issued.

Article 11.

Each Contracting Party shall keep, and transmit to the Commission, according to a standard procedure, records of the nature and the quantities of the substances and materials dumped under permits or approvals issued by that Contracting Party, and of the dates, places and methods of dumping.

Article 12.

The Contracting Parties agree to establish complementary or joint programmes of scientific and technical research, including research on alternative methods of disposal of harmful substances, and to transmit to each other the information so obtained. In doing so they will have regard to the work carried out by the appropriate international organizations and agencies.

Article 13.

The Contracting Parties agree to institute, in co-operation with appropriate international organizations and agencies, complementary or joint programmes for monitoring the distribution and effects of pollutants in the area to which this Convention applies.

Article 14.

The Contracting Parties pledge themselves to promote, within the competent specialized agencies and other international bodies, measures concerning the protection of the marine environment against pollution caused by oil and oily wastes, other noxious or hazardous cargoes, and radioactive materials.

Article 15.

1) Each Contracting Party undertakes to ensure compliance with the provisions of this Convention:

a) by ships and aircraft registered in its territory;

b) by ships and aircraft loading in its territory the substances and materials which are to be dumped;

c) by ships and aircraft believed to be engaged in dumping within its territorial sea.

2) Each Contracting Party undertakes to issue instructions to its maritime inspection vessels and aircraft and to other appropriate services to report to its authorities any incidents or conditions on the high seas which give rise to suspicions that dumping in contravention of the provisions of the present Convention has occurred or is about to occur. That Contracting Party shall, if it considers it appropriate, report accordingly to any other Contracting Party concerned.

3) Each Contracting Party shall take in its territory appropriate measures to prevent and punish conduct in contravention of the provisions of this Convention.

4) The Contracting Parties undertake to assist one another as appropriate in dealing with pollution incidents involving dumping at

sea, and to exchange information on methods of dealing with such incidents.

5) The Contracting Parties further agree to work together in the development of co-operative procedures for the application of the Convention, particularly on the high seas.

6) Nothing in this Convention shall abridge sovereign immunity to which certain vessels are entitled under international law.

Article 16.

A Commission, made up of representatives of each of the Contracting Parties, is hereby established. The Commission shall meet at regular intervals and at any time when, due to special circumstances, it is so decided in accordance with the Rules of Procedure.

Article 17.

It shall be the duty of the Commission:

a) To exercise overall supervision over the implementation of this Convention;
b) To receive and consider the records of permits and approvals issued and of dumping which has taken place, as provided for in Articles 8, 9 and 11 of this Convention, and to define the standard procedure to be adopted for this purpose;
c) To review generally the condition of the seas within the area to which this Convention applies, the efficacy of the control measures being adopted, and the need for any additional or different measures;
d) To keep under review the contents of the Annexes to this Convention, and to recommend such amendments, additions or deletions as may be agreed;
e) To discharge such other functions as may be appropriate under the terms of this Convention.

Article 18.

1) The Commission shall draw up its own Rules of Procedure which shall be adopted by unanimous vote. The Government of Norway shall call the first meeting of the Commission as soon as practicable after the coming into force of this Convention.

2) Recommendations for modification of the Annexes to this Convention in accordance with Article 17 (d) shall be adopted by a unanimous vote in the Commission, and the modifications contained therein shall enter into force after unanimous approval by the Governments of the Contracting Parties.

Article 19.

For the purpose of this Convention:

1) «Dumping» means any deliberate disposal of substances and materials into the sea by or from ships or aircraft other than:

a) any discharge incidental to or derived from the normal operation of ships and aircraft and their equipment;
b) the placing of substances and materials for a purpose other than the mere disposal thereof, if not contrary to the aim of this Convention.

2) «Ships and aircraft» means sea-going vessels and air-borne craft of any type whatsoever. This expression includes air-cushion craft, floating craft whether self-propelled or not, and fixed or floating platforms.

Article 20.

This Convention shall be open for signature at Oslo until 15th August 1972 by the States invited to participate in the Conference on Marine Pollution, held there from 19th to 22nd October, 1971.

Article 21.

This Convention shall be subject to ratification. The instruments of ratification shall be deposited with the Government of Norway.

Article 22.

This Convention shall be open for accession by any State referred to in Article 20. The Contracting Parties may unanimously invite other States to accede to the Convention. The instruments of accession shall be deposited with the Government of Norway.

Article 23.

1) This Convention shall enter into force on the thirtieth day following the date of deposit of the seventh instrument of ratification or accession.

2) For each State ratifying or acceding to the Convention after the deposit of the seventh instrument of ratification or accession, the Convention shall enter into force on the thirtieth day after deposit by such State of its instrument of ratification or accession.

Article 24.

At any time after two years from the date on which this Convention has come into force with respect to a Contracting Party, that Party may withdraw from the Convention by means of a notice in writing addressed to the depositary Government. Any such withdrawal shall take effect twelve months after the date of its receipt.

Article 25.

A conference for the purpose of revising or amending this Convention may be convened by the depositary Government at the request of the Commission adopted by a two-thirds majority.

Article 26.

The depositary Government shall inform the Contracting Parties and the States referred to in Article 20:

a) of signatures to this Convention, of the deposit of instruments of ratification or accession, and of the receipt of a notice of withdrawal, in accordance with Articles 20, 21, 22 and 24;
b) of the date on which this Convention will come into force in accordance with Article 23;
c) of the receipt of notification of approval relating to modifications of the Annexes to this Convention and of the entry into force of such modifications in accordance with Article 18.

Article 27.

The original of this Convention, of which the English and French texts are equally authentic, shall be deposited with the Government of Norway, which shall send certified copies thereof to the Contracting Parties and to the States referred to in Article 20, and which shall transmit a certified copy to the Secretary-General of the United Nations for registration and publication in accordance with Article 102 of the Charter of the United Nations.

IN WITNESS WHEREOF the undersigned, being duly authorized by their respective Governments, have signed this Convention.

Done at Oslo, this fifteenth day of February 1972.

Annex I.

The following substances are listed for the purposes of Article 5 of the Convention:

1. Organohalogen compounds and compounds which may form such substances in the marine environment, excluding those which are non-toxic, or which are rapidly converted in the sea into substances which are biologically harmless;

2. Organosilicon compounds and compounds which may form such substances in the marine environment, excluding those which are non-toxic, or which are rapidly converted in the sea into substances which are biologically harmless;

3. Substances which have been agreed between the Contracting Parties as likely to be carcinogenic under the conditions of disposal;

4. Mercury and mercury compounds;

5. Cadmium and cadmium compounds;

6. Persistent plastics and other persistent synthetic materials which may float or remain in suspension in the sea, and which may seriously interfere with fishing or navigation, reduce amenities, or interfere with other legitimate uses of the sea.

Annex II.

1. The following substances and materials requiring special care are listed for the purposes of Article 6:

a) Arsenic, lead, copper, zinc and their compounds, cyanides and fluorides, and pesticides and their by-products not covered by the provisions of Annex I;
b) Containers, scrap metal, tar-like substances liable to sink to the sea bottom and other bulky wastes which may present a serious obstacle to fishing or navigation;
c) Substances which, though of a non-toxic nature, may become harmful due to the quantities in which they are dumped, or which are liable to seriously reduce amenities.

2. The substances and materials listed under paragraph 1 (b) above should always be deposited in deep water.

3. In the issuance of permits or approvals for the dumping of large quantities of acids and alkalis, consideration should be given to the possible presence in such wastes of the substances listed in paragraph 1) above.

4. When, in the application of the provisions of Annexes II and III, it is considered necessary to deposit waste in deep water, this should be done only when the following two conditions are both fulfilled:

a) that the depth is not less than 2000 metres,
b) that the distance from the nearest land is not less than 150 nautical miles.

Annex III.

Provisions governing the issue of permits and approvals for the dumping of wastes at sea.

1. *Characteristics of the waste*

a) Amount and composition;
b) Amount of substances and materials to be deposited per day (per week, per month);
c) Form in which it is presented for dumping, i.e. whether as a solid, sludge or liquid;
d) Physical (especially solubility and specific gravity), chemical, biochemical (oxygen demand, nutrient production) and biological properties (presence of viruses, bacteria,yeasts, parasites, etc.);
e) Toxicity;
f) Persistence;
g) Accumulation in biological materials or sediments;
h) Chemical and physical changes of the waste after release, including possible formation of new compounds;
i) Probability of production of taints reducing marketability of resources (fish, shellfish, etc.).

2. *Characteristics of dumping site and method of deposit*

a) Geographical position, depth and distance from coast;
b) Location in relation to living resources in adult or juvenile phases;
c) Location in relation to amenity areas;
d) Methods of packing, if any;
e) Initial dilution achieved by proposed method of release;
f) Dispersal, horizontal transport and vertical mixing characteristics;
g) Existence and effects of current and previous discharges and dumping in the area (including accumulative effects).

3. *General considerations and conditions*

a) Interference with shipping, fishing, recreation, mineral extraction, desalination, fish and shellfish culture, areas of special scientific importance and other legitimate use of the sea;

b) In applying these principles the practical availability of alternative means of disposal or elimination will be taken into consideration.

NORWAY: REGULATIONS CONCERNING THE DISCHARGE OR DUMPING OF CERTAIN SUBSTANCES HAVING HARMFUL EFFECT ON MARINE LIFE OR HUMAN HEALTH, JUNE 11, 1971

(given by Royal Decree)

Pursuant to (Sec.) 18 and (Sec.) 3, paragraph 4 of the Water Pollution Law of June 26, 1970, the following regulations are laid down concerning the discharge or dumping of certain substances which are capable of having harmful effects on marine life or human health:

Section 1.

In accordance with the prohibition on water pollution set out in (Sec.) 3 and (Sec.) 4 (of the Law), Norwegian ships shall be prohibited from discharging the following substances in international waters, provided that such substances were taken on board for the purpose of being discharged:-

1. Persistent organic substances i.e. organic compounds which can only be broken down slowly in organisms or by natural chemical processes.

2. Waste which is composed of the above mentioned substances or of organic or inorganic compounds of heavy metals or other toxic metals.

Similarly Norwegian nationals and companies shall be prohibited from taking action with the object of causing such discharge.

Section 2.

The supervisory authorities set up under (Sec.) 13 of the Water Pollution Law may draw up lists of the substances prohibited in (Sec.) 1 of this Decree, and may at any time amend or add to these lists.

Section 3.

These regulations enter into force immediately.

SINGAPORE

THE ENVIRONMENTAL PUBLIC HEALTH (PROHIBITION ON DISCHARGE OF TRADE EFFLUENTS INTO WATER COURSES) REGULATIONS, 1971.

In exercise of the powers conferred by section 141 of the Environmental Public Health Act, 1968, the Minister for Health hereby makes the following Regulations:-

1. These Regulations may be cited as the Environmental Public Health (Prohibition on Discharge of Trade Effluents into Water Courses) Regulations, 1971, and shall come into operation on the 1st day of March, 1971.

2. In these Regulations, unless the context otherwise requires -

"authorised person" means a person who has obtained the written consent of the Commissioner as provided in regulation 4 of these Regulations or the further consent in writing of the Commissioner under paragraph (4) of regulation 5 of these Regulations:

"Director" means the Director of Public Works appointed under section 13 of the Local Government Integration Ordinance, 1963, and includes a Deputy Director of Public Works and an Assistant Director of Public Works appointed under the said section:

"trade effluent" means the liquid waste of any trade, manufacture or business or of any building construction or other operation;

"water course" includes any reservoir, lake, river, stream, canal, drain, spring or well or any part of the sea abutting on the foreshore and any other body of natural or artificial surface or sub-surface water.

3.--(1) Any Public Health Engineer may carry out all or any of the powers conferred on the Commissioner by these Regulations.

(2) The Commissioner may delegate to any public officer, subject to such limitations as he may deem fit to impose, all or any of the powers conferred on him by these Regulations.

(3) For the purposes of these Regulations, "public officer" includes any officer of any statutory board or body who has been authorised in writing by the Commissioner to

carry out all or any of the powers conferred on the Commissioner by these Regulations.

4. No person shall discharge, or cause or permit to be discharged, any trade effluent into any water course without first obtaining the written consent of the Commissioner who, in giving such consent, may impose such conditions as he may deem fit.

5.--(1) Every application to the Commissioner for permission to discharge any trade effluent into a water course shall be made in writing to the Commissioner in such form as he may require and shall be in respect of specified premises.

(2) Every applicant shall in such application--

(a) specify particulars of the trade, manufacture, business, building construction or other operation carried on or intended to be carried on by him;

(b) provide details of any process used by him which is likely to result in the creation of any trade effluent;

(c) provide particulars of the raw materials and chemicals used in such process;

(d) show details of the layout of various units of machinery and plant used in the premises concerned and the direction of the flow of any liquid or trade effluent issuing from, or produced by, such machinery or plant;

(e) give an estimate of the amount of water consumed;

(f) state particulars of the physical and chemical nature of the waste products as well as the organic content expressed in terms of Biochemical Oxygen Demand; and

(g) provide such other particulars as the Commissioner may deem necessary or the applicant may consider relevant.

(3) Every authorised person shall notify the Commissioner in writing immediately upon the occurrence of any change in the particulars or information given in his form of application.

(4) Where, in any case, after the written consent of the Commissioner has been given under regulation 4 of these Regulations, the nature and content of the trade effluent has undergone any alteration, the authorised person in question shall obtain further consent in writing from the Commissioner before discharging the same into any water course. The Commissioner may, in giving such further consent, impose such conditions as he may think fit.

6. An authorised person shall comply with the conditions and requirements set out in the Schedule to these Regulations and such other conditions as the Commissioner may have imposed under regulation 4 or paragraph (4) of regulation 5 of these Regulations, as the case may be.

7.--(1) The Commissioner may withdraw, or suspend for such period as he thinks fit, any consent given by him under regulation 4 or paragraph (4) of regulation 5 of these Regulations if any authorised person fails to comply with any condition or requirement set out in the Schedule to these Regulations or with any condition imposed by the Commissioner under regulation 4 or paragraph (4) of regulation 5 of these Regulations.

(2) The Commissioner shall inform the authorised person in writing of such withdrawal or suspension, but in so doing need not assign any reason therefor.

8. The Commissioner may, with the concurrence of the Director, by notice in writing, direct any person to discharge the trade effluent of his trade, manufacture or business into a public sewer, and such person shall comply with such notice within such period as may be specified therein.

9. Any certificate or document purporting to be a report under the hand of a chemist or analyst in the service of the Government upon any matter or thing submitted to him for examination, analysis of report shall be admissible as evidence in any proceedings under these Regulations and shall be _prima facie_ evidence of the facts stated therein, unless the court or the accused requires him to be called as a witness:

Provided that in any case in which the prosecutor intends to give in evidence any such report, he shall deliver a copy thereof to the accused not less than ten clear days before the commencement of such proceedings.

10. Any person who contravenes the provisions of regulation 4, paragraph (3) or (4) of regulation 5, regulation 6 or regulation 8 of these Regulations shall be guilty of an

offence under these Regulations and shall be liable on conviction--

(a) for a first offence, to a fine not exceeding one thousand dollars and to a further fine not exceeding twenty-five dollars for every day during which the offence is continued after conviction; and

(b) for a second or subsequent offence, to a fine not exceeding two thousand dollars and to a further fine not exceeding fifty dollars for every day during which the offence is continued after conviction.

THE SCHEDULE.

(Regulation 6).

1. The authorised person shall, if the Commissioner so requires, treat the trade effluent of his trade, manufacture, business, building construction or other operation before it is discharged into any water course.

2. The authorised person shall install such sampling and test points, inspection chambers and recording and other apparatus as the Commissioner may, from time to time, require.

3.--(1) The authorised person shall, in addition to any consent given under regulation 4 or paragraph (4) of regulation 5 of these Regulations, obtain the prior approval in writing of the Commissioner before he makes or causes to be made any drain or connection into a water course for the purpose of discharging any trade effluent; and in every such case the position and design of the outlet for the discharge of the trade effluent shall be approved by the Commissioner and shall not be altered or changed without the prior approval from the Commissioner.

4. The authorised person shall submit returns, at such times as the Commissioner may deem necessary in the circumstances of his case, concerning the trade effluent emanating from his trade, manufacture, business, building construction or other operation.

5. The authorised person shall not discharge into a water course the trade effluent of his trade, manufacture, business, building construction or other operation at a rate exceeding the rate of discharge authorised by the Commissioner in his case nor exceed the maximum quantity of the trade

effluent permitted to be discharged by him in any period of twenty-four hours.

6. The temperature of the trade effluent at the point of entry into a water course shall not exceed 43° Centigrade.

7. The pH value of the trade effluent at the point of entry into a water course shall not be less than 6 nor more than 9.

8. The trade effluent discharged into a water course shall not include the following substances in a proportion greater than that stated below:-

(a) the five-day Biochemical Oxygen Demand (B.O.D.) at 20°C shall not exceed 50 milligrams per litre;

(b) the Chemical Oxygen Demand (C.O.D.) shall not exceed 100 milligrams per litre;

(c) the oxygen absorbed from N/80 acid permanganate in 4 hours at 29°C shall not exceed 40 milligrams per litre;

(d) the total suspended solids shall not exceed 50 milligrams per litre;

(e) the concentration of the following metals shall not exceed 0.1 milligram per litre individually and 0.5 milligram per litre collectively:-

cadmium; chromium (trivalent or hexavalent); copper; lead; mercury; nickel; silver; and zinc;

(f) the cyanide content (as HCN) shall not exceed 0.1 milligram per litre;

(g) the arsenic expressed as metal shall not exceed 0.5 milligram per litre;

(h) beryllium - 0.5 milligram per litre;

(i) boron - 0.5 milligram per litre;

(j) iron - 5 milligrams per litre;

(k) sulphide expressed as sulphur shall not exceed 0.2 milligram per litre;

(l) sulphate expressed as sulphur (SO) shall not exceed 50 milligrams per litre;

(m) detergents shall not exceed 15 milligrams per litre;

(n) grease, oil, tar and all other liquids immiscible with water shall not exceed 5 milligrams per litre;

(o) chloride expressed as chlorine shall not exceed 400 milligrams per litre;

(p) total dissolved solids shall not exceed 1,000 milligrams per litre;

(q) chlorine shall not exceed 1 milligram per litre;

(r) colour shall not exceed 7 Lovibond units.

9. The trade effluent discharged into any water course shall not include any of the following:-

(a) any radio-active material;

(b) phenol;

(c) any pesticide, fungicide, herbicide, insecticide or rodenticide;

(d) any fumigant; or

(e) any refuse, garbage, sawdust, timber, human or animal waste or any solid matter.

Made this 22nd day of February, 1971.

TAN TECK KHIM,
Permanent Secretary (Special Duties),
Ministry of Health,
Singapore

/PH./035/17; AG./L./63/68 Pt./

(To be presented to Parliament under section 141 (4) of the Environmental Public Health Act, 1968).

An Act

84 STAT. 91

To amend the Federal Water Pollution Control Act, as amended, and for other purposes.

Be it enacted by the Senate and House of Representatives of the United States of America in Congress assembled,

Federal Water Pollution Control Act, amendments.

TITLE I—WATER QUALITY IMPROVEMENT

Citation of title.

SEC. 101. This title may be cited as the "Water Quality Improvement Act of 1970".

Repeal. 80 Stat. 1252. 33 USC 466m, 466n. 33 USC 466 note. 70 Stat. 506; 79 Stat. 903. 33 USC 466h-1.

SEC. 102. Existing sections 17 and 18 of the Federal Water Pollution Control Act, as amended, are hereby repealed. Section 19 of such Act is redesignated as section 27. Sections 11 through 16 of such Act are redesignated as sections 21 through 26, respectively. Such Act is further amended by inserting after section 10 the following new sections:

"CONTROL OF POLLUTION BY OIL

Definitions.

"SEC. 11. (a) For the purpose of this section, the term—

"(1) 'oil' means oil of any kind or in any form, including, but not limited to, petroleum, fuel oil, sludge, oil refuse, and oil mixed with wastes other than dredged spoil;

"(2) 'discharge' includes, but is not limited to, any spilling, leaking, pumping, pouring, emitting, emptying or dumping;

"(3) 'vessel' means every description of watercraft or other artificial contrivance used, or capable of being used, as a means of transportation on water other than a public vessel;

"(4) 'public vessel' means a vessel owned or bare-boat chartered and operated by the United States, or by a State or political subdivision thereof, or by a foreign nation, except when such vessel is engaged in commerce;

"(5) 'United States' means the States, the District of Columbia, the Commonwealth of Puerto Rico, the Canal Zone, Guam, American Samoa, the Virgin Islands, and the Trust Territory of the Pacific Islands;

"(6) 'owner or operator' means (A) in the case of a vessel, any person owning, operating, or chartering by demise, such vessel, and (B) in the case of an onshore facility, and an offshore facility, any person owning or operating such onshore facility or offshore facility, and (C) in the case of any abandoned offshore facility, the person who owned or operated such facility immediately prior to such abandonment;

"(7) 'person' includes an individual, firm, corporation, association, and a partnership.

"(8) 'remove' or 'removal' refers to removal of the oil from the water and shorelines or the taking of such other actions as may be necessary to minimize or mitigate damage to the public health or welfare, including, but not limited to, fish, shellfish, wildlife, and public and private property, shorelines, and beaches;

"(9) 'contiguous zone' means the entire zone established or to be established by the United States under article 24 of the Convention on the Territorial Sea and the Contiguous Zone; 15 UST 1606.

"(10) 'onshore facility' means any facility (including, but not limited to, motor vehicles and rolling stock) of any kind located in, on, or under, any land within the United States other than submerged land;

"(11) 'offshore facility' means any facility of any kind located in, on, or under, any of the navigable waters of the United States other than a vessel or a public vessel;

"(12) 'act of God' means an act occasioned by an unanticipated grave natural disaster;

"(13) 'barrel' means 42 United States gallons at 60 degrees Fahrenheit.

"(b)(1) The Congress hereby declares that it is the policy of the United States that there should be no discharges of oil into or upon the navigable waters of the United States, adjoining shorelines, or into or upon the waters of the contiguous zone.

"(2) The discharge of oil into or upon the navigable waters of the United States, adjoining shorelines, or into or upon the waters of the contiguous zone in harmful quantities as determined by the President under paragraph (3) of this subsection, is prohibited, except (A) in the case of such discharges into the waters of the contiguous zone, where permitted under article IV of the International Convention for
12 UST 2989. the Prevention of Pollution of the Sea by Oil, 1954, as amended, and (B) where permitted in quantities and at times and locations or under such circumstances or conditions as the President may, by regulation, determine not to be harmful. Any regulations issued under this subsection shall be consistent with maritime safety and with marine and navigation laws and regulations and applicable water quality standards.

"(3) The President shall, by regulation, to be issued as soon as possible after the date of enactment of this paragraph, determine for the purposes of this section, those quantities of oil the discharge of which, at such times, locations, circumstances, and conditions, will be harmful to the public health or welfare of the United States, including, but not limited to, fish, shellfish, wildlife, and public and private property, shorelines, and beaches, except that in the case of the discharge of oil into or upon the waters of the contiguous zone, only those discharges which threaten the fishery resources of the contiguous zone or threaten to pollute or contribute to the pollution of the territory or the territorial sea of the United States may be determined to be harmful.

"(4) Any person in charge of a vessel or of an onshore facility or an offshore facility shall, as soon as he has knowledge of any discharge of oil from such vessel or facility in violation of paragraph (2) of this subsection, immediately notify the appropriate agency of the United
Penalty. States Government of such discharge. Any such person who fails to notify immediately such agency of such discharge shall, upon conviction, be fined not more than $10,000, or imprisoned for not more than one year, or both. Notification received pursuant to this paragraph or information obtained by the exploitation of such notification shall not be used against any such person in any criminal case, except a prosecution for perjury or for giving a false statement.

Penalty. "(5) Any owner or operator of any vessel, onshore facility, or offshore facility from which oil is knowingly discharged in violation of paragraph (2) of this subsection shall be assessed a civil penalty by the Secretary of the department in which the Coast Guard is operating of not more than $10,000 for each offense. No penalty shall be assessed unless the owner or operator charged shall have been given notice and opportunity for a hearing on such charge. Each violation is a separate offense. Any such civil penalty may be compromised by such Secretary. In determining the amount of the penalty, or the amount agreed upon in compromise, the appropriateness of such penalty to the size of the business of the owner or operator charged, the effect on the owner or operator's ability to continue in business, and the gravity of the violation, shall be considered by such Secretary. The Secretary of the

Treasury shall withhold at the request of such Secretary the clearance required by section 4197 of the Revised Statutes of the United States, as amended (46 U.S.C. 91), of any vessel the owner or operator of which is subject to the foregoing penalty. Clearance may be granted in such cases upon the filing of a bond or other surety satisfactory to such Secretary.

"(c) (1) Whenever any oil is discharged, into or upon the navigable waters of the United States, adjoining shorelines, or into or upon the waters of the contiguous zone, the President is authorized to act to remove or arrange for the removal of such oil at any time, unless he determines such removal will be done properly by the owner or operator of the vessel, onshore facility, or offshore facility from which the discharge occurs.

"(2) Within sixty days after the effective date of this section, the President shall prepare and publish a National Contingency Plan for removal of oil pursuant to this subsection. Such National Contingency Plan shall provide for efficient, coordinated, and effective action to minimize damage from oil discharges, including containment, dispersal, and removal of oil, and shall include, but not be limited to— National Contingency Plan.

"(A) assignment of duties and responsibilities among Federal departments and agencies in coordination with State and local agencies, including, but not limited to, water pollution control, conservation, and port authorities;

"(B) identification, procurement, maintenance, and storage of equipment and supplies;

"(C) establishment or designation of a strike force consisting of personnel who shall be trained, prepared, and available to provide necessary services to carry out the Plan, including the establishment at major ports, to be determined by the President, of emergency task forces of trained personnel, adequate oil pollution control equipment and material, and a detailed oil pollution prevention and removal plan;

"(D) a system of surveillance and notice designed to insure earliest possible notice of discharges of oil to the appropriate Federal agency;

"(E) establishment of a national center to provide coordination and direction for operations in carrying out the Plan;

"(F) procedures and techniques to be employed in identifying, containing, dispersing, and removing oil; and

"(G) a schedule, prepared in cooperation with the States, identifying (i) dispersants and other chemicals, if any, that may be used in carrying out the Plan, (ii) the waters in which such dispersants and chemicals may be used, and (iii) the quantities of such dispersant or chemical which can be used safely in such waters, which schedule shall provide in the case of any dispersant, chemical, or waters not specifically identified in such schedule that the President, or his delegate, may, on a case-by-case basis, identify the dispersants and other chemicals which may be used, the waters in which they may be used, and the quantities which can be used safely in such waters.

The President may, from time to time, as he deems advisable, revise or otherwise amend the National Contingency Plan. After publication of the National Contingency Plan, the removal of oil and actions to minimize damage from oil discharges shall, to the greatest extent possible, be in accordance with the National Contingency Plan.

"(d) Whenever a marine disaster in or upon the navigable waters of the United States has created a substantial threat of a pollution hazard to the public health or welfare of the United States, including, but not limited to, fish, shellfish, and wildlife and the public and private shorelines and beaches of the United States, because of a discharge, or an imminent discharge, of large quantities of oil from a vessel the United States may (A) coordinate and direct all public and private efforts directed at the removal or elimination of such threat; and (B) summarily remove, and, if necessary, destroy such vessel by whatever means are available without regard to any provision of law governing the employment of personnel or the expenditure of appropriated funds. Any expense incurred under this subsection shall be a cost incurred by the United States Government for the purposes of subsection (f) in the removal of oil.

"(e) In addition to any other action taken by a State or local government, when the President determines there is an imminent and substantial threat to the public health or welfare of the United States, including, but not limited to, fish, shellfish, and wildlife and public and private property, shorelines, and beaches within the United States, because of an actual or threatened discharge of oil into or upon the navigable waters of the United States from an onshore or offshore facility, the President may require the United States attorney of the district in which the threat occurs to secure such relief as may be necessary to abate such threat, and the district courts of the United States shall have jurisdiction to grant such relief as the public interest and the equities of the case may require.

"(f)(1) Except where an owner or operator can prove that a discharge was caused solely by (A) an act of God, (B) an act of war, (C) negligence on the part of the United States Government, or (D) an act or omission of a third party without regard to whether any such act or omission was or was not negligent, or any combination of the foregoing clauses, such owner or operator of any vessel from which oil is discharged in violation of subsection (b)(2) of this section shall, notwithstanding any other provision of law, be liable to the United States Government for the actual costs incurred under subsection (c) for the removal of such oil by the United States Government in an amount not to exceed $100 per gross ton of such vessel or $14,000,000, whichever is lesser, except that where the United States can show that such discharge was the result of willful negligence or willful misconduct within the privity and knowledge of the owner, such owner or operator shall be liable to the United States Government for the full amount of such costs. Such costs shall constitute a maritime lien on such vessel which may be recovered in an action in rem in the district court of the United States for any district within which any vessel may be found. The United States may also bring an action against the owner or operator of such vessel in any court of competent jurisdiction to recover such costs.

"(2) Except where an owner or operator of an onshore facility can prove that a discharge was caused solely by (A) an act of God, (B) an act of war, (C) negligence on the part of the United States Government, or (D) an act or omission of a third party without regard to whether any such act or omission was or was not negligent, or any combination of the foregoing clauses, such owner or operator of any such facility from which oil is discharged in violation of subsection (b)(2) of this section shall be liable to the United States Government for the actual costs incurred under subsection (c) for the removal of such oil by the United States Government in an amount not to exceed $8,000,000, except that where the United States can show that such discharge was the result of willful negligence or willful misconduct within the privity and knowledge of the owner, such owner or operator shall be liable to the United States Government for the full amount of such costs. The United States may bring an action against the owner or operator of such facility in any court of competent jurisdiction to recover such costs. The Secretary is authorized, by regulation, after consultation with the Secretary of Commerce and the Small Business Administration, to establish reasonable and equitable classifications of those onshore facilities having a total fixed storage capacity of 1,000 barrels or less which he determines because of size, type, and location do not present a substantial risk of the discharge of oil in violation of subsection (b)(2) of this section, and apply with respect to such classifications differing limits of liability which may be less than the amount contained in this paragraph.

"(3) Except where an owner or operator of an offshore facility can prove that a discharge was caused solely by (A) an act of God, (B) an act of war, (C) negligence on the part of the United States Government, or (D) an act or omission of a third party without regard to whether any such act or omission was or was not negligent, or any combination of the foregoing clauses, such owner or operator of any such facility from which oil is discharged in violation of subsection (b)(2) of this section shall, notwithstanding any other provision of law, be liable to the United States Government for the actual costs incurred under subsection (c) for the removal of such oil by the United States Government in an amount not to exceed $8,000,000, except that where the United States can show that such discharge was the result of willful negligence or willful misconduct within the privity and knowledge of the owner, such owner or operator shall be liable to the United States Government for the full amount of such costs. The United States may bring an action against the owner or operator of such a facility in any court of competent jurisdiction to recover such costs.

"(g) In any case where an owner or operator of a vessel, of an onshore facility, or of an offshore facility, from which oil is discharged in violation of subsection (b)(2) of this section proves that such discharge of oil was caused solely by an act or omission of a third party, or was caused solely by such an act or omission in combination with an act of God, an act of war, or negligence on the part of the United States Government, such third party shall, notwithstanding any other provision of law, be liable to the United States Government for the actual costs incurred under subsection (c) for removal of such oil by the United States Government, except where such third party can prove that such discharge was caused solely by (A) an act of God, (B) an act of war, (C) negligence on the part of the United States Government, or (D) an act or omission of another party without regard to whether such act or omission was or was not negligent, or any combination of the foregoing clauses. If such third party was the owner or operator of a vessel which caused the discharge of oil in violation of subsection (b)(2) of this section, the liability of such third party under this subsection shall not exceed $100 per gross ton of such vessel or $14,000,000, whichever is the lesser. In any other case the liability of such third party shall not exceed the limitation which would have been applicable to the owner or operator of the vessel or the onshore or offshore facility from which the discharge actually occurred, if such owner or operator were liable. If the United States can show that the discharge of oil in violation of subsection (b)(2) of this section was the result of willful negligence or willful misconduct within the privity and knowledge of such third party, such third party shall be liable to the United States Government for the full amount of such removal costs. The United States may bring an action against the third party in any court of competent jurisdiction to recover such removal costs.

"(h) The liabilities established by this section shall in no way affect any rights which (1) the owner or operator of a vessel or of an onshore facility or an offshore facility may have against any third party whose acts may in any way have caused or contributed to such discharge, or (2) the United States Government may have against any third party whose actions may in any way have caused or contributed to the discharge of oil.

"(i) (1) In any case where an owner or operator of a vessel or an onshore facility or an offshore facility from which oil is discharged in violation of subsection (b) (2) of this section acts to remove such oil in accordance with regulations promulgated pursuant to this section, such owner or operator shall be entitled to recover the reasonable costs incurred in such removal upon establishing, in a suit which may be brought against the United States Government in the United States Court of Claims, that such discharge was caused solely by (A) an act of God, (B) an act of war, (C) negligence on the part of the United States Government, or (D) an act or omission of a third party without regard to whether such act or omission was or was not negligent, or of any combination of the foregoing clauses.

"(2) The provisions of this subsection shall not apply in any case where liability is established pursuant to the Outer Continental Shelf Lands Act.

67 Stat. 462. 43 USC 1331 note.

"(3) Any amount paid in accordance with a judgment of the United States Court of Claims pursuant to this section shall be paid from the fund established pursuant to subsection (k).

Regulations.

"(j) (1) Consistent with the National Contingency Plan required by subsection (c) (2) of this section, as soon as practicable after the effective date of this section, and from time to time thereafter, the President shall issue regulations consistent with maritime safety and with marine and navigation laws (A) establishing methods and procedures for removal of discharged oil, (B) establishing criteria for the development and implementation of local and regional oil removal contingency plans, (C) establishing procedures, methods, and requirements for equipment to prevent discharges of oil from vessels and from onshore facilities and offshore facilities, and (D) governing the inspection of vessels carrying cargoes of oil and the inspection of such cargoes in order to reduce the likelihood of discharges of oil from such vessels in violation of this section.

"(2) Any owner or operator of a vessel or an onshore facility or an offshore facility and any other person subject to any regulation issued under paragraph (1) of this subsection who fails or refuses to comply with the provisions of any such regulation, shall be liable to a civil penalty of not more than $5,000 for each such violation. Each violation shall be a separate offense. The President may assess and compromise such penalty. No penalty shall be assessed until the owner, operator, or other person charged shall have been given notice and an opportunity for a hearing on such charge. In determining the amount of the penalty, or the amount agreed upon in compromise, the gravity of the violation, and the demonstrated good faith of the owner, operator, or other person charged in attempting to achieve rapid compliance, after notification of a violation, shall be considered by the President.

Appropriation.

"(k) There is hereby authorized to be appropriated to a revolving fund to be established in the Treasury not to exceed $35,000,000 to carry out the provisions of subsections (c), (i), and (l) of this section and section 12 of this Act. Any other funds received by the United States under this section shall also be deposited in said fund for such purposes. All sums appropriated to, or deposited in, said fund shall remain available until expended.

Post, p.98.

"(l) The President is authorized to delegate the administration of this section to the heads of those Federal departments, agencies, and instrumentalities which he determines to be appropriate. Any moneys in the fund established by subsection (k) of this section shall be available to such Federal departments, agencies, and instrumentalities to carry out the provisions of subsections (c) and (i) of this section and section 12 of this Act. Each such department, agency, and instrumentality, in order to avoid duplication of effort, shall, whenever appropriate, utilize the personnel, services, and facilities of other Federal departments, agencies, and instrumentalities. Post, p.98.

"(m) Anyone authorized by the President to enforce the provisions of this section may, except as to public vessels, (A) board and inspect any vessel upon the navigable waters of the United States or the waters of the contiguous zone, (B) with or without a warrant arrest any person who violates the provisions of this section or any regulation issued thereunder in his presence or view, and (C) execute any warrant or other process issued by an officer or court of competent jurisdiction.

"(n) The several district courts of the United States are invested with jurisdiction for any actions, other than actions pursuant to subsection (i)(1), arising under this section. In the case of Guam, such actions may be brought in the district court of Guam, and in the case of the Virgin Islands such actions may be brought in the district court of the Virgin Islands. In the case of American Samoa and the Trust Territory of the Pacific Islands, such actions may be brought in the District Court of the United States for the District of Hawaii and such court shall have jurisdiction of such actions. In the case of the Canal Zone, such actions may be brought in the United States District Court for the District of the Canal Zone.

"(o)(1) Nothing in this section shall affect or modify in any way the obligations of any owner or operator of any vessel, or of any owner or operator of any onshore facility or offshore facility to any person or agency under any provision of law for damages to any publicly-owned or privately-owned property resulting from a discharge of any oil or from the removal of any such oil.

"(2) Nothing in this section shall be construed as preempting any State or political subdivision thereof from imposing any requirement or liability with respect to the discharge of oil into any waters within such State.

"(3) Nothing in this section shall be construed as affecting or modifying any other existing authority of any Federal department, agency, or instrumentality, relative to onshore or offshore facilities under this Act or any other provision of law, or to affect any State or local law not in conflict with this section.

"(p)(1) Any vessel over three hundred gross tons, including any barge of equivalent size, using any port or place in the United States or the navigable waters of the United States for any purpose shall establish and maintain under regulations to be prescribed from time to time by the President, evidence of financial responsibility of $100 per gross ton, or $14,000,000 whichever is the lesser, to meet the liability to the United States which such vessel could be subjected under this section. In cases where an owner or operator owns, operates, or charters more than one such vessel, financial responsibility need only be established to meet the maximum liability to which the largest of such vessels could be subjected. Financial responsibility may be established by any one of, or a combination of, the following methods acceptable to the President: (A) evidence of insurance, (B) surety bonds, (C) qualification as a self-insurer, or (D) other evidence of financial responsibility. Any bond filed shall be issued by a bonding company authorized to do business in the United States.

Effective date.

"(2) The provisions of paragraph (1) of this subsection shall be effective one year after the effective date of this section. The President shall delegate the responsibility to carry out the provisions of this subsection to the appropriate agency head within sixty days after the date of enactment of this section. Regulations necessary to implement this subsection shall be issued within six months after the date of enactment of this section.

"(3) Any claim for costs incurred by such vessel may be brought directly against the insurer or any other person providing evidence of financial responsibility as required under this subsection. In the case of any action pursuant to this subsection such insurer or other person shall be entitled to invoke all rights and defenses which would have been available to the owner or operator if an action had been brought against him by the claimant, and which would have been available to him if an action had been brought against him by the owner or operator.

"(4) The Secretary of Transportation, in consultation with the Secretaries of Interior, State, Commerce, and other interested Federal agencies, representatives of the merchant marine, oil companies, insurance companies, and other interested individuals and organizations, and taking into account the results of the application of paragraph (1) of this subsection, shall conduct a study of the need for and, to the extent determined necessary—

"(A) other measures to provide financial responsibility and limitation of liability with respect to vessels using the navigable waters of the United States;

"(B) measures to provide financial responsibility for all onshore and offshore facilities; and

"(C) other measures for limitation of liability of such facilities;

for the cost of removing discharged oil and paying all damages resulting from the discharge of such oil. The Secretary of Transportation shall submit a report, together with any legislative recommendations, to Congress and the President by January 1, 1971.

Report and recommendations to Congress and the President.

"CONTROL OF HAZARDOUS POLLUTING SUBSTANCES

"SEC. 12. (a) The President shall, in accordance with subsection (b) of this section, develop, promulgate, and revise as may be appropriate, regulations (1) designating as hazardous substances, other than oil as defined in section 11 of this Act, such elements and compounds which, when discharged in any quantity into or upon the navigable waters of the United States or adjoining shorelines or the waters of the contiguous zone, present an imminent and substantial danger to the public health or welfare, including, but not limited to, fish, shellfish, wildlife, shorelines, and beaches; and (2) establishing, if appropriate, recommended methods and means for the removal of such substances.

Ante, p. 91.

"(b) Sections 551 through 559, inclusive (other than section 553 (c)), and 701 through 706, inclusive, of title 5, United States Code, shall apply to regulations issued under authority of this section.

80 Stat. 381; 81 Stat. 54.

"(c) In order to facilitate the removal, if appropriate, of any hazardous substance any person in charge of a vessel or of an onshore or offshore facility of any kind shall, as soon as he has knowledge of any discharge of such substance from such vessel or facility, immediately notify the appropriate agency of the United States of such discharge.

"(d) Whenever any hazardous substance is discharged into or upon the navigable waters of the United States or adjoining shorelines or the waters of the contiguous zone, unless removal is immediately undertaken by the owner or operator of the vessel or onshore or offshore facility from which the discharge occurs or which caused the discharge, pursuant to the regulations promulgated under this section, the President, if appropriate, shall remove or arrange for the removal thereof in accordance with such regulations. Nothing in this subsection shall be construed to restrict the authority of the President to act to remove or arrange for the removal of such hazardous substance at any time.

"(e) Nothing in this section shall affect or modify in any way the obligations of any owner or operator of any vessel, onshore or offshore facility to any person or agency under any provision of law for damages to any publicly- or privately-owned property resulting from a discharge of any hazardous substance or from the removal of any such substance.

"(f)(1) For the purpose of this section the definitions in subsection (a) of section 11 of this Act shall be applicable to the provisions of this section, except as provided in paragraph (2) of this subsection: Ante, p. 91.

"(2) For the purpose of this section, the term— Definitions.

"(A) 'remove' or 'removal' refers to removal of the hazardous substances from the water and shorelines or the taking of such other actions as may be necessary to minimize or mitigate damage to the public health or welfare, including, but not limited to, fish, shellfish, wildlife, and public and private property, shorelines, and beaches;

"(B) 'owner or operator' means any person owning, operating, chartering by demise, or otherwise controlling the operations of, a vessel, or any person owning, operating, or otherwise controlling the operations of an onshore or offshore facility; and

"(C) 'offshore or onshore facility' means any facility of any kind and related appurtenances thereto which is located in, on, or under the surface of any land, or permanently or temporarily affixed to any land, including lands beneath the navigable waters of the United States and which is used or capable of use for the purpose of processing, transporting, producing, storing, or transferring for commercial purposes any hazardous substance designated under this section.

"(g) The President shall submit a report to the Congress, together with his recommendations, not later than November 1, 1970, on the need for, and desirability of, enacting legislation to impose liability for the cost of removal of hazardous substances discharged from vessels and onshore and offshore facilities subject to this section including financial responsibility requirements. In preparing this report, the President shall conduct an accelerated study which shall include, but not be limited to, the method and measures for controlling hazardous substances to prevent this discharge, and the most appropriate measures for (1) enforcement (including the imposition of civil and criminal penalties for discharges and for failure to notify) and (2) recovery of costs incurred by the United States if removal is undertaken by the United States. In carrying out this study, the President shall consult with the interested representatives of the various public and private groups that would be affected by such legislation as well as other interested persons.

Presidential report and recommendations to Congress.

"(h) Any moneys in the funds established by section 11 of this Act shall be available to the President to carry out the purposes of this section. In carrying out this section the President shall utilize the personnel, services, and facilities of Federal departments, agencies, and instrumentalities in such manner as will avoid duplication of effort.

"CONTROL OF SEWAGE FROM VESSELS

Definitions.

"SEC. 13. (a) For the purpose of this section, the term—

"(1) 'new vessel' includes every description of watercraft or other artificial contrivance used, or capable of being used, as a means of transportation on the navigable waters of the United States, the construction of which is initiated after promulgation of standards and regulations under this section;

"(2) 'existing vessel' includes every description of watercraft or other artificial contrivance used, or capable of being used, as a means of transportation on the navigable waters of the United States, the construction of which is initiated before promulgation of standards and regulations under this section;

"(3) 'public vessel' means a vessel owned or bareboat chartered and operated by the United States, by a State or political subdivision thereof, or by a foreign nation, except when such vessel is engaged in commerce;

"(4) 'United States' includes the States, the District of Columbia, the Commonwealth of Puerto Rico, the Virgin Islands, Guam, American Samoa, the Canal Zone, and the Trust Territory of the Pacific Islands;

"(5) 'marine sanitation device' includes any equipment for installation on board a vessel which is designed to receive, retain, treat, or discharge sewage, and any process to treat such sewage;

"(6) 'sewage' means human body wastes and the wastes from toilets and other receptacles intended to receive or retain body wastes;

"(7) 'manufacture' means any person engaged in the manufacturing, assembling, or importation of marine sanitation devices or of vessels subject to standards and regulations promulgated under this section;

"(8) 'person' means an individual, partnership, firm, corporation, or association, but does not include an individual on board a public vessel;

"(9) 'discharge' includes, but is not limited to, any spilling, leaking, pumping, pouring, emitting, emptying, or dumping.

Standards.
Post, p. 112.

"(b) (1) As soon as possible, after the enactment of this section and subject to the provisions of section 5(j) of this Act, the Secretary, after consultation with the Secretary of the department in which the Coast Guard is operating, after giving appropriate consideration to the economic costs involved, and within the limits of available technology, shall promulgate Federal standards of performance for marine sanitation devices (hereafter in this section referred to as 'standards') which shall be designed to prevent the discharge of untreated or inadequately treated sewage into or upon the navigable waters of the United States from new vessels and existing vessels, except vessels not equipped with installed toilet facilities. Such standards shall be consistent with maritime safety and the marine and navigation laws and regulations and shall be coordinated with the regulations issued under this subsection by the Secretary of the department in which the Coast Guard is operating. The Secretary of the department in which the Coast Guard is operating shall promulgate regulations, which are consistent with standards promulgated under this subsection and with maritime safety and the marine and navigation laws and regulations, governing the design, construction, installation, and operation of any marine sanitation device on board such vessels.

"(2) Any existing vessel equipped with a marine sanitation device on the date of promulgation of initial standards and regulations under this section, which device is in compliance with such initial standards and regulations, shall be deemed in compliance with this section until such time as the device is replaced or is found not to be in compliance with such initial standards and regulations.

"(c)(1) Initial standards and regulations under this section shall become effective for new vessels two years after promulgation; and for existing vessels five years after promulgation. Revisions of standards and regulations shall be effective upon promulgation, unless another effective date is specified, except that no revision shall take effect before the effective date of the standard or regulation being revised.

Effective dates of standards and regulations.

"(2) The Secretary of the department in which the Coast Guard is operating with regard to his regulatory authority established by this section, after consultation with the Secretary, may distinguish among classes, types, and sizes of vessels as well as between new and existing vessels, and may waive applicability of standards and regulations as necessary or appropriate for such classes, types, and sizes of vessels (including existing vessels equipped with marine sanitation devices on the date of promulgation of the initial standards required by this section), and, upon application, for individual vessels.

"(d) The provisions of this section and the standards and regulations promulgated hereunder apply to vessels owned and operated by the United States unless the Secretary of Defense finds that compliance would not be in the interest of national security. With respect to vessels owned and operated by the Department of Defense, regulations under the last sentence of subsection (b)(1) and certifications under subsection (g)(2) of this section shall be promulgated and issued by the Secretary of Defense.

"(e) Before the standards and regulations under this section are promulgated, the Secretary and the Secretary of the department in which the Coast Guard is operating shall consult with the Secretary of State; the Secretary of Health, Education, and Welfare; the Secretary of Defense; the Secretary of the Treasury; the Secretary of Commerce; other interested Federal agencies; and the States and industries interested; and otherwise comply with the requirements of section 553 of title 5 of the United States Code.

80 Stat. 383.

"(f) After the effective date of the initial standards and regulations promulgated under this section, no State or political subdivision thereof shall adopt or enforce any statute or regulation of such State or political subdivision with respect to the design, manufacture, or installation or use of any marine sanitation device on any vessel subject to the provisions of this section. Upon application by a State, and where the Secretary determines that any applicable water quality standards require such a prohibition, he shall by regulation completely prohibit the discharge from a vessel of any sewage (whether treated or not) into those waters of such State which are the subject of the application and to which such standards apply.

"(g)(1) No manufacturer of a marine sanitation device shall sell, offer for sale, or introduce or deliver for introduction in interstate commerce, or import into the United States for sale or resale any marine sanitation device manufactured after the effective date of the standards and regulations promulgated under this section unless such device is in all material respects substantially the same as a test device certified under this subsection.

"(2) Upon application of the manufacturer, the Secretary of the department in which the Coast Guard is operating shall so certify a marine sanitation device if he determines, in accordance with the provisions of this paragraph, that it meets the appropriate standards and regulations promulgated under this section. The Secretary of the department in which the Coast Guard is operating shall test or require such testing of the device in accordance with procedures set forth by the Secretary as to standards of performance and for such other purposes as may be appropriate. If the Secretary of the department in which the Coast Guard is operating determines that the device is satisfactory from the standpoint of safety and any other requirements of maritime law or regulation, and after consideration of the design, installation, operation, material, or other appropriate factors, he shall certify the device. Any device manufactured by such manufacturer which is in all material respects substantially the same as the certified test device shall be deemed to be in conformity with the appropriate standards and regulations established under this section.

Recordkeeping.

"(3) Every manufacturer shall establish and maintain such records, make such reports, and provide such information as the Secretary or the Secretary of the department in which the Coast Guard is operating may reasonably require to enable him to determine whether such manufacturer has acted or is acting in compliance with this section and regulations issued thereunder and shall, upon request of an officer or employee duly designated by the Secretary or the Secretary of the department in which the Coast Guard is operating, permit such officer or employee at reasonable times to have access to and copy such records. All information reported to or otherwise obtained by, the Secretary or the Secretary of the department in which the Coast Guard is operating or their representatives pursuant to this subsection which contains or relates to a trade secret or other matter referred to in section 1905 of title 18 of the United States Code shall be considered confidential for the purpose of that section, except that such information may be disclosed to other officers or employees concerned with carrying out this section. This paragraph shall not apply in the case of the construction of a vessel by an individual for his own use.

62 Stat. 791.

"(h) After the effective date of standards and regulations promulgated under this section, it shall be unlawful—

"(1) for the manufacturer of any vessel subject to such standards and regulations to manufacture for sale, to sell or offer for sale, or to distribute for sale or resale any such vessel unless it is equipped with a marine sanitation device which is in all material respects substantially the same as the appropriate test device certified pursuant to this section;

"(2) for any person, prior to the sale or delivery of a vessel subject to such standards and regulations to the ultimate purchaser, wrongfully to remove or render inoperative any certified marine sanitation device or element of design of such device installed in such vessel;

"(3) for any person to fail or refuse to permit access to or copying of records or to fail to make reports or provide information required under this section; and

"(4) for a vessel subject to such standards and regulations to operate on the navigable waters of the United States, if such vessel is not equipped with an operable marine sanitation device certified pursuant to this section.

"(i) The district courts of the United States shall have jurisdictions to restrain violations of subsection (g)(1) and subsections (h)(1) through (3) of this section. Actions to restrain such violations shall be brought by, and in, the name of the United States. In case of contumacy or refusal to obey a subpena served upon any person under this subsection, the district court of the United States for any district in which such person is found or resides or transacts business, upon application by the United States and after notice to such person, shall have jurisdiction to issue an order requiring such person to appear and give testimony or to appear and produce documents, and any failure to obey such order of the court may be punished by such court as a contempt thereof.

"(j) Any person who violates subsection (g)(1) or clause (1) or (2) of subsection (h) of this section shall be liable to a civil penalty of not more than $5,000 for each violation. Any person who violates clause (4) of subsection (h) of this section or any regulation issued pursuant to this section shall be liable to a civil penalty of not more than $2,000 for each violation. Each violation shall be a separate offense. The Secretary of the department in which the Coast Guard is operating may assess and compromise any such penalty. No penalty shall be assessed until the person charged shall have been given notice and an opportunity for a hearing on such charge. In determining the amount of the penalty, or the amount agreed upon in compromise, the gravity of the violation, and the demonstrated good faith of the person charged in attempting to achieve rapid compliance, after notification of a violation, shall be considered by said Secretary. Penalty.

"(k) The provisions of this section shall be enforced by the Secretary of the department in which the Coast Guard is operating and he may utilize by agreement, with or without reimbursement, law enforcement officers or other personnel and facilities of the Secretary, other Federal agencies, or the States to carry out the provisions of this section.

"(l) Anyone authorized by the Secretary of the department in which the Coast Guard is operating to enforce the provisions of this section may, except as to public vessels, (1) board and inspect any vessel upon the navigable waters of the United States and (2) execute any warrant or other process issued by an officer or court of competent jurisdiction.

"(m) In the case of Guam, actions arising under this section may be brought in the district court of Guam, and in the case of the Virgin Islands such actions may be brought in the district court of the Virgin Islands. In the case of American Samoa and the Trust Territory of the Pacific Islands, such actions may be brought in the District Court of the United States for the District of Hawaii and such court shall have jurisdiction of such actions. In the case of the Canal Zone, such actions may be brought in the District Court for the District of the Canal Zone.

"AREA ACID AND OTHER MINE WATER POLLUTION CONTROL DEMONSTRATIONS

"SEC. 14. (a) The Secretary in cooperation with other Federal departments, agencies, and instrumentalities is authorized to enter into agreements with any State or interstate agency to carry out one or more projects to demonstrate methods for the elimination or control, within all or part of a watershed, of acid or other mine water pollution resulting from active or abandoned mines. Such projects shall demonstrate the engineering and economic feasibility and practicality of various abatement techniques which will contribute substantially to effective and practical methods of acid or other mine water pollution elimination or control.

"(b) The Secretary, in selecting watersheds for the purposes of this section, shall (1) require such feasibility studies as he deems appropriate, (2) give preference to areas which have the greatest present or potential value for public use for recreation, fish and wildlife, water supply, and other public uses, and (3) be satisfied that the project area will not be affected adversely by the influx of acid or other mine water pollution from nearby sources.

"(c) Federal participation in such projects shall be subject to the conditions—

"(1) that the State or interstate agency shall pay not less than 25 per centum of the actual project costs which payment may be in any form, including, but not limited to, land or interests therein that is needed for the project, or personal property or services, the value of which shall be determined by the Secretary; and

"(2) that the State or interstate agency shall provide legal and practical protection to the project area to insure against any activities which will cause future acid or other mine water pollution.

Appropriation.

"(d) There is authorized to be appropriated $15,000,000 to carry out the provisions of this section, which sum shall be available until expended. No more than 25 per centum of the total funds available under this section in any one year shall be granted to any one State.

"POLLUTION CONTROL IN GREAT LAKES

Demonstration projects, Federal aid to States.

"SEC. 15. (a) The Secretary, in cooperation with other Federal departments, agencies, and instrumentalities is authorized to enter into agreements with any State, political subdivision, interstate agency, or other public agency, or combination thereof, to carry out one or more projects to demonstrate new methods and techniques and to develop preliminary plans for the elimination or control of pollution, within all or any part of the watersheds of the Great Lakes. Such projects shall demonstrate the engineering and economic feasibility and practicality of removal of pollutants and prevention of any polluting matter from entering into the Great Lakes in the future and other abatement and remedial techniques which will contribute substantially to effective and practical methods of water pollution elimination or control.

"(b) Federal participation in such projects shall be subject to the condition that the State, political subdivision, interstate agency, or other public agency, or combination thereof, shall pay not less than 25 per centum of the actual project costs, which payment may be in any form, including, but not limited to, land or interests therein that is needed for the project, and personal property or services the value of which shall be determined by the Secretary.

Appropriation.

"(c) There is authorized to be appropriated $20,000,000 to carry out the provisions of this section, which sum shall be available until expended.

"TRAINING GRANTS AND CONTRACTS

Colleges, water quality control.

"SEC. 16. The Secretary is authorized to make grants to or contracts with institutions of higher education, or combinations of such institutions, to assist them in planning, developing, strengthening, improving, or carrying out programs or projects for the preparation of undergraduate students to enter an occupation which involves the design, operation, and maintenance of treatment works, and other facilities whose purpose is water quality control. Such grants or contracts may include payment of all or part of the cost of programs or projects such as—

"(A) planning for the development or expansion of programs or projects for training persons in the operation and maintenance of treatment works;

"(B) training and retraining of faculty members;

"(C) conduct of short-term or regular session institutes for study by persons engaged in, or preparing to engage in, the preparation of students preparing to enter an occupation involving the operation and maintenance of treatment works;

"(D) carrying out innovative and experimental programs of cooperative education involving alternate periods of full-time or part-time academic study at the institution and periods of full-time or part-time employment involving the operation and maintenance of treatment works; and

"(E) research into, and development of, methods of training students or faculty, including the preparation of teaching materials and the planning of curriculum.

"APPLICATION FOR TRAINING GRANT OR CONTRACT; ALLOCATION OF GRANTS OR CONTRACTS

"SEC. 17. (1) A grant or contract authorized by section 16 may be made only upon application to the Secretary at such time or times and containing such information as he may prescribe, except that no such application shall be approved unless it— Conditions.

"(A) sets forth programs, activities, research, or development for which a grant is authorized under section 16, and describes the relation to any program set forth by the applicant in an application, if any, submitted pursuant to section 18;

"(B) provides such fiscal control and fund accounting procedures as may be necessary to assure proper disbursement of and accounting for Federal funds paid to the applicant under this section; and

"(C) provides for making such reports, in such form and containing such information, as the Secretary may require to carry out his functions under this section, and for keeping such records and for affording such access thereto as the Secretary may find necessary to assure the correctness and verification of such reports. Reports to Secretary.

"(2) The Secretary shall allocate grants or contracts under section 16 in such manner as will most nearly provide an equitable distribution of the grants or contracts throughout the United States among institutions of higher education which show promise of being able to use funds effectively for the purposes of this section. Equitable distribution.

"(3) (A) Payment under this section may be used in accordance with regulations of the Secretary, and subject to the terms and conditions set forth in an application approved under subsection (a), to pay part of the compensation of students employed in connection with the operation and maintenance of treatment works, other than as an employee in connection with the operation and maintenance of treatment works or as an employee in any branch of the Government of the United States, as part of a program for which a grant has been approved pursuant to this section. Compensation of employed students.

"(B) Departments and agencies of the United States are encouraged, to the extent consistent with efficient administration, to enter into arrangements with institutions of higher education for the full-time, part-time, or temporary employment, whether in the competitive or excepted service, of students enrolled in programs set forth in applications approved under subsection (a).

"AWARD OF SCHOLARSHIPS

"SEC. 18. (1) The Secretary is authorized to award scholarships in accordance with the provisions of this section for undergraduate study by persons who plan to enter an occupation involving the operation and maintenance of treatment works. Such scholarships shall be awarded for such periods as the Secretary may determine but not to exceed four academic years.

"(2) The Secretary shall allocate scholarships under this section among institutions of higher education with programs approved under the provisions of this section for the use of individuals accepted into such programs, in such manner and according to such plan as will insofar as practicable—

"(A) provide an equitable distribution of such scholarships throughout the United States; and

"(B) attract recent graduates of secondary schools to enter an occupation involving the operation and maintenance of treatment works.

Program approval, conditions.

"(3) The Secretary shall approve a program of an institution of higher education for the purposes of this section only upon application by the institution and only upon his finding—

"(A) that such program has as a principal objective the education and training of persons in the operation and maintenance of treatment works;

"(B) that such program is in effect and of high quality, or can be readily put into effect and may reasonably be expected to be of high quality;

"(C) that the application describes the relation of such program to any program, activity, research, or development set forth by the applicant in an application, if any, submitted pursuant to section 16 of this Act; and

"(D) that the application contains satisfactory assurances that (i) the institution will recommend to the Secretary for the award of scholarships under this section, for study in such program, only persons who have demonstrated to the satisfaction of the institution a serious intent, upon completing the program, to enter an occupation involving the operation and maintenance of treatment works, and (ii) the institution will make reasonable continuing efforts to encourage recipients of scholarships under this section, enrolled in such program, to enter occupations involving the operation and maintenance of treatment works upon completing the program.

Payments to recipient of scholarship and his college.

"(4)(A) The Secretary shall pay to persons awarded scholarships under this section such stipends (including such allowances for subsistence and other expenses for such persons and their dependents) as he may determine to be consistent with prevailing practices under comparable federally supported programs.

"(B) The Secretary shall (in addition to the stipends paid to persons under subsection (a)) pay to the institution of higher education at which such person is pursuing his course of study such amount as he may determine to be consistent with prevailing practices under comparable federally supported programs.

"(5) A person awarded a scholarship under the provisions of this section shall continue to receive the payments provided in this section only during such periods as the Secretary finds that he is maintaining satisfactory proficiency and devoting full time to study or research in the field in which such scholarship was awarded in an institution of higher education, and is not engaging in gainful employment other than employment approved by the Secretary by or pursuant to regulation.

"(6) The Secretary shall by regulation provide that any person awarded a scholarship under this section shall agree in writing to enter and remain in an occupation involving the design, operation, or maintenance of treatment works for such period after completion of his course of studies as the Secretary determines appropriate.

"DEFINITIONS AND AUTHORIZATIONS

"SEC. 19. (1) As used in sections 16 through 19 of this Act—

"(A) The term 'State' includes the District of Columbia, Puerto Rico, the Canal Zone, Guam, the Virgin Islands, American Samoa, and the Trust Territory of the Pacific Islands.

"(B) The term 'institution of higher education' means an educational institution described in the first sentence of section 1201 of the Higher Education Act of 1965 (other than an institution of any agency of the United States) which is accredited by a nationally recognized accrediting agency or association approved by the Secretary for this purpose. For purposes of this subsection, the Secretary shall publish a list of nationally recognized accrediting agencies or associations which he determines to be reliable authority as to the quality of training offered. Accreditation. 79 Stat. 1269; 82 Stat. 1051. 20 USC 1141.

"(C) The term 'academic year' means an academic year or its equivalent, as determined by the Secretary.

"(2) The Secretary shall annually report his activities under sections 16 through 19 of this Act, including recommendations for needed revisions in the provisions thereof. Annual report.

"(3) There are authorized to be appropriated $12,000,000 for the fiscal year ending June 30, 1970, $25,000,000 for the fiscal year ending June 30, 1971, and $25,000,000 for the fiscal year ending June 30, 1972, to carry out sections 16 through 19 of this Act (and planning and related activities in the initial fiscal year for such purpose). Funds appropriated for the fiscal year ending June 30, 1970, under authority of this subsection shall be available for obligation pursuant to the provisions of sections 16 through 19 of this Act during that year and the succeeding fiscal year. Appropriations.

"ALASKA VILLAGE DEMONSTRATION PROJECTS

"SEC. 20. (a) The Secretary is authorized to enter into agreements with the State of Alaska to carry out one or more projects to demonstrate methods to provide for central community facilities for safe water and the elimination or control of water pollution in those native villages of Alaska without such facilities. Such projects shall include provisions for community safe water supply systems, toilets, bathing and laundry facilities, sewage disposal facilities, and other similar facilities, and educational and informational facilities and programs relating to health and hygiene. Such demonstration projects shall be for the further purpose of developing preliminary plans for providing such safe water and such elimination or control of water pollution for all native villages in such State.

"(b) In carrying out this section the Secretary shall cooperate with the Secretary of Health, Education, and Welfare for the purpose of utilizing such of the personnel and facilities of that Department as may be appropriate.

"(c) The Secretary shall report to Congress not later than January 31, 1973, the results of the demonstration projects authorized by this section together with his recommendations, including any necessary legislation, relating to the establishment of a statewide program. Report to Congress.

"(d) There is authorized to be appropriated not to exceed $1,000,000 to carry out this section." Appropriation.

SEC. 103. Redesignated section 21 of the Federal Water Pollution Control Act, as amended, is amended to read as follows: Ante, p.

"COOPERATION BY ALL FEDERAL AGENCIES IN THE CONTROL OF POLLUTION

"SEC. 21. (a) Each Federal agency (which term is used in this section includes Federal departments, agencies, and instrumentalities) having jurisdiction over any real property or facility, or engaged in any Federal public works activity of any kind, shall, consistent with the paramount interest of the United States as determined by the President, insure compliance with applicable water quality standards Federal agencies, alleged pollution, hearings.

70 Stat. 504; 79 Stat. 903, 907. 33 USC 466g.

79 Stat. 907; 80 Stat. 1251.

and the purposes of this Act in the administration of such property, facility, or activity. In his summary of any conference pursuant to section 10(d)(4) of this Act, the Secretary shall include references to any discharges allegedly contributing to pollution from any such Federal property, facility, or activity, and shall transmit a copy of such summary to the head of the Federal agency having jurisdiction of such property, facility, or activity. Notice of any hearing pursuant to section 10(f) of this Act involving any pollution alleged to be effected by any such discharges shall also be given to the Federal agency having jurisdiction over the property, facility, or activity involved, and the findings and recommendations of the hearing board conducting such hearing shall include references to any such discharges which are contributing to the pollution found by such board.

Federal license, State certification.

"(b)(1) Any applicant for a Federal license or permit to conduct any activity including, but not limited to, the construction or operation of facilities, which may result in any discharge into the navigable waters of the United States, shall provide the licensing or permitting agency a certification from the State in which the discharge originates or will originate, or, if appropriate, from the interstate water pollution control agency having jurisdiction over the navigable waters at the point where the discharge originates or will originate, that there is reasonable assurance, as determined by the State or interstate agency that such activity will be conducted in a manner which will not violate applicable water quality standards. Such State or interstate agency shall establish procedures for public notice in the case of all applications for certification by it, and to the extent it deems appropriate, procedures for public hearings in connection with specific applications. In any case where such standards have been promulgated by the Secretary pursuant to section 10(c) of this Act, or where a State or interstate agency has no authority to give such a certification, such certification shall be from the Secretary. If the State, interstate agency, or Secretary, as the case may be, fails or refuses to act on a request for certification, within a reasonable period of time (which shall not exceed one year) after receipt of such request, the certification requirements of this subsection shall be waived with respect to such Federal application. No license or permit shall be granted until the certification required by this section has been obtained or has been waived as provided in the preceding sentence. No license or permit shall be granted if certification has been denied by the State, interstate agency, or the Secretary, as the case may be.

Public notification procedures.

Standards, enforcement.

"(2) Upon receipt of such application and certification the licensing or permitting agency shall immediately notify the Secretary of such application and certification. Whenever such a discharge may affect, as determined by the Secretary, the quality of the waters of any other State, the Secretary within thirty days of the date of notice of application for such Federal license or permit shall so notify such other State, the licensing or permitting agency, and the applicant. If, within sixty days after receipt of such notification, such other State determines that such discharge will affect the quality of its waters so as to violate its water quality standards, and within such sixty-day period notifies the Secretary and the licensing or permitting agency in writing of its objection to the issuance of such license or permit and requests a public hearing on such objection, the licensing or permitting agency shall hold such a hearing. The Secretary shall at such hearing submit his evaluation and recommendations with respect to any such objection to the licensing or permitting agency. Such agency, based upon the recommendations of such State, the Secretary, and upon any additional evidence, if any, presented to the agency at the hearing, shall condition such license or permit in such manner as may be necessary to insure compliance with applicable water quality standards. If the imposition of conditions cannot insure such compliance such agency shall not issue such license or permit.

"(3) The certification obtained pursuant to paragraph (1) of this subsection with respect to the construction of any facility shall fulfill the requirements of this subsection with respect to certification in connection with any other Federal license or permit required for the operation of such facility unless, after notice to the certifying State, agency, or Secretary, as the case may be, which shall be given by the Federal agency to whom application is made for such operating license or permit, the State, or if appropriate, the interstate agency or the Secretary, notifies such agency within sixty days after receipt of such notice that there is no longer reasonable assurance that there will be compliance with applicable water quality standards because of changes since the construction license or permit certification was issued in (A) the construction or operation of the facility, (B) the characteristics of the waters into which such discharge is made, or (C) the water quality standards applicable to such waters. This paragraph shall be inapplicable in any case where the applicant for such operating license or permit has failed to provide the certifying State, or if appropriate, the interstate agency or the Secretary, with notice of any proposed changes in the construction or operation of the facility with respect to which a construction license or permit has been granted which changes may result in violation of applicable water quality standards.

Prior inspection.

"(4) Prior to the initial operation of any federally licensed or permitted facility or activity which may result in any discharge into the navigable waters of the United States and with respect to which a certification has been obtained pursuant to paragraph (1) of this subsection, which facility or activity is not subject to a Federal operating license or permit, the licensee or permittee shall provide an opportunity for such certifying State or, if appropriate, the interstate agency or the Secretary to review the manner in which the facility or activity shall be operated or conducted for the purposes of assuring that applicable water quality standards will not be violated. Upon notification by the certifying State or, if appropriate, the interstate agency or the Secretary that the operation of any such federally licensed or permitted facility or activity will violate applicable water quality standards, such Federal agency may, after public hearing, suspend such license or permit. If such license or permit is suspended, it shall remain suspended until notification is received from the certifying State, agency, or Secretary, as the case may be, that there is reasonable assurance that such facility or activity will not violate applicable water quality standards.

Standards violation, license suspension.

"(5) Any Federal license or permit with respect to which a certification has been obtained under paragraph (1) of this subsection may be suspended or revoked by the Federal agency issuing such license or permit upon the entering of a judgment under section 10(h) of this Act that such facility or activity has been operated in violation of applicable water quality standards.

70 Stat. 504; 79 Stat. 903, 907. 33 USC 466g.

"(6) No Federal agency shall be deemed to be an applicant for the purposes of this subsection.

"(7) In any case where actual construction of a facility has been lawfully commenced prior to the date of enactment of the Water Quality Improvement Act of 1970, no certification shall be required under this subsection for a license or permit issued after the date of enactment of such Act of 1970 to operate such facility, except that any such license or permit issued without certification shall terminate at the end of the three-year period beginning on the date of enactment of such Act of 1970 unless prior to such termination date the person having such license or permit submits to the Federal agency which issued such license or permit a certification and otherwise meets the requirements of this subsection.

"(8) Except as provided in paragraph (7), any application for a license or permit (A) that is pending on the date of enactment of the Water Quality Improvement Act of 1970 and (B) that is issued within one year following such date of enactment shall not require certification pursuant to this subsection for one year following the issuance of such license or permit, except that any such license or permit issued shall terminate at the end of one year unless prior to that time the licensee or permittee submits to the Federal agency that issued such license or permit a certification and otherwise meets the requirements of this subsection.

"(9)(A) In the case of any activity which will affect water quality but for which there are no applicable water quality standards, no certification shall be required under this subsection, except that the licensing or permitting agency shall impose, as a condition of any license or permit, a requirement that the licensee or permittee shall comply with the purposes of this Act.

Failure to comply, license suspension.

"(B) Upon notice from the State in which the discharge originates or, as appropriate, the interstate agency or the Secretary, that such licensee or permittee has been notified of the adoption of water quality standards applicable to such activity and has failed, after reasonable notice, of not less than six months, to comply with such standards, the license or permit shall be suspended until notification is received from such State or interstate agency or the Secretary that there is reasonable assurance that such activity will comply with applicable water quality standards.

"(c) Nothing in this section shall be construed to limit the authority of any department or agency pursuant to any other provision of law to require compliance with applicable water quality standards. The Secretary shall, upon the request of any Federal department or agency, or State or interstate agency, or applicant, provide, for the purpose of this section, any relevant information on applicable water quality standards, and shall, when requested by any such department or agency or State or interstate agency, or applicant, comment on any methods to comply with such standards.

"(d) In order to implement the provisions of this section, the Secretary of the Army, acting through the Chief of Engineers, is authorized, if he deems it to be in the public interest, to permit the use of spoil disposal areas under his jurisdiction by Federal licensees or permittees, and to make an appropriate charge for such use. Moneys received from such licensees or permittees shall be deposited in the Treasury as miscellaneous receipts."

Ante, p. 91.

SEC. 104. Redesignated section 22 of the Federal Water Pollution Control Act, as amended, is amended by adding at the end thereof the following:

"(f)(1) It is the purpose of this subsection to authorize a program which will provide official recognition by the United States Government to those industrial organizations and political subdivsions of States which during the preceding year demonstrated an outstanding technological achievement or an innovative process, method or device in their waste treatment and pollution abatement programs. The Secretary shall, in consultation with the appropriate State water pollution control agency, establish regulations under which such recognition may be applied for and granted, except that no applicant shall be eligible for an award under this subsection if such applicant is not in total compliance with all applicable water quality standards under this Act, and otherwise does not have a satisfactory record with respect to environmental quality.

"(2) The Secretary shall award a certificate or plaque of suitable design to each industrial organization or political subdivision which qualifies for such recognition under regulations established by this subsection.

Awards.

"(3) The President of the United States, the Governor of the appropriate State, the Speaker of the House of Representatives, and the President pro tempore of the Senate shall be notified of the award by the Secretary, and the awarding of such recognition shall be published in the Federal Register."

Notification to President of U.S., etc.

Publication in Federal Register.

SEC. 105. Section 5 of the Federal Water Pollution Control Act, as amended, is amended as follows:

70 Stat. 499; 75 Stat. 205; 79 Stat. 903; 80 Stat. 1247. 33 USC 466c.

(1) by redesignating subsections (g) and (h) as (m) and (n), respectively, including all references thereto;

(2) by inserting after subsection (f) the following new subsections:

"(g) (1) For the purpose of providing an adequate supply of trained personnel to operate and maintain existing and future treatment works and related activities, and for the purpose of enhancing substantially the proficiency of those engaged in such activities, the Secretary shall finance a pilot program, in cooperation with State and interstate agencies, municipalities, educational institutions, and other organizations and individuals, of manpower development and training and retraining of persons in, or entering into, the field of operation and maintenance of treatment works and related activities. Such program and any funds expended for such a program shall supplement, not supplant, other manpower and training programs and funds available for the purposes of this paragraph. The Secretary is authorized, under such terms and conditions as he deems appropriate, to enter into agreements with one or more States, acting jointly or severally, or with other public or private agencies or institutions for the development and implementation of such a program.

"(2) The Secretary is authorized to enter into agreements with public and private agencies and institutions, and individuals to develop and maintain an effective system for forecasting the supply of, and demand for, various professional and other occupational categories needed for the prevention, control, and abatement of water pollution in each region, State, or area of the United States and, from time to time, to publish the results of such forecasts.

"(3) In furtherance of the purposes of this Act, the Secretary is authorized to—

"(A) make grants to public or private agencies and institutions and to individuals for training projects, and provide for the conduct of training by contract with public or private agencies and institutions and with individuals without regard to sections 3648 and 3709 of the Revised Statutes;

31 USC 529; 41 USC 5.

"(B) establish and maintain research fellowships in the Department of the Interior with such stipends and allowances, including traveling and subsistence expenses, as he may deem necessary to procure the assistance of the most promising research fellowships; and

"(C) provide, in addition to the program established under paragraph (1) of this subsection, training in technical matters relating to the causes, prevention, and control of water pollution for personnel of public agencies and other persons with suitable qualifications.

"(4) The Secretary shall submit, through the President, a report to the Congress within eighteen months from the date of enactment of this subsection, summarizing the actions taken under this subsection and the effectiveness of such actions, and setting forth the number of persons trained, the occupational categories for which training was

Report to President and Congress.

provided, the effectiveness of other Federal, State, and local training programs in this field, together with estimates of future needs, recommendations on improving training programs, and such other information and recommendations, including legislative recommendations, as he deems appropriate.

Contract authority.

"(h) The Secretary is authorized to enter into contracts with, or make grants to, public or private agencies and organizations and individuals for (A) the purpose of developing and demonstrating new or improved methods for the prevention, removal, and control of natural or manmade pollution in lakes, including the undesirable effects of nutrients and vegetation, and (B) the construction of publicly owned research facilities for such purpose.

Functions.

"(i) The Secretary shall—

"(A) engage in such research, studies, experiments, and demonstrations as he deems appropriate, relative to the removal of oil from any waters and to the prevention and control of oil pollution;

"(B) publish from time to time the results of such activities; and

"(C) from time to time, develop and publish in the Federal Register specifications and other technical information on the various chemical compounds used as dispersants or emulsifiers in the control of oil spills.

In carrying out this subsection, the Secretary may enter into contracts with, or make grants to, public or private agencies and organizations and individuals.

"(j) The Secretary shall engage in such research, studies, experiments, and demonstrations as he deems appropriate relative to equipment which is to be installed on board a vessel and is designed to receive, retain, treat, or discharge human body wastes and the wastes from toilets and other receptacles intended to receive or retain body wastes with particular emphasis on equipment to be installed on small recreational vessels. The Secretary shall report to Congress the results of such research, studies, experiments, and demonstrations prior to the effective date of any standards established under section 13 of this Act. In carrying out this subsection the Secretary may enter into contracts with, or make grants to, public or private organizations and individuals.

Report to Congress.

Ante, p. 100.

"(k) In carrying out the provisions of this section relating to the conduct by the Secretary of demonstration projects and the development of field laboratories and research facilities, the Secretary may acquire land and interests therein by purchase, with appropriated or donated funds, by donation, or by exchange for acquired or public lands under his jurisdiction which he classifies as suitable for disposition. The values of the properties so exchanged either shall be approximately equal, or if they are not approximately equal, the values shall be equalized by the payment of cash to the grantor or to the Secretary as the circumstances require.

"(l)(1) The Secretary shall, after consultation with appropriate local, State, and Federal agencies, public and private organizations, and interested individuals, as soon as practicable but not later than two years after the effective date of this subsection, develop and issue to the States for the purpose of adopting standards pursuant to section 10(c) the latest scientific knowledge available in indicating the kind and extent of effects on health and welfare which may be expected from the presence of pesticides in the water in varying quantities. He shall revise and add to such information whenever necessary to reflect developing scientific knowledge.

79 Stat. 907.
33 USC 466g.

"(2) For the purpose of assuring effective implementation of standards adopted pursuant to paragraph (1) the President shall, in consultation with appropriate local, State, and Federal agencies, public and private organizations, and interested individuals, conduct a study and investigation of methods to control the release of pesticides into the environment which study shall include examination of the persistency of pesticides in the water environment and alternatives thereto. The President shall submit a report on such investigation to Congress together with his recommendations for any necessary legislation within two years after the effective date of this subsection." Pesticide release control study. Report to Congress.

(3) in redesignated subsection (m) (4) by striking out the words "and June 30, 1969," and inserting in lieu thereof "June 30, 1969, June 30, 1970, and June 30, 1971,"; 80 Stat. 1248.

(4) by amending the first sentence of redesignated subsection (n) to read as follows: "There is authorized to be appropriated to carry out this section, other than subsection (g) (1) and (2), not to exceed $65,000,000 per fiscal year for each of the fiscal years ending June 30, 1969, June 30, 1970, and June 30, 1971. There is authorized to be appropriated to carry out subsection (g) (1) of this section $5,000,000 for the fiscal year ending June 30, 1970, and $7,500,000 for the fiscal year ending June 30, 1971. There is authorized to be appropriated to carry out subsection (g) (2) of this section $2,500,000 per fiscal year for each of the fiscal years ending June 30, 1970, and June 30, 1971.". Ante, p. 111.

SEC. 106. Section 6(e) of the Federal Water Pollution Control Act (33 U.S.C. 466c–1) is amended as follows: Research and development appropriation. 80 Stat. 1247.

(1) Paragraph (1) is amended by striking out "three succeeding fiscal years" and inserting in lieu thereof "five succeeding fiscal years,".

(2) Paragraph (2) is amended by striking out "two succeeding fiscal years," and inserting in lieu thereof "four succeeding fiscal years,".

(3) Paragraph (3) is amended by striking out "two succeeding fiscal years," and inserting in lieu thereof "four succeeding fiscal years,".

SEC. 107. Redesignated section 24 of the Federal Water Pollution Control Act, as amended, is amended by deleting the following: "the Oil Pollution Act, 1924, or". Ante, p. 91.

SEC. 108. The Oil Pollution Act, 1924 (43 Stat. 604), as amended (80 Stat. 1246–1252), is hereby repealed. Repeal. 33 USC 431.

SEC. 109. The Secretary of the Interior shall conduct a full and complete investigation and study of the feasibility of all methods of financing the cost of preventing, controlling, and abating water pollution, other than methods authorized by existing law. The results of such investigation and study shall be reported to Congress no later than December 31, 1970, together with the recommendations of the Secretary for financing the programs for preventing, controlling, and abating water pollution for the fiscal years beginning after fiscal year 1971, including any necessary legislation. Prevention and control study. Report to Congress.

SEC. 110. (a) The first sentence of section 2 of the Federal Water Pollution Control Act (33 U.S.C. 466–1) is amended by striking out "Federal Water Pollution Control Administration" and inserting in lieu thereof "Federal Water Quality Administration". 79 Stat. 903.

(b) Any other law, reorganization plan, regulation, map, document, record, or other paper of the United States in which the Federal Water Pollution Control Administration is referred to shall be held to refer to the Federal Water Quality Administration. "Federal Water Quality Administration."

SEC. 111. Section 8(c) of the Federal Water Pollution Control Act is amended in the fourth sentence by inserting after "because of lack 75 Stat. 206; 79 Stat. 903. 33 USC 466e.

of funds" the following: "including States having projects eligible for reimbursement pursuant to the sixth and seventh sentences of this subsection".

Water quality standards. 79 Stat. 908. 33 USC 466g.

SEC. 112. Section 10 of the Federal Water Pollution Control Act, as amended, is amended by adding at the end of subsection (c)(3) the following new sentence: "In establishing such standards the Secretary, the hearing board, or the appropriate State authority shall take into consideration their use and value for navigation."

TITLE II—ENVIRONMENTAL QUALITY

SHORT TITLE

SEC. 201. This title may be cited as the "Environmental Quality Improvement Act of 1970."

FINDINGS, DECLARATIONS, AND PURPOSES

SEC. 202. (a) The Congress finds—

(1) that man has caused changes in the environment;

(2) that many of these changes may affect the relationship between man and his environment; and

(3) that population increases and urban concentration contribute directly to pollution and the degradation of our environment.

(b)(1) The Congress declares that there is a national policy for the environment which provides for the enhancement of environmental quality. This policy is evidenced by statutes heretofore enacted relating to the prevention, abatement, and control of environmental pollution, water and land resources, transportation, and economic and regional development.

(2) The primary responsibility for implementing this policy rests with State and local governments.

(3) The Federal Government encourages and supports implementation of this policy through appropriate regional organizations established under existing law.

(c) The purposes of this title are—

(1) to assure that each Federal department and agency conducting or supporting public works activities which affect the environment shall implement the policies established under existing law; and

Office of Environmental Quality. Authorization. 83 Stat. 852.

(2) to authorize an Office of Environmental Quality, which, notwithstanding any other provision of law, shall provide the professional and administrative staff for the Council on Environmental Quality established by Public Law 91–190.

OFFICE OF ENVIRONMENTAL QUALITY

Establishment.

SEC. 203. (a) There is established in the Executive Office of the President an office to be known as the Office of Environmental Quality (hereafter in this title referred to as the "Office"). The Chairman of the Council on Environmental Quality established by Public Law 91–190 shall be the Director of the Office. There shall be in the Office a Deputy Director who shall be appointed by the President, by and with the advice and consent of the Senate. 83 Stat. 852.

(b) The compensation of the Deputy Director shall be fixed by the President at a rate not in excess of the annual rate of compensation payable to the Deputy Director of the Bureau of the Budget. Pay.

(c) The Director is authorized to employ such officers and employees (including experts and consultants) as may be necessary to enable the Office to carry out its functions under this title and Public Law 91–190, except that he may employ no more than ten specialists and other experts without regard to the provisions of title 5, United States Code, governing appointments in the competitive service, and pay such specialists and experts without regard to the provisions of chapter 51 and subchapter III of chapter 53 of such title relating to classification and General Schedule pay rates, but no such specialist or expert shall be paid at a rate in excess of the maximum rate for GS–18 of the General Schedule under section 5332 of title 5. Duties. 5 USC 5101-5115; 5331-5338. 34 F.R. 9605. 5 USC 5332 note.

(d) In carrying out his functions the Director shall assist and advise the President on policies and programs of the Federal Government affecting environmental quality by—

(1) providing the professional and administrative staff and support for the Council on Environmental Quality established by Public Law 91–190;

(2) assisting the Federal agencies and departments in appraising the effectiveness of existing and proposed facilities, programs, policies, and activities of the Federal Government, and those specific major projects designated by the President which do not require individual project authorization by Congress, which affect environmental quality;

(3) reviewing the adequacy of existing systems for monitoring and predicting environmental changes in order to achieve effective coverage and efficient use of research facilities and other resources;

(4) promoting the advancement of scientific knowledge of the effects of actions and technology on the environment and encourage the development of the means to prevent or reduce adverse effects that endanger the health and well-being of man;

(5) assisting in coordinating among the Federal departments and agencies those programs and activities which affect, protect, and improve environmental quality;

(6) assisting the Federal departments and agencies in the development and interrelationship of environmental quality criteria and standards established through the Federal Government;

(7) collecting, collating, analyzing, and interpreting data and information on environmental quality, ecological research, and evaluation.

(e) The Director is authorized to contract with public or private agencies, institutions, and organizations and with individuals without regard to sections 3648 and 3709 of the Revised Statutes (31 U.S.C. 529; 41 U.S.C. 5) in carrying out his functions. Contract authority.

REPORT

SEC. 204. Each Environmental Quality Report required by Public Law 91–190 shall, upon transmittal to Congress, be referred to each standing committee having jurisdiction over any part of the subject matter of the Report. Referral to congressional committees.

AUTHORIZATION

Appropriations. SEC. 205. There are hereby authorized to be appropriated not to exceed $500,000 for the fiscal year ending June 30, 1970, not to exceed $750,000 for the fiscal year ending June 30, 1971, not to exceed $1,250,000 for the fiscal year ending June 30, 1972, and not to exceed $1,500,000 for the fiscal year ending June 30, 1973. These authorizations are in addition to those contained in Public Law 91–190. 83 Stat. 852.

Approved April 3, 1970.

LEGISLATIVE HISTORY:

HOUSE REPORTS: No. 91-127 (Comm. on Public Works) and No. 91-940 (Comm. of Conference).
SENATE REPORT No. 91-351 accompanying S. 7 (Comm. on Public Works).
CONGRESSIONAL RECORD:
Vol. 115 (1969): Apr. 15, 16, considered and passed House.
Oct. 7, 8, considered and passed Senate, amended, in lieu of S. 7.
Vol. 116 (1970): Mar. 24, Senate agreed to conference report.
Mar. 25, House agreed to conference report.

UNION OF SOVIET SOCIALIST REPUBLICS: STATUTE OF THE ADMINISTRATION OF THE NORTHERN SEA ROUTE ATTACHED TO THE MINISTRY OF THE MARITIME FLEET*

[Confirmed by the Council of Ministers of the Union of Soviet Socialist Republics, September 16, 1971]

1. The Administration of the Northern Sea Route attached to the Ministry of the Maritime Fleet has been established for the purpose of ensuring the safety of arctic navigation, as well as of taking measures to prevent and eliminate the consequences of pollution of the marine environment and the northern coast of the Union of Soviet Socialist Republics.

2. The basic tasks of the Administration of the Northern Sea Route shall be:

the implementation of state supervision over the rational use of the Northern Sea Route as the major national transport route of the Union of Soviet Socialist Republics in the Arctic;

the organization of Arctic navigation, taking measures to ensure the safety of navigation on the lanes of the Northern Sea Route and on the lanes of adjacent areas (providing icebreaker escort and pilotage for vessels and navigational and hydrographic services for them, ensuring air navigation, rendering aid to vessels and aircraft in distress);

taking measures to prevent and eliminate the consequences of pollution of the marine environment and the northern coast of the Union of Soviet Socialist Republics and effectuating supervision of vessels for this purpose and of other floating means which may be a source of pollution.

3. The Administration of the Northern Sea Route shall:

(a) regulate the movement of vessels and other floating means along the Northern Sea Route and coordinate marine ice operations;

(b) establish, proceeding from considerations of ensuring the safety of navigation, areas of compulsory icebreaker escort or pilotage of all vessels and determine their conditions;

(c) organize icebreaker escort and pilotage of vessels along the Northern Sea Route, as well as air reconnaissance, and provide guidance for the purpose of creating the most favorable navigational conditions;

(d) organize the rendering of assistance to vessels and aircraft in distress, enlisting for this purpose any necessary transport and technical means in the area of the Northern Sea Route;

(e) carry out the navigational and hydrographic servicing of vessels sailing the Northern Sea Route;

(f) organize the drafting and preparation for publication in the established procedure of navigational aids, cartographic materials, and other technical documents necessary for navigation along the Northern Sea Route;

(g) work out and effectuate measures to improve methods of ice navigation along the Northern Sea Route, as well as prevent pollution of the marine atmosphere and the northern coast of the Union of Soviet Socialist Republics by vessels and other floating means which may be a source of pollution, and to eliminate the consequences of pollution;

(h) establish rules for the navigation of vessels and other floating means, work out instructions and directions for navigation along the Northern Sea Route proceeding from ice, navigational, and meterological conditions and of increased requirements for the equipping and supplying of

---

*[Translated for <u>International Legal Materials</u> by W.E. Butler, Reader in Comparative Law, University of London, from the orginal Russian text which appeared in the <u>Sobranie postanovlenii soveta ministrov SSSR</u> (1971), No. 17, item 124.

vessels in order to ensure safety of navigation and to prevent pollution of the marine environment and the northern coast of the Union of Soviet Socialist Republics;

(i) determine the condition of vessels and other floating means before they sail along the Northern Sea Route in order to establish the conformity of such vessels and floating means to the increased requirements of safe navigation in ice;

(j) organize scientific research in the domain of the development of navigation and ensuring the safety of navigation in ice conditions, improving methods of icebreaker escort and pilotage of vessels, preventing and eliminating the consequences of pollution of the marine environment and the northern coasts of the Union of Soviet Socialist Republics;

(k) determine the periods of Arctic navigation.

4. Instructions of the Administration of the Northern Sea Route on questions relating to the safety of navigation along the Northern Sea Route, icebreaker escort and pilotage of vessels, rendering aid to vessels or aircraft in distress, preventing and eliminating the consequences of pollution of the marine environment and the northern coast of the Union of Soviet Socialist Republics, shall be subject to fulfillment by organizations and persons, as well as vessels sailing along the Northern Sea Route.

5. The Administration of the Northern Sea Route shall be headed by a Chief appointed by the Council of Ministers of the Union of Soviet Socialist Republics.

6. The Chief of the Administration of the Northern Sea Route, his deputies, the chief state inspectors, and the state inspectors shall have the right:

(a) to visit vessels and other floating means for the purpose of determining their condition as provided for by Article 3(i) of the present Statute, and if such vessels and floating means do not conform to the increased requirements of the safety of navigation in ice, to prohibit them from sailing the Northern Sea Route;

(b) to suspend icebreaker escort and pilotage and the navigation of vessels and other floating means in individual portions of the Northern Sea Route if this is called for by ice, navigation, or meterological conditions or threatens pollution of the Marine environment and the northern coasts of the Union of Soviet Socialist Republics;

(c) to impose penalties provided for by existing legislation on masters and other officers of vessels and floating means sailing the Northern Sea Route for violation of rules of navigation or of rules for the prevention of pollution of the marine environment and the northern coasts of the Union of Soviet Socialist Republics, unless these rules entail criminal responsibility under prevailing legislation. Bringing the said persons to administrative or criminal responsibility does not preclude the bringing of a suit in the established procedure in connection with the causing of damage in consequence of the failure to fulfill the said rules.

7. The Administration of the Northern Sea Route shall operate on the rights of the Chief Administration of the Ministry of the Maritime Fleet (on economic accountability) and shall exercise direction over organizations and enterprises subordinate to it.

8. Officials of the Administration of the Northern Sea Route shall, in execution of their official duties, wear the established dress and insignia of the Administration of the Northern Sea Route.

9. The Administration of the Northern Sea Route attached to the Ministry of the Maritime Fleet shall have a seal depicting the State Seal of the Union of Soviet Socialist Republics and its own name.

STOCKHOLM DECLARATION
Declaration on the Human Environment

The United Nations Conference on the Human Environment having met at Stockholm from 5 to 16 June 1972, and having considered the need for a common outlook and for common principles to inspire and guide the peoples of the world in the preservation and enhancement of the human environment, proclaims:

1. Man is both creature and moulder of his environment which gives him physical sustenance and affords him the opportunity for intellectual, moral,social and spiritual growth. In the long and tortuous evolution of the human race on this planet a stage has been reached when through the rapid acceleration of science and technology, man has acquired the power to transform his environment in countless ways and on an unprecedented scale. Both aspects of man's environment, the natural and the man-made, are essential to his well-being and to the enjoyment of basic human rights - even the right to life itself.

2. The protection and improvement of the human environment is a major issue which affects the well-being of peoples and economic development throughout the world; it is the urgent desire of the peoples of the whole world and the duty of all governments.

3. Man has constantly to sum up experience and go on discovering, inventing, creating and advancing. In our time man's capability to transform his surroundings, if used wisely, can bring to all peoples the benefits of development and the opportunity to enhance the quality of life. Wrongly or heedlessly applied, the same power can do incalculable harm to human beings and the human environment. We see around us growing evidence of man-made harm in many regions of the earth: dangerous levels of pollution in water, air, earth and living beings; major and undesirable disturbances to the ecological balance of the biosphere; destruction and depletion of irreplaceable resources; and gross deficiencies harmful to the physical, mental and social health of man, in the man-made environment, particularly in the living and working environment.

4. In the developing countries most of the environmental problems are caused by under-development. Millions continue to live far below the minimum levels required for a decent human existence, deprived of adequate food and clothing, shelter and education, health and sanitation. Therefore, the de-

veloping countries must direct their efforts to development, bearing in mind their priorities and the need to safeguard and improve the environment. For the same purpose, the industrialized countries should make efforts to reduce the gap between themselves and the developing countries. In the industrialized countries, environmental problems are generally related to industrialization and technological development.

5. The natural growth of population continuously presents problems on the preservation of the environment, and adequate policies measures should be adopted as appropriate to face these problems. Of all things in the world, people are the most precious. It is the people that propel social progress, create social wealth, develop science and technology and through their hard work, continuously transform the human environment. Along with social progress and the advance of production, science and technology, the capability of man to improve the environment increases with each passing day.

6. A point has been reached in history when we must shape our actions throughout the world with a more prudent care for their environmental consequences. Through ignorance or indifference we can do massive and irreversible harm to the earthly environment on which our life and well being depend. Conversely, through fuller knowledge and wiser action, we can achieve for ourselves and our posterity a better life in an environment more in keeping with human needs and hopes. There are broad vistas for the enhancement of environmental quality and the creation of a good life. What is needed is an enthusiastic but calm state of mind and intense but orderly work. For the purpose of attaining freedom in the world of nature, man must use knowledge to build in collaboration with nature a better environment. To defend and improve the human environment for present and future generations has become an imperative goal for mankind - a goal to be pursued together with, and in harmony with, the established and fundamental goals of peace and of worldwide economic and social development.

7. To achieve this environmental goal will demand the acceptance of responsibility by citizens and communities and by enterprises and institutions at every level, all sharing equitably in common efforts. Individuals in all walks of life as well as organizations in many fields, by their values and the sum of their actions, will shape the world environment of the future. Local and national governments will bear the greatest burden for large scale environmental policy and action within their jurisdictions. International cooperation is also needed in order to raise resources to support the developing countries in carrying out their responsibilities in this field.

A growing class of environmental problems, because they are regional or global in extent or because they affect the common international realm, will require extensive cooperation among nations and action by international organizations in the common interest. The conference calls upon the governments and peoples to exert common efforts for the preservation and improvement of the human environment, for the benefit of all the people and for their posterity.

Principles

States the common conviction that --

1. Man has the fundamental right to freedom, equality and adequate conditions of life, in an environment of a quality which permits a life of dignity and well being, and bears a solemn responsibility to protect and improve the environment for present and future generations. (In this respect, policies promoting or perpetuating apartheid, racial segregation, discrimination, colonial and other forms of oppression and foreign domination stand condemned and must be eliminated.)

2. The natural resources of the earth including the air, water, land, flora and fauna and especially representative samples of natural ecosystems must be safeguarded for the benefit of present and future generations through careful planning or management as appropriate.

3. The capacity of the earth to produce vital renewable resources must be maintained and wherever practicable restored or improved.

4. Man has a special responsibility to safeguard and wisely manage the heritage of wildlife and its habitat which are now gravely imperilled by a combination of adverse factors. Nature conservation including wildlife must therefore receive importance in planning for economic development.

5. The non-renewable resources of the earth must be employed in such a way as to guard against the danger of their future exhaustion and to ensure that benefits from such employment are shared by all mankind.

6. The discharge of toxic substances or of other substances and the release of heat, in such quantities or concentrations as to exceed the capacity of the environment to render them harmless, must be halted in order to ensure that serious or irreversible damage is not inflicted upon ecosystems. (The just struggle of the peoples of all countries against pollution should be supported.)

7. States shall take all possible steps to prevent pollution of the seas by substances that are liable to create hazards to human health, to harm living resources and marine life, to damage amenities or to interfere with other legitimate uses of the sea.

8. Economic and social development is essential for ensuring a favorable living and working environment for man and for conditions on earth that are necessary for the improvement of the quality of life.

9. Environmental deficiencies generated by the conditions of underdevelopment and natural disasters pose grave problems and can best be remedied by accelerated development through the transfer of substantial quantities of financial and technological assistance, as a supplement to the domestic effort of the developing countries and such timely assistance as may be required.

10. For the developing countries, stability of prices and adequate earnings for primary commodities and raw material are essential to environmental management since economic factors as well as ecological processes must be taken into account.

11. The environmental policies of all states should enhance and not adversely affect the present or future development potential of developing countries, nor should they hamper the attainment of better living conditions for all, and appropriate steps should be taken by states and international organizations with a view to reaching agreement on meeting the possible national and international economic consequences resulting from the application of environmental measures.

12. Resources should be made available to preserve and improve the environment, taking into account the circumstances and particular requirements of developing countries and any costs which may emanate from their incorporating environmental safeguards into their development planning and the need for making available to them, upon their request, additional international technical and financial assistance for this purpose.

13. In order to achieve a more rational management of resources and thus to improve the environment, states should adopt an integrated and coordinated approach to their development planning so as to ensure that development is compatible with the need to protect and improve the human environment for the benefit of their population.

14. Rational planning constitutes an essential tool for

reconciling any conflict between the needs of development and the need to protect and improve the environment.

15. Planning must be applied to human settlements and urbanization with a view to avoiding adverse effect on the environment and obtaining maximum social, economic and environmental benefits for all. In this respect projects which are designed for colonialist and racist domination must be abandoned.

16. Demographic policies which are without prejudice to basic human rights and which are deemed appropriate by governments concerned, should be applied in those regions where the rate of population growth or excessive population concentrations are likely to have adverse effects on the environment or development, or where low population density may prevent improvement of the human environment and impede development.

17. Appropriate national institutions must be entrusted with the task of planning, managing or controlling the environmental resources of states with the view to enhancing environmental quality.

18. Science and technology, as part of their contribution to economic and social development, must be applied to the identification, avoidance and control of environmental risks and the solution of environmental problems and for the common good of mankind.

19. Education in environmental matters, for the younger generation as well as adults, giving due consideration for the underprivileged, is essential in order to broaden the basis for an enlightened opinion and responsible conduct by individuals, enterprises and communities in protecting and improving the environment in its full human dimension. It is also essential that mass media of communications avoid contributing to the deterioration of the environment, but, on the contrary, disseminate information of an educational nature on the need to protect and improve the environment in order to educate man to develop in every respect.

20. Scientific research and development in the context of environmental problems, both national and multinational must be promoted in all countries, especially the developing countries. In this connection, the free flow of up to date scientific information and experience must be supported and assisted, to facilitate the solution of environmental problems; environmental technologies should be made available to developing countries on terms which would encourage their wide dissemination without constituting an economic burden on the developing countries.

21. States have, in accordance with the Charter of the United Nations and the principles of international law, the sovereign right to exploit their own resources pursuant to their own environmental policies, and the responsibility to ensure that activities within their jurisdiction or control do not cause damage to the environment of other states or of areas beyond the limits of national jurisdiction.

22. States shall cooperate to develop further the international law regarding liability and compensation for the victims of pollution and other environmental damage caused by activities within the jurisdiction or control of such states to areas beyond their jurisdiction.

23. Without prejudice to such general principles as may be agreed upon by the international community, or to the criteria and minimum levels which will have to be determined nationally, it will be essential in all cases to consider the systems of values prevailing in each country, and the extent of the applicability of standards which are valid for the most advanced countries but which may be inappropriate and of unwarranted social cost for the developing countries.

24. International matters concerning the protection and improvement of the environment should be handled in a cooperative spirit by all countries, big or small, on an equal footing. Cooperation through multilateral or bilateral arrangements or other appropriate means is essential to prevent, eliminate or reduce and effectively control adverse environmental effects resulting from activities conducted in all spheres, in such a way that due account is taken of the sovereignty and interests of all states.

25. States shall ensure that international organizations play a coordinated, efficient and dynamic role for the protection and improvement of the environment.

26. Man and his environment must be spared the effects of nuclear weapons and all other means of mass destruction. States must strive to reach prompt agreement, in the relevant international organs, on the elimination and destruction of such weapons.

DECISIONS OF THE UNITED NATIONS CONFERENCE ON THE HUMAN ENVIRONMENT (5-16 JUNE 1972) RELATING TO THE PRESERVATION OF THE MARINE ENVIRONMENT AND MARINE POLLUTION

A. DECLARATION OF THE UNITED NATIONS CONFERENCE ON THE HUMAN ENVIRONMENT (See preceeding document)

B. MARINE POLLUTION RECOMMENDATIONS

Recommendation 86

It is recommended that Governments, with the assistance and guidance of appropriate United Nations bodies, in particular the Joint Group of Experts on the Scientific Aspects of Marine Pollution (GESAMP):

(a) Accept and implement available instruments on the control of the maritime sources of marine pollution;

(b) Ensure that the provisions of such instruments are complied with by ships flying their flags and by ships operating in areas under their jurisdiction and that adequate provisions are made for reviewing the effectiveness of, and revising, existing and proposed international measures for control of marine pollution;

(c) Ensure that ocean dumping by their nationals anywhere, or by any person in their jurisdiction, is controlled and that Governments shall continue to work towards the completion of, and bringing into force as soon as possible of, an over-all instrument for the control of ocean dumping as well as needed regional agreements within the framework of this instrument, in particular for enclosed and semi-enclosed seas, which are more at risk from pollution;

(d) Refer the draft articles and annexes contained in the report of the intergovernmental meetings at Reykjavik, Iceland, in April 1972 and in London in May 1972 to the United Nations Committee on the Peaceful Uses of the Seabed and the Ocean Floor beyond the Limits of National Jurisdiction at its session in July/August 1972 for information and comments and to a conference of Governments to be convened by the Government of the United Kingdom of Great Britain and Northern Ireland in consultation with the Secretary-General of the United Nations before November 1972 for further consideration, with a view to opening the proposed convention for signature at a place to be decided by that Conference, preferably before the end of 1972;

(e) Participate fully in the 1973 Intergovernmental Maritime Consultative Organization (IMCO) Conference on Marine Pollution and the Conference on the Law of the Sea scheduled to be held in 1973, as well as in regional efforts, with a view to bringing all significant sources of pollution within the marine environment, including radioactive pollution from nuclear surface ships and submarines, and in particular in enclosed and semi-enclosed seas, under appropriate controls and particularly to complete elimination of deliberate pollution by oil from ships, with the goal of achieving this by the middle of the present decade;

(f) Strengthen national controls over land-based sources of marine pollution, in particular in enclosed and semi-enclosed seas, and recognize that, in some circumstances, the discharge of residual heat from nuclear and other power-stations may constitute a potential hazard to marine ecosystems.

Recommendation 87

It is recommended that Governments:

(a) Support national research and monitoring efforts that contribute to agreed international programmes for research and monitoring in the marine environment, in particular the Global Investigation of Pollution in the Marine Environment (GIPME) and the Integrated Global Ocean Station System (IGOSS);

(b) Provide to the United Nations, the Food and Agriculture Organization of the United Nations and the United Nations Conference on Trade and Development, as appropriate to the data-gathering activities of each, statistics on the production and use of toxic or dangerous substances that are potential marine pollutants, especially if they are persistent;

(c) Expand their support to components of the United Nations system concerned with research and monitoring in the marine environment and adopt the measures required to improve the constitutional, financial and operational basis under which the Intergovernmental Oceanographic Commission is at present operating so as to make it an effective joint mechanism for the Governments and the United Nations organizations concerned (United Nations Educational, Scientific and Cultural Organization, Food and Agriculture Organization of the United Nations, World Meteorological Organization, Intergovernmental Maritime Consultative Organization, United Nations) and in order that it may be able to take on additional responsibilities for the promotion and co-ordination of scientific programmes and services.

Recommendation 88

It is recommended that the Secretary-General, together with the sponsoring agencies, make it possible for the Joint Group of Experts on the Scientific Aspects of Marine Pollution (GESAMP):

(a) to re-examine annually, and revise as required, its "Review of Harmful Chemical Substances", with a view to elaborating further its assessment of sources, pathways and resulting risks of marine pollutants;

(b) To assemble, having regard to other work in progress, scientific data and to provide advice on scientific aspects of marine pollution, especially those of an interdisciplinary nature.

Recommendation 89

It is recommended that the Secretary-General ensure:

(a) That mechanisms for combining world statistics on mining, production, processing, transport and use of potential marine pollutants shall be developed along with methods for identifying high-priority marine pollutants based in part on such data;

(b) That the Joint Group of Experts on the Scientific Aspects of Marine Pollution (GESAMP), in consultation with other expert groups, propose guidelines for test progammes to evaluate toxicity of potential marine pollutants;

(c) That the Food and Agriculture Organization of the United Nations, the World Health Organization, the Intergovernmental Oceanographic Commission and the International Atomic Energy Agency encourage studies of the effects of high-priority marine pollutants on man and other organisms, with appropriate emphasis on chronic,low-level exposures;

(d) That the Intergovernmental Oceanographic Commission, with the Food and Agriculture Organization of the United Nations and the World Health Organization, explore the possibility of establishing an international institute for tropical marine studies, which would undertake training as well as research.

Recommendation 90

It is recommended that the Intergovernmental Oceanographic Commission, jointly with the World Meteorological Organization and, as appropriate, in co-operation with other interested intergovernmental bodies, promote the monitoring of marine pollution, preferably within the framework of the Integrated

Global Ocean Station System (IGOSS), as well as the development of methods for monitoring high-priority marine pollutants in the water, sediments and organisms, with advice from the Joint Group of Experts on the Scientific Aspects of Marine Pollution (GESAMP) on intercomparability of methodologies.

Recommendation 91

It is recommended that the Intergovernmental Oceanographic Commission:

(a) Ensure that provision shall be made in international marine research, monitoring and related activities for the exchange, dissemination, and referral to sources of data and information on baselines and on marine pollution and that attention shall be paid to the special needs of developing countries;

(b) Give full consideration, with the Food and Agriculture Organization of the United Nations, the World Meteorological Organization, the Intergovernmental Maritime Consultative Organization, the World Health Organization, the International Atomic Energy Agency, the International Hydrographic Organization and the International Council for the Exploration of the Sea and other interested and relevant organizations to the strengthening of on-going marine and related data and information exchange and dissemination activities;

(c) Support the concept for development of an interdisciplinary and inter-organizational system primarily involving centres already in existence;

(d) Initiate an interdisciplinary marine pollution data and scientific information referral capability.

Recommendation 92

It is recommended:

(a) That Governments collectively endorse the principles set forth in paragraph 197 of Conference document A/CONF.48/8 as guiding concepts for the Conference on the Law of the Sea and the Intergovernmental Maritime Consultative Organization (IMCO) Marine Pollution Conference scheduled to be held in 1973 and also the statement of objectives agreed on at the second session of the Intergovernmental Working Group on Marine Pollution as follows:

"The marine environment and all the living organisms which it supports are of vital importance to humanity, and all people have an interest in assuring that this environment is so managed that its quality and resources are not impaired. This applies especially to coastal area resources. The capacity of the sea to assimilate wastes and render them harmless and its ability to regenerate natural resources are not unlimited. Proper management is required and measures to prevent and control marine pollution must be regarded as an essential element in this management of the oceans and seas and their natural resources.",

and that, in respect of the particular interest of coastal States in the marine environment and recognizing that the resolution of this question is a matter for consideration at the Conference on the Law of the Sea, they take note of the principles on the rights of coastal States discussed but neither endorsed nor rejected at the second session of the Intergovernmental Working Group on Marine Pollution */and refer those principles to the 1973 Intergovernmental Maritime Consultative Organization Conference for information and to the 1973 Conference on the Law of the Sea for such action as may be appropriate;

---

*/ 1. A State may exercise special authority in areas of the sea adjacent to its territorial waters where functional controls of a continuing nature are necessary for the effective prevention of pollution which could cause damage or injury to the land or marine environment under its exclusive or sovereign authority.

2. A coastal State may prohibit any vessel which does not comply with internationally agreed rules and standards or, in their absence, with reasonable national rules and standards of the coastal State in question, from entering waters under its environmental protection authority.

3. The basis on which a State should exercise rights or powers, in addition to its sovereign rights or powers, pursuant to its special authority in areas adjacent to its territorial waters, is that such rights or powers should be deemed to be delegated to that State by the world community on behalf of humanity as a whole. The rights and powers exercised must be consistent with the State's primary responsibility for marine environmental protection in the areas concerned: they should be subject to international rules and standards and to review before an appropriate international tribunal.

(*b*) That Governments take early action to adopt effective national measures for the control of all significant sources of marine pollution, including land-based sources, and concert and co-ordinate their actions regionally and where appropriate on a wider international basis;

(*c*) That the Secretary-General, in co-operation with appropriate international organizations, endeavor to provide guidelines which Governments might wish to take into account when developing such measures.

Recommendation 93

It is recommended that any mechanism for co-ordinating and stimulating the actions of the different United Nations organs in connection with environmental problems include among its functions over-all responsibility for ensuring that needed advice on marine pollution problems shall be provided to Governments.

Recommendation 94

It is recommended that the Secretary-General, with the co-operation of United Nations bodies, take steps to secure additional financial support to those training and other programmes of assistance that contribute to increasing the capacity of developing countries to participate in international marine research, monitoring and pollution-control programmes.

C. OTHER RECOMMENDATIONS

Recommendation 32

It is recommended that Governments give attention to the need to enact international conventions and treaties to protect species inhabiting international waters or those which migrate from one country to another:

(a) A broadly-based convention should be considered which would provide a framework by which criteria for game regulations could be agreed upon and the over-exploitation of resources curtailed by signatory countries;

(b) A working group should be set up as soon as possible by the appropriate authorities to consider these problems and to advise on the need for, and possible scope of, such conventions or treaties.

Recommendation 47

It is recommended that Governments and the Secretary-General of the United Nations, in co-operation with the Food and Agriculture Organization of the United Nations and other United Nations organizations concerned, as well as development assistance agencies take steps to ensure close participation of fishery agencies and interests in the preparations for the United Nations Conference on the Law of the Sea. In order to safeguard the marine environment and its resources through the development of effective and workable principles and laws, the information and insight of international and regional fishery bodies, as well as the national fishery agencies, are essential.

Recommendation 99

1. It is recommended that Governments should:

(a) Noting that the draft convention prepared by the United Nations Educational, Scientific and Cultural Organization concerning the protection of the world natural and cultural heritage marks a significant step towards the protection, on an international scale, of the environment, examine this draft convention with a view to its adoption at the next General Conference of UNESCO;

(b) Whenever appropriate, sign the Convention on Conservation of Wetlands of International Importance.

2. <u>It is recommended</u> that the Secretary-General, in consultation with the competent agencies of the United Nations system and the non-governmental organizations concerned make arrangements for a detailed study of all possible procedures for protecting certain islands for science;

3. <u>It is recommended</u> that a plenipotentiary conference be convened as soon as possible, under appropriate governmental or intergovernmental auspices, to prepare and adopt a convention on export, import and transit of certain species of wild animals and plants.

RESOLUTION VI-13
Passed at the 6th Session of the Intergovernmental Oceanographic Commission, 1969

PROMOTING FUNDAMENTAL SCIENTIFIC RESEARCH

The Intergovernmental Oceanographic Commission,

Recognizing that in accordance with Article 1, para. 2 of the Commission's Statutes its main function is: ". . . to promote scientific investigation. . . of the oceans, through the concerted action of its members",

Taking into account that physical, chemical, biological and geological phenomena are closely interrelated throughout the ocean and observe the laws of nature,

Bearing in mind the interests of mankind in the field of scientific research, with particular reference to the interests and needs of the developing countries,

Taking into account that specific cases of obtaining consent for conducting scientific research in areas falling under the national jurisdiction of coastal States are usually resolved between the interested States,

Taking note of the Summary Report of the IOC Working Group on Legal Questions Related to Scientific Investigations of the Ocean, established by Resolution V-6,

Being of the opinion that it is desirable that the procedures to obtain the consent of a coastal State for the carrying out of fundamental scientific research in the areas over which jurisdiction is exercised be simple and effective,

Observing that any steps which might be taken in this regard are not intended to impair the sovereign rights of States,

Considers that the Commission should assist in promoting fundamental scientific research that is carried out either in the framework of the long-term and expanded programme of oceanic research or within Declared National Programmes. This assistance regarding areas of national jurisdiction will be subject to the following principles:

(a) As soon as a tentative decision to carry out a research programme is made, the coastal State shall be informed in a preliminary manner to ensure that it may, if it so desires, be associated, from the preliminary steps, with the planning of the programme and arrange for early con tact between interested scientists;

(b) A formal description of the nature and location of the research programme shall be submitted to the coastal State and to the Commission as soon as possible in order to enable the coastal State to respond formally as far in advance as possible and in order to enable the coastal State to participate effectively in the research programme;

(c) The Secretary of the Commission shall transmit the formal description so received to the coastal State within twenty days of receipt together with the Commission's request for favourable consideration and, if possible, with a factual description of the international scientific interest in the subject prepared by the requesting State, supplemented, if he considers this desirable, by the Secretary;

(d) The coastal State, if it so desires, will participate in such research programmes as arranged between the interested States;

(e) The coastal State will have available to it as soon as possible all data from such research, including data and samples not feasible to duplicate; special arrangements shall be made regarding the custody of data and samples not feasible to duplicate;

(f) The results of such research programmes shall be published as soon as possible in an open internationally distributed scientific publication;

Invites interested Member States to act in a spirit of international co-operation, to consider favourably and to facilitate within the framework of national laws and regulations the requests for vessels conducting fundamental scientific research to make port calls;

Recommends that the Working Group continue examining the question in the terms of the above-mentioned resolution, and report back on it at the VIIth session.

UNITED NATIONS
GENERAL ASSEMBLY

A/AC.138/SC.III/L.23
3 August 1972

COMMITTEE ON THE PEACEFUL USES OF THE SEA-BED AND THE OCEAN FLOOR BEYOND THE LIMITS OF NATIONAL JURISDICTION. SUB-COMMITTEE III

Working Paper submitted by the People's Republic of Bulgaria, the Ukrainian Soviet Socialist Republic and the Union of Soviet Socialist Republics

Basic principles concerning international co-operation in marine scientific research

It could be stated in the preamble that:

- Further progress in marine scientific research for peaceful purposes is in the common interest of all mankind;
- Knowledge of all aspects of the natural processes and phenomena occurring in the ocean, including the sea-bed and the ocean floor, is of great significance;
- Marine scientific research will promote the practical utilization of marine areas and resources and will facilitate action to deal with natural disasters;
- Marine scientific research should be conducted for the benefit of all countries irrespective of their degree of economic and technological development;
- Assistance to marine scientific research would help to increase the well-being of the peoples of the world, particularly in the developing countries;
- A comprehensive knowledge of the oceans can only be acquired by uniting the scientific capacities and combining the efforts of States;
- It is essential to extend international co-operation in marine scientific research and to establish the most favourable conditions for conducting such research.

The basic principles might be formulated as:

1. Inter-State co-operation in the further development of marine scientific research and the combined efforts of scientists in studying the nature and interrelationships of oceanic phenomena and processes are an essential condition for the efficient and rational exploitation of the wealth and resources of the seas and the oceans in the interests of all countries.

2. International co-operation in conducting marine scientific research shall serve peaceful purposes and help to increase the well-being of the peoples of all countries.

3. Marine scientific research shall be conducted in conformity with the universally-recognized principles and standards of international law, including the United Nations Charter.

The high seas are open to the unhampered pursuit of scientific research work by all States on a basis of equality, without discrimination of any kind.

4. States shall co-operate with one another in providing favourable conditions for the conduct of marine scientific research and in the removal of obstacles to such research. In particular, in the interests of international co-operation, States shall, within the framework of their national laws and regulations, facilitate the entry into their ports of ships conducting marine scientific research by simplifying the relevant procedure.

5. States shall co-operate in adopting measures designed to extend the research opportunities of developing and land-locked countries, including the participation of the nationals of such countries in scientific research work, the provision of scientific training and the exchange of experience in the conduct of scientific research work.

6. All States may take part in international marine scientific research programmes and will encourage the participation of their own scientists in the work envisaged under those programmes.

7. States and international organizations shall co-operate under the auspices of the UNESCO Intergovernmental Oceanographic Commission in conducting marine scientific research in accordance with the long-term and expanded programme of oceanic exploration and research.

8. States shall endeavour in every way to stimulate the mutual exchange of scientific data, and shall make such data available to the developing countries as part of the scientific and technical assistance they provide to those countries.

9. States shall adopt and encourage measures to ensure the publication and wide dissemination of the results of marine scientific research, inter alia, through the system of world and regional data centres.

10. All States shall co-operate with each other in preventing hindrances to the normal functioning and safe preservation of stationary and mobile, manned and unmanned, equipment and installations on the high seas carrying scientific apparatus and intended for making scientific measurements and experiments.

11. Marine scientific research shall be carried out without causing damage to the environment which might entail the disturbance of ecological balances therein.

12. Marine scientific research shall be conducted without causing danger to navigation or unwarranted interference with fishing. Where necessary, appropriate notifications of when and where experiments are to be conducted shall be provided in good time.
13. States shall bear international responsibility for national activities connected with marine scientific research, whether such activities are conducted by government bodies or by individuals or bodies corporate under their jurisdiction.
14. No such activity shall constitute legal grounds for any claims to any part of the seas or oceans or their resources.
15. These principles shall extend equally to scientific research carried out on the sea-bed and the ocean floor beyond the limits of the continental shelf.

UNITED NATIONS
GENERAL ASSEMBLY

A/AC.138/SC.III/L.18
25 July 1972

COMMITTEE ON THE PEACEFUL USES OF THE SEA-BED AND OCEAN FLOOR BEYOND THE LIMITS OF NATIONAL JURISDICTION.
SUB-COMMITTEE III

Working Paper submitted by the
Canadian Delegation

PRINCIPLES ON MARINE SCIENTIFIC RESEARCH

For the Third Law of the Sea Conference

PREAMBLE

1. All mankind has an interest in the facilitation of marine scientific research and the publication of its results.

2. Marine scientific research is any study, whether fundamental or applied, intended to increase knowledge about the marine environment, including all its resources and living organisms, and embraces all related scientific activity.

3. The objectives of marine scientific research include achievement of a level of understanding which allows accurate assessment and prediction of oceanic processes and provide the basis for the development of a management policy which will ensure that the quality and resources of the marine environment are not impaired, and for the rational use of this environment, in the service of human welfare, international equity and economic progress and, in the interest of peace and international co-operation among States.

PRINCIPLES

1. Knowledge resulting from marine scientific research is part of the common heritage of all mankind, and such knowledge and information of a non-proprietary or non-military nature should be exchanged and made available to the whole world.

2. Marine scientific research constitutes a legitimate activity within the marine environment. Every State, whether coastal or not, and every competent international organization has the right to conduct or authorize the conduct of scientific research

in the marine environment, in accordance with the rules and recognized principles of international law and subject to the provisions of the present principles.

3. Marine scientific research as such shall not form the legal basis for any claims of exploitation rights or any other rights in areas beyond the limits of national jurisdiction.

4. Marine scientific research shall be conducted in a reasonable manner, and shall not result in any unjustifiable interference with other uses of the marine environment; nor shall other uses of the marine environment result in any unjustifiable interference with marine scientific research.

5. Marine scientific research shall not entail excessive collection of specimens and samples, nor cause pollution or undue disturbance of the marine environment.

6. The availability to every State of information and knowledge resulting from marine scientific research shall be facilitated by effective international communication of proposed major programmes and their objectives, and by publication and dissemination through international channels of their results.

7. States shall take steps to further the development and growth of marine scientific research and to obviate interference with its progress, and shall co-operate in the elaboration of international rules to facilitate such research. States shall promote arrangements and agreements to advance marine scientific research and the exchange of data and information on a regional, as well as on a global basis, in co-operation with other States and with international organizations, whether governmental or non-governmental.

8. States shall, both individually and in co-operation with other States and with competent international organizations, promote the flow of scientific data and information and the transfer of experience resulting from marine scientific research to developing countries and the strengthening of the marine research capabilities of these countries to a level corresponding to their needs and resources, including programmes to provide adequate training of the technical and scientific personnel of these countries.

9. Marine scientific research in areas within the jurisdiction of a coastal State shall be conducted with the consent of the coastal State. If such consent is granted, the coastal State shall have the right to participate or to be represented in such marine scientific research and shall have the right of utilizing samples, the right of access to data, and results,

and the right to require that the results be published.

10. The coastal State prior to determining whether it will grant consent to marine scientific research in areas within its jurisdiction, may require information such as the period, location, nature and purpose of the proposed investigations, the observations to be made, the proposed disposition of all material collected, the means to be employed and, where applicable, the name of the ship with its full description, including tonnage, type and class, the name of the agency sponsoring the investigations and the names of the Master of the vessel, the proposed scientific leaders and members of the scientific party and particulars of any proposed entry into a coastal State port. The coastal State shall be kept informed of any changes in the above information.

11. The coastal State shall reply promptly to a request accompanied by information required by it in accordance with the provisions of Principle 10. The coastal State shall facilitate the conduct of marine scientific research to which it has consented by extending necessary facilities to ships and scientists while they are operating in areas within its jurisdiction wherever possible.

12. Marine scientific research shall comply with all coastal State's laws and regulations when carried out in areas within the jurisdiction of the coastal State, including the resource management regulations and directions in areas where the coastal State has authority over resources appertaining to its continental shelf, the environmental protection regulations in areas where the coastal State has a primary responsibility for environmental protection, the management regulations in areas under fishery management, where in addition all information resulting from such research shall be made available to the authority managing such area, and the regulations and directions necessary to protect the security of the coastal State.

13. Marine scientific research concerning the sea-bed and ocean floor, and the subsoil thereof, beyond the limits of national jurisdiction shall comply with any regulations developed by a competent international organization to minimize disturbance and prevent pollution of the marine environment and interference with exploration and exploitation activity.

14. States shall devise means to enable responsibility to be fixed with States or international organizations that have caused damage in the course of marine scientific research or where such damage has been caused by the activities of persons under their jurisdiction, to the marine environment or to any other State or to its nationals.

III. UNITED NATIONS CONFERENCE ON THE LAW OF THE SEA

("MORATORIUM" Resolution. Adopted by the 24th Session of the United Nations General Assembly by a vote of 62 in favor, 28 against with 28 abstaining.)

2574 (XXIV). Question of the reservation exclusively for peaceful purposes of the sea-bed and the ocean floor, and the subsoil thereof, underlying the high seas beyond the limits of present national jurisdiction, and the use of their resources in the interests of mankind.

THE GENERAL ASSEMBLY,

RECALLING its resolution 2467 A (XXIII) of 21 December 1968 to the effect that the exploitation of the resources of the sea-bed and the ocean floor, and the subsoil thereof, beyond the limits of national jurisdiction should be carried out for the benefit of mankind as a whole, irrespective of the geographical location of States, taking into account the special interests and needs of the developing countries,

CONVINCED that it is essential, for the achievement of this purpose, that such activities be carried out under an international regime including appropriate international machinery,

NOTING that this matter is under consideration by the Committee on the Peaceful Uses of the Sea-Bed and the Ocean Floor beyond the Limits of National Jurisdiction,

RECALLING its resolution 2340 (XXII) of 18 December 1967 on the importance of preserving the sea-bed and the ocean floor, and the subsoil thereof, beyond the limits of national jurisdiction from actions and uses which might be detrimental to the common interests of mankind,

DECLARES that, pending the establishment of the aforementioned international regime:

(a) States and persons, physical or juridical, are bound to refrain from all activities of exploitation of the resources of the area of the sea-bed and ocean floor, and the subsoil thereof, beyond the limits of national jurisdiction;

(b) No claim to any part of that area or its resources shall be recognized.

1833rd plenary meeting,
15 December 1969.

UN GENERAL ASSEMBLY RESOLUTION 2750 (XXV), DECEMBER 17, 1970

2750 (XXV). Reservation exclusively for peaceful purposes of the sea-bed and the ocean floor, and the subsoil thereof, underlying the high seas beyond the limits of present national jurisdiction and use of their resources in the interests of mankind, and convening of a conference on the law of the sea

C

The General Assembly,

Recalling its resolutions 798 (VIII) of 7 December 1953, 1105 (XI) of 21 February 1957 and 2574 A (XXIV) of 15 December 1969,

Recalling further its resolutions 2340 (XXII) of 18 December 1967, 2467 (XXIII) of 21 December 1968 and 2574 (XXIV) of 15 December 1969,

Taking into account the results of the consultations undertaken by the Secretary-General[42] in accordance with paragraph 1 of resolution 2574 A (XXIV), which indicate widespread support for the holding of a comprehensive conference on the law of the sea,

Conscious that the problems of ocean space are closely interrelated and need to be considered as a whole,

Noting that the political and economic realities, scientific development and rapid technological advances of the last decade have accentuated the need for early and progressive development of the law of the sea, in a framework of close international co-operation,

Having regard to the fact that many of the present States Members of the United Nations did not take part in the previous United Nations conferences on the law of the sea,

Convinced that the elaboration of an equitable international régime for the sea-bed and the ocean floor, and the subsoil thereof, beyond the limits of national jurisdiction would facilitate agreement on the questions to be examined at such a conference,

Affirming that such agreements on those questions should seek to accommodate the interests and needs of all States, whether land-locked or coastal, taking into account the special interests and needs of the developing countries, whether land-locked or coastal,

Having considered the report of the Committee on the Peaceful Uses of the Sea-Bed and the Ocean Floor beyond the Limits of National Jurisdiction,[43]

Convinced that a new conference on the law of the sea would have to be carefully prepared to ensure its success and that the preparatory work ought to start as soon as possible after the conclusion of the twenty-fifth session of the General Assembly, drawing on the experience already accumulated in the Committee on the Peaceful Uses of the Sea-Bed and the Ocean Floor beyond the Limits of National Jurisdiction and using fully the opportunity provided by the United Nations Conference on the Human Environment, to be held in 1972, to further its work,

1. *Notes with satisfaction* the progress made so far towards the elaboration of the international régime for the sea-bed and the ocean floor, and the subsoil thereof, beyond the limits of national jurisdiction through the Declaration of Principles Governing the Sea-Bed and the Ocean Floor, and the Subsoil Thereof, beyond the Limits of National Jurisdiction, adopted by the General Assembly on 17 December 1970;[44]

2. *Decides* to convene in 1973, in accordance with the provisions of paragraph 3 below, a conference on the law of the sea which would deal with the establishment of an equitable international régime—including an international machinery—for the area and the resources of the sea-bed and the ocean floor, and the subsoil thereof, beyond the limits of national jurisdiction, a precise definition of the area, and a broad range of related issues including those concerning the régimes of the high seas, the continental shelf, the territorial sea (including the question of its breadth and the question of international straits) and contiguous zone, fishing and conservation of the living resources of the high seas (including the question of the preferential rights of coastal States), the preservation of the marine environment (including, *inter alia,* the prevention of pollution) and scientific research;

3. *Decides further* to review, at its twenty-sixth and twenty-seventh sessions, the reports of the Committee referred to in paragraph 6 below on the progress of its preparatory work with a view to determining the precise agenda of the conference on the law of the sea, its definitive date, location and duration, and related arrangements; if the General Assembly, at its twenty-seventh session, determines the progress of the preparatory work of the Committee to be insufficient, it may decide to postpone the conference;

4. *Reaffirms* the mandate of the Committee on the Peaceful Uses of the Sea-Bed and the Ocean Floor beyond the Limits of National Jurisdiction set forth in General Assembly resolution 2467 A (XXIII) as supplemented by the present resolution;

5. *Decides* to enlarge the Committee by forty-four members, appointed by the Chairman of the First Committee in consultation with regional groups and taking into account equitable geographical representation thereon;

6. *Instructs* the enlarged Committee on the Peaceful Uses of the Sea-Bed and the Ocean Floor beyond the Limits of National Jurisdiction to hold two sessions in Geneva, in March and in July-August 1971, in order to prepare for the conference on the law of the sea draft treaty articles embodying the international régime—including an international machinery—for the area and the resources of the sea-bed and the ocean floor, and the subsoil thereof, beyond the limits of national jurisdiction, taking into account the equitable sharing by all States in the benefits to be derived therefrom, bearing in mind the special interests and needs of developing countries, whether coastal or land-locked, on the basis of the Declaration of Principles Governing the Sea-Bed and the Ocean Floor, and the Subsoil Thereof, beyond the Limits of National Jurisdiction, and a com-

42 See A/7925 and Add.1-3.

43 *Official Records of the General Assembly, Twenty-fifth Session, Supplement No. 21* (A/8021).

44 Resolution 2749 (XXV).

prehensive list of subjects and issues relating to the law of the sea referred to in paragraph 2 above, which should be dealt with by the conference, and draft articles on such subjects and issues;

7. *Authorizes* the Committee to establish such subsidiary organs as it deems necessary for the efficient performance of its functions, bearing in mind the scientific, economic, legal and technical aspects of the issues involved;

8. *Requests* the Committee to prepare, as appropriate, reports to the General Assembly on the progress of its work;

9. *Requests* the Secretary-General to circulate those reports to Member States and to observers to the United Nations for their comments and observations;

10. *Decides* to invite other Member States which are not appointed to the Committee to participate as observers and to be heard on specific points;

11. *Requests* the Secretary-General to render the Committee all the assistance it may require in legal, economic, technical and scientific matters, including the provision of relevant records of the General Assembly and specialized agencies for the efficient performance of its functions;

12. *Decides* that the enlarged Committee, as well as its subsidiary organs, shall have summary records of its proceedings;

13. *Invites* the United Nations Educational, Scientific and Cultural Organization and its Intergovernmental Oceanographic Commission, the Food and Agriculture Organization of the United Nations and its Committee on Fisheries, the World Health Organization, the Inter-Governmental Maritime Consultative Organization, the World Meteorological Organization, the International Atomic Energy Agency and other intergovernmental bodies and specialized agencies concerned to co-operate fully with the enlarged Committee on the Peaceful Uses of the Sea-Bed and the Ocean Floor beyond the Limits of National Jurisdiction in the implementation of the present resolution, in particular by preparing such scientific and technical documentation as the Committee may request.

1933rd plenary meeting,
17 December 1970.

* * *

The Chairman of the First Committee subsequently informed the Secretary-General[45] *that, in pursuance of paragraph 5 of resolution C above, he had appointed forty-three of the forty-four additional members of the Committee on the Peaceful Uses of the Sea-Bed and the Ocean Floor beyond the Limits of National Jurisdiction, namely:* AFGHANISTAN, ALGERIA, BOLIVIA, *the* BYELORUSSIAN SOVIET SOCIALIST REPUBLIC, COLOMBIA, *the* CONGO (DEMOCRATIC REPUBLIC OF), CYPRUS, DENMARK, ECUADOR, ETHIOPIA, GABON, GHANA, GREECE, GUATEMALA, GUINEA, GUYANA, HUNGARY, INDONESIA, IRAN, IRAQ, *the* IVORY COAST, JAMAICA, LEBANON, MALI, MAURITIUS, MOROCCO, NEPAL, *the* NETHERLANDS, NEW ZEALAND, PANAMA, *the* PEOPLE'S REPUBLIC OF THE CONGO, *the* PHILIPPINES, SENEGAL, SINGAPORE, SOMALIA, SPAIN, SWEDEN, TUNISIA, TURKEY, *the* UKRAINIAN SOVIET SOCIALIST REPUBLIC, URUGUAY, VENEZUELA *and* YEMEN.

As a result of the above appointments, the Committee is composed of the following Member States: AFGHANISTAN, ALGERIA, ARGENTINA, AUSTRALIA, AUSTRIA, BELGIUM, BOLIVIA, BRAZIL, BULGARIA, BYELORUSSIAN SOVIET SOCIALIST REPUBLIC, CAMEROON, CANADA, CEYLON, CHILE, COLOMBIA, CONGO (DEMOCRATIC REPUBLIC OF), CYPRUS, CZECHOSLOVAKIA, DENMARK, ECUADOR, EL SALVADOR, ETHIOPIA, FRANCE, GABON, GHANA, GREECE, GUATEMALA, GUINEA, GUYANA, HUNGARY, ICELAND, INDIA, INDONESIA, IRAN, IRAQ, ITALY, IVORY COAST, JAMAICA, JAPAN, KENYA, KUWAIT, LEBANON, LIBERIA, LIBYAN ARAB REPUBLIC, MADAGASCAR, MALAYSIA, MALI, MALTA, MAURITANIA, MAURITIUS, MEXICO, MOROCCO, NEPAL, NETHERLANDS, NEW ZEALAND, NIGERIA, NORWAY, PAKISTAN, PANAMA, PEOPLE'S REPUBLIC OF THE CONGO, PERU, PHILIPPINES, POLAND, ROMANIA, SENEGAL, SIERRA LEONE, SINGAPORE, SOMALIA, SPAIN, SUDAN, SWEDEN, THAILAND, TRINIDAD AND TOBAGO, TUNISIA, TURKEY, UKRAINIAN SOVIET SOCIALIST REPUBLIC, UNION OF SOVIET SOCIALIST REPUBLICS, UNITED ARAB REPUBLIC, UNITED KINGDOM OF GREAT BRITAIN AND NORTHERN IRELAND, UNITED REPUBLIC OF TANZANIA, UNITED STATES OF AMERICA, URUGUAY, VENEZUELA, YEMEN *and* YUGOSLAVIA.

---

[45] See *Official Records of the General Assembly, Twenty-fifth Session, Annexes,* agenda item 25, document A/8273.

UN GENERAL ASSEMBLY RESOLUTION 2749 (XXV), DECEMBER 17, 1970

2749 (XXV). Declaration of Principles Governing the Sea-Bed and the Ocean Floor, and the Subsoil Thereof, beyond the Limits of National Jurisdiction

The General Assembly,

Recalling its resolutions 2340 (XXII) of 18 December 1967, 2467 (XXIII) of 21 December 1968 and 2574 (XXIV) of 15 December 1969, concerning the area to which the title of the item refers,

Affirming that there is an area of the sea-bed and the ocean floor, and the subsoil thereof, beyond the limits of national jurisdiction, the precise limits of which are yet to be determined,

Recognizing that the existing legal régime of the high seas does not provide substantive rules for regulating the exploration of the aforesaid area and the exploitation of its resources,

Convinced that the area shall be reserved exclusively for peaceful purposes and that the exploration of the area and the exploitation of its resources shall be carried out for the benefit of mankind as a whole,

Believing it essential that an international régime applying to the area and its resources and including appropriate international machinery should be established as soon as possible,

Bearing in mind that the development and use of the area and its resources shall be undertaken in such a manner as to foster the healthy development of the world economy and balanced growth of international trade, and to minimize any adverse economic effects caused by the fluctuation of prices of raw materials resulting from such activities,

Solemnly declares that:

1. The sea-bed and ocean floor, and the subsoil thereof, beyond the limits of national jurisdiction (hereinafter referred to as the area), as well as the resources of the area, are the common heritage of mankind.

2. The area shall not be subject to appropriation by any means by States or persons, natural or juridical, and no State shall claim or exercise sovereignty or sovereign rights over any part thereof.

3. No State or person, natural or juridical, shall claim, exercise or acquire rights with respect to the area or its resources incompatible with the international régime to be established and the principles of this Declaration.

4. All activities regarding the exploration and exploitation of the resources of the area and other related activities shall be governed by the international régime to be established.

5. The area shall be open to use exclusively for peaceful purposes by all States, whether coastal or land-locked, without discrimination, in accordance with the international régime to be established.

6. States shall act in the area in accordance with the applicable principles and rules of international law, including the Charter of the United Nations and the Declaration on Principles of International Law concerning Friendly Relations and Co-operation among States in accordance with the Charter of the United Nations, adopted by the General Assembly on 24 October 1970,[38] in the interests of maintaining international peace and security and promoting international co-operation and mutual understanding.

7. The exploration of the area and the exploitation of its resources shall be carried out for the benefit of mankind as a whole, irrespective of the geographical location of States, whether land-locked or coastal, and taking into particular consideration the interests and needs of the developing countries.

8. The area shall be reserved exclusively for peaceful purposes, without prejudice to any measures which have been or may be agreed upon in the context of international negotiations undertaken in the field of disarmament and which may be applicable to a broader area. One or more international agreements shall be concluded as soon as possible in order to implement effectively this principle and to constitute a step towards the exclusion of the sea-bed, the ocean floor and the subsoil thereof from the arms race.

9. On the basis of the principles of this Declaration, an international régime applying to the area and its resources and including appropriate international machinery to give effect to its provisions shall be established by an international treaty of a universal character, generally agreed upon. The régime shall, *inter alia,* provide for the orderly and safe development and rational management of the area and its resources and for expanding opportunities in the use thereof, and ensure the equitable sharing by States in the benefits derived therefrom, taking into particular consideration the interests and needs of the developing countries, whether land-locked or coastal.

10. States shall promote international co-operation in scientific research exclusively for peaceful purposes:

(*a*) By participation in international programmes and by encouraging co-operation in scientific research by personnel of different countries;

(*b*) Through effective publication of research programmes and dissemination of the results of research through international channels;

(*c*) By co-operation in measures to strengthen research capabilities of developing countries, including the participation of their nationals in research programmes.

No such activity shall form the legal basis for any claims with respect to any part of the area or its resources.

11. With respect to activities in the area and acting in conformity with the international régime to be established, States shall take appropriate measures for and shall co-operate in the adoption and implementation of international rules, standards and procedures for, *inter alia*:

(*a*) The prevention of pollution and contamination, and other hazards to the marine environment, including the coastline, and of interference with the ecological balance of the marine environment;

38 Resolution 2625 (XXV).

(*b*) The protection and conservation of the natural resources of the area and the prevention of damage to the flora and fauna of the marine environment.

12. In their activities in the area, including those relating to its resources, States shall pay due regard to the rights and legitimate interests of coastal States in the region of such activities, as well as of all other States, which may be affected by such activities. Consultations shall be maintained with the coastal States concerned with respect to activities relating to the exploration of the area and the exploitation of its resources with a view to avoiding infringement of such rights and interests.

13. Nothing herein shall affect:

(*a*) The legal status of the waters superjacent to the area or that of the air space above those waters;

(*b*) The rights of coastal States with respect to measures to prevent, mitigate or eliminate grave and imminent danger to their coastline or related interests from pollution or threat thereof or from other hazardous occurrences resulting from or caused by any activities in the area, subject to the international régime to be established.

14. Every State shall have the responsibility to ensure that activities in the area, including those relating to its resources, whether undertaken by governmental agencies, or non-governmental entities or persons under its jurisdiction, or acting on its behalf, shall be carried out in conformity with the international régime to be established. The same responsibility applies to international organizations and their members for activities undertaken by such organizations or on their behalf. Damage caused by such activities shall entail liability.

15. The parties to any dispute relating to activities in the area and its resources shall resolve such dispute by the measures mentioned in Article 33 of the Charter of the United Nations and such procedures for settling disputes as may be agreed upon in the international régime to be established.

1933rd plenary meeting,
17 December 1970.

UNITED NATIONS
GENERAL ASSEMBLY

Distr.
GENERAL

A/RES/2881 (XXVI)
13 January 1972

Twenty-sixth session
Agenda item 35

RESOLUTION ADOPTED BY THE GENERAL ASSEMBLY
(on the report of the First Committee (A/8623, A/L.670))

2881 (XXVI). Reservation exclusively for peaceful purposes of the sea-bed and the ocean floor, and the subsoil thereof, underlying the high seas beyond the limits of present national jurisdiction and use of their resources in the interests of mankind, and convening of a conference on the law of the sea

The General Assembly,

Recalling its resolutions 2340 (XXII) of 18 December 1967, 2467 (XXIII) of 21 December 1968, 2574 (XXIV) of 15 December 1969 and 2750 (XXV) of 17 December 1970,

Having considered the report of the Committee on the Peaceful Uses of the Sea-Bed and the Ocean Floor beyond the Limits of National Jurisdiction, 1/

1. Notes with satisfaction the encouraging progress of the preparatory work of the Committee on the Peaceful Uses of the Sea-Bed and the Ocean Floor beyond the Limits of National Jurisdiction towards a comprehensive conference on the law of the sea, in conformity with its mandate contained in General Assembly resolution 2750 C (XXV), in particular with regard to the elaboration of the international regime and machinery for the sea-bed and the ocean floor, and the subsoil thereof, beyond the limits of national jurisdiction;

2. Notes also the consideration by the Committee of the reports submitted by the Secretary-General 2/ pursuant to resolutions 2750 A and B (XXV) and of the study of possible methods and criteria for the sharing of benefits derived from the exploitation of the resources of the area, 3/ undertaken in accordance with the Committee's request of March 1970;

3. Decides to add to the membership of the Committee China and four other members to be appointed by the Chairman of the First Committee in consultation with regional groups with due regard to the interests of under-represented groups;

4. Requests the Committee, in the discharge of its mandate in accordance with resolution 2750 C (XXV), to hold two sessions, one in New York during March-April and one at Geneva during July-August 1972

2029th plenary meeting,
21 December 1971.

1/ Official Records of the General Assembly, Twenty-sixth Session, Supplement No. 21 (A/8421).

2/ A/AC. 138/36 and A/AC.138/37 and Corr. 1 and 2, which are summarized in Supplement No. 21.

3/ A/AC. 138/38 and Corr. 1.

*

* *

At the 2031st plenary meeting, on 22 December 1971, the Chairman of the First Committee announced that, in pursuance of paragraph 3 of the above resolution, he had appointed the following States members of the Committee on the Peaceful Uses of the Sea-Bed and the Ocean Floor beyond the Limits of National Jurisdiction: Fiji, Finland, Nicaragua and Zambia.

As a result, the Committee is composed of the following Member States: Afghanistan, Algeria, Argentina, Australia, Austria, Belgium, Bolivia, Brazil, Bulgaria, Byelorussian Soviet Socialist Republic, Cameroon, Canada, Ceylon, Chile, China, Colombia, Congo, Cyprus, Czechoslovakia, Denmark, Ecuador, Egypt, El Salvador, Ethiopia, Fiji, Finland, France, Gabon, Ghana, Greece, Guatemala, Guinea, Guyana, Hungary, Iceland, India, Indonesia, Iran, Iraq, Italy, Ivory Coast, Jamaica, Japan, Kenya, Kuwait, Lebanon, Liberia, Libyan Arab Republic, Madagascar, Malaysia, Mali, Malta, Mauritania, Mauritius, Mexico, Morocco, Nepal, Netherlands, New Zealand, Nicaragua, Nigeria, Norway, Pakistan, Panama, Peru, Philippines, Poland, Romania, Senegal, Sierra Leone, Singapore, Somalia, Spain, Sudan, Sweden, Thailand, Trinidad and Tobago, Tunisia, Turkey, Ukrainian Soviet Socialist Republic, Union of Soviet Socialist Republics, United Kingdom of Great Britain and Northern Ireland, United Republic of Tanzania, United States of America, Uruguay, Venezuela, Yemen, Yugoslavia, Zaire and Zambia.

COMMITTEE ON THE PEACEFUL USES OF THE SEA-BED AND THE OCEAN FLOOR BEYOND THE LIMITS OF NATIONAL JURISDICTION

LIST OF SUBJECTS AND ISSUES RELATING TO THE LAW OF THE SEA*

1. International Regime for the Sea-Bed and the Ocean Floor Beyond National Jurisdiction
   - 1.1 Nature and Characteristics
   - 1.2 International Machinery: Structure, Functions, Powers
   - 1.3 Economic Implications
   - 1.4 Equitable Sharing of Benefits Bearing in Mind the Special Interests and Needs of the Developing Countries, whether Coastal or Land-Locked.
   - 1.5 Definition and Limits of the Area.
     (To be considered in the light of the procedural agreement as set out in paragraph 22 of the report of the committee (A/8421).)
   - 1.6 Use Exclusively for Peaceful Purposes

2. Territorial Sea
   - 2.1 Nature and Characteristics, Including the Question of the Unity or Plurality of Regimes in the Territorial Sea
   - 2.2 Historic Waters
   - 2.3 Limits
   - 2.3.1 Question of the Delimitation of the Territorial Sea: Various Aspects Involved
   - 2.3.2. Breadth of the Territorial Sea. Global or Regional Criteria. Open Seas and Oceans, Semi-Enclosed Seas and Enclosed Seas
   - 2.4 Innocent Passage in the Territorial Sea
   - 2.5 Freedom of Navigation and Overflight Resulting From the Question of Plurality of Regimes in the Territorial Sea

3. Contiguous Zone
   - 3.1 Nature and Characteristics
   - 3.2 Limits
   - 3.3 Rights of Coastal States with Regard to National Security, Customs and Fiscal Control, Sanitation and Immigration Regulations

---

*Editor's Note: Adopted by the Committee on August 16, 1972. It is anticipated that this list will form the basis for the agenda of the Third Conference on the Law of the Sea presently scheduled to commence in 1973.

4. Straits Used for International Navigation
  4.1 Innocent Passage
  4.2 Other Related Matters Including the Question of the Right of Transit

5. Continental Shelf
  5.1 Nature and Scope of the Sovereign Rights of Coastal States Over the Continental Shelf. Duties of States
  5.2 Outer Limit of the Continental Shelf: Applicable Criteria
  5.3 Question of the Delimitation Between States: Various Aspects Involved
  5.4 Natural Resources of the Continental Shelf
  5.5 Regime for Waters Superjacent to the Continental Shelf
  5.6 Scientific Research

6. Exclusive Economic Zone Beyond the Territorial Sea
  6.1 Nature and Characteristics, Including Rights and Jurisdiction of Coastal States in Relation to Resources, Pollution Control and Scientific Research in the Zone. Duties of States
  6.2 Resources of the Zone
  6.3 Freedom of Navigation and Overflight
  6.4 Regional Arrangements
  6.5 Limits: Applicable Criteria
  6.6 Fisheries
  6.6.1 Exclusive Fishery Zone
  6.6.2 Preferential Rights of Coastal States
  6.6.3 Management and Conservation
  6.6.4 Protection of Coastal States' Fisheries in Enclosed and Semi-Enclosed Seas
  6.6.5 Regime of Islands Under Foreign Domination and Control in Relation to Zones of Exclusive Fishing Jurisdiction.
  6.7 Sea-Bed Within National Jurisdiction
  6.7.1 Nature and Characteristics
  6.7.2 Delineation Between Adjacent and Opposite States
  6.7.3 Sovereign Rights Over Natural Resources
  6.7.4 Limits: Applicable Criteria
  6.8 Prevention and Control of Pollution and Other Hazards to the Marine Environment
  6.8.1 Rights and Responsibilities of Coastal States
  6.9 Scientific Research

7. Coastal State Preferential Rights or Other Non-Exclusive Jurisdiction Over Resources Beyond the Territorial Sea
   7.1 Nature, Scope and Characteristics
   7.2 Sea-Bed Resources
   7.3 Fisheries
   7.4 Prevention and Control of Pollution and Other Hazards to the Marine Environment
   7.5 International Cooperation in the Study and Rational Exploitation of Marine Resources
   7.6 Settlement of Disputes
   7.7 Other Rights and Obligations

8. High Seas
   8.1 Nature and Characteristics
   8.2 Rights and Duties of States
   8.3 Question of the Freedoms of the High Seas and Their Regulation
   8.4 Management and Conservation of Living Resources
   8. 5 Slavery, Piracy, Drugs
   8.6 Hot Pursuit

9. Land-Locked Countries
   9.1 General Principles of the Law of the Sea Concerning the Land-Locked Countries
   9.2 Rights and Interests of Land-Locked Countries
   9.2.1 Free Access To and From the Sea: Freedom of Transit, Means and Facilities for Transport and Communications
   9.2.2. Equality of Treatment in the Ports of Transit States
   9.2.3. Free Access to the International Sea-Bed Area Beyond National Jurisdiction
   9.2.4. Participation in the International Regime, Including the Machinery and the Equitable Sharing in the Benefits of the Area
   9.3 Particular Interests and Needs of Developing Land-Locked Countries in the International Regime
   9.4 Rights and Interests of Land-Locked Countries in Regard to Living Resources of the Sea

10. Rights and Interests of Shelf-Locked States and States with Narrow Shelves or Short Coastlines
   10.1 International Regime
   10.2 Fisheries

10.3 Special Interests and Needs of Developing Shelf-Locked States and States with Narrow Shelves or Short Coastlines
10.4 Free Access To and From the High Seas

11. Rights and Interests of States with Broad Shelves

12. Preservation of the Marine Environment
12.1 Sources of Pollution and Other Hazards and Measures to Combat Them
12.2 Measures to Preserve the Ecological Balance of the Marine Environment
12.3 Responsibility and Liability for Damage to the Marine Environment and to the Coastal State
12.4 Rights and Duties of Coastal States
12.5 International Cooperation

13. Scientific Research
13.1 Nature, Characteristics and Objectives of Scientific Research of the Oceans
13.2 Access to Scientific Information
13.3 International Cooperation

14. Development and Transfer of Technology
14.1 Development of Technological Capabilities of Developing Countries
14.1.1 Sharing of Knowledge and Technology Between Developed and Developing Countries
14.1.2 Training of Personnel from Developing Countries
14.1.3 Transfer of Technology to Developing Countries

15. Regional Arrangements

16. Archipelagoes

17. Enclosed and Semi-Enclosed Seas

18. Artificial Islands and Installations

19. Regime of Islands:
(A) Islands Under Colonial Dependence or Foreign Domination or Control:
(B) Other Related Matters

20. Responsibility and Liability for Damage Resulting From the Use of the Marine Environment

21. Settlement of Disputes

22. Peaceful Uses of the Ocean Space: Zones of Peace and Security

23. Archaeological and Historical Treasures on the Sea-Bed and Ocean Floor Beyond the Limits of National Jurisdiction

24. Transmission from the High Seas

25. Enhancing the Universal Participation of States in Multilateral Conventions Relating to the Law of the Sea

United States Policy for the Seabed

STATEMENT BY PRESIDENT NIXON [1]

The nations of the world are now facing decisions of momentous importance to man's use of the oceans for decades ahead. At issue is whether the oceans will be used rationally and equitably and for the benefit of mankind or whether they will become an arena of unrestrained exploitation and conflicting jurisdictional claims in which even the most advantaged states will be losers.

The issue arises now—and with urgency—because nations have grown increasingly conscious of the wealth to be exploited from the seabeds and throughout the waters above and because they are also becoming apprehensive about ecological hazards of unregulated use of the oceans and seabeds. The stark fact is that the law of the sea is inadequate to meet the needs of modern technology and the concerns of the international community. If it is not modernized multilaterally, unilateral action and international conflict are inevitable.

This is the time, then, for all nations to set about resolving the basic issues of the future regime for the oceans—and to resolve it in a way that redounds to the general benefit in the era of intensive exploitation that lies ahead. The United States, as a major maritime power and a leader in ocean technology to unlock the riches of the ocean, has a special responsibility to move this effort forward.

Therefore, I am today proposing that all nations adopt as soon as possible a treaty under which they would renounce all national claims over the natural resources of the seabed beyond the point where the high seas reach a depth of 200 meters (218.8 yards) and would agree to regard these resources as the common heritage of mankind.

The treaty should establish an international regime for the exploitation of seabed resources beyond this limit. The regime should provide for the collection of substantial mineral royalties to be used for international community purposes, particularly economic assistance to developing countries. It should also establish general rules to prevent unreasonable interference with other uses of the ocean, to protect the ocean from pollution, to assure the integrity of the investment necessary for such exploitation, and to provide for peaceful and compulsory settlement of disputes.

I propose two types of machinery for authorizing exploitation of seabed resources beyond a depth of 200 meters.

First, I propose that coastal nations act as trustees for the international community in an international trusteeship zone comprised of the continental margins beyond a depth of 200 meters off their coasts. In return, each coastal state would receive a share of the international revenues from the zone in which it acts as trustee and could impose additional taxes if these were deemed desirable.

As a second step, agreed international machinery would authorize and regulate exploration and use of seabed resources beyond the continental margins.

The United States will introduce specific proposals at the next meeting of the United Nations Seabeds Committee to carry out these objectives.

Although I hope agreement on such steps can be reached quickly, the negotiation of such a complex treaty may take some time. I do not, however, believe it is either necessary or desirable to try to halt exploration and exploitation

[1] Issued on May 23 (White House press release).

of the seabeds beyond a depth of 200 meters during the negotiating process.

Accordingly, I call on other nations to join the United States in an interim policy. I suggest that all permits for exploration and exploitation of the seabeds beyond 200 meters be issued subject to the international regime to be agreed upon. The regime should accordingly include due protection for the integrity of investments made in the interim period. A substantial portion of the revenues derived by a state from exploitation beyond 200 meters during this interim period should be turned over to an appropriate international development agency for assistance to developing countries. I would plan to seek appropriate congressional action to make such funds available as soon as a sufficient number of other states also indicate their willingness to join this interim policy.

I will propose necessary changes in the domestic import and tax laws and regulations of the United States to assure that our own laws and regulations do not discriminate against U.S. nationals operating in the trusteeship zone off our coast or under the authority of the international machinery to be established.

It is equally important to assure unfettered and harmonious use of the oceans as an avenue of commerce and transportation and as a source of food. For this reason the United States is currently engaged with other states in an effort to obtain a new law-of-the-sea treaty. This treaty would establish a 12-mile limit for territorial seas and provide for free transit through international straits. It would also accommodate the problems of developing countries and other nations regarding the conservation and use of the living resources of the high seas.

I believe that these proposals are essential to the interests of all nations, rich and poor, coastal and landlocked, regardless of their political systems. If they result in international agreements, we can save over two-thirds of the earth's surface from national conflict and rivalry, protect it from pollution, and put it to use for the benefit of all. This would be a fitting achievement for this 25th anniversary year of the United Nations.

SUMMARY OF PROVISIONS OF DRAFT "UNITED NATIONS CONVENTION ON THE INTERNATIONAL SEABED AREA"

(Prepared by John R. Stevenson, Legal Adviser, Department of State)

On May 23, 1970, President Nixon announced a new oceans policy for the United States and stated that the United States would make specific proposals at the UN Seabeds Committee in August with regard to the proposed regime for the seabeds beyond national jurisdiction which he set forth in broad outline in his announcement. The submission of a draft "United Nations Convention on the International Seabed Area" to the Seabeds Committee as a working paper for discussion within that Committee as well as with other governments and within the United States, implements the President's announcement. The draft Convention and its appendices raise a number of questions with respect to which further detailed study is clearly necessary and do not necessarily represent the definitive views of the United States Government.

The basic structure of the Convention reflects the President's proposals that States should by international agreement renounce their sovereign rights in the seabed under the high seas* beyond a water depth of 200 meters; establish an

*The President also referred to the U.S. proposals to fix the boundary between the territorial sea and the high seas at a maximum of 12 nautical miles with free transit through international straits and carefully defined preferential fishing rights for coastal states on the high seas.

international regime for the area beyond with certain basic principles and general rules applicable throughout this area; authorize coastal States as Trustees for the international community to carry out the major administrative role in licensing the exploration and exploitation of natural resources from the limit of coastal State national jurisdiction to the edge of the continental margin, and to share in the international revenues from the Trusteeship Area which they administered; and establish international machinery to perform similar functions in the area beyond the continental margin.

Basic Principles

Among the basic principles which would become applicable to the entire International Seabed Area (including the International Trusteeship Area) under the Convention would be the following:

The International Seabed Area would be the common heritage of mankind and no State could exercise sovereignty or sovereign rights over this area or its resources, or, except as provided in the Convention, acquire any right or interest therein.

The International Seabed Area would be open to use by all States without discrimination, except as otherwise provided in the Convention, and would be reserved exclusively for peaceful purposes.

Provision would be made for the collection of revenues from mineral production in the Area to be used for international community purposes including economic advancement of developing countries and to promote the safe, efficient and economic exploitation of the mineral resources of the seabed.

Exploration and exploitation of the natural resources of the Area must not result in unjustified interference with other activities in the marine environment and all activities in the Area must be conducted with adequate safeguards against pollution and for the protection of human life and the marine environment.

A Contracting Party would be responsible for ensuring that those authorized by it (as Trustee in the Trusteeship Area) or sponsored by it (in the area beyond) complied with the Convention. Contracting Parties would also be responsible for any damage caused by those authorized or sponsored by them.

The general rules would be as follows:

Mineral Resources

All exploration and exploitation of the mineral deposits in the Area would be licensed by the appropriate Trustee in the Trusteeship Area and by the International Seabed Resource Authority in the area beyond subject to general provisions relating to the terms of licenses included in Appendices forming part of the Convention, a number of which allow greater discretion to the Trustee State in the case of the Trusteeship Area. The Contracting Parties would have primary responsibility for inspecting activities licensed or sponsored by them. The International Seabed Resource Authority would also have authority to inspect and determine if a licensed operation violates the Convention. Licenses would be revoked only for cause and in accordance with the Convention. Expropriation of investments made, or unjustifiable interference with operations conducted pursuant to a license, would be prohibited.

Living Resources of the Seabed

All Contracting Parties would have the right to explore and exploit these resources (e.g., king crab) subject to necessary conservation measures and the right of the Trustee in the Trusteeship Area to decide whether and by whom such resources should be exploited.

Protection of the Marine Environment, Life and Property

The International Seabed Resource Authority would be authorized to prescribe rules to protect against pollution of the marine environment and injury to persons and resources resulting from exploration and exploitation and to prevent unjustifiable interference with other activities in the marine environment.

Scientific Research

Each party would agree to encourage and to obviate interference with scientific research and to promote international cooperation in scientific research.

International Trusteeship Area

The provisions of the Convention relating to the International Trusteeship Area would define the outer limit of this area as a line beyond the base of the continental slope where the downward inclination of the seabed reaches a specified gradient. Such gradient would be determined by technical experts who would take into account, among other factors, ease of determination, the need to avoid dual administration of single resource deposits and the avoidance of including excessively large areas in the Trusteeship Area. Other provisions would limit the Trustee's rights to those set forth in the Convention. These rights of the Trustee State would include the issuing, suspending and revoking of mineral exploration and exploitation licenses subject to the rules set forth in the Convention and its Appendices, full discretion to decide whether a license should be issued and to whom a license should be issued, exercise of criminal and civil jurisdiction over its licensees, and retention of a portion (a figure between 33-1/3% and 50% is suggested for consideration) of the fees and payments required under the Convention for activities in the Area. The Trustee State would also be able to collect and retain additional license and rental fees to defray its administrative expenses and to collect other additional payments, retaining the same portion as indicated above of such other additional payments.

International Seabed Resource Authority

The principal organs of the proposed International Seabed Resource Authority would be an Assembly of all Contracting Parties; a Council of 24 members, including the six most industrially advanced Contracting States, at least twelve developing countries and at least two landlocked or shelf-locked States; and a Tribunal of from five to nine judges elected by the Council.

The Assembly, which would meet at least once every three years, would elect members of the Council, approve budgets proposed by the Council, approve proposals of the Council for changes in allocation of net income within the limits prescribed in an Appendix to the Convention, and make recommendations.

The Council, which would make decisions only with the approval of a majority of both the six most industrially advanced Contracting States and of the eighteen other Contracting States, would appoint the Commissions provided for in the Convention, submit to the Assembly budgets and proposals for changes in the allocation of net income within the limits prescribed in an Appendix, and could issue emergency orders at the request of a Contracting Party to prevent serious harm to the marine environment.

The Tribunal would decide all disputes and advise on all questions relating to the interpretation and application of the Convention. It would have compulsory jurisdiction in respect of any complaint brought by a Contracting Party against another Contracting Party for failure to fulfill its obligations under the Convention, or whenever the Operations Commission, on its own initiative or at the request of any licensee, considered that a Contracting Party or licensee had failed to fulfill its obligations under the Convention. If the Tribunal found the Contracting Party or licensee in default, such Party or licensee would be obligated to take the measures required to implement the Tribunal's judgment. The Tribunal would have the power to impose fines of not more than $1,000 for each day of an offense as well as to award damages to the other Party concerned. Where the Tribunal determined that a licensee had committed a gross and persistent violation of the provisions of the Convention and within a reasonable time had not brought its operations into compliance, the Council could either revoke the license or request the Trustee Party to do so. Where a Contracting Party failed to perform the obligations incumbent on it under a judgment of the Tribunal, the Council, on application of the other Party to the case, could decide upon measures to give effect to the judgment, including, when appropriate, temporary suspension of the rights of the defaulting Party under the Convention (the extent of such suspension to be related to the extent and seriousness of the violation). In addition, any Contracting Party, and any person directly affected, could bring before the Tribunal the question of the legality of any measure taken by the Council, or one of its Commissions, on the ground of violation of the Convention, lack of jurisdiction, infringement of important procedural rules, unreasonableness, or misuse of powers; and the Tribunal could declare such measure null and void.

The Convention also provides for the establishment of three Commissions, each of from five to nine members. The Rules and Recommended Practices Commission would consider and recommend to the Council adoption of Annexes as described below. The Operations Commission would issue licenses for mineral exploration and exploitation in the area beyond the International Trusteeship Area and supervise the operations of licensees in cooperation with the Trustee or Sponsoring Party, but not itself engage in exploration or exploitation. The International Seabed Boundary Review Commission would review the delineation of boundaries submitted by the Contracting Parties for approval in accordance with the Convention, negotiate differences among the Parties and if the differences were not resolved initiate appropriate proceedings before the Tribunal, and render advice to Contracting Parties on boundary questions.

The members of the Rules and Recommended Practices Commission and the International Seabed Boundary Review Commission would not be full-time employees of the Authority.

The Secretariat of the Authority would consist of a Secretary-General appointed by the Council and a staff appointed by the Secretary-General under the general guidelines established by the Council.

Any amendment of the Convention or the Appendices would require the approval of the Council and a two-thirds vote of the Assembly and would come into force only when ratified by two-thirds of the Contracting Parties, including each of the six most industrially advanced Contracting States.

Appendices, which are integral parts of the Convention, are included in the draft Convention by way of example only as they require extensive consideration of the questions involved by technically qualified experts.

The illustrative Appendices included in the draft Convention relate to (a) terms and procedures applying to all licenses in the International Seabed Area; (b) terms and procedures applying to licenses in the International Seabed Area beyond the International Trusteeship Area; (c) terms and procedures for licenses in the International Trusteeship Area; (d) division of revenue; and (e) designation of members of the Council representing the six most industrially advanced States.

Appendix A, applicable to the entire International Seabed Area, would provide for non-exclusive exploration licenses not restricted as to area authorizing geophysical and geochemical measurements and bottom sampling and exclusive exploitation licenses including the right to undertake deep drilling which would expire at the end of fifteen years if no commercial production were achieved. Deep drilling for purposes other than exploration or exploitation of seabed minerals would be authorized under a permit issued at no charge by the Authority provided the proposed drilling would not pose an uncontrollable hazard to human safety and the environment. Appendix A also provides for certification by the Trustee or Sponsoring Party of the Operator's technical and financial competence. Minimum and maximum limits on required license fees (the applicable fee to be specified in an Annex to the Convention with authorization to the Trustee or Sponsoring Party to impose additional fees within specified limits to help cover its administrative costs) are set out. Provision is also made for the categories of minerals and areas covered by licenses and relinquishment of part of the licensed area when production commences. Maximum and minimum required rental fees prior to and after attaining commercial production (the applicable fee to be specified in an Annex to the Convention) and minimum annual work requirements are provided for. Submission of work plans and data under exploitation licenses prior to commercial production and submission of production plans and reports is required. Rules are set forth with regard to unit operations. Appendix A further contains minimum and maximum required payments on production, the applicable amount to be specified in an Annex to the Convention (such payments to be percentages of the gross value at the site of oil and gas or minerals, to be proportional to production, and to be in the nature of payments ordinarily made to governments under similar conditions). The levels of payments on production and work requirements would be graduated to take account of probable risk and cost to the investor, including such factors as water depth, climate, volume of production, vicinity to existing production, or other factors affecting the economic rent that can reasonably be anticipated from mineral production in a given area. Finally, the operator and the Authorizing or Sponsoring Party, as appropriate, would be liable for damage to other users of the environment, and operators would be required to subscribe to an insurance plan or provide other means of guaranteeing responsibility.

Appendix B, applicable to the area beyond the International Trusteeship Area, would permit Contracting Parties to obtain exploration and exploitation licenses from the Authority if they designate a specific agency to act as operator on their behalf and to authorize persons they sponsor to apply for licenses. It would require the Sponsoring Party to certify as to the technical and financial competence of the operator and would require the Authority to grant licenses on proper application unless another application for the same block had been received at the monthly intervals at which applications were opened. If more than one application had been received, the license would be awarded in accordance with competitive bidding among the applicants. There would also be provision for award of a license by competitive bidding in the event of termination, forfeiture, or revocation of an exploitation license, or sale of a block contiguous to a block on which production had begun, or of a block from which hydrocarbons or other fluids were being drained. Appendix B would authorize transfer of an exploitation license with the approval of the Sponsoring Party and the Authority and the payment of a transfer fee. It would provide limits on the duration of exploitation licenses and would set out minimum and maximum work requirements, the applicable amount of such work requirements to be stipulated in an Annex to the Convention.

Appendix C, applicable solely to the International Trusteeship Area, would reaffirm the Trustee's exclusive right, in its discretion, to approve or disapprove applications for exploration and exploitation licenses and to use any system for this purpose. It would establish the term of the exploitation license and conditions, if any, under which it might be renewed, provided that continuance after the first 15 years is contingent upon achieving commercial production. Finally, Appendix C would impose proration and set work requirements above the minimums specified in Appendix A.

Appendix D would provide that the net income, after administrative expenses of the Authority, would be devoted to the economic advancement of developing States Parties to the Convention and would be divided among a list of stipulated international and regional development organizations, the list to indicate the percentages assigned to each organization.

Appendix E would stipulate the formula for determining the six most industrially advanced Contracting Parties for purposes of designation to the Council.

Annexes to the Convention would be prepared by the Rules and Recommended Practices Commission, submitted for comments to the Contracting Parties and to the Council for adoption and would come into force unless more than one-third of the Contracting Parties disapproved within three months. In addition to fixing the level, basis and accounting procedures for determining international fees and other forms of payment within the ranges specified in Appendix A and establishing work requirements for the area beyond the Trusteeship Area within the ranges specified in Appendix B, Annexes could establish criteria for defining the technical and financial competence of applicants for licenses and would assure that all exploration and exploitation activities and deep drilling would be conducted with strict and adequate safeguards for the protection of human life and safety, the marine environment and living marine organisms. Annexes would be drawn up to prevent or reduce to acceptable limits interference arising from exploration and exploitation activities with other uses and users of the marine environment, assure safe design and construction of fixed exploration and exploitation installations and equipment, and other related matters. Any Contracting Party believing that a provision of an Annex could not be reasonably applied to it because of special circumstances might seek a waiver from the Operations Commission.

The Convention would provide for due protection of the integrity of investments in the International Seabed Area made prior to the coming into force of the Convention. Authorizations by a Contracting Party to exploit mineral resources of the

International Seabed Area granted prior to July 1, 1970, would be continued without change after the coming into force of the Convention, with the Contracting Parties being obligated to pay the production requirements provided under the Convention. New activities under such authorizations would be subject to the regulatory requirements of the Convention relating to pollution and unjustifiable interference with other uses of the marine environment. With respect to authorizations granted after July 1, 1970, the authorizing Contracting Party would be bound either to issue a new license in its capacity as Trustee or, in the area beyond, to sponsor the licensee's application for a new license from the International Seabed Resource Authority. A new license issued by a Trustee would include the same terms and conditions as the previous authorization, and the Trustee would be responsible for compliance with the increased obligations resulting from the application of the Convention. Moreover, any Contracting Party authorizing activities after July 1, 1970, would be required to compensate the licensee for any investment losses resulting from the application of the Convention.

August 3, 1970

###

Schematic Representation of the Seabeds and Ocean Floor
(Showing the U.S. Proposal)

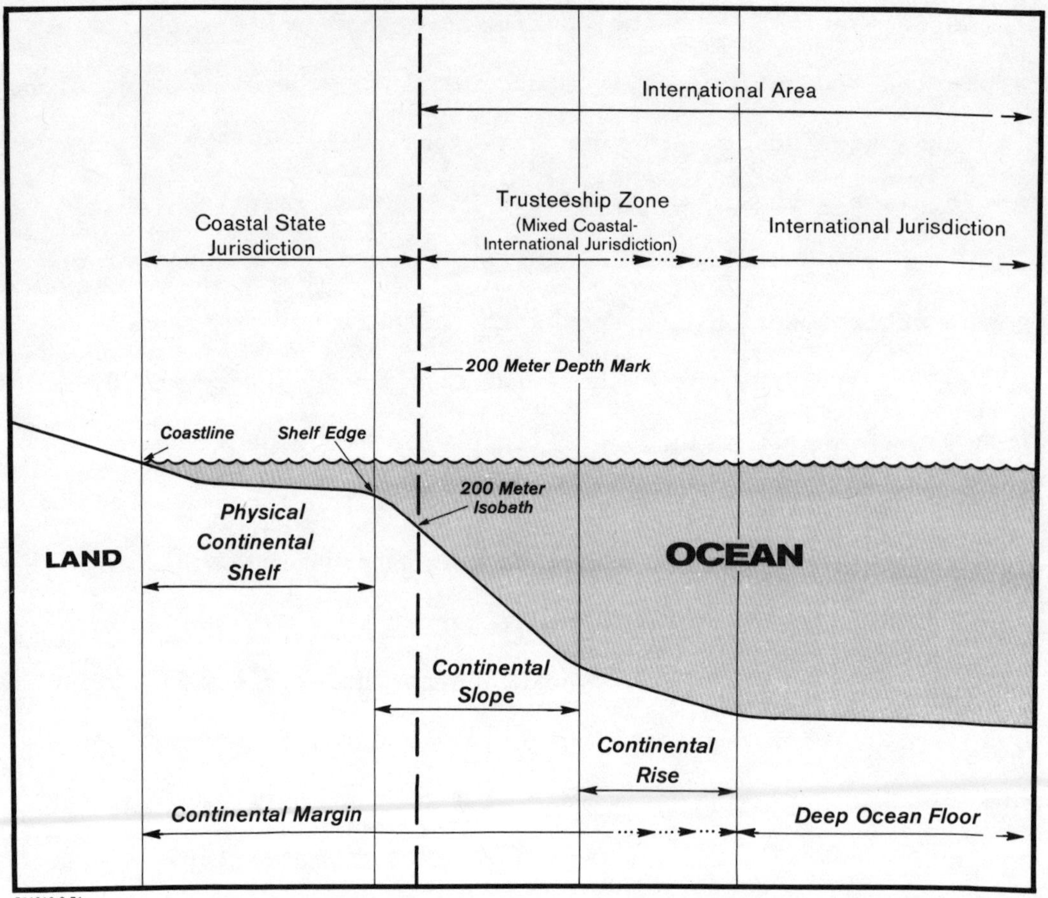

511616 6-71

IV. REFERENCE MATERIALS ON THE LAW OF THE SEA

Editor's Note:

LIST OF TREATIES RELATING TO THE LAW OF THE SEA.

There follows a list of treaties relating to the Law of the Sea concluded since 1945. A few pre-1945 treaties have also been included, either because their text is given in Parts I or II of this book, or because an agreement relating to them or amending them has been concluded since 1945. Only those treaties which are still in force are listed. The treaties listed under "Miscellaneous Conventions" are a selection: in general all treaties relating to commerce, trade and navigation, rivers, canals and the Great Lakes, and bilateral treaties relating to tonnage measurements and the safety of life at sea, have been omitted. Agreements concerning technical co-operation in fisheries have also been excluded. Even within these limitations it is realised that the list is not complete, although every attempt has been made to ensure that it is.

The list has been broken down into a number of headings and sub-headings (although some treaties appear under more than one heading). Within each sub-heading the treaties have been arranged chronologically after the date of signature. The information given is: title of treaty, date and place of signature, and date of entry into force. Reference is also made to where the text of the treaty may be found. If it is in the League of Nations Treaty Series (LNTS), United Nations Treaty Series (UNTS), United States Treaties and other International Agreements (UST), Treaties and Other International Acts Series (TIAS) or United Kingdom Treaty Series (UKTS), these references are given. Where it is not in any of them, another reference is given if known. Many of the treaties may be found in the UN collections referred to in the Introduction: separate references to them are not given here.

In general the information is correct to August 1, 1972.

TERRITORIAL SEA

1. Convention on International Civil Aviation. Signed at Chicago, December 7, 1944. In force April 4, 1947. 15 UNTS 295; 61 Stat. 1180; TIAS 1591; 1953 UKTS 8. (There have been a number of subsequent protocols amending the Convention: details are not given here).

2. Chile-Ecuador-Peru. Agreements signed at the First Conference on the Exploitation and Conservation of the Maritime Resources of the South Pacific, Santiago, August 18, 1952: (i) Declaration on the Maritime Zone; (ii) Organisation of the Standing Committee of the Conference on the Use and Conservation of the Marine Resources of the South Pacific; (iii) Joint Declaration of Fishery Problems in the South Pacific; (iv) Regulations governing Whaling in the Waters of the South Pacific.

Agreements signed at the Second Conference on the Exploitation and Conservation of the Maritime Resources of the South Pacific, Lima, December 4, 1954: (i) Agreement Supplementary to the Declaration of Sovereignty over the Maritime Zone of Two Hundred Miles; (ii) Agreement relating to Penalties; (iii) Agreement relating to Measures of Supervision and Control in the Maritime Zones of the Signatory Countries; (iv) Agreement relating to the Issue of Permits for the Exploitation of the Maritime Resources of the South Pacific; (v) Agreement relating to a Special Maritime Frontier Zone.

3. Norway-USSR. Agreement concerning the Sea Frontier between Norway and the USSR in the Varanger-fjord. Signed at Oslo, February 15, 1957. In force April 24, 1957. 312 UNTS 289.

Descriptive Protocol (with Annexes) relating to the Sea Frontier between Norway and the USSR in the Varanger-fjord, demarcated in 1957. Signed at Moscow, November 29, 1957. In force March 17, 1958. 312 UNTS 289.

4. Poland-USSR. Protocol (with annexed maps) concerning the Delimitation of Polish and Soviet Territorial Waters in the Gulf of Gdansk in the Baltic Sea. Signed at Warsaw, March 18, 1958. In force July 29, 1958. 340 UNTS 94.

5. Convention on the Territorial Sea and Contiguous Zone. Signed at Geneva, April 29, 1958. In force September 10, 1964. 516 UNTS 205; 15 UST 1606; TIAS 5639; 1965 UKTS 3.

6. Argentine-Uruguay. Declaration on the Outer Limit

of the Rio de la Plata. Signed at Montevideo, January 30, 1961. (1964) Annuaire Francais de Droit International 736.

7. Finland-USSR. Agreement concerning the Boundaries of Sea Areas and of the Continental Shelf in the Gulf of Finland. Signed at Helsinki, May 20, 1965. In force May 25, 1966. 566 UNTS 31.

8. Finland-USSR. Protocol Description of the Sea Boundary Line between Finland and the Soviet Union in the Gulf of Finland to the Northeast of Gogland Island. Signed at Helsinki, April 5, 1967. Soviet Statutes and Decisions, VI (1970), 265.

9. Kuwait-Saudi Arabia. Agreement relating to Partition of the Neutral Zone. Signed July 7, 1965. In force July 25, 1966. (1966) 60 American Journal of International Law 744.

10. Norway-Sweden. Declaration concerning the Territorial Sea of Norway and Sweden in the North-Eastern Skagerrak. Signed at Oslo, April 5, 1967. In force June 29, 1967. (1967) Overenskomster med Fremmede Stater 547.

11. Brazil-Uruguay. Agreement on the Delimitation of the Territorial Sea. Signed May 10, 1969.

12. Argentine-Uruguay. Declaration of March 15, 1970.

13. Malaysia-Indonesia. Agreement on Territorial Waters in the Malacca Straits. Signed March 17, 1970.

14. Declaration of Montevideo on the Law of the Sea, May 8, 1970. (1970) 9 International Legal Materials 1081.

15. Declaration of the Latin American States on the Law of the Sea, Lima, August 8, 1970. (1971) 10 International Legal Materials 207.

16. Mexico-USA. Treaty to resolve pending Boundary Differences and maintain the Rio Grande and Colorado River as the International Boundary between the United States and Mexico, with Maps. Signed at Mexico City, November 23, 1970. In force April 18, 1972. TIAS 7313.

CONTINENTAL SHELF

Baltic

1. Finland-U.S.S.R. Agreement concerning the Boundaries

of Sea Areas and of the Continental Shelf in the Gulf of Finland. Signed at Helsinki, May 20, 1965. In force May 25, 1966. 566 UNTS 31.

2. Finland-U.S.S.R. Protocol Description of the Sea Boundary Line between Finland and the Soviet Union in the Gulf of Finland to the Northeast of Gogland Island. Signed at Helsinki, April 5, 1967. Soviet Statutes and Decisions, VI (1970), 265.

3. Finland-U.S.S.R. Agreement concerning the Boundary of the Continental Shelf between Finland and the Soviet Union in the Northeastern Part of the Baltic Sea (with annexed maps). Signed at Helsinki, May 5, 1967. In force March 5, 1968. 640 UNTS 111.

4. German Democratic Republic-Poland-U.S.S.R. Declaration on the Continental Shelf of the Baltic Sea. Signed at Moscow, October 23, 1968. (1968) 7 International Legal Materials 1393.

5. German Democratic Republic-Poland. Agreement on the Delimitation of the Continental Shelf. 1968.

6. Poland-U.S.S.R. Agreement concerning the Course of the Continental Shelf Boundary in the Gulf of Gdansk and the Southeastern Part of the Baltic Sea. Signed at Warsaw, August 28, 1969. In force May 13, 1970. (1970) 9 International Legal Materials 697.

North Sea

1. Federal Republic of Germany-Netherlands. Treaty concerning the Lateral Delimitation of the Continental Shelf in the Vicinity of the Coast. Signed at Bonn, December 1, 1964. In force September 18, 1965. 550 UNTS 123.

2. Norway-United Kingdom. Agreement relating to the Delimitation of the Continental Shelf between the Two Countries (with annexed chart). Signed at London, March 10, 1965. In force June 29, 1965. 551 UNTS 213; 1965 UKTS 71.

3. Denmark-Federal Republic of Germany. Agreement (with Protocol) concerning the Delimitation, in the Coastal Regions, of the Continental Shelf of the North Sea. Signed at Bonn, June 9, 1965. In force May 27, 1966. 570 UNTS 91.

4. Netherlands-United Kingdom. Agreement relating to the Delimitation of the Continental Shelf under the North Sea

between the Two Countries (with annexed chart). Signed at London, October 6, 1965. In force December 23, 1966. 595 UNTS 113; 1967 UKTS 23.

Protocol amending the Agreement. Signed at London, November 25, 1971. Not yet in force. Cmnd. 4875.

5. Netherlands-United Kingdom. Agreement relating to the Exploitation of Single Geological Structures extending across the Dividing Line on the Continental Shelf under the North Sea. Signed at London, October 6, 1965. In force December 23, 1966. 595 UNTS 105; 1967 UKTS 24.

6. Denmark-Norway. Agreement relating to the Delimitation of the Continental Shelf (with annexed map). Signed at Oslo, December 8, 1965. In force June 22, 1966. 634 UNTS 71.

Exchange of Notes constituting an Agreement amending the Agreement. Signed at Copenhagen, April 24, 1968. In force April 24, 1968. 643 UNTS 414.

7. Denmark-United Kingdom. Agreement relating to the Delimitation of the Continental Shelf between the Two Countries (with annexed chart). Signed at London, March 3, 1966. In force February 6, 1967. 592 UNTS 207; 1967 UKTS 35. (This Agreement will terminate when Agreement 17 comes into force).

8. Denmark-Netherlands. Agreement concerning the Delimitation of the Continental Shelf under the North Sea between the Two Countries (with annexed map). Signed at The Hague, March 31, 1966. In force August 1, 1967. 604 UNTS 209. (This Agreement will terminate when Agreement 15 comes into force).

9. Denmark-Federal Republic of Germany. Special Agreement for the Submission to the International Court of Justice of a difference between the Kingdom of Denmark and the Federal Republic of Germany concerning the Delimitation, as between the Kingdom of Denmark and the Federal Republic of Germany, of the Continental Shelf in the North Sea. Signed at Bonn, February 2, 1967. In force February 2, 1967. 606 UNTS 97.

10. Federal Republic of Germany-Netherlands. Special Agreement for the Submission to the International Court of Justice of a difference between the Kingdom of the Netherlands and the Federal Republic of Germany concerning the delimitation, as between the Kingdom of the Netherlands and the Federal Republic of Germany, of the Continental Shelf in the North Sea. Signed at Bonn, February 2, 1967. In force February 2, 1967. 606 UNTS 105.

11. Denmark-Federal Republic of Germany-Netherlands. Protocol concerning the Submission of a Case to the International Court of Justice (with annexed Protocol). Signed at Bonn, February 2, 1967. In force February 2, 1967. 606 UNTS 89.

12. Norway-Sweden. Agreement on the Delimitation of the Continental Shelf. Signed at Stockholm, July 24, 1968. In force March 18, 1969. (1968) Overenskomster med Fremmede Stater 324.

13. Denmark-Federal Republic of Germany. Treaty relating to the Delimitation of the Continental Shelf under the North Sea. Signed at Copenhagen, January 28, 1971. Not yet in force. (1971) 10 International Legal Materials 603.

14. Federal Republic of Germany-Netherlands. Treaty relating to the Delimitation of the Continental Shelf under the North Sea. Signed at Copenhagen, January 28, 1971. Not yet in force. (1971) 10 International Legal Materials 607.

15. Denmark-Federal Republic of Germany-Netherlands. Protocol to the Agreements delimiting the Continental Shelf in the North Sea. Signed at Copenhagen, January 28, 1971. Not yet in force. (1971) 10 International Legal Materials 600.

16. Federal Republic of Germany-United Kingdom. Agreement relating to the Delimitation of the Continental Shelf under the North Sea between the Two Countries. Signed at London, November 25, 1971. Not yet in force. Cmnd. 4881.

17. Denmark-United Kingdom. Agreement relating to the Delimitation of the Continental Shelf between the Two Countries. Signed at London, November 25, 1971. Not yet in force. Cmnd. 4882.

Persian Gulf

1. Bahrain-Saudi Arabia. Agreement for the Definition of their Respective Rights in the Offshore Areas lying between their Territories. Signed at Riyadh, February 22, 1958. In force February 26, 1958. (1958) 7 International and Comparative Law Quarterly 519.

2. Qatar-Saudi Arabia. Agreement on Marine Boundaries. Signed June 27, 1965. In force December 1965.

3. Kuwait-Saudi Arabia. Agreement relating to Partition of the Neutral Zone. Signed July 7, 1965. In force July 25,

1966. (1966) 60 American Journal of International Law 744.

4. Iran-Kuwait. Agreement on the Delimitation of the Continental Shelf. Signed January 13, 1968.

5. Abu Dhabi-Dubai. Agreement on Offshore Boundaries. Signed February 18, 1968.

6. Iran-Saudi Arabia. Agreement concerning Sovereignty over Al-'Arabiyah and Farsi islands and Delimitation of Boundary Line separating Submarine Areas between the Kingdom of Saudi Arabia and Iran. Signed at Teheran, October 24, 1968. In force January 29, 1969. (1969) 8 International Legal Materials 493.

7. Abu Dhabi-Qatar. Agreement for the Settlement of the Offshore Boundary and Ownership of Islands. Signed March 20, 1969. In force March 20, 1969. (1970) 74 Revue Générale de Droit Internationale Publique 565.

8. Iran-Qatar. Agreement on Marine Boundaries. Signed June 30, 1969.

Other Agreements

1. Great Britain-Venezuela. Treaty relating to the Submarine Areas of the Gulf of Paria. Signed at Caracas, February 26, 1942. In force September 22, 1942. 205 LNTS 121; 1942 UNTS 10.

2. Convention on the Continental Shelf. Signed at Geneva, April 29, 1958. In force June 10, 1964. 499 UNTS 311; 15 UST 471; TIAS 5578; 1964 UKTS 39.

3. Italy-Yugoslavia. Agreement relating to the Delimitation of the Continental Shelf between the Two Countries. Signed at Rome, January 8, 1968. In force January 21, 1970. (1968) 7 International Legal Materials 547.

4. Indonesia-Malaya. Agreement relating to the Delimitation of the Continental Shelves between the Two Countries. Signed at Kuala Lumpur, October 27, 1969. In force November 7, 1969. (1970) 9 International Legal Materials 1173.

5. Uruguay-Argentine. Declaration of March 15, 1970.

6. Australia-Indonesia. Agreement establishing Certain Seabed Boundaries. Signed at Canberra, May 18, 1971. (1971) 10 International Legal Materials 830.

7. To the section on the Continental Shelf: (other agreements) Italy - Tunisia. Agreement on the boundaries of the Continental Shelf. Signed August 20th, 1971.

FISHING LIMITS

Baltic

1. Denmark-Federal Republic of Germany. Agreement regarding Common Fishery Rights in the Flensborg Fjord. Signed May 29, 1958. U. N. Registry No. 9731.

2. Finland-USSR. Agreement (with annexes) regarding Fishing and Sealing. Signed at Moscow, February 21, 1959. In force April 4, 1959. 338 UNTS 3.

Protocol extending the Agreement to an Area in the Gulf of Finland to the East of the Island of Suusaari (Gogland). Signed at Helsinki, May 20, 1965. In force May 25, 1966. 566 UNTS 350.

3. Finland-USSR. Agreement on Fishing and Sealing. Signed at Moscow, June 13, 1969. (1970) 9 International Legal Materials 507.

4. To the section on Fishing Limits (Baltic): Poland - Sweden. Agreements on fisheries. Signed 1970.

5. Denmark-Poland. Fisheries Agreement. Signed at Warsaw, February 26, 1971.

North Sea and North-East Atlantic

1. Great Britain-France. Convention for Defining and Regulating the Limits of the Exclusive Rights of the Oyster and other Fishery on the Coasts of Great Britain and France. Signed August 2, 1839. British and Foreign State Papers (1838-1839) Vol. 27, 983.

2. Great Britain-France. Regulations for the Guidance of the Fishermen of Great Britain and of France in the Seas lying between the Coasts of the Two Countries. Signed at London, May 24, 1843.

Declaration approving these Regulations. London, June 23, 1843. British and Foreign State Papers (1842-1843), Vol 31, 190.

3. France-Ireland-United Kingdom. Agreement regarding the Limits of French Fisheries in Granville Bay. Signed at London, December 20, 1928. In force January 20, 1929. 86 LNTS 429; 1929 UKTS 2.

4. France-United Kingdom. Agreement (with two annexed charts) regarding rights of fishery in areas of the Ecrehos and Minquiers. Signed at London, January 30, 1951. In force September 24, 1951. 121 UNTS 97; 1952 UKTS 4.

5. France-United Kingdom. Exchange of Notes concerning the Status of Previous Fisheries Agreements in relation to the Fisheries Convention open for signature at London from March 9 to April 10, 1964. Signed at London, April 10, 1964. In force April 10, 1964. 648 UNTS 73; 1968 UKTS 54.

6. France-Spain. Convention relating to Fishing in the Bidassoa and the Bay of Figuier. Signed July 14, 1959. Journal Officiel de la République Française, 1965, No. 57.

7. Norway-United Kingdom. Fishery Agreement (with annexes, exchange of letters and related note). Signed at Oslo, November 17, 1960. In force March 3, 1961. 398 UNTS 189; 1961 UKTS 25.

8. Iceland-United Kingdom. Exchange of Notes constituting an Agreement settling the Fisheries Dispute. Signed at Reykjavik, March 11, 1961. In force March 11, 1961. 397 UNTS 275; 1961 UKTS 17.

9. Federal Republic of Germany-Iceland. Exchange of Notes constituting an Agreement concerning the Fishery Zone around Iceland. Signed at Reykjavik, July 19, 1961. In force July 19, 1961. 409 UNTS 47.

10. Denmark-Iceland. Exchange of Notes constituting an Agreement on the Access for Faeroese fishermen to engage in handline fishing off Iceland. Signed at Reykjavik, August 1, 1961. In force August 1, 1961. 425 UNTS 191.

11. Norway-USSR. Agreement on Fishing. Signed at Moscow, April 16, 1962. In force August 1, 1962. 437 UNTS 175.

12. Fisheries Convention. Signed at London, March 9, 1964. In force March 15, 1966. 581 UNTS 57; 1966 UKTS 35.

13. Protocol of Provisional Application of the Fisheries Convention and Two Agreements as to Transitional Rights. Signed at London, March 9, 1964. In force March 18, 1964. 581 UNTS 57; 1965 UKTS 29.

14. Poland-United Kingdom. Exchange of Notes regarding the Rights to be accorded to Polish Vessels within the British Fishery Limits to be established on September 30, 1964. Signed at Warsaw, September 26, 1964. In force September 30, 1964. 539 UNTS 153; 1964 UKTS 64.

15. Norway-United Kingdom. Agreement for the Continuance of Fishing by Norwegian Vessels within the Fishery Limits of

the United Kingdom of Great Britain and Northern Ireland (with Exchange of Notes). Signed at London, September 28, 1964. In force March 11, 1965. 548 UNTS 63; 1965 UKTS 43.

16. United Kingdom-USSR. Exchange of Notes on Matters arising from the Establishment by the United Kingdom of the Fishery Regime provided for by the Fishery Limits Act 1964. Signed at Moscow, September 30, 1964. In force September 30, 1964. 539 UNTS 159; 1964 UKTS 63.

17. Denmark-Norway-Sweden. Agreement on Reciprocal Access to Fishing in the Skagerrak and the Kattegat (with Protocol). Signed at Copenhagen, December 19, 1966. In force August 7, 1967. 605 UNTS 313.

18. Denmark-Norway. Exchange of Notes constituting an Agreement on Traditional Norwegian Sprat Fishing in the Kattegat. Signed at Copenhagen, December 19, 1966. In force August 7, 1967. 606 UNTS 3.

19. France-Spain. Exchange of Notes constituting a General Agreement on Fisheries. Signed at Paris, March 20, 1967. In force March 20, 1967. Journal Officiel de la Republique Française 1967, p. 7806.

20. Norway-Sweden. Agreement concerning the Delimitation of the Fishery Areas of Norway and Sweden in the North-Eastern Skagerrak. Signed at Oslo, April 5, 1967. In force June 29, 1967. (1967) Overenskomster med Fremmede Stater 545.

21. Denmark-Norway. Agreement concerning the East Greenland Fisheries (with Additional Protocol). Signed at Oslo, April 20, 1967. In force July 10, 1967. 604 UNTS 103.

22. Denmark-Belgium. Exchange of Letters constituting an Agreement regarding the Fishing Rights of Belgian Fishermen in the Fishery Zones of Danish Waters. Signed at Brussels, June 29, 1967. In force July 1, 1967. 606 UNTS 113.

23. Denmark-Federal Republic of Germany. Exchange of Notes constituting an Agreement concerning German Fishing Rights in the Danish Fishery Zone. Signed at Bonn, November 30, 1967. In force November 30, 1967. 632 UNTS 153.

24. Denmark-Norway. Exchange of Letters constituting an Agreement concerning Fishing Rights within the Danish Fishery Zone. Signed at Oslo, April 24 and 26, 1968. In force April 26, 1968. 644 UNTS 149.

25. Denmark-Netherlands. Exchange of Notes constituting

an Arrangement concerning Fishing Rights within Danish Fishery Areas. Signed at The Hague, May 30, 1968. In force May 30, 1968. 645 UNTS 147.

26. Portugal-Spain. Fisheries Agreement. Signed December 10, 1969.

27. Treaty concerning the Accession of the Kingdom of Denmark, Ireland, the Kingdom of Norway and the United Kingdom of Great Britain and Northern Ireland to the European Economic Community and the European Atomic Energy Community (with Final Act). Signed at Brussels, January 22, 1972. Not yet in force. Cmnd. 4862

Other Agreements

1. Japan-New Zealand. Fisheries Agreement. Signed at Wellington, July 12, 1967. In force July 26, 1968. (1967) 6 International Legal materials 736.

2. Mexico-USA. Agreement on Traditional Fishing in the Exclusive Fishery Zones contiguous to the Territorial Seas of Both Countries. Signed At Washington, October 27, 1967. In force January 1, 1968. 18 UST 2724; TIAS 6359.

3. Argentine-Brazil. Agreement concerning Fishing. December, 1967. Revista de Derecho Internacional y Ciencias Diplomaticas, XV and XV1, No's 29-32, p. 146.

4. Japan-Mexico. Agreement concerning the Right of Japanese Vessels to fish in the waters contiguous to the Territorial Sea of Mexico. Signed at Mexico City, March 7, 1968. In force June 10, 1968. (1970) 74 Revue Générale de Droit Internationale Publique 845.

5. Indonesia-Japan. Fisheries Agreement. Signed July 20, 1968. (This Agreement expired on July 26, 1972).

6. Australia-Japan. Fisheries Agreement. Signed November 27, 1968.

7. Morocco-Spain. Fisheries Convention. Signed January 4, 1969.

8. Italy-Yugoslavia. Agreement relating to Fishing in Yugoslav Waters. Signed April 16, 1969. In force September 1, 1969.

9. Argentine-Uruguay. Declaration on Provisional Fishing Rights. Signed March 15, 1970.

10. Canada-USA. Agreement on Reciprocal Fishing Privileges in Certain Areas off their Coasts. Signed at Ottawa, April 24, 1970. In force April 24, 1970. TIAS 6879

11. Canada-USSR. Agreement on Co-operation in Fisheries off the Coast of Canada in the North-Eastern Pacific Ocean. Signed at Moscow, January 22, 1971. In force February 19, 1971.

12. Canada-Norway. Exchange of Notes concerning Fishing by Norwegian Nationals off Canada's Atlantic Coast. Signed at Ottawa, July 15, 1971. In force July 15, 1971. (1971) Overenskomster med Fremmede Stater 350.

13. Italy - Tunisia. Fisheries Agreement. Signed August 20th 1971; Libya - Tunisia. Fisheries Agreement. Signed September 8th 1971.

14. Canada-United Kingdom. Exchange of Notes concerning Fishing by British Vessels off the Atlantic Coast of Canada. Signed at Ottawa, March 27, 1972. In force March 27, 1972.

15. Canada-France. Agreement on their mutual Fishing Relations with annex. Signed at Ottawa, March 27, 1972. In force March 27, 1972.

16. Brazil-USA. Agreement concerning Shrimp. Signed at Brazilia, May 9, 1972. (State Dept. Press release 111, 1972).

17. Trinidad and Tobago-Brazil. Agreement concerning Shrimp. Signed on May 19, 1972.

18. Canada-Portugal. Agreement concerning Fisheries Relations, with exchange of notes and annex, signed Ottawa March 27, 1972. In force March 27, 1972.

19. Canada-Denmark. Exchange of Notes concerning Fisheries Relations, with annexes, done at Ottawa March 27, 1972. In force March 27, 1972.

OTHER AGREEMENTS RELATING TO FISHERIES

Atlantic

1. Convention (with annexes) for the Regulation of the Meshes of Fishing Nets and the Size Limits of Fish. Signed at London, April 5, 1946. In force April 5, 1953. 231 UNTS 199; 1956 UKTS 8.

Amendment of paragraph 2 of Article 7 of the Convention. Adopted at the 7th meeting of the Permanent Commission, Dublin, November 1958. In force January 30, 1959. 354 UNTS 408; 1959 UKTS 38.

Amendments to the Convention. Adopted at the 8th meeting of the Permanent Commission, London, May 3-6, 1960. In force May 12, 1961. 431 UNTS 304; 1960 UKTS 66.

Amendments to the Convention. Adopted at the 9th meeting of the Permanent Commission, Copenhagen, May 9-12, 1961. 1962 UKTS 39.

Amendments to the Convention. Adopted at the 10th meeting of the Permanent Commission, Hamburg, May 8-11, 1962. In force May 11, 1962. 456 UNTS 496.

Amendments to the Convention. Adopted at the 11th meeting of the Permanent Commission, London, May 8-10, 1963. In force June 1, 1963. 482 UNTS 372; 1963 UKTS 85.

2. Denmark-Belgium. Exchange of Notes constituting an Arrangement to facilitate the Settlement of Disputes arising at Sea between Belgian and Danish Fishermen outside Territorial Waters. Signed at Copenhagen, December 30, 1948. In force January 1, 1949. 25 UNTS 173.

3. Norway-Sweden. Convention concerning the Establishment of Joint Regulations for Salmon and Sea Trout Fishing, etc. in Iddefjord and Svinesund. Signed at Oslo, January 28, 1949. In force April 1, 1949. 196 UNTS 3.

4. International Convention for the Northwest Atlantic Fisheries (with annex). Signed at Washington, February 8, 1949. In force July 3, 1950. 157 UNTS 157; 1 UST 477; TIAS 2089; 1950 UKTS 62.

Protocol to the Convention relating to the Holding of Annual Meetings. Signed at Washington, June 25, 1956. In force January 10, 1959. 331 UNTS 388; 10 UST 59; TIAS 4170; 1959 UKTS 22.

Declaration of Understanding regarding the Convention concerning Mollusks. Signed at Washington, April 24, 1961. In force June 5, 1963. 480 UNTS 334; 14 UST 924; TIAS 5380; 1963 UKTS 71.

Protocol to extend the Provisions of the Convention to Harp and Hood Seals. Signed at Washington, July 15, 1963. In force April 29, 1966. 590 UNTS 292; 17 UST 635; TIAS 6011; 1966 UKTS 40.

Protocol to the Convention relating to Entry into Force of Proposals adopted by the Commission. Signed at Washington, November 29, 1965. In force December 19, 1969. 21 UST 567; TIAS 6840; 1970 UKTS 73.

Protocol to the Convention relating to Measures of Control. Signed at Washington, November 29, 1965. In force December 19, 1969. 21 UST 576; TIAS 6841; 1970 UKTS 74.

Protocol to the Convention relating to Panel Membership and to Regulatory Measures. Signed at Washington, October 1, 1969. In force December 15, 1971. 1972 UKTS 26.

Protocol to the Convention relating to Amendments to the Convention. Signed at Washington, October 6, 1970. Not yet in force. Cmnd. 4601.

5. Federal Republic of Germany-Norway. Agreement regarding Claims in Respect of Damage to Fishing Gear. Signed at Bonn, May 7, 1951. In force June 4, 1951. 92 UNTS 51.

6. Denmark-Norway. Agreement regarding Claims in Respect of Damage to Fishing Gear. Signed at Copenhagen, January 14, 1952. In force January 14, 1952. 120 UNTS 119.

7. Denmark-Norway-Sweden. Agreement concerning Measures for the Protection of the Stocks of Deep-Sea Prawns (pandalus borealis), European Lobsters (homarus vulgaris), Norway Lobsters (nephrops norvegicus) and Crabs (cancer pagurus). Signed at Oslo, March 7, 1952. In force January 26, 1953. 175 UNTS 205.

Protocol amending Article 4. Signed at Oslo, October 14, 1959. In force October 14, 1959. 427 UNTS 366.

8. North-East Atlantic Fisheries Convention. Signed at London, January 24, 1959. In force June 27, 1963. 486 UNTS 157; 1963 UKTS 68.

9. Norway-USSR. Agreement concerning the Handling of Claims in Connection with Damage to Fishing Gear. Signed at Moscow, December 9, 1959. In force January 1, 1960. 361 UNTS 93.

10. International Convention for the Conservation of Atlantic Tunas. Signed at Rio de Janeiro, May 14, 1966. In force March 21, 1969. 673 UNTS 63; 20 UST 2887; TIAS 6767.

11. Convention on Conduct of Fishing Operations in the North Atlantic. Signed at London, June 1, 1967. Not yet in force. Cmnd. 3645.

12. Denmark-Sweden. Exchange of Notes constituting an Agreement concerning Swedish Direct Landings of Fish in Denmark. Signed at Copenhagen, December 5, 1967. In force December 5, 1967. 631 UNTS 257.

13. Norway-USSR. Exchange of Notes concerning an Arrangement for Mutual Communication with Regard to the Capture of Fishing and Similar Vessels. Signed at Moscow, July 9, 1968. In force July 9, 1968. (1968) Overenskomster med Fremmede Stater 352.

14. Convention on the Conservation of the Living Resources of the South-East Atlantic. Signed at Rome, October 23, 1969. In force October 24, 1971.

15. France-Spain. Agreement relating to the Creation of Fishing Sectors in the Bay of Gascony. Signed at Foutarbie, November 14, 1969.

16. Poland-USA. Agreement regarding Fisheries in the Western Region of the Middle Atlantic Ocean. Signed at Washington, June 13, 1970. In force June 13, 1970. TIAS 6890.

Agreement extending the Agreement. Signed at Warsaw, October 1, 1971. In force October 1, 1971. (TIAS 7264 - terminated). Agreement signed at Warsaw, June 28 and 30, 1972 extending Agreement of June 13, 1970. In force June 30, 1972.

17. USSR-USA. Agreement on Certain Fishery Problems on the High Seas in the Western Areas of the Middle Atlantic Ocean. Signed at Washington, December 11, 1970. In force January 1, 1971. 21 UST 2664; TIAS 7009.

Protocol to the Agreement. Signed at Washington, February 2, 1971. In force February 7, 1971. 22 UST 113; TIAS 7043.

18. Iceland-Norway-USSR. Agreement on the Regulation of the Fishing of Atlanto-Scandian Herring. Signed at Moscow, February 25, 1972. In force February 25, 1972.

Pacific

1. Canada-USA. Convention for the Protection, Preservation and Extension of the Sockeye Salmon Fisheries in the Fraser River System. Signed at Washington, May 26, 1930. In force July 28, 1937. 184 LNTS 305.

Exchange of Notes (with appendices) constituting an Agreement relating to Sockeye Salmon Fisheries in the Fraser River System. Signed at Washington, July 21 and August 5, 1944. In force August 5, 1944. 121 UNTS 299.

Protocol to the Convention for Protection, Preservation

and Extension of the Sockeye Salmon Fisheries in the Fraser River System. Signed at Ottawa, December 28, 1956. In force July 3, 1957. 290 UNTS 103.

2. Convention for the Extension of Port Privileges to Halibut Fishing Vessels on the Pacific Coasts of the USA and Canada. Signed at Ottawa, March 24, 1950. In force July 13, 1950. 200 UNTS 211.

3. Chile-Ecuador-Peru. Agreements signed at the First Conference on the Exploitation and Conservation of the Maritime Resources of the South Pacific, Santiago, August 18, 1952: (i) Declaration on the Maritime Zone; (ii) Organisation of the Standing Committee of the Conference on the Use and Conservation of the Marine Resources of the South Pacific; (iii) Joint Declaration of Fishery Problems in the South Pacific; (iv) Regulations governing Whaling in the Waters of the South Pacific.

Agreements signed at the Second Conference on the Exploitation and Conservation of the Maritime Resources of the South Pacific, Lima, December 4, 1954; (i) Agreement Supplementary to the Declaration of Sovereignty over the Maritime Zone of Two Hundred Miles; (ii) Agreement relating to Penalties; (iii) Agreement relating to Measures of Supervision and Control in the Maritime Zones of the Signatory Countries; (iv) Agreement relating to the Issue of Permits for the Exploitation of the Maritime Resources of the South Pacific; (v) Agreement relating to the Regular Annual Meeting of the Standing Committee; (vi) Agreement relating to a Special Maritime Frontier Zone

4. USA-Canada-Japan. International Convention (with annex and protocol) for the High Seas Fisheries of the North Pacific Ocean. Signed at Tokyo, May 9, 1952. In force June 12, 1953. 205 UNTS 65; 4 UST 380; TIAS 2786.

Amendments of Paragraphs 1(a) and (b) of the Annex to the Convention. Adopted at Seattle, November 17, 1962. 14 UST 953; TIAS 5385.

5. Canada-USA. Convention for the Preservation of the Halibut Fishery of the Northern Pacific Ocean and Bering Sea. Signed at Ottawa, March 2, 1953. In force October 28, 1953. 222 UNTS 77.

6. Japan-USSR. Convention concerning Fishing on the High Seas in the Northwest Pacific Ocean. Signed at Moscow, May 14, 1956. In force December 12, 1956. Soviet Statutes and Decisions, VI (1970), 359.

7. Agreement on Co-operation in Conducting Fishery, Oceanological and Limnological Research in the Western Pacific Ocean. Signed at Peking, June 12, 1956.

8. Japan-USSR. Agreement on King Crab. Signed on April 16, 1970. In force April 16, 1970.

9. Japan-USA. Agreement concerning Certain Fisheries off the Coast of the United States, with Agreed Minutes. Signed at Tokyo, December 11, 1970. In force December 11, 1970.

10. Japan-USA. Agreement relating to Salmon Fishing in Waters Contiguous to the United States Territorial Sea, with Agreed Minutes. Signed at Tokyo, December 11, 1970. In force December 11, 1970.

11. Japan-USA. Agreement regarding the King and Tanner Crab Fisheries in the Eastern Bering Sea, with Agreed Minutes. Signed at Tokyo, December 11, 1970. In force December 11, 1970. TIAS 7019 .

12. Canada-USSR. Agreement on Provisional Rules of Navigation and Fisheries Safety in the Northeastern Pacific Ocean off the Coast of Canada (with Provisional Rules of Navigation and Fisheries Safety). Signed at Moscow, January 22, 1971. In force April 15, 1971.

13. Canada-USSR. Agreement on Co-operation in Fisheries off the Coast of Canada in the Northeastern Pacific Ocean. Signed at Moscow, January 22, 1971. In force February 19, 1971.

14. USSR-USA. Agreement relating to Fishing Operations in the Northeastern Pacific Ocean. Signed at Washington, February 12, 1971. In force February 12, 1971.

15. USSR-USA. Agreement relating to Fishing for King and Tanner Crab. Signed at Washington, February 12, 1971. In force February 12, 1971. TIAS 7044.

16. USSR-USA. Agreement on Certain Fisheries Problems in the Northeastern Part of the Pacific Ocean off the Coast of the United States of America. Signed at Washington, February 12, 1971. In force February 12, 1971. TIAS 7046.

Agreement amending the Agreement. Effected by Exchange of Aide-mémoire, Moscow, February 22 and March 15, 1972. In force March 15, 1972. TIAS 7328 .

Other Agreements

1. Agreement for the Establishment of the Indo-Pacific Fisheries Council. Formulated at Baguoi, February 26, 1948. Approved by the Conference of FAO, Washington, November 15-29, 1948. In force November 9, 1948. 120 UNTS 59; 1949 UKTS 73.

Amendment of Paragraph 2 of Article VI of the Agreement. Done at Quezon City, October 23-November 7, 1952. In force December 9, 1952. 190 UNTS 383.

Amendments to the Agreement. Done at Tokyo, September 30-October 14, 1955. In force October 31, 1955. 227 UNTS 322.

Amendments to Articles II, III and VI of the Agreement. Adopted at Colombo, December 6-22, 1958. In force December 17, 1958. 343 UNTS 343.

Amendments to the Agreement. Adopted at Karachi, January 20, 1961. In force November 23, 1961. 418 UNTS 348; 13 UST 2511; TIAS 5218.

2. Mexico-USA. Convention relating to the Establishment of an International Commission for the Scientific Investigation of Tuna (with an Exchange of Notes). Signed at Mexico City, January 25, 1949. In force July 11, 1950. 99 UNTS 3.

3. Convention for the Establishment of an Inter-American Tropical Tuna Commission. Signed at Washington, May 31, 1949. In force March 3, 1950. 80 UNTS 3; 1 UST 230; TIAS 2044.

Costa Rica-USA. Exchange of Notes relating to the Agreement. Signed at Washington, March 3, 1950. In force March 3, 1950. 80 UNTS 3.

4. Agreement for the Establishment of a General Fisheries Council for the Mediterranean. Signed at Rome, September 24, 1949. In force February 20, 1952. 126 UNTS 337; 1952 UKTS 15.

Amendments to the Agreement. Adopted at Rome, May 22, 1963. In force December 3, 1963. 490 UNTS 444; 1963 UKTS 40.

5. Canada-USA. Convention on the Great Lakes Fisheries. Signed at Washington, September 10, 1954. In force October 11, 1955. 238 UNTS 97. 6 UST 2836.

6. Convention on Fishing and Conservation of the Living Resources of the High Seas. Signed at Geneva, April 29, 1958. In force March 20, 1966. 559 UNTS 285; 17 UST 138; TIAS 5969; 1966 UKTS 39.

7. Cuba-USA. Convention for the Conservation of Shrimp. Signed at Havanna, August 15, 1958. In force September 4, 1959. 358 UNTS 63.

8. Bulgaria-Romania-USSR. Convention concerning Fishing in the Black Sea. Signed at Varna, July 7, 1959. In force March 21, 1960. 377 UNTS 203.

9. Agreement concerning Co-operation in Marine Fishing. Signed at Warsaw, July 28, 1962. In force February 22, 1963. 460 UNTS 219.

10. Agreement concerning the Protection of the Salmon Population in the Baltic Sea. Signed at Stockholm, December 20, 1962. In force March 1, 1966.

11. Japan-USSR. Agreement between the Great Japan Fisheries Association and the USSR Ministry of Fisheries concerning the Collection of Sea Kale in Areas around the Kaigara Islands by Japanese Fishermen. Signed at Moscow, June 10, 1963. Soviet Statutes and Decisions, VI (1969/70), 170.

12. Japan-Republic of Korea. Agreement on Fisheries (with annex, exchange of notes, agreed minutes and record of discussions). Signed at Tokyo, June 22, 1965. In force December 18, 1965. 583 UNTS 51.

13. Agreement establishing the Southeast Asian Fisheries Development Centre. Signed at Bangkok, December 28, 1967. In force December 28, 1967. 651 UNTS 19.

Protocol amending the Agreement. Signed at Bangkok, January 13, 1968. In force January 13, 1968. 651 UNTS 19.

14. Argentine-Brazil. Agreement on the Conservation of Natural Resources in the Sea adjacent to the Argentinian Coasts of the South Atlantic. Signed December 1967. Revista de Derecho Internacional y Ciencias Diplomaticas, XV and XVI, 1966-67, No's 29-32, p. 147.

WHALING

1. International Convention for the Regulation of Whaling (with annexed Schedule). Signed at Washington, December 2, 1946. In force November 10, 1948. 161 UNTS 72; 62 Stat. 1716; TIAS 1849; 1949 UKTS 5.

Protocol to the Convention. Signed at Washington,

November 19, 1956. In force May 4, 1959. 338 UNTS 366; 10 UST 952; TIAS 4228; 1959 UKTS 68.

The Schedule to the Convention is amended annually. The latest amendments are: Amendments adopted at the 23rd Meeting of the International Whaling Commission, Washington, June 21-25, 1971. In force October 5, 1971 and January 3,1972. 1972 UKTS 30.

2. Japan-Norway-USSR. Arrangements for the Regulation of Antarctic Pelagic Whaling. Signed at Tokyo, September 29, 1971. (Lays down arrangements for 1971-72 season).

3. USSR-USA. Agreement on the Regulation of North Pacific Whaling. Signed 1970. TIAS 7081.

4. Japan-USSR-USA. Agreement on the Regulation of North Pacific Whaling. Signed at Tokyo, July 30, 1971. In force July 30, 1971. TIAS 7188.

SEALING

1. Canada-USA. Exchange of Notes constituting a Provisional Agreement relating to Fur Seals. Signed at Washington, December 8 and 19, 1942. In force May 30, 1944. 26 UNTS 363.

Exchange of Notes constituting an Agreement amending the Agreement. Signed at Washington, December 26, 1947. In force December 26, 1947. 27 UNTS 29.

2. Canada-Japan-USA. Exchange of Notes constituting an Agreement relating to Scientific Investigation of Fur Seals in the North Pacific Ocean. Signed at Tokyo, January 31 and February 8, 1952; at Ottawa, February 7 and March 1, 1952. In force February 8, 1952 (for Japan and USA) and March 1, 1952 (Canada). 168 UNTS 9.

3. Interim Convention (with Schedule) on Conservation of North Pacific Fur Seals. Signed at Washington, February 9, 1957. In force October 14, 1957. 314 UNTS 105; 8 UST 2283; TIAS 3948.

Protocol amending the Interim Convention. Signed at Washington, October 8, 1963. In force April 10, 1964. 494 UNTS 303; 15 UST 316; TIAS 5558.

Agreement extending the Interim Convention. Signed

September 3, 1969. In force September 3, 1969. 20 UST 2992; TIAS 6774.

4. Norway-USSR. Agreement (with annex) on Measures for Regulating the Catch and Conserving Stocks of Seals in the Northeastern Part of the Atlantic Ocean, Signed at Oslo, November 22, 1957. In force June 27, 1958. 309 UNTS 269.

5. Canada-Norway. Exchange of Notes constituting an Agreement to ensure Compliance with Sealing Regulations. Signed at Oslo, April 2 and 26, 1968. In force April 26, 1963. (1968) Overenskomster med Fremmede Stater 298.

6. Canada-Norway. Agreement on Sealing and the Conservation of the Seal Stocks in the Northwest Atlantic. Signed at Ottawa, July 15, 1971. In force December 22, 1971.

7. Convention for the Conservation of Antarctic Seals. Signed at London, June 9, 1972. Not yet in force. (1972) 11 International Legal Materials 251.

POLLUTION

Oil Pollution

1. International Convention for the Prevention of Pollution of the Sea by Oil. Signed at London, May 12, 1954. In force July 26, 1958. 327 UNTS 3; 12 UST 2989; TIAS 4900; 1958 UKTS 56.

Amendments to the Convention. Adopted at London, April 11, 1962. In force (except amendment to Article 14) May 18, 1967; amendment to Article 14, June 28, 1967. 600 UNTS 332; 17 UST 1523; TIAS 6109; 1967 UKTS 59.

Amendments to the Convention. Adopted at London, October 21, 1969. Not yet in force. Cmnd. 4347.

Amendments to the Convention. Adopted at London, October 15, 1971. Not yet in force. (1972) 11 International Legal Materials 267.

2. International Convention relating to Intervention on the High Seas in Cases of Oil Pollution Casualties. Signed at Brussels, November 29, 1969. Not yet in force. Cmnd. 4403.

3. International Convention on Civil Liability for Oil Pollution Damage, Signed at Brussels, November 29, 1969. (Not yet in force.) Cmnd. 4403.

4. International Convention on the Establishment of an International Fund for Compensation for Oil Pollution Damage. Signed at Brussels, December 18, 1971. Not yet in force. (1972) 11 International Legal Materials 284.

5. Agreement for Co-operation in Dealing with Pollution of the North Sea by Oil. Signed at Bonn, June 9, 1969. In force August 9, 1969. 1969 UKTS 78.

6. Denmark-Finland-Norway-Sweden. Agreement concerning Co-operation in taking Measures against Pollution of the Sea by Oil. Signed at Copenhagen, September 16, 1971. In force October 16, 1971.

Pollution from Nuclear Waste

1. Convention on the Liability of Operators of Nuclear Ships. Signed at Brussels, May 25, 1962. Not yet in force. (1963) 57 American Journal of International Law 268.

2. USA-Greece. Exchange of Notes (with annex) constituting an Agreement relating to the Use of Greek Ports and Territorial Waters by N. S. Savannah. Signed at Athens, April 23 and 24, 1962. In force April 24, 1962. 459 UNTS 3.

3. USA-Federal Republic of Germany. Agreement on the Use of Territorial Waters and Ports by the N. S. Savannah. Signed at Washington, November 29, 1962. In force November 29, 1962. 460 UNTS 169.

4. USA-Netherlands. Agreement on Public Liability for Damage caused by the N.S. Savannah (with annex). Signed at the Hague, February 6, 1963. In force May 22, 1963. 487 UNTS 113.

5. USA-Netherlands. Operational Agreement on Arrangements for a Visit of the N.S. Savannah to the Netherlands. Signed at The Hague, May 20, 1963. In force May 22, 1963. 487 UNTS 123.

6. USA-Norway. Agreement on the Use of Norwegian Ports and Territorial Waters by the N.S. Savannah. Signed at Oslo, March 1, 1963. In force May 8, 1964. 524 UNTS 185.

7. USA-Belgium. Agreement (with annex) on the visit of the N.S. Savannah to Belgian Ports. Signed at Brussels, April 19, 1963. In force November 27, 1963. 493 UNTS 83.

8. USA-Ireland. Exchange of Notes constituting an Agree-

ment relating to Public Liability for Damage caused by the N.S. Savannah. Signed at Dublin, June 18, 1964. In force June 18, 1964. 530 UNTS 217.

9. USA-UK. Exchange of Notes (with annexes) constituting an Agreement relating to the Use of United Kingdom Ports and Territorial Waters by the N.S. Savannah. Signed at London, June 19, 1964. In force June 19, 1964. 530 UNTS 99; 1964 UKTS 37.

Exchange of Notes constituting an Agreement modifying the Agreement. Signed at London, June 12, 1967. In force June 12, 1967. 610 UNTS 350; 1967 UKTS 68.

10. USA-Denmark. Agreement concerning Visits of the N.S. Savannah. Signed at Copenhagen, July 2, 1964. In force July 2, 1964. 529 UNTS 277.

11. USA-Sweden. Exchange of Notes (with enclosure) constituting an Agreement relating to the Use of Swedish Ports and Waters by the N.S. Savannah. Signed at Stockholm, July 6, 1964. In force July 6, 1964. 529 UNTS 287.

12. USA-Spain. Exchange of Notes (with Annex) constituting an Agreement relating to the Use of Spanish Ports and Territorial Waters by the N.S. Savannah. Signed at Madrid, July 16, 1964. In force July 16, 1964. 529 UNTS 187.

13. USA-Portugal. Exchange of Notes (with Annex) constituting an Agreement relating to the Use of Portugese Ports and Territorial Waters by the N.S. Savannah. Signed at Lisbon, November 12, 1964. In force November 12, 1964. 541 UNTS 251.

14. USA-Italy. Agreement on the Use of Italian Ports by the N.S. Savannah (with annexes). Signed at Rome, November 23, 1964. In force November 23, 1964. 532 UNTS 133.

15. USA-Italy. Exchange of Notes constituting an Agreement concerning Liability during Private Operations of N.S. Savannah. Signed at Rome, December 16, 1965. In force December 16, 1965. 574 UNTS 139.

16. USA-Greece. Agreement relating to United States Liability during Operation of the N.S. Savannah by a Private Company. Signed at Athens, November 22, 1966 and January 12, 1967. In force January 12, 1967.

17. USA-Yugoslavia. Agreement relating to United States Liability during Operation of N.S. Savannah by a Private Company. Signed at Belgrade, January 23 and April 24, 1967. In force April 24, 1967.

18. USA-China. Agreement relating to United States Liability during Operation of the N.S. Savannah by a Private Company. Signed at Taipei, March 24 and June 8, 1967. In force June 8, 1967.

19. Convention on Third Party Liability in the Field of Nuclear Energy. Signed at Paris, July 29, 1960. In force April 1, 1968. 1968 UKTS 69.

Additional Protocol. Signed at Paris, January 28, 1964. In force April 1, 1968. 1968 UKTS 69.

Supplementary Convention. Signed at Brussels, January 31, 1963. (1963) 2 International Legal Materials 685.

20. Convention on Civil Liability for Nuclear Damage. Signed at Vienna, May 21, 1963.(1963) 2 International Legal Materials 727.

21. Convention relating to Civil Liability in the Field of Maritime Carriage of Nuclear Material. Signed at Brussels, December 17, 1971. Not yet in force. (1972) 11 International Legal Materials 277.

Other Agreements

1. European Agreement on the Restriction of the Use of Certain Detergents in Washing and Cleaning Products. Signed at Strasbourg, September 16, 1968. In force February 16, 1971. European Treaty Series No. 64.

2. Finland-USSR. Protocol on Co-operation in checking Pollution in the Gulf of Finland. Signed at Helsinki, 1970.

3. Convention for the Prevention of Marine Pollution by Dumping from Ships and Aircraft. Signed at Oslo, February 15, 1972. Not yet in force. (1972) 11 International Legal Materials 262.

4. USA-Canada. Great Lakes Water Quality Agreement. Signed at Ottawa, April 15, 1972. In force April 15, 1972. TIAS 7312 .

INTERNATIONAL ORGANISATIONS

1. Convention on the Inter-Governmental Maritime Consultative Organisation. Signed at Geneva, March 6, 1948. In force March 17, 1958. 289 UNTS 3; 9 UST 621; TIAS 4044; 1958 UKTS 54.

Amendments to Articles 17 and 18 of the Convention. Adopted at London, September 15, 1964. In force October 6, 1967. 607 UNTS 276; 18 UST 1299; TIAS 6285; 1967 UKTS 92.

Amendment to Article 28 of the Convention. Adopted at Paris, September 28, 1965. In force November 3, 1968. 19 UST 4855; TIAS 6490; 1968 UKTS 105.

2. UK-IMCO. Agreement regarding the Headquarters of the Organisation. Signed at London, November 28, 1968. In force November 28, 1968. 1969 UKTS 18.

Exchange of Notes to amend Article 10 of the Agreement. Signed at London, October 28, and November 1, 1971. In force February 5, 1972. 1972 UKTS 25.

3. Convention on the International Council for the Exploration of the Sea. Signed at Copenhagen, September 12, 1964. In force July 22, 1968. 652 UNTS 237. 1968 UKTS 67.

4. Denmark-ICES. Agreement on the Privileges, Immunities and Facilities to be granted to the International Council for the Exploration of the Sea. Signed at Copenhagen, July 24, 1968. In force July 24, 1968. 657 UNTS 159.

5. Convention on the International Hydrographic Organisation. Signed at Monaco, May 3, 1967. In force September 22, 1970. 21 UST 1857; TIAS 6933; 1971 UKTS 30.

CONVENTIONS CONCLUDED UNDER THE AUSPICES OF IMCO

1. International Convention for the Safety of Life at Sea. Signed at London, June 17, 1960. In force May 26, 1965. 536 UNTS 271; 16 UST 185; TIAS 5780; 1965 UKTS 65.

Procés-Verbal of Rectification of Annexes to the Convention. Signed at London, February 15, 1966. 18 UST 1289; TIAS 6284.

Amendments to Chapter II of the Regulations annexed to the Convention. Adopted at London, November 30, 1966. Not yet in force. Cmnd. 3187.

Amendments to the Regulations annexed to the Convention. Adopted at London, October 25, 1967. Cmnd. 4048.

Amendments to Chapter V of the Regulations annexed to the Convention. Adopted at London, November 26, 1968. Not yet in force. Cmnd. 4016.

Amendments to the Convention. Adopted at London, October 21, 1969. Not yet in force.

Amendments to the Convention. Adopted in London, October 12, 1971. Not yet in force.

2. International Regulations for Preventing Collisions at Sea. Signed at London, June 17, 1960. In force September 1, 1965. 16 UST 794; TIAS 5813; 1966 UKTS 23.

3. Convention on Facilitation of International Maritime Traffic (with annex). Signed at London, April 9, 1965. In force March 5, 1967. 591 UNTS 265; 18 UST 411; TIAS 6251; 1967 UKTS 46.

Amendment to the Annex of the Convention. In force August 12, 1971. Cmnd. 4745.

4. International Convention on Load Lines (with annexes). Signed at London, April 5, 1966. In force July 21, 1968. 640 UNTS 133; 18 UST 1857; TIAS 6331; 1968 UKTS 58.

Procès-Verbaux of Rectification. Signed at London, January 30 and May 5, 1969. 20 UST 17 and 2577; TIAS 6629 and 6720; 1969 UKTS 108.

Amendments to the Convention. Adopted at London, October 12, 1971. Not yet in force.

4. International Convention on Tonnage Measurement of Ships. Signed at London, June 23, 1969. Not yet in force. Cmnd. 4332.

MISCELLANEOUS CONVENTIONS

1. Convention regarding the Régime of the Straits, with Annexes and Protocol. Signed at Montreux, July 20, 1936. In force November 9, 1936. 173 LNTS 213; 1937 UKTS 30.

2. Convention (with Final Protocol and International Regulations and Figures) for a Uniform System of Tonnage Measurement of Ships. Signed at Oslo, June 10, 1947. In force December 30, 1954. 208 UNTS 3.

3. International Convention on Certain Rules concerning Civil Jurisdiction in Matters of Collision. Signed at Brussels, May 10, 1952. In force September 14, 1955. 439 UNTS 217; 1960 UKTS 47.

4. International Convention relating to the Arrest of Seagoing Ships. Signed at Brussels, May 10, 1952. In force February 24, 1956. 439 UNTS 193; 1960 UKTS 47.

5. International Convention for the Unification of Certain Rules relating to Penal Jurisdiction in Matters of Collision or Other Incidents of Navigation. Signed at Brussels, May 10, 1952. In force November 20, 1955. 439 UNTS 233; 1960 UKTS 47.

6. Agreement (with Annexed Chart) regarding Financial Support of the North Atlantic Ice Patrol. Signed at Washington, January 4, 1956. In force July 6, 1956. 256 UNTS 171; 7 UST 1969; TIAS 3597; 1956 UKTS 43.

7. International Convention relating to the Limitation of the Liability of Owners of Sea-going Ships (with Protocol of Signature). Signed at Brussels, October 10, 1957. In force May 31, 1968. 1968 UKTS 52.

8. Convention on the High Seas. Signed at Geneva, April 29, 1958. In force September 30, 1962. 450 UNTS 11; 13 UST 2312; TIAS 5200; 1963 UKTS 5.

9. Optional Protocol of Signature concerning the Compulsory Settlement of Disputes arising from the Law of the Sea Conventions. Signed at Geneva, April 29, 1958. In force September 30, 1962. 450 UNTS 169; 1963 UKTS 60.

10. Denmark-Finland-Norway-Sweden. Agreement concerning Co-operation in Ice-breaking. (with Protocol). Signed at Helsinki, December 20, 1961. In force December 20, 1961. 419 UNTS 79

11. Denmark-Finland-Norway-Sweden. Agreement concerning Uniform Rules for the Marking of Navigable Waters. Signed at Helsinki, September 18, 1962. In force October 18, 1962. 442 UNTS 215.

12. Treaty banning Nuclear Weapon Tests in the Atmosphere, in Outer Space, and under Water. Signed at Moscow, August 5, 1963. In force October 10, 1963. 480 UNTS 43; 14 UST 1313; TIAS 5433; 1964 UKTS 3.

13. European Agreement for the Prevention of Broadcasts transmitted from Stations outside National Territories. Signed at Strasbourg, January 22, 1965. In force October 19, 1967. 634 UNTS 239; 1968 UKTS 1.

14. Convention on Transit Trade of Land-locked States.

Signed at New York, July 8, 1965. In force June 9, 1967. 597 UNTS 3; 19 UST 7383; TIAS 6592.

15. International Convention for the Unification of Certain Rules relating to Carriage of Passenger Luggage by Sea. Signed at Brussels, May 27, 1967. Not yet in force.

16. Treaty on the Prohibition of the Emplacement of Nuclear Weapons and Other Weapons of Mass Destruction on the Seabed and Ocean Floor and in the Subsoil thereof. Signed at London, Moscow and Washington, February 11, 1971. In force May 18, 1972. Cmnd. 4678. (1971) 10 International Legal Materials 146.

TABLES OF RATIFICATION OF THE MAJOR MULTILATERAL CONVENTIONS ON THE LAW OF THE SEA

The date given is the date of the deposit of the instrument of acceptance. States have been arranged in geo-political groupings, with land-locked States underlined. The Conventions dealt with are set out in the following tables:

1. The Geneva Conventions.

2. Oil Pollution Conventions.

3. Other Conventions concluded under the auspices of IMCO.

4. Conventions regulating fisheries in the North Atlantic and North Sea.

5. Miscellaneous Conventions in Western Europe.

6. Miscellaneous Fisheries Conventions.

7. Miscellaneous Conventions.

TABLE 1. THE GENEVA CONVENTIONS

AFRICA

Convention	Convention on the Territorial Sea and Contiguous Zone	Convention on the High Seas	Convention on Fishing and Conservation of the Living Resources of the High Seas	Convention on the Continental Shelf	Optional Protocol of Signature concerning the Compulsory Settlement of Disputes.
Date of Signature	29.4.1958.	29.4.1958.	29.4.1958.	29.4.1958.	29.4.1958.
Date of Entry into Force	10.9.1964.	30.9.1962.	20.3.1966.	10.6.1964.	30.9.1962.
Algeria					
Botswana					
Burundi					
Cameroon					
Central African Republic		15.10.1962.			
Chad					
Congo, Republic of					
Dahomey					
Equatorial Guinea					
Ethiopia					
Gabon					
Gambia					
Ghana					29.4.1958.
Guinea					
Ivory Coast					
Kenya	20.6.1969.	20.6.1969.	20.6.1969.	20.6.1969.	
Lesotho					
Liberia					27.5.1958.
Libya					
Malagasy Republic	31.7 1962.	31.7.1962	31.7.1962.	31.7.1962.	10.8.1962.
Malawi	3.11.1965.	3.11.1965.	3.11.1965.	3.11.1965.	17.12.1965.
Mali					
Mauritania					
Mauritius	5.10.1970.	5.10.1970.	5.10.1970.	5.10.1970.	5.10.1970.

AFRICA (cont.)

Convention	Convention on the Territorial Sea and Contiguous Zone	Convention on the High Seas	Convention on Fishing and Conservation of the Living Resources of the High Seas	Convention on the Continental Shelf	Optional Protocol of Signature concerning the Compulsory Settlement of Disputes.
Morocco					
Niger					
Nigeria	26.6.1961	26.6.1961.	26.6.1961.	28.4.1971.	
Rwanda					
Senegal	25.4.1961.(1)	25.4.1961.	25.4.1961.(1)	25.4.1961.	
Sierra Leone	13.3.1962.	13.3.1962.	13.3.1962.	25.11.1966.	14.2.1963.
Somalia					
South Africa	9.4.1963.	9.4.1963.	9.4.1963.	9.4.1963.	
Sudan					
Swaziland	16.10.1970.	16.10.1970.		16.10.1970.	
Tanzania					
Togo					
Tunisia					
Uganda	14.9.1964.	14.9.1964.	14.9.1964.	14.9.1964.	15.9.1964.
United Arab Republic					
Upper Volta		4.10.1965.	4.10.1965.		
Zaire					
Zambia					

ASIA AND THE FAR EAST

Convention	Convention on the Territorial Sea and Contiguous Zone	Convention on the High Seas	Convention on Fishing and Conservation of the Living Resources of the High Seas	Convention on the Continental Shelf	Optional Protocol of Signature concerning the Compulsory Settlement of Disputes.
Afghanistan		28.4.1959.			
Bahrein					
Bangladesh					
Bhutan					
Burma					
Cambodia	18.3.1960.	18.3.1960.	18.3.1960.	18.3.1960.	22.1.1970.
China, People's Republic of					
China, Republic of				12.10.1970.	29.4.1958.

ASIA AND THE FAR EAST (cont.)

Convention	Convention on the Territorial Sea and Contiguous Zone	Convention on the High Seas	Convention on Fishing and Conservation of the Living Resources of the High Seas	Convention on the Continental Shelf	Optional Protocol of Signature concerning the Compulsory Settlement of Disputes.
Fiji	19.3.1971.	19.3.1971.	19.3.1971.	19.3.1971.	
India					
Indonesia		10.8.1961.			
Iran					
Iraq					
Israel	6.9.1961.	6.9.1961.		6.9.1961.	
Japan	10.6.1968.	10.6.1968.			
Jordan					
Korea, North					
Korea, Republid of					
Kuwait					
Laos					
Lebanon					
Malaysia	21.12.1960.	21.12.1960.	21.12.1960.	21.12.1960.	1.5.1961.
Maldives					
Mongolia					
Nauru					
Nepal		28.12.1962.			29.4.1958.
Oman					
Pakistan					6.11.1958.
Philippines					
Qatar					
Saudi Arabia					
Singapore					
Southern Yemen					
Sri Lanka					30.10.1958.
Syria					

ASIA AND THE FAR EAST (cont.)

Convention	Convention on the Territorial Sea and Contiguous Zone	Convention on the High Seas	Convention on Fishing and Conservation of the Living Resources of the High Seas	Convention on the Continental Shelf	Optional Protocol of Signature concerning the Compulsory Settlement of Disputes
Thailand	2.7.1968.	2.7.1968.	2.7.1968.	2.7.1968.	
Tonga	29.6.1971.	29.6.1971.	29.7.1971.	29.6.1971.	
Vietnam, North					
Vietnam, Republic of					
Yemen					
			EASTERN EUROPE		
Albania		7.12.1964.		7.12.1964.	
Bulgaria	31.8.1962.	31.8.1962.		31.8.1962.	
Byelorussian SSR	27.2.1961.	27.2.1961.		27.2.1961.	
Czechoslovakia	31.8.1961.	31.8.1961.		31.8.1961.	
German Democratic Republic					
Hungary	6.12.1961.	6.12.1961.			
Poland		29.6.1962.		29.6.1962.	
Romania	12.12.1961.	12.12.1961.		12.12.1961.	
Ukrainian SSR	12.1.1961.	12.1.1961.		12.1.1961.	
USSR	22.11.1960.	22.11.1960.		22.11.1960.	
Yugoslavia	28.1.1966.	28.1.1966.	28.1.1966.	28.1.1966.	28.1.1966.
			LATIN AMERICA AND THE CARIBBEAN		
Argentine					
Barbados					
Bolivia					17.10.1958.
Brazil					
Chile					
Colombia			3.1.1963.	8.1.1962.	29.4.1958.
Costa Rica		16.2.1972.		16.2.1972.	29.4.1958.

LATIN AMERICA AND THE CARIBBEAN (cont.)

Convention	Convention on the Territorial Sea and Contiguous Zone	Convention on the High Seas	Convention on Fishing and Conservation of the Living Resources of the High Seas	Convention on the Continental Shelf	Optional Protocol of Signature concerning the Compulsory Settlement of Disputes
Cuba					29.4.1958.
Dominican Republic	11.8.1964.	11.8.1964.	11.8.1964.	11.8.1964.	29.4.1958.
Ecuador					
El Salvador					
Guatemala		27.11.1961.		27.11.1961.	
Guyana					
Haiti	29.3.1960.	29.3.1960.	29.3.1960.	29.3.1960.	29.3.1960.
Honduras					
Jamaica	8.10.1965.	8.10.1965.	16.4.1964.	8.10.1965.	
Mexico	2.8.1966.	2.8.1966.	2.8.1966.	2.8.1966.	
Nicaragua					
Panama					2.5.1958.
Paraguay					
Peru					
Trinidad and	11.4.1966.	11.4.1966.	11.4.1966.	11.7.1968	
Uruguay					29.4.1958.
Venezuela	15.8.1961.	15.8.1961.	10.7.1963.	15.8.1961.	

WESTERN EUROPE AND OTHERS

Australia	14.5.1963.	14.5.1963.	14.5.1963.	14.5.1963.	14.5.1963.
Austria					
Belgium	6.1.1972.	6.1.1972.	6.1.1972.		6.1.1972.
Canada				6.2.1970.	
Cyprus					
Denmark	26.9.1968.	26.9.1968.	26.9.1968.	12.6.1963.	26.9.1968.
Finland	16.2.1965.	16.2.1965.	16.2.1965.	16.2.1965.	16.2.1965.
France			18.9.1970.	14.6.1965.	30.10.1958.
Germany, Federal Republic					30.10.1958.
Greece					

WESTERN EUROPE AND OTHERS (cont.)

Convention	Convention on the Territorial Sea and Contiguous Zone	Convention on the High Seas	Convention on Fishing and Conservation of the Living Resources of the High Seas	Convention on the Continental Shelf	Optional Protocol of Signature concerning the Compulsory Settlement of Disputes
Holy See					30.4.1958.
Iceland					
Ireland					
Italy	17.12.1964.	17.12.1964.			
Luxembourg					
Malta	19.5.1966.			19.5.1966.	19.5.1966.
Monaco					
Netherlands	18.2.1966.	18.2.1966.	18.2.1966.	18.2.1966.	18.2.1966.
New Zealand				18.1.1965.	29.4.1958.
Norway				9.9.1971.	
Portugal	8.1.1963.	8.1.1963.	8.1.1963.	8.1.1963.	8.1.1963.
San Marino					
Spain	25.2.1971.	25.2.1971.	25.2.1971.	25.2.1971.	
Sweden				1.6.1966.	28.6.1966.
Switzerland	18.5.1966.	18.5.1966.	18.5.1966.	18.5.1966.	18.5.1966.
Turkey					
United Kingdom	14.3.1960.	14.3.1960.	14.3.1960.	11.5.1964.	9.9.1958.
United States of America	12.4.1961.	12.4.1961.	12.4.1961.	12.4.1961.	
Total number of ratifications	43	51	34	50	36

TABLE 2. OIL POLLUTION CONVENTIONS

AFRICA

Convention	International Convention for the Prevention of Pollution of the Sea by Oil (2)	Amendments to the Convention	Amendments to the Convention	International Convention relating to Intervention on the High Seas in Cases of Oil Pollution Casualties	International Convention on Civil Liability for Oil Pollution Damage	International Convention on the Establishment of an International Fund for Compensation for Oil Pollution Damage
Date of Signature	12.5.1954.	21.10.1969	15.10.1971.	29.11.1969.	29.11.1969.	18.12.1971.
Date of Entry into Force	26.7.1958.	(3)	(3)	(4)	(5)	(6)
Algeria	20.1.1964.					
Botswana						
Burundi						
Cameroon						
Central Africa Republic						
Chad						
Congo, Republic of						
Dahomey						
Equatorial Guinea						
Ethiopia						
Gabon						
Gambia						
Ghana	17.7.1962.					
Guinea						
Ivory Coast	17.3.1967.					
Kenya						
Lesotho						
Liberia	28.3.1962.					
Libya						
Malagasy Republic	1.2.1965.	22.1.1971.				
Malawi						
Mali						

AFRICA (cont.)

Convention	International Convention for the Prevention of Pollution of the Sea by Oil	1969 Amendments	1971 Amendments	Public Law Convention 1969	Private Law Convention 1969	1971 Convention
Mauritania						
Mauritius						
Morocco	29.2.1968.					
Niger						
Nigeria	22.1.1968.					
Rwanda						
Senegal				27.3.1972	27.3.1972.	
Sierra Leone						
Somalia						
South Africa						
Sudan						
Swaziland						
Tanzania						
Togo						
Tunisia						
Uganda						
United Arab Republic	22.4.1963.					
Upper Volta						
Zaire						
Zambia						

ASIA AND THE FAR EAST

Convention	International Convention for the Prevention of Pollution of the Sea by Oil	1969 Amendments	1971 Amendments	Public Law Convention 1969	Private Law Convention 1969	1971 Convention
Afghanistan						
Bahrein						
Bangladesh						
Bhutan						
Burma						
Cambodia						
China, People's Republic						
China, Republic of						

ASIA AND THE FAR EAST (cont.)

Convention	International Convention for the Prevention of Pollution of the Sea by Oil	1969 Amendments	1971 Amendments	Public Law Convention 1969	Private Law Convention 1969	1971 Convention
Fiji						
India						
Indonesia						
Iran						
Iraq						
Israel	11.11.1965.					
Japan	21.8.1967.	6.4.1971.		6.4.1971.		
Jordan	8.5.1963.					
Korea, North						
Korea, Republic of						
Kuwait	27.11.1961.					
Laos						
Lebanon	31.5.1967.					
Malaysia						
Maldives						
Mongolia						
Nauru						
Nepal						
Oman						
Pakistan						
Philippines	19.11.1963.					
Qatar						
Saudi Arabia	30.12.1971.	30.12.1971.				
Singapore						
Southern Yemen	20.5.1969.					
Sri Lanka						
Syria	24.12.1968.					

ASIA AND THE FAR EAST (cont.)

Convention	International Convention for the Prevention of Pollution of the Sea by Oil	1969 Amendments	1971 Amendments	Public Law Convention 1969	Private Law Convention 1969	1971 Convention
Thailand						
Tonga						
Vietnam, North						
Vietnam, Republic of						
Yemen						
EASTERN EUROPE						
Albania						
Bulgaria						
Byeloruss-SSR						
Czechoslovakia						
German Democratic Republic						
Hungary						
Poland	28.2.1961.					
Romania						
Ukrainian SSR						
USSR	3.9.1969.	2.11.1971.				
Yugoslavia						
LATIN AMERICA AND THE CARIBBEAN						
Argentine						
Barbados						
Bolivia						
Brazil						
Chile						
Colombia						
Costa Rica						
Cuba						
Dominican Republic	29.5.1963.					

LATIN AMERICA AND THE CARRIBEAN (cont.)

Convention	International Convention for the Prevention of Pollution of the Sea by Oil	1969 Amendments	1971 Amendments	Public Law Convention 1969	Private Law Convention 1969	1971 Convention
Ecuador						
El Salvador						
Guatemala						
Guyana						
Haiti						
Honduras						
Jamaica						
Mexico	10.5.1956.					
Nicaragua						
Panama	25.9.1963.					
Paraguay						
Peru						
Trinidad and Tobago						
Uruguay						
Venezuela	12.12.1963.					

WESTERN EUROPE AND OTHERS

Convention	International Convention for the Prevention of Pollution of the Sea by Oil	1969 Amendments	1971 Amendments	Public Law Convention 1969	Private Law Convention 1969	1971 Convention
Australia	20.8.1962.					
Austria						
Belgium	16.4.1957.			21.10.1971.		
Canada	19.12.1956.					
Cyprus						
Denmark	26.11.1956.	22.3.1971.				
Finland	30.12.1958.					
France	26.7.1957.	4.2.1972.				
Germany, Federal Republic	11.6.1956.					
Greece	28.3.1967.					
Holy See						
Iceland	23.2.1962.	5.3.1970.				

WESTERN EUROPE AND OTHERS (cont.)

Convention	International Convention for the Prevention of Pollution of the Sea by Oil	1969 Amendments	1971 Amendments	Public Law Convention 1969	Private Law Convention 1969	1971 Convention
Ireland	13.2.1957.					
Italy	25.5.1964.					
Luxembourg						
Malta						
Monaco	25.3.1970.					
Netherlands	24.7.1958.					
New Zealand	1.6.1971.					
Norway	26.1.1957.	29.6.1971.				
Portugal	28.3.1967.					
San Marino						
Spain	22.1.1964.					
Sweden	24.5.1955.					
Switzerland	12.1.1966.					
Turkey						
United Kingdom	6.5.1955.	10.5.1971.		12.1.1971.		
U.S.A.	8.9.1961.	14.10.1971.		14.10.1971.		
Total number of Ratifications	44	10	0	5	1	0

TABLE 3. OTHER CONVENTIONS CONCLUDED UNDER THE AUSPICES OF IMCO.

AFRICA

Convention	International Convention for the Safety of Life at Sea.	Amendments to the Convention.	Amendments to the Convention.	Amendments to the Convention.	Amendments to the Convention.	Amendments to the Convention.	Regulations for the Prevention of Collisions of Vessels at Sea.	Convention on Facilitation of International Maritime Traffic.(7)	International Convention on Load Lines.	Amendments to the Convention.	International Convention on Tonnage Measurement of ships.
Date of Signature	17.6.1960.	30.11.1966.	25.10.1967.	26.11.1968.	21.10.1969.	12.10.1971.	17.6.1960.	9.4.1965.	5.4.1966.	12.10.1971	23.6.1969.
Date of Entry into force	26.5.1965.	(3)	(3)	(3)	(3)	(3)	1.9.1965.	5.3.1967.	21.7.1968.	(3)	(8)
Algeria	20.1.1964.										
Botswana											
Burundi											
Cameroon							10.7.1961.				
Central African Repub.											
Chad											
Congo, Rep.											
Dahomey											
Equatorial Guinea	3.3.1972.										
Ethiopia											
Gabon											
Gambia	1.11.1966.						1.2.1967.				
Ghana	22.3.1962.	1.11.1967.					22.3.1962.	5.11.1965.	25.9.1968.		
Guinea	5.9.1968.										
Ivory Coast	2.11.1965.						2.12.1965.	16.2.1967.	19.7.1971.		
Kenya											

AFRICA (cont.)

Convention	SOLAS Convention	1966 Amendments	1967 Amendments	1968 Amendments	1969 Amendments	1971 Amendments	Regulations	Facilitation Convention	Loadlines Convention	Amendments	Tonnage Convention
Lesotho											
Liberia	26.5.1964.	25.2.1969.	29.1.1970.				26.5.1964.		8.5.1967.		
Libya											
Malagasy Republic	13.9.1962.	9.8.1967.		29.9.1969.			8.11.1963.	8.7.1970.	16.1.1967.		
Malawi											
Mali											
Mauritania	4.12.1967.								4.12.1967.		
Morocco	28.11.1962.	28.6.1968.					28.6.1965.		19.1.1968.		
Niger											
Nigeria	28.11.1965.						30.11.1965.	24.1.1967.	14.11.1968.		
Rwanda											
Senegal	9.4.1970.										
Sierra Leone											
Somalia	30.3.1967.								30.3.1967.		
South Africa	13.12.1967.	2.12.1968.	31.1.1972.	31.1.1972.	31.1.1972.		7.1.1966.		14.12.1966.		
Sudan											
Swaziland											
Tanzania											
Togo											
Tunisia	20.5.1963.	23.11.1971.	23.11.1971.					27.1.1969.	23.8.1966.		
Uganda											
U.A.R.	27.7.1965.	15.7.1970.					29.5.1964.		6.12.1968.		
Upper Volta											

AFRICA (cont.)

Convention	SOLAS Convention	1966 Amendments	1967 Amendments	1968 Amendments	1969 Amendments	1971 Amendments	Regulations	Facilitation Convention	Loadlines Convention	Amendme
Zaire	20.5.1968.									
Zambia	2.9.1970.	2.9.1970.	2.9.1970.	2.9.1970.				14.12.1965.	2.9.1970.	
ASIA AND THE FAR EAST										
Afghanistan										
Bahrein										
Bangladesh										
Bhutan										
Burma	12.7.1965.						27.1.1961.			
Cambodia	24.11.1970.									
China, Peoples Rep.										
China, Rep.	23.2.1965.	16.4.1968.					21.11.1966.	19.7.1968.	24.7.1968.	
Fiji										
India	28.2.1966.						28.7.1964.		19.4.1968.	
Indonesia	28.10.1966.						7.5.1968.			
Iran	31.5.1966.									
Iraq										
Israel	5.10.1965.	13.10.1967.	22.4.1969.				5.8.1964.	13.10.1967.	5.7.1967.	
Japan	24.3.1963.						7.8.1964.		15.5.1968.	
Jordan										
Korea N.										
Korea, Rep.	21.5.1965.	6.12.1968.					8.12.1965.		10.7.1969.	
Kuwait	14.5.1965.		7.7.1969.				14.5.1965.		28.8.1968.	
Laos										

ASIA AND THE FAR EAST (cont.)

Convention	SOLAS Convention	1966 Amendments	1967 Amendments	1968 Amendments	1969 Amendments	1971 Amendments	Regulations	Facilitation Convention	Loadlines Convention	Amendments	Tonnage Convention
Lebanon	27.4.1966	25.1.1968.	8.10.1968.	8.7.1969.			22.9.1969.		7.7.1970.		
Malaysia	16.8.1965.								12.1.1971.		
Maldives	29.1.1968.	20.12.1968.	6.11.1968.	16.7.1969.	1.4.1970.		21.7.1969.		29.1.1968.		
Mongolia											
Nauru	19.1.1970.										
Nepal											
Oman											
Pakistan	24.2.1966.	6.7.1967.	7.6.1968.				14.5.1963.		5.12.1968.		
Philippines	11.8.1965.			9.9.1969.			25.1.1962.		4.3.1969.		
Qatar											
Saudi Arabia	3.5.1965.										
Singapore	12.2.1969.						23.8.1968.	21.9.1971.			
S. Yemen	20.5.1969.	20.5.1969.	20.5.1969.	20.5.1969.					20.5.1969.		
Syria	24.12.1968.										
Thailand											
Tonga											
N. Vietnam											
Vietnam,Rep.	8.1.1962.	14.3.1968.					8.1.1962.		14.6.1968.		
Yemen											

EASTERN EUROPE

Convention	SOLAS Convention	1966 Amendments	1967 Amendments	1968 Amendments	1969 Amendments	1971 Amendments	Regulations	Facilitation Convention	Loadlines Convention	Amendments	Tonnage Convention
Albania											
Bulgaria	16.10.1967.						1.7.1966.		30.12.1968.		
Byelorussian SSR											

EASTERN EUROPE (cont.)

Convention	SOLAS Convention	1966 Amendments	1967 Amendments	1968 Amendments	1969 Amendments	1971 Amendments	Regulations	Facilitation Convention	Loadlines Convention	Amendments	Tonnage Convention
Czechoslovakia	5.7.1967.						5.7.1967.	19.12.1966.	16.6.1969.		
German Democratic Rep.											
Hungary	24.3.1970.										
Poland	29.4.1966.						14.3.1963.	25.7.1969.	28.5.1969.		
Romania	12.12.1967.	23.12.1970.	23.12.1970.				6.2.1964.		3.6.1971.		
Ukrainian SSR											
USSR	4.8.1965.						24.5.1961.	25.10.1966.	4.7.1966.		20.11.1969.
Yugoslavia	23.2.1965.	22.11.1968.					26.7.1961.	18.7.1966.	25.10.1968.		29.4.1971.
LATIN AMERICA AND THE CARIBBEAN											
Argentine	27.4.1966.						27.4.1966.		3.6.1971		
Barbados											
Bolivia											
Brazil	8.3.1967.	9.12.1971.	9.12.1971.				8.3.1967		12.9.1969.		30.11.1970.
Chile	7.9.1966.										
Colombia											
Costa Rica											
Cuba	22.8.1963.								6.2.1969.		
Dominican Republic								11.7.1966.			
Ecuador											
El Salvador											
Guatemala											

LATIN AMERICA AND THE CARIBBEAN (cont.)

Convention	SOLAS Convention	1966 Amendments	1967 Amendments	1968 Amendments	1969 Amendments	1971 Amendments	Regulations	Facilitation Convention	Loadlines Convention	Amendments	Tonnage Convention
Guyana											
Haiti	17.3.1961.										
Honduras	18.2.1969.										
Jamaica	22.2.1968.						5.9.1968.				
Mexico	22.6.1966.								25.3.1970.		
Nicaragua	9.10.1967.										
Panama	12.10.1965.	30.5.1968.							15.5.1966.		
Paraguay	11.9.1963.						11.9.1963.				
Peru	25.7.1962.	14.7.1967.					15.11.1961.		18.1.1967.		
Trinidad & Tobago	6.9.1966.						6.9.1966.	16.3.1967.	24.8.1966.		
Uruguay	19.9.1968.										
Venezuela	23.1.1969.										

WESTERN EUROPE AND OTHERS

Convention	SOLAS Convention	1966 Amendments	1967 Amendments	1968 Amendments	1969 Amendments	1971 Amendments	Regulations	Facilitation Convention	Loadlines Convention	Amendments	Tonnage Convention
Australia	20.12.1967.						13.1.1967.		29.7.1968.		
Austria											
Belgium	10.2.1966.						29.3.1961.	4.1.1967.	22.1.1969.		
Canada	26.5.1965.	23.4.1968.	2.6.1969.				24.3.1963.	18.7.1967.	14.1.1970.		
Cyprus	26.7.1965.						11.8.1966.		5.5.1969.		
Denmark	1.12.1964.	24.7.1969.					10.7.1961.	9.1.1968.	28.6.1967.		
Finland	11.5.1965.	25.11.1971.					12.4.1962.	20.3.1967.	15.5.1968.		
France	16.10.1961.	6.6.1967.	14.1.1969.	18.6.1969.	14.4.1970.		18.5.1961.	29.11.1967.	30.11.1966.		
Germany, Fed. Rep.	25.5.1965.	25.6.1969.					25.5.1965.	26.7.1967.	9.4.1969.		

WESTERN EUROPE AND OTHERS (cont.)

Convention	SOLAS Convention	1966 Amendments	1967 Amendments	1968 Amendments	1969 Amendments	1971 Amendments	Regulations	Facilitation Convention	Loadlines Convention	Amendments	Tonnage Convention
Greece	13.2.1963.	31.7.1968.					16.4.1963.		12.6.1968.		
Holy See											
Iceland	11.12.1964.	15.5.1967.					22.1.1965.	24.1.1967.	24.6.1970.		17.6.1970.
Ireland	14.2.1967.						6.4.1964.	18.6.1971.	28.8.1968.		
Italy	26.5.1966.	9.12.1968.					6.7.1966.		19.4.1968.		
Luxembourg											
Malta											
Monaco	25.3.1970.	25.3.1970.	25.3.1970.	25.3.1970.			25.3.1970.	9.4.1965.	25.3.1970.		19.1.1971.
Netherlands	16.10.1964.	29.12.1967.					4.3.1963.	21.9.1967.	21.7.1967.		
New Zealand	14.2.1966.						17.9.1965.		5.2.1970.		
Norway	23.8.1961.	18.3.1969.	31.10.1969.	17.9.1970.	23.7.1971.		23.8.1961.	8.9.1966.	18.3.1968.		26.8.1971.
Portugal	14.6.1966.						9.4.1962.		22.12.1969.		
San Marino											
Spain	22.1.1963.		9.12.1969.	25.7.1969.			21.4.1964.		1.7.1968.		
Sweden	23.12.1965.	18.8.1967.					12.7.1961.	28.7.1967.	28.7.1967.		
Switzerland	12.1.1966.	16.12.1971.					27.8.1965.	23.4.1968.	23.4.1968.		
Turkey	2.6.1966.						2.6.1966.		5.8.1968.		
UK	11.6.1964.	13.9.1967.	(21)	1.2.1971.	1.2.1971.		28.8.1963.	24.2.1966.	11.7.1967.		8.1.1971.
USA	2.8.1962.	7.4.1967.	10.6.1968.				12.3.1964.	17.3.1967.	17.11.1966.		
Total number of Ratifications	84	36	19	12	5	0	59	30	62	0	7

TABLE 4. CONVENTIONS REGULATING FISHERIES IN THE NORTH ATLANTIC AND NORTH SEA

Convention	International Convention for the Northwest Atlantic Fisheries	Protocol to the Convention relating to the holding of annual meetings	Declaration of Understanding regarding the Convention concerning Mollusks	Protocol to extend the Provisions of the Convention to Harp and Hood Seals	Protocol relating to Entry into Force of Proposals adopted by the Commission	Protocol relating to Measures of Control	Protocol relating to Panel Membership and to Regulatory Measures	Protocol relating to Amendments to the Convention	North-East Atlantic Fisheries Convention	Convention on Conduct of Fishing Operations in the North Atlantic	Fisheries Convention
Date of Signature	8.2.1949.	25.6.1956.	24.4.1961.	15.7.1963.	29.11.1965.	29.11.1965.	1.10.1969.	6.10.1970.	24.1.1959.	1.6.1967.	9.3.1964.
Date of Entry into force	3.7.1950.	10.1.1959.	5.6.1963.	29.4.1966.	19.12.1969.	19.12.1969.	15.12.1971.	(9)	27.6.1963.	(10)	15.3.1966.
Belgium									15.9.1961.		10.2.1966.
Canada	3.7.1950.	27.3.1957.	15.9.1961.	23.1.1964.	1.4.1966.	1.4.1966.	29.10.1970.				
Denmark	14.12.1950.	23.11.1956.	5.2.1961.	27.7.1964.	14.8.1968.	14.8.1968.	18.8.1970.	27.10.1970.	14.7.1960.		9.10.1964.
France	27.1.1953.	10.1.1959.	5.5.1961.	21.7.1964.	15.2.1967.	15.2.1967.	23.12.1970.	6.4.1971.	20.3.1962.		5.7.1965.
Germany, Federal Republ-	27.6.1957.	27.6.1957.	8.5.1961.	26.5.1965.	29.5.1969.	29.5.1969.	15.12.1971.	15.12.1971.	27.6.1963.		
Iceland	13.2.1950.	23.11.1956.	8.5.1961.	23.3.1964.	7.12.1965.	7.12.1965.	14.11.1969.		12.4.1960.	12.5.1969.	
Ireland									2.10.1962.		20.9.1965.
Italy	19.8.1952.	7.6.1957.	14.9.1961.	29.4.1966.	19.12.1969.	19.12.1969.	18.11.1971.				25.3.1966.
Japan	1.7.1970.	1.7.1970.	1.7.1970.	1.7.1970.	1.7.1970.	1.7.1970.	1.7.1970.				
Netherlands									21.4.1960.		20.7.1971.
Norway	2.7.1952.	15.5.1957.	8.5.1961.	3.12.1963.	9.3.1967.	9.3.1967	10.7.1970.	8.1.1971.	12.1.1960.	20.8.1968.	
Poland	21.11.1961.	21.11.1961.	5.6.1963.	5.1.1966.	7.1.1969.	7.1.1969.	30.11.1971.	30.11.1971.	22.2.1961.		7.6.1966.
Portugal	19.7.1952.	17.1.1957.	8.5.1961.	2.10.1964.	19.12.1960.	19.12.1969.	19.10.1971.		13.12.1962.	28.10.1968.	15.3.1966.
Romania	21.3.1967.	21.3.1967.	21.3.1967.	21.3.1967.	21.3.1967.	21.3.1967.	10.4.1970.				
Spain	17.1.1952.	2.5.1957.	5.5.1961.	17.8.1964.	29.3.1967.	30.3.1967.	3.3.1971.		7.11.1960.		15.9.1965.

TABLE 4. CONVENTIONS REGULATING FISHERIES IN THE NORTH ATLANTIC AND NORTH SEA (cont.)

Convention	International Convention for the Northwest Atlantic Fisheries	Protocol to the Convention relating to the holding of annual meetings	Declaration of Understanding regarding the Convention concerning Mollusks	Protocol to extend the Provisions of the Convention to Harp and Hood Seals	Protocol relating to Entry into Force of Proposals adopted by the Commission	Protocol relating to Measures of Control	Protocol relating to Panel Membership and to Regulatory Measures	Protocol relating to Amendments to the Convention	North-East Atlantic Fisheries Convention	Convention on Conduct of Fishing Operations in the North Atlantic	Fisheries Convention
Sweden									31.3.1960.	6.2.1970.	16.2.1966.
USSR	10.4.1958.	11.8.1958.	8.5.1961.	13.4.1964.	23.10.1967.	23.10.1967.	21.11.1969.	13.10.1971.	25.8.1960		
UK	15.12.1949.	2.4.1957.	2.8.1961.	8.5.1964.	15.8.1966.	15.8.1966.	12.1.1971.	14.6.1971.	27.8.1959.	2.6.1970	11.9.1964.
USA	1.9.1949.	22.5.1957.	9.2.1962.	13.7.1964.	16.8.1966.	16.8.1966.	17.4.1970.			(10 A)	
Total	15	15	15	15	15	15	15	7	14	5	11

TABLE 5. MISCELLANEOUS CONVENTIONS IN WESTERN EUROPE

Convention	Agreement for Co-operation in Dealing with Pollution of the North Sea by Oil	Convention for the Prevention of Marine Pollution by Dumping from Ships and Aircraft	European Agreement for the Prevention of Broadcasts transmitted from Stations outside National Territories
Date of signature	9.6.1969.	15.2.1972.	22.1.1965.
Date of entry into force	9.8.1969.	(11)	19.10.1967.
Belgium	9.6.1969.		18.9.1967.
Cyprus			1.9.1971.
Denmark	9.6.1969.		22.9.1965.
Finland			
France	9.6.1969.		5.3.1968.
Germany, Federal Republic of	9.6.1969.		30.1.1970.
Iceland			
Ireland			22.1.1969.
Netherlands			
Norway	28.9.1970	2.6.1972.	16.9.1971.
Portugal			6.8.1969.
Spain			
Sweden	9.6.1969.		15.6.1966.
United Kingdom	9.6.1969.		2.11.1967.
Total number of ratifications	7	1	10

TABLE 6. MISCELLANEOUS FISHERIES CONVENTIONS

Convention	International Convention for the Regulation of Whaling.	Protocol to the Convention.	Convention for the Establishment of an Inter-American Tropical Tuna Commission.	International Convention for the Conservation of Atlantic Tunas.	Convention on the Conservation of the Living Resources of the South-East Atlantic.	Agreement for the Establishment of the Indo-Pacific Fisheries Council	Agreement for the Establighment of a General Fisheries Council for the Mediterranean.
Date of signature	2.12.1946.	15.11.1956.	31.5.1949.	14.5.1966.	23.10.1969.	26.2.1948.	24.9.1949.
Date of entry into force	10.11.1948.	4.5.1959.	3.3.1950.	21.3.1969.	24.10.1971.	9.11.1948.	20.2.1952.
Algeria							11.12.1967.
Argentine	18.5.1960.	18.5.1960.					
Australia	1.12.1947.	8.4.1957.				10.3.1949.	
Brazil	(12)	(12)		1.4.1969.			
Bulgaria					24.4.1972.		
Burma						7.1.1949.	
Cambodia						19.1.1951.	
Canada	25.2.1949.	14.6.1957.	3.10.1967.	20.8.1968.			
China, Republic of							(13)
Costa Rica			3.3.1950.				
Cyprus							10.6.1965.
Denmark	23.5.1950.	26.7.1957					
Ecuador			(20)				
France	3.12.1948.	14.4.1958.		7.11.1968.		30.6.1948.	8.7.1952.
Ghana				17.4.1968.			
Greece							7.4.1952.
Iceland	10.3.1947.	23.11.1956.					
India						9.11.1948.	
Indonesia						29.3.1950.	
Israel							20.2.1952.
Italy							29.5.1950.
Japan	21.4.1951.	24.5.1957.	25.6.1970.	24.8.1967.	22.6.1970.	3.10.1952.	
Korea						19.1.1950.	
Lebanon							14.11.1960.
Libya							13.5.1963.
Malaysia						15.9.1958.	

TABLE 6. MISCELLANEOUS FISHERIES CONVENTIONS (cont.)

Convention	International Convention for the Regulation of Whaling.	Protocol to the Convention.	Convention for the Establishment of an Inter-American Tropical Tuna Commission.	International Convention for the Conservation of Atlantic Tunas.	Convention on the Conservation of the Living Resources of the South-East Atlantic.	Agreement for the Establishment of the Indo-Pacific Fisheries Council	Agreement for the Establishment of a General Fisheries Council for the Mediterranean.
Malta							29.4.1965.
Mexico	30.6.1949.	9.3.1959.	29.1.1964.				
Monaco							14.5.1954.
Morocco				26.9.1970.			17.9.1956.
Netherlands	(14)	(14)				12.11.1948.	
New Zealand	(15)	(15)				6.9.1966.	
Norway	3.3.1948[16]	15.4.1957.					
Pakistan						1.8.1949.	
Panama	(17)	(17)	21.9.1953.				
Peru							
Philippines						23.7.1948.	
Poland					2.3.1972.		
Portugal					22.1.1971.		
Senegal				25.8.1971.			
South Africa	5.5.1948.	25.4.1957.		17.10.1967.	2.10.1970.		
Spain				21.3.1969.	6.12.1971.		19.10.1953.
Sri Lanka						21.2.1949.	
Sweden	(18)	(18)					
Thailand						6.10.1948.	
Tunisia							22.6.1954.
Turkey							6.4.1954.
USSR	11.9.1948.	3.7.1957.			24.9.1971.		
UAR							19.2.1951.
UK	17.6.1947.	23.5.1957.				28.2.1949	(19)
USA	18.7.1947.	30.8.1957.	3.3.1950.	18.5.1967.		3.9.1948	
Vietnam						3.2.1951.	
Yugoslavia							12.10.1951.
Total number of ratifications	13	13	6	10	7	18	16

TABLE 7. MISCELLANEOUS CONVENTIONS

AFRICA

Convention	Treaty Banning Nuclear Weapons Tests in the Atmosphere, in Outer Space, and Under Water. (23)	Treaty on the Prohibition of the Emplacement of Nuclear Weapons and Other Weapons of Mass Destruction on the Seabed and the Ocean Floor and in the Subsoil thereof. (26)	Convention on Transit Trade of Land Locked State.	Convention on the Inter-Governmental Maritime Consultative Organisation. (22)	Convention on the International Hydrographic Organisation.	Convention on the International Council for the Exploration of the Sea.
Date of Signature	5.8.1963.	11.2.1971.	8.7.1965.	6.3.1948.	3.5.1967.	12.9.1964.
Date of Entry into Force	10.10.1963.	18.5.1972.	9.6.1967.	17.3.1958.	22.9.1970	22.7.1964.
Algeria				31.10.1963.		
Botswana	10.10.1963.					
Burundi			1.5.1968.			
Cameroon				1.5.1961.		
Central African Republic	24.8.1965					
Chad			2.3.1967.			
Congo,Rep.						
Dahomey	22.5.1965.					
Equatorial Guinea						
Ethiopia						
Gabon	4.3.1964.					
Gambia	10.10.1963.					
Ghana	27.11.1963.			6.7.1959.		
Guinea						
Ivory Coast		14.1.1972.		4.11.1960.		
Kenya	10.6.1965.					
Lesotho			28.5.1969.			
Liberia	22.5.1964.			6.1.1959.		
Libya	15.7.1968.			16.2.1970.		
Malagasy Rep.				8.3.1961.		
Malawi	10.10.1963.		12.12.1966.			
Mali			11.10.1967.			
Mauritania	15.4.1964.			8.5.1961.		

AFRICA (cont.)

Convention	Nuclear Test. Ban Treaty	Seabed Arms Limitation Treaty	Land Locked States Convention	IMCO Convention	IHO Convention	ICES Convention
Mauritius	10.10.1963.	23.4.1971.				
Morocco	1.2.1966.	5.8.1971.		30.7.1962.		
Niger	6.7.1964.	9.8.1971.	3.6.1966.			
Nigeria	17.2.1967.		16.5.1966.	15.3.1962.		
Rwanda	22.10.1963.		13.8.1968.			
Senegal	6.5.1964.			7.11.1960.		
Sierra Leone	21.2.1964.					
Somalia						
S. Africa	10.10.1963.				16.8.1968.	
Sudan	4.3.1966.					
Swaziland	29.5.1969.	9.8.1971.	26.5.1969.			
Tanzania	6.2.1964.					
Togo		28.6.1971.				
Tunisia	26.5.1965.	29.10.1971.		23.5.1963.		
Uganda	24.3.1964.					
UAR	10.1.1964.			17.3.1958.	13.12.1968.	
Upper Volta						
Zaire						
Zambia	10.10.1963.		2.12.1966.			
			ASIA AND THE FAR EAST			
Afghanistan	12.3.1964.	21.5.1971.				
Bahrein						
Bangladesh						
Bhutan						
Burma	15.11.1963.			6.7.1951.		
Cambodia				3.1.1961.		
China, People's Rep. of				(24)		
China, Rep.		22.2.1972.		1.7.1958.(24)	18.11.1968.	
Fiji						
India	10.10.1963.			6.1.1959.	24.6.1968.	
Indonesia	8.5.1964.			18.1.1961.	28.11.1968.	

ASIA AND THE FAR EAST (cont.)

Convention	Nuclear Test. Ban Treaty	Seabed Arms Limitation Treaty	Land Locked States Convention	IMCO Convention	IHO Convention	ICES Convention
Iran	5.5.1964.	26.8.1971.		2.1.1958.	16.9.1968.	
Iraq	30.10.1964.					
Israel	15.1.1964.			24.4.1952.		
Japan	15.6.1964.	21.6.1971.		17.3.1958.	12.6.1969.	
Jordan	29.5.1964.	17.8.1971.				
Korea, North						
Korea, Rep.	24.7.1964.			10.4.1962.	21.7.1969.	
Kuwait	21.5.1965.			5.7.1960.		
Laos	10.2.1965.	3.11.1971.	29.12.1967.			
Lebanon	20.5.1965.			3.5.1966.		
Malaysia	16.7.1964.			17.6.1971.		
Maldives				31.5.1967.		
Mongolia	7.11.1963.		26.7.1966.			
Nauru						
Nepal	7.10.1964.	9.8.1971.	22.8.1966.			
Oman						
Pakistan				21.11.1958.	17.6.1968.	
Philippines	10.11.1965.			9.11.1964.		
Qatar						
Saudi Arabia				25.2.1969.		
Singapore	16.7.1964.			17.1.1966.		
S. Yemen						
Sri Lanka	13.2.1964.			6.4.1972.		
Syria	1.6.1964.			28.1.1963.		
Thailand	15.11.1963.				13.3.1972.	
Tonga	10.10.1963.					
Vietnam, N.						
Vietnam, Rep.						
W. Samoa	19.1.1965.					
Yemen						

EASTERN EUROPE

Convention	Nuclear Test Ban Treaty	Seabed Arms Limitation Treaty	Land Locked States Convention	IMCO Convention	IHO Convention	ICES Convention
Albania						
Bulgaria	2.12.1963.	7.5.1971.		5.4.1960.		
Byelorussian SSR						
Czechoslovakia	14.10.1963.	11.1.1972.	8.8.1967.	1.10.1963.		
German Democratic Rep.						
Hungary	21.10.1963.	13.8.1971.	20.9.1967.	10.6.1970.		
Poland	14.10.1963.	15.11.1971.		16.3.1960.		25.11.1966.
Romania	12.12.1963.			28.4.1965.		
Ukrainian SSR						
USSR	10.10.1963.	18.5.1971.		24.12.1958.		28.10.1965.
Yugoslavia	15.1.1964.		10.5.1967.	12.1.1960.	20.9.1968.	

LATIN AMERICA AND THE CARIBBEAN

Convention	Nuclear Test Ban Treaty	Seabed Arms Limitation Treaty	Land Locked States Convention	IMCO Convention	IHO Convention	ICES Convention
Argentine				18.6.1953.	4.4.1968.	
Barbados				7.1.1970.		
Bolivia	25.1.1966.					
Brazil	4.3.1965.			4.3.1963.		
Chile	6.10.1965.			17.2.1972.	11.6.1961.	
Colombia						
Costa Rica						
Cuba				6.5.1966.		
Dominican Rep.	18.6.1964.	11.2.1972.		25.8.1953.		
Ecuador	8.5.1964.			12.7.1956.		
El Salvador	7.12.1964.					
Guatemala					26.1.1971.	
Guyana						
Haiti				23.6.1953.		
Honduras	2.12.1964.			23.8.1954.		
Jamaica						

LATIN AMERICA AND THE CARIBBEAN (cont.)

Convention	Nuclear Test Ban Treaty	Seabed Arms Limitation Treaty	Land Locked States Convention	IMCO Convention	IHO Convention	ICES Convention
Mexico	27.12.1963.			21.9.1954.		
Nicaragua	26.1.1965.					
Panama				31.12.1958.		
Paraguay						
Peru	4.8.1964.			15.4.1968.		
Trinidad and Tobago	16.7.1964.			27.4.1965.		
Uruguay	25.2.1969.			10.5.1968.		
Venezuela	3.3.1965.					

WESTERN EUROPE AND OTHERS

Australia	12.11.1963.		2.5.1972.	13.2.1952.	25.11.1968.	
Austria	17.7.1964.					
Belgium	1.3.1966.		21.4.1970.	9.8.1951.		20.7.1967.
Canada	28.1.1964.	17.5.1972.		15.10.1948.	26.8.1968.	22.6.1967.
Cyprus	15.4.1965.	17.11.1971.				
Denmark	15.1.1964.	15.6.1971.	26.5.1969.	3.6.1959.	22.6.1970.	20.4.1965.
Finland	9.1.1964.	8.6.1971.	22.1.1971.	21.4.1959.	16.2.1968.	10.6.1965.
France				9.4.1952.	4.4.1968.	19.1.1965.
Germany, Federal Republic	1.12.1964.			7.1.1959.	12.6.1969.	13.5.1965.
Greece	18.12.1963.			31.12.1958.	15.2.1971.	
Holy See						
Iceland	29.4.1964.			8.11.1960.	7.5.1968.	4.12.1964.
Ireland	18.12.1963.	19.8.1971.		26.2.1951.		10.6.1965.
Italy	10.12.1964.			28.1.1957.		28.12.1967.
Luxembourg	10.2.1965.					
Malta	10.10.1963.	4.5.1971.		22.6.1966.		
Monaco						
Netherlands	14.9.1964.		30.11.1971.	31.3.1949.	6.6.1969.	13.2.1967.
New Zealand	10.10.1963.	24.2.1972.		9.11.1960.		
Norway	21.11.1963.	28.6.1971.	17.9.1968.	29.12.1958.	12.3.1969.	26.5.1965.

WESTERN EUROPE AND OTHERS (cont.)

Convention	Nuclear Test Ban Treaty	Seabed Arms Limitation Treaty	Land Locked States Convention	IMCO Convention	IHO Convention	ICES Convention
Portugal					27.11.1968.	18.2.1966.
San Marino	3.7.1964.		12.6.1968.			
Spain	17.12.1964.			23.1.1962.	2.6.1969.	9.9.1965.
Sweden	9.12.1963.	28.4.1972.	16.6.1971.	27.4.1959.	11.10.1971.	30.11.1964.
Switzerland	16.1.1964.			20.7.1955.		
Turkey	8.7.1965.		25.3.1969.	25.3.1958.	6.9.1971.	
UK	10.10.1963.	18.5.1971.		14.2.1949(25)		4.5.1965.
USA	10.10.1963.	18.5.1971.	29.10.1968.	17.8.1950.	10.6.1968.	
Total number of ratifications	93	31	26	74	29	17

FOOTNOTES

1. Senegal announced in June 1971 that it no longer considered itself as being a party to this Convention.

2. The Convention was amended by Amendments adopted on April 11, 1962. The Amendments to Articles 1-10, 16 and 17, and to Annexes A and B, came into force on May 18, 1967; the Amendments to Article 14 came into force on June 28, 1967.

3. These amendments will come into force for all parties to the Convention when they have been ratified by two-thirds of the States Parties to the Convention.

4. The Convention will come into force when it has been ratified by 15 States.

5. The Convention will come into force when it has been ratified by 8 states, of which 5 must have not less than 1 million gross tons of tanker tonnage each.

6. The Convention will come into force when it has been ratified by 8 States (who must be parties to the International Convention on Civil Liability for Oil Pollution Damage) and whose total quantity of imported oil in the preceding year must be not less than 750 million metric tons.

7. Amendments to the Annex of the Convention entered into force on August 12, 1971.

8. The Convention will come into force 24 months after it has been accepted by 25 States with combined merchant fleets of not less than 65% of the gross tonnage of the world's merchant shipping.

9. These Amendments will come into force when they have been ratified by all the States Parties to the Convention.

10. The Convention will come into force when it has been ratified by 10 States.

10A. The Senate gave its advice and consent to ratification on October 22, 1969. It was ratified by the President on November 12, 1969. The deposit of instrument of ratification is awaiting enactment of implementing legislation.

11. The Convention will come into force when it has been

FOOTNOTES (cont.)

ratified by 7 States.

12. Brazil ratified the Convention on May 9, 1950 and the Protocol to the Convention on May 4, 1959. It denounced the Convention with effect from June 30, 1966.

13. Republic of China ratified the Convention on January 31, 1949 and withdrew with effect from July 21, 1952.

14. Netherlands ratified the Convention on November 10, 1948 and the Protocol to the Convention on December 23, 1957. It denounced the Convention with effect from June 30, 1959, re-acceded on May 4, 1962, but subsequently denounced the Convention again with effect from June 30, 1970.

15. New Zealand ratified the Convention on August 2, 1949 and the Protocol to the Convention on June 21, 1957. It denounced the Convention with effect from June 30, 1969.

16. Norway denounced the Convention with effect from June 30, 1959, but re-acceded on September 28, 1960.

17. Panama ratified the Convention on September 30, 1948 and the Protocol to the Convention on February 9, 1959. It denounced the Convention with effect from June 30, 1969.

18. Sweden ratified the Convention on January 28, 1949 and the Protocol to the Convention on June 6, 1957. It denounced the Convention with effect from June 30, 1964.

19. United Kingdom ratified the Convention on November 20, 1950 and withdrew on March 25, 1968.

20. Ecuador adhered to the Convention on April 7, 1961 and denounced it on August 21, 1967, effective August 21, 1968.

21. United Kingdom accepted the Amendments to Annexes I, II, IV and V on October 14, 1969 and the Amendments to Annex VI on February 1, 1971.

22. The Convention was amended by Amendments adopted on September 15, 1964 (Articles 17 and 18) and on September 28, 1965 (Article 29). They came into force on October 6, 1967 and November 3, 1968 respectively.

FOOTNOTES (cont.)

23. The list of ratifications refers to those ratifications deposited with the Government of the United Kingdom.

24. On May 24, 1972 the Council of IMCO adopted a resolution recognising the People's Republic of China as the only government having the right to represent China in IMCO.

25. Hong Kong became an associate member of IMCO on June 7, 1967.

26. The list of ratifications refers to those ratifications deposited with the government of USA.

CLAIMS TO TERRITORIAL SEA, EXCLUSIVE FISHING ZONES, CONTINENTAL SHELF AND OTHER EXCLUSIVE ZONES.

This table sets out the claims made by States to the Territorial Sea, Exclusive Fishing Zones, Continental Shelf and other zones as they appear from their national legislation and relevant treaties to which they are parties. States have been arranged according to geographical location under the following headings:-

1. Africa South of the Sahara
2. Arctic
3. Asia (excluding the Middle East)
4. Baltic
5. Black Sea
6. Gulf of Aqaba
7. Latin America and the Caribbean
8. Mediterranean
9. North Atlantic (including the English Channel)
10. North Pacific
11. North Sea (including the Skagerrak and Kattegat, but excluding the English Channel)
12. Pacific (Islands)
13. Persian Gulf
14. Red Sea

Some States appear under more than one heading. Where a State appears under more than one heading but information relating to its claims is relevant to only one of these headings, that information will only be given under the relevant heading,eg. Sweden appears under both the Baltic and North Sea; in the Baltic Sweden does not claim an exclusive fishing zone, but claims a 12 fishing zone in the North Sea. Consequently this claim is shown only under the North Sea heading and not under the Baltic.

Unless otherwise stated, all distances are given in nautical miles. "Exclusive fishing zone" refers to a zone beyond the outer limit of the territorial sea in which the coastal state claims the exclusive right to fish, subject to any concessions which may be granted to foreign fishermen. The dates in brackets refer to the year in which the claim was made. Only the current position (as of 8.1.1972) is given: thus for example, where nationals of one State have had transitional rights in the exclusive fishing zone of another State and these rights have expired, this will not normally be shown. Bilateral agreements appear in general only with the date and names of the parties.

a. indicates that a State is a party to the Convention on the Territorial Sea and Contiguous Zone 1958.

b. indicates that a State is a party to the Convention on the Continental Shelf.

"EEC Treaty of Accession" refers to Treaty concerning the Accession of the Kingdom of Denmark, Ireland, the Kingdom of Norway and the United Kingdom of Great Britain and Northern Ireland to the European Economic Community and the European Atomic Energy Community (with Final Act) of January 22, 1972.

While every attempt has been made to ensure that this table is as complete and accurate as possible, there are inevitably bound to be some errors.

AFRICA SOUTH OF THE SAHARA

State	Territorial Sea	Exclusive Fishing Zone	Fishery Conservation Zone	Other Zones	Continental Shelf
CAMEROON	18 (1967)				"Continental Platform" (1967)
CONGO	15 (1970) unconfirmed				
DAHOMEY	12 (1968)				Subsoil of area stretching 100 miles from the low tide level or from the first obstacle to navigation. (1968)
EQUATORIAL GUINEA	12 (1970)				
ETHIOPIA	12 (1953) In the case of pearl and other sedentary fisheries, the seaward limit of the territorial sea extends to the limit of these fisheries.				
GABON	100 (1972)				
GAMBIA	50 (1971)			In a six mile zone beyond the outer limit of the territorial sea, control may be exercised to punish any infringements of Gambian legislation. (1969)	
GHANA	12 (1963)		100 (1963)		Seabed and subsoil to a depth of 100 fathoms, and such further parts beyond that depth capable of exploitation. (1968)
GUINEA	130 (1964)				

AFRICA SOUTH OF THE SAHARA (continued)

State	Territorial Sea	Exclusive Fishing Zone	Fishery Conservation Zone	Other Zones	Continental Shelf
IVORY COAST	6 (1967)	12 (1967)			Subsoil of ocean floor or area lying between the low water line and the isobath of 200 metres. (1967)
KENYA	[a] 12 (1969)	(1)			[b]
LIBERIA	12 (1967)				Seabed and subsoil to 200 metres, or beyond to where depth admits of exploitat-ion. (1969)
MADAGASCAR	[a] 12 (1963)				[b]
MAURITANIA	30 (1972)	Foreign vessels wishing to fish in the zone contiguous to the territorial sea must obtain the consent of the Minister of Fisheries (1966)	Reserves the right to reg-ulate fishing in a zone contiguous to the terri-torial sea. (1967)		200 metres, or beyond to where depth admits of exploitation. (1971)
MAURITIUS	[a] 12 (1970)				[b] Seabed and subsoil less than 200 metres below the surface of the sea, or beyond where the natural resources are capable of exploitation. (1970)
NIGERIA	[a] 30 (1971)				[b] 200 metres, or beyond to where depth admits of exploitation. (1969)
SENEGAL	[a] 12 (1968)	110 (1972)			[b] 200 metres. (1961)
SIERRA LEONE	[a] 200 (1971)				[b]

AFRICA SOUTH OF THE SAHARA (continued)

State	Territorial Sea	Exclusive Fishing Zone	Fishery Conservation Zone	Other Zones	Continental Shelf
SOMALIA	12 (1967)				
SOUTH AFRICA	[a] 6 (1963)	12 (1963)		In a six mile zone beyond the outer limit of the territorial sea, the right to exercise any powers which may be considered necessary to prevent contravention of any fiscal law or any customs, emigration, immigration or sanitary law. (1963)	[b] as defined in the Convention on the Continental Shelf. (1963)
SUDAN	12 (1960)			6 miles beyond the territorial sea for customs and security purposes. (1970)	200 metres, or beyond where depth admits of exploitation. (1970)
TANZANIA	12 (1967) (1)				
TOGO	12 (1964)				
ZAIRE	12 (1971)				

ARCTIC

State	Territorial Sea	Exclusive Fishing Zone	Fishery Conservation Zone	Other Zones	Continental Shelf
CANADA	12 (1970)	Prescribed areas adjacent to the coast of Canada. (1970) (2)		Power to exercise pollution control within 100 miles of the Canadian coast or upto the median line where the distance between Canada and Greenland is less than 200 miles. (1970) (3)	[b]
GREENLAND (Danish)	[a] 3 (1950)	12 (1963) (4), (5)			[b]

ARCTIC (continued)

State	Territorial Sea	Exclusive Fishing Zone	Fishery Conservation Zone	Other Zones	Continental Shelf
SPITSBERGEN (Norwegian)	a 4 (1812) (6)				b
USSR	a 12 (1909) (7)			Pollution control in the Northern Sea Route. (1971)	b Seabed and subsoil to a depth of 200 metres, or beyond to where depth admits of exploitation. (1968)
USA	a 3 (1793)	12 (1966)	Power to set up explicitly bounded conservation zones in areas of the High Seas where fisheries are developed and maintained by US nationals alone, (1945)	12 mile custom zone.(1930) 300 mile defence zone. (1939) 100 mile zone from vessels suspected of smuggling. (1935) Aircraft approaching USA are to identify themselves 500 miles from land.	b Natural resources of the seabed and subsoil of the continental shelf contiguous to the coast of USA. (1945)

ASIA (excluding the Middle East)

State	Territorial Sea	Exclusive Fishing Zone	Fishery Conservation Zone	Other Zones	Continental Shelf
BANGLADESH	12 (1971)				
BURMA	12 (1968)				
CAMBODIA	a 12 (1969)				b To 50 metre isobath, including sovereignty over superjacent waters. (1957)
CHINA, PEOPLE'S REPUBLIC	12 (1958)				
CHINA, REPUBLIC OF	3 (1930)			12 mile custom zone.(1934)	b
INDIA	12 (1967)		112 (1956)		Seabed and subsoil to a depth of 200 metres or to where depth admits of exploitation. (1959)
INDONESIA	12 (1957) (8)				To whatever depth resource can be exploited. (1969) (10), (11)

ASIA (excluding the Middle East) (continued)

State	Territorial Sea	Exclusive Fishing Zone	Fishery Conservation Zone	Other Zones	Continental Shelf
JAPAN	[a] 3 (1870)	(9)			
KOREA, NORTH	12				
KOREA, REPUBLIC OF		20-200 (1952-54) (9)			
MALAYSIA	[a] 12 (1969)				[b] Seabed and subsoil to a depth of 200 metres or to where depth admits of exploitation. (1966) (12)
MALDIVES	Less than 3 to nearly 55 (retangular) (1968)	(12)			
PAKISTAN	12 (1966)		112 (1966)		Seabed to a depth of 100 fathoms. (1950)
PHILIPPINES	(1961) (13)				Seabed and subsoil to where depth admits of exploitation. (1968)
SINGAPORE	3 (1878) (14)				
SRI LANKA	12 (1971)		112 (1957)		Seabed and subsoil of continental or insular shelf. (1957)
THAILAND	[a] 12 (1966)				[b]
VIETNAM, NORTH	12 (1964) (15)				
VIETNAM, REPUBLIC OF	3 (1965) (16)		20 kilometres (1936)	Upto 12 miles from the base line of the territorial sea, the control necessary to prevent or punish infringements of the customs, fiscal, immigration and sanitary regulations effective within the territory or territorial sea. (1965)	200 metres or where the depth admits of exploitation. (1970)

ASIA (excluding the Middle East (continued)

State	Territorial Sea	Exclusive Fishing Zone	Fishery Conservation Zone	Other Zones	Continental Shelf
UK DEPENDENCIES: in general:	a 3				b
specific legislation for: SEYCHELLES	a 3	12 (1972)			b Seabed and subsoil over which Seychelles is entitled by international law to exercise sovereign rights for exploring and exploiting its natural resources. (1962)
BALTIC					
DENMARK	a 3 (1966) (27)	12 miles around Bornholm (1971) (25)(29)		Customs authorities have supervisory powers in a zone one mile beyond the outer limit of the territorial sea. (1967)	b 200 metres, or to where depth admits of exploitation (1963) (26)
FINLAND	a 4 (1956) (17)(31)			Customs zone two miles beyond the outer limit of the territorial sea. (1939)	b Seabed and subsoil adjacent to the territorial sea out to the boundary line determined by Articles 1 and 6 of the Convention on the Continental Shelf or by agreements with a foreign state. (1965) (17)
GERMANY, DEMOCRATIC REPUBLIC OF	3				200 metres, or to where the depth of superjacent waters admits of exploitation. (1964) (18) (19)
GERMANY, FEDERAL REPUBLIC OF	In accordance with international law (3 miles). (1956) (27)	(25)(30)			200 metres, or to where depth of superjacent waters admits of exploitation. (1964) (26)
POLAND	3 (1932) (21)	12 (1970) (22)(28)		6 mile customs and security zone (1932)	b (18)(19)(20)
SWEDEN	4 (1779) (31) Passage may be restricted in certain parts of the territorial sea for security reasons.	12 (1968)			b As defined in the Convention on the Continental Shelf. (1966)

BALTIC (continued)

State	Territorial Sea	Exclusive Fishing Zone	Fishery Conservation Zone	Other Zones	Continental Shelf
USSR	a 12 (1909) (9)(17)(21)	(24)			b Seabed and subsoil to a depth of 200 metres, or to where depth admits of exploitation. (1968) (17)(18)(20)
BLACK SEA					
BULGARIA	a 12 (1951) (34)				b (1962)
ROMANIA	a 12 (1951) (34)				b (1961)
TURKEY	6 (1964) (32) 12 (1964) in Black Sea	12 (1964)			(33)
USSR	a 12 (1909) (9)				b Seabed and subsoil to a depth of 200 metres, or to where depth admits of exploitation. (1968)
GULF OF AQABA					
EGYPT	12 (1958)				
ISRAEL	a 6 (1956)				b Submarine areas contiguous to coasts outside the territorial sea and to the extent depth admits of exploitation. (1952)
JORDAN	3 (1943)				
SAUDI ARABIA	12 (1958)			For assuring compliance with laws relating to security, navigation, fiscal and health matters, maritime surveillance may be exercised in a contiguous zone extending 6 miles beyond the outer limit of the territorial sea. (1958)	

LATIN AMERICA AND CARIBBEAN

State	Territorial Sea	Exclusive Fishing Zone	Fishery Conservation Zone	Other Zones	Continental Shelf
ARGENTINA (35)(36)	200 (1967) Freedom of navigation and overflight are not affected. (37)(38)(39)(50)				Seabed and subsoil of submarine zones adjacent to its territory to a depth of 200 metres, or to where depth permits of exploitation. (1966)
BARBADOS	3				
BRAZIL (35)(36)	200 (1970) (38)(40)(41)(49)				"Continental Shelf" (1950)
CHILE (35)(36)(42)	3	200 (1947)		100 kilometre customs and security zone. (1948)	"Continental Shelf" (1947)
COLOMBIA (36)	12 (1970)			Zone of 20 kilometres from the coast for enforcing customs legislation. (1931) Control for the purposes of maritime vigilance, national security and protection of national interests in a zone upto 12 miles from the coast. (1952)	b
COSTA RICA (43)	12 (1972)		200 (1949)		b 200 (1949) (45)
CUBA	3 (1942)		Legal, administrative or technical measures necessary for the protection and conservation of the marine resources in the high seas contiguous to the Cuban territorial sea. (1955)	12 mile customs zone from the high water mark. (1942)	

LATIN AMERICA AND CARIBBEAN (continued)

State	Territorial Sea	Exclusive Fishing Zone	Fishery Conservation Zone	Other Zones	Continental Shelf
DOMINICAN REPUBLIC (36)	[a] 6 (1967)	12 (1967)	In a zone extending 6 miles from the outer limit of the territorial sea, the powers of jurisdiction and control necessary for the protection and conservation of fisheries and other natural resources of the sea (1967)	In a zone extending 6 miles from the outer limit of the territorial sea, the powers of jurisdiction and control necessary for preventing contraventions of Cominican legislation governing public health, public revenue and customs (1967).	[b] 200 metres, or to where depth admits of exploitation. (1967)
ECUADOR (35)(36)(42)	200 (1966) Ships not bound for an Ecuador port may not come within three miles of the coast. (1966)	Under certain conditions foreign vessels may be permitted to fish in Ecuador's territorial sea.			200 metres, including the conservation of resources. (1951)
EL SALVADOR (35)(36)	200 (1950)				
GUATEMALA (36)	12 (1940)				[b] "Continental Shelf" (1956)
GUYANA	3 (1878)				Seabed and subsoil lying beneath the high seas contiguous to Guyana's territorial sea. (1954)
HAITI	[a] 12 (1972)	12 & 3 (1972)			[b]
HONDURAS (36)	12 (1965)				200 metres, or to where depth admits of exploitation. (1965)
JAMAICA	[a] 12 (1971)				[b] "Continental Shelf" (1948)
MEXICO (36)	[a] 12 (1969) (51)	(46)(47)			[b] "Continental Shelf" (1945)

LATIN AMERICA AND CARIBBEAN (continued)

State	Territorial Sea	Exclusive Fishing Zone	Fishery Conservation Zone	Other Zones	Continental Shelf
NICARAGUA (35)(36)		200 (1965)			"Continental Shelf" (1950)
PANAMA (35)(36)	200 (1967)				
PERU (35)(36)(42)		200 (1947)			"Continental Shelf: (1947)
TRINIDAD AND TOBAGO	a 12 (1969)				b 200 metres, or to where depth admits of exploit-ation. (1969) (48)
URUGUAY (35)(36)	200 (1969) (41) Right of innocent (50) passage in inner 12 miles. Full freedom of navigation in outer 188 miles. Full free-dom of overflight.	Fishing in the outer 188 miles by foreign vessels may be permitted under certain conditions. (39)			200 metres, or to where depth admits of exploit-ation. (1963)
VENEZUELA	a 12 (1956)	Exploration and exploita-tion of fixed fishing grounds in the continental shelf shall be subject to prior authorisation and control of the National Executive. (1956)	Outside the territorial sea and contiguous zone the State shall determine the maritime zones over which it shall exercise its authority and be respons-ible for the development, conservation and rational exploitation of the living resources. (1956)	Contiguous zone 3 miles beyond the outer limit of the territorial sea for the purposes of maritime control and vigilance. (1956)	b (48) Seabed and subsoil to a depth of 200 metres, or beyond to where depth admits of exploitation of the resources of the seabed. (1956)

LATIN AMERICA AND CARIBBEAN (continued)

State	Territorial Sea	Exclusive Fishing Zone	Fishery Conservation Zone	Other Zones	Continental Shelf
UK DEPENDENCIES: in general:	a 3				b
specific legislation for: BAHAMAS	a 3	12 (1969)			b Continental shelf beneath the sea contiguous to the coast of Bahamas. (1948)
FALKLAND ISLANDS	a 3				b Seabed and subsoil contiguous to the coasts of the Falkland Islands, but not beyond 100 fathoms. (1950)
DUTCH DEPENDENCIES	a 3				b
			MEDITERRANEAN		
ALBANIA	12 (1970)				b (1970)
ALGERIA	12 (1963)				
CYPRUS	12 (1964)				
EGYPT	12 (1958)				
FRANCE	12 (1971 (52)	(53)(54)			b Exercises the rights conforming to the Convention on the Continental Shelf. (1968)
GIBRALTAR (UK Dependency)	3 (1878)				
GREECE	6 (1936) 10 for the purposes of aviation			10 mile security zone (1913)	

MEDITERRANEAN (continued)

State	Territorial Sea	Exclusive Fishing Zone	Fishery Conservation Zone	Other Zones	Continental Shelf
ISRAEL	a 6 (1956)				b Submarine areas contiguous to the coast outside the territorial sea and to the extent depth admits of exploitation. (1952)
ITALY	a 6 (1942)	(28)(55)		12 mile custom zone (1940) 10 mile security zone (1912)	200 metres or to where depth admits of exploitation. (1967) (56)(61)
LEBANON		6 (1921)		20 kilometre customs zone (1935)	
LIBYA	12 (1959)				
MALTA	a 6 (1971)	12 (1971)			b (1966)
MONACO	3 (1967)	12 (1967)			
MOROCCO	(57)	12 (1967) (57) 6 in the Straits of Gibraltar			
SPAIN	a 6 (1957)	12 (1967) (54)(57)		Customs jurisdiction upto 12 miles from the baseline of the territorial sea. (1968)	b "Continental Shelf" (1958)
SYRIA	12 (1964)			Customs and security zone 6 miles beyond the outer limit of the territorial sea. (1964)	200 metres, or beyond to where depth admits of exploitation. (1964)
TUNISIA	6 (1962)	12 (1962 (58)(62)			(61)
TURKEY	6 (1964) (32) 12 (1964) Black Sea	12 (1964)			(33)

MEDITERRANEAN (continued)

State	Territorial Sea	Exclusive Fishing Zone	Fishery Conservation Zone	Other Zones	Continental Shelf
YUGOSLAVIA	a (59)(60) 10 (1965)			In a zone two miles beyond the outer limit of the territorial sea, control for the purpose of preventing violations of customs, fiscal, immigration and sanitary regulations, and for punishing violations of these regulations. (1965)	b (56) 200 metres, or to where depth admits of exploitation. (1965)

NORTH ATLANTIC (including the English Channel)

State	Territorial Sea	Exclusive Fishing Zone	Fishery Conservation Zone	Other Zones	Continental Shelf
CANADA	12 (1970) (63)	Prescribed areas adjacent to the coast of Canada. (1970) (64)(65)		Pollution control in all Canadian waters South of 60^{0} North and in all fishing zones. (1971)	b
FAEROES (Danish)	a 3	12 (1963)			b
FRANCE	12 (1971) (52)(54) (66)(67)(68)(69)	(28)			b Exercises the rights conforming to the Convention on the Continental Shelf. (1968)
GREENLAND	a (6)(7) 3 (1950)	12 (1963)			b
ICELAND	4 (1859)	12 (1958) (70)(79) 50 (on September 1, 1972)	Power to establish explicitly bounded conservation zones within the limits of the continental shelf where in all fisheries are subject to Icelandic rules and control. (1948)		As far out as it may be exploited. (1969)
IRELAND	3 (1959)	12 (1964) (28)(71)	May adopt conservation measures in any area of the High Seas adjacent to its exclusive fishing limits. (1964)		(1968)

NORTH ATLANTIC (continued)

State	Territorial Sea	Exclusive Fishing Zone	Fisheries Conservation Zone	Other Zones	Continental Shelf
NORWAY	4 (1812) (72) In certain areas of the territorial sea navigation is restricted.	12 (1961)		Customs supervision 6 miles beyond the outer limit of the territorial sea. (1921)	b Seabed and subsoil to where depth admits of exploitation. (1963)
PORTUGAL	a (74)	12 (1966) (73)		The powers conferred by international law, particularly the control necessary to prevent and punish infringements of customs, fiscal, sanitary or immigration regulations within its territory or territorial sea or to provide for self-defence, 12 miles from the baselines of the territorial sea. (1966)	b 200 metres, or to where the depth admits of exploitation. (1969)
SPAIN	a	12 (1967) (28)(54)(57) (67)(73)		Customs jurisdiction upto 12 miles from the baseline of the territorial sea. (1968)	b "Continental Shelf" (1968)
SPITSBERGEN (Norwegian)	a (8) 4				b
USSR	a (9)(72) 12 (1909)		(78)		b Seabed and subsoil to a depth of 200 metres or to where depth admits of exploitation. (1968)
UK	a 3 (1878)	12 (1964) (28)(68)(75)(76)		Power to take action against foreign vessels on the high seas which are liable to cause oil pollution in UK or its territorial sea. (1971)	b "Designated areas" (1964)

NORTH ATLANTIC (continued)

State	Territorial Sea	Exclusive Fishing Zone	Fishery Conservation Zone	Other Zones	Continental Shelf
USA	a 3 (1793) (51)	12 (1966) (47)(63)(77)(78)(80)	Power to set up explicitly bounded conservation zones in areas of the high seas where fisheries are developed and maintained by US nationals alone. (1945) (78)(80)	12 mile custom zone (1930) 300 mile defence zone. (1939) 100 mile zone from vessels suspected of smuggling. (1935) Aircraft approaching USA are to identify themselves 500 miles from land.	b Natural resources of the subsoil and seabed of the continental shelf adjacent to the coast of USA. (1945)

NORTH PACIFIC

State	Territorial Sea	Exclusive Fishing Zone	Fishery Conservation Zone	Other Zones	Continental Shelf
CANADA	12 (1970 (63)(81)	Prescribed areas adjacent to the coast of Canada. (1970) (82)		Pollution control in all Canadian waters South of 60° North and in all fishing zones. (1971)	b
JAPAN	a 3 (1870)				
USSR	a 12 (1909) (9)	(83)	(84)		b Seabed and subsoil to a depth of 200 metres, or to where depth admits of .exploitation. (1968)
USA	a (51)	12 (1966) (47)(63)(77)(84)	Power to set up explicitly bounded conservation zones in areas of the high seas where fisheries are developed and maintained by US nationals alone. (1945) (84)	12 mile custom zone. (1930) 300 mile defence zone. (1939). 100 mile zone from vessels suspected of smuggling. (1935) Aircraft approaching USA are to identify themselves 500 miles from land.	Natural resources of the subsoil and seabed of the continental shelf adjacent to the coast of USA. (1945) (85)(86)

NORTH SEA (INCLUDING THE SKAGERRAK AND KATTEGAT, BUT NOT INCLUDING THE ENGLISH CHANNEL)

State	Territorial Sea	Exclusive Fishing Zone	Fishery Convervation Zone	Other Zones	Continental Shelf
BELGIUM	a	12 (28)(30)(87A)		Customs authorities have supervisory powers in a zone 10 kilometres from the base line from which the territorial sea is measures. (1832) (87B)	Seabed and subsoil of submarine areas adjacent to the coast but not extending beyond the median line between Belgium and opposite or adjacent coasts. (1969)
DENMARK	a (27) 3 (1966) (87C)	12 (1965-in force 1967) (28)(29)(87D)(88)		Customs authorities have supervisory powers in a zone one mile beyond the outer limit of the territorial sea. (1928) (87B)	b 200 metres, or to where the depth admits of exploitation. (1963) (89)(90)(91)(92)
FRANCE	12 (1971) (52)(53) (69)	(28)		(87B)	b Exercises the rights conforming to the Convention on the Continental Shelf. (1968)
GERMANY, FEDERAL REPUBLIC	In accordance with international law (3 miles). (27)	(30)		(87B)	200 metres, or to where the depth admits of exploitation, (1964) (90)(97) (98)
NETHERLANDS	a 3 (1889)	(28)(30)(87A)			b (91)(97)(99) Sovereign rights in accordance, <u>inter alia</u>, with the Convention on the Continental Shelf. (1965)
NORWAY	4 (1812) (94) In certain areas of the territorial sea navigation is restricted.	12 (1961) (87D)(93) (95)		Customs supervision 6 miles beyond the outer limit of the territorial sea. (1921) (87B)	Seabed and subsoil to where depth of superjacent waters admits of exploitation. (1963) (89)(100) b (101)
SWEDEN	4 (1779) (87C)(94) Passage may be restricted in certain parts of the territorial sea for security reasons.	12 (1968) (28)(87D) (93)(102)		(87B)	As defined in the Convention on the Continental shelf. (1966) (100) b

NORTH SEA (continued)

State	Territorial Sea	Exclusive Fishing Zone	Fishery Conservation Zone	Other Zones	Continental Shelf
UNITED KINGDOM	a 3 (1878)	12 (1964) (28)(96)(103)		Power to take action against foreign ships on the high seas which are liable to cause oil pollution in United Kingdom or its territorial sea. (1971) (87B)	b "Designated areas" (1964) (92)(98)(99)(101)
PACIFIC (ISLANDS)					
AUSTRALIA	a 3 (1878)	12 (1967) (104)		An area adjacent to Australia may be declared an area for gunnery, bombing, mine-laying etc. practice. (1960)	b (13) Continental shelf within the meaning of the Convention on the Continental Shelf. (1967)
FIJI	a 3 (1878)				b
NAURU	3 (1968)	12 (1968)			
NEW ZEALAND	3 (1878)	12 (1965)			b Seabed and subsoil less than 200 metres below the surface of the sea, or beyond to where the natural resources are capable of exploitation, (1964)
TONGA	a 12 (1972) (106)				b
WESTERN SAMOA	3				
UK DEPENDENCIES: in general:	a 3				b

PERSIAN GULF

State	Territorial Sea	Exclusive Fishing Zone	Fishery Conservation Zone	Other Zones	Continental Shelf
BAHRAIN	3 (107)				Seabed and subsoil beneath the high seas of the Persian Gulf contiguous to the territorial sea of Bahrein (1949) (107)
IRAN	12 (1959) The territorial sea shall not exceed the median line between the coast of Iran and opposite or adjacent coasts. (105)(110) (112)				Seabed and subsoil of the continental shelf. (1955) (105)(110)(112)
IRAQ	12 (1958)				Seabed and subsoil of the maritime zone contiguous to the territorial sea. (1957)
KUWAIT	12 (1967) (109)(110)				Seabed and subsoil of the sea adjoining the coastal territorial sea of Kuwait (1949) (109)(110)
OMAN	12 (1972)	38 (1972)			(1968)
QATAR	3 (108)(112) (113)				Seabed and subsoil beneath the high seas of the Persian Gulf contiguous to the territorial sea of Qatar. (1949) (108)(112) (113)
SAUDI ARABIA	12 (1958) (105) (107)(108) (109)			For assuring compliance with laws relating to security, navigation, fiscal and health matters, maritime surveillance may be exercised in a contiguous zone extending 6 miles beyond the outer limit of the territorial sea. (1958)	Subsoil and seabed of those areas of the Persian Gulf seaward from the coastal sea of Saudi Arabia but contiguous to its coasts. (1949) (105)(107)(108)(109)

PERSIAN GULF (continued)

State	Territorial Sea	Exclusive Fishing Zone	Fishery Conservation Zone	Other Zones	Continental Shelf
UNITED ARAB EMIRATES ABU DHABI	3 (111)(113)				Seabed and subsoil beneath the high seas of the Persian Gulf contiguous to the territorial sea of Abu Dhabi. (1949) (111)(113)
AJMAN	3				Seabed and subsoil beneath the high seas of the Persian Gulf contiguous to the territorial sea of Ajman. (1949)
DUBAI	3 (111)				Seabed and subsoil beneath the high seas of the Persian Gulf contiguous to the territorial sea of Dubai. (1949) (111)
FUJAIRAH	3				(1966)
SHARJAH	12 (1970)				Seabed and subsoil beneath the high seas of the Persian Gulf contiguous to the territorial sea of Sharjah (1949)
UMM AL QAIWAIN	3				Seabed and subsoil beneath the high seas in the Persian Gulf contiguous to the territorial sea of Umm al Qaiwain. (1949)
RAS AL KHAIMAH	3				Seabed and subsoil beneath the high seas of the Persian Gulf contiguous to the territorial sea of Ras al Khaimah. (1949)

RED SEA

State	Territorial Sea	Exclusive Fishing Zone	Fishery Conservation Zone	Other Zones	Continental Shelf
EGYPT	12 (1958)				
ETHIOPIA	12 (1953) In the case of pearl and other sedentary fisheries, the seaward limit of the territorial sea extends to the limit of these fisheries.				
SAUDI ARABIA	12 (1958)			For assuring compliance with the laws relating to security, navigation, fiscal and health matters, maritime surveillance may be exercised in a contiguous zone extending 6 miles beyond the outer limit of the territorial sea. (1958)	Red Sea bed adjacent to the continental shelf of Saudi Arabia. (1968)
SOMALIA	12 (1967)				
SUDAN	12 (1960)			A customs and security zone 6 miles beyond the outer limit of the territorial sea. (1970)	
YEMEN (Aden)	12 (1970)			A customs and security zone 6 miles beyond the outer limit of the territorial sea. (1970)	300 metres or to where depth admits of exploitation. (1970)
YEMEN (Sana)	12 (1967)			A customs and security zone 6 miles beyond the outer limit of the territorial sea. (1967)	200 metres (1967)

FOOTNOTES

1. In the Pemba Channel between Kenya and Tanzania where the width is less than 24 miles, the outer limit of the territorial sea is the median line between the two States.

2. No such areas have yet been prescribed adjacent to the Arctic coast of Canada.

3. Under the Arctic Waters Pollution Prevention Act 1970. This Act was brought into force on July 25, 1972.

4. Any Danish national may fish in the 3-12 mile zone, but regulations may be made providing that only Danish nationals domiciled in Greenland may fish in the innermost zone of 3 miles. Under the EEC Treaty of Accession, Danish vessels not coming from Greenland may only fish in the Greenland exclusive fishing zone until December 31, 1977.

5. The Denmark-Norway Agreement concerning the East Greenland Fisheries of April 20, 1967 grants the same fishing rights to Norwegian nationals as to Danish nationals until July 10, 1977 in the waters off the coast of Greenland between Lindenovsfjord and Nordostruningen.

6. Under the Treaty concerning the Archipelago of Spitsbergen of February 9, 1920, all Parties to the Treaty enjoy equal freedom of access to, and fishing in, the territorial sea of Spitsbergen.

7. Navigation may sometimes be temporarily restricted in certain coastal areas of USSR. Special rules govern passage by foreign merchant ships through certain areas contiguous to USSR, known as fortified zones.

8. The breadth of the territorial sea is measured from straight lines drawn between the outermost points of the islands forming part of the Indonesian archipelago. The Indonesia-Japan Agreement of July 20, 1968 authorises Japanese vessels to fish in designated areas of the Indonesian territorial sea. The Agreement, originally concluded for one year, has since been extended until July 26, 1972.

9. The Japan-Republic of Korea Fisheries Agreement of June 22, 1965 makes no mention of the Korean fishing zone established under the Presidential Proclamation of January 18, 1952. Instead it establishes a joint conservation zone off

the Korean coast and recognises that each contracting party has the right to establish an exclusive fishing zone of 12 miles. It is questionable whether the Korean Proclamation is still in force.

10. The Indonesia-Malaysia Agreement of October 27, 1969 established the boundaries of the continental shelves of the two countries in the Straits of Malacca and the South China Sea.

11. The Australia-Indonesia Agreement of May 18, 1971 establishes a partial delimitation of the respective continental shelves.

12. In a letter of May 11, 1969, addressed to FAO, the Directorate of Fisheries described the "fishing territory" of the Maldive Islands as being: "A line drawn from a point at 7°42' 30" North latitude and 70°53'30" East longitude, due south along 70°53'30" East longitude to 2°22'30" South latitude, thence due East to 75°23' East longitude, thence due North along 75°23' East longitude to 7°28' North latitude, thence in a northwesterly direction to a point at 75°10'10" East longitude and 7°42'30" North latitude, due west to the original point."

13. The territorial sea is determined from straight baselines joining appropriate points of the outermost islands forming the Philippines archipelago. (For a statement of the Philippine view of the territorial sea, see Yearbook of the International Law Commission, 1956, Vol. II, p. 69-70).

14. The widest territorial sea claim which Singapore's geography would permit would be between 3 and 4 miles.

15. Based on a radio broadcast.

16. New legislation on the territorial sea and contiguous zone is under consideration.

17. The Finland-USSR Agreement concerning the Boundaries of Sea Waters and of the Continental Shelf in the Gulf of Finland of May 20, 1965 establishes a sea boundary line between the two States, as well as the boundary lines of their respective territorial sea in the Gulf of Finland in the northeast section of Sursari (Gogland) Island.

The Finland-USSR Agreement of May 5, 1967 provides for the delimitation on the median line principle of the continental shelf between the two countries.

18. Signatory to the Declaration on the Continental Shelf of the Baltic Sea, Moscow, October 23, 1968. This says

inter alia, that the continental shelf in the Baltic Sea should be delimited in accordance with the principles of the Convention on the Continental Shelf, and in particular Article 6.

19. The German Democratic Republic-Poland Agreement of 1968 delimits the continental shelf between the two countries.

20. The USSR-Poland Agreement of August 28, 1969 adopts the median line as the boundary between the respective continental shelves.

21. The Poland-USSR Protocol of March 18, 1958 delimits the Polish and Soviet territorial sea in the Gulf of Gdansk.

22. The Denmark-Poland Fisheries Agreement of February 26, 1971 permits Danish fishermen to fish indefinitely in the outer six miles of the Polish fishing zone. Fishermen who have traditionally fished for salmon can continue to fish in 3-6 mile zone until July 1, 1972.

23. The Sweden-Poland Fisheries Agreement of 1970 gives Swedish fishermen certain rights in the Polish fishing zone.

24. The Finland-USSR Agreement of June 13, 1969 grants to Finnish nationals the right to engage in fishing and sealing in certain areas of the territorial sea of USSR in the Gulf of Finland.

25. The Denmark-Federal Republic of Germany Agreement of May 29, 1958 regulates certain common fishery rights in the Flensborgfjord.

26. The Protocol to the Denmark-Federal Republic of Germany Agreement of June 9, 1965 provides that the median line principle should be adopted in delimiting the continental shelf between the two countries in the Baltic.

27. The boundary between the Federal Republic of Germany and Denmark was established in 1921 by a Commission set up under the Treaty of Versailles.

28. Party to the Fisheries Convention, March 9, 1964.

29. Denmark is a signatory to the EEC Treaty of Accession: when this comes into force, (probably on January 1, 1973), other States Parties to the Treaty will be able to fish in the outer six miles of the Danish fishing zone, except between Thyborøn and Blaavandshuk where the 12 mile limit will remain.

30. Between February 1, 1971 and the coming into force of the EEC Treaty of Accession (probably January 1, 1973), present members of EEC have the right to fish in the maritime waters coming under its sovereignty or jurisdiction. After the Treaty has come into force, it may claim a six mile exclusive fishing zone if it so wishes.

31. The boundary between the territorial seas of Finland and Sweden is laid down in the Topographical Description signed on January 19, 1811 at Tornea after the peace of Frederikshamn, as revised in 1926-27.

32. "In relation to States whose territorial sea is of greater breadth, the breadth of Turkey's territorial sea shall be determined in accordance with the principle of reciprocity." (Article 2 of Law No. 476 of May 15, 1964.) "Where the distance between Turkey's land territory and the land territory of a neighbouring State is less than the total breadth of the territorial seas of each of the two States, the median line shall, failing agreement to the contrary, constitute the outer limit of Turkey's territorial sea." (Article 3). Navigation through the Dardanelles and Bosphorus is regulated by the Montreux Convention of July 20, 1936.

33. No legislation at present exists in Turkey on the continental shelf and on exploitation procedures and research in natural resources of the seabed, ocean floor and subsoil. According to current regulations, permission for oil drilling within the continental shelf is subject to a decision by the Council of Ministers. In granting such permission, it is normally stipulated that those undertaking the drilling should conform to the provisions of the Convention on the Continental Shelf.

34. The legislation of Bulgaria and Romania each provides that the boundary between their respective territorial seas shall be the parallel of latitude passing through the point where the land frontier reaches the coast.

35. Signatory to the Declaration of Montevideo on the Law of the Sea, May 8, 1970.

36. Signatory to the Declaration of Lima on the Law of the Sea, August 4-8, 1970.

37. Argentina claims exclusive fishing rights in the inner 12 miles. Fishing in the outer 188 miles by foreign vessels is permitted if the necessary authorisation has been obtained. However parts of the outer 188 mile zone may from

time to time be set aside for exclusive exploitation by Argentinian vessels (1967).

38. The Argentina-Brazil Fishing Agreement of December 1967 provides that nationals of one country may fish in the territorial sea of the other beyond a 6 mile limit measured from the baseline of the said area.

39. The Argentina-Uruguay Declaration on Provisional Fishing Rights of March 15, 1970 gives Argentina and Uruguay fishermen reciprocal rights in the innermost 12 miles of the territorial sea of each State.

40. Decree No. 68.458 of April 1, 1971 provides that within the territorial sea up to 100 miles, fishing shall be reserved for vessels owned or chartered by Brazilian nationals. Exceptions may be granted in favour of foreign vessels in special circumstances. Foreign vessels may fish in the area between 100 and 200 miles subject to licensing.

41. In a Declaration of May 10, 1969, the Governments of Brazil and Uruguay adopted the median line principle as delimiting the maritime boundary between the two countries.

42. Signatory to the Declaration on the Maritime Zone, 1952. This provides that signatory States possess sole sovereignty and jurisdiction over the area of the sea adjacent to the coast and extending not less than 200 miles from the coast.

43. Costa Rica adhered to the Declaration on the Maritime Zone 1952 on October 3, 1955. However in a Declaration of November 31, 1966, the President of the Republic explained his veto of a draft law submitted for his approval, the purpose of which was the ratification of Costa Rica's adherence to the Declaration on the Maritime Zone. The draft law, in expressly adopting the provisions of the Declaration proclaiming sole sovereignty and jurisdiction over the sea to a distance of 200 miles from the coastline, was in violation of Article 6 of the Costa Rican Constitution of 1949, which provided for complete and exclusive sovereignty over the territorial sea and the continental shelf in accordance with the principles of international law.

44. By a judgment delivered on December 14, 1950 in Jonas Boden v. Han Daniëls, the Costa Rican Sala de Casacion defined the breadth of the territorial sea as being 3 miles. (Colleccion de Sentencias, Vol. 2, 2nd. semester, 1950. p. 1220.)

45. This is according to Article 6 of the Constitution of 1949. However Decree-Law No. 803 of November 2, 1949 proclaims sovereignty over "the whole submarine platform or continental and insular shelf adjacent to the continental and insular coasts of the national territory, at whatever depth it is found."

46. The Japan-Mexico Fisheries Agreement of March 7, 1968 allows Japanese fishing vessels to fish for specified species and within certain limits, in the 9-12 mile zone off Mexico's Pacific coast until December 31, 1972.

47. The Mexico-USA Fisheries Agreement of October 27, 1967 provides for reciprocal fishing rights for US and Mexican fishermen in the 9-12 mile zone off each other's coasts until December 31, 1972.

48. The United Kingdom-Venezuela Agreement of 1942 delimits the submarine area between Venezuela and Trinidad and Tobago.

49. The Brazil-USA Agreement concerning Shrimp of May 9, 1972 provides that USA may fish for shrimp within Brazil's claimed territorial sea and shall pay part of the cost of the enforcement of shrimp conservation measures made under the Agreement. There is a similar Brazil-Trinidad and Tobago Agreement of May 19, 1972.

50. The Argentina-Uruguay Declaration of January 30, 1961 fixes the outer limit of the Rio de la Plata for the purposes of forming the baseline for the delimitation of the territorial sea. The Declaration of March 15, 1970 establishes the boundary between the territorial seas of the two countries from this baseline.

51. The USA-Mexico Agreement of November 23, 1970 establishes the maritime boundaries on the principle of equidistance, between the two countries to a distance of 12 miles from their respective baselines.

52. In the case of opposite or adjacent coasts, the outer limit does not extend beyond the median line. Where the distance between the French baselines and the baselines of an opposite or adjacent coast is less than 24 miles "or does not allow any longer the existence of a zone of high sea sufficient for navigation, regulations may be issued in order to ensure a free maritime and aerial navigation." (Article 3 of Law No. 71-1060 of December 24, 1971.)

53. France is a signatory to the EEC Treaty of Accession: when this comes into force (probably on January 1, 1973), other States Parties to the Treaty will be able to fish in the outer six miles of the French territorial sea. Between February 1, 1971 and the coming into force of the Treaty, present members of EEC have the right to fish in the maritime waters coming under French sovereignty or jurisdiction.

54. The France-Spain Fisheries Agreement of March 20, 1967 authorises each contracting party's fishermen to fish indefinitely for all species in certain parts of the 6-12 mile zone of their respective territorial sea and fishing zone. Local fishermen have certain rights in the 0-3 mile zone.

55. Between February 1, 1971 and the coming into force of the EEC Treaty of Accession (probably January 1, 1973), present members of EEC have the right to fish in the maritime waters coming under Italian sovereignty or jurisdiction. After the Treaty has come into force, Italy will revert to having a 6 mile exclusive fishing zone.

56. The Italy-Yugoslavia Agreement of January 8, 1968 establishes the line of delimitation of the respective continental shelves.

57. The Morocco-Spain Convention of January 4, 1969 authorises the nationals of each country to fish in the "territorial sea" of the contracting parties subject to specified conditions. For the purposes of the Convention, "territorial sea" is taken to mean, in relation to fisheries, a zone adjacent to the coast extending to a distance of 12 miles from the baseline of the territorial sea.

58. Under the Tunisia-Italy Fisheries Agreement of February 1, 1963, Italian fishermen had the right to fish in designated areas of the Tunisian fishing zone until December 31, 1970. This Agreement was extended on August 20, 1971 according to an Agreement of February 1971.

59. For reasons of security, certain parts of the territorial sea may be closed to innocent passage by foreign vessels.

60. The Italy-Yugoslavia Agreement of April 16, 1969 authorises, subject to specified conditions, fishing by Italian vessels in Yugoslav waters for a period of three years.

61. The Italy-Tunisia Agreement of August 20, 1971 delimits the continental shelf between the two countries.

62. The Libya-Tunisia Fisheries Agreement of September 8, 1971 gives Libyan fishermen certain fishing rights in the Tunisian fishing zone.

63. The Canada-USA Agreement of April 24, 1970 sets out reciprocal fishing privileges for designated species and areas over a period of two years.

64. The areas prescribed under the Territorial Sea and Fishing Zones Act 1970 are, in the Atlantic, the Gulf of St. Lawrence and the Bay of Fundy. These areas are delimited by "fishery closing lines" drawn across their entrance pursuant to Order in Council P.C. 1971-366.

65. The Canada-Norway Agreement of July 15, 1971 permits up to 20 Norwegian vessels to fish with lines for cod in the Gulf of St. Lawrence between August 15 and December 15 each year until January 1, 1975. The Canada-Norway Agreement on Sealing of July 15, 1971 gives Norwegian vessels the right to take seals indefinitely in certain areas of the Canadian territorial sea.

The Canada-UK Agreement of March 27, 1972 gives British vessels the right to fish for demersal species in the outer 9 miles of the territorial sea off most of the East coast until January 1, 1978 and within certain parts of the Gulf of St. Lawrence outside the territorial sea until January 1, 1973.

The Canada-France Agreement of March 27, 1972 gives French vessels certain fishing rights in the Gulf of St. Lawrence until 1986.

66. France is a signatory to the EEC Treaty of Accession: when this comes into force (probably on January 1, 1973), other States Parties to the Treaty will be able to fish in the outer six miles of the French territorial sea off its Atlantic coasts, except for parts of Brittany and Normandy where the limit will remain 12 miles. Between February 1, 1971 and the coming into force of the Treaty, present members of EEC have the right to fish in the maritime waters coming under French sovereignty or jurisdiction.

67. The Franco-Spain Agreement of July 14, 1959 regulates fishing by French and Spanish nationals in the Bidassoa and the Bay of Figuier. A French decree of January 2, 1970 and a similar Spanish decree, implementing an Agreement of November 14, 1969 between representatives of the French and Spanish fishing industries, divide up the Bay of Gascony into sectors in which all fishing is forbidden except surface fishing for tuna.

68. The France-UK Agreement of September 24, 1951 interpreted a Convention of August 2, 1839 as offering British and French nationals equal fishing rights in areas of the Ecrehos and Minquiers between the limit of three miles from the low-water mark off the coast of Jersey and the limit under which exclusive rights of fishing are reserved to French nationals by that Convention, as redefined by a Declaration regarding the limit of French fisheries in Granville Bay of September 20, 1928.

69. Decree No. 70-292 of March 25, 1970 permits British vessels to fish for herring, mackerel and demersal fish in the 6-12 mile zone between Dunkirk and Cap d'Alprech.

70. On February 15, 1972 the Althing (Parliament) of Iceland adopted a resolution under which the fishing limits of Iceland will be extended to 50 miles on September 1, 1972. Regulations implementing this resolution were published on July 14, 1972.

71. By order under section 5(2) of the Maritime Jurisdiction Act 1964, the fishing vessels of Belgium, France, the Federal Republic of Germany, Netherlands, Spain and the United Kingdom are authorised to fish particular stocks of fish in certain parts of the 6-12 mile zone.

Ireland is a signatory to the EEC Treaty of Accession. When this comes into force (probably on January 1, 1973), other States Parties to the Treaty will be able to fish in the outer six miles of the Irish fishing zone except between Lough Foyle and Cork harbour, and between Carlingford Lough to Carnsore Point (in the case of the latter, only fishing for crustaceans and molluscs is not allowed).

72. The Norway-USSR Agreement of February 15, 1957 defined the Norwegian-USSR frontier in the Varangerfjord as a straight line from an agreed frontier mark to the intersection of the outer limits of the USSR and Norwegian territorial seas. Neither of the parties is to extend its territorial sea beyond the straight line extending from the said intersection to the median point of the line between Cape Nemetsky and Cape Kibergnes.

73. The Spain-Portugal Agreement of December 10, 1969 defines the area of exclusive fishing rights between the two countries.

74. The outer limit of the territorial sea shall not extend beyond the median line between the baselines of Portugal and opposite or adjacent States (1966).

75. The Norway-United Kingdom Agreement of September 28, 1964 permits Norwegian fishermen to fish for dogfish and basking sharks in the 6-12 mile zone off the Outer Hebrides, Orkneys and Shetland until December 31, 1984.

The USSR-United Kingdom Agreement of September 30, 1964 permits Soviet fishing vessels and depot ships to anchor, navigate, transship fish, and perform other activities ancillary to fishing operations in the 3-12 mile zone around the Shetland Islands.

The Poland-United Kingdom Agreement of September 26, 1964 permits Polish mother ships to enter the outer 6 mile zone for purposes ancillary to fishing.

A number of statutory instruments permit fishing vessels of Belgium, France, Federal Republic of Germany and Ireland to fish for certain species of fish in certain parts of the 6-12 mile zone.

76. The United Kingdom is a signatory to the EEC Treaty of Accession. When this comes into force (probably on January 1, 1973), other States Parties to the Treaty will be able to fish in the outer six miles of the United Kingdom fishing zone, except around the Orkneys and Shetlands, County Down, and between Lyme Regis and Hartland Point.

77. The Japan-USA Agreement of December 11, 1970 (replacing an earlier Agreement of May 9, 1967) provides for Japanese fishing vessels to fish for certain species in certain areas of the US fishing zone.

78. The USA-USSR Agreement on Certain Fishery Problems on the High Seas in the Western Areas of the Middle Atlantic Ocean of December 11, 1970 (replacing an earlier Agreement of November 25, 1967) authorises inter alia fishing vessels of USSR to fish during a specified period in specifically designated areas of the US exclusive fishing zone. The Agreement also establishes a conservation zone on the High Seas in which fishermen of USA and USSR are not to fish for certain species at certain times of the year.

79. Under the Denmark-Iceland Agreement of August 1, 1961, fishing vessels registered in the Faeroe Islands have the right to engage in hand-line fishing in certain areas of the Icelandic exclusive fishing zone at certain times of the year.

80. The Poland-USA Agreement regarding Fisheries in the

the Western Region of the Middle Atlantic Ocean of June 13, 1970, extended on October 1, 1971, (replacing an earlier Agreement of June 12, 1969), provides that Polish fishermen will not fish for certain species at certain times of the year in specified areas of the High Seas. In return, USA permits Polish fishermen to transfer their catch between vessels in three designated areas of the US exclusive fishing zone.

81. The Canada-USSR Agreement on Co-operation in Fisheries in North-Eastern Pacific Ocean off the Coast of Canada of January 22, 1971, allows, inter alia, fishing vessels of USSR to conduct fishing with trawls in specified areas in the 3-12 mile zone of the Canadian territorial sea.

82. The areas prescribed under the Territorial Sea and Fishing Zones Act 1970 are, in the Pacific, Queen Charlotte Sound, Dixon Entrance and Hecate Strait. These areas are delimited by "fishery closing lines" drawn across their entrance pursuant to Order in Council P.C. 1971-366.

83. The Japan-USSR King Crab Agreement of April 11, 1969 regulated fishing for king crabs and tanner crabs in the North-western Pacific and in the Okhotsk Sea for a period of one year. The Agreement was renewed on April 7, 1970 and May 18, 1971.

84. The USSR-USA Agreement on Certain Fishery Problems in the North-Eastern Part of the Pacific Ocean off the Coast of USA of February 12, 1971, (replacing an earlier Agreement of February 13, 1967), establishes specifically designated areas of the High Seas off the coast of USA in which Soviet vessels' fishing activities are restricted. In return, Soviet vessels are authorised to fish for certain species in specifically designated areas of the US exclusive fishing zone.

85. The Japan-USA Agreement regarding the King and Tanner Crab Fisheries in the Eastern Bering Sea of December 11, 1970, (replacing an earlier Agreement of November 25, 1964), grants Japanese vessels the right to fish for King and Tanner Crabs on the US continental shelf in the Eastern Bering Sea, subject to conditions relating to catch limits. Both Governments reserve their positions with regard to the question of whether the King Crab is a High Sea fishery resource (the Japanese view) or is a natural resource of the continental shelf (the US view).

86. The USA-USSR Agreement relating to Fishing for King and Tanner Crab of February 12, 1971 (replacing an earlier Agreement of February 5, 1965), recognises that the King Crab is a resource of the continental shelf. The Agreement fixes

quotas and size limits for the number of king and tanner crabs which may be taken by Soviet fishermen on US continental shelf off Alaska in the Bering Sea.

87A. Article 2(ii)(b) of the Treaty instituting the Benelux Economic Union of February 3, 1958 provides for the common access of Dutch and Belgian fishermen to each other's territorial sea. The Convention containing the Transitional Provisions of the same date provides for a five year delay in bringing this provision into force.

87B. Under the Agreement for Co-operation in Dealing with Pollution of the North Sea by Oil of June 9, 1969, the North Sea is divided up into zones. Any Contracting Party observing oil in its zone is to inform the other Contracting Parties.

87C. The Boundary between Danish and Swedish waters in the Sound is laid down in the Declaration concerning the Boundaries of the Sound of January 30, 1932.

87D. The Denmark-Norway-Sweden Agreement of December 19, 1966 provides that the three countries may fish up to a line 4 miles from the baseline of their territorial sea in the Skagerrak and Kattegat.

88. Under the Denmark-Norway Agreement of April 26, 1968 Norwegian fishermen can fish indefinitely for sprat at certain times of the year in certain areas of the Danish exclusive fishing zone.

Under the Denmark-Belgium Agreement of June 29, 1967, Belgian fishermen may fish indefinitely for flatfish in the outer six miles of the Danish exclusive fishing zone between Lyngvig and the German-Danish frontier.

Under the Denmark-Federal Republic of Germany Agreement of November 30. 1967, German fishermen may fish indefinitely for certain kinds of fish in certain parts of the outer six miles of the Danish exclusive fishing zone. This Agreement also provides that the southern boundary of the Danish fishing zone shall provisionally be the line established by the Denmark-Federal Republic of Germany Agreement on the Delimitation of the Continental Shelf of June 9, 1965.

Under the Denmark-Netherlands Agreement of May 30, 1968, Dutch fishermen may fish indefinitely for plaice and sole in the outer six miles of the Danish fishing zone between Bovbjerg and the German-Danish frontier.

Under the Denmark-Poland Agreement of February 26, 1971, Polish fishermen may fish indefinitely in certain parts of the outer six miles of the Danish fishing zone.

89. The Denmark-Norway Agreement of December 8, 1965, as amended by the Agreement of April 24, 1968, delimits the continental shelf between the two countries on the basis of the median line principle.

90. The Denmark-Federal Republic of Germany Agreement of June 9, 1965 delimits between the two countries that part of the continental shelf nearest the coast. The remainder is delimited by the Agreement of January 28, 1971.

91. The Denmark-Netherlands Agreement of March 31, 1966 delimits the continental shelf between the two countries on the basis of the median line principle. This Agrement will cease to have effect when the Agreements between Denmark and the Federal Republic of Germany and between the Federal Republic of Germany and Netherlands of January 28, 1971 come into force.

92. The Denmark-United Kingdom Agreement of March 3, 1966, (which will be replaced by the Agreement of November 25, 1971 when the latter comes into force), delimits the continental shelf between the two countries on the basis of the median line principle.

93. The Norway-Sweden Agreement of April 5, 1967 delimits Norwegian and Swedish fishing zones in the North-Eastern Skagerrak.

94. An arbitral award of October 23, 1909 and the Norway-Sweden Declaration of April 5, 1967 establish the boundary between the Norwegian and Swedish territorial seas.

95. Norway is a signatory to the EEC Treaty of Accession: when this comes into force (probably on January 1, 1973), other States Parties to the Treaty will be able to fish in the outer 6 miles of the Norwegian fishing zone between Egersund and the Norwegian-Swedish frontier.

96. A number of Statutory Instruments permit Belgian and French vessels to fish for demersal fish and West German and Dutch vessels to fish for herring in certain parts of the 6-12 mile zone.

United Kingdom is a signatory to the EEC Treaty of Accession: when this comes into force (probably on January 1, 1973), other States Parties to the Treaty will be able to fish in the outer six miles of the United Kingdom fishing zone between Berwick and River Coquet and between Flamborough Head and the Straits of Dover.

97. The Federal Republic of Germany-Netherlands Agreement of December 1, 1964 delimits between the two countries that part of the continental shelf nearest the coast. The remainder is delimited by the Agreement of January 28, 1971.

98. The Federal Republic of Germany-United Kingdom Agreement of November 25, 1971 delimits the continental shelf between the two countries.

99. The Netherlands-United Kingdom Agreement of October 6, 1965, as amended by the Protocol of November 25, 1971, delimits the continental shelf between the two countries on the basis of the median line principle.

100. The Norway-Sweden Agreement of July 24, 1968 delimits the continental shelf between the two countries on the basis of the median line principle.

101. The Norway-United Kingdom Agreement of March 10, 1965 delimits the continental shelf between the two countries on the basis of the median line principle.

102. Notes of the Swedish Foreign Ministry of September 18, 1970 and September 14, 1971 give vessels of the Federal Republic of Germany the right of fish for certain species in certain areas of the Swedish fishing zone.

103. Under the Norway-United Kingdom Agreement of September 28, 1964, Norwegian vessels may fish for dogfish and basking sharks in the 6-12 mile zone off the Orkneys and Shetlands until December 31, 1984.

Under the Poland-United Kingdom Agreement of September 26, 1984, Polish mother ships are permitted to enter the 6-12 mile zone for purposes ancillary to fishing.

Under the USSR-United Kingdom Agreement of September 30, 1964, Soviet fishing vessels and depot ships are permitted to anchor, navigate, transship fish and perform other activities ancillary to fishing operations in 3-12 mile zone around the Shetlands.

104. The Australia-Japan Agreement of November 27, 1968 authorises, for a period of 7 years with regard to Australia and three years with regard to Papua and New Guinea, tuna longline fishing by Japanese vessels in specified areas of the Australian fishing zone.

105. The Iran-Saudi Arabian Agreement of October 24, 1968 establishes a boundary line separating the submarine areas appertaining to Iran from those appertaining to Saudi Arabia.

106. Contained in Minera Reef Annexation Proclaimation.

107. The Bahrein-Saudi Arabia Agreement of February 22, 1958 delimits the submarine boundaries between the two countries.

108. The Qatar-Saudi Arabian Agreement of June 27, 1965 delimited the submarine boundaries between the two countries. It is uncertain whether this Agreement is still in force.

109. The Kuwait-Saudi Arabian Agreement of July 7, 1965 delimits the submarine boundaries between the two countries.

110. The Iran-Kuwait Agreement of January 13, 1968 delimits the submarine boundaries between the two countries.

111. The Abu Dhabi-Dubai Agreement of February 18, 1968 delimits the submarine boundaries between the two countries.

112. The Iran-Qatar Agreement of June 30, 1969 delimits the submarine boundaries between the two countries.

113. The Abu Dhabi-Qatar Agreement of March 20, 1969 delimits the submarine boundaries between the two countries.

SUMMARY OF CLAIMS TO THE OUTER LIMIT OF THE CONTINENTAL SHELF

The following table is a summary of claims to the outer limit of the continental shelf. States parties to the Convention on the Continental Shelf are underlined. Shelf-locked States (i.e. States whose continental shelf is cut off from the seabed beyond national jurisdiction by the continental shelf of one or more other States) are in [].

Claim	State	
In accordance with the Convention, 200 metres or beyond to where depth admits of exploitation	Australia, [Belgium], [Denmark], Dominican Republic, [Finland, France, [Democratic Republic of Germany], [Federal Republic of Germany], Ghana, Honduras, India, Italy, Liberia, [Malaysia], Mauritania, Mauritius, [Netherlands], New Zealand, Nigeria, Portugal, South Africa, [Sudan], [Sweden], Syria, Trinidad and Tobago, USSR, Venezuela, Republic of Vietnam, [Yugoslavia].	(Total: 29)
50 metres	[Cambodia]	(Total: 1)
200 metres	Ivory Coast, Pakistan, Senegal, [Yemen].	(Total: 4)
300 metres	[Southern Yemen]	(Total: 1)
12 miles	Colombia	(Total: 1)
100 miles	Dahomey	(Total: 1)
200 miles (1)	Argentina, Brazil, Chile, Costa Rica, Ecuador, El Salvador, Nicaragua, Panama, Peru, Sierra Leone, Uruguay.	(Total: 11)
To where depth admits of exploitation	Iceland, Indonesia, Israel, Philippines, Norway	(Total: 5)
No precise claim made, claim not known	Albania, Algeria, Bahrein, Bangladesh, Barbados, Bulgaria, Burma, Cameroon, Canada, People's Republic of China, Republic of China, Congo, Cuba, Cyprus, Equatorial Guinea, [Ethiopia], Fiji, Gabon, Gambia, Greece, Guatemala, Guinea, Guyana, Haiti, [Iran], [Iraq], Ireland, Jamaica, Japan, [Jordan], Kenya, North Korea, Republic of Korea, [Kuwait], Lebanon, Libya, Malagasy Republic, Maldive Islands, Malta, Mexico, Monoco, Morocco, Nauru, Oman [Poland], Qatar, Ras al Khaimah, Romania, [Saudi Arabia], [Singapore], Somalia, Spain, Sri Lanka, Tanzania, [Thailand], Togo, Tonga, Tunisia, Turkey, United Arab Emirates, United Arab Republic, UK, USA, [North Vietnam], Western Samoa, Zaire.	(Total: 65)

(1) Some of these States have not specifically claimed a 200 mile continental shelf but have claimed a 200 mile territorial sea. Others have claimed a 200 mile territorial sea, but have used different criteria for establishing the outer limit of their continental shelf.

CHANGES IN CLAIMS TO THE TERRITORIAL SEA

The following table shows how the number of claims to different breadths of the territorial sea has altered between 1958 and 1972. The totals only include independent States. The fact that a considerable number of States have achieved independence since 1958 accounts for the fact that the total number of claims for each year varies.

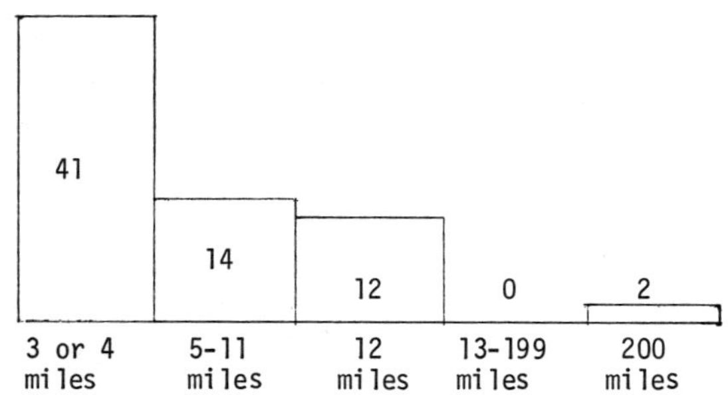

1. The position at 1.1.1958.

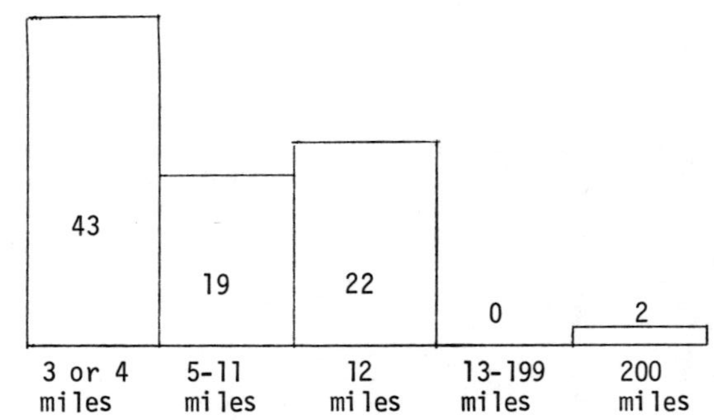

2. The position at 1.1.1964.

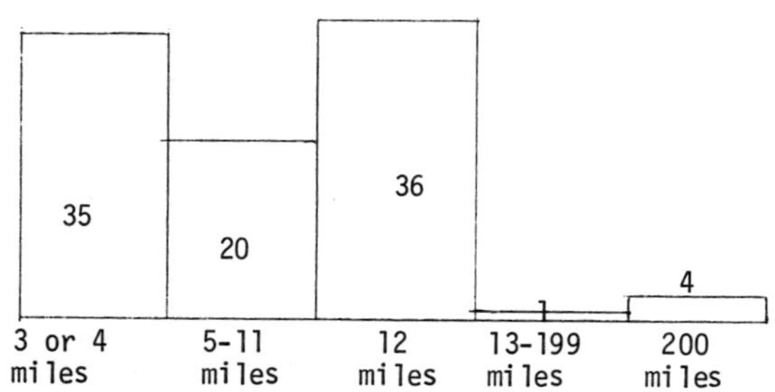

3. The position at 1.1.1968.

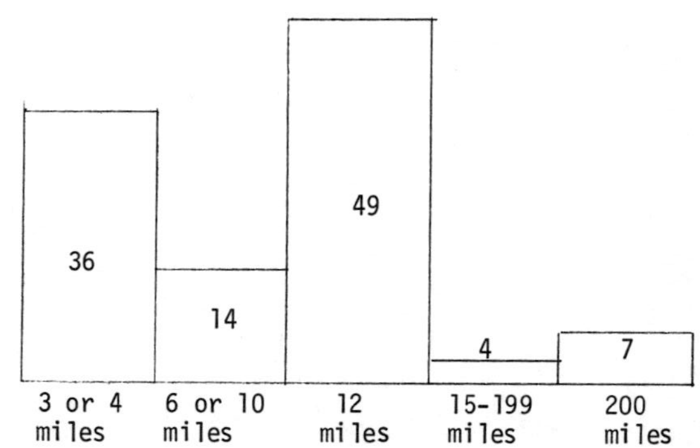

3. The position at 1.1.1972.

CHANGES IN THE CLAIMS TO AN EXCLUSIVE FISHING ZONE

The following table shows how the number of claims to an exclusive fishing zone beyond the territorial sea has altered between 1958 and 1972.

a: States with less than 12 miles territorial sea claiming a 12 mile exclusive fishing zone.

b: States with less than 200 mile territorial sea claiming a 200 mile exclusive fishing zone.

1. The position at 1.1.1958.

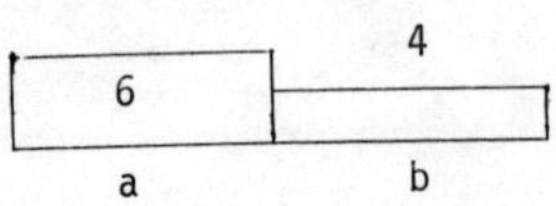

2. The position at 1.1.1964.

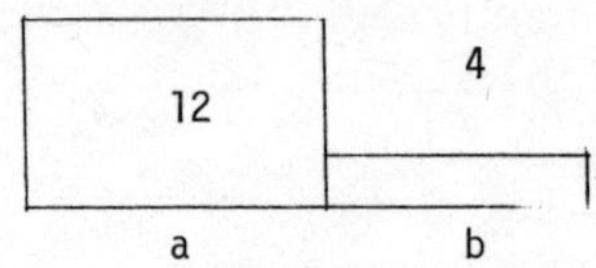

3. The position at 1.1.1968.

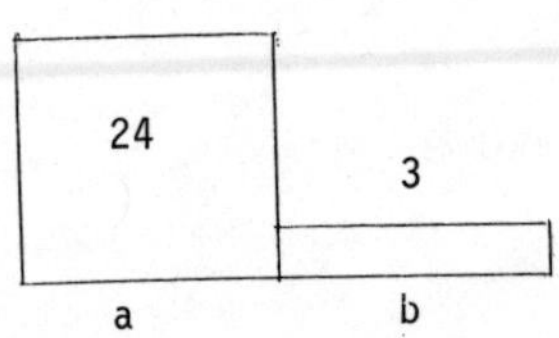

4. The position at 1.1.1972.

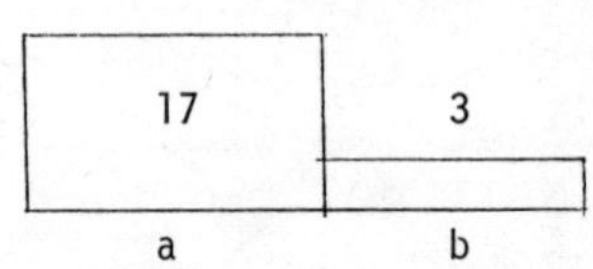

In addition:

At 1.1.1958: one State with 3 miles territorial sea claimed a 10 mile fishing zone.
" " " " " " " " " 6 " " "
1.1.1964: " " " " " " " " " 10 " " "
1.1.1972: " " " " " " " " " 18 " " "

TABLE OF FISHERY ARRANGEMENTS IN THE NORTH SEA. 1960-1972.

Before 1960 no North Sea State claimed any exclusive fisheries jurisdiction beyond its territorial sea (which was either three or four miles). With a number of claims to a 12 mile exclusive fishing zone coming in the North-East Atlantic from Iceland (1958), Norway (1961) and the Faeroes (1963), the necessity for some kind of regional arrangement arose. The result was the Fisheries Convention of March 9, 1964. The Convention provides that States Parties may claim a 12 mile exclusive fishing zone. Other States Parties may continue to fish indefinitely in the outer six miles of this zone for species which they have traditionally caught there. Transitional arrangements may be made for fishing in the 3-6 mile zone. Table 1 shows the extension to 12 miles of the exclusive fishing zone and the resulting transitional arrangements effected by bilateral agreements, either pursuant to the Fisheries Convention or independently of it. Table 2 shows the position after the expiry of the transitional provisions and indicates where and for what species of fish the fishermen of one State may fish in the outer six miles of another State's exclusive fishing zone. In this table a number of other regional arrangements are shown - those of Benelux and EEC (both of which provide for free access to maritime waters) and the Scandinavian Agreement of 1966 (which provides for rather wider access in the Skagerrak and Kattegat than under the Fisheries Convention). The whole position will be substantially modified when the EEC Treaty of Accession comes into force. This is shown in Table 3. For this purpose it is assumed that the Treaty will come into force on January 1, 1973 for all 10 signatory States i.e. all the North Sea States except Sweden, but with addition of Ireland, Italy and land-locked Luxembourg. It is also assumed that Belgium, Federal Republic of Germany and the Netherlands will not extend their exclusive fishing limit to 6 miles, although they are entitled to do so.

For the purpose of these Tables, the North Sea includes the Skagerrak and Kattegat, but does not include the English Channel.

In each Table, the States in the extreme left-hand vertical column represent the States granting concessions to foreign fishermen in their exclusive fishing zone. The States in the uppermost horizontal column are those whose fishermen have obtained concessions in another State's exclusive fishing zone. Thus in Table 1; if we take Denmark in the extreme left-hand column and Belgium in the uppermost horizontal column, reading across and down we find that Denmark granted Belgium fishermen the right to fish in the 3-6 mile zone between Lyngvig and the German-Danish frontier until 1.7.1968.

In Tables 1 and 2 States which are underlined are parties to the Fisheries Convention. The date and figure given under States in the extreme left-hand vertical column represent the year in which a claim to an exclusive fishing zone was made and the breadth claimed. In Table 3 only the breadth of the exclusive fishing zone is given. The dates given in brackets in the boxes represent the dates of signature of bilateral agreements granting the fishing rights in question; those dates which are underlined indicate that the Agreement has been concluded pursuant to the Fisheries Convention. Where no date is given, the fishing rights in question have been granted as a result of domestic legislation. Where fishing rights have been given, all species may be fished for unless otherwise stated.

1. Claims to a 12 mile exclusive fishing zone and the resulting transitional arrangements.

STATE	BELGIUM	DENMARK	FRANCE	FEDERAL REPUBLIC OF GERMANY	NETHERLANDS	NORWAY	SWEDEN	UNITED KINGDOM
BELGIUM (1)								
DENMARK (1965) (12)	3-6 mile zone between Lyngvig and German-Danish frontier until 1.7.1968. (1967)			In certain parts of the 3-6 mile zone for certain species until 1.7. 1968. (1967) (8)	3-6 mile zone between German-Danish frontier and Bovbjerg for plaice and sole until 1.7.1968. (1968)	6-12 mile zone between German-Danish frontier and Hanstholm until 31.10.1970 (1968)		
FRANCE (1967) (12)								3-6 mile zone between Dunkirk and Cap d'Alprech for herring, mackerel and demersal fish until 31.12.71.
(1) FEDERAL REPUBLIC OF GERMANY								
NETHERLANDS (1)								
NORWAY (1961) (2) (12)		6-12 mile zone until 31.5.1968. Thereafter 6-12 mile zone between Lindesnes and USSR-Norwav frontier until 31.10. 1970.					6-12 mile zone until 31.5.1968. Thereafter 6-12 mile zone between Lindesnes and USSR-Norway frontier until 31.10.1970.	6-12 mile zone until 31.12 1970. (1960)
SWEDEN (1968) (12)								
UNITED KINGDOM (1964) (3) (12)	3-6 mile zone until 31.12. 1965. or 31.12. 1966 (where straight baselines) (1964)		3-6 mile zone until 31.12.1965 or 31.12.1966. (where straight baselines.) (1964)	3-6 mile zone until 31.12.1965. or 31.12.1966. (where straight baselines). (1964)	3-6 mile zone until 31.12.1965 or 31.12.1966. (where straight baselines). (1964)	Dogfish and Basking sharks in 3-6 mile zone off Orkneys and Shetland until 31.12. 1965. or 31.12. 1966. (where straight baselines). (1964)		

2. The position after the expiry of transitional arrangements i.e. as of January 1, 1972.

STATE	BELGIUM	DENMARK	FRANCE	FEDERAL REPUBLIC OF GERMANY	NETHERLANDS	NORWAY	SWEDEN	UNITED KINGDOM
BELGUIM (1)(6)			All maritime waters between 1.2.1971. and 31.12.1972. (5)	All maritime waters between 1.2. 1971. and 31.12. 1972. (5)	Under the Benelux Convention can fish in the territorial sea. (1963)			
DENMARK (1965) (12)	6-12 mile zone between Lyngvig and German-Danish frontier for flat fish. (1967)			In certain parts of the 6-12 mile zone for certain species. (1967) (8)	6-12 mile zone between German-Danish frontier and Bovbjerg for plaice and sole. (1968)	4-12 mile zone between Hanstholm and Skagen. (1966) Sprats in Oct., Nov. and Dec. in certain areas. (1966)	4-12 mile zone between Hanstholm and Skagen. (1966)	
FRANCE (1967) (6) (12)	All maritime waters between 1.2.1971. and 31.12.1972. (5)			All maritime waters between 1.2.1971. and 31.12.1972. (5)	All maritime waters between 1.2.1971 and 31.12.1972. (5)			6-12 mile zone between Dunkirk and Cap d'Alprech for herring, mackerel and demersal fish.
FEDERAL REPUBLIC OF GERMANY (1) (6)	All maritime waters between 1.2.1971. and 31.12.1972 (5)		All maritime waters between 1.2.1971. and 31.12.1972. (5)		All maritime waters between 1.2.1971. and 31.12.1972. (5)			
NETHERLANDS (1) (6)	Under the Benelux Convention can fish in the territorial sea. (1963)		All maritime waters between 1.2.1971. and 31.12.1972. (5)	All maritime waters between 1.2. 1971. and 31.12. 1972. (5)				
NORWAY (1961) (12)		4-12 mile zone between Lindesnes and Norway-Sweden frontier. (1966)					4-12 mile zone between Lindesnes and Norway-Sweden frontier. (1966)	
SWEDEN (1968) (12)		4-12 mile zone between Tistlarna and Norway-Sweden frontier. (1966)		Certain species in certain areas. (1970)		4-12 mile zone between Tistlarna and Norway-Sweden frontier. (1966)		

2. The position after the expiry of transitional arrangements i.e. as of January 1, 1972 (continued)

STATE	BELGIUM	DENMARK	FRANCE	FEDERAL REPUBLIC OF GERMANY	NETHERLANDS	NORWAY	SWEDEN	UNITED KINGDOM
UNITED KINGDOM (1964) (4) (12)	6-12 mile zone between North Foreland and Cromer and between Troup Head and Noss Head for demersal fish.		6-12 mile zone between North Foreland and Lowestoft for demersal fish.	6-12 mile zone between Whitby and Longstone and around Shetlands and Fair Isle for herring.	6-12 mile zone between Flamborough Head and Longstone and around Shetlands and Fair Isle for herring.	Dogfish and Basking sharks in 6-12 mile zone off Orkneys and Shetlands until 31.12.1984.(1964)		

3. The position as at January 1, 1973.

STATE	BELGIUM	DENMARK	FRANCE	FEDERAL REPUBLIC OF GERMANY	NETHERLANDS	NORWAY	SWEDEN	UNITED KINGDOM
BELGIUM 3					Under the Benelux Convention can fish in the territorial sea (1963)			
DENMARK (7) 12	6-12 mile zone except between Thyborøn and Blaavandshuk (1972)		6-12 mile zone except between Thyborøn and Blaavandshuk (1972)	6-12 mile zone except between Thyborøn and Blaavandshuk (1972)	6-12 mile zone except between Thyborøn and Blaavandshuk (1972)	6-12 mile zone except between Thyborøn and Blaavandshuk. (1972) 4-6 mile zone between Hanstholm and Skagen (1966)	4-12 mile zone between Hanstholm and Skagen (1966	6-12 mile zone except between Thyborøn and Blaavandshuk (1972)
FRANCE (7) 12	6-12 mile zone (1972)	6-12 mile zone (1972)		6-12 mile zone (1972)	6-12 mile zone (1972)	6-12 mile zone (1972)		6-12 mile zone (1972)
FEDERAL REPUBLIC OF GERMANY 3								
NETHERLANDS 3	Under the Benelux Convention can fish in the territorial sea (1963)							
NORWAY (7) 12	6-12 mile zone between Egersund and Norway-Sweden frontier (1972)	6-12 mile zone between Egersund Lindesnes (1972). 4-12 mile zone between Lindesnes and Norway-Sweden frontier (1966)	6-12 mile zone between Egersund and Norway-Sweden frontier (1972)	6-12 mile zone between Egersund and Norway-Sweden frontier (1972)	6-12 mile zone between Egersund and Norway-Sweden frontier (1972)		4-12 mile zone between Lindesnes and Norway-Sweden frontier (1966)	6-12 mile zone between Egersund and Norway-Sweden frontier (1972)

3. The position as at January 1, 1973. (continued)

STATE	BELGIUM	DENMARK	FRANCE	FEDERAL REPUBLIC OF GERMANY	NETHERLANDS	NORWAY	SWEDEN	UNITED KINGDOM
SWEDEN 12		4-12 mile zone between Tistlarna and Norway-Sweden frontier (1966)		Certain species in certain areas (1970)		4-12 mile zone between Tistlarna and Norway-Sweden frontier (1966)		
UNITED KINGDOM 12 (7)	6-12 mile zone between Berwick and River Coquet and between Flamborough Head and Straits of Dover (1972)	6-12 mile zone between Berwick and River Coquet and between Flamborough Head and Straits of Dover (1972)	6-12 mile zone between Berwick and River Coquet and between Flamborough Head and Straits of Dover (1972)	6-12 mile zone between Berwick and River Coquet and between Flamborough Head and Straits of Dover (1972)	6-12 mile zone between Berwick and River Coquet and between Flamborough Head and Straits of Dover (1972)	6-12 mile zone between Berwick and River Coquet and between Flamborough Head and Straits of Dover (1972)		

TABLE OF BILATERAL AGREEMENTS DELIMITING THE BED OF THE NORTH SEA

STATE	BELGIUM (1969)	DENMARK [1963] (1963)	FRANCE [1965] (1968)	FEDERAL REPUBLIC OF GERMANY (1964)	NETHERLANDS [1966] (1965)	NORWAY [1971] (1963)	SWEDEN [1966] (1966)	UNITED KINGDOM [1964] (1964)
BELGIUM (1960)								
DENMARK [1963](1963)				1965 (applies only to coastal regions) 1971	1966 (will terminate when the 1971 Agreement with the Federal Republic of Germany comes into force)	1965 (amended 1968)		1966 1971 (this will replace the 1966 Agreement when it comes into force)
FRANCE [1965](1968)								
FEDERAL REPUBLIC OF GERMANY (1964)		1965 (applies only coastal regions) 1971			1964 (applies to coastal regions) 1971			1971
NETHERLANDS [1966] (1965)		1966 (will terminate when the 1971 Agreement with the Federal Republic of Germany comes into force)		1964 (applies only to coastal regions) 1971				1965 (amended by the Protocol of 1971)
NORWAY [1971](1963)		1965 (amended 1968)					1968	1965
SWEDEN [1966](1966)						1968		
UNITED KINGDOM [1964](1964)		1966 1971 (this will replace the 1966 Agreement when it comes into force)		1971	1965 (amended by Protocol of 1971)	1965		

States which are underlined are parties to the Geneva Convention on the Continental Shelf, the date in [] being the date of ratification. The date in () is the date a claim was made to the Continental Shelf. The date in the box represents the date of the signature of the agreement. Agreements which are underlined represent delimitation in accordance with the principle of equidistance.

FOOTNOTES

1. No claim has been made to an exclusive fishing zone beyond the territorial sea. A three mile territorial sea is claimed.

2. Vessels of the Soviet Union were allowed to fish in the outer six miles until 31.10.1970: in certain areas they were limited to fishing with fixed nets and handtackle (1962).

3. Irish vessels were allowed to fish in the 3-6 mile zone until 31.12.1965 or 31.12.1966. (where straight baselines were drawn) (1964). Polish vessels were allowed to fish for herring in the 6-12 mile zone between Longstone Lighthouse and River Tyne North Pier Lighthouse until 31.12.1967. (1964).

4. Polish mother ships are permitted to enter the outer six mile zone for purposes ancillary to fishing (1964). Soviet fishing vessels and depot ships are permitted to anchor, navigate, transship fish and perform other activities ancillary to fishing operations in the 3-12 mile zone around the Shetlands (1964).

5. Under EEC Regulation 2141/70 of October 20, 1970.

6. Italy can fish in the maritime waters coming under its sovereignty or jurisdiction between 1.2.1971. and 31.12. 1972. (EEC Regulation 2141/70).

7. Ireland and Italy can fish in the 6-12 mile zone except in the areas specified under the agreement with Belgium.

8. The species and areas are as follows:

shrimp: between the German-Danish frontier and Skalligen.
flounder: between the German-Danish frontier and Bovbjerg.
flounder and Norway lobster: around Laesø.
flounder, Norway lobster and herring: around Anholt.
flounder, herring and sprat: north of Sjaelland.

Widths of Selected Straits and Channels

Passage (arranged clockwise by major regions)	*Sovereignty (on either side)*	*Geographical situation*	*Least width (in nautical miles)*
ANGLO-AMERICA			
Robeson Channel	Canada/Denmark	Between Ellesmere Island and Greenland.	10
Hudson Strait	Canada	Entrance to Hudson Bay	[1] 55
Strait of Belle Isle	Canada	Between Labrador and Newfoundland.	9
Jacques Cartier Passage	Canada	Between Quebec Coast and Anticosti Island.	15
Gaspé Passage	Canada	Between Anticosti Island and Gaspé Peninsula.	38

See footnotes at end of table.

Passage (arranged clockwise by major regions)	*Sovereignty (on either side)*	*Geographical situation*	*Least width (in nautical miles)*
Cabot Strait	Canada	Between Newfoundland and Cape Breton Island.	57
Northumberland Strait	Canada	Between New Brunswick and Prince Edward Island.	7
Florida Strait	United States/Cuba	Between Key West and Cuba	[2] 82
Santa Barbara Channel	United States	Between Channel Islands and California Coast.	11
Strait of Juan de Fuca	United States/Canada	South of Vancouver Island	9
Hecate Strait	Canada	Between Queen Charlotte Islands and Mainland.	24
Dixon Entrance	United States/Canada	Between Alexander Archipelago and Queen Charlotte Islands.	27
Amukta Pass	United States	Aleutian Islands: West of Amukta Island.	37
Unimak Pass	United States	Aleutian Islands: West of Unimak Island.	10
Shelikof Strait	United States	Between Alaska Peninsula and Kodiak Island.	20
Bering Strait	United States/U.S.S.R	Between Alaska and Siberia	[3] 19
LATIN AMERICA			
Yucatan Channel	Cuba/Mexico	Between Cuba and Yucatan Peninsula	[4] 105
Northwest Providence Channel.	United Kingdom	Bahamas: Southwest of Great Abaco	26
Northeast Providence Channel.	United Kingdom	Bahamas: Between Great Abaco Island and Eleuthera.	[5] 29
Crooked Passage	United Kingdom	Bahamas: Between Long Island and Crooked Island.	26
Mayaguana Passage	United Kingdom	Bahamas: Between Acklins Island and Mayaguana Island.	[6] 39
Caicos Passage	United Kingdom	Bahamas Area: Between Mayaguana Island and Caicos Islands.	35
Windward Passage	Cuba/Haiti	Between Cuba and Hispaniola	45
Turks Island Passage	United Kingdom	Between Turks Islands and Caicos Islands.	13
Mouchoir Passage	United Kingdom	Near Turks Islands	23
Mona Passage	U.S./Dominican Rep	Between Dominican Republic and Mona Island (P.R.).	33
Virgin Passage	United States	Between Culebra (P.R.) and Virgin Islands.	[7] 8
Anegada Passage	United Kingdom	Between Anegada and Sombrero	[8] 48
Guadeloupe Passage	France/United Kingdom.	Between Guadeloupe and Montserrat	28
Dominica Channel	France/United Kingdom.	Between Marie Galante (Guadeloupe) and Dominica.	16
Martinique Passage	France/United Kingdom.	Between Dominica and Martinique	22

See footnotes at end of table.

Passage (arranged clockwise by major regions)	Sovereignty (on either side)	Geographical situation	Least width (in nautical miles)
LATIN AMERICA—Continued			
St. Lucia Channel	France/United Kingdom.	Between Martinique and St. Lucia	17
St. Vincent Passage	United Kingdom	Between St. Lucia and St. Vincent	23
Dragon's Mouth	Trinidad and Tobago/ Venezuela.	Between Trinidad (Chacachacare Island) and Peninsula of Paria.	6
Serpent's Mouth	Trinidad and Tobago/ Venezuela.	Between Trinidad and Coast of Venezuela.	8
Aruba-Paraguana Passage.	Netherlands/Venezuela	Between Aruba and Paraguana Peninsula.	15
Estrecho de la Maire	Argentina	Between Tierra del Fuego and Isla de los Estados.	16
Strait of Magellan	Argentina/Chile	Between Tierra del Fuego and Mainland South America.	2
EUROPE			
Bosporus	Turkey	Between Turkey in Europe and Anatolia.	([8a])
Dardanelles	Turkey	Between Gallipoli Peninsula and Anatolia.	([8a])
Kårpathos Strait	Greece	Dodecanese: Between Kårpathos and Rhodes.	23
Kásos Strait	Greece	Dodecanese: Between Kásos and Crete.	26
Strait of Otranto	Albania/Italy	Between Albania and Italian Peninsula.	41
Strait of Messina	Italy	Between Sicily and Italian Peninsula	2
Malta Channel	Italy/United Kingdom	Between Malta (Gozo) and Sicily	44
Strait of Sicily	Italy	Between Pantelleria and Sicily	55
Strait between Elba and Italy.	Italy	Between Elba and Italian Peninsula	5
Strait between Corsica and Elba.	France/Italy	Between Corsica and Elba	27
Strait of Bonificio	France/Italy	Between Corsica and Sardinia	6
Freu de Minorca	Spain	Between Majorca and Minorca	20
Strait of Gibraltar	Morocco/Spain	Between Morocco and Spain	8
Strait of Dover	France/United Kingdom.	Between England and France	18
The Solent	United Kingdom	Between Isle of Wight and English Mainland.	2
St. George's Channel	Ireland/United Kingdom.	Between Ireland and Wales	[9] 42
North Channel	United Kingdom	Between Northern Ireland and Scotland.	11
Little Minch	United Kingdom	Between Outer Hebrides and Island of Skye.	10
North Minch	United Kingdom	Between Outer Hebrides and Mainland of Scotland.	[10] 20

See footnotes at end of table.

Passage (arranged clockwise by major regions)	*Sovereignty (on either side)*	*Geographical situation*	*Least width (in nautical miles)*
EUROPE—Continued			
Pentland Firth	United Kingdom	Between Orkneys and Mainland of Scotland.	[11] 5
The Hole	United Kingdom	Between Orkneys and Shetland Islands (Fair Isle).	23
Skagerrak	Denmark/Norway	Between Denmark (Jutland) and Norway.	61
Ore Sund	Denmark/Sweden	Between Sjaelland and Sweden	2
Bornholmsgat (Hambarne).	Denmark/Sweden	Between Bornholm and Sweden	19
Kalmar Sund	Sweden	Between Öland Island and Swedish Mainland.	2
Entrance to Gulf of Bothnia.	Finland/Sweden	Between Aland Islands and Sweden	[12] 17
Entrance to Gulf of Finland.	Estonia/Finland	Between Estonia and Finland	17
FAR EAST			
Kuril Strait	U.S.S.R	Between Kamchatka and Kuril Islands.	6
Etorofu Kaikyo	U.S.S.R./U.S.S.R. Administration.	Between Etorofu and Uruppu	22
Kunashiri Suido	U.S.S.R. Administration.	Between Etorofu and Kunashira	12
Shikotan Suido	U.S.S.R. Administration.	Between Shikotan and Taraku (Habomai Islands).	12
Taraku Suido	U.S.S.R. Administration.	Habomai Island: Between Taraku and Shibotsu.	6
Notsuke	Japan/U.S.S.R. Admin	Between Hokkaido and Kunashira	9
Soya Kaikyo (La Perouse Strait).	Japan/U.S.S.R	Between Hokkaido and Sakhalin	[13] 23
Tsugara Kaikyo	Japan	Between Honshu and Hokkaido	10
Eastern Chosen Strait	Japan	Between Iki (Off coast of Kyushu) and Tsushima.	25
Western Chosen Strait	Japan/Korea	Between Korea and Tsushima	[14] 23
Cheju Haehyop	Korea	Off Southern Coast of Korea (Cheju Do to Haem Sō).	12
Maemul Suido	Korea	Off Southwest Coast of Korea (Maemul To to Yōngsan Do).	13
Huksan Chedo	Korea	Off Southwest Coast of Korea	8
Pohai Strait	China	Entrance to Pohai Bay	22
Osumi Kaikyo (Van Dieman Strait).	Japan	Between Kyushu and Ryukyus	16
Tokara Kaikyo (Colnett Strait).	Japan	Ryukyus: Between Osumi Gunto and Tokara Gunto.	22
Formosa Strait	China	Between Taiwan and Mainland China	[15] 74
P'enghu Shuitao (Pescadores Channel).	China	Between Taiwan and P'enghu (Pescadores).	17

See footnotes at end of table.

Passage (arranged clockwise by major regions)	Sovereignty (on either side)	Geographical situation	Least width (in nautical miles)
FAR EAST—Continued			
Lema Channel	China/United Kingdom	Between Hong Kong and Lema Islands.	6
Hainan Strait	China	Between Hainan Island and Mainland China.	10
SOUTHEAST ASIA			
Babuyan Channel	Philippines	Between Babuyan Islands and Luzon	15
Polillo Strait	Philippines	Between Polillo Island and Luzon	10
Maqueda Channel	Philippines	Between Cataduanes and Luzon	4
Verde Island Passage	Philippines	Between Luzon and Mindoro (Verde Island to Mindoro).	[16] 4
San Bernardino Passage	Philippines	Between Luzon and Samar	8
Mindoro Strait	Philippines	Between Calamian Islands and Mindoro (from Apo I. to outermost of Calamian Islands).	[17] 20
Surigao Strait	Philippines	Between Leyte and Mindanao	10
Basilan Passage	Philippines	Between Mindanao and Sulu Archipelago.	7
Balabac Passage	Malaysia/Philippines	Between Palawan and Sabah (Island of Borneo).	[18] 27
Sibutu Passage	Philippines	In Sulu Archipelago near Borneo	18
Bangka Passage	Indonesia	Between Bangka Island and offshore islands to north.	19
Selat Grehund	Indonesia	Between offshore islands of Celebes to east.	10
Makassar Strait	Indonesia	Between Borneo and Celebes (without regard to offshore islands).	[19] 62
Koti Passage	Indonesia	Off northwest coast of Borneo	10
Serasan Passage	Indonesia	Off northwest coast of Borneo	23
Api Passage	Indonesia	Off northwest coast of Borneo	16
Selat Ombai	Indonesia/Portugal	Between Alor and Portuguese Timor	16
Selat Roti	Indonesia	Between Roti and Timor	6
Selat Sape	Indonesia	Between Komoda and Sumbawa	8
Selat Alas	Indonesia	Between Lombok and Sumbawa	5
Selat Lombok	Indonesia	Between Bali and Lombok	11
Selat Bali	Indonesia	Between Bali and Java	2
Selat Sunda	Indonesia	Between Java and Sumatra (not taking into account Pulau Sangiang in middle of strait).	12
Gaspar Strait	Indonesia	Between Bangka and Billiton	[20] 8
Selat Bangka	Indonesia	Between Bangka and Sumatra	8
Berhala Strait	Indonesia	Between Singkep and Sumatra	[21] 9
Strait of Malacca (North)	Indonesia/Malaysia	Between Malaysia and Sumatra	20
Strait of Malacca (South)	Indonesia/Malaysia	Between Malaysia and Sumatra opposite Singapore.	8

See footnotes at end of table.

Passage (arranged clockwise by major regions)	*Sovereignty (on either side)*	*Geographical situation*	*Least width (in nautical miles)*
OCEANIA			
Alenuihaha Channel	United States	Between Hawaii and Maui	25
Alalakeiki Channel	United States	Between Kahoolawe and Maui	6
Kealaikahiki Channel	United States	Between Kahoolawe and Lanai.	15
Auau Channel.	United States	Between Lanai and Maui	8
Pailolo Channel	United States	Between Molokai and Maui	8
Kalohi Channel	United States	Between Lanai and Molokai	8
Kaiwi Channel	United States	Between Oahu and Moloaki	22
Kauai Channel	United States	Between Kauai and Oahu	63
Kaulakahi Channel	United States	Between Kauai and Niihau	15
Apolima Strait	Western Samoa	Between Savai'i and Upolu (not taking into account Apolima Island in center of strait).	4
Indispensable Strait	United Kingdom	Between Guadalcanal and Malaita	[22] 19
Manning Strait	United Kingdom	Between Choisel and Santa Isabel	6
Bougainville Strait	United Kingdom	Between Bougainville and Choiseul	15
St. George's Channel	Australia	Between New Britain and New Ireland.	8
Goschen Strait	Australia	Between New Guinea and D'Entrecasteaux Islands.	7
Dampier Strait	Australia	Between New Britain and Umboi	13
Vitiaz Strait	Australia	Between New Guinea and Bismarck Archipelago.	24
Cook Strait	New Zealand	Between North Island and South Island.	12
Banks Strait	Australia	Between Australia and offshore islands (near Tasmania).	8
Floveaux	New Zealand	Between South Island and Stewart Island.	[23] 15
MISCELLANEOUS			
Kara Strait	U.S.S.R.	Between Novaya Zemlya and Ostrov Vaygach.	19
Palk Strait	Ceylon/India	Through Adams Bridge	3
Strait of Hormoz	Iron/Muscat and Oman	Entrance to Persian Gulf	21
Bab el Mandeb	France/Yemen	Southern Entrance to Red Sea	[24] 14

[1] Entrance to Hudson Strait between Resolution Island and Button Islands (off Labrador Coast), 37 miles.

[2] Distance between Bimini (Bahamas) and Florida, 43 miles.

[3] Distance given in table is that between Big Diomede Island (U.S.S.R.) and Mainland Siberia. Other distances: (1) Between Little Diomede Island (U.S.) and Big Diomede Island, 2 miles. (2) Between Little Diomede Island and Mainland Alaska, 20 miles. (3) Between Mainland Alaska and Mainland Siberia, 45 miles.

[4] Distance given is that from Contoy, an island about 6 miles off the Yucatan coast.

[5] Distance between Great Abaco Island and Royal Island, off Eleuthera coast, 26 miles.

[6] Distance between Acklins Island and Plana Cays, 12 miles; between Plana Cays and Mayaguana Island, 21 miles.

[7] Distance given in table is from Culebrita, an islet east of Culebra.

[8] Distance between Sombrero and Horse Shoe Reef, a breaking reef running southeast of Anegada and attached thereto, is 42 miles.

[8a] Less than a nautical mile.

[9] Distance given in table is between mainlands; between South Bishop Rock (Wales) and Tuskar Rock (Ireland), 36 miles.

[10] Between Shiant Island and mainland of Scotland, 17 miles.

[11] Between Pentland Skerries and mainland of Scotland,

4 miles. Stroma Island, which also lies in Pentland Firth, is not considered in the computation.

[12] Distance given in table approximately correct; several small islands in strait makes precise measurements difficult.

[13] Distance between Hokkaido and Ostrov Kamen' Opasnosti, 20 miles; on to Sakhalin, 9 miles.

[14] Measured from island off the coast of Korea.

[15] Distance is 68 miles if offshore islands are taken into consideration.

[16] Distance between Luzon and Verde Island, 3 miles.

[17] Distance between Mindoro to Apo Reef, 15 miles.

[18] Distance given in table is that measured between Balabac, largest of the major islands south of Palawan, and Balambangan, closest of the major islands of Sabah.

[19] Distance between Borneo and Pulau Tuguan, 55 miles.

[20] Distance given in table is that measured across Macclesfield Strait portion of Gaspar Strait.

[21] Distance from Sumatra to Berhala, in middle of strait, 9 miles; from Berhala to Singkep, 10 miles.

[22] Distance given in table is that measured between Malaita and Nura Islands, the latter 10 miles from Guadalcanal.

[23] Distance between Centre Island (4 miles off South Island) and Stewart Island at west end of strait, 13 miles. At east end of strait the recommended channel for ships between Dog Island on the north and Ruapuke on the south, the channel is 11 miles wide.

[24] Distance given in table is between mainlands; between Perim Island and African continent, 11 miles; between Perim Island and French islets to south, 9 miles.

FISHERY STATISTICS

1. World Catches

Year	1958	1966	1967	1968	1969	1970
Total World Catch (1)	33.3	57.5	61.1	64.3	62.9	69.3
For Human Consumption:	27.9	38.6	39.6	40.3	40.4	42.8
Marketing (fresh)	14.8	18.5	18.7	18.5	18.0	19.0
Freezing	2.8	6.9	7.6	8.1	8.6	9.5
Curing	7.3	8.2	8.0	8.1	8.0	8.1
Canning	3.0	5.0	5.3	5.6	5.8	6.2
For Other Purposes	5.4	18.9	21.5	24.0	22.5	26.5

The Totals are given in million metric tons and do not include whale catches.

(1) The total world catch in 1938 was 21.0 and in 1948 19.6.

Source: FAO Yearbook of Fishery Statistics 1970, Vol. 31.

2. Catches of Leading Countries (only those countries catching more than 1 million metric tons in 1970 are listed)

Year	1958	1966	1967	1968	1969	1970
Peru	900.2	8712.1	10,034.1	10,440.5	9143.4	12,481.1
Japan	5506.0	7102.6	7850.9	8670.1	8613.4	9314.3
Norway	1438.9	2871.9	3264.9	2838.1	2437.0	2855.7
U.S.A.	2703.4	2542.9	2430.4	2479.4	2495.7	2758.3
India	1064.4	1367.4	1400.2	1525.9	1605.0	1745.9
Thailand	196.3	708.1	847.2	1089.0	1270.1	1594.9
Spain	844.9	1352.8	1432.1	1500.1	1481.7	no figure given
Canada	992.2	1315.9	1258.5	1452.2	1351.2	1323.0
Denmark (excluding Faeroes)	598.1	850.7	1068.4	1463.7	1277.3	1228.7
Chile	220.9	1383.3	1052.8	1376.1	1076.9	1161.0
United Kingdom	1136.3	1052.6	1004.5	1017.9	1062.4	1075.3

The totals are given in thousand metric tons and do not include whale catches.

Source: FAO Yearbook of Fishery Statistics 1970, Vol. 31.

Note: The figures for USSR and the People's Republic of China are not known, but almost certainly they are among the world's leading fishing countries.

3. Leading exporters of fish in 1969.

State	Value in $ million	Volume in thousand metric tons
Japan	281.8	458.5
Canada	247.4	379.7
Norway	231.6	752.6
Peru	220.4	1890.1
Denmark and Faeroes	164.3	497.8
U.S.A.	97.7	153.5
Iceland	86.0	324.5
U.S.S.R.	84.9	305.0

4. Leading importers of fish in 1969.

State	Value in $million	Volume in thousand metric tons
U.S.A.	735.9	1078.7
United Kingdom	271.8	865.6
Federal Republic of Germany	230.0	979.5
Japan	219.4	323.3
France	165.9	354.4
Italy	131.7	311.9
Netherlands	82.5	403.9
Belgium and Luxembourg	76.2	224.6
Sweden	65.0	170.4

The totals do not include whale catches.

Source: FAO Yearbook of Fishery Statistics 1969, Vol. 30.

INTERGOVERNMENTAL ORGANIZATIONS CONCERNED WITH THE LAW OF THE SEA

This is a selected list of Intergovernmental Organizations concerned with the Law of the Sea with particular emphasis on fisheries bodies. The date in parenthesis is the year in which the organization was established. Acronyms, addresses, and members are provided in certain instances.

I. United Nations General Assembly

A. Committee on the Peaceful Uses of the Sea-Bed and the Ocean Floor Beyond the Limits of National Jurisdiction. Australia, Algeria, Argentina, Afghanistan, Austria, Belgium, Bulgaria, Brazil, Bolivia, Chile, Canada, China (P.R.C. Colombia, Cyprus, Cameroon, Czechoslovakia, Denmark, Fiji, Guyana, Japan, New Zealand, Nicaragua, Poland, Singapore, United Kingdom, United States, Greece, Finland, Iceland, Norway, Sweden, Italy, Ivory Coast, Malta, Spain, Tunisia, Turkey, Yugoslavia, Egypt, India, Indonesia, Iran, Iraq, Jamaica, Kenya, Kuwait, Liberia, Libya, Madagascar, Malaysia, Mauritius, Mexico, Morocco, Somalia, Sri Lanka, Sudan, Tanzania, Thailand, Trinidad & Tobago, Ukrainian SSR, Union of Soviet Socialist Republics, Venezuela, Yemen (San'aa), Zaire, Mauritania, Nigeria Bagon, Guinea, Ecuador, El Salvador, Panama, Peru, Sierra Leone, Uruguay, Byelorussia SSR, Hungary, Mali, Nepal, Zambia.

B. International Atomic Energy Agency (IAEA) (1957)
Address: 9-13 Kaerntner Ring, Vienna. Members:
Afghanistan, Albania, Algeria, Argentina, Australia, Austria, Belgium, Bolivia, Brazil, Bulgaria, Burma, Byelorussia SSR, Cameroon, Canada, Ceylon, Chile, Colombia, Costa Rica, Cuba, Cyprus, Czechoslovakia, Denmark, Domican Republic, Ecuador, Egypt, El Salvador, Ethiopia, Federal Republic of Germany, Finland, France, Gabon, Chana, Greece, Guatemala, Haiti, Holy See, Hungary, Iceland, India, Indonesia, Iran, Iraq, Ireland, Israel, Italy, Ivory Coast, Jamaica, Japan, Jordan, Kenya, Khmer Republic, Kuwait, Lebanon, Liberia, Libyan Arab Republic, Liechtenstein, Luxembourg, Madagascar, Malaysia, Mali, Mexico, Monaco, Morocco, Netherlands, New Zealand, Niger, Nigeria, Norway, Pakistan, Panama, Paraguay, Peru, Philippines, Poland, Portugal, Republic of Korea, Republic of Viet-Nam, Romania, Saudi Arabia, Senegal, Sierra Leone, Singapore, South Africa, Spain, Sudan, Sweden, Switzerland, Syrian Arab Republic, Thailand, Tunisia, Turkey, Uganda, Ukrainian Soviet Socialist Republic, Union of Soviet Socialist Republics, United Kingdom, United States, Uruguay, Venezuela, Yugoslavia, Zaire, Zambia

C. U.N. Conference on Trade and Development (UNCTAD) (March-June 1964) Members:

135 Members. (The 126 UN Members and the 9 members of the SA's... (Fed. Rep. of Germany, Holy See, Liechtenstein, Monaco, Republic of Korea, Republic of Viet-Nam, San Marino, Switzerland, Western Samoa)

Geographical distribution:
As per original arrangements - 1964

<u>A Countries</u> -

Afghanistan	Gabon	Liberia	Rep of Viet-Nam	Tanzania
Algeria	Ghana	Libya	Rwanda	Upper Volta
Burma	Guinea	Madagascar	Saudi Arabia	Western Samoa
Burundi	India	Malaysia	Senegal	Yemen
Cambodia	Indonesia	Mali	Sierra Leone	Yugoslavia
Cameroon	Iran	Mauritania	Somalia	
Cent. Af. Rep.	Iraq	Mongolia	South Africa	
Ceylon	Israel	Morocco	Sudan	
Chad	Ivory Coast	Nepal	Syria	
China	Jordan	Niger	Thailand	
Congo (b)	Kenya	Nigeria	Togo	
Congo (Dem Rep)	Kuwait	Pakistan	Tunisia	
Dahomey	Laos	Philippines	Uganda	
Ethiopia	Lebanon	Korea	UAR	

A decision of 23rd GA added to List A - Botswana, Gambia, Lesotho, Malawi, Maldive Islands, Mauritius, Singapore, Southern Yemen and Zambia

B Countries -

Australia	Fed Rep Germany	Ireland	Netherlands	Sweden
Austria	Finland	Italy	New Zealand	Switzerland
Belgium	France	Japan	Norway	Turkey
Canada	Greece	Liechtenstein	Portugal	UK
Cyprus	Holy See	Luxembourg	San Marino	US
Denmark	Iceland	Monaco	Spain	

23rd GA added Malta

C Countries -

Argentina	Costa Rica	Guatemala	Nicaragua
Bolivia	Cuba	Haiti	Panama
Brazil	Dominican Republic	Honduras	Paraguay
Chile	Ecuador	Jamaica	Peru
Colombia	El Salvador	Mexico	Trinidad & Tobago
			Uruguay
			Venezuela

23rd GA added Barbados and Guyana

D Countries -

Albania	Hungary	USSR
Bulgaria	Poland	
Byelorussian SSR	Romania	
Czechoslovakia	Ukrainian SSR	

D. Economic and Social Council (ECOSOC) Members:

[Advisory Committee on Science and Technology]

Argentina (70)	India (70)	Peru (72)
Brazil (72)	Indonesia (71)	Sudan (71)
Bulgaria (70)	Ireland (70)	Tunisia (72)
Ceylon (72)	Italy (72)	USSR (71)
Chad (70)	Jamaica (71)	UK (71)
Congo (B) (70)	Japan (70)	US (70)
France (72)	Kenya (72)	Upper Volta (70)
Ghana (72)	Norway (71)	Uruguay (71)
Greece (72)	Pakistan (71)	Yugoslavia (71)

U.N. Development Program (UNDP) Address:
United Nations, New York, (Nov. 22, 1965) Members (of Governing Council):

Algeria	70	Malaysia	70
Austria	70	Mauritania	71
Belgium	70	Mexico	72
Cameroon	72	Netherlands	71
Canada	70	Pakistan	70
Chile	71	Panama	71
Congo (B)	71	Peru	71
Cuba	72	Philippines	72
Czechoslovakia	71	Poland	70
Denmark	72	Romania	70
Federal Republic of Germany	71	Sweden	71
		Switzerland	71
Finland	70	Syria	71
France	70	USSR	72
India	72	UAR	70
Italy	72	UK	72
Japan	72	Tanzania	71
Jordan	70	United States	72
		Venezuela	70

II. United Nations - Specialized Agencies

A. U. N. Educational Scientific and Cultural Organization (UNESCO) (Nov. 4, 1946), Members: See page 900.

1. Office of Oceanography

2. Intergovernmental Oceanographic Commission (IOC)*
Address: 16 bd. de Suisse, Montecarlo, Monaco.
Members: Algeria, Argentina, Australia, Austria, Belgium, Brazil, Bulgaria, Canada, Chile, China (Republic of), Colombia, Congo (Brazaville), Cuba, Denmark, Dominican Republic, Egypt, Greece, Guatemala, Iceland, India, Indonesia, Iraq, Israel, Italy, Ivory Coast, Jamaica, Japan, Korea (Republic of), Lebanon, Madagascar, Malaysia, Malta, Mauritania, Mexico, Monaco, Morocco, Netherlands, New Zealand, Norway, Pakistan, Panama, Peru, Philippines, Poland, Portugal, Romania, Senegal, Singapore, South Africa, Spain, Sweden, Switzerland, Syria, Tanzania, Thailand, Trinidad, Tobago, Tunisia, Turkey, Ukrainian SSR, Union of Soviet Socialist Republics, United Kingdom, Uruguay, United States of America, Venezuela, Viet-Nam (Republic of), Yugoslavia.

B. Food and Agriculture Organization (1945). FAO.**
Address: Via dell Terme di Caracalla, 00100 Rome, Italy. See page 900.

1. Committee of Fisheries (1965). (OFI)
Members: Argentina, Australia, Bahrain, Belgium, Brazil, Bulgaria, Cameroon, Canada, Central African Republic, Ceylon, Chile, Costa Rica, Cuba, Czechoslovakia, Denmark, Ecuador, Egypt, Ethiopia, Finland, France, Gabon, Germany (Federal Republic of), Ghana, Greece, Honduras, Hungary, Iceland, India, Indonesia, Iran, Iraq, Ireland, Israel, Italy, Ivory Coast, Japan, Kenya, Korea (Republic of), Kuwait, Liberia, Libya, Madagascar, Malaysia, Malta, Mexico, Morocco, Netherlands, New Zealand, Nicaragua, Niger, Nigeria, Norway, Pakistan, Panama, Peru, Philippines, Poland, Portugal, Romania, Senegal, Sierra Leone, Somali, Spain, Sudan, Sweden, Tanzania, Thailand, Trinidad and Tobago, Tunisia, Turkey, Uganda, United Kingdom, United States of America, Uruguay, Venezuela, Vietnam (Republic of), Zaire and Zambia.

2. Advisory Committee on Marine Resources and Research.
(Private individuals who advise FAO)

3. Working Party of Fishery Statistics in the North Atlantic Area.
(Private individuals who advise FAO)

4. Panel of Experts for the Facilitation of Tuna Research.
(Private individuals who advise FAO)

C. World Meteorological Organization (WMO) (March 23, 1950)
Address: 41 Avenue Guiseppe Motta, Geneva.
Members: See page 900.

[Commission on Maritime Meteorology (CMM)]

D. Intergovernmental Maritime Consultative Organization (1958). IMCO.
Address: 101-104 Piccadilly, London WIV OAE, United Kingdom.
Members: See page 900.

E. International Bank for Reconstruction and Development (IBRD)
Address: 1818 H Street, N.W. Washington, D.C. 20433
Members: See page 900.

F. International Telecommunication Union (ITU) (1865)
Address: Place des Nations, Geneva. U.S. Participation 1912 International Radio Telegraph Union.
Members: See page 900.

G. World Health Organization (WHO) (April 7, 1948) - U.S. Participation 1948 (TIAS) 1808
Address: Avenue Appia, Geneva
Members: See page 900.

* See following list of subsidiary bodies.
** See following list of regional bodies.

H. Regional U.N. Economic Commissions

1. Economic Commission for Europe (ECE)
Address: Palais des Nations, Geneva
The Economic Commission for Europe was established by the ECOSOC in March 1947. It now has thirty-one members, the European members of the UN, including the Union of Soviet Socialist Republics, the Federal Republic of Germany, and the United States. Switzerland is an observer.

2. Economic Commission for Latin America (ECLA)
Address: Av. Providencia 871, Santiago, Chile
Established: ECOSOC RES 106(VI) of February 25, 1948
Members: Membership is open to members of the UN in North, Central and South America and in the Caribbean Area, France, Netherlands and the United Kingdom. Argentina, Barbados, Bolivia, Brazil, Canada, Chile, Colombia, Costa Rica, Cuba, Dominican Republic, Ecuador, El Salvador, France, Guatemala, Guyana, Haiti, Honduras, Jamaica, Mexico, Netherlands, Nicaragua, Panama, Paraguay, Peru, Trinidad & Tobago, United Kingdom, United States of America, Uruguay, Venezuela.
Associate Members: British Honduras (Belize), the Associated States of Antigua, Dominica, Grenada, St. Kitts-Nevis-Anguilla and St. Lucia and the Territories of Montserrat and St. Vincent. The Federal Republic of Germany and Switzerland take part in a consultative capacity.

3. Economic Commission for Africa (ECA)
Address: Addis Ababa
Members: Non-Self-Governing territories in Africa (including African islands) and powers other than Portugal responsible for the international relations of those territories (France, Spain, United Kingdom) are associate members. The Federal Republic of Germany and Switzerland take part in a consultative capacity. Algeria, Botswana, Burundi, Cameroon, Central African Republic, Chad, Congo(B), Congo(K), Dahomey, Equitorial Guinea, Ethiopia, Gabon, Gambia, Ghana, Guinea, Ivory Coast, Kenya, Madagascar, Malawi, Mali, Mauritania, Mauritius, Morocco, Niger, Rwanda, Senegal, Sierra Leone (South Africa), Sudan, Swaziland, Togo, Tunisia, Uganda, United Arab Republic, Tanzania, Upper Volta, Zambia.

4. Economic Commission for Asia and the Far East (ECAFE)
Address: (Temporary) Sala Santitham (Peace Hall), Bangkok, Thailand
Established: By ECOSOC Resolution 37(IV) of March 28, 1947. Includes Committee for Coordination of Joint Prospecting for Mineral Resources in Asian Offshore Areas (1965)
Members: Commission has 27 members: Afghanistan, Australia, Burma, Cambodia, Ceylon, China, France, India, Indonesia, Iran, Japan, Laos, Malaysia, Mongolia, Nepal, Netherlands, New Zealand, Pakistan, Republic of Korea, Republic of Viet-Nam, Singapore, Thailand, Union of Soviet Socialist Republics, United Kingdom, the United States of America, Western Samoa. Among these countries, France, Netherlands, Union of Soviet Socialist Republics, United Kingdom and the United States of America are considered non-regional members. Bhutan, Nauru, Tonga and Philippines have been added to the membership since 1970. The Commission also has seven associate members: British Solomon Islands, Brunei, Cook Islands, Fiji, Hong Kong, Papua, and New Guinea.

Member Nations of U.N. Specialized Agencies (keyed to Sections II.A through II.G)

Afghanistan, A,B,C,E,F,G
Albania, A,C,F,G
Algeria, A,B,C,D,E,F,G
Angola (Portuguese West Africa), C
Argentina, A,B,C,D,E,F,G
Australia, A,B,C*,D,E,F,G
Austria, A,B,C,E,F,G
Bahamas, C
Bahrain, B,G
Bangladesh, G
Barbados, A,B,C,D,F,G
Belgium, A,B,C,D,E,F,G
Bolivia, A,B,C,E,F,G
Botswana, B,C,E,F
Brazil, A,B,C,D,E,F,G
British Eastern Caribbean Group, A,C
Bulgaria, A,B,C,D,F,G
Burma, A,B,C,D,E,F,G
Burundi, A,B,C,E,F,G
Byelorussian Soviet Socialist Republic, A,C,F,G
Cambodia, A,B,C,D,E,F,G
Cameroon, A,B,C,D,E,F,G
Canada, A,B,C,D,E,F,G
Central African Republic, A,B,C,E,F,G
Ceylon, A,B,C,E,F,G
Chad, A,B,C,E,F,G
Chile, A,B,C,E,F,G
China, A,C,D,E,F,G
Colombia, A,B,C,E,G

Comoro Islands, C
Congo (Brazzaville), A,B,C,E,F,G
Costa Rica, A,B,C,E,G
Cuba, A,B,C,D,F,G
Cyprus, A,B,C,E,F,G
Czechoslovakia, A,B,C,D,F,G
Dahomey, A,B,C,E,F,G
Denmark, A,B,C,D,E,F,G
Dominican Republic, A,B,C,D,E,F,G
Ecuador, A,B,C,D,E,F,G
Egypt, A,B,C,D,E,F,G
El Salvador, A,B,C,E,G
Equitorial Guinea, E,F
Ethiopia, A,B,C,E,F,G
Fiji, B,E,F,G
Finland, A,B,C,D,E,F,G
France, A,B,C,D,E,F,G
French Polynesia, C
French Somaliland, C
French Territory of Afars and Issa, C
Gabon, A,B,C,E,F,G
Gambia, The, B,E,G
Germany, Federal Republic, A,B,C,D,E, F,G
Ghana, A,B,C,D,E,G
Greece, A,B,C,D,E,F,G
Guatemala, A,B,C,E,G
Guinea, A,B,C,E,F,G
Guyana, A,B,C,E,F,G
Haiti, A,B,C,D,E,G
Honduras, A,B,C,D,E,G
Hong Kong, C, D*
Hungary, A,B,C,D,F,G
Iceland, A,B,C,D,E,F,G
India, A,B,C,D,E,F,G
Indonesia, A,B,C,D,E,F,G
Iran, A,B,C,D,E,F,G
Iraq, A,B,C,E,F,G
Ireland, A,B,C,D,E,F,G
Israel, A,B,C,D,E,F,G
Italy, A,B,C,D,E,F,G
Ivory Coast, A,B,C,D,E,F,G
Jamaica, A,B,C,E,F,G
Japan, A,B,C,D,E,F,G
Jordan, A,B,C,E,F,G
Kenya, A,B,C,E,F,G
Korea, A,B,C,D,E,F,G
Kuwait, A,B,C,D,E,F,G
Laos, A,B,C,E,F,G
Lebanon, A,B,C,D,E,F,G
Lesotho, A,B,E,F,G
Liberia, A,B,D,E,G
Libya, A,B,C,D,E,G
Liechtenstein, F
Luxembourg, A,B,C,E,F,G
Madagascar, A,B,C,D,E,F,G
Malawi, A,B,C,E,F,G
Malaysia, A,B,C,D,E,F,G
Maldive Islands, B,D,F,G
Mali, A,B,C,E,F,G
Malta, A,B,D,F,G
Mauritania, A,B,C,D,E,F,G
Mauritius, A,B,C,E,F,G
Mexico, A,B,C,D,E,F,G
Monaco, A,F,G
Mongolian People's Republic, A,C,G
Morocco, A,B,C,D,E,F,G
Mozambique, (Portuguese East Africa),C
Nauru, F
Nepal, A,B,C,E,F,G
Netherlands, A,B,C,D,E,F,G
Netherlands Antilles (Curaçao), C
New Caledonia, C
New Zealand, A,B,C,D,E,F,G
Nicaragua, A,B,C,E,F,G
Niger, A,B,C,E,F,G
Nigeria, A,B,C,D,E,F,G
Norway, A,B,C,D,E,F,G
Oman, B,E,G
Pakistan, A,B,C,D,E,F,G
Panama, A,B,C,D,E,F,G
Papua-New Guinea, G
Paraguay, A,B,C,E,F,G
Peru, A,B,C,D,E,F,G
Philippines, A,B,C,D,E,G
Poland, A,B,C,D,F,G
Portugal, A,B,C,E,F,G
Qatar, A*, B,G
Romania, A,B,C,D,F,G
Rwanda, A,B,C,E,F,G
St. Pierre and Miquelon, C
Saudi Arabia, A,B,C,D,E,F,G
Senegal, A,B,C,D,E,F,G
Sierra Leone, A,B,C,E,G
Singapore, A,C,D,E,F,G
Somalia, A,B,C,E,F,G
South Africa, C,E,F,G
Southern Rhodesia, C,G*
Spain, A,B,C,D,E,F,G
Sudan, A,B,C,E,G
Surinam, C
Swaziland, B,E,F
Sweden, A,B,C,D,E,F,G
Switzerland, A,B,C,D,F,G
Syrian Arab Republic, A,B,C,D,E,F,G
Tanzania, A,B,C,E,F,G
Thailand, A,B,C,E,F,G
Togo, A,B,C,E,F,G
Trinidad and Tobago, A,B,C,D,E,F,G
Tunisia, A,B,C,D,E,F,G
Turkey, A,B,C,D,E,F,G
Uganda, A,B,C,E,F,G
Ukrainian Soviet Socialist Republic, A,C,F,G
Union of Soviet Socialist Republic, A,C,D,F,G
United Arab Emirate, G
United Kingdom, A,B,C,D,E,F,G
United States, A,B,C,D,E,F,G
Upper Volta, A,B,C,E,F,G
Uruguay, A,B,C,D,E,F,G
Vatican City, F
Venezuela, A,B,C,E,F,G
Viet-Nam, A,B,C,E,F,G
Western Samoa, G
Yemen (Aden), A,B,C,E,F,G
Yemen (San'ā'), A,B,C,E,G
Yugoslavia, A,B,C,D,E,F,G
Zaire, A,B,C,E,F,G
Zambia, A,B,C,E,F,G

---

* Associate Member

III. Other Intergovernmental Marine Science Organizations

A. International Council for the Exploration of the Sea (1902).
Address: Charlottenlund Slot, Dk-2920 Charlottenlund, Denmark.
Members: Belgium, Canada, Denmark, Finland, France, Germany (Federal Republic of), Iceland, Ireland, Italy, Netherlands, Norway, Poland, Portugal, Spain, Sweden, Union of Soviet Socialist Republics and United Kingdom.

B. International Hydrographic Organization (1970). (Successor to International Hydrographic Bureau (1921).
Address: 7 Avenue President J. F. Kennedy, Montecarlo, Monaco.
Members: Argentina, Australia, Brazil, Burma, Canada, Chile, China (Republic of), Cuba, Denmark, Dominican Republic, Egypt, Finland, France, Germany (Federal Republic of), Greece, Guatemala, Iceland, India, Indonesia, Iran, Italy, Japan, Korea (Republic of), Monaco, Netherlands, New Zealand, Norway, Philippines, Poland, Portugal, South Africa, Pakistan, Paraguay, Spain, Sweden, Thailand, Turkey, United Kingdom, United States of America, Venezuela, Yugoslavia

C. International Commission for Scientific Exploration of Mediterranean Sea (1919).
Address: 16 bd. de Suisse, Montecarlo, Monaco.
Members: Algeria, Egypt, France, Greece, Israel, Italy, Monaco, Morocco, Romania, Spain, Tunisia, Turkey and Yugoslavia.

IV. International Fisheries Commissions

A. International Pacific Halibut Commission (1953). IPHC.
Members: Canada and United States of America

B. International Pacific Salmon Fisheries Commission (1937). IPSFC.
Members: Canada and United States of America

C. Inter-American Tropical Tuna Commission (1950). IATTC.
Address: c/o. Scripps Institution of Oceanography, La Jolla, California 92037, USA.
Members: Canada, Costa Rica, Japan, Mexico, Panama and United States of America.

D. International Commission for the Northwest Atlantic Fisheries (1950). ICNAF.
Address: Bedford Institute, P.O. Box 638, Dartmouth, Nova Scotia, Canada
Members: Canada, Denmark, France, Germany (Federal Republic of), Iceland, Italy, Japan, Norway, Poland, Portugal, Romania, Spain, United Kingdom, United States of America and Union of Soviet Socialist Republics.

E. International Whaling Commission (1948). IWC.
Address: Room 276, Great Westminster House, Horseferry Road, London, SW1, United Kingdom.
Members: Argentina, Australia, Canada, Denmark, France, Iceland, Japan, Mexico, Norway, Panama, South Africa, United Kingdom, United States of America and Union of Soviet Socialist Republics.

F. Great Lakes Fishery Commission (1955).
Members: Canada and United States of America.

G. International North Pacific Fisheries Commission (1953). INPFC.
Address: 6640 Northwest Marine Drive, Vancouver 8, British Columbia, Canada.
Members: Canada, Japan and United States of America.

H. North Pacific Fur Seal Commission (1957). NPFSC.
Address: National Marine Fisheries Service, Department of Commerce, Washington, D.C. 20240, USA
Members: Canada, Japan, Union of Soviet Socialist Republics and United States of America.

I. International Commission for the Conservation of Atlantic Tunas (1969). ICCAT.
Members: Brazil, Canada, France, Ghana, Japan, Korea (Republic of), Morocco, Portugal, Senegal, South Africa, Spain and United States of America.

J. North-East Atlantic Fisheries Commission (1963). NEAFC.
Address: Room 275, Great Westminster House, Horseferry Road
London SW1, United Kingdom.
Members: Belgium, Denmark, France, Germany (Federal Republic of), Iceland, Ireland, Netherlands, Norway, Poland, Portugal, Spain, Sweden, United Kingdom, and Union of Soviet Socialist Republics.

K. Mixed Commission for the Black Sea Fisheries (1960). MCBSF.
Members: Bulgaria, Romania and Union of Soviet Socialist Republics.

L. Mixed Fisheries Commission (1963). MFC.
Members: Bulgaria, German Democratic Republic, Poland, Romania and Union of Soviet Socialist Republics.

M. International Commission for the South-East Atlantic Fisheries (1971). ICSEAF.
Members: Bulgaria, Japan, Poland, Portugal, South Africa, Spain and Union of Soviet Socialist Republics.

N. Permanent Commission of the Conference on the Use and Conservation of the Marine Resources of the South Pacific (1951). PCSP.
Members: Chile, Ecuador and Peru.

O. Baltic Sea Salmon Standing Committee. (1966) BSSC.
Members: Denmark, Germany (Federal Republic of), Poland, and Sweden.

P. Shellfish Commission for the Skagenak-Kattegat. SCSK.
Members: Denmark, Norway and Sweden

Q. Commission on Deep-Sea Prawns, European Lobsters, Norway Lobsters and Crabs. (1953).
Members: Denmark, Norway and Sweden.

R. Japan-Korea Joint Fisheries Commission (1965). JKFC.

S. Japanese-Soviet Commission for the Northwest Pacific Fisheries (1956). JSFC.

T. International Joint Commission (for the Great Lakes) (1909).
Address: 1717 Street N.W., Washington, D.C. 2044-, USA.
Members: Canada and United States of America.

U. Southeast Asian Fisheries Development Center (1967).
Members: Japan, Malaysia, Philippines, Singapore, Thailand and Vietnam (Republic of).

V. Sealing Commission for the Northeast Atlantic (1958). SCNEA.
Members: Norway and Union of Soviet Socialist Republics.

W. Canada-Norway Sealing Commission (1971).

V. IOC Intergovernmental Subsidiary Bodies

A. Working Groups (WG)

WG on Training, Education and Mutual Assistance in Marine Science

WG on Oceanographic Data Exchange (ODE)

WG on Legal Questions Related to Scientific Investigations of the Ocean (LEG)

B. International Coordination Groups (ICG)

ICG for the Cooperative Study of the Kuroshio and Adjacent Regions

ICG for the Tsunabi Warning System in the Pacific (TSU)

ICG for the Southern Ocean (SOC)

ICG for the Cooperative Investigations of the Caribbean and Adjacent Regions (CKAR)

ICG for the Global Investigation of Pollution in the Marine Environment (GIPME)

Working Committee for an Integrated Global Ocean Station System (IGOSS)

C. International Coordination Groups Sponsored Jointly with Other Intergovernmental Organizations

Joint IOC/ICSEM/GFCM Group for the Technical Coordination (GTC) of the Cooperative Investigations in the Mediterranean (CIM)

Joint ICES/FAO/IOC Coordinating Group for the Planning and Execution of the Cooperative Investigations of the Northern Part of the Eastern Central Atlantic (CINECA)

Joint ICES/ICNAF/IOC Coordinating Group for the Systematic Studies in the North Atlantic (NAT)

Joint IOC/WMO Planning Group for IGOSS (IPLAN)

VI. FAO Regional Bodies

A. General Fisheries Council for the Mediterranean (1952). GFCM.
Members: Algeria, Bulgaria, Cyprus, Egypt, France, Greece, Israel, Italy, Lebanon, Libya, Malta, Monaco, Morocco, Romania, Spain, Tunisia, Turkey, and Yogoslavia.

B. Indo-Pacific Fisheries Council (1948). IPFC.
Address: FAO Regional Office, Maliwan Mansion, Phra Atit Road, Bangkok 2, Thailand.
Members: Australia, Burma, France, India, Indonesia, Japan, Khmer Republic, Korea (Republic of), Malaysia, Netherlands, New Zealand, Pakistan, Philippines, Sri Lanka, Thailand, United Kingdom, United States of America and Vietnam (Republic of).

C. Fisheries Committee for the Eastern Central Atlantic (1967). CECAF.
Members: Cameroon, Congo, Cuba, Dahomey, France, Gabon, Gambia, Ghana, Greece, Guinea, Italy, Ivory Coast, Japan, Korea (Republic of), Liberia, Mauritania, Morocco, Nigeria, Poland, Romania, Senegal, Sierra Leone, Spain, Togo, United Kingdom, United States of America and Zaire.

D. Regional Fisheries Advisory Commission for the Southwest Atlantic (1962). CARPAS.
Members: Argentina, Brazil, Uruguay.

E. Indian Ocean Fisheries Commission (1967). IOFC.
Members: Australia, Bahrain, Cuba, Ethiopia, France, Greece, India, Indonesia, Iraq, Israel, Japan, Jordan, Kenya, Korea (Republic of), Kuwait, Madagascar, Malaysia, Mauritius, Netherlands, Oman, Pakistan, Portugal, Qatar, Sri Lanka, Tanzania, Thailand, United Kingdom, United States of America and Vietnam (Republic of).

WORLD PETROLEUM STATISTICS

WORLD CRUDE OIL PRODUCTION 1971

	Thousand Barrels per Day	Percent of Total
Total	**48,211.2**	**100.0**
EASTERN HEMISPHERE	32,244.4	66.9
Middle East	16,383.6	34.0
Saudi Arabia	4,769.8	9.9
Iran	4,535.0	9.4
Kuwait	3,198.2	6.6
Iraq	1,712.0	3.6
Others	2,168.6	4.5
Africa	5,592.0	11.6
Libya	2,761.7	5.7
Nigeria	1,522.6	3.2
Algeria	720.6	1.5
Others	587.1	1.2
Asia-Pacific	1,598.8	3.3
Indonesia	888.0	1.8
Others	710.8	1.5
Western Europe	355.0	0.7
Communist countries	8,315.0	17.2
USSR	7,440.0	15.4
Others	875.0	1.8
WESTERN HEMISPHERE	15,966.8	33.1
North America	11,329.7	23.5
United States	9,544.1	19.8
Canada	1,358.2	2.8
Mexico	427.4	0.9
South America	4,637.1	9.6
Venezuela	3,547.7	7.4
Argentina	423.6	0.9
Columbia	227.4	0.5
Brazil	167.6	0.3
Others	270.8	0.6

GROWTH IN WORLD CRUDE OIL PRODUCTION, BY MAIN AREAS

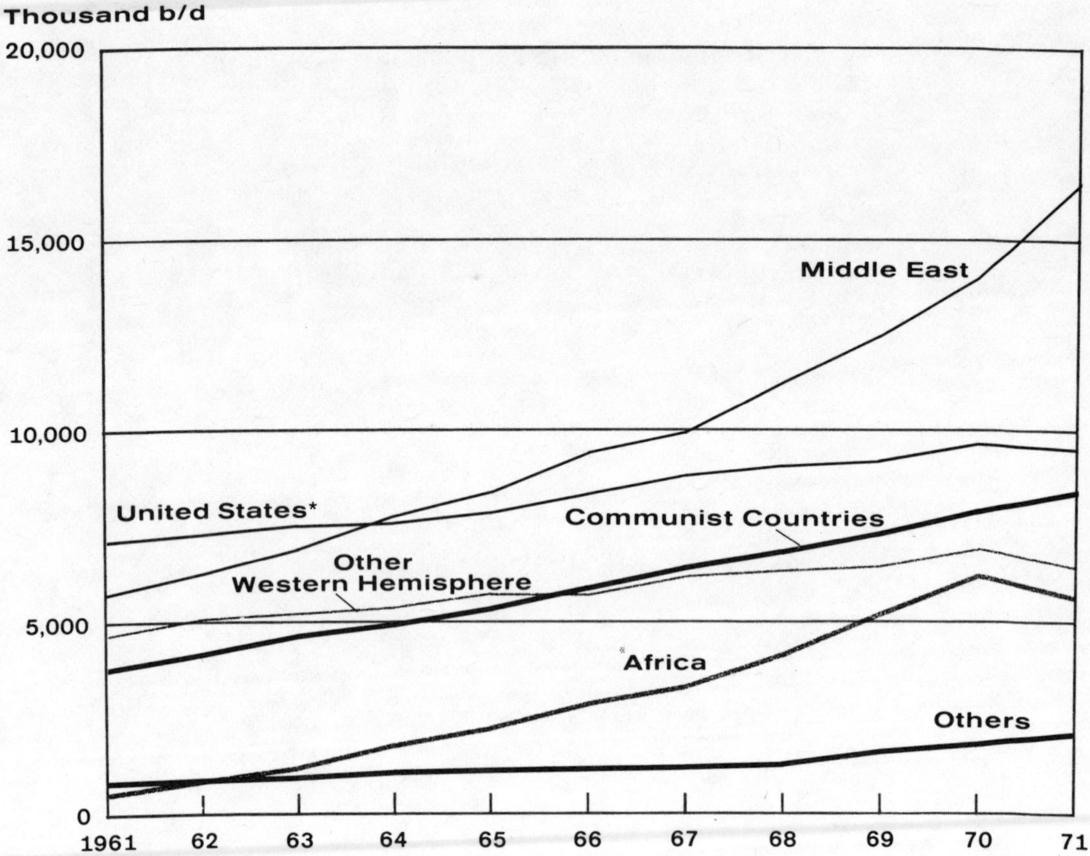

*Excluding natural gas liquids.

513760 6-72

WORLD PROVED OIL RESERVES
Year-end 1971

	Billion Barrels	Percent of Total
Total	**590.0**	**100.0**
EASTERN HEMISPHERE	512.7	86.9
Middle East	367.4	62.3
Abu Dhabi	18.9	3.2
Iran	55.5	9.4
Iraq	36.0	6.1
Kuwait	78.0	13.2
Saudi Arabia	157.3	26.7
Others	21.7	3.7
Africa	58.9	10.0
Libya	25.0	4.2
Algeria	12.3	2.1
Nigeria	11.7	2.0
Egypt	4.0	0.7
Congo	3.3	0.6
Angola	0.8	0.1
Gabon	0.8	0.1
Tunisia	0.6	0.1
Others	0.4	0.1
Asia-Pacific	15.6	2.6
Indonesia	10.4	1.8
Others	5.2	0.9
Western Europe	14.2	2.4
Norway	7.0	1.2
United Kingdom	5.0	0.8
Others	2.2	0.4
Communist countries	56.6	9.6
USSR	36.0	6.1
Eastern Europe	1.0	0.2
People's Republic of China	19.6	3.3
WESTERN HEMISPHERE	77.3	13.1
North America	50.2	8.5
United States	37.3	6.3
Canada	8.4	1.4
Mexico	4.5	0.8
South America	27.1	4.6
Venezuela	13.9	2.4
Ecuador	5.7	1.0
Others	7.5	1.3

INTERNATIONAL FLOW OF CRUDE

Importing Areas	Exporting Areas						
	United States	Canada	Mexico	Caribbean	Other Western Hemisphere	Non-Communist Europe	North Africa
United States							
Region I-IV	...	623	28	1,487	527	130	87
Region V	...	235	...	130	3	...	3
Canada	30	...	...	575	...	2	...
Mexico	32	...	...	21	...	...	...
Caribbean	2	...	...	...	...	3	55
Other Western Hemisphere	20	...	...	853	...	30	125
Non-Communist Europe							
Northwest	40	...	...	400	20	...	2,065
Mediterranean	20	...	...	95	...	...	1,240
North Africa	1	...	...	2	...	35	...
West Africa	2	...	...	25	...	35	...
Near East	...	...	...	...	...	20	...
Middle East	...	...	...	...	...	5	50
South and East Africa	...	...	...	2	...	5	5
Japan	51	...	...	25	...	...	30
Other Eastern Hemisphere	20	...	...	5	...	5	...
USSR and Eastern Europe	...	...	...	...	...	20	40
Total	**218**	**858**	**28**	**3,620**	**550**	**290**	**3,700**

SELECTED BIBLIOGRAPHY[1]

ALEXANDER, L. (Ed.), *The Law of the Sea: Offshore Boundaries and Zones.* [Columbus: Ohio University Press. 1967. 321pp.]

______________ *The Future of the Sea's Resources.* [Kingston: University of Rhode Island. 1968. 155pp.]

______________ *International Rules and Organisation for the Sea.* [Kingston: University of Rhode Island. 1969. 464pp.]

______________ *National Policy Recommendations.* [Kingston: University of Rhode Island. 1970. 533pp.]

______________ *The United Nations and Ocean Management.* [Kingston: University of Rhode Island. 1971.]

______________ *The Law of the Sea: a New Geneva Conference.* [Kingston: University of Rhode Island. 1972.]

______________ *The Law of the Sea: the Needs and Interests of the Developing Countries.* [Kingston: University of Rhode Island. 1971.]

ANDRASSY, J., *International Law and the Resources of the Sea.* [New York: Columbia University Press. 1970. 191pp.]

BARABOLYA, P.D. et al., *Manual of International Maritime Law,* 2 vols. (translated from Russian) [Springfield: Clearing House for Scientific and Technical Information. 1966, English translation 1968. 475pp.]

BAXTER, R.R., *The Law of International Waterways.* [Cambridge: Harvard University Press. 1964. 371pp.]

BORGESE, E.M., *The Ocean Regime.* [Santa Barbara: Center for the Study of Democratic Institutions. 1968.]

BOUCHEZ, L., *The Regime of Bays in International Law.* [The Hague: Nijhoff. 1963. 330pp.]

BOWETT, D.W., *The Law of the Sea.* [Dobbs Ferry and Manchester: Oceana and Manchester University Press. 1967. 117pp.]

BRITISH INSTITUTE OF INTERNATIONAL AND COMPARATIVE LAW, *Developments in the Law of the Sea, 1958-1964.* [London: British Institute of International and Comparative Law. 1965. 208pp.]

BRITTIN, B., *International Law for Seagoing Officers.* [Annapolis: U.S. Naval Institute. 1972. 536pp.]

BROWN, E.D., *Arms Control in Hydrospace: Legal Aspects.* [Washington: Woodrow Wilson International Center for Scholars. 1971. 131pp.]

______________ *The Legal Regime of Hydrospace.* [London: Stevens. 1971. 236pp.]

BRUEL, E., *International Straits,* 2 vols. [London: Sweet and Maxwell. 1947. 278 and 426pp.]

[1]This is a very short bibliography containing some of the more important publications on the Law of the Sea of recent years. For more comprehensive bibliographies the reader is referred to Woodrow Wilson International Center for Scholars, *Ocean Affairs Bibliography* [1971. 201pp.] and Law of the Sea Institute, Rhode Island, *Marine Policy, Law and Economics Bibliography* [1970, with annual supplements].

BURKE, W.T., *Some Thoughts on Fisheries and a New Conference on the Law of the Sea*. Law of the Sea Institute, University of Rhode Island, Occasional Paper No. 9. [Kingston: University of Rhode Island. 1971.]

BUTLER, W.E., *The Soviet Union and the Law of the Sea*. [Baltimore: The Johns Hopkins Press. 1971. 245pp.]

CHRISTY, F.T. and SCOTT, A., *The Common Wealth in Ocean Fisheries: Some Problems of Growth and Economic Allocation*. [Baltimore: The Johns Hopkins Press. 1965. 281pp.]

COLOMBOS, C.J., *International Law of the Sea*. [London: Longmans. 1967. 886pp.]

COULL, J.R., *The Fisheries of Europe: an Economic Geography*. [London: Bell. 1972. 240pp.]

FRIEDMANN, W., *The Future of the Oceans*. [New York: Braziller. 1971. 132pp.]

GAMBLE, J.K., *Index to Marine Treaties*. [Washington: University of Washington Press. 1972, 438pp.]

GARCIA AMADOR, F., *The Exploitation and Conservation of the Resources of the Sea*. [Leyden.: Sijthoff. 1963. 240pp.]

GLASSNER, M.I., *Access to the Sea for Developing Land-locked States*. [The Hague: Nijhoff. 1970. 298pp.]

HENKIN, L., *Law for the Sea's Mineral Resources*. [New York: Institute for the Study of Science in Human Affairs, Columbia University. 1968. 75pp.]

JENNINGS, R.Y., "The United States Draft Treaty on the International Seabed Area-Basic Principles" in (1971) 20 *International and Comparative Law Quarterly* 433.

JOHNSTON, D.M., *The International Law of Fisheries: a Framework for Policy-Oriented Inquiries*. [New Haven and London: Yale University Press. 1965. 554pp.]

KOERS, A.W., *The Enforcement of Fisheries Agreements on the High Seas: a Comparative Analysis of International State Practice*. Law of the Sea Institute, University of Rhode Island, Occasional Paper No. 6. [Kingston: University of Rhode Island. 1970.]

KRUEGER, R.B., *Study of the Outer Continental Shelf Lands of the United States*. Public Land Law Review Commission, Vols. I and II, 1968.

McDOUGAL, M.S. and BURKE, W.T., *The Public Order of the Oceans: a Contemporary International Law of the Sea*. [New Haven and London: Yale University Press. 1962. 1226pp.]

MERO, J., *The Mineral Resources of the Sea*. [New York: Elsevier. 1965. 312pp.]

ODA, S., *International Control of Sea Resources*. [Leyden: Sijthoff. 1963. 215pp.]

_______________ *The International Law of the Ocean Development: Basic Documents*. [Leyden: Sijthoff. 1972. 519pp.]

OXMAN, B., "The Preparation of Article 1 of the Convention on the Continental Shelf" in (1972) 3 *Journal of Maritime Law and Commerce* 245.

PROCEEDINGS OF THE PACEM IN MARIBUS CONFERENCE. [Dodd, Mead. 1971.]

SCHACHTER, O. and SERWER, D., "Marine Pollution Problems and Remedies" in (1971) 65 *American Journal of International Law* 84.

SHALOWITZ, A., *Shore and Sea Boundaries.* [Washington: U.S. Government Printing Office. Vol I, "Boundary Problems associated with the Submerged Lands Acts". 1962. 420pp. Vol II, "Interpretation and Use of Coast and Geodetic Survey Data". 1964. 749pp.]

SLOUKA, Z., *International Custom and the Continental Shelf: A Study in the Dynamics of Customary Rules of International Law.* [The Hague: Nijhoff. 1968. 186pp.]

STOCKHOLM INTERNATIONAL PEACE RESEARCH INSTITUTE, *Towards a Better Use of the Ocean.* [Stockholm: Almquist and Wiksell. 1969. 231pp.]

STROHL, M., *The International Law of Bays.* [The Hague: Nijhoff. 1963. 426pp.]

SZTUCKI, J. (Ed.), *Symposium on the International Regime of the Seabed, Proceedings.* [Rome: Academia Nazionale dei Lincei. 1970. 767pp.]

U.S. CONGRESS, *Laws of the United States relating to Water Pollution Control and Environmental Quality.* Compiled by the Committee on Public Works, House of Representatives, July 1970. 91st Congress, 2d Session, Committee Print 91-33. [Washington: U.S. Government Printing Office. 265pp.]

______________ *Legislation on Foreign Relations.* Printed for the Use of the Committee on Foreign Affairs and Foreign Relations of the House of Representatives and Senate respectively, July 1972. 92d Congress, 2d Session. [Washington: U.S. Government Printing Office.]

______________ *Treaties and Other International Agreements on Oceanographic Resources, Fisheries, and Wildlife to which the United States is a Party.* Prepared for the Use of the Committee on Commerce, U.S. Senate, December 1970. 91st Congress, 2d Session. [Washington: U.S. Government Printing Office. 672pp.]

U.S. DEPARTMENT OF STATE, *Sovereignty of the Sea.* [Geographical Bulletin No. 3, revised. 1969. 33pp.]

WHITEMAN, M., *Digest of International Law.* [Washington: Department of State. Vol. III, 1964, 1261pp. Vol. IV, 1965, 1240pp.]

WINTON, H., *Seabed.* [New York: Worldmark Press. 1968, 1969, 1970 and 1971.]

NEW DIRECTIONS IN THE LAW OF THE SEA

NEW DIRECTIONS IN THE LAW OF THE SEA

Collected Papers—Volume III

Edited by
Robin Churchill
K. R. Simmonds
Jane Welch

1973
THE BRITISH INSTITUTE
OF INTERNATIONAL AND COMPARATIVE LAW
LONDON

OCEANA PUBLICATIONS INC.
DOBBS FERRY, NEW YORK

Library of Congress Catalogue Card No. 72-12713

Printed in Great Britain by The Eastern Press Ltd., London and Reading

73 10100

Preface

THIS volume completes the three-volume collection of documents and papers on *New Directions in the Law of the Sea* sponsored by the British Institute of International and Comparative Law and co-published by the Institute together with Oceana Publications Inc. The first two volumes of the set, compiled and edited by S. Houston Lay, Robin Churchill and Myron Nordquist, were devoted to a collection of basic documents and were published in 1972. The present volume is made up of a selection from the working papers, now presented in a revised and edited form, which were prepared by leading participants in an International Conference on "New Directions in the Law of the Sea" which was organised by the Institute in London on February 2, 3 and 4, 1973. This volume also contains tables and a reference index to the three-volume collection as a whole, for the preparation of which the Institute is most grateful to Mrs. A. Sarup.

The British Institute of International and Comparative Law is greatly indebted to the work of all those who, either in the research or the administrative field, have contributed to the successful initiation and implementation of this project. This has been a truly international exercise, in which, as will be seen from a glance at the table of contents of any of the volumes, international lawyers have been aided throughout by specialists from other disciplines. The Institute believes that such a multi-disciplinary approach to this field of study is essential and that the materials and commentaries presented to the reader in this group of volumes deserve wide attention at the present juncture, on the eve of what is generally expected to be the most critical international conference ever held to determine the future direction and content of the law of the sea. At no time has the conflict between national control and international regulation interests been so direct or so diverse. This work seeks to present, in juxtaposition, some of those interests against a background of the most significant contemporary source materials.

THE BRITISH INSTITUTE OF INTERNATIONAL AND COMPARATIVE LAW,
32, FURNIVAL STREET,
LONDON, EC4A 1JN

K. R. SIMMONDS.

June, 1973

Contents

PART V. NAVIGATION

PART VI. JURISDICTIONAL QUESTIONS

PART VII. SOME REGIONAL APPROACHES

PART VIII. NATIONAL PRACTICE

PART IX. THE UNITED NATIONS AND THE EUROPEAN ECONOMIC COMMUNITY

Table of Treaties

Table of Municipal Legislation

UNITED KINGDOM

U.S.A.

YUGOSLAVIA

TABLE OF MUNICIPAL LEGISLATION

[illegible] (continued)

[illegible] Act 19[illegible] . . . . . II, 49[illegible], 298
[illegible] Prevention of Pollution [illegible] Acts 1951 and 19[illegible] . . . . . II, [illegible]
[illegible] Act 19[illegible] . . . . . II, 294
[illegible] 1960 . . . . . [illegible]
[illegible] . . . . . II, 294
Continental Shelf Act 1964 . . . . . I, 2[illegible], II, 2[illegible], 2[illegible]
[illegible] Act 1967 . . . . . II, 29[illegible]
Territorial Waters Order in Council 1964 . . . . . II, 2[illegible]
[illegible] Act [illegible] . . . . . II, [illegible], 2[illegible]
Marine, &c. Broadcasting (Offences) Act 1967 . . . . . I, 1[illegible]
[illegible] Control [illegible] Act 1967 . . . . . II, [illegible]
[illegible] (Shell[illegible]) Act 1967 . . . . . II, 89
Sea Fish Industry Act 1970 . . . . . II, 2[illegible]
[illegible] Navigable Waters Act 1951 . . . . . I, 2[illegible], II, [illegible]
[illegible] Navigation Waters [illegible] Order 1971 . . . . . I, 2[illegible]
[illegible] Workings (Offshore Installations) Act 1971 . . . . . II, 29[illegible], 29[illegible]
[illegible] (Oil Pollution) Act 1971 . . . . . I, 2[illegible], II, 2[illegible]
[illegible] of Oil Pollution Act 1971 . . . . . II, 19[illegible], 2[illegible], 2[illegible]

U.S.A.

Presidential Proclamation No. 2667 on the Policy of the United States with respect to the Natural Resources of the Subsoil and Seabed of the Continental Shelf, September 28, 1945 . . . . . I, 1[illegible]; II, 75
Presidential Proclamation No. 2668 concerning the Policy of the United States with Respect to Coastal Fisheries in certain areas of the High Seas, September 28, 1945 . . . . . I, 1[illegible]
[illegible] Submerged Lands Act, 1953 . . . . . I, 1[illegible]
Outer Continental Shelf Lands Act, 1953 . . . . . I, 1[illegible]
U.S. Federal Water Pollution Control Act 1948 as amended in 1970 . . . . . III, [illegible]
Act establishing a Fisheries Zone Contiguous to the Territorial Sea of the United States, October 14, 1966 . . . . . [illegible]
Water Quality Improvement Act, 1970 . . . . . [illegible]

[illegible]

Law of [illegible] 1964 [illegible] Maritime [illegible] Continental Shelf [illegible] . . . . . [illegible]

Table of Cases

Table of Cases

Introduction

WHEN the British Institute of International and Comparative Law began work in 1971 to prepare the programme of, and the documentation for, an International Conference on " New Directions in the Law of the Sea," eventually to be held in London in February 1973, the intention was to focus attention in the Conference itself on a selection of topics which were considered to be of critical importance, but to support the work of the Conference with the prior publication of a general collection of basic source materials. The Institute also considered, in consequence of earlier experience, that the work of the Conference would be greatly enhanced by the preparation of a range of background papers that would be deliberately wider in scope and in content than the Conference programme; a selection from these papers, with the addition of the key Conference addresses, would then be prepared for subsequent general publication.

The first part of the Institute's publication programme was, in the event, happily combined with a project that had been separately initiated in the United States; the two-volume collection of documents, edited by S. Houston Lay, Robin Churchill and Myron Nordquist and published as a set together with this volume of papers, is the result of this combined enterprise and was produced in time for study and comment by the delegates to the International Conference.

The present volume contains a selection only from the large number of background papers which were commissioned by the Institute for use at the Conference and which are now made available to a wider audience. They are not " Conference papers " in the generally accepted sense but are concise, up to the moment surveys of significant problems and problem areas. They are not, for varied reasons, comprehensive in their geographical range or in their scientific coverage of source materials. Certain anticipated national reports and regional surveys were not in the end forthcoming. The papers do, however, reflect fairly the principal expectations and concerns that were expressed by the speakers and the delegates at the Conference and that have emerged during the course of the Institute's work in this field over the past years.

It should be added that the delegates themselves, in keeping with the Institute's intention to adopt throughout a multi-disciplinary approach to the examination of new directions in the law of the sea, brought to the Conference an exceptionally wide and diverse variety of interests and attitudes. They came from government ministries, from many sectors of trade and industry, from the universities, from non-governmental organisations, from both public and private research agencies, and, of course, from professional practice of various kinds. They came from many different countries and included, for example, marine biologists, economists, marine engineers and geologists as well as lawyers. Conference sessions were devoted to addresses and discussions on three principal themes: (i) *fisheries*—including the special problems of coastal fishing, conservation on the high seas, and fish farming; (ii) *pollution*—including an examination of the nature of marine pollutants and surveys of pollution from vessels, from rivers and outfalls, and from seabed operations; and (iii) *jurisdictional problems*—including a review of the current condition of national claims to increasing jurisdiction and an inquiry into the enforcement and regulation of claims. In addition, the Conference delegates had the advantage of hearing two important " guide-line " addresses, by Professor Louis Henkin and Professor R. Y. Jennings, each of which is printed, in a revised form, in this volume.

What conclusions emerge from the papers in this volume and the discussions at the Conference? As far as fisheries are concerned, the most basic and urgent need is for the establishment of an effective and rational system of fisheries management. For, as in so many other areas of the law of the sea, the present law is outdated and inadequate. The Geneva Convention on the High Seas gives everyone the right to fish on the high seas. Fine and fair though this principle may sound in theory, it has in practice three unfortunate consequences. First, it can lead to overfishing and the consequent depletion or even extinction of stocks. Secondly, because access to high seas fisheries is unrestricted, it may be economically wasteful if too many fishermen are chasing too few fish. Thirdly, the freedom to fish has become a licence for the distant-water, factory fishing fleets of some of the developed States to wipe out stocks, often off the coasts of developing States, thus tending to increase the gap between developed and developing States.

Faced with the need to develop new law in this area, the international community appears to be offered broadly two choices—either a much more comprehensive system of international regulation through international agreements and international fisheries commissions, or a system of national regulation through a much greater extension of the rights of coastal States. Indeed with the present profusion of every kind of claim to more exclusive maritime jurisdiction (surveyed by Dr. Brown in Chapter 14), it may not be long before the international community has no option left at all. Outside Latin America, there were, until recently, no claims to an exclusive fishing zone beyond 12 miles (and, as Professor Johnson usefully reminds us in Chapter 5, the concept of an exclusive fishing zone is of recent origin). But now what once seemed the exaggerated position of Latin America has been taken up in claims by a number of African States and Iceland, and in two sets of important proposals before the UN Seabed Committee. The African and Latin American States have put forward the idea that coastal States should be entitled to a broad exclusive economic zone or patrimonial sea. The other set of proposals, put forward by Canada and supported by Australia, New Zealand, and, in a rather modified form by the U.S.A., is based on a species approach. Rather than give the coastal State a specificially defined geographical area in which it would exercise exclusive fishing rights, these proposals would give the coastal State exclusive or preferential rights over sedentary, coastal and anadromous species, with wide-ranging oceanic species being regulated by international commissions. Both sets of proposals have received wide attention, both in this volume (in particular, in the chapters of Dr. Brown and Professor Johnson), and at the Conference. From the Conference discussion a number of interesting points emerged.

Professor Alexander gave us a salutary reminder that many of the developing countries would not benefit from either of these proposals, either because they are landlocked or because they have a short coastline. And even if developing coastal States are given extensive exclusive fishing rights off their coasts, many of them, as a Nigerian participant rightly pointed out, will not benefit, because they do not have the vessels, manpower or technical knowledge to exploit such fisheries fully. A number of speakers were worried about the future of existing international fisheries commissions should these proposals be adopted by the Santiago Conference. They pointed out that, while the proposals would make it easier for a coastal State to adopt a more rational economic approach to fishing, existing examples of broad fishing zones did not encourage the belief that fish stocks would be any better conserved. The value of having representatives of many different interests at the Conference was shown when a number of marine biologists present criticised the species approach advocated by Canada as being difficult to operate in practice.

The alternative to extensive coastal State rights is international regulation. Again, past practice does not encourage hope for the future, as can be seen in Dr. Koers' charting in Chapter 3 of the slow progress and limited successes of the North-East Atlantic Fisheries Commission. One of the more notable failures of the Commission, the drastic decline of North Sea herring stocks, was the subject of one of the working sessions of the fisheries group. From this a rather gloomy conclusion emerged that, even where the number of States in the fishery is limited and these States in their general international relations are on good terms with one another, it is still very difficult to reach agreement on conservation measures of any kind, let alone the rather stringent measures for which the seriousness of the situation calls. The attraction of an effective system of international regulation is that, by means of national quota arrangements, it is possible to ensure that the fishery is exploited only to its maximum sustainable yield and for States to introduce a greater degree of economic rationality in the fishing activities of their nationals.

It will be up to the Santiago Conference to choose one of these alternatives. From the way the debate is moving at the time of writing, it looks as though extensive coastal State rights will form the basis of the new legal régime of fisheries management. There may, of course, be room for a good deal of regional variation, and Dr. Koers in his paper puts forward a possible outline of arrangements in the North-East Atlantic.

One, though as yet relatively unexplored, way of increasing fish production may be through the growth of fish farms, moving from the concept of hunting to herding. This, too, challenges the traditional freedom of the seas and the notion of unrestricted access to a common resource. Again a new approach is called for, and as Miss Newton and Mr. Richardson show in Chapter 7, the essential change in this area, amounting to no less than a minor legal revolution, is to make it possible for a person to acquire an exclusive property right in the fish itself.

One of the popular myths surrounding the subject of marine pollution, which was exploded by speakers at the Conference and by papers in this volume, is that most pollution is caused by spectacular oil disasters such as the *Torrey Canyon* or the Santa Barbara oil spill. In fact, as Michael Hardy points out in Chapter 8, " land-based sources are estimated to account for between 50 to 90 per cent." of the oil which enters the sea each year, while " the disposal of domestic and industrial wastes from the shore . . . is by far the largest single source of marine pollution." It is unfortunate that the attention which has been focused on pollution caused by sea-based activities has inevitably meant that little has been done to regulate the continuous flow of pollution from domestic sources. Undue emphasis has also been placed on oil pollution, although, as Professor Fleischer shows, oil is to some extent broken down by natural processes in the sea, while persistent synthetic chemicals coming from land-based sources are known to accumulate in fish and sea animals and to threaten the future existence of several species. It was, however, argued by Professor R. B. Clark, at the Conference, that in many areas our present knowledge of all the effects of pollution is simply inadequate: States are therefore faced with the dilemma of waiting until scientific evidence accumulates, by which time it may be too late to act, or of passing sweeping preventative legislation, *e.g.*, the Canadian Arctic Waters Pollution Prevention Act, and thereby arousing international hostility.

Given, however, that we have reached a level of knowledge where there are some clearly recognisable areas of potential damage, what are the most practical means of prevention and regulation of marine pollution? Principle 21 of the Stockholm Declaration on the Human Environment, while positive in its aspirations, has yet to be transformed into a specific international legal obligation—" States have the sovereign right to exploit their own resources . . . and the responsibility to ensure that activities within their jurisdiction or control do not cause damage to the environment of other States or of areas beyond the limits of national jurisdiction." In the light of this, it remains to be seen to what extent the principle of freedom of the high seas is compatible with the preservation of the marine environment.

The problem, too, remains as to where pressure for action should be concentrated—at the national, regional or international levels? The disadvantages of relying solely on national efforts are all too obvious. Likewise, international regulation is defective because of the immense difficulties of enforcement. A more positive hope for the future would therefore seem to be offered by regional arrangements, *e.g.*, those established by the 1972 Oslo Convention for the Prevention of Marine Pollution. Here self-interest should provide the necessary incentive for effective co-operation. The importance of regional schemes was again emphasised by Article VIII of the London Convention on the Dumping of Wastes at Sea 1972.

It is to be hoped that the Santiago Conference will concentrate on the problem of marine pollution from land-based sources which has not yet received adequate attention. What is needed is a framework of general principles of international law on marine pollution which regional authorities and UN agencies can then implement.

Time and again in these papers reference is made to aspects of the mounting conflict between national jurisdictional claims and international regulation interests and standards. In Dr. Brown's survey of current State practice, which also contains an interesting categorisation and analysis of differing regional expectations, emphasis is laid upon the possibility of seeking the foundations of a new legal order through the evolution of the concept of an " exclusive economic zone "; this view is adverted to, with varying emphasis, by a number of other contributors, including Dr. Ajomo.

Is this really the avenue toward a truly international law of the sea and toward a lasting reconciliation of interests which have largely become polarised through the progressive debilitation of the original concept of the freedom of the seas? As Dr. Brown points out, the attractiveness of this concept will hardly be enhanced by its confused and emotional advocacy, as in the Dissenting Opinions of Judge Padilla Nervo in the Interim Measures of Protection and Jurisdictional phases of the *Fisheries Jurisdiction Cases* (1972 and 1973). Indeed, an uncritical adherence to this concept by certain coastal States may well lead to a new polarisation of interests and materially retard the building up of consensus views upon the use of ocean space beyond the limits of national jurisdiction in the interests of the international community as a whole.

The basic new direction in the law of the sea, and the fundamental difference between the traditional law of the sea as reflected in the Geneva Conventions and what one hopes will emerge from the current movement to make new law, is the change from an essentially *laissez-faire* approach to marine activities to the perception that a system of proper and effective regulation of all activities in, on or under the sea is required. This change results from a number of factors. Technological developments have led to the sea being used in new ways; at the same time many of the traditional uses of the sea have increased. In a world whose resources are clearly finite and in some cases near to exhaustion in the foreseeable future, the need to exploit non-renewable resources carefully is readily apparent, and the need to conserve renewable resources vital. The need for regulation also arises from competing uses of the sea. Drilling rigs may interfere with navigation; the use of the sea for the disposal of waste may have an adverse effect on fishing. The developing States see a greater regulation of the sea, whether it be through an international authority for the exploitation of the wealth of the seabed beyond national jurisdiction or through an extension of the rights of coastal States to the natural resources in the waters adjacent to their coasts, as one way of redressing the present inequalities in the distribution of the world's wealth.

In legal terms, the change from *laissez-faire* to the proper regulation of marine activities means supplementing the rights and freedoms, to use the rather glib language in which the Geneva Conventions are couched, by spelling out in detail the duties and obligations which complement those rights and freedoms. New rules are necessary to deal with the new uses and abuses of the sea, to regulate competing uses so as to avoid conflict, and to effect a redistribution of the wealth of the seas.

There appears to be broad agreement that this is the new direction in which the law of the sea ought to move. How this is to be done is the challenge facing the Santiago Conference. At the time of writing, it is very difficult to predict what the outcome of the Conference will be and whether any agreement will be reached at all. Indeed, at this stage, it is difficult to envisage exactly what kind of conference it will be. Will the Conference be presented with draft conventions to be discussed and voted on, or will it be presented with much less concrete proposals which, in order to be transformed into conventions, will require several sessions of what will in effect become a standing conference? And if agreements are concluded, how long will it be before they are ratified and come into force? What will be the effect, in the intervening period, of State practice and agreements concluded in other international fora? If the Conference does produce a new law of the sea, there is the big question of to what extent this will be genuinely international in character. Even if the end result is that coastal States obtain exclusive exploitation rights over the natural resources of a very extensive belt of waters adjacent to their coasts—and this is the way developments now appear to be moving—international law will still have an important role to play. For as Professor Jennings points out in Chapter 2, the national jurisdiction of the coastal State will need to be penetrated by international rules providing uniform standards in such matters as the regulation of shipping and pollution control. An oil tanker, for example, cannot change specifications as to tank size each time it moves from one coastal State's exclusive zone to another.

As is stressed many times in this volume, if there is to be a successful outcome to the Santiago Conference, this will only take the form of a package deal on all the unsettled major issues of the law of the sea. Whether such a package deal can accommodate all the interests involved remains to be seen. There is a danger that coastal State interests, which, it is important to remember, are not synonymous with developing State interests, will triumph at the expense of the interests of States which are land-locked or shelf-locked or which have only a short coastline. The fact that so many controversial issues are the subject of negotiation probably makes it harder to arrive at agreement, but there is nevertheless a good deal of sense in this approach, for all the issues to be discussed are interlocking. And when the international community is plainly embarked on a full-scale reform of the international law of the sea, the range of issues involved is hardly surprising. We therefore feel entirely justified in having included a wide number of themes in the present volume, although we do of course realise that many subjects, such as marine research and military activities, have not been dealt with at all, and that other subjects are touched on only briefly.

At the final session of the Conference, the Legal Adviser to the Canadian Department of External Affairs, Mr. J. A. Beesley, quite rightly described the Conference as a gathering of the conservatives. But he went on to say that the conservatives have moved a long way in the last two or three years. This observation was borne out in much of the discussion at the Conference, and is reinforced by many of the papers in this volume. That the many interests in the reshaping of the law of the sea are now beginning to speak the same language, is perhaps one of the most hopeful signs for the future.

Part I

The Law of The Sea: Evolution and Expectation

CHAPTER 1

Old Politics and New Directions

By Louis Henkin *

THE title of this volume implies that the law of the sea is headed in new directions. The title of these remarks may be read to imply that the changing law is due to unchanging politics. But whether the law of the sea is being redirected by old politics or by new politics, or by some of each, the future law of the sea—like all law—will be made not by lawyers but by politicians, by governments and the individuals who constitute them, impelled by political forces within, between, and among States.

The Third United Nations Law of the Sea Conference is scheduled for 1973–74.[1]† That Conference will differ from the previous ones in critical respects. The 1958 Conference was convened after more than six years of intensive and careful preparation. Before the Conference was a draft, prepared by experts and revised by them several times in the light of the comments of governments.[2] The provisions in the draft, moreover, reflected general agreement: on the whole these conventions were declaratory of existing law; in so far as they developed new law, the directions and largely the degrees of change had already been generally agreed. Indeed on the one issue on which there was basic disagreement when the Conference began—the width of the territorial sea—agreement was never reached.

The forthcoming Conference will be different. There will be more than 120 States represented and the some 40 additional participants, with greater political variegation, will render negotiation more complicated and agreement more difficult to achieve. There will be no single draft, only numerous small pieces of paper of varying significance, none of which, I guess, will be accepted without basic changes. In a word, the next Conference faces sharp divisions and fundamental issues, and one would be hardy to prognosticate how the political forces playing at the Conference will resolve themselves, what agreements—if any—will result.

I use the metaphor of forces and of a vector of forces, but unlike those in basic physics, political forces are not simple and their interplay does not produce a clean, sharp arrow of clear direction and defined magnitude. The influence on a particular issue of particular governments or even of groups of governments is difficult to measure, and the probable combinations of governments still difficult to anticipate. The positions of governments, moreover, are still highly uncertain and fluid: five years after Ambassador Pardo forced the subject on the attention of the world,[3] many governments have not yet determined their varying interests in the seas, which of competing interests they would prefer, what laws for the sea they will therefore favour. The Conference will see bargaining on particular issues and among issues, with nations also sacrificing their preferences in the sea for larger causes beyond it.

The vector of forces is not simple for another reason. Within some countries, *e.g.*, the United States, the national position is itself a vector of domestic forces that are

* Professor of International Law, Columbia University, New York.

† For references, see p. 10.

variable and of uncertain outcome. In our field there are also forces difficult to characterise as either strictly national or international, *e.g.*, major companies with transnational interests which exercise various influence upon governments, their own and others, and upon the future law.

Without pretence to precision, however, one can discern trends, tendencies and influences directing the law of the sea generally, and relevant, therefore, to the law of fishing and pollution that are our principal concern here.

THE OLDER DIRECTIONS

One should begin, perhaps, with a glance at the law's earlier directions. Until the early 1960s, I believe, the law reflected largely the traditional notions of freedom. The freedom of the seas meant essentially *laissez-faire*, and seemed to imply freedom both to use the seas (including its use for indiscriminate dumping of waste) and to take its resources (including, principally, free competition for its fish). There was, we know, a major exception to such freedom in favour of coastal States[4]: effective sovereignty and property in the territorial sea; in recent years, also, exclusive rights to resources of the seabed of the continental shelf; and peripheral rights of law enforcement in a " Contiguous Zone," in related air-defence identification zones, other defence zones in time of war (*cf.* the Declaration of Panama), and, more recently, Canada's claim to an Arctic anti-pollution zone.[5]

Until recently, however—as the 1958 Conventions reflect—the aspirations of coastal States generally were restrained by the international law of freedom and the inchoate " commonage " that underlay that law. There were indeed efforts to expand coastal fishing zones, but they were tentative and effectively resisted. There was some burgeoning concern about pollution, but the principal perpetrators of pollution, the coastal States, continued in old ways without international concern. There was no serious effort at the 1958 Conference, for example, to redistribute fishing rights, or to regulate pollution, whether by coastal States or others, whether in coastal areas or beyond.[6]

Now, we know, there has been notable change. The changing law reflects, of course, transformations in the facts of the sea, primed by transformed technologies, in its uses and in their economic significance. The changing law, I believe, reflects also change in the political forces that determine law-making in contemporary international society.

THE POLITICS OF LAW-MAKING

One can make a plausible case that the traditional law of the sea reflected the laws of power; powerful nations had to be naval Powers and they achieved a law of the sea that supported their naval needs as well as their commercial maritime interests. But even those who continue to see international politics essentially in terms of the interplay of military power would be hard-pressed to argue that military prowess will determine the future law of the sea. Military power means—has always meant—military power effectively applicable; but, for our purposes at least, the military power of the truly mighty today is often not effectively applicable. The use of force is illegal[7] and usually, also, otherwise impolitic. The threshold of perceived national interest that would lead a big Power to use force against a small one is much higher than it used to be[8]; and few issues in the law of the sea are likely to rise to that threshold.

Military prowess has not become irrelevant but the future law of the sea, I believe, will be shaped as well by other forces and sources of political influence—by the proliferation of new States, by the solidarity of the poor, by geography and technology as they relate to peaceful uses of the sea. There are now many States in the international society and most of them are poor; their poverty is a bond, a basis for political action and a base for political power. Unlike the "egoism" of the rich, moreover, the egoism of the poor—the drive to advance their particular national interests—is a human ideal accepted even by the rich, in part, perhaps, from guilt for their present wealth or past imperialism.

Their numbers, too, give the poor nations power to shape the law of the sea. In principle, we know, new nations coming into international society are bound by the law as they find it. In fact, we know, law cannot survive if it is rejected by many States. In principle, we know, the laws of law-making are based on the equality of States and their unanimity: new law is binding on States only with their acquiescence, and cannot be imposed on dissenters. In fact, we know, majorities, focused at the United Nations or at multilateral conferences, can press the few recalcitrant States—even, or perhaps especially, if they are rich and powerful—and make them accept something other than what they would really like. In addition to resolutions overwhelmingly adopted, there are other devices, some legal, some non-legal or even illegal—by interpretation, by *ipse dixit*, by collective declarations, by what to some, surely, are violations, but violations repeated and supported by others and condoned by some powerful sponsor, so that in time violation is transmuted into legislation.

NEW DIRECTIONS IN THE SEA

The declining relevance of military power, and the solidarity of the many poorer States, have not enabled them to remould international society and international law to their hearts' desire, even when they are agreed on the changes they would like. Existing law enjoys powerful inertia and is supported by powerful interests resisting change. But the developments I have described have, I believe, given to the many poor States new influence in the international political system and therefore in international law-making. In the seas, moreover, that influence is magnified, and geography has provided these States with additional and more effective weapons. The result is two major new directions in the law of the sea: the expansion of coastal State jurisdiction at the expense of the commonage; and, beyond any plausible coastal State jurisdiction, a transformed concept of commonage reflecting regulation rather than *laissez-faire*, and the principle of welfare rather than wholly-free enterprise.[9]

COASTAL STATE EXPANSION

Most States are coastal States. Most coastal States are poor. All coastal States are tempted to claim monopoly in the sea's resources as far as economically interesting, but the temptation of the poor coastal States is, of course, strongest. They need the resources. The States they would exclude are usually interlopers, distant and rich (having the capital, the technology, the enterprise, for distant fishing or other long-range exploitation). Often, the distant "intruder" is also a former (or present) "imperialist."

And the poor have had instruction and example. It was President Truman who achieved that coastal State expansion which is now the doctrine of the continental shelf, and justified it as "reasonable and just." [10] Now other coastal States insist, if it is reasonable and just that the resources of the continental shelf belong to the coastal State, why not those of the continental slope and the continental rise? If coastal minerals, why not coastal fish? If—as the 1958 Convention provides—sedentary fish,[11] why not swimming fish? If 12 mile fishing zones (now claimed even by the United States),[12] why not 25 miles (which some consider the average width of the continental shelf), or 50 miles, or 200? And if it is reasonable and just that the coastal State have a monopoly over resources, why not authority to act there to protect her security or the environment, or to regulate all other uses?

The Latin American countries in particular, in a series of declarations,[13] and through diverse diplomatic actions, have asserted the right of the coastal State to exclusive economic interests in a "Patrimonial Sea." African States have supported similar claims to an "Exclusive Economic Zone." [14] Together they have tried to make coastal State monopoly over resources a banner for the solidarity of the poor—all poor, not only those that are coastal States—and for their economic self-determination against the economic imperialism of distant invaders.

Finally, and not least, the political influence of coastal States, their arguments and symbols, are supported by the facts of geography and the effective irrelevance of military power. If possession is nine points of the law, it is at least that many in law-making. The coastal States have effective "possession" of the coastal areas. And, today, who will take it from them? Which government will use force to protect distant fishing or other economic interests against coastal governments? I do not know what the United Kingdom is prepared to do if Iceland persists in its cod claims; but the United States, we know, has not sent its Navy to protect its tuna boats from expansionist assertions by Ecuador and Peru.

What is more, those who might be most strongly tempted to resist the expansion of other coastal States are themselves coastal States, and also interested in expanding. In the past, countries like the United Kingdom and the United States, though they have extensive coasts, firmly resisted coastal State expansion because the advantages to them of expanding into the sea meant less than did keeping their other interests in the seas free from invasion by other coastal States. (The United States and the United Kingdom have long been major bulwarks of a narrow territorial sea.) Today, not only are their means of resistance circumscribed, but their desire to resist is ambivalent, selective and half- or quarter-hearted.

Consider, for a crucial example, the United States, and the national forces which are pushing and pulling to achieve a national policy, especially as regards seabed mining. Despite her firm insistance on a narrow territorial sea, the United States led the expansion on the continental shelf in order to reduce her dependence on foreign petroleum for civilian as well as military uses. For that same reason, there are forces in the United States today (compare the Reports of the National Petroleum Council and of the Metcalf Subcommittee in the United States Senate),[15] that are asserting and pressing the national interest in an ever-wider continental shelf. On the other hand, the Department of Defense opposed such further expansion, apparently from fear of "creeping jurisdiction," that a wide shelf for the United States meant also a wide shelf for others, and their jurisdiction over resources will lead effectively to a wide territorial sea, and will close large expanses to United States military uses. The result in 1970 was the Nixon Plan,[16] a compromise between the desires of the oil companies and those of the Defense Department, between the interests of the United States in the resources of a wide shelf and her interest in keeping as much of the sea as possible, including foreign coastal areas, free for her navigation and military uses. There are, however, reports that this compromise may not emerge as national policy, that there are efforts to persuade the Department of Defense that resistance to coastal State expansion is hopeless, and that the United States could further all her interests by pressing for wide coastal State jurisdiction over resources, for others as well as for herself, in exchange for reaffirmation by all of the freedom of military uses outside a narrow territorial sea.

There is a different, less ambivalent resistance to expanded coastal State jurisdiction over minerals. The same majority of united poor States has succeeded in establishing, in international rhetoric and perhaps in international law, that the seabed is " the common heritage of mankind." [17] (Not only President Truman but the other American President who died recently also deserves a memorial in the law of the sea: President Johnson was apparently the first to insist that the deep seas and the ocean bottoms are "the legacy of all human beings"). [18] If the seabed beyond national jurisdiction is the common heritage, and if, as we shall see, mankind is prepared to claim it for all, every inch of it claimed by a coastal State does not deprive some distant imperialist but is at the expense of mankind. If most coastal States do not seem to have noticed that inescapable fact, the land-locked and the " shelf-locked " countries of the world have noted it well. Invoking the solidarity of the anti-imperialist poor to a different end, they may yet be prepared to fight to protect " the common pot " against depredation even by poor coastal States.[19]

There are some 50 land-locked and shelf-locked States, enough, if united, to prevent the two-thirds majority that is usually required at international conferences, but not enough to get their way. Might they be joined even by some coastal States, which, consulting the best guesses of the best geologists, conclude that their particular coasts are not richly endowed, and that, therefore, they have more to gain if all coastal States are restrained, and more seabed (especially the immediately rewarding, petroleum-rich continental margins of the world) is left for the common pot? Or will even the land- and shelf-locked bow to the will of coastal States and accept that the common heritage begins where the interests of coastal States end? Or, might there be a compromise, giving the coastal States more than they have but less than they might wish? It is perhaps of some significance that a plurality in the General Assembly recently voted to request a study of the significance for the common heritage of various proposals as to the limits of coastal State jurisdiction, while a minority strongly objected to having that question studied.[20]

A different kind of resistance to coastal State expansion may result from the dichotomy of coastal State interests, principally in fishing and mining. Few States have major interests in both coastal fish and coastal minerals, and the expansion of coastal State jurisdiction over either will not occur without the solidarity of fishing States with mining States in a common political front for a wide, exclusive zone for both—hence the Latin American "Patrimonial Sea" and the African "Exclusive Economic Zone." But while the resistance to coastal State expansion over mining is uncertain, there are influential States with vested distant fishing interests (*e.g.*, the United Kingdom, but also the U.S.S.R., Japan, even the U.S.) which will resist a wide fishing zone. If there is to be a single economic zone, then, the distant fishing States will insist that it be narrower than a zone for mining alone might be If, thereupon, some coastal States abandon the single zone and ask to continue to enjoy a wider mining zone, as at present, they might lose the support of the coastal fishing States; might these, then, join with the land- and shelf-locked to contain coastal State mining rights in favour of a larger area for the common heritage?

OTHER USES IN COASTAL AREAS

Whether in the name of national security, the environment or "principle," there will also be some pressure by coastal States for larger and more comprehensive control over other uses. A 12 mile territorial sea is virtually inevitable, though the U.S. and U.S.S.R. are insisting on free transit (not merely "innocent passage") through international Straits.[21] In general, again, coastal State claims will be supported in the name of anti-imperialism against powerful, distant users. The United States and Russia (and their allies) will resist, perhaps even forcefully, interference with their military uses of the sea; and other States, too, might recognise that such freedom today supports the principal strategic deterrent on which strategic stability depends. There will be strong, if less strong, resistance to interference with shipping in the name of the environment, but coastal States might achieve substantial anti-pollution authority in wide zones if they do not interfere unduly with major shipping, *e.g.*, of oil.[22]

BEYOND NATIONAL JURISDICTION

Somewhere, at some distance from shore, coastal State jurisdiction will end, and the "international sea" begin. There we find the second new direction, the changing significance of "commonage" in the seas beyond national jurisdiction.

The principal area of change is the seabed. The seabed "beyond national jurisdiction" has been unanimously declared to be the "common heritage of mankind."[23] Clearly rejected, then, is any notion of *res nullius*, that the seabed belongs to no one and can be seized by the first comer; all are agreed now that the international seabed is not subject to national appropriation. It is also widely agreed that the international seabed should provide some revenue for some international purposes, notably for development of the under-developed countries, including the land-locked.

These two points of agreement apart, there is sharp disagreement as to what else "common heritage" implies. Some international companies, for example, urge that if they are allowed to proceed in freedom, under "free enterprise" protected by their national laws and by simple treaties, they will make these resources available to mankind quickly and cheaply. What is more, they might add, if they are not released and encouraged to proceed in freedom, the resources will remain on the seabed and mankind will enjoy neither the minerals nor any revenue from their exploitation. At the other extreme are those who say that "common heritage" necessarily implies that mankind should own, exploit and dispose of these resources; and, some add, mankind means the existing States acting equally by majority vote, whether in the UN or in some body specially created for the purpose. Between these two extremes are numerous permutations as to the amount of regulation, the authority of international institutions, and the system of voting and other elements in their governance.[24]

As regards this new direction in the law, the political forces, I suggest, are different, and differently arrayed. If, as regards coastal areas, most States will be moved by their particular coastal interests, the majority of States voting a régime for the international seabed will be vindicating the interests of "mankind," or, perhaps, their undivided common interest in the common pot. And some States that have national mining industries might be concerned less to profit from exploitation of the commonage than to assure that the seabed not be "unduly" exploited, that its minerals do not compete with their national product, taking away their markets or reducing the price of their ore. Some States may rise above money to "principle," seeking collective political authority over the seabed, with a view perhaps eventually to authority over the seas.

The relevant realities in the international seabed are also different from those shaping the future law of coastal areas. Principally, here " possession " is not in the hands of the many small coastal States; it is rather in the hands of the few developed States which have the essential initiative, capital and technology, and can proceed to dig at will. They have voted to give up the right to acquire national sovereignty over the seabed [25]; they have not given up the right to dig, and keep the minerals. (States, they point out, can fish freely in the deep seas and keep the fish.) Inevitably there is the implicit threat that if the majority insists on a régime unacceptable to the developed States, they will proceed to dig unilaterally; and who will prevent them?

These are the implications of the controversy between the United States and the majority in the UN General Assembly about the " Moratorium Resolution." [26] The majority sought to tie the hands of the developed countries by asserting that no one may dig in the deep seabed until a new international régime has been established and only in accordance with its terms. The United States rejected both the terms of the resolution and its implications. In the Congress of the United States, Bills have been introduced that would authorise Americans to dig in the international seabed, and would protect them as well as nationals of any other State that accepted reciprocal arrangements.[27] The Executive Branch has asked the Congress not to adopt such legislation at this time, but, it is clear, it might support some such unilateral action if an acceptable régime is not achieved at an early date.[28]

The new direction in the law of deep-sea mining, I believe, will have to be acceptable to the United States. Again, the Nixon Plan is instructive. Again, it was the result of competing forces. The Department of Defense, I surmise, pressed for an enlightened régime with international revenue and some international authority, in order to appeal to the mass of States and to induce even some coastal States not to expand too far (and, especially, to leave military uses alone). Again, industry spokesmen favoured less international authority,[29] but the oil companies are not particularly interested in the international régime if it governs only the deep seabed, not the continental margins where petroleum seems to be concentrated. Hard-mineral companies do have substantial interests in the manganese nodules of the deep seabed and might also prefer less international " meddling," but these companies are less united and less influential. The resultant compromise, closer to what the Department of Defense wished, was a proposal providing, essentially, for international licensing on the basis of competitive bidding, international revenue, and an international authority governed by weighted voting. Some such proposal has, I believe, good prospects. Surely, the developed States will not accept (and would effectively frustrate) any scheme for exclusive exploitation of the deep seabed by an international operating agency. Nor will they accept equal voting by all States, and unqualified majority rule, in any body that has substantial authority in the seas: roughly, the degree of " democracy " in an international sea agency will vary inversely with the amount and kind of its authority.

These, then, are the principal new directions in the sea, and the political forces that, in my view, will determine them and fix their reach. They will affect particularly the exploitation of resources, especially mineral resources; but they are relevant, too, for fishing and for protection against pollution.

The exclusive jurisdiction of coastal States over fishing will extend farther than it has, perhaps in an exclusive economic zone; but such a zone will not be as wide as a mining zone alone might be. The jurisdiction of coastal States to impose conservation measures may extend farther than its exclusive right to fish. Beyond national jurisdiction, freedom to fish will apparently continue, subject to group arrangements governing particular species. In a long time, perhaps, the concept of the common heritage might extend also to fish but that direction is not now apparent.

The disposition of political forces will be resolved differently, I believe, with regard to pollution and environmental protection. Here there are, in a sense, three different confrontations of forces. In coastal areas, the coastal State is asserting the right to protect herself against maritime " interlopers " threatening her environment. If the maritime powers do not do more to satisfy the coastal States, more even than the recent Conventions,[30] the latter—a majority of the States, many of which are not themselves maritime States—will make the law, whether formally or by concerted unilateral action.

The principal source of sea pollution in coastal areas, however, is the coastal State itself. It seems commonly overlooked that such pollution is the consequence of a valid, valuable human use of the sea: waste has to be disposed of, and the seas have been an accessible, inexpensive, apparently harmless receptacle. Now we have become aware that it is not harmless and that the harm is not only to the coastal State itself. Here, then, it is the coastal State against mankind, against the " common heritage," and, unhappily, the common interest has yet no effective champion. But the coastal State's claim for protection against other polluters should exert some influence to restrain her as well.

Beyond coastal areas, the issue is between polluter—various maritime Powers (and consider also the continued nuclear testing in the air by France)—and the rest of us, mankind, the common interest. Here the resistance to *laissez-faire* is weakest, and even the strong and growing environmentalist forces in the developed countries are not yet concerned and effective champions in that environment. It will take time and growing laws and institutions, with jurisdiction, in the first instance, over resources and other uses, before the common environment of the common seas can find effective protection.

These, I believe, are the influences upon and between governments that will determine the new directions in the law of the sea and their reach and consequence. In the next months, States will be studying geography and economics, politics and strategy, pondering the consequences for themselves and for others of various proposals for coastal State jurisdiction and for international régimes, and the consequences, too, of failure to reach agreement. Before and during the conference there will be hard bargaining involving sea issues and other issues, and international relations generally. The result of this political process of international legislation, one must hope, will be new law that wisely accommodates particular to common interests, reflects enlightened new directions, and is " reasonable and just."

REFERENCES

1. UN General Assembly Resolution 3029A (XXVII), Dec. 18, 1972.

2. Report of the International Law Commission, 1956. 11 UNGAOR, Supp. No. 9, UN Doc. A/3159 (1956).

3. UN Doc. A/6695 (1969).

4. Compare the 1958 Convention on the Territorial Sea and the Contiguous Zone, 516 U.N.T.S. 205; the Convention on the Continental Shelf, 499 U.N.T.S. 311.

5. On Air Defence Identification Zones, see Murchison, *The Contiguous Air Space Zone in International Law* (1956); for the Declaration of Panama, see (1939) 1 *Department of State Bulletin* 331. Canada's anti-pollution action was proclaimed in the Arctic Waters Pollution Prevention Act, June 26, 1970, 2nd Session, 28th Parliament, 18–19 Elizabeth II, 1969–70.

6. Compare Art. 24 of the Convention on the High Seas; Art. 5 (7) of the Convention on the Continental Shelf. Also, the International Convention for the Prevention of Pollution of the Sea by Oil, 1954, and related conventions.

7. UN Charter, Art. 2 (4).

8. See L. Henkin, *How Nations Behave* (1968), pp. 128–141.

9. Compare L. Henkin, " The Once and the Future Law of the Sea " in W. Friedmann, L. Henkin and O. Lissitzyn (eds.), *Transnational Law in a Changing Society* (1972).

10. Presidential Proclamation No. 2667, Sept. 28, 1945, 10 Fed.Reg. 12303 (1945).

11. See the Convention on the Continental Shelf, Art. 2 (4).

12. Pub.L. 89–658, 1–3, 80 Stat. § 908 (1966), 16 U.S.C. 1091–1093 (1970).

13. See, for example, the Declarations of Montevideo ((1970) 9 Int.Leg.Mat. 1081), Lima ((1971) 10 Int.Leg.Mat. 207) and Santo Domingo ((1972) 11 Int.Leg.Mat. 892).

14. See the Kenya proposal in the UN Seabed Committee, A/AC.138/80, July 26, 1972, repeating recommendations of the Yaoundé Seminar of June 1972, A/AC.138/79, July 21, 1972.

15. Compare *National Petroleum Council Report on Petroleum Resources under the Ocean Floor* (1969); *Report of the Special Committee on Outer Continental Shelf*, U.S. Senate Committee on Interior and Insular Affairs, Dec. 21, 1970, 91st Cong., 2d Sess.

16. Statement of May 23, 1970 (1970) 9 Int.Leg.Mat. 806; draft Convention submitted as working paper to UN Seabed Committee, A/AC.138/25, Aug. 3, 1970 (1970) 9 Int.Leg.Mat. 1046.

17. See Declaration of Principles Governing the Seabed and the Ocean Floor and the Subsoil thereof Beyond the Limits of National Jurisdiction, UN General Assembly Resolution 2749 (XXV), Dec. 17, 1970, unanimously adopted.

18. President's remarks at the commissioning of the new research ship, *The Oceanographer*, July 13, 1966 (1966) 2 *Weekly Compilation of Presidential Documents* 930, 931.

19. Compare n. 20.

20. See UN General Assembly Resolution 3029B (XXVII), Dec. 18, 1972. The Resolution was adopted by 69–15, with 41 abstentions. Compare Res. 3029C (XXVII), Dec. 18, 1972, adopted 100–0–28.

21. Compare the Nixon statement, n. 16 above.

22. Compare L. Henkin, "Arctic Anti-Pollution: Does Canada Make—or Break—International Law?" (1971) 65 A.J.I.L. 131.

23. See n. 17 above.

24. See, *e.g.*, L. Henkin, *Law for the Sea's Mineral Resources* (1968), pp. 49–68.

25. See n. 17 above.

26. UN General Assembly Resolution 2574D (XXVII), Dec. 15, 1969.

27. S. 2801, 92d Cong., 1st Sess. (1971), reintroduced as S. 1134, 93d Cong., 1st Sess. (1973); also H.R. 9, *ibid.*

28. Letter of Acting Legal Adviser to Senator Fulbright, Chairman, Committee on Foreign Relations, U.S. Senate, Mar. 1, 1973.

29. See n. 15 above.

30. Compare the Convention on the Prevention of Marine Pollution by Dumping of Wastes and Other Matter, Dec. 29, 1972. Compare n. 6 above.

CHAPTER 2

The Santiago Conference and The Future

By R. Y. Jennings*

I SHALL not attempt in this paper any soothsaying exercise about the international law of the future, and I must be at pains to disclaim any great degree of prescience, not to say assurance, but it might serve a useful purpose if I attempt, in however amateur a fashion, to bring together the different aspects of the law of the sea, and to see if we can now get a sort of bird's-eye view of the whole subject-matter that will go to the Santiago Conference.

I wonder whether we might first look at a question which, I think, has not been considered, or hardly at all, in this volume, but a matter which, all the same, will govern the whole operation. I mean the question of the procedures that are in fact available for making this attempt to reshape the international law of the sea. In calling the forthcoming Santiago Conference, I suppose the United Nations was taking a calculated risk, and it is a risk, because at Santiago we shall see an assembly of the society of States very different and far more varied than has ever been assembled before at such a Conference. Its programme will be, again, unprecedentedly large and varied and, furthermore, it will not, as the 1958 Conference did, have the very great benefit of draft articles prepared after years of careful scientific labour and negotiation by the International Law Commission. Indeed, how could it, for the codification and development element promises to be very small. This is an attempt to make new law which will, in many essential respects, be absolutely novel.

Yet, on the other hand, it is also true, I think, that the new law is already taking shape. I do not, with great respect, think that I altogether agree with Professor Henkin's observation that the new law will be fashioned by the politicians. On the contrary, it seems to me that the choices are already very restricted, that the tendencies are already being fashioned strongly by the pressures and the logic of events, and, indeed, the choices may become more restricted before the Conference meets. So the tendencies are already quite strong and, in some respects, fairly clear. Nor, I think, do I agree—if I may venture to disagree again with Professor Henkin, though he knows I agree with him on many other aspects of this subject—that it is altogether a question of rich and poor, developed and undeveloped. Quite frankly, I think we are deceiving ourselves if we think it is so simple.

The movements and tendencies, and the identification of interests by States already form an extremely complex pattern, and I do not think it can be usefully analysed now in very simple terms.

So it seems to me the crucial question now is how far the movements and tendencies that already exist can be harnessed into an international system, instead of fragmented, as they otherwise might be, into regional and even unilateral assertion. To take the recent Declaration of Santo Domingo, this is but one example of a steady flow of

* Whewell Professor of International Law, University of Cambridge.

regional or group declarations, working papers, whatever you like to call them. One introductory phrase in that Declaration has not, I think, received much attention. I mean the assertion at the beginning of the Declaration that the Caribbean States are in a peculiar situation calling for special criteria. It is true the Declaration goes on to ask other Latin American States to join. The implication is clear: this is a working paper for a general scheme, but it is also a fall-back position on a regional basis.

This can be paralleled in many other examples from all sides. One hears murmurs about semi-enclosed seas and about the peculiar position of a particular region. Apart from the great oceans, where is there a sea which is not semi-enclosed?

There was a time when I doubted the wisdom of calling a Conference to reopen the law of the sea, but for some time now there really has been no alternative. The failure of the forthcoming Conference would not mean that the old law, and it seems to be odd to be thinking of 1958 as the old law, but that is what we have to do, would remain in force, but rather that the international law of the sea would be in serious danger of falling into fragments before our eyes. This cannot be allowed to happen, and if we are to prevent it, the only right thing to do, it seems to me, is to take tendencies and movements as they strongly exist and inject into them the leaven of general international law.

But, of course, this is generally appreciated, I think, in the United Nations. As Miss Gutteridge in her excellent paper points out, the summer 1972 meeting of the Seabed Committee was relatively businesslike, and the chairman at the end of it was able to commit himself to the view that a compromise on the basic issues is definitely within reach, and that when this compromise has been worked out, the process of drafting treaty articles should not be a matter of insuperable difficulty.

What, then, is the shape of this compromise likely to be? Everybody seems to be agreed that the principal issues at the Conference will be interdependent. This is what is meant, I think, by the compromise which has just been referred to. It is a whole package. There is no inherent logic in this. It would be perfectly possible in theory to deal with, say, the territorial sea quite separately and in isolation. But in real life at present, it is not. In fact, the only part of the law of the sea that is not involved in package negotiation seems to be bays and other purely national waters.

We have all moved quite a long way in a very short time in our thinking about the law of the sea. Hardly anyone is heard today to assert the simple principle of the freedoms of the high seas as immutable and essential, though even two years ago that would have been the stock-in-trade of a very large proportion of writers. Now we all recognise that the freedoms have to be sublimated into more or less complicated régimes, whether we are thinking of hydrocarbons or of fishing or of pollution or even of navigation. If, then, it is a question of a package deal on régimes, this means that the question of limits is of the essence. Under limits, I mean to discuss not only the question of measurement but also the question of the content, the question, if you like, of zones.

Here the outline of the possible compromise seems to me to be already fairly clear. There will, of course, be the territorial sea. Its basic régime is already established. As to the question of breadth, there is a strong tendency towards 12 miles as it were from both directions, from smaller claims and from larger claims. In that case, if the agreed figure were to be 12 miles, that would leave to be secured the rights of transit, which cannot be swept under the carpet and will have to be dealt with, though there may be more than one way of accomplishing that. I hope we shall not lose sight of the very attractive, if unofficial, suggestion that a beautifully simple solution would be that perhaps a three mile territorial sea would be as much as anybody wants if they have also a patrimonial sea.

Then there is the continental shelf, the régime of which I suppose will stay very much as it is. The long-debated question of the breadth of the continental shelf is now qualified or, perhaps, made more complicated by the proposal for a patrimonial sea or economic zone, and this latter idea—the patrimonial sea—seems to me to be here to stay in one form or another. This is, perhaps, for two main reasons, though one could think of others. In the first place, I think it is inherently reasonable that a coastal State's resource interests in the adjacent sea beyond the territorial sea, whatever they amount to in terms of jurisdiction, should not be confined to the resources of the seabed and subsoil. We have been reminded in the discussion that the Truman proclamation on the continental shelf excited emulation and no protest. That is so and that is of great importance juridically. But I have sympathy with those who point out that it did also provoke a rather different view of the matter from three Latin American countries. It is true that their claim did excite protest, and it is also true that as a matter of legal history there were excellent grounds for making a sharp distinction, as the Truman declaration did, between the resources of the seabed and subsoil on the one hand and the resources of the water column on the other. But, in equity, the case was not, after all, quite so good, and equity has tended, as it often does, in the long run to prevail.

In the second place, the patrimonial sea idea is of prime importance because, if I am not mistaken, it is the factor which promises to make some compromise, some negotiation, at a forthcoming conference possible. It makes a general agreement on a territorial sea of 12 miles or perhaps even less a matter of practical politics for the first time for quite a long while. For this reason alone, the patrimonial sea idea is of great importance.

The question of breadth is one that will be discussed and debated and negotiated. We may have to get used to the idea that there is great power in the figure of 200 miles, because, after all, 200 mile territorial sea claims have tended to breed fast in the last decade or so. But apart from the question of width, surely the important point is that the indications are that the jurisdictional content of the patrimonial sea notion is negotiable.

Beyond the continental shelf, which may well, in some cases, be beyond the patrimonial sea, will then be the area of seabed and subsoil which is described as being beyond national jurisdiction, an area clearly tending to recede in terms of immediate importance for exploitable resources. Nevertheless it is an area which still poses difficult and important questions. A régime for it can doubtless be articulated on the basis of the General Assembly's statement of principles, but then there is also that strong desire, particularly among developing countries, to see established a strong international agency with power itself, perhaps, even to explore and exploit as well as to manage the régime of the area beyond national jurisdiction.

The idea of a strong international agency to do all these things is easily expressed in general terms, but it will not be so easy to design the structure of it (especially the voting structure) and to organise the controls of power within it in such a way that it will both secure sufficiently wide acceptance to make it viable and also to produce a body that really can work and do things. The novelty of this kind of organisation has not, it seems to me, been sufficiently stressed. There is no really useful existing pattern even among the present proliferation of international organisations. It is not possible to say more at present about this problem, but I would just like to make this observation: that the problem of the actual structure of an international organisation of this kind is one that needs far more study than has so far been given to it, and unless this is forthcoming, the agency may turn out to be no more than a pious proposal.

Such, then, will be the range of zones as I believe—territorial sea, continental shelf, patrimonial sea or economic zone, high seas, international seabed. How will this scheme cope with the particular problems that are discussed in this volume, and how will they fit into this general scheme of jurisdiction? As soon as one begins to think of particular uses of the seabed or the sea, one comes right up against the question of pluralities and conflicts of user, and of determining priorities. It must be allowed here, I think, that the idea of a patrimonial sea, assuming it would give management jurisdiction of some sort to the coastal State, would in some ways simplify the problem, but not a great deal. Let us look, for example, at the most elementary user of the seas, for communications by merchant vessels. I leave aside the question of naval vessels which is not discussed in this volume at all but which obviously is of great importance. The elementary right of navigation and transit must clearly be secured. It must be secured indeed if the resources are themselves to be properly exploited and marketed. Yet vessels may be required, it appears, in fairly extensive zones of municipal jurisdiction, to observe regulations designed, for example, to prevent pollution, to protect resources, installations and, above all, for their own safety in narrow or treacherous waters.

Obviously, there must here be a high degree of uniformity of regulation attained in some way, because as it has been pointed out, it simply is not possible to change the design of a tanker as it passes from one jurisdiction to another. So we have the seeming paradox that the more coastal State jurisdiction is extended, the more it needs itself to be controlled and penetrated by a régime of international law and international standards. And maybe indeed, also, inspected and even overseen by an international agency or international agencies. In fact, if one looks at things in the right perspective, we may find that, after all, creeping national jurisdiction is very fertile material in which to plant the seeds of international law.

There is also the difficult question of the potential conflict of coastal and flag jurisdiction. This is not a new problem, as a glance at any old textbook of international law will testify. But, again, conflicting jurisdiction becomes overlapping and reinforcing jurisdiction where uniform laws and standards can be applied. Here, I think, I must voice my own great fear about the preparation for the Santiago Conference. My fear is that the attention of commentators and even perhaps of legal advisers will have been so concentrated on the much publicised question of an international régime beyond national jurisdiction that they will fail adequately to notice the urgent need for more thinking about the international régime that will be needed forthwith in the area within national jurisdiction. My only quarrel with the phrase "the common heritage of mankind" is that it obscures the fact that it is the whole of the sea that is the common heritage of mankind, including that part that is subject to national jurisdiction. But we have become so mesmerised by this dichotomy of national and so-called international jurisdiction that we are in danger of forgetting that the essential role of international law is performed within and through the medium of national jurisdiction whether on the sea or, indeed, on land.

The emphasis on the need for general international standards may require qualification in one respect, that of fishery control. It would seem that many fishery problems including even some forms of fish farming, may best be solved on a regional basis. It is clear, therefore, that the general international pattern of the Convention ought to admit of regional variations, not only perhaps in this respect but also in some others. There is a strong regionalist tendency, as I have already pointed out. It must be accommodated and controlled, but still accommodated; and, of course, regional arrangements possibly provide one way in which land-locked States could also have their needs accommodated. But that is merely a suggestion in passing.

Thus, in conclusion, one might perhaps sum it up in this way. We probably have now to accept some sort of economic or patrimonial sea in addition to the territorial sea and a more or less extensive continental shelf. In these areas the coastal State will want management jurisdiction over resources. The coastal State will also accordingly wish to exercise its pollution jurisdiction. This will include some regulation of navigation lanes, safety practices, and so on. But the content is negotiable, and this may well be the chief focus of the necessary compromise. This extension of national jurisdiction, including even the continental shelf, must be brought within the context of a strong international convention which will specify and limit the jurisdictional competences of the coastal State in this area, both jurisdiction to prescribe and jurisdiction to enforce, and will lay down some uniform rules and standards so as to make international sense of the whole structure.

There must also be good methods of settling international disputes that arise, and some measure of compulsory jurisdiction is highly desirable. We have tended for political reasons to run away from that in recent years, but we must come back to it especially if we are to develop a complex international law.

The Convention will also no doubt provide some kind of international régime for the area beyond national jurisdiction, but it seems to me that this is less urgent as a problem, though I do not mean to suggest that it is, for that reason, any less important in the longer run.

Finally, one ought to mention the important matter of islands which is difficult and delicate and greatly affects practically everything else that I have mentioned. If I merely refer to the problem and hurriedly pass on, I can plead that this hitherto has been the firmly established practice in the United Nations Seabed Committee.

I would like to end on a note of hopefulness. Everyone, I think, must have felt gloomy sometimes at the prospect before them. For a long time it seemed that the erosion of the old law was the only certainty. But a law of the high seas, after all, that was expressed simply in terms of freedoms is inadequate and inapt to the present world and its needs. This is where it all began, of course, with the realisation that the old law of the high seas was practically useless when it came to the problem of exploiting the resources of the deep seabed beyond national jurisdiction. Now a more elaborate and adequate régime is beginning to take shape. We can already see the outlines. The task at Santiago will be immensely difficult, but I believe we have perhaps within our grasp a new law of the sea which, in its elaboration and suitability to modern needs, could be greatly superior to the old.

Part II

Living Resources

CHAPTER 3

The Freedom of Fishing in Decline: The Case of the North-East Atlantic

By Albert W. Koers*

I. SOME BASIC FACTS

THE North-East Atlantic Ocean may be delineated roughly as the waters between Cape Farewell at the north-west and Novaya Zemlya at the north-east to the latitude of Gibraltar (36° N.) in the south.[1]† It is an area that includes some of the most productive fishing grounds in the world: in 1970 the North-East Atlantic produced 10·5 million tons of fish, which is approximately 14 per cent. of the 1970 total world catch of 69·3 million tons. In that year the total catch in the North-West Atlantic Ocean was about 4·2 million tons, *i.e.*, 6 per cent. of the total world catch. As a fishing area the North-East Atlantic is surpassed only by the North-West Pacific Ocean (15·4 million tons in 1970) and the South-East Pacific Ocean (13·7 million tons in 1970).[2] The most important species that support the North-East Atlantic fisheries are: herring (2·2 million tons in 1968), cod (2 million tons in 1968), mackerel (0·9 million tons in 1968), capelin (0·6 million tons in 1968), Norway pout (0·46 million tons in 1968), haddock (0·38 million tons in 1968) and saithe (0·3 million tons in 1968).[3] Other species include whiting, sandeels, redfish, plaice and hake. The number of nations participating in these fisheries is almost as large as the number of species under exploitation, although the catches of Norway exceed by far those of any other nation fishing in this area: in 1970 it caught 2·85 million tons of fish in the North-East Atlantic alone. Other North-East Atlantic fishing nations are: the U.S.S.R. (1·56 million tons in 1970), Denmark (1·2 million tons in 1970), the U.K. (1 million tons in 1970), Iceland (0·73 million tons in 1970), Spain (0·65 million tons in 1970), France (0·55 million tons in 1970), the Federal Republic of Germany (0·39 million tons in 1970), the Netherlands (0·29 million tons in 1970), Sweden (0·28 million tons in 1970), Portugal (0·23 million tons in 1970) and Poland (0·2 million tons in 1970).[4] Other States involved in these fisheries are: Belgium, Finland, the German Democratic Republic, Ireland, Japan and Roumania.

If these are the basic facts of the fisheries of the North-East Atlantic, what, then, are the specific problems facing the international law of marine fisheries in this area?

II. FIVE MAJOR PROBLEM AREAS

Generally, the international law of marine fisheries must deal with these five questions: (1) how to use the living resources of the sea as fully as is desirable; (2) how to prevent exploitation of these resources beyond biologically acceptable levels; (3) how to

* Institute of International Law, University of Utrecht.
† For references, see p. 32.

allocate catches among fishing nations; (4) how to ensure the economic efficiency of fishing operations; and (5) how to provide an adequate body of knowledge upon which decisions can be based. In the following sections these five questions will be examined briefly with a view to the particular problems of the North-East Atlantic fisheries.[5]

The world fish catch has expanded rapidly since the Second World War: from a total catch of about 20 million tons in 1950 to about 69 million tons in 1970.[6] This expansion is largely the result of the growth of distant water fishing operations—a growth made possible by technological advances that enable fishermen to operate efficiently far from their home base.[7] Estimates concerning the maximum *potential* productivity of the sea's living resources vary widely, but assuming that no radical changes will occur in catching techniques and taste preferences, the FAO sets the maximum potential catch of world fisheries at 120 million tons annually.[8] Thus, it would be possible to expand the present total annual yield of 70 million tons without infringing upon the biological limits of the living resources of the sea. In a world faced with critical nutritional problems,[9] it must be a function of the international law of marine fisheries to assist in bringing about such an expansion to the extent that it is both economically desirable and biologically possible. However, it appears that this general task is of relatively little significance for the North-East Atlantic: most stocks in this area are already subject to full exploitation. Only a few North-East Atlantic species would produce larger yields if the fishing effort were increased—many more would yield higher catches as a result of more effective conservation measures.[10] Accordingly, while in many other fishing areas special arrangements for fishery development and expansion are a major concern of the international law of marine fisheries, such arrangements are not a priority in the North-East Atlantic. Nevertheless, legal arrangements applicable to the fisheries of this area should not form an impediment to the fullest possible and desirable utilisation of its living resources, and if these resources can yield higher catches, such legal arrangements should assist in expanding the fisheries concerned.

"Conservation" is the term commonly used to refer to the problem of limiting catches to biologically acceptable limits.[11] Conservation measures are generally designed to restrict the catch of a stock of fish to the maximum sustainable yield of that stock, *i.e.*, to the maximum catch that can be maintained year after year. Each stock has a specific maximum sustainable yield depending upon such factors as rate of recruitment, rate of growth and rate of mortality.[12] As these factors may vary from year to year, the maximum sustainable yield of a stock may also fluctuate in time. Obviously, this is the first difficulty in adjusting actual catches to the maximum sustainable yield level. A second problem is caused by the fact that taking the maximum sustainable yield from one species may affect the catch that is available from another species.[13] For example, increasing the size of the fur seal herds for the purpose of achieving their maximum sustainable yield may have an adverse effect on the catches of those species on which fur seal feed. Thirdly, the determination of the maximum sustainable yield of a stock requires a great deal of information[14] which in many cases does not yet exist. Thus, apart from political problems involved in reaching international agreement on conservation measures, there is also a great deal of scientific uncertainty that makes conservation a very difficult problem. Fortunately, experience shows that most stocks of fish are quite resilient to overfishing,[15] and that they usually recover from a reduction in stock size.[16] Nevertheless, it is undoubtedly an extremely important task of the international law of marine fisheries to limit catches in the North-East Atlantic to the maximum sustainable yield level. This is illustrated by a map[17] produced by the 1949 United Nations Scientific Conference on the Conservation and Utilisation of

Resources which shows that in 1949 such important North-East Atlantic stocks as herring and cod were still under-exploited. All these stocks are now in need of proper management—often rather urgently. As will be discussed in section III, existing arrangements have not been very successful in this respect.

Very difficult problems exist in connection with the allocation of the catch of marine fisheries among the nations of the world. It is with respect to allocation that a most intensive political confrontation among fishing nations occurs. Essentially, four categories of States are involved in this confrontation: (1) distant water fishing States; (2) coastal fishing States; (3) developing fishing States; and (4) developed fishing States. It has been mentioned that in the past distant water fishing States have expanded their catches much more rapidly than coastal fishing States.[18] This has led to a great deal of friction among these two categories of States concerning questions of allocation. Similar problems exist between developed and developing fishing States: developing States—often not yet able to participate actively in marine fisheries—find it difficult to accept the increasingly intensive distant water fisheries of some developed States in the waters off their coasts.[19] The momentum existing in the international community in favour of an extension of exclusive fishery limits is largely the result of this dual confrontation: it is an attempt by coastal States and developing States to alter the allocation of the sea's living resources to their advantage. As far as the allocation of high seas fisheries *per se* is concerned, there are essentially two alternatives[20]: (1) allocation by international agreement,[21] or (2) allocation on the basis of free competition among fishing States. Under the first alternative fishing nations reach agreement on the distribution of either the total catch or of the total fishing effort (measured, for example, in standard fishing days). Since a distribution of fishing effort is quite difficult to achieve,[22] allocation usually refers to catches: each fishing nation obtains a right to a certain tonnage. In the second approach[23] the share of a nation in the total catch of a stock is a function of the effort which that nation applies to the fishery in question. Allocation on the basis of free competition still prevails in the North-East Atlantic fisheries, although there exist a few national quota agreements. As a result, there is a great deal of friction among the nations participating in these fisheries with respect to allocation, particularly since all commercially attractive stocks are subject to full exploitation.[24] Apart from the undesirability of such a confrontation, allocation on the basis of free competition is also at the root of economic efficiency problems.

Fishing operations are carried out not only to produce food, but—at least for most countries[25]—also in order to make a profit.[26] Such a profit will be made only if the income from marine fisheries is higher than the costs involved in such fisheries. It is with respect to the costs of fishing operations—or their economic efficiency—that existing international legal arrangements have become subject to severe criticism.[27] Under the freedom of fishing on the high seas all fishermen have free access to marine fisheries. Consequently, as long as the fishermen participating in a certain fishery make a profit, new fishermen will be tempted to enter this fishery, which process will continue until the fishery is no longer profitable.[28] Thus, open access tends to result in the over-capitalisation of marine fisheries, *i.e.*, in a situation in which too much manpower and capital is applied to a specific fishery in relation to the amount of fish it produces. Problems of over-capitalisation may become particularly serious in free competition fisheries for fully exploited and over-exploited stocks.[29] In these fisheries States are forced to apply more and more manpower and capital for the sole purpose of maintaining their share in the overall catch. As a result, most such fisheries suffer from over-capitalisation. The North-East Atlantic fisheries are no exception. It has, for example, been estimated that in the cod and haddock fisheries of the North

Atlantic as a whole, substantially the same catch could be taken with about one-half to two-thirds of the present fishing effort.[30] Economic rationalisation could result in annual savings ranging from $50 million to $100 million.[31] Thus, legal arrangements applicable to the North-East Atlantic fisheries must assist in solving over-capitalisation problems. Such action is desirable not only for its own sake, but also because it would eliminate a major obstacle to more effective international co-operation in other problem areas of marine fisheries: nations are, for example, very reluctant to accept conservation measures if these measures would aggravate their over-capitalisation problems.[32] On the other hand, the North-East Atlantic fishing nations should not be forced to carry out their fishing operations with a minimum of manpower and capital. They might have other priorities—*e.g.*, the protection of employment opportunities—which do not conflict with the interests of other States. This provides another strong argument for national quota arrangements. Not only do they eliminate the confrontation among fishing nations with respect to the allocation of the catch, but they also enable nations to rationalise their fisheries economically without forcing them to do so: as a national quota arrangement essentially eliminates competition, each fishing nation can decide for itself how much fishing effort it wishes to apply for the purpose of catching its fixed share of the total catch.

It will be evident that international action with respect to the above problem areas requires a great deal of information, and that special arrangements may be necessary to make such information available. In the case of full utilisation and conservation problems, this refers particularly to biological data of an economic, legal and social nature. Such information enhances, first of all, the rationality[33] of regulatory decisions and, secondly, may increase their political acceptability.[34] If a certain measure is strongly supported by scientific evidence, nations will find it more difficult to resist its adoption. However, this acceptability effect depends to a large extent upon the impartiality of the scientific findings. If these findings are the result of research carried out by a certain State,[35] other nations may take the view that such findings reflect the specific interests of that State, and, as a result, they might not be willing to accept the regulatory implications of the scientific evidence.[36] Such problems can be avoided by organising research internationally.[37] If a neutral group of internationally recruited experts draws certain scientific conclusions from the available data base, no State can take the view that such conclusions reflect the partial interests of a specific nation. It appears that the urgent nature of the fishery problems of the North-East Atlantic makes it mandatory to adopt such procedures.

Obviously, the foregoing does not examine all questions facing the international law of marine fisheries in the North-East Atlantic Ocean. It does, for example, not deal with the enforcement of regulatory measures, with the avoidance of incidents among fishermen and with conflicts between marine fisheries and other ocean uses. Nevertheless, it provides a framework for reviewing the existing international legal arrangements applicable to the North-East Atlantic fisheries.

III. EXISTING ARRANGEMENTS

A great variety of international legal arrangements is concerned with the problems of the North-East Atlantic fisheries as outlined above.[38] Generally speaking, they fall within two broad categories: (1) non-institutionalised arrangements; and (2) institutionalised arrangements. Examples of non-institutionalised arrangements are: (1) the European Fisheries Convention of London 1964, which deals primarily with exclusive fishery limits and, thus, with matters of allocation[39]; (2) agreements concerning claims in connection with damage to fishing gear[40]; and (3) the Convention on Conduct of Fishing Operations in the North Atlantic of London 1967.[41] Institutionalised arrangements are: (1) the International Council for the Exploration of the Sea; (2) the North-East Atlantic Fisheries Commission; and (3) such broader organisations as the European Economic Community and the Organisation for Economic Co-operation and Development. The following sections will review these organisations in more detail.

The International Council for the Exploration of the Sea was established in 1902 and is the oldest international fisheries organisation.[42] Although its Statutes have been changed from time to time, the Council's main function throughout its existence has been to encourage and co-ordinate the scientific investigations of its member States; only occasionally did it conduct its own investigations. In order to formalise the status of the Council, a new Convention was signed in 1964, which entered into force in July 1968.[43] The present members of ICES are: Belgium, Canada, Denmark, the Federal Republic of Germany, Finland, France, Iceland, Ireland, Italy, the Netherlands, Norway, Poland, Portugal, Spain, Sweden, the United Kingdom and the U.S.S.R.[44] Under the new Convention the functions of the Council are: (1) to promote research for the study of the sea, particularly with respect to the sea's living resources; (2) to draw up research programmes; and (3) to publish the results. These functions must be carried out in the Atlantic Ocean and especially in the North Atlantic. The International Council conducts its business through a number of committees and working groups; at present there are 12 standing committees, each of which deals with a specific area or with a specific topic. A Consultative Committee co-ordinates their activities. In addition to its committee structure, ICES has a Bureau with certain executive functions and a Secretariat with about 18 full-time officials. Apart from co-ordinating the research work of its member States, the Council's main activities are: (1) the collection and publication of hydrographic data; (2) the standardisation of research methods; (3) the collection and publication of statistical information concerning the fisheries of the member States; and (4) the publication of a wide variety of studies. It is generally agreed that within its terms of reference the International Council has been a most successful organisation. It has drawn a great number of marine scientists into its work, which has been instrumental in bringing about effective international co-operation among the member States. Through its relationship with the North-East Atlantic Fisheries Commission, ICES has also made an indirect, but substantial, contribution towards the regulation of the fisheries of the North-East Atlantic. Thus, it appears that the International Council essentially solves the problems of scientific research as outlined in the previous section. Most important, it screens the data collected by the member States and places the impartiality of the scientific findings above question. Nevertheless, there are a few problems. First of all, ICES restricts its work primarily to biological and oceanographical investigations. Consequently, it does not provide all the economic, legal and social information required for the international regulation of marine fisheries. However, although it would be a break with tradition, its terms of reference do not seem to prevent the Council from carrying out such studies. Other difficulties may arise from the fact that it is necessary to adjust the work of the Council to the informational needs of the North-East Atlantic Fisheries Commission. Although a special ICES liaison committee is quite effective in this respect, it remains questionable whether the rather complex ICES–NEAFC structure is the most efficient solution to the problem of providing the information upon which North-East Atlantic fisheries regulation depends.

In April 1946 the fishing nations of Northern Europe signed a convention for the purpose of restricting the catch of young and immature fish.[45] A Permanent Commission was created whose main function was to keep the provisions of the Convention up to date. Largely because the 1946 Convention proved to be an impediment to the development of fisheries for smaller species, it was replaced in 1959 with the North-East Atlantic Fisheries Convention. This Convention established the North-East Atlantic Fisheries Commission.[46] Its present members are: Belgium, Denmark, France, the Federal Republic of Germany, Iceland, Ireland, the Netherlands, Norway, Poland, Portugal, Spain, Sweden, the United Kingdom and the U.S.S.R. Unlike ICES, the North-East Atlantic Fisheries Commission is a body with regulatory functions: it is responsible for making recommendations to the member States for the purpose of achieving a " rational exploitation " of the fisheries in the North-East Atlantic Ocean. These recommendations, which are based upon the scientific advice of the International Council, may provide for a variety of conservation measures. Most regulations adopted under NEAFC continue to be concerned with minimum mesh sizes and minimum fish sizes. These measures undoubtedly contributed to the consistently high yields of several North-East Atlantic stocks. On the other hand, the North-East Atlantic Fisheries Commission has been unable to prevent the overfishing of all species for which it is responsible[47] and, as a result, some stocks of the North-East Atlantic Ocean have been seriously depleted. A most important reason for NEAFC's ineffectiveness lies in the political unwillingness of its member States to accept strict conservation measures, but some responsibility can be traced back to its terms of reference. The general objective of its recommendations—to achieve a rational exploitation of the stocks of fish of the North-East Atlantic—has been formulated broadly enough to allow the Commission to deal with all five problem areas outlined in section II. In this respect NEAFC is in a better position than those regional fisheries commissions that are explicitly restricted to the single objective of achieving a maximum sustainable yield. However, NEAFC's powers are not proportionate to the scope of its objectives: the original Convention did not grant the Commission the power to make recommendations concerning measures for regulating the total amount of the catch or the total amount of fishing effort and their allocation among fishing nations.[48] This severely limited the effectiveness of the Commission in matters of conservation and made it virtually impossible to deal with questions of allocation and economic efficiency. However, the Commission has recently taken steps to enhance its authority by invoking a provision in the Convention authorising it to request additional powers, provided that a proposal to that effect is adopted by a two-thirds majority vote.[49] At its eighth meeting NEAFC adopted a resolution in which it requested its member States to grant it the authority to make recommendations concerning the regulation of the total catch, the total fishing effort and their allocation among the member States.[50] In addition, its constitutional limitations have not prevented the Commission from discussing matters of allocation and economic efficiency. This contributed to agreement on national quota arrangements outside the Commission.[51] If the amendment of its constitution becomes effective, such quota arrangements could be recommended by NEAFC itself. This could make the North-East Atlantic Fisheries Commission more effective not only with respect to the problems of allocation and economic efficiency, but also with respect to conservation. A remaining difficulty is that NEAFC's dependence upon ICES in scientific matters implies that it lacks adequate economic, social and legal advice in respect of allocation and economic efficiency.

Several other specialised fisheries bodies are concerned with the North-East Atlantic Ocean and its adjacent seas.[52] Generally speaking, they follow the general pattern of the ICES–NEAFC complex: they are responsible for making recommendations to member States for the purpose of promoting and co-ordinating scientific research or for the purpose of adopting conservation measures. Apart from such fishery bodies, there are other, more general, organisations which are either directly or indirectly concerned with the North-East Atlantic fisheries.[53] The Common Fisheries Policy[54] of the European Economic Community has major implications in this respect, although its primary purpose is to set up a system of price controls. However, since marine fisheries are a commercial activity, such price-related measures have a direct impact on the utilisation of the resources. More important, the Common Fisheries Policy also provides for a reciprocal right of free access to exclusive fishery waters by the fishermen of the member States. In the negotiations concerning the entry of Denmark, Ireland and the United Kingdom into the Common Market this proved to be a difficult issue. It has been resolved by an agreement providing for a transitional period in which member States may reserve fisheries in a specified zone for their own fishermen; after the expiration of this period, the EEC Council will examine the arrangements to follow the temporary derogations from the Common Fisheries Policy. Although these Common Market actions are extremely important, it must be kept in mind that such major North-East Atlantic fishing nations as Norway, the U.S.S.R., Spain, Sweden, Portugal and Poland do not participate in them. Therefore, there will remain a need for special fisheries organisations whose membership is larger than that of the Common Market.

Without implying that the above discussion of existing arrangements is complete, the question must be asked of how effective they are in coping with the problems of the North-East Atlantic fisheries. It has already been mentioned that several stocks have been depleted, that only a few allocation agreements exist, and that many fisheries continue to suffer from severe over-capitalisation problems. Thus, the conclusion must be drawn that existing arrangements have not been very successful, except in the area of research. However, the essential question is whether this ineffectiveness is due to these arrangements themselves or to the wider context within which they function. More specifically: are the shortcomings of the North-East Atlantic Fisheries Commission due to factors within its control or to factors outside its control? Apart from a politically motivated unwillingness of the members to make concessions, it seems that there is at least one other factor beyond the Commission's control that is directly at the root of its problems: the freedom of fishing on the high seas. Freedom of fishing has essentially three basic characteristics: (1) all States have a right of free and unrestricted access to the living resources of the high seas; (2) the only way in which States can share in the wealth of these resources is by participating in marine fisheries; and (3) the living resources of the high seas are not subject to formal ownership until they have been captured. In evaluating the implications of these characteristics for the North-East Atlantic, the most fundamental fact is that virtually all stocks in this area are subject to exploitation at or above the level of their maximum sustainable yield. A first point is that, in this case, free and unrestricted access to the resources does not serve the interests of full utilisation: new States entering the fisheries of the North-East Atlantic do not increase the productivity of its fully exploited stocks. Secondly, since, under the freedom of fishing, outsiders can reap the benefits from conservation measures adopted by the North-East Atlantic fishing States, it is not very attractive for these States to accept such measures; freedom of fishing does not guarantee that they will be the only ones to benefit if a stock recovers as a result of the conservation measures they have accepted. Thirdly, freedom of fishing is also a major reason why the North-East Atlantic fisheries suffer from all the problems associated with allocation on the basis of free competition. It is difficult for the States participating in the fisheries of this region to accept a national quota agreement that restricts their catches to a very specific level as long as outsiders can freely enter the fisheries to which such an agreement applies. Although some national quota arrangements contain special provisions for the purpose of dealing with this question,[55] the fact remains that the problem of new entrants is the single most serious obstacle to international agreement concerning national quotas. Freedom of fishing has also another implication with respect to allocation: if a State wishes to share in the wealth of a stock it has no choice but to engage in the fisheries for that stock. Freedom of fishing fully assimilates the allocation of the wealth of the sea's living resources with the allocation of the catch; a State's share in the wealth is a function of its share in the catch.[56] Obviously, this also complicates reaching agreement on national quotas for the North-East Atlantic fisheries since it makes it difficult for outsider States to give up their right to enter these fisheries. Fourthly, the above suggests that freedom of fishing is also at the basis of the over-capitalisation problems of the North-East Atlantic, primarily because it is incompatible with limitations upon entry into marine fisheries. Thus, the conclusion must be that if existing arrangements have not been able to cope with the problems of the North-East Atlantic fisheries, such ineffectiveness is not only the result of their own shortcomings, but also of the fact that the freedom of fishing on the high seas is a liability, rather than an asset, in regulating the fisheries for the fully exploited stocks of the North-East Atlantic Ocean. Freedom of fishing is directly responsible for the inadequate and piecemeal fashion in which existing arrangements attempt to solve the problems of the North-East Atlantic fisheries.

IV. ALTERNATIVES

Essentially, there are two basic alternatives for changing the legal arrangements applicable to the North-East Atlantic fisheries: (1) more authority could be given to the coastal States of the region; or (2) the international organisations and agreements of the region could be made to function more effectively. Each basic alternative has a number of different variations.

The most extreme form of the first alternative would occur if coastal States were to divide up the waters of the North-East Atlantic and their resources among themselves.[57] Less extreme variations would involve an extension of certain coastal State regulatory controls to a wider distance from the coast or internationally agreed upon coastal State preferential rights with respect to certain stocks of fish in the waters of the high seas adjacent to that coastal State's exclusive fishery waters.[58] However, the most vital questions concern the effects of a possible extension of the exclusive fishery rights of the North-East Atlantic coastal States. A first aspect of such action is that coastal States may act more effectively with respect to the conservation of the area's living resources than international organisations. Conservation measures would no longer depend upon the ability to reach agreement among all States participating in the North-East Atlantic fisheries, but could be enacted under the coercive powers of the coastal States.[59] In addition, since a coastal State would have exclusive rights over its offshore living resources, it would be in its self-interest to protect these resources. Secondly, extending the exclusive rights of coastal States would also establish the conditions for rationalising fishing operations economically: on the basis of their exclusive rights coastal States could regulate access to the fisheries in order to match fishing effort with catch. Thirdly, an extension of exclusive fishery rights would also eliminate most of the allocation problems of coastal States. Their fishermen are often dependent upon particular species, either because they lack the equipment to exploit other stocks, or because they do not have a market for such other stocks.[60] An extension of coastal State exclusive fishery rights would enable a coastal State to protect these special allocation interests of its fishermen. On the other hand, an extension of exclusive fishery rights would have several disadvantages. First of all, coastal State fishermen usually do not exploit all resources in their offshore waters. Thus, unless special arrangements were made that would allow foreign fishermen to continue to exploit stocks not, or not fully, exploited by the coastal States' fishermen, an extension of exclusive fishery rights could very well have an adverse effect from the point of view of full utilisation.[61] It could be difficult for coastal States to accept such special arrangements since they would conflict with the very reason why a coastal State wishes to extend its jurisdiction, *i.e.*, to eliminate foreign fishing. Secondly, there is no *a priori* guarantee that coastal States would act more effectively with respect to conservation than international organisations. If in the past coastal States were able to adopt conservation measures independently from other nations, they have often been as ineffective as international fisheries commissions.[62] Moreover, some species would migrate beyond the limits of the area in which a coastal State would have its extended exclusive rights, which suggests that international co-operation would remain a necessity.[63] Thirdly, although an extension would create the conditions for economic rationalisation, it is doubtful whether coastal States would use this opportunity: most coastal States have demonstrated little inclination to take such action regarding the fisheries that are presently subject to their exclusive rights.[64] Finally, even with respect to allocation it is doubtful whether extending exclusive fishery limits would be a panacea for all the problems of coastal States. For example, many coastal States consider the present allocation of salmon unacceptable. But the highly migratory characteristics of this species [65] make it unlikely that an extension of exclusive fishery limits could solve this problem, unless such action were to extend to an unrealistically large area. Finally, since in many respects it is the most drastic option, an extension of coastal State exclusive fishery rights will lead to a maximum of conflict among all States concerned.

The above observations regarding an extension of coastal State exclusive rights apply *mutatis mutandis* to the other variations of the first basic alternative. Granting coastal States additional [66] powers with regard to the conservation of the living resources in the waters of the high seas adjacent to their coast would, for example, be of the same questionable effectiveness with respect to conservation as an extension of their exclusive fishery rights. Moreover, it would fail to deal with the more urgent dissatisfaction of coastal States in the area of allocation. Coastal State preferential rights over certain high seas stocks, on the other hand, could eliminate a coastal State's specific allocation problems, but they would have little effect on questions of conservation and economic efficiency.

The second basic alternative—improving the effectiveness of international arrangements—also presents a range of options. For example, the request of the North-East Atlantic Fisheries Commission for additional powers with respect to total and national quotas falls within this category—but so do proposals for a world wide organisation with full authority over all living resources of the sea.[67] However, the most important aspects of this alternative can be clarified by reference to a special fisheries organisation that would have full authority over all the living resources of the North-East Atlantic.[68]

A North-East Atlantic fisheries body with such authority could, first of all, be responsible for ensuring the fullest possible and desirable use of the resources. It could have at its disposal the required knowledge and the technological means, while its exclusive rights over the stocks would constitute a strong incentive for utilising them as fully as possible.[69] Secondly, such an organisation could adopt and enforce all necessary conservation measures: its forcible powers would replace a variety of commissions dependent upon the voluntary co-operation of States. Thirdly, with regard to allocation, the organisation could ensure that all States of the region would share equitably in the wealth of the fish stocks of the North-East Atlantic, if not in the fisheries themselves. However, even more important, the organisation would be capable of solving the economic efficiency problems of the North-East Atlantic fisheries. It could, for example, operate these fisheries itself and buy the necessary manpower and capital in the cheapest market, while selling the fishery products in the dearest market. The organisation's profit could be redistributed among the States of the region. Alternatively, it could auction off the right to fish in the North-East Atlantic to the highest bidders; revenues could again be redistributed.[70] In a more modest approach the organisation would issue licences either to States or to fishing companies and thus restrict the waste of manpower and capital. On the other hand, a North-East Atlantic fisheries organisation with full authority over the living resources of that region would also have several disadvantages. First of all, since it would operate on the basis of economic rationality, the organisation would most probably limit fishing to the level at which it would maximise profits, rather than to the level at which it would maximise the catch.[71] Although, as a group, the States of the region do not suffer from problems of malnutrition, the resulting reduction of the area's catch appears to be undesirable, particularly in view of the fact that the world community as a whole has a shortage of animal protein. Secondly, a number of questions may be raised with regard to the most important justification for the organisation, *i.e.*, the fact that it could ensure the economic efficiency of fishing operations.[72] As has been stated, nations may have priorities other than carrying out marine fisheries with a minimum of manpower and capital, *e.g.*, the protection of employment opportunities. Thirdly, the organisation's goal of maximising profits could lead to a situation in which the poorest nations, or parts of nations, carry out all the fishing operations of the North-East Atlantic, while only the richest nations, or parts of nations, can afford to buy the fish they produce. This would certainly be an undesirable way of allocating the living resources of the North-East Atlantic Ocean. Other problems may arise in connection with the fact that the organisation—even though it would have full authority—would be regional in scope.[73] This leads to such questions as: what are the States of the region? Only coastal States or also States which have traditionally fished in the North-East Atlantic? Who shares in the revenues generated by the organisation? Only the member States or also the other States of the world community? However, the most fundamental difficulty of such an organisation appears to be that its creation would constitute a radical departure from existing international structures—a departure for which the world community does not seem to be prepared, not even on a regional basis. The establishment of an organisation with full authority over all living resources of the North-East Atlantic must be deemed beyond present political realities.[74]

Other variations of the second basic alternative may be politically more feasible. This applies in particular to the strengthening of the existing regional fisheries organisations of the North-East Atlantic Ocean. Recent developments in the North-East Atlantic Fisheries Commission support this point of view. Gradual improvements in existing international arrangements also offer the advantage that no proposals are implemented that may be sound in theory, but that would fail the ultimate test of reality.

A choice between the above two basic alternatives is extremely difficult, largely because of the fact that the ultimate outcome of either alternative is a secret of the future. Nevertheless, the nations participating in the North-East Atlantic fisheries have come to a juncture in time at which they must decide whether they will attempt to solve the problems of these fisheries by enhancing the authority of coastal States or by making international arrangements more effective. The fishery-related aspects of this choice have been briefly discussed in the foregoing. It appears that they generally favour the second alternative, provided that international arrangements can be made responsive to the special allocation problems of coastal States. Internationally agreed upon coastal State preferential rights could accomplish this. A choice in favour of international solutions is also suggested by non-fishery related considerations. In a period in which in other areas the nations of the North-East Atlantic region are gradually moving in the direction of a larger role for international structures,[75] it would be a lost opportunity if fishery problems were to be dealt with along strictly national lines. The interdependence of the States of the region has progressed to such a point that exclusive reliance upon coastal State based solutions appears to conflict with reality. However, regardless of the fishery and non-fishery arguments in favour of international solutions, there is one fundamental factor that supports the first basic alternative: enhancing the powers of coastal States can be achieved not only by international agreement, but also through the growth of customary law initiated by the unilateral action of these States. International solutions, on the other hand, depend upon agreement among the States concerned—and States will accept such agreements only if they deem this in their self-interest. The final observations of the preceding section suggest that under the freedom of fishing on the high seas it is not in the self-interest of the North-East Atlantic fishing nations to choose international solutions. Thus, enhancing the effectiveness of the international arrangements applicable to the North-East Atlantic fisheries requires more than anything else changes in the concept of freedom of fishing on the high seas.[76]

V. SOME SUGGESTIONS FOR FUTURE ARRANGEMENTS

It seems that most problems of the North-East Atlantic fisheries could be accommodated in a future régime that would be based upon two interrelated distinctions: (1) in order to recognise differences in the fishing activities of nations, future arrangements could make a distinction between coastal State fisheries and common fisheries; and (2) in order to recognise differences in the condition of stocks, such future arrangements could make a distinction between fisheries for under-exploited, fully exploited and over-exploited stocks.[77]

Coastal fisheries would be fisheries for stocks over which a coastal State would have either exclusive rights or internationally agreed upon preferential rights. If a future régime for the North-East Atlantic accepted preferential rights, it could attempt to prevent a further extension of coastal State exclusive fishery rights beyond their present limits—whatever those present limits may be. Generally, preferential rights would give the fisherman of the coastal State a certain preference over distant water State fishermen. This could be a higher share in a national quota scheme; it could be an exclusive right to use certain fishing grounds during a specified period; it could be the right to use a particular kind of gear that non-coastal fishermen would not be allowed to use, etc. Any arrangement that would be capable of solving the special allocation problems of a coastal State in a manner acceptable [78] to distant water fishing States could serve as a preferential rights arrangement. However, all such schemes could have a few essential characteristics. First of all, coastal States would acquire preferential rights only if certain internationally agreed upon criteria were to justify these rights. These criteria could refer to the dependence of coastal State fishermen upon specific stocks; the dependence of a coastal State upon marine fisheries in general; its past record with respect to conservation; the proximity of stocks to the coast and their migratory patterns; etc. If, under these criteria, a coastal State were to have a prima facie case for preferential rights, future arrangements could make international negotiations among the States concerned mandatory. These negotiations could take place with the North-East Atlantic Fisheries Commission. If they should fail, the States in question or the Commission itself could submit the dispute to arbitration by a group of qualified fishery experts and lawyers. A second basic characteristic of coastal State preferential rights could be that coastal States would enjoy such rights as agents of those States which originally granted them. This would reflect the fact that coastal State preferential rights would apply to a high seas resource of the North-East Atlantic, *i.e.*, a resource which in principle may be harvested by other nations. This agent status of coastal States could have a number of consequences. For example, the international agreement granting the preferential rights could require a coastal State to regulate its preferential right fisheries in a certain way, particularly with respect to conservation. Moreover, coastal States could be required to report on their preferential right fisheries to the North-East Atlantic Fisheries Commission, which would expose their activities to the scrutiny of the other member nations. Finally, a last basic characteristic of any preferential rights scheme could be that since such rights would be justified only under certain conditions, it would be necessary to determine from time to time whether or not these conditions still prevailed. Accordingly, the original agreement would have to be renegotiated periodically.

Such preferential right arrangements would not be a radical departure from present practice. For example, the recommendations of the North-East Atlantic Fisheries Commission concerning restrictions on high seas salmon fisheries may contribute to defining the critieria that would justify coastal State preferential rights *vis-à-vis* this species. Another example may be found in the special arrangements concerning access to exclusive fishery waters that will apply during a transitional period among the member States of the European Economic Community. It is suggested that such developments indicate the direction that should be taken in elaborating future arrangements for the North-East Atlantic fisheries.

Reaching agreement on coastal State preferential rights could be easier if future arrangements were also to accept distant water fishing State preferential rights. However, as distant water fishermen are not very dependent upon specific fisheries, there appears to be less justification for such rights. Nevertheless, it is conceivable that a distant water fishing country has developed certain fisheries by its own efforts and that only its fishermen have harvested the stocks in question. In this case there might be justification for distant water fishing State preferential rights. Moreover, since negotiations concerning preferential rights would usually take place between distant water fishing States and coastal States, accepting distant water fishing State preferential rights, as well as coastal State preferential rights would greatly increase the possibilities for trade-offs between these two categories of States.

It has been stressed that preferential rights would be justified only under specific conditions. Thus, a considerable number of stocks would not be subject to such rights. The fisheries for these stocks would be common fisheries, *i.e.*, fisheries in which a number of North-East Atlantic fishing States participate on an equal footing. In such common fisheries the condition of the stocks could be a major element in determining future legal arrangements. As far as common fisheries for under-exploited stocks would be concerned, these legal arrangements could leave the freedom of fishing on the high seas essentially uncompromised. Accordingly, any interested State would have a right of free and unrestricted access to the fisheries for such under-exploited stocks, which would be in the interest of full utilisation. However, as has been mentioned, most North-East Atlantic stocks are already subject to full exploitation or even over-exploitation. The conclusion of sections III and IV was that freedom of fishing has become a fundamental obstacle to a more effective international regulation of the fisheries for such stocks. Thus, a future legal régime applicable to common fisheries for fully exploited North-East Atlantic stocks would have to transform the freedom of fishing, and particularly open access. This could be accomplished by restricting access to those States that had participated in such common fisheries for fully exploited stocks during a certain base period. This would close access on the basis of the past record of fishing States, which would ensure that States could reap the benefits from their efforts in developing certain fisheries. However, the most fundamental advantage of closing access to fisheries for fully exploited stocks would be that *as a group* States with a right of access would have an exclusive title to the stock or stocks in question. Thus, it would be in their self-interest to regulate the fisheries in such a way that they would maximise their benefits. This would apply to conservation measures, as well as to questions of allocation, economic efficiency and research.

North-East Atlantic fishing States with a right of access to common fisheries for fully exploited stocks would not only acquire additional rights, but additional responsibilities as well. First of all, States with such a right of access could be required to transfer this right to other interested States if they were no longer to use it or if they were no longer to fully participate in the fisheries to which the right in question referred. Such a requirement would prevent the degree of utilisation of a stock dropping as a result of States keeping a right of access without fully using it. Secondly, States with a right of access to common fisheries could be required to adopt all the necessary regulatory measures. This obligation would reflect the fact that they—like coastal States in preferential right fisheries—would be agents of the other States of the region or even of the world community as a whole. In order to expose their actions to the scrutiny of other nations, these States could be required to report to the North-East Atlantic Fisheries Commission on the regulations adopted by them. In the case of over-exploited stocks they could be required to take measures for the purpose of rebuilding those stocks to their former level of abundance, unless a stock had been deliberately over-exploited for the purpose of increasing the productivity of a more desirable species. This obligation of rational regulation would refer in particular to conservation; as far as questions of economic efficiency and allocation are concerned fishing States could have more freedom to act in accordance with their own priorities.[79] They could also be obliged to carry out all necessary investigations. A third and more substantial obligation of States with a right of access to the common fisheries of the North-East Atlantic could involve certain financial requirements. One characteristic of the present freedom of fishing is that it enables all States to share in the wealth of the sea's living resources by allowing them to participate in marine fisheries. Thus, if future arrangements for the North-East Atlantic were to close access to the fisheries, these arrangements could incorporate special provisions for the purpose of enabling nations to share in the wealth of the stocks of this area in return for losing the right to fish for them. A levy system could accomplish this. Essentially, it would require that States with a right of access to specific fisheries pay levies which would be made available to States without such a right. Levies could be proportionate to a variety of factors, but probably the most direct solution would be to set them as a percentage of the dockside value of the catch of each nation. Revenues could be redistributed on the basis of a formula which would give the largest shares to the States with the smallest catches in the North-East Atlantic. However, there is one important difficulty in establishing such a levy system for that region alone: it is clear which States should pay the levies,[80] but it is less evident which States must share in the revenues. The answer to this last question depends upon the answer to the question of who owns the living resources of the North-East Atlantic. If the answer were that these resources belong to the States of the region, those States only should share in the revenues from the levies. But if the answer were that these resources belong to the world community as a whole, all nations of the world should share in these revenues. A practical reason for supporting the second alternative is that with the present mobility of fishing vessels even distant States are capable of entering the North-East Atlantic fisheries.[81] Thus, if a levy system were confined to the States of the region only, non-region States would continue to pose the threat of new entrants.

The above suggests, in outline form at least, some essential elements of a future legal régime for the North-East Atlantic fisheries that might be able to cope better with the problems of these fisheries than existing arrangements. Such a future régime will not come about as a result of a single act, but rather as the result of a process of informal growth characterised not only by success and agreement, but also by failure and conflict. One of the most important instruments for making desirable changes in existing arrangements could be the North-East Atlantic Fisheries Commission. It could, for example, impose levies on fisheries for fully exploited stocks, provided that no new States entered the fisheries concerned. This could give the States fishing for such stocks a *de facto* right of exclusive access, which could be a basis for more effective regulatory measures. Revenues could be used for generally acceptable purposes. However, like any other international organisation, the North-East Atlantic Fisheries Commission is dependent upon the co-operation of its member States. Thus, in the final analysis, the responsibility of creating more satisfactory international legal arrangements for the fisheries of the North-East Atlantic Ocean rests in the hands of those persons who determine the courses of action of States.

REFERENCES

1. This corresponds with the ICES statistical area; see FAO, *The Fish Resources of the Ocean*, J. A. Gulland (ed.), FAO Fisheries Technical Paper No. 97 (Rome, 1970), p. 23.

2. FAO, *Yearbook of Fishery Statistics 1970* (Rome, 1971), p. 436.

3. FAO, *op. cit.* n. 1, p. 41.

4. FAO, *op. cit.* n. 2, p. 450.

5. For a more general analysis, see A. W. Koers, *The International Regulation of Marine Fisheries. A Study of Regional Fisheries Organisations* (London: Fishing Books Ltd., 1973).

6. FAO, *op. cit.* n. 2, pp. 4–5; 1970 salt water catches amounted to about 60 million tons.

7. Japan and the Soviet Union, two of the most active distant water fishing nations, expanded their catches in the period 1948–70 respectively from 2·5 to 9·3 and from 1·5 to 7·2 million tons annually; of all coastal fishing countries only Peru achieved a similar rate of growth: from 0·8 in 1948 to 12·6 million tons in 1970; see FAO, *op. cit.* n. 2, pp. 4–11.

8. FAO, *The Prospects of World Fishery Development in 1975 and 1985*, FAO Fisheries Circular No. 118 (Rome, 1969), p. 8.

9. C. P. Idyll, *The Sea against Hunger* (New York, 1970).

10. See the table in FAO, *op. cit.* n. 1, p. 41.

11. Art. 2 of the 1958 Geneva Convention on Fishing and Conservation of the Living Resources of the High Seas, 559 U.N.T.S. 286, defines " conservation of the living resources of the high seas " as " the aggregate of the measures rendering possible the optimum sustainable yield from those resources so as to secure a maximum supply of food and other marine products "; it is generally understood that " optimum sustainable yield " stands for " maximum sustainable yield."

12. J. A. Gulland, *The Concept of the Maximum Sustainable Yield and Fishery Management*, FAO Fisheries Technical Paper No. 70 (Rome, 1968).

13. FAO, *The Management of Fishery Resources* (Rome, 1967), pp. 14–15.

14. *Ibid.* p. 23.

15. In most fisheries the fishermen go bankrupt before the fish; see W. M. Chapman, " Fishery Resources in Offshore Waters," in L. M. Alexander (ed.), *Offshore Boundaries and Zones* (Kingston, R.I. 1967), p. 102.

16. An exception may occur if other species take over the ecological niche occupied by the over-fished stock; this may have been the case with the California sardines which did not recover from over-exploitation; see FAO, *op. cit.* n. 13, p. 7.

17. Reproduced in FAO, *op. cit.* n. 13, p. 2; see also p. 6.

18. See n. 7.

19. A comparison of the total catch figures of developing States and developed States would give the misleading impression that the catch of developing States has grown more rapidly than the catch of developed States; however, most of the increase in the catch of developing States must be attributed to a single State, *i.e.*, Peru; the total share of all other developing States remained about the same; see F. T. Christy, Jr., " Fisheries and the New Conventions on the Law of the Sea " (1970) *San Diego Law Review* 464–465.

20. S. Oda, " Distribution of Fish Resources of the High Seas: Free Competition or Artificial Quotas?," in L. M. Alexander (ed.), *The Future of the Sea's Resources* (Kingston, R.I., 1968), pp. 29–32.

21. J. A. Crutchfield, " National Quotas for the North Atlantic Fisheries: An Exercise in Second Best," in L. M. Alexander (ed.), *International Rules and Organisation for the Sea* (Kingston, R.I., 1969), pp. 263–275.

22. J. A. Gulland, *Fisheries Management and the Limitation of Fishing*, FAO Fisheries Technical Paper No. 92 (Rome, 1969), pp. 13–15.

23. Implicitly incorporated in the 1958 Geneva Convention on Fishing and Conservation of the Living Resources of the High Seas.

24. If stocks are not fully exploited, nations are capable of expanding their catches without endangering the resources.

25. Communist countries, for example, may be an exception.

26. These dual objectives of marine fisheries have been the object of an exhaustive discussion between biologists and economists, biologists insisting that the objective of international fisheries regulation should be to maximise the food production from the ocean (maximum sustainable yield), and economists insisting that its objective should be to maximise the economic returns from marine fisheries (maximum economic yield); see, *e.g.*, W. M. Chapman, " The Theory and Practice of International Fishery Development-Management " (1970) *San Diego Law Review*, 412–413; F. T. Christy, Jr., " The Distribution of the Sea's Wealth in Fisheries," in L. M. Alexander (ed.), *Offshore Boundaries and Zones* (Kingston, R.I., 1967), pp. 106–122. In reality both concepts seem to be less mutually exclusive than their theoretical extremes may suggest.

27. Christy, *op. cit.* n. 26. F. T. Christy, Jr., and A. Scott, *The Common Wealth in Ocean Fisheries. Some Problems of Growth and Economic Allocation* (Baltimore, 1965), pp. 6–17; H. S. Gordon, " The Economic Theory of a Common Property Resource: the Fishery " (1954) *Journal of Political Economy*, 124–142.

28. Christy, *op. cit.* n. 26, p. 112.

29. For a detailed study of the over-capitalisation of a specific fishery, see J. A. Crutchfield and G. Pontecorvo, *The Pacific Salmon Fisheries. A Study of Irrational Conservation* (Baltimore, 1969).

30. FAO, *op. cit.* n. 13, p. 6.

31. International Commission for the Northwest Atlantic Fisheries, *Annual Proceedings for the year 1966–1967* (Dartmouth, 1968), p. 56.

32. If there is one single reason for the failure of the International Whaling Commission, it was the unwillingness of the Antarctic whaling nations to endanger the investment in whaling fleets by limiting catches.

33. FAO, *op. cit.* n. 13, p. 3.

34. Chapman, *op. cit.* n. 26, p. 446.

35. Most international fisheries commissions depend upon the investigations of their member States; in this case the major guarantee for the impartiality of the scientific evidence presented to the commission lies in the integrity of the scientists involved.

36. This has occurred in the International Whaling Commission; a special Committee of Three Scientists from non-Antarctic whaling countries was needed to establish the scientific facts in an unquestionable manner; see International Whaling Commission, *Twelfth Report of the Commission* (London, 1961), p. 16.

37. The International Pacific Salmon Fisheries Commission, the International Pacific Halibut Commission and the Inter-American Tropical Tuna Commission are the only international fisheries organisations with an independent international research staff.

38. Obviously, *national* legal arrangements are concerned with the same problems.

39. (1964) 3 Int.Leg.Mat. 476.

40. An example is the Agreement Concerning the Handling of Claims in Connection with Damage to Fishing Gear which was signed by Norway and the U.S.S.R. on Dec. 9, 1959, at Moscow, 361 U.N.T.S. 93.

41. (1967) 6 Int.Leg.Mat. 760.

42. For more information, see C. E. Lucas, *International Fishery Bodies of the North Atlantic*, Law of the Sea Institute, University of Rhode Island, Occasional Paper No. 5, April 1970, pp. 2–13. United Nations Economic and Social Council, *Non-United Nations Intergovernmental Organisations*, UN Doc.E/4487, annex XII, Apr. 24, 1968, pp. 2–10. FAO, *International Fisheries Bodies*, FAO Fisheries Technical Paper No. 64 (Rome, 1966), p. 18; M. K. Whiteman, *Digest of International Law*, Vol. 4 (Washington, DC, 1965), pp. 1070–1072.

43. (1968) 7 Int.Leg.Mat. 302.

44. *I.e.*, all States substantially engaged in the North-East Atlantic fisheries.

45. Convention for the Regulation of the Meshes of Fishing Nets and the Size Limits of Fish, 231 U.N.T.S. 200.

46. 486 U.N.T.S. 158. The convention entered into force in June 1963. For more information on the Commission, see Lucas, *op. cit.* n. 42, pp. 13–18.

47. North-East Atlantic Fisheries Commission, *Report of the Ninth Meeting* (London, 1971), pp. 1–10.

48. Art. 7, para. 1.

49. Art. 7, para. 2.

50. North-East Atlantic Fisheries Commission, *Report of the Eighth Meeting* (London, 1970), p. 12.

51. *E.g.*, with respect to the Atlanto-Scandian herring; see North-East Atlantic Fisheries Commission, *Report of the Ninth Meeting* (London, 1971), p. 17. Other agreements are being negotiated.

52. *E.g.*, the Sealing Commission for the North-East Atlantic and the Shellfish Commission for the Skagerrak-Kattegat.

53. *E.g.*, FAO, OECD and the EEC.

54. *Journal Officiel des Communautés européennes*, L 236.1, Oct. 27, 1970.

55. Usually, such arrangements set aside a certain percentage of the total allowance catch for new entrants; the rest is divided among the established fishing nations.

56. Christy, *op. cit.* n. 26, p. 112.

57. By extending, as from Sept. 1, 1972, its exclusive fishery limits to 50 miles from its coast, Iceland is making an important step in this direction: see Ministry for Foreign Affairs of Iceland, *Fisheries Jurisdiction in Iceland* (Reykjavik, 1972). Much will depend upon the proceedings instituted by the United Kingdom and the Federal Republic of Germany against Iceland before the International Court of Justice. The Court issued Interim Measures of Protection on Aug. 17, 1972.

58. An example of an extension of coastal State regulatory controls may be found in Art. 7 of the 1958 Geneva Convention on Fishing and Conservation of the Living Resources

of the High Seas, 559 U.N.T.S. 286. An example of internationally agreed upon preferential rights can be found in the Agreement on Certain Fishery Problems on the High Seas in the Western Areas of the Middle Atlantic which was originally signed in Nov. 1967 and which has been renewed annually, (1968) 7 Int.Leg.Mat. 144; this Agreement gives U.S. coastal fishermen certain preferences over Soviet fishermen in specific high seas fisheries off the American coast.

59. W. C. Herrington, "The Convention on Fisheries and Conservation of Living Resources: accomplishments of the 1958 Geneva Conference," in L. M. Alexander (ed.), *Offshore Boundaries and Zones* (Kingston, R.I., 1967), p. 32.

60. The result is that coastal State fishermen are less flexible than distant water fishermen who can easily move from stock to stock.

61. Chapman, *op. cit.* n. 15, p. 104.

62. W. M. Chapman, *Some Problems and Prospects for the Harvest of Living Marine Resources to the Year 2000*, paper at a meeting of experts at UNITAR, Feb. 25–27, 1970, p. 38.

63. Chapman, *op. cit.* n. 15, p. 96.

64. R. W. Johnson, "State and Federal Laws which retard High Seas Fishing Development," in *Transactions of the Second Annual Marine Technology Society Conference and Exhibit* (supplement), June 27–29, 1966.

65. Pacific salmon, for example, migrate over such a distance that even an extremely large extension of U.S. coastal jurisdiction would fail to solve the special allocation problems of American coastal fishermen.

66. *I.e.*, beyond the powers of Art. 7 of the 1958 Geneva Convention on Fishing and Conservation of the Living Resources of the High Seas.

67. Christy and Scott, *op. cit.* n. 27, pp. 239–240.

68. It has also been proposed to vest such powers in an organisation concerned with a particular species, *e.g.*, whales; see F. T. Christy, Jr., and D. B. Brooks, "Shared Resources of the World Community," in Commission to study the Organisation of Peace, *New Dimensions for the United Nations* (New York, 1966), p. 155.

69. Christy, *op. cit.* n. 26, p. 119.

70. *Ibid.* pp. 116–117.

71. In most fisheries the former level is lower than the latter; see M. B. Schaefer, "Biological and Economic Aspects of the Management of Commercial Marine Fisheries," in [1959] *Transactions of the American Fisheries Society* 103.

72. Christy, *op. cit.* n. 26, pp. 118–120.

73. Most proposals for such a comprehensive international fisheries organisation envisage vesting full authority over the sea's living resources in the United Nations or an affiliated agency.

74. H. Kasahara, "Future Régime for High Seas Fisheries," in L. M. Alexander (ed.), *The Future of the Sea's Resources* (Kingston, R.I., 1968), p. 134. However, the limits of political realities are vague and subject to change.

75. Particularly within the context of the EEC.

76. These suggestions are not solely based upon considerations of political acceptability, but take a more idealised approach.

77. The degree of exploitation is here defined in biological terms: full exploitation means that catches are at the maximum sustainable yield level.

78. The acceptability of coastal State preferential rights to distant water fishing States will be greatly increased if an extension of coastal State exclusive rights appears to be the alternative.

79. If fishing States decide to fish inefficiently, they do not gain at the expense of other States; by over-exploiting a certain high seas stock they cause damage to a resource that may be utilised by all States.

80. *I.e.*, States fishing in the North-East Atlantic Ocean.

81. Japan, for example, participates already in these fisheries.

CHAPTER 4

Fisheries Conservation in the North-East Atlantic and the North Sea: Biological Aspects

By G. Saetersdal*

INTRODUCTION

The utilisation of living marine resources presents problems which in many respects are unique compared to other natural resource uses. The identification and assessment of the resources both in space, time and extent is difficult. The resources are subject to considerable changes, both with regard to their potential yield and location. Because of the general remote and secluded life of sea fish, the science on which a proper and safe use of these resources must be based has only been developed relatively recently. These factors have, no doubt, contributed to the general unsatisfactory state of management in which we at present find the North-East Atlantic fish resources, although it may probably be argued quite forcefully that the main obstacle to progress has been the undefined ownership of the resources.

The various biological aspects of marine fishery resources, which are important from the point of view of conservation and management policies, may be grouped under a few key concepts as follows: the identification of units of resources in terms of fish stocks or fisheries; the geographical distribution of fish stocks, and particularly of its fishable parts; the main life history features, migrations, behaviour, reproduction, and phenomena of concentration in relation to catch potential and economy of harvesting; natural fluctuations in stock size; the state of exploitation, particularly as it relates to the maximum sustainable yield (MSY), reproduction at a normal level and economic factors influencing the use of the resource.

The North Atlantic, and particularly the North Sea, is, relatively speaking, an intensively investigated area, and important items of the information listed above are available for the major stocks in this area. A very brief review of the most relevant features of this great mass of information is presented in the following sections.

BRIEF REVIEW OF SOME INFORMATION ON FISHERIES AND MAJOR STOCKS

(1) Distribution and recent trends of yields

Figure 1 shows the 1971 landings distributed in the main catch regions. The North Sea and Arctic areas are the most productive grounds. Pelagic and demersal fish contribute in roughly equal proportions. The main pelagic species are herring, capelin and mackerel, while cod, haddock, saithe, Norway pout and sandeels dominate the demersal categories.

* Institute of Marine Research, Bergen, Norway.

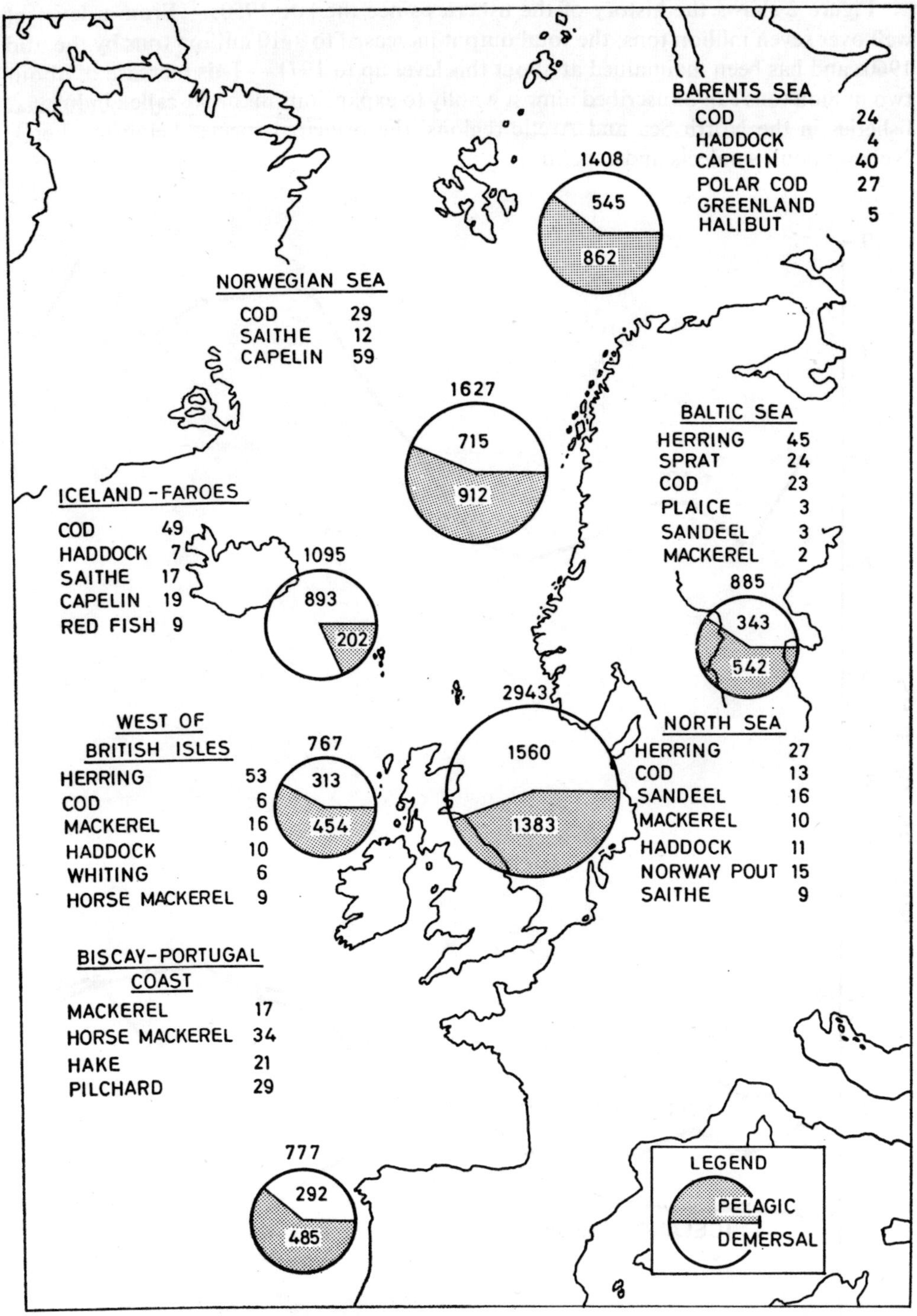

FIGURE 1. Landings in 1971 distributed in main fishing regions and by main species. *Note:* The yield is given in thousands of metric tons and the areas of the circles are proportional to the yields. The relative importance of pelagic and demersal fish is also indicated, as well as the principal species and their percentage shares in the zone's catch. (For Biscay–Portugal coast the figures refer to the year 1970.) *Source:* International Council for the Exploration of the Sea, Copenhagen.

Figure 2 shows the history of the fisheries since the late 1950s. From a level of well over seven million tons, the total output increased to 9–10 million tons by the mid 1960s and has been maintained at about this level up to 1971. This increase of about two million tons can be ascribed almost wholly to expansions in the so-called industrial fisheries in the North Sea and Arctic regions, the principal species being mackerel, Norway pout, sandeels and capelin.

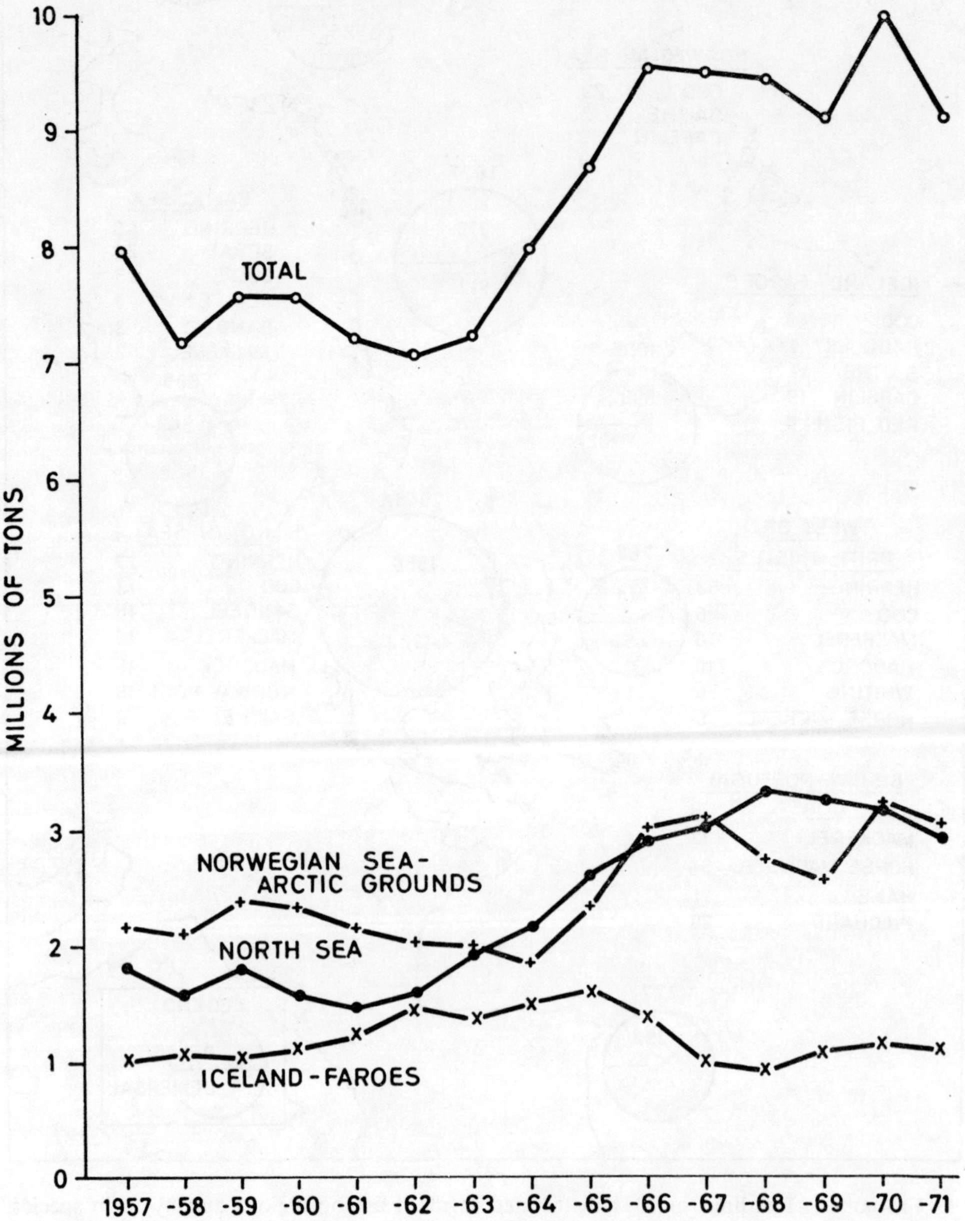

FIGURE 2. Development of sea fisheries in the North-East Atlantic 1957–71. *Source:* International Council for the Exploration of the Sea, Copenhagen.

The figures emerging from this type of overall regional analysis do not, however, reveal much of the true processes and changes which have occurred in the fisheries. These can only be demonstrated by considering unit stocks of the fisheries, and some of the major stocks will be discussed below. But the quite considerable increase that has recently occurred in the total yield from the North Sea grounds, the world's perhaps oldest fishing region, is in itself quite remarkable.

(2) Stock identification

A unit stock is usually defined with reference to common features of reproduction, migration, distribution and other aspects of its life history. The most prominent phenomenon in the life history of the fish populations in the North-East Atlantic is the spawning season, usually preceded by a migration and resulting in a concentration of the adult part of the stock in a relatively restricted area. This feature is therefore often used as the principal means of identification and classification.

There may be a tendency for demersal fish to be more stationary than pelagic species, and thus split into a greater number of population units. At higher latitudes the migrations tend to be more extensive and the areas of distribution greater, but also more variable. Towards the limits of distribution of a species, changes may occur which may even affect the identity of the stocks in the areas, such as the periodical mixing between the Icelandic and Greenland cod stocks.

(3) Distribution, migrations, natural fluctuations and other life history features of major stocks

The whereabouts of the fish stocks, their main areas of concentration and their life cycle are aspects of considerable significance for fishery management problems, particularly in the international context. Commercial fish populations exist in all parts of the oceans, but fish production is usually much higher in the shallow parts of the sea over the continental shelf, reflecting the distribution of primary production and the feeding and spawning habits of the fish.

In the preparatory discussions for the next UN Conference on the Law of the Sea, attempts have been made to create a framework for fishery management based on a classification of the resources into four basic ecological groups: sedentary species, coastal species, anadromous species and wide-ranging oceanic species. If these ideas are further pursued, problems will no doubt arise concerning points of definition of some of these categories, particularly as between coastal and wide-ranging oceanic species. Increasing attention may therefore in the future be directed towards ecological and distributional characteristics of fish stocks.

The life cycle of marine fish is to a large part determined by the dynamics of their environmental system, principally the main ocean currents. The currents are used to transport the eggs, larvae and young fish from the spawning area and spread them out over the feeding grounds.

In the Arctic regions of the North Atlantic, the main stocks such as Arcto-Norwegian cod and haddock, capelin, Atlanto-Scandian herring, saithe and halibut, all have their spawning grounds located along the coast of mid- and north Norway in the southern part of their area of distribution, and their offspring spend about six months drifting in the north-bound current. The areas of total distribution are extensive for these northern species, particularly cod, and capelin, and cover the shallow Barents Sea up to the polar fronts. The Atlanto-Scandian herring is, however, the only one of these species which also ranges far into the Norwegian Sea beyond the continental shelf, where summer grazing takes place in the productive frontal zones between Atlantic and Arctic water masses.

In the Icelandic area the predominantly anti-cyclonic current system keeps the larvae and young fish largely within the continental shelf regions, but a varying degree of intermixing occurs between the cod stock at Iceland and the East and West Greenland stocks.

The distribution and spawning migrations of the fish stocks in and around the North Sea is dominated by the largely cyclonic current system and eddies. Herring stocks spawn along the north-west and eastern coasts of the British Isles and the young herring aggregate in the southern and central parts of the area, while adult herring move west and north. The North Sea mackerel spawn in the central parts in early summer and adult fish move north and north-west in summer and mix with similar components of Irish Sea mackerel in the northern North Sea and around the Shetlands. Demersal species in the North Sea also keep within this relatively shallow basin throughout their life, with more or less well-defined spawning locations inside the system.

Fisheries are traditionally related to the concentration phenomena of spawning and feeding. The Norwegian " skrei " fishery is a typical example, and similar use is made of spawning stocks of cod around Iceland, capelin in the Arctic, herring in the North Sea and others. Distant water trawler fleets seek the large concentrations of young feeding cod in the Barents Sea, Spitsbergen, Greenland, etc. Changes may take place in the distribution of fish, as natural processes are brought about by fishing. In the North Sea an important fishery for adult herring took place on the north-eastern grounds, but following the expansion of the fishery by the Norwegian purse seine fleet in the mid 1960s, this part of the stock was depleted, and continued fishing pressure has so far prevented a rebuilding of this older part of the stock. The purse seine fishery is now concentrated on younger age groups in the more western parts of the northern North Sea.

Fluctuations in stock size and in the yields from the fisheries is a phenomenon of great importance in the area. There are perhaps two different types of such natural fluctuations: short term variations from a few up to six or eight years' duration brought about by apparently random variations in survival success of the broods; and long term fluctuations ranging from 10 to perhaps 50 or 70 years involving periods of extremely low or high productivity of the stock. These long term periods seem to be related to marked changes in the biology and distribution of the fish stock. Periods of this kind are known from the Atlanto-Scandian herring and the Arcto-Norwegian cod. The former stock has probably just entered a period of low production, which has, no doubt, been further accentuated by high fishing pressure towards the end of the productive period, resulting in an extremely low level of present stock size.

" Normal " variations in year class strength may be of the order of 10 times or more, but the effect on the fisheries depends on the age structure of the fishable stock. In the Arctic cod, variations in the total yield are of the order of three times the basic yield. Such changes in the resource base of fisheries naturally create economic problems for harvesting and marketing and complicate conservation systems. The necessary forecasting of recruitment strength places great demands on fishery scientists.

(4) State of fisheries in the North-East Atlantic

The impressive total yields and increasing trends referred to under (1) above are unfortunately not a demonstration of a sound industry and a rational resource usage for European fisheries as a whole. A combination of increases in investment in fishing fleets and technological innovations in fishing methods and techniques has resulted in a great expansion of the total effort in fisheries. This additional effort has been applied without any overall planning in the international sense. Stocks have been attacked when and where available and in accordance with marketing possibilities for the various products. Stock depletion has often been the result of this lack of management. A typical example is the invasion of the Norwegian purse seine fleet into North Sea herring fishing, a stock which was already nearly fully utilised. Another example is the excessive fishing by trawlers of the northern stocks of cod. A large part of the expanding effort in industrial fisheries has, however, been spent on unused resources such as sandeels, Norway pout and capelin. In some of these fisheries by-catches of valuable food fish present a serious conservation problem. There are still some unused or underexploited resources within the area, such as blue whiting in the Norwegian Sea, squids and others. But all the stocks of highly valued fish such as cod, herrings, etc., are now heavily fished and many stocks are overfished with reduced total yields, waste of fishing effort and risks of reduced potential for reproduction as a result. Effective management of such stocks is badly needed. Some international regulation measures of limited nature have been agreed on and introduced, but for practical purposes the main sea fisheries of Europe are without any planned international management.

FISHERIES CONSERVATION IN THE NORTH-EAST ATLANTIC IN THEORY AND PRACTICE: SELECTED CASE HISTORIES

(1) Main conservation aims

A simple and repeated aim of fisheries conservation has been to maximise the yield on a long-term sustained basis. In practice, the maximum sustainable yield is, however, often only taken as a guiding principle since economic and social arguments and market choices may make it preferable to aim at other levels of resource utilisation. The maximum sustainable yield is, however, not in itself an entirely simple concept from the point of view of the fishery scientist. An assessment of the maximum yield *per recruit* (MSY) can usually be made, but since our knowledge about the relationship between parent stock and recruitment is incomplete, it is in general not possible to state definitely the relation between amount of fishing and long-term yield. Or, in other words, with the relatively high fishing effort needed to produce the MSY per recruit, the possibility exists that recruitment itself may be reduced. Since, however, any stock-recruitment relationship must function between the adult mature fish and the recruits, factors other than the total amount of fishing may also be significant, *e.g.*, the minimum size of the fish in the catches. Regulatory measures such as minimum sizes of fish and meshes of fishing gear may thus have the important effect of increasing the spawning stock and indirectly controlling the recruitment.

The research gap, which may be said to exist in our knowledge of the stock and recruitment relationship, represents an important impediment to conservation, but so far the effects in practice have perhaps not been as serious as one might have feared. Most fish stocks react relatively quickly to reduced fishing pressure, in contrast to, for instance, marine mammals. And a recommendation from fishery scientists to exploit stocks at lower levels than that which corresponds to the MSY per recruit, in order to reduce the risks of a failure of recruitment, is usually supported by very strong arguments of an economic nature, since a simultaneous effect will be an increase of catch per vessel or other units of effort.

Effective conservation depends on reliable and timely information on the state of the resources. In this respect the situation in the North-East Atlantic has perhaps been better than in most other parts of the world, thanks mainly to the existence for about 70 years of the International Council for the Exploration of the Sea with its Secretariat in Copenhagen. There is, however, still much room for advance and improvement in our state of knowledge of fish stocks, and also in the contact and understanding between the scientists and the decision-makers, both nationally and internationally.

(2) Selected case histories

(a) *Cod stocks*

The conservation of the cod stocks of the North Atlantic has been the centre of attention both of fishery scientists and administrators over the last 10–20 years. The state of these stocks was reviewed recently by a working group of scientists set up by the International Council for the Exploration of the Sea and the International Commission for the North-West Atlantic Fisheries.[1]† This Group found that by about 1960 the North-East Atlantic stocks were fully exploited, but the North-West Atlantic less so. The further developments in the 1960s reduced this " imbalance." Prior to 1960, during the expanding phase, one or more lightly fished cod stocks existed which could absorb excessive fishing effort diverted from other areas. This is no longer the case, and, for virtually all stocks, fishing mortality has reached a level where further increases of fishing at best will produce very small increases, or actually will decrease the yield per recruit. Furthermore, in the actual words of the working group:

> " There is a probability that spawning stocks as low as, or lower than the present could lead to a recruitment failure and consequently to a very large drop in total catch. Taking this into account, and to some extent the economic benefits implied by an improved catch per unit effort, a desirable level of fishing mortality (effort) would be approximately half the present level. This would not affect the average long-term yield."

Another effect of intensive fishery is that of reducing the average age of fish in the stocks, making short-term fishing prospects over the whole Atlantic cod resources more dependent on the strength of new year classes; when these appear, they attract the mobile fleet causing " pulse fishing." The intensive pulse fishing also depletes the older age groups of the stock.

Various alternative schemes for the management of cod stocks have been made available by fishery scientists over the last 10–15 years. So far, the only regulations that have been introduced at the international level are minimum sizes of fish and the net meshes to control the size at first capture. In addition, control of the amount of fishing is necessary, and so far this has only been attempted to a limited extent at the national level by some countries.

Up till now, the conservation problems for cod stocks have not been of the urgent and dramatic nature which we have seen, for instance, in the Georges Bank haddock. Although exposed to high fishing pressures, the stocks do not appear to have been brought down to permanent low-production levels. The situation may, however, change for the worse unless fishing is further controlled in the future. There are no longer any alternative unfished resources to which the mobile fleets can turn when the stocks pass through low natural levels of abundance. The relative high value of fish

† For references, see p. 45.

and advances in technology make it possible to continue fishing even at very low catch rates. There is thus an increasing danger of reducing the abundance of the stocks still further, down to levels where there could be serious risks of recruitment failures.

(b) *Barents Sea capelin*

Up until the late 1960s fishing for this stock was grossly wasteful because it only made use of a small fraction of its potential yield. Following the failures of the herring fisheries, it became an alternative resource for the Norwegian fish meal and oil industry. After a few years, the fishery developed to its present level of 1–1·5 million tons. It seems probable, however, that the stock is now in a particularly productive period.

Fishery scientists have had difficulties in keeping pace with this rapid development and in providing the much-needed information for management. By making use of direct methods of abundance estimation (based on acoustic techniques), estimates of total stock size were, however, provided and a management scheme was developed and introduced which included the following aspects:

Minimum size. Assessments showed that fishing for capelin younger than about two years of age would be wasteful. Young fish are therefore protected by a minimum landing size.

Closed seasons. Because the quality and fat content is inferior in spring and early summer, the fishing season is only opened in late summer.

Closed areas are used to protect young fish and, in part, the demersal spawning grounds after spawning has occurred.

Catch quotas are used to limit both the offshore summer fishery and the coastal winter fishery of the spawning capelin. Since the capelin dies after spawning, the object of the restrictions on winter fishing is to allow a sufficient number of fish to spawn for reproduction to remain normal and unaffected.

The adequacy of this system of management of the capelin fishery has yet to be proved, since it has only been in operation for a few years. It is important to note, however, that in these new and large scale fisheries, a number of restrictive regulation measures have been introduced and accepted at short notice. At some stages in the development of the fisheries, the demands from fishermen and industry for action aiming at the conservation of resources were considerably more drastic and restrictive than the advice offered by the fishery scientists. This is simply a confirmation of a widely recognised axiom: that the main obstacles to a proper use of the fishery resources of the oceans are not inherent in the resources industry science complex, but must be sought mainly at the level of international relationships. The next example, which is the North Sea herring stock, will demonstrate some of the difficulties which may arise in a typical international fishery.

(c) *North Sea herring*

The North Sea herring fisheries are unusually composite and complex. The fisheries involve more than a dozen nations using a variety of fishing gear: drift nets, purse seines, bottom and pelagic trawls. The stock itself is a complex of more or less well-defined sub-populations which mix at some life stages, and the fisheries exploit nearly all age groups of the herring. A great amount of research effort has, however, been devoted to herring problems, and through the co-ordinating function of the International Council for the Exploration of the Sea, the information basis for better management of the fishery has been available for some time. The latest assessments date from a mid-1972 meeting of the ICES herring working group.[2]

In brief, the recent history of the fishery is as follows: Prior to the mid-1950s the fishery was based on the adult herring with total landings of the order of 600–700 thousand tons. The development of industrial fishing for small herring then increased the yield, which levelled off at roughly 800–900 thousand tons. In the mid-1960s Norwegian purse seiners, diverted from a declining winter herring stock, started fishing the adult components of the stock. This increased the yield to an all time maximum of about 1·4 million tons in 1965, but it then declined and from 1969 onwards the catch dropped below the previous level. The last available figure is that of 1971 with a catch of 574 thousand tons. This 1971 catch is close to the catch level of the period 1948–50 when the main fisheries in the North Sea were the traditional adult herring fisheries for human consumption and the effort was probably less than half the recent level. These drastic events in the fisheries may still represent too optimistic a picture of the state of the North Sea stocks proper. This is because the structure of the stocks is not well defined and it is likely that fishing in later years has to a greater degree exploited previously little fished or unfished sub-stocks.

On the basis of an analysis of extensive biological and biostatistical data, the ICES Assessment Working Group concluded that the maximum sustainable yield of North Sea herring would be obtained with a fishing effort of about half of that used at present. A further conclusion was that more severe selective restrictions on fisheries for young fish would lead to higher gains in terms of quantity of landings, without even considering the higher value of herring for human consumption, as compared to industrial use.

Most of the reduction in stock sizes has taken place in the adult stock, and a result of this is that the estimated spawning potential has been reduced by about three times in later years. The effect of this is uncertain. Recruitment has apparently not been reduced in this period, at least not by the same proportion, but since recruitment is measured by the combined contribution to young herring stocks from a number of sub-stocks, contributions from north-western stocks, which have only been lightly fished up till now, may have masked depleted recruitment from other stock components.

The North Sea herring fisheries present a number of largely unsolved management problems. The present fisheries are wasteful in several ways: the fishing of young herring is wasteful both because it reduces the total yield and because it contributes to an unwanted and unnecessary reduction of the spawning potential; the invasion of the Norwegian ring net fleet into the North Sea fisheries proper, a fisheries which already made use of the resource near its maximum level, was wasteful to the extent that it introduced excessive effort into the fisheries and reduced the level of exploitation below that of the MSY; the use of herring for products of inferior economic value in competition with more highly valued products is wasteful. It should be noted, however, that most of the information on which these conclusions are drawn has only become available over the last few years.

Regulation at the international level has so far been limited to seasonal closures resulting in minor reductions of the total fishing effort. Considerably more far-reaching measures are required to bring the stocks up to full productive levels.

CONCLUSION

In this very brief review of the biological problems of fishery management in the North-East Atlantic, it has clearly only been possible to refer to a relatively small number of fisheries and to draw attention to selected aspects of fishery problems. A number of important stocks and fisheries have been omitted, such as the demersal species of the North Sea—haddock, cod, plaice and others—which now have seemingly passed into an unexpected productive period; the important North Sea mackerel fishery; the " industrial " fisheries for Norway pout and other species with their special problems of by-catches of fish for human consumption and so on. A comprehensive review of all the fisheries in the area and their problems has thus not been intended. It is thought, however, that the presentation which has been made warrants the following main conclusions:

Nearly all stocks of highly valued fish such as cod, herring, etc. are now heavily fished. Many stocks are overfished with reduced total yield, waste of fishing effort and risks of reduced potential for reproduction.

The scientific basis for fishery resource management is in many cases complex by nature and difficult to provide. In spite of this, the information base for the basic regulation of the major fish stocks in the area has been made available.

Adequate management programmes have, in many cases, been put into force at the national level, and the main obstacles to efficient management of sea fisheries are not inherent in the resources industry science complex, but must be sought at the level of international relationships.

REFERENCES

1. Report of the ICES/ICNAF Working Group on cod stocks in the North Atlantic. CM 1972/F:4 International Council for the Exploration of the Sea, Copenhagen, 1972.

2. Report of the North Sea Herring Assessment Working Group. International Council for the Exploration of the Sea, Copenhagen, 1972.

CHAPTER 5

The Special Interests of Coastal States

By D. H. N. Johnson*

I RECEIVED my baptism in international law, just over 20 years ago, in the case generally referred to as the *Anglo-Norwegian Fisheries Case*, although described in the list of the International Court of Justice merely as the *Fisheries Case.*[1]† That was the case in which the Court decided that Norway was not bound to adhere to the low-water mark rule but was entitled to delimit its territorial sea by reference to base lines which, though they had to "follow the general direction of the coast," were subject to no fixed limit as regards length. The breadth of the territorial sea, or exclusive fisheries zone, in that case was not in dispute: it was agreed by both parties to be four miles in Norway's case. If the relatively specific yet anonymous description given to that case in the Court's list was intended to convey the hope that disputes about fisheries would not again trouble the Court, that hope has been belied because the Court now has before it two more cases concerning fisheries; one between the United Kingdom and Iceland,[2] the other between the Federal Republic of Germany and Iceland.[3] This time both cases are described in the Court's list simply as *Fisheries Jurisdiction Cases.*

The decision of the Court in the original *Fisheries Case* of 1951 is generally regarded as having been one of the most important yet rendered by the present Court. Coming as it did just after the Second World War, when for a variety of reasons the law relating to the delimitation of maritime areas was in a state of uncertainty, it has been described by Sir Hersch Lauterpacht as "a significant contribution to the theory and practice of judicial legislation."[4] The same authority said of the judgment that, while it could be criticised on account of its subjectivity and generality, such criticism should "be tempered by the consideration that innovation by way of legislative judicial action cannot properly aim at full elaboration and exhaustiveness."[5] The innovation involved consisted in the Court employing "a judicial method which declines to treat a widely adopted practice (the low-water mark rule) as constituting accepted international law and which elevates the attitude of a small number of States (*i.e.*, those adopting the base line method) to the authority of a practice entitled to equal—or greater—respect."[6] However, Sir Hersch was prepared to allow that "when faced with a situation in which practice is not uniform and in which the preponderant practice does not yield a rule which, in the case before it, renders possible a solution deemed to be in accordance with justice and economic or geographic reality, the Court may deem itself justified in adopting a solution which, although far from achieving certainty, is deemed to embody the rational principle best suited to provide the basis of the general rule."[7] Be that as it may—and this is the important thing—the Court's decision to accept the validity of the base line method was vindicated by events and this method was written into Article

* Professor of International and Air Law, University of London.

† For references, see p. 51.

4 of the Geneva Convention on the Territorial Sea and the Contiguous Zone 1958, in words borrowed largely from the Court's own language. Consequently, although many questions relating to coastal fisheries remain to be settled, the problem of base lines is no longer one of them.

In the *Fisheries Case* the Court referred to certain fishing grounds as " known to Norwegian fishermen and exploited by them from time immemorial," said of " these barren regions " that the inhabitants " derive their livelihood essentially from fishing " and finally commented that " such are the realities which must be borne in mind in appraising the validity of the United Kingdom contention that the limits of the Norwegian fisheries zone laid down in the 1935 Decree are contrary to international law." [8] Even so the case was not, strictly speaking, about fisheries at all. As the Court said: "Although the Decree of July 12, 1935, refers to the Norwegian fisheries zone and does not specifically mention the territorial sea, there can be no doubt that the zone delimited by this Decree is none other than the sea area which Norway considers to be her territorial sea. That is how the Parties argued the question and that is the way in which they submitted it to the Court for decision." [9] In other words, the case was argued and decided at a time when a State's exclusive fisheries zone was still considered to be equivalent to its territorial sea. The idea that a State should have an exclusive fisheries zone different in extent from, and wider than, its territorial sea became fashionable at the Geneva Conferences on the Law of the Sea of 1958 and 1960. The idea was not new. In early times States had often claimed exclusive jurisdiction in respect of fisheries over areas different from those claimed as their limits for purposes of neutrality in time of war. The notion of having a single limit for all purposes was never realised in practice and existed only as an ideal for about a hundred years, the century preceding 1950 in fact.

At the Geneva Conference of 1958, so far as the territorial sea was concerned, the main contention was between those who favoured three miles and those who favoured 12 miles. It was realised by all that, if agreement was to be reached at all, it would not be on a simple compromise such as six or nine miles, but on a " package deal."

The elements of such a package were the " six plus six " formula (*i.e.*, six miles of territorial sea plus a further exclusive fisheries zone of six miles, subject to the exception that, if a State could show that its vessels had been fishing regularly in the " outer six " zone for the previous five years, they should be allowed to go on fishing there). The exclusive fisheries zone was thus to be separated from the territorial sea but neither problem could be solved without agreement on the other, and unfortunately the package proposal put forward by the United States received only 45 votes instead of the 52 required for a two-thirds majority.

It was hoped in 1958 that States favouring a broad exclusive fisheries zone would be won over by conceding to them in Article 6 of the Convention on Fishing and Conservation of the Living Resources of the High Seas " a special interest " in the maintenance of the productivity of the living resources in any area of the high seas adjacent to the territorial seas of such States. This concession, however, proved to be insufficient because, while under it the coastal State obtained a right to take part in conservation arrangements even though its nationals were not yet fishing in the area concerned, it gave to the coastal State no preferential, still less exclusive, rights in such areas. The nearest these States came to receiving acknowledgment of their special claims was in a Resolution on Special Situations Relating to Coastal Fisheries adopted at Geneva on April 26, 1958. This recorded that a special situation existed for countries " whose people are overwhelmingly dependent upon coastal fisheries for their livelihood or economic development" and recommended that under conservation schemes there should be recognition of "any preferential requirements of the coastal State resulting from its dependence upon the fishery concerned while having regard to the interests of the other States."

The entire fate of the 1960 Geneva Conference hung, and as it turned out unsuccessfully, on a more sophisticated version of the 1958 package proposal. This time Canada, instead of opposing the United States, joined with them in submitting a "six plus six" proposal which would allow States whose vessels had been fishing in the "outer six" zone for five years to continue doing so for ten years only; and, as amended, the proposal would allow for preferential rights for coastal States in areas of the high seas adjacent to the "outer six" zone. This proposal obtained 54 votes instead of the 55 required for a two-thirds majority. Despite this failure, the two Geneva Conferences proved decisive in developing the law along the lines of recognition of exclusive fishing zones of 12 miles accompanied by a "phase-out" period for States whose vessels had hitherto been fishing in the area now to be reserved exclusively for the coastal State. Solutions along these general lines, although varying from case to case, were arrived at in agreements between the United Kingdom and Denmark (April 27, 1959), the United Kingdom and Norway (November 17, 1960) and the United Kingdom and Iceland (March 11, 1961); in the general European Fisheries Convention (March 9, 1964); and between the United Kingdom and Poland (September 26, 1964), and between the United Kingdom and Norway (September 28, 1964). Nor was this kind of solution confined to the European area. Japan made a similar agreement with the United States on May 9, 1967 and with New Zealand on July 12, 1967. It is true that the agreement between the United States and Japan contained the qualification that "Nothing in the present arrangements shall be deemed to prejudice the claims of either Government in regard to the jurisdiction of a coastal State over fisheries." However, in a letter dated May 18, 1966 and addressed to the Chairman of the Committee on Commerce of the United States Senate, the Department of State had been bold enough to say the following:

> "Since the 1960 Law of the Sea Conference there has been a trend toward the establishment of a 12 mile fisheries rule in international practice. Many States acting individually or in concert with other States have extended or are in the process of extending their fisheries limits to 12 miles. Such actions have no doubt been accelerated by the support for the proposals made at the Geneva Law of the Sea Conferences in 1958 and 1960, of a fisheries zone totalling 12 miles as part of a package designed to achieve international agreement on the territorial sea. In view of recent developments in international practice, action by the United States at this time to establish an exclusive fisheries zone extending nine miles beyond the territorial sea would not be contrary to international law."

Acting on this advice the Congress enacted a 12 mile fisheries limit for the United States in October 1966.

We are now in the period immediately prior to yet another United Nations Conference on the Law of the Sea and, as before, the principal contestants are jockeying for position. It is already evident that, if agreement is to be reached, there will have to be put forward and discussed package proposals even more complex and sophisticated than those tried out in 1958 and 1960.

One of the most elaborate proposals to emerge so far is that of the Government of Canada [10] which distinguishes between the following groups of species of fish (a) sedentary, (b) coastal, (c) anadromous, and (d) wide-ranging. Following the language of

Article 2 (4) of the 1958 Convention on the Continental Shelf, sedentary species are defined as " those organisms which, at the harvestable stage, either are immobile on or under the seabed or are unable to move except in constant physical contact with the seabed or the subsoil." Such species are therefore not to be confused with the other possible definition of " sedentary fisheries," *i.e.*, those " fisheries conducted by means of equipment embedded in the floor of the sea," for which a different régime is provided in Article 13 of the 1958 Convention on Fishing and Conservation of the Living Resources of the High Seas. The Canadian Government is satisfied with the régime of Article 2 of the Continental Shelf Convention, which provides that " the coastal State exercises over the continental shelf sovereign rights for the purpose of exploring it and exploiting its natural resources." Sedentary species as defined in this Article are thus subject to the exclusive and sovereign control of the coastal State. This approach, the Canadian Government considers, " is appropriate and adequate in that it recognises the interrelationship between the management of living and mineral resources and assigns to the coastal State unitary and full authority over all the resources appertaining to its continental shelf."

" Coastal species " are defined by the Government of Canada as " non-sedentary, free-swimming species which inhabit nutrient-rich areas adjacent to the coast." For such species it is maintained that the coastal State has a *special responsibility* as well as a *special interest* in the maintenance of their productivity, and this responsibility and this interest, which arise because the productivity of the species is dependent in large part on land-related factors, should be fully reflected by assigning to the coastal State the authority to manage the species as well as a preferential—but apparently not exclusive—position as regards their utilisation.

" Anadromous species " are said to represent a special component of the " coastal species." Of these the Government of Canada says: " They are bred and spend their early life in the rivers of the state of origin. Even though they may travel far to sea away from their rivers of origin, they return to these rivers to reproduce. If the State of origin did not take special measures to maintain these rivers in fit condition, the most important stocks of anadromous species would soon disappear." Moreover, in the case of these species, so the argument runs, " the State of origin has virtually sole responsibility for the continued existence of the stocks " and, in the Canadian view, " these heavy and unique responsibilities and the high cost of exercising them . . . can be justified only if management authority is vested in the state of origin and if that State, in principle, has the sole right to harvest the anadromous species bred in its own rivers." The argument seems to be overstated in so far as the stocks can be depleted by irresponsible fishing by other nations on the high seas almost as much as by irresponsible management by the coastal State. That the Canadian Government is aware of this danger, however, is clear from its proposal that fishing for these species should not be conducted on the high seas at all.

Finally, according to the Canadian classification, there are the " wide-ranging species," which include " most of the large pelagic fish such as tunas and most of the marine mammals." For these species the Canadian Government proposes management by " an international authority composed of interested States " except that, in so far as some of these species depend on coastal waters to a certain extent, " consideration should be given to the provision that might be made to accommodate coastal State interests in these species during the period in which they inhabit coastal waters."

To sum up, the Canadian proposal is as follows: for " sedentary species," exclusive control by the coastal State as far as the extent of the continental shelf; for " coastal species," exclusive management by the coastal State in " areas adjacent to the coast " together with a preferential position as regards utilisation; for " anadromous species," exclusive control by the coastal State, accompanied by a complete ban on fishing for these species by other nations on the high seas; and for " wide-ranging species," management by an international authority accompanied by some accommodation of coastal State interests to the extent that some of these species depend on coastal waters.

The Governments of Australia and New Zealand have jointly submitted a working paper [11] which adopts the Canadian classification. These governments suggest that " the coastal State shall have exclusive jurisdiction . . . over the living resources of the sea in an adequately wide zone of the high seas adjacent to its territorial sea." " Adequately wide " is not defined, but " the basic concept would be to establish coastal State responsibility and control over the coastal species." It would be for the coastal State to determine " the allowable catch " of any particular species, and to allocate to itself that portion of the allowable catch, up to 100 per cent., that it could harvest. However " where the coastal State is unable to take 100 per cent. of the allowable catch of a species . . . it shall allow the entry of foreign fishing vessels with a view to maintaining the maximum possible food supply," and " such access shall be granted up to the level of allowable catch on an equitable basis without the imposition of unreasonable conditions and without discrimination between nationals of other States, except as may be provided for under phasing-out arrangements. . . ." It is a feature of the Australian and New Zealand proposal that measures adopted by the coastal State shall take account of " traditional subsistence fishing " carried out by other States in any part of the fisheries zone; and as regards " anadromous species " and " wide-ranging species," these two governments agree with the Government of Canada.

Not surprisingly the proposals of one of the world's greatest fishing nations, Japan,[12] are less far-reaching in the concessions they would make to coastal States. Beyond the 12 mile limit a developing coastal State would, according to the Japanese proposal, be allowed annually a preferential allocation of resources corresponding to its harvesting capacity; but apparently this allocation would never exceed 50 per cent. As for developed coastal States, they would be allowed preferential rights only to the extent necessary to maintain " locally conducted small-scale coastal fisheries."

Particular interest attaches to the proposals of the Soviet Union.[13] In 1958 that country was foremost among those pressing for at least a 12 mile limit, and possibly even greater limit, for the territorial sea. However, it now adopts a rather guarded attitude towards the rights of coastal States in the matter of fisheries. Beyond the 12 mile zone a coastal State—provided it is a developing country—is, according to the Soviet proposal, to be allowed to reserve to itself annually " such part of the allowable catch of fish as can be taken by vessels navigating under that State's flag." Coastal States, whether developed or not, are also to be allowed to reserve to themselves such part of the stock of anadromous fish spawning in their rivers as can be taken by their own vessels. However, as regards what the Canadian Government calls " coastal specie " generally, the Soviet view is that, while " the coastal State may establish fishing regulatory measures on the basis of scientific findings," such measures must be established " by the coastal State in agreement with the States also engaged in fishing in the same areas." Moreover, as regards enforcement, where foreign vessels are concerned, the coastal State is restricted to stopping and inspecting them and drawing up a statement. Punishment, if necessary, is a matter to be left entirely within the hands of the flag State.

To sum up: it is far too early yet to predict whether agreement on coastal fisheries will be reached at the forthcoming Conference on the Law of the Sea. But it already seems clear that, if agreement can be arrived at at all, it will be on the basis of an exclusive fisheries zone of 12 miles; the classification of species along functional lines (*e.g.*, sedentary, coastal, anadromous, wide-ranging); some notion of "allowable catch"; and an amalgam of "exclusive," "preferential" and "traditional subsistence" rights, coupled with an ingenious balancing of interests of developing countries on the one hand and phase-out periods for developed countries on the other hand.

REFERENCES

1. [1951] I.C.J.Rep. 16.
2. [1972] I.C.J.Rep. 12.
3. [1972] I.C.J.Rep. 30.
4. *The Development of International Law by the International Court* (1958), p. 199.
5. *Ibid.* p. 195.
6. *Ibid.* pp. 191–192.
7. *Ibid.* pp. 195–196.
8. [1951] I.C.J.Rep. 127–128.
9. *Ibid.* p. 125.
10. Working Paper on Mangement of the Living Resources of the Sea, submitted by Canada (A/AC.138/SC.II/L.8).
11. A/AC.138/SC.II/L.11.
12. A/AC.138/SC.II/L.12.
13. A/AC.138/SC.II/L.6.

CHAPTER 6

The Economics of Fishing

By J. R. Coull*

INTRODUCTION

FISHERIES in the modern world present an unusual phenomenon in that they are generally an activity at the most primitive economic level of hunting, while (at least in advanced countries) a range of sophisticated technical equipment is employed in their pursuit. Fishing is an expanding industry, and the total world catch more than trebled between 1938 and 1970; in the latter year it stood at over 69 million metric tons. However, it is a minor industry in the world economy, and in no country is fish more than about 5 per cent. of the total food intake.

The character and importance of fisheries vary very widely, and the priorities within the industry itself show prominent contrasts as between different nations. Comprehensive analysis of these differences is difficult, as fisheries are still one of the most poorly recorded economic sectors. The assessments of economic viability which are available are nearly all for the more highly developed countries, and even for those there are serious limits on the possibility of systematic comparison.

It is, however, possible to state that the fishing industry is in a weak position economically. It depends on a natural resource with biological ceilings on yield, and on which there is little control of exploitation. At the same time, the prices of the capital equipment of vessels and equipment have been rising more rapidly than those of fish, and this has made it very difficult to raise the productivity of the industry to that of other sectors in the modern economy. Also there is the increasing problem of conserving fish stocks in the long term with the growing efficiency of catching methods. On the marketing side, too, there are difficulties: in developed countries demand for fish is flagging, while in the developing world purchasing power is often inadequate to sustain demand. The modern situation is also complicated by the trend of growing economic interdependence between countries. Fisheries have long persisted as largely isolated sectors in different national economies, but there is increasing international trade now in specialised capital goods used in fishing, as well as in fish products.

FISHERIES IN DEVELOPED, DEVELOPING AND CENTRALLY PLANNED COUNTRIES

The position of the industry in the three groups of countries recognised by international organisations (*i.e.*, those with developed market economies, centrally planned economies, and developing economies) shows prominent contrasts. In the developed countries there were phases of vigorous expansion during the Industrial Revolution, but the

* Senior Lecturer in Geography, University of Aberdeen.

accent is now on consolidation and rationalisation in production. This is linked to a situation in which the market has tended to stagnate, and in which other protein foods tend to be preferred to fish, although fish (especially quality products) do retain a sector of the market through the variety they provide. In some cases, however, developing scarcities, which have resulted from reduced fish stocks, have driven up the prices even of common varieties. In production, the emphasis is on increasing the returns on capital and labour. However, landings values tend to increase considerably more slowly than costs of capital equipment, and this is seldom made good through increases in turnover. In addition, fishing tends still to be labour-intensive and sheds labour relatively slowly. The overall result is that efficiency in fishing increases more slowly than in other sectors in the economy, and this leads to demands for aid among producers. This, most generally, has been given in the form of investment aids, especially to improve vessels and equipment. It has taken the form of grant and loan schemes, *e.g.*, in Britain and Canada, but more commonly is in the form of loans at low interest rates, as in Spain and Norway. In addition, direct production subsidies, based on landed weights or days at sea, have also been given in some countries. Often such measures of aid have been first envisaged as temporary, to allow the industry to stand on its own feet; but all too often they have become effectively a permanent expedient, due basically to the inherent economic weaknesses of the industry.

In the developing countries, there are basic differences both in production and marketing. In production, it is more important to give men employment than to save labour; but the poorer countries are short of capital in this, as in other fields, and it is difficult to provide the necessary boats and gear. There have not been lacking attempts to improve the traditional fisheries in the developing world, many of them with international funds, although success has been sparing. Some of the better results have come with unsophisticated schemes installing engines in the boats for greater mobility, and providing gear of better materials. Nearly all the developing countries are short of protein in their diets, and in many cases the source from which this can most economically come is fish. If fish can be marketed in good condition and at a satisfactory price, there is no shortage of demand. In these countries, however, there is the lack of an adequate economic infrastructure—to provide the training, transport and other necessary facilities, and this hamstrings both production and marketing. However, the potential for development in some parts of the developing world—particularly South-East Asia and South America—is high, and has been partially realised in the industrial fisheries of Peru and Chile. Landed tonnages have increased thirty-fold in Chile since 1938, and in Peru by the spectacular figure of 400 times. Peru, with an annual production of around 10 million metric tons, now leads the world's landings.

Countries with centrally planned economies have in fact achieved the most comprehensive expansion in the industry in the post-war period. This has been especially noteworthy in the Soviet Union, where production has multiplied nearly five times since 1938, to over seven million metric tons. Although generally behind the countries of the western world in level of development, these countries have had the necessary technology and economic infrastructure to allow expansion. Promotion of fisheries appears to have been primarily motivated by the fact that they give the most rapid and least expensive method of increasing protein food supplies, especially in countries where climatic factors create difficulties for stock rearing. However, the programmes have involved heavy expenditure in distant-water fleets, port terminals and transport facilities, in a manner difficult to see as viable in the western world.

INDUSTRIAL FISHERIES

While the main goal in fisheries is still, as it has always been, to produce human food, a very important post-war development has been the rapid rise of fisheries for reduction (or industrial fisheries), to the point that they now account for 37 per cent. (1970) of total landings by volume, although the proportion by value is much lower. Industrial fisheries are of interest to economists not only for their scale, but also for the fact that they allow to the greatest extent the deploying of the modern techniques of mechanisation and mass-handling. This gives economies of scale in an industry in which a great many traditional features survive even in developed countries, and these features contribute to low levels of economic efficiency. An important point about industrial fisheries is that their products now constitute the biggest items in the international fish trade, and they involve the linking of the developing countries with the developed and (to a lesser extent) with those with centrally planned economies. Peru is by far the leading producer, and the great bulk of production goes to export. Although the world market for fish meal and oil has expanded vigorously in the last 20 years, supply and demand have on occasion got seriously out of step. This led to the institution of the International Association of Fish Meal Manufacturers in 1959, and there is more international co-operation to stabilise conditions for producers than in any other sector of the fishing industry. Peru, as the leading producer, has been especially prominent in the regulation of both the production and marketing sides of its industry. The great quantities caught for industrial fisheries have generated increased pressure on certain stocks, and resulted in increased danger of over-fishing in species like the North Sea herring and South African pilchard.

FISH STOCKS IN RELATION TO BIOLOGICAL AND ECONOMIC PRODUCTIVITY

Of basic importance in the fishing industry is the relationship between biological productivity and the economics of operation. The essentials of this are best seen by a graph [1] to show the extreme simple case.

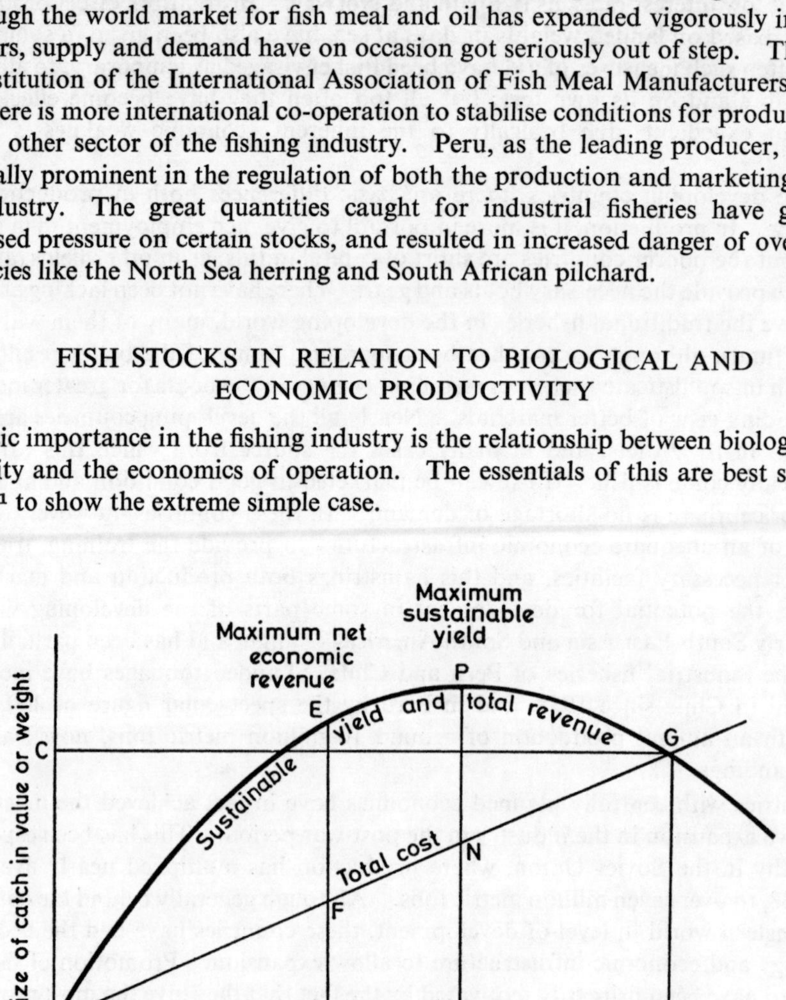

[1] This graph is reproduced by permission of the Johns Hopkins Press.

This shows the changes as the exploitation of a new fish stock proceeds, there being a progressive flow of boats into the fishery. The curve shows the yield of the fishery, and this tapers off as the breeding stock is reduced, till the point of maximum sustainable yield (P) is reached—the point where the total growth in the stock is equal to the catch. This is the *biological* optimum, and any increase in effort means a decrease in total yield.

However, the economic optimum necessarily occurs at a different point. If prices are constant, the curve will represent also the revenue from the fishery; while if each boat has equal operating costs, the line OG will represent the graph of aggregate cost.

The important point is that the maximum vertical distance EF between the curve (revenue) and the line OG (costs) gives the maximum net revenue, or the maximum *economic* yield. In a privately owned resource, the number of boats would be halted at this point; but with the common ownership of the fish stock, there is a strong tendency for more and more boats to join the fishery, and for the level of exploitation to be pushed beyond both the economic and biological optima.

In these circumstances, there are strong pressures towards over-exploitation, especially with the modern improvement in equipment for locating and catching fish. Vessels must continually aim to catch more to make good the widening gap between costs and prices.

In the face of the resulting increasing pressure on resources, a number of measures have been introduced in the more intensively fished seas of the world. These have generally begun as national arrangements, but have expanded into a number of international conventions, especially in the North Atlantic and North Pacific. The measures taken have included mainly regulation of net mesh sizes and the establishment of closed seasons, although with various other restrictions. From the economist's point of view, however, these restrictions are undesirable in that they obstruct the free deployment of capital and labour. The only way of achieving the economic optimum would be to limit the catching effort by restricting the number of boats. While some steps in this direction have been taken within territorial waters, the practical difficulties for anything of the kind on the high seas are immense. There is such a range of vessels of different types using different catching methods, catering for separate markets, and frequently operating in different sea areas according to the time of year or availability of fish.

An important result of the pressure on resources has been the outward extension of the intensely exploited zone from such early areas as the North Sea and Sea of Japan, to cover a great part of the world's continental shelves. A significant part of this expanded production has been achieved through distant-water fleets working off foreign shores—first by British trawlers—but now in large measure also by vessels from Japan, the U.S.S.R., Spain and West Germany, among others. Such distant-water working depends essentially on rich grounds, as it is not uncommon for half the time at sea to be spent in making the return passage, with consequent higher overhead costs. An example of this difference in productivity which affects Britain is that the Irish Sea yields per year about 550 kg. of fish per square kilometre while the Icelandic shelf yields around 5,000 kg. of fish per square kilometre. Even this, however, pales by comparison with the productivity of the Humboldt Current off Peru, which is the best of any open sea area, and which has been computed at 37,500 kg. per square kilometre. In the great part of the area of the world's oceans, however, biological productivity is so low that there is no effective contribution to fishery resources.

As well as big variations in the biological productivity of fishing grounds, there are also big contrasts in the returns to labour and capital. For the developing world, available data suggests that the yearly production is seldom much in excess of one ton per man. In the developed world it is usually above 10 tons, while in the Peruvian anchovy fishery it exceeds 600 tons per man. Data on values of landings are less complete, but in the leading developed countries yearly production now exceeds U.S. $5,000 per man, although in developing countries it is generally a small fraction of this. Returns to capital cannot be directly assessed from available data, but when catches are related to the indirect measure of fleet tonnage, the leading nations are in general the same group that lead in labour productivity, and include such countries as Iceland, Denmark, France, the Netherlands and Norway.

The modern tendency—especially in distant-water and industrial fisheries—is for operation to become more capital-intensive. This applies especially to the shooting and hauling of gear, where the power winch can be used to the greatest effect: the trawl and purse-seine are becoming the dominant gears, the former predominating for ground fish and the latter for pelagic species. Inshore vessels use these methods to an increasing extent, although here there is a greater survival of more labour-intensive methods, including the use of lines, drift and set nets, and seines. It is inevitably more difficult to mechanise operation completely on small boats, and this applies especially in such matters as the use of gutting machines and conveyors which are appearing on bigger vessels.

INSHORE AND DISTANT-WATER FISHERIES

In many countries there are divergent interests between inshore and distant-water fisheries. The former are often prosecuted by fishermen owning their own boats, while the latter are very generally organised by companies. This distinction highlights the difficulties of the position at national level with regard to fishing limits. The interests of inshore fleets are best served by the maximum extent of fishing limits to exclude foreign competitors, and there has also been pressure exerted to exclude or restrict the operations of bigger vessels of the home nation in the inshore zone: this has been especially prominent in Norway. On the other hand, distant-water fleets favour minimal limits, to allow access to grounds off foreign coasts, and some such fisheries have been operated for centuries—particularly around Iceland, which is now in the thick of the argument over fishing limits.

With the general increase in exploitation of fish stocks, and the growing range and catching power of the bigger vessels, it is inevitable that there should be conflict between inshore and distant-water operators. As well as the cases from the North Atlantic, it can be seen, for example, in the North Pacific salmon fisheries on both sides of the ocean. Of increasing scale, too, is the concern of nations in the developing world to protect their stocks against the onslaught of well equipped distant-water fleets. The most prominent case here is the friction caused between the U.S.A. and the nations of Ecuador, Peru and Chile in the post-war period; these nations have claimed a 200 mile fishing limit, and have restricted the operations of the American tuna fleet. More recently, Brazil, Argentina and Guinea have claimed 200 mile limits. Many of these developing nations do not yet fully exploit their own waters, and such claims arise from long-term considerations.

The modern phenomenon of factory fishing is very much an accompaniment to distant-water operation. Such is the perishability of fish that minimal delay in processing is required, even if this involves the extra cost and complications of processing at sea. Processing at sea is not, in fact, a modern development; in the North Sea and the North Atlantic the pickle-curing of herring and wet-salting of cod are centuries old.

However, " factory fishing " implies the deployment of improved and more sophisticated methods of preservation, including freezing, canning and reduction as well as salting. Such methods can only be economically justified on rich distant-water grounds, as the building of floating units is inevitably considerably more costly than the construction of plant of equivalent capacity on land. Among the majority of developed countries, processing at sea takes place on big catching vessels, especially on trawlers equipped to fillet and freeze white fish; and freezing of tuna and shellfish aboard boat is practised by both U.S. and French vessels. " Factory fishing " has most far-reaching connotations for the U.S.S.R. and Japan, and, to some extent, Poland and East Germany. These countries have big fleets operating at several thousand miles from base, and the U.S.S.R. and Japan now fish all the world's oceans. At extremely long ranges, it would not be economic for the catching vessels to return to base with their fish. For this reason, fleet systems have been developed, whereby floating factories and base ships (some of which are over 30,000 tons) are accompanied by fleets of catchers, together with other support vessels like fish carriers, supply ships and tugs. Another innovation is the use of helicopters to help locate fish shoals. Such fleet systems do allow a fuller use of capital equipment, although there can be considerable problems of trans-shipment at sea, and both the U.S.S.R. and Japan make some use of foreign land bases.

In factory fishing, freezing is now the dominant process employed for preserving catches, and this involves links with freezer chains on land. While both the U.S.S.R. and Japan have floating canneries, a big section of the canning industry consists of shore units which process pelagic species temporarily preserved aboard by freezing. The U.S.S.R. also operates floating salting plants, although these are being rapidly displaced by freezing units. For the most part, reduction aboard factory ships is operated only as a by-product industry. Despite the much lower unit value of the products of reduction, both the Norwegians and Japanese have experimented with floating meal and oil plants, with fleets of attendant catchers. The viability of such ventures, however, remains to be proved.

SEASONAL FLUCTUATIONS IN FISHERIES

A feature which limits economic rationalisation in fisheries—as in agriculture—is seasonal availability of resources, which does not allow a regular flow of the product to the market. In the past, a fisherman often required part of the year to work a small holding, and the seasonal laying up of simple boats and gear was of limited economic consequence. Many important traditional fisheries—such as the Newfoundland summer cod or the Norwegian winter herring—were very much seasonal employments of men otherwise occupied at other seasons. This pattern persists to some extent in developed countries, and is still common in the developing world. With modern capital investment in bigger and more effective catching units, seasonal lay-ups become a serious matter. The effects of seasonal fluctuations for inshore craft may be minimised by switching to other fisheries for the remainder of the year, as is common in Norway. It may be minimised, too, by moving to distant bases, as is still done to a considerable extent in the herring fisheries of Britain. It is distant-water vessels, however, which can best accommodate their operation to seasonal fluctuations in fish stocks by moving to different grounds. This is well exemplified by the distant-water trawler fleets of Britain and West Germany, which may range over the whole North Atlantic at different seasons.

The consequences of seasonal fisheries are transmitted to the processing and servicing centres on land. Processing plants geared to dealing with seasonal peaks in landings have excess capacity for the rest of the year, and also have seasonal demands for labour. There are various means by which these seasonal effects may be minimised. It is possible to encourage distant-water vessels to provide supplies outside the peak season, as is done in North Norway and parts of Newfoundland; fluctuations may also be buffered by cold stores, to hold the raw material for processing; and it is possible to concentrate on a higher degree of processing outside the peak season. However, all such expedients involve extra costs, and may indeed become holding operations while the peak season may be the only period of real profit.

POLLUTION

Pollution is a modern problem on a global scale. For the fishing industry its most concentrated effects are seen on inland waters, but it is increasingly affecting the seas also. There are already cases where aquatic eco-systems have been strongly altered, with adverse effects on fish productivity and the welfare of fishermen. The most prominent example is the Great Lakes of North America, where most of the commercial species have disappeared from Lake Erie, and where fishing has been banned from Lake St. Clair. Levels of harmful chemicals are also building up in such near-enclosed seas as the Baltic and Mediterranean. While it is very difficult to assess and to distribute the costs of polluting water bodies, it is obviously a field in which international action and financing is required to formulate measures to monitor and control pollution.

MARKETING, DISTRIBUTION AND CONSUMPTION

The arrangements for the marketing and distribution of fish reflect its character as a perishable commodity. In many countries, streamlining of distribution systems has been slow to develop, and a high margin between prices at first sales and to the customer is characteristic.

While price systems vary in detail between all countries, it is general for densely populated industrial countries to have auction systems. These were usually developed during the Industrial Revolution, as the best means of gearing supply and demand for a perishable commodity at a time when the railway allowed the innovation of delivery of fresh fish in quantity to inland markets. Some of the main fishing nations like Iceland and Norway are, however, thinly populated, and much of their effort is geared to serving distant export markets. Here fixed price systems are general, and average prices considerably lower. Systems of this kind are also usual in the developing world, where limitations of infrastructure and market demand inhibit the development of efficient links between producer and consumer. In the developed countries, the unfettered interplay of supply and demand, with the inevitable accompanying uncertainties, is now tending to be modified—especially when fish is frozen at sea and it is essential that the cold chain be unbroken. Yet the auction system remains dominant in Western Europe, and the methods of transfer of fish from the auction market floor to processing plants are often antiquated and inefficient.

The structure of the processing industry has changed considerably in recent years. The traditional preservation methods—drying, salting and smoking—are still used everywhere, although they are stagnating or declining in developed countries. Filleting, freezing and pre-cooking command higher-value levels in the market; but the biggest processing sector by far now is that of reduction, although it operates on a big scale in only a few countries.

Modernisation of processing and marketing has been hindered by the general survival of big numbers of small concerns, although the more modern processing methods tend to be dominated by big units. While national policies now tend to encourage the amalgamation of small units, this may be otherwise an occasion where regional policies aim at retaining employment in small scattered communities, as occurs in Norway. In the developing countries there are schemes for the establishment of fishing terminals and distribution chains which are meeting with some success, notably in Peru.

Demand for fish is characteristically greatest in countries with long-established fisheries, and levels of consumption are highest at the sea-board and decline inland. Per capita consumption on the national scale appears to be greatest in Iceland with around 100 kg. per year, although only a minority of countries have levels of over 25 kg. per capita. Consumption is rising fastest in developing and centrally planned countries, where it is the cheapest source of additional protein.

In any detailed consideration of demand for fish, it becomes apparent that the total market consists of a series of markets for individual species, with limited overlap or possibility for substitution. The greater part of the market, even in developed countries, is for a limited number of common varieties like cod, haddock and herring. At a higher level of market value are prime fish like sole and halibut, and the highest value is realised by salmon and shellfish. In nearly all countries, the main part of the market is still for fresh fish; but in developed countries this sector of the market is stagnating or declining, along with the sector of those preserved by drying, salting and smoking. The expanding part of the market is for the more valuable varieties, usually preserved by freezing. Market expansion was inhibited for a time by the difficulty of preserving and packaging in a suitable manner for sale in such modern outlets as supermarkets, but expansion is often now quite vigorous, and these quality products are being increasingly traded on the international market. The American market, especially, absorbs frozen shellfish, white fish fillets and salmon from a great range of countries, and the U.S.A. now imports more than one-half of the total fish it consumes.

THE IMPORTANCE OF FISHERIES TO DIFFERENT COUNTRIES

It is now general for fisheries to be of minor importance in national economies; and like other activities in the primary sector, their importance continues to decrease. At the same time the industry may be vital to the welfare of individual communities, and its importance can be crucial at regional (and even national) level.

Iceland is unique in being a country in which fishing is the foundation of the whole economy, but even here the value of fish landings is now less than 20 per cent. of the Gross National Product; such is the importance of the secondary and tertiary sectors of the economy in an advanced country that primary production necessarily contributes a limited share to the GNP. In the case of Peru, a developing country with a major fishing industry, the proportional value of fish landings in the GNP is *c.* $3\frac{1}{2}$ per cent., while in Norway it is now *c.* 2 per cent. For Japan, the country with by far the highest value of fish landings, their proportional value in the GNP is about 1 per cent.; and in countries like the United Kingdom, Canada and the U.S.A. which are still major fishing nations, the proportion is a small fraction of 1 per cent. Naturally when value added by processing in the secondary sector is considered, fish have higher proportions in the GNP than such figures indicate; no comprehensive figures are available, but it appears likely that the value added is very generally less than the initial landed value.

Fish can be considerably more important to countries in their export economies: in the case of Iceland, they constitute *c.* 80 per cent. of exports by value, and in the case of the Faroe Islands (which are linked to Denmark) over 90 per cent. In Peru, the mushroom rise in the fish meal industry has led to fish products being the main export with over 25 per cent. by value of the total. In Norway, although declining, fish are still *c.* 12 per cent. of exports by value, and in Denmark about 4 per cent.

Despite the big imports of fish to industrial countries like the U.S.A., Britain and West Germany, the share in the total imports is always a very minor proportion of national imports.

Even in the major fishing nations, fishermen are only a small proportion of the labour force. A 1960 estimate for Iceland indicates that *c.* 30 per cent. of the labour force were in fisheries, while in Norway the proportion is now down to *c.* 4 per cent. At a regional level, however, the importance of the fisheries component in the labour force is greater. It appears to account for nearly one-half in the Faroe Islands, while in North Norway the proportion is nearly 20 per cent.

CONCLUSION

The fishing industry in the modern world is faced with a series of major problems, and there is a strong economic component in them all. It is the familiar situation in the modern world of an industry—and often a way of life—which evolved under conditions of a simpler economy, trying to adjust in an age when economic development is proceeding at an unprecedented rate. It is increasingly clear that the resolution of the problems of the industry depends on a greater measure of co-ordination of different interests than has yet been achieved. It may be that in the long-term the industry may pass in large measure to a stage of husbandry rather than hunting, in which case controls would be easier to apply. Fish farming is already practised on a commercial basis for valuable species like trout in inland waters, and oysters and mussels in lagoons and estuaries, but the effective farming of the open sea still presents more of a dream than a prospect to the technology and organisation of even the most highly developed societies. At the present time there is still a formidable challenge to the world's fishing nations and fishermen to promote an industry which is economically viable and yet allows the long-term conservation of the resources on which it depends.

CHAPTER 7

Marine Fish Farming—Some Legal Problems

By L. K. Newton* and I. D. Richardson†

I. SOME GENERAL PROBLEMS

A NUMBER of writers have discussed the need for effective conservation and management of the natural resources of fish and shellfish in international waters. Without adequate resource management policies agreed and observed by the various national fleets fishing, the maximum economic or biological sustainable yield cannot be achieved. It is admittedly extremely difficult, but not impossible, to formulate management techniques which will allow catches from a particular area of stock to be stabilised. But, as experience has shown, it is difficult in practice to obtain the agreement of all countries participating in the particular fishery, to accept and observe the necessary management policy. Consequently, and there are many examples which may be quoted, the stock of a particular species may be severely depleted, possibly beyond the point of recovery and often beyond the point at which it remains economically attractive to fish the stock, before effective management policies are accepted and enforced. In addition to a reduction in catches due to over-exploitation of the stock, supplies of fish can be dramatically reduced as a result of unilateral action on the part of countries bordering certain traditional fishing grounds to extend their fishing limits, with a consequent loss of catches to those countries which traditionally relied on those fishing grounds.

In short, whether we like it or not, and in spite of considerable government support provided to the fisheries biologists to obtain the scientific evidence on which management policies can be formulated, and in spite of the well established International Commissions set up for the purpose of designing, agreeing and ensuring the enforcement of international management policies, the possibility of any dramatic increase in domestic supplies of more popular fish and shellfish from home based fishing fleets fishing the traditional fishing grounds, is remote. Indeed, a decline in supplies is more likely to occur.

To make up the anticipated short-fall in supplies, the options are to encourage fishing on the more distant non-traditional fishing grounds where, as yet, stocks are not heavily exploited, or to create a new resource by means of farming. The former solution is likely to be short-lived for obvious reasons: the high cost of exploiting fishing grounds at a considerable distance from the home port or market compared with fishing the nearer grounds, and the fact that the species caught are unlikely to be recognised or command a premium price on the established home market.

* Formerly Assistant Secretary, United Kingdom White Fish Authority.
† Formerly Research Secretary, United Kingdom White Fish Authority.

Against this background the White Fish Authority in the United Kingdom, mindful of its duty to maintain an adequate supply of marine fish to the consumer, determined to examine the feasibility of farming marine fish and also to devote some of its limited research and development funds to improving the existing systems and techniques used for farming molluscs, particularly oysters and clams. Unfortunately there were insufficient funds to support work on the development of farming techniques for the third attractive group of marine animals, namely crustacea, such as prawns. In the context of discussion on the legal problems associated with marine farming, the requirements will be broadly similar whatever the species farmed and the purpose of this paper is to point out the type of problem which faces the fish and shellfish farmer now and, by reference to the likely shape and form of the fish farm of the future, to indicate the type of problem which might arise and for which some legal provision will have to be made. There is something of a chicken and egg situation developing. The research worker and the technician can, and will, provide the data on the biological, engineering and economic feasibility of fish and shellfish farming, but when these are available and it is attractive to the investor, commercial fish farming is unlikely to be practised until the operator has the necessary protection and recourse to law without which his investment is not secure.

We may be wrong, but we believe that, in the foreseeable future, commercial investment in marine fish farming will be in systems which involve the stock being held throughout the whole of its life from egg or at least early juvenile stage, through to marketable size. At no stage will the stock be liberated into the open sea. This being so, fish farming can be considered for all practical purposes, as confined essentially to the immediate coastal waters up to high-water mark and the land immediately adjacent to the shore where hatcheries, nursery facilities and even fattening units such as tanks, lagoons or ponds may be constructed. We will describe the nature of the installations which we believe will be found in the future fish farm, and we will indicate some of the possible problems, problems concerned with access to the farm installations and stock, the ownership of the stock, etc. But before doing so, we should point out that there is, in theory, and some evidence in practice, that there may be merit in restocking the seas through the establishment of hatcheries and associated nursery facilities in which the fry is taken through the period of high mortality which occurs naturally in the open sea and is then liberated to supplement the natural stocks. Some success has been reported from Norway where cod and certain species of flat fish have been reared and liberated at late larval stage. It has also been the practice, for instance in Canada where some 20 hatcheries exist, to establish salmon hatcheries to release fingerlings which enter the rivers to support an offshore fishery as well as fisheries in the river systems to which the fingerlings return as adult salmon. Similarly attempts have been made to supplement the natural stocks of lobsters by hatching and rearing to late potslarval stage before liberation into the open sea. Eels are also farmed but because of the nature of their life cycle, it is the young naturally-spawned eel which is caught at the start of its migration from sea to freshwater, and the eels are then raised in freshwater farms.

Apart from the difficulty of proving the effectiveness and the economic benefits of such activities, there is no way at present, as the stock is available to all who fish on the high seas, of ensuring that the economic benefit accrues to the company or government providing the original finance for the hatcheries. (The exception is the salmon which returns to the river of origin and is therefore only exposed to public or international fishing in the open sea migratory phase.) Also when the fish or shellfish are liberated as juveniles into the open sea, they are at the mercy of natural predators. These, the lack of food and mortalities inflicted by man are strong arguments why, assuming the economics to be attractive, the stock should be held in captivity to marketable size. This introduces the first legal problem—the right of private property in international or coastal waters.

Here we would like to make a topical point. Under regulations made under the Rome Treaty, access for fishing purposes is granted to the fleets of member nations up to the shore line. It is true that before the U.K. signed the Treaty of Accession modifications were made which provide that until December 31, 1982, U.K. coastal waters within the six mile limit are restricted to British vessels and waters between six and 12 miles, where there is a danger of over-fishing, to British vessels plus those with historic rights to fish for certain species. Are all fish or shellfish whether farmed or wild, therefore to be freely available to the EEC fleets after 1982? There would appear to be a requirement to exercise jurisdiction in favour of the farmer over the farmed stock from high-water mark to a predetermined distance off shore.

Before describing in detail some possible types of coastal fish farm of the future, we should touch on another possible way in which protein production from the sea might be increased. Although it is unlikely that farming will be practised in offshore waters for some considerable time, the possibility must be recognised. Certain areas of the ocean are not rich in terms of productivity, principally because the essential nutrients required for photosynthesis are "locked-up" in the deep water away from the surface and sunlight. Up-welling of the water rich in nutrients occurs naturally in certain sea areas and results in highly productive fishing grounds. Theoretically up-welling could be created artificially by suitable engineering works. But who would pay for such installations when the product in the form of fish is freely available to all comers?

Fish farms have to be stocked. Ideally they would be stocked from hatcheries which offer the possibility of a regular supply of the chosen species at known cost. They also offer the possibility of breeding new genetic strains combining the characters of fast growth, disease resistance, etc., desired by the fish farmer—the Aberdeen Angus of the marine farm. But at present the technique for hatching many of the more desirable species is not available, and juvenile fish from natural spawning have to be caught from the open sea. This is the basis of the Japanese Yellow Tail farming, the Chanos farms of Taiwan, and many other marine fish and shellfish farms throughout the world. If turbot are to be farmed in this country, and turbot are most attractive subjects for fish farming, the young of naturally spawned wild fish may have to be caught on the beaches because as yet there is no known method of hatching this species in quantity or of rearing them through metamorphosis. Present international regulations in the North Sea and North Atlantic, which have rightly been framed to prohibit the capture and landing of young immature fish of certain species in the interest of conservation, would have to be modified to allow the farmer to obtain supplies of young fish with which to stock his farm. In United Kingdom coastal waters Sea Fisheries Committees are also empowered to introduce by-laws regulating the fishery in their area, and they may well prohibit the use of fishing gear of the mesh size and design required to catch the young fish destined to stock the fish farm.

A distinction must be made between the farming of molluscs, and, particularly, oysters, and the farming of free swimming fish. The former has been prosecuted in this country and elsewhere for centuries and is regulated by legislation (although the legislation is specific to certain species and may require extension to cover other molluscan species as these become attractive to farm), whereas the cultivation of marine fish is still under development. Although we believe that a convincing case can be made that, in the not too distant future, given adequate funding of the development programme, the farming of free swimming marine fish will be an attractive commercial possibility and will be prosecuted on a substantial scale in the U.K., there is at present no legislation specifically designed to enable commercial fish farming to be undertaken. The state of development is such, however, that consideration must be given, as suggested by the Cameron Report, to appropriate legislation now, or the potential investor will find himself unable to proceed, not because of the lack of technical and economic data, but because of the restrictions placed on his operations by existing law or the absence of it. Not only is the present legal framework inadequate, but the responsibility for its administration is divided between a large number of organisations with ill-defined and conflicting allegiances.

Traditionally molluscs have been cultivated on the seabed, usually below low-water mark, where they are laid on previously prepared beds as small seed molluscs of a size sufficient to be resistant to predators such as crabs. The mollusc is then harvested, usually by means of dredging from specially designed vessels, after two or more years when the animal is of market size. During this period of growth, the molluscs may be thinned and relaid and various measures taken to reduce predation by starfish and various parasitic animals. The seed may be naturally settled seed, taken from the beds where it has settled for relaying on the fattening grounds, which may be some distance away—mussels are usually treated in this way. Alternatively seed may be obtained by means of erecting suitable structures—ropes, tiles, etc. on which the naturally spawned spat settles and is later stripped and transferred to the fattening beds or on-growing structures, or as a result of a technique recently developed by the White Fish Authority in this country, seed may be available from hatcheries. As mentioned earlier, seed may be harvested from natural beds some distance away from the location of the on-growing beds, *e.g.*, mussel seed transferred from Morecambe Bay to the Menai Straits or from Southern Ireland, or it may be purchased from suppliers in areas where natural settlement is abundant, as in the case of the seed oyster which was traditionally imported from France and Portugal, and which more recently has been imported into France from Japan.

The questions so far raised are (1) allocations of seed areas for the exclusive use of the farmer; (2) the ownership of the seed, and in the case of naturally settled seed beds where there may be no right of private ownership, these will be, in the interests of the user, the requirement to establish some conservation measures which may include a limitation of the exploitation of the beds; (3) the need to monitor the movement of seed and exercise control on such movements so as to prevent the introduction of disease and predators into areas previously unaffected; and (4) the requirement, when the stock is laid on fattening beds, to ensure that adequate husbandry is exercised, including adequate control of predators such as starfish and slipper limpets within the designated area. Furthermore, there may be a requirement to exercise control and revoke licences to farm a particular area, if as a result of negligence, mismanagement of a farm is prejudicial to the well-being of its neighbour.

In several countries, including France and Japan, the system adopted commercially for rearing oysters or mussels from seed to market size involves the use of structures fixed to the seabed or anchored rafts from which ropes are suspended and to which the molluscs are attached. The use of such structures clearly introduces problems which are not encountered in the traditional systems of mollusc cultivation presently prosecuted in the U.K. These rely on fattening the mollusc to market size on the seabed and harvesting the adults for market by means of dredges operated from vessels. However, with the advent of a supply of seed from hatcheries, there is likely to be a considerable expansion and change in the system of mollusc cultivation in the U.K.

This will involve the use of structures offshore affecting the rights of free navigation and requiring to be fixed or anchored to the seabed. A greater variety of molluscan species than presently catered for within existing legislation will also be reared. Briefly, and this will be dealt with in more detail when considering the farming of marine fish, the farmer will require to be able to erect structures on the seabed or anchor structures offshore either to the seabed or to the shore, or to have access to the structures from the land directly or by vessel. The conflicting interests of farming and navigation will have to be resolved, and the rights of the neighbouring landlord and of the public or others to use the inter-tidal zone will have to be clarified in the context of farming.

Above all, the farmer will require security of property and some right of redress against poachers and others who remove or damage either his stock or farm equipment or installations. It is of interest to note, in this context, that one of the reasons why the full potential of mussel cultivation in the Wash has not been realised is that the areas allocated to individual growers by means of a number of Statutory Instruments are small and scattered. The result is that an individual grower cannot effectively police his lays, nor is a grower willing to introduce more efficient cultivation techniques when the benefits can be reduced by malpractices on neighbouring lays.

The physical form of marine fish farms is difficult to state at present, as no system is yet fully developed. In so far as marine fish farms will involve the use of offshore structures, although not of precisely the same design as those used in shellfish cultivation, similar problems to those already mentioned will undoubtedly exist. From first-hand experience over the last five or six years during which the White Fish Authority has been working on marine fish farming, and from experience in Japan, the U.S.A. and other countries, it is possible to speculate on what shape and form a fish farm might take. It is unlikely that there will be one standard design of fish farm—the economics of one system will be more attractive than another depending on the species to be farmed. Other variables include the local topography, the availability and nature of the fish food, the local labour situation, and above all, whether the farm utilises natural water or thermal discharge from an electrical generating station or other industrial complex.

Assuming the stock is not caught in the open sea but is provided from a hatchery, each farm may have its own hatchery. It is more likely, however, that because of the degree of expertise required to operate a hatchery, a few hatcheries will supply the growers with stock. There are certain requirements to be met in the siting and operation of hatcheries. Ideally a hatchery should be located in an area where little or no known contamination or pollution of the intake water is likely to occur. Some protection against the development of industrial complexes upstream from the intake point would be welcomed by the hatchery operator. At present, at least as far as the United Kingdom is concerned, the only known recourse the operator has to such a development is by objection at public inquiries dealing with applications for planning permission. The ability to claim damages or loss of earnings resulting directly from pollution, whether accidental or not, would be an advantage. One of the principal difficulties in substantiating objections, whether made through existing channels or any new channels which may be provided, is the inability to specify precisely what discharges, or what chemical compounds in what concentrations, are harmful to the animals and therefore likely to endanger the success or economics of the operation. The effect of low level concentrations of pollutants may lead to mortalities or cause the animal to be stressed and result in poor growth or mortality from secondary causes, but the effect may not be seen for a considerable time after first exposure to the contamination. Whilst on the subject of pollution—the presence of the wrong substance in the wrong place and the wrong time—due regard must also be paid to chemical, bacterial or viral concentrations being built up by the animal itself. This may not be harmful to the animal but could be injurious to the health of the ultimate consumer. Examples which come to mind are the ability of certain animals to concentrate zinc, mercury compounds and radio-active material. The establishment of health standards and certification of the product destined for the human foodstuffs market is one approach, but control at source by regulation of discharge of the contaminant is more attractive. In the United Kingdom the Closing Order Procedure in the Public Health Acts precludes shellfish being taken from pulluted areas. There are many Closure Orders in force where shellfish may not be farmed.

Marine fish farms, or at least that part of the farm concerned with rearing the animal from the juvenile post-hatchery and nursery stage to marketable size, may involve the use of one of the following systems or a mixture of them.

(1) Low density, free range rearing of fish in a large area of water such as a Scottish loch, bay or inlet, or artificially created lagoon formed by bunds constructed offshore from which the fish are prevented from migrating either by means of solid barriers—*e.g.*, concrete dams, nets—or perhaps in the future, by means of some sort of electrical field, acoustic barrier or bubble curtain.

(2) High density culture involving the use of netting, floating or submerged cages utilising a rigid or flexible frame-work and covered to prevent the entry of predators, anchored to the seabed or sea shore or suspended from rafts, pontoons, cat-walks or piers. Such structures would require service facilities in the form of floating pontoons, cat-walks, piers or vessels to allow the necessary husbandry, feeding and inspection of fish for disease, etc., to be undertaken and to allow for the cleaning and maintenance of the rearing structures. Provision would have to be made in the design of the holding facilities or associated equipment for harvesting the fish.

(3) Structures constructed on the shore taking the form of excavated pools, ponds, tanks or raceways—essentially narrow tanks offering access for servicing—through which a flow of water is maintained either by gravity feed through the use of sluices from the open sea directly, or via reservoirs, or by pumping. Pumped water circulation is likely to be acceptable where fish are reared in the thermal discharge of a plant such as an electrical generating station where a " head " of water is available, but provision would have to be made to bypass the thermal discharge and to introduce sea water directly at times of the year when the temperature of the thermal discharge was too high for the well-being of the fish. Again provision for servicing, maintenance and harvesting the fish would be required.

Systems of high density culture similar to those described in (2) and (3) above show promise for marine fish in the development work being undertaken by the White Fish Authority, and most encouraging production rates are being obtained using a variety of species of fish and fish mixed with molluscs. Cage cultivation in the sea is also being used on a commercial scale in Japan and for Salmonid species in the U.K. and the U.S.A., as well as Norway.

The first system described, that of low-density, free-range culture, is, at our present state of knowledge, the least attractive because of the difficulty of exercising the necessary husbandry over the stock: it also raises quite severe problems of harvesting the stock cheaply and efficiently. It is, however, theoretically the most attractive because all other systems depend on the fish being supplied with virtually all their food requirements, whereas in the large stretch of water some natural food will be available, and if non-permeable barriers are used, *e.g.*, a concrete dam with sluices to form the enclosed body of water and to limit the interchange of water between the " pond " and sea, productivity might be increased by the use of artificial fertilisers and so reduce or eliminate the need for supplementary feeding. Furthermore, the total cost of enclosing a single large area of water in the manner described might be less than the cost of constructing and anchoring a number of small discrete holding facilities.

Although at present there is neither the requirement nor the technical know-how to utilise open waters further offshore for fish culture, provision should be made, when considering the legal requirements, to provide for the possibility of an extension of fish farms to offshore areas.

Finally, the capital works associated with a fish farm are likely to include processing, cold storage and packaging facilities, as well as hatchery buildings, nursery tanks, fish food stores and preparation rooms, pump houses and intake and outfall pipes. Fish farming buildings and land should enjoy the same taxation and rating concessions as agricultural land and buildings.

Inevitably there will be a conflict of interests between fish farmers and those wishing to use the area for other purposes. Because virtually no legislation has been enacted in support of fish farming (with the exception of farming oysters and certain other molluscs), the " other interests " are in a stronger position.

Fish farmers are, for example, already beginning to be faced with encroachment on their existing interests and curtailment of their extension by water sportsmen and naturalists. Recreation in the form of yachting and boating has a very strong lobby, which is understandably supported by the commercially interested boat builders and constructors and operators of marinas. The creation of nature reserves, for example, that proposed for the Swale in Kent, could effectively stop the extension of oyster-rearing grounds. In South Wales a commercially important cockle bed is subject to heavy predation by protected birds. Both shellfish and fish farmers have either to accept heavy losses of their stock, or to adopt expensive methods of protecting their stock from predation by a variety of birds and animals which are at present protected by law.

Depending on the system of fish farming which is adopted, and more than one system may be incorporated within a single fish farm complex, the fish farmer will require:

(1) To exercise complete control over his stock, whether that stock is sedentary or free-swimming and whatever the nature of the facilities used to contain that stock, and to have all rights of private property over his stock.

(2) To have access to the stock whensoever required.

(3) To be able to enclose a bay or inlet or other area of sea with a permeable or non-permeable barrier, and if necessary maintain a head of water permanently at or near high-water spring tide level.

(4) To have the right of access over the adjacent land and foreshore, be free to use the foreshore and be able to construct jetties, walkways or other structures on the beach and between high- and low-water mark as well as over the inter-tidal zone to the open water beyond.

(5) To be able to affix structures, *e.g.*, the ends of enclosures, dams or other forms of barriers in the inter-tidal zone or to the shore above high-water spring—the

height may be appreciably higher than normal high-water spring level to enable the barrier to function in periods of exceptional tides and to fix anchoring points ashore.

(6) To have the right to prohibit access by unauthorised persons to any part of the farm, be this below or above high-water mark, and to those areas of open water and and seabed which are an integral part of the " farm."

(7) To have the right to erect structures in the open sea or anchor floating or submerged structures offshore, and if necessary, to be able to use the inter-tidal area or shore for anchoring purposes. Such structures would comprise hazards to navigation. There should be freedom from liability for damage by collision.

(8) To be able to erect or build enclosures or anchor cages and carry out the necessary servicing in such a way that the conflicting interest of freedom of navigation and anchorage rights etc. are satisfied. The fish farmer would have to have the right to deny access to strange vessels, *e.g.*, yachts using his structures for berthing, anchoring, access to shore, etc.

(9) In the interest of good husbandry and to reduce the risk of disease and spread of predators, controls may be required on the movement of stock, and for the purpose of ensuring wholesomeness of the product destined for human consumption, quality standards may be required to be devised by and enforced by a recognised authority. Such regulations must be acceptable to both the farmer and the consumer and be updated in line with changing practices and techniques. For example, the existing prohibition on the sale of oysters at certain times of the year when the oysters are developing gonads, which was introduced to conserve natural regeneration of the oyster beds, is not applicable to non-indigenous species of oyster which do not reproduce naturally in the U.K. and are supplied from hatcheries.

II. SPECIFIC LEGAL PROBLEMS IN THE UNITED KINGDOM

The public has, generally speaking, a right to fish in the sea within the three mile territorial waters (or possibly now, within the 12 mile exclusive fishing zone of the United Kingdom), in arms of the sea and in tidal reaches of rivers and estuaries. This right may be exercised by laying lines, drawing nets or adopting any other ordinary method of fishing. There is an attendant public right, at places appropriated by usage to the purpose, to pass and repass across the foreshore for the purpose of fishing.

The public also has, generally speaking, a right of navigation in the sea and in tidal waters. This right extends to the foreshore between high- and low-water mark, and it is irrelevant that at certain states of the tide the water is too shallow for a vessel to float. It also comprises rights attendant to the right of navigation, such as mooring and anchoring. Although the right of navigation does not, in general, include a right to land persons or goods on the foreshore or banks, such a right may exist at places which usage has appropriated to the purpose. While the public right must be exercised reasonably and with due regard to the rights which the owner of the foreshore may have, the owner of the foreshore may do nothing (except under statutory authorisation) to interfere with the right of navigation.

As a general rule there is no absolute property in living fish. In their natural state they are wild creatures and, as such, are not owned by anyone. At common law, they can be the subject of larceny if reduced into possession. They can also be the subject of the offence of theft if kept in captivity or reduced into possession. " Wild creatures, tamed or untamed, shall be regarded as property; but a person cannot steal a wild creature not tamed nor ordinarily kept in captivity unless it has been reduced into possession by or on behalf of another person and possession of it has not since been lost or abandoned or another person is in course of reducing it into possession." [1†]

Under the Coast Protection Act 1949, the construction of any works on, under or over any part of the seashore requires the consent of the Minister if their construction would be likely to cause or would cause obstruction or danger to navigation. The "seashore" is defined as the bed and shore of the sea and of every channel, creek, bay or estuary and every river as far up that river as the tide flows and any cliff, bank, barrier, dune, beach, flat or other kind adjacent to the shore. The Act empowers the Minister to publish notice of an application for consent, to provide for receipt of objections and, if he thinks fit, to direct that a local inquiry be held. The Minister, if of the opinion that obstruction or danger to navigation will or is likely to result, is required either to refuse his consent or to attach to his consent conditions designed to mitigate the obstruction or danger otherwise resulting or likely to result: the period for which any consent given is to remain in force may also be restricted.

The Sea Fish (Conservation) Act 1967 prohibits a fishing vessel from either landing or carrying sea fish of less than the minimum size prescribed by an Order of the appropriate Ministers. An Order may confer exemptions from this prohibition: these exemptions may be general or subject to conditions and may relate to all fish covered by the Order or to fish of specified descriptions. The Act also empowers the Ministers by Order to prescribe minimum sizes of mesh for nets carried by fishing vessels. These Orders may provide for exemptions either generally or in relation to particular fishing vessels, or classes of fishing vessel. The Act exempts from both the prohibitions on the carrying of undersized fish and the terms of any Order relating to mesh sizes any fishing operations conducted for the purpose of transplanting fish from one fishing ground to another, provided those operations are carried on under the authority of one of the Ministers.

The sizes of fish which may be caught and the methods of catching which may be used may also be the subject of by-laws made by local fisheries committees under powers now contained in the Sea Fisheries Regulation Act 1966.

Under nineteenth-century legislation, now consolidated in the Sea Fisheries (Shellfish) Act 1967, the appropriate Minister may by Order grant exclusive rights of fishery within an area of the shore or seabed or of an estuary or tidal river, above or below or partly above and partly below low-water mark and within so much of the exclusive fishery limits of the British Islands as is adjacent to Great Britain. These rights may relate to oysters, mussels and cockles and, under an amending statute of 1968, to clams and any other molluscs of a kind specified in ministerial regulations. The Act provides for notification to interested persons of the intention to make an Order, for receipt of objections and for the holding of a local inquiry. The making of an Order confers upon the grantee exclusive rights within the area of the fishery to deposit, propagate and take shellfish of the species covered by the Order, to make and maintain beds and to take all necessary steps for the operation of the fishery. The grant may be for any period up to 60 years: it is, however, subject to determination if the Minister is not satisfied that that grantee is properly cultivating the area of the fishery for shellfish of the description to which the Order relates. The Act provides that shellfish covered by the Order within the area of the fishery shall be the absolute property of the grantee and deemed to be in his actual possession. The Act also protects the grantee

† For references, see p. 70.

against interference by unauthorised persons, by making it an offence, involving liability to a fine and to make compensation for damage done, to fish for shellfish within the area of the fishery (provided that this is sufficiently marked out), or (subject to the same proviso), to disturb or injure the shellfish other than in the exercise of lawful rights of navigation and anchorage.

Marine fish farming was among the subjects considered by the Scottish Inshore Fisheries Committee, appointed by the Secretary of State for Scotland to review the law governing the methods of sea fishing in Scottish coastal waters. In their Report,[2] the Committee expressed the view that, having regard to the rights which would be affected if marine fish farmers were afforded legal status and protection, the establishment of fish farms should be strictly regulated by law. At the same time they accepted that for the successful prosecution of fish farming the farmer must be afforded certain rights of exclusive possession and control. The Committee accordingly recommended that new legislation should:

(a) define sea fish farming and the rights of sea fish farmers;
(b) empower the Secretary of State to grant, conditionally, to any person or persons a right, including an exclusive right, to use any defined area of sea or seabed for the purpose of fish farming;
(c) require all persons wishing to establish sea fish farms to make application to the Secretary of State;
(d) require that such applications shall be publicly intimated and that objectors be given a suitable opportunity to make representations before a decision is taken on any application.

REFERENCES

1. Theft Act 1968, s. 4 (4).
2. Department of Agriculture and Fisheries for Scotland, *Regulation of Scottish Inshore Fisheries: Report of the Scottish Inshore Fisheries Committee* (Edinburgh: HMSO, 1970, Cmnd. 4453).

Part III

Pollution

CHAPTER 8

Definition and Forms of Marine Pollution

By Michael Hardy*

In considering the topic of marine pollution, it is first necessary to refer to the question of its definition. Despite its seeming scientific sound, "marine pollution" is not a single, precisely determined, biological, chemical or physical process. It may take any one of these forms, and the exact chain of cause and effect may require most complex scientific inquiries—indeed, as has been remarked, the seas may constitute the most difficult substance that science has yet been called upon to study. The definition of marine pollution supplied by expert United Nations bodies is:

> "Introduction by man, directly or indirectly, of substances or energy into the marine environment (including estuaries) resulting in such deleterious effects as harm to living resources, hazard to human health, hindrance to marine activities including fishing, impairment of quality for use of sea water and reduction of amenities." [1]†

What man may consider damage to the marine environment may thus take many different harmful forms and be produced, possibly cumulatively and over a lengthy period of time, as a result of many different human activities. The multiplicity of factors involved may in turn affect the nature of the regulatory measures to be taken and the question of apportionment of responsibility, if damage is found to have occurred.

Without going into the scientific aspects as to exactly what form of harm may be caused in each instance—an inquiry which, in any case, tends to run across categories, as chemical, physical and biological consequences impinge on one another—marine pollution may, for present purposes, be divided under six main headings, relating chiefly to the nature of the human activities involved: (1) marine pollution caused *via* the atmosphere by land-based activities; (2) the disposal of domestic and industrial wastes; (3) radioactive pollution; (4) the disposal of military materials; (5) ship-borne pollutants; and (6) pollution resulting from offshore mineral exploitation.[2] Of these headings, sources (1), (2) and (5) are the most important in the sense that they constitute the principal causes of marine pollution now encountered. It should, however, be

* Senior Legal Officer, Office of Legal Affairs, United Nations. Any views expressed are those of the author in a personal capacity and do not purport to represent those of the Organisation.

This paper is an extract from a longer study entitled "Offshore Development and Marine Pollution" prepared for a Regional Conference on the Petroleum Industry in Africa, organised by the Economic Commission for Africa and scheduled to be held in September 1973. The full study is to be published in (1973) *Ocean Development and International Law Journal.*

† For references see p. 76.

noted at the outset that land-based sources of all kinds (*e.g.*, outflow from rivers and outfalls, industrial wastes, agricultural run-off, air-borne pollutants such as vaporised hydrocarbons, and direct sewage discharge) provide the largest amounts of pollutants to the marine environment. In the specific case of petroleum, land-based sources are estimated to account for between 50 to 90 per cent. of the two to five million metric tons of oil which enter the seas each year.[3] The extent to which natural seepage of oil from the seabed contributes to marine pollution is not known, although there are indications that (at least in some areas) it may be significant. There is, of course, no known means of controlling this source. So far as sea-based activities are concerned, offshore exploration and exploitation of oil is thought to produce less than 2 per cent. of the total marine pollution caused by oil at the present time. Divided solely between marine activities, seabed oil activities are estimated to make up about 5 per cent. of oil pollution of the seas and vessels the remaining 95 per cent.[4] As seabed activities are intensified, however, the proportion of marine pollution from this source may be expected to increase, so as to require that further measures of national and international control be adopted.

(1) Marine pollution caused via the atmosphere

This is the source of marine pollution of which least is known.[5] The scientific evidence indicates three areas of particular concern: the use of various synthetic chemicals (especially chlorinated hydrocarbons) for agricultural purposes; the release of heavy metals (notably lead and mercury) in industrial and other processes; and the passage into the atmosphere of petroleum hydrocarbons from the use of petroleum to provide energy. The proposals made within the framework of the United Nations Conference on the Human Environment,[6] based on the work done by WMO, to establish a network of stations whereby atmospheric pollution may be measured, will constitute a significant means whereby the international community can guard against a deterioration in marine conditions from this source.

(2) The disposal of domestic and industrial wastes

The disposal of domestic and industrial wastes from the shore—whether by means of rivers, by sewage outlets, or by dumping—is by far the largest single source of marine pollution[7] and, from the nature of the case, the most varied in composition and in effect. Essentially the control measures taken are national: many of them are public health ordinances, others relate to controls over industrial processes, others again, including some of the most recent, deal with the matter within overall plans for the maintenance of water quality. The multiplicity of authorities involved, the large number of enactments, both local and national, and the absence hitherto of international consequences, appear to be responsible for the lack of a detailed comparative study of the regulations in question. There are indications that efforts are being made, both nationally and more widely, to improve the regulatory body of law in question.[8]

(3) Marine pollution caused by radioactivity

Marine pollution of this kind may result from natural radioactivity or from various human activities. The two major instances of the latter are the "fall out" from the testing of nuclear weapons and the dumping of radioactive wastes, the first being by far the most significant.[9] The 1963 Nuclear Test Ban Treaty placed a general ban on the testing of nuclear weapons. However, as is well known, not all nuclear States are parties to the Treaty. The dumping of radioactive wastes has not, so far as is known, produced any adverse effects.[10] If the volume of such wastes were to increase substantially, the matter would have to be re-examined and, in any case, is one which needs to be kept under careful review.

(4) The disposal of military materials

This source of marine pollution may be regarded as, on the one hand, an aspect of the military uses of the seas and, on the other, as a particular form of ocean dumping. The United Nations Committee on the Peaceful Uses of the Seabed has expressed its concern over this practice and appealed to all governments to refrain from using the seabed as a dumping ground for such materials.[11] It is to be hoped that the growth of nascent " community " or " general " interest in this sphere will continue, so as to keep this source of pollution at a minimum.

(5) Ship-borne pollutants

Pollution from this source may take many forms—as many forms as there are ships and cargoes—but attention has been concentrated on the loss of oil. A distinction may be drawn between pollution resulting from acts performed in the course of normal ship operations and pollution resulting from accidents. The first largely concerns the practice, hitherto prevalent but now, it is to be hoped, on the decline, of filling or flushing empty tanks with sea water[12] and emptying the resulting mixture into the ocean. The International Convention for the Prevention of Pollution of the Sea by Oil, which was concluded in 1954 and amended, under the auspices of IMCO, in 1962, 1969 and 1971, places steadily increased controls on ship practices in this regard. Under the 1954 and 1962 versions of the convention, the discharge of oil or of oily mixture was prohibited within specified zones[13]; the 1969 and 1971 amendments do away with the system of prohibited zones and in principle prohibit oil discharge (except under carefully limited conditions) more stringently than those previously applicable.

A Conference, to be held under IMCO auspices from October 8 to November 2, 1973, will consider the adoption of a more comprehensive instrument. The draft " International Convention for the Prevention of Pollution from Ships 1973 " contains a number of general principles and a series of technical annexes relating to the prevention of pollution caused by oil from ships, by noxious substances other than oil carried in bulk or in packages, or by ship-generated sewage and garbage.[14] As regards oil pollution from ships, the draft Convention contains provisions relating to all the aspects covered by the 1954 Convention, as subsequently amended, which it would effectively supersede. The new provisions are more stringent than existing requirements, in particular as regards the deliberate discharge of oil. In the case of noxious substances other than oil, some 450 substances carried by ships have been evaluated, with the help of experts from GESAMP, in terms of the hazards they pose with respect to bio-accumulation characteristics, harm to human health, marine life or amenities. Based on this evaluation, three main categories of harmful substances have been identified. For each of these, the discharge of tank washings, dirty ballast and other residues and mixtures will be prohibited except in accordance with very strict criteria. The issue of certificates, recording that ships satisfy the conditions laid down with respect to the nature of their equipment and the maintenance of records, is intended to ensure the effective application of the convention and to enable inspection by national authorities to proceed smoothly and in a uniform manner.[15]

Marine pollution arising out of normal ship operations may be distinguished from that which may result when a bulk carrier—typically a tanker—loses its cargo as a result of an accident,[16] whether because of a storm, a collision, or by running aground.

Tankers have increased greatly in size over the past 10–15 years and though there may now be a levelling out, the size is large enough to entail a risk of substantial harm; the case of the *Torrey Canyon* is well known.[17] The measures to be taken include provision of improved navigation aids, increased training for ships' officers, changes in ship construction methods, and limitations on the size of individual tanks, all of which are under active consideration by IMCO and by various technical and industrial bodies. Regionally, arrangements have been made for regional co-operation and, internationally, for the possibility of intervention by governments on the high seas to avert the dangers of a catastrophic accident threatened by a ship or its cargo, under the terms of the International Convention Relating to Intervention on the High Seas in Cases of Oil Pollution Casualties, drawn up under IMCO auspices in 1969.[18] The nature and extent of the obligation incurred by the ship owner to compensate for any pollution damage caused is regulated by an accompanying instrument, the International Convention on Civil Liability for Oil Pollution Damage.[19]

The 1973 IMCO Conference, besides considering the proposed Convention for the Prevention of Pollution from Ships, will also have before it a draft Protocol to the 1969 Intervention Convention. The Protocol would extend the principles and procedures of the 1969 Convention to noxious and hazardous substances other than oil carried by ships. States would thus be able to take action with respect to pollution threatened or caused by substances other than oil, following a marine casualty or threat of a casualty, in the same way as they can now do with respect to accidents involving tankers. The main instances which would be covered by the new instrument would be accidents involving ships transporting chemicals in bulk.

REFERENCES

1. Definition adopted by the Inter-governmental Oceanographic Commission (based on a definition originally prepared by a SCOR/ACMRR/Working Group) and accepted by the Joint IMCO/FAO/UNESCO/WMO/WHO/IAEA/UN Group of Experts on the Scientific Aspects of Marine Pollution (GESAMP). See doc. A/7750, Part I, 3, Nov. 10, 1969, and GESAMP I/II, para. 12. See also principle 7 of the Declaration of the United Nations Conference on the Human Environment.

2. This last source is considered separately below, see *infra*, Lay, pp. 103–105.

3. *Marine Environment Quality*, U.S. National Research Council, 1971; *Man's Impact on the Global Environment*, Report of the Study of Critical Environmental Problems, Massachusetts Institute of Technology, 1970; "Tankers and ecology," *Transportation*, Vol. 79, 1971. Cited in working paper presented by the United States to the Committee on the Peaceful Uses of the Seabed and the Ocean Floor beyond the Limits of National Jurisdiction, doc. A/AC.138/SC.III/L.36.

4. "Tankers and ecology," n. 3 above.

5. Two documents prepared by WMO for GESAMP (GESAMP II/2/4 and II/2/1) describe respectively the role of the atmosphere in hydrological cycles which contributes to marine pollution as a result of run off from land contaminated by industrial dust or agricultural pesticides, and atmospheric pollution in general and the establishment of a network of stations, whereby atmospheric pollution may be measured. WMO has sponsored, by resolution 11 (EC–XXI) of its Executive Committee, the establishment of a network of stations to measure background pollution. Pollution of the sea by transfer from the atmosphere and the dispersal and transport of surface pollution by natural physical processes, such as winds, waves and currents, are under examination by GESAMP.

6. See *infra*, Fleischer, pp. 93–94.

7. Atmospheric deposition and natural seepage (as opposed to deliberate disposal) may be responsible for larger amounts of material entering the oceans in a significant number of cases, including hydrocarbons and possibly lead and mercury. These sources, however, do

not appear (at least so far as available evidence goes) to contribute to marine pollution to the same extent as materials directly disposed of in the seas as a result of immediate human activities. Further investigations in the future may of course show a different, and more complex, picture. There are so many unknown factors that few conclusive statements are possible; since the seas have not previously had to cope with the entry of so large a volume of hydrocarbons and heavy metals it is difficult to say what the consequences will be, of a substantial increase in the amounts concerned, coming from a variety of sources.

8. As regards international measures, reference may be made to the conclusion of the Convention on the Prevention of Marine Pollution by Dumping of Wastes and Other Matter (the 1972 Ocean Dumping Convention). See *infra*, Fleischer, pp. 86–88.

9. According to IAEA " By far the larger contribution to the radioactivity burden of the seas has come from nuclear weapon tests," " The Sea: International Co-operation in Questions relating to Oceans," doc. E/4836, May 12, 1970, para. 44.

10. So stated by the IOC Working Group on Marine Pollution; see the recommendations of its first meeting, Aug. 14, 1967, n. 10 to Table of Major Categories of Pollution. The deliberate dumping of radioactive material is covered by the 1972 Ocean Dumping Convention, see *infra*, Fleischer, p. 92.

11. The dumping of materials produced for biological and chemical warfare is also covered by the 1972 Ocean Dumping Convention. See *infra*, Fleischer, pp. 86–87.

12. The main reason why this is done is to provide ballast for an otherwise empty ship, so as to prevent it moving violently in rough weather. Besides the IMCO Convention mentioned in the text, the use of " load on top " procedures has also been instrumental in reducing marine pollution caused by routine oil spills. See Hardy " International Control of Marine Pollution " (1971) 11 *Natural Resources Journal*, 296 at 321 *et seq.*, and works there cited.

13. Under the 1962 amendments the prohibited area extends generally 50 miles from the coast of all countries and may be extended by a State party to 100 miles; special consideration was given to particular regions, such as the Mediterranean. Under the 1969 amendments, there is a ban on the discharge of oil in excess of a rate of 60 litres of oil for each mile travelled.

14. The dumping of shore-generated waste and the release of harmful substances in the course of seabed mineral development are excluded.

15. Among other new requirements, contracting States would be obliged to ensure the provision of adequate port facilities, particularly oil-loading terminals and repair ports, for the reception of oily residues. This is a particularly important aspect in enclosed or semi-enclosed seas, where ships engaged on short-haul voyages may have difficulty in complying with the new limitations on operational discharges. Such areas are regarded as " special areas " for which certain other restrictions are also envisaged.

16. For relative frequencies and other data see *Environmental Conservation, The Oil and Gas Industries*, a report by a committee of the U.S. Natural Petroleum Council, Vol. 2, Feb. 1972, pp. 241 *et seq.*, especially figure 59 at p. 242 and table 32 at p. 249. According to the information given there, 75% of past major oil spills were associated with vessels and less than 10% from refineries and offshore drilling (the latter being assessed at approximately 5%). 70% of the spills were greater than 5,000 barrels and 90% involved crude or residual oils. 80% occurred within 10 miles of the shore and 75% within 25 miles from the nearest port. 80% contaminated less than 20 miles of coastline and 85% occurred off recreational areas.

17. See *infra*, Fleischer, pp. 80, 89.

18. For details see Hardy, *op. cit.*, at pp. 324–325, and also *infra*, Fleischer, pp. 90–91.

19. See Hardy, *op. cit.* pp. 325–327. There is a ceiling of $14 million as regards the compensation payable by a ship-owner with respect to any one incident. Neither of these conventions has yet entered into force. It may be noted that arrangements have since been made under IMCO auspices for the creation of a supplementary international compensation fund for oil pollution damage; see the final Act of the Conference held at Brussels, Nov. 29–Dec. 18, 1971, IMCO doc. LEG/CONF. 2/9, Dec. 16, 1971. The tanker owners have established a fund (Tanker Owners' Voluntary Agreement on Oil Pollution), with a ceiling of $9,600,000 per accident, intended to compensate governments directly. Another body, the Oil Companies International Marine Forum, was set up with the intention of providing the higher " cover " with which the new international compensation fund is concerned.

CHAPTER 9

Pollution from Seaborne Sources

By Carl August Fleischer*

1. INTRODUCTION

THIS paper will be limited to the discussion of pollution which has its source in acts which take place on the sea itself and therefore often outside the ordinary limits of national jurisdiction. An observation of a general character, which should be made at the outset, is that the problems of the "international" and the "municipal" sources are interrelated. Dumping in the ocean is just one of the methods by which the industry on the continent can get rid of its waste—including by-products which cannot today be marketed at a sufficiently attractive price. The same substances will reach the sea and contribute to the often alarming state of marine pollution, whether they are dumped from barges outside territorial limits or carried by rivers after being pumped directly into them.

Against this background it must be a priority, when action is undertaken to prohibit or limit a certain activity which leads to marine pollution, to avoid the possible effects of transferring the pollution from one source to another. Little is achieved if prohibition of ocean dumping just implies that the same substances will be dumped in rivers or territorial waters instead. In this connection reference may be made to the principles adopted by the United Nations Intergovernmental Working Group on Marine Pollution in November 1971 and endorsed by the 1972 United Nations Conference on the Human Environment at Stockholm (Recommendation No. 92), in particular, principle No. 13: "Action to prevent and control marine pollution (particularly direct prohibitions and specific release limits) must guard against the effect of simply transferring damage or hazard from one part of the environment to another."

Another observation is that many of the "international" types of pollution result from activities which intentionally are carried out by a party beyond the limits of national jurisdiction, because of the advantage it gives the party to escape from the ordinary exercise of jurisdiction within the limits of State territory.

Ocean dumping of waste has become a practical alternative as a result of the fact that no State would want the same substances or articles disposed of on its own territory. Outside the territorial limit the question of jurisdiction is more complex. In many cases, pollution is the result of ships sailing under flags of convenience.

* Professor of Law at the University of Oslo, Special Consultant in International Law to the Royal Ministry of Foreign Affairs, Oslo.

2. POLLUTION AND THE FREEDOM OF THE SEA: GENERAL VIEWPOINTS

International as well as national measures to control marine pollution have today become a matter of paramount importance for the world community.

In earlier years writers on the law of the sea used to spend a lot of time and paper discussing whether the area beyond national jurisdiction should be regarded as *res nullius*—belonging to no one—or as *res communis*; a term which has been adopted in considering the oceans as the "common heritage of mankind." But the important aspects are not those of legal terminology. The principal factor is that the nations of the world are dependent, and will become increasingly dependent, on the sea for transport, for the exploitation of its living resources and even for their supply of oxygen; resources which today are threatened with serious damage and in some cases even extermination as a result of uncontrolled use of the sea, *inter alia* as a dumping-ground for toxic materials from the chemical industry.

The principle of the freedom of the sea, according to which no State can prescribe legislation or take action against a foreign vessel on the high seas, may to some extent be considered as being in opposition to these considerations. On the one hand, the high seas still comprise by far the greatest portion of the world's marine resources, despite efforts by some States to extend their national sovereignty over large areas hitherto considered as high seas, *e.g.*, the claims for jurisdiction over a 200 mile zone. On the other hand, for purposes of regulating traffic on the high seas themselves, freedom of the seas represents a division of competence among nations. The term "freedom" is a misnomer in the sense that no person or ship is free to travel the high seas without carrying the flag of some country. And there is no such thing as a "freedom" in relation to the legislation of the flag State and the exercise thereof. While each State, as a general rule, can exercise jurisdiction only against a ship under its own flag, it has a perfect right and often even a clear obligation to do so, as set out in the 1958 Convention on the High Seas, Article 5 (1), and in particular as regards pollution, Articles 24 and 25. As in the area of non-marine pollution, the authorities of all States taken together are competent to take the action which is required. But they have refrained from doing so in practice. The steps each State has taken until now in its own sphere of sovereignty have not been sufficient.

The reason is obvious. Measures taken by one single State to restrict the freedom to perform acts which alone, or together with other acts, constitute hazards to the marine environment, would only affect its own ships. The freedom of the seas, which *de jure* is solely a division of competence among the authorities of different States, has therefore become a *de facto* freedom for the individual to disregard the interests of others in their continued exercise of the freedom of the seas. It becomes clear that a State's unilateral regulation of the relatively narrow belt, which is recognised as territorial waters, and its regulation of its own ships on the high seas, can never be effective as a means to protect the marine environment. Here I might associate myself with Professor Richard A. Falk, who rightly points out that the existing threat to the human environment is closely linked to the sovereignty of States.[1]†

But this does not mean that national sovereignty or the legal principle of the freedom of the seas should be abolished or replaced by another general rule which gives one or more nations a prerogative to visit and search vessels from other nations while on the high seas. Schemes of control on the high seas *vis-à-vis* ships of other nations

† For references, see p. 101.

must be restricted to certain specific fields and specific types of vessels where such schemes are found practicable. No single nation can perform the task of policing the sea, and a mutual right of control might easily lead to serious conflicts in practice.

It may well be said that we cannot expect to save the marine environment by applying the present international law of the sea, the main principles of which were developed in the age of sailing ships. However, the freedom of the sea or the division of competence is not inadequate as such. What is needed is co-operation among States to develop rules which supplement the existing but imprecise standard of reasonableness in the use of the sea, and above all the exercise of effective jurisdiction by all States to prevent such acts or activities which are carried out without " reasonable regard to the interests of other States in their exercise of the freedom of the high seas," to use the words of Article 2, paragraph 2 of the Geneva Convention on the High Seas.

3. EXISTING RULES OF INTERNATIONAL LAW: GENERAL SURVEY

The existing body of law, which may be applied to the activities which are the subject of the present paper, may be divided in three:

1. General principles of international law; not specifically related to the law of the sea.
2. General principles of the law of the sea; such as Article 2 of the Geneva Convention on the High Seas.
3. Rules specifically dealing with pollution of the sea.

Under item 3 we may also present a subdivision: (a) general rules on pollution, such as Articles 24 and 25 of the Geneva Convention, (b) specific conventions on pollution, such as the 1954, 1969 and 1971 IMCO Conventions, and (c) rules and regulations which, though not dealing specifically with pollution, are designed to or have the effect of preventing pollution or reducing the risk thereof, such as rules to prevent collision. As for the latter category, it goes beyond the purpose of the present paper to consider such rules in detail, or even to list the existing conventions which have a more or less direct bearing on the prevention of pollution. It should be borne in mind, however, that marine pollution and the question of the safety of life at sea in general are interrelated. In several cases marine pollution caused by accident may be considered as a result of the ship's failure to comply with general navigational standards, as was the case for the stranding of the *Torrey Canyon* on March 18, 1967. Indeed, after this accident and the ensuing spillage of oil, the then British Prime Minister, Harold Wilson, proposed a series of measures to the Intergovernmental Maritime Consultative Organisation in order to avoid similar happenings in the future. Mr. Wilson's list was not restricted to questions of high seas intervention or civil liability for oil pollution damage, but included items such as: sea lanes, restrictions of speed within a specified distance from land, whether masters and/or crew should be specially trained and qualified to use additional equipment, whether there should be some limitation on the use of automatic pilots, whether certain routes should be specifically surveyed and marked, etc.[2]

4. GENERAL PRINCIPLES OF INTERNATIONAL LAW

The " international " sources of marine pollution must be subject to the same general principles of law which were applied *inter alia* in the *Trail Smelter Case*.[3] To a large extent these general principles, which are not limited to the law of the sea, were set out in that case in the following wording:

"The Tribunal, therefore, finds that the above decisions,[4] taken as a whole, constitute an adequate basis for its conclusions, namely, that under the principles of international law, as well as of the law of the United States, no State has the right to use or permit the use of its territory in such a manner as to cause injury by fumes on or to the territory of another or the properties or persons therein, when the case is of serious consequence and the injury is established by clear and convincing evidence.

"The decisions of the Supreme Court of the United States which are the basis of these conclusions are decisions in equity and a solution inspired by them, together with the regime hereinafter prescribed, will, in the opinion of the Tribunal, be 'just to all parties concerned', as long, at least, as the present conditions in the Columbia River Valley continue to prevail.

"Considering the circumstances of the case, the Tribunal holds that the Dominion of Canada is responsible in international law for the conduct of the Trail Smelter. Apart from the undertakings in the Convention, it is, therefore, the duty of the Government of the Dominion of Canada to see to it that this conduct should be in conformity with the obligation of the Dominion under international law as herein determined."

The same basic principle, as stated by the *Trial Smelter Arbitration*, is applied to water pollution, and, in particular, to rivers, in the preamble of a draft European Convention on the Protection of Fresh Waters against Pollution, at present under preparation under the auspices of the Council of Europe.

The tenth preambular paragraph has the following wording: "Considering that it is a general principle of international law that no country is entitled to exploit its natural resources in a way that may cause substantial damage in a neighbouring country."

There can be no doubt that these general principles apply to the sea as well, and that a State may consequently be responsible both for its own activities and for its lack of effective jurisdiction *vis-à-vis* nationals and vessels when pollution of the sea has been caused. The wording of the award on the *Trail Smelter* certainly deals with activities which took place in the territory of Canada and which caused damage "in or to the territory" of another State, namely the United States. But it is difficult to find any convincing material to support a conclusion that the State's obligation to control vessels under its registry is in principle different from the obligation to control its territory (even if the fiction of regarding a ship as *territoire flottant* is not generally accepted).

Nor is there sufficient reason to deny to States a claim that their "common heritage," the seas, should be protected from damage caused by other States or by their failure to exercise effective jurisdiction, on the same basis as a State can protest against violations of its own territory according to the wording of the *Trail Smelter* decision. This is the case even if damage to territory may imply a "violation of sovereignty," which is not present when the damage caused is limited to the high seas. The obligation of States to refrain from *culpa* is not limited to acts which may infringe upon the sovereignty of another State. And even if the aspect of "violation of sovereignty" was presented by the claimant in the *Trail Smelter Case*, it was not on this basis that the tribunal came to its conclusions.[5] In this connection reference may also be made to the principle of Article 2, paragraph 2, of the Geneva Convention, declaratory of international law, which sets out that the high seas shall be open to all nations and reiterates the international obligation to respect the right of every nation to its use. It may also be pointed out that all activities which contribute to the pollution of the high seas, will also in time to some extent contribute to the pollution of territorial waters and thereby to a violation of sovereignty.

In this connection the 1949 *Corfu Channel Case* is of particular interest. In this case the International Court of Justice *expressis verbis* laid down Albania's obligation to prevent the use of its territory in such a way as to infringe upon the rights of other States to navigate through the Channel. The pollution which exists today has mainly effects with regard to the common right of usage in relation to fisheries and recreational values. But there can be no doubt that the same protection under international law applies here as with regard to the common freedom to navigate and the common right to make use of the sea as a *res communis* for this purpose. The Court said:

> "Such obligations are based, not on the Hague Convention of 1907, No. VII, which is applicable in time of war, but on certain general and well-recognised principles, namely: elementary considerations of humanity, even more exacting in peace than war; the principle of the freedom of maritime communication; and every State's obligation not to allow knowingly its territory to be used for acts contrary to the rights of other States." [6]

It goes beyond the scope of the present paper to pursue any detailed analysis of the general principles of law and the extent to which they may be applied in pollution cases. In addition to what has been said, however, one should mention that we are here in a field which may also be looked upon from the angle of "State responsibility." In the second report to the International Law Commission, the Commission's special rapporteur, Mr. Ago, has suggested an article laying down the principle that every "internationally wrongful act by a State gives right to international responsibility." [7] As to what constitutes an "internationally wrongful act", I personally find the formula chosen by the Harvard Law School in its 1961 draft Convention on the international responsibility of States for injuries to aliens, attractive:

> "1. An act or omission which is attributable to a state and causes an injury to an alien is 'wrongful' as the term is used in this Convention:
>
> (a) if, without sufficient justification, it is intended to cause, or to facilitate the causing of, injury;
> (b) if, without sufficient justification, it creates an unreasonable risk of injury through a failure to exercise due care;
> (c) if it is an act or omission defined in Articles 5 to 12; or
> (d) if it violates a treaty.
>
> 2. The wrongfulness of such an act or omission may be the result of the fact that the law of the State does not conform to international standards or of the fact that the law, although conforming to international standards, has been misapplied." (Article 3.)

Although the authors evidently have not intended specifically to cover cases of pollution, or seem to have had these in mind, the proposed article would support a conclusion that a party which pollutes the sea and thereby causes a risk to the use of the sea by other parties for fishing and other purposes, acts contrary to international law unless that party can invoke "sufficient justification" for its conduct.

5. GENERAL RULES OF THE LAW OF THE SEA

As stated in the preamble of the 1958 High Seas Convention, its provisions are meant to be "generally declaratory of established principles of international law." This clearly is the case as regards the fundamental rule of Article 2.

On the one hand, Article 2, paragraph 1, lays down the very principles of the freedom of the sea itself: The high seas being open to all nations, no State may validly purport to subject any part of them to its sovereignty. It comprises, *inter alia*, for all States the freedoms of "navigation," "fishing," "to lay submarine cables and pipe lines" and "to fly over the high seas." As shown by the wording "*inter alia*" the enumeration is not exhaustive. And paragraph 2 of the same article speaks of "others" (*i.e.*, "freedoms") which are "recognised by the general principles of international law."

On the other hand the exercise of the freedom is not unlimited. Article 2, paragraph 1, states that "freedom of the high seas is exercised under the conditions laid down by these articles and by the other rules of international law." In paragraph 2 we find the obligation to respect the right of others to enjoy the same freedoms and the well-known test of reasonableness: "These freedoms ... shall be exercised by all States with reasonable regard to the interests of other States in their exercise of the freedom of the high seas."

From time to time the view has been advanced that the positive part of Article 2 also implies a licence to pollute, or that a right to dump harmful materials is one of the freedoms of the sea. This view is obviously unsound. There can be no such thing as a right to pollute, or to cause a permanent degradation of the waters to which all nations have an equal right. If dumping should be considered as an exercise of the freedom of the seas on the basis of Article 2, it must be restricted to cases where it has been established that the dumping may take place without harmful consequences of any significance.

More important are the restrictions which follow from Article 2, especially the second paragraph: this must imply a general obligation for States to refrain from activities which cause a greater risk of pollution than can be justified according to the test of reasonableness, and to see that such activities are not undertaken by persons or ships having their nationality.

Nationality—or in other words the questions of registry or flag State—is the key factor in regard to maritime jurisdiction. Article 5 of the convention departs from the principle that it is up to each State to fix the conditions for the grant of its nationality to ships, for the registration of ships in its territory, and for the right to fly its flag. As we know, this freedom has led to the use of flags of convenience, which again has become one of the most serious obstacles to an effective and modern regulation of the law of the sea in general and of marine pollution in particular. For this reason the practice of flags of convenience threatens the very existence of the principle of the freedom of the seas: the lack of effective jurisdiction and of the political will to establish the necessary regulations by international agreement will inevitably lead to unilateral action by some States, as was evidenced in the case of the Canadian action in 1970 and the establishment of a 100 mile anti-pollution zone by virtue of the Arctic Waters Pollution Prevention Act. The continued practice that a ship-owner can seek shelter from effective legislation by using any country he chooses as the State of registry is not only damaging to the regulation of world shipping as a whole. If the practice is to be pursued, it will also serve as an ever-present justification for unilateral measures on the part of coastal States.

Article 5 also requires a " genuine link " between the ship and the State of registry. And " in particular the State must effectively exercise its jurisdiction and control in administrative, technical and social matters over ships flying its flag." However, despite the grave hazards of marine pollution and the danger which today's practice presents to the freedom of the seas itself, both maritime and coastal States seem to have refrained from taking effective steps to secure the observance of Article 5. It should be added that the provisions of the article have met with serious criticism, and that it seems uncertain what consequences other States might draw from the fact that Article 5 has not been observed.[8]

The importance of these jurisdictional considerations is also borne out by the fact already mentioned, that the freedom of the high seas, or rather the division of competence among the flag States, is not inadequate as such. Maritime pollution is not a result of the jurisdictional monopoly of the flag State, but of its unwillingness to exercise effective jurisdiction and to take part in effective measures which are agreed on the international level. In principle, the jurisdictional monopoly which present international law accords to the flag State, is a corollary to the territorial jurisdiction which must be applied to prevent pollution coming from national territory. It may, however, be noted that the flag State's jurisdiction as it today is exercised by most countries does not respond satisfactorily to the needs of the international community to preserve both the marine environment as such and the coastline of other States against contamination. A Canadian film (*Who owns the Sea?*), which was shown to the participants at the 1972 July–August Session of the United Nations Committee on the Peaceful Uses of the Seabed and the Ocean Floor beyond the Limits of National Jurisdiction put it this way: " As the ship goes down, flag State jurisdiction goes down with it. And it is left for others to clean up the mess."

Articles 24 and 25 of the High Seas Convention are also of a fairly general character, even if limited to certain types of pollution. Article 24 concerns the duty " to draw up regulations " to prevent pollution of the seas by the discharge of oil from ships or pipelines or resulting from activities regarding the seabed and its subsoil. Article 25, paragraph 1, concerns the special problem of " dumping of radioactive waste." Every State shall " take measures " to prevent pollution from this source. Paragraph 2 of the same article has a broader scope, as it prescribes a general obligation for all States to " co-operate with the competent international organisations " in taking measures for the prevention of pollution from " any activities with radio-active materials or other harmful agents."

The wording of these articles appears somewhat casuistical and one may question the justification for their limited scope, *e.g.*, why Article 25, paragraph 2, concerns only a duty to co-operate with organisations in opposition to States. However, it goes without saying that Articles 24 and 25 cannot be interpreted *a contrario* so as to exclude, *e.g.*, an obligation on States to draw up regulations to prevent the discharge of substances other than oil, which is the only one mentioned in Article 24.

Obviously the standards in Article 2 and Articles 24 and 25 are far too imprecise to form any practical deterrent. They need to be supplemented by detailed regulations for different types of pollution and for different activities. One must, however, guard against the fact that such detailed rules will be regarded as the sole basis for controlling pollution: even if the detailed rules of other conventions are complied with, States must also conform to the general obligations of the Geneva Convention to avoid any unjustified pollution.

6. OCEAN DUMPING

General

The dumping of toxic or other hazardous or noxious substances in the sea will, to a great extent, be covered by the general principles which are expressed in Articles 2, 24 and 25 of the Geneva Convention. These standards have, however, not been able to prevent the widespread practice whereby land-based industries dispose of their waste by this method. Some firms have even been set up for the specific purpose of dumping industrial waste.

The dumping of industrial waste, which very often contains toxic material, such as heavy metals and certain hydrocarbons, must be distinguished from the more innocuous cases, such as the dumping of sand, mud or clay. In some parts of the world ocean dumping is also being used as one of the methods to get rid of ordinary sewage. This seems to represent just one part of the general problem of municipal sewage, and does probably not require special consideration from the angle of ocean dumping as such.

It may be that the material to be dumped contains oil or substances which are of the kind to fall under the definitions of the 1954 London Convention for the Prevention of Pollution of the Sea by Oil, which prohibits the discharge of oil or "oily mixture" into the sea (with amendments of 1962 and 1969). This is not unusual, especially as regards waste from the petrochemical industry, which uses oil as a basic raw material.

The Oslo Convention of February 15, 1972

The Oslo Convention is a regional arrangement for the north-east part of the Atlantic Ocean. In the original discussions the attention was centred around the North Sea. It was obvious, however, that it would not be possible to restrict the convention area to the North Sea, as this would only mean that the dumping which otherwise would have taken place in the North Sea itself, would be transferred to other parts of the North-East Atlantic area.

The convention is directed against marine pollution by dumping from ships and aircraft. In the preamble it is stated that concerted action by governments at "national, regional and global levels is essential to prevent and combat marine pollution." The preamble also refers to the fact that pollution of the sea has many sources, including dumping from ships and aircraft and discharges through rivers, estuaries, outfalls and pipelines within national jurisdiction. It is important that States use the best practical means to prevent such pollution. Products and processes which will minimise the amount of harmful waste requiring disposal should be developed. At the same time the participating States are convinced that international action to "control" the pollution of the sea by the dumping of harmful substances can and should be taken without delay. But this should not preclude discussions of measures to control other sources of marine pollution as soon as possible. The parties consider that the States bordering the North-East Atlantic have a particular responsibility to protect the waters of this region.

In Article 1 the parties have undertaken a duty to take all possible steps to prevent pollution of the sea by harmful substances in general. The substances referred to are those "that are liable to create hazards to human health, to harm living resources and marine life, to damage amenities or to interfere with other legitimate uses of the sea." This general obligation is not restricted to the question of dumping.

In Article 3 the parties agree to apply the measures which they adopt, in such a way as to prevent diversion of dumping into seas outside the convention area. Article 4 lays down an obligation to harmonise the policies of States, and generally to " introduce, individually and in common," measures to prevent the pollution of the sea by dumping.

The more specific obligations with regard to ocean dumping are divided into three. In Article 5 we find a total prohibition of the dumping of certain substances listed in Annex I to the convention. This Annex contains such substances as " organohalogen compounds and compounds which may form such substances in the marine environment, excluding those which are non-toxic, or which are rapidly converted in the sea into substances which are biologically harmless," and mercury and mercury compounds, cadmium and cadmium compounds, persistent plastics and other persistent synthetic materials which may float and remain in the sea, etc. In addition to this " black list " we have a " grey list," regulated by Article 6 and Annex II. Here there is no absolute prohibition, but dumping shall be subject to special control. The " grey list " contains such substances as arsenic, lead, copper, zinc, cyanides and fluorides, and pesticides and their by-products not covered by the provisions of Annex I. Annex II also mentions " substances which, though of a non-toxic nature, may become harmful due to the quantities in which they are dumped, or which are liable to seriously reduce amenities." The dumping of these substances, in quantities which the commission defines as significant, shall be subject to a permit granted in each specific case from the appropriate national authority. Article 7 contains a general rule that no dumping of substances or materials shall take place without the approval of the appropriate national authority or authorities. Annex III to the convention contains important considerations and conditions which shall be taken account of when the authorities decide, *inter alia,* where the dumping should take place.

Article 15 deals with the aspect of jurisdiction. The specific provisions of Article 15, paragraph 1, are not directed towards the real source of the pollution, namely certain industries in most cases, but towards ships and aircraft. On the other hand, the parties have to take measures not only against ships and aircraft registered in their territories. A State must also ensure compliance with the convention by ships and aircraft " loading in its territory the substances and materials which are to be dumped," and by ships and aircraft " believed to be engaged in dumping within its territorial sea." In practice this will also place the duty to exercise effective jurisdiction upon the State in whose territory the production is taking place, and where the waste is taken on board for the purpose of ocean dumping. Article 16 establishes an international commission, whose duty it shall be to supervise the implementation of the convention, to review generally the condition of the seas to which the convention applies, and consider the efficacy of the control measures being adopted, and the need for any additional or different measures. It shall keep under review the contents of the Annexes to the convention, and recommend such amendments, additions or deletions as may be agreed.

The Intergovernmental Conference on the Convention of the Dumping of Wastes at Sea; the London Convention of December 29, 1972

A world-wide multilateral convention being based on the same principles as the Oslo Convention was agreed to at the Intergovernmental Conference in London from October 13 to November 13, 1972. In addition to what is said in the Oslo Convention, the preamble of the London Convention restates principle 21 of the Stockholm Declaration on the Human Environment: States have a sovereign right to exploit their own resources, and the responsibility to ensure that activities within their jurisdictional control do not cause damage to the environment of other States or of areas beyond the limits of national jurisdiction. Also, the preamble points to the need for appropriate regional arrangements supplementary to the general convention.

In Article I the contracting parties declare that they shall " individually and collectively promote the effective control of all sources of pollution of the marine environment." They pledge themselves especially to take all practical steps to prevent the pollution of the sea by " the dumping of waste and other matter that is liable to create hazards to human health, to harm living resources and marine life, to damage amenities or to interfere with other legitimate uses of the sea." Also Article II gives a fairly general statement of the obligation to prevent the pollution caused by dumping, by taking effective measures individually and collectively. States shall harmonise their policies in this regard.

Article III contains a definition of the word " dumping " as used in the convention. According to Article III, paragraph (1), dumping means " any deliberate disposal at sea of wastes and other matter from vessels, aircraft, platforms or other man-made structures at sea." Dumping does not include the disposal of wastes or other matter incidental to, or derived from, the normal operations of vessels, aircraft, etc. Disposal of waste directly related to exploration and exploitation of the continental shelf is not covered by the convention.

Article IV divides the specific obligations along the same lines as the Oslo Convention: the dumping of waste or other matter listed in Annex I is prohibited. The dumping of waste or other matter listed in Annex II, *i.e.*, the " grey list," requires a prior special permit, and the dumping of all other waste or matter requires a prior general permit. Article IV, paragraph 2, says that " any permits shall be issued only after careful consideration of all the factors set forth in Annex III, including prior studies of the characteristics of the dumping site, as set forth in Sections B and C of that Annex." No provision of the convention shall be interpreted so as to prevent the contracting parties from prohibiting, in so far as that party is considered, the dumping of waste or other matter not mentioned in Annex I.

Article VII, on jurisdiction, states that each contracting party shall apply the measures required to implement the Convention to: (a) vessels and aircraft registered in its territory or flying its flag, (b) vessels and aircraft loading in its territory or territorial sea matter which is to be dumped, and (c) vessels and aircraft and fixed or floating platforms under its jurisdiction believed to be engaged in dumping. Article VII, paragraph 5, has the same *ex tuto* reservation as Article IV, namely that nothing in the Convention shall affect the right of each party to adopt other measures, in accordance with the principles of international law, to prevent dumping at sea.

Article X contains an interesting provision on the question of State responsibility and liability for damage. The parties undertake " to develop procedures " for the assessment of liability and the settlement of disputes regarding dumping. This shall be " in accordance with the principles of international law regarding State responsibility for damage to the environment of other States or to any other area of the environment, caused by dumping of wastes and other matter of all kinds." This seems to imply a clear recognition of the principle that State responsibility and liability for damage also applies to damage which is caused to the sea as the " common heritage of mankind," and in particular by the activities of dumping.

Article XIII states that nothing in the Convention shall prejudice the codification and development of the law of the sea by the UN Conference scheduled for 1973, nor the present or future claims and legal view of any State concerning " the law of the sea and the nature and extent of coastal and flag State jurisdiction." A rather more complex and controversial issue is dealt with in the second sentence of this article, namely the question of an adjacent anti-pollution zone outside territorial waters. The contracting parties have agreed "to consult at a meeting to be convened by the Organisation after the Law of the Sea Conference, and in any case not later than 1976, with a view to defining the nature and extent of the right and the responsibility of a coastal state to apply the Convention in a zone adjacent to its coast." Of course this is no recognition of any right under present international law to establish such a zone on a unilateral basis. It should also be noted that the type of contiguous zone which is foreseen by this article is limited to the question of applying internationally agreed measures, *i.e.*, the London Convention, within a zone which otherwise belongs to the high seas and is subject to the rules thereof.

Finally, it should be mentioned that according to Article VII, paragraph 3, the parties shall co-operate in the development of procedures "for the effective application of this Convention, particularly on the high seas, including procedures for the reporting of vessels and aircraft observed dumping in contravention of the Convention." A similar rule is found in the Oslo Convention, Article 15, paragraph 5, according to which the parties shall work together in the development of co-operative procedures for the application of the convention, "particularly on the high seas." Here there is no specific mention of, or possible limitation to, reporting, etc., as opposed to the boarding and seizure of vessels. It seems clear, however, that any agreed measures might also include such action under the London Convention. A useful precedent here is the procedures which have been agreed under the North-East Atlantic Fisheries Convention, whereby inspection vessels of one party may board and inspect vessels of other parties in order to ascertain whether the provisions of the convention have been complied with. Such measures may also be found appropriate in regard to vessels suspected of dumping or of having taken aboard a cargo for this purpose. But any measure against a foreign ship on the high seas would have to be based on a future agreement to which the flag State is a party. The provisions of the Oslo and the London Conventions may only be regarded as a *pactum de contrahendo*, or an obligation to consider whether such measures should be adopted.

7. SHIPPING

General

Until the adoption, as late as in 1972, of the two dumping Conventions, the conventional regulation of marine pollution was to a very large extent restricted to pollution which was a result of shipping, and even more specifically to pollution by oil from tankers. And even after the two 1972 Conventions the international regulation of marine pollution is still very much restricted to pollution by discharges from ships. Although pollution by oil from ships is a serious problem, it may be said that the present regulation, which, to a large extent, is a result of the valuable work carried out by IMCO, has caused something of a disequilibrium as far as international legislation is concerned. While oil is broken down by natural process (with some reservations for spills in the Arctic and Antarctic regions), persistent synthetical chemicals coming from land-based sources are known to accumulate in fish and sea animals, and to threaten the further existence of several species thereof. It is believed that the attention of world opinion and the efforts for international co-operation may, until now, to a disproportionate extent have been focused on the special aspects of the carriage of oil, at the expense of the other and equally dangerous ecological imbalances which result from the continuous flow and accumulation of toxic materials. Indeed it seemed to be one of the achievements of the Conference in London on " New Directions in the Law of the Sea " that it was clearly recognised that the hazards presented by land-based sources of pollution present the major problem where marine pollution is concerned. This does not, of course, mean that pollution from ships is no longer worthy of attention, but the efforts of the world community must be concentrated to a greater extent on land-based sources. Generally speaking there are two types of pollution, *i.e.*, accidental and deliberate pollution. Deliberate pollution, which is probably the most important source with respect to the state of the sea itself, and the danger to the life of the sea and to coastlines, is to a large extent a result of the cleaning of oil tanks in the open sea. Attempts to eliminate and to reduce this form of pollution were made by the International Convention for the Prevention of Pollution of the Sea by Oil of 1954, whose regulations in this regard were modified in 1962 and 1969.

Before 1969, accidental pollution had not been subject to international regulation to the same extent as the intentional discharge of oil. This type of pollution is mainly the result of the collision or stranding of ships, and may lead to catastrophic consequences in the form of contamination of coastlines. The best-known case, and the one having the gravest consequences until now, is that of the *Torrey Canyon*, a Liberian tanker which stranded on the south-west coast of England on March 18, 1967. Approximately 100,000 tons of crude oil were spilled into the sea. The steps taken by the British Government against the wreck could not prevent the contamination of a large part of the British as well as the French coast. The total damage has been estimated at some £6 million. Today the structure of the oil transport system is becoming increasingly dependent on the VLCCs (Very Large Crude Carriers). Compared to ships of 200,000 tons deadweight and even up to 500,000 tons the *Torrey Canyon*, of 118,000 tons, may be considered as small.

The 1954 Convention for the Prevention of Pollution of the Sea by Oil; with amendments of 1962 and 1969

The Convention of May 12, 1954 was amended on April 11, 1962. It prohibits the discharge of " oil " (defined to include " crude oil ") and " oily mixture " within certain zones. " Oily mixture " is defined as a mixture with an oil content of 100 parts or more in 1,000,000 parts of the mixture. According to Annex A, the prohibited zones shall extend to all sea areas within 50 miles from the nearest land, and shall also include such waters as the whole of the North Sea and the Baltic Sea, and a 100 mile zone around Iceland and along the coast of Norway.

New amendments, which have not yet entered into force, were adopted by the Assembly of IMCO on October 21, 1969. The amendments will, according to Article XVI, come into force 12 months after they have been ratified by two-thirds of the contracting governments.

By the 1969 amendments the system of prohibited zones has been substituted for what is, in principle, a total prohibition of all discharges of " oil " or " oily mixture." The definition of " oily mixture " has been changed to include " a mixture with any oil content." The main rule will be found in Article III, with the following wording:

" Subject to the provisions of Articles IV and V:

(a) the discharge from a ship to which the present Convention applies, other than a tanker, of oil or oily mixture shall be prohibited except when the following conditions are all satisfied:

(i) the ship is proceeding en route,

(ii) the instantaneous rate of discharge of oil content does not exceed 60 litres per mile,

(iii) the oil content of the discharge is less than 100 parts per 1,000,000 parts of the mixture,
(iv) the discharge is made as far as practicable from land,

(b) the discharge from a tanker to which the present Convention applies of oil or oily mixture shall be prohibited except when the following conditions are all satisfied:
(i) the tanker is proceeding en route,
(ii) the instantaneous rate of discharge of oil content does not exceed 60 litres per mile,
(iii) the total quantity of oil discharged on a ballast voyage does not exceed 1/15,000 of the total cargo-carrying capacity,
(iv) the tanker is more than 50 miles from the nearest land;

(c) the provisions of sub-paragraph (b) of this Article shall not apply to:
(i) the discharge of ballast from a cargo tank which, since the cargo was last carried therein, has been so cleaned that any effluent therefrom, if it were discharged from a stationary tanker into clean calm water on a clear day, would produce no visible traces of oil on the surface of the water; or
(ii) the discharge of oil or oily mixture from machinery space bilges, which shall be governed by the provisions of sub-paragraph (a) of this Article."

The 1969 Convention relating to Intervention on the High Seas in Cases of Oil Pollution Casualties

As a direct result of the *Torrey Canyon* incident, the British Government proposed that IMCO should consider, as a matter of urgency, several topics connected with the need to protect potential victims against oil pollution. The matters to which attention and efforts were mainly directed, and which led to the diplomatic conference at Brussels from November 10 to 29, 1969, and to the adoption of two international conventions, were those concerned with the coastal State's right to intervene against a ship on the high seas in cases similar to that of the *Torrey Canyon*, and civil liability for damage caused by pollution.

Of the two conventions, the Public Law Convention was the one which seemed to receive the larger degree of universal acceptance. Agreement had also been reached on the main principles and on the formulation of articles pertaining thereto during the preparatory work of IMCO, through its Legal Committee.

The main principle of the convention is found in Article I, which gives a coastal State the right to take such measures on the high seas as may be necessary to prevent, reduce or eliminate the danger of pollution to its coastline. The right which is conferred upon the coastal State by Article I is, however, strictly limited to extreme circumstances, in which the parties have found it necessary to provide for exceptional measures. There must be a "grave and imminent danger," which follows upon a "maritime casualty," and this "casualty" or acts related thereto must "reasonably be expected to result in major harmful consequences."

Article I does not specify the measures which may be taken against a foreign ship on the high seas. The measures range from the towing away of an abandoned ship from the zone where an oil spill can cause serious damage, to the use of bombs to destroy the oil by fire (which was indeed tried in the case of the *Torrey Canyon*, but with slight success). However, Article V lays down the principle that measures taken by the coastal State must be proportionate to the damage threatened to it. In the test of proportionality, account shall be taken both of the likelihood of the measures being effective and of the damage which they may cause to the ship or otherwise.

A coastal State which takes measures in contravention of the convention is obliged to pay compensation (*cf.* Article VI).

The convention does not apply to a ship which is within a State's territorial limits after the stranding or collision. This does not, of course, mean that no measures can be taken. Here the solution must be sought on the basis of three general principles of law; the sovereignty of the coastal State over its territorial waters, which, in principle, gives it the right to prescribe rules and to take measures, the right of innocent passage, and the principle of proportionality. The importance of the latter principle is borne out by the case of the *I'm Alone*. Here the U.S.A. was considered responsible for excessive measures in its exercise of jurisdiction against a foreign vessel engaged in smuggling (which was sunk by the Coast Guard), even though the U.S.A. was competent to exercise jurisdiction.[9] As to the more severe measures against a foreign ship, the rights of the coastal State in its territorial waters will, therefore, probably not be considerably greater than those which can be exercised on the high seas according to the convention. Other steps may be taken, *e.g.*, the ordering of a ship which presents a special danger of oil pollution to proceed along a certain route, even if the conditions of the convention (such as the occurrence of a " casualty ") are not fulfilled.

The 1969 Convention on Civil Liability for Oil Pollution Damage

See below, on Civil Liability.

Pollution from shipping by agents other than oil

IMCO planned to pursue its successful work for the prevention of pollution from ships through a conference on marine pollution due to be held in October 1973. At this conference it is proposed to extend the principles of the 1969 Public Law Convention to other casualties where there is a similar grave and imminent risk to the coastline because of spillage of substances other than oil. Indeed, such accidents may imply an even greater danger than oil, especially if the vessel is carrying toxic chemicals. Further, IMCO has been working on a draft of a general International Convention for the Prevention of Pollution from Ships. This convention is meant to replace the 1954 Convention, and at the same time extend the application of the same principles to other agents. Or, possibly, the proposals with regard to other agents, etc., may be adopted in the form of amendments to the 1954 Convention, thereby extending its scope to pollutants other than oil. Irrespective of the form which may eventually be chosen, the 1973 Convention will cover deliberate, negligent or accidental release of oil and other harmful substances from ships. The aim will be to " achieve the complete elimination of intentional pollution by oil and other harmful substances and the minimisation of accidental release of such substances."

8. FISHING

Pollution from the activities of fishing may seem to be one of the lesser sources of marine pollution.

Annex V, rule 4, of the 1967 Convention on Conduct of Fishing Operations in the North Atlantic prohibits the dumping of articles or substances which may interfere with fishing or cause damage to fish, fishing gear or fishing vessels. The prohibition is directed against a " vessel," which is defined as a vessel engaged in fishing or the processing of fish, etc. (see Article 1 of the convention). The reason for this limitation is, of course, that the whole convention is restricted to fishing operations, and that it would be beyond its scope to regulate the conduct of vessels other than those engaged in fishing or related operations.

Strong reasons seem to suggest that the principle of rule 4 may be applied to other vessels as well, as declaratory of general principles of international law.

9. NUCLEAR MATERIAL

International co-operation for the prevention of pollution of the sea by nuclear material, as well as co-operation in the disposal of such material, has been undertaken by the International Atomic Energy Agency and by the Nuclear Energy Agency of OECD for several years, but so far no general convention on the matter has emerged.

Pollution of the sea from nuclear material is dealt with by the provisions of Article 25, paragraphs 1 and 2, of the Geneva Convention on the High Seas, which has been mentioned above.

Dumping of radioactive material is covered by the 1972 London Convention on Dumping. Annex I, which covers the substances of which dumping shall be prohibited, includes the following items:

> " High-level radioactive wastes or other high-level radioactive matter, defined on public health, biological or other grounds, by the competent international body in this field, at present the International Atomic Energy Agency, as unsuitable for dumping at sea."

The dumping of radioactive wastes or radioactive matter not included in this text is covered by Annex II of the same convention; which means that a specific permit is necessary in each case (Article IV).

The Oslo Convention has not included nuclear material in its annexes. In Article 14 " the Contracting Parties pledge themselves to promote, within the competent specialised agencies and other international bodies, measures concerning the protection of the marine environment against pollution caused by oil and oily wastes, other noxious or hazardous cargoes, and radioactive materials."

Another source of pollution may be nuclear-powered vessels or the carriage of nuclear material as cargo. Although there are safety standards on the handling and transport of nuclear material, and even if there have been some attempts to settle questions of safety and pollution on a bilateral basis (*e.g.*, with bilateral negotiations concerning the nuclear-powered vessel the N.S. *Otto Hahn* of the Federal Republic of Germany), it seems that the international protection against this risk of pollution is at the moment not sufficient. A complicating factor is to be found in the large number of military vessels using nuclear power, especially submarines.

Another military aspect is the testing of nuclear weapons. The 1963 Test Ban Treaty prohibits, *inter alia*, the use of the sea for this purpose. As France (and China) is not a party to the treaty, there is at present a controversy in the Pacific area as a result of tests being carried out by France. Whether such tests are legitimate or infringe upon the rights of other States, would seem to depend on the test of reasonableness prescribed in Article 2, paragraph 2, of the Geneva Convention. As the general political situation is now somewhat different than it was in the years before the Test Ban Treaty, there may be reasons to invoke the view that the French tests—in order to make France an " independent nuclear power "—are not in conformity with the principles of the freedom of the sea, even if one should accept the legality of tests earlier carried out by the U.S.A., the U.S.S.R. and by the United Kingdom. An even greater risk of pollution is presented by the aspects of a nuclear war; but this lies far beyond what we can expect to prevent by international law alone, or by discussions concerning solely the aspects of marine pollution.

10. THE STOCKHOLM CONFERENCE ON THE HUMAN ENVIRONMENT

The Stockholm Conference from June 5 to 16, 1972, adopted both a general Declaration on the Human Environment, consisting of 26 Principles, and nine recommendations relating specifically to marine pollution. Among the general Principles the following may be of a special interest also in the context of marine pollution:

The point of departure is Principle No. 1, stating that "man has the fundamental right to freedom, equality and adequate conditions of life, in an environment of a quality which permits a life of dignity and well-being," and also a responsibility to "protect and improve the environment for present and future generations."

Principle No. 6 contains a general rule on pollution, applicable to the sea as well as to the non-marine environment:

> "The discharge of toxic substances or of other substances and the release of heat, in such quantities or concentrations as to exceed the capacity of the environment to render them harmless, must be halted in order to ensure that serious or irreversible damage is not inflicted upon ecosystems. The just struggle of the peoples of all countries against pollution should be supported."

Principle 7 is a special rule on the obligation to prevent pollution of the sea:

> "States shall take all possible steps to prevent pollution of the seas by substances that are liable to create hazards to human health, to harm living resources and marine life, to damage amenities or to interfere with other legitimate uses of the sea."

In Principle 13 the Declaration draws attention to the important aspect of planning (with special reference to development planning). Pollution control is not only a matter of direct prohibition or restrictions, but depends on planning and on the rational management of resources in general.

Principle 21 may also be mentioned. States are considered to have the responsibility to ensure that activities "within their jurisdiction or control" do not cause damage to "the environment of other States or of areas beyond the limits of national jurisdiction." Thus Principle No. 21 confirms the view of the 1949 *Corfu Channel Case* that the rights and duties of States also comprise the protection of international interests such as the common use of international waterways and the obligation to exercise effective jurisdiction in order to avoid damage to these interests.

Principle 22 contains an obligation for States to co-operate "to develop further the international law regarding liability and compensation for the victims of pollution and other environmental damage caused by activities within the jurisdiction or control of such States to areas beyond their jurisdiction."

As for the special recommendations on marine pollution, these are to a great extent directed towards further research and assessment of potential damage, and co-operation for this purpose. This is, *inter alia*, the case for Recommendation No. 88. Here the Secretary-General is instructed to make it possible for the Joint Group of Experts on the Scientific Aspects of Marine Pollution (GESAMP) to re-examine annually and to revise as required, its "Review of Harmful Chemical Substances."

This shall be done with a view to elaborate further its assessment of sources, pathways and resulting risks of marine pollution. Even if this Recommendation is directly concerned only with the work of a certain scientific body, it should be noted that the findings of this body and its collection of material may have an important impact on rules of international law. This is especially the case with regard to a possible revision of the annexes to the dumping conventions and the extent of the prohibitions therein contained.

Recommendation No. 86, especially its paragraphs (a), (b) and (c), has a more direct relationship to the international law of the sea:

"*It is recommended* that Governments, with the assistance and guidance of appropriate United Nations bodies, in particular the Joint Group of Experts on the Scientific Aspects of Marine Pollution (GESAMP):

(a) Accept and implement available instruments on the control of the maritime sources of marine pollution;

(b) Ensure that the provisions of such instruments are complied with by ships flying their flags and by ships operating in areas under their jurisdiction and that adequate provisions are made for reviewing the effectiveness of, and revising, existing and proposed international measures for control of marine pollution;

(c) Ensure that ocean dumping by their nationals anywhere, or by any person in areas under their jurisdiction, is controlled and that Governments shall continue to work towards the completion of, and bringing into force as soon as possible of, an over-all instrument for the control of ocean dumping as well as needed regional agreements within the framework of this instrument, in particular for enclosed and semi-enclosed seas, which are more at risk from pollution."

According to Recommendation No. 92 of the Stockholm Conference, governments should collectively endorse certain principles earlier adopted by the Intergovernmental Working Group on Marine Pollution[10] as "guiding concepts" for the 1973 Conference on the Law of the Sea and the IMCO Conference on Marine Pollution. In addition to these "guiding concepts" the resolution also referred to certain "Canadian" principles on a coastal State's possible environmental protection authority in waters adjacent to its territorial sea. These latter principles have, however, been accorded a somewhat lower status. The parties have "taken note" of such principles, which were "neither endorsed nor rejected" at the second session of the Working Group, as "a matter for consideration" at the Law of the Sea Conference.

Among the Principles adopted as guiding principles and actively endorsed by the Stockholm Conference one may quote the following as particularly important:

"(1) Every State has a duty to protect and preserve the marine environment and, in particular, to prevent pollution that may affect areas where an internationally shared resource is located.

"(2) Every State should adopt appropriate measures for the prevention of marine pollution, whether acting individually or in conjunction with other States under agreed international arrangements.

"(3) States should use the best practicable means available to them to minimise the discharge of potentially hazardous substances to the sea by all routes, including land-based sources such as rivers, outfalls and pipelines within national jurisdiction, as well as dumping by or from ships, aircraft and platforms.

"(4) States should ensure that their national legislation provides adequate sanctions against those who infringe existing regulations on marine pollution.

"(5) States should assume joint responsibility for the preservation of the marine environment beyond the limits of national jurisdiction. . . .

"(17) In addition to its responsibility for environmental protection within the limits of its territorial sea, a coastal State also has responsibility to protect adjacent areas of the environment from damage that may result from activities within its territory.

"(18) Coastal States should ensure that adequate and appropriate resources are available to deal with pollution incidents resulting from the exploration and exploitation of seabed resources in areas within the limits of their national jurisdiction. . . .

"(20) All States should ensure that vessels under their registration comply with internationally agreed rules and standards relating to ship design and construction, operating procedures and other relevant factors. States should co-operate in the development of such rules, standards and procedures, in the appropriate international bodies.

"(21) Following an accident on the high seas which may be expected to result in major deleterious consequences from pollution or threat of pollution of the sea, a coastal State facing grave and imminent danger to its coastline and related interests may take appropriate measures as may be necessary to prevent, mitigate, or eliminate such danger, in accordance with internationally agreed rules and standards."

11. LIABILITY AND COMPENSATION

General

Basically the question of civil liability for pollution and compensation to victims is one of internal law and is settled through procedure before internal courts. Usually the damage is caused by a private operator. The State whose national he is or the flag State of the vessel is not liable to pay compensation under general international law. Exceptions to this rule may, of course, be found, *inter alia* where the Government has not exercised due diligence in controlling its shipping or in establishing the necessary anti-pollution regulations (*cf.* Articles 24 and 25 of the Geneva Convention on the High Seas). As a general rule it is left for the victim to pursue his claim for damage by the means of an ordinary civil lawsuit before the tribunals of some country or other, against the private tortfeasor as such. Usually the State is not involved on either side.

The wording "some country or other" is particularly relevant where the international aspects of pollution damage are concerned. As a rule the victim and the vessel causing the damage will have different nationalities. The victim will in practice often have to sue the guilty party in a foreign court, a fact which places an additional burden upon him in addition to the difficulties presented by the gathering of proof in what is virtually "troubled waters." On the other hand there is a widespread practice in relation to shipping which allows for civil arrest and lawsuits in any port where the vessel may chance to be present. And there is a great variety of national rules.

The variety of national legislation combined with the very nature of international shipping and the mobility of vessels accounts for the well-known practice of "forum shopping": the claimant trying to find the forum and the legislation which will give him the best possible position *vis-à-vis* the defendant. On the other hand it also accounts for the need to draw up international rules to limit the freedom of the different legislatures and to unify the rules which are in force in different countries. The need for international or unified rules applies with regard to questions of substantive law as well as to those of jurisdiction.

It has been usual in internal legislation or in practice to limit the ship-owner's liability. The same has been done by international agreements, which also serve to unify the different national rules in this respect, such as the 1957 Brussels Convention Relating to the Limitation of the Liability of Owners of Seagoing Ships. The ship-owner's liability is not limited when the damage is a result of his own personal "fault or privity" (as opposed to that of his servants).

For the more ordinary cases of pollution these existing rules would seem to be sufficient. The 1967 *Torrey Canyon* disaster proved that a major accident involving a huge tanker might easily cause damage which goes far beyond the amount of liability which is allowed under the limitations prescribed by national law and by international conventions. Indeed, the Convention on the Limitation of Liability, binding upon the participating States under international law, would prohibit States and their courts from awarding the victims full compensation in accordance with the losses suffered and the special risk to which they were exposed.

On the other hand, the accident also served to show that it is impossible to expect a full coverage of the risks of modern oil transport through the traditional system of maritime law, based on ship-owner's liability. It should be borne in mind that, after all, the carrier has only a part of the economic interest, namely, that corresponding to the freight rate, in the potentially dangerous cargo which he is carrying.

It is a sound principle both legally and economically that all expenses of oil production and distribution, including the damage caused, should be paid by the party who has the economic interest in the goods as such, and eventually by the consumers. The discussions undertaken by IMCO, with the assistance of the CMI (Comité Maritime International) after the *Torrey Canyon* incident also proved that it would not be possible to make ship-owners pay for the total damage which might be caused by the cargo in major pollution accidents. Nor could the necessary amount be covered by maritime insurance within the capacity which exists in the present markets for such insurance. In this situation new principles of liability and insurance, different from those of traditional maritime law, had to be found.

The most important questions which suggested themselves after the *Torrey Canyon* were the following:

1. Nature of liability. While traditional maritime law is based on the fault of the ship-owner or of his servants, the need to protect the victim and the difficulties of proof may be invoked in favour of strict liability.
2. Who should be liable? The traditional principle of ship-owner's liability is unable to supply a satisfactory solution in practice, and a system of cargo liability and insurance would correspond better to the fact that pollution damage is due to the cargo as such (with an exception for cases where the spill comes from the ship's own fuel tanks, etc.).
3. Limitation of liability. In addition one is faced with questions of jurisdiction; compulsory insurance, or whether the owner of the cargo or the vessel should be required to put up some other kind of security; and sanctions, by the flag State or by other States, in ports, etc.

The solution proposed by the CMI was meant as a compromise in so far as question No. 1 was concerned: liability based on fault, but with a reversion of the burden of proof in favour of the victim. When liability was to be based on fault, it must, according to the CMI's view, be borne by the ship-owner. This implied that question No. 2 was solved as a consequence of No. 1, and that the final solution would depend on the order in which the different questions were put (or solved).

The 1969 Convention on Civil Liability for Oil Pollution Damage, and the 1969 Resolution on an International Fund

The CMI solution was not accepted by the 1969 Brussels Conference. Instead the Conference based itself on a system of strict liability, and a hybrid solution with respect to the person liable.

According to Article III the ship-owner shall be liable for any pollution damage. The liability is not based on the fault of any person, but certain exceptions have been made, *inter alia*, with regard to acts of war, and the failure of governments to maintain lights or other navigational aids, etc. The maximum liability is, with the usual exception for the fault or privity of the owner, 2,000 francs per ton, which is double the amount of the maximum liability for damage to property under the general Convention on Shipowners' Liability of 1957. The victim may not simultaneously claim up to 1,000 francs per ton under the 1957 and up to 2,000 francs under the 1969 Convention. The total sum which can be claimed in respect of any one incident is limited to 210 million francs, *i.e.*, approximately 15 million U.S. dollars.

According to a resolution passed at the Conference, the convention shall function in conjunction with an International Fund which shall be used both to compensate victims for damage, which they have suffered in excess of the convention limits, and to relieve the ship-owner of the increased burden imposed by the convention. The fund shall be built up by contributions from the cargo-owners.

The 1971 Convention on the Establishment of an International Fund for Compensation for Oil Pollution Damage

The second part of the Brussels compromise was finished in 1971, by the Convention of December 18, 1971, which is supplementary to the 1969 Convention. The 1971 Convention has a double purpose. On the one hand it provides for compensation to victims where the total damage exceeds the limitation of the 1969 Convention on the ship-owner's liability (and, to a certain extent, where the damage is not subject to compensation at all under the latter convention). On the other hand, it relieves the ship-owner of the additional financial burden which he has to carry as a result of the increased liability of the Convention of 1969 as compared to that of traditional maritime law (the Convention of 1957).

The compensation which can be awarded by the Fund is limited to a maximum of 450 million gold (Poincaré) francs, or approximately 33 million U.S. dollars (including the amount which shall be paid by the ship-owner according to the 1957 Convention or national legislation). The Assembly of the Fund may, by a three-quarters majority of the participating States, raise the amount of this liability to 900 million francs.

Reference may also be made to the voluntary agreements by oil companies and tanker owners for a similar system of liability, in the so-called TOVALOP and CRISTAL agreements of January 7, 1969, and January 14, 1971, respectively. The maximum liability of the Compensation Fund established under CRISTAL is set to 30 million U.S. dollars.

Agents other than oil

It remains to be seen whether the complex solution of the two (or rather three: of

1957, 1969 and 1971) Brussels Conventions, which apply to pollution caused by the carriage of oil in ships, can be applied to other types of marine pollution: from sources other than ships, and from agents other than oil.

Under the general rules of private international law which are applied by most countries it would seem feasible for a country, affected by pollution from land-based sources of another State, to apply its rules on civil liability to the damage caused. The execution of such a judgment by the courts of the State of the victim may, however, easily meet with difficulties in practice; depending on the rules and treaties in force between the two States with regard to the recognition and execution of judgments.

Civil liability for the damage by nuclear material has been regulated by, *inter alia*, the Brussels Convention of May 25, 1962, on the Liability of Operators of Nuclear Ships, the Vienna Convention on Civil Liability for Nuclear Damage of May 21, 1963, and—within the auspices of the OECD—the Paris Convention on Third Party Liability in the Field of Nuclear Energy of July 29, 1960, with a supplementary Convention of January 31, 1963.

As for dumping, the question of liability and compensation was touched upon by the 1972 London Convention (see above), but only as a subject for further study and negotiation.

Besides the civil liability of the private party actually causing the damage, there may be good reasons for engaging the responsibility of States. Since the *Trail Smelter Case* States have (surprisingly enough) been reluctant to press claims against one another for pollution damage and for the (not wholly unknown) negligence of authorities. There can be no doubt that present international law lays an obligation upon States to establish and enforce legislation to control and reduce pollution and thereby to protect the freedom of the seas. The rules of the Geneva High Seas Convention, in particular Articles 2, paragraph 2, 24 and 25, may be taken as evidence of this obligation. With the grave consequences of pollution this responsibility cannot be taken lightly. In particular, there may be grounds for international responsibility on the part of a State whose position as a State of registry is merely of a formal character, and which does not exercise effective control, as is the case for the typical flags of convenience.

12. REGIONAL ARRANGEMENTS

In many cases action against pollution can most effectively be taken at a regional level. The need for appropriate regional arrangements to supplement the general international conventions is, *inter alia*, stressed by the 1972 London Convention on the Dumping of Wastes at Sea (Article VIII, see above).

An example is found in the Agreement of June 9, 1969, for Co-operation in Dealing with Pollution of the North Sea by Oil. For the purpose of this agreement the North Sea has been divided into zones. Each coastal State shall in the zone which is its responsibility, for this "sole" purpose, make the necessary assessments of the nature and extent of any casualty or, as the case may be, of the type and approximate quantity of the oil floating on the sea, and the direction and speed of movement of the oil. The contracting party concerned shall immediately inform all the other contracting parties through their competent authorities of its assessments and of any action which it has taken to deal with the floating oil. It shall keep the oil under observation as long as it is drifting in its zone. A party requiring assistance to dispose of oil floating on the sea or polluting its coast may call on the help of the other contracting parties, starting with those which also seem likely to be affected by the floating oil. Contracting parties called upon for help in accordance with this provision shall " use their best endeavours to bring such assistance as is within their power " (see Articles 6 and 7).

13. THE QUESTION OF AN ADJACENT ZONE FOR ANTI-POLLUTION MEASURES

The application of anti-pollution measures in a contiguous zone, in particular a 12 mile fishery zone or a 12 mile contiguous zone established according to Article 24 of the 1958 Geneva Convention on the Territorial Sea and the Contiguous Zone, is known from statutes recently passed by the United States and by Canada.[11] To what extent contiguous zones are admitted in contemporary international law is open to some doubt.

As long as the zone does not go beyond the limit of 12 miles prescribed in Article 24, paragraph 2, of the Geneva Convention on the Territorial Sea and the Contiguous Zone, it seems that no serious objection is likely to be advanced from the point of international law, or by the protests of other States. Even if not mentioned in Article 24, the anti-pollution zone is closely related to the other "protective" zones which are listed in the convention. The objective is not, as is the case for a fishery zone, to obtain some kind of ownership in regard to the zone itself, but to protect the State's own territory from damage which might otherwise result from activities taking place in the zone. It might also be argued that, if a 12 mile limit is accepted in relation to the territorial sea, which is in fact the case in the contemporary practice of States, it follows *a fortiori* that a 12 mile zone for anti-pollution measures may be accepted as a lesser evil from the view of foreign States, when the territorial limit is less than 12 miles.

A more controversial issue is that of a pollution zone which goes beyond the limit of 12 miles and which allows for measures against foreign vessels in this area, which is regarded as high seas by most nations. A zone extending to 100 miles from the nearest land has been provided for in the so-called Arctic Waters in the Arctic Waters Pollution Prevention Act of Canada. The Act defines Arctic Waters as all waters between the parallel of 60° N. latitude on the Eastern coast and the Alaskan border. The adoption of such unilateral measures will inevitably lead to disputes concerning jurisdiction, and it is doubtful to what extent the special interests and obligations of the coastal State in certain situations may justify such measures. In the interest of the international community, it would, of course, be preferable if the necessary regulation to protect the ecological situation of the Arctic areas (as the preamble points to) could be worked out on an international level and with the consent of all States concerned.

Whether a contiguous zone for anti-pollution should be established, is also one of the questions which may be solved by the forthcoming Law of the Sea Conference.

A special zone under the jurisdiction of the coastal State will always be something of a " half-way-house " as far as pollution control is concerned. It cannot prevent pollution which arrives from the high seas outside the limits of the pollution zone or from sources within the jurisdiction of other States. To take the parallel case of air pollution, it seems obvious that, practically speaking, it all derives from sources which are within the jurisdiction of some State or other. Yet few steps have been taken to limit the international effects of such pollution. Also with regard to marine pollution, the situation is, in fact, that even the rules of contemporary international law place the sources of pollution within the jurisdiction of one or more States. Pollution either comes from land-based sources, or from vessels (or aircraft), which are under the jurisdiction of the flag State. If a ship is not registered anywhere, it is subject to the jurisdiction of all States.[12] In other words, the necessary jurisdictional competence exists thereof. If the so-called freedom of the high seas were to be abolished and substituted for a division of the sea into jurisdictional zones, we would still be faced with the one problem which is the crux of the matter: the need for effective exercise of the jurisdiction of all States, each within their own jurisdictional monopoly (land, sea or vessels), and the need for internationally agreed measures and co-ordination of action.

The second disadvantage of extended coastal State jurisdiction is found in the interference with the freedom of navigation and other legitimate uses of the sea.

As far as terminology is concerned, the situation would not be serious. The special pollution zone adjacent to territorial waters would retain its character of " high seas." While it may be dubious whether the term " high seas " is appropriate for the special fishery zone,[13] the character of " high seas " should in principle be unaffected by a zone whose purpose is only the protection of the coastal State's territory as such. But the practical consequences of a pollution zone—and, in particular, of different zones and different systems established by different States—might even be more serious in relation to the interests of other States and their common right to use the high seas.

Unilateral measures in large areas of what is otherwise regarded as high seas may also lead to abuse in practice and to discrimination between ships of different nations. And even if the legislative measures taken by each coastal State were reasonable enough *per se*, international navigation would meet with serious difficulties if it had to comply with different safety standards when passing from the zones of State A to those of State B (with regard to ship's design and equipment, insurance, etc.). To some extent the reasons for this criticism of the idea of the special pollution zone would disappear if the competence of the coastal State were to be restricted to the enforcement of internationally agreed measures (*e.g.*, by inspecting vessels and drawing up reports of infringements, as was provided as early as 1882 in the Convention for Regulating the Police of the North Sea Fisheries).

14. THE UNITED NATIONS CONFERENCE ON THE LAW OF THE SEA—WHAT SHOULD BE DONE?

Marine pollution is one of the topics of the Law of the Sea Conference. It is relevant both in the specific connection of the régime for the seabed and ocean floor beyond the limits of national jurisdiction (see paragraph 11 of the General Assembly's Declaration of Principles of December 17, 1970) and as one of the items with regard to the law of the sea in general. Marine pollution is, indeed, the main topic of the third sub-committee of the UN Seabed Committee, which is charged with the task of preparing the Conference.

As to what the Seabed Committee and the Conference should do, the following consideration may be relevant:

As mentioned above, it seems that the question of pollution from ships, in particular from ships carrying oil, is to a great extent covered by international regulation. Important action has also been taken with respect to dumping. One may wonder whether the aspects of shipping, which is after all not the most dangerous source of ocean pollution, have not been the subject of too much attention and work by the international community, at the expense of those types of marine pollution which derive from land-based sources, and which hitherto have been virtually without any international regulation or control whatsoever. And it is only a small part of the marine pollution by industrial waste which is dumped from ships in the sea itself. While valuable and important work has been carried out and is going on with respect to pollution from activities at sea, especially in IMCO, little has been done to reduce the continuous outflow of chemical waste and untreated municipal sewage from domestic sources.

On the other hand, the present "legal imbalance," with existing international legislation concentrated on the aspects of shipping, also has its explanations in the very extensive and effective work which has been and is still being done by IMCO. IMCO's practical results may indeed be said to be both amazing and impressive. In his statement of August 2, 1972, the United States representative to the United Nations Seabed Committee, the Hon. John R. Stevenson, pointed out that the work of IMCO should be "strongly supported," and that IMCO has been a forum in which great achievements in this field have been realised.

In my opinion it is equally important that the achievements of IMCO should not divert the attention from the even more dangerous problems of pollution from other sources. On the contrary, the same type of international co-operation and the same elaboration of concrete regulation which has been practised within IMCO with such results, should also be instituted with respect to other types of pollution which do not derive from the operation of vessels. IMCO's competence is restricted to maritime operations as such *i.e.*, in respect of pollution, which derives from the operation of vessels or other floating craft. It would not seem acceptable if the forthcoming Law of the Sea Conference, which has marine pollution on its agenda, without any such limitation, should restrict its own competence or mainly concern itself with pollution from shipping. The Conference would thereby serve to focus the world's attention on this aspect, which has after all now been brought under control and is fairly well regulated as compared to pollution from other sources, and thereby perhaps contribute to even a further postponement of the necessary international regulation of marine pollution from domestic outlets.

As for shipping, it seems that the Law of the Sea Conference should, in any event, restrict itself to the formulation of the more general principles of marine pollution. The more detailed and technical regulations relating to shipping should be left to the work of IMCO, which has the expertise required for this purpose.

On the other hand, the principles adopted by the Stockholm Conference seem to form a useful basis for a codification of the general international law on marine pollution, to be adopted by the Law of the Sea Conference. Such a codification of the general principles should not be restricted to pollution from ships and aircraft, but must cover land-based activities as well.

REFERENCES

1. Falk, "Toward Equilibrium in the World Order System" (1970) *Proceedings of the American Society of International Law* 217, *et seq.*

2. Note presented by the Government of the United Kingdom, circulated to the IMCO Council on Apr. 18, 1967.

3. *Trail Smelter Case*, U.N.R.I.A.A., Vol. III, pp. 1905 *et seq.*

4. By internal courts, but used as a basis for analogy from municipal to international law, *loc. cit.* p. 1964.

5. See above, and U.N.R.I.A.A., Vol. III, pp. 1932–1933 and 1965–1966.

6. [1949] I.C.J.Rep. 22.

7. [1970] I.L.C.Rep., Vol. II, p. 187.

8. See McDougal and Burke, *The Public Order of the Oceans*, pp. 1013 *et seq.*

9. U.N.R.I.A.A., Vol. III, pp. 1609 *et seq.*

10. Doc. A/CONF.48/8, para. 197.

11. See U.S. Federal Water Pollution Control Act 1956, as amended by Public Law 91–224, 1970, 11, paras. (a) and (b), and the Canada Shipping Act 1970.

12. See Art. 6 of the Geneva Convention on the High Seas and *Molvan* v. *Attorney General for Palestine*, 81 Ll.L.R. 277.

13. See my article in *Developments in the Law of the Sea 1958–1964*, p. 106, with n. 25 and the Geneva Convention on the Territorial Sea and the Contiguous Zone, Art. 24, which clearly regards the zone as a part of the high seas.

CHAPTER 10

Pollution from Offshore Oil Wells

By S. Houston Lay *

OFFSHORE oil drilling activities are certain to increase rapidly as land-based resources are exhausted, technology improves the ability to exploit undersea petroleum reserves and as more of the world becomes industrialised and increased populations must be supported. The comments and suggestions contained herein are almost equally applicable to mining of the seabed for hard minerals such as manganese nodules.

Customary international law and the 1958 Territorial Sea Convention gives a coastal State sovereignty over its territorial sea and the possible development of economic zones are treated elsewhere in this volume.

The 1958 Continental Shelf Convention gives a coastal State the equivalent of sovereign control over the seabed and subsoil of its continental shelf, for purposes of exploration and exploitation of natural resources. The extent of the shelf is open-ended in that the convention extends national control to a water depth of 200 metres or beyond where the depth of the superjacent waters still permits the exploitation of the natural resources. Natural islands probably have their own continental shelf areas.

There are thus under the high seas vast expanses of the seabed and subsoil subject to national control amounting to sovereignty, and such areas are steadily expanding in size as technology extends the ability of man to exploit the resources of the seabed at ever-increasing depths. There is currently, on an experimental basis, the ability to drill into the bed of the sea in water of several thousand metres depth, although the commercially producing oil wells are in shallow water. There is nothing in customary international law or in any treaty, or record of negotiations, to indicate any intent to freeze the extent of the continental shelf by the technology existing in 1958 or at any other particular time in history. However, there are numerous proposals to internationalise control of exploitation of seabed resources, but these deal only to a limited extent with pollution from such activities.

Following the existing rules, there is very little, if any, of the seabed of the North Sea, the Red Sea or the Persian Gulf not subject to national control of one of the riparian States. To avoid controversy, the nations adjacent to these seas have undertaken to divide the continental shelf beneath between themselves by several treaties and protocols. The International Court of Justice has assisted by setting forth principles to be used in making these delimitations.[1]†

Numerous treaties, referred to in other papers in this volume, have been adopted regulating pollution of the sea by oil discharged or spilled from ships and several coastal States have enacted legislation relating to discharge or spillage of oil under circumstances where it may pollute the shore or territorial waters or water over which the State thinks it has special interest or responsibility. Examples of this are Canada's

* Professor of International Law, California Western Law School, San Diego.

† For references, see p. 105.

Arctic Waters Pollution Prevention Act, and the British Prevention of Oil Pollution Act, but these laws and treaties relate almost exclusively to shipping rather than to the extractive process itself.

Article 24 of the 1958 High Seas Convention requires States to: " draw up regulations to prevent pollution of the seas . . . resulting from the exploitation and exploration of the seabed and its subsoil, taking account of existing treaty provisions on the subject."

Article 5 of the 1958 Continental Shelf Convention provides that exploration and exploitation must not " result in any interference with fundamental oceanographic or other scientific research carried out with the intention of open publication. . . ." The coastal State is also required to take " all appropriate measures for the protection of the living resources of the sea from harmful agents. . . ." There are no special enforcement procedures and standards of care are no more than those of customary international law. They are no more than pious expressions of good intentions and hope. As set forth in the *Trail Smelter Arbitration* " no State has the right to use or permit the use of its territory in such a manner as to cause injury by fumes in or to the territory of another or the property or persons therein. . . ." [2] The *Corfu Channel Case* is also in point.[3]

In accordance with the existing legal régime, almost all petroleum extractive activities on the seabed will take place pursuant to licence of an adjacent coastal State. The licence may contain such terms and conditions as the adjacent State wishes to impose but very little has been done internationally to require special safeguards for an extra-hazardous activity, or to provide for expeditious international recovery for damage caused. It seems doubtful that any uniform engineering rules suitable for world-wide application could be prepared because of geologic differences.

Everyone is familiar with the Santa Barbara oil spill of a few years ago. This was close to shore and the readily observable damage which resulted therefrom was limited almost entirely to the western coast of California. Similar blow-outs or leakages have occurred in the Gulf of Mexico and elsewhere. These accidents have damaged the world as a whole, because of the loss of wild life, pollution of the atmosphere and the unknown climatic effects as well as the dispersion of some parts of the oil slick over the oceans by winds and water currents.

What would be the international legal consequence if an oil well, being drilled on the U.K. continental shelf by a U.S.-U.K. consortium of private oil companies, blew out and the winds and ocean currents eventually carried the crude oil to the Danish and Norwegian coasts, doing substantial damage, while migratory wild fowl that usually flew to Sweden to the great pleasure of tourists, birdwatchers, hunters and others, disappeared? The international legal régime provides, at best, vague and uncertain answers.

It is recommended that a multilateral treaty, or treaties, borrowing ideas from the 1967 Space Treaty and the 1972 Convention on International Liability for Damage Caused by Space Objects as well as the various treaties relating to liability for nuclear activities, be negotiated and brought into force. Such a treaty or treaties should provide for absolute liability of the State from whose continental shelf the oil leakage occurred. Where the activity is beyond national control on the basis of a continental shelf, the nation whose flag flies over the enterprise should bear the responsibility. *Force majeure* or act of God should be no defence since the damage could not have occurred but for the existence of the seabed activity. Provisions should be made in the treaty so that the State primarily liable could recover from any State whose activities had negligently or deliberately contributed to or actually caused the oil spill. The

State liable could have such reimbursement provisions etc. in licences granted by it as it might desire, but the injured State should be given its option to proceed against the State or the actual private petroleum activity, or both, with concepts of joint and several liability. A world-wide treaty has some appeal, but it seems likely that initially a series of regional agreements would be more acceptable.

Consideration should be given to providing that the United Nations could bring an action to recover for generalised damage to the world environment, with any funds recovered to be used for environmental and health research in connection with products of the sea.

On an overall basis, the petroleum industry as represented by the State authorising the particular activities should bear the risk as a part of the cost of producing petroleum products. To the extent that the amount of damages, including expenses of clean-up operations, can be established, there should be no limit to the amount of recovery. As an added incentive for the exercise of great national care, there might be an automatic assessment of so many dollars or pounds or francs penalty for each ton of petroleum leaked or spilled into the sea. This proposal suggests absolute, or close to absolute, liability of States. Consequently, it follows that each State should prescribe the engineering safety rules applicable to the geologic conditions existing in the area over which that State exercises control.

Western-style arbitral commissions should be set up to hear claims presented under the basic treaty or treaties above proposed. Claims by nationals of the State liable should be handled in domestic courts, as at present, but international claims should not require exhaustion of local remedies, although a period of time for direct negotiation between claimant and respondent should be provided.

Traditionally, only States may be parties to international litigation, but this rule is not immutable and consideration should be given to allowing private parties who have suffered damage to bring their own actions: see, for example, the jurisdiction of the Court of Justice of the European Communities. Costs of such litigation will prevent frivolous claims from being presented and also will usually result in consolidation of claims for presentation by a government. Awards made should be paid in a hard currency of the claimant's choice.

It is believed that a régime of law, such as proposed here, will result in nations substantially increasing the care and supervision exercised over offshore petroleum activities without the necessity of setting up under the aegis of the United Nations a huge unwieldy regulatory and supervisory agency. The liability régime proposed, as a comparatively minor item not overly contentious, can be fitted easily into the framework of the comprehensive law of the sea treaties to be negotiated by governments in conferences, scheduled to commence late in 1973. Acceptance of these proposals through adoption of a world-wide treaty or a series of regional treaties would lessen substantially the economic incentive presently existing to allow oil drilling and exploitation under inadequate controls.

It is believed that the proposals given will not unnecessarily inhibit exploration and exploitation of petroleum resources existing under the sea, but will provide a measure of protection to the world environment, which does not at present exist and will provide a means by which injured States can receive prompt and adequate compensation for the damage suffered.

REFERENCES

1. See [1969] I.C.J.Rep. 3.
2. See also Fleischer, *supra*, pp. 80–81.
3. See Fleischer, *supra*, p. 82.

Part IV

The Seabed and the Ocean Floor

CHAPTER 11

Geo-Physical Characteristics

By André Guilcher *

INTRODUCTION

THE enormous amount of new information which has been gathered in this field during the last 25 years has come from the increase in size and number of oceanographical ships, especially in the United States and the U.S.S.R. and by improvements in investigation techniques, such as echo-sounding, dredging, coring, seismic refraction and reflection, magnetic field measurement, gravimetry, underwater photography and television, scientific submarine navigation and aqualung diving at shallow depths. The JOIDES programme, sponsored by the National Science Foundation of the United States, has been performed by means of the *R.V. Glomar Challenger*, which is able to penetrate more than 1,000 metres into the seafloor in a short time; its world-wide programme, one century after the *H.M.S. Challenger* expedition, is now bringing about a second revolution in ocean knowledge.

The material thus available gives more and more accuracy in classifying and describing the geo-physical characteristics of the seafloor. Most of the main subdivisions were already discovered in previous decades, but their real nature has been unknown until recent geo-physical investigation. These subdivisions are the following:

A. The continental margin, which borders the continents and also the larger islands (in which case it is an insular margin), includes the continental shelf, slope and rise.

B. The deep seafloor, which covers a much larger area than the continental margin, includes the mid-oceanic ridge, and some minor seismic ridges; deep-sea trenches; basins comprising abyssal plains and abyssal hills.

C. A third class of features may include banks, other ridges and seamounts rising from the deep seafloor, which are aseismic contrary to the mid-oceanic ridge.

The aim of this paper is to review the above-mentioned features and to indicate the probable or proven mineral resources lying on them or buried beneath their surface, in so far as they are known at the present time. The possibilities for exploitation will be kept in mind, although the economic implications will not be discussed in detail.

A. The Continental Margin

The continental margin covers 20·6 per cent. of the seafloor. According to proposals made in previous conferences (Rome, 1969; Strasbourg, 1970), the following definitions may be accepted for the shelf, slope, and rise.

Continental shelf: the zone around the continent extending from the low waterline to the depth at which there is usually a marked increase of declivity to greater depth. Where this increase occurs, the term " shelf edge " is appropriate. This shelf

* University of Western Brittany, Brest.

edge ranges in depth from less than 60 metres to more than 500 metres and it averages 130 metres. Where the zone below the low-water line is highly irregular and contains depths in excess of those typical of continental shelves (as off southern California), the term "continental borderland" is appropriate.

Continental slope: the zone bordering the continental shelf that extends seawards from the shelf edge at declivities that average about 4° 15′ down to the depths of 1,200–3,500 metres. Its outer edge approximately marks the boundary between the low density rocks of the continents and the high density ones of the deep ocean floor or the intermediate ones of the enclosed or marginal seas.

Continental rise: the zone that borders the base of many continental slopes and has a smooth declivity that averages 30′ to depths of 3,500–5,500 metres.

If the conventional limit of 200 metres is accepted, the shelf covers 7·6 per cent. of the seafloor. The area covered by the slope amounts to 7·7 per cent.; by the rise, 5·3 per cent. The combined continental shelf and slope are sometimes called the continental terrace.

The word "continental" is really adequate to qualify the margin, or, at least, the terrace, because this part of the ocean is actually an extension of the same nature as the continents themselves. This point has now been verified by the geo-physical research carried out in extremely numerous areas in the world. Whereas the deep seafloor is made of very dense rocks such as basalt and ultra-basic rocks, with only a thin veneer of sediment, the continents consist of granite and sedimentary rocks; and so the margin is too.

A further result is that, when the continent is an old shield made of crystalline or old, highly indurated sedimentary or metamorphic rocks, the margin consists for the most part of more recent, unconsolidated or semi-consolidated sediment resting awkwardly on the old shield and dipping in an offshore direction. For example, the old rocks outcropping in South-West England and in Brittany on either side of the western English Channel quickly disappear under sea beneath a cover of secondary and tertiary rocks. The situation is the same on the western side of the British Isles, on the southern side of the Armorican Massif in the Bay of Biscay, along the Atlantic coasts of Spain and Portugal, North-West Africa, and so on. The geo-physical records show that the sedimentary strata thicken as the distance from the coast increases, the dip remaining variable in detail. On the east coast of the United States, the sedimentary cover begins inside the present coastline, in other words, the boundary between the Appalachian basement and its cover has now shifted to the East. The case of eastern England is similar. The sedimentary beds result from the deposit of terrigenous material originating on the continents, eroded and carried to the sea by rivers, and from organogenic deposits favoured by suitable conditions of life provided for organisms in shallow areas surrounding the emerged lands. A minor contribution comes from coastal erosion. Subsidence accounts for the thickness, frequently averaging several thousands of metres as, for example, in the North Sea basin.

In many areas this sediment settled freely around the continents, *i.e.*, without protection on the outer side. In other regions, however, the deposit was favoured by the existence of submerged ridges behind which the sediment was piled. K. O. Emery has shown that such has been the case in the East China Sea and the Yellow Sea, where a series of dams running north-east and south-west enclose three basins (the Yellow Sea Basin, Taiwan Basin and Okinawa Depression) elongated in the same direction and including sediment exceeding 2,000 metres in thickness in the Taiwan Basin.

Emery has applied the dam concept to many other areas, and he distinguishes three kinds of dams: tectonic dams, formed by geological uplift or upwelling of lava; reef dams, created by marine organisms; and diapir dams, pushed upward by salt domes. The margins off the western coasts of the Americas are nearly all classified by him in the dam type.

A large part of the dams derive from the folding or the faulting of sediments formerly deposited on the margins. When such ridges originated by folds or faults are not yet buried beneath more recent sediments, the shelf consists of parallel rises and falls. An example is found off southern California, previously mentioned in the definition of the shelf.

The sedimentary nature of the larger part of the continental margin is most important, since, combined with the thickness, it involves the possibility of oil and gas resources trapped in its strata (see below).

Considering now the *shelf*, we can hold as certain that it has been alternately dry land and sea-covered during the last million years, as a result of glaciations and deglaciations which modified the water content in the ocean and consequently the sea-level. These fluctuations, amounting approximately to 100–150 metres and perhaps more, fall largely within the range of depth of the most usual shelves. The unconsolidated sediments which cover generally the solid rock, and also the topographical features, bring evidence of these alterations.

Off the east coast of the United States, drowned shorelines testified by former coastal deposits have been discovered and dated, so that a curve of sea-level fluctuations, down to 120 metres lower than now, has been proposed for the last 35,000 years. In other areas, data are generally not so complete, but they point to the same pattern. Old shorelines have been found on the shelves off western Europe and other continents. Submerged peat is reported at various depths. Drowned valleys, continuing the emerged fluvial patterns on the shelf are one of the main features in the same line of evidence. Those which remained free of sediment have often been noted in a number of areas; those which have been filled with deposits can be recognised today by geophysical prospecting. In regions where icecaps extended over the shelf during glaciations, *i.e.*, north-western Europe and north-eastern North America, glacial deposits and related landforms (moraines, drumlins, etc.) have been described, as, for example, in the North Sea, the Irish Sea, and off New England. In places where the climate was cold without glaciers, as off Brittany, frost shattered cobbles are dredged on the shelf. Off the coast of Provence, the marine regression during the last glacial period resulted in the production of solution features in limestone, scree and talus deposits, sand dunes, and the growth of coastal biocoenoses, including a cold fauna, then living in shallow water and now found at more than 100 metres depth. As a rule, the river discharge was larger than now in a wide range of climates, so that coarse deposits were laid down on shelves in large quantities. Such evidence, and others, may be quoted from areas as various as the Gulf of Mexico, South America shelves, Portuguese Guinea and the Republic of Guinea, South-West Africa, Madagascar, the Sunda shelf, Malacca Strait, North-West Australia, etc. It has been stated that about 70 per cent. of the area of the continental shelves of the world are presently covered by relict sediments which settled during lower Quaternary sea-levels.

Some authors, however, have suggested that the sediment considered as "relics" on shelves are often not exactly in the place in which they settled initially. They have been more or less reworked since the sea-level rose as a result of the melting of the glaciers. This is particularly true in areas surrounding the British Isles. Moreover, new material has been added to the shelves since the marine transgression and after.

Detrital shells and calcareous algae have been supplied everywhere and continue to increase the calcium carbonate content of the loose fraction. In areas where tidal currents are strong, *e.g.*, the English Channel and the Irish Sea, sand waves, sand ribbons and sand streams have been built, and their elongated patterns, directly controlled by the tidal régime, have been mapped. Another extensive sand wave field is found off the coast of Holland, covering 15,000 square kilometres and also related to tidal currents. Some of these hydraulic dunes are exclusively skeletal as off western Brittany, so that their calcium carbonate content is especially interesting for exploitation. These areas contrast sharply with others, as off the north coast of the Cotentin Peninsula in the central English Channel, where sediments are swept, and coarse residual cobbles and the solid rock outcrop on the seabed. As a whole, however, the strata deposited on shelves during the last million years, either in sub-aerial conditions or under water, are thin when compared with the previous shelf deposits, except for a restricted number of places where some glacial moraines or submarine sand dunes may reach tens of metres in thickness.

In the slope and rise, the outstanding features are the *submarine canyons* which are deeply cut into the seafloor in a great number of places, although not everywhere. They are steep-sided valleys several hundred metres deep, often branching, and ranging from a few kilometres to several hundred kilometres in length. The longest known submarine canyon is the Bering Canyon in the Bering Sea, which is 400 km. long, with a volume of 4,300 cubic kilometres; not far away the Zhemchug Canyon has a volume of 8,500 cubic kilometres. The usual volume of large canyons is less than 500 cubic kilometres, a figure that is still considerable. Off the coasts of Europe, such canyons occur in groups on the north-eastern side of the Bay of Biscay, off the coasts of Languedoc and Provence, and off western Corsica. The most accurately charted in the world lie on the slope of the eastern United States and in southern California. A few cut their upper courses into the shelf which they deeply penetrate, as the Cap Breton Canyon in the Bay of Biscay, the Trou Sans Fond off Ivory Coast, and the Cayar Canyon off Senegal. The Congo Canyon is exceptional in that it enters even the estuary of the river. The outer reaches of the canyons extend as deep as 4,000 metres or sometimes more, in the continental rise. These outer ends appear often not as deeply cut valleys, but as deep sea fans, widely extended, in which sets of shallow valleys are moderately incised and bounded by lateral levees. A typical example of this is the Astoria deep sea fan, off the mouth of the Columbia River in western North America.

Among the various opinions expressed on the origin of the submarine canyons, only two seem to deserve attention in the present state of knowledge. According to the first, they would have been cut by sub-aerial rivers, and drowned at great depths by a large flexure depressing the continental margin and the adjoining portion of the continent. This hypothesis may account for some canyons cutting across the whole shelf, as the Congo Canyon, and some others carved into very hard rocks as granite, as in Corsica, for which processes other than sub-aerial erosion by continental rivers seem difficult to accept. The second explanation, which is considered as the more accurate by a large majority of geologists, especially in America, relates the carving of canyons to slumping and turbidity currents, *i.e.*, water loaded with suspended sediment, flowing with rising velocity (perhaps several tens of knots) down the continental slope, and depositing their load as fans on the rise and even on the adjacent deep seafloor. Turbidity currents have never been observed directly by man, and such an observation is quite impossible if the velocity of the currents is as high as assumed. But some evidence has been presented, including tank experiments, structure of deposits in canyons and in their outer reaches (the so-called graded bedding with multiple recurrences of coarse and fine beds), rupture of submarine cables ascribed to earthquakes (*e.g.*, the Grand Banks earthquake off Newfoundland in 1929, or the Orléansville earthquake in Algeria in 1954), or to big floods of rivers discharging large amounts of sediment on the shelf (*e.g.*, Magdalena River in Colombia, South America). Another line of evidence is the common existence on many geophysical records of the continental slope, of highly contorted and disturbed stratifications, pointing to sliding and slumping. As a matter of fact, the turbidity currents seem to be generated by large landslides on the slope, suspending sediment in the water. They are thought to have occurred more frequently than now during the Quaternary low sea-levels, when the rivers were more heavily loaded and flowed into the sea directly at the outer edge of the shelf. In several areas (*e.g.*, Coral Sea, Bering Sea, Bay of Biscay), it seems that tectonic lineations have played a part in canyon initiation. This part may sometimes have been considerable (Cap Breton Canyon).

A related, although somewhat different process which has been invoked is the sliding of sand from beaches into the inner heads of canyons starting not far from the coastline. Such sand-slides occur at low velocity and, consequently, were observed and photographed by divers in California. It is quite proved that big sand-slides occur also from time to time at Trou Sans Fond on the Ivory Coast, engulfing tremendous amounts of sand supplied by the beach. In Calfornia, finer material consisting of silt and clay is thought to travel slowly across the shelf, and to fall into the canyons where it joins the sand and continues to migrate with it down to greater depths.

Although everything is not yet clear, one point seems to be certain: the continental slope and rise is not a fossil feature; it is alive, it continues to be moulded and modified by submarine processes. Even if a part of the canyons are former sub-aerial valleys, sediment travels through them; if some canyons have been completely filled up, as shown by geo-physical records, others have remained open because of currents. Not only the canyons but also the intervening divides are subject to modifications by submarine forces of erosion and deposit. The sedimentary nature of the slope, which is built as an apron in front of the continents as seen above, favours the theory of canyon carving by submarine currents, since these sediments are only moderately consolidated and thus easily eroded. The rise, on the other hand, appears to be for a very large part the result of the accumulation of deposits at the foot of the slope. A general consequence of this is that the texture of the sediments is partly coarse down to depths of thousands of metres. Shelf, slope and rise as sedimentary units are interrelated since the same processes of transportation are acting on them.

It happens in some areas that the continental slope is broken into two sections by a wide terrace which repeats more or less the shelf at an unusual depth. The best example of this type is the Blake Plateau lying at 800–1,000 m. off Georgia and Florida, south-eastern United States. It seems to be related to a lower rate in sedimentation during subsidence than the adjacent shelf, owing to the slackening action of the Gulf Stream throughout the Tertiary.

Another peculiarity is the great depth of the shelf surrounding Antarctica, which reaches 500 m. and is often very uneven.

The *mineral resources* useful to man and lying on and into the continental margin form certainly the most important submarine resources in the present time and for the forseeable future, in spite of the fact that the continental margin covers only one fifth of the whole seafloor. They are the only ones to be exploited so far. Oil and natural gas form approximately 90 per cent. in value of the exploited submarine resources; and the submarine oil and gas amount in turn to 15–18 per cent. of the total production, continents and seabed included, of these raw materials. The second proportion tends to increase. Oil and gas are now exploited in a number of shelves, as, for example, the Gulf of Mexico, the Persian Gulf, the North Sea, Venezuela, Nigeria. They certainly exist in many other shelves where they have already been discovered or are most probable. Their presence is related to the sedimentary structure of most continental margins (see above), since pervious rocks included between impervious layers are needed to trap hydrocarbons in natural reservoirs. Although a large proportion has escaped through the slope and submarine canyons in the course of time, the remaining reserves must be enormous.

Drilling in shelves for oil is now a current technique. It can be carried out from artificial platforms or islands supported on legs resting on the seafloor, or from floating structures which take their buoyancy from chambers at 20 metres below the sea surface and are thus largely independent of the swell. The loose structure of the seabed cover in large areas of the shelf generally presents no great difficulty, or, at least, the difficulties can be overcome except in a few special cases. But other kinds of problems should be kept in mind.

The main point is the difference between technical feasibility and economic possibility. Drilling is technically possible everywhere for exploration, but it quickly becomes very expensive with increasing depth: so that oil and gas exploitation are economically interesting only if very large resources are proved in a given place. The distance offshore also greatly increases the costs in production. The consequence is that almost all the offshore oil and gas exploitation is presently made at depths not reaching 100 metres. If resources are found on slopes and rises, the costs in present conditions are likely to prevent exploitation. But the improvements in techniques may, of course, change the terms of the problem in the more or less near future, so that present time exploration in areas deeper than 100 metres may appear as wise. Other problems arise from the competition with other marine activities, such as fisheries and navigation, not only for drilling, but also for transportation to land. These problems, and those related to pollution, will not be treated here.

Other valuable resources now exploited on the continental shelf are, in order of value, sand and gravel, tin, and diamonds. Sand and gravel are dredged off the United States and western Europe from very shallow water, mostly less than 10 metres at low tide, and their value is reckoned to be 8 per cent. of the dry land production of these raw materials. It is expected that this type of production will increase rapidly in the next few years to meet the needs of coastal cities and industries, and that the dredging will be extended to greater depths, although probably not exceeding several dozen metres. Tin is exploited in South-East Asia and the production amounts to 1 per cent. of the output on dry land or a little more. Diamond is collected off the coast of South-West Africa (Namibia), in shallow water not far from the shore, but this exploitation is made difficult by the heavy swell. Phosphorites could be mined on some outer shelves (California, north-western Africa, South Africa, Peru and Chile).

To sum up, the exploitation of mineral resources of the continental shelf is already considerable in so far as oil, gas, sand and gravel are concerned. Increase in output is to be expected, since reserves are certainly enormous, technical problems are solved or are not insoluble, but improvements in techniques and lowerings of costs will be indispensable to make further operations profitable. In the near future, mining and drilling of these products are not expected to be extended to the slope and rise.

B. The Deep Seafloor

The floor of the deep sea, 3,000 to 11,000 m., is the *oceanic crust*, which is thin and quite different in nature from the continental crust underlying the continents and continental shelves and slopes. The Oceanic crust includes three layers, similar to one another except in the mid-oceanic ridge (see below): layer one, averaging 0·45 km. in thickness, in which the velocity of seismic waves is small and probably close to 2 km/s; layer two, 1·75 km. thick, velocity 5·00 km/s; layer three, 4·7–4·9 km. thick, velocity 6·7 km/s. Layer one is made up of sediment ranging from Cretaceous to Recent; layer two must consist mostly of basalt; layer three includes ultrabasic rocks (peridotites) or metamorphised basalt. Below layer three is the Mohorovicic discontinuity and upper mantle rocks in which the velocity is 8·1 km/s. The upper mantle is thus at 7 km. beneath the seabed, or 12 km. beneath the sea-level; whereas below the continents, it lies at more than 30 km. beneath the sea-level.

The *mid-oceanic ridge* covers 32·7 per cent. of the seabed, that is much more than the continental margin. It is essential to analyse it in order to understand the mechanism of the whole deep seafloor. The mid-oceanic ridge is a huge and rugged mountain system, 60,000 km. long, 1,000 to 2,500 km. wide, and 1,000 to 3,000 m. high above the surrounding seafloor. It begins in the North Polar Sea near the Lena Delta, runs towards the Norwegian Sea which it crosses through Jan Mayen Island, includes Iceland, which is its only extensive area above sea-level, stretches in the Atlantic through Ascension Island to the Southern Ocean, and, round South Africa, enters the Indian Ocean in which it forms an inverted Y: one of the branches penetrates the Gulf of Aden, while the other stretches south of Australia into the Pacific where it finally links with North America in California. Easter Island lies on its Pacific section. Smaller ridges, structurally similar to the mid-oceanic ridge, are the Scotia Ridge, running north-east and south-west at the south-east of Cape Horn, and the Chile Ridge, linking the mid-oceanic ridge and South America at the latitudes of 35–45° S.

The characteristics of the mid-oceanic ridge are the following. In the Atlantic and Indian Oceans (but not in the Pacific, however) it bears in its median crest a long steep-sided axial valley or rift, 25 to 50 km. wide, 1,000 to 2,500 m. below the summits of the walls, much resembling the sub-aerial rift valleys of East Africa. On the other hand, the ridge is accompanied by a belt of shallow earthquake epicentres which is also found on the Scotia Ridge and the Chile Ridge. It is almost completely devoid of sediment (layer one of the oceanic crust), which appear on its flanks and increase in thickness and in age from the axis of the ridge to the continental margins bordering the continents on both sides of the ocean. Layer three disappears generally under the ridge, except in the East Pacific, and is replaced at 2 or 3 km. beneath the seabed by an abnormal mantle, with velocities ranging from 7·1 to 7·5 km/s.

The interpretation of these facts, and also of the distribution of magnetic anomalies in rocks, is that the mid-oceanic ridge is the rising place of sub-crustal materials, which expand laterally on both sides and travel to the continents at the rate of 1 to 6 cm. per year according to place and time. This explanation is known as the spreading seafloor. The Chile and Scotia Ridges are secondary spreading axes. The evidence is so great that the spreading seafloor, a theory which was proposed for the first time by Dietz in 1961, appears not to be theoretical but reality. The existing oceans were formed and enlarged by spreading since the Jurassic or the Cretaceous Ages. The process has stopped in areas such as the Labrador Sea; as a rule, it is still going on, and is found at an incipient stage in the Red Sea which is an ocean in the making, and in the East African rift, which may be an ocean of the future.

The movement of the seafloor has been accompanied by large fracture zones, which run perpendicular to the ridge and displace it to the right or to the left. The Mendocino, Murray, Clipperton and Eltanin fracture zones may be quoted in the

Pacific, and the Romanche, Vema and Gibbs fracture zones in the Atlantic. The Chile Ridge and Scotia Ridge are also affected by fracture zones.

From an economic point of view it must be kept in mind that the mid-oceanic ridge bears no sediment or only very little, because its volcanic floor is too young to have been fossilised.

Deep sea trenches and plates. The deep sea trenches, which occupy about 1 per cent. of the total seafloor, are long, narrow features in which the deepest places in the ocean are found. Several of them exceed 10,000 m. in depth: the Marianas Trench (11,022 m.), the Kuril, Philippine, Tonga and Kermadec trenches. All but three are located in the Pacific, where they lie on the oceanic side of the island arcs stretching in the western Pacific from the Aleutian Islands to the Kermadec Islands, and along the mountains of western North and South America. In Melanesia, three trenches are exceptionally situated on the inner, western side of island arcs. The three trenches which are not in the Pacific are the Puerto-Rico Trench in the Atlantic, the South Sandwich Trench in the Southern Ocean, and the Java Trench in the Indian Ocean. The bottom of the trenches, although narrow, is usually flat and occupied by sediments, which seem to be supplied for a large part by turbidity currents originated on the slope.

All trenches are highly seismic, even more than the mid-oceanic ridge. All these earthquakes are not generated at shallow depths: some of them originate on planes sloping deeply to hundreds of kilometres from the bottom of the trenches towards the continents. It is most probable that these oblique megafaults along which the earthquakes occur are thrust planes allowing the floor of the ocean, which has appeared in the mid-oceanic ridge and hence travelled in opposite directions, to be engulfed again into the earth's interior. A difficulty arises, however, from the fact that trenches are uncommon on the sides of the Atlantic and Indian Oceans. This difficulty is likely to be solved by the theory of plates, according to which the earth's crust, either continental or oceanic, is divided into a small number of stiff plates: the large displacements, accompanied by earthquakes, are restricted to the boundaries of the plates. There would be no such boundary on the sides of the Atlantic, except in the Caribbean area, since the Americas are a part of the same plate as the western Atlantic, and Eurafrica is similarly tied to the eastern Atlantic. Around the Pacific, the seafloor, on the contrary, is underthrusted beneath the adjoining plate (*e.g.*, Asian plate, Philippine Sea plate). This theory seems to have been recently checked by the study of what happens during great earthquakes in South-West Japan, which is uplifted and laterally displaced at the rate of 8 cm./year.

Abyssal plains and hills are the largest submarine unit, since they cover 41·8 per cent. of the seafloor according to Menard and Smith. These areas occupy wide oceanic basins at the foot of the mid-oceanic ridge. The plains are flat-bottomed and their slope is less than 1:1,000. They alternate with hills where the topography is gently undulated, the height of the hills ranging from a few metres to several dozen metres. Although sediment is considerably thinner in these areas than in the continental margin, it often reaches several hundred metres in thickness, since it had time to settle since the volcanic oceanic crust upon which it lies was extruded from the mid-oceanic ridge. This sediment falls into two classes: turbidites, and pelagic sediment.

Turbidites have been deposited in parts of the oceanic basins lying within the reach of the turbidity currents generated on continental slopes. They have the same structure (graded bedding) as those existing at the lower course of the canyons, and this process explains how coarse particles may be found at great depths. In the Indian Ocean, the abyssal plains of Indus and Ceylon have been fed by turbidites from the rivers Indus, Ganges and Brahmaputra: these areas include 40 per cent. of the total amount of the deep sediment of this ocean. In some regions, as in the North-East Pacific, turbidites were formerly laid down, and in more recent times ceased to arrive, because the abyssal plain was cut from the source of the turbidity currents by modifications in the shape of the seafloor. Turbidites may spread from one abyssal plain to another if these plains are interlinked, as the Biscay and Iberia plains in the North-East Atlantic. Deep sea channels bounded by levees are thought to be turbidite feeders. A larger feature of this kind is the so-called mid-ocean canyon, discovered in the Labrador Sea and the Irminger Sea, North-West Atlantic, three to seven kilometres wide, 50 to 200 metres deep, containing sand on its floor, and possibly (?) fed by currents generated by cold masses of water sinking to the bottom when freezing conditions occur at the surface. Other deep currents are more probably the cause of the Blake-Bahama outer ridge, a giant spit rising from the seabed at a depth of 4,000 m. off South Carolina and Georgia, and other deep accumulations reported from the south of Greenland and the surroundings of Rockall Plateau off the British Isles. Deep sea currents are thus able to build landforms and not only to bury older structures.

Pelagic sediments are those deriving from the showering on the bottom of fine particles suspended in the sea. These consist either of organogenic oozes, calcareous or siliceous, or of still finer mineral particles, such as red clay. This class of sediment prevails in regions which are inaccessible to turbidity currents coming from shallower water (in areas that are reached by turbidity currents, pelagic sediments do also settle but are superseded by the mass of the turbidites). Red clay is found in the deepest parts, from 4,000 to 4,800 metres down; because of these depths the calcareous tests (the most common in oozes) are dissolved before reaching the seabed. Red clay is thus a residual deposit of sedimentation. The average accretion rate of pelagic sediment is exceedingly low. For organogenic sediment the figure of 1 cm. per 1,000 years has been put forward, and, for red clay, 1 mm. per 1,000 years.

Another type of deposit which is widespread on the deep seafloor is *manganese nodules*, consisting of granules, cobbles and slabs scattered over the surface of finer material, and weighing from a few grams to hundreds of kilograms. Manganese nodules have attracted considerable interest, since their industrial exploitation could possibly become feasible in the not too distant future. The interest comes from their composition. According to Mero, their average content in the Pacific would be 24·2 per cent. in manganese, 0·35 per cent. in cobalt, 0·99 per cent. in nickel, and 0·53 per cent. in copper. In the Atlantic the composition does not seem so favourable. An estimate of the tonnage by Mero for the Pacific alone amounts to 1,656 thousand million tons. Even if this figure is much too large, it is quite sure that huge accumulations of manganese nodules exist on the deep seafloor, and that their formation is continuing so that although they generally occur at depths of between 3,000 and 5,000 metres, some mining companies have started preliminary studies in this respect, and the French have decided to make experimental dredgings in the Tahiti region.

So far, manganese nodules appear to be the only mineral deep sea resource which could be competitive with dry land ores in the near future. Oil has been discovered, it is true, at a depth of 3,600 m. in the abyssal plain of the Gulf of Mexico, that is, in an adjacent sea and not in the ocean. Other discoveries of the same kind are possible elsewhere, in the western Mediterranean for example. In the ocean itself, the thinness of the sedimentary cover is not promising, but nothing seems impossible, especially far away from the mid-oceanic ridge. In any event it would be necessary to find enormous reserves to meet the equally enormous expenses of exploitation at such depths, and it appears that the deep seafloor is not on the way to competing for oil and gas with the margins, and even less so with the continents.

C. Banks, Other Ridges, and Seamounts in the Deep Sea

Shallow banks rise from abyssal depths in the Caribbean Sea, in the Bahamas, in the Coral Sea, in the North-East Atlantic, and elsewhere. Some of them bear islands or islets, as the Bahamas; some others are entirely submerged, as in the Caribbean and between Ireland, Scotland and Iceland, so that problems of property may be raised for them. Their nature is not always the same: they may be volcanic, or made of continental rocks (as Rockall Bank in the North-East Atlantic, or Flinders and Holmes Banks in the Coral Sea), or built up by prolonged calcareous sedimentation (Bahamas). The Seychelles Bank in the Indian Ocean is, as Rockall, a remnant of continent or isolated raft following the expansion of the seafloor. Sedimentation continues to go on at their tops.

Aseismic ridges, in contrast to the ridges shaken by frequent earthquakes, are the largest feature to be considered in this section. Most of them lie in the Pacific, where they run north-west and south-east, as the Hawaiian Ridge, the Marshall Ridge, the Samoa Ridge, the Tuamotu Ridge, the Cook and Austral Ridge. All are volcanic, and volcanism has migrated from one end to the other in the course of time. Other aseismic ridges are the Lomonosov and Mendeleev Ridges in the North Polar Sea, which they divide into deep basins, and the Walvis and Rio Grande Ridges in the South Atlantic.

Seamounts rising from the deep seafloor are almost always volcanoes. Some are associated with seismic or aseismic ridges, others are independent. According to Menard, there must be ten thousand volcanoes rising at least one kilometre above the seabed in the Pacific Ocean alone. A part of these volcanoes have retained their conical shape, while others, which are called guyots, are flat-topped since they have been truncated by marine erosion after emersion and have subsequently subsided down to various depths, for example in the Mid-Pacific and in the Gulf of Alaska.

Approximately 430 seamounts in the intertropical belt are capped by *atolls*, which are coral rings that grew upon volcanic mountains during their slow subsidence. The formation of atolls has taken millions to tens of millions of years, and was complicated during the Quaternary by oscillations of the sea-level. Atoll evolution has been associated with the history of the Pacific aseismic ridges (the Tuamotu Ridge bears 75 atolls), and, more widely, with the long-continued subsidence of the Darwin Rise, a huge structure which is thought to have existed in a Proto-Pacific before the spreading of the seafloor now in progress.

Scattered banks, seamounts and atolls, either submerged or slightly emerged, may have an economic interest if the surrounding seafloor is exploited in the future.

CHAPTER 12

Future Régimes: A Survey of Proposals

By L. M. Alexander *

THE bed of the world ocean, comprising over 70 per cent. of the earth's surface, represents a new geographic frontier for the world community—a frontier about which little is yet known in terms of potential wealth, or, for much of the area, of even the basic physical environment itself within which international rules and regulations are eventually to be established. Only in recent years has technology offered the possibility of utilising the floor of the ocean beyond shallow coastal depths. Only in recent years have questions of jurisdiction and control over the deep seabed come to assume major international proportions. Nearly a dozen national or multinational proposals have, in recent months, been put forward regarding future jurisdiction over this vast area.[1]† This paper is intended to discuss aspects of these proposals in the light of current developments taking place with respect to ocean affairs.

The terms " seabed " and " ocean floor " are not clearly defined in United Nations documents. The 1958 Geneva Convention on the Continental Shelf made reference to the " seabed and subsoil of submarine areas," but 12 years later the UN alluded to the " area of the seabed and the ocean floor, and the subsoil thereof, beyond the limits of national jurisdiction . . ." without differentiating between " seabed " and " ocean floor." The considerable literature on the subject which has appeared in recent years also fails to make clear any meaningful distinction, leading one to conclude that the two terms are somewhat redundant. For the purposes of this paper, the term " seabed " will be used as referring both to the floor of the ocean and to the subsoil thereof, everywhere seaward of the tideline. In this sense the seabed consists of two general categories: (1) the continental margin, including the continental shelf, the slope, and the rise[2]; and (2) the deep seabed, beyond the limits of the margin. This division is important in terms of possible future international régimes.

The 1958 Geneva Conventions failed to mention specifically the status of the deep seabed, thus leaving open the questions, first, whether it, like the high seas, is free to the use of all nations; and second, whether in time it may be subject to gradual appropriation by coastal States on the grounds of the exploitability criterion.[3] In the years following the 1958 Law of the Sea Conference there was much discussion of the possible effects of the exploitability clause of the Continental Shelf Convention[4] so far as jurisdiction over the outer continental margin (*i.e.*, beyond the 200 metre isobath) is concerned; but there was relatively little discussion of any new types of régime for the seabed beyond national limits until nine years after the First Geneva Conference had ended. In August 1967 Ambassador Pardo of Malta brought the seabed issue into the limelight with his request that there be included in the UN General Assembly agenda an item entitled " Declaration and treaty concerning the reservation exclusively for

* Director, Law of the Sea Institute, Kingston, Rhode Island.

† For references, see p. 131.

peaceful purposes of the seabed and of the ocean floor underlying the seas beyond the limits of present national jurisdiction, and the use of their resources in the interests of mankind." [5] The memorandum accompanying the Maltese *note verbale* suggested that the seabed and ocean floor be declared the common heritage of mankind, and that an international agency be established to assume jurisdiction over the area and to control the activities taking place thereon. The impact of Dr. Pardo's suggestion on the world community was heightened, several months later when, in a statement before the First Committee, he estimated that given certain assumptions, a seabed agency, five years after its establishment, might have at least $5 billion annually to further the development of poor countries.[6] Shortly after this, the General Assembly, acting on the report of the First Committee, established a 35-member *ad hoc* Committee to study the Peaceful Uses of the Seabed and the Ocean Floor Beyond the Limits of National Jurisdiction.[7] The following December, the *ad hoc* Committee was replaced by a standing Committee with 42 members, later expanded to 86, and still later to 91. It is this Committee which has been preparing the groundwork for a Third Law of the Sea Conference, hopefully to start in 1974.[8]

In addition to creating and supporting the so-called "Seabed Committee," the United Nations also responded to the suggestions of Dr. Pardo by adopting in December 1970 a "Declaration of principles governing the seabed and the ocean floor and the subsoil thereof beyond the limits of national jurisdiction." [9] The Declaration proclaimed that the seabed and subsoil beyond the limits of national jurisdiction, as well as the resources thereof, are the common heritage of mankind, that the area shall not be subject to appropriation or the exercise of sovereignty by States, and that an international régime shall be established to govern all activities related to the exploration and exploitation of the area's resources.

Although the Declaration was adopted with 108 votes in favour, none against, and 14 abstentions (including the Soviet bloc), it tended almost to raise more questions than it resolved. How were these principles to be translated into operational realities? Where, for example, were the "limits of national jurisdiction"? What sort of international régime should be set up for the seabed beyond national limits which could accommodate the interest of all independent States of the world, including land-locked, shelf-locked, developed and developing?

Since the time of the Declaration of Principles, a series of proposals for an international seabed régime have been put before the Seabed Committee. An analysis of these proposals indicates at least four basic issues associated with them. These are:

1. Where are the limits of national jurisdiction beyond which an international seabed régime applies?

2. What is the legal status of the international area?

3. What type of administrative structure is to be created to handle the international régime? What will its powers and functions be?

4. What would the impact be of alternative régimes on the interests of individual countries and groups of countries?

There are, of course, many other questions. How soon, for example, will technology permit the exploitation of the mineral resources of the outer continental margin and the deep seabed? What, in fact, is a realistic estimate of the potential wealth of the seabed which would be available within the foreseeable future for distribution by an international agency? Does the 1969 UN Moratorium Resolution [10] bind the developed countries to a policy of blocking the exploitation of seabed resources by their own nationals beyond the 200 metre isobath for what may be many years pending the coming into force of an international arrangement for the seabed? These questions are an integral part of the total régime syndrome; rather than speculate on such issues, however, this paper will confine itself to consideration of how the major proposals, now before the Seabed Committee, compared with one another in terms of their general outlines. The 11 proposals to be considered here are those of (1) the United States [11]; (2) the United Kingdom [12]; (3) France [13]; (4) Tanzania [14]; (5) the Soviet Union [15]; (6) Poland [16]; (7) the 13-Power Working Paper [17]; (8) Malta [18]; (9) the 7-Power Working Paper [19]; (10) Canada [20]; (11) Japan.[21] The texts of the first three of these proposals are annexed to the 1970 Report of the Seabed Committee.[22] Those of the other proposals, except for Japan's, are annexed to the 1971 Report of the Seabed Committee,[23] while the Japanese proposal was reproduced as a Seabed Committee Document.[24]

Three points should be noted with respect to the proposals. A first is that they differ considerably in their form. Six consist of draft treaty articles,[25] while the remainder were submitted as working papers, or as commentaries on principles, with considerations or suggestions advanced on different issues. A second point is that the working paper submitted by Malta was for a comprehensive draft treaty covering all aspects of the ocean space rather than just the seabed. In its *Comparative Table of Draft Treaties* the UN Secretariat included only those parts of the Maltese proposal which seemed germane to seabed issues. Finally, it should be noted that the proposals covered in this paper are those which the UN Secretariat had received and tabulated by January 1972. They have been listed here in the chronological order in which they were submitted, and in subsequent references any two or more proposals will continue to be listed in that order.

THE LIMITS OF NATIONAL JURISDICTION

Of the 11 proposals, four make no mention in the texts of the question of where the limits of national jurisdiction should be [26]; three take note of the problem, but without specifying the limits,[27] while the remaining four have definite suggestions. The United States proposes that the International Seabed Area comprise all areas of the high seas seaward of the 200 metre isobath, adjacent to the coast of continents and islands. Coupled with this is the suggestion that an International Trusteeship Area be established between the 200 metre isobath and some line beyond the base of the continental slope where the downward inclination of the surface of the seabed declines to a yet-unspecified gradient. Within this Trusteeship Area the coastal State will be responsible for issuing, suspending and revoking mineral exploration and exploitation licences, and for other regulatory activities.[28]

The Soviet Union feels that the international seabed area should begin at the limits of the continental shelf.[29] Since the U.S.S.R. has ratified the 1958 Continental Shelf Convention, these limits presumably are the 200 metre isobath, or beyond where the depth of the superjacent waters admits of the exploitation of the area's natural resources.

Malta's proposal calls for extension of national jurisdiction to a belt of ocean space, 200 nautical miles in breadth adjacent to the coast. The Maltese also suggest that portions of the continental shelf less than 200 metres in depth, which extend more than 200 miles from shore, be surrendered by the coastal State to become part of the internationalised area.[30]

A fourth suggestion, that in the 7-Power Working Paper, is that the limits of national jurisdiction should be placed either at the 200 metre isobath or 40 nautical miles from the coast, whichever alternative the coastal State chooses to use. Seaward of these limits is a 40 mile wide "coastal State priority zone" in which the International Seabed Authority cannot explore and exploit directly, or license exploration and exploitation by a non-littoral State without the consent of the coastal State.

It is surprising, perhaps, that not more attention was paid in the proposals to where the geographic boundaries of the international seabed area should be, considering the potential differences which would result in terms of availability of revenues depending on whether the limits were close to the coast, or at or beyond the continental margin. The Japanese proposal suggested that the international seabed régime "should have, as its scope of application, an area large enough so that the establishment of the régime would not be devoid of economic significance." As will be noted later, the question of national limits could have considerable impact on the interests both of the international régime itself, and of individual States and groups of States.

THE STATUS OF THE INTERNATIONAL SEABED AREA

There is little variation among the proposals regarding conditions within the international seabed area, as outlined in items 1–11 of the 1970 Declaration of Principles. The salient provisions are as follows:

1. The international seabed area, and the resources thereof, are the common heritage of mankind.

2. The area shall not be subject to appropriation, and no State shall claim or exercise sovereignty or sovereign rights over any part thereof.

3. All activities regarding the exploration and exploitation of the resources of the area and other related activities shall be governed by the international régime to be established.

4. No State or person shall claim, exercise or acquire rights to the area or its resources incompatible with the international régime and the principles of this Declaration.

5. The area shall be open to use exclusively for peaceful purposes by all States, whether coastal or land-locked, without discrimination.

6. States shall act in the international seabed area in accordance with the applicable principles and rules of international law.

7. The exploration of the area and the exploitation of its resources shall be carried out for the benefit of mankind as a whole. There will be equitable sharing of the benefits taking into particular consideration the interests and needs of the developing countries, whether land-locked or coastal.

8. States shall promote international co-operation in scientific research exclusively for peaceful purposes.

9. States shall take appropriate measures for the adoption and implementation of international rules for the prevention of pollution and contamination, and other hazards of the marine environment, and for protection and conservation of the natural resources of the area.

10. Due regard shall be paid to the rights and legitimate interests of coastal States in the region where seabed activities are taking place.

11. The legal status of the waters superjacent to the international seabed area or of the air space above those waters shall not be affected by the new régime nor the rights of coastal States to protect against danger from pollution or other hazardous occurrences.

The only important variations among the proposals so far as the status of the international seabed area are concerned involve scientific research, and coastal State rights.[31] Both the Soviet Union and the United Kingdom mention freedom of scientific research relating to the seabed as a continuing international right, subject to reasonable constraints, and the United States suggests that the contracting parties should agree to encourage and to obviate interference with such research. Malta, on the other hand, feels that the right to undertake scientific research in ocean space is subject to such regulations as may be prescribed by the international authority. Here then is an issue about which considerable debate may at some future time take place. The 1958 Convention on the High Seas does not specifically mention scientific research as one of the basic freedoms, although some countries have argued that it is subsumed under the provisions for other freedoms "which are recognised by the general principles of international law." When and if a new international seabed régime comes into force, must it cope with an already existing situation in which freedom of scientific research with respect to the seabed is recognised by international law, or can it formulate its own rules relating to freedom of research inasmuch as such freedom does not in fact currently exist?

As regards coastal State rights it has already been noted that the U.S. proposal (which is supported by the U.K.) calls for a Trusteeship Area to be established beyond the limits of national jurisdiction, while the 7-Power proposal recommends a Coastal State Priority Zone seaward of national limits. The only other comment on this topic is by the Canadians who suggest that "there should be some mechanism to allow coastal States a degree of special rights within an adjacent zone beyond the limits of national jurisdiction at least with regard to the prevention of pollution from seabed resource operations." Although the idea of some sort of "intermediate" zone between the area of the seabed subject to national jurisdiction, and that area under an international authority, would seem to make sense from the standpoint of accommodating a broad spectrum of national interests, the concept as yet seems to have found little support among members of the Seabed Committee.

THE NATURE AND FUNCTIONS OF THE INTERNATIONAL SEABED AUTHORITY

1. Organisation

All of the proposals, except that of the 7-Power Working Paper, provide for specific organs for the international Authority. First there is to be an Assembly (France refers to it as a "Conference of Plenipotentiaries") which is open to all member States.[32] Decisions in the Assembly are generally based on a simple majority, although the Soviet Union favours decisions based on a two-thirds majority.

A second body is the Council, or "Executive Board" as the Russians term it. The membership varies from 18 to 35 according to different proposals[33] and decisions may be by simple majority (U.S., U.K., Malta), by a two-thirds majority (Tanzania, 13 Powers, Canada, Japan) or by general consensus (U.S.S.R., Poland). The membership of the Council is a highly important element in the functioning of the Authority, and proposals on its composition will be discussed shortly.

Third is the Secretariat, headed by the Secretary-General. There seems to be little variation in the proposals concerning this organisation. A fourth body called for in some proposals is a Tribunal to which disputes can be referred. The U.S. suggestion for inclusion of such a body is echoed by the Maltese in their recommendation for an International Maritime Court, as well as by Canada. Japan feels that the Tribunal should be established on an *ad hoc* basis, while the U.K. notes "it could also be agreed that the Convention should provide for a Tribunal" which would be an entirely independent agency. The other seven proposals, however, are silent on the Tribunal question.

There are also suggestions for subsidiary organs. The United States feels that there should be a Rules and Recommended Practices Commission, an Operations Commission, and an International Seabed Boundary Review Commission; and Tanzania recommends a Distribution Agency and a Stabilisation Board. Poland is in favour of such subsidiary organs of the Council as a Technical Board, Economic Board, and Registration and Licensing Board, while Malta proposes an Ocean Management and Development Commission, a Scientific and Technical Commission, and a Legal Commission. In time other types of subsidiary bodies will, in all likelihood, be recommended.

The composition of the Council is a topic to which several of the proposals address themselves. The Council is responsible for the functioning of the Authority, including in particular the issuing of licences for seabed exploration and exploitation. The U.S. proposal provides for a Council of 24 States, including the six most industrially advanced countries,[34] plus an additional 18, at least 12 of which are developing States. At least two of the 24 members are to be land-locked or shelf-locked States. Decisions of the Council would require not only a majority of all its members, but also concurrent majorities among the most industrially advanced States, and among the 18 others.

The composition of Council membership is not spelled out in either the British or French proposals, although the British suggest that "membership of the Council should reflect the diverse interests of States parties to the Convention, including those of the developing and land-locked countries." A limited number of industrialised countries which have, or develop, a substantial seabed technology should be designated as Council members.

Tanzania recommends an 18-member Council, elected by the Seabed Assembly "with due regard to geographic distribution" and including not less than three land-locked States. Procedural decisions of the Council would be based on a simple majority vote, but substantive issues would require a two-thirds majority of the members for passage.

The U.S.S.R. feels that the Executive Board of the International Seabed Resources Agency should have 30 members with an allocation of five seats to each of the following: (a) the socialist countries; (b) the countries of Asia; (c) the countries of Africa; (d) the countries of Latin America; and (e) the Western European and other countries not coming within the four previous categories. In addition there would be one land-locked country represented from each of the five groups. Decisions on questions of substance should be made by agreement. Poland's proposal follows along much the same lines, although the Poles would have only a 25-member Council, with five members each from the first five groups listed by the Soviet Union. Within the Council "the principle of consensus should be applied as generally as possible." Regarding the views on voting by the Soviets and the Poles, Sohn writes, "While one can agree with the need for adequate protection of the rights of each important group of States, the system adopted should be sufficiently flexible to permit decision by a preponderant majority, whenever an inaction should threaten world community interests more than an action objected to by a small group of states."[35]

The 13-Power proposal of Latin American States is for a 35-member Council "having due regard to the principle of equitable geographical representation." Substantive decisions would be made by a two-thirds majority of Council members present and voting.

The provisions in the Maltese proposal for representation on the Council by members of the three categories of States have already been noted. According to Malta, States belonging to category A shall be coastal and either (a) have a population exceeding 90 million inhabitants; or (b) possess six of the following qualifications:

1. have a population greater than 45 million; 2. have a length of coastline exceeding 5,000 kilometres; 3. possess more than one million gross tons of merchant shipping; 4. own and operate more than 20 ships and submersibles aggregating no less than 30,000 gross tons for scientific and rescue purposes; 5. have produced more than one million metric tons of fish annually over the previous three years; 6. have produced annually over the previous three years more than one million tons of hydrocarbons or other minerals from the seabed of ocean space; 7. own submarine pipelines or cables in International Ocean Space; 8. have expended more than $20 million annually from State funds over the previous three years for scientific research in ocean space; 9. have contributed annually over the previous three years more than $25 million to the international authority in respect of revenue obtained from the exploitation of natural resources in national ocean space.

Coastal States which do not qualify for Category A shall be in Category B, while non-coastal States are in Category C.

The 7-Power proposal does not mention the number of members of the Council, but suggests that all countries be divided into two categories—one consisting of primarily coastal States, and the other of primarily non-coastal States. At the time of ratification of the Treaty, each State should indicate to which category it belongs. Representation on the Council should be divided equally between the two categories, with the developing countries adequately represented within each category.[36]

The Canadian proposal, like the British, does not include specific recommendations on membership. In achieving the proper balance of national interests Canada feels "the essential criteria could be the level of state expertise in offshore technology and resource management, the length of the coastline, area of continental shelf, land-locked or shelf-locked status, and level of economic development." The Council should probably not exceed a maximum of 30 States, divided into two classes of membership; those designated by the Assembly, and those elected by the Assembly. Decisions should be based on a two-thirds majority vote.

A final proposal, by Japan, is for a 24-member Council, some members of which would be designated and some elected by the Assembly. At least 12 of the Council members would be developing countries and at least three would be land-locked or shelf-locked States. Account should be taken by the Assembly in electing members of equitable geographical distribution. Voting on non-procedural matters would be by a two-thirds majority of those present and voting.

2. Powers of the Authority

A basic dichotomy exists among the proposals between recommendations for an international Authority which is primarily a licensing agency, and for an Authority which has jurisdiction over all activities relating to the seabed within the international area. The U.S., U.K., France and Japan support the concept of the Authority as largely a regulatory body, issuing licences, protecting the marine environment, and collecting and distributing revenues. The U.S.S.R., while noting the licensing issue as one aspect of the Authority's organisation, is of the opinion that specifics on licensing procedures should await settlement of certain other ocean problems (see note 29). Poland feels that during a transitional period the functions of the Authority might be limited to co-ordination of the activities of States and exchange of information, but that later its functions might comprise certain forms of supervision and regulation including licensing. The Canadians note the possibility of conflict of interests between the Authority's role as a regulatory body, and its possible role as an operating unit, and urge that expansion of its functions proceed very slowly.

There are, on the other hand, the much more comprehensive proposals of Malta ("all activities in International Ocean Space shall be governed by the régime"), Tanzania ("All activities regarding exploration and exploitation . . . and other related activities shall be subject to regulation by the Authority") and the 13-Power proposal ("Exclusive jurisdiction over the area and administration of its resources shall be exercised . . . by the Authority"). The 13-Power Draft goes on to suggest that the Authority itself may undertake exploration and exploitation activities in the international area or avail itself of the services of other organisations for this purpose. Tanzania also feels that the Authority should have this option, as does the 7-Power proposal. Here, then, as in the case of the composition of the Council, a wide diversity of positions exists among the proposals.

3. Other provisions

Several proposals are concerned with the possible effects deep sea exploitation may have on prices for land-based minerals. Tanzania suggests a Price Stabilisation Board which, among other duties, can fix prices for raw materials obtained from the seabed, and regulate rates of production. The 13-Power proposal provides for the Authority to regulate production of seabed resources if there is a threat of adverse economic effects in developing countries, and Malta feels that the Council must manage the resources of the international area in a way which is non-prejudicial to the interests of States exporting minerals or raw materials obtained from land sources. The 7-Power Draft mentions the need for avoiding possible adverse effects of exploitation in any part of the international area on the interests of developing countries; and Canada notes that a seabed resource management system must be created, which, among others, regulates production, marketing and distribution of raw materials from the seabed in order to minimise adverse economic effects caused by the fluctuation of prices of raw materials. The Japanese feel that due regard should be paid "to the need for minimising adverse effects of the development of the seabed resources on the prices of land-based minerals."

Another issue concerns settlement of disputes. As noted earlier, a Tribunal is provided for in the proposals of the U.S., Malta and Japan (on an *ad hoc* basis) and is suggested as a possibility by the U.K., Poland and Canada. Tanzania recommends the submission of disputes to the International Court of Justice, and several other proposals mention this as an alternative to a Tribunal. The U.S.S.R., however, feels that disputes should be referred to the Executive Board (Council) which will "Assist in settling disputes . . . by applying the means for peaceful settlement listed in Article 33 of the United Nations Charter, and establish, at the request of parties to a dispute, organs of conciliation, arbitration, etc., for settling the dispute;" (Article 22). The traditional Soviet aversion to compulsory arbitration can be clearly seen here.

Still another issue regards the interim period before an international Authority is established. Few proposals take cognisance of this problem, one of the exceptions being the U.S. which holds that there shall be due protection for the integrity of investments made in the international seabed area prior to the coming into force of the convention. The Maltese and Canadian proposals carry similar provisions. Poland, on the other hand, recognises the need for a transitional period, once the Authority has been established, within which the various organs of the Authority are given time to establish themselves.

The matter of the ultimate distribution of revenues received from seabed activities is alluded to only in general terms. While there is no question of the use of revenues for the benefit primarily of the developing countries, there are also suggestions that a part be utilised to defray administrative costs of the international organisation, and both the U.S. and the U.K. feel that a portion might be devoted to activities relating to the marine environment, such as research or pollution control. Equally important is the issue of where the decisions will be made on allocation of revenues among States. Some proposals suggest the Assembly; others the Council. In still other cases, neither organ is specifically mentioned, although reference is made to the international organisation *per se* as the deciding body. The U.S.S.R. feels that the issue of revenue distribution procedures is premature. But whether decision-making on revenue allocations takes place in the Assembly, the Council, or by some other means, it is clear that the issue itself may be a difficult one to resolve.

THE IMPACT OF ALTERNATIVE RÉGIMES ON NATIONAL INTERESTS

There are various means for assessing what the impact of international seabed régimes might be on the interests of countries or groups of countries. Some of the technologically advanced States, which have the capacity to explore and exploit the resources of the deep seabed, might experience a loss of certain elements of freedom of operations. For some, if not all, of the developing States, the régime could, in time, mean an inflow of much-needed revenue without the expenditure of development effort on their part. The administrative machinery of any proposed régime will mean, for some countries at least, a series of costs over and above those normally associated with the operations of the United Nations. For our purposes here, only three categories of impact will be considered: (1) the geographic limits of the international seabed area; (2) the possible competition of seabed minerals with those produced on land; and (3) the " developed " countries which might gain little from an international seabed régime.

1. The geographic limits of the international seabed area

The 1970 Declaration of Principles speaks of the area " beyond the limits of national jurisdiction " and, as noted above, where these limits are is an issue which most of the proposals do not even attempt to resolve. There are, in fact, four criteria which, alone or in combination with one another, might be used to determine the limits of coastal State jurisdiction over the seabed.

First, there is the criterion of geology. Seaward from the coast are several physical features which might be utilised for marking national limits. One is the outer edge of the continental shelf, a feature which the 200 metre isobath is taken to represent.[37] Beyond the shelf is the continental slope, extending down to the deep ocean floor. The boundary between the slope and the continental rise which abuts on it may vary from 1,000 to 4,000 metres, but in some areas, as along the west coast of South America, the slope may descend to depths of 8,000 metres. Thus it is difficult to equate a fixed depth with the point of contact between slope and rise.[38]

The continental rise descends very gently seaward from the slope to merge with the abyssal plain. Its width may be as great as 500–600 miles although in some regions it is extremely narrow or completely absent, and its outer limit may occur at depths ranging from 1,000 to 5,000 metres. Here again, the outer limit of the continental rise represents a physical feature showing wide variation from place to place both as to depth and to distance from shore.

A basic geomorphic division exists between the continental platform or block and the ocean basins. This division is represented by the differences in rock types. The rocks of the continental block have greater thickness, lesser density, lower seismic velocity, and more acidic composition than do the rocks of the ocean basins. "The change from continental to oceanic crust is the most distinctive, recognizable lateral change in the earth's lithologic character . . . the base of the continental slope, coinciding approximately with the other limits of the continental crust, constitutes . . . the only natural surface feature which can be used as a guideline to the outer limits of the continent." [39]

If any of these geologic criteria beyond the 200 metre isobath are accepted as valid for determining the outer boundary of the national jurisdiction, should the physical differences themselves be used, or should some approximate depth be taken as corresponding to them? If the latter, what depth or depths should be chosen?

The criterion of depth is an alternative to geology, whether or not such depth actually conforms to any geologic feature. One difficulty of this criterion is that, like geology, it may vary considerably in terms of distance from shore. The 200 metre isobath, which represents one of the two cornerstones of the 1958 Geneva Convention provisions, is highly uneven in terms of the distance offshore at which it occurs. Using this criterion a few States gain very large areas of shelf, and many gain very little.[40] The U.S. proposal that this isobath represent the outer limits of national jurisdiction, would result in the closing off of only 7·6 per cent. of the seabed, leaving the remainder (including all of the continental slopes and rises) for the international seabed area. Another depth which is sometimes cited is 3,000 metres, corresponding to some extent with the outer portions of the continental rise. Using the 3,000 metre isobath would result in 22·8 per cent. of the total seabed being within the limits of national jurisdiction. Moving seaward, the outer limits of national jurisdiction from the 200 to the 3,000 metre isobath would benefit much the same States which now control large seabed areas under the 200 metre criterion.[41]

A basic issue here is the question of which States might stand to lose through this movement seaward of national limits to include the continental slope and all or most of the rise. The 30 land-locked States, and the 20 shelf-locked ones would be denied the opportunity for gaining a share of the revenue derived from the future exploitation of resources on other countries' slopes and rises. At least 19 other States, with small areas of outer continental margin, might also feel it to be within their best interests to press for as extensive an international seabed area as possible; the resulting bloc would represent nearly half the States of the world whose interests would be in as narrow a zone of national jurisdiction over the seabed as possible. Opposing them might be some 50 countries whose outer continental margins measure 20,000 square nautical miles or more, and which might be expected to opt for placing the seabed areas at least out to the 3,000 metre isobath, under the jurisdiction of the coastal State.

Since the criterion of depth like that of geology results in a considerable variation because of the distances from shore at which such depths occur, an alternative criterion might be *distance* itself, used either alone, or in combination with depth or geology. The 200 metre isobath averages worldwide some 42 nautical miles from the coast and one suggestion is that a distance of 40 nautical miles be taken to represent this isobath. Used alone, such a distance criterion would close off 11·8 per cent. of the total seabed area within national jurisdiction. More realistically, however, it would have to be used as a distance equivalency, combined with the 200 metre isobath in fixing national limits. Another distance equivalency might be 100 nautical miles from shore, which would close off 21·6 per cent. of the total seabed area within national limits. This distance might be equated with the 3,000 metre isobath.

Still another distance figure, frequently mentioned, is 200 nautical miles. If this were used for defining the limits of national jurisdiction, 35·9 per cent. of the total seabed area of the world would be closed off. The countries gaining the most additional seabed area beyond the 200 metre isobath, through adoption of the 200 mile criterion, would correspond fairly closely with those which gain the most from the 3,000 metre standard.[42]

A final criterion might be exploitability, as provided for in the 1958 Geneva Convention. One difficulty here is that the exploitability criterion benefits primarily the developed countries which can lead the way for the extension seaward of national limits. Another difficulty is the "elastic" nature of this criterion; as long as it continues to be utilised, the geographic limits of the international seabed area will remain in doubt.[43] It would seem improbable that the international community at this time would elect the exploitability test as the final determinant of where the outer limits of national jurisdiction would ultimately be placed.

2. Competition of seabed minerals with those produced on land

One of the difficulties often mentioned in connection with future seabed exploitation is its possible impact on existing commodity production patterns, particularly those involving the minerals anticipated from manganese nodule production—*i.e.*, manganese, cobalt, copper and nickel. It was noted earlier that several of the proposals have referred to the need for machinery to handle this situation. But what, in fact, are the probable dimensions of the issue?

The UN Secretariat in 1971 prepared a report, *Possible Impact of Seabed Mineral Production in the Area Beyond National Jurisdiction on World Markets, with Special Reference to the Problems of Developing Countries: a Preliminary Assessment* (UN Doc.A/AC. 138/36). This was followed in May 1972 by *Additional Notes on the Possible Economic Implication of Mineral Production from the International Seabed Area* (UN Doc.A/AC. 138/73). The latter report hypothesises that annual production from a one million ton/year operation of manganese nodules might be approximately 16,000 tons of nickel, 13,000 tons of copper, 2,800 tons of cobalt, and 270,000 tons of manganese. It was felt that the cobalt market might be the first to be affected by seabed production, since the quantity derived from the one million ton/year operation would constitute about 8 per cent. of total world requirements by 1980. The African State of Zaire normally produces over half the world's cobalt, followed—at much lower percentages—by Morocco, Finland, Canada and Zambia. Demand for cobalt, however, might expand rapidly if prices were lower.

Nickel was seen in the UN reports as the mainstay of the nodule industry, accounting for over half the gross revenues. Demand for nickel is expected to grow rapidly over the coming decades, even at the present high prices. Canada produces over half the world's nickel, followed by the Soviet Union (about 20 per cent. of the total), and New Caledonia.

Manganese may not be recovered, at least in the foreseeable future, because the processes now being considered are not commercially attractive. But when and if commercial production is undertaken, seabed resources could have an impact on prices, since demand for manganese is quite inelastic, and no new uses are foreseen to absorb any increased supplies. The Soviet Union produces about half the world's manganese;

India, South Africa, Brazil and Gabon each account for less than 10 per cent. of the total supply.

Copper production from seabed nodules is expected to have little immediate effect on the world commodity market. The demand for copper is about 10 times that for nickel; if rates of production of nodules are geared to the demand for nickel, the actual percentage of total copper demand which is produced from the seabed would be minimal. The United States produces about a quarter of the world's copper, while the Soviet Union, Zambia and Chile each produce about an eighth.

From the above it would seem that adverse economic impacts on developing countries as a result of commercial mining of seabed nodules would fall most heavily on Zaire (cobalt) and to a much lesser degree on Morocco (cobalt); Zambia (cobalt, copper); India, Brazil and Gabon (manganese); and Chile (copper). If indeed the prospects of adverse impacts from seabed production in the areas of copper and manganese are not serious at least over the next few decades, this leaves only Zaire, Morocco and Zambia among the seriously affected developing countries.[44]

3. The position of developed countries with respect to the proposed régime

The Declaration of Principles, and the proposals themselves, when alluding to the eventual benefits to be derived from the exploitation of seabed resources, refer to the need for special consideration to be given to the interests and needs of developing countries. The implication seems to be that it is the developed countries which primarily will carry out exploitation activities, and the developing countries which will have priority in the distribution of revenues from the international fund.

The United Nations has in the past accepted the dividing line between developed and developing countries at $1,000 per capita gross national product,[45] and while up to date statistics on the gross national product of some countries are frequently difficult to obtain, the $1,000 figure might be taken as a general yardstick for the division. According to the 1971 estimates there are some 33 States of the world with per capita GNP figures above this level. Of these, perhaps eight or ten (*i.e.*, the U.S., U.S.S.R., Japan, U.K., Sweden, France, Federal Republic of Germany, Australia) may be in the vanguard of development of seabed resources within the international seabed area. They will presumably share with the international régime the revenues derived from such exploitation. But what of the 25 or so developed countries, which on the one hand do not now have the capability for such exploitation and on the other would seem to have little chance of sharing in the ultimate benefits from such activities?[46] The Tanzanian proposal even goes so far as to suggest that the sharing of revenues among members should be according to the inverse ratio of their respective contributions to the annual budget of the United Nations.[47]

SUMMARY

It is a formidable, if not impossible, task to accommodate the needs and interests of nearly 150 States within a régime which governs activities throughout 70 per cent. of the earth's surface. Although the 1970 Declaration of Principles lays down certain agreed guidelines for the régime, the interpretation of these guidelines is subject to a wide disparity of views, as evidenced by the diversity of the proposals considered here. Eventually some means must be found for achieving a compromise between suggestions for minimal régimes (as exemplified, perhaps, in the Soviet proposal) and the comprehensive régimes recommended by such countries as Malta and Tanzania. Without such a compromise it is difficult to imagine any one international seabed régime proposal gaining the necessary acceptance to be universally adopted by the world community.

It is unfortunate that many of the law of the sea debates have become politicised and that some delegations appear to perceive the seabed issues in terms of non-marine matters, such as the growing gap between the rich and poor countries, or the creation of regional interest blocs to deal with economic, social or military problems. To the extent that these " exogenous " elements enter into the seabed question, the international régime deliberations would seem to become much more complex and probably much less effective.

REFERENCES

1. The salient aspects of these proposals are summarised in *Comparative Table of Draft Treaties, Working Papers and Draft Articles* (UN Doc. A/AC.138/L.10, Jan. 28, 1972), prepared by the Secretariat for the Committee on the Peaceful Uses of the Seabed and the Ocean Floor Beyond the Limits of National Jurisdiction.

2. For a discussion on the continental margin, see, among others, K. O. Emery, " Geological Aspects of Sea-Floor Sovereignty," in L. M. Alexander (ed.), *The Law of the Sea: Offshore Boundaries and Zones* (Kingston, R.I., University of Rhode Island, 1967), pp. 139–160.

3. For a concise summary of the current status of the bed and subsoil of the deep sea, see E. D. Brown, *The Legal Regime of Hydrospace* (London: Stevens & Sons, 1971), Chap. 3, pp. 81–130.

4. See Art. 1 of the Convention on the Continental Shelf (UN Doc. A/CONF.13/L.55) which states that the term " continental shelf " is used as referring " . . . (a) to the seabed and subsoil of the submarine areas adjacent to the coast but outside the area of the territorial sea, to a depth of 200 metres or, beyond that limit, to where the depth of the superjacent waters admits of the exploitation of the natural resources of the said areas. . . ."

5. UN Doc. A/6695. Actually there had been informal suggestions for some kind of international régime for the deep seabed prior to Dr. Pardo's request. See, for example, Scelle, " Plateau continental et Droit international " (1955) 59 *Revue Générale de Droit International Public* 5; and two publications of the Commission to Study the Organisation of Peace, *Strengthening the United Nations* (1957) and *New Dimensions for the United Nations* (1966).

6. Statement of Nov. 1, 1967. Reproduced in *H.R.999, 90th Congress*, 1st Session (1967), p. 285. Among Dr. Pardo's assumptions was that the continental shelf under national jurisdiction be defined approximately at the 200 metre isobath or at 12 miles from the nearest coast.

7. A/RES/2340 (XXII).

8. The decision to convene a new Conference on the Law of the Sea was included in A/RES/2750 C (XXV) adopted by the UN General Assembly in Dec. 1970 by a vote of 108 to seven with six abstentions. The three U.S.S.R. votes and those of Bulgaria, Czechoslovakia, Hungary and Poland were cast against the Resolution.

9. A/RES/2749 (XXV).

10. A/RES/2574 D (XXIV). The Resolution provides that, pending the establishment of an international régime for the seabed beyond national limits, States and individuals are bound to refrain from all activities of exploitation of the resources of the area; and that no claims to any part of the area or its resources shall be recognised.

11. *Draft United Nations Convention on the International Seabed Area; Working Paper Submitted by the United States of America* (A/AC.138/25).

12. *International Seabed Régime: Proposals of the United Kingdom for Elements of a Convention* (A/AC.138/46). Also included are portions of an earlier proposal—*International Régime: Working Paper Submitted by the United Kingdom* (A/AC.138/26).

13. *Establishment of a Régime for the Exploration and Exploitation of the Seabed: Proposals Submitted by France* (A/AC.138/27).

14. *Draft Statute for an International Seabed Authority, Submitted by the United Republic of Tanzania* (A/AC.138/33).

15. *Provisional Draft Articles of a Treaty on the Use of the Seabed for Peaceful Purposes, Submitted by the Union of Soviet Socialist Republics* (A/AC.138/43).

16. *Working Paper Concerning an International Organisation to be Established to Deal with the Problems of the Exploration and Exploitation of the Mineral Resources of the International Area of the Seabed and the Subsoil Thereof, the Limits of which are to be Determined, Submitted by Poland* (A/AC.138/44).

17. *Working Paper on the Régime for the Seabed and Ocean Floor and the Subsoil Thereof Beyond the Limits of National Jurisdiction, Submitted by Chile, Colombia, Ecuador, El Salvador, Guatemala, Guyana, Jamaica, Mexico, Panama, Peru, Trinidad and Tobago, Uruguay and Venezuela* (A/AC.138/49).

18. *Draft Ocean Space Treaty: Working Paper Submitted by Malta* (A/AC.138/53).

19. *Preliminary Working Paper Submitted by Afghanistan, Austria, Belgium, Hungary, Nepal, Netherlands and Singapore* (A/AC.138/55).

20. *International Seabed Régime and Machinery: Working Paper Submitted by the Delegation of Canada* (A/AC.138/59).

21. *Outline of a Convention on the International Seabed Régime and Machinery, Working Paper Submitted by Japan* (A/AC.138/63).

22. *Official Records of the General Assembly, Twenty-fifth Session, Supplement No. 21.*

23. *Official Reports of the General Assembly, Twenty-sixth Session, Supplement No. 21.*

24. UN Doc. A/AC.138/63 (Nov. 1971).

25. Those of the U.S.A., Tanzania, the U.S.S.R., the 13-Power Working Paper, Malta and Japan.

26. U.K., France, 13 Powers and Canada.

27. Tanzania, Poland, Japan.

28. See Art. 27, the main thrust of which is that only nationals of the coastal State, or its licensees, would be permitted to carry out exploration and exploitation activities in the Trusteeship Area.

29. Art. 3 of the Soviet proposal, dealing with the limits of national jurisdiction, has no specific text, pending solution of such issues as the breadth of the territorial sea, freedom of passage through international straits, and fishing in waters adjacent to the territorial sea. The Sovet Union also omitted specific texts for Art. 9, dealing with licensing procedures, and with Art. 14 on the distribution of benefits from seabed exploitation.

30. Unlike the other proposals, that of the Maltese spells out in considerable detail suggested baseline procedures, modelled rather closely along the lines of the 1958 Geneva Convention on the Territorial Sea and the Contiguous Zone.

31. Differences in the nature and operations of the international authority itself are discussed later in this paper.

32. According to the Maltese the original members of the Authority shall be those States which, having participated at the Third Law of the Sea Conference, sign the convention and ratify it. Thereafter, any State with a population exceeding 75,000, recognised as independent by not less than 30 other States which sign the convention and ratify it, may become a member.

33. Malta suggests that the Council consist of all members belonging to category A, an equal number belonging to category B, and five members belonging to category C. These categories are discussed below. According to the allocation of States in category A, this proposal might mean that well over 35 States are members of the Council.

34. They must be developed countries having the highest gross national product, and would include the U.S., Soviet Union, Japan, Federal Republic of Germany, France and the U.K. For a discussion of alternative proposals for Council membership, see Louis Sohn, " The Council of an International Seabed Authority " (1972) 9 *The San Diego Law Review* 404–432.

35. *Ibid.* p. 410. Sohn also notes that prior to 1971 the Soviet Union had contended that no new machinery for the seabed was needed.

36. Of approximately 148 independent States of the world, only 30 are land-locked (25 of these are in the UN), and another 20 are shelf-locked (of which 16 are in the UN). A few " open-ocean " countries such as Zaire, Gambia and Togo, with very short coastlines, might also feel themselves justified for inclusion in the " primarily non-coastal " category, but certainly two-thirds or more of the world's States are " primarily coastal."

37. The actual depth of the shelf edge throughout the world ranges from 20 to 550 metres, with an average of 133 metres (see Emery, *op. cit.* p. 149). The figure of 200 metres was based on the terminology adopted by the International Committee on the Nomenclature of Ocean Bottom Features at its meeting in Monaco in 1952. There are, of course, cases where a " clean " break of slope at the edge of the shelf does not exist.

38. Dr. Hollis Hedberg has recently suggested that the base of the continental slope is a valid natural guide to the limits of national jurisdiction, the base itself to be determined by the beginning of the most prominent and most persistent flattening in angle of slope beyond the shelf edge. See Hedberg, " National-International Jurisdictional Boundary on the Ocean Floor," *Law of the Sea Institute Occasional Paper* (in press) (Kingston, R.I., University of Rhode Island, 1973).

39. *Petroleum Resources Under the Ocean Floor* (Washington: The National Petroleum Council, 1969), p. 10.

40. The principal beneficiaries in terms of shelf area are, in order of rank: Canada, Indonesia, Australia, U.S., U.S.S.R., Argentina, People's Republic of China, Brazil, U.K. and Japan. Between them, these 10 comprise 51% of the total shelf area of the world ocean included within the 200 metre isobath. (Data on seabed allocation from *International Boundary Study, Series A, Limits in the Seas,* No. 46, " Theoretical Area Allocations of Seabed to Coastal States. . . ." (Aug. 12, 1972), Washington: U.S. Department of State, Office of the Geographer, Aug. 12, 1972.)

41. The 10 States which would benefit the most are, in order of rank: Australia, New Zealand, Norway, Indonesia, Canada, U.S.S.R., U.S., Japan, Argentina, Mexico. Between them, these States comprise 53% of the total seabed area which would be added to national control by the movement seaward of national limits from 200 metres to 3,000 metres. (Data from *International Boundary Study, Series A, Limits in the Seas,* No. 46, " Theoretical Area Allocations of Seabed to Coastal States. . . ." (Aug. 12, 1972), Washington: U.S. Department of State, Office of the Geographer, Aug. 12, 1972.)

42. The 10 leading States, in order of rank, are: the U.S.A., Australia, New Zealand, Japan, U.S.S.R., Indonesia, Mexico, Brazil, Chile, Norway. These 10 States, between them, account for 56% of the additional seabed area acquired by the shift seaward of the limits of national jurisdiction from the 200 metre isobath to 200 miles from shore.

43. On the other hand the International Court of Justice, in the *North Sea Continental Shelf Cases,* ruled that Art. 1 of the 1958 Continental Shelf Convention (which contains the exploitability principle) has the status of customary international law. See *North Sea Continental Shelf, Judgment,* (1969) I.C.J.Rep. 3.

44. As well as the developed States of Canada, U.S.S.R., Finland and France.

45. Sohn, for example, notes that this criterion has been applied by the UN Committee on Contributions since its early years. (See Sohn *op. cit.* p. 419.)

46. Among the countries in this category might be: Argentina, Austria, Belgium, Bulgaria, Canada, Czechoslovakia, Denmark, Finland, German Democratic Republic, Hungary, Iceland, Ireland, Israel, Italy, Kuwait, Libya, Luxembourg, Netherlands, New Zealand, Norway, Poland, Romania, Switzerland, Uruguay, Venezuela.

47. There may also, of course, be one or more countries in the " developing " category—such as the People's Republic of China or the Republic of South Africa—which may, before long, engage in seabed mineral exploitation.

Part V

Navigation

CHAPTER 13

The Regulation of Navigation

By Colin Warbrick*

I. INTRODUCTION

THE purpose of this paper is to consider contemporary problems of the freedom of navigation.[1]† This freedom embraces two notions: one is the right to make progress over the surface of (and in) the sea—the area of the operation of the right; the other is the duty to make progress only in an orderly way, as to speed, steering, lights and so on—the manner of the operation of the right. The first is the freedom to sail the high seas free from the jurisdictional authority of any State other than that of the flag and the more limited right of innocent passage through the territorial waters of coastal States. These rights can be limited by an extension of territorial waters to reduce correspondingly the area of the high seas and by restrictions on the right of passage imposed by the littoral State. For the high seas, the right can also be infringed by the extension of jurisdictional claims, other than to territorial waters, to exclude or regulate non-flag shipping and by the necessary effects of competing uses of the seas which involve the emplacement of obstructions to navigation in the sea, whether or not accompanied simultaneously by extended jurisdictional prerogatives. The second part is the duty which derives from the general maritime law and is at least as old as the international law right of the freedom of navigation. For its implementation, it requires that directions be given to mariners. The imposition of these duties is a function of the flag State. Their formulation has become increasingly the task of international organisations. Frequently, it creates international legal obligations for the States when the standards are contained in international agreements. The trend of international and national activity is to restrict the area of the freedom of navigation and to increase the duties of the control of its exercise.

II. THE CONTROL OF NAVIGATION

The traditional idea of the freedom of the seas comprehended both a public and a private aspect. As a principle of public international law, it meant that vessels on the high seas were subject, save in the most exceptional circumstances, to the authority of the State of the flag and of no other. The private concept entailed that it was the absolute right and total responsibility of the master to choose how that public right be exercised by his ship. This private notion amounted to this: that it was desirable that even the single jurisdiction of the flag State be not exerted to inhibit the navigational autonomy of the master, for it was in the unrestrained practice of good seamanship, which had itself developed the only necessary regulation, that safety at sea was best

* Lecturer in Law, University of Durham.
† For references, see p. 149.

assured.[2] Accordingly, even national regulation of navigation has been slow in developing; but more than that, such legislation, as did come about, has been industry-orientated. It has met, or at the most compromised with, the commercial demands of the shipping industry and it has done so in isolation of the impact these activities have on interests outside the industry. The hankering of the industry after retaining this position remains.[3] However, both the independence of the masters[4] and the self-regulation by the industry are being increasingly broken down by national and international regulation.

It is difficult to say when the risk of collision with another vessel became a more present maritime hazard to a ship than the chance of stranding on some natural impediment to navigation; certainly, that is now the reality. The accuracy and availability of charts, the provision and maintenance of warnings, the assistance to be gained from shipboard equipment have consistently improved and have consistently operated to diminish the dangers from geographical obstacles.[5] On the other hand, the increase in the density of traffic, the speed at which it moves and the restrictions on manoeuvrability have multiplied the collision risk, especially in bad weather, to the extent that one ship in 14 is involved in a collision with another vessel every year. It may, of course, be that the stationary obstacle is beginning to be of increasing significance again to mariners because of the rise in the number of artificial structures being placed in the seas, although this does not diminish the risk of ship-ship collisions. However, and hopefully, this will be at worst a temporary phenomenon because the techniques required to avoid ships running into, say, offshore drilling rigs are much the same as those which now, by and large successfully, keep ships off shoals and rocks.[6]

The elementary collision rules have their origins in the practice of seamen and were accepted as a legal code without any national or international legal authority.[7] The reason is not far to find: there is a natural imperative for consistent rules of steering and so on when ships meet at sea, whatever their flags, a need which arose long in advance of any international legal arrangements which could provide an authoritative pattern. The new parameters of present-day navigation equally demand appropriate rules but the customary processes which produced the general maritime law are not able to supply them (and the intervening expedient of dealing with technical advance, the general acceptance of unilateral national standards, is no longer a political alternative). The present version of the collision rules was annexed to the 1960 SOLAS Convention.[8] The Collision Regulations are an anomalous legal creature. Breach of them, even without damage, is a criminal offence under the law of the flag, but this is a sanction of uncommon application, especially where manoeuvring is concerned, because of the substantial discretions that rest with a master.[9] On the other hand, failure to comply with the Regulations raises no presumption of civil liability; the standard of the maritime law is actual negligence.[10] The Regulations rather savour of an attempt to codify the law of negligence relating to road traffic. Only the most blatantly reckless conduct can be clearly condemned in advance; terms like "moderate speed" have no objective meaning. The importance of the Regulations is as a guide to mariners, to establish common standards as to lights and signals and to achieve some degree of predictability of manoeuvring in collision situations. The rules can be no more than a guide; even the most rigorous policing of the most perfect set of Regulations could not lead to the abolition of collisions (quite apart from "pure" accidents).

The Regulations and actual maritime practice must never be far apart, because there is a real danger that practice will begin to supplant the rules and undermine the uniformity which is their object.[11] The 1960 Conference could not agree to incorporate a complete set of rules on the use of radar and the provisions were reduced to the ambiguous status of an annex. Even with this compromise, the Regulations did not enter into force until 1965, although the United Kingdom Government did try to encourage their earlier acceptance by instructing its mariners to apply the new Regulations at once. Partly, but not wholly, because of the failure to deal adequately with the radar question, the 1960 Regulations have been assailed from one quarter to another almost from the time that they came into force. Technical developments have revealed further deficiencies in the Regulations as they now stand.[12] In response to the criticism, revision of the rules has been undertaken at an IMCO-convened Conference in October, 1972.[13]

The critics of the rules appear to divide into three camps: those who think that only minor tinkering is required and that perhaps some account need be taken of recent advances[14]; those who would have the rules rewritten and reordered in the interests of logic and clarity, but who adhere to the basic principles[15]; and those who require a thoroughgoing reconsideration of the fundamental basis for the rules and whose views are usually founded on mathematical studies of the theories of collision avoidance.[16] The fundamental attack on the Regulations is that they are based on collision avoidance *responsibility* rather than on collision avoidance *action*; and that they put responsibility on a *single* ship rather than on both or all the vessels engaged in a potential collision situation. Put another way, the complaint is that the Regulations tell *which* vessel should take action but they do not tell it *what* action that it should take; and that because they are restricted to single vessel responsibility, they do not utilise all the resources for avoiding a collision and are vastly deficient in bad weather, when mutual awareness cannot be assumed.[17] Less iconoclastic but still highly critical, others would take the view that there are no errors of principle in the Regulations but that there are deficiencies of organisation—not enough priority to the good seamanship principle, for example, and in accommodating technical advance.[18]

In the light of these divisions among expert opinion, it was hardly to be anticipated that the Revision Conference would come up with root and branch solutions. The Conference had before it IMCO's own proposals for a new set of Regulations and, although these had been subject to extensive governmental comment, no State had called for a more radical general approach.[19] In the event, the new Regulations follow the general form that the Organisation had suggested. They are appended to a new and separate convention, which sets the earliest coming-into-force date as January 1, 1976, and which has interesting provision for future revision and amendments.[20] The most common complaint against the old Regulations has been met and the new version reordered to give proper priority to the Steering and Sailing Rules. Next, technical developments have been accommodated. New Rules are included on radar and traffic separation schemes, provision is made for deep-draught vessels and those of limited manoeuvrability, technical annexes establish higher standards for light and sound signals; and the Regulations as a whole apply to "non-displacement craft," which will include hovercraft and hydrofoils.[21]

However, on matters of substance, the Rules remain much the same. The "stand-on" principle is preserved and although the action to avoid collision is spelled out in more detail, it is still in quite general terms and, in the context of the old directions, almost unamended.[22] However, priorities between different kinds of vessels are usefully detailed.[23] Deep-draught vessels and ships of limited manoeuvrability are given special consideration, but while other ships must "keep out of the way" of the latter, they are constrained only "not to impede the safe passage" of the former: a curious compromise which may cause some difficulties in practice.[24] And this is typical of the dilemma in revising the Regulations. The lawyer may be happier with the increased detail of definition and responsibility, whereas the mariner may find his instructions increasingly impracticable. Whatever the utility of the stand-on principle in ample sea-room, one must doubt whether it remains adequate in congested shipping areas, particularly in bad weather. It may be that the answer in these congested areas is much closer short-based control under a legal régime separate from the Collision Regulations. The drafting of adequate controls within the Regulations may well not be commensurate with the mariners' demand for easily applicable instructions. Thus while technical deficiencies have been largely met by the Revision Conference, the new Regulations do not go to meeting the furthest criticisms levelled against the old version.

And this is perhaps no bad thing: the revision of the Regulations ought to proceed cautiously for there is a quite amazing dearth of information on what causes collisions and, in particular, to what extent the Regulations themselves contribute to accidents. Governmental inquiries are held only infrequently; many disputes are settled before arbitrators whose detailed findings are not published; and those cases which reach the courts are both far too few and too specialised to provide any useful evidence.[25] Even if we were able to get more complete data on the causes of collisions, there is a crucial question which remains to be asked: that is, what is the function of the collision rules?[26] Is it, can it be, the absolute avoidance of collisions? Or is it less ambitious —merely the reduction of accidents? If it is the latter, then there are two further questions: how many collisions do we want to prevent, and do we want to prevent all kinds of collisions equally or are some especially to be avoided? The first is a question of cost, like the so-called "5 m.p.h." principle in municipal road traffic law. Given that an increase in speed (and/or a decrease in other precautions) means an increase in economic return, is it possible to discover the economic maximisation point, where delays caused by accidents, increases in insurance premiums, etc., begin to outweigh the cost advantages of higher speeds and lower running costs? While the determination of such a point might satisfy the industry, it cannot possibly take into account other interests. It may be necessary to sort out priorities, for example, of passenger ships over cargo ships[27] or to decide that ships with high damage-doing capacity by reason of size and nature of cargo ought to be privileged over those which will sink with a minimum of deleterious effects upon third parties. There may be some areas where collisions must be reduced as far as possible, such as in narrow shipping lanes or where collisions between particular kinds of ships ought not to occur at all, for example involving oil-carrying vessels off areas of important wild-life resources.[28]

Once any of these questions gets a positive answer, a new consideration has entered into the control of navigation; the prospect is raised of the regulation of shipping on grounds other than the safety of the ships themselves, and of the introduction of varying controls, depending on the nature of the ship, or its cargo, or its geographical location. At this point, we have reached the stage where regulation can no longer be left to the industry, for the policy decisions that have to be taken are not ones in which the industry has special competence, or indeed would even recognise as valid at all.

Traffic routeing schemes are the most important present example of this kind of control.[29] They illustrate the furthest departure from the "independent-master-industry-orientated" approach of the traditional law, for the discretion of the master and the ship-owner becomes limited as to the area and the direction in which ships are to be navigated. Not that traffic schemes are at all new[30]; it is the making compulsory of the routeing schemes that is the important recent development. IMCO took the initiative with respect to these schemes when the demand was heard for their widespread introduction shortly after the stranding of the *Torrey Canyon*.[31] The Organisation maintains that its competence over high seas routeing schemes is exclusive[32] to the extent that it will not recommend any arrangement operated by national authorities until it has been looked at by the Navigation Sub-Committee. Up to the present, IMCO has recommended 50 schemes of one kind or another.[33] The 1971 session of the Assembly adopted a revised Regulation to the SOLAS Convention recommending the routeing schemes and urging States to " use their influence " to have their ships follow the established routes.[34] Given IMCO's limited competence, this is all that it could do, but the matter has now been brought within the revised Collision Regulations.[35] It is important to understand the ambit of " compulsory " traffic systems. Under the present IMCO Assembly recommendation, States have the power to make it a criminal offence to fail to obey an IMCO approved routeing scheme, wherever that scheme may be.[36] Once the revised Collision Regulations enter into force, States parties to them will be under an international obligation to make deviation from the traffic schemes by their own flagships a criminal offence under their respective national laws. There will, however, be no power to proceed against delinquent ships of another flag, nor for any State to perform police functions on the high seas. The most a State can do towards enforcement will be to report the miscreant master to the State of the flag.[37] Nor does any of this activity have much impact on civil liability. When routes were first introduced in the Dover Straits, it was suggested that deviation from these wholly recommendatory lanes would be of significance in inquiries and civil proceedings.[38] It is difficult to see how this could be so. Even when the routes are incorporated in the revised Regulations, failure to obey them will no more raise presumptions of civil responsibility than would any other breach of the rules.[39]

Although they have been operating only for a few years, the working of the traffic schemes has not been free from disputes. In particular, this is true of the Dover Straits scheme and its associated systems.[40] The differences have been about the measure of success the scheme has achieved and whether alternatives would be more likely of success.[41] However, even if traffic routeing and separation are much extended, even if they improve hugely with experience, the need for collision avoidance rules will remain. It would be most regrettable of all if traffic schemes had the effect of reducing the precautions taken by ships sailing in accordance with them.[42] These routes will be safer, if at all, only if ships proceed with at least as much care as they do at present. On the most favourable estimates, at least half the collisions in the Dover Straits must occur between ships that are observing the routeing arrangements. On the other hand, not even radical improvements in the collision rules will totally abolish accidents. Nor will this be achieved by advances in equipment. As navigational aids become more sophisticated and helpful, they also become more difficult to understand and operate. In both the application of the collision rules and the working of equipment, the most significant advances might come in lifting the standards of training of officers and seamen. Although the number of cases in the reports are small and they are doubtless not a typical sample, one cannot help being impressed by the number of occasions on which errors of seamanship have contributed to maritime accidents. International progress in this field has been far from extensive[43] and it is currently bedevilled by being one of the focus points of the on-going flags of convenience dispute. Two kinds of activity are required: one, the elaboration of adequate standards of training, the other, the provision of assistance to ensure that seamen under all flags can receive those levels of instruction. There is a quite impressive unanimity of opinion of the inadequacies of training, particularly in the use of modern apparatus.[44] What is needed is international agreement and international co-operation to fill out, in a way that means something, the obligation in the High Seas Convention.[45] After a hesitant start, IMCO and the ILO are taking steps jointly and severally to repair long-standing deficiencies in this area of international activity.[46] It is an area where international co-operation is required not so much to obtain uniformity as to set minimum standards.

III. PROVISION OF NAVIGATIONAL SERVICES

Once agreement has been reached on the desirability of traffic control, the implementation of any scheme requires the provision of extensive services by the coastal States. These include shore-based radar facilities, the removal and marking of wrecks, the buoying of channels, the supplying or resiting of lights and lightships and, if progress is to be made in identifying and convicting masters who ignore the routeing arrangements, the means of monitoring the systems once they are operational. The duty of a coastal State to lay on any services at all is very limited in the absence of an international agreement. Under the Territorial Waters Convention, the most that is required is that the State should " give appropriate publicity to any dangers to navigation, of which it has knowledge. . . ." [47] This duty is limited to the territorial sea. Of course, States do have the right to set up navigational aids or remove wrecks in their territorial waters or in the high seas, but there is no duty upon them to do so. Whether a coastal State will take on the onerous task of supplying sophisticated aids and services depends upon its interest in ship safety. Since most accidents occur around the entrances to ports[48] and come within the jurisdiction of the coastal State, the need to safeguard its own shipping and the trade of its own ports will likely combine sufficient legal authority with an adequate practical incentive to provide protective measures. Thus the coastal State may be expected to clear wrecks and will have the power to insist upon compulsory pilotage.[49] Beyond territorial waters, the coastal State may have an interest in providing services, either because a substantial part of the trade is carried in its own bottoms or is destined for its own ports,[50] or because the risk of an accident which may pollute its shores is sufficiently pressing. Also, lights which serve intra-territorial waters traffic may be of utility to ships on the high seas. On the other hand, the coastal State will not be able to demand that any traffic take a pilot[51] or follow a specific course or travel at a regulated speed. The interests of the coastal State may be substantial enough for it to undertake large-scale activities beyond its territorial waters. The most spectacular example of this is the dredging of a deep sea canal, the Euroguel, by the Netherlands some 20 miles out into the North Sea in order that deep-draught vessels may enter Rotterdam and the Europoort.[52] Where the coastal State has no interest in the destination of passing traffic, not only may it be without inclination to supply navigational services, but it may feel justified in demanding that that traffic bear the cost of such services as are required to prevent damage to its coasts as a result of accidents of navigation.[53]

From time to time, various *ad hoc* international arrangements have been devised to supply services of particular utility to shipping. The North Atlantic Ice Patrol, administered by the United States Coastguard and paid for by contributions from the governments of the shipping nations in proportion to their flag tonnages using the North Atlantic, has been most successful.[54] The United Kingdom has administered the lighthouses at the southern entrance to the Red Sea,[55] although with less success in collecting contributions. It may be that similar activity is necessary to make the fullest use of traffic schemes. It is desirable that there be a uniformity of standards or equipment on shore and in marking at sea, as well as in the surveillance of the routes. The standards might be established by IMCO, the administration undertaken by the coastal States and the costs borne by the flag States, either on a global basis or system by system. This would leave it to the flag States to decide how much of the cost ought to be passed on to the shipping industry [56] and how much would be absorbed by the national exchequer as a " social " charge. Arrangements of the above type would head off attempts by the coastal States to levy charges themselves, which could mean unnecessary interference with passing traffic, and it would allow some degree of international supervision by IMCO, albeit of an advisory kind, of the adequacy of the national services. They would not, however, satisfy those coastal States which would regard the raising of contributions from passing ships as a device for producing funds beyond those needed specifically for the navigation services.

IV. COMPETING USES

It is not possible within the short scope of this paper to give more than the most cursory consideration to this substantial topic.[57] What follows will be some general principles baldly stated, and their application to the most pertinent present example of a competing use from the point of view of the freedom of navigation. First, each competing claim to a use must be established in the law of the sea before there can be any question of a legal conflict between them.[58] On the other hand, even legally recognised uses of the seas are not absolute but must be exercised " with reasonable regard to the interests of other States." [59] Whether the exercise of such a use is reasonable cannot be decided *a priori* but will depend on an examination of all the circumstances of the conflict. In some cases, the standard of what is reasonable may be laid down in an international agreement.[60] To look at this problem in terms of the derogation from, or interference with, the right of navigation is not to postulate the juristic superiority of that use over any other.[61] It is a recognition that, in the absence of legally accepted competing uses, the right of sailing over the seas was once an almost plenary right—almost, but not absolutely so. Conflicts were not unknown, for instance, between fishing and navigation, and priority for ships engaged in fishing over those merely navigating has been legally recognised in the Collision Regulations.[62]

For shipping, there are two kinds of claim to competing use which derogate from the right of sailing. The first are those that pose a collision risk to navigation, that involve the erection of structures in the sea.[63] Once the right to place the installations in the seas is admitted, then it follows that the freedom to sail over the surface is curtailed; ships cannot, and knowingly will not, sail over an occupied part of the sea. The right to explore and exploit the continental shelf is clearly the most important existing competing use. The right to erect rigs, inevitable in the present state of the exploitation art, must affect ships. However, the right is limited: exploitation " must not result in any unjustifiable interference with navigation . . ." [64] The restriction is intensified by Article 5 (6) which provides that: " Neither the installations or devices, nor the safety zones around them, may be established where interference may be caused to the use of recognised sea lanes essential to international navigation." Perhaps it may be put this way: the rigs must be established in such a way that the right of sailing between points A and B remains possible, but the right to sail over point X is not guaranteed unless traversing point X is essential for navigation between A and B.

National legislation on the régime of the continental shelf is not always solicitous of the right of navigation.[65] The older laws make almost no provision whatever.[66]

Legislation that has provision for safety zones is frequently prompted more by considerations of the protection of the installations than for the safety of shipping.[67] Even where the protection of shipping is well provided for,[68] it is not always obvious that shipping interests would have the standing to challenge what is invariably an administrative decision to issue a licence for a rig to operate in a particular location. The IMCO recommendation on the establishment of fairways through exploitation fields, rather surprisingly, seems to water down the Article 5 (6) obligation, suggesting as it does only that operations ought not "seriously to obstruct" sea approaches and shipping routes.[69] Equally, surprisingly, the hazards of negotiating offshore fields do not seem to have been of much concern to the professional bodies.

While the *de facto* collision sanction may stop ships damaging the rigs, the convention provides a wider area of protection than mere minimal avoidance by allowing the drawing of 500 metre safety zones round the rigs which must be respected by "ships of all nationalities."[70] It has been suggested that safety zones are irrelevant,[71] but this is based on the premise that collision is the only danger. There may be others, such as the risk of sparks from ships in the oily atmosphere, which require that ships keep further away than the minimum distance necessary to avoid collision. Even in a collision, structural damage to the ship and installation is not the only kind of harm that might result. The possibility that substantial oil leakages would occur could justify the coastal State in laying down a protective régime based on rather different considerations than the safety zones, with the design of limiting the risk of collisions below the mere collision avoidance discretion of mariners.

In the Gulf of Mexico, the United States has established fairways through the intensive oil-rig sites far out into the Gulf over the American continental shelf, presently the most decisive example of shelf exploitation interfering with navigation. Ships are required to keep to the designated routes, marked in the sea and on charts, except in emergencies; drilling operations will not take place in the fairways.[72] It is by no means clear, however, that, if it became desirable to drill in these areas, new fairways would not be established and drilling permitted in the once prohibited areas. The fairways are established through the drilling operations, rather than the exploitation conducted out of the way of shipping routes. The situation on the Dutch continental shelf appears somewhat different. Regulations issued there have created "restricted" areas where drilling is subject to conditions which take account of existing shipping patterns.[73] These include not only the major routes into Rotterdam but also those across the Dutch offshore areas from the southern North Sea to the Elbe and the Skagerrak. Also, the restricted areas cover deep sea anchorages and the traffic scheme north of the Maas.[74] The conditions of traffic in the Gulf of Mexico and the North Sea differ sufficiently to legitimise these differences in approach. The intensity of traffic in the North Sea is very much greater than off the southern United States and, in particular, is still circumscribed as to routes by the presence of mines. In terms of the convention, the Gulf of Mexico may be described as coming within Article 5 (1), the North Sea within Article 5 (6).

Not only are there powers of establishing installations on the shelf and proclaiming safety zones around them, but States are under a duty to make sure that the rigs are adequately lighted and marked on charts and removed when finally out of use.[75]

The erection of artificial structures in the sea creates one kind of interference with navigation, that of collision hazard. The extent to which it is necessary to protect the installations from risks other than collision is an indication of the second kind of interference by competing use. These are claims to regulate or to exclude shipping.

They are based on jurisdictional claims and they lack the *de facto* sanction of threatening damage to the ship as well as to the devices of the competing use. Of this kind is Canada's claim to exclude from or regulate entry into the Arctic waters, not that this is so much a competing use as a non-use. The creation of fish farms under the high seas with the need to exclude polluting surface navigation would be a more obvious competing use.[76]

V. INNOCENT PASSAGE

So far, we have been dealing mainly with the right of navigation over the high seas and broadly assuming that the high seas start at the seaward limit of the territorial sea. That is to say, that any extension of the territorial waters is *ipso facto* an infringement of the freedom of the high seas because the area of the latter is diminished as that of the former is increased.[77] The further from the baselines the limits of territorial waters spread, the more important becomes the content of the right to sail within them—the right of innocent passage. This right has long been recognised as subject to some limitations beyond the " reasonable use " criterion of the high seas.[78] Even the restrictions laid down in the Geneva Convention have not satisfied all coastal States, most especially because of the identity of the rights of merchant vessels and warships.[79] The Soviet Union and several other States, not all of them coastal, have entered reservations requiring coastal State permissions for the passage of warships; other States have similar limitations in their national legislation.[80] And, since the régime of territorial waters is sovereignty-based, it is not inconceivable that a coastal State would use this to formulate an extensive claim to regulate passage or to exclude ships altogether.[81]

An exact definition of the powers of the coastal State becomes of yet more importance as the extension of territorial waters has the effect of bringing within such a régime, of one or of opposite States, straits used for the passage of ships. The right of passage through such straits, it is maintained, is essential if the freedom of navigation over what remain high seas is to survive as a useful right. Because the convention definition of innocent passage has been contested for territorial waters, maritime States fear that this is even more likely for the wide guarantees of passage through straits laid down in the convention.[82] Within the terms of the Geneva Convention, the issue ought to be clear. Article 16 (4) lays down that the right of passage through straits used in international navigation is not to be suspended and the location of this Article makes it quite clear that it applies to straits that are wholly or partly within the territorial waters of one of more States. The mere extension of territorial waters cannot change the status of international straits, although additional rights of regulation (and duties for the provision of services, small as they are) will accrue to the coastal State.

However, the United States, in particular among maritime States, was not content with the régime provided for by the convention. At one time, it seemed as though the *quid pro quo* which the United States would demand for an agreement recognising the width of the territorial sea as 12 miles was a more certain guarantee of the right of innocent passage, especially for its warships, through straits that came within national jurisdiction as a result of that extension.[83] That would appear to be no longer enough. What the United States has now proposed is an entirely new concept, that of a right of transit, which, in the American view, would avoid the limitations of the present right of innocent passage.[84] The right of transit implies that ships passing through straits would have the same rights of navigating as they do over the high seas and under them.[85] This latter is of special importance. Under the Geneva Convention, submarines must navigate on the surface,[86] a somewhat disadvantageous method of proceeding for nuclear submarines. The importance of the secrecy of the location of missile-carrying submarines has increased since the arms limitation agreements between the United States and the Soviet Union.[87] Although the right would serve the American military purpose well enough, the obligation on coastal States to accept the unimpeded passage of foreign warships would not be the only disadvantage for these States. Attempts to control shipping by coastal States have not been founded solely or even primarily on considerations of military security. The Canadian claims to exercise control over areas of the Arctic seas, including the North-West Passage, are based on a desire to prevent absolutely the pollution by oil of those waters.[87a] It is a claim that does not admit of the right of transit of unregulated ships. The United States' proposal does acknowledge these additional consequences, but only to a limited extent. Ships in transit must, for example, comply with navigation rules of the coastal State. This would reduce the risk of collision and hence of pollution, but hardly to the level that Canadian policy demands. Again, the right of transit is not compatible with the kind of claims being made by Indonesia and Malaysia for the Straits of Malacca. In view of the secrecy of their deliberations, it is somewhat difficult to disentangle all their claims, but the coastal States require the total exclusion of very large ships (those over 200,000 tons) because of the risks of pollution from a grounded vessel. Those ships that it is considered can safely make the passage will have to pay a levy to the coastal States (which tribute would be increased if the ship did not call at a port of either of the coastal States). Warships, at least of the super-Powers, would be excluded.[88] An alternative passage for very deep-draught vessels would be allowed through the Straits of Maccassar but there would be no right of passage here either, because this involves crossing the waters of the Indonesian archipelago, which Indonesia regards as internal waters.

It is interesting that one passage that would come within territorial waters if there was a mutual extension to 12 miles is the English Channel. In making a unilateral extension to that distance, France has provided that the rights of free maritime and aerial passage will be ensured, subject to international conventions and any necessary agreements with States opposite.[89] This, of course, would be an undertaking in municipal law, and apart from an agreement of the latter kind or possible considerations of estoppel, would not impose any international legal duties on France which could be enforced, say, by the United States. The right of transit would secure the United States' position and it is notable for being the first attempt *to extend* rather than merely resist encroachment upon, the right of navigation, that has been made in the law of the sea for a very long time.

Claims of the kind posited by Canada and Indonesia-Malaysia are aimed directly against shipping; they involve prohibited areas and the close regulation of maritime traffic. Many other of the proliferation of claims to extended maritime jurisdiction do not of themselves involve any necessary interference with shipping but the natural development of those claims can easily lead to this. Almost all the claims are to protect natural resources. Where those resources are living ones, the presence of shipping is a potential polluting threat. It is a short step from excluding fishing vessels to excluding all ships, even without any reformulation of the nature of the exclusive claim. The earliest and most famous incident in the Peruvian 200 mile zone was the arrest and detention of the Onassis whaling fleet at a time when the Peruvian claim was certainly only to do with fishing. The whaling fleet was engaged in sailing to the whaling grounds: no fishing right was in issue. The consequences of recent collective declarations by certain Latin American States, confirmed by contemporaneous national legislation, are that the coastal States are not seeking claims over a wider area of the seas but that, within the areas that they have already claimed, they are seeking more extensive rights of control, up to and including claims to a very wide territorial sea.[90] Although the Declarations of Montevideo [91] and Lima [92] affirm that the claims made are without prejudice to the freedom of navigation, in the second of these, the States mention the "grave dangers of contamination of the waters and disturbance of the ecological balance" and assert the right to prevent these harmful results arising out of the "use" of "areas adjacent" to the coast—more or less the rationale of the Canadian claim over the Arctic seas with the very considerable degree of interference that that assertion involves.

All these kinds of claims imply wide extra-territorial jurisdiction both of the application and the enforcement of the law of the coastal State. In the present state of the law, justification for the one is hard to find [93]; the consequences of the other may create dangers to shipping of a different kind to the legislative ones.[94]

VI. METHODS OF CONTROL

Where the claim of the State is to regulate the entry into or exclude from areas of the high seas the ships of other flags, the issue presents itself squarely as one of public international law. The conduct that is sought to be influenced is that of States and the remedies that are available are the traditional ones of international law. On the other hand, where the matter is one of the control of the navigation of ships, the conduct sought to be influenced is that of the officers and crews of ships. Directions are issued to them through the flag States. Breach of the individual's duty under the law of the flag will not necessarily mean that the flag State is in breach of its international duty. The matter could hardly be otherwise. International law is not possessed of the institutions or the rules to deal with individual conduct. Proposals for the internationalisation of this area of the law, with the panoply of an International Mariners' Court are too ambitious in the short run.[95] What ought to be more immediately possible is a raising of standards and a better means of supervision of the discharge by States of their obligations to safeguard these standards.[96]

We are faced in each case with two questions: what is the jurisdictional reach of the law-making authority to legislate, and what methods may be used to enforce its legislative competence? In the present state of the law, the following conclusions may be hazarded. On the high seas, no State other than the flag has legislative jurisdiction over a ship that is navigating normally. Jurisdiction may arise if, after an incident of navigation, a ship poses an "imminent" threat to the coastal State by reason of the actual or anticipated release with polluting effects of its cargo.[97] Such jurisdiction is restricted to taking action against the ship; it does not allow the bringing of disciplinary or criminal charges against the master arising out of the cause of the threat, although it could conceivably do so if the master infringes orders from the coastal State after the threat has materialised.[98] There can, however, be no threat earlier than an "imminent" one sufficient to found this special jurisdiction. Mere potential possibility of doing damage as a result of some yet unfulfilled disaster is not enough. If this latter kind of jurisdiction can be justified, then it ought to be acknowledged that the status of the waters within which it may operate is something other than high seas. It avails nothing to go on describing such areas as high seas when one of their essential juridical characteristics has been withdrawn.

International agreement could extend the legislative jurisdiction of States to include criminal liability for actions on the high seas, but this hardly seems a present political possibility.[99] Instead, international agreements have been used to establish uniform or minimum standards and to rely on the flag State to enforce these standards where they relate to conduct on the high seas. The flag State has certain general obligations under the High Seas Convention.[100] This and other international conventions place varying obligations on it to enforce its law when it is breached on the high seas, but the obligations will usually be restricted to punishing infractions rather than to interfering with shipping on the high seas; it is an obligation to control rather than to police.[101] Since the infractions may take place many miles from its own territory, other parties may report breaches to the flag State. There are real difficulties of policing high seas conduct, even if it were obligatory. The surveillance of traffic routes quite close to coasts may be inadequate to identify offenders spotted on radar in bad weather or at night. More than that could be counter-productive. There is little to be gained in directing a ship proceeding against a traffic scheme out of that lane unless it can get into the right one, something that may be rendered impossible by geographical obstacles, as in the Dover Straits.[102]

What all States may do is to use the sanction of exclusion from or detention in their ports of ships with those standards of safety or with whose masters' certificates of competence the coastal State is not satisfied.[103] It has been maintained that this is available for ships passing through territorial waters[104] but this is a controverted position.[105] The weakness of these sanctions is that they can apply only to an offence committed within territorial waters in order to found a legitimate exercise of legislative authority of the coastal State and not merely to conduct on the high seas by a ship which subsequently enters territorial waters. The sanction of detention means that the ship may be kept in port until the defects have been repaired. It is useful when combined with a right of inspection of foreign flag vessels while they are in port. Exclusion is more difficult to apply. The requirements of allowing innocent passage and the right of entry in distress must be taken into account. It probably operates best against all ships under a particular flag, perhaps if that State is not a party to an international agreement, because verification of the flag at sea is a simpler task than checking on complex technical details. Operated on a regional basis, say by the States surrounding the North Sea, it could have a potent effect on regulating the standards of vessels sailing into the area.

While this discretion does remain with a coastal State, its unco-ordinated exercise would strangle the maritime industry as ships tried to satisfy incompatible standards. The need for common standards has long been recognised and there has been a continuous improvement in the institutional arrangements for achieving them. Another reason for international action is to avoid retaliatory action by flag States against ships of the detaining or excluding State. This is a consideration of the greatest importance for States like the United Kingdom with high interests in merchant marine and in protecting long and busy offshore areas.[106] International activity can be prompted by unilateral action but only in the exceptional case when a State is peculiarly dominant[107] or influential.[108] International regulation is of two kinds: by full international treaty or recommendatory action under the auspices of an international organisation, almost invariably IMCO. In IMCO's case, this regulatory action can have no quasi-legislative effect.[109] Treaties have the advantage of creating international obligations but the disadvantages that they invariably take a long time to prepare and even longer to come into force and that their amendment is an equally cumbersome process. Although the revision of the Collision Regulations will make routeing schemes as fully "compulsory" as is conceivable when the subsequent treaty enters into force, the need for a more expeditious amending procedure has been pressed.[110] The flexibility of organisational control is its most attractive feature, both as to speed and ease of amendment.

The Rochdale Report warned that there was a danger that international minimum standards might become the maxima in practice but that the danger might be mitigated because the requirements of marine insurers would limit the degree of evasion.[111] It is not clear that States ought to rely on private commercial organisations to supplement the deficiencies of their own supervisory systems but it is certainly the case that the "insurance sanction" is peculiarly potent in the control of international shipping. Insurance premiums are the highest operating costs in running a super-tanker and increasingly the insurance industry is assessing the risk, not as traditionally in terms of the past safety record of the client but in the light of compliance with safety standards and making distinctions between different types of ships.[112] The insurance industry has been brought increasingly into the formulation of international standards.[113] It is a co-operation that could be as helpful in the enforcement of safety standards as it could be profitable to the companies.[114]

REFERENCES

1. It will be obvious that I have tried to raise problems and to indicate choices that must be made rather than to provide answers, an approach dictated by the orders of the Editors and considerations of space. The following abbreviations are used:
SOLAS—International Convention for the Safety of Life at Sea, 1960; J.I.N.—*Journal of the Institute of Navigation*, London; S.S.R.—*Shipbuilding and Shipping Record.*

2. It is a view that persists. See, *e.g.*, in the U.K., the *Report from the Select Committee of the House of Commons on Science and Technology on Coastal Pollution, 1967–68*, para. 18. Like so many other fundamentals of maritime law and practice, this principle came under critical scrutiny after the stranding of the *Torrey Canyon.* Perhaps the most significant aspect of the whole calamity was that the ship was such a good ship and the Seven Stones were such a notorious hazard. The disaster was laid plainly at the feet of a certified and experienced mariner. But see Oudet, "The *Torrey Canyon* Commission of Inquiry" (1970) J.I.N. 238.

3. "... the shipping industry (in the broadest sense of the word) must make a concerted effort if it is to convince governments and through them IMCO that it is capable of operating shipping in an orderly and responsible manner." Maybourn, "What Constitutes an Acceptable Risk at Sea (Summary)" (1971) J.I.N. 415, 418. The major oil companies in particular have made important contributions, notably the development of load-on-top by Shell, Gulf's skim-clean system for the prevention of explosions in empty tanks and Esso's work on the berthing of very large ships.

4. Anthony Grant, Minister of State at the U.K. Department of Trade and Industry at the opening of the IMCO Assembly, 1971: "It may be that we are entering into a new phase in the history of navigation; a phase in which the masters of ships will expect to receive and will receive precise guidance as they traverse the waters of international straits of a kind which has not in the past been thought necessary."

5. Beattie, "Marketing a New Radar" (1970) J.I.N. 212.

6. *Infra*, s. IV.

7. Marsden, *The Law of Collisions at Sea* (ed. McGuffie), Chap. 23; Colombos, *Law of the Sea* (6th ed.), Chap. IX.

8. International Convention for the Safety of Life at Sea, 1960, Cmnd. 2812.

9. Rules 21, 27 and 29.

10. The presumption of liability in the Merchant Shipping Act 1894 was abolished by the Maritime Conventions Act 1911, which gave effect to the Brussels Convention of the previous year. Until that treaty, there had been no international uniformity in standards and limitations of liability as had existed for the collision rules.

11. For an example of a *de facto* rule that has developed in current practice, see Garcia-Frias; "The Revision of the Rules" (1970) J.I.N. 71.

12. ". . . there now seems to be general dissatisfaction amongst seafarers with the lack of guidance provided in the Rules." Garcia-Frias, *ibid.* States have found it necessary to supplement the rules, *e.g.*, Provisional Rules for Navigation and Fisheries Safety in the North-East Pacific Ocean off the coast of Canada; Agreement between Canada and the Soviet Union, 1971.

13. Final Act of the International Conference on Revision of the International Regulations for Preventing Collisions at Sea, 1972.

14. Thompson, "Revised Rules for Preventing Collisions at Sea" (1970) J.I.N. 188.

15. Oudet, "How to Prevent Collisions at Sea" (1971) J.I.N. 60.

16. Revision of the Collision Regulations (An Interim Report), Institute of Navigation's Expert Working Group (1970) J.I.N. 448; Jones, "Manoeuvres to Avoid Collisions at Sea" (1971) J.I.N. 60.

17. Garcia-Frias, *op. cit*.

18. The divisions are, to some extent, reflected in the Institute of Navigation's Working Group.

19. IMCO/CR/CONF. 3.

20. Final Act, *op. cit.* n. 13, Arts. IV (1) (a), V, VI.

21. Radar Rules 6 (b), 7 (b); Traffic Separation Schemes, Rule 10; Deep-Draught Vessels, Rule 3 (b); Vessels of Limited Manoeuvrability, Rule 3 (g); Lights and Sounds, Annexes 1–111; Non-Displacement Craft, Rule 3 (a).

22. Rule 8. There are also more detailed provisions on safe speed (Rule 6) and the risk of collision (Rule 7).

23. Rule 18.

24. Rule 18 (d). The Institute of Navigation has spoken out against allowing the demands of these exceptional vessels to distort traffic patterns beyond the extent that their relatively small members justify: Interim Report, *supra*.

25. *Ibid.* But now see Wheatley, "Circumstances of Collisions and Groundings" (1973) J.I.N. 92.

26. Maybourn, *op. cit.*, and "A question of Cost-Effectiveness: An Interview with Captain Maybourn," 115 S.S.R. No. 5, p. 19. Captain Maybourn is an articulate defender of an industry-orientated approach but his attitudes cannot in other respects be said to be conservative. The challenge he raises, particularly in the first article, must be answered first by those who would go on to impose additional controls on ships' owners and masters.

27. It is a fallacy that legislation must apply equally to all vessels. The SOLAS Convention distinguishes between passenger ships and other vessels; the Channel Routeing Scheme makes special provision for deep-draught vessels. In neither case is there any difficulty of definition.

28. IMCO has adopted certain prohibited areas off the Aghulas Bank and Cape Terpenia.

29. Three-quarters of all marine casualties are traffic accidents. Toyoda and Fujii, "Marine Traffic Engineering in Japan" (1971) J.I.N. 24.

30. They have operated on the North Atlantic passenger routes since 1868, but the States have forborne to make them compulsory, being content to leave it to the operating companies to lay down routes. The failure of the 1960 SOLAS Conference to accede to the French demand to make these routes compulsory was particularly unlaudable because both the *Stockholm* and the *Andrea Doria*, in the wake of whose collision the Conference had been summoned, belonged to companies that were not parties to the North Atlantic Track Agreement and were sailing on exactly the reciprocal courses which it is the purpose of routeing arrangements to avoid.

31. IMCO/C/ES.III/5, point 9. It is ironic that so much impetus has come from the sinking of the *Torrey Canyon*, which was a stranding rather than a traffic accident, and that the area of the Seven Stones, far from being excluded to ships, is one of the routed areas approved by IMCO.

32. Amendments to the SOLAS Convention, 1960, Res. A/205 (VII), Annex VI, pp. 9–10. The emphasis is on national or regional initiatives. Before the approval of the latest Dover Straits scheme by IMCO, there was a meeting of representatives of Belgium, France, the Netherlands and the U.K.

33. IMCO, *Ships Routeing and Traffic Separation Schemes* (2nd ed.).

34. *Supra*, n. 32.
35. *Supra*, p. 139.
36. The State would have the power in any event. This was a co-ordinated exercise. See U.K., The Collision Regulations (Traffic Separation Schemes) Order 1972 S.I. 1972 No. 809.
37. *Infra*, s. VI. The opportunity does not seem to be much used.
38. Lord Shackleton, *The Times*, Apr. 6, 1967.
39. Murphy, " Comparison of Four Different Rules of the Road " (1970) Int. Bar Ass. 545.
40. IMCO A/VII/Res. 227.
41. Trinity House and the Master Mariners' Association have been especially critical of the existing scheme: (1970) J.I.N. 780.
42. The fear that routed ships in the North Atlantic would be careless of fishing boats on the Grand Banks was one of the reasons why those routes never became compulsory. The warning still remains in the SOLAS Convention.
43. For the work of the ILO, see " Seven Maritime Sessions of the International Labour Conference," 78 Int.Lab.Rev. 429.
44. Maybourn, *op. cit.*; Wepster, " The Future of Merchant Marine Navigation " (1969) J.I.N. 92; " Marine Safety: A New Look Needed," 117 S.S.R. No. 19, p. 35; Rochdale Report (Cmnd. 4337), Chap. 14; Liberian Maritime Board of Investigation into Collision between the *Pacific Glory* and the *Allegro*; Willmer, "*Pacific Glory* and *Allegro* Collision," 165 *Shipbuilding World* 827.
45. High Seas Convention, Art. 10 (i) (b).
46. Document for Guidance—1970. An International Maritime Training Guide, JCST/2/1970/3; Int. Labour Conference, Recommendation 137, concerning vocational training for seafarers. Both Organisations are widely engaged in technical assistance programmes.
47. Art. 15 (2). The obligation undertaken by parties to the SOLAS Convention is: " to arrange for the establishment and maintenance of such aids to navigation, including radio beacons and electronic aids, *as in their opinion*, the volume of traffic justifies and the degree of risk requires, and to arrange for information relating to these aids to be made available to all concerned." (Italics added: the phase makes any obligation nugatory.)
48. Beattie, *op. cit.*
49. U.K. Pilotage Act 1913. Compulsory pilotage may be demanded under by-laws issued by Local Pilotage Authorities. By implication, these powers cannot be exercised beyond territorial waters, s. 7.
50. However, even where ships would be destined for a State's ports, " Harbour authorities are showing an understandable lack of enthusiasm for the prospect of dredging for the half-million ton ships ": 115 S.S.R. No. 10/11, p. 29.
51. But Queensland does take such powers.
52. Koele and Don, " Manoeuvring Large Tankers in the Approach Channels to the Europoort " (1971) J.I.N. 301.
53. *Infra*, p. 146. Malaysia-Indonesia claims and Straits of Malacca.
54. SOLAS, Chap. V, Regulation 8 (d). Since it was inaugurated, following the sinking of the *Titanic*, no passenger lives have been lost due to collision with icebergs in the North Atlantic.
55. International Agreement regarding the Maintenance of Certain Lights in the Red Sea (1967) U.K.T.S. No. 8.
56. A similar system operates in the U.K. for the payment of light dues by ships, which go into the General Lighthouse Fund for the maintenance of coastal lights.
57. On this particularly, McDougal and Burke, *The Public Order of the Oceans*, Chap. 1.
58. Jennings, " A Changing International Law of the Sea " [1972B] C.L.J. 32, 44. *Re* the notion of custodianship of the coastal State over the high seas: " it will need to find its justification not only in the reason of the thing but also in received international law." See also U.S. protest to Canada about Arctic waters legislation: " other countries could assert the right to claim and exercise jurisdiction for other purposes, some reasonable and some not, but all equally invalid according to international law " (1970) 9 Int.Leg.Mat. 605.
59. High Seas Convention, Art. 2.
60. The traditional example is the International Convention for the Protection of Submarine Telegraph Cables 1884. The Continental Shelf Convention contains many examples in Art. 5.

61. But see the statement of the Government of Sweden doubting whether the right to deploy Ocean Data Stations was on an equal footing with the right of navigation, International Oceanographic Commission, Second Session of the Working Group on Legal Questions relating to Scientific Investigations of the Ocean, SC/IOC/WG4/2 Annex V, p. 4.

62. Rule 26.

63. On structures in general, see Consultative Assembly of the Council of Europe, Rec. 653 (1972) on the Legal Status of Artificial Islands built in the High Seas, and Report, *ibid.* Doc. 3054.

64. Art. 5 (1) of the Convention on the Continental Shelf. It was the inevitable interference with the established right of navigation that caused writers such as Scelle and Schwarzenberger to doubt the legitimacy of exclusive claims to exploit the continental shelf in the early days of their promulgation by coastal States.

65. In *U.S.* v. *Ray*, 294 F.Supp. 532 (1969) the U.S. Government justified moving a structure on the continental shelf not erected under licence and not for the purpose of exploiting the shelf on the grounds that it interfered with navigation.

66. National Legislation and Treaties relating to the Territorial Sea, the Contiguous Zone, the Continental Shelf, the High Seas and to Fishing and Conservation of the Living Resources of the Sea, UN/ST/LEG/SER.B/15, *e.g.*, Guatemala, Petroleum Code 1955, p. 360.

67. *Ibid.*, *e.g.*, Australia, Petroleum (Submerged Lands) Act 1967, p. 319.

68. *Ibid.*, *e.g.*, Malaysia, Continental Shelf Act 1966, s. 6 (1) (*b*), p. 375; Norway, Safe Practice Regulations 1967, s. 6, p. 395.

69. IMCO Assembly Res. A. 179 (VI) Oct. 28, 1969.

70. *Ships* are instructed to respect the safety zones. This is an example, and there are others in the Geneva Conventions, of an international duty being addressed to a non-international person. It may carry the implication here that a State can act to keep out of a safety zone which it has designated a ship of another flag rather than merely putting on the flag State a duty to legislate against such infractions by its own ships.

71. See the U.S. statement in n. 61, *supra*, p. 11.

72. Griffin, "Accommodation of Conflicting Uses of Ocean Space with Special Reference to Navigation Safety Lanes," in *Proceedings of Second Law of the Sea Institute Conference* (ed. Alexander).

73. Other restricted areas are those used for national defence purposes. Under the Continental Shelf Mining Act, in some areas, exploration is prohibited altogether (Art. 3), while in others, the installation of exploitation equipment requires the approval of the Ministry of Transport and Defence. Letter from Director of Rijkswaterstaat, Feb. 13, 1973. These areas are marked on a map published by British Petroleum, Licences in the North Sea, the Celtic Sea, and British Coastal Waters, 4358/19.

74. The Netherlands are considering the possibility of enacting binding rules of regulation for ships negotiating the Deep Sea Canal, whether inside or outside its territorial waters, *ibid.*

75. See, Canada: Off-Shore Information and Procedures, Department of Energy, Mines and Resources, Ottawa, which requires 60 days' notice (90 days in territorial waters) of any operations in licensed areas to be given to the Aids to Navigation Division of the Ministry of Transport in order that notices to mariners can be issued and aids to navigation positioned.

76. Some protection for in-shore shellfisheries is provided in the U.K. Sea Fisheries (Shellfish) Act 1967, s. 7 (4). Its scope would need to be extended geographically and to the nature of the damage to cover high seas fisheries endangered by pollution.

77. Equally important, especially where claims to a narrow band of territorial waters is made, is the delimitation of baselines, which may have the effect, not only of closing off wider areas of the high seas but of denying shipping any access at all since the waters behind the baselines will be internal waters and not subject to a right of innocent passage.

78. Territorial Waters Convention, s. III, Arts. 14–23.

79. *Ibid.*, s. III, subs. A.

80. *E.g.*, Sudan, Act 106/1970 in *National Claims to Maritime Jurisdictions*, Department of State, 1972.

81. Territorial Waters Convention, Arts. 1 (1) and 14 (4).

82. *Ibid.* Art. 16 (4).

83. See the U.S. protest to Canada (1970) 9 Int.Leg.Mat. 606.

84. Statement of Legal Adviser to the State Department before Sub-Committee II of the UN Committee on the Peaceful Uses of the Seabed and Ocean Floor Beyond the Limits of National Jurisdiction (1972) 66 A.J.I.L. 133.

85. The U.S. proposal would also give the same protection to the right of overflying.

86. Territorial Waters Convention, Art. 14 (6).

87. For accounts of the military significance of the seas, see Brown, *Arms Control in Hydrospace: Legal Aspects*, pp. 13–17; O'Connell, "International Law and Contemporary Naval Operations" (1970) 45 B.Y.I.L. 19.

87a. See *infra*, pp. 248–251.

88. *The Times*, Mar. 7 and Jul. 4, 1972 and *Guardian*, Mar. 28 and Jul. 3, 1972.

89. (1972) 11 Int.Leg.Mat. 153, and see *infra*, pp. 259–260.

90. Brazil (1971) 10 Int.Leg.Mat. 1224.

91. (1970) 9 Int.Leg.Mat. 1081.

92. (1971) 10 Int.Leg.Mat. 207.

93. Jennings, *op. cit.* n. 58, p. 47; Johnson, *Rechtsgeleerde Adviezen* (REM Opinion), p. 6, para. 7 (b).

94. See O'Connell, n. 87, *supra*, pp. 76–79, for the navigational difficulties of arresting fishing vessels. U.K. fishermen have been making it difficult for Icelandic boats to take any measures against them to enforce Iceland's claim to an extended fishing zone.

95. For such a proposal, see Buzek and Wepster, "The Master in Changing Times" (1971) J.I.N. 35.

96. An example of a marginal improvement to this end is Art. X of the 1962 Amendments to the International Convention for the Prevention of Pollution of the Sea by Oil 1954. States could, under the unamended Convention, report breaches of the Convention by non-flag ships to the State of the flag; the amendment puts an obligation on the flag State to inform IMCO what action it has taken on any such reports.

97. This is the standard whether the action is taken in the exercise of the right of self-defence or under the International Convention relating to Intervention on the High Seas in Cases of Oil Pollution Casualties 1969, Art. 1 (in Final Act of the International Legal Conference on Marine Pollution Damage, 1969, Cmnd. 4403); and see Brown, *The Legal Régime of Hydrospace*, pp. 139–154.

98. The same would seem to be true about a collision between a ship and an offshore installation. Since the status of the superjacent waters of the continental shelf is preserved, the collision will be "an accident of navigation on the high seas" within Art. 11 of the High Seas Convention.

99. *E.g.*, Statement of the U.S.A. that it would not accept any jurisdictional provisions which would expose a U.S. master to personal accountability in a foreign court, IMCO/LEG/WP/1.

100. High Seas Convention, Art. 10; Meyers, *The Nationality of Ships*, pp. 114–118.

101. Boczek, *Flags of Convenience*, p. 259, would appear to put too high a duty on the flag State if he is suggesting that it must exercise its authority on the high seas.

102. Draper and Bennett, "Maritime Traffic Engineering Conference" (1972) *Journal of the Royal Institution of Naval Architects* 375.

103. SOLAS, Chap. I, Regulation 19.

104. Beesley, Legal Adviser to the Canadian Government, quoted in Jennings, n. 58, p. 43.

105. Verzijl, *International Law in Historical Perspective*, Vol. IV, p. 183: "simple non-observance by passing vessels of duly published regulations of the coastal State on navigation does not deprive an otherwise inoffensive passage of its 'innocent' character."

106. Grant, Minister of State at the Department of Trade and Industry, inaugurating the Channel Routeing Scheme, *Trade and Industry*, 7/9/1971, p. 24.

107. The U.S.A. was able to secure compliance with improved fire precautions in the construction of passenger vessels before the achievement of agreement within IMCO because almost all the ships concerned were being built for the cruise trade out of U.S. ports.

108. The U.K. recommended premature but cautious application of the 1960 revised Collision Regulations.

109. On this whole problem, see Alexandrowicz, *The Law of Global Communications*.

110. Both the Netherlands and Canada pressed for one to be built into the revised Collision Regulations. It appears as Art. VI of the Convention to which the Revised Regulations are attached.

111. Para. 194.

112. "Tanker Problems Dominate Marine Safety Field," 117 S.S.R., Annual Marine Design International, 1971, p. 43.

113. The levels of maximum liability in the International Convention on Civil Liability for Oil Pollution Damage were fixed after consultation with the insurance industry about the capacity of the market.

114. The marine insurance industry is reported to have enjoyed good financial years since this co-operation got off the ground, *The Times*, Aug. 25, 1972.

Part VI

Jurisdictional Questions

CHAPTER 14

Maritime Zones: A Survey of Claims

By E. D. Brown*

THE purpose of this paper is to present a balance-sheet of claims to jurisdiction over the seas; to identify current trends; to understand the forces lying behind these claims and trends; to assess the viability and desirability of various proposals *de lege ferenda* and, where appropriate, to offer alternative suggestions.

The variety and complexity of current claims are such that it may be useful to begin by providing a sense of historical perspective in which to view the analysis which follows.

MARITIME JURISDICTION IN HISTORICAL PERSPECTIVE

The history of the modern international law of the sea can perhaps be best understood by perceiving it as a continual conflict between two opposing, yet complementary, fundamental principles—territorial sovereignty and the freedom of the high seas.

Certainly at most times in the development of the modern system, there has been a geographical area at one extreme where the freedom of the high seas was the predominant principle and other areas at the other extreme, where the predominant principle was that of sovereignty. The boundary between the two areas has never been a stable one, however, and its precise position at any one time has been largely determined in accordance with the selfish interests of the most powerful maritime States of the day.

" Freedom " being such an emotive word and the doctrine of the freedom of the high seas having been so clearly advantageous to a small island power with an extensive overseas Empire, it is all the more necessary for the British international lawyer today to be reminded that one State's freedom frequently implies another's restraint and that perhaps the most powerful defence of the doctrime of *mare clausum* ever written came from the pen of an English writer [1]† in support of claims to the possession of the " British Seas " which had been made as early as the tenth century,[2] were strongly reasserted by the Stuart kings in the seventeenth century,[3] and extended in 1674 " from Cape Finisterre to Cape Staten in Norway." [4] The reasons behind the policy were not far to seek. The Elizabethan desire for a share in the East Indies trade and the consequent deployment of the doctrine of the freedom of the seas against the monopolist claims of the Iberian powers had given way, nearer home, to the preoccupation of James I with the British fisheries [5] and the need to minimise the benefits to the United Provinces of their superior merchant and fishing fleets.

A few other well known examples, illustrate the same theme. Sweeping claims were made by the Scandinavian rulers, Denmark even claiming sovereign rights in all the northern seas between Norway, Iceland and Greenland,[6] as well as the right to levy tolls on passage through the Danish Sound.

* Ph.D., B.L., Reader in International Law, University College, London.
† For references, see p. 186.

In the Mediterranean, competing sovereign claims by the Italian States contending for a monopoly of trade with the Levant, meant that "the freedom of the Seas . . . was altogether lost between the eleventh and the sixteenth centuries."[7] Even more ambitious, in 1493, was the attempted allocation of spheres of influence in the Atlantic to Spain and Portugal by Pope Alexander VI, confirmed by the Treaty of Tordesillas in 1494.[8] The Elizabethan rejection of such claims, already noted, was strenuously supported by the United Provinces and supplied with theoretical justification by the Grotian *magnum opus*, *Mare Liberum*, published in 1609.[9]

As Colombos has noted, "Up to the end of the eighteenth century there was no part of the seas surrounding Europe free from the claims of proprietary rights by individual Powers, nor were there any seas over which such rights were not exercised in varying degrees."[10]

From the beginning of the nineteenth century, Britain, as the leading maritime State, continued to pursue and consolidate a policy of freedom of the seas. Thus, in 1821 she helped the United States against Russia's attempt to debar foreign shipping from all waters up to 100 miles from Alaska but opposed the United States in 1886 when that Power too attempted to extend its jurisdiction over the seal fishery in the Behring Sea.

In the present century, sharing the United Kingdom's established economic and security interest in freedom of the high seas, the United States, as the new leading maritime power, has carried on the traditional British policies.

Even this very brief résumé of the history of the freedom of the sea suffices to show that the notion of freedom is used as an ideological tool where the national interest so requires. Freedom is good when it allows Elizabeth to challenge Spain's and Portugal's "freedom" of monopoly; freedom is bad when it prevents James from excluding the Dutch from the North Sea fisheries.

With the benefit of hindsight, it is not difficult to identify trends in the law of the sea and recognise the policy interests of the Powers which lie behind them. The task is made easier by the relatively small number of States involved, the relatively simple interests they had in the sea and the relatively straightforward political milieu in which they operated. At the present time, the situation is very different. There are now about 113 coastal States—not to mention the 31 land-locked States which also have an interest in the sea and its products; there are considerably more complex interests in the sea; there are a multiplicity of types of maritime zone over which jurisdiction may be asserted; and the political milieu is quite different, given the voting strength of the developing States and the currency of new concepts such as the common heritage of mankind and the patrimonial sea or exclusive economic zone.

It is accordingly much more difficult—indeed, in the nature of present circumstances it is probably not possible—to examine State practice and find that the law is likely to crystallise around a set of maritime boundaries which reflect the interests of the most powerful maritime power or class of powers. All than one can probably do is to identify trends in different regions or among similarly placed sets of States; seek to understand them in the light of their differing interests; and consider whether there are any possibilities for reconciliation, or compromise, including the possibility of the reluctant necessity for recognition of a plurality of limits—in the sense of different States being entitled to different limits for the same functions.

The political milieu today

Between the beginning of the nineteenth century and the era of decolonisation in the wake of the Second World War the freedom of the sea was firmly established as a fundamental principle of international law. The two most important freedoms were, of course, freedom of fishing and freedom of navigation. Given the fishing technology of the period, there was little significant conflict between the interests of coastal communities in fish stocks adjacent to the coast and those of foreign distant-water fishing States; and, in any case, even if there had been an awareness of such conflict, the numbers of independent coastal States so affected would have been so small and their power and lack of co-ordination such that no serious challenge to freedom of fishing could possibly have been mounted. Similarly, in relation to freedom of navigation, the conflict was not over the desirability of the principle or even its geographical scope but over which State should, by virtue of its maritime supremacy, enjoy the fruits of "freedom" in terms of overseas trade and naval security.

Since the Second World War there has been a radical change in the international political background against which the freedom of the seas has to be seen and re-assessed. Since 1943, 69 States have achieved independence, of which 55 are coastal States.[11] A very large proportion of these States are very small in terms of either area or population, or both, and it is some measure of their stage of development to note that of a list of 25 "hard-core" least-developed countries adopted by the General Assembly on November 18, 1971,[12] no less than 19 were among these 69 new States. If they are relatively powerless in terms of population and wealth, they share two other features which make their views important in the present context: they have voting strength in the United Nations and, in common with the older developing States, they are often conscious of their group solidarity and of the need to review traditional international legal doctrines to ensure their compatability with their own interests. The freedom of the sea and the delimitation of maritime zones are high on the list of their priorities for reconsideration.

The theme will be developed further below[13] but, briefly stated, the basic questions which are being asked are these: has freedom of the seas become tantamount to a freedom to overfish; a freedom to pollute; a freedom to monopolise the exploitation of submarine resources; a freedom of deployment of nuclear-armed submarines; and, if so, is the traditional acceptance of the desirability of maximising the area of the high seas any longer justifiable or has the time come for a swing back to *mare clausum*?

Before returning to these questions, it is necessary to examine current State practice.

CURRENT STATE PRACTICE

The seas may be divided into five jurisdictional zones. In the first two zones, internal waters and the territorial sea, the predominant principle is that of sovereignty but, already in the territorial sea, the existence of a right of innocent passage reflects the landward reach of the principle of the freedom of the seas. In the next two zones, the various functional zones and the continental shelf, the position is reversed; the basic principle is that of the freedom of the seas but certain limitations on that freedom reflect the seaward extension of sovereign rights. Finally, in the zone beyond the continental shelf, in the high seas proper, the reach of territorial sovereignty is practically exhausted and jurisdictional claims are in the main limited to quasi-territorial jurisdiction over national vessels.

Current State practice is analysed below in relation to the first four of these five jurisdictional zones.

1. Internal waters and the question of archipelagos

The rules governing the outer limit of internal waters—or the baseline from which the territorial sea is measured—are now fairly well established and, as formulated in the Geneva Convention on the Territorial Sea and the Contiguous Zone (1958)[14] are probably generally accepted even by non-parties to the Convention. While it is unnecessary, for this reason, to discuss these rules in this context, it may be useful to be reminded of one aspect of the Geneva régime, since it may have some bearing on the problem of archipelagos.

Article 5 (2) of the Geneva Convention provides that where the adoption of a straight baseline system has the effect of enclosing as internal waters areas previously forming part of territorial waters or of the high seas, a right of innocent passage is to be preserved in such waters. Already, therefore, the international community has recognised a category of internal waters which, in all but name, shares the nature of the territorial sea.

This rule does of course apply to coastal, as opposed to oceanic, archipelagos. But, since the claims persistently made by Indonesia and the Philippines have been opposed by the major Powers hitherto mainly because the application of the straight baseline system to enclose the entire area of inter-island waters would prejudice freedom of navigation, there is no reason in principle why general recognition of these claims could not be coupled with a conventional limitation akin to that in Article 5 (2) of the Geneva Convention. Since freedom of innocent passage is already provided for in at least Indonesian legislation,[15] such a proviso would not seem to present any problem for the archipelago States. The major Powers might object that they require more than a right of innocent passage through some of the more important of the inter-island passages. If so, such counterclaims might be considered together with the problem of territorial sea straits which is referred to below.[16] The United States delegation in the UN Seabed Committee has indicated a readiness to consider how coastal and international interests may best be reconciled in the case of island nations.[17]

There is increasing evidence of sympathy for the arguments skilfully deployed by Indonesian and Philippino spokesmen[18] and the time seems ripe for the settlement of this problem. If the will is there, such problems as those of defining an archipelago in such a way as not to invite abuse of the new rules or of imposing a maximum limit on the length of closing lines are surely not insuperable.[19]

2. The territorial sea and functional zones

At the present time, when State practice exhibits such a variety of claims and such a lack of stability, it is not practicable to examine claims in watertight compartments employing the traditional terminology. Some States are asserting traditional territorial sea claims, supplemented by claims to various functional zones, whereas others have dispensed with such refinements and are making comprehensive territorial sea claims of very considerable dimensions. Others again are experimenting *de lege ferenda* with new compromise formulae such as "the patrimonial sea" or the "exclusive economic zone." In this section, therefore, the writer's object has been to analyse and show the interrelation between the various claims now made. Part of the picture—the changing dimensions of the various categories of claim—can best be revealed by a tabular analysis. This has to be supplemented, however, by an examination of the nature of some of these claims—to show, for example, that Latin America is not the homogeneous region one is sometimes tempted to imagine it to be in terms of its 200 mile claims. A complete picture must also reflect the doctrines which seem to be in the course of crystallisation in the current international debate.

(1) *Prospects for 12 mile territorial sea*

Looking first at the bare figures, the data presented in Tables I–V [20] largely speak for themselves but a few comments may be helpful.

On the basis of Tables I and II alone (and other evidence, considered later, supports the same conclusion), it would seem reasonable to conclude that, provided States can be dissuaded from making general territorial sea claims when more limited functional claims would suffice, the prospects seem good for general agreement on a 12 mile territorial sea.

In the relatively short period of 12 years since the Geneva Conference in 1960 there has been no less than a 25 per cent. increase in the number of States claiming a 12 mile territorial sea, an increase from 22 to 47 per cent. of all recorded claims. Nevertheless, one has also to be conscious of a secondary trend. As Table I shows, there are an increasing number of more extended claims and the prospects of reaching a settlement on a 12 mile limit will certainly deteriorate if agreement is unduly delayed and yet more States feel obliged to secure their special interests by making general claims.

There are at present two major groups whose interests must be catered for if general agreement is to be reached on a 12 mile territorial sea. Firstly, the major maritime Powers, including the Soviet Union, the United Kingdom and the United States, will continue to press for a satisfactory settlement of the problem of international straits; and, secondly, a large group of developing States will continue to make their agreement conditional upon recognition of some kind of extended functional zone beyond the territorial sea.

TABLE I

Territorial Sea Claims 1960 and 1972

Breadth in Miles	3	4	5	6	9	10	12	18	30	50 km.	50	130	170	200	Archipelago
1960	26	4	1	10	1	1	13			1				1	2
1972 (October)	27	4		12		1	50	1	2		1	1	1	7	2

TABLE II

Percentage of Reported State Claims to Territorial Sea of Breadth of:

	3 Miles	6 Miles	12 Miles	18–170 Miles	200 Miles	12 Miles and Over
1960	43	17	22	2	2	26
1972 (October)	25	11	47	6	7	59
Percentage Change	−18	−6	+25	+4	+5	+33

(2) *The question of international straits*

A vital condition of agreement on a 12 mile territorial sea is a satisfactory settlement of the straits problem.

As Tables I and II show, 50 States (47 per cent. of recorded claims) now claim a territorial sea of 12 miles and a further 13 States (12 per cent.) claim between 18 and 200 miles. Nevertheless, 44 States (41 per cent.) still maintain claims to less than 12 miles and, of these, 27 States (25 per cent.) claim only 3 miles. The 3-milers include such important maritime States as Australia, Japan, the Netherlands, the United Kingdom and the United States.

It is still possible—though increasingly difficult—for States claiming less than 12 miles to decline to recognise 12 mile claims. Their concern is due to the fact that there are some 116 straits which would become entirely territorial sea straits if a 12 mile breadth were to be accepted, whereas, at the moment, there exists a central belt of high seas waters in which the freedom of the high seas may be enjoyed. These straits include the Dover Straits; the Strait of Gibraltar; the Bering Straits; various passages between the islands of the Kuril and the Aleutian chains; the Kara Strait in the Soviet Arctic and Barrow Strait in the Canadian Arctic; Bab-el-Mandeb (southern entrance to Red Sea) and Strait of Hormuz (Persian Gulf); and various passages between Malaysia and the islands of Indonesia and the Philippines, including the Malacca Straits.[21]

The status of territorial sea straits is regulated *inter partes* by Section III of the Geneva Convention on the Territorial Sea and the Contiguous Zone (Right of Innocent Passage) and in particular by Article 16 (4), in terms of which:

> " 4. There shall be no suspension of the innocent passage of foreign ships through straits which are used for international navigation between one part of the high seas and another part of the high seas or the territorial sea of a foreign State."

This, however, is felt by some States to be less than satisfactory because (i) the applicability of the convention's rules on innocent passage to warships is not beyond dispute; (ii) under Article 14 (6), " Submarines are required to navigate on the surface and to show their flag "; (iii) the coastal State is free in the first instance to categorise a particular passage as non-innocent—*e.g.*, the passage of nuclear-powered vessels or of oil tankers; and (iv) there is no right of innocent passage for aircraft through the air-space above the territorial sea.

If anything, the position under international customary law is even less satisfactory since there is even more doubt about the position of warships, some States demanding prior notification and/or authorisation as a condition of passage.[22]

In order to avoid these difficulties, it is United States policy to press for a new treaty which, in the language of President Nixon's Oceans Policy Statement of May 23, 1970, " would establish a 12-mile limit for territorial seas and provide for free transit through international straits." [23]

Similarly the Soviet Union has expressed the view that " it is necessary to preserve in . . . [such straits] the freedom of passage which existed before the extension of the territorial sea " [24] and the United Kingdom has stressed the serious defence implications of any system under which international straits would be closed.[25]

The term " free transit " does of course represent a new concept in relation to the territorial sea and is designed to give the same rights of navigation and overflight in territorial sea straits as are now enjoyed as part of the freedom of the high seas in the area beyond territorial waters.

Prima facie " free transit " would apparently therefore permit complete freedom of passage for warships, including nuclear-armed submarines, on the surface or submerged, without notification and irrespective of mission. It would permit freedom of civilian and military flight through the superjacent air-space. Finally, it would seem to deprive the coastal State of the power to categorise certain passages, such as those of nuclear-powered or nuclear-armed vessels and mammoth oil-tankers, as non-innocent.

At first sight, it also seemed to be the intention of the United States to apply the new rule not only to the territorial sea lying beyond the old three mile limit but to the whole of that part of the territorial sea which constitutes the strait, or part of the strait, with the exception of straits such as the Turkish Straits which are subject to a special treaty régime. However, the draft Articles submitted to the Seabed Committee in August 1971 [26] are more modest and would permit the coastal State to "designate corridors suitable for transit by all ships and aircraft," provided that, in "the case of straits where particular channels of navigation are customarily employed by ships in transit, the corridors, so far as ships are concerned, shall include such channels." In a supporting statement,[27] the U.S. delegation emphasised that the right claimed was one of transiting the straits only and that shipping engaged in other activities contrary to coastal State law would be subject to appropriate enforcement action. In a subsequent statement,[28] the United States emphasised that safety standards must be internationally prescribed; proposed that there should be a treaty obligation to respect international traffic separation schemes [29] in accordance with the Rules and Procedures established by IMCO and in the International Regulations for Preventing Collisions at Sea; and that aircraft would normally respect ICAO standards, recommended practices and procedures.

On the question of pollution, it was said that "Specific international agreements are required to insure appropriate protection from the hazards of pollution," [30] thus again playing down the scope of the coastal State's discretion. On the other hand, coastal States may take some comfort from the further proposal that there should be strict liability for all vessels, including warships, for accidents caused by deviations from traffic separation schemes established by IMCO as well as for State aircraft exercising the right of free transit.[31]

The United Kingdom has expressly supported the American draft Article.[32]

The Soviet Union has also tabled draft articles on international straits,[33] which are very similar to the United States proposals, but more detailed on the question of threats to the security of the coastal State. In addition to a general duty on all ships to "take all necessary steps to avoid causing any threat to" security, "warships in transit through such straits shall not in the area of the straits engage in any exercises or gunfire, use weapons of any kind, launch their aircraft, undertake hydrographical work or engage in other acts of a nature unrelated to the transit." There is, however, no mention of passage by submarines and the intention clearly is that submerged passage should be permitted.

It is perhaps not going too far to describe as gentle blackmail the tactics adopted by the Soviet Union and the United States to persuade coastal States to entertain such proposals. Thus, the United States has strongly hinted that "Those nations, like the United States, which attach particular importance to freedom of navigation may be prepared to give greater support to coastal States' legitimate claims to the resources adjacent to their shores, if States primarily concerned with resources can recognise the problems and needs of those nations deeply concerned about freedom of movement over the oceans." [34]

Similarly, the Soviet Union has made it clear that it would be prepared to support provisions in a seabed régime for a system of licensing and distribution of revenue only provided that solutions were forthcoming on freedom of passage through international straits and on the question of fishing.[35]

At a time when 59 per cent. of coastal States claim a territorial sea of 12 miles or more, a rise of 33 per cent. since 1960, the United States interest is not perhaps best served by such statements as that:

> "We do not recognise the 12 mile territorial sea and it is doubtful that if we fail to obtain the necessary protection through international straits at a conference, that we could accept the 12 mile territorial sea. We would as a matter of high national security priority have to maintain that we are only bound to recognise the three mile limit if we were unable to obtain the necessary protection through straits." [36]

The response of many States is likely to be similar to that of the Egyptian representative who said that "Such a freedom which allows submerged submarines, nuclear or otherwise, to pass unseen cannot be called anything other than licensing for the spread of terror." [37]

Equally strongly-worded statements made by Spain[38] and Tanzania[39] reflect a widespread hostility to any proposal to allow more than the innocent passage through straits already provided for in the Geneva Convention.

The position of the archipelago States is also quite firm. Indonesia (which, in co-operation with Malaysia has purported to deprive the Straits of Malacca of their international waterway status)[40] has made it quite clear that it will not agree to a right of free transit as opposed to innocent passage through its national waters.[41]

It is also significant that, in its original form, the list of issues prepared for Seabed Sub-Committee II by members of the Group of 77 developing States, included a reference to innocent passage through straits but omitted any reference to free transit[42] —an omission regarded by the United States as unfair and biased.[43] The amended list, adopted by the Seabed Committee in August 1972,[44] only grudgingly acknowledges the need to discuss "free transit" by including in item 4 not only "Innocent Passage" but also "Other Related Matters Including the Question of the Right of Transit." The United States accepted this compromise as providing an opportunity for a presentation of their views.[45]

If negotiations for a generalised rule reach deadlock, a solution may be found by distinguishing different classes of straits.

One approach along these lines might be to examine the 116 straits which would lose their belt of high seas if agreement were reached on a 12 mile territorial sea, with a view to identifying (a) those which form the only link between two expanses of high seas and (b) those which provide the only or main access to internal seas or gulfs of particular importance for navigation or international security. The feasibility might then be explored of preserving in these straits a high seas type of freedom of navigation and overflight in the belt previously recognised as high seas or, alternatively, in the waters of the strait lying beyond six miles of either coast. If such a proposal is not negotiable in relation to (a) and (b) it may be negotiable in relation to (a) or even to particular straits in either or both categories which could then be identified in the convention.

It must be said, however, that there is much evidence of sensitivity on this subject, partly caused by the less than delicate diplomacy of the United States in the earlier stages of formulating its policy and partly by the realisation that defence interests are the paramount issue behind the policy of the major powers.

(3) *Functional zones beyond the territorial sea*

It was suggested above that a second question which would have to be settled as a condition of agreement on a 12 mile territorial sea was that of recognition of some kind of functional zone beyond the territorial sea which would satisfy the interests of the coastal State.

An examination of the functional zone claims presently asserted, as analysed in Tables III–V, and a comparison of this data with that on the territorial sea (Tables I–II) [46] show just how confused and complex the present position is; and it is of course further complicated by the problem of the outer limit of the continental shelf (or the inner limit of the zone beyond national jurisdiction).

The position is, however, less complicated and more amenable to simplification when it is reduced to its essentials. The following facts should be noted: (i) only 13 States claim a *territorial sea* in excess of 12 miles; (ii) the functions for which *exclusive zones* in excess of 12 miles are claimed are very few. With few and insignificant exceptions, they relate to fishing; fishery conservation; pollution; and natural resources exploitation; (iii) it appears to be a matter of chance in many cases whether a particular State opts for an extended territorial sea or an extended functional zone and, where the former is chosen, it is also a matter of chance whether a " pure " territorial sea claim is asserted or whether freedom of navigation and overflight is preserved.

TABLE III

Functional Zone Claims and Territorial Sea Claims in Excess of Three Miles (Excluding Archipelago and Continental Shelf Claims)

(Functional Zone Claims are entered only if they are in excess of the Territorial Sea claims of the States concerned)

Breadth in Miles	4	6	10	12	18	20 km.	30	50	100	110	100–112	130	170	20–200	200
Territorial Sea	4	12	1	50	1		2	1				1	1		7
Exclusive Fishing				17				1		1				1	4
Fishery Conservation						1			1		4				1
Pollution									1						

Civil Jurisdiction
Customs
Penal Jurisdiction
Sanitary
Security
Neutrality

Special zones have been established from time to time for these purposes.

With a few and, for present purposes, insignificant exceptions, they have not exceeded 12 miles.

This feature is especially noticeable if a closer examination is made of the 11 200 mile claims presented in Table IV. The only African State in this group, Sierra

TABLE IV

Exclusive Fishing Zones in Excess of 12 Miles—Including Comprehensive Territorial Sea Claims as at October 1, 1972*

Breadth	18 miles	30 miles	50 miles	110 miles	130 miles	170 miles	20–200 miles	200 miles
Africa	Cameroon (TS)	Congo (Brazzaville) (TS) (?) Nigeria (TS)	Gambia (TS)	Senegal (FZ)	Guinea (TS)	Gabon (TS)		Sierra Leone (TS)
Asia							Rep. of Korea (FZ)	
Europe			Iceland (FZ)					
Latin America								Argentina (TS) Brazil (TS) Chile (FZ) Ecuador (TS) El Salvador (TS) Mexico (FZ) (?) Nicaragua (FZ) Panama (TS) Peru (FZ) Uruguay (TS)

*Note too that under the Territorial Sea and Fishing Zones Act 1970, Canada has drawn " fishery closing lines " across the entrances to the Gulf of St. Lawrence, Bay of Fundy, Queen Charlotte Sound, Dixon Entrance and Hecate Strait.

FZ = FISHING ZONE; TS = TERRITORIAL SEA;
? = unconfirmed report

TABLE V

Fishery Conservation Zones in Excess of 12 Miles

	State	*Breadth (miles)*
Africa	Ghana	100
Asia	Bangladesh	12+100 (?)
	India	12+100
	Pakistan	12+100
	Rep. of Vietnam	20 km.
	Sri Lanka	6+100
Latin America	Costa Rica	200

Leone, has opted for a 200 mile traditional territorial sea.[47] Of the 10 Latin American States, six have claimed a 200 mile territorial sea, the remainder favouring the functional zone approach. But, whereas the territorial sea claims of Brazil, Ecuador, El

Salvador and Panama are unqualified by reference to freedom of navigation or overflight, those of the other two territorial sea claimants (Argentina and Uruguay), in common with the four States making functional zone claims (Chile, Mexico, Nicaragua and Peru), do recognise the right of freedom of navigation (as distinct from innocent passage) and of overflight, either expressly or by implication.[48] Thus, in essence, six of the 11 200 mile claims are functional zone claims rather than classical territorial sea claims. The writer has not yet been able to examine the scope in this respect of the other six territorial sea claims in excess of 12 miles but, even if they are of the classical variety, they would not add very substantially to the influence of the four hard-core Latin Americans.

The evidence seems to lead to the conclusion that, with the exceptions noted, there has been no felt need for extended comprehensive territorial sea claims; and that even in Africa, Asia and Latin America (see Tables IV and V), where the extensive claim trend predominates, there are still good prospects for recognition of a 12 mile territorial sea, coupled with a functional zone beyond. However, a large number of questions remain: is there to be one unified zone for all functions; if so, of what dimensions and will it include continental shelf claims?; if not, what dimensions will be recognised for what functions?; and will they be decided upon universally or regionally in accordance with universal guidelines or by individual States in the light of geographical, geological, biological, ecological, etc., criteria?

THE EXCLUSIVE ECONOMIC ZONE

Many of these questions have been raised, if not answered, and evidence of the formation of a consensus has been apparent in the current debate on what has come to be known as the Exclusive Economic Zone or the Patrimonial Sea. In this writer's view, the compromise formula offered by the modified version of the already familiar notion of the functional zone is one of the most promising developments in the international law of the sea for many years. Originating in the developing world and catering for the interests of developing coastal States, it is nevertheless formulated with moderation and based on a realistic appreciation of political feasibility. If handled diplomatically and in a spirit of reasonable flexibility, it may well prove to be the key to a solution of not only the problem of the breadth of the territorial sea but of those of fishery limits, pollution zones and even of the delimitation of the continental shelf.

Perhaps the main reason for this guarded optimism is that the notion of the exclusive economic zone is a reflection in jurisdictional terms of the contemporary political balance. The international community has been passing through a very confused and dynamic period in *inter alia* the international law of the sea as a new post-colonial order was evolving and it may not be over-fanciful to hope that, in the marine arena at least, a point of balance is in sight. Earlier in this paper,[49] reference was made to the manner in which the fundamental rules of the law of the sea were fashioned to reflect the interests of the contemporarily most powerful States. Returning to this theme, it is possible today to identify four main interest groups and it will be seen that the last of these groups to be considered lies somewhere between the extremes represented by the other three and is the group from which the main support for the new order is initially forthcoming.

1. Group 1—the developed, satisfied States

This group, which includes Japan, the Soviet Union, the United Kingdom and the United States, together with most of the European States, is the predominant interest group of the historical phase now drawing to a close, a phase summed up in the term "freedom of the high seas." This was a freedom which, for good or for ill, enabled these powers to enjoy freedom of navigation in practically the whole of ocean space for three main purposes: trade (specialisation and exchange on an international level, with overseas possessions integrated into the metropolitan economic system); high seas fishing, often in areas adjacent to the coasts of distant countries (an interest greatly expanded more recently with the advent of scientific fishing and marketing methods); and security (in relation both to metropolitan and overseas dominions).

Times and, with them, interests have changed. As regards trade, overseas empires have been run down; the Third World has emerged; and, despite statements made particularly by the Soviet Union and the United States,[50] no-one surely fears that commercial navigation will be seriously prejudiced by jurisdictional claims—except perhaps in relation to the protection of the environment.

As regards fishing, the two basic facts are not difficult to recognise. Firstly, the developed States have enjoyed till now the exploitation (in a non-pejorative sense) of fisheries near the coasts of what are now developing States and economic and political vested interests demand that their traditional " rights " based on the traditional law, should be vigorously defended. Secondly, the coastal developing States are in the course of developing their fishing capacity.[51] Having done so, they will clearly be better placed to exploit the adjacent zones than the distant-water fleets of the developed States; and, not without reason, they find it a little difficult to understand the equity of a law which allows a coastal State to exploit the mineral resources of the natural prolongation of its territory into and under the sea, but forbids a similar monopoly situation in relation to the living resources in the superjacent waters.

Finally, as regards security, the traditional objectives remain important but they have been given an added dimension by the fact that the nuclear deterrent has " gone to sea " and the submarine world is therefore a strategic area of prime importance.[52] Maximum areas of deployment and freedom of undetected and unregulated manoeuvre are regarded as essential by the nuclear super-powers. Jurisdictional claims by coastal States may well conflict with this interest and, security being the *sine qua non* of practically every other goal, it follows that, whether expressly so stated or not, it is this interest which will supply the main motive power of the developed States even when the argument is being deployed by non-nuclear powers in terms of trade and fish.

Indeed, all the evidence suggests that the developed States are fully aware that, over the medium to long term, their interest in middle- and distant-water fishing is quite indefensible against the concerted attacks of the developing States; that freedom of commercial navigation is perceived as advantageous by the developing States and is not therefore endangered in its substance [53]; and that, accordingly, the objective should be to concentrate on securing the defence interest by a reluctant, grudging and as protracted as possible trade-off of coastal economic zones. The fact that such an accommodation would leave undisturbed the jurisdiction of the developed States over their own continental shelf resources is a factor which will commend it to strong lobbies in some of these States.[54]

2. Group 2—the extended territorial sea States

At the other extreme from Group 1 are those States which have decided, or seem to be in the course of deciding, that their interests can be adequately protected only by the assumption of full sovereignty over an extended belt of territorial waters and are dissatisfied with limited functional rights in these areas. For the purpose of this analysis, it would be quite proper either to include or exclude from this group those

States, mentioned above, which, while claiming extended territorial seas, do nevertheless make provision for freedom of navigation and overflight. It is, however, more appropriate to classify them with Group 4, those States which would be content with some kind of exclusive economic zone. On this assumption, the States in Group 2 are:

(1) *In Latin America*: *Brazil, Ecuador, El Salvador and Panama, all of which claim a territorial sea of 200 miles.* Ecuador is perhaps the most forceful advocate of this point of view and a recent speech by an Ecuadorian spokesman does not reveal any softening of his country's attitude. The irrelevance of United States non-recognition of the Ecuadorian 200 mile claim was stressed and it was asserted that the big powers should realise that international law is now intended to defend the developing world, 95 of the current 132 United Nations members being developing States.[55] On the other hand, even this State may be prepared to modify its attitude in certain circumstances. Speaking in the Seabed Committee in July 1972, Mr. Benites stated that "Ecuador would not be able to negotiate any changes in its position on [its claim to sovereignty out to 200 miles] . . . as long as the United States continued to apply sanctions to his country," [56] thus implying the possibility that it might change otherwise. Mr. Benites also stressed the need for the developing States to unify their efforts and attitudes prior to the Law of the Sea Conference.

(2) *In Africa*: *Cameroon, the Congo (Brazzaville), Gabon, Gambia, Guinea, Nigeria and Sierra Leone.* Cameroon's extension of its territorial sea from six to 18 miles is reported to have been finalised [57] but its representative has recently spoken in favour of a 200 mile territorial sea as being preferable to a 200 mile exclusive economic zone.[58] Gabon too (territorial sea recently extended first from 25 to 30 miles and then to 170 miles) has stated that it would oppose a 12 mile territorial sea settlement and favours the conventional establishment of minimum and maximum figures for the breadth of the territorial sea.[59] The Congo (Brazzaville), Gambia, Guinea and Nigeria, which claim territorial seas of respectively 30 miles, 50 miles, 130 miles and 30 miles would also seem to favour the comprehensive territorial sea concept. Finally, Sierra Leone [60] became the first African State to join the 200 mile club, previously confined to Latin American States, when it extended its territorial sea to 200 miles in 1971.

3. Group 3—Land-locked States, shelf-locked States and States with short coastlines

The voting strength of these States is sometimes overlooked. According to a recent calculation, of a total of 146 States, 31 are land-locked and 23 are shelf-locked [61] and of course quite a few others possess only a short frontage to the sea. They had already made their presence felt in 1970 in relation to the seabed. As the Afghanistan delegation noted in the General Assembly's First Committee, the interest of land-locked States in the seabed beyond national jurisdiction is twofold, as it relates, first, to a right of participation and, secondly, a right to benefits.[62] From both points of view, it is clearly in the interests of these States to maximise the area to which the international régime will apply and recognition of this fundamental fact obliged Bolivia to cast a negative vote against the Lima Declaration of Latin American States on the Law of the Sea, adopted in August 1970.[63]

On December 17, 1970, the General Assembly adopted Resolution A/RES/2750B (XXV), *inter alia* requesting the Secretary-General to "report on the special problems of land-locked countries relating to the exploration and exploitation of the resources of the seabed and the ocean-floor, and the subsoil thereof, beyond the limits of national jurisdiction." The inclusion in the resolution of the passage quoted above was opposed by the delegations of Cameroon [64] and Nigeria [65] on the grounds that it discriminated in favour of a certain group—land-locked States—and constituted a dangerous precedent of differentiating between different groups of developing States. The fact that only two States voted against this clause [66] and that both were African developing countries understandably caused some bitterness.

The great majority preferred the view expressed by Mr. Koh (Singapore) that the resolution was not discriminatory because it justifiably differentiated two categories of countries that are different.[67] The resolution also enjoyed the support of the shelf-locked States and of what the Belgian delegate called the sea-locked States, that is, small island States such as Haiti which have no opportunity to extend their territorial sea because of the presence of other States in their immediate vicinity.[68]

As the Austrian [69] and Singapore [70] delegations have pointed out, land-locked and shelf-locked countries have no means of balancing the unilateral extensions of jurisdiction which are open to both States with broad continental shelves and even to States which do not have broad shelves but do face the open oceans and can therefore envisage extensive seabed claims.

Although their voting strength is not negligible, the population and power of these States are not great and, given also their weak negotiating base in the present law, their opposition to wide national limits could probably be assuaged by adequate provision for limitations on the exclusive rights of coastal States in the form of some recognition of their right to participate in either the exploitation of seabed resources or the benefits arising therefrom.

The position is similar in the field of coastal fisheries. Nepal, for example, argues that the special interest of the coastal State can be recognised without establishing an exclusive zone and suggests the setting up of an international or regional arrangement under which land-locked States might have a fair share in the fisheries.[71] Similarly, Iraq, while not hostile to the concept of an exclusive economic zone, stressed that it should not be detrimental to the interests of land-locked countries and those with limited coastlines.[72]

As will be seen, the advocates of the exclusive economic zone concept have tried to make provision for such interests through regional arrangements.[73]

4. Group 4—States advocating an Exclusive Economic Zone

As has been noted above, the notion of coastal State jurisdiction in a functional zone beyond the territorial sea is scarcely a new one. The same idea lies behind the " contiguous zone " in either its traditional or more recent conventional form [74] and, of course, fishery zones, pollution control zones and even the concept of the legal continental shelf embody the same idea. Nonetheless, as the following analysis will make clear, the concept of the Exclusive Economic Zone (EEZ) is much more comprehensive than any of its forerunners and its adoption would mark a radical change in the international law of the sea. Perhaps the most useful approach to a full understanding of this concept is, first, to analyse it as expounded particularly by Kenyan, Mexican, Tanzanian and Venezuelan spokesmen [75]; secondly, to note its essential compatibility with the claims already made by two different groups of Latin American States and with the thinking of Iceland, India and Pakistan; thirdly, to draw attention to the sympathetic response which has been forthcoming from a broad cross-section of the international community, including States such as the United Kingdom which appreciate the need for a reasonable compromise between what they would ideally prefer and what is currently being claimed by the more extreme States. The concept is still of course in a formative stage and the following analysis is based on a composite account abstracted from the expositions of its chief advocates.

(1) *Purpose of EEZ concept*

The purpose of the EEZ has been succinctly stated by Mr. Njenga of Kenya:

"... the economic zone concept offers a good basis for resolving the impasse between those who believe in a narrow and those who believe in a broad belt of territorial sea. Basically, the purpose of the exclusive economic zone concept is to safeguard the economic interests of the coastal States in the waters and seabed adjacent to their coasts without unduly interfering with other legitimate uses of the sea by other States." [76]

As Mr. Njenga pointed out,

"... Freedom of any kind is meaningful only if there is equality of opportunity to make use of it. ... [It] is ... hypocritical to praise freedom of the high seas when the great majority of nations have no means of enjoying those freedoms. In such a situation such freedom amounts to freedom to exploit others which is what is hoped to be curbed through the concept of an exclusive economic area." [77]

(2) *Scope of EEZ ratione loci*

While no firm agreement yet exists among advocates of an EEZ, most of them assume that (i) there will be a territorial sea of 12 miles and (ii) an EEZ beyond the territorial sea of a breadth not exceeding 200 miles from the baseline of the territorial sea and extending vertically through the entire water column to include the subjacent seabed and subsoil.

In the *Draft Articles on Exclusive Economic Zone Concept* prepared by Kenya, the limits were to be fixed in accordance with " criteria which take into account [the coastal State's] ... own geographical, geological, biological, ecological, economic and national security factors " (Article I). Article VII further provided that the limits should be fixed " in accordance with criteria in each region, which take into consideration the resources of the region and the rights and interests of developing land-locked, near land-locked, shelf-locked States and States with narrow shelves and without prejudice to limits adopted by any State within the region." The Economic Zone was not, however, in any case to exceed 200 miles.[78]

Some of the African States at least consider that no EEZ should attach to islands under colonial dependence or foreign domination or control [79] but any such limitation would clearly cause considerable difficulties.

It is clear that one of the main considerations favouring the figure of 200 miles is that EEZ advocates recognise that the Latin American and other States which have already made 200 mile fishery or territorial sea claims will not be won over to support the EEZ concept if anything less is envisaged. The fact that 200 miles is also gaining ground as a reasonable distance criterion for the outer limit of the continental shelf is a further factor to be taken into account.[80]

(3) *Scope of EEZ ratione materiae*

Positively, it is envisaged that the EEZ should give the coastal State (i) exclusive jurisdiction over all the living and non-living resources of the Zone, including in particular fish and continental shelf resources; (ii) jurisdiction for the prevention and control of pollution. The degree of freedom to be allowed to the coastal State to promulgate and enforce anti-pollution legislation remains to be formulated in detail but EEZ advocates will clearly insist on effective national powers; (iii) effective powers of enforcement of EEZ rights over foreign vessels.[81] It has been made clear by, for example, Tanzania that effective powers of enforcement are demanded not only in relation to pollution but also in relation to fishery jurisdiction. Responding to Japanese proposals which would have preserved the right of prosecution for the flag State,[82] the Tanzanian representative said that " To cling to the old rule of inspection and arrest and then handing over to the flag State is to defend an anachronism." [83]

Negatively, it has been made clear that the EEZ would not interfere with the legitimate interests of other States, " particularly in navigation and overflight and laying of submarine cables [and pipelines [84]] *i.e.*, in all aspects of international communication for which the sea is used." [85]

It is in this area that the major maritime Powers will have to be satisfied if the EEZ is to attract their support. Jurisdiction in relation to fisheries and pollution is of course already an interference with navigation and the major Powers will wish to be convinced not only that such jurisdiction will be clearly delimited but also that such jurisdiction will be an exception—to be restrictively interpreted—to the general principle that the waters of the EEZ remain subject to the fundamental régime of the high seas except where conventionally limited by the régime of the EEZ.

(4) *Scope of EEZ ratione personae*

Reference has already been made to the view that islands under colonial dependence or foreign control should not be accorded an EEZ. In addition, the Kenyan representative in the Seabed Committee made it clear that no State was obliged to claim an EEZ and, indeed, it would be welcomed if the developed States did not.[86] Similarly, Mexico, responding to statements by European delegations that the EEZ concept would be difficult to apply in Europe, stressed that there was no question of imposing this concept on States satisfied with other arrangements.[87]

(5) *Scope of EEZ ratione temporis*

Although one of the arguments deployed in support of the EEZ is that it is necessary for the protection of the infant fishing industries of developing coastal States, there is no suggestion that the exclusive rights of the coastal State should be phased out once these industries are independently viable. There has however been a suggestion by Mexico that, since the establishment of an EEZ or patrimonial sea would entail changes in traditional fishing practices, it would be desirable to make provision for a transitional period.[88] This is of course an established practice, especially in Europe, whenever the reluctant recognition of expanded fishery claims involves the sacrifice of established fishing rights.[89]

(6) *Criticism of EEZ concept*

Five main criticisms have been levelled against the EEZ concept:

(a) *The creeping jurisdiction argument* is that experience suggests that maritime jurisdictional rights granted for one purpose are likely to expand either *ratione loci* or *ratione materiae* and that there is no guarantee that the 200 mile line will not " creep " out further into the high seas or that the freedom of navigation will not be further eroded within the EEZ.

The answer which Kenya has given to this criticism is that the EEZ concept cannot lead to such a result if the EEZ is well defined and the rights in such zones properly specified.[90] It might have added that claims are creeping forward in any event and one of the important advantages of the EEZ is that it might halt this trend at a reasonable line.

(b) *Interference with navigation and an increase in freight charges* are other results feared by opponents of the EEZ concept.

The Tanzanian representative countered this argument by asserting that, " Commercial shipping is so vital to all coastal States that I cannot imagine a State interfering with it. The truth is, States will seek to facilitate it more than hinder it." [91]

The fact remains, however, that shipping States must guard themselves against the possibility of irresponsible legislation imposing unfair burdens on their shipping, on the pretext that they are required in the interests of fishery protection, environmental protection, national security or safety of navigation. Once again, the EEZ concept provides a framework for a compromise solution—perhaps by empowering the local State to enforce internationally prescribed and carefully specified standards.

(c) *Under-utilisation, especially of living resources*,[92] is perhaps the favourite criticism levelled against the EEZ. The argument, based on the admitted present incapacity of many of the developing coastal States to take and utilise the optimum catch from their offshore waters, is usually deployed to show that this is a wasteful, inefficient proposal which will not only prejudice the traditional rights of distant-water fishermen but will also reduce the supply of protein to an impoverished world.

The answer given by the developing States is that their intention is not necessarily to exclude the fishing fleets of other States from their EEZ but to ensure that they fish under licence from, and in accordance with regulations made by, the coastal State and on payment of licence fees or other payments.[93]

If the oil of the less-developed countries can be utilised under concession arrangements, why, they ask, cannot similar arrangements be made for fish.

The Mexican Government's position [94] on this question is rather interesting. In 1971, they had proposed a system of preferential rights under which the coastal State would have been entitled to take whatever it could catch in its adjacent waters, a share which it could expand as its fishing capacity was developed. The remainder of the stock (after making allowance for the demands of conservation) would be available to the fishermen of other States. The idea was, of course, to prevent under-utilisation. In 1972, however, Mexico came to the conclusion that under-utilisation could be provided against by the grant of concessions and espoused the patrimonial sea concept. In so doing, however, they stressed the desirability of devising a formula which would oblige the coastal State not to refuse to grant such concessions without valid reason if it was not fully fishing the resource itself. The idea is a good one but its implementation would probably involve a willingness to vest considerable powers in an international fishery commission or arbitral tribunal—devoutly to be wished but unlikely to be realised.

(d) A fourth argument, that *the developing States are selfishly grabbing what belongs to mankind* comes ill from the mouths of those who were quite ready in the quarter century following 1945 to " grab " the resources of the continental shelf. As a Tanzanian spokesman put it, " The same thing is now happening with regard to fisheries—only that the world is more civilised now and we want this to come by negotiations! " [95]

(e) Finally, there is the *land-locked States' argument*, already alluded to. The EEZ, it is contended, is clearly contrary to the interests of the land-locked States and to States with short coastlines, in that it deprives them of any opportunity to benefit from the exploitation of marine resources within 200 miles of land.[96]

A short and persuasive reply has been given by Mr. Njenga (Kenya). After pointing out that such States were seriously handicapped under the present régime and had no hope of improving their situation, he went on to say that . . .

> " Those proposing an exclusive economic zone were prepared to enter into regional arrangements—entailing preferential granting of licences and jointly undertaken

activities—to alleviate the disadvantages imposed on certain countries by geography and also by colonialism and imperialism." [97]

Elsewhere, Mr. Njenga explained further the view that:

> ". . . the best solution for land-locked countries, particularly in Africa, would be along the basis of regional arrangements, along the lines of the joint Kenya, Tanzania, Uganda and Zambia shipping line which would enable these countries to engage in fishery within the economic zone of neighbouring countries. Within the African Group this idea of regional multilateral and bilateral arrangements, not only for the land-locked countries but also for countries like the Republic of Zaire and adjoining Congo which have extremely narrow coasts was very well received. It would also suit countries like Sudan [98] and Ethiopia, bordering on a relatively narrow sea. . . ." [99]

Such regional co-operative schemes, holding out a promise of participation either in exploitation or the benefits therefrom, would certainly seem more attractive to land-locked and similarly placed States than either the present position or the still very vague plans of more universal scope.

(7) *International response to EEZ concept*

The response to the EEZ concept from the international community has varied from warm support through qualified interest to downright opposition. While attitudes within regions have by no means been uniform, the concept has been particularly well received in the developing countries of Latin America, Africa and Asia. At the other extreme, three major maritime powers, Japan, the Soviet Union and the United States have consistently opposed the EEZ notion. Somewhere between these two extremes lie the views of States like Canada, Australia and New Zealand, which have put forward detailed proposals on coastal fisheries, claiming them to be capable of incorporation in a EEZ régime but laying rather more stress on compliance with internationally prescribed standards than advocates of the EEZ envisage. Finally, mention must also be made of the views of a number of States which are at least in favour of further investigation of the feasibility of the EEZ concept. This spectrum of responses is presented below in descending order from enthusiastic support to complete rejection.

(a) *Latin American and the Caribbean.* As has been noted above, two of the six Latin American States claiming a 200 mile territorial sea, Argentina and Uruguay,[100] expressly recognise freedom of navigation and overflight and their claims are therefore more akin to EEZ claims than classical territorial sea claims. The relevant Uruguayan legislation is particularly clear on this point, since it provides for a right of innocent passage in a 12 mile coastal zone but states that "Beyond that 12 mile zone the provisions of this law do not affect free navigation and overflight." [101]

The four Latin American States claiming functional zones of 200 miles (Chile, Mexico, Nicaragua and Peru) are of course even more akin to the EEZ concept. It is true that a Peruvian representative has recently made it clear that his country would prefer an extensive territorial sea (the breadth of which, not exceeding 200 miles, could vary according to local circumstances) rather than an EEZ. He went on to say, however, that it was foreseeable that agreement could be reached on the distance from which coastal States may consent to "the establishment of a system of ensuring the liberties of international communication and trade, without flag discrimination." [102]

Even those remaining Latin American States (Brazil, Ecuador, El Salvador and

Panama) which claim a classical territorial sea of 200 miles may not be intransigent if the EEZ concept seems generally acceptable. The Kenyan representative's prediction seems well based:

> "Even the minority who like Brazil insist on innocent passage in the whole of the 200 miles do not and cannot really enforce it. Consequently the economic zone concept would be the way out for them at the Conference though one suspects that, for tactical reasons, they would continue to insist on a territorial sea of 200 miles, finally making their acceptance of the economic zone *provided* it extended to 200 miles, look like a big compromise on their part." [103]

The majority of Latin American States have of course been acting in concert and issuing joint declarations on the law of the sea for some time. One of the six "Basic Principles" of the Montevideo Declaration (1970) of nine Latin American States included "the right to establish the limits of their maritime sovereignty and jurisdiction in accordance with their geographical and geological characteristics and with the factors governing the existence of marine resources and the need for their rational utilisation." [104] This principle was confirmed in broadly similar language in one of the five "common principles" incorporated in a Declaration of Latin American States on the Law of the Sea issued at the Lima Conference attended by 20 Latin American States and eight observer States in August 1970.[105]

More recently, a Specialised Conference of the Caribbean Countries on Problems of the Sea met in Santo Domingo in May/June 1972 and was attended by 15 States of the region, together with observers from other Latin American countries. The Conference adopted the Santo Domingo Declaration by a vote of 10 in favour, with five abstentions.[106] The main principles of the Declaration referred to a 12 mile territorial sea; a "patrimonial sea" not exceeding 200 miles, with sovereign rights over all resources, the rights to regulate scientific research and adopt pollution prevention measures. Provision was made for freedom of navigation, overflight and submarine cable and pipe laying. In short, on all these points, the patrimonial sea is merely another name for the EEZ. There is however one point of some importance on which the authors of the Santo Domingo Declaration have gone further than the EEZ advocates. Under the heading "Continental Shelf," after incorporating the definition of the continental shelf as formulated in the Geneva Convention on the Continental Shelf, it is declared that the Conference considered that the Latin American States "should promote a study concerning the advisability and timing for the establishment of precise outer limits of the Continental Shelf *taking into account the outer limits of the continental rise*." [107] The implication that the continental shelf may thus extend beyond a 200 mile patrimonial sea is confirmed by a further declaration that, "With respect to the part [of the continental shelf] beyond the patrimonial sea, the régime established for the continental shelf by International Law shall apply." [107a]

If this attitude prevails, it would of course diminish the attraction of the EEZ concept as a compromise formula for settling most of the problems of maritime limits. It may be that this matter will be clarified when the Declaration is further considered at the regional level by all Latin American States.

The Jamaican delegate, explaining his country's abstention, referred to a lack of enthusiasm for the "patrimonial sea" because of its geographical situation, with other island States situated comparatively near. Jamaica was not, however, rejecting the concept and would consider with sympathy some form of preferential treatment based on regional solidarity.[108]

(b) *The African States*. On the international institutional level, the FAO has helped the African States in the shaping of their policies, not least through the Consultation with the African States on the Conservation of Fishery Resources and on the Control of Fishing in Africa (Casablanca, May 1971). The developing countries in general have also noted the views of the FAO in the report of its 16th Conference on Fishery Problems:

> "... the Conference recognised that certain disturbing features of fishery exploitation and utilisation had nevertheless remained in evidence. These related to the comparatively small share of many developing countries in world fisheries, the effect of long-range fishing operations of certain countries with developed fisheries, and the generally increasing need for resource management, particularly of stocks exploited by a number of nations." [109]

The Organisation of African Unity (OAU) has also adopted resolutions bearing on this subject. In particular, a Resolution on Territorial Waters was adopted by the OAU Educational, Scientific, Cultural and Health Commission in December 1971.[110] The Resolution endorses a recommendation of the Scientific Council for Africa (SCA)[111] that African States should extend their territorial waters to 200 miles; establish a 212 mile non-pollution zone; and create a restricted national fishery zone in the 12 mile belt adjacent to the baseline of the territorial sea. It was commented that "The 212 nautical miles limit would thus constitute the national economic limit in the oceans and seas surrounding Africa." [112]

Although the Thirteenth Session of the Asian-African Consultative Committee (January 1972) did not adopt any resolutions on the EEZ, it did have before it a Working Paper on the EEZ prepared by Mr. Njenga of Kenya[113] and, as the citations throughout the present paper bear witness, the concept attracted widespread support in the Conference proceedings.

In June 1972, very similar proposals were incorporated in unanimous Recommendations made by the African States Regional Seminar on the Law of the Sea attended in Yaoundé by representatives of 16 African States.[114] Stress was again put on the proposals for a regional accommodation of the interests of land-locked States, referred to above.

Finally, these same elements of the EEZ doctrine were incorporated in the Draft Articles on Exclusive Economic Zone Concept tabled in the Seabed Committee by Kenya in August 1972.[115]

(c) *The Indian Sub-Continent*. The position of Bangladesh has not yet been made clear but the other States of the Indian Sub-Continent, India, Pakistan and Sri Lanka, now support the EEZ concept.

India, even as late as January 1972, was still thinking in terms of a 12 mile territorial sea; a contiguous zone of unspecified dimensions for fiscal, health and other matters; a 200 mile seabed area; an exclusive fishery zone (limit not yet specified); and a fishery protection or preferential zone if the exclusive zone was not sufficiently wide.[116] In August 1972, however, the Indian delegation in the Seabed Committee described the Kenyan draft articles on the EEZ as "a timely and useful contribution providing for a realistic restructuring of international law." A 12 mile territorial sea, with an EEZ out to 200 miles "would solve the question of jurisdiction realistically." [117]

Pakistan has shown similar sympathy for the EEZ, and the Sri Lanka delegation in the Seabed Committee has not only commended the Kenyan draft articles as one of the most important contributions to the work of the Committee, but has described the

EEZ concept as one of the " two cornerstones of the over-all compromise necessary for the future Conference " on the law of the sea.[118]

(d) *Iceland.* Iceland's policy is particularly interesting, being that of the only State in the European region which has embraced a doctrine similar to the EEZ concept. Not only has its Government unilaterally extended its fishery limits to 50 miles. It has also been authorised by the Althing (in the same Resolution which dealt with this extension) " to declare unilaterally a special jurisdiction with regard to pollution in the seas surrounding Iceland." [119] The EEZ advocates clearly see Iceland as a good example of a State attempting to act in accordance with the EEZ doctrine in difficult political circumstances and as fixing its fishery limits in accordance with local " geographical, geological, biological, ecological, economic and national security factors." [120]

(e) *Canada, Australia and New Zealand.* The United States delegation in the Sea-bed Committee has criticised the Santo Domingo Declaration and the Yaoundé recommendations *inter alia* because of their failure to make any reference to international standards and dispute settlement procedures applicable to coastal State resources jurisdiction.[121] The detailed working papers on fishery management prepared by Canada [122] and by Australia and New Zealand [123] are interesting in this context because, while sympathetic to the EEZ concept [124] and clearly designed to emphasise the comprehensive jurisdictional powers of the coastal State, they also provide for a minimal international element and, in the Australia/New Zealand proposals, for phasing-out of the rights of non-coastal State interests. Either or both of these ideas may help to make the EEZ concept more palatable.

The Canadian position may be summed up in this quotation:

> " The responsibilities which the coastal State must assume in maintaining resource productivity and quality, and the costs it bears in meeting this responsibility, must be balanced by the authority to manage and the *preferential right to utilise* adjacent living marine resources subject to internationally agreed principles." [125]

The Working Paper goes on to suggest basic principles for coastal State management but prefaces their elaboration with a recognition of the special interest of the coastal State as "an overriding principle." [126] *Inter alia*, the coastal State could reserve for itself a share—even up to 100 per cent.—proportionate to its needs and its capacity to exploit the stock in question (after allowing for conservation).[127] The minimal role envisaged for international institutions is reflected in the statement that

> " The concept of coastal state management of coastal species as ' custodian ' for the international community would not imply some form of close supervision over the exercise of powers and the discharge of responsibilities by the coastal state, but rather that the exercise of powers in accordance with internationally agreed criteria would be subject to appropriate dispute-settlement procedures." [128]

Thus, for example, if the coastal State were to reserve an entire stock to meet its own special needs, it might be required to submit a dispute to such procedures if it were alleged that the stock was as a result being under-utilised.[129]

The Australia/New Zealand Working Paper is partly based on, and is broadly similar to, the Canadian paper and, like it, provides for compulsory jurisdiction over allegations of under-exploitation or departures from conservation principles. It is, however, more explicit as regards jurisdiction over foreign vessels and contains proposals for " phasing out."

On the first point, the coastal State is to have powers to board, arrest and detain foreign fishing vessels and to institute proceedings in its own courts for breach of licence conditions or of laws or regulations applying in the zone.[130]

The "phasing out" proposal would apply where the coastal State intended to allocate to itself the whole allowable catch of a species and another State could show that its vessels had fished the stock on a substantial scale for not less than—tentatively—10 years. In such cases, there would be an obligation to negotiate special arrangements for phasing out the foreign vessels, with a mandatory phasing out period of—tentatively—five years if no agreement was reached.[131]

Whether even these modest proposals for compulsory jurisdiction will be acceptable to EEZ advocates must be regarded as extremely doubtful. They may, however, recognise, as Mexico has done,[132] the desirability of a phasing-out provision.

(f) *Other sympathetic States.* Space will permit reference to only a few representative views, some of which are less sympathetic to the EEZ concept than others.

CHINA has not made any extensive claims herself, but has given vigorous support to those States which have made 200 mile claims and has spoken in favour of it being the sovereign right of each State to determine its own territorial sea.[133] China is clearly vitally concerned with the submarine resources of the seas bordering the Chinese mainland.

INDONESIA considers that the EEZ "merits serious consideration" and favours its extension for 200 miles from the *outer* limit of the territorial sea.[134] Considering the difficulties already experienced in winning recognition of its archipelago claims, this is nothing if not a bold initiative.

IRAN has noted a growing tendency to link the extent of fishery zones with the extent of the continental shelf and regards this trend as justified since many of the most productive fisheries are in the relatively shallow shelf waters. Iran for this reason finds the idea of the EEZ attractive.[135]

Finally, the views of the UNITED KINGDOM may be noted. The United Kingdom feels that a consensus is emerging on a 12 mile territorial sea and that many of the claims greatly in excess of 12 miles, being claims to rights falling well short of sovereignty, are not necessarily incompatible with a 12 mile settlement.[136] It must also be said, of course, that the United Kingdom is vitally concerned with passage through straits and freedom of navigation generally and that it is opposed to control of fisheries being vested in the coastal State.[137] It is, however, well disposed towards a differentiation between the territorial sea and a functional zone or zones beyond and may be prepared to compromise if navigational rights are secured and reasonable transitional arrangements can be worked out on the fisheries question.

(g) *Japan, the Soviet Union and the United States.* JAPAN is ready to agree to a 12 mile territorial sea, provided that other problems directly related to it are satisfactorily solved.[138] The most important of these is, of course, the fisheries problem. Briefly, Japan's proposal is that preferential fishing rights should be recognised for coastal States (i) to help promote expansion of the infant coastal fisheries of the *developing States* by allocating to them the maximum annual catch obtainable on the basis of their individual fishing capacity; and (ii) to minimise or redress certain disruptive socio-economic effects of competition on the small-scale coastal fisheries of *developed States* by allocating to them the minimum annual catch required for the continued operation on the existing scale of clearly and precisely defined small-scale coastal fisheries. Coastal States enjoying such preferential rights would be entitled to inspect or arrest vessels of distant-water fishing States violating the regulatory measures in their respective adjacent waters; *but*, the arrested vessel would be promptly delivered to the duly authorised officials of the flag State concerned.[139]

The Japanese proposals, being clearly designed to preserve as much of the interests of distant-water fishing fleets as is now politically possible, are unlikely to provide even a starting point for negotiation with the EEZ advocates.

The SOVIET UNION has quite specifically rejected 200 mile fishery claims and even the concept of extensive, exclusive fishing zones, arguing that scientific data shows this approach to be wasteful and that losses due to the under-catch of vast fish resources are particularly intolerable when a considerable part of the world population is starving.[140]

The Soviet recommendations—supported by a Soviet Bloc Declaration[141]—are that *developing States* should have the preferential right, in areas adjacent to a 12 mile territorial sea or fishing zone, to reserve for themselves a given share of the fish stock which their national fleets could harvest, this share to expand as their fishing capacity expands. Distant-water fleets would have the right to fish for the unreserved share of the stock, with proper regard for the needs of conservation.[142]

The UNITED STATES served notice of its attitude to the EEZ by proposing that the reference to the EEZ in the original version of the list of issues drafted by the developing States for Sub-Committee II of the Seabed Committee should be amended to include, in addition, the concepts of economic jurisdiction or economic rights beyond the territorial sea, thus keeping all options open.[143] As a result, the final list adopted by the Seabed Committee included an additional item on "Coastal State preferential rights or other non-exclusive jurisdiction over resources beyond the territorial sea."[144]

Instead of an EEZ, the United States has advocated the "species approach" to fisheries. A first draft of an Article embodying this approach was tabled in the Seabed Committee in August 1971[145] but it was revised twice in 1972 in response to the needs, economic and social, of coastal States and amended to allow for a greater role for the coastal State. In introducing the first set of revisions in March 1972, Ambassador McKernan summarised the species approach to coastal stocks as follows:

> "Overall three-quarters of the world's marine fish catch is composed of coastal and anadromous species. Effective management and conservation of these species may be provided by granting coastal States clear and effective control over all such species, in the context of protecting other uses of the high seas. This concept includes inspection and arrest authority. The control exercised by the coastal States would follow such stocks as far offshore as the stock ranges. The coastal State would reserve to itself that portion of the allowable catch that it could utilise. The remaining portion of the allowable catch would be open to harvest on a non-discriminatory basis by fishermen of other nations but would be subject to the coastal State's non-discriminatory conservation measures, and reasonable management fees fixed in accordance with an international standard. The extent to which the coastal State preference should diminish traditional distant water fisheries—or vice versa—would be dealt with under a reasonable compromise provision in the treaty. . . ."[146]

The revised version made provision for the regulatory authority of the coastal State over coastal species; for non-discriminatory management fees; for a right of inspection and arrest. It was also made clear that "Non-discriminatory access to coastal stocks on the part of distant-water fishermen should not preclude reciprocal and other special arrangements among States in a region."[147]

In August 1972, the United States introduced in the Seabed Committee a "Revised

Draft Fisheries Article"[148] which goes further to meet the needs of the developing coastal States. Very briefly, the five main points to note are these: (1) the coastal State may annually reserve to itself such portion of coastal resources as it can harvest; (2) in disputes over the validity of the coastal State's conservation measures, such measures would remain in force pending settlement of the dispute; (3) the coastal State would grant access under reasonable conditions to the share of the stock not fully utilised by its vessels on the basis of these priorities: (i) traditional fishing States; (ii) other States in the region, particularly land-locked States and others with limited access to the resource, and (iii) other States, without discrimination; (4) the coastal State may punish foreign fishermen for infringement of its regulations provided that the flag State does not have machinery to punish the offender for that infringement; (5) finally, provision is made for compulsory jurisdiction and binding awards in any dispute arising under this article.

Once again, it seems unlikely that points (4) and (5) will be acceptable to EEZ advocates even if the remaining points are.

In an earlier statement it was claimed that the species approach:

> " more closely reflects the biological and economic realities upon which any sound accommodation of interests should be based. While a basic rule of law would be established, the effects of its application would vary with different economic conditions in different parts of the world. The fact that different coastal States have different interests in fisheries itself commends a certain flexibility, but does not mean that there can be no universal rules. It merely means that the rules should require a balancing of interests and not forejudge what the particular result should be with respect to every stock of fish in every part of the world. Such rules could be formulated to make maximum use of international or regional fisheries organisations."[149]

A concrete application of the American approach may be seen in the U.S.–Brazilian Agreement on Shrimp, signed on May 9, 1972,[150] without prejudice to the position of the two States on Brazil's 200 mile territorial sea claim. The United States agreed to license and control the numbers of American shrimp boats in specified areas within the 200 mile zone; authorised Brazil to board and search American vessels in that zone and to seize and detain any such vessel reasonably believed to have violated the Agreement. The institution of proceedings against such vessels is, however, reserved to the United States, to which Brazil is bound to hand over detained vessels as soon as practicable. The United States further agreed to pay the Brazilian Government for its part in enforcing the agreement the sum of $200,000 per annum and $100 for each day an American shrimping boat is under the control of the Brazilian enforcement authorities.[151]

It is hoped by the American government that this experiment, which allows conservation, while at the same time protecting at a reasonable level the interests of foreign fishermen, will commend itself to Peru and Ecuador and provide a model for similar accommodations with other States. It is, however, not at all certain that even this Agreement will last beyond January 1, 1974,[152] and there appears to be no evidence that other States find the formula attractive. Failing its adoption by other States, this model may still, however, be useful as an example of how competing interests may be accommodated during a transitional period before the establishment of an EEZ.

A further point to note about the Shrimp Agreement is that it affects only two States. It is clearly easier to reach agreement on a formula for allocating shares in a fishery when only two States are involved. It was perhaps for this reason that the

Icelandic Ambassador to the Seabed Committee was able to give only a qualified welcome to the American proposals of August 1971. Referring to the proposal that the allocation should be negotiated between coastal and distant water fishing States, Mr. Andersen commented that:

> "... the final solution would then depend on to what extent the distant water fishing nations in the region were willing to allocate to the coastal State.... Perhaps some formula can be found, which would clearly establish in what manner the general principle should be implemented, *i.e.*, of allocating to the coastal State that portion of the allowable catch that can be harvested by that State.... But in the meantime we do not see that the problem can be solved in any other way than through fishery limits beyond the territorial sea...." [153]

Earlier he had pointed out too that:

> "The real problem indeed does arise when the other nations of a given region do not want to give up their claims—when they perhaps all want to fish off the coasts of one nation in the region." [154]

(8) *The "Natural Law" argument*

It is, of course, quite possible to regard the EEZ concept as a helpful key to the whole question of maritime boundaries, without subscribing to many of the arguments of a somewhat natural law flavour advanced in its support. In view of the fact, however, that a judge of the International Court of Justice has now expressed opinions very much in line with the natural law approach, it may be worthwhile to examine the argument briefly. To state the conclusion first, it is the writer's view that the virtues of the EEZ concept can only be obscured by some of the pseudo-scientific arguments deployed in its support.

"Bioma" or "Ecosystem" theories. The "bioma" or "ecosystem" theories used to justify Latin-American claims are too well known to need more than passing reference. Some of the earlier statements of these theories have been criticised as pseudo-scientific. A typical example is to be found in a Peruvian statement in 1956. After explaining the circumstances brought about by the Humboldt Current (which flows along the coast of Peru, Chile and Ecuador), the Peruvian spokesman went on to say that:

> "Owing to the occurrence of these circumstances, Peru depends for its food supply mainly on the sea, that is to say directly on fish and indirectly on the guano which is essential to the farmers in the small coastal valleys. This is Peru's underlying motivation; the close relationship between man, the mainland and the sea in a particular country where the ecology is such that the biological balance must not be upset...." [155]

The United States has countered such arguments by pointing out that:

> "The communities that live in the sea do not in any sense require the coastal human populations to support their life.... Conversely while coastal communities, in some cases may depend upon the products of the sea for their sustenance, the relationship is first of all limited, and secondly, is far from an intimate biological relationship as suggested. The relationship of coastal communities to the sea is ... one of economic rather than biological character." [156]

It is perhaps less than the whole truth to say that coastal fish "do not in any sense require the coastal human populations to support their life." A Guyanese representative has recently argued, for instance, that the coastal State's exclusive right to exploit the living resources of its adjacent ocean space is justified "not only by the interrelationship of the land, its people and the adjacent ocean space *but also by the costs of keeping the adjacent ocean environment in a condition conducive to the survival and generation of fish.*" [157] More generally, however, the charges of pseudo-science seem justified. It is one thing to recognise "the natural relationship existing between the sea, the land and man who dwells on it, as well as . . . the economic, social and political implications resulting from this relationship." [158] It is quite another to accept such a relationship and its implications as justifying the particular legal claims made by *inter alia* the CEP States. The economic, social and political implications of this relationship may well be a very strong metalegal formative factor in bringing about a change in the law. Neither the natural relationship, however, nor its implications are a source of legal rights.

The related arguments that (1) "living resources closely related to the marine ecosystem of a particular country must be recognised as part of its natural resources" [159]; (2) that limits must be determined by geographical, geological, ecological and socio-economic factors [160]; and (3) that it would therefore be "an arbitrary act, *contra natura*" to establish a single limit all over the world [161] are no more convincing.

Iceland's case. It is one of the more refreshing features of the arguments deployed by the chief proponents of the EEZ concept that they eschew such thinking and base their case squarely on selfish interest and political calculation. It is, however, not only the Latin-American school which is expounding the "natural law" fallacy. Iceland, has also deployed this argument with skill—so skilfully indeed, it would appear, as to have persuaded the Mexican judge in the World Court (already open to persuasion in view of his country's policy) of the merits of the case.

The most comprehensive recent statement of Iceland's case is contained in *Fisheries Jurisdiction in Iceland*, published by the Ministry for Foreign Affairs in February 1972. This 46-page booklet refers time and time again to "Nature" and "natural resources." The following quotations represent the substance of Iceland's case:

1. "Marine products constitute between 80 and 90 per cent. of the exports of the country." [162]

2. "The coastal fisheries are the *conditio sine qua non* for the Icelandic economy; without them the country would not have been habitable. It is indeed as if Nature had intended to compensate for the barrenness of the country itself by surrounding it with rich fishing grounds." [163]

3. "Already . . . [in 1948] the fundamental proposition was that the coastal fisheries formed a part of the natural resources of the country within a reasonable distance from the coast in view of the relevant local considerations. Such considerations are evident in the case of Iceland. It is the continental shelf, the platform upon which the country rests, which provides the environment and the biological conditions required for the spawning areas, nursery grounds and food reservoirs for the fishstocks." [164] ". . . That environment is an integral part of the natural resources of the country." [165]

4. "We consider that the submarine platform on which Iceland rests is a natural continuation of the country itself, and the right of exploiting the continental seabed by the coastal State has achieved recognition. It is our opinion that the seabed of the continental shelf and the waters above it, together with the country itself form one physical and organic unit . . . and we consider it unnatural

that . . . [vessels of other nations] should be able without our permission to prosecute fishing in the sea above our continental shelf." [166]

In a speech in the Seabed Committee on August 6, 1971, Mr. Andersen sought to invoke the authority of the World Court in support of this position:

> " The basic principle should be that the coastal fisheries formed part of the natural resources of the coastal State. In other words, the principles laid down by the International Court of Justice in the Anglo-Norwegian Fisheries Case should apply. The Court had said that it was the land that conferred upon the coastal State the right to the waters off its coast. More recently, the Court had stressed the fact that the continental shelf was a natural prolongation of the territory." [167]
>
> 5. " [We] hope that . . . [the] reaction [of other nations] will be to recognise the proper place of Iceland—to assume her role in the international division of labour which has been allotted to Iceland by Nature, *i.e.* to produce the goods which are derived from the only available natural resources for the benefit of the Icelandic nation and her friends." [168]
>
> 6. " Account must be taken of the fact that many new states have emerged who rightly consider that coastal fishing resources are a part of the natural resources of the coastal nation and that is, indeed, the predominant view of the international community today." [169]
>
> 7. " The essential thing is to recognise the basic principle that to the extent that the coastal State is willing and able to utilise its coastal fishery resources it should be allowed to do so." [170]
>
> 8. " [Iceland] considers that it is unrealistic that foreigners can be prevented from pumping oil from the continental shelf but that they cannot in the same manner be prevented from destroying other resources which are based on the same seabed." [171]

Many of these statements and invocations of " Nature " do of course contain forceful arguments *de lege ferenda* and sympathy for the Icelandic case and recognition of the need for preferential treatment of some kind are practically universal. When the case is examined *de lege lata*, however, there are really only two arguments of any substance at all. The first argument starts from the respectable premise that the continental shelf is the natural prolongation of the land territory [172]; the next step is already suspect —the statement that " the right of exploiting the continental seabed by the coastal State has achieved recognition." This is only a half-truth because, of course, such recognition is limited to the natural resources of the continental shelf which the great majority of States, including the 51 parties to the Continental Shelf Convention (1958), do not interpret to include the living resources in the superjacent waters.[173] The third step is to state that the country, the seabed of the continental shelf and the superjacent waters are one unit and it is " unnatural " that others should fish those waters. The failure to claim that it would be not only " unnatural " but actually " illegal " is significant. Finally, the fourth step in the argument is equally imperfect. Two isolated dicta of the World Court are cited in support of the principle which " should apply." The references are brief and unelaborated for the very good reason that they do not on closer examination support the case being argued. No one denies that " the land . . . confers upon the coastal state a right to the waters off its coasts " [174] but the obvious rejoinder is to refer to another dictum from the same *Anglo-Norwegian Fisheries Case* —where the Court emphasised that the validity of a unilateral act of delimitation with regard to other States depends upon international law.[175] Similarly, the reference to the Court's "natural prolongation" dictum in the *North Sea Continental Shelf Case* has really no bearing on jurisdiction over living resources in the waters above the continental shelf.[176]

The only other legal argument is that it is the predominant view of the international community today that coastal fishery resources are a part of the natural resources of the coastal nation (quotation 6 above). It should be obvious from the tables and analysis presented earlier in this paper that the scope *ratione loci* of this view is very much in dispute and that such views are clearly in many cases *de lege ferenda*.

The Padilla Nervo opinion. As mentioned above, the Icelandic argument received a sympathetic response from Judge Padilla Nervo in his Dissenting Opinion in the *Interim Measures of Protection* phase of the *Fisheries Jurisdiction Case* (1972). Thus, he referred to the "natural prolongation" dictum of the Court in the *North Sea Continental Shelf Case* as supporting the claim of Iceland that its continental shelf must be considered to be a part of the country itself.[177] This woolly proposition once established, he was then in a position to criticise the Order of the majority of the Court ordering interim measures as being "obviously against Iceland, interfering with its indisputable rights to legislate over its own territory as it considers essential."[178] The lack of precision in the original proposition which alone permitted the later criticism to be made hardly needs to be underlined. To describe the continental shelf *simpliciter* as "part of the country itself" is to invite confused thinking.

Again, he spoke of the "well-founded reasons and explanations of [Iceland's] sovereign right to extend its fisheries jurisdiction to the entire continental shelf area"[179] and paraphrased the above-quoted Icelandic arguments. It became clear, however, from later passages in his Opinion that its foundation lay in his adherence to the concept of the patrimonial sea. In one passage he stated that:

> "The international community has increasingly recognised that the coastal fishery resources are to be considered as a part of the natural resources of the coastal State. The special situation of countries who are overwhelmingly dependent on coastal fisheries was generally recognised at both Geneva Conferences in 1958 and 1960. Since then this view has found frequent expression both in the legislation of various countries and in important political statements. The course of events is decidedly progressing in this direction."[180]

In a later passage, Judge Padillo Nervo referred to "the living resources of the sea covering their continental shelf and in the fishery zone contiguous to their territorial sea" as being "the most essential asset of coastal States,"[181] thus implying their exclusive jurisdiction over such resources. He went on to say that:

> "The progressive development of international law entails the recognition of the concept of the patrimonial sea, which extends from the territorial waters to a distance fixed by the coastal State concerned, in exercise of its sovereign rights, for the purpose of protecting the resources on which its economic development and the livelihood of its people depends [*sic*].
>
> This concept is not a new one. It has found expression in declarations by many governments proclaiming as their international maritime policy, their sovereignty and exclusive fisheries jurisdiction over the sea contiguous to their shores."[182]

The only evidence specified consisted of nine 200 mile exclusive fishery claims and the Santiago Declaration signed by the CEP States in 1952.[183]

Once again, the comment seems justified that the cause of the progressive development of international law would be better served if the argument proceeded from a bona fide analysis of the present law, through current trends, to reasoned recommendations for changes in the law.

(9) *The continental shelf and the EEZ*

It is of course less easy to tabulate continental shelf claims than the other claims considered above since, in a great many cases, States have adopted a formula for determination of the outer limit which does not lend itself to simple quantification in terms of distance from the coast. The writer has commented extensively elsewhere on the problem of the limits of the continental shelf[184] and, since 1968, has argued the merits of attempting to agree upon 200 miles as the outer limit of the continental shelf.[185] Although this proposal was arrived at primarily on the basis of an analysis of the legal problem of the outer limit of the continental shelf and of the metalegal factors affecting its determination, it was also considered:

> " desirable that any new régime should be capable of facilitating a settlement with the Latin-American States over the question of delimitation of maritime areas. Agreement on a 200 mile limit would go someway in this direction though, in itself, it would not of course deal with the more extreme claims to exclusive fisheries and rights of jurisdiction over the superjacent high seas."[186]

It was hoped when this suggestion was made that it might still be possible to settle the continental shelf limit as a separate question and to work towards recognition of different limits for other functions such as fishing and pollution control. This hope no longer seems justifiable in the light of the recent trends considered above and the more realistic view would now appear to be to recognise that the arguments favouring a continental shelf of a maximum of 200 miles are now reinforced by strong arguments for an exclusive zone of the same extent for other economic functions also. There might be an argument for stressing that this is a maximum limit and that the actual permissible extent of the zone would have to be justified in each case by reference to "geographical, geological, ecological and socio-economic factors."[187] This would certainly be more acceptable to States such as the United Kingdom which is already finding difficulty in accepting Iceland's 50 mile claim. The difficulties inherent in such a flexible formula are also very obvious, however. In the almost certain absence of a generally accepted means of compulsory settlement of disputes, claims would tend to be unilateral assertions and to be highly inflationary.

The opposition of the satisfied States to any such formula is of course predictable. Their long-term interests might, however, be better served by recognising now what they may well be obliged to recognise fairly soon in any event and by concentrating on such questions as phasing out arrangements for the surrender of fishing rights in the offshore waters of foreign States and the negotiation of concession-rights in such waters; satisfaction on the territorial sea straits question; careful delimitation of the anti-pollution jurisdiction of the coastal State; and the establishment of a mechanism to ensure that "the heritage of mankind," the resources of the seabed and subsoil in part at least of the 200 mile zone, is shared with the international community. The prospects of agreement on any such sharing have not been improved by the poor reception accorded to the concept of an intermediate zone, as proposed by the United States.[188] Whether the EEZ advocates can be persuaded to contribute to an international fund in some other form seems doubtful. However, the kind of regional co-operation which some of them envisage, involving co-operative ventures with land-locked States,[189] may in practice be just as useful, if only because more practicable.

Failing such a compromise solution, it seems only too likely that it will not be found possible to agree upon a revision of the unsatisfactory definition of the continental shelf in the Geneva Convention on the Continental Shelf (1958) and that, in the words of preambular Paragraph 2 of the Declaration of Principles Governing the Seabed, it will be possible only to affirm "that there is an area of the seabed and the ocean floor, and the subsoil thereof, beyond the limits of national jurisdiction, the precise limits of which are yet to be determined."[190]

In assessing the political feasibility of a 200 mile EEZ in the light of previously expressed opposition to recognition of an extensive distance limit, the following factors should be borne in mind: (1) nine States[191] already claim either a continental shelf or, more comprehensively, a territorial sea of 200 miles; (2) four more States have expressed a preference for a 200 mile territorial sea or seabed area (Cameroon, France, India and Pakistan)[192]; (3) a large and growing group of Asian, African and Latin American States favour a 200 mile EEZ and their views can be seen to be gradually crystallising in the proceedings of a number of regional conferences on the law of the sea[193]; (4) China is actively supporting the 200 mile claim of other States[194]; (5) finally, many States such as the United Kingdom already enjoy very extensive continental shelves under the 200 metre formula in the Geneva Convention.

CONCLUSION

The slow progress being made in the preparations for the United Nations Conference on the Law of the Sea and the profusion of proposals on every aspect of maritime limits which are still on the table make prediction of new directions in the law of the sea a hazardous occupation. The strength of the opposition of some of the leading maritime Powers to the EEZ concept is obviously formidable and undue optimism that a solution can be arrived at on this basis is not to be encouraged. It would, however, seem fair to conclude that the prospects for a successful conference are extremely dim and that, accordingly, the present chaotic situation can only worsen in the future if this concept is not adopted as the foundation upon which a new order may be constructed.

REFERENCES

1. J. Selden, *Mare Clausum*, 1635. See too S. de Freitas, *De Justo Imperio Lusitanorum Asiatico*, 1625 and C. G. Alexandrowicz, "Freitas Versus Grotius" (1959) 35 B.Y.I.L.
2. C. J. Colombos, *The International Law of the Sea*, 1967, p. 48.
3. *Ibid.* p. 52.
4. *Ibid.* p. 53.
5. It is of topical interest to recall that "The claims of England were partly due to the assistance which the British Navy rendered to international commerce, but in the seventeenth century, when they were warmly disputed by the Dutch, they were based principally on the right to the fisheries in the North Sea. Thus James I forced foreigners to apply for fishing licences in that sea, and the omission by the Dutch to do so in 1636 enabled Charles I to extract the payment of £30,000 from them" (*Ibid.* p. 55).
6. *Ibid.* p. 49.
7. *Ibid.*
8. *Ibid.*
9. H. Grotius, *Mare Liberum*, 1609.

10. *Op. cit.* n. 2 *supra*, p. 48.

11. U.S. Dept. of State, " Status of the World's Nations " (*Geographic Bull.*, No. 2, revised Aug. 1969), App. II, updated from other sources.

12. A/RES/2768 (XXVI).

13. See below, text following n. 49.

14. 516 U.N.T.S. 205; U.K.T.S. No. 3 (1965), Cmnd. 2511.

15. Law No. 4 (1960) and Government Regulation No. 8 (1962).

16. *Cf.* statement by delegation of Fiji in Seabed Committee on Mar. 10, 1972: "... oceanic archipelagic waters would be subject to the general principle of the law of the sea set out in Article 5, paragraph 2, of the 1958 Convention on the Territorial Sea and Contiguous Zones, namely that the right of communication should be preserved. The best way of guaranteeing that right to other States would be to equate archipelagic waters with international straits." (A/AC.138/SR.73, p. 5.)

17. Mr. Stevenson's statement of Aug. 3, 1971 ((1971) 10 Int.Leg.Mat. 1013, at p. 1015) specifically referred to an earlier statement by the delegation of Fiji.

18. See, *e.g.*, Japanese statement in *Asian-African Legal Consultative Committee*, *Report of the Thirteenth Session*, Lagos, Jan. 1972 (Hereafter *Asian-African Report* (*1972*)), p. 329, at pp. 331–332. The expected independence of the Bahamas in 1973 will introduce another strategically placed archipelago into the picture.

19. The following passage appears in the Report of Sub-Committee II of the Seabed Committee on the work of its 1972 session:

> " It was also added that the special interests and needs of archipelagic States with regard to economic development, political stability and national security would require a special régime which would also accommodate other interests by providing for the innocent passage of foreign ships through designated sealanes in archipelagic waters." (A/AC.138/83, p. 16.)

The following symbols are used in this and subsequent notes to refer to the Documents and Summary Records of the UN Committee on the Peaceful Uses of the Seabed and the Ocean Floor beyond the Limits of National Jurisdiction (Seabed Committee) and its three Sub-Committees:

Plenary Committee: Documents: A/AC.138/1 *et seq.*
Summary Records: A/AC.138/SR.1 *et seq.*

Sub-Committee I: Documents: A/AC.138/SC.I/L.1 *et seq.*
Summary Records: A/AC.138/SC.I/SR.1 *et seq.*

Sub-Committees II and III. Mutatis mutandis, as for Sub-Committee I.

20. On Tables III–V, see also text below, following n. 46.

21. The Office of the Geographer, U.S. Dept. of State has published a very useful map: " World Straits Affected by a 12 Mile Territorial Sea " (510376 2–71). On the Malacca Straits, see also n. 40 below.

22. See further on the straits question, E. D. Brown, *Arms Control in Hydrospace: Legal Aspects* (Woodrow Wilson International Center for Scholars, 1971), pp. 21–22 and 92–94.

23. (1970) 9 Int.Leg.Mat. 807 at 809.

24. *Asian-African Report* (*1972*), p. 298.

25. *Ibid.* p. 30.

26. A/AC.138/SC.II/L.4; (1971) 10 Int.Leg.Mat. 1018.

27. (1971) 10 Int.Leg.Mat. 1013 at 1015.

28. A/AC.138/SC.II/SR.37 (July 31, 1972), pp. 2–5.

29. On IMCO's work on traffic separation schemes, see statement by T. A. Mensah in Seabed Sub-Committee III on July 26, 1972.

30. *Loc. cit.* in n. 26 above. On U.S. attitude to archipelagic straits, see n. 16 above.

31. A/AC.138/SC.II/SR.37 (July 31, 1972), p. 5.

32. A/AC.138/SC.II/SR.27 (Mar. 24, 1972), p. 6.

33. U.S.S.R., *Draft articles on straits used for international navigation*, A/AC.138/SC.II/L.7 (July 25, 1972).

34. *Asian-African Report* (*1972*), p. 237. See too Mr. Stevenson's firm statement of Aug. 10, 1972 in Seabed Committee.

35. *Asian-African Report* (*1972*), p. 303.

36. L. Ratiner, Chairman, Defense Advisory Group on Law of the Sea, U.S. Department of Defense, in Hearings on Territorial Sea Boundaries before Sub-Committee on Sea-Power of House of Representatives Committee on Armed Services, June 25, 1970 (H.A.S.C. No. 91–61) at p. 9291.

37. *Asian-African Report* (*1972*), p. 320.

38. A/AC.138/SC.II/SR.42 (Aug. 10, 1972), pp. 2–3.

39. A/AC.138/SC.II/SR.40 (Aug. 7, 1972), pp. 4–6.

40. In a joint statement issued on Nov. 16, 1971 by Indonesia, Malaysia and Singapore (*Lloyd's List*, Nov. 17, 1971).

41. A/AC.138/SC.II/SR.31 (Apr. 3, 1972), p. 20. See also on U.S. policy on archipelagic straits, text above at n. 16 and nn. 16 and 17.

42. "List of subjects and issues relating to the law of the sea to be submitted to the Conference of the Law of the Sea," A/AC.138/66 (Mar. 24, 1972).

43. *Per* Mr. Stevenson in A/AC.138/SC.II/SR.29 (Mar. 29, 1972), p. 14. U.S. proposed amendments to List are in A/AC.138/68 (Mar. 29, 1972).

44. The List is reproduced in Report of Sub-Committee II, A/AC.138/83 (Aug. 18, 1972), at pp. 17–22.

45. *Per* Mr. Stevenson's statement of Aug. 16, 1972 in Sub-Committee II.

46. See above, p. 161.

47. Decree of Nov. 6, 1971.

48. In the case of Ecuador, provision is made for the establishment of "different zones of the territorial sea by executive decree . . . [which] shall be subject to the régime of free maritime navigation or of innocent passage for foreign ships" (F. V. Garcia-Amador, *Latin America and the Law of the Sea* (Law of the Sea Institute, University of Rhode Island, Occasional Paper No. 14, July 1972), p. 2. The position of the Latin American States is discussed further below, at pp. 169, 174–175 and 181–182.

49. At pp. 157–159.

50. See, *e.g.*, Soviet statement in *Asian-African Report* (*1972*) at p. 37.

51. The "comparatively small share of many developing countries in world fisheries, the effect of long-range fishery operations of certain countries with developed fisheries" was recognised as a "disturbing feature" in a recent FAO report. See statement by Observer for the FAO in *Asian-African Report* (*1972*), at p. 307.

52. See further E. D. Brown, *op. cit.* in n. 22 above.

53. Environmental protection and safe navigation may of course impose further controls, some of which may be unilaterally prescribed and abusively administered.

54. *E.g.*, the National Petroleum Council in the U.S.A. See their report on *Petroleum Resources Under the Ocean Floor*, 1969 and *Supplemental Report*, 1971.

55. A/AC.138/SC.II/SR.31 (Apr. 3, 1972), p. 31.

56. Press Release SB/70, July 27, 1972.

57. Until recently, the change awaited Presidential confirmation. See (1971) 10 Int.Leg. Mat. 1272, n. 5.

58. *Asian-African Report* (*1972*), p. 259.

59. A/AC.138/SC.II/SR.31 (Apr. 3, 1972), p. 2.

60. By decree dated Nov. 6, 1971.

61. L. M. Alexander and E. W. S. Hull, *The Law of the Sea. A Statistical Summary of the Practice of States*, Nautilus Press, 1971.

62. A/C.1/PV.1781 (Dec. 2, 1970), p. 42.

63. A/C.1/PV.1783 (Dec. 3, 1970), p. 82.

64. A/C.1/PV.1799 (Dec. 15, 1970), pp. 42, 47, 63 and 66.

65. *Ibid.* p. 51.

66. *Ibid.* pp. 69–70.

67. *Ibid.* pp. 52–55.

68. See Belgium, *ibid.* p. 56, and Haiti, A/C.1/PV.1798 (Dec. 15, 1970), pp. 18–26.

69. A/C.1/PV.1776 (Nov. 30, 1970), p. 41.

70. A/AC.138/SR.50 (Mar. 18, 1971), p. 7.

71. *Asian-African Report* (*1972*), p. 318.

72. *Ibid.* p. 284. The Soviet Union has repeatedly tried to win the support of the land-locked States by stressing that the establishment of an Exclusive Economic Zone would jeopardise their economic position. See *e.g.*, Byelorussian statement in A/AC.138/SC.II/SR.43 (Aug. 18, 1972), pp. 13–16.

73. See below, text following n. 95.

74. As provided for in Geneva Convention on the Territorial Sea and the Contiguous Zone 1958, Art. 24.

75. See especially KENYA: statement by Mr. Njenga in *Asian-African Report (1972)*, pp. 209–214 and his Working Paper on *The Exclusive Zone Concept*, *ibid.* pp. 369–374; Mr. Njenga in A/AC.138/SC.II/SR.29 (Mar. 28, 1972), pp. 5–8 and in A/AC.128/SC.II/SR.42 (Aug. 10, 1972), pp. 3–4, and the *Draft Articles on Exclusive Economic Zone Concept*, A/AC. 138/SC.II/L.10 (Aug. 7, 1972). MEXICO: statements by Mr. Castañeda in A/AC.138/SC.II/SR.30 (Mar. 29, 1972), pp. 6–12 and in A/AC.138/SC.II/SR.42 (Aug. 10, 1972), pp. 5–6. TANZANIA: statements by Mr. Warioba in *Asian-African Report (1972)*, pp. 35–36 and in A/AC.138/SC.II/SR.28 (Mar. 24, 1972). VENEZUELA: statement by Mr. Aguilar in A/AC. 138/SR.64 (Aug. 12, 1971).

76. *Asian-African Report (1972)*, p. 210.

77. *Ibid.* p. 373.

78. A/AC.138/SC.II/L.10 (Aug. 7, 1972).

79. A/AC.138/SC.II/SR.29 (Mar. 31, 1972), p. 7 and Kenyan Draft Article XI.

80. See, *e.g.*, French statement in A/AC.138/SC.II/SR.27 (Mar. 22, 1972), p. 11 and statements by Indian and Pakistani spokesmen in *Asian-African Report (1972)*, pp. 273 and 323.

81. Kenyan Draft Article V. On legal problems of marine scientific research see E. D. Brown, "Freedom of Scientific Research and the Legal Regime of Hydrospace" (1969) 9 *Indian Journal of International Law* 327–380.

82. Japan, Working Paper on *Proposed Régime concerning Fisheries on the High Seas*, *Asian-African Report (1972)*, pp. 339–367.

83. *Asian-African Report (1972)*, p. 285.

84. Kenyan Draft Article III.

85. *Asian-African Report (1972)*, p. 371.

86. A/AC.138/SC.II/SR.29 (Mar. 31, 1972), p. 7.

87. Seabed Committee, Aug. 14, 1972 (Press Release SB/82).

88. A/AC.138/SC.II/SR.30 (Mar. 31, 1972), p. 11. See too text following n. 129 for reference to "phasing-out" proposals in an Australian–New Zealand Working Paper.

89. See further E. D. Brown, "British Fisheries and the Common Market" (1972) 25 *Current Legal Problems* 37–73.

90. *Asian-African Report (1972)*, p. 214.

91. *Ibid.* p. 286.

92. *E.g.*, Soviet statement in A/AC.138/SC.II/SR.27 (Mar. 22, 1972), pp. 7–11.

93. Tanzanian statement in *Asian-African Report (1972)*, pp. 285–286, Kenyan statement in A/AC.138/SC.II/SR.29 (Mar. 31, 1972), p. 7 and Kenyan Draft Article V.

94. As outlined in A/AC.138/SC.II/SR.30 (Mar. 31, 1972), pp. 6–12.

95. *Asian-African Report (1972)*, pp. 284–285.

96. See text above, at n. 61 and following.

97. A/AC.138/SC.II/SR.29 (Mar. 31, 1972), p. 8.

98. Footnote added. Sudan responded favourably to Kenyan Draft Article VI in Seabed Committee on Aug. 14, 1972 (Press Release SB/82, p. 5).

99. *Asian-African Report (1972)*, pp. 372–373.

100. *Supra*, following n. 47.

101. Law 13.833 of Dec. 23, 1969 (*Diario Oficial*, Jan. 5, 1970) Art. 3, reproduced in Garcia-Amador, *loc. cit.* in n. 48 above, at p. 39.

102. *Asian-African Report (1972)*, pp. 265 and 423–424.

103. *Ibid.* p. 371.

104. (1970) 64 A.J.I.L., 1021, or (1970) 9 Int.Leg.Mat. 1081.

105. (1971) 10 Int.Leg.Mat. 207.

106. A/AC.138/80 (July 26, 1972); (1972) 11 Int.Leg.Mat. 892.

107. Emphasis added. On the meaning of continental rise and related terms, see E. D. Brown, *The Legal Regime of Hydrospace*, 1971, "Note on Submarine Geology," pp. 74–78.

107a. The Venezuelan statement on the patrimonial sea made in 1971 (see n. 75 above) also envisaged the possibility of the continental shelf extending beyond 200 miles.

108. Seabed Committee, July 24, 1972 (Press Release SB/67). See too the reserved attitude of Ecuador in Seabed Committee, July 27, 1972 (Press Release SB/70).

109. *Asian-African Report* (*1972*), pp. 306–307.

110. *Asian-African Report* (*1972*), p. 433 (Appendix V).

111. See *Report of 4th CSA Meeting* (*ibid.* Appendix VI), p. 435, at p. 452.

112. *Ibid.*

113. *Loc. cit.* in n. 75 above.

114. *Conclusions in the General Report of the African States Regional Seminar on the Law of the Sea, held in Yaoundé*, June 20–30, 1972, A/AC.138/79 (July 21, 1972). It should be emphasised that this was a seminar rather than a high level intergovernmental conference.

115. *Loc. cit.* in n. 75 above.

116. *Asian-African Report* (*1972*), pp. 271–277.

117. Seabed Committee, Aug. 14, 1972 (Press Release SB/82, p. 1).

118. *Ibid.* p. 4.

119. For text, see Icelandic Ministry for Foreign Affairs, *Fisheries Jurisdiction in Iceland*, Feb. 1972, p. 19.

120. See text above, at n. 78.

121. Seabed Committee, Aug. 10, 1972 (Press Release SB/80).

122. A/AC.138/SC.II/L.8 (July 27, 1972).

123. A/AC.138/SC.II/L.11 (Aug. 11, 1972).

124. Thus a Canadian spokesman emphasised (Press Release SB/71, July 28, 1972, p. 5) that the Canadian management concept was not inconsistent with, nor an alternative to the EEZ concept. Similarly, it is stressed in the Australia/New Zealand Working Paper that the fishery zone proposed " could be readily incorporated in, for example, an economic zone concept covering all resources, non-living as well as living " (*Loc. cit.* in n. 123, at p. 2).

125. *Loc. cit.* in n. 122 above, at p. 4.

126. *Ibid.* p. 5.

127. *Ibid.* pp. 6–8.

128. *Ibid.* p. 8.

129. *Ibid.*

130. A/AC.138/SC.II/L.11 (Aug. 11, 1972), p. 4 (VIII).

131. *Ibid.* p. 4 (VII).

132. See above, n. 88.

133. See, *e.g.*, first statement made by Chinese representative in Seabed Committee on Mar. 3, 1972 (1972) 11 Int.Leg.Mat. 654–661.

134. *Asian-African Report* (*1972*), pp. 327–328.

135. *Ibid.* p. 84.

136. A/AC.138/SC.II/SR.27 (Mar. 22, 1972), p. 5.

137. A/AC.138/SC.II/SR.31 (Apr. 3, 1972), p. 26.

138. *Asian-African Report* (*1972*), p. 202.

139. See Japanese statement in *Asian-African Report* (*1972*), pp. 200–208 and Working Paper on *Proposed Régime concerning Fisheries on the High Seas*, *ibid.* pp. 339–367; and statements in A/AC.138/SC.II/SR.31 (Apr. 3, 1972), pp. 3–8 and A/AC.138/SC.II/SR.43 (Aug. 18, 1972), pp. 2–4 and *Proposals for a Régime of Fisheries on the High Seas*, A/AC.138/SC.II/L.12 (Aug. 14, 1972).

140. *Asian-African Report* (*1972*), pp. 295–304.

141. *Declaration on Principles of Rational Exploitation of the Living Resources of the Seas and Oceans in the Common Interests of All Peoples of the World*, A/AC.138/85, Aug. 17, 1972.

142. A/AC.138/SR.27 (Mar. 24, 1972), pp. 9–10 and Draft Article on Fishing introduced in Seabed Committee on July 21, 1972 (A/AC.138/SC.II/L.6).

143. A/AC.138/SC.II/SR.29 (Mar. 31, 1972), pp. 13–15.

144. The list adopted is that approved by Sub-Committee II on Aug. 16, 1972. See text in *Report of Sub-Committee II* (A/AC.138/83, Aug. 18, 1972), pp. 17–22, especially items 6 and 7 which (*ibid.* p. 22) are to be treated simultaneously.

145. Text in General Assembly *Official Records:* Twenty-sixth Session, Supplement No. 21 (A/8421), Annex IV.

146. Text of Mr. McKernan's speech at p. 7; also reported in A/AC.138/SC.II/S.R.30 (Apr. 3, 1972), p. 12, at pp. 17–18.

147. *Ibid.* at p. 16.

148. A/AC.138/SC.II/L.9 (Aug. 4, 1972).

149. Text of Mr. Stevenson's speech in Seabed Committee on Mar. 18, 1971; also reported in A/AC.138/SR.51, at p. 9.

150. (1972) 11 Int.Leg.Mat. 453.

151. In terms of Exchange of Notes of May 9, 1972 (*ibid.* pp. 463–465).

152. Agreement, Art. XI.

153. *Loc. cit.* in n. 119 above, at p. 44.

154. *Ibid.* p. 38.

155. A/C.6/SR.486 (1956), cited by L. F. E. Goldie, " International Law of the Sea. A Review of States' Offshore Claims and Competences " (1972) XXIV *Naval War College Review* 43 at 50.

156. U.S. Dept. of State, *Santiago Negotiations on Fishery Conservation Problems*, 1955, p. 37, cited by Goldie, *loc. cit.* in n. 155 above, at p. 51.

157. A/AC.138/SC.II/SR.30 (Mar. 31, 1972), p. 6.

158. Address by Peruvian Observer in *Asian-African Report* (*1972*), at p. 421.

159. *Ibid.* p. 425.

160. *Ibid.* p. 421.

161. *Ibid.* pp. 422–423.

162. *Loc. cit.* in n. 119 above, at p. 13.

163. *Ibid.* at p. 7.

164. *Ibid.* at p. 29.

165. *Ibid.* at p. 32.

166. *Ibid.* at p. 35.

167. A/AC.138/SC.II/SR.9 (Aug. 12, 1971), p. 4.

168. *Loc. cit.* in n. 119, at p. 30.

169. *Ibid.* p. 37.

170. *Ibid.* p. 43.

171. *Ibid.* p. 38.

172. *North Sea Continental Shelf, Judgment* [1969] I.C.J.Rep. 3, at 22 (" natural prolongation " dictum).

173. See definition of natural resources in Art. 2 (4) of Geneva Convention on the Continental Shelf (1958).

174. *Anglo-Norwegian Fisheries Case* [1951] I.C.J.Rep. 116 at 133.

175. *Ibid.* 132.

176. *Loc. cit.* in n. 172 above. For an analysis of this case, see E. D. Brown, *The Legal Régime of Hydrospace*, 1971, esp. at pp. 32–35 and 41–73.

177. *Fisheries Jurisdiction* (*United Kingdom of Great Britain and Northern Ireland* v. *Iceland*), *Interim Protection Order of 17 August 1972* [1972] I.C.J.Rep. 12. Dissenting Opinion of Judge Padilla Nervo, 20–28, at 22.

178. *Ibid.* at 27.

179. *Ibid.* at 23.

180. *Ibid.*

181. *Ibid.* at 27.

182. *Ibid.*

183. *Ibid.*

184. *Op. cit.* in n. 176, esp. at pp. 36–40, 114–123 and 208–210.

185. E. D. Brown, *Report on the Legal Régime of Deep-Sea Mining* (British Branch of International Law Association, 1968), pp. 42–43, or " Deep-Sea Mining: The Legal Régime of Inner Space " (1968) 22 *Year Book of World Affairs*, at p. 180.

186. *Op. cit.* in n. 176 above, at p. 39.

187. N. 160 above.

188. In essence, the proposal was that in the zone between the 200 metre isobath and the edge of the continental margin, the coastal State would act as trustee for the international community and that part of the proceeds of exploitation of the resources of the seabed of this zone would accrue to an International Seabed Resources Authority. See further *Draft*

United Nations Convention on the International Seabed Area, General Assembly *Official Records:* Twenty-Fifth Session, Supplement No. 21 (A/8021), Annex V, esp. Chap. III and Appendix D.

189. See above, text following n. 95.

190. A/RES/2749 (XXV) (Dec. 17, 1970).

191. Argentina, Brazil, Chile, Ecuador, El Salvador, Panama, Peru, Sierra Leone and Uruguay.

192. See above, at n. 80.

193. See above, text following n. 103.

194. See above, at n. 133.

CHAPTER 15

Policing on the High Seas: With Special Reference to the North Sea

By A. De Smet *

I. INTRODUCTION

THIS paper is not a study of the provisions of international treaties or of customary international law establishing the legal régime of the high seas, but rather a general outline of the ways of ensuring on the high seas what might be called public order. It deals only with the position in time of peace. Freedom of the high seas is a fundamental principle of public international law; it may be regarded as constitutional law in the field of public international law.[1]† Consequently, by analogy with the state of affairs in the field of constitutional liberties in municipal law, there should be a tendency to limit police powers in a restrictive manner. This is all the more true since the high seas are not subject to national sovereignty.

The basic rule of policing the high seas, and which results from the principle of the freedom of the high seas, is that a State may only exercise jurisdiction over ships flying its flag, and may not interfere with ships flying any other flag. There are a number of general exceptions to this rule, provisions relating to which are found in the Geneva Convention on the High Seas. These are the repression of piracy and slavery, hot pursuit, and cases where a ship, though flying a foreign flag or refusing to show its flag, is, in reality, of the same nationality.[2] Traditionally a State exercises its jurisdiction and policing powers through its warships, although the Geneva Convention does provide for exceptions to this rule in the case of piracy and hot pursuit.

A number of particular and limited exceptions to the general rule of non-interference by States over ships flying the flags of other States have been established by international agreements, particularly between the States of the North Sea and North-East Atlantic. These relate to, *inter alia*, fisheries regulation, pollution control and the protection of submarine cables, and it is with these that this paper is chiefly concerned.

II. PARTICULAR CASES OF HIGH SEAS POLICING

(a) Fisheries regulation

An initial distinction must be drawn between, on the one hand, the high seas, where the freedom to fish is expressly recognised by Article 2 of the Geneva Convention on the High Seas, and, on the other, the exclusive fishing zone, territorial sea and internal waters, where States claim a monopoly of policing powers.

* Director-General of Administration, Ministry of Defence, Brussels.
† For references, see p. 204.

1. *The Prevention of Overfishing and the North-East Atlantic Fisheries Convention*

Overfishing is becoming a prime concern of mankind in search of means of subsistence adapted to the increasing needs of an expanding world population. As Colombos points out,[3] our knowledge of the living resources of the sea shows that it is absolutely necessary to adopt conservation measures: this leads to the necessity for international conventions.

The prevention of overfishing formed the subject of the Convention for the Regulation of the Meshes of Fishing Nets and the Size Limits of Fish of April 5,1946. This convention was replaced by the North-East Atlantic Fisheries Convention, which was signed at London on January 24, 1959, and came into force on June 27, 1963.[4] The North-East Atlantic Fisheries Commission, which is set up by the convention, may make recommendations concerning, *inter alia*, the size of meshes of fishing nets, minimum size of fish, closed seasons and closed areas.[5] Unless objected to, these recommendations are binding on the States parties to the convention.

The supervision and enforcement of these recommendations are organised at both the national and international level. Article 13 states:

> " (1) Without prejudice to the sovereign rights of States in regard to their territorial and internal waters, each Contracting State shall take in its territories and in regard to its own nationals and its own vessels appropriate measures to ensure the application of the provisions of this Convention and of the recommendations of the Commission which have become binding upon that Contracting State and the punishment of infractions of the said provisions and recommendations.
>
> " . . .
>
> " (3) The Commission may by a two-thirds majority make recommendations for, on the one hand, measures of national control in the territories of the Contracting States and, on the other hand, national and international measures of control on the high seas, for the purpose of ensuring the application of the Convention and the measures in force thereunder. . . ."

These provisions relating to control are obviously of the utmost importance since experience shows that " the fear of the gendarme is the beginning of wisdom." Therefore the Dutch and Belgian Governments, on depositing their instruments of ratification, declared that they would accept measures concerning closed periods, closed areas and the regulation of equipment, on the express understanding that an international control system be introduced at the same time.

The necessity for international control in order to attain the objects of this convention has been stated thus:

> " If the Commission is not in a position to utilise the new means of intervention that have been placed at its disposal, the elaboration of a new convention will prove useless. . . .
>
> " The adoption of [conservation] measures implies a preliminary international control. As a matter of fact, in the case of fishing on the high seas, for instance, it is obvious that the control must be exercised at international level. Otherwise there would be the risk of encountering paradoxical situations in which a supervisory ship of a given country would have the right to sanction a ship of the same nationality, but would have to allow a ship of another nationality to go on fishing quietly. International control is thus the foundation on which it is necessary to build the new system of conservation measures which the Commission has to adopt if it really wants to attain the objects the Convention has set for it." [6]

In order to answer this need for control, an International Control Committee was set up following a decision of the Commission. Year after year the necessity for international control on the high seas became more and more evident, and it was at the Sixth Meeting of the Commission at Reykjavik in May 1968 that an international control system was approved. This control system has formed the subject of a recommendation in pursuance of Article 13 (3) of the convention, to be applicable outside the territorial sea and exclusive fishing zone.[7]

The recommendation provides for the inspection of catches and nets. The truly international character of the control should be underlined: inspectors of the authorities responsible for the control of fisheries in the contracting States, sailing on board ships flying a special flag or pennant approved by the Commission and holding an identity document issued by the flag State in conformity with a form approved by the Commission, may board any fishing boat, accompanied by a witness. They may inspect the catches, nets and other equipment and any document connected therewith. Inspections must be executed so as to interfere with the activities of the ship as little as possible. Resisting an inspector or refusing to obey his directions shall be regarded by the flag State as equivalent to resisting an inspector of that State or refusing to conform to his directions.

The recommendation further provides for the drawing up of an inspection report: during his inspection, the inspector is authorised to ask the captain for any assistance he may require. He shall draw up his inspection report in the form approved by the Commission. He shall sign this report in the presence of the captain; the latter may cause any remarks he considers to be necessary to be added with his signature. Copies of this report shall be delivered to the captain and to the government of the inspector's State. This government shall send a duplicate to the competent authorities of the flag State of the inspected ship and to the Commission. When the inspector ascertains a violation of the regulations he shall also, as far as possible, notify the competent authorities of the flag State as well as any control ship of the flag State, the presence of which in the vicinity is known to him.

Contracting States shall consider the reports drawn up by foreign inspectors and comply with them as if these reports were issued by their own inspectors. These provisions, however, shall not constrain any contracting State to assign to a report issued by a foreign inspector a probative value superior to that which this report would have in the inspector's State. Contracting States are also to collaborate in facilitating the legal or other proceedings following upon a report issued in pursuance of these provisions.

It should be noted that the inspectors are to perform their tasks according to the rules established by the recommendation, but that they remain under the operational control of their national authorities to whom they are accountable.

It should further be noted that the fishing boat must stop when ordered to do so by a ship having an inspector aboard. This obligation does not exist, however, when the fishing boat is engaged in fishing, shooting or hauling in its nets: it must be added that, in general, inspections must be executed so as to interfere with the activities of the controlled ship as little as possible.

This limitation on inspection and control was criticised by the Belgian delegation at the Second Meeting of the International Control Committee, held at London on March 29–31, 1966, on the grounds that it makes avoidance of inspection relatively easy.

It must be added that it was not easy to prepare a text which would give satisfaction to everybody. In any case, reservations have been made to the recommendation.

At this Sixth Meeting of the Commission, the delegates of the contracting States agreed that, subject to the approval of their respective governments which was to be notified to the Secretariat of the Commission, and without prejudice to the rights of the contracting States derived from the provisions of paragraph 9 (ii) of the recommendation:

(a) the provisions of the recommendation relating to the inspection of equipment stowed under deck and of catches should not be operative between the Soviet Union and the other contracting States;

(b) the provisions of the recommendation relating to the inspection of equipment on catches under deck should not be operative between Poland and the other contracting States;

(c) the provisions of the recommendation relating to the inspection of equipment or catches under deck should not be operative between Sweden and the other contracting States before January 1, 1972, or at an earlier date if the Commission was notified thereof by the Swedish Government.

It was agreed that by reason of the legislative and administrative difficulties encountered by some States, the draft recommendation would not come into effect until January 1, 1970, and that the contracting States should submit their programme of participation in the scheme before March 1, 1969. On the other hand, the agreement of the delegations on the pattern of the special pennant flown by ships carrying international inspectors was deferred to the next meeting held at London in May 1969.

At this meeting, the delegations of Ireland, the Federal Republic of Germany and the Netherlands stated that there was a risk that they would be unable to put the system into operation on January 1, 1970, because of legislative difficulties. The Swedish delegation, which at the Sixth Meeting had drawn attention to the fact that it was necessary for Sweden to modify its national law, made it known that the problem would probably be solved within the time limits specified at the Sixth Meeting. Other delegations stated that they expected to be able to participate in the system of international control as from January 1, 1970. The Commission accepted the reservations submitted by the Soviet Union, Poland and Sweden at the previous meeting. The Polish delegation stated that the system would not be operative between Poland and those States with which it did not entertain diplomatic relations. The Portugese delegation reminded the Commission that their Government had submitted a similar reservation. The Spanish delegation stated that the system would not be operative between Spain and those countries which did not authorise Spanish inspectors to effect control on board their ships.

Those delegations which made it known that they were unable to bring the international control system into operation within the required time also stated that they upheld their agreement in principle to the system and that they still wanted to carry it into effect as soon as possible. Some delegations, however, raised the question as to whether the date of its coming into effect was to be maintained since some States were unable to participate in the system on this date. The Commission considered the possibility of postponing the date of the recommendation's coming into effect and examined whether countries with legislative difficulties might still be able to fulfil these obligations and participate in the international control system on January 1, 1970. After a discussion, the Commission confirmed its decision to maintain the coming into effect of the international control system on January 1, 1970. Those countries which were not able to put the system into operation on that date should attempt to resolve their legislative difficulties immediately and notify the Secretariat of the date on which they would be able to bring the international control scheme into operation.

At the Eighth Meeting, held at London in May 1970, the Commission heard the reports prepared by those States which had not been able to put the international control scheme into operation on January 1, 1970, and noted that some States would apply the system earlier than had been decided and that all States believed they would be ready in 1971. It expressed the hope that these States would join those which were already applying the international control system in the shortest possible time.

The number of inspections effected in connection with the scheme seems to have been small up to the present time, but it does not appear that serious practical difficulties have been encountered. It has also been agreed that inspection reports should be returned directly to the competent authorities of the flag State rather than through diplomatic channels, to avoid wasting time.

Finally, a word about the kind of ships undertaking control. We have seen above that policing on the high seas normally falls to warships. The conventional régime of policing as regards fisheries regulation has not followed the same pattern: according to the above-mentioned recommendation, any kind of ship may be specially assigned to surveillance.

2. *Policing of fishing activities on the high seas and the Convention on Conduct of Fishing Operations in the North Atlantic of 1967*

It is the policing of fishing operations as such, and not the avoidance of overfishing, which is aimed at here, *i.e.*, it is a question of maintaining order amongst the fishermen of different States.

The 1967 Convention, which is intended to replace the 1882 Convention for Regulating the Police of the North Sea Fisheries, contains provisions concerning the identification of fishing boats, especially as concerns the indication of fishing activities, and the marking of nets, lines and other fishing devices.

Unlike the Convention of 1882, the Convention of 1967 applies within the territorial sea. The convention has deliberately departed from a special régime applying to the territorial sea, but nevertheless reserves a right of policing for the coastal State within an area which is not the territorial sea but " the area where a coastal State has jurisdiction over fisheries." [8]

Because of divergent opinions, it was felt that to make the convention applicable only outside fishing limits would have been unreasonable; but to try and establish a system of international control (Art. 9) within these limits would have doomed the Convention to failure. It was therefore necessary to set up a system taking into account fishing limits in such a way that the relevant provisions would not be interpreted as interfering with the " rights, claims or views of any Contracting Party in regard to the limits of territorial waters or national fishery limits, or of the jurisdiction of a coastal State over fisheries " (Art. 2). However, it would be a mistake to overlook the fact that the equivocal situation covered by Article 2 is liable to create control rivalry within the fishing areas.

The 1967 Convention lays down the duties of control on the " authorised officers." Under Article 9 (4),

> "Authorised officers shall observe whether the provisions of the Convention are being carried out, inquire and report on infringements of the provisions of the Convention, seek information in cases of damage, where desirable draw the attention of vessels of Contracting Parties to the provisions of the Convention, and

co-operate for these purposes with the authorised officers of other Contracting Parties."

Like the 1882 Convention, the 1967 Convention provides that resistance to the instructions of commanders of vessels in charge of policing fishing or of those which are acting by their order should be considered as resistance to the national authorities of the fishing boat. The 1967 Convention also establishes within the sphere of international control the authorised officer's power to stop a ship, and even to go on board in two cases. Article 9 provides:

"... (5) If an authorised officer has reason to believe that a vessel of any Contracting Party is not complying with the provisions of the Convention, he may identify the vessel, seek to obtain the necessary information from the vessel and report. If the matter is sufficiently serious, he may order the ship to stop and, if it is necessary to verify the facts of the case, he may board the vessel for inquiry and report.

"(6) If an authorised officer has reason to believe that a vessel or its gear has caused damage to a vessel or fishing gear and that this may be due to a breach of the Convention, he may, under the same conditions as in the preceding paragraph, order any vessel concerned to stop and board it for inquiry and report."

Unlike the 1882 Convention, there is no mention of conducting the ship into port. This is hardly an improvement in the system of international control.

Other limitations on the international right of policing are imposed by the 1967 Convention. Thus Article 9 prescribes that:

"... (7) An authorised officer shall not order a fishing vessel to stop while it is actually fishing or engaged in shooting or hauling gear except in an emergency to avoid damage to vessels or gear.

"(8) An authorised officer shall not pursue his inquiries further than is necessary to satisfy him either that there has been no breach of the Convention or, where it appears to him that a breach has occurred, to secure information about the relevant facts, always acting in such a manner that vessels suffer the minimum interference and inconvenience.

"...

"(12) An authorised officer shall not exercise his powers to board a vessel of another Contracting Party if an authorised officer of that Contracting Party is available and in a position to do so himself."

Needless to say, these restrictions are likely to interfere to a considerable extent with international police control: on the one hand, the fishing boat actually engaged in fishing enjoys a kind of immunity, and on the other hand, the foreign authorised officer might be reluctant to act in all cases of uncertainty if there is the possibility of intervention by an authorised officer of the same nationality as the fishing boat.

It should also be stated that when the 1967 Convention intends to assign to a foreign authorised officer's reports the same value as to reports from national officers, it immediately lessens the effect of this international police measure by adding that no obligation may be derived therefrom "to give the report of a foreign authorised officer a higher evidential value than it would possess in the authorised officer's own country." We may therefore conclude that the 1967 Convention has been rather timid in organising a system of international control.

3. *Fishing Zones and the Fisheries Convention of 1964*

The convention enables the States parties to establish off their coasts two zones, the first going from nought to six miles, the second from six to 12 miles. In the inner zone, the coastal State has exclusive fishing rights and the jurisdiction relating thereto, it being understood that a transitional régime may be adopted for fishing by the other contracting parties who have been in the habit of fishing there (Arts. 2 and 9). In the outer zone, fishing rights are exercised by the coastal State and by the other contracting parties, the fishing boats of which have been accustomed to fish in this zone between January 1, 1953, and December 31, 1962.

The 1964 Convention does not alter the status of the territorial sea. That part of the fishing zone which extends beyond the territorial sea still pertains to the high seas. This means that the coastal State is invested with exclusive policing competence, even on the high seas, up to six miles, as far as fisheries are concerned, and, moreover, it has a monopoly of fishing there. In fact, the consequence of the 1964 Convention could be, strangely enough, that a coastal State having a territorial sea of only three miles would exercise on the high seas up to six miles a policing authority which it does not have under customary international law: in order to solve this difficulty, it should extend its territorial waters, thereby depriving Article 2 of the convention of its object. This would reduce the high seas to the same extent. As to the outer zone, the situation is even stranger. Here the convention grants the coastal State a limited policing competence: it may enforce on foreign fishermen the obligation to confine themselves to their habitual fishing and may, furthermore, regulate fishing there. But monopoly is out of the question here, and a State other than the coastal State might very well claim policing competence according to customary international law, as far as the ships flying its flag are concerned. This would lead to an overlapping of competence.[9] Here again, the coastal State could easily solve the question by extending its territorial waters to 12 miles. But this would once more be a reduction of the high seas. The 1964 Convention penalises coastal States which stick to a breadth of three miles for their territorial sea, establishing on their behalf within the three to six mile zone a policing authority contrary to customary international law, and which could be rejected by States not signatories to the convention. The convention also penalises such coastal States by making their policing authority in the outer zone coincide with that of other States, even if they have signed the convention. It goes without saying that the powers granted to the coastal State by Article 24 of the Geneva Convention on the Territorial Sea and the Contiguous Zone only concern policing powers extraneous to the policing of high seas fisheries: the establishment of a fishing zone beyond the territorial sea does not constitute an enlargement of the concept of the contiguous zone.[10]

As far as Western Europe is concerned, attention must also be paid to the Common Fisheries Policy of the EEC as laid down in Regulation No. 2141/70 of the Council of October 20, 1970.[11] This Regulation provides for equality of access to fishing zones, a principle from which the special provisions brought about by the enlargement of the European Communities only depart in a limited way and for a limited period. As a matter of fact, the co-existence of the EEC régime with the régime laid down by the 1964 Convention, together with the régime established by the four Geneva Conventions, where those enjoying the right to fish on the high seas may not have recognised the fishing zones of the 1964 Convention, may create a confused situation from the point of view of the exercise of policing rights: the law of the sea has no interest in allowing the existence of overlapping régimes. The simplest solution would be that the States parties to the 1964 Convention extend their territorial sea to six or even

12 miles, thus preventing any interference by non-signatory States in the fishing zones; foreign fishermen traditionally fishing there could be protected by a system similar to that of the present convention.

It is interesting to notice how the kinds of ships in charge of policing exclusive fishing zones vary. In the course of the different incidents that have been recorded from 1970 to 1972, the territorial sea and exclusive fishing zone have been policed by patrol-ships, escort vessels, coastguard vessels and revenue-cutters.[12]

In the face of the trend to increasing unilateral claims to maritime jurisdiction, we should be aware of the necessity of guiding this development so as to strengthen in a twofold manner policing on the high seas: first, by proceeding solely by agreement when extending any reserved policing zone and, secondly, by giving a marked international character to policing on the high seas outside reserved zones.

(b) The prevention of pollution

The necessity of taking action against pollution has induced some States to take unilateral measures, *e.g.*, Canada, the United Kingdom and the United States,[13] even for pollution taking place outside the territorial sea or contiguous zone. It may be observed, however, that the contiguous zone concept enables the coastal State to exercise its national policing rights so as to take action against pollution: although the contiguous zone is part of the high seas, the coastal State may intervene there in sanitary matters, following Article 24 (1) of the Convention on the Territorial Sea and the Contiguous Zone. This Article, however, only applies to action taken by the coastal State to prevent pollution of its territory or of its territorial sea.

But it is obvious that a satisfactory solution to the problem of pollution can only be found, as far as the high seas are concerned, through international agreement. When considering what has been achieved and what has been planned, we can make a distinction between pollution by oil and pollution by other waste.

The first international act which is important in this respect is the International Convention for the Prevention of Pollution of the Sea by Oil, signed at London on May 12, 1954, and amended in 1962, 1969 and 1971.[14] This convention prohibits the discharge of oil in certain zones or from certain ships. But it would be in vain to look in this convention for the organisation of a policing competence on the high seas. The convention is scrupulously respectful of the traditional régime of sovereignty. Nevertheless, it would have been perfectly possible for the maritime community to agree to a reciprocal control of ships suspected of causing oil pollution. Besides, Article 24 of the Convention on the High Seas enjoins every State "to draw up regulations to prevent pollution of the seas by the discharge of oil from ships. . . ." As far as the 1954 Convention is concerned, "the flag State alone remains competent to pursue and punish breaches of the Convention; this is one of the basic reasons for the inefficacy of its provisions, together with the difficulty of proving that the pollution originates from a particular ship."[15] The system of sanctions is scarcely adequate, since they are to be determined unilaterally by the contracting States (Art. 6 of the convention). The convention does not enjoin warships to inspect, verify or conduct suspected ships into a port of their nationality.

The Agreement for Co-operation in Dealing with Pollution of the North Sea by Oil, signed at Bonn on June 9, 1969, compels the parties to give mutual information as to accidents or the presence of oil slicks which might constitute a serious threat to their coasts or related interests, and to render mutual aid in combating such pollution. But however laudable the intention of this convention may be, it does not provide for any policing measures on the high seas: there are no provisions concerning the inspection or verification of suspected ships. This is a serious gap.

Real policing measures, which go very far and transcend traditional notions of policing rights, are provided for by a convention of an entirely new type, namely the Brussels Convention of November 29, 1969. Article I provides that, except for warships or other State-owned non-commercial ships,

> " [p]arties to the Convention may take such measures on the high seas as may be necessary to prevent, mitigate or eliminate grave and imminent danger to their coastline or related interests from pollution or threat of pollution of the sea by oil, following upon a maritime casualty or acts related to such casualty, which may reasonably be expected to result in major harmful consequences."

It is clear that these excessive powers, which allow the coastal State to board, divert or even bomb a ship on the high seas, may only be exercised under certain conditions of consultation and notification; intervention is limited to what is necessary and may possibly give rise to reparation. Moreover, the coastal State may only intervene in the case of an accident and should be as careful as possible to " avoid any risk to human life, and to afford to persons in distress any assistance of which they may stand in need, and in appropriate cases to facilitate the repatriation of ships' crews " (Art. III (e)). Even with these limitations, the Convention involves completely new powers of policing. " It is undeniably an exception to customary international law concerning the intervention of States on the high seas, since it permits a State, in time of peace, to take action against a foreign ship." [16]

It is, however, regrettable that the intervention of States entirely depends on national initiative—as a rule it is up to each coastal State to defend its own coasts. This leads us to the realisation that ultimately we must arrive at a common international policing and punishment agency. This would reinforce the idea that the freedom of the high seas is curtailed in the interests of the international community as a whole.

Pollution from dumping is the subject of the Oslo Convention of February 15, 1972, for the Prevention of Marine Pollution by Dumping from Ships and Aircraft. This convention does not set up an international policing agency on the high seas, but provides for a system for the mutual provision of information and co-operation. A Commission is set up in order to supervise the observance of the provisions of the convention prohibiting dumping. Article 15 (2) provides that:

> " each Contracting Party undertakes to issue instructions to its maritime inspection vessels and aircraft and to other appropriate services to report to its authorities any incidents or conditions on the high seas which give rise to suspicions that dumping in contravention of the provisions of the present Convention has occurred or is about to occur. That Contracting Party shall, if it considers it appropriate, report accordingly to any other Contracting Party concerned."

In the same way, paragraphs 4 and 5 of Article 15 provide that

> " (4) The Contracting Parties undertake to assist one another as appropriate in dealing with pollution incidents involving dumping at sea, and to exchange information on methods of dealing with such incidents.
>
> " (5) The Contracting Parties further agree to work together in the development of co-operative procedures for the application of the Convention, particularly on the high seas."

Notwithstanding the great moderation of these very general declarations of principle, the Oslo Convention deems it necessary not to hurt national susceptibilities by providing in Article 15 (6) that "nothing in this Convention shall abridge sovereign immunity to which certain vessels are entitled under international law."

This last provision will only acquire importance if the Commission set up in pursuance of Article 16 of the Convention is able to supervise the efficacy of control measures which are to be decided upon, or deems that additional control measures are necessary, in pursuance of Article 17 (c).

(c) The protection of submarine telegraph cables

Telegraph cables laid on the bed of the high seas, being outside the area subject to territorial sovereignty, are in need of legal protection. The Convention of March 14, 1884, on the Protection of Submarine Cables deals with this question. From the point of view of policing, this convention is interesting for three reasons.

First, enforcement is entrusted to the national authorities for offences committed on board ships flying their flag. Secondly, since enforcement remains national, it was necessary to lay down rules as to the reports drawn up by the competent international policing agencies. After a long exchange of views, it was finally admitted that it was better to leave it to each State to decide about the probative value to be granted to these reports. Finally, the exercise of the right of policing itself is very limited: it merely consists of nationality control. Proposals tending to the admission of a right of visitation or examination, necessary to discover on board foreign ships evidence of the offence committed, were rejected.

In short, the 1884 Convention is relatively timid as regards policing on the high seas. To all appearances the general principle is as formulated by Professor Louis Renault. "As to the general spirit of the proposed articles, it can be summarised thus: the sovereignty and legislation of the Contracting States are respected to the greatest extent possible."[17]

(d) The suppression of traffic in spirits in the North Sea

This subject is dealt with by the Convention of November 16, 1887, for the Prohibition of the Liquor Traffic in the North Sea. The difficulties once more concern the respect of sovereign rights on the high seas. The drafters of the convention had the choice of two régimes: that of the 1882 Convention on the policing of fishing, containing the right of visitation, or that of the Convention on the Protection of Submarine Cables, which is limited to checking the nationality of the ship and drawing up reports. It was the latter system which was adopted. Hence the international right of policing was limited to checking the nationality and drawing up reports; nevertheless, following the pattern of the 1882 Convention, the commanders of warships entrusted with policing had the right to conduct a suspected ship into a port of its nationality.

III. GENERAL CHARACTERISTICS OF THE RIGHT OF POLICING ON THE HIGH SEAS

Let us try to deduce from an examination of the different conventions some general rules. These will be classified in the order in which they are most in conformity with national sovereignty, *i.e.*, most in conformity with the rule of non-interference and of respect for the flag. The different rules of policing are not applicable in all cases: most of them cannot be formulated as principles without exceptions. One might say that each convention, other than the Geneva Convention on the High Seas, which claims to be a statement of established principles of international law (see its preamble), constitutes a particular regulation drawn up to meet a definite need. We may nevertheless extrapolate the following principles which show the large range of possibilities already existing for the policing of the high seas, and from which the negotiators, confronted with the necessity to go further into the control of the application of the various conventions regulating the use of the high seas, may choose.

1. The right of policing is concerned with national sovereignty, either by reference to an exclusively national control or by reserving punishment to the authorities of the offender's flag. An example of national inspection may be found in Rule 6 of Chapter I, General Provisions, of the Rules appended to the 1960 Convention for the Safety of Life at Sea. The reference to punishment by the national authorities, even in the case of international policing, is a constant principle. We can find it in the 1882 Convention (policing of fisheries in the North Sea), in Articles 8 and 9 of the 1884 Submarine Cables Convention, in Article 4 *et seq.* of the 1887 Convention, in Articles VI and X of the amended 1954 Oil Pollution Convention, and in Article 8 of the recommendation on the Scheme of Joint Enforcement of the North-East Atlantic Fisheries Commission; the same principle is also recognised in the 1967 Convention. An exception to this rule is provided by Article 19 of the 1958 Convention on the High Seas in favour of the arresting State in the case of piracy.

2. The conventions examined do not regulate policing in the territorial sea or exclusive fishing zone. Most of them restrict their field of application to the high seas. The 1959 and 1967 Conventions, although they apply to the territorial sea and exclusive fishing zone, limit their international policing provisions to the high seas.

3. The immunity of warships (and in certain cases of other State-owned ships) is always respected.

4. In case of war each State may be released from its treaty obligations. The influence of hostilities on treaties (*i.e.*, as a ground for either abrogation or suspension) is a controversial question in international law. The 1884 Convention provides in Article 15 that the freedom of action of belligerent States is not prejudiced. Article XIX of the 1954 Convention provides that the provisions of the convention may be suspended in time of war. The Convention for the Safety of Life at Sea allows the total or partial suspension of the Rules appended to the convention in time of war or other hostilities (Art. VI (a)).

5. Contrary to what might be expected, policing on the high seas is not the monopoly of warships. The 1882 Convention in Article 26 only deals with warships, although it makes an exception for Belgium. The 1887 Convention in Article 7 (1) limits itself to designating the cruisers in charge of fisheries policing—in fact, the system of the 1882 Convention. On the other hand, the 1884 Convention assigns policing to warships or to ships specially commissioned for that purpose. The 1958 Convention on the High Seas, when dealing with arrest for piracy and with the right of hot pursuit, provides that warships or military aircraft, or other ships or aircraft assigned to public service and authorised for that purpose, may be used (Arts. 21 and 23 (4)). But the same convention provides that only warships have the right of boarding (Art. 22). The North-East Atlantic Fisheries Commission's recommendation deals with ships specially assigned to control: these may even include fishing boats. The 1967 Convention does not refer to a specific class or classes of ship, but to the authorised officer.

6. Policing may be carried out by a number of different methods:

(a) A very widespread practice is that of information. This takes the form of reports addressed to the national authorities in charge of enforcement.

(b) Certain conventions expressly lay down an obligation to co-operate. This is the case with the Bonn Convention of 1969 (Art. 7) and with the Oslo Convention of 1972 (Art. 15 (4)).

(c) Control on the high seas, limited to the checking of nationality, is provided for in the 1884 Convention (Art. 10 (ii)), and in the 1887 Convention (Art. 7 (ii)).

(d) A right of visitation, going further than a mere checking of nationality, is provided for in the 1882 Convention (Art. 29), in the 1954 Convention, and in the cases of slavery, piracy and hot pursuit under the Convention on the High Seas. The recommendation of the North-East Atlantic Fisheries Commission permits a fishing vessel to be stopped and searched, more particularly for the inspection of its catches and nets, and of its documents. The 1967 Convention permits a ship to be stopped and boarded in cases where there is a presumption that the provisions of the Convention have been infringed or in cases where damage has been caused (Art. 9 (5) and (6)).

(e) The 1882 Convention (Art. 30) allows a warship to conduct a suspected ship into a port where law enforcement competence may be exercised.

(f) The 1969 Brussels Convention grants the most extensive right of policing, since it permits a State to take on the high seas absolutely all measures necessary "to prevent, mitigate or eliminate . . . pollution."

7. The probative value of reports is not equal in all cases. The fact that enforcement is reserved to the national authorities involves communication to them of the reports drawn up by the policing agencies. The 1884 and 1887 Conventions provide that the reports may serve as proof for the authorities responsible for enforcement. This means that the national authorities are free to decide what probative value shall be attached to them. Another system is that provided for in the recommendation of the North-East Atlantic Fisheries Commission (Art. 8), and in the 1967 Convention (Art. 9 (11)). Here reports have the same probative value as if they emanated from officers of the State responsible for enforcement, it being understood, however, that the latter should not assign to a report emanating from a foreign authorised officer a probative value superior to that which the report would have had in the country of that foreign officer.

8. A genuinely international system of policing puts resistance to the foreign policing agency on the same footing as resistance to national policing authorities; see the 1882 Convention (Art. 32), the 1887 Convention (Art. 7 (v)), recommendation of the North-East Atlantic Fisheries Commission (Art. 6), and the 1967 Convention (Art. 9 (10)).

From this examination it appears that we are far from having achieved a homogeneous régime of policing on the high seas. However, in the present state of international law and political realities, a more effective and genuinely international system of policing the high seas appears to be out of the question.

REFERENCES

1. Georg Dahm, *Völkerrecht*, Vol. I, p. 666.
2. Convention on the High Seas, Arts. 22 and 23.
3. C. J. Colombos, *The International Law of the Sea*, p. 367.
4. For further details of these two conventions, see Koers, p. 24, *supra*.

5. North-East Atlantic Fisheries Convention, Art. 7.

6. *La Pêche Maritime*, June 20, 1967, p. 54.

7. North-East Atlantic Fisheries Commission. Scheme of Joint Enforcement. For text, see Vol. I, pp. 484–487.

8. Art. 8 of the Convention.

9. Jean de Breucker, *La Belgique et le Problème de la Police de la Pêche*, p. 120.

10. F. Monconduit, " L'extension des zones de pêche réservées aux pêcheurs français, application de la Convention de Londres du 9 mars 1964 " (1967) *Annuaire Français de Droit International* 685 *et seq*.

11. For further details, see Vignes, pp. 342–344, *infra*.

12. Some 15 incidents have been reported for this period in " Chronique des faits internationaux," in the *Revue Générale de Droit International Public* for 1970–72. The qualification " warship " hardly ever appears.

13. For details of the Canadian and United Kingdom legislation, see Morin and Churchill, pp. 248–251 and 294–295 respectively, *infra*.

14. For further details, see Fleischer, pp. 89–90, *supra*.

15. E. du Pontavice, *Le Droit Maritime Français*, p. 331.

16. L. Lucchini, " La pollution des mers par les hydrocarbures: les Conventions de Bruxelles de novembre 1969 ou les fissures du droit international classique " (1970) *Journal du Droit International* 809.

17. F. de Pauw, " L'exercise de mesures de police en haute mer en vertu des traités ratifiés par la Belgique," in *La Belgique et le Droit de la Mer*, p. 113.

Part VII

Some Regional Approaches

CHAPTER 16

The Baltic

By Bo Johnson *

INTRODUCTION

IN political debates the expression "the Sea of Peace" sometimes appears. The Baltic Sea has occasionally been termed a "Sea of Peace."

It goes without saying that States situated along the coastline of one and the same sea regard peaceful co-operation as essential. The water that separates them geographically should be the very factor linking them together. States bordering on the same sea have nowadays every reason to direct their co-operation towards safeguarding the resources of the sea and the purity of the water. Formerly, and perhaps rightly so, the sea was considered big enough to accommodate everyone and in those days it aroused little attention if somebody occasionally used the expanse of the oceans to the detriment of others. But our era has witnessed an industrial and technological revolution. The consequences have been enormous, also for the sea as such. The wealth of the seabed is being revealed—oil, minerals, gas. Methods of fishing are being improved. But all this technological progress is accompanied by all kinds of risks. Oil-wells on the continental shelf and the seabed may burst, enormous tankers may be wrecked causing severe damage to the marine environment. The calculated risks ought to give indications in one and the same direction: towards new and effective norms for the use of the oceans, norms taking proper consideration of the fundamental fact that the legal nature of the high sea is built upon the criterion "an object open to the public use." An object that in the interest of the community must remain accessible to everyone; a legal régime characterised by the conception of *usus publicus*.[1]†

In theory it is always easy to formulate abstract norms for the purpose of ensuring that the sea is used in conformity with the interests and needs of mankind. Is perhaps an internationalised régime the best solution? Should the element of supranationality dominate or is it, perhaps, preferable to let the old concept of "condominium" constitute the basis of universal or regional co-operation, the concept of which does not contain the element of supranationality but more the elements of equality and equal rights between co-operating States? It is well known that during the past it has been difficult to get the international community to take unified action on measures for regulating the use of the sea. A more limited, or regional, co-operation seems, on the other hand, to be fruitful. The riparian States along a certain area of water join in common efforts to regulate outstanding questions, *i.e.*, fishing, the prevention of pollution and oil damage, an overall policy of active environmental protection.[2] Regional development of the kind described undoubtedly consolidates countries, and

* LL.D., Ministry of Foreign Affairs, Stockholm.

† For references, see p. 218.

the area concerned thus becomes an area of peace in the real sense. The powers embark on the road of peaceful settlement of outstanding questions and problems, which otherwise could have resulted in serious frictions that become more and more threatening.

The foregoing indicates how positive co-operation guides development onto the paths of peace. This aspect will be dealt with in more detail with regard to the Baltic Sea.

In this connection I should also like to mention that the geographical area to which I will generally refer is the Baltic Sea proper, *i.e.*, the Gulf of Bothnia and the Gulf of Finland are in the main excluded from the discussion in this paper, although occasionally mentioned when necessary.

REGIONAL CO-OPERATION

A sea having the geographical configuration of the Baltic Sea encourages the riparian States to take part in regional co-operation. The distances from shore to shore are not of a scale tending to diminish common interests, an obvious risk in the case of vast oceans. Partly because of this proximity, the neighbouring States are forced into each others' hands and, more or less automatically, their common interests assume an intrinsic identity. It is worth repeating that the Baltic waters are surrounded by highly industrialised countries. Intensive exploitation impoverishes the hydrospace. The sophisticated techniques of advanced industries produce serious pollution.

The necessary prerequisites for fruitful co-operation exist, and no doubt all countries concerned are of the opinion that the time is ripe to commence. However, it is well known that one of the great political issues of our time—the German question—has prevented a deeper and more extensive co-operation between the States along the Baltic Sea. The German Democratic Republic has, since its coming into being, not been in a position to conclude treaties with the majority of the neighbouring States, because of its lack of diplomatic recognition. It is no secret, however, that the Powers, which for more than 20 years withheld their official recognition, have carried out practical collaboration on a lower level with the German Democratic Republic. But the solution of more extensive problems and important questions of principle has had to be postponed for a considerable time. The German question is now in the process of being solved and diplomatic recognition is extended to the German Democratic Republic by a majority of States. The political factors that for years have prevented an overall solution of outstanding Baltic Sea questions have disappeared. Regional co-operation could begin, without delay, co-operation on a wider and more extensive scale than earlier. A list of items for regional co-operation of specific importance to the future settlement of common problems would most certainly be headed by the general regulation of fishing, the conclusion of multilateral treaties preventing marine pollution, marine damage from oil waste, and, perhaps, the regulation and unification of the rules of navigation for supertankers in the Baltic. There are already a number of international treaties and conventions in these fields. Together they form a certain pattern of relations between States and might serve as models for the riparian States of the Baltic Sea when they start working on these issues. Activities of different kinds pertaining to a specific geographical area of water are regulated in detail by these conventions. A factor of great importance is that the provisions laid down in the treaties referred to are combined with a system of supervision, which ensures the implementation in practice of normative rules. The direct responsibility for implementation rests with special commissions invested with varyingly extensive authority. Besides regional agreements of the above-mentioned type, there are, of course, others of a more universal character to take into consideration, some perhaps already applicable to the Baltic Sea, and some which might come into force after accession by the riparian States. There are no longer any legal obstacles to the German Democratic Republic acceding to multilateral treaties. Allow me to give a few examples.

The North-East Atlantic Fisheries Convention of January 24, 1959, regulates fishing in specific regions of the Atlantic and Arctic Oceans.[3] As a matter of fact, this convention also covers a very small part of the south-western Baltic Sea and the Danish Belts. The area is defined as the Baltic Sea and Belts lying to the north and west of lines drawn from Hasenore Head to Gniben Point, from Korshage to Spodsbierg and from Gilbierg Head to the Kullen. The North-East Atlantic Fisheries Commission supervises the implementation of the provisions of the convention. An agreement of a similar nature is the Convention on Conduct of Fishing Operations in the North Atlantic, signed at London on June 1, 1967.[4] It comprises the North Sea and the Baltic within the area just defined. The European Fisheries Convention of March 9, 1964, contains detailed rules of rights and obligations between the contracting parties, especially when one party is fishing inside the other party's exclusive fishing zone.[5] On February 8, 1949, the International Convention for the Northwest Atlantic Fisheries was signed; 16 countries are now parties. The Pacific Ocean is also covered by multi- and bilateral agreements on fisheries. The International Convention for the High Seas Fisheries of the North Pacific Ocean of 1952 between the United States, Canada and Japan regulates the halibut, herring and salmon fisheries in the said region. The observance in practice of rules and regulations laid down is, as stated earlier, supervised by international commissions. A quick recapitulation of existing authorities gives a global perspective: the North-East Atlantic Fisheries Commission, the Northwest Atlantic Fisheries Commission, the International North Pacific Fisheries Commission, the International Commission for the South-East Atlantic Fisheries, the Japanese-Soviet Commission for the Northwest Pacific Fisheries, the Inter-American Tropical Tuna Commission, the Indo-Pacific Fisheries Council, the Latin American General Fisheries Council, the General Fisheries Council for the Mediterranean.

The absence of regional co-operation and regulation for the Baltic Sea is conspicuous in the global perspective just presented. It is obvious that this region should also have its place in the global pattern now prevailing. A Baltic Sea Fisheries Convention, perhaps coupled with a supervisory commission, is now a real possibility in the near future. Some of the existing agreements, as indicated above, could be made applicable to the Baltic Sea through a simple accession procedure. This is also true of those agreements now coming into force in the field of environmental protection. As an example, I should like to mention the so-called Oslo Convention (Convention for the Prevention of Marine Pollution by Dumping from Ships and Aircraft), which was signed on February 15, 1972, by Belgium, Denmark, the Federal Republic of Germany, Finland, France, Iceland, the Netherlands, Norway, Portugal, Spain, Sweden and the United Kingdom.[6] Other States may, however, be invited to accede to the convention. This multilateral agreement opens with a solemn promise by the contracting parties to take all possible steps to prevent the pollution of the sea by substances that are liable to create hazards to human health, to harm living resources and marine life, to damage amenities or to interfere with other legitimate uses of the sea. A remarkable fact is also that the IMCO Convention of 1954 on the prevention of discharge of oil by ships into the open sea includes the entire Baltic Sea. The so-called prohibited zones are defined in Annex A as extending to the whole of the Baltic Sea and its gulfs.[7]

TREATIES IN FORCE FOR THE BALTIC SEA

This attempt to arrange systematically examples from the field of international legal relations, although by no means exhaustive, may have given some valuable information as to the possible nature of future co-operation between the riparian States of the Baltic Sea. It is quite natural that treaties of a multilateral character predominate here, and have claimed our exclusive attention. But even though regional agreements are of great importance, they do not, of course, exclude bilateral agreements from regulating certain areas between neighbouring States—often pertaining to the boundary-lines between States on terra firma, on the continental shelf or between territorial seas and contiguous zones. On the establishment of exclusive fishing zones contiguous to the territorial sea, it is usual and necessary to settle problems which may materialise through bilateral agreements. By definition, an extensive fishing zone necessarily comprises waters that were formerly designated as the high seas. These areas may formerly have been used frequently by foreign fishing boats that are suddenly excluded. This is the kind of problem which has to be solved.

Let us leave the models for the future and pay a little attention to existing agreements directly bearing on the Baltic Sea.

It is worth repeating that several treaties mentioned above are applicable to a small part of the Baltic, *i.e.*, the areas around the Danish straits. Article 2 of the 1972 Dumping Convention contains an identical definition of the area to which the convention applies. As also indicated above, the Convention of 1954 on prevention of discharge of oil by ships into the open sea applies to the whole of the Baltic Sea including its gulfs. This is an important agreement having direct practical relevance since all the riparian States, with the exception of the German Democratic Republic, have acceded to it. Other steps taken in the field of environmental protection include an agreement of October 16, 1971, between the Nordic countries—Denmark, Finland, Norway and Sweden—on co-operation to prevent oil pollution of the sea.[8] The parties declared their intention to co-operate in combating oil pollution threatening their coasts or substantial interests of theirs, and, further, to promote the implementation of the Convention of 1954 just mentioned. The "Nordic" agreement does not contain any specific bearing on the Baltic. In this context it is worth noting that there exists a special regional agreement for co-operation in dealing with pollution of the North Sea by oil, dated June 9, 1969, and concluded between Belgium, Denmark, the Federal Republic of Germany, France, Norway, Sweden and the United Kingdom.[9] This can perhaps serve as a model for a regional agreement pertaining to the Baltic. As is well known, but worth pointing out, the Convention on the High Seas, adopted at Geneva in 1958, contains a special provision in Article 25 (2) concerning pollution of the high seas. This provision is obviously also applicable to the Baltic Sea.

When turning to the field of fisheries, we have previously noted that only the south-western part of the Baltic waters is included in regional fisheries conventions. There are, of course, certain lasting principles and important rules as to fishing and the conservation of living resources laid down in the Geneva Conventions of 1958. This is a basis but we lack more precise rules on the conduct of fishing in our own region and on the protection of the resources of our own sea. However, there is one exception, namely, the agreement between Denmark, the Federal Republic of Germany, Sweden and Poland of December 20, 1962, concerning the protection of salmon in the Baltic Sea.[10] This agreement is open to new signatories without any changes having to be made in the text. The area of applicability is defined as comprising the Baltic Sea, including the Gulf of Bothnia and the Gulf of Finland.

An instance of another kind of collaboration of practical importance we should consider is the agreement of December 10, 1961, between Denmark, Finland, Norway and Sweden on co-operation in ice-breaking.[11] The area of co-operation is defined as extending to the Gulf of Bothnia, the Sea of Aaland and the Baltic Sea north to the latitude through Dueodde on the island of Bornholm, and also the Sound. An agreement between the same parties on the unification of the rules for erecting seamarks was concluded in Helsinki on September 18, 1962.[12] In the Preamble, reference is made to the "Nordic Waters," a term applicable *per se* to parts of the Baltic Sea.

Another question of great urgency is life-saving at sea. Quite obviously this subject must be given high priority in the forthcoming regional Baltic co-operation. As far back as 1954, on September 29, Sweden and the Soviet Union concluded an agreement on co-operation for the salvage of life in the Baltic Sea. The agreement aims to ensure quick and effective assistance to crews and passengers of ships and aircraft in distress in the said area.[13]

During the period between the world wars, a number of conventions on the prevention of smuggling were concluded. In this context I wish merely to mention the agreement of 1934 between Sweden and Finland on prevention of smuggling of alcohol, which is still in force.[14]

It goes without saying that a number of bilateral treaties could be taken into consideration, especially those pertaining to boundary-lines and lines of delimitation in the sea. In fact, in the Baltic area the existing borders often constitute the only remaining visible sign of military entanglements of wars. These demarcations are solemnly laid down in peace treaties, often several centuries old. It is by no means my intention to get involved in a discussion of these interesting questions that could lead us too far from the subject in hand. But there is, however, a question of delimitation that cannot be disregarded, a subject of an urgent nature, namely, the delimitation between States of the continental shelf.

As we know, the concept of the "continental shelf" is legally defined as the seabed and subsoil of the submarine areas adjacent to the coast, but outside the area of the territorial sea, to a depth of 200 metres. The second flexible criterion in the definition may be ignored in this connection, since the seabed of the Baltic Sea *in toto* constitutes a continental shelf as defined above. Further, the narrow configuration of the sea gives as result that the claims of the riparian States meet somewhere in the middle of the sea. It follows thus, that the solution of the whole problem pertaining to the continental shelf in this region is entirely dependent on a system of treaties between the neighbouring States. It is worth adding that according to Article 6 (2) of the Convention on the Continental Shelf, in the absence of agreement or so-called special circumstances, the boundary shall be determined by applying the principle of equidistance from the nearest points of the base lines from which the breadth of the territorial sea of each State is measured.

The situation at present with regard to the continental shelf is as follows: Sweden has not yet concluded any treaty with the Soviet Union. The negotiations that were opened in 1969 have so far failed to give results. Bilateral talks between Sweden and Poland will begin. It is also assumed that talks may commence in the near future with representatives of the German Democratic Republic. Sweden and Finland concluded on September 29, 1972, an agreement on the delimitation of the continental shelf in the Gulf of Bothnia, the Sea of Aaland and the northern part of the Baltic. The boundary largely follows the old line of demarcation already laid down in the Peace Treaty of Fredrikshamn (1809) between Imperial Russia and Sweden.[15] That line, too, was drawn in accordance with the principle of equidistance, although nobody in those days envisaged new legal doctrines such as the continental shelf.

The East European countries—the Soviet Union, Poland and the German Democratic Republic—have adopted a special declaration on the delimitation of the continental shelf in the Baltic Sea, the "Moscow Declaration" of October 23, 1968. The Soviet Union and Poland concluded on August 28, 1968, an agreement on the delimitation of the continental shelf in the Gulf of Gdánsk and the south-eastern part of the Baltic. There is a similar agreement between the Soviet Union and Finland pertaining to the Gulf of Finland, dated May 5, 1967.

A subject that also comes under the present heading comprises those treaties that are of an indispensable character when States establish exclusive fishing zones contiguous to their territorial seas. Foreign fishing boats are thereby excluded from waters which they have perhaps used for a considerable period of time. There are no longer any legal obstacles to claiming a fishing zone of reasonable extension, but to avoid unnecessary trouble States usually find it appropriate to regulate these matters by agreement. However, it would be a grave exaggeration to say that this is an acute problem in the Baltic. Up to now, the demarcation of exclusive fishing zones has not often been used in this region. In any case, there is nothing to prevent States from claiming a zone, and when this happens, we shall most certainly have an urgent question to solve.

For the time being, only the Soviet Union claims a territorial sea of 12 nautical miles. Formerly, this was a matter of controversy, but hardly now. Foreign fishing boats are prohibited within Soviet territorial waters. A brief observation as to the conditions in the Gulf of Finland may be relevant here: Finnish fishermen are allowed by agreement to fish in Soviet territorial waters in the Gulf. No treaties exist between the Soviet Union and Sweden in this respect.

Another East European country, namely Poland, has, since February 12, 1970, claimed an exclusive fishing zone extending 12 nautical miles from the base lines. Poland and Sweden are parties to a special agreement of October 5, 1970, concerning the rights of Swedish fishing boats to fish within the Polish zone. On the same date both the countries entered into an agreement on salvage activities and recovery of property from Swedish and Polish internal waters and territorial seas.[16]

The purpose of this rudimentary exposition of treaties and agreements has been to give some idea of the range of the relations now existing between the riparian States of the Baltic. In addition, some models for the future have been reviewed. In my opinion it is more than obvious that these relations, as they stand at present, are insufficient and inadequate, especially in the light of the fact that highly industrialised societies are to be found everywhere along the coasts of the Baltic Sea. It is to be hoped that in a few years' time the situation will have changed into one characterised by intensive regional co-operation between all the States concerned and in all the fields discussed here.

THE BALTIC BETWEEN EAST AND WEST

The foregoing has shown how fruitful co-operation has positive effects on development towards peace. Hopefully, in the time to come we will witness how this identity of interests contributes to the consolidation of peace in our region.

However, it should not be forgotten that the concept of " the Sea of Peace " has been given more than one interpretation, often influenced by political factors of various kinds, at times even factors of military policy. As the reader will understand, I here refer to the contradiction between two fundamental concepts in legal theory, namely " high sea " and " closed sea." The latter concept has above all found support in the doctrines of the Soviet Union and other East European countries. The essential meaning of the term " closed sea " is, in short, that a certain kind of sea is meant to be closed to the military units of a third Power. A *mare clausum*, a term that can also be used, is an area of water where only military units belonging to the riparian States are said to be allowed to operate. But the question as to whether such an area genuinely and *ipso facto* constitutes a " Sea of Peace " is surely open to question. Definitions of peace are multifarious. And peace in one part of the world is basically dependent on and influenced by the political situation prevailing globally. In periods of détente between the nations of the world, direct threats diminish. In periods of increasing tension the Great Powers, in particular, immediately become more eager to keep the potential enemy at a distance from their own coasts.

Since, in Soviet and East European legal and political doctrines, the Baltic has been classified as a *mare clausum* or in later periods as a " Sea of Peace " there may be reason to touch upon this question from the Swedish point of view and in so doing to try to present such facts as are decisive from the Swedish standpoint as regards the legal status of the Baltic Sea. In this respect there might, theoretically at least, be a conflict of interests between the riparian States.[17]

The literature of the Soviet Union and other East European countries in the fields of politics and public international law presents as an obvious fact that the Baltic constitutes a " closed sea " or a *mare clausum.* Only naval and air-force units belonging to Denmark, the Federal Republic of Germany, Finland, the German Democratic Republic, Poland, the Soviet Union and Sweden would be allowed to operate in this area. Forces belonging to third Powers are to be excluded from the Baltic region, in fact from all seas, which, according to the doctrines referred to, are regarded as "closed." In this context it is important to note that shipping of a commercial character has nothing to do with the concept of *mare clausum.* Commercial vessels, and aircraft too, are in no way affected. Therefore the issue is limited to the rights of navigation for military forces in the sea and the air above. But limiting the range of discussion solely to the military sector confronts us with a wide spectrum of very delicate issues like military balance, strategic importance, freedom of navigation on and over the high seas, etc., etc.

The policy of the Soviet Union to " claim " the Baltic as a *mare clausum* is a tradition dating from the days of Imperial Russia. The subject attracted little attention for a considerable period, although some Soviet proposals for the " closing " of both the Black and the Baltic Seas were tabled during a conference on marine disarmament in Rome in 1924. During the period 1917–40, the Soviet Union was not one of the riparian States of the Baltic. Not until the late fifties was the question raised again; for instance, Prime Minister Khruschev's speech at Riga in 1959, in which he coupled the question of " foreign " military presence with more far-reaching ideas regarding the future status of the whole Baltic area. On this particular occasion and on several others, it became evident that the " old " formula of *mare clausum* was just a small part of a new, more comprehensive legal régime, comprising elements such as " nuclear-free zones," " neutralisation," " demilitarisation " and " pacification." The elements would together constitute a " Sea of Peace." As the reader most probably remembers, certain aspects of this subject were discussed during the Geneva Conference on the

Law of the Sea in 1958. Roumania and the Ukraine suggested a special formulation having a direct impact on this kind of sea: " For certain seas a special régime of navigation may be established for historical reasons or by virtue of international agreements." Proposals of the same nature have often been put forward since: the Baltic Sea should be closed to third parties' naval and air-force units.[18]

The legal and political literature, for instance the official *Mezhdunarodnoye Pravo*, explains these conceptions by invoking the notion of " life interest." [19] It is a simple and generally applicable fact that only the riparian States have a " life interest " in their region. Why not also in the Baltic? Accordingly, in a special area of sea the Powers concerned have every right to take all measures designed to protect their " interests." The concept of *mare clausum* corresponds to these basic elements. A most essential factor in all discussion in any way allied to these doctrines is that very often arguments like " historical tradition," " basic facts of history," etc., are used to support the official standpoint. These basic facts, by which are mainly meant ancient treaties, are usually interpreted as bearing witness to the nature of the legal status of the Baltic Sea. According to this, these waters have for centuries been " closed " to the naval units of third parties. The legal régime in a *mare clausum* is purported to have been laid down by the riparian States in concert.

What are the " basic historical facts " in this respect? Do they contain anything to this effect? Even if the answer is in the positive, is this sufficient? It is a well-known fact in international law that ancient treaties must be interpreted in close accord with the situation prevailing at their time of adoption, the so-called inter-temporal interpretation. Adhering to this principle, nothing prevents us from confirming that several treaties dating from the eighteenth century are based upon the assumption that the Baltic was a *mare clausum* open solely to the warships of the Baltic States. Before commenting upon this subject in more detail, however, it is worth noting that the formula of *mare clausum* was first applied after the conclusion of the Peace Treaty of Nystad in 1721, when Russia acquired new territories along the coast of the Baltic Sea proper and was thereby allowed to take active part in the protection of the region against foreign intrusion. Before then the responsibility of protection had from time immemorial rested with Denmark and Sweden, the so-called *Dominium maris Baltici.* As early as the beginning of the fourteenth century it appears that the Danish monarchy took over the *Dominium* from the Hanseatic cities and it rested with the Danish King for centuries to come, although due consideration was generally paid to Swedish interests. As master of the Baltic straits, Denmark was then in an excellent position to guard the waters. During the first part of the seventeenth century the power of Denmark was broken by the Emperor of Germany and the *Dominium* over the Baltic passed to Sweden and stayed there until 1721, when the one-Power domination gave place to a kind of " condominium " between the riparian States—Denmark, Germany, Russia and Sweden. They acted in concert to protect the Baltic from the intrusion of foreign hostile navies, all in accordance with the formula of *mare clausum.* Treaties from this period mention specifically the Baltic as " *une mer fermée.*" In the Declaration of St. Petersburg on July 21, 1780, the foundation of the so-called armed neutrality of the Baltic States, the following sentence appears:

> " Comme Sa Majesté . . . et Sa Majesté . . . sont toujours également intéressées à veiller à la sûreté et à la tranquillité de la Mer Baltique . . . Elles sont mutuellement convenues à soutenir, que c'est une mer fermée, . . . où toutes les nations doivent et peuvent naviguer en paix . . . et de prendre pour cette effet entre Elles des

mesures capables de garantir cette mer et ses côtes de toutes hostilités, pirateries et violences."[20]

Similar wording was also used in other treaties from the same period. There is, though, one indispensable factor not to be forgotten. All treaties pertaining to the Baltic as a " closed sea " aimed at the protection of the *neutrality* of the riparian States and the consolidation of peace in the Baltic region. The Powers acted in common, through their " League of Armed Neutrality," to uphold their own neutral status and that of the sea itself. There are further grounds for believing that other States, if reluctantly, accepted this special régime as long as the Baltic States strictly adhered to their declared neutrality. The factor of neutrality was thus a *sine qua non* for the whole construction of *mare clausum*. When the Powers along the Baltic coast actively became involved in military entanglements or wars—as was the case from the early 1800s—the concept of *mare clausum* was impossible to maintain. If one of the riparian States was at war with Powers outside the region, it seemed neither in accordance with international law, nor with national interests, for a neutral State to take active part in the " closing " of the sea concerned, thereby protecting one of the belligerent parties.

The fact is that, as early as 1807, Sweden had obviously come to share this view. In an exchange of notes with Russia, Sweden argued along these lines: it was not prepared to take part in measures aiming at the " closing " of the Baltic. A message to the same effect was dispatched to Denmark in 1834, which in practice came to take the same attitude. The Belts and the Sound would be free for passage, also for foreign warships. As a matter of fact, even whole navies were allowed to pass through the straits during the Crimean War (1835–56). These navies, seeking contact with Russian forces, were not denied passage as both Sweden and Denmark had declared themselves neutral. The policy of the " open sea " was established. Ever since, Sweden and Denmark have adhered to this policy and always tried to implement it also in practice. In proclamations of neutrality and decrees regulating admission to territorial waters and the air space above for foreign warships and military aircraft—dating from 1834 to 1966—both Sweden and Denmark have meticulously followed the principle of " free passage " to and from the Baltic for all kinds of traffic. It is worth noting in this context that the Convention of 1857 on the Abolition of Rights over the Sound and the Belts between Denmark on the one hand and Sweden–Norway, Austria–Hungary, Belgium, France, the Netherlands, the United Kingdom, Germany and Russia on the other, contains rules on free passage through the straits with regard to fiscal duties and fees. It is believed that the convention in the first place apertains to commercial shipping, but a paragraph of a wider nature could, I repeat could, have some general bearing on the question of the rights of passage: " Aucun navire quelconque ne pourra désormais, sous quelque prétexte, que ce soit, étre assujetti au passage du Sund et des Belts à une détention ou entrave quelconque."[21]

As just mentioned, the " strait-owning " States, Denmark and Sweden, have for a long time applied the principle of free passage through the straits. It goes without saying that action taken by these two countries in this respect is of the greatest importance to the whole question of the status of the Baltic Sea. The decrees in force in respective countries declare specifically that the Swedish part of the Sound, and the Great Belt, are totally free for passage without any form of " homage " to the States through which territorial waters the passage is made. No notification is necessary, not even for passage in the air above the territorial waters of Sweden and Denmark in the Sound and the Great Belt. The free entrance to the Baltic is, thus, a reality and has been so for more than 160 years. The right of passage is based on national legislation and on principles of public international law. Custom has made the free entrance through the straits part of a recognised " European legal order," as well as the principle of the " open sea " with regard to the Baltic is also part of the same order. The " order " referred to has no doubt contributed to the stability of the Baltic region.

REFERENCES

1. See Bo Johnson, *Suveränitet i havet och luftrummet/Souveraineté sur la Mer et dans les Airs. Etudes sur les droits de souveraineté en haute mer et les limites de la juridiction nationale sur la mer et dans l'espace aérien. Avec un condensé en français*, pp. 44–77, 373–389, Stockholm, 1972.
2. *Ibid.*
3. See Sveriges Överenskommelser med främmande makter, cited as SÖ (Sweden's Agreements with Foreign Powers) 1960:4.
4. See SÖ 1970:14.
5. SÖ 1966:29–30.
6. Kungl. Maj:ts prop. 1972:71 (Royal Proposition).
7. SÖ 1956:15, 1963:15.
8. SÖ 1971:23.
9. SÖ 1969:21.
10. SÖ 1963:13, 1972:2.
11. SÖ 1961:45.
12. SÖ 1962:21.
13. SÖ 1954:46.
14. SÖ 1934:1.
15. Kungl. Maj:ts prop. 1972:123.
16. SÖ 1971:13–14.
17. See Johnson, *Suveränitet i havet och luftrummet*, pp. 278–287.
18. See UN Doc. A/CONF.13/C.2/L.26; also Gerhard Reintanz, " Ostsee—Meer des Friedens " (1971) Aussenpolitik 706 *et seq.*
19. Comp. *Völkerrecht*. Akademie der Wissenschaften der UdSSR, p. 234 (Hamburg, 1960).
20. See *Recueil des Principaux Traités Conclus par les Puissances de l'Europe. Tome IV 1761–1790*, p. 357 *et seq.* (Gottingen, 1795). Also *Danske Tractater 1751–1800* (Copenhagen, 1882), p. 386 *et seq.*
21. See Sten Lewenhaupt, *Recueil des Traités de la Suède I.* (Stockholm, 1926), p. 23 *et seq.*

CHAPTER 17

The Baltic—Special Pollution Problems

By G. Reintanz *

APART from the Mediterranean and the North Sea, the Baltic Sea is one of the most polluted and endangered marine areas. The research programmes of the "1969–70 International Baltic Sea Year," in which all the Baltic States took part, have considerably increased our knowledge of the hydrology, pollution and fish stocks of the Baltic.

The Baltic Sea is a small and shallow basin containing brackish water. Its surface area is 386,000 square kilometres, as compared with 360 million square kilometres for the surface of the oceans. Its average depth is only 60 metres, as against 3,700 metres for the oceans. With its 22,000 cubic kilometres against 1·4 million cubic kilometres for the oceans, the volume of water it contains is quite small. The input and output of its waters through the Danish straits is of minor importance. The residence time for Baltic water has been estimated to be about 20 years. Other scientists believe the residence time to be up to about 30 or 40 years. Be that as it may, all these circumstances make the Baltic very susceptible to every change affecting its natural status.

The seven countries on the Baltic Sea have played an important role in European history. At the present time they are of great political, economic and cultural importance for Europe. These countries are of differing socio-economic structures: besides three socialist States, there are four capitalist countries, all of them being highly developed industrial countries with intensive agriculture, forestry and fisheries. Some 140 million people producing about 15 per cent. of the world's industrial output live on the shores of the Baltic.

Unfortunately from some areas of the Baltic coast considerable amounts of impure industrial waste waters and domestic sewage with synthetic detergents from washing agents are dumped into the sea. Scientists estimate that every year the 200 rivers flowing into the Baltic Sea carry nearly half a million tons of waste waters into it. Phosphates originating from domestic sewage and from fertilisers cause eutrophication. As a result of eutrophication, the oxygen dissolved in the water diminishes and the living resources diminish too, with fishing becoming more difficult and yields decreasing.

Packing materials dropped from ships, especially from the large ferry-boats, are another source of pollution. It is estimated that the ferry-boats, which carry more than 30 million passengers a year, dump 50,000 tons of refuse into the Baltic Sea annually.

Some parts of the Baltic Sea bottom are littered with objects thrown overboard, so that trawling has become difficult or even impossible.

Almost 40 years ago concrete containers with 7,000 tons of arsenic, mercury and various acids were dumped off the Swedish coast. Now it is feared that these containers may leak and their contents escape.

* Professor of Law, Martin Luther University, Halle.

Moreover, plant protectives like DDT, aldrin, dieldrin and endrin are carried from land into the open sea. Sweden and the U.S.S.R. have forbidden the use of DDT, and other Baltic countries, *e.g.*, the G.D.R., have gradually been reducing the use of these agents.

In the Bornholm Deep Nazi mustard-gas bombs from the Second World War make fishing difficult. Danish fishermen operating in that part of the Baltic Sea have been poisoned from fish contaminated with this mustard gas.

Oil spills from ships are another source of pollution. The danger of this kind of pollution has increased as a result of the construction of supertankers. According to an estimate by Professor Simenov, of the Oceanographic Institute of the Soviet Union, oil pollution of the Baltic Sea has already reached such an extent that it will take at least 15 years until the last oil traces decompose, even if from now on no more oil is discharged into the Baltic Sea.

Oil pollution from oil drilling in the open sea is also possible. Underwater prospecting for oil and gas in the Baltic Sea is planned by some countries, but for the time being there seems to be no imminent danger of oil pollution from this source. Nevertheless, if an accident involving oil occurs in the Baltic Sea, the consequences would be extremely grave. It is therefore necessary to arrange in time for all Baltic States to co-operate in minimising those consequences.

Fortunately, radioactive and thermal pollution is not a pressing problem in the waters of the Baltic.

Summing up, one may say that many areas of the Baltic Sea, especially the central areas, are seriously polluted by industrial waste waters, domestic sewage, oil and toxic substances, and this pollution is growing. Some parts of the Baltic Sea, *e.g.*, the waters near Bornholm and Gotland, are to a large extent already biologically dead. This pollution depletes the living resources of the Baltic Sea, especially salmon. Growing eutrophication and the negative development in the availability of oxygen over the past few years make it an urgent necessity to undertake international action towards keeping the Baltic Sea clean and preserving its stocks of fish.

All States bordering on the Baltic Sea are responsible for keeping it clean. All the coastal States are engaged in scientific research on pollution and have taken measures against the pollution of their coastal waters. All Baltic States have adequate legal powers to fight against the pollution of their own waters.

In the G.D.R. the Environmental Policy Act of 1970 [1]† enjoins the competent government offices to pay special attention, among other things, to the protection of water. This applies in particular to the discharge of waste waters by industrial enterprises. Cases of oil pollution are covered by the Decree for the Prevention and Control of Oil Accidents of 1969,[2] which is of particular importance for the coastal waters of the German Democratic Republic. This Decree enjoins the owners and users of facilities by means of which oil is prospected for, extracted, transhipped or transported to act in such a way that oil leakage is avoided, and contains far-reaching measures of supervision and control. Violations of this Decree are prosecuted.

In Poland, the Water Act of 1962 [3] also provides the legal foundations for comprehensive measures for protecting the coastal waters from pollution. Apart from this Act, there are in Poland more than 20 other legal provisions of various kinds concerning the protection of maritime waters from pollution.

It is also generally known, and this is shown, *e.g.*, by a decision of the Supreme

† For references, see p. 222.

Soviet of the U.S.S.R. taken on September 20, 1972, on measures to continue improving environmental protection and the rational use of natural resources, that the Soviet Union is making a great effort to keep its inland and maritime waters clean and that it has tightened penal provisions for water polluters.

Actions by individual States to keep the Baltic clean are very important, but they alone are not enough to protect it, for they only cover the maritime internal waters and the territorial sea. The 1954 IMCO Convention on the Prevention of Oil Pollution, as amended in 1962 and 1969, alone is not enough to prevent the continued pollution of the Baltic. There is an urgent need now for more comprehensive joint action by all Baltic States on an international scale. This has to be done on the basis of the equality of all Baltic States. They should form a regional community of co-operation to make the protection of the Baltic against pollution effective by pooling their efforts and resources.

In order to work out effective international legal provisions it is necessary to find out by way of scientific research what are the best measures for preventing further pollution of the Baltic and for preserving and propagating the stocks of living resources. At a conference of Baltic oceanographers in Helsinki in May 1970, wide-ranging research on these questions was recommended and has subsequently begun. Similarly, at the conference of fishermen and oceanographers held in Stockholm in June 1972 emphasis was laid on the urgent need for all Baltic States to take joint measures to protect stocks of fish.

There is already a network of multilateral agreements on maritime pollution. But this network has many gaps. To secure a clean Baltic Sea and propagate the stocks of living resources we are particularly in need of international agreements between all Baltic States to establish technical standards to define pollution of the Baltic Sea by oil, industrial waste and domestic sewage; to provide for methods to detect water pollution; to establish regular and routine surveillance of the cleanliness of the Baltic waters and provide for an exchange of information and reports on instances of pollution; to provide for arrangements on the carrying out of checks; and to establish rules governing the co-operation between all Baltic States to combat jointly, *e.g.*, an oil disaster caused by a collision of tankers. These rules might be similar to those laid down in the Agreement for Co-operation in Dealing with Pollution of the North Sea by Oil of 1969. Moreover, rules might be established saying what concerted action Baltic States might take to obtain compensation, *e.g.*, for damage caused by oil pollution, from the party that caused the pollution. This catalogue of proposals on the problem of pollution in the Baltic is incomplete, but it may suffice to point out that the problems involved are of a complex nature. As regards protection of the living resources in the Baltic, ideas have already been put forward as to possible legal arrangements for fisheries and the protection of fish stocks. The Polish People's Republic has drawn up a draft convention which *inter alia* contains the following principles: increasing the stocks of fish in the interest of all Baltic States; joint responsibility of all Baltic States for the protection of fish stocks and their rational use; expanding complex international co-operation; and setting up an International Commission to recommend, on the basis of scientific research and information, measures to regulate the catch and preserve the stocks for all varieties of fish in the Baltic Sea.

In conclusion I wish to underline three more points:

First, I believe that the international law of the sea will be extended to include new branches, such as law regarding the exploitation of the deep seabed, law for the protection of the sea from pollution and law for the protection and use of the living resources of the sea. These new branches must rest on the basic principles of international law as laid down in the Charter of the United Nations and in Resolution A/2625 (XXV). The law must be an instrument to protect the human environment and its living resources. I believe that the international law of the sea, which, among other things, has to protect the oceans from pollution and the living resources from extermination, must be based on the existing principles of the law of the sea as contained in the 1958 Geneva Convention and on the common interests of all peoples. Within the framework of the existing principles of the law of the sea special rules and regulations against maritime pollution and for the preservation of living resources must be devised.

Secondly, the elaboration of the above-mentioned agreements, rules and regulations calls for the co-operation of lawyers, oceanographers, ichthyologists and economists. The protection of the human environment and its living resources in the sea in general, and in the Baltic Sea in particular, confronts jurists with problems of an entirely new dimension and complexity. Jurists must therefore tackle these problems jointly with oceanographers, ichthyologists and economists.

Thirdly, the agreements I have mentioned can only become effective if, in accordance with international law, all Baltic States, regardless of their differing political, economic and social systems, take part in their elaboration and implementation. During the last few years, Finland, Poland and Sweden have sought to prepare multilateral agreements with all Baltic States to combat marine pollution and protect living resources. In 1969 and 1970 representatives from all the Baltic States meeting in Visby, capital of the island of Gotland, worked out the draft of a convention on co-operation in combating oil pollution in the Baltic. However, the signing and entry into force of this convention has not been possible so far because the Federal Republic of Germany has not been prepared to sign this convention as a treaty concluded between governments. I believe it is necessary for such agreements to be concluded on a high intergovernmental level because of their importance. Such regional agreements should be signed between governments and not between local authorities or scientific institutions.

The protection of the Baltic Sea from pollution and the preservation of its living resources is undoubtedly a grave international problem. Because of its complex nature it can only be solved by way of the close interstate co-operation of all Baltic States. The problems of the Baltic Sea are a sample or a cross-section of the problems affecting the oceans, problems which numerous committees of the UN and many international organisations are concerned with. These regional and global problems require for their solution the co-operation of all interested States.

REFERENCES

1. *Official Gazette* I, p. 67.
2. *Official Gazette* II, p. 145.
3. Dz. Ustaw, No. 34/1962.

CHAPTER 18

The Great Lakes

By Don C. Piper *

BECAUSE the Great Lakes of Canada and the United States are national waters subject to the exclusive jurisdiction and ownership of the two riparian States, it is beneficial and instructive to examine the international legal régime of the lakes. Indeed, the optimal utilisation of the lakes by the riparian States and by third States is dependent upon a network of conventional and customary rules of international law. In many cases, these rules are particular rules of international law that are applicable to the unique situation presented by the Great Lakes. In other instances, customary rules of international law that can appropriately be applied to the Great Lakes are utilised.[1]† The importance of the international legal régime as instructive precedent for the new directions in the law of the sea should not be discounted. National policy-makers seeking precedent and possible guidance on the difficult issue of the width of the territorial sea will not likely find an example in the Great Lakes, but policy-makers seeking a precedent applicable to the question of rights of passage through national waters that are part of an important international navigation route will find instructive precedent in the conventional rules formulated to guarantee navigation on the Great Lakes.

Although the Great Lakes may be small in contrast to the expanse of the high seas, the importance of the lakes to the riparian States and the significance of the international legal régime should not be minimised.

The physical and economic facts of the lakes illustrate their importance and the need for the application of rules and principles of international law. The Great Lakes are the largest body of fresh water in the world. They encompass 95,000 square miles of which approximately two-thirds is within the jurisdiction of the United States and one-third within Canadian jurisdiction. Since the opening of the St. Lawrence Seaway in 1959, there has been a continuous waterway of 2,347 miles into the North American continent with a channel of sufficient depth to accommodate ocean-going vessels. The ports along the lakes have become major centres of international commerce with shipments of wheat and containerised cargo. Water diverted from the American side of the Niagara River produces annually more than 50 million dollars' worth of hydro-electric power for consumption in the populous north-eastern states with an equal, if not greater, amount of power generated on the Canadian side. Two-thirds of the Canadian population resides within the Great Lakes basin; on the American side, such populous cities as Chicago, Cleveland, Detroit, Milwaukee and Buffalo circle the shoreline.

Since, as a general rule of international law, each State has exclusive jurisdiction over the land and water within its territorial limits, the resources of the Great Lakes

* Chairman, Department of Government and Politics, University of Maryland.
† For references, see p. 230.

could have been developed independently by each sovereign as a purely internal matter without reference to the rights and interests of the other riparian State or without any reciprocal extension of rights to the nationals of the other State. Such an approach would certainly have frustrated the full development and optimal utilisation of the resources of the lakes. Fortunately, since the days of American independence, there has been an awareness by the policy-makers that their mutual interests in realising the potential of the lakes' resources could only be accomplished by the utilisation of applicable customary rules of international law and the formulation of special conventional rules.

A survey of the international law of the Great Lakes supports the conclusion that the greater portion of the international legal régime consists of particular conventional rules. This is not surprising since the topographical characteristics of the lakes are unique and require specially focused rules. Consequently, there are treaty provisions governing the rights of navigation, the use and control of boundary waters, the preservation of fisheries, the definition and delineation of the international boundary, the scope of salvage rights, and the use of radiotelephone installations on vessels for safety purposes. Notwithstanding this preponderance of conventional law, general principles of customary international law have also been utilised in the legal régime. This is particularly the case with regard to the exercise of criminal and admiralty jurisdiction. Reciprocal legislation enacted by the national legislative bodies has also been effective, *e.g.*, rules of the road and pilotage requirements.

In the context of the broad inquiry of new directions in the law of the sea, it is instructive to examine the international legal régime of the Great Lakes in the areas of navigation, control of fisheries, control and prevention of pollution and international machinery for the control and use of the water resources.

NAVIGATION RIGHTS

With regard to navigation, it should be recalled that the complete Great Lakes–St. Lawrence River navigation system lies solely within the territory of the national States. The international boundary between Canada and the United States in the area mentioned is approximately a median line through the upper portion of the St. Lawrence River, the Lakes Ontario, Erie, Huron and Superior, and the connecting rivers. The lower portion of the St. Lawrence River is located solely within Canadian jurisdiction and Lake Michigan is located solely within the jurisdiction of the United States.[2]

Notwithstanding the national jurisdiction, the riparian States have established a significant international legal régime which pertains not just to the nationals and vessels of the riparian States but also to the nationals and vessels of third States. Until the construction of the St. Lawrence Seaway, the primary focus of the legal régime was upon the establishment of rights of navigation for the nationals and vessels of the two riparian States. At the present time, however, attention must be directed to the policies and rules that assure to nationals and vessels of third States navigation rights along the entire system. Indeed, it is this subject that may provide a precedent for rights of transit through former parts of the high seas that become national waters as a result of national or international decisions to increase the width of the territorial sea.

The present bilateral régime respecting rights of navigation for the riparian States is the result of negotiation and compromise rather than the application of *a priori* legal principles. Moreover, the régime was not accomplished by a single treaty arrangement; rather there is a series of bilateral arrangements that together establish the legal régime. Although some of the treaties are not in force at the present time, this legal régime includes provisions of the Jay Treaty 1794[3]; the Webster-Ashburton Treaty 1842[4]; the Treaty of Washington 1871[5]; and the Boundary Waters Treaty 1909.[6] In addition there are some exchanges of notes between the two Governments regarding joint co-operation in the construction of the St. Lawrence Seaway project.[7] Although there are some variations in particular instruments, the significant consequence of the network of international instruments is that the entire Great Lakes–St. Lawrence River system is open to navigation by the inhabitants and vessels of either riparian.[8]

As an instructive lesson for the new directions in the law of the sea, it is more appropriate to examine the arrangements that have been established by the two riparians to facilitate navigation by vessels of third States. Since the waters of the waterway system are national and not international, vessels of third States have no legal right of transit without the permission of the two riparian States. The treaties mentioned above pertain only to navigation rights for Canadian or United States vessels. Moreover, navigation of the entire waterway system requires transit through both Canadian and United States waters. Hence the two riparians must co-operate together if the Seaway is to be optimally utilised and if third party vessels are to enjoy navigation privileges.

Both Canada and the United States are parties to numerous commerical treaties that permit vessels of the contracting parties to enter national waters and ports. The standard of treatment generally set forth in such treaties is most-favoured-nation treatment, national treatment, or both. These bilateral treaties, however, do not authorise vessels of the treaty party to transit the waters of the co-riparian State. As a matter of public policy, both riparian States permit transit by commercial vessels of third States in time of peace. There is, however, no specific understanding between Canada and the United States whereby each agrees to permit the transit of vessels of third States in order to call at ports of the co-riparian State. As a matter of policy, it is unlikely that either riparian would undertake any action that would seek to exclude all third party vessels from transit on the waterway system. To do so would certainly frustrate the purpose of the St. Lawrence Seaway and the co-operative arrangements.

The obligation of each riparian to the other regarding third party vessels is considered in the exchange of notes relative to the St. Lawrence Seaway, but not definitively resolved.[9] In the notes, the two Governments agree to consult with one another before promulgating any regulations applicable to a national section of the Seaway that might affect third party shipping proceeding to or from either party. The requirement of consultation does not, however, bar subsequent unilateral action by either party. Discriminatory exclusion of certain third party vessels by either riparian would appear to be in conflict with the spirit of Article 16 (3) of the Convention on the Territorial Sea and the Contiguous Zone.[10]

A possible bar to unilateral action by either State to preclude transit of third party vessels is Article V of the General Agreement on Tariffs and Trade.[11] That Article assures freedom of transit through the territories of the member States for traffic in transit to or from the territory of another contracting party. Accordingly one may conclude that neither riparian could exclude vessels from a third State carrying cargo from one contracting party to the other co-riparian, also a contracting party. Although this Article would appear to limit the legal right of either riparian to exclude certain third party vessels from the waterway system, it does not assure that all third party vessels will enjoy freedom of transit. This right of transit applies only to those vessels carrying cargo from one GATT contracting party to either riparian.

The author is not aware of any public dispute between the two riparians regarding the transit of third party vessels or vessels from any particular State. Because of the close relationship between the two States, the requirement of consultation may be adequate to preclude any difficulties. One must acknowledge, however, that the international legal régime is incomplete on this matter. In a larger context, the legal régime would appear to be strengthened by the conclusion of a specific agreement that sets forth for both riparians the obligations to the other regarding the rights of transit of third party vessels. One might suggest that a basic instrument should reaffirm what appears to be existing policy, *i.e.*, that both riparians in time of peace will pursue a national treatment policy regarding third party vessels seeking to utilise any portion of the Great Lakes–St. Lawrence River system.

REGULATION OF FISHERIES

Regulation of fisheries on the Great Lakes, while important to the nationals of the riparian States, does not appear to offer an instructive lesson for application to other areas. Since the waters are national and not international, commercial fishing by third party nationals or vessels is excluded. The numerous efforts to establish an international legal régime for fisheries have been complicated by the fact that the legal ownership and authority to promulgate regulations for fisheries resides individually with the eight American states that encircle the Lakes and both the Canadian Federal Government and the Province of Ontario. The effort of the American Federal Government to nationalise the fishery regulations and play a significant rôle has been consistently rejected by the local governmental units. Although the fish appear not to have recognised either international, state or provincial boundaries, regulation of fishing activities is conducted essentially at the local level. As a consequence, specific regulations such as those regulating licences and size of catch are issued by the eight American states and the Canadian Federal Government in co-operation with the Province of Ontario. With the exception of a few of the American states that permit Canadian nationals to purchase a commercial fishing licence, the right of commercial fishing within the territory of each State is restricted to nationals.

After two unperfected treaties and several joint studies, the two Federal Governments were finally able in 1954 to conclude and perfect a treaty establishing an international régime with limited authority.[12] The primary focus of this régime is the Great Lakes Fishery Commission with equal representation from the two riparian States. The basic purpose of the Commission is to promote and co-ordinate research activities relating to the conservation of the fishery and to formulate and implement a comprehensive programme for the control and eradication of the parasitic sea lamprey. The Commission may offer recommendations to the American states and the Province of Ontario but it has no regulatory authority.

Although the Commission may be able to alleviate the existing problem of destruction by the sea lamprey, the long-range problem of the gradual depletion of the fish available for human consumption will probably require a more ambitious international régime. Whether such a régime will be established depends, not so much upon international considerations, as upon the domestic problem of obtaining agreement among the eight American states as to the nature and scope of such a régime. One may speculate that the difficulties and problems inherent in facilitating and completing negotiations and co-operation among the eight American states probably equal those accompanying international negotiations relating to the high seas fishery.

NON-NAVIGATION PRINCIPLES AND WATER USE

Having resolved the fundamental legal issues regarding free and open navigation during the nineteenth century, the two Governments in this century have concentrated upon the establishment of an effective international legal régime to facilitate the optimal use of the Great Lakes for non-navigation purposes. Because the Great Lakes–St. Lawrence River system is one watershed, co-operation in non-navigable uses is just as essential as for navigation use. In this regard, the two Governments have not looked to existing, generally accepted principles of customary international law relating to the non-navigable use of flowing waters; rather they have pursued treaty law and the bilateral formulation of basic principles governing the use of the common water resources. They have indeed been in the forefront in the establishment of treaty rules in this matter. The specific rules that have been formulated to fulfil the requirements of the Great Lakes system will not necessarily meet the requirements of other international waterways. The basic purpose of the rules is, however, universally applicable: to develop the waterway system for the optimal benefit of the community notwithstanding the division of political authority. Accordingly, the general approach and perspective adopted by the two Governments is instructive and possibly applicable to other waterway systems.

The basic document that regulates the non-navigable uses of the water is the Boundary Waters Treaty concluded between Great Britain and the United States in 1909.[13] This instrument sets forth the principles that are applicable to the boundary waters and establishes the International Joint Commission to exercise jurisdiction over the use, obstruction or diversion of the waters. Within the terms of the treaty, boundary waters are those through which the international boundary passes. Tributary waters are those that flow into boundary waters. In general the treaty permits each State to undertake unilateral action in its tributary waters but requires joint co-operation in the use of boundary waters. The specific principles that govern the use of boundary waters are the following:

1. With the exception of existing arrangements or special agreements, any use, diversion or obstruction of waters on either side of the boundary line affecting the natural flow of waters on the other side of the boundary line requires the approval of the International Joint Commission. This principle is not intended, however, to interfere with ordinary use of the water for domestic and sanitary purposes.

2. Each Government may construct works in boundary waters for the improvement of commerce and navigation provided such works are wholly on its side of the boundary and do not " materially affect " the flow or level of the boundary waters on the other side of the boundary line.

3. Except in cases of special agreement, the parties will not construct any works or obstructions in the waters flowing from boundary waters or in waters at a lower level than the boundary in rivers flowing across the boundary that would raise the level of the waters on the other side without the approval of the International Joint Commission.

4. Boundary waters and waters flowing across the boundary line shall not be polluted on either side to the injury of health or property on the other side of the boundary line.

5. Each party shall have equal and similar rights in the use of boundary waters on its respective side of the boundary line. The International Joint Commission may suspend this rule for temporary diversions.

6. The following order of precedence is to be observed in the use of the boundary

waters and no use shall be permitted which tends " materially " to conflict with or restrain any other use which has precedence: (a) uses for domestic and sanitary purposes; (b) uses for navigation including the service of navigation canals; (c) uses for power and irrigation purposes.

Viewing the Commission's 60 years of experience, one can conclude that the principles outlined above and their application by the International Joint Commission have promoted the wide utilisation of the boundary waters with a minimum of disagreement. In contrast there has been continuous controversy regarding the treaty principle that permits each party to undertake unilateral actions in its tributary waters.[14] The then Canadian Prime Minister, Wilfrid Laurier, believed that this principle was contrary to international law and considered rejecting the treaty prior to its ratification.

Indeed one of the lessons of the treaty is that the international régime is vulnerable and incomplete when not all parts of the waterway system are subject to the same general principles regarding use and diversion.

Because it may be an instructive example for other riparian States, it is appropriate to mention briefly the functions and purposes of the International Joint Commission. The Commission, consisting of six members, primarily engineers and technicians, has both investigatory and quasi-adjudicatory tasks. With regard to the latter tasks, it approves all projects involving the use, obstruction or diversion of boundary waters. In performing this task it utilises the principles mentioned above and renders decisions that are binding upon the parties. These projects have varied from major hydroelectric power projects to private projects involving small scale construction activities. As an international tribunal, the Commission adheres to the adjective rule that a private applicant does not enjoy direct access to the Commission. Rather the private applicant must apply to the government within whose territory the project will be developed.

In its investigatory role, the Commission, at the request of either Government, undertakes studies of matters that involve the rights of either State towards the other or the inhabitants of the other along the common boundary. The investigative reports are advisory to the Governments and are not legally binding or required. The Governments have requested studies relating to pollution in the boundary waters and the atmosphere, the preservation of Niagara Falls, power and navigation development in the St. Lawrence River, the regulation of the level of Lake Ontario, and the potential for oil pollution in Lake Erie with the introduction of lake-bed drilling operations.

A survey of the Commission's dockets, decisions and reports supports the conclusion that the Commission's contribution to the development and utilisation of the waterway resources has been very substantial.[15]

POLLUTION CONTROL

The Great Lakes, perhaps more so than the high seas, have experienced substantial pollution problems within the past decades. Unlike the high seas, where the concern with pollution may centre upon shipping activities, pollution on the Great Lakes is caused by metropolitan and industrial centres that are along the waterline as well as by shipping activities. Indeed the pollution is so extensive that some critics have characterised Lake Erie as a " dead " lake because of its polluted condition.

The international legal régime for the Great Lakes is concerned with problems of trans-boundary pollution. One of the principles of the Boundary Waters Treaty, mentioned above, is that the boundary waters shall not be polluted to the injury of health or property on the other side of the international boundary. Whatever the causes and wherever the origin, it is evidence that the entire waterway system is suffering from varying degrees of water pollution. Pollution, like fish, does not manifest any respect for international boundaries or agreements.

To investigate the causes and extent of pollution and to make recommendations for its alleviation, the riparian States have relied upon the International Joint Commission. The Commission in one of its first reports recommended that the two Governments conclude an agreement authorising the Commission to regulate and prohibit the pollution of boundary waters and waters crossing the boundary. At the request of the Governments, the Commission prepared a draft treaty that would give it such authority, but the instrument was never perfected. One may speculate that, if the Commission had been granted the regulatory authority to prohibit pollution activities, the extensive pollution existing today might have been prevented.

Notwithstanding its lack of regulatory authority, the Commission has been actively investigating and monitoring water pollution. In 1946 and 1948 both Governments asked the Commission to investigate water pollution in the connecting rivers and in the Niagara River. The Commission identified the primary causes of the pollution as the municipal and industrial centres along the rivers and offered appropriate recommendations to the Governments.

In 1964 the two Governments requested the Commission to undertake a study of the extent, causes and location of pollution in Lakes Ontario and Erie and the international section of the St. Lawrence River. Following an extensive investigation, the Commission reported in 1970 that the waters of the lower Great Lakes were being seriously polluted on both sides of the international boundary to the detriment of both countries and to an extent that was causing injury to health and property on the other side of the boundary.[16] The Commission again identified the primary cause of the pollution as the wastes discharged by municipalities and industrial centres along the lakes. In its detailed and comprehensive report to the Governments, the Commission recommended specific water quality objectives and programme to achieve the objectives.

In 1969 the Commission undertook at the request of both Governments an urgent examination of the adequacy of existing procedures to prevent a serious oil-spill on Lake Erie as a consequence of the oil and gas exploration and development. After investigation, the Commission reported that the existing regulations of the Province of Ontario and the states of New York and Pennsylvania, if effectively enforced, were adequate to protect the water resources of the lake.

A focused international régime to combat pollution using the work of the International Joint Commission was established on April 15, 1972, when President Nixon and Prime Minister Trudeau signed the Great Lakes Water Quality Agreement.[17] This agreement, relying substantially upon the I.J.C. report, is a comprehensive document that sets forth both general and specific water quality objectives for the improvement of the lakes. The specific action to accomplish the objectives will be undertaken by the two Federal Governments, the Province of Ontario and the eight American states. Programmes will be established to combat pollution from municipal, industrial, agricultural, forestry and other land uses, shipping activities and eutrophication. In addition, the agreement calls for the formulation of a joint contingency plan to respond to oil-spills and the identification of hazardous polluting substances. Annexes specify steps for both implementation and study.

The majority of the programmes will pertain to national activities and will not have any direct impact upon third States. However, some parts of the programme to combat pollution from shipping activities will affect third parties. In this regard the

Governments will consider compatible regulations regarding vessel design, construction and operation to prevent harmful discharges of oil. In addition, studies will be initiated of traffic patterns and of foreign competence standards for manning of vessels to ascertain that the foreign standards meet the Canadian and United States standards.

Although the primary concern of the agreement is the control of pollution in the boundary waters, the agreement recognises that the programmes mentioned above should be applied to tributary waters where necessary or desirable to achieve the water quality objectives for the boundary waters.

In establishing this international régime, the two Governments have also set forth a number of responsibilities for the International Joint Commission. The Commission is specifically requested to undertake studies of pollution in boundary waters caused by agricultural, forestry and land use activities and of the actions necessary to enhance the water quality of Lakes Huron and Superior. In addition, the Commission has the very broad responsibility of monitoring the water quality activities, including investigations and analysis of data and the preparation of specific recommendations to the Governments for implementation. Indeed, it is not difficult to speculate that the major activities of the Commission in the near future will relate almost exclusively to the control of pollution and the enhancement of water quality.

In summary, the new direction in the law of the sea for the Great Lakes clearly is the route of pollution control and the improvement of water quality in the waterway. Perhaps this experience will provide instructive precedent for other States and waterways.

REFERENCES

1. For a detailed analysis of the international legal régime, see Don C. Piper, *The International Law of the Great Lakes* (Durham, N.C.: Duke University Press, 1967).

2. The Canadian International Boundary, Apr. 11, 1908: 35 *Stat*. 2003.

3. 8 *Stat*. 116.

4. 8 *Stat*. 572.

5. 18 *Stat*. 335.

6. 36 *Stat*. 2448.

7. 5 U.S.T. 1784.

8. It should be noted that the freedom of navigation applies not to nationals and vessels but to *inhabitants* and vessels. See Art. 1 of the Boundary Waters Treaty.

9. 5 U.S.T. 1784.

10. This article provides that if the right of innocent passage through the territorial sea is temporarily suspended it must be accomplished on a non-discriminatory basis: 15 U.S.T. 1606.

11. 61 *Stat*. (5) (6).

12. 6 U.S.T. 2836.

13. 36 *Stat*. 2448.

14. The primary disagreement has centred on the diversion at Chicago of water out of Lake Michigan into the Mississippi River watershed. See Piper, *op. cit.*, pp. 90–103; and Don C. Piper, "A Significant Docket for the International Joint Commission" (1965) A.J.I.L. 593–597.

15. The Commission's dockets are conveniently summarised in Marjorie M. Whiteman, *Digest of International Law* (Washington: Government Printing Office, 1964), III, pp. 826–871.

16. International Joint Commission: Canada and the United States, *Pollution of Lake Erie, Lake Ontario, and the International Section of the St. Lawrence River* (1970).

17. T.I.A.S. 7312. For the U.S.A., this is an executive agreement and does not require the consent of the Senate for its approval. The Agreement entered into force on the date of its signature.

CHAPTER 19

The Persian Gulf

By Richard Young *

1. THE GEOGRAPHICAL SETTING

THE Persian Gulf, that arm of the Indian Ocean lying between the Arabian peninsula and Iran, has an area of some 241,000 square kilometres—slightly larger than the Gulf of St. Lawrence and about two-thirds the size of the Baltic. From its head at the mouth of the Shatt al-Arab river system to its entrance at the Strait of Hormuz, its length is about 430 nautical miles and its maximum width about 160 nautical miles. Generally shallow, its greatest depth is about 100 metres and its average no more than 40. The deeper waters are found mostly in the lower part of the Gulf and along the mountainous Iranian coast, which contrasts markedly with the generally low-lying shore on the Arabian side. Throughout the Gulf, but particularly on the Arabian side, are numerous islands, reefs, banks and shoals which constitute hazards not only to the navigator but also to the political geographer and the international lawyer.

The narrowest part of the Gulf is at its entrance in the Strait of Hormuz. This is bounded on its northerly side by the coast of Iran, including the close inshore Iranian islands of Qishm, Henjam, Larak and Hormuz. The southerly side is formed by the great promontory of Oman, terminating in the Musandam Peninsula under the sovereignty of the Sultanate of Oman. Three small islets, known as Salamah Wa Binatahan or the Quoins, lie in the Strait within nine miles of the Musandam Peninsula, and the most constricted part of the Strait, 20¾ miles wide, is that between these islands and Larak to the north. In this area about 16½ miles of the Strait's length is 26 miles or less in width.[1]†

Particularly significant because of their strategic location in the area where the Strait widens out into the Gulf proper are the islands of Great Tumb (Tanb-e-Bozorg), Little Tumb (Nabiyu Tumb) and Abu Musa. Great Tumb, the easternmost, lies about 15 miles from the island of Qishm and 40 miles from the Arabian mainland. Little Tumb, about eight miles west of its big brother, lies about 20 miles from Qishm and 45 miles from the Arabian side. Abu Musa, about 23 miles south-west of Little Tumb, is about 32 miles from the Arabian mainland and 40 miles from Iran.

Within the Gulf are eight littoral States. Counter-clockwise from the Strait of Hormuz they are Iran; Iraq, with a narrow frontage west of the Shatt al-Arab; Kuwait; Saudi Arabia; Bahrain (the only island State); Qatar; the Union of Arab Emirates (the seven former Trucial States) [2]; and Oman.[3] Since the termination in December 1971 of the United Kingdom's special relationship with the Trucial sheikhdoms, all the Gulf States are fully independent and are members of the United Nations.

* Attorney, Van Hornesville, New York.
† For references, see p. 239.

2. OFFSHORE JURISDICTIONAL CLAIMS

Except for belts of territorial sea along the mainland coast and around islands, the waters of the Persian Gulf have traditionally been regarded as part of the high seas. This view is to be found, for example, in the opinion of a special committee of jurists consulted at the International Conference on Trade in Arms held at Geneva in 1925. Asked specifically about the "present status of the Persian Gulf from the point of view of international law," the committee answered: "The status of the Persian Gulf from the point of view of international law is the same as that of the open sea. The same applies to the Strait of Hormuz and to the Gulf of Oman."[4] There is no reason to think that this status has altered in the intervening years, but it has been affected by two developments. One is the trend, evident in the Persian Gulf as elsewhere, towards wider territorial sea claims. The other is the general acceptance in the last quarter of a century of the continental shelf doctrine, which authorises a coastal State to exercise, for resource exploitation purposes, sovereign rights over the seabed and subsoil beneath the high seas adjacent to its coast out to at least the 200 metre isobath.

(a) Territorial sea and contiguous zone

Of the eight Gulf States, five have taken positive steps to claim a belt of territorial sea 12 miles in width: Saudi Arabia (1958), Iraq (1958), Iran (1959), Kuwait (1967) and Oman (1972).[5] Bahrain and Qatar appear thus far to have made no change in the three mile limit originally established under British influence. The position in the new Union of Arab Emirates is somewhat unclear: of the seven constituent sheikhdoms, six appear to have adhered in the period before the Union to the three mile standard, but Sharjah in March 1970 published a claim to a 12 mile limit. The Union itself has as yet taken no position, although the power to define territorial waters is expressly conferred on the federal authorities by the Constitution.[6]

Despite this variation in existing claims, it may be surmised that, once they come to deal with the subject, the three mile States in the Gulf will adopt the broader limit already claimed by their larger neighbours. For all practical purposes 12 miles may be regarded as the general Gulf standard at present; but the possibility of a still more extended claim, perhaps 18 miles, cannot be ruled out.

A contiguous zone beyond the territorial sea has been claimed expressly only by Saudi Arabia, which asserts authority to conduct "maritime surveillance" in a six mile zone for the purpose of assuring compliance with its laws relating to security, navigation, fiscal and health matters.[7] In its 1967 decree Kuwait reserved its right to a contiguous zone to be later delineated, but this does not appear yet to have been done. Both countries make it clear that any rights they may have to control fishery resources are not restricted by this legislation.

(b) Continental shelf

Under the continental shelf doctrine referred to above, all the Gulf States have expressly laid claim to the seabed and subsoil of areas adjacent to their coasts but beyond the limit of their territorial seas. Because of the shallowness of the Gulf, these claims dispose of its entire seabed and subsoil and consequently adjoin one another. Recognising this geographical situation, the claims made have not been specific as to limits, but have affirmed instead the need to establish seabed boundaries in accordance with equitable principles by agreement with neighbouring States. All the claims have recognised the character of the superjacent waters as high seas.

Since 1958, when Saudi Arabia and Bahrain concluded the first offshore boundary agreement in the Gulf, a number of the required offshore boundary lines have been definitively settled. In the case of Iran, for example, which has the longest offshore boundary in the Gulf, the delineation of such lines has been agreed upon with Saudi Arabia (1968), Bahrain (1971) and Qatar (1969). A line with Abu Dhabi was reportedly initialled in 1971, and the line with Kuwait has been said to be in an advanced stage of negotiation. Still to be finally determined, however, are the boundaries between Iran and Iraq, the Neutral Zone, and the Union of Arab Emirates; and on these progress may be delayed by strained Iraqi-Iranian relations and by Arab concern over Iran's occupation, mentioned in the next section, of the Tumbs and Abu Musa.

Also completed are the boundaries between Qatar and Abu Dhabi (1969), and a number of those between the States of the Union of Arab Emirates, which are no longer international boundaries properly speaking. The Qatar-Saudi Arabian boundary in the Bay of Salwa has been reported as agreed upon in principle, but the line between Qatar and Bahrain remains unsettled because of disagreement over the Hawar islands between the two States. The course of the Kuwait-Iraq boundary is understood to be still unresolved, as is also the case with the boundary between Kuwait and the Neutral Zone. The southern offshore boundary of the Neutral Zone, between the Zone and Saudi Arabia, has not yet been formally determined throughout its length; but the segment nearer the shore, which runs through the Safaniya and Khafji offshore oilfields, has been established *de facto* for a number of years.

Certain common features can be identified in the various agreements so far reached. Despite the fact that none of the Gulf States is a party to the 1958 Continental Shelf Convention, there has been a clear tendency to rely for guidance on Article 6 of that Convention, which specifies that, in the absence of agreement or " special circumstances," the boundary shall follow a line equidistant from the nearest points on the base lines from which the territorial sea of each State is measured. This concept of equidistance appears in almost all cases to have been the starting-point for negotiations, but it can be seen in some cases to have undergone adjustments in the course of the bargaining process.

It is also evident that, in the construction of median lines along the axis of the Gulf, small outlying islands have generally been disregarded, with the result that the lines tend to reflect a " true " median between the opposite mainlands. (But it should be pointed out that none of the agreed boundaries has required a coming to grips with the question of the effect to be given to an " important " island—for example, Kharg, of which Iran on occasion has urged that account be taken.) In the case of boundaries not involving the main axis, islands and shoals have more often been given weight, notably between Abu Dhabi and Qatar.

Where islands lie on or near the agreed line they have usually been recognised as possessing a belt of territorial sea; and provision has been made for the seabed boundary to deviate from its normal course to follow the limit of this belt around the island until it rejoins that course. Examples are the treatment of the islands of al-Arabiyah and al-Farisiyah, which lie athwart the median line, in the Saudi Arabia-Iran agreement, and Dayyinah between Abu Dhabi and Qatar. In constricted waters, however, where there is no room for a territorial belt, this has not always been possible: thus on the Saudi Arabia-Bahrain boundary, two points on the line are located on the tips of islets, the islets themselves being allocated one to each party.

Another factor influencing modifications in a strictly equidistant line is the presence of offshore oil deposits. Thus the northerly segment of the Saudi Arabia-Iran boundary deviates from the median in order to achieve a more equitable division of the

Marjan-Fereydoon reservoir. In the case of Abu Dhabi and Qatar, one of the non-equidistant boundary points is well no. 1 in the al-Bunduq field. This effects a division of that field between the two parties, but provision was made for the entire field to be operated by Abu Dhabi's concessionaire and for revenues to be split equally.

Lastly, it may be observed that on the whole the offshore boundaries so far determined in the Gulf conform remarkably well to the guidelines laid down by the International Court of Justice in the *North Sea Continental Shelf Cases*.[8] The agreements have been worked out on equitable principles, and the factors of geographical configuration, ascertainable resources and proportionality cited as relevant by the Court have generally been taken into account.

(c) Islands

Of some 130 islands and islets in the Gulf, the great majority are barren and uninhabited. But barren or not, they present two types of legal problems. First, since every island is normally entitled to a belt of territorial sea, the large number in the Gulf raise complicated questions of delimitation. Second, those islands whose sovereignty has been in dispute have been subjects of controversies which in some cases are still continuing.

The first point is particularly important in relation to freedom of navigation, especially in view of the trend towards a wider territorial sea limit. The effect of such an enlargement, taken in conjunction with the large number of islands not more than 24 miles distant from each other or from the mainland, is to include within the territorial sea a much larger area of the Gulf than formerly was the case. For example, off the coast of Saudi Arabia, the Saudi Arabian islands of Jana, al-Jurayd, Kurayn, Karan, Harqus and al-Arabiyah are so located that their territorial belts merge to form a continuous expanse of territorial sea reaching from the mainland more than 60 miles out to the centre of the Gulf. So also, in the narrower part of the Strait of Hormuz, the 12 mile claims by Iran and Oman more than meet, thus making the entrance to the Gulf territorial waters of the two States.

With respect to questions of sovereignty, a number of once troublesome disputes have now been settled by tacit understandings or express agreements; but some unresolved problems still exist. The status of islands off the Saudi Arabia-Kuwait Neutral Zone is one instance. But the most significant recent case has involved the two Tumb islands and Abu Musa in the lower Gulf.

During the period of British ascendancy, Britain regarded the two Tumbs as appertaining to Ras al-Khaimah and Abu Musa as appertaining to Sharjah. On November 30, 1971, however, Iranian forces landed on all three islands in furtherance of a long-standing but long-dormant Iranian claim to sovereignty. The landing on Abu Musa was made by agreement with the then ruler of Sharjah, which apparently reserved certain rights to Sharjah in somewhat ambiguous terms [9]; but no such agreement existed in the case of the Tumbs.

Reaction on the Arab side to the Iranian occupation was angry and frequently vociferous, but the only serious concrete consequence was Libya's nationalisation of British Petroleum properties in that country, allegedly in retaliation for Britain's failure to resist the Iranian move. Various mediatory efforts have thus far had no effect; the Iranian occupation of the islands continues, although Iran announced in January 1972 that it had no more territorial claims in the Gulf and would not use its position to interfere with free transit.[10]

In the case of Abu Musa, additional complications over oil arose from a conflict between Sharjah and Umm al-Qaiwain. In late 1969 the holder of Umm al-Qaiwain's offshore concession, Occidental Petroleum Corporation, announced the discovery of an " extensive structure " in Umm al-Qaiwain's offshore area about nine miles east of Abu Musa and thus six miles beyond the three mile limit originally claimed around that island. In March 1970, however, Sharjah announced that by an unpublished decree of September 10, 1969, it had fixed its limit at 12 miles—thus encompassing the site and bringing it within the Sharjah offshore concession held by Buttes Gas and Oil Company. This claim was subsequently endorsed by Iran in its 1971 understanding with Sharjah.

Considerable furore followed the Sharjah announcement, including litigation between the concessionaires,[11] and the matter has not yet been finally resolved. While Buttes is reported to be proceeding with development work at the scene, Occidental has announced that it will continue to pursue all recourses open to it, including possible attachment in other jurisdictions of any oil produced.

3. FISHERIES

For many centuries the one world-famous fishery in the Persian Gulf was that for the pearl oyster, which flourished in its waters and produced natural pearls of unexcelled quality. As late as 1946 Bahrain alone sent 192 boats and 7,100 divers to the fishery, which yielded a harvest that year valued at over three million rupees.[12] But in recent years the competition of cultured pearls and the lure of better and easier jobs in the oil industry have reduced this once major activity to negligible proportions. For practical commercial purposes pearling in the Gulf must now be regarded as defunct.

Just the reverse promises to be true of commercial fishing for edible species. Until very recent years, fishing for such species was carried on predominantly by local inhabitants using fish traps, small boats and simple methods; even trawling was rare because of a lack of craft with sufficient power to handle heavy nets. The result was a total catch representing only a fraction of the potential yield to be obtained from the more than 200 edible species which have been identified in the area. But this traditional pattern has now been breaking down for some years, and the process of change may be expected to accelerate. Fishing craft from outside the Gulf, particularly Japanese, have made their appearance; at the same time, local capital and foreign technical advice have become available to stimulate the growth of a local fishing industry using modern methods and equipment.

Among the edible species are mackerel, several varieties of grouper (including the bass-like *hamur*), and tuna. Commercially most important, however, is an abundance of shrimp. In recent years the catch has been estimated to average more than 20,000 tons annually—a rate said to be far below the possible optimum amount. With the installation of modern processing facilities, an export trade in shrimp from the Gulf has begun, and this will in all likelihood increase. But much additional scientific study needs to be done before the potential of the Gulf shrimp fishery can be accurately assessed.

Scientific information on all the Gulf fisheries is fragmentary, and fishery statistics are still regrettably approximate. Estimates suggest that the average annual catch has amounted to no more than two or three kilogrammes per hectare, as contrasted with six or seven times that amount in the North Atlantic. Considering the apparent richness of the Gulf stocks, the current production of 40,000 to 50,000 tons could probably be raised to perhaps 250,000 tons a year.[13]

Up to the present time, the Gulf States appear to have made no effort to police or control fishing in the Gulf beyond the limits of their territorial seas. The pearl fishery, which could come in law within the continental shelf doctrine as the exploitation of a sedentary species, has traditionally been regarded as open to all the peoples of the Gulf; and assurances of continued free access were given in a number of the instruments announcing shelf claims. Although, as noted above, some States have reserved their positions on other fisheries, no novel or unusual claims have yet been advanced with respect to these. At the moment the high seas fisheries in the Gulf remain in general open to all comers.

4. OIL PRODUCTION AND TRANSPORT

There is no need in this paper to restate well-known facts about the oil resources in general of the Persian Gulf region. Amounting by current estimates to more than half of the world's presently known total reserves, their existence has the most far-reaching economic, political and strategic implications. Production has continued to escalate each year, reaching some 16 million barrels per day in 1971 or about one-third of the world total.[14] By October 1972 the rate had gone to over 19 million barrels per day, and the end is not in sight.[15]

Of this amount about 3·6 million barrels, or a trifle less than 20 per cent., are currently being produced from offshore fields in the Gulf. Some 25 such fields are presently known, scattered throughout most of the Gulf's length, and in all probability there will be more. Some lie immediately adjacent to the coast; others, such as Iran's Cyrus, Rostam and Sassan fields, are almost in the centre. But wherever they are, they are relatively accessible because of shallow water depths and weather conditions which, though not wholly innocuous, are less severe than those found in many offshore areas elsewhere. On the whole, the engineering problems of offshore operations in the Gulf are probably simpler than those encountered, for example, in the North Sea.

One consequence of this large-scale activity has been the proliferation of offshore installations of all kinds in many parts of the Gulf. These include not merely drilling platforms but also a wide variety of ancillary facilities—pipeline systems, huge underwater storage tanks, gas-oil separating units, loading terminals miles offshore, mooring complexes for both storage and transport vessels, and other novel devices. Many of these installations are located in areas of no great importance to shipping; but some necessarily present new hazards for navigation and for fishing and new problems for the international lawyer.

Offshore production activities, however, are not the only source of new problems in the utilisation of the waters of the Gulf for diverse purposes. The increased oil production of the Gulf States has as a corollary the fact that this vast quantity of oil and related products must be moved continuously to market. Except for the amounts used locally or dispatched through pipelines to the Mediterranean, which constitute perhaps 10 per cent. of the total, oil from the Gulf region must go out by tanker. It is not difficult to imagine the growth in tanker traffic needed to handle a production volume which has more than tripled in 10 years.

Not only are there more vessels, but they are constantly growing in size. Twenty-five years ago a tanker of 26,000 dead-weight tons was considered big; today tankers of 100,000 to 300,000 tons are common. And early in 1973 will come the maiden voyage of the Japanese-built *Globtik Tokyo*, a vessel of 477,000 tons with an oil cargo capacity of 3,000,000 barrels. The problems of handling such craft in narrow and shallow seas such as the Persian Gulf, amid an assortment of islands, shoals, installations and small craft, are obvious.

As a final comment, it should be noted also that maritime traffic in the Gulf is by no means limited to tankers. The prosperity generated by oil income is already reflected in increased trade, the bulk of it seaborne, which means in turn a growth in non-oil commercial shipping. This trend, which can be expected to continue, adds still another element to the activities for which room must be found in Gulf waters.

5. POLLUTION

Pollution of the seas can come from many sources, and the increase in population and human activity around the Gulf will bring additional risks of pollution from sewage, fertilisers, industrial wastes, and other sources. Oil pollution is only the most conspicuous of these hazards, made so by the combination of extensive offshore production operations and heavy maritime traffic within a limited geographical area. Thus it is obvious that a major mishap at a drill site, to a storage facility or to a loaded supertanker could conceivably result in oil discharges amounting to many thousands of barrels. Even without a major accident, insufficient care in the course of normal operations could lead to troublesome accumulations of oil on the waters and shores of the Gulf. While much of the Gulf's coastline is desolate and uninhabited, thus reducing some types of potential damage, it is nevertheless true that serious harm could be be done in some areas, particularly to marine life.

Thus far few steps have been taken by the Gulf States, on either the national or international level, to establish legal requirements with respect to pollution. There is as yet, for example, nothing comparable to the United Kingdom's Prevention of Oil Pollution Act of 1971. This does not mean, of course, that liability may not now exist in delict or tort under ordinary municipal law for the wilful or negligent discharge of oil which does damage to others. But it does mean that specific guidelines in such cases have yet to be prescribed.

General international standards for the control of oil pollution at sea are still fragmentary, though much effort is now under way to enlarge and implement them. This effort has been most advanced with respect to discharges from ships, which are now regulated for many countries by the 1954 Convention for the Prevention of Pollution of the Sea by Oil and its amendments. Yet for a decade Kuwait was the only Gulf State to have become a party to this instrument. This situation may now be changing: Saudi Arabia became bound by the Convention in 1972, and it seems probable that other Gulf States may follow. But no Gulf State has yet taken action on other multilateral anti-pollution measures, including the Ocean Dumping Convention signed at London in December 1972. Nor has there yet been, on the intergovernmental level, any joint action of a regional character by the States of the Gulf.

Most steps to counter possible pollution problems in the Gulf thus far have been the result of private initiatives by oil producers and tanker operators. Thus, for example, the 1969 Tanker Owners' Voluntary Agreement on Liability for Oil Pollution (TOVALOP), together with its 1971 supplement, is applicable to occurrences in the Gulf which fall within its terms. The agreement in effect provides an insurance fund to cover, up to specified limits, direct clean-up costs caused by oil spills from tankers belonging to participating owners; but it does not extend to consequential or ecological damage. Despite its limitations, the protection afforded by TOVALOP is substantial in view of the fact that it covers well over half of the world's privately owned tanker tonnage.

Arrangements to deal with oil spills resulting from offshore operations have been slower to develop than those relating to tankers, but significant progress is now being made in the Gulf on this problem also. Under an agreement made on July 11, 1972,

13 oil-producing companies in the region joined in establishing the Gulf Area Oil Companies Mutual Aid Organisation for the purpose of providing a joint capability to clean up oil spills larger than could be dealt with by a single party. Each participant is understood to have accepted obligations to submit oil spill contingency plans and to keep on hand specified amounts of equipment and supplies to be made available to other participants in emergencies. The Organisation itself thus has a co-ordinating rather than an operating function. Membership is open to all companies in the Gulf region.

6. QUESTIONS FOR THE FUTURE

The Persian Gulf is a leading example of an enclosed sea subjected to an increasing intensity of use for a variety of purposes. Navigation, fishing and offshore oil production are all major activities, each essential to the economic well-being of the region and each with its own demands on the environment. To reconcile these interests in such a way as to assure the functioning of each safely, efficiently and economically is not an easy task. Nor is it made simpler by political differences among the littoral States and by the geographical characteristics of the Gulf itself. Precisely what answers will emerge in the future it is impossible to say; but it may be possible to identify some of the questions which must be solved.

If one asks what is required from a practical point of view to establish harmony and stability for the interests at stake, certain steps can be readily suggested by way of example. In areas of prime value for oil production, navigation (at least by large vessels) should be discouraged. Access to ports and loading terminals should be afforded by adequately designed fairways, with separation schemes for inbound and outbound traffic where necessary. Possibly such a system of defined navigation routes should also be extended to any area of constricted waters, or even to the Gulf as a whole. The ongoing improvement in navigational aids and information to mariners should be encouraged. On both vessels and offshore installations the use of up-to-date safety and accident-control devices should be a continuing obligation. And where fishing is important, this fact should be given recognition and other activities so conducted as to minimise interference. At the same time, the possibility that fishing itself may require regulation to prevent over-exploitation must be borne in mind.

The mutual adjustment of these activities is complicated by the fact that they are carried on under different legal régimes which attribute varying rights and duties to the coastal State. Thus substantial water areas of the Gulf are subject to national authority under the régime of the territorial sea, but with the corollary right of innocent passage for foreign vessels.[16] Other waters are high seas, traditionally open to all comers for navigation, fishing and other purposes. Yet the seabed beneath these high seas falls within the régime of the continental shelf, with the result that the bed is divided into areas of exclusive national jurisdiction for certain purposes.

There can be no doubt that a coastal State has ample powers under international law to prescribe within its territorial sea reasonable rules for all uses applicable to all comers, although it must not impede unduly the transit through its waters of vessels in innocent passage. So far few municipal measures of this kind have been enacted by the Gulf States except with regard to customs enforcement and like matters. But this is now changing as a result of need: fairways for approaching some ports, such as Ras Tanura in Saudi Arabia, are already in the process of being established, and similar developments will no doubt occur elsewhere.

In areas beyond the territorial sea it becomes more difficult to determine priorities among rights arising under different régimes. The orthodox method for resolving such problems is by international agreements, yet this is not a wholly satisfactory answer. Even if such agreement could be achieved among the Gulf States on, say, maritime traffic routes or fishery conservation, it would not in strict law be binding on non-parties who presumably could exercise their customary high seas freedoms of navigation and fishing as they saw fit. Troublesome conflicts might ensue, which could invite, in turn, more drastic actions by one or more Gulf States, such as efforts to declare the Gulf a " closed sea " or to assert special forms of jurisdiction over activities within its limits. Objectionable though such moves might be under traditional law of the sea principles, the possibility of their taking place cannot be ignored if other solutions are not found.[17] As in other parts of the world, the problems are real and the feeling is widespread that existing doctrines do not provide adequate answers.

What the answers eventually will be will depend in large part on what shape the general law of the sea assumes as a result of the current tumultuous efforts in the United Nations and elsewhere to revise and update it. These efforts, even if successful, will take some time to become effective. In the meantime, voluntary co-operation can do much to achieve the necessary harmonisation of diverse uses. Observance by shipowners of agreed-upon traffic patterns, recognition by producers of the need for safe shipping lanes, attention by both to the needs of fishermen, concern on the part of all to prevent injury to the environment, can greatly reduce the hazards of operations within the confines of the Gulf. The progress already made on some of these problems is encouraging for the future—particularly the notable fact that up to the present time, despite increased activity, no major accident—on the scale of the *Torrey Canyon* or larger—has yet occurred in Gulf waters.

REFERENCES

1. For a detailed description of the Strait, see Kennedy, "A Brief Geographical and Hydrographical Study of Straits which Constitute Routes for International Traffic," 1958 UN Conference on the Law of the Sea, 1 *Official Records* 114 at 129–130.
2. The States are Abu Dhabi, Dubai, Sharjah, Ajman, Umm al-Qaiwain, Ras al-Khaimah and Fujaira. Fujaira, on the east side of the Oman promontory, has no coastline in the Gulf.
3. The Neutral Zone between Kuwait and Saudi Arabia was partitioned between them by an agreement of 1965; but the precise boundary line on land established in 1969 ends at the coast and has not been prolonged offshore. An English translation of the 1965 agreement appears in (1966) 60 A.J.I.L. 744; of the 1969 agreement, in a supplement to (1970) 13 *Middle East Economic Survey*. Offshore areas associated with the former Zone on land thus appear to be still under joint control of the two States.
4. League of Nations Doc. A.13.1925.IX, 377–378. The committee included American, British, Colombian, French, German, Italian and Persian experts.
5. Saudi Arabia, Royal Decree No. 33 of Feb. 16, 1958; Iraq, Ordinance No. 435 of Nov. 4, 1958; Iran, constitutional amendment of Apr. 16, 1959; Kuwait, Decree of Dec. 17, 1967; Oman, Decree of July 18, 1972. Data in this section are taken chiefly from a compilation issued by the Geographer of the U.S. Department of State, National Claims to Maritime Jurisdictions (International Boundary Study Series A, Limits in the Seas No. 36, Jan. 3, 1972).
6. Art. 121 of the Constitution of July 18, 1971, English translation in (1972) 26 *Middle East Journal* 307 at 321. The matter is further complicated by Art. 4, which obligates the Union not to abandon its sovereignty over any part of its lands or waters, which latter are in turn defined in Art. 2 as those within the international boundaries of the member emirates.
7. Decree No. 33, Art. 9.

8. [1969] I.C.J.Rep. 3 at 53–54.

9. The English text of a " Memorandum of Understanding " between Iran and Sharjah, together with related documents, was published in (1972) 15 *Middle East Economic Survey* Supplement (May 5, 1972).

10. (1972) 26 *Middle East Journal* 167. If the three islands are attributed to Iran, the effect is to establish in that vicinity an area of Iranian territorial sea extending continuously to within some 20 miles of the Arabian coast and embracing most of the normal shipping routes up and down the Gulf.

11. *e.g., Occidental Petroleum Corp.* v. *Buttes Gas & Oil Co.*, 331 F.Supp. 92 (U.S. District Court, Central District of California, 1971), a private anti-trust suit dismissed primarily on the ground that the act of State doctrine forbade inquiry into acts of foreign sovereigns even if allegedly procured by the defendants. The dismissal was affirmed on appeal, 461 F. 2d 1261 (1972), and further review refused by the U.S. Supreme Court in October 1972.

12. Report of the Government of Bahrain for the Year 1365 (Dec. 1945–Nov. 1946), p. 14. See also Bowen, " Pearl Fisheries of the Persian Gulf " (1951) 5 *Middle East Journal* 161–180.

13. The figures given in these paragraphs are based largely on a survey by Wallen, " Non-Oil Trade and Resources " (paper presented at Princeton University Conference on the Persian Gulf, 1968).

14. For rough conversion purposes, one barrel per day is approximately equal to 50 tons per year. Recent production and reserve figures are authoritatively reviewed in Barger, " Middle Eastern Oil since the Second World War " (1972) 401 *Annals of the American Academy of Political and Social Science* 31–44.

15. *Oil and Gas Journal*, Dec. 18, 1972.

16. A special situation within this category arises with respect to the Strait of Hormuz, which as a result of Oman's recent move to a 12 mile limit now appears to be territorial waters of Oman and Iran. As a strait used for international navigation, it could not under the rule in the *Corfu Channel Case* [1949] I.C.J.Rep. 4, be closed to innocent passage.

17. Suggestions have already been made in the Iranian Press along these lines, *e.g.*, in *Kayhan International* (Teheran), May 13, 1970, where it was proposed that the Gulf be made an " inland sea," like the " Bay of St. Lawrence," in order to control shipping and " keep out foreign fishermen."

Part VIII

National Practice

CHAPTER 20

Canada

By J.-Y. Morin *

THE evolution of Canadian law in the areas of the territorial sea, fishing zones, continental shelf and prevention of pollution has been remarkable in the last 20 years or so. There was a time when Canada adhered without difficulty to the rules of the law of the sea which it derived from Great Britain and it started to revise these rules with reference to its own needs only after the Second World War. Furthermore, it was only at that period that it started to prepare a truly autonomous foreign policy.

One will remember the very active participation of Canada in the Conferences on the Law of the Sea in 1958 and 1960, and particularly the diplomatic activity which it displayed in order to rally the States advocating a narrow territorial sea and those asserting a 12 mile limit, to reach a compromise solution. This solution, sometimes called the " six-plus-six " formula, would have given to each coastal State a six mile belt of territorial waters, beyond which would have extended an exclusive six mile fishing zone.[1]†

This compromise failed to achieve by one vote [2] the two-thirds majority required for its insertion in the Convention on the Territorial Sea.

Following this effort in favour of a multilateral solution, the law of the sea nevertheless continued to be transformed by State action, but henceforth this was to be done through unilateral acts or bilateral agreements. Canada certainly could not stand aloof from the evolution which took shape in the first few years following the failure of the 1960 Conference. Technical progress, notably in the area of maritime transport, the increasingly extensive exploration of the Arctic regions, the continental shelf and the seabed, which soon opened up prospects of exploitation, as well as the development of fisheries, raised the question of the adequacy of the existing rules as regards the new situation.

In addition, these problems, tied up with technical progress and economic development, arose at the very moment when a large number of former colonies were achieving Statehood and were asserting the right to take part in the preparation of international rules which would take into consideration their interests and their needs. Canada then discovered that its interests, particularly as regards fisheries and the exploitation of the seabed, were perhaps closer to the interests of the developing countries than to those of the developed countries.

Without renouncing multilateral solutions, despite these considerations, Canada has thus, in the last few years, carried out a certain number of unilateral acts concerning the territorial sea, fisheries and the prevention of pollution. Moreover, the positions which it adopted during the negotiations preceding the IMCO Conventions and

* Professor of Law, University of Montreal, Associate Editor of the *Canadian Yearbook of International Law*.

† For references, see p. 251.

within the UN Committee on the Seabed, as well as its numerous interventions in all the debates concerning the future of the law of the sea, constitute a contribution which cannot be disregarded in the definition of new directions of this law.

I. THE TERRITORIAL SEA

The rules concerning the width and régime of Canadian territorial waters originate in U.K. law, both written and customary. At the Conference for the Codification of International Law which took place at The Hague in 1930, the Canadian attitudes were never, in this field, very far from the British positions: " The base line for the calculation of the breadth of territorial waters is the line of low water following the sinuosities of the coast." [3] And later on, concerning the breadth of the territorial sea, the Canadian Government representative, Mr. L. B. Pearson, was categorical: " The breadth of the belt of territorial waters subject to the sovereignty of the coastal State is three nautical miles. The claim of any foreign State to exercise sovereignty on any grounds whatever over a greater breadth of territorial waters than three nautical miles is not admitted." [4]

Moreover, a few years previously, the British Ambassador in Washington had signed on behalf of Canada an agreement in which it was said that the United Kingdom and the United States had the " firm intention to uphold the principle that three marine miles . . . constitute the proper limits of territorial waters." [5]

Under the patronage of such sponsors, the rules of English law could only become deeply embedded in Canadian law. They were, however, to give way quickly under the strain of the problems raised by the protection of coastal fisheries, especially from the moment when it became possible to rely on the authority of the conclusions of the International Court of Justice in the *Anglo-Norwegian Fisheries Case*.[6] From this time onwards, Canada considered the advantage it could obtain by adopting the system of straight base lines, taking into consideration the extremely indented configuration of its coastline, and the extension of its territorial waters. As early as 1956, the Prime Minister, L. S. St.-Laurent, declared that the decision of the Court had " set a principle which (he thought) should be applicable to our own shores " [7] and, in the " note verbale " that the Ministry of External Affairs forwarded to the Secretary-General of the United Nations in 1957, concerning the project of the International Law Commission relating to the codification of the law of the sea, it was stated:

> " The three-mile limit is not adequate for all purposes. It is not adequate for the enforcement of customs, fiscal and sanitary regulations. It is also not adequate for the protection and control of fisheries. . . . One way of providing for this would be by accepting, for general application, the twelve-mile breadth for the territorial sea." [8]

Afterwards, at the two Conferences in 1958 and 1960, Canada proposed the abovementioned " six-plus-six " compromise. The failure of this compromise, which was at the same time the failure of the 1960 Conference, put the Canadian Government in an awkward position in the face of the ever-increasing demands of the coastal population whose subsistence was tied up with the protection of fisheries against the incursions of foreign trawlers.

As a first step, in 1964, it was decided to create an exclusive nine mile fishing zone beyond territorial waters, which maintained their traditional breadth. Parliament thus adopted an " Act respecting the Territorial Sea and the Fishing Zones of Canada," which not only extended the Canadian jurisdiction towards the high seas, but also authorised the federal executive to determine by order the straight base lines from which would be measured, from then on, the breadth of the territorial waters and the fishing zone.[9]

The legislature indeed considered that the Canadian coastline fulfilled all the conditions required by the International Court of Justice in its judgment in the *Fisheries Case*, and consolidated in 1958 in Article 4 of the Convention on the Territorial Sea, for the application of the straight base lines method, since one could find there both a " deeply indented and cut into " coastline and " a fringe of islands along the coast in its immediate vicinity."

The first order defining the base lines was published on October 27, 1967. It applied to Labrador and to the island of Newfoundland.[10] On the whole, the lines defined by this order never stray in any perceptible way from the general direction of the coast, but the vast bays of Newfoundland are all included in the area of internal waters.[11] The second order, applicable to Nova Scotia and to the Pacific coast, was published on May 29, 1969; there, the straight base lines follow closely the general direction of the coast.[12]

The second step, which saw the extension of the territorial sea to 12 nautical miles (and consequently entailed the disappearance of the fishing zone), was taken in 1970.[13] The Government deemed it opportune to extend to that zone the whole of the rights and powers which constitute territorial jurisdiction, taking into consideration the necessity to regulate not only fisheries, but also the discharge of polluting substances into the sea.[14] It is worth noting that the straight base lines delimited by the 1967 and 1969 orders remain in force.[15]

Some large marine areas remain, such as the Gulf of St. Lawrence, the Bay of Fundy, Queen Charlotte Sound and Hecate Strait, for which the Government has not yet fixed any base lines. Canada indeed claims these arms of the sea as forming part of its historical (internal) waters, but for various reasons, including the opposition of the United States, has not yet initiated the " closing " by straight lines of the straits which give access to them.[16] Parliament has nevertheless delegated to the Government the power to convert these areas into " adjacent " fishing zones, which we shall consider later.

The internal waters and the territorial sea of Canada have thus been extended considerably since 1964. It is very unlikely, however, that the extension of the territorial waters will exceed the present 12 miles in the foreseeable future. If it proves necessary to regulate certain activities beyond that limit, it is probable that the Government will resort to the creation of " functional zones " over which it would only exercise a jurisdiction limited to certain precise purposes.

II. THE CONTINENTAL SHELF

Canada has the second largest continental shelf in the world. Indeed, it amounts to almost 40 per cent. of the surface of its emerged territory, that is, approximately two million square miles.[17]

The " sovereign rights " of the country over these immense underwater stretches have not been the subject of any special proclamation, but the Federal Government intends to avail itself of all the advantages conferred upon it by the 1958 Convention on the Continental Shelf, to which it is a party, including the criterion of " exploitability," according to which the shelf extends up to the point where the depth of the superjacent waters allows the exploitation of the natural resources. It is estimated that the oil reserves of the Canadian shelf exceed 56 billion barrels (the figure is 65 billion for the emerged land).

The federal Oil and Gas Production and Conservation Act is based on the double criterion of depth and exploitability; it recognises the power of the Government to make regulations respecting the exploration and drilling for, and the production and conservation of, as well as the processing and transportation of, oil and gas.[18]

No map has been published which shows the precise extent of the Canadian claims regarding the continental shelf, but there are many departmental documents describing the location of the exploration permits for oil and gas.[19] Off the coast of Newfoundland these permits cover the area of the Grand Banks up to 425 miles to the east of the coast, and up to 320 miles to the south. In Nova Scotia, it is possible to obtain a permit over 150 miles from the coast. In the Labrador Sea, the permits cover a marine area extending approximately 100 to 200 miles from the coast. Finally, on the Pacific coast, the permits cover the whole of Hecate Strait and Queen Charlotte Sound, and extend, depending on the area, from 20 to 50 miles from the coast of Vancouver Island and the Queen Charlotte Archipelago.

In several places, the Canadian continental shelf overlaps with the shelf of the neighbouring States: the United States, Denmark (Greenland) and France (St. Pierre and Miquelon islands). According to Article 6 of the Convention on the Continental Shelf, the delimitation, in the absence of any agreement, is, in principle, determined by the median line, the points of which are equidistant from the nearest points to the base lines. In most of the cases concerning Canada, the equidistance principle is difficult to apply and does not settle all the problems. So negotiations are now proceeding with those countries with a view to delimiting by common consent the partition line in the straits which separate Ellesmere Island from Greenland, in the Strait of Juan de Fuca, the Dixon Entrance, the Beaufort Sea, the George Bank (between Nova Scotia and Maine) and in the Sound between Newfoundland and the French islands. These negotiations seem to be progressing very slowly.

In conformity with the 1958 Convention, Canada recognises that the " sovereign rights " which it exercises over the continental shelf do not apply to the superjacent waters, which form part of the high sea (beyond the 12 mile territorial sea).

As for the limit between the continental shelf and the seabed beyond national jurisdiction, Canada is of the opinion that it should be fixed at the point where the continental margin ends, the whole area situated beyond it being part of the " geological shelf." According to a map published in the 10th report of the Science Council of Canada, that limit coincides, in most areas, with the 1,000 fathoms isobath (1,830 metres).[20]

III. FISHING ZONES

From 1966 to 1970, as we have seen, Canadian law had established fishing zones along all the coasts of Canada, except in the Arctic regions. These exclusive zones extended nine miles beyond the territorial sea, so that the marine area reserved for Canadian fishermen extended to 12 miles from the base lines. The Canadian Government reached, at that time, agreements with foreign countries holding conventional or historic fishing rights in these waters, with a view, either to securing for their nationals fishing rights, subject to reciprocity, or to excluding them gradually (*phasing out* technique).

In 1970, these " contiguous " fishing zones were integrated into the new 12 mile territorial sea, whose outer limit coincides exactly with that of the former fishing zone, the base lines not having been modified.

New " adjacent " fishing zones have been created by the 1970 Act, the limits of which, the so-called " fisheries closing lines," have been fixed by order.[21] Three distinct zones are subject to the new régime, without however extending the internal waters or the territorial sea of the country.

Zone 1 consists of the Gulf of St. Lawrence, whose mouths are bounded by two series of straight lines. The first series of straight lines crosses Cabot Strait, from Money Point to Cape Ray, passing through St. Paul Island, while the second series passes through the mouth of the Strait of Belle-Isle, from Eastern White Island to Double Island, through the *Northeast Ledge*, off Belle-Isle. Hence, these lines join the ends of the base lines of Labrador and Nova Scotia to those of Newfoundland, but it is important to note that they are not themselves base lines, but " closing lines "; they cannot thus be used to determine the position or the breadth of the territorial sea.

Zone 2 includes the Bay of Fundy, the two entrances of which are closed by a single broken line constituted by 11 straight lines. The line leaves Whipple Point (on Brier Island on the south side of the Bay) and crosses the principal entrance up to *Gannet Rock*. From there, it extends seawards to join *Yellow Ledge* and Machinas Seal Island around which it turns to come back then towards Grand Manan Channel.

Zone 3 joins together Queen Charlotte Sound, Hecate Strait and Dixon Entrance. The two arms of the sea which give access to this zone have been closed respectively by a series of straight lines. The former encloses Queen Charlotte Sound, from Winifred Island to Kunglit Island. The latter directly connects Langara Island to Cape Muzon.

If these three " adjacent " zones are different, from a geographical point of view, from the former " contiguous " fishing zones, are they the same thing from a juridical point of view? We are inclined to think so. Indeed, the 1964 Act has not been modified on this point, so it follows that " the laws of Canada respecting fishing and the exploitation of the living resources of the sea apply to the fishing zones of Canada in the same way and to the same extent as they apply to the territorial sea of Canada." [22]

The Minister of External Affairs has specified that the arms of the sea transformed into " adjacent " fishing zones shall not constitute territorial waters.[23] Do they then form part of the high seas? The Minister has stated that the closing lines " will establish areas of the same kind as are now enclosed by the fishing zones " which have extended till now beyond the territorial sea. It will, he adds rightly, " have the same effect." [24]

Now the legal definition of the former fishing zones, as given by the Government, has not always been clear. The 1964 Act itself described them as including " those areas of the sea contiguous to the territorial sea " and it has frequently happened that States' representatives designate them under the name of " contiguous fishing zones." [25]

It is true that the geographical surface covered by the 1964 fishing zones coincided with that of the contiguous zone recognised by Article 24 of the 1958 Convention on the Territorial Sea and that its distance from the base line never exceeded 12 miles. Nevertheless, the geographical correspondence does not necessarily mean that the fishing zones constitute contiguous zones in the eyes of the law.

If the fishing zones proclaimed by States were legally identical to the contiguous zone, they could not extend their legislation to these zones; *a fortiori* they could not ban foreign fishermen from these zones. These are, however, precisely the objectives which they mean to realise through the creation of fishing zones. In Canada, as we have seen, the laws respecting fishing apply to the fishing zone, whether contiguous or adjacent, in the same way as in the territorial sea.

The following conclusion emerges: the fishing zones are areas subject to the territorial jurisdiction of the coastal State for the restricted purposes of fishing. They are " prohibited zones," so called by S. Hsu at the International Law Commission. Even so they are not territorial waters, for the coastal State does not pretend to assert its complete jurisdiction over these zones, which remain subject to the régime of the high seas for the purposes of navigation. It must be made clear, however, that the inclusion of Hecate Strait and Dixon Entrance into the fishing zone does not modify in any way, in the opinion of the Canadian Government, the status claimed for these marine areas: they are still, in its opinion, historic waters.

Canada thus extends its jurisdiction beyond its territorial waters in the Gulf of St. Lawrence, Queen Charlotte Sound and the other areas mentioned above. If we had to define the legal nature of the powers so claimed, we could establish an analogy with the " sovereign rights " exercised by the States over their continental shelf, with this exception, that these rights do not depend on any declaration. Such rights must not be confused with full and complete sovereignty, and the fishing zones do not constitute territorial waters, but in the regions which are subject to their jurisdiction for the purposes of fishing, the traditional freedom of other States is reduced accordingly; it is no more the high seas of classical international law.

Canada's unilateral action is not without precedent, for the Icelandic " fishing limits " (1958) include vast arms of the sea, because its straight base lines are up to 62 nautical miles in length.[26] Moreover, the claims of many Latin American countries over areas called " territorial sea," " patrimonial sea " or " national fisheries zone " whose breadth generally reaches up to 200 miles constitute, in reality, extensions of particular jurisdictions, notably with respect to the biological resources of these zones.[27] If these claims differ from Canada's demands from a geographical point of view, they do, to some extent, resemble them from a legal point of view.

IV. ZONES FOR THE PREVENTION OF POLLUTION

The wrecks of the *Torrey Canyon*, off the shore of Britain, and the *Arrow*, in the Bay of Chedabucto in Nova Scotia, have led the Canadian legislature to a growing awareness of the dangers which the great number of tankers imposes on the marine environment. Furthermore, it was in Canada that, in September 1970, the first deep water oil-receiving port in the western hemisphere was inaugurated and two new ports intended for the giant tankers have been opened since then. To that must be added the proximity of the large urban centres of the United States, whose energy needs are constantly increasing.

In the report, which it submitted to the Canadian Government in 1970, the group of experts entrusted with the fight against the pollution created by the stranding of the *Arrow* urges the legislature not to rely any longer solely upon the mechanisms provided for in the IMCO Convention on the Prevention of Oil Pollution (1954, modified in 1962 and 1969). This Convention established " prohibited zones " in relation to the discharge of oil, oily mixtures or ballast from tankers, but relies on the flag States for the punishment of the infractions committed beyond territorial waters. It would be advisable, says the Report on the *Arrow*, to establish vast pollution control zones, 100 miles in width, along the whole of the Canadian coast, within which Canadian jurisdiction would apply.[28]

The Government has not been willing to go as far as the Report recommended, except in the Arctic, where special reasons have prompted it to introduce changes in the matter of the prevention of pollution. Before we deal with this question, it is appropriate to cast a glance over prevention in territorial waters and fishing zones.

The Canada Shipping Act was modified in 1969 with the purpose of prohibiting the discharge of polluting substances by ships, except where authorised.[29] This law and the regulations established in accordance with it are applicable, in the first place, to all Canadian waters situated south of the 60th parallel latitude north. This description relates to the whole of the Pacific coast and the whole of the Atlantic coasts, from Cape Kakkiviak (Labrador) to the Bay of Fundy. In the second place, the law is applicable to all the adjacent fishing zones, as delimited by the orders which have been adopted by the Government.[30] To the " sovereign right " to regulate fishing in the Gulf of St. Lawrence, Hecate Strait and Queen Charlotte Sound must thus be added the right to prevent and punish pollution offences. This jurisdiction supports fisheries conservation and can thus be justified for the same reasons. One could also stress the point that, in areas surrounded by land, such as the Gulf of St. Lawrence or Hecate Strait, any pollution risks ending up on either coast, hence the necessity of a very strict control from the coastal State.

Thirdly, the Act applies to all Canadian waters situated north of the 60th parallel of latitude, in other words, to the whole of the islands of the Arctic Archipelago, within the limits of the territorial waters, but with the exception of the waters situated within the so-called " shipping safety control zones," considered below.

The Act empowers the federal executive to make regulations concerning the various categories of polluting substances, the quantities conveyed, the loading methods, the registers which must be kept on board ships, the compulsory shipping routes and any other rules considered necessary to secure the safety of navigation.[31] It is worth noticing that the Act also enables it to regulate and prevent the discharge of polluting substances outside Canadian waters, but no definition is given as to the zones and areas contemplated. The inspectors commissioned to combat pollution have very extensive powers, including the power to divert ships or the power to exclude them from Canadian waters (or from the fishing zones) if they do not comply with the standards. The Department of Transport may order any ship in distress, stranded or abandoned to be destroyed if it risks polluting the sea. As for the civil liability resulting from an act of pollution, it is " absolute and not subordinated to the proof of fault or negligence "; liability falls on the owner of a ship and, in some cases provided for in the regulations, both on him and on the owner of the cargo.[32]

In the Arctic, ecological considerations have persuaded the Government to create a special prevention zone, 100 nautical miles in width and extending all around the Archipelago. The journey of the *Manhattan*, which had no follow-up, was not unrelated to the adoption of the Arctic Waters Pollution Prevention Act (1970) for it was then thought that tankers would pass in large numbers through the North-West Passage. However, the new law is not restricted to hydrocarbons; it applies to waste, of which a very comprehensive definition is given in section 2.[33]

Parliament gives the executive the power to make regulations respecting the discharge and deposit of polluting substances and the construction of works likely to result in a risk of water pollution. The Government may also require any person who engages in exploring for or exploiting any natural resources within the zone to provide evidence of financial responsibility. It may designate inspectors and impose fines of up to $5,000 if the offender is a ship. The officials entrusted with the prevention of pollution may seize, with the consent of the Governor-in-Council, a ship that contravenes the law, and its cargo, anywhere in the prevention zone: in the case of a ship in distress, wrecked or abandoned, the Government may cause the ship to be destroyed or removed, if there is a risk of pollution.[34]

Within the prevention zone, the Government may establish, by order, " shipping safety control zones," and it may prohibit access to these by any ship which does not comply with the prescribed standards relating to:

" (i) Hull and fuel tank construction, including the strength of materials used therein, the use of double hulls and the subdivision thereof into watertight compartments,
(ii) the construction of machinery and equipment and the electronic and other navigational aids and equipment and telecommunications equipment . . .,
(iii) the nature and construction of propelling power and appliances and fittings for steering and stabilising,
(iv) the manning of the ship, including the number of navigating and look-out personnel . . .,
(v) with respect to any type of cargo . . ., the maximum quantity thereof that may be carried, the method of stowage thereof and the nature . . . of supplies and equipment to be carried for use in repairing or remedying any condition that may result from the deposit of any such cargo in the Arctic waters,
(vi) the freeboard to be allowed and the marking of load lines . . .,
(vii) . . .,
(viii) the maps, charts, tide tables and any other documents . . . to be carried." [35]

Moreover, the regulations can prescribe criteria of competence for the pilots for ice navigation or impose ice-breaker assistance. These provisions leave nothing to chance and, in addition, the Government intends to restrict navigation in places and at times of particular danger.

The United States have seen in these measures an infringement of the principle of the freedom of the sea. In a Press Release dated April 15, 1970, the American Government declared that it could " neither accept nor acquiesce " in the establishment of such a zone, lest the Canadian law should be taken as a precedent in other parts of the world.[36] Washington says that it is " acutely aware " of the peculiar ecological nature of the Arctic region, but that this area concerns all nations in " its increasing significance as a world trade route."

Canada replied to that criticism saying that the United States themselves had had no hesitation in extending their jurisdiction seawards when they had deemed it necessary to do so and that the new law constituted " a lawful extension of a limited form of jurisdiction to meet particular dangers, and is of a different order from unilateral interferences with the freedom of the high seas such as, for example, the atomic tests carried out by the U.S.A. and other States. . . ." [37]

The Canadian Government readily admits that there are few rules of international law in the field of pollution. The Legal Adviser to the Department of External Affairs went so far as to say that in this field a kind of anarchy prevailed, rather than deadlock. The law of the sea has been so far too strongly influenced by the interests of " the conservative States which are the ones that tend to be the major shipping maritime nations " and, for this reason, takes absolutely no account of the point of view of the States who are facing the problems of pollution.[38] The system of the IMCO Convention does not answer the needs, especially in an area such as the Arctic, where *preventive* measures must be taken. We are, adds the Legal Adviser, in " an area of non-law " where, having fallen behind the development of technology, the law has become out of date.

The new Canadian law thus stands on the very edge of international law,[39] but the Government considered that it was its duty to act and to contribute to the development of that law. It has done so, the Minister of External Affairs stated, not by proclaiming its complete sovereignty over the high seas, but merely by asserting " the limited jurisdiction required to achieve a specific and vital purpose." There is, added the Minister, a distinction between a limited competence and the whole of the powers which together constitute sovereignty; the Arctic Waters Pollution Prevention Act, similar in this respect to the measures adopted for the conservation of fisheries resources, is a " constructive and functional approach to environmental preservation." [40]

REFERENCES

1. A/CONF.19/L.11 in Second UN Conference on the Law of the Sea 1960, Official Records, p. 173. The proposal, endorsed by the U.S.A., also provided for the gradual phasing out of the foreign States holding fishing rights within these zones.
2. *Ibid.* p. 30. The voting was as follows: 54 votes in favour; 28 against and 5 abstentions.
3. Replies of Canada in Conference for the Codification of International Law, Bases of Discussion, supplement to Vol. II, L. of N., 1929, Vol. 9. See J.-Y. Morin, " Les eaux territoriales du Canada au regard du droit international " (1963) 1 *Canadian Yearbook of International Law* (hereafter, C.Y.I.L.) 82–87.
4. Replies of Canada, *supra*, n. 3, p. 2 (point III).
5. Convention between the U.K. and the U.S.A. respecting the Regulation of the Liquor Traffic, Jan. 23, 1924, Art. 1.
6. Judgment of Dec. 18, 1951 [1951] I.C.J.Rep. 116.
7. House of Commons Debates, 1956, Vol. VII, p. 6702.
8. Note verbale, in UN Conference on the Law of the Sea (1958), Vol. 1, p. 76.
9. Statutes of Canada, 1964, Chap. 22, in force on July 23, 1964. See J.-Y. Morin, " La zone de pêche exclusive du Canada " (1964) 2 C.Y.I.L. 77.
10. Territorial Sea and Fishing Zones Geographical Co-ordinates (Areas 1, 2 and 3) Order, P.C. 1967–2025, SOR/67 no. 543, *The Canada Gazette*, Part II, Vol. 101, No. 21, p. 1701.
11. On this subject, see J.-Y. Morin, " Les zones de pêche de Terre-Neuve et du Labrador à la lumière de l'évolution du droit international " (1968) 6 C.Y.I.L. 91.
12. Territorial Sea and Fishing Zones Geographical Co-ordinates (Areas 3, 4 and 6) Order, P.C. 1969–1109, SOR/69 no. 278, *The Canada Gazette*, Part II, Vol. 103, No. 11, p. 822.
13. Statutes of Canada, 1969–70, Chap. 68, in force on June 26, 1970.
14. See J.-Y. Morin, " Le progrès technique, la pollution et l'évolution récente du droit de la mer au Canada, particulièrement à l'égard de l'Arctique " (1970) 7 C.Y.I.L. 158–164.
15. Except for some minor modifications which could result from the new provisions of the law (s. 5) in respect of low-tide elevations.
16. See on this subject J.-Y. Morin, *supra*, n. 14, pp. 173, 186.
17. See J. A. Beesley, " The Law of the Sea Conference: Factors behind Canada's Stance " (1972) Jul., Aug. *International Perspectives* 28.
18. Revised Statutes of Canada, 1970, Vol. V, Chap. O–4.
19. Maps published by the Department of Energy, Mines and Resources (Resources Management and Conservation Branch) in *Offshore Exploration, Information and Procedures* (ed. Aug. 1970).
20. Map entitled " The Continental Margin of Canada," in *Canada, Science and the Oceans* (10th report of the C.S.C.).
21. Fishing Zones of Canada (Zones 1, 2 and 3) Order, *The Canada Gazette*, Part I, Vol. 104, p. 3036 (Dec. 26, 1970), in force 60 days later.
22. *Op. cit., supra*, n. 9, s. 4 (2).
23. Standing Committee on Fisheries and Forestry (House of Commons), session 1969–70, Minutes of Proceedings, No. 16, p. 12 (Apr. 21, 1970).
24. *Ibid.*

25. See in particular the commentary annexed to the Bill on the Territorial Sea (Bill C-203), s. 2.

26. See on this subject J.-Y. Morin, *op. cit.*, *supra*, n. 14, p. 204. The most important Icelandic juridical instruments are Law No. 66, Aug. 17, 1956, and Regulation No. 70, June 30, 1958.

27. See F. V. Garcia-Amador, *Latin America and the Law of the Sea* (Organisation of American States, 1972).

28. Report of the Task-Force " Operation Oil " (clean up of the *Arrow* oil spill in Chedabucto Bay) to the Minister of Transport, Sept. 1, 1970, Vol.1, pp. 7, 37, 39. See also, Report of the Royal Commission on the Pollution of Canadian Waters by Oil and Formal Investigation into the Grounding of the Steam Tanker *Arrow* (July 1970).

29. Statutes of Canada, session 1968–69, Chap. 53, s. 24; 1969–70, Chap. 51, s. 1.

30. See Standing Committee, *supra*, n. 23, No. 16, p. 29 (Apr. 21, 1970).

31. Act, *supra*, n. 29, s. 739.

32. *Ibid.* ss. 743 and 744.

33. Statutes of Canada, session 1969–70, Chap. 47.

34. *Ibid.* ss. 4, 8, 10, 13, 18 and 23.

35. *Ibid.* s. 12 (1).

36. U.S. Press Release on Canada's Claim to Jurisdiction over Arctic Pollution and Territorial Sea Limits, House of Commons Debates, session 1969–70, Vol. 114, p. 5923.

37. Summary of the Canadian Note handed to the U.S. Government on Apr. 16, 1970, in House of Commons Debates, session 1969–70, Vol. 114, p. 6027.

38. Standing Committee on External Affairs and National Defence, Minutes of Proceedings, session 1969–70, No. 25, p. 43.

39. Standing Committee on Indian Affairs and Northern Development, Minutes of Proceedings, session 1969–70, No. 15, pp. 7, 29 (Apr. 30, 1970).

40. House of Commons Debates, session 1969–70, Vol. 114, p. 5951 (Apr. 16, 1970).

CHAPTER 21

Federal Republic of Germany

By F. Münch *

AT the time this report was written, the German authorities had hardly begun to define their position in regard to all the problems to be discussed at the forthcoming Conference on the Law of the Sea. Having only an observer status on the United Nations Committee on the Peaceful Uses of the Seabed, Germany has not presented a draft convention nor offered an opinion on any document submitted to that committee. But a fairly consistent doctrine may be derived from her interests, from her former attitudes to maritime law and from precedents, and that doctrine is likely to become the guideline for her delegation.

One observation must nevertheless be made here: while belonging to the traditional seafaring nations, Germany has not presumed to have sufficient weight to pursue alone a strictly conservative maritime policy. She has been, and probably will be, anxious to march in line with the Great Western Powers, and these have shown, since 1945, tendencies to deviate from the former international law and to seek a compromise with new lines of thought. Such trends are also to be found in German non-official writings.

Germany, by her geographical position, does not control any important stretch of the sea. Since the loss of her colonies in the First World War, she is confined to the remotest corner of the North Sea and to a coast along the still more secluded Baltic. On the other hand, her maritime trade is important, and her fisheries must provide for a population of over 60 million. The new prospects of deep sea mining have aroused much interest, since Germany depends heavily on the importation of raw materials.

All this would urge her to advocate the maximum freedom of the sea, defined as a regulated freedom equal for all, with the self-evident limitations protecting the marine environment from pollution and the living resources of the sea from depletion.

The precedents of German maritime policy bear out these conclusions. Germany still limits her territorial waters to three miles and has not yet followed the trend towards extension of this zone or towards claims to special fisheries or economic zones. She invariably protests against such extensions by other States, and, with much reluctance, on a few occasions has given in to pressures exerted, for instance, by Iceland to obtain recognition of a 12 mile exclusive fishery zone. Together with the United Kingdom, she is contesting before the International Court the most recent Icelandic demands. In this, the German authorities are determined to apply and to maintain general international law.

At the Codification Conference of the League of Nations in 1930, the German position did not exclude certain concessions. Thus the delegation was willing to admit exceptions to the three mile rule in certain areas with historical peculiarities,

* Professor of Law, Max-Planck-Institut für Ausländisches Öffentliches Recht und Völkerrecht, Heidelberg.

especially in Scandinavia, and a contiguous zone with limited rights for the coastal State was considered as a possible compromise.[1]† At the Geneva Conferences in 1958 and 1960, Germany followed the lead of the United States and the United Kingdom on the way to compromise. But since no understanding on the width of territorial waters was reached, she continued to adopt her former attitude.

As to the status of internal, territorial waters and the high seas, German practice also relied on the general rules of international law. It is true that she has not yet ratified the 1958 Convention on Territorial Waters and that only in 1972 did the Act ratifying the 1958 Convention on the High Seas obtain the consent of the legislature,[2] but this indicates no divergence of view on the contents of these texts. Perhaps it is worthwhile to recall that there was a prolonged dispute with France during the Algerian troubles when France visited and arrested German ships on the high seas on suspicion of smuggling weapons to North Africa.[3]

The German Shipowners' Association have not yet discussed the actual questions of public international law of the sea, but they issued a statement in February 1958 on the then draft of the International Law Commission. That statement was essentially in line with what has become the 1958 Convention on the High Seas, except that it condemns more strictly the misuse of flags of convenience. This would indicate that German shipping interests tend to support the public international law of maritime traffic. On the other hand, commercial maritime law and its development is under constant review by the interested parties.[4]

German fisheries extend to the Baltic, the North Sea and the North Atlantic. Tentative moves have been made recently in the South Atlantic, but it is not clear whether they will be pursued. The fishing industry is, in principle, opposed to broad territorial waters and exclusive zones, and the third Geneva Convention of 1958 has not been ratified by Germany. This is not to say that conservation problems are neglected in Germany. As early as 1876–77 a German Law and an Ordinance instituted a closed season for sealing for German fishing craft in an area north of Iceland.[5] Conservation arrangements were concluded with States on the Baltic, and Germany is a party to the important general and regional fisheries conventions.[6] The Law by which the German legislature consented to several regional conventions confers ordinance powers on the Minister for Food and Agriculture so that the regulations laid down by the international commissions can be transformed into German law.[7] In fact, the German fishing industry and the authorities will co-operate in any reasonable scheme to maintain and protect the living resources of the sea, and to consider the interest of the coastal State, provided the scheme is non-discriminatory.

As to mineral resources, the continental shelf idea did not find, at first, much sympathy. When the German delegation was preparing for the Geneva Conference in 1958, only the Ministry of Economic Affairs was inclined to accept the proposals worked out by the International Law Commission. The result of the debates was a German memorandum to the Conference which recommended a liberal régime under the supervision of the adjacent coastal State.[8] The Conference however adopted the other proposal and Germany signed the Continental Shelf Convention on October 30, 1958, but did not ratify it.

Nevertheless, when foreign enterprises were approaching the North Sea with drilling gear, the Federal Government proclaimed on January 20, 1964,[9] rights on the continental shelf in the North Sea. The exact delimitation of the shelf area created difficulties with her neighbours, as Germany denied that she was bound by Article 6

† For references, see p. 256.

of the 1958 Continental Shelf Convention. It was only after repeated negotiations and an appeal to the International Court of Justice (*North Sea Continental Shelf Cases, Fed. Rep. of Germany* v. *Denmark, Fed. Rep. of Germany* v. *Netherlands*, Judgment of February 20, 1969) that the limits of the respective parts were settled.[10] Moreover, as in other federal States, there were questions about the competences of federal and member states, and the Law of July 24, 1964, only solved them provisionally.[11] In fact, the German portion of the North Sea shelf has not been productive up to now, and activity has been limited to exploration.

Deep sea mining concerns areas where Germany could not under any known rule affirm rights as a coastal State. Her interest in raw materials and in the activity of her specialised industries would press her to advocate a very liberal régime; but co-operation with underdeveloped countries with long coastlines or with States obtaining mining concessions from an international body for deep sea mining could also be considered. Germany can therefore discuss the problems with an open mind, and the important points are the effectiveness and impartiality of any régime which might be agreed upon.[12] As far as is known, a German firm is interested in a consortium working on hot brines in the Red Sea.

The international organisation to be set up for deep sea mining or for the use of the oceans generally is expected to be of the usual type without supranational or executive powers; and it is therefore essential that the material régime of the oceans be fixed in detail by treaty. On this point Germany is in line with the proposals made by Western countries and by the Deep Sea Mining Committee of the International Law Association.

Pollution of the sea is a big problem for Germany, for almost the entire North Sea coast and a great part of the Baltic coast are dotted with seaside resorts, and the fisheries in the narrow and intensely navigated North Sea are seriously threatened. Public concern was aroused some years ago when the Press discussed plans for pipelines discharging waste from the big urban and industrial centres on the Rhine and the Ruhr into the North Sea.

Germany is a party to the anti-pollution Convention of May 12, 1954, and to the Regional Agreement for the North Sea of June 9, 1969. The Law of September 21, 1972, ratifying the 1958 Convention on the High Seas authorises the Transport Minister to take anti-pollution measures by Ordinance.[13] Germany has also signed the Oslo Convention for the Prevention of Marine Pollution by Dumping from Ships and Aircraft, of February 15, 1972.

In this connection it may be noted that Germany is to become a party to the convention prohibiting the emplacement of nuclear weapons on the seabed of February 11, 1971.[14] Possessing a reactor-driven ship, she has agreements with several States insuring against the resulting danger,[15] but is not a party to the Convention of 1962. Shipowners are still discussing the arduous problem of liability for pollution damages.[16]

Pirate broadcasting was, for a while, a problem for the German authorities. The Federal Republic is now a party to the European Agreement for the Prevention of Broadcasts transmitted from Stations outside National Territories, of January 22, 1965. The penal sanctions of the concomitant Law of September 26, 1969,[17] apply to fixed stations as well but not to every sort of collaboration described in Article 2 of the Agreement.

Germany attaches much importance to ocean research and it is regretted that the 1958 Continental Shelf Convention in Article 5, para. 8, unduly restricts freedom of research. This seems to be the general feeling, and it is hoped that the revision of the public international law of the sea will amend that clause. In the meantime German research is proceeding on the basis of friendly understanding with the interested foreign authorities.

Germany is not a party to the Convention on Transit Trade of Land-Locked States of July 8, 1965. The problem of transit trade is well known to Germany, depending as she does, on the one hand, on the transit facilities of Dutch, Belgian, French and Italian ports, while, on the other, offering seaport facilities herself to Switzerland, Austria and central Europe. But as the European delegations were able to point out at the 1958 Geneva Conference, the problem is solved by existing régimes and agreements to the satisfaction of everyone. This state of affairs seems likely to continue.[18]

REFERENCES

1. W. Schücking, *Der Kodifikationsversuch betreffend die Rechtsverhältnisse des Küstenmeeres und die Gründe seines Scheiterns* (1931), p. 18 *et seq.*

2. Law of Sept. 21, 1972, Bundesgesetzblatt 1972 II, p. 1089.

3. On these incidents, see S. Vollmar, *Das Durchsuchungsrecht im Frieden aus Gründen des Selbstschutzes* (Law Thesis, Bonn, 1966).

4. See A. Krieger, *Der gegenwärtige Stand der Arbeiten zur Modernisierung des Seerechts.*

5. Reichsgesetzblatt 1876, p. 233, 1877, p. 409, Bundesgesetzblatt III 793–2 and 793–2–1.

6. For details, see Beilage zum Bundesgesetzblatt II, Fundstellennachweis B, Dec. 31, 1971, p. 319.

7. Seefischerei-Vertragsgesetz 1971 of Aug. 25, 1971, Bundesgesetzblatt 1971 II, p. 1057, with the Ordinances of Aug. 26, 1971, and Jan. 25, 1972, Bundesgesetzblatt 1971 II, p. 1065, and 1972 II, p. 34.

8. A/Conf.13/C.4/L.1.

9. Bundesgesetzblatt 1964 II, p. 104.

10. Treaties between Germany and the Netherlands of Dec. 1, 1964, and Jan. 28, 1971, between Germany and Denmark of June 9, 1965, and Jan. 28, 1971, between Germany and the United Kingdom of Nov. 25, 1971 (Bundesgesetzblatt 1965 II, p. 1141, 1966 II, p. 205, 1972 II, p. 881).

11. With an amendment of June 25, 1969, Bundesgesetzblatt 1964 I, p. 497, 1969 I, p. 581.

12. There are memoranda by the industrial associations Wirtschaftsvereinigung Industrielle Meerestechnik and Wirtschaftsvereinigung Bergbau; the important part of the latter is reprinted in W. Graf Vitzthum, *Der Rechtsstatus des Meeresbodens* (1972), pp. 364–372.

13. Law of Sept. 21, 1972; see n. 2, *supra.*

14. Law of May 12, 1972, Bundesgesetzblatt 1972 II, p. 325.

15. See the document quoted *supra*, n. 6, at p. 318, left column.

16. A. Krieger *op. cit.* n. 4, *supra*, at p. 10 *et seq.*

17. Bundesgesetzblatt 1969 II, p. 1939.

18. See D. Schröder, *Der freie Zugang der Binnenstaaten zum Meer* (1966), esp. p. 31 *et seq.*

CHAPTER 22

France

By Jean-Pierre Quéneudec *

THE French position in relation to the law of the sea can be discussed under four main headings: the legal régime of the territorial sea, the régime of the continental shelf, the regulation of fishing and the prevention of marine pollution.

1. THE TERRITORIAL SEA

(a) The 12 mile rule

The Law of December 24, 1971, concerning the Delimitation of the French Territorial Sea extended the breadth of the territorial sea to 12 miles.[1]† France thus broke with a long tradition and a long adherence to the old rule of three miles.

However, until 1971 French law contained no general provision expressly relating to the breadth of the territorial sea. All that existed were various pieces of legislation governing the different powers exercised by France in a belt of varying width adjacent to the coastal waters.

Thus the Law of March 1, 1888, prohibited foreign vessels from fishing in the territorial sea within three miles of the low-water mark. It was assumed that this Law prescribed a three mile territorial sea, when all it did was to lay down an exclusive fishing limit for French nationals; it did not lay down any general rule on the limits of the territorial sea. Moreover in an advisory opinion of April 25, 1928, the Conseil d'Etat was of the opinion that " the Law of March 1, 1888, had neither as its object nor effect to lay down a three mile limit . . . for the breadth of the territorial sea over which France exercises sovereignty and the right of police." [2]

Thus for a very long time the breadth of the French territorial sea, regarded as being three miles, was determined by custom, attested by continuous practice and the position repeatedly adopted by the French authorities. In particular, the Minister of Foreign Affairs said in June 1959: " The French Government remains firmly attached to the principle that the breadth of the territorial sea does not exceed three nautical miles, measured from the base line, and it considers that any modification of this rule can only occur as a result of general international agreement." [3]

Following the failure of the United Nations Conference to agree on the breadth of the territorial sea, the French Government, which had supported proposals for a six mile territorial sea at Geneva, announced that it was not envisaging unilaterally extending its own territorial sea beyond three miles. The Minister of Public Works declared in the National Assembly on January 16, 1963: " Moreover, such an extension falls within the province of international law and the Government does not at present

* Professor, Faculty of Law, University of Montpellier.
† For references, see p. 265.

envisage such an extension by unilateral decree when it has constantly protested against the taking of similar measures by other States." [4]

Nevertheless the idea began to gain ground that France, yielding to the general tendency in this field, ought to abandon the three mile rule.

The abandonment of this traditional position is easily explained. In fact, after the extension to 12 miles of the exclusive fishing zone (Decree of June 7, 1967) and the adoption of the same limit for the Maritime Customs Zone (Law of July 31, 1968), France was exercising more and more jurisdiction in this 12 mile zone, and was tending to acquire again all the attributes of territorial sovereignty.

With the approach of the third United Nations Conference on the Law of the Sea, France wanted to show that the most traditionalist maritime States, if they are prepared to compromise, also intend to fix a reasonable limit for the breadth of the territorial sea, that is, a limit which, while satisfying the legitimate interest of the protection of coastal States, also satisfies the general interest of the international community.

Faced with a general trend towards increasing the breadth of the territorial sea, France considers that 12 miles is a reasonable breadth which ought to persuade the members of the international community to agree on the establishment of a limit to unilateral encroachments on the high seas. This breadth, which is observed in the practice of a majority of States and which represents a fair balance between the interests of coastal States and the interests of the international community, has the added advantage of being in conformity with Article 24 of the Geneva Convention on the Territorial Sea and the Contiguous Zone, which fixes at 12 miles the outer limit of the territorial sea and contiguous zone taken together. Although the French Government refused to sign the Convention in 1958 because it did not fix the outer limit of the territorial sea, it considers that Article 24 means that a State cannot extend its exercise of sovereignty beyond 12 miles.

Apart from these considerations of international order, there have been a number of other motives behind the extension of French territorial waters.

First, the demands of the fight against pollution have been largely responsible for making the French Government, aware of the problems of pollution since the *Torrey Canyon* episode, decide to extend the scope of its jurisdiction over a larger area of the sea. The new conditions of navigation resulting from the progress of technology and the risks arising from the carriage of oil by very large ships justify a State, which borders sea routes carrying a large quantity of traffic, in exercising its policing power over a wider area. In this connection, the extension of French territorial waters is interesting as a way of dealing with the dangers of coastal pollution. The Brussels Convention on Civil Liability for Oil Pollution Damage of November 29, 1969, provides that oil tankers carrying more than 2,000 metric tons of oil should be insured and carry an insurance certificate on board (Art. 7). The French authorities have let it be known on several occasions that they are considering making the carrying of an insurance certificate obligatory for tankers exercising the right of passage through the French territorial sea, and that in cases where no certificate is carried or there is a refusal to show the certificate the passage would no longer be considered as "innocent."

Secondly, the planned construction of an oil terminal outside Le Havre for giant tankers will be made easier, from the legal point of view, by the extension of the territorial sea, to the extent that the structure lies more than three miles from the French coast. Building an artificial terminal for giant tankers would have raised, in fact, insuperable problems if it had taken place on the high seas, even though adjacent to the territorial sea. In particular, the legal régime to be applied to this installation and to ships coming to berth there would have been rather difficult to define and put into operation. It is only with difficulty that such installations on the high seas could be placed under the jurisdiction of the coastal State where there is no question of making the legal régime governing the exploration or exploitation of the continental shelf applicable. This is the reason why France, being unable for technical reasons to construct this installation within a three mile territorial sea, managed to place them legally within the territorial sea by extending it to 12 miles. This extension also made it possible to exercise in respect of all oil tankers using the terminal the control provided for in Article 7 (xi) of the 1969 Brussels Convention: " Each Contracting State shall ensure, under its national legislation, that insurance or other security . . . is in force in respect of any ship, wherever registered, entering or leaving a port in its territory, or arriving at or leaving an off-shore terminal in its territorial sea." This consideration is related to the previous one.

Finally, military considerations have also played their part in the French decision. The extension of the territorial sea has also been dictated for reasons of national defence and, more particularly, by the safety requirements of nuclear submarines manoeuvring near the French coast. There is no doubt, in fact, that the new breadth of the territorial sea will make it easier to adopt surveillance measures over navigation in the approaches to Brest, at the time of the entry and exit of submarines belonging to the strategic force which are compelled to navigate on the surface to pass the Brest Channel roadsteads. Since the base line of the territorial sea in this area consists of a straight line drawn across the Iroise (Decree of October 19, 1967), nuclear submarines will thus be able to submerge before leaving the territorial sea and therefore will be less easy to detect.

It should be pointed out that there was no question of the French territorial sea being extended in order to protect the interests of inshore fisheries. In the French view, the régime of the territorial sea serves no real economic purpose. The territorial sea is considered above all as a protective zone and not as a zone designed to give particular economic rights. France therefore tends to keep the idea of the territorial sea separate from that of an exclusive fishing zone or, more generally, a zone of economic rights claimed by certain States.

(b) The problem of straits

According to Article 2 of the 1971 Law, " unless otherwise provided in some particular convention the breadth of the territorial sea does not extend beyond a median line, every point of which is equidistant from the nearest point on the base lines of the French coast and the base lines of the foreign coasts opposite or adjacent to the French coast." Nevertheless this median line principle may be modified in the case of certain international straits where France is one of the coastal States. This applies particularly in the case of the Straits of Dover, the Straits of Bonifacio between Corsica and Sardinia, and the Straits of Bab-el-Mandeb between French Somaliland and the island of Perim in the entrance to the Red Sea.

With the aim of maintaining and safeguarding the most complete freedom of navigation through these straits, and pending the conclusion of a special international convention laying down the legal régime for passage through straits lying within the territorial waters of the coastal State, France has decided to set an example. Thus Article 3 of the Law of December 24, 1971, provides for the possibilities of taking measures " in order to insure free maritime and aerial navigation, subject to the provisions of international conventions and, if need be, after agreement has been reached with the States concerned," when the distance between the French base lines and those of an opposite foreign State is equal to or less than 24 miles, or when this distance no longer allows the existence of a zone of high seas adequate for navigation.

Thus the extension of the French territorial sea keeps a navigation zone (in international straits) in which the principle of the freedom of the high seas is to be applied, and not the more restricted right of innocent passage. It can therefore be seen that the French view is that the right of passage through straits should be regarded as an indispensable complement to the right of navigation and overflight of the high seas.

2. THE CONTINENTAL SHELF

Being opposed to the criterion of exploitability used in the Geneva Convention to define the continental shelf, France had refused to sign the Convention in 1958 and only acceded to it, under the pressure of events, on June 14, 1965. Its instrument of accession is, however, accompanied by two declarations and three reservations concerning the definition and delimitation of the continental shelf and the conditions under which it may be exploited.[5]

(a) Definition and delimitation of the continental shelf

The interpretative declaration made by the French Government with regard to Article 1 of the Geneva Convention aims to limit the disadvantages arising from the lack of precision involved in the criterion of exploitability and to keep for the term " continental shelf " the meaning of a submarine zone near the coast. According to the French view, the idea of adjacency, used by the convention, refers to a " notion of geo-physical, geological and geographical dependence which *ipso facto* rules out an unlimited extension of the continental shelf." The French Government, therefore, refuses to recognise as legal excessive claims to almost limitless seabed areas by coastal States. The 1965 declaration thus aims to prevent such claims being binding on France, whether they result from unilateral action or as the results of division by agreement.

As regards the division of the continental shelf, the French Government has made a triple reservation to Article 6 of the Geneva Convention, so as to guard against improper divisions resulting from the automatic use of the equidistance principle; neighbouring States will not be able to invoke against France, unless it be by special agreement, delimitation of the seabed beyond the 200 metre isobath, nor delimitation based on base lines drawn after April 29, 1958. Moreover, the French Government has made a reservation in the case of areas where " special circumstances " exist of the kind to modify the rules of delimitation of neighbouring continental shelves: the Bay of Biscay where fishing interests predominate, the Straits of Dover, because of the interests of navigation, and Granville Bay, because of the existence of the Channel Islands which come under British jurisdiction.

(b) Exploitation of the continental shelf

At the Geneva Conference of 1958, the French delegation voted for the term " exclusive rights," in preference to the term " sovereign rights " which was thought to be ambiguous, to define the right of the coastal State over its continental shelf. Nevertheless the Law of December 30, 1968, relating to the Exploration of the Continental Shelf and to the Exploitation of its Natural Resources restricts itself to repeating the expression used in Article 2 of the Geneva Convention.[6] When the Law was enacted, it was nevertheless made clear that the rights of France over its continental shelf were limited and that there was no question of any territorial acquisition. It is, moreover, for this reason that the French Government has been led to protest against claims made by certain States to sovereignty over the continental shelf.[7]

In addition, when acceding to the Geneva Convention on the Continental Shelf, the French Government showed its concern for keeping the widest freedom of fishing in epicontinental waters. With this aim, it made an interpretative declaration to Article 2 (iv) of the convention. According to this, the expression " living organisms belonging to the sedentary species " must be interpreted as excluding crustaceans, with the exception of the species of crab termed " barnacle." This declaration was largely motivated by memories of the differences which arose on this score in 1962–63 between France and Brazil, when the latter denied to French fishermen the right to fish for lobsters on the Brazilian continental shelf because they were considered as being natural resources over which Brazil possessed sovereign rights.

With the same aim, the French Government has propounded the principle of the right to compensation for restrictions placed on the exercise of acquired fishing rights in waters above the continental shelf, even if these restrictions constitute a justifiable interference within the meaning of Article 5 of the Convention on the Continental Shelf. France considers, in fact, that the provisions of this Article ought to be applied in such a way as to guarantee the reasonable exercise of other uses of the sea lying over the continental shelf.

Following the Law of December 30, 1968, three Decrees of June 6, 1971, have been made in order to render French domestic law more precise as regards conditions for exploiting the continental shelf.[8] In particular, they provide that permits to explore or exploit the continental shelf shall only be granted to persons having a place of business in France. This rule does not have as its effect the reservation exclusively to French nationals of the exercise of exploitation activities on the continental shelf. This provision is quite compatible with the Treaty establishing the European Economic Community and, in particular, with the prohibition of any discrimination on grounds of nationality and with the principle of the freedom of establishment. The Commission of the European Communities is of the opinion that the Treaty of Rome is applicable to the continental shelf.[9] In applying the French legislation, it will not be possible to discriminate and so Community principles will be respected.

The possession of a place of business in France is not, however, a requirement for the granting of a permit to conduct purely scientific research concerning the physical or biological characteristics of the shelf; this is quite in conformity with Article 5 (viii) of the Geneva Convention.

(c) The seabed beyond the continental shelf

In a document presented in August 1970 to the Committee on the Peaceful Uses of the Seabed and Ocean Floor beyond the Limits of National Jurisdiction,[10] France stressed that the future legal régime of the seabed and ocean floor ought to fulfil the double requirement of economic efficiency and international equity, and that extreme solutions should be avoided—both appropriation pure and simple by States of more or less extensive areas of the seabed, as well as the simple taking over of all seabed exploration and exploitation activities by an international organisation invested with considerable powers. The French proposal was for a solution between these two extremes and advocated the making of a distinction between the exploitation of mineral substances lying on the ocean floor (manganese nodules) and the exploitation of mineral substances found in the subsoil (oil and gas). Since the former can be exploited from mobile equipment, the legal régime should take the form of simple registration with an international organisation, and without any exclusive rights of exploration or exploitation. On the other hand, in the case of the latter, which can only be exploited from fixed installations, rights of exploration and exploitation should be exclusive and should take the form of the granting of areas to States, who would thus be the link between the international organisation and the companies engaging in the exploitation of seabed resources. Under the French proposal, States would thus be given areas within which they themselves would license exploitation: this would exclude any system of direct management by an international agency, as was pointed out by the French delegate at the meeting of the Seabed Committee held in New York in March 1972.

In the course of this same meeting, the French delegation also let it be known that it was in principle in favour of the recognition of jurisdiction being exercised by the coastal State over the seabed and its subsoil beyond the limits of national jurisdiction up to a distance of 200 miles from its coast. This position represents an important concession to States which claim the exclusive right to issue exploitation licences in the areas adjacent to their continental shelf.

3. FISHING

Following the London Fisheries Convention of March 9, 1964, a Decree was promulgated in France on June 7, 1967, extending the outer limit of the French exclusive fishing zone to 12 miles, measured from the base lines of the territorial sea, and prohibiting foreigners from fishing in this zone. Then within the framework of agreements provided for by Article 9 of the London Convention, France concluded a General Agreement on Fisheries with Spain on March 20, 1967, under which nationals of both countries are given the reciprocal right to fish indefinitely in the outer 6 mile zone.[11] This agreement is noteworthy for widening the geographical scope of the London Convention since it applies to both the Atlantic and Mediterranean coasts of both countries. The French and Spanish Governments have also extended their co-operation by jointly adopting several measures of conservation of the living resources of the sea, in order to limit the risks of over-exploitation of certain fish stocks. After an agreement of this nature had been signed at Fontarabie on November 14, 1969, sectors, *i.e.*, zones where fishing is forbidden, were established in the Bay of Biscay in 1970.[12]

This concern for the conservation of fishery resources recently led France to enact the Law of July 5, 1972, relating to the Conservation of the Living Resources of the Sea adjacent to French Guiana, which has as its object the extension of the outer limit of the exclusive fishing zone of this overseas *département* to 80 miles.

The importance of the fishing industry for the economy of French Guiana necessitated measures to conserve shrimp stocks, which are one of its chief resources. The application of the provisions of the Decree of June 7, 1967, establishing a 12 mile exclusive fishing zone was ineffective as far as shrimps are concerned because they are caught up to 80 miles from the coast. The decision of the Brazilian authorities to extend their territorial sea to 200 miles profoundly affected the situation in this region. Fishermen, no longer able to fish off the Brazilian coast, came to fish off the coasts of French Guiana and subjected the stock to intensive fishing. Negotiations begun with Brazil in July 1971 to safeguard the activities of French fishermen off its coasts failed to reach a solution which was legally acceptable in practice. Finally the numerous discussions to which the planned UN Conference on the Law of the Sea has given rise on the international level have revealed a more and more widespread trend towards extensive claims by coastal States to marine areas adjacent to their coasts.

All these new factors taken together made urgent the adoption of conservation measures which would reconcile the need to maintain a reasonable legal position with the fishing interests of French Guiana. It is in order to fulfil this double requirement that the 1972 Law establishes an 80 mile exclusive fishing zone.

By doing this, France did not intend to identify with the extreme legal positions adopted by many States, notably those of the Latin American countries. On the general level, the French Government continues not to recognise as valid unilateral claims to extensive areas of the sea and does not envisage having recourse to a new extension of its territorial sea merely to deal with the problem of the conservation of the living resources of the sea.

The exclusive fishing zone established in French Guiana has been done on a temporary basis and is a simple safeguard measure until rules of international law acceptable to all interested States have established an agreed régime in this region. Indeed Article 1 of the Law explicitly states that this exclusive fishing limit has been created " pending the entry into force of appropriate international agreements." Thus this legislation is of limited scope and does not prejudice the general position taken by France on the limitation of exclusive fishing zones.

Basing itself on the special interest of every coastal State in the maintenance of the productivity of the living resources in any area of the high seas adjacent to its territorial sea, recognised by Article 6 of the Geneva Convention on Fishing and Conservation of the Living Resources of the High Seas (which France ratified on September 18, 1970), the French Government assumes the right to regulate and limit the catching of various marine species within the 80 mile zone. This regulation will be valid *erga omnes*, but its application to fishermen of foreign States will depend on " the geographical position of these States and the fishing traditions of their nationals " (Art. 2). This 80 mile zone will, in fact, remain open to States which do not invoke against France fishing limits in excess of 12 miles and which share French views on the principles laid down in the Geneva Convention, according to which the demands of the conservation of living resources alone justify a restriction by coastal States on fishing activities adjacent to their coasts. *A fortiori*, this zone will be open to member States of the European Economic Community in conformity with the Regulation on the Establishment of a Common Structural Policy for the Fishing Industry.

The measures for preventing fishing which France can take within the 80 mile zone off the coast of French Guiana will thus only be applied against States which claim exclusive fishing zones in excess of 12 miles. Article 2 (ii) of the Law of July 5, 1972, states explicitly that within the 80 mile zone " decrees may be made prohibiting fishing to the vessels of States which do not allow French vessels to fish under comparable conditions." France could not allow Brazilian trawlers to fish freely off the coast of French Guiana, when this same right is denied to French fishermen in the Brazilian 200 mile zone. But it is not really a measure of retorsion taken against Brazil, since the wording of Article 2 of the French Law is such that it does not allow the prohibition of fishing to be applied automatically if it appears that new negotiations with the Brazilian authorities have some chance of leading to an acceptable agreement on the problems of access to fishing grounds and the conservation of living resources in this region.

In the view of the French authorities, this limited and temporary fishing zone is only justified by its exceptional character and its establishment does not undermine the general position on the law of the sea taken by the French Government.

France wants, in fact, to safeguard the principle of freedom of fishing on the high seas as far as possible, subject to the restrictions and controls laid down by international agreements for preserving and conserving living resources. In order to ensure the effective putting into operation of this control, France enacted the Law of December 23, 1970, relating to the Procedure to be Followed regarding International Inspection of Sea Fisheries provided for by International Conventions.[13] This Law, which implements the London Convention on Conduct of Fishing Operations in the North Atlantic of June 1, 1967, also has as its aim to allow the carrying out of international inspection of regulations on the protection of species which are laid down in the Recommendations adopted in May 1967 by the North-East Atlantic Fisheries Commission and in June 1970 by the International Commission for the Northwest Atlantic Fisheries. In this context, the French authorities are of the view that international supervision of sea fishing ought to become more widespread.

In general, the French Government never refuses to take into consideration proposals made to it concerning restrictions on the freedom of fishing, when these restrictions are based on the need to conserve resources and are aimed at concerted action on the international level. The Agreement between France and Canada on their Mutual Fishing Relations, signed at Ottawa on March 27, 1972, is one example.[14] This originated from a proposal for negotiations based on the need to adapt fishing efforts to the present state of stocks off the coasts of Canada.

In the French view, the concern of certain States to protect the living resources in the waters adjacent to their coasts, where these are regarded as a resource whose exploitation is a factor in economic development, may sometimes justify derogations from the principle of the freedom of fishing, particularly when the prosperity and economic well-being of a country depends on coastal fisheries. However, these exceptions would not form the basis of a general legal rule.

In this connection, the French Government is of the view that the rules of the international law of fisheries ought to take account, not only of the particular problems of developing States, but also those of States which have long possessed distant water fleets. Countries which suffer from the disadvantage of having the waters adjacent to their coasts being poorly stocked with fish and which have had to build up distant water fleets deserve legal protection in the same way as States whose fishermen have the advantage of having coastal waters rich in living resources.

Even though France has gone so far in the Seabed Committee as to contemplate the possibility of the extension of the jurisdiction of the coastal State over economic interests to a limit beyond 12 miles, she is of the view that this jurisdiction ought to be exercised in such a way that it has regard to the interests of foreign fishermen and to the conditions for a rational exploitation of the resources of the sea.

4. THE PREVENTION OF MARINE POLLUTION

France, which is a signatory to all the conventions drawn up in recent years for preventing pollution of the marine environment, has enacted in its municipal law provisions which will ensure effective means for tackling such pollution.

Thus, under the Law of December 16, 1964, relating to the Régime and Repartition of Water and the Prevention of its Pollution, " the discharge or placing in the sea of any substances whatever, particularly industrial and radioactive waste, which is detrimental to public health, marine flora and fauna, and the economic and touristic development of coastal areas, is prohibited." In furtherance of this Law, a Decree of September 25, 1970, prohibits more particularly the discharge into the sea of detergents which are not 80 per cent. biodegradable. This Law and Decree, however, only apply to internal waters and the territorial sea.

The Law of December 26, 1964, on the Prevention of Pollution of the Sea by Oil lays down a fine of between 2,000 and 20,000 francs for the captain of any ship contravening the provisions of the London Convention of May 12, 1954. For a second offence, the penalty is a fine of between 5,000 and 50,000 francs and imprisonment between 10 days and six months. These penalties apply to the captains of French vessels covered by the London Convention, and to the captains of foreign vessels causing pollution in French internal or territorial waters, even if these vessels are not registered in a State party to the London Convention.[15]

The same penalties are laid down by the 1968 Law on the Continental Shelf when pollution results from exploitation on the continental shelf.

All these provisions, however, only deal with intentional pollution of the sea. To deal with accidental pollution to French coasts caused by oil, a Ministerial Circular of December 23, 1970, established the so-called POLMAR plan (Emergency Organisation for Dealing with Marine Pollution). Under this plan, action can be taken against the ship or installation causing the pollution, without regard to its position (whether it be on the high seas or in territorial waters). Even before the entry into force of the Brussels Convention relating to Intervention on the High Seas in Cases of Oil Pollution Casualties of November 29, 1969, France has equipped itself to utilise this right of intervention.

REFERENCES

1. (1972) 11 Int.Leg.Mat. 153.

2. G. Gidel, *Le droit international public de la mer* (1934), Vol. 3, p. 466, n. 1.

3. (1959) *Annuaire français de droit international* 899.

4. (1963) *Annuaire français de droit international* 1058.

5. See F. de Hartingh, " La position française à l'égard de la Convention de Genève sur le plateau continental " (1965) *Annuaire français de droit international* 725–734.

6. See J. P. Quéneudec, " Chronique du droit de la mer " (1969) *Annuaire français de droit international* 737–746.

7. *e.g.*, protest of Feb. 1, 1967, against the promulgation by Argentina of a Law of Dec. 29, 1966, extending its sovereignty to the continental shelf and superjacent waters (1967) *Revue générale de droit international public* 389.

8. See J. P. Quéneudec, " Chronique du droit de la mer " (1971) *Annuaire français de droit international* 778–780.

9. Memorandum concernant l'applicabilité du Traité de la C.E.E. au plateau continental, SEC (70) 3095 final, Sept. 18, 1970. See also *infra*, p. 336.

10. Establishment of a Régime for the Exploration and Exploitation of the Seabed, A/AC. 138/27.

11. (1967) *Revue générale de droit international public* 839–842.

12. See J. P. Quéneudec, " Chronique du droit de la mer " (1970) *Annuaire français de droit international* 736–737. A new French-Spanish agreement, signed at Paris on Aug. 28, 1972, relating to the supervision of zones where fishing is forbidden, provides for international control of fishing operations and vessels in accordance with the recommendations of the North-East Atlantic Fisheries Commission (see *Journal Officiel de la République française*, Nov. 8, 1972, p. 11630).

13. (1970) *Annuaire français de droit international* 734–735.

14. *Journal Officiel de la République française*, July 27, 1972, p. 7998. Through this Agreement, Canada has phased out the fishing rights and privileges conferred on French fishermen according to the Convention of April 8, 1904, with the U.K.

15. The French Government has recently proposed raising the initial fine to a higher level of between 5,000 and 50,000 francs.

CHAPTER 23

Italy

By Francesco Durante *

ITALY, on account of her lack of natural resources in raw materials and commodities, is particularly interested in the recent developments in the Law of the Sea, and especially in the tendency towards a greater protection, by the maritime States, of the natural resources of the sea, the seabed and subsoil, especially those resources located in the seas adjacent to the coast.

It must be pointed out, however, that Italy, unlike some maritime States, has not taken a position or adopted acts with the intention of subordinating the traditional principle of freedom of the seas to the protection of solely national interests.

Even though the Italian Government has accepted the general tendency to extend, within certain limits, some exclusive rights, in favour of coastal States, over areas of the sea much larger than those previously contemplated by international law, it has abstained from taking up an extremist position even though, in actual international practice, such positions have been assumed.

The Italian Government has, on the other hand, followed the prevailing tendency to combine the protection of legitimate national interests and the general principle of freedom of the seas. This tendency develops along three lines: (a) the first leads to the progressive merging of the territorial sea and the contiguous zone on account of the general tendency to stretch the limit of the territorial sea to 12 nautical miles from the coast; (b) the second provides for more restrictive fishing regulations, either dictated by the coastal State or established through agreements between the States having the strongest interests in the fishing of a certain area. The adoption of national and international rules pertaining to pollution of the sea is closely associated with fishing regulations and the conservation of the sea's biological resources in general. (c) The third line of development concerns the exploitation of the mineral resources of the sea bottom (continental shelf, deep sea mining).

We may now consider, in more detail, Italy's position in respect of each of these three aspects of the evolution of the law of the sea.

TERRITORIAL SEA

As regards the tendency to extend the width of that part of the sea subject to sovereignty of the coastal State, we may recall that Italy, for some time now, has recognised the inadequacy of the territorial sea's outward limit of three nautical miles. In fact, Italian law (Art. 2 of the Code of Navigation) fixes the limit of the territorial sea at six nautical miles from the low-water mark along the coast. Straight base lines are only used for the measurement of such distances, should the case arise, where the actual

* Professor of International Law, University of Catania.

coastal formation creates gulfs, coves and bays whose natural mouths do not exceed, in straight lines, the distance of 20 nautical miles, measured from their outer points.

Without a doubt, a territorial sea of this size more fairly satisfies the necessities of protection of the State and its citizens in relation to the new exigencies arising in the international community. Italy, however, has not assumed the position taken by some other States which have claimed sovereignty over much vaster areas of the sea (from 25 to 200 nautical miles) on the assumption that the safeguarding of the primarily national interests located in these zones necessitates such an action.

Nevertheless, the present outward limit of the territorial sea, fixed by Italian law at six miles, and the fact that Italy has ratified the Geneva Convention on the Territorial Sea and the Contiguous Zone does not exclude the possibility, in the near future, of the Italian State's extension of its territorial sea to a distance, by now recognised legitimate by most States, of 12 nautical miles from the coast.

At present, this distance is provided for by Italian law (Customs Law of September 25, 1940 n. 1424) for the purpose of customs control; in other words, with a view to preventing violations of customs laws in Italian customs' territory.

FISHING

Considering the local population's pre-eminent interests, fishing in the territorial sea is reserved to nationals and national fishing vessels (Art. 221, Code of Navigation). Nevertheless, according to special provisions by the State or international agreements, foreigners may be permitted to fish in Italian territorial waters (Art. 221, Code of Navigation).

By international agreements Italy has, nevertheless, permitted some coastal States to exclude foreign fishermen from an area extending up to 12 miles from their coasts or has recognised the right to regulate unilaterally fishing in the said stretch of sea, compulsory for all foreign fishermen (Fisheries Convention, London, March 9, 1964).

The regulations on maritime fishing, established by the Italian State, apply to all fishermen authorised to fish in the territorial waters but only to Italian fishermen fishing on the high seas (Art. 1, Law no. 963 of 1965 on the regulation of sea fishing).

The freedom to fish outside the zone reserved for Italian fishermen is guaranteed not only by the explicit limits imposed on the application of Italian law, but also by the express re-confirmation of that freedom as contained in the provisions which, anticipating Italian claims to the high seas, could be interpreted as ideal for establishing a limit to that freedom (see Art. 2, para. 3 of Law no. 613 of 1967 on the continental shelf).

Strict respect for the principle of freedom of the seas does not preclude Italy from sharing the concern shown by many other States, that indiscriminate exercise of the freedom to fish on the high seas can deny, in an unjustifiable way, the very possibility of enjoying that same freedom, thus leading to the extinction of some species of fish now being fished, and damaging fishing in the coastal areas reserved to nationals of coastal States.

Consequently, although Italy has not yet ratified the Geneva Convention on Fishing and the Conservation of the Living Resources of the High Seas, she has adhered to many international conventions which aim at regulating fishing on the high seas for the purpose of permitting improved exploitation of marine resources.

Among those agreements on the regulation of fishing to which Italy is a contracting party, we might mention:

—Convention for the Northwest Atlantic Fisheries (Washington, February 8, 1949) and the protocols which modify or supplement it.

—European Fisheries Convention (London, March 9, 1964), already mentioned. Italy's interest in regulating high seas fishing and in safeguarding the general interest in the conservation of the biological resources of the sea, has also been confirmed recently by the issuing of a regulation regarding sea fishing (Order of the President of the Republic, October 2, 1968 n. 1639). This order contains compulsory rules not only for those fishing in those areas of the sea which are under Italy's control and jurisdiction but also on the high seas, even though applying only to Italian fishermen. This regulation is dedicated, for the main part (Arts. 86–144), to regulating the period and means of fishing in such a way that the conditions for reproduction and the actual existence of the biological resources will not be jeopardised.

The Regions too, within the limits of their competence, have made provisions for the protection of fishing against the indiscriminate practice of marine livestock destruction in such a way as to co-ordinate their work with that of the Italian State in this field. Worth mentioning in this respect are the Presidential and Assessorial Orders no. 810 of November 28, 1956 and no. 194 of March 17, 1967 of Sicily which regulate fishing in regional waters and the Presidential Order no. 10285/3403 of August 8, 1968 of Sardinia which limits trawl fishing with mechanically propelled boats.

POLLUTION

The problem of the pollution of the sea, for its serious economic repercussions, possibly resulting in damage to maritime activities (fishing, navigation) or to indirect activities, must concern a country which, like Italy, has more than 8,000 kilometres of coast bordering on an inland sea, the Mediterranean. The damaging direct and indirect effects of pollution can be more noticeable here than in the open seas.

On an international level, Italy contributed to setting up a legal system for pollution under the dual profile of both pollution prevention and regulation of the consequences of pollution, when it adhered to the London Convention of 1954 on the Prevention of Oil Pollution (in the text amended in 1962) and the Brussels Convention of 1969 on the Liability for Oil Pollution of the Sea.

On the level of national legislation, Italy has recently issued provisions aiming at prohibiting any form of marine pollution that could harmfully affect the biological resources of the sea. This legislation combines the preceding national regulations which, even though in a disorganised way, aimed at preventing and punishing any activities that could lead to pollution of the sea. As an example we might mention that the Code of Navigation prohibits the disposal of wastes in the sea (Art. 71) and the muddying of sea water (Art. 76) even though it is limited to particular areas and applies only to limited categories of operators.

Only recently, as already mentioned, has the Italian legislature considered the problem of pollution of the sea in a more coherent and specific way. Regulations more suited to pollution prevention have been laid down, even though their effectiveness has been limited by the fact that they are included in fishing regulations. Articles 14–15 of the above-mentioned Law no. 963 of July 14, 1965 prohibit, or at least tend to limit, activities that might pollute the sea in such a way as to harm, directly or on account of alterations in the environment, the biological resources of the sea. Article 25 of the same law imposes heavy penalties on offenders.

Article 2, para. 3 of Law no. 613 of 1967, already mentioned, also refers indirectly to pollution where it states that activities relating to the exploration and exploitation of hydrocarbons in the sea's subsoil must not constitute a restriction on the traditional uses of the high seas, among which fishing and other biological resources of the sea are expressly mentioned.

CONTINENTAL SHELF

Among the most interesting aspects of the new uses of the seas which require adequate national and international legal regulation are certainly those of exploration and exploitation of the natural resources of the seabed and subsoil beyond the limits of the territorial sea.

Given the present and potential importance, from an economic point of view, of the activities concerned with utilising the submarine resources, all the major maritime States have taken a stand on the legal regulations that they intend to carry out in safeguarding their respective national interests, even where conflicts with the interests of other States arise.

Although Italy has not yet ratified the Geneva Convention on the Continental Shelf, Italian law has followed the leading trends as concerns the definition of the continental shelf, the nature of the coastal State's rights and the limits within which these rights may be enforced.

Even on the subject of the delimitation of that part of the shelf common with other States, Italian law conforms to the international rules codified by the Geneva Convention in the sense confirmed, subsequently, by the decision of the International Court of Justice in the *North Sea Continental Shelf Cases*. Article 1 of the above-mentioned Law no. 613 of 1967 established, in fact, that the outward limit of the continental shelf, where it is in common with another State whose coast faces the Italian coast, will be fixed according to bilateral agreements with the said State. Until these agreements are concluded, exploration and exploitation of the natural resources of the seabed and subsoil may only be permitted on this side of the median line between the Italian coast and the coast of the State facing it. Italian law has not, however, taken directly into consideration the possibility of delimiting the continental shelf which it shared with States having adjacent coasts.

In this line of action Italy has concluded two international agreements, one with Yugoslavia and the other with Tunisia, for the delimitation of the continental shelf common in the Adriatic Sea and the Sicilian Channel respectively. These two agreements do not deviate from the criteria used for this kind of agreement, already generally accepted in practice. The criteria assumed for the delimitation are those provided by the Geneva Convention: the median line between the two coasts with corrections in relation to the presence of islands at variable distances from the coasts themselves. In the case of deposits forming a geological unit, straddling the line of demarcation of the respective sections of common continental shelf, the agreements provide for bilateral consultations on the ways of using these common deposits.

As regards the area of the seabed delimited, as already mentioned, Italy claims not only exclusive rights in international law, which exclude the existence of other State's rights or the possibility of creating them, but has attributed to itself, in municipal legislation, the exclusive right to carry out any activity of exploitation of the continental shelf's natural resources.

All who intend to carry out activities of exploration and exploitation of the sea's natural resources are subject to Italian national regulations, which presuppose that the above-mentioned activities are, in principle, within the competence of the State. It follows that any other person, national or foreign, who intends to undertake the said activities must be authorised by the State.

Even though it is not to be excluded that the Italian State can directly exercise such activities (through its various organs), Italian legislation provides for the concession of licences to public bodies and private individuals for the purpose of carrying out the same activities under the conditions established by the law itself.

Law no. 613, repeatedly cited herein, makes a distinction between direct activities of exploration and exploitation of oil and other mineral substances in the sea bottom of the continental shelf and the activities which, with reference to the same area of the seabed, are directly concerned with the exploration and exploitation of other natural resources. Although Law no. 613 refers questions pertaining to mineral resources to the general regulations provided by the Code of Navigation where applicable, and to the competence of maritime authorities, the regulation of activities concerning mineral resources and, in particular, the exploitation of hydrocarbons is contained in the Law itself.

This statute distinguishes three particular types of activities (prospecting, exploration and exploitation) and establishes, for each of these, the conditions under which they may be carried out by persons other than the State and its organs. Furthermore, the rights and duties of authorised persons or persons possessing concessions concerning the continental shelf are also established in detail.

Among the rules of particular interest contained in this law, we feel it necessary to single out that rule which permits, on conditions of reciprocity, foreign persons and organisations to obtain prospecting permits (Art. 9), exploration permits (Art. 16) and concessions for the exploitation of deposits discovered (Art. 27).

The possibility of granting permits and concessions to foreign organisations for the exploitation of the mineral resources of the Italian continental shelf is counter-balanced by the rule, according to which the products extracted from the continental shelf must be destined, first for the national market and require authorisation by the State before being exported (Art. 55).

CHAPTER 24

Union of Soviet Socialist Republics

By W. E. Butler *

The 1960–70's are a different time, even in comparison with the period preceding the Second World War, not to mention earlier times: the arrangement of forces in the international arena has changed, and international law has changed.

O. N. Khlestov (1973).

THE cumulative change in Soviet maritime power during the past two decades has been responsible for recent modifications of long-standing and fundamental attitudes toward the law of the sea. Soviet doctrines and practices in the past reflected (1) pre-revolutionary Russian attitudes and policies; (2) profound Soviet naval weakness and the relegation of the Navy to an auxiliary coastal-defence role in Soviet strategic doctrine; (3) predominantly coastal and inland commercial fishing operations; and (4) the need for foreign vessels to carry seaborne trade.[1]† Current Soviet policy now mirrors world-wide operations of its high seas fishing fleet, its modern merchant fleet, immense oceanographic research fleet, and augmented naval capabilities.

MARINE JURISDICTION

The Statute on the Protection of the State Boundary of the U.S.S.R. enacted on August 5, 1960, and amended on June 10, 1971, provides:

> " Coastal sea waters, twelve nautical miles in breadth, computed from the line of lowest ebb-tide both on the mainland and also around islands, or from the seaward line of internal sea waters of the U.S.S.R. and in those localities where the coastline is deeply indented and cut into or if there is a fringe of islands along the coast in its immediate vicinity—from straight base lines joining appropriate points, shall constitute the territorial waters of the U.S.S.R." [2]

Exceptions to the 12 mile rule exist pursuant to Soviet–Finnish treaties in certain areas of the Gulf of Finland and north of Suursaari Island;[3] a median line serves as the State frontier in the Bering Strait and on the straits between the Japanese island of Hokkaido and the Soviet Kurile islands.

The geographic co-ordinates on the points through which straight base lines shall pass for the purpose of delimiting the territorial sea of the U.S.S.R. are not yet a matter of public record. Under the 1960 Statute on the State Boundary, the closing line for bays, inlets, coves and estuaries should not exceed 24 nautical miles, excluding historic bays. Although nothing is said in this Statute about the length of straight base lines generally, several Soviet jurists have expressed the view that the 24 mile rule should

* Reader in Comparative Law, University of London.
† For references, see p. 279.

apply here as well.[4] There also is doctrinal support for the view that integral permanent port installations are to be regarded as part of the coast for the purpose of delimiting territorial waters; Soviet legislation is silent on the point.

The Soviet Union has no contiguous zones, as that term is commonly understood. Special legislation concerning the passage of warships, regulation of navigation, the use of wireless radio equipment, customs, sanitary protection, sunken property and salvage, hydrographic research, cabotage, and coastal fishing all appertains to activities conducted within the territorial sea.

An Edict of February 6, 1968, defines the Soviet continental shelf as the:

> ". . . seabed and subsoil of the submarine areas adjacent to the coast or to islands of the U.S.S.R. but outside the area of the territorial sea, to a depth of 200 metres or, beyond that limit, to where the depth of the superjacent waters admits of the exploitation of the natural resources of these areas.
>
> "The seabed and subsoil of depressions situate in the continuous mass of the continental shelf of the U.S.S.R., irrespective of their depth, shall be part of the continental shelf of the U.S.S.R."[5]

A number of views about the seaward limit of the shelf have been expressed in Soviet legal media, but the majority maintain that, under the 1958 Geneva Convention on the Continental Shelf, to which the U.S.S.R. is a party, the legal concept of the shelf cannot be deemed to exceed the geophysical shelf.[6] Soviet geologists regard the so-called " continental rise " as an oceanic rather than a continental formation.[7] Two Soviet jurists recently have concluded after examining the *travaux préparatoires* of the Geneva Convention that ". . . it is obvious that the conference participants were not inclined to include the slope in the legal concept of the continental shelf."[8]

Article 4 of the 1960 Statute on the Protection of the State Boundary defines the internal *sea* waters of the U.S.S.R. as waters of ports, of " bays, inlets, coves, and estuaries " whose aperture does not exceed 24 nautical miles, and of " bays, inlets, coves, and estuaries, seas, and straits, historically belonging to the U.S.S.R." There is no uniform view in Soviet legal doctrine as to what criteria historic waters must meet. One Soviet jurist has suggested that a State must have exercised authority over such waters for an extended period of time and that the overwhelming majority of States have not objected to the coastal State declaration that such waters are historic. In the case of an historic bay, the body of water must additionally possess the geographic configuration of a bay and, above all, be of " economic and defence significance " to the coastal State.[9]

Which bodies of water washing Soviet coasts fall into the category of historic waters is not wholly clear. Soviet doctrinal literature has classified some bodies of water as both closed seas and historic waters. The White Sea, for example, has been variously depicted as a closed sea, an internal Russian sea, and an historic bay. On various occasions since the Second World War, Soviet international lawyers have mentioned the Gulf of Riga, the Sea of Azov, and the Kara, Laptev, East Siberian and Chukotsk Seas as historic waters. The latest discussions of the subject in Soviet legal media list the White Sea, Cheshskaia Bay and Peter the Great Bay in the category of historic waters, as well as the Laptev and Sannikov Straits linking the Laptev and East Siberian Seas.[10] The claim to the straits apparently originated in an exchange of diplomatic notes with the United States concerning a contemplated voyage by an American oceanographic research vessel through the North-East Passage.[11]

The Soviet Union has long sought international recognition of a special status for certain other contiguous seas through the " closed " or " regional " sea doctrine.

The two bodies of water which have figured most prominently in Soviet diplomatic practice in this regard are the Baltic and Black Sea. Proposals to other littoral Powers of these seas have been made directly and at international conferences, but without success. Soviet doctrine from time to time has included the Sea of Azov and the Caspian, Japan, Okhotsk, Kara, Laptev, East Siberian and Chukotsk Seas in this category.

While there is no unanimity in Soviet doctrinal literature on the nature of a closed sea and it is difficult to ascertain how much vitality the doctrine has today, it would seem that a closed sea must possess a coastline of a particular geographic configuration, a limited number of littoral States whose land territory fully encloses the particular sea, a comparatively narrow entrance to the sea, and the absence of significant international sea lanes through the sea. All vessels flying the flag of a littoral State would have free and equal access to the use of the sea beyond the territorial waters of other Powers. Warships of non-littoral States would be excluded, though non-littoral merchant shipping would be freely admitted. The right of non-coastal States to fish has been left open.[12]

A recent treatment of the closed sea doctrine returns to the view, stressed in the late 1940s, that the legal nature of straits leading to a particular sea is conclusive in determining whether such a sea should enjoy a special juridical status. Straits leading to closed seas are said to be distinctive in that they are apart from the basic world sea lanes and have economic importance for only a small number of States. Such straits would be open to foreign merchant and fishing vessels, just as the high seas. Only one limitation would be imposed: warships of non-littoral Powers would be excluded. Among the straits which would fall into this category are the Black Sea and Baltic Straits and the Korean, Sangar, La Perouse and Kuril Straits leading into the Sea of Japan and the Okhotsk Sea.[13]

The extensive high seas fishing operations by the Soviet Union off the coasts of other States, coupled with apprehensions for the fate of maritime commerce, naval deployment, and oceanographic research, have led the Soviet Government generally to oppose claims of other States to marine jurisdiction beyond 12 miles or to areas of shelf or seabed that involve sovereign claims over the superjacent water column. Such claims have been the object of official protests at the governmental level,[14] of official censure in Soviet media,[15] and of severe criticism by Soviet jurists.[16] Although these expressions of concern usually have been muted and diplomatically phrased in an understandable effort to avoid giving offence to less developed countries, the general Soviet view is that claims to a territorial sea or contiguous zone in excess of 12 miles are inadmissible under international law. Argentina, Brazil, Chile, Costa-Rica, Ecuador, Honduras, Mexico, Panama, Peru, Salvador and Uruguay have been expressly named in Soviet legal media as examples of States whose claims to seabed have been extended unlawfully to the superjacent waters. Presumably the recent Soviet practice of paying licence fees to some Latin American countries for the privilege of fishing within the 200 mile limit is under protest and not intended to signify recognition of the legality of such limits.[17]

ACCESS TO FISHERIES

Soviet fisheries policy has two distinct aspects. So far as her own coastal fisheries are concerned, Soviet policy has been as protectionist as possible. Article 19 of the 1960 Statute on the Protection of the State Boundary provides that:

"The conduct of maritime trade (catching fish, crabbing, killing of marine fur-bearing animals, and any other trade) in the territorial and internal sea waters of the U.S.S.R. by a foreign vessel shall be prohibited, except in instances when such trade has been authorised by agreement of the U.S.S.R. with the respective States."

Finland has obtained authorisation for their nationals to fish in certain areas of the Gulf of Finland within the Soviet 12 mile limit, as has Japan for the collection of sea kale in Soviet territorial waters near Kaigara Island. Except for these very minor concessions, the U.S.S.R. has effectively asserted exclusive fishing jurisdiction within its 12 mile limit.

Soviet fisheries activity on the high seas has been accompanied by greater participation in international agreements which regulate the seasons, conditions and locales for nations to fish. Accession to the relevant multilateral agreements or the conclusion of bilateral arrangements has tended to correlate with the movement of the Soviet fishing fleet into the respective areas. But the 1958 Geneva Convention on Fishing and Conservation of the Living Resources of the High Seas continues to be unacceptable because of the compulsory procedure for the settlement of certain fishing disputes, reservations to this procedure being prohibited.

The U.S.S.R. joined the International Council for the Exploration of the Sea in 1955, is a party to the North-East Atlantic Fisheries Convention and an active member of the North-East Atlantic Fisheries Commission; a member of the International Commission for the Northwest Atlantic Fisheries; and a member of the smaller fishing commissions for the Western Pacific (with North Korea, North Vietnam and Mongolia), for the Black Sea (with Bulgaria and Rumania), and for the Baltic Sea (with the German Democratic Republic and Poland).

Bilateral fishing commissions have been created with Chile, Cuba, Ghana, the United Arab Republic, Japan and others. The Soviet–Japanese Northwest Pacific Fisheries Commission, created pursuant to a fisheries convention of May 14, 1956, takes decisions on catch quotas, fishing areas and inspection procedures, with regard to both pelagic fishing and crabbing.[18] The other commissions are essentially concerned with co-operation and mutual assistance in the development and expansion of fishing operations.

To support its widely dispersed fishing operations, the Soviet Government has concluded fishing assistance agreements with Cuba, Yemen, Senegal, Somalia, Bulgaria, Poland, the German Democratic Republic, Iran, Ghana, the United Arab Republic, Indonesia, Chile and others in return for servicing, loading, port and other privileges essential for the maintenance of a high seas fishing fleet.[19]

When Soviet fishing operations have brought the U.S.S.R. into conflict with States whose fishing interests are chiefly coastal, the normal pattern has been to strike a balance among its incontestable right to fish on the high seas, its desire to avoid precipitate unilateral action by the coastal State, and its desire to minimise conflict. Thus, the U.S.S.R. has firmly asserted its right to fish in such areas but has concluded bilateral agreements, particularly with the United States and Canada,[20] wherein the Soviet Union consents to reduce its catch and abstain from fishing certain areas or species in return for the right to conduct loading operations in contiguous fishing zones, to have access to ports under certain conditions, and to carry out joint fishing research.

Recent Soviet proposals in regard to fisheries attempt to accommodate the interests of developing countries and the need to conserve and rationally exploit coastal species.

The Soviet Union would acknowledge a preferential right for developing States to fish stocks in the areas adjacent to a 12 mile territorial sea or fishing zone which these States are capable of harvesting. The balance of the stock would be available to distant-water fleets, having due regard to conservation requirements.[21]

Soviet commercial fishing is carried on almost entirely by State agencies or enterprises and fishing collectives.[22] There is an extensive network of All-Union Republic legislation governing fisheries, violation of which can involve administrative or criminal penalties. Soviet citizens who violate the fishing laws of foreign States or international agreements to which the U.S.S.R. is a party are subject to disciplinary and possibly criminal sanctions at home, in addition to whatever liability they may incur at the place where the offence was committed.

EXPLOITATION OF SEABED RESOURCES

Depending on what criteria are employed to determine the seaward limit of the continental shelf, the Soviet shelf comprises from five to almost 10 per cent. of the world shelf area. The broadest shelf areas adjacent to Soviet coasts tend to be in the regions climatically most adverse; *e.g.*, the Arctic seas and the Bering Sea. Until comparatively recently, Soviet exploitation of the shelf has been confined to offshore oil production in the Caspian Sea, which has been severely polluted in consequence. For the past six years or so, the Soviet press has been full of reports about various forms of mineral wealth that geological surveys are said to have discovered in the shelf. Iron and manganese nodules have been located in the Baltic Sea; deposits of rutile and zircon in the Baltic and Black Seas and the Sea of Japan; iron ore in the Black Sea and Sea of Azov; and assorted precious metals in the Laptev, East Siberian and Chukotsk Seas. Some Soviet geologists are optimistic about large natural gas deposits in the Arctic shelf. Actual exploitation of this wealth, however, is evidently at any early, chiefly experimental stage. The emphasis is still on prospecting rather than production.

Exploitation of living organisms is another matter. The seas washing the far eastern coasts are unusually rich in flora and fauna of commercial value. Crabbing is a major activity (the U.S.S.R. considers the crab to be a creature of the shelf), and there is much experimentation in mariculture. On October 29, 1968, the U.S.S.R. Ministry of Fisheries approved a " List of Living Organisms which are Natural Resources of the Continental Shelf of the U.S.S.R." containing 52 species of marine life.[23]

According to the 1968 Edict on the Continental Shelf, foreign individuals and companies are prohibited from engaging in research, exploration and exploitation of natural resources or other work on the shelf unless authorisation has been granted expressly in an international agreement to which the U.S.S.R. is a party, or unless a special permit has been issued by competent authorities. There are no reports of such permits being issued. In a Declaration on the Continental Shelf of the Baltic Sea of October 23, 1968, the U.S.S.R., Poland and the German Democratic Republic agreed not to give over parcels of that shelf for exploration, exploitation or other use to non-Baltic States' citizens or firms.[24]

Soviet policy toward jurisdiction over and exploitation of the resources of the ocean floor beyond the continental shelf has developed cautiously. From the outset, Soviet diplomats have stressed in the UN Seabed Committee that the seabed and ocean floor are not a legal vacuum; existing principles of general international law extend to this region of the globe and any future activities or régime must conform thereto.

The most elaborate exposition of how the U.S.S.R. conceptualises these principles at this stage of seabed deliberations is the " Provisional Draft Articles of a Treaty on the Use of the Seabed for Peaceful Purposes," submitted on July 22, 1971, to the Seabed Committee.[25] Its provisions reflect Soviet attitudes consistently upheld from the earliest UN General Assembly debates of the issue and others forged during the exchange of views in the Assembly and Seabed Committee.

Demilitarisation of the seabed is strongly emphasised in Soviet seabed diplomacy. The U.S.S.R. played a leading role in initiating and drafting the Treaty on the Prohibition of the Emplacement of Nuclear Weapons and Other Weapons of Mass Destruction on the Seabed and the Ocean Floor and in the Subsoil Thereof, now in force. The provisional draft articles would go further by establishing that the seabed would be " open to use exclusively for peaceful purposes by all States . . ." and prohibited " for military purposes " (Articles 1 and 5). Precisely how this language, if accepted, would constrain naval activities of the U.S.S.R. and the United States has not been commented upon in Soviet legal media.

The limits of the seabed are left open in the provisional draft articles. Within the seabed area States would be proscribed from claiming or exercising sovereignty or sovereign rights over any part of the seabed or its subsoil, nor would States or juridical or natural persons be permitted to appropriate this area by any means. Within the seabed area, States are to act in conformity with the United Nations Charter, the Declaration on Principles of International Law concerning Friendly Relations and Co-operation among States, the Declaration on the Granting of Independence to Colonial Countries and Peoples, and other applicable principles of general international law. Among the latter are the principles of freedom of navigation, fishing, research and other activities on the high seas.

Commercial exploration and exploitation of seabed resources is to be carried out " for the benefit of mankind as a whole," irrespective of whether States are coastal or land-locked, in accordance with some sort of licensing scheme. Special consideration is to be accorded to the needs and interests of the developing countries.

To supervise the implementation of the proposed treaty, the provisional draft articles would establish an International Seabed Resources Agency comprised of a Conference of member States and an Executive Board. The inclusion of an international organisation in the draft is a modification of no small importance in original Soviet attitudes toward a seabed régime. The antipathy of the U.S.S.R. toward schemes to internationalise issues or dispute settlement is well known; one must hasten to add that in this case the compromise with past attitudes is very minimal, for the powers that would devolve on the contemplated Conference and Executive Board are not far-reaching.

The Conference would consist of representatives of all member States. Meeting biannually, unless an extraordinary session were convened, it would establish and consider reports of the Executive Board, approve the budget, consider general questions relating to the exploitation of the seabed resources, adopt resolutions on the recommendation of the Executive Board or the UN Security Council depriving member States of their rights and privileges, appoint the Executive Secretary of the Agency, draft general principles and recommendations to States concerning the prevention of pollution and contamination of the marine environment as a result of the exploration and exploitation of seabed resources, and certain other matters. Decisions in the Conference would be taken by a two-thirds majority on substantive questions and a simple majority on procedural, each State having one vote.

The proposed Executive Board would be dominated by the developing countries. It is to consist of 30 States, six (including one land-locked Power) to be elected for a four-year term from each of the following groups of countries: (a) socialist; (b) Asia; (c) Africa; (d) Latin America; (e) Western Europe and others not falling within the aforesaid categories. It would be the function, *inter alia*, of the Board to " supervise " implementation of the Treaty and seabed activities, to " co-ordinate " seabed exploration and exploitation by member States and " evaluate " reserves of proven resources on the basis of data submitted by States, to " consider " specific problems arising for the land-locked countries, to " promote " exchanges of relevant scientific and technical information, to " recommend " ways of preventing pollution of the marine environment and damage to living resources caused by seabed activities, to " assist " in settling disputes between States concerning implementation of the Treaty, to " supervise " compliance with certain Treaty provisions, and to exercise unspecified functions regarding the issuance of licences and the distribution of benefits. The Executive Board is to meet at least once annually. Substantive decisions shall be taken " by agreement "; procedural, by majority.

The draft provisional articles show considerable concern for the freedom of the seas. The legal status of the superjacent high seas or the air space above those waters is not to be affected, nor is the International Seabed Resources Agency permitted to look upon the seabed or subsoil thereof as " owned, possessed or used by it, or at its disposal." The freedom of research on the seabed is to remain unimpaired, activities conducted " in accordance with the generally recognised principles of international law " are not to be unjustifiably impeded by seabed exploration or exploitation, and rules for the protection of human life at sea are to be observed. Stationary and mobile installations are not to be placed where they may obstruct passage on sea lanes of vital importance for international shipping or at points of intense fishing activities. Appropriate safety zones established around such installations are to be in a configuration such that they do not together form a belt barring the access of shipping to particular maritime zones or cutting across international sea lanes.

Whether these draft provisional articles will bear any resemblance to the instruments that emerge from the forthcoming Law of the Sea Conference remains to be seen. The Soviet approach at this stage favours the adoption of standards to avoid unreasonable interference with other uses of the seas, to prevent pollution of the marine environment, and to share equitably the benefits derived from seabed exploitation. But the U.S.S.R. clearly is sceptical that large-scale seabed exploitation beyond the continental shelf will be a reality in the near future. Protection of investment is a lesser consideration in comparison with apprehension over international machinery becoming a " tool of monopolies " and operating independently in seabed exploitation. Compulsory procedures for the settlement of disputes continue to be objectionable as well.

MILITARY USES OF THE SEA

Considerable stress has been placed in Soviet legal literature, to some extent reflected in Soviet legislation, on abuses of the law of the sea by powerful maritime States. Pursuant to Rules enacted June 25, 1960, the Soviet Government permits foreign warships to traverse its territorial waters only if authorisation in each case has been sought at least 30 days prior to the contemplated visit.[26] Foreign submarines which enter Soviet territorial waters without authorisation and in a submerged position risk destruction.[27]

The creation of zones near foreign coasts or international sea lanes for use as naval or air ranges or the conducting of naval manoeuvres for extended periods of time has been severely condemned by Soviet jurists. Although this sentiment has been muted in recent years, the proximity of Western naval exercises to Soviet coasts continues to draw sharp protests. In a development symbolic of growing use of the high seas by Soviet naval vessels, the United States and the U.S.S.R. have concluded an agreement to reduce incidents arising out of mutual surveillance activities.[28]

POLLUTION CONTROL

Preventing pollution of the sea has been a theme of some prominence in Soviet international legal literature, though less so in treaty practice. Soviet jurists continue to castigate the United States for its earlier nuclear tests in contravention of international law and for poisoning marine life. A similar argument is put forward when aircraft accidents occur involving planes carrying nuclear weapons. The practice of disposing of radioactive wastes at sea in special containers also is criticised on the same ground.[29]

Anti-pollution measures applied to seas washing Soviet coasts are of recent origin. In October 1968 the U.S.S.R. Council of Ministers adopted a decree on measures for the prevention of pollution of the Caspian Sea, impelled in part by reports of very serious oil pollution.[30] Less than one year later the Soviet Government acceded to the 1954 London Convention for the Prevention of Pollution of the Sea by Oil, as amended in 1962, with a reservation objecting to compulsory jurisdiction of the International Court of Justice.[31] At about the same time, the Soviet Government agreed to participate in meetings with other Baltic powers with a view to devising means to reduce pollution in the Baltic Sea. The recent normalisation of relations with the German Democratic Republic has removed a major political obstacle to a regional arrangement, and an agreement is expected in early 1973.[32]

In September 1971, the U.S.S.R. Council of Ministers established a Northern Sea Route Administration attached to the U.S.S.R. Ministry of the Maritime Fleet "for the purpose of ensuring the safety of Arctic navigation, as well as of taking measures to prevent and eliminate the consequences of pollution of the marine environment and the northern coast of the U.S.S.R." The Administration is empowered to draft and implement anti-pollution requirements, including minimum technical standards for vessels intending to sail the Northern Sea Route, the suspension of navigation in areas where pollution may be a problem, and the imposition of penalties.[33]

LAW OF THE SEA CONFERENCE

The Soviet Union has long preferred that seabed issues ought to be dealt with in specialised technical bodies less susceptible to the vagaries of General Assembly politics. In April 1967 the U.S.S.R. proposed that the Intergovernmental Oceanographic Commission organise a special working group on legal aspects of ocean studies and utilisation of oceanic resources with a view to preparing draft conventions on the basic principles of conducting scientific research on the high seas and on international rules for the exploration and exploitation of the mineral resources of the high seas. An international conference was contemplated at a later stage to discuss and adopt the draft conventions.

In late 1967 Soviet diplomats reportedly were sounding out opinion in other capitals toward convening an international conference for the purpose of reaching agreement on a 12 mile territorial sea.[34]

When the Maltese proposal to place the issue of the seabed on the agenda of the UN General Assembly was raised, the Soviet representative stressed the avoidance of precipitate action and the need to identify and eventually to agree upon the most appropriate ways of studying matters. In subsequent seabed deliberations the same frame of mind has been evident. Soviet diplomats emphasise that the technology required for commercial seabed development is years away. Revision of the 1958 Geneva Conventions is strenuously opposed.[35] Most urgent, in the Soviet view, is agreement on the breadth of the territorial sea, passage through and flight over international straits, a rational allocation of fishery resources, and a more precise definition of the continental shelf.

Many Soviet jurists are frankly apprehensive over the extensive agenda that undoubtedly will confront the next Law of the Sea Conference. The years of preparing drafts in the International Law Commission prior to the 1958 and 1960 Geneva Conferences, they point out, has no analogue in the 1970s, though many of the questions proposed for consideration are more far-reaching.

On the other hand, the prospect of no agreement is similarly daunting. The Soviet legal adviser commented in early 1973: " History teaches that in attempts to resolve international questions not on the basis of law, but by ignoring it, unilateral actions lead to chaos, open the way for similar actions on the part of other States, and all this complicates relations between States and damages international co-operation."[36]

REFERENCES

1. See W. E. Butler, *The Soviet Union and the Law of the Sea* (1971).

2. Art. 3 (1960) no. 34, *Vedomosti verkhovnogo soveta SSSR*, item 324; (1971), no. 24, *ibid.*, item 254 (hereinafter cited as *Vedomosti SSSR*).

3. See the Soviet–Finnish Peace Treaty, signed on Mar. 12, 1940, and the Soviet–Finnish Agreement of May 20, 1965.

4. See Butler, " New Soviet Legislation on Straight Base Lines " (1971) 20 I.C.L.Q. 750–752.

5. Art. 1 (1968), no. 6, *Vedomosti SSSR*, item 40. English texts in (1968) 7 Int.Leg.Mat. 392; (1970) 6 *Soviet Statutes and Decisions* 258 (hereafter cited as SS&D).

6. 3 V. M. Chkhikvadze *et al.* (eds.), *Kurs mezhdunarodnogo prava v shesti tomakh*, p. 208 (1967); also see I. I. Cheprov, " Mezhdunarodnopravovoi rezhim morskogo dna " (1968), no. 10, *Sovetskoe gosudarstvo i pravo* 81.

7. A Soviet representative noted in the UN Seabed Committee that scientists in the U.S.S.R. refer to the so-called continental rise as the " sloping oceanic plain." See UN Doc. A/AC.135/WG.2/SR.11, July 3, 1968.

8. See S. N. Smirnov, in M. I. Lazarev and L. V. Speranskaia (eds.), *Okean, tekhnika, pravo*, p. 97 (1972); V. F. Tsarev, " Mezhdunarodnopravovye voprosy kontinental'nogo shel'fa," in M. I. Lazarev *et al.* (eds.), *Aktual'nye problemy sovremennogo mezhdunarodnogo morskogo prava*, p. 51 (1972).

9. See B. N. Nechaev, in Lazarev and Speranskaia, *Okean, tekhnika, pravo*, p. 46.

10. *Ibid.* at p. 51.

11. See Butler, *The Soviet Union and the Law of the Sea*, pp. 66–70; R. Petrow, *Across the Top of Russia* (1967); D. Pharand, " Soviet Union Warns United States Against Use of Northeast Passage " (1968) 72 A.J.I.L. 927–935.

12. On the closed sea, see Butler, *The Soviet Union and the Law of the Sea*, pp. 116–133; K. Grzybowski, " The Soviet Doctrine of Mare Clausum and Politics in Black and Baltic Seas " (1955) 14 *Journal of Central European Affairs* 339–353.

13. See P. D. Barabolia, in Lazarev and Speranskaia, *Okean, tekhnika, pravo*, pp. 19–21.

14. The Soviet Government pointed out the illegality of a territorial sea exceeding 12 nautical miles in a Statement dated Jan. 25, 1967, to Argentina. See L. V. Speranskaia, in *ibid.* at pp. 56–57.

15. (1967) no. 3, *Rybnoe khoziaistvo* 1; English translation in (1969) 6 SS&D 45–49.

16. See A. A. Volkov, *Morskoe pravo*, p. 102 (1969); also see A. L. Kolodkin, " Territorial Waters and International Law " (1969) 8 *International Affairs* 81; A. N. Nikolaev, *Territorial'noe more* (1969). V. A. Serkov describes the 12 mile limit as " optimal." See Serkov, " Pravovoi rezhim spetsial'nykh morskikh zon," in Lazarev *et al.* (eds.), *Aktual'nye problemy sovremennogo mezhdunarodnogo morskogo prava*, p. 34.

17. An English text of the Soviet–Chilean fisheries agreement of Sept. 7, 1971, appears in (1972) 11 Int.Leg.Mat. 1. For the text of the Soviet–Chilean contract regarding the use of Soviet fishing vessels, see (1972) 11, *ibid.* at 947, and a summary of debate in the Chilean Senate at p. 1156.

18. A Russian text of the 1970 Soviet–Japanese crabbing arrangement appears in (1971) 15 *Japanese Annual of International Law* 380.

19. Citations to and further information regarding these agreements are given in Butler, *The Soviet Union and the Law of the Sea*, pp. 189–194.

20. On Jan. 22, 1971, Canada and the Soviet Union concluded an Agreement on Co-operation in Fisheries in the Northeastern Pacific Ocean Off the Coast of Canada and an Agreement on Provisional Rules of Navigation and Fisheries Safety in the Northeastern Pacific Ocean Off the Coast of Canada. The latter Agreement will be extended automatically for a further two years on Apr. 22, 1973, but the former is subject to review before its date of expiry on Feb. 18, 1973.

21. See the draft articles on fishing submitted on July 21, 1972, by the U.S.S.R. to Sub-Committee II of the UN Seabed Committee. UN Doc. A/AC.138/SC.II/L.6. Similar views are set forth in a Declaration on Principles of Rational Exploitation of the Living Resources of the Seas and Oceans in the Common Interests of All Peoples, adopted at a Conference of Ministers of Eastern European States in Moscow on July 6–7, 1972, and circulated to the Seabed Committee as Doc. A/AC.138/85. Also see O. Khlestov, " Mezhdunarodno-pravovye problemy mirovogo okeana," *Mezhdunarodnaia zhizn'*, no. 2 (1973), p. 56.

22. Useful data on the organisation of the Soviet fisheries industry is to be found in Volkov, *Maritime Law*, translated by E. D. Gordon (1971).

23. (1969) no. 2, *Rybnoe khoziaistvo* 4–5; English text in (1970) 6 SS&D 282.

24. *Izvestia*, Oct. 24, 1968, p. 3; English text in (1970) 6 SS&D 261.

25. Text in (1971) 10 Int.Leg.Mat. 994.

26. English text in (1969) 6 SS&D 65.

27. *Pravda*, Aug. 29, 1961; English text in (1969) 6 SS&D 74.

28. English text in (1972) 11 Int.Leg.Mat. 778.

29. Ia. A. Ostrovskii, in Lazarev and Speranskaia (eds.), *Okean, teknika, pravo*, pp. 171–193.

30. Translated in (1969/70) 6 SS&D 197.

31. Effective for the U.S.S.R. on Dec. 3, 1969. See *Vodnyi transport*, Sept. 23, 1969, p. 3.

32. See (1972) 3 *World Ecology 2000*, no. 25, p. 4.

33. See Butler, " Pollution Control and the Soviet Arctic " (1972) 21 I.C.L.Q. 557–560.

34. (1968) 10 *Ocean Science News* no. 30, p. 1.

35. The Soviet legal adviser, O. Khlestov, said to the Seabed Committee in Nov. 1970: " It was sometimes alleged that in a changing world, with the emergence of new States and the rapid advance in science and technology, the rules of the law of the sea contained in the Geneva Conventions of 1958 were obsolete and needed revision. In fact, the existing rules of the law of the sea had not come into being overnight, but had been shaped over centuries of co-operation between States. The Geneva Conventions of 1958 merely contained, in treaty form, a number of generally recognised principles of the law of the sea which had proved their value in practice." UN Doc. A/AC.138/SR.56, p. 149.

36. Khlestov, " Mezhdunarodno-pravovye problemy mirovogo okeana," p. 53.

CHAPTER 25

United Kingdom

By R. R. Churchill *

INTRODUCTION

ITS geographical position as an island lying off the continent of Europe has given the United Kingdom a heightened awareness of the importance of the sea, both as a means of communication with the outside world and, until the invention of the aircraft, as a natural defensive barrier against its enemies. From the time of Elizabeth I, in the latter half of the sixteenth century, until the early twentieth century, the United Kingdom has, with one or two exceptions,[1]† been one of the foremost champions of the doctrine of the " Freedom of the Seas." The United Kingdom was interested in the fewest restrictions possible being placed on the use of the seas, because this suited best its military and trade interests, its colonial exploitation of Africa, Asia and the Far East and its fishing industry. In the twentieth century there have been a number of changes in the United Kingdom's interests in the use of the sea, and consequently a reassessment, if sometimes an unconscious one, of the traditional doctrine of the freedom of the seas. The United Kingdom has lost its Empire, but it is still a major trading nation with a large merchant fleet. In spite of the invention of aircraft, the Navy is an important element in the defensive capabilities of the United Kingdom, and all the United Kingdom's nuclear weapons are carried by polaris submarines. Unhampered navigation thus remains an important consideration. But elsewhere old interests have changed and new interests have emerged which have led to a questioning of former ideas about the unregulated use of the high seas. In fisheries, the emphasis has changed somewhat from distant water fishing to near and middle water fishing. Valuable mineral deposits have been found in the extensive shallow continental shelf surrounding the United Kingdom. As a highly developed, industrialised country, the United Kingdom has been made aware of the dangers and far-reaching extent of the pollution of the seas, and the consequent need for greater control over the entry of pollutants into the sea, whether they come from the land or from ships.

The object of this paper is to give an account of the various zones of exclusive jurisdiction claimed by the United Kingdom and the marine activities carried on within these zones and on the high seas, to try and point up the interests which lie behind United Kingdom policy in this field, and to see how far British legislation has been influenced by, and is in accordance with, international law. It is hoped that this will provide some insight into the position which the United Kingdom is taking and may be expected to take in the current reshaping of the international law of the sea. For this reason, emphasis will be placed on recent developments, and some aspects of United Kingdom law and practice will be highly compressed.

* LL.M. (Lond.), Research Officer in International Law, British Institute of International and Comparative Law.

† For references, see p. 296.

TERRITORIAL SEA

The United Kingdom has always been one of the strongest advocates of a three mile territorial sea, its own claim being first formally made in 1878.[2] Nevertheless it seems that the United Kingdom would be prepared to abandon this principle in favour of a wider limit, if this was capable of receiving general acceptance. Thus at both the 1958 and 1960 Geneva Conferences on the Law of the Sea, the United Kingdom supported compromise proposals which would have fixed the breadth of the territorial sea at more than three miles. However failure to agree on the breadth of the territorial sea led the United Kingdom delegate to make a statement emphasising that the United Kingdom would continue to regard the three mile limit as the only breadth recognised under international law.[3]

This is almost certainly still the official position of the United Kingdom and it is most unlikely that the United Kingdom will unilaterally extend its territorial sea in the near future. However, reference must be made to one or two recent events which may indicate a greater flexibility in United Kingdom attitudes. A series of collisions in the English Channel in the winter of 1970–1971 showed up the risk of serious pollution resulting from collisions in this narrow waterway, so long as the regulation of shipping there is only on a non-binding basis. It also showed that the principle of freedom of navigation—which lies behind the United Kingdom's desire for a narrow territorial sea—does have disadvantages for the United Kingdom. This series of collisions coincided with the passage of the Oil in Navigable Waters Act through Parliament. During debates on the Act, a number of Members of Parliament called for the extension of the United Kingdom territorial sea to 12 miles. Similar action by France would have meant that parts of the Straits of Dover would have ceased to be high seas. The Government rejected these demands and stressed that any solution to these problems must be based on international agreement. No doubt it feared that unilateral action in the Channel could lead to retaliation in other international waterways. However the opposition Labour Party has proposed that the United Kingdom should extend its territorial sea to the median line in the Channel in order to control shipping.[4] At the time these demands for an extension of the United Kingdom territorial sea to 12 miles were made, France claimed a three mile territorial sea, so that the question of the Straits of Dover ceasing to be high seas was entirely theoretical. However, in December 1971 France did extend her territorial sea to 12 miles.[5] So far as is known, there has been no adverse comment on this action from the British Government. There has been an even more positive acquiescence in the Canadian action extending its territorial sea to 12 miles in 1970. In an agreement phasing out the rights of British vessels to fish in the Canadian territorial sea and exclusive fishing zones, the United Kingdom has explicitly accepted the Canadian 12 mile territorial sea and the base line from which it is measured.[6] There has been little direct reaction by the United Kingdom to the claims of the Latin American States, probably because there is virtually no fishing by United Kingdom vessels in the South Atlantic or South Pacific.

As far as concerns the way in which the breadth of the territorial sea is measured, the United Kingdom's position before the 1958 Geneva Conference was that the base line from which the outer limit of the territorial sea is measured was the low-water mark on permanently dry land and, in the case of bays, a line drawn across the mouth not exceeding 10 miles in length. In particular, it was strongly opposed to the use of straight base lines. So confident was it that straight base lines were contrary to international law, that it submitted its dispute with Norway over this question to the International Court of Justice. To the United Kingdom's great surprise, the Court found in Norway's favour.[7] At the Geneva Conference, the United Kingdom's views received a further setback. An article (Article 4 of the Convention on the Territorial Sea and the Contiguous Zone) was adopted, permitting the use of straight base lines in certain circumstances. The United Kingdom tried to secure a maximum limit on the length of such base lines, but this proposal was not accepted. The use of low-tide elevations as base lines in certain circumstances was agreed by the Conference[8] as was a 24 mile closing line for bays.[9] In spite of certain initial dissatisfaction with these provisions,[10] the United Kingdom was the first State to ratify the Convention on the Territorial Sea and the Contiguous Zone,[11] and with the coming into force of the Convention in 1964, it adopted these provisions into its national law. In particular, Article 3 of the Territorial Waters Order in Council[12] provides for the creation of a series of straight base lines between Cape Wrath and the Mull of Kintyre off the West Coast of Scotland. This has the important effect of enclosing as internal waters all the sea between the Outer Hebrides and the mainland of Scotland, a very rich fishing ground. This action has undoubtedly given a boost to inshore fishing in the area. Although the Convention on the Territorial Sea and the Contiguous Zone has now more or less settled the problems relating to the way in which the territorial sea is delimited, there is one outstanding question which the United Kingdom has expressed its views on, namely, the way the territorial seas of archipelagoes are delimited. Specifically, the United Kingdom has objected to the way in which Indonesia has defined the base lines of its territorial sea as being the straight lines joining the outermost islands of the archipelago.[13]

Article 24 of the Convention on the Territorial Sea and Contiguous Zone permits States parties to the convention to claim a contiguous zone beyond their territorial sea. The United Kingdom has never availed itself of this possibility. At the time of the stranding of the *Torrey Canyon* (which lay outside the United Kingdom's territorial sea but within 12 miles of its base line), there was some discussion as to whether the United Kingdom ought to have claimed a contiguous zone in accordance with the convention, and if it had done so, whether the convention would have given it the necessary authority to take the measures that were taken to deal with the oil pollution from the ship, which included bombing it.[14] Since then, there has been no serious discussion about the United Kingdom's claiming a contiguous zone. Those who advocate an extension of the United Kingdom's jurisdiction, for example, in the English Channel, are pressing for an extension of the territorial sea and not a claim to a contiguous zone.

FISHERIES

(a) Exclusive fishing zone

Before the two Geneva Conferences on the Law of the Sea, the United Kingdom did not accept that coastal States could claim an exclusive fishing zone beyond the territorial sea. At Geneva the United Kingdom did vote in favour of such zones, but only as a compromise designed to obtain general agreement on the breadth of the territorial sea. With the failure to reach agreement on this compromise, the United Kingdom reverted to its former position. The situation did not remain stable for long. In the North-East Atlantic, in some of the United Kingdom's most productive distant water fishing grounds, there was a series of claims to a 12 mile exclusive fishing limit coming from Iceland (1958), Norway (1961) and the Faeroes (1963). The United Kingdom at first objected to all these claims, but was eventually compelled to accept them.[15] At the same time the United Kingdom's middle water and inshore fishing fleets came under increasing competition because of extensive fishing by foreign vessels in waters close to the United Kingdom and immediately beyond the outer limit of its territorial sea. The United Kingdom was thus getting the worst of both worlds.[16] It therefore took the initiative and called a European Fisheries Conference to try and work out a regional solution for this problem. The Conference met in London between December 1963 and March 1964 and produced the Fisheries Convention.[17]

The convention provides that States parties may claim a 12 mile exclusive fishing zone. The vessels of other States parties may continue indefinitely to fish in the outer six miles for species which they have traditionally caught there. The United Kingdom lost little time in implementing the convention and in September 1964 made its claim to a 12 mile exclusive fishing zone.[18] At the same time, as we have already seen,[19] part of the base line from which the territorial sea and fishing zone are measured was redrawn. As a result, a large area was added to that where British fishermen already had exclusive rights, and there is no doubt that this action has given a considerable boost to inshore fishing.[20] At the same time, fishermen of a number of other convention countries were given the right to fish indefinitely in the outer six miles for certain species, following a brief transitional period during which they were also allowed to fish in the three to six mile zone. The countries in question, Belgium, France, Ireland and Netherlands, are designated by Order under section 1 of the Fishery Limits Act. These Orders[21] also specify the areas in which vessels may fish and the species which may be taken. The Federal Republic of Germany, which is not a party to the convention, but which did sign the Protocol of Provisional Application of the Fisheries Convention,[22] is similarly designated by Order.[23] A number of other States which are not parties to the Fisheries Convention have been given certain rights in the outer six miles by virtue of special bilateral agreements. Norwegian fishermen can fish for dog fish and basking sharks around the North-West Scottish coast until the end of 1984.[24] Soviet fishing vessels and depot ships are not permitted to fish, but may perform other activities ancillary to fishing, such as trans-shipment, around the Shetlands.[25] Polish ships have similar rights.[26] Following the expiry of transitional rights for British fishermen in Icelandic and Norwegian waters, the only foreign fishing zone in which British fishermen now have any fishing rights under the Fisheries Convention, is that of France.[27]

The welcome stability which was provided by the Fisheries Convention is now being disturbed by three factors: first by claims to an exclusive fishing zone beyond 12 miles, secondly by the adoption of a common fisheries policy by the European Communities, and thirdly by the forthcoming UN Conference on the Law of the Sea.

There have recently been two claims to an exclusive fishing zone beyond 12 miles which affect the areas fished in by United Kingdom fishermen. The first is by Canada, the second by Iceland. In 1970 Canada extended its territorial sea to 12 miles and at the same time claimed the power to make Orders creating exclusive fishing zones beyond the territorial sea.[28] The first such Orders were duly made in early 1971,[29] enclosing vast tracts of High Seas on both Canada's Atlantic and Pacific coasts within the exclusive fishing zone. Whatever initial doubts the United Kingdom Government might have had about the propriety of this claim, it has now firmly accepted it, since an exchange of notes has been concluded phasing out the rights of British fishermen in the exclusive fishing zone on Canada's Atlantic coast.[30] The case of Iceland is very much less straightforward, probably because there is more at stake here.[31] On September 1, 1972, Iceland extended its fishing limits to 50 miles. Its intention to do so was communicated to the British Government many months beforehand. The British Government objected to the proposed Icelandic course of action and the two sides entered into negotiations to try and avoid a dispute. The negotiations seems to have been particularly fruitless, and at the time of writing (March 1973) the two sides are as far from reaching agreement as ever. The British Government would be prepared to restrict the amount of fish taken by British fishermen, though not to the extent demanded by Iceland. Iceland would also want all British fishing in the 50 mile limit to be gradually phased out, and the 50 mile limit recognised. The British Government cannot accept either of these demands. Its position was clearly stated by Lady Tweedsmuir, Minister of State at the Foreign Office, in a debate in the House of Lords on March 2, 1972.

> " We have stated very clearly and on several occasions that we cannot accept any extension of Iceland's fishing limits beyond 12 miles as being compatible with international law . . . It is true that a few States have claimed fisheries jurisdiction beyond 12 miles in recent years, but we have consistently maintained that all such claims are contrary to international law. We recognise, of course, that the question of any special position a coastal State may have, or ought to have, as regards fisheries in adjacent areas of the high seas is one which requires further international consideration." [32]

Although negotiations between the two sides are still continuing, the dispute has to some extent been taken out of the hands of the parties by the decision of the British Government on April 14, 1972, to refer the case to the International Court of Justice in accordance with the penultimate paragraph of the 1961 Exchange of Notes. This reads:

> " The Icelandic Government will continue to work for the implementation of the Alting Resolution of May 5, 1959, regarding the extension of fisheries jurisdiction around Iceland, but shall give to the United Kingdom Government six months' notice of such extension and in case of a dispute in relation to such extension, the matter shall, at the request of either party, be referred to the International Court of Justice."

In a judgment of February 2, 1973, the Court, by 14 votes to one, held that this paragraph did give it jurisdiction to hear the merits of the dispute and it dismissed what it assumed were Iceland's objections to its jurisdiction.[33] Earlier the Court had held that it had enough prima facie jurisdiction to grant the United Kingdom's request for interim measures of protection. In an order of August 17, 1972, the Court, again by 14 votes to one, indicated the following provisional measures: the parties must take no action to aggravate the dispute or to prejudice the rights of the other party; Iceland should take no action to enforce its claim to a 50 mile exclusive fishing zone; the United Kingdom should take no more than 170,000 tons of fish per annum, the average for the last five years.[34]

The second factor threatening the stability of the régime for fishing limits laid down by the Fisheries Convention is the common fisheries policy adopted by the European Communities in the latter part of 1970. The policy is divided into two parts—structural and marketing. The structural part of the policy is concerned directly with the question of limits. Article 2 of EEC Council Regulation 2141/70 of October 20, 1970,[35] provides for the access of a fishing vessel registered in one Community member State to the " maritime waters coming under [the] sovereignty or within [the] jurisdiction " of any other Community member State. At the time this policy was adopted, the United Kingdom was beginning its negotiations for membership of the European Communities, together with Denmark, Ireland and Norway. The provisions on common access were not acceptable to any of the candidate countries, and a protracted series of negotiations took place to try and modify the policy. In these negotiations the United Kingdom Government tended to suffer from schizophrenia. On the one hand a powerful inshore fishing lobby was pressing for nothing less than a 12 mile limit, in other words, a maintenance of the *status quo*, while an equally vociferous distant water fishing lobby wanted fishing zones opened up so that its members could go trawling in the rich Norwegian fishing grounds. The resulting compromise seems to have been as much a compromise between these two interests as between the United Kingdom and its negotiating partners. What has been agreed is that for a period of 10 years, a derogation from Article 2 of Regulation 2141/70 will be allowed and member States will be authorised to claim a six mile exclusive fishing zone, which in certain places will be extended to 12 miles. These are areas where the local population is primarily dependent on fishing for its livelihood. Before the end of the 10 year transitional period, the Council will decide, on the basis of a report from the Commission, what arrangements are to follow the transitional period.[36] According to Mr. Rippon, Britain's chief Common Market negotiator, the effect of these provisions is that there is no change at all in the protection offered to areas from which about 95 per cent. by value of the total inshore catch is now taken.[37]

The third factor affecting the stability of the present régime of fishing limits is the forthcoming UN Conference on the Law of the Sea. This is discussed in further detail below.

It is perhaps appropriate to point out here that although the United Kingdom claims an exclusive fishing zone, it has never claimed an exclusive fishery conservation zone.

(b) Size, structure and regulation of the United Kingdom fishing industry

Like most primary industries in the developed countries, the United Kingdom fishing industry provides a very small contribution to the country's Gross National Product.[38] In spite of this, the industry is important, both as a means of providing employment, particularly in some of the poorer areas of the United Kingdom where possibilities of alternative employment are slight, and as an important source of animal protein for the population of the United Kingdom.[39]

The size of catch taken by United Kingdom fishermen has remained fairly constant for most of the present century. In 1971, 965,000 tons of fish were caught, worth £92 million, thus putting the United Kingdom about 13th in the list of the world's leading fishing nations.[40] The most important species caught are, by weight, cod (32 per cent. of the total catch), haddock (18 per cent.) and herring (15 per cent.), and, by value, cod (44 per cent.), haddock (19 per cent.), shellfish and plaice (8 per cent. each), and herring (6 per cent.).[41] The most notable feature here is the decline in the importance of the herring in recent years. The most important fishing grounds are the North Sea (39 per cent. of the total catch by weight), Iceland and the West of Scotland (18 per cent. each).[42] The distant water fleet accounts for 27 per cent. of the catch by weight, and 32 per cent. by value.[43] There has been a decline in recent years in the proportion taken by the distant water fleet: this is due partly to the extension of fishing limits by countries such as Iceland, Norway and the Faeroes, and partly by the recovery of the middle and near water fleets, which is due in no small measure to the extension by the United Kingdom of its own fishing limits.

Of the fish caught by United Kingdom fishermen, the vast majority goes to human consumption as either fresh or frozen fish. In spite of its large catches, the United Kingdom imports considerable quantities of fish. In 1971, 173,000 tons were imported, worth £82 million, nearly half of which came from the EFTA countries. Only about a quarter of these imports were fresh fish. In addition, a further £50 million worth of fish and marine mammal products (oil, meals and flour etc.) were imported.[44] In this connection it is interesting to note that the Cameron Committee recommended that industrial fishing by the United Kingdom should be considerably increased, so enabling it to become largely self-sufficient in fish meal and fish oil.[45] The United Kingdom is also a modest exporter of fish: 119,000 tons, worth £26 million, in 1971. Of this total, about two-thirds was in the form of fresh fish, and about two-thirds going to the EEC and EFTA countries.[46]

About 18,000 people are employed in the United Kingdom fishing industry, with a further 4,000 part-time workers.[47] This is a decline of about 50 per cent. on the total employed in 1948. Of course, many more people are employed in allied industries such as fish-processing and ship-building. Although these figures are a minute fraction of the total United Kingdom labour force, fishing is an important source of employment in parts of the United Kingdom, notably north-east and north-west Scotland. Fishing is carried out in 6,071 vessels, of which 164 are over 140 feet (including 37 freezer trawlers), 326 between 80 and 140 feet, and no less than 3,785 under 40 feet.[48] Trawling is the most important method of fishing and accounts for about 70 per cent. of the total wet fish catch.

In spite of increasing rationalisation, large parts of the fishing industry continue to operate at a loss or at a marginal profit. To assist it, the State provides a subsidy on fishing operations and a system of grants and loans for modernising fishing vessels. This assistance is administered by the White Fish Authority and Herring Industry Board. These two bodies also have a number of other general supervisory functions in relation to the fishing industry.[49] The recent entry of the United Kingdom into the European Communities, with the consequent application of the Communities' common fisheries policy, is bound to have considerable impact on the United Kingdom fishing industry. It will mean the end of subsidies. The Communities' system of guidance and withdrawal prices will replace the present United Kingdom's price-fixing system which is based on auctions, and, in some cases, on the seasonal fixing of minimum prices. The Communities' marketing policy is also designed to be operated through producer organisations: these scarcely exist in the United Kingdom at present.

(c) Conservation

The United Kingdom is a member of both the North-East Atlantic Fisheries Commission and the International Commission for the Northwest Atlantic Fisheries, and has accepted all the recommendations of these two bodies. Between them, the two Commissions cover virtually all the areas fished by United Kingdom vessels. The legislative framework for fisheries conservation in the United Kingdom is two-fold. First, under the Sea Fish (Conservation) Act 1967 (which consolidates earlier legislation), orders can be made prescribing minimum sizes for fish (ss. 1 and 2); regulating the type and size of nets and other fishing gear (s. 3); prescribing closed areas and closed seasons (s. 5); and prohibiting the landing of fish caught in certain areas (s. 6). Exceptions can be made for the purpose of scientific investigation (s. 9). These orders may be applied to United Kingdom vessels anywhere and to all ships within United Kingdom fishing limits. A large number of orders have been made under this Act, most of which implement Recommendations of the North-East Atlantic Fisheries Commission and the International Commission for the Northwest Atlantic Fisheries. Those that do not are concerned mainly with salmon and trout fishing and with minimum sizes for shellfish. Two recent orders are particularly interesting. The Beam

Trawl Regulations Order 1972[50] and the Sea Fishing (North Norfolk Coast) (Prohibition of Trawling) Order 1972[51] are concerned to protect inshore fishermen from increased competition resulting from the greater opening up of the United Kingdom's exclusive fishing zone to EEC vessels, and to avoid conflict between different methods of fishing.[52]

Ultimately the only way of conserving the living resources of the sea, together with their more rational economic exploitation, may be to restrict access to high seas fishing grounds by a system of licensing and national quotas. Legislation already exists on the United Kingdom statute book for doing just that. Under section 4 of the Sea Fish (Conservation) Act 1967, orders may be made providing that vessels may only fish in certain areas under licence " for the purpose of preventing overfishing." Conditions may be attached to the licence, and these presumably would include the imposition of quotas, although they are not specifically mentioned. In the case of fishing on the high seas, orders may only be made under this section if " measures substantially equivalent . . . are being taken by the governments of other countries interested in fishing in that area." So far this power has been used four times. The Sea Fishing (Specified Northern Waters) Licensing Order 1972[53] implements the Order of the International Court of Justice of August 17, 1972, laying down an interim quota to be taken by United Kingdom vessels in the waters around Iceland. Orders have been made implementing the North-East Atlantic Fisheries Commission's Recommendations on closed seasons in the North Sea for herring, together with a small excepted quota, in 1971 and 1972.[54] Interestingly enough, none of these Orders mention quotas, although concerned with them: presumably the Minister allocates quotas when issuing licences under the Order. The other two occasions on which this power has been used have been to license salmon fishing[55] and to implement quotas laid down by the International Commission for the Northwest Atlantic Fisheries.[56] Another piece of legislation also provides for a system of licensing. Under section 9 of the Sea Fish Industry Act 1970, all vessels over 40 feet engaged in sea fishing require a licence from the White Fish Authority. At present this seems to be largely a formality (at least as concerns the restriction of access to fishing grounds), but it need not be so. The White Fish Authority can grant a licence subject " to such conditions as the Authority think fit to impose—(i) for preventing overfishing." It is also interesting to note that a recent government report recommended that the public right of sea fishing should be limited to rod and line fishing, with licences, which could be limited in number, for other methods of sea fishing.[57]

The Sea Fish (Conservation) Act 1967 is one part of the United Kingdom legislative framework for fisheries conservation. The other is the Sea Fisheries Regulation Act 1966 (consolidating earlier legislation). Under sections 5 and 7 of this Act, Sea Fisheries Committees in England and Wales (and in Scotland, the Department of Agriculture and Fisheries for Scotland) can make by-laws to regulate and conserve fishing in the territorial sea or internal waters. Such by-laws require the confirmation of the relevant Minister.[58]

As far as enforcement of conservation measures is concerned, the United Kingdom has accepted both the North-East Atlantic Fisheries Commission and the International Commission for the Northwest Atlantic Fisheries Schemes of Joint Enforcement. In the case of the enforcement of conservation measures lying outside these two Schemes, British sea fishing officers can enforce conservation regulations against United Kingdom registered or British owned boats anywhere, and against foreign boats in the United Kingdom's exclusive fishing zone.[59] Sea Fisheries Committees can appoint fishery officers to enforce their by-laws. Such officers may also examine the nets of United Kingdom boats in the territorial sea or internal waters of the United Kingdom.[60] The United Kingdom has ratified the Convention on Conduct of Fishing Operations in the North Atlantic 1967,[61] although the Convention has not yet come into force.

CONTINENTAL SHELF

(a) Area and jurisdiction claimed

The United Kingdom was one of the first States to recognise claims to explore and exploit the seabed beyond the territorial sea. Initially this was done only in the case of overseas territories for whose foreign relations the United Kingdom was responsible. Thus as early as 1942, the United Kingdom concluded an agreement with Venezuela, on behalf of Trinidad and Tobago, which delimited the seabed in the Gulf of Paria.[62] Seven years later, claims to the seabed beyond the territorial sea were made on behalf of the Persian Gulf territories for whose foreign relations the United Kingdom was responsible.[63] Not until 1964 did the United Kingdom formally claim rights over the seabed surrounding its own shores. This was the year in which exploration for oil and gas in the North Sea began in earnest, and the same year in which the United Kingdom ratified the Convention on the Continental Shelf 1958.

The United Kingdom adheres strictly to the dualist theory of international law. This means that the provisions of the convention have to be transformed by Act of Parliament in order to become part of British municipal law. In the light of this situation, the Continental Shelf Act 1964, together with certain subsequent legislation and subsidiary legislation, is an interesting and, at times, curiously worded statute. Perhaps the most bizarre part of the Act is that which deals with the definition and extent of the area claimed by the United Kingdom. Section 1 (7) provides that " Her Majesty may from time to time by Order in Council designate any area as an area within which the rights mentioned in subsection (1) of this section are exercisable, and any area so designated is in this Act referred to as a designated area." Section 1 (1) reads: " Any rights exercisable by the United Kingdom outside territorial waters with respect to the seabed and subsoil and their natural resources, except in so far as they are exercisable in relation to coal, are hereby vested in Her Majesty." In other words, the United Kingdom is claiming to exercise certain rights in certain " designated areas " beyond the territorial sea. There is no mention of the kind of rights which are being claimed, and no mention of either of the criteria referred to in Article 1 of the convention for determining the outer limit of the continental shelf. As of March 1973, four Orders had been made under section 1 (7).[64] The area claimed relates to the continental shelf around the whole of the United Kingdom. Although virtually none of the area claimed lies beyond the 200 metre isobath, much of the area lies at a considerable distance from the coast, the farthest point being some 160 miles from land.[65] Nor should it be overlooked that at the beginning of 1972 the island of Rockall was formally incorporated into the United Kingdom.[66] The main reason for this was because the United Kingdom hopes at some time in the future to be able to exploit what are believed to be considerable quantities of oil and gas lying under the seabed around Rockall.

In practical terms, the problem of the outer limit of the United Kingdom continental shelf has largely been solved because of the presence of the continental shelves of other States. In the North Sea the boundary between the United Kingdom's continental shelf and the continental shelves of the other littoral States has been determined by a series of bilateral agreements.[67] With the exception of the agreement with the

Federal Republic of Germany, all these agreements are based on the principle of delimitation in accordance with the equidistance principle. In the case of the United Kingdom continental shelf in the English Channel and Irish Sea, the United Kingdom has not claimed any area lying beyond the median line between the United Kingdom and France, and the United Kingdom and Ireland respectively. In the case of the North Sea, it is fortunate that the seabed was divided up at a very early stage in the process of oil and gas exploration, because many of the most promising subsequent finds lie very close to the boundary line. A serious conflict situation has therefore been avoided. In this context it is interesting to note that in each of the agreements with the other North Sea littoral States, there is a provision for joint consultation over the exploitation of geological structures straddling the boundary line. This provision has not yet been invoked, but it is possible that it may be in the not-too-distant future. Already talks have begun between United Kingdom and Norwegian officials over the question of bringing oil from the Norwegian sector of the North Sea continental shelf ashore in the United Kingdom.[67a]

As has already been mentioned, the Continental Shelf Act 1964 is very vague about the kind of rights the United Kingdom has in its designated areas. In contrast, Article 2 of the Convention is fairly precise in talking about sovereign rights for the purpose of exploring and exploiting the natural resources of the continental shelf. When it comes to the question of jurisdiction, the Act again differs from the Convention. Where the Convention speaks of States having " jurisdiction " over installations on the continental shelf[68] and having the power to take in a 500 metre safety zone around such installations " measures necessary for their protection,"[69] the Act extends in blanket fashion all criminal and civil legislation of the United Kingdom to such installations and to a 500 metre zone around them.[70] Article 5 (iii) of the Convention states that ships shall " respect " 500 metre safety zones. Section 2 of the Act, on the other hand, provides that Orders may be made prohibiting ships from entering such zones and that failure to observe such orders is a criminal offence.[71] Section 8 (4) of the Mineral Workings (Offshore Installations) Act 1971 goes quite beyond the convention by providing that Orders may be made, making it possible for foreign aircraft to be prohibited from flying over or " in the neighbourhood " of seabed installations. Finally, there are two matters which the Convention deals with, but on which the Act is silent, sedentary species and the legal status of the waters lying over the continental shelf.[72]

(b) Activities on the United Kingdom continental shelf

The continental shelf claimed by the United Kingdom is playing an increasingly important part in the provision of the country's mineral resources. Four gas fields in the southern North Sea provide 70 per cent. of the country's natural gas needs.[73] Seven million tons of sand and gravel, representing 10 per cent. of United Kingdom output, are dredged each year in shallow water near the coast. Potentially detrimental effects on the nearshore environment are likely to limit an increase in production.[74] Nine per cent. of the United Kingdom's coal output comes from the seabed. The coal is mined from shafts driven under the sea from mines on land, the longest such shaft being four miles.[75] Oil is not yet being exploited, although a number of promising looking fields have been discovered in the North Sea. One of the most recent forecasts is that North Sea oilfields will produce about 75 per cent. of the United Kingdom's oil requirements by the early 1980s.[76] The importance of this is likely to be very great, both on the economy and environment of Scotland and as a lessening of dependence on Middle East oil supplies. In addition, the seabed may produce other minerals in the future. Alluvial tin has been found in the sea off Cornwall and lime deposits have been found in the Minches. The seafloor beneath the North Sea is also thought to hold huge reserves of potash. Deposits lying along the Yorkshire coast are already being worked from land. Sand with a magnetic equivalent of 4 per cent. iron content has been found off West Scotland.

The legal régime regulating exploitation activities on the continental shelf varies somewhat, depending on the substance being exploited. Under section 1 (1) of the Continental Shelf Act 1964, all rights for exploiting mineral resources, except coal, vest in the Crown. The right to mine coal vests in the National Coal Board.[77] Of the other substances, sand and gravel mining is regulated by the Crown Estate Commissioners, and oil and gas by the Department of Trade and Industry. The Crown Estate Commissioners issue licences for sand and gravel mining, after consulting the Department of Environment about the effects of dredging on coastal erosion, and the Ministry of Agriculture, Fisheries and Food about the danger to fisheries.[78] The provisions governing oil and gas exploitation are more complex. The Department of Trade and Industry issues licences for exploration and exploitation.[79] Only persons who are citizens of the United Kingdom and Colonies and who are resident in the United Kingdom, or who are bodies corporate incorporated in the United Kingdom, may apply for such licences.[80] The licence is governed by model clauses[81] which not only deal with such questions as the length of licence, keeping of accounts, provision of samples and so on, but also certain provisions regulating the safety of installations and the safety and welfare of those employed on drilling rigs. The latter rather general provisions have recently been greatly strengthened by the Mineral Workings (Offshore Installations) Act 1971 and orders made under that Act.[82] Originally a uniform rate was charged for exploration and production licences, but in 1971 an experimental system of auctions was introduced. Recently the Government has come under increasing criticism for being over-generous to the oil companies and for not doing enough to allow British businesses to reap the benefits of North Sea oil and gas.[83] What has been said so far applies to both oil and gas. But there is one important distinction to be made between them. Whereas a company can dispose of any oil won from the seabed as it likes, any gas obtained which is brought to land must, as a general rule, be sold to the nationalised Gas Council.[84]

Apart from mineral resources, there is one other quite different use of the seabed which may be important for the future tunnelling. After 170 years of deliberation, it seems as if the idea of a tunnel under the English Channel may become a concrete reality in the foreseeable future. A final set of feasibility studies was approved by the British and French Governments in August 1972, and on the basis of these studies, a definite decision as to whether to build the tunnel is expected to be made in 1973.

NAVIGATION

With one of the largest merchant shipping fleets in the world[85] and with naval power forming an important part of its military capabilities, the United Kingdom has traditionally been in favour of there being as little interference as possible in the movement of shipping. However the wreck of the *Torrey Canyon* and the increasing number of collisions in the English Channel and Straits of Dover have caused a change of attitude. The United Kingdom took an important initiative within IMCO to press, first for a system of traffic separation schemes[86] and secondly, that the observance of such schemes should be made mandatory.[87] Throughout, the Government has made it clear that it will not be pressurised into acting unilaterally, but will only act internationally through the medium of IMCO. Nevertheless the Government, in collaboration with the French, Belgian and Dutch Governments, set up a surveillance scheme for the English Channel and Straits of Dover in September 1971. Under this scheme, vessels travelling in contravention of the Traffic Separation Scheme are identified and information about their presence passed on to other ships in the area. In addition, details are also given to the authorities of the State in which the offending ship is registered.[88] About 10 per cent. of all shipping has been found to be travelling in contravention of the Scheme. The Government is also contemplating the possibility, again in collaboration with the French, Belgian and Dutch Governments, of instituting a navigation service to assist the movement of ships through the Straits of Dover.[89]

A rather different problem is the danger to navigation posed by such things as drilling rigs. Under the Coast Protection Act 1949 [90] and the Continental Shelf Act 1964 [91] the consent of the Secretary of State for the Environment is required before any works which may cause a danger to navigation are undertaken in United Kingdom territorial waters or on the United Kingdom continental shelf.

POLLUTION

As a highly industrialised and island country, the United Kingdom has until very recently tended to use the seas around its coasts as a bottomless sink for the disposal of waste. As a result, the seas around the United Kingdom are polluted to a considerable extent, although there seems to be general agreement—at least from official sources—that the situation is some way from reaching crisis point.[92] Just as the sources of marine pollution are many and varied, so is United Kingdom legislation to control pollution contained in a large number of instruments. It is convenient to divide the subject up as follows:

(i) dumping from ships and aircraft
(ii) oil pollution from ships
(iii) pollution from seabed activities
(iv) pollution from outfalls and shore-based industry
(v) pollution from rivers and estuaries
(vi) airborne pollution.

(i) Dumping from ships and aircraft

At present, only radioactive waste is covered by legislation. The Radioactive Substances Act 1960, by making it an offence to use radioactive materials without registration, creates what amounts to a licensing system for the dumping of radioactive waste at sea.[93] Such dumping is also carried out in accordance with the recommendations of the International Commission on Radiological Protection, the International Atomic Energy Agency and the Nuclear Energy Agency of OECD. For other substances, the Ministry of Agriculture, Fisheries and Food operates a voluntary system of control. The Ministry recommends sites and methods for dumping to companies engaged in waste disposal.[94] The United Kingdom is a signatory to the Oslo Convention [95] and the Government has said that legislation will be introduced in the current (1972–73) session of Parliament to allow the United Kingdom to ratify the Convention. This legislation would replace the present voluntary system. The United Kingdom is also a signatory to the London Convention on Dumping of December 1972.[95a]

(ii) Oil pollution from ships

The United Kingdom is a party to the International Convention for the Prevention of Pollution of the Sea by Oil 1954, as amended, and has ratified the 1969 amendment to the Convention.[96] Although the latter have not yet come into force, they have been applied to British ships since January 1973.[97] As regards civil liability for oil pollution damage, the United Kingdom has ratified the International Convention on Civil Liability for Oil Pollution Damage 1969. Again, although this Convention has not yet come into force, it has been implemented in United Kingdom law by the Merchant Shipping (Oil Pollution) Act 1971 and this Act is partially in force.[98] The Act is interesting in that it departs from the Convention in several places, notably in its requirement of a valid insurance certificate for the visit to British ports of tankers registered in States which are not parties to the Convention.

(iii) Pollution from seabed activities

There have as yet been no serious pollution problems arising from the exploration or exploitation of oil on the United Kingdom continental shelf. Section 3 of the Prevention of Oil Pollution Act 1971 makes it an offence punishable with a fine of up to £50,000 to allow oil to be discharged from a pipeline or any seabed operation. Under the Petroleum (Production) Regulations 1966, the holder of a production or exploration licence is also under an obligation to see that no oil escapes into the sea.[99]

(iv) Pollution from outfalls and shore-based industry

A number of different sources of pollution fall under this heading. First there is sewage. In England and Wales the sewage refuse of six million people living near the coast is discharged, in most cases in partially treated or untreated form, directly into the sea through pipelines, many of which do not extend beyond the low-water mark.[100] Secondly, there is waste from shore-based industries: these include oil refineries, aluminium smelting, coal-mining and mining for china clay and potash.[101] Thirdly, there is the warm water returned from power stations to the sea. Finally, pollution may result from the discharge of radioactive waste from shore-based power stations. The legislative provisions for controlling these sources of pollution are rather inadequate. Under section 5 of the Sea Fisheries Regulation Act 1966, the 12 Sea Fisheries Committees of England and Wales can make by-laws " prohibiting or regulating the deposit or discharge of any solid or liquid substance detrimental to sea fish or sea fishing " in United Kingdom territorial waters adjacent to the coast.[102] In the case of sewage, a certain control is exercised by the central government, since any new local authority sewage discharge requires loan sanction from the Department of the Environment, and is examined to ensure that there is no risk to public health or amenity. The Jeger Committee recommended that the Sea Fisheries Committees should be replaced by a new body which would combine its functions with those of the river authorities. This new body should be able to control all discharge of sewage by pipeline to the sea.[103] In the case of waste from shore-based industry, the fact that local authority planning permission is necessary for new factories, may lead to certain conditions being imposed on effluents discharged to the sea.

(v) Pollution from rivers and estuaries

The principal sources of pollution in rivers and estuaries are sewage (which may also contain industrial effluent), industrial waste discharged directly, and run-offs of various substances from the land. The latter may include pesticides, and this is one of the ways that highly noxious PCBs enter the sea. Under existing legislation[104] River Authorities (River Purification Authorities in Scotland) can impose conditions regarding the treatment, composition and quality of effluent before granting consents to discharges. Nevertheless these powers are inadequate in several respects, and a recent Report[105] has recommended that the Authorities should be given powers to control those discharges which at present lie outside their control.[106] River Authorities are due to be replaced in 1974 by multi-purpose regional water authorities.[107] The present Government has made the cleaning-up of rivers one of the major projects in its programme to improve the quality of the environment, and is pressing for more international discussion and action on this aspect of marine pollution.

(vi) Airborne pollution

This kind of pollution is not often discussed in connection with marine pollution, and yet it is clear that many pollutants in the air eventually find their way into the sea, either because they are precipitated over the sea or rivers, or because they fall on the land and run off into rivers. There is comparatively little legislation in the United Kingdom for controlling air pollution. The Alkali and Clean Air Inspectorate supervises emissions from factories in many industries, but has been widely criticised for lacking effective powers to control much of the pollution from this source. The Clean Air Act 1956 enables local authorities to prohibit the emission of smoke from all premises within specified areas: at present, about one-third of all premises in the United Kingdom come within these smokeless zones and the Act has, on the whole, been very successful. There is little control over air pollution emanating from motor vehicles, but on the other hand, there has been a substantial reduction in the use of the more noxious pesticides.[108]

Pollution control zone

The idea that a State may claim the right to exercise control over ships causing pollution in an area of the sea adjacent to its coast but beyond its territorial sea is a recent one.[109] Certainly it was not seriously mooted at the time of the *Torrey Canyon* incident. Canada appears to have been the first State to claim pollution control jurisdiction beyond the territorial sea, with the Arctic Waters Pollution Prevention Act enacted in 1970. The United Kingdom is reported to have protested to Canada about the enactment of this legislation,[110] yet less than a year later, we find the British Parliament enacting legislation which, although not as far-ranging as the Canadian Act, does undoubtedly go beyond the provisions of existing international law. A series of collisions and strandings in the English Channel, many of them taking place outside British territorial waters, during the winter of 1970–71, caused the Government to make a last-minute addition to the Oil in Navigable Waters Bill.[111] Under section 16 (1) of the Prevention of Oil Pollution Act, an Order may be made applying the Act to foreign ships on the high seas. Such an order has been made.[112] This means that the Secretary of State has powers to take certain action against any foreign ship on the high seas where, as a result of an accident to that ship, he is of the opinion that there is a need to protect the coast or territorial sea of the United Kingdom against " grave and imminent danger of oil pollution."[113] The action the Secretary of State may take includes taking over the control of the ship or sinking or destroying it. These provisions go beyond existing international law on a number of counts. Although they are similar to the provisions of the International Convention relating to Intervention on the High Seas in Cases of Oil Pollution Casualties 1969,[114] they differ in important ways from the terminology used in the Convention and do not provide the same safeguards, such as prior consultations, as the Convention.[115] Secondly, the Act applies not only to ships of States parties to the convention, but also to ships of States not parties to the Convention.[116] Finally, it is doubtful whether the power of the Minister to take over control of a ship is compatible with Article 11 of the Convention on the High Seas.

It seems permissible to refer to this claim as a pollution control zone, even though no very precise geographical area is defined in which jurisdiction to control oil pollution is claimed. Much more precise geographically, although quite different legally, are various pollution surveillance schemes. Under the Agreement for Co-operation in Dealing with Pollution of the North Sea by Oil 1969,[117] the United Kingdom is allocated a zone of the North Sea in which it is to report any serious oil slicks, and any action it takes to deal with such slicks, to the other States parties to the Agreement. It is made quite clear, however, that the division of the North Sea into zones shall not " be invoked as a precedent or agreement in any matter concerning sovereignty or jurisdiction." [118] Similar surveillance agreements between the United Kingdom and France and Belgium for the English Channel and Straits of Dover were concluded in August 1972.[119]

TOWARDS THE UNITED NATIONS CONFERENCE ON THE LAW OF THE SEA

The earlier part of this paper should have given some idea of the kind of interests which will motivate the negotiating position of the United Kingdom at the forthcoming UN Conference on the Law of the Sea. Nevertheless it may be worth summarising briefly the British reactions to some of the proposals which have so far been made in the Seabed Committee. On the general question of limits, the United Kingdom is very keen that agreement should be reached, so that uncertainties over the future of the freedom of navigation and the future of distant water fisheries may be allayed. On the question of the breadth of the territorial sea, the United Kingdom is very much in agreement with the United States position, namely that it would accept a 12 mile territorial sea if there were satisfactory agreement on the question of navigation through straits.[120] On the question of fisheries, the United Kingdom recognises that the problem is one of " striking a fair balance between the claims of individual States to an exclusive right to exploit the waters in the vicinity of their coasts, and the general freedom of all States to fish in the high seas." [121] Nevertheless, the United Kingdom might not be totally opposed to the idea of a broad economic zone adjacent to the territorial sea, if freedom of navigation were assured and reasonable transitional arrangements made for foreign fishermen traditionally fishing in this zone.

As far as the international régime to govern the seabed beyond the limits of national jurisdiction is concerned, the United Kingdom supports the United States proposal for an intermediate trusteeship zone between the continental shelf and the international area. The international area would be administered by an international organisation which would be limited to a licensing function: licences would be allocated to States parties so as to lead to an equitable distribution of the wealth of the seabed. The revenue from licences would cover the administrative costs of the organisation: any revenues left over would be available for distribution for the benefit of States parties. The institutional framework of the organisation would be very simple.[122]

CONCLUSION

In an area of law which is in the course of considerable change and upheaval, the United Kingdom—even though one of the most traditionalist States in law of the sea questions—has by no means stood still. Unlike earlier periods in its history, the United Kingdom is now having much less influence on how the law of the sea develops: indeed, it is rather in the position of being forced to adapt to changing trends by the pressure of external events. It is being partly swept along by the practice of the newer States, and partly being forced to re-evaluate its own maritime interests by the realisation that the rationale for many of its earlier policy stands no longer holds good. Pollution threats to its own coast no longer make complete freedom of navigation such an attractive proposition. The Icelandic fisheries dispute has shown up the inconsistency, even if not a legal one, between claiming a broad zone for coastal State jurisdiction over seabed resources, but denying such a zone for fisheries. In a rather typical British way, United Kingdom policy-makers in this area of international law and international relations have reacted in a haphazard, piecemeal and somewhat unconscious manner—particularly in relation to claims to the seabed and pollution control—and on the eve of the Santiago Conference, it would be difficult to say that the United Kingdom had a comprehensive and properly thought-out policy.

REFERENCES

1. The most famous being Selden's doctrine of *mare clausum*, current in the first half of the seventeenth century.
2. Territorial Waters Jurisdiction Act 1878. Before this date a three mile limit had been accepted in a number of judicial decisions and bilateral agreements. For examples, see C. J. Colombos, *International Law of the Sea*, 6th ed. (London: Longmans, 1967), pp. 92–95.
3. See *UN Conference on the Law of the Sea, Official Records, 1958 and 1960* and also *Report on the First United Nations Conference on the Law of the Sea* (London: HMSO, 1958. Cmnd. 584), p. 6. For U.K. statements made after both these Conferences, see H.C.Deb., Vol. 587, col. 24 (Apr. 28, 1958) and Vol. 622, col. 402 (Apr. 28, 1960).
4. There is further discussion on the question of control of navigation in the English Channel below, in the sections on a pollution control zone and navigation. See also Laurance Reed, *An Ocean of Waste* (London: Conservative Political Centre, 1972), pp. 61–62 and H.C.Deb., Vol. 815, col. 621 *et seq.* (Apr. 8, 1971).
5. *Loi no. 71–1060 du 24 décembre 1971, relative à la délimitation de la mer territoriale française*. Further on this, see Chap. 22, *supra*.
6. Exchange of Notes between the Government of the United Kingdom of Great Britain and Northern Ireland and the Government of Canada concerning Fishing by British Vessels off the Atlantic Coast of Canada, Ottawa, Mar. 27, 1972 ((1972) U.K.T.S. 68). For further details of the Canadian action, see Chap. 20, *supra*.
7. *Anglo-Norwegian Fisheries Case* [1951] I.C.J.Rep. 116.
8. Art. 11 of the Convention.
9. Art. 7 of the Convention.
10. Cmnd. 584 *op. cit.*, in n. 3, *supra*.
11. On Mar. 14, 1960.
12. (1964) 98 Statutory Orders and Regulations 771 (no. 291).
13. United Kingdom objection to the statement made by Indonesia when ratifying the Convention on the High Seas. See *Multilateral Treaties in respect of which the Secretary-General Performs Depositary Functions: List of Signatures, Ratifications, Accessions, etc. as at 31st December 1968* (St/LEG/SER.D/2), p. 343.
14. Further on this, see E. D. Brown, "The Lessons of the *Torrey Canyon*," in (1968) 21 Current Legal Problems 113.

15. The dispute with Iceland, which was the most bitter and protracted, was settled by an Exchange of Notes of Mar. 11, 1961 (397 U.N.T.S. 275; (1961) U.K.T.S. 17), which gave United Kingdom fishermen a three-year transitional period in the outer six miles. In the case of Norway, an Anglo-Norwegian Agreement of Nov. 17, 1960 (398 U.N.T.S. 189; (1961) U.K.T.S. 25) gave British fishermen a 10-year transitional period in the outer six miles. For further details, see Colombos, *op. cit.* in n. 2, *supra*, pp. 118–119, 155–159.

16. Further on this, see E. D. Brown, " British Fisheries and the Common Market " in (1972) 25 Current Legal Problems 37 and D. H. N. Johnson, " European Fishery Limits " in *Developments in the Law of the Sea 1958–1964* (London: British Institute of International and Comparative Law, 1965), pp. 48–74.

17. Fisheries Convention, Mar. 9, 1964 (581 U.N.T.S. 57; (1966) U.K.T.S. 35).

18. Fishery Limits Act 1964.

19. See p. 283 above.

20. See, *e.g.*, the Adjournment Debate of Mar. 6, 1972, on Fishery Limits in the Irish Sea: H.C.Deb., Vol. 832, col. 1200.

21. Fishing Boats (Belgium) Designation Order 1965 (S.I. 1965 No. 1569). Fishing Boats (France) Designation Orders 1965 (S.I. 1965 Nos. 1241 and 1667). Fishing Boats (Ireland) Designation Order 1965 (S.I. 1965 No. 1448). Fishing Boats (European Economic Community) Designation Order 1972 (S.I. 1972 No. 2026).

22. Protocol of Provisional Application of the Fisheries Convention, London, Mar. 9, 1964 (581 U.N.T.S. 57; (1965) U.K.T.S. 29).

23. Fishing Boats (European Economic Community) Designation Order 1972 (S.I. 1972 No. 2026) (revoking and replacing an earlier Order).

24. Norway–United Kingdom. Agreement for the Continuance of Fishing by Norwegian Vessels within the Fishing Limits of the United Kingdom of Great Britain and Northern Ireland (with Exchange of Notes), London, Sept. 28, 1964 (548 U.N.T.S. 63; (1965) U.K.T.S. 43).

25. U.S.S.R.–United Kingdom. Exchange of Notes on Matters arising from the Establishment by the United Kingdom of the Fishery Régime provided for by the Fishery Limits Act 1964, Moscow, Sept. 30, 1964 (539 U.N.T.S. 159; (1964) U.K.T.S. 63).

26. Poland–United Kingdom. Exchange of Notes regarding the Rights to be accorded to Polish Vessels within the British Fishery Limits to be established on Sept. 30, 1964, Warsaw, Sept. 26, 1964 (539 U.N.T.S. 153; (1964) U.K.T.S. 64). Polish fishermen were also given the right to fish for herring in the outer six miles until the end of 1967.

27. Decree No. 70–292 of Mar. 25, 1970. The United Kingdom also has certain fishing rights under a series of earlier agreements. See Exchange of Notes concerning the Status of Previous Fisheries Agreements in relation to the Fisheries Convention open for Signature at London from Mar. 9 to Apr. 10, 1964, London, Apr. 10, 1964 (648 U.N.T.S. 73; (1968) U.K.T.S. 54). Following the new French Law on the Territorial Sea (*op. cit.* n. 5, *supra*), the former 12 mile fishing zone has become subsumed in the territorial sea: the rights of foreign fishermen in the former fishing area are expressly preserved however.

28. Territorial Sea and Fishing Zones Act 1970.

29. Fishing Zones of Canada (Zones 1, 2 and 3), Order P.C. 1971–366.

30. See n. 6, *supra*.

31. About 18% of all fish landed in the United Kingdom come from the waters around Iceland.

32. H.L.Deb., Vol. 328, col. 1258, 1260–1 (Mar. 2, 1972).

33. *Fisheries Jurisdiction Case* (*United Kingdom* v. *Iceland*). Jurisdiction of the Court, Judgement of Feb. 2, 1973 [1973] I.C.J.Rep. 3. Iceland was not represented before the Court and the Court therefore had to infer Iceland's objections to its jurisdiction.

34. *Fisheries Jurisdiction Case* (*United Kingdom* v. *Iceland*). Request for the Indication of Interim Measures of Protection, Order of Aug. 17, 1972 [1972] I.C.J.Rep. 12.

35. Official Journal of the European Communities, No. L 236/1, of Oct. 27, 1970.

36. Arts. 100–103 of the Treaty concerning the Accession of the Kingdom of Denmark, Ireland, the Kingdom of Norway and the United Kingdom of Great Britain and Northern Ireland to the European Economic Community and the European Atomic Energy Community (with Final Act), Brussels, Jan. 22, 1972 ((1973) U.K.T.S. 1).

37. H.C.Deb., Vol. 828, col. 52 (Dec. 13, 1971).

38. 0·17% according to J. R. Coull, *The Fisheries of Europe: An Economic Geography* (London: Bell, 1972), p. 229.

39. See, *e.g.*, the United Kingdom's pleadings before the International Court of Justice in the *Fisheries Jurisdiction Case* (*United Kingdom* v. *Iceland*), Request for the Indication of Interim Measures of Protection, as reported in *Guardian*, Aug. 2, 1972, p. 4.

40. Ministry of Agriculture, Fisheries and Food. *Sea Fisheries Statistical Tables 1971* (London: H.M.S.O., 1972), p. 3.

41. *Ibid.* pp. 4–5.

42. *Ibid.* pp. 16–18.

43. *Ibid.* p. 22.

44. *Ibid.* pp. 32–38.

45. Department of Agriculture and Fisheries for Scotland. *Regulation of Scottish Inshore Fisheries: Report of the Scottish Inshore Fisheries Committee* (Edinburgh: H.M.S.O., 1970, Cmnd. 4453), p. 110.

46. *Sea Fisheries Statistical Tables 1971*, p. 39.

47. *Ibid.* p. 27.

48. *Ibid.* pp. 28–29.

49. For details, see the Sea Fish Industry Act 1970 (consolidating earlier legislation). For further information on the regulation of the industry, see D. H. N. Johnson, " Background to the Sea Fish Industry Act 1962," in *Developments in the Law of the Sea 1958–1964* (*op. cit.*, n. 16, *supra.*), pp. 110–132, and the Annual Reports of the White Fish Authority and the Herring Industry Board (published by H.M.S.O.).

50. S.I. 1972 No. 23.

51. S.I. 1972 No. 1662.

52. Further discussion on this point is contained in the Cameron Committee's Report, *op. cit.* n. 45, *supra*, Chap. 9.

53. S.I. 1972 No. 1477.

54. Herring (North Sea Fishing) Licensing Order 1971 (S.I. 1971 No. 687); Herring (North Sea Fishing) Licensing Order 1972 (S.I. 1972 No. 470).

55. Salmon and Migratory Trout (Drift-Net Fishing) Licensing Order 1962 (S.I. 1962 No. 1393) (extended by S.I. 1966 No. 1546 and S.I. 1968 No. 1974); Salmon and Migratory Trout (Sea Fishing) Licensing Order 1971 (S.I. 1971 No. 181).

56. Sea Fishing (Northwest Atlantic) Licensing Order 1972 (S.I. 1972 No. 1857).

57. *Sinews for Survival: a Report on the Management of Natural Resources* (London: H.M.S.O., 1972), p. 24.

58. For a list of by-laws in force for Scotland, see the Cameron Committee's Report, *op. cit.* n. 45, *supra*, pp. 180–181.

59. Sea Fish (Conservation) Act 1967, s. 15 and Sea Fisheries Act 1968, s. 8.

60. Sea Fisheries Regulation Act, 1966, s. 10 and Sea Fish (Conservation) Act 1967, s. 17. For a general discussion on the enforcement of conservation measures within the United Kingdom's exclusive fishing zone, see Cameron Committee's Report, *op. cit.* n. 45, *supra*, pp. 141–163.

61. Cmnd. 3645.

62. Great Britain–Venezuela. Treaty relating to the Submarine Areas of the Gulf of Paria, Caracas, Feb. 25, 1942 (205 U.N.T.S. 121; (1942) U.K.T.S. 10). This agreement is the first delimiting the seabed between two States.

63. For details of these claims, see *Laws and Regulations on the Régime of the High Seas*, Vol. 1 (UN Legislative Series ST/LEG/SER.B/1. 1951), pp. 23–29.

64. Continental Shelf (Designation of Areas) Order 1964 (S.I. 1964 No. 697). Continental Shelf (Designation of Additional Areas) Order 1965 (S.I. 1965 No. 1531). Continental Shelf (Designation of Additional Areas) Order 1968 (S.I. 1968 No. 891). Continental Shelf (Designation of Additional Areas) Order 1971 (S.I. 1971 No. 594).

65. For a map of the area covered, see *Continental Shelf Act, 1964: Report for the Year 1971–72* (H.M.S.O. 1972. H.C. 47 (1972–73)) between pp. 4–5.

66. Island of Rockall Act 1972.

67. United Kingdom–Norway. Agreement relating to the Delimitation of the Continental Shelf between the Two Countries (with annexed chart), London, Mar. 10, 1965 (551 U.N.T.S. 213; (1965) U.K.T.S. 71).

United Kingdom–Netherlands. Agreement relating to the Delimitation of the Continental Shelf under the North Sea between the Two Countries (with annexed chart), London, Oct. 6, 1965 (595 U.N.T.S. 113; (1967) U.K.T.S. 23). Protocol amending the Agreement, London, Nov. 25, 1971 ((1972) U.K.T.S. 130). United Kingdom–Denmark. Agreement relating to the delimitation of the Continental Shelf between the Two Countries, London, Nov. 25, 1971 ((1973) U.K.T.S. 6) (this replaces an earlier agreement of 1966). United Kingdom–Federal Republic of Germany. Agreement relating to the Delimitation of the Continental Shelf under the North Sea between the Two Countries, London, Nov. 25, 1971 ((1973) U.K.T.S. 7).

It is interesting to note that the Agreement with Norway implicitly recognises the Norwegian claim to the continental shelf. This claim is based on the criterion of exploitability and ignores the Norwegian Trench which is over 200 metres in depth and which lies between the Norwegian coast and the United Kingdom–Norway boundary.

67A. According to *Aftenposten* of Apr. 9, 1973, p. 13, a draft agreement on this question was initialled on Mar. 29, 1973.

68. Art. 5 (iv).

69. Art. 5 (ii).

70. ss. 3, 6 and 7 of the Act, read together with the Continental Shelf (Jurisdiction) Order 1968: (S.I. 1968 No. 892) and the Mineral Workings (Offshore Installations) Act 1971, s. 8.

71. Continental Shelf (Protection of Installations) No. 6 Order 1973 (S.I. 1973 No. 284). S. 2, as well as differing from the Convention on the Continental Shelf, is also contrary to Art. 11 of the Geneva Convention on the High Seas, 1958.

72. Arts. 2 (iv) and 3 of the Convention. Although the Act says nothing about the legal status of superjacent waters, one of the bilateral delimitation agreements, that with Norway, reproduces the provisions of Art. 3.

73. Reed, *op. cit.* n. 4, *supra*, p. 21. See also *Continental Shelf Act, 1964: Report for the Year 1971–72*, *op. cit.* n. 65, *supra*, p. 3, and map between pp. 34 and 35.

74. Reed, p. 21 and *Marine Science and Technology* (London: H.M.S.O., 1969. Cmnd. 3992), p. 14.

75. Reed, p. 21.

76. *Guardian*, Feb. 21, 1973, p. 16.

77. Continental Shelf Act 1964, s. 1 (2). The consent of the Minister of Power (now the Secretary of State for Trade and Industry) is required for any mining activities undertaken by the Coal Board on the continental shelf.

78. Reed, p. 51.

79. Continental Shelf Act 1964, s. 1 (3). The details of this system of licensing are contained in the Petroleum (Production) Regulations 1966 (S.I. 1966 No. 898) as amended by the Petroleum (Production) (Amendment) Regulations 1971 (S.I. 1971 No. 814), and Petroleum (Production) (Amendment) Regulations 1972 (S.I. 1972 No. 1522).

80. Petroleum (Production) Regulations, Art. 4.

81. *Ibid.* Art. 10, Sched. 4 (production licences) and Sched. 5 (exploration licences).

82. Offshore Installations (Registrations) Regulations 1972 (S.I. 1972 No. 702); Offshore Installations (Managers) Regulations 1972 (S.I. 1972 No. 703); Offshore Installations (Logbooks and Registration of Death) Regulations 1972 (S.I. 1972 No. 1542).

83. Apart from the press and individuals, serious criticism has been made in two official reports. The International Management and Engineering Group of Britain Ltd., in its *Study of Potential Benefits to British Industry from Offshore Oil and Gas Developments* (London: H.M.S.O., 1973), which was commissioned by the Government, criticised the modest role so far played by British companies. The Government has said that it accepts the Report's recommendations (see *Guardian*, Jan. 17, 1973, pp. 1, 11, 15). The Report of the Public Accounts Committee (London: H.M.S.O., 1973. H.C. 122 (1972–1973)) criticises successive governments for having been far too generous in the financial conditions attached to exploration and exploitation licences. One immediate result of this Report was the announcement by the Chancellor of the Exchequer in his Budget Speech on Mar. 6, 1973, that legislation governing taxation of North Sea oil profits is to be made much stricter, with a substantial increase in revenue for the Treasury.

84. Continental Shelf Act 1964, s. 9.

85. According to the latest figures published by Lloyd's Register, the U.K. with its 28·6 million tons comes third after Liberia and Japan in the list of the world's leading merchant shipping tonnages. See *Guardian*, Nov. 8, 1972, p. 4.

86. For a list of such schemes, see IMCO, *Ships Routeing and Traffic Separation Schemes*, 1971.

87. This will be the case when the Amendments to the International Convention for the Safety of Life at Sea which were adopted on Oct. 12, 1971 (Cmnd. 5095) come into force. The United Kingdom has already made the observance of traffic separation schemes mandatory for its own ships—Collision Regulations (Traffic Separation Schemes) Order 1972 (S.I. 1972 No. 809), as amended by the Collision Regulations (Traffic Separation Schemes) (Amendment) Order 1972 (S.I. 1972 No. 1267).

88. For further details, see 263 *Baltic and International Maritime Conference Bulletin* 1642 and H.C.Deb., Vol. 822, col. 747 (July 29, 1971).

89. H.C.Deb., Vol. 822, col. 748 (July 29, 1971).

90. ss. 34–36.

91. s. 4.

92. See, *e.g.*, *Sinews for Survival: A Report on the Management of Natural Resources*, *op. cit.* n. 57, *supra*, pp. 24–25. *Pollution: Nuisance or Nemesis? a Report on the Control of Pollution* (London: H.M.S.O., 1972), pp. 23, 53. (These two reports were prepared for the Stockholm Conference on the Environment). *First Report of the Royal Commission on Environmental Pollution* (London: H.M.S.O., 1971, Cmnd. 4585), pp. 25–26, and H.C.Deb., Vol. 820, cols. 1675–6, 1682–5 (July 8, 1971).

93. Reed, *op. cit.* n. 4, *supra*, p. 45. See also *First Report of the Royal Commission on Environmental Pollution*, *supra*, pp. 25, 27 and *The Protection of the Environment: the Fight against Pollution* (London: H.M.S.O., 1970, Cmnd. 4373), pp. 26–27.

94. Reed, *op. cit.* p. 44.

95. Convention for the Prevention of Marine Pollution by Dumping from Ships and Aircraft, Oslo, Feb. 15, 1972. Cmnd. 4984.

95A. Convention on the Prevention of Marine Pollution by the Dumping of Wastes and Other Matter, London, Dec. 29, 1972. Cmnd. 5169.

96. The Convention and its amendments have been implemented into U.K. law by Prevention of Oil Pollution Act 1971 (consolidating earlier legislation). In 1971 the penalties for oil pollution were drastically increased, the maximum fine being raised from £1,000 to £50,000. The Act also covers oil pollution in U.K. territorial waters.

97. Oil in Navigable Waters (Exceptions) Regulations 1972 (S.I. 1972 No. 1928), and Oil in Navigable Waters (Records) Regulations 1972 (S.I. 1972 No. 1929).

98. The Merchant Shipping (Oil Pollution) Act 1971 (Commencement) Order 1971 (S.I. 1971 No. 1423).

99. Petroleum (Production) Regulations 1966 (S.I. 1966 No. 898), Sched. 4, Cl. 16 and Sched. 5, Cl. 9. See also G. Victory, " Avoidance of Accidental and Deliberate Pollution," in *Coastal Water Pollution: Pollution of the Sea by Oil Spills*, Proceedings of a NATO Colloquium held in Brussels, Nov. 1970, pp. 2.7–2.9.

100. For further details, see *Report of the International Council for the Exploration of the Sea Working Group on Pollution of the North Sea* (Copenhagen: International Council for the Exploration of the Sea, 1969. Co-operative Research Report Series A, No. 13), pp. 8 and 40 (hereafter referred to as *I.C.E.S. Report*).

101. For further details, see *I.C.E.S. Report*, pp. 15–16, and *Third Report of the Royal Commission on Environmental Pollution* (London: H.M.S.O., 1972), pp. 87–89, Chaps. III and IV and Appendix 1.

102. There are no Sea Fisheries Committees in Scotland. The River Purification Authorities have somewhat similar powers in estuaries and certain coastal waters.

103. *Taken for Granted: Report of the Working Party on Sewage Disposal* (London: H.M.S.O., 1970), p. 33. As yet, no action has been taken to implement the Committee's proposals. See the comments on these proposals in *Third Report of the Royal Commission on Environmental Pollution*, *supra*, pp. 11–12.

104. Rivers (Prevention of Pollution) Acts 1951 and 1961, and Clean Rivers (Estuaries and Tidal Waters) Act 1960. The equivalent legislation for Scotland is Rivers (Prevention of Pollution) (Scotland) Acts 1951 and 1965. For a more detailed description of this legislation and the position at common law, see *Nuisance or Nemesis? op. cit.* n. 92, *supra*, pp. 58–59, 60–62.

105. *Third Report of the Royal Commission on Environmental Pollution*, *op. cit.* n. 101, *supra*, pp. 10–11.

106. These include certain discharges to estuaries, discharge of sewage from vessels in estuaries and discharge to sewers.

107. Under the Water Bill, published on Jan. 23, 1973.

108. For further information on this topic, see *Nuisance or Nemesis? op. cit.* n. 92, *supra*, pp. 38–40; Cmnd. 4373, *op. cit.* n. 93, *supra*, pp. 8–13; and *I.C.E.S. Report*, *op. cit.* n. 100, *supra*, pp. 19–21.

109. It does not seem permissible to interpret Art. 24 of the Convention on the Territorial Sea and the Contiguous Zone as covering pollution control. See the discussion above under the territorial sea and the reference in n. 14.

110. According to *Svenska Dagbladet* of Feb. 13, 1971.

111. This Act has been repealed and replaced by the consolidating Prevention of Oil Pollution Act 1971. Some 25% of the world's oil traffic passes through the English Channel.

112. The Oil in Navigable Waters (Shipping Casualties) Order 1971 (S.I. 1971 No. 1736).

113. *Ibid.* Art. 5. At the time of writing, none of the powers under the Act have yet been used.

114. Cmnd. 4403. The United Kingdom ratified the Convention on Jan. 12, 1971.

115. On this, see M. J. Forster, " The Prevention of Oil Pollution Act 1971" (1972) 21 I.C.L.Q. 771.

116. It has been argued by some writers that the Convention is no more than a codification of already existing customary international law. If this were true, then the point made here would lose much of its force. Considerations of space unfortunately preclude a discussion as to how far the Convention, and indeed the Act, merely reflect existing customary international law. The writer is, however, of the opinion that both the Convention and the Act do go beyond existing customary international law.

117. (1969) U.K.T.S. 78.

118. Art. 6 (v) of the Agreement.

119. As reported in the *Guardian*, Aug. 10, 1972, p. 7.

120. A/AC.138/SC.II/SR.27, p. 6.

121. A/AC.138/SC.II/SR.14, p. 3.

122. International Régime, Working Paper 1970, A/AC.138/26. Proposals for the Elements of a Convention for an International Seabed Régime 1971, A/AC.138/46.

CHAPTER 26

Third World Expectations

By M. A. Ajomo *

We must begin with an *a priori* assumption that the rules of general international law apply to the Third World,[1]† as well as to the highly developed countries of Europe and America. But international law, like any other law of a given legal order, is moving according to the development of new social and political conditions in the community where it operates. Africa and Asia, being the newest of the continents which have entered the international community, have a duty to enrich international law with their own experiences, their own values and ideas in defence of their legitimate interests.

The interdependence of States in the international community makes imperative the existence of a system of legal norms for the conduct of inter-State relations. Nowhere is this more desirable than in the law concerning the rights of States over the waters of the world.

Two cardinal questions are at issue as regards the attitude of countries of the Third World to international law in general and the law of the sea in particular. The first is whether or not countries of the Third World ought to accept all of existing customary international law; and the second is that, if they desire any modifications in the existing norms, which method of approach should be adopted in seeking the changes required?

With regard to the first issue it must be realised that existing norms governing rights on the sea, like most norms of customary international law, were formed from practice among Western European States before the accession of the new African and Asian States to independence. Many countries of the Third World were not parties to the development of these norms. Further, some of these norms have been considered as unfavourable to many countries of Africa and Asia and their aspirations. It is therefore not surprising that over and over again at various world forums, countries of the Third World have started to query many of the assumptions of customary international law which they did not participate in formulating and have gone even further, as at the Bandung Conference of 1955, to regard some of the existing norms of international customary law formed before their emergence as of doubtful validity.[2]

Countries of the Third World have therefore felt the need to change some of these norms, since international law, after all, is not an immutable, but rather a constantly changing, system.

It is the view of the present writer that certain modifications are desirable to meet the situations of countries of the Third World. However, modifications, where necessary, must be approached in a spirit of gradual evolution in preference to a revolutionary approach which might lead to chaos. In fact countries of the Third

* Ph.D. (Manchester), of the Faculty of Law, University of Lagos.
† For references, see p. 309.

World are already adopting the evolutionary approach, and by it have been able to effect changes in the existing rules by their active participation in the work of the United Nations and other international organisations.[3]

Although the expression " Third World " refers to the less developed areas of the world, namely, Africa, Asia, and, to some extent, Latin America, throughout this paper emphasis will be on the law in relation to Africa with which the writer is more familiar.

In this paper it is intended to discuss the legal status of maritime jurisdictions and the problems connected with them under the following main headings: (1) Territorial Sea and Contiguous Zone; (2) Fishery Limits; (3) Continental Shelf and Seabed Resources; (4) Pollution.

(1) *Territorial sea and contiguous zone*

Following the failure of the Geneva Conferences to agree on the breadth of the territorial sea, many States, including the majority of the major maritime Powers, continued to maintain their former positions, the three mile limit they have been maintaining since the eighteenth century. Countries of the Third World on the other hand, being newcomers in the international arena, felt free to determine new limits for their marginal sea in accordance with their national interests and within limits which they regarded as reasonable. And so in recent years many nations have made claims to extended maritime jurisdiction and exclusive control and sometimes of sovereignty over areas of the sea far beyond the three mile territorial sea traditionally claimed by many nations.

It was against this background that Nigeria by virtue of its Territorial Waters Decree 1967[4] extended its territorial sea from three to 12 nautical miles and again to 30 miles in 1971.[5] In 1966,[6] the Argentine Government claimed as territorial sea adjacent waters out to 200 nautical miles, measured from an extreme system of straight base lines. Pursuant to an accompanying Presidential Decree,[7] regulations on foreign fishing within the area were also issued which considerably stiffened control over foreign fishing vessels within the permitted limit and provided for heavy penalties for offenders in case of infringement. The provisions of the Decree have been rigidly enforced ever since. Ecuador has made claims similar to those of Argentina,[8] Guinea has laid claim to 130 miles[9] whilst a majority of other States of the Third World have since 1958 laid claim to a territorial sea of 12 nautical miles, thus equating their contiguous zone with their territorial sea, and initiating the development of a new rule of customary international law.[10]

Herein lies the conflict. The varied claims to different widths of the territorial sea is a reflection of each State trying to correct what it regards as the imbalance in the utilisation of the seas.

Most of the wider claims are by developing countries, *i.e.*, the countries of Africa, Asia and Latin America, while, on the whole, the developed maritime Powers favour the narrower limits. The reason for this is easy to understand. The major characteristic of the territorial sea is that the coastal State has complete jurisdiction over it with one exception, *i.e.*, the right of innocent passage of other nations' ships therein. Moreover, no foreign vessel may engage in fishing activities within the territorial sea. The interest of the major maritime Powers is to keep this zone of coastal State jurisdiction to the minimum. In this way, as large a portion of the sea as possible would be regarded as *res communis omnium*. The developing countries on the other hand, with barely any navies except for coastal defence, few, if any, ocean-going commercial vessels, fledgling fishing fleets, and little or no marine technology of the scale enjoyed by advanced countries, have an interest in a broad belt of territorial sea where they would be free from competition, particularly from the sophisticated fishery fleets of the developed countries. They insist that a doctrine of *res communis* can scarcely be maintained any longer in this changed situation.

It is significant to note also that a majority of countries of the Third World, as has been mentioned, insist that the present régime of the high seas, like much of customary international law, is a by-product of western culture and European institutions and therefore benefits only the countries which established the rules. Coupled with this is the added fear, to some extent justified, of the smaller States that it would be unrealistic and unsafe under the conditions of modern warfare to permit only a narrow belt of sea along national coasts. Armed with these arguments, developing countries tend to conserve a large portion of the sea as a reservoir of economic resources whose exploitation must be jealously guarded and protected. This is why many of these States have resorted to a broad unilateral extension of their coastal waters in order to create a buffer zone of security against external aggression.

Naturally the major traditional maritime nations like the U.K., France, the United States, Japan and the Federal Republic of Germany are reluctant to admit any pressure in favour of a much wider area of territorial sea than they claim themselves. Notwithstanding this, I think it is right to say that the majority of States have abandoned the traditional limit of three miles for the territorial sea and claim extended territorial seas of up to 12 miles. At the forthcoming Santiago Law of the Sea Conference, therefore, a compromise will inevitably be needed to secure general acceptance of a uniform breadth of territorial sea and States will need to view their own interests in the larger context of the interest of international society as a whole. In fact, the United States has recently taken a renewed initiative in favour of a 12 mile territorial sea.[11] The issue continues to be of international concern. There is nothing incompatible between the continued exercise of the freedom of the seas and recognition of the legitimate concern of the coastal State with security, resources, pollution and the like, provided this recognition is within reasonable limits. However, the OAU resolution endorsing the recommendation of its Scientific Commission that African States should extend their territorial waters to 200 nautical miles, which would thus come under their individual national sovereignty and jurisdiction, is extravagant.[12] Such an extension might not in the long run be in the interest of African States themselves. Experience has shown that, with very few exceptions, many African nations may need to fish from areas outside those adjacent to their coasts because of the prevailing oceanographic conditions which are not favourable to fisheries development in waters off their coasts.

(2) *Fishing*

The traditional basic assumption about the high seas has always been that the concept of freedom of the high seas involved freedom of fishing.[13] On the assumption that these resources were unlimited, there seemed to be no reason to qualify this attitude, for complete freedom had as its corollary the maximum utilisation of the sea resources.

Experience has shown that the living resources of the high seas may not be inexhaustible unless wisely husbanded and protected; fishing stocks are endangered by overfishing using sophisticated catching methods. The States parties to the 1958 Geneva Convention on Fishing and Conservation of the Living Resources of the High Seas stated in the Preamble to that convention that " the development of modern techniques for the exploitation of the living resources of the sea, increasing man's ability to meet the need of the world's expanding population for food, has exposed some of these resources to the danger of being over-exploited." Herein lies the special interest of a coastal State, an interest which is well recognised in the Geneva Convention itself where it is stated that " a coastal State has a special interest in the maintenance of the productivity of the living resources in any area of the high seas adjacent to its territorial sea."[14] The convention endeavoured to institute a system of conservation measures which might be adopted on a multilateral, bilateral or unilateral basis by interested States. This is particularly important because of " the preponderant influence of distant water fishery nations, who wished to fish as close as possible to the shores of other nations, frequently destroying one area and proceeding to another."[15]

The only logical deduction from this brief analysis is that the principle of freedom of the seas can no longer be treated as a rigid dogma. Regional arrangements, as instanced by the European Fisheries Convention of March 9, 1964,[16] for example, bear eloquent testimony to the practice of States recognising the fact that the theory of freedom of fishing has to be restricted in order to prevent a decline of fish stocks and that the coastal State, more than any other, has a special responsibility to maintain the productivity of living resources in the high seas contiguous to its territorial sea, because its economic interests are particularly at stake. Judge Padilla Nervo recently gave classic expression to the present state of affairs in his dissenting opinions in the Icelandic Fisheries case.[17]

The international wind of change is decidedly blowing against the traditional concept of freedom of the seas and the modern trend is to give primacy of place to the interest of a coastal State to preserve its fishery resources.

In recent years, claims by many nations, in Africa and Asia in particular, to extended maritime jurisdiction or exclusive control have as their primary objective control over fishing in coastal waters, with the purpose of reserving for the exclusive use of the fishermen of the coastal State the fish resources in the waters claimed, or of controlling the activities of foreign fishermen in order to prevent overfishing. Since the middle of this century technological advances have led to the intensification of long-distance operations and many States which were not formerly engaged in large-scale fishing have entered the industry.[18]

As with the territorial sea, efforts in 1958 and 1960 by the UN Conference on the Law of the Sea to determine internationally acceptable limits of restricted fisheries, failed. States have come to regard themselves free to create exclusive fisheries zones in order to preserve their economic resources. More than 30 States which have kept to limits of three, four or six miles have recently claimed an additional fishing zone, as a rule up to 12 miles. These include some of the traditional maritime Powers such as the United Kingdom (1964), Denmark (1965), Canada (1964), New Zealand (1965), United States (1966), Australia (1968) and France (1967). Iceland, from September 1972, unilaterally extended her exclusive fishing zone to 50 miles.[19] Among the countries of the Third World the claim is much more extravagant, as witnessed by the following claims made by States: Chile—200 miles, Peru—200 miles, Nicaragua—200 miles, Sri Lanka—106 miles, Ghana—100 miles, India—112 miles and Pakistan—112 miles.

The concept of the Patrimonial Sea[20] found in the Declaration of Santa Domingo of the Specialised Conference of Caribbean Countries, Concerning the Problems of the Sea, June 9, 1972,[21] the Montevideo Declaration on the Law of the Sea signed by nine Latin American States,[22] the Declaration of Latin American States on the Law of the

Sea of August 8, 1971, and the various recommendations of OAU organs and Specialised Commissions on permanent sovereignty of African countries over the fishery resources off the shores of Africa,[23] all revolve around the difficulty of the countries of the Third World to compete successfully on the same scale with developed countries in the efficient use of long distance fishery fleets. Advanced maritime nations have superior technological, scientific and financial means for fishery exploitation. On the other hand, the developing countries wish to participate in the exploitation of fishery resources in the waters adjacent to their territories and thus to avail themselves of the living resources of these waters in order to promote the maximum development of their economies and to raise the living standards of their peoples.

All the above-mentioned declarations have urged the countries of the Third World to extend their national sovereignty or exclusive rights of jurisdiction over the maritime area adjacent to their coasts, its soil and subsoil to a distance of 200 nautical miles from the base line of the territorial sea. It is this impasse which the forthcoming United Nations Law of the Sea Conference will be called upon to resolve.

Although conservation is necessary in the development of a rational exploitation of the living resources of the sea, yet basically exclusive fishing zones, of whatever size, may not be an efficient method of conservation. Exclusive fishing zones may prove valueless if the stocks of fish are exhausted by activities outside the zones, while, if claims to such zones are substantial enough to conserve stocks, not only will this lead to loss of marine resources through under-utilisation, but they may also prove too much of a limitation on the major fishing fleets which have also a vital role to play in providing food for the world's ever-growing population.

A way out at the Third Law of the Sea Conference may be the adoption of the " Economic Zone Concept " put forward and discussed extensively at the Colombo meeting of the Asian-African Legal Consultative Committee in January 1971. This would have the advantage of safeguarding the economic interests of coastal States without interfering unduly with the rights of other States to enjoy the freedom of the high seas.[24]

Surprisingly even now, although the 1958 Geneva Convention has remained the only multilateral instrument of potential general application, resort to it has been infrequent. In practice, recourse has more often been had to the more particular agreements referred to in its first Article, some of which provide for the establishment of standing bodies to deal with questions of management and conservation.

(3) *Continental shelf and seabed resources*

Since 1958, technological and scientific progress has shown that exploration and exploitation can be carried out at depths considerably greater than the 200 metres which the International Law Commission and the Law of the Sea Conference in 1958 considered to be sufficient. For example, the continental shelf of Nigeria extends to a depth of 2,500 metres and seawards up to about 140 nautical miles at its widest point. A failure to take into account the pace of scientific progress may result in technologically equipped countries claiming vast areas of the ocean depths as part of their continental shelves, on the basis of their newly developed capacity to exploit those deeper areas.

Many problems therefore remain before the world community, including both developed and developing countries, in dealing with the seabed and the utilisation of its resources. Some of those questions are expected to be dealt with in 1974 by the Conference on the Law of the Sea, which will take up such issues as the establishment of an international seabed régime and the demarcation line between national and international waters. A clear and certain delimitation of national jurisdiction can, however, only be reached by the establishment of a rule of international law which is accepted by the overwhelming majority of States, *e.g.*, by agreements on a certain isobath or certain distance from the coast, or a combination of the two. Attempts to fix an outer limit to the national shelf area in this way deserve support.[25]

Ocean floor and subsoil of the seabed

The legal status of the seabed should not present any difficulty as there is general agreement that the ocean floor beyond national jurisdiction is governed by the same régime as the high seas. As a result it is subject to Article 2 of the Convention on the High Seas, by which no State may assert its sovereignty over any part of the high seas. The ocean floor and subsoil may therefore not be occupied by a State or otherwise subjected to national jurisdiction, either temporarily or permanently. It is *res communis*. *A fortiori* the natural resources of the ocean floor and the subsoil are the common heritage of mankind. This view has found expression in several resolutions of the General Assembly of the United Nations [26] and recently in the Declaration and Resolution of the Third Conference of Heads of State or Government of Non-aligned Countries at Lusaka in 1970.[27]

These resolutions have urged States to establish a universal and an equitable international régime for the use and exploitation of the seabed and ocean floor beyond the limits of national jurisdiction.

By Resolution 2467A (XXIII) of December 21, 1968, the General Assembly set up a Committee on the Peaceful Uses of the Seabed and Ocean Floor beyond the Limits of National Jurisdiction, composed of 42 members including Nigeria and some other countries of the Third World.[28] On the basis of the work of the Committee, including that of its Legal Sub-Committee, the General Assembly adopted under Resolution 2749 (XXV) of December 17, 1970, a Declaration of Principles Governing the Seabed and the Ocean Floor, and the Subsoil thereof, beyond the Limits of National Jurisdiction. In another resolution at the same time, the General Assembly decided to convene a Conference on the Law of the Sea.[29]

In addition to the work of the Committee on Peaceful Uses of the Seabed and the Ocean Floor, international conferences have been held at various levels to discuss the United Nations Law of the Sea Conference scheduled for 1974. Of particular importance is the contribution to the debate by countries of the Third World through the work of the Asian-African Legal Consultative Committee (AALCC). The AALCC held its 12th Session in Colombo in January 1971[30] and its 13th Session at Lagos in January 1972.[31]

Following on from the activities of the United Nations Committee earlier mentioned and the various regional conferences, an international convention of a universal character on the seabed régime, including appropriate machinery to give effect to its provisions, is being recommended to the forthcoming Santiago Conference. The aim will be the establishment of an international Seabed Authority to be brought into a special relationship with the United Nations and concerned with the establishment of basic rules for the development of seabed resources. If concluded, the convention would provide for an orderly and safe development of seabed resources, ensure an equitable sharing by all States in the benefits derived from such development, taking into particular consideration the interests and needs of the developing countries, whether land-locked or coastal. In other words all States will have a joint interest in the resources of the ocean floor which will entitle them to benefit in the proceeds of exploitation even though, in the case of countries of the Third World, they may not be able to contribute *pro rata* to the costs of exploration and exploitation. According to Ambassador Alfonso Arias Schreiber of Peru, the interests of the international community lie in promoting the economic and social development of less advanced countries and in reducing the existing imbalance between the rich and poor nations, because, without justice and welfare for everyone, there will hardly be peace and security for anyone.[32] It is a view with which this writer is in accord. It is evident, however, that a substantial body of new law will be required if progress is to be made towards the elaboration of the international régime in order to provide for the orderly development of the natural resources of the seabed and its subsoil.

(4) *Pollution*

We may finally turn to one problem which is of concern not only to the developed countries but also to countries of the Third World, namely, pollution. The problem of pollution is a transnational one, and an international endeavour is therefore necessary if the problem is to be solved adequately.

As a matter of necessity, every State has the obligation to take the necessary legislative and administrative measures to ensure that ships, installations and persons subject to its jurisdiction do not engage in activities which endanger the quality of the waters of the sea or the substance of its resources and, in particular, the marine environment in the neighbourhood of its territory which might disturb its ecological balance as well as the health and other interests of its population.[33]

Articles 24 and 25 of the Geneva Convention on the High Seas [34] already impose on States obligations to this effect. Article 24 of the High Seas Convention requires States to " draw up regulations to prevent pollution of the seas by the discharge of oil from ships or pipelines or resulting from exploitation and exploration of the seabed and its subsoil . . ."; Article 25 creates an obligation to take steps to prevent the contamination of the sea by dumping radioactive waste or other noxious substances.

The general nature of these provisions is scarcely sufficient to achieve the desired goal. They must be transformed into more specific obligations by means of international agreement and enforced by international control mechanisms. In the field of pollution, the Inter-Governmental Maritime Consultative Organisation (IMCO) has spearheaded the adoption of many conventions designed to prevent the discharge of oil at sea.

As a matter of urgency, international co-operation and control in these and other spheres will need to be greatly intensified if practical results are to be achieved. Unless this problem is tackled in a concerted manner the international community will again be faced with a situation where, as in other areas of ocean jurisdiction, initiative will be assumed by national authorities with the inevitable consequence of further extending national jurisdiction into the high seas. Two recent examples illustrate this attitude. Not long ago the Scientific Commission of Africa (SCA), an agency of the OAU, recommended that a zone of 212 miles earlier suggested as a territorial sea and contiguous zone for African countries should also be made into a non-pollution zone for Africa. And recently the United States protested vigorously over the Canadian Arctic Waters Pollution Prevention Act 1970,[35] which established a control zone 100 miles wide off the Canadian Arctic coast to prevent oil pollution of the sea in the course of oil transportation through the North-West Passage.[36]

Whatever international arrangements are made can only be successful if the primary and over-riding interest of the neighbouring coastal State is recognised by giving it jurisdiction to enforce such pollution legislation as may be enacted by it or by the international community. In this, the countries of the Third World share common concern and expectations in the elaboration of new doctrines on the international law of the sea. This is because they follow similar paths towards the consolidation of their political independence, economic and social development and raising the standard of living of their vast populations.

CONCLUSION

Countries of the Third World are of the view that it is futile to insist on freedom of the high seas while such freedom primarily benefits the developed nations, who have all the means to utilise such freedoms effectively. Freedom of any kind, they suggest, is meaningful only if there is equality of opportunity to make use of it. It is to be hoped, therefore, that any juridical régime or régimes created at Santiago in 1974 to alter the existing *status quo* will confer on the coastal peoples legitimate priority in the utilisation of the natural resources provided by their marine environment and take account of the geographical realities of the coastal States and the special needs and economic and social responsibilities of developing countries. It is only this that can ensure peace, equity and progress to all nations of the world. This position can be reached at Santiago in 1974 if claims to freedom of navigation by the leading maritime Powers and claims to exploitation of ocean resources by the developing countries are faced and reconciled.

REFERENCES

1. Third World here meaning Africa and Asia in the main, *i.e.*, newly emerging countries of the world, including the South American Republics.

2. See generally, G. M. Kahin, *The Asian-African Conference, Bandung, Indonesia, April 1955* (Cornell Univ. Press).

3. See generally, T. O. Elias, *Africa and the Development of International Law* (Sijthoff, 1972), Preface and Chap. 3.

4. No. 5 of 1967.

5. Decree No. 38 of 1971; Official Gazette of Nigeria, Suppl. Vol. 58, No. 44, Sept. 2, 1971, Part A; (1972) 11 Int.Leg.Mat. 154.

6. Law No. 17, 094-M 24 of Dec. 29, 1966.

7. Decree No. 5106 of Jan. 4, 1967.

8. The Ecuadorian Civil Code of Aug. 20, 1960, Registro Official No. 1202 of Aug. 20, 1960 (Supplement) and as amended by Decree No. 1542 of Nov. 10, 1966, published in Registro Official, No. 158, Nov. 11, 1966.

9. Decree No. 224/PRG of June 3, 1964.

10. For national legislation establishing these claims, see UN Legislative Series, Doc. ST/LEG/SER.B/15 of Apr. 1970.

11. See Message of the U.S. President to Congress on the Foreign Policy of the U.S. in the Seventies of Feb. 18, 1970 ((1970) 9 Int.Leg.Mat. 434–40) where he said: " As a result of our consultations we believe the time is right for the conclusion of a new international treaty fixing the limitation of the territorial sea at 12 miles, and providing for freedom of transit through and over international straits and carefully defined preferential fishing rights for coastal States on the high seas."

12. Report of the 13th Session of Asian-African Legal Consultative Committee, Lagos, 1972, p. 433. The 200 mile zone was to be followed by the internationally accepted contiguous zone of 12 miles.

13. Art. 2 (1) of the Geneva Convention on the High Seas, Apr. 29, 1958 (1963) U.N.T.S., Vol. 450, p. 11.

14. Art. 6 (1) of the Convention on Fishing and Conservation of the Living Resources of the High Seas (1966) U.N.T.S., Vol. 559, p. 285.

15. As *per* dissenting opinion of Judge Padilla Nervo in the Fisheries Jurisdiction (*U.K.* v. *Iceland*), Interim Protection, Order of Aug. 17, 1972 [1972] I.C.J.Rep. 12 at 23.

16. (1966) U.N.T.S., Vol. 581, p. 57; (1964) 3 Int.Leg.Mat. 476.

17. [1972] I.C.J.Rep. 12 at 23, 27.

18. For a general review of the present situation and trends, see the statement made by the FAO representative before the Committee on the Peaceful Uses of the Seabed and the Ocean Floor beyond the Limits of National Jurisdiction, Doc. A/AC.138/32.

19. Regulations concerning the Fishery Limits Off Iceland, July 14, 1972 ((1972) 11 Int.Leg.Mat. 1112); for the Icelandic Althing Resolution on Fisheries Jurisdiction, Feb. 15, 1972, see (1972) 11 Int.Leg.Mat. 643.

20. See dissenting opinion of Judge Padilla Nervo in the Fisheries Jurisdiction (*U.K.* v. *Iceland*), Interim Protection, Order of Aug. 17, 1972 [1972] I.C.J.Rep. 12, reported in (1972) 11 Int.Leg.Mat. 1073 at 1076.

21. Doc. CCM/RC/5 (1972), pp. 918–20; (1972) 11 Int.Leg.Mat. 892; (1972) 66 A.J.I.L. 918.

22. UN Press Release, NV/185 of June 9, 1970.

23. See Problem of Seabed and Fisheries Resources in Africa (Doc. CSA(71)3/6); Resolution of the Council of Ministers of OAU in its 16th Ordinary Session on Problem of Seabed (Doc. CM/Res.238 (xvi)); Resolution of the Council of Ministers of OAU in its 17th Ordinary Session on the Permanent Sovereignty of African Countries over their Fishery Resources off the Shores of Africa (Doc. CM/Res.250 (xvii)).

24. See *Report of Asian-African Legal Consultative Committee, 13th Sess. Lagos, 1972*, p. 369.

25. For text of U.S. suggestion of May 23, 1970, see (1970) 9 Int.Leg.Mat. 806–830.

26. G.A. Res. 2158 (XXI) of Nov. 26, 1966 (Y.U.N., 1966, p. 333); 2430 (XXII) of Dec. 18, 1967; 2467C (XXIII) of Dec. 21, 1968; 2602D (XXIV) of Dec. 15, 1969; 2574D (XXIV) of Dec. 15, 1969; 2749 (XXV) of Dec. 17, 1970 (UN Press Release No. GA/4355 (1971) 10 Int.Leg. Mat. 220). See for a reproduction of most of the above resolutions (1969) 8 Int.Leg.Mat. 201–208.

27. Lusaka Declaration of Sept. 8–10, 1970; Doc. NDC/CONF.3/RES.11 (1971) 10 Int.Leg.Mat. 215; see also the Lima Declaration of Latin American Countries of Aug. 4–8, 1970 (1971) 10 Int.Leg.Mat. 208.

28. See also Doc. A/RES/2667 (XXIII). The membership has now been enlarged to 86; see Doc. A/CN.4/245 of Apr. 23, 1971, p. 162.

29. Res. 2750 (XXV) of Dec. 17, 1970. Subjects and issues relating to the law of the sea prepared by the Committee is contained in the UN Doc. A/AC/138/66/Rev. 1.

30. Some of the topics discussed at Colombo include international machinery for the seabed, fisheries, archipelagoes, etc.

31. In Lagos seven topics were exhaustively discussed, these were: international machinery for the seabed, fisheries, economic zone, territorial sea and straits, regional arrangements, archipelagoes and the position of land-locked countries.

32. *Report of the 13th Sess. of the Asian-African Legal Consultative Committee*, p. 420.

33. For UN Resolution on Prevention of Marine Pollution, see Res. 2467B (XXIII) of Dec. 21, 1968; and for Res. 2566 (XXIV) of Dec. 13, 1969, see (1970) 9 Int.Leg.Mat. 424.

34. (1963) U.N.T.S. Vol. 450, p. 11.

35. 18 and 19 Eliz. 2, c. 47 (Can. 1970).

36. (1970) 9 Int.Leg.Mat. 543–552, 600–615. See *supra*, J.-Y. Morin, pp. 248–251.

Part IX

The United Nations and the European Economic Community

CHAPTER 27

The U.N. and the Law of the Sea

By Joyce A. C. Gutteridge *

INTRODUCTION

On December 17, 1970 the General Assembly of the United Nations decided, by a vote of 108 to seven with six abstentions, to convene a conference on the law of the sea:

> " which would deal with the establishment of an equitable international régime—including an international machinery—for the area and the resources of the sea-bed and the ocean floor, and the subsoil thereof, beyond the limits of national jurisdiction, a precise definition of the area, and a broad range of related issues including those concerning the régimes of the high seas, the continental shelf, the territorial sea (including the question of its breadth and the question of international straits) and contiguous zone, fishing and conservation of the living resources of the high seas (including the question of the preferential rights of coastal States), the preservation of the marine environment (including, *inter alia*, the prevention of pollution) and scientific research." [1†]

In the Resolution so adopted, the General Assembly expressed its consciousness that the problems of ocean space are interrelated and need to be considered as a whole.

This recognition that the problems of ocean space " form a unit that should be considered as a whole " [2] has resulted in the enlargement of the United Nations Committee on the Peaceful Uses of the Seabed and the Ocean Floor beyond the Limits of National Jurisdiction into what has become, in effect, a Preparatory Committee for the Conference on the Law of the Sea. Indeed, in the last two years some of its members have urged that its name should be changed to give a more realistic idea of its scope and terms of reference.

The Seabed Committee, as so enlarged, set up three Sub-Committees. Sub-Committee I was entrusted with the preparation of draft treaty articles embodying the international régime—including an international machinery—for the area and the resources of the seabed and the ocean floor, and the subsoil thereof beyond the limits of national jurisdiction.[3] Sub-Committee II was charged with the preparation of a comprehensive list of subjects and issues relating to the law of the sea which should be revised or developed, and the preparation of draft articles on such subjects and issues. Sub-Committee III was charged with considering the preservation of the marine environment (including the prevention of pollution) and scientific research, and with the preparation of draft articles thereon. Both of the first two Sub-Committees were

* This paper is based on a paper presented in the New York Conference (1972) of the International Law Association by the present writer as Chairman and Rapporteur of the British Branch Committee on Deep Sea Mining. She is therefore indebted to other members of that Committee for advice and suggestions.

† For references, see p. 330.

accorded the right to consider the question of the limits of the area beyond national jurisdiction, but it was agreed that the main Committee would take no decision on this matter until it had received the recommendations of Sub-Committee II on the definition of the area.[4]

The catalyst which produced the present movement towards a radical revision of the law of the sea was the tabling by Malta at the XXIInd Session of the United Nations General Assembly of an item which was inscribed on the agenda as " Examination of the question of the reservation exclusively for peaceful purposes of the seabed and the ocean floor, and the subsoil thereof, underlying the high seas beyond the limits of present national jurisdiction, and the use of their resources in the interests of mankind." On December 18, 1967, the General Assembly, after some preliminary consideration of this item, adopted a Resolution establishing, *inter alia*, an Ad Hoc Committee of 33 States " to study the scope and various aspects of this item." [5]

The Ad Hoc Committee held three sessions during the spring and summer of 1968, and established working groups on the economic and technical aspects and on the legal aspects, respectively. Substantially, its mandate was transferred by the General Assembly of the United Nations on December 21, 1968, to a permanent Committee composed of 42 States and entitled the Committee on the Peaceful Uses of the Seabed and the Ocean Floor beyond the Limits of National Jurisdiction.[6] The Seabed Committee (as it came to be known) held a number of further meetings in New York and in Geneva in 1969 and 1970. It established two Sub-Committees—the Economic and Technical Sub-Committee and the Legal Sub-Committee, both of which produced reports, and it also studied reports produced by the United Nations Secretariat under the Resolution of December 1967 and subsequent Resolutions of the General Assembly.[7] A number of working papers were tabled by delegations representing members of the Committee; one of the earliest of these was a draft convention introduced by the United States delegates at the 29th meeting of the Committee on August 3, 1970.[8] On the basis of the discussions which had taken place, and despite doubts and reservations expressed by some of its members, the Seabed Committee produced at the XXVth Session of the General Assembly a Declaration of Principles which was adopted by the General Assembly as Resolution 2749 (XXV). This Declaration, which was based on the concept of the seabed and the ocean floor beyond the limits of national jurisdiction as " the common heritage of mankind," disclosed certain areas of agreement, but left a number of questions, including the extent of the area beyond the limits of national jurisdiction, unresolved.

The debates in the Seabed Committee during 1969 and 1970 had, however, shown both the difficulty and the unfruitfulness of considering certain aspects of the Law of the Sea in isolation from other aspects. For instance, the question of the limits of national jurisdiction could not be raised without touching on such matters as the breadth of the territorial sea, the definition of the continental shelf, and the concept of the freedom of the high seas. It is therefore not surprising that the adoption of the General Assembly Resolution embodying the Declaration of Principles was immediately followed by the Resolution referred to at the beginning of this paper—Resolution 2750C (XXV)—which enlarged the Committee, extended its scope and mandate, and converted it, in effect, into the preparatory Committee for the Law of the Sea Conference which the same Resolution decided should be convened in 1973.

Resolution 2750C (XXV) expanded the membership of the Seabed Committee to 86. Under Resolution 2881 (XXVI) it was enlarged still further by the decision to add to its membership China and four other members to be appointed by the Chairman of the First Committee of the General Assembly. Fiji, Finland, Nicaragua and

Zambia have been so appointed. Since it was originally enlarged and its mandate broadened at the end of 1970, the Seabed Committee has, as already noted in the present paper, set up three Sub-Committees, and has considered a number of proposals —some of which are in the form of a draft convention or draft treaty articles— submitted by members of the Committee.[9] In March 1972, Sub-Committee I set up a working group to study the scope and basic provisions of an international seabed régime, and the first meetings of this working group were held during the Committee's summer session in 1972. The group have produced texts, illustrating areas of agreement and disagreement, drawn up during these meetings.[10] Sub-Committee II adopted " by acclamation " on August 18, 1972, a lengthy list of subjects and issues relating to the law of the sea which should be revised or developed.[11] A list drawn up privately during the 1972 spring session of the Committee by a group of developing States[12] formed the basis of subsequent negotiations which resulted in the list adopted at the end of the summer session. That list has 25 main items, most of which have a number of sub-items. The list is preceded by an explanatory note stating that " sponsorship or acceptance of the list does not prejudice the position of any State or commit any State with respect to the items on it or to the order, form or classification according to which they are presented." Sub-Committee III set up a working group on marine pollution during the Committee's summer session in 1972.[13] None of the three Sub-Committees has so far produced agreed proposals for treaty articles.

The Report of the Seabed Committee on its work in the spring and summer of 1972 was discussed by the First Committee of the United Nations General Assembly at its XXVIIth Session, particularly, during its later meetings, with a view to a decision being reached by the General Assembly as to the time and place at which the Law of the Sea Conference should be convened. A draft Resolution[14] submitted by the First Committee to the General Assembly in Plenary Session was unanimously adopted on December 18, 1972.[15]

The Resolution so adopted embodies *inter alia*, the following decisions. Two further sessions of the Seabed Committee were to be held in the spring and summer of 1973, and the Committee is to submit a report " with recommendations " to the General Assembly at its XXVIIIth Session. An organisational session of the Law of the Sea Conference is to be held in New York in November/December 1973; and the second session of the Conference, " for the purpose of dealing with substantive work " is to be convened at Santiago, Chile, in April/May 1974 for a period of eight weeks, with a possibility of further sessions if so decided by the Conference and approved by the General Assembly.

Before proceeding to a more detailed examination of some of the issues discussed by the Seabed Committee it is necessary to ask, and to try to answer, the question of why, little more than a decade after the adoption of the four 1958 Geneva Conventions on the Law of the Sea, a demand should have arisen in the United Nations for a radical reconsideration of the traditional law of the sea. In examining this question the following considerations appear to be relevant:

(1) *The adequacy of the 1958 Conventions.* During the discussions in the Seabed Committee many different views have emerged on the adequacy, or otherwise of the 1958 Conventions. There are, on the one hand, those States who, in general, support the established norms of international law and in particular, those contained in the 1958 Geneva Conventions. Among such States are to be found the Soviet Union and other Eastern European States who have argued, for instance, that the present approach to questions of the law of the sea " need not be fundamentally different from

the one underlying the Geneva Conventions " although, they concede, " the legal régime developed for the seabed must take account of scientific and technical progress." [16] At the other extreme are those States who hold that the principles set forth in the Geneva Conventions have served their purpose and should now " yield to the new aspirations of mankind." [17] In between are those who would not throw the 1958 Conventions completely overboard, but consider that "... a number of subjects would inevitably involve some change in the 1958 Conventions, and the changes required might be so substantial as to necessitate the drafting of an entirely new convention or conventions, at least with regard to fisheries." [18] Other States do not seek any significant departure from the existing rules set out in the Geneva Conventions, but consider that they are not sufficiently clear in certain respects; for example, Fiji is mainly interested in obtaining confirmation of the integration of the archipelagic principle in existing international law.[19]

(2) *The emergence of new States.* There has come into being since 1958 [20] " a large body of new national States inevitably concerned about their own sovereignty." [21] These new States are conscious of the fact that most of them had no share in drawing up the 1958 Geneva Conventions or in the development of the customary law of the sea. Dissatisfaction with the law of the sea as it stands has increased " particularly among States which have gained their independence since the signature of the 1958 Conventions," [22] and many, though not all, new States share the belief, expressed by Indonesia in Sub-Committee II, that " The freedoms mentioned in the 1958 Convention . . . are more advantageous for the developed maritime countries than for the developing countries." [23] A large number of these new States consider that they should have extensive jurisdiction over natural resources adjacent to their coasts and, whether coastal or land-locked States, claim a substantial share in the exploitation of resources lying beyond the limits of national jurisdiction. Such States believe that " The next Conference on the law of the sea will . . . provide the first opportunity for the developing countries of Asia, Africa and Latin America to mould an equitable and just system to govern the sea." [24]

(3) *Extensions of jurisdiction.* Even if a large number of new States had not emerged between the First Conference on the Law of the Sea in 1958 and the present time, the tendency towards an extension of jurisdiction for certain purposes, of which the 1958 Convention on the Continental Shelf is an example, would have continued. The question of an extension of fisheries jurisdiction which was raised at the 1958 and 1960 Conferences on the Law of the Sea was left unresolved by those Conferences. Consequently a number of States, including those who claimed only a three mile limit for their territorial waters, have since 1958 extended their fishery limits to 12 miles. The older States have preferred to do this in agreement with their neighbours and the latters' traditional fishing rights have been respected in the arrangements reached, for example, in the 1964 Fisheries Convention to which a number of European States are parties. Nevertheless, such agreed extensions have not normally exceeded 12 miles from the base lines from which the territorial sea is measured, and Iceland's unilateral decision to extend on September 1, 1972, its fishery limits to 50 miles has not gone unchallenged.[25]

There have, however, been other unilateral assertions of extended jurisdiction. For example, 10 of the Latin American States have for some time been committed to a limit of national jurisdiction of 200 nautical miles, although the legal character of these extended claims and the motives underlying them vary in different cases.[26] Some of these claims, for example, the claims of Peru and Ecuador to a territorial sea of 200 miles, have been made because the States concerned wish within that area to maintain an exclusive fishery jurisdiction. Other claims to a national jurisdiction of 200 miles are primarily directed to the resources of the seabed; for example those asserted by Brazil, Argentina and Uruguay.

Another example, although of a different type, of the assertion of extended jurisdiction for a specific purpose, is the unilateral action taken by Canada in enacting the Arctic Waters Pollution Act of 1970 by which jurisdiction to make and enforce measures against pollution was established up to a distance of 100 miles from every point of the Canadian coast north of the sixtieth parallel.

(4) *Advances in technology*. One of the reasons for which it is asserted that the 1958 Geneva Conventions are now out of date is that the principles embodied in them are "incompatible with recent technological developments."[27] Even though this statement cannot be accepted in full, it is undeniable that there have been since 1958 very rapid advances in technology which affect the marine environment and the exploitation of its living and mineral resources. This is particularly so in respect of the exploitation of the seabed and the subsoil thereof. At the Law of the Sea Conference in 1958, exploitation beyond a depth of 550 metres seemed to be unlikely in the immediately foreseeable future.[28] But in the last decade exploitation beyond this depth has become a possibility, and the fear that the largely unknown resources of the oceanic depths would be exploited only by, and for the benefit of, technologically developed States led to Malta's initiative in the General Assembly of the United Nations in 1967. This initiative was, however, also supported by developed States who considered that a régime governed only by the principle of the freedom of the high seas gave inadequate protection to high risk and high cost mining ventures beyond the limits of national jurisdiction.

It is not, however, the purpose of the present paper to examine in depth the factors which have led to the demand for a radical re-examination of the traditional law of the sea, but to indicate and examine certain trends which have emerged and developed during the discussions in the United Nations Seabed Committee during the last two years. In the second part of this paper these trends will be examined under the following headings:

A. The Territorial Sea (including the question of International Straits)
B. The Question of Fisheries
C. Special Jurisdiction
D. The International Régime for the Seabed outside the Limits of National Jurisdiction
E. Preservation of the Marine Environment (including the prevention of Pollution) and Scientific Research.

These headings are not scientific categories and to a lesser or greater extent the subject-matter overlaps, but they are convenient to describe the way in which discussion in the United Nations Seabed Committee has developed. Running through these discussions, like a connecting thread, is the theme of the limits of national jurisdiction.

PRESENT TRENDS

A. The Territorial Sea (including the Question of International Straits)

The breadth of the territorial sea

Since the failure of the 1960 Conference on the Law of the Sea to agree upon a uniform breadth for the territorial sea there have been a number of unilateral claims to limits of 12 miles and beyond. Recent figures show that over 50 States have claimed a territorial sea of 12 miles; 38 States are still claiming less than 12 miles; and 13 States have claimed more than 12 miles.[29] It has therefore been argued in the United Nations Seabed Committee that there can now be said " to be a sufficient international consensus of opinion for the 12 mile limit of the territorial sea to be regarded as a customary rule."[30]

Further support for a 12 mile limit for the territorial sea is to be found in two documents drawn up outside the United Nations in the summer of 1972, but now circulated as documents for the use of the Seabed Committee. These are the Declaration of Santo Domingo approved by representatives of the Caribbean States (including Mexico) on June 7, 1972[31]; and the Conclusions of the African States Regional Seminar held in Yaoundé from June 20–30, 1972.[32] The Declaration of Santo Domingo states that " The breadth of the territorial sea and the manner of its delimitation should be the subject of an international agreement, preferably of a world wide scope," but that in the meantime " Each State has the right to establish the breadth of its territorial sea up to a limit of 12 nautical miles to be measured from the applicable base line." The Yaoundé Conclusions state that " The Territorial Sea should not extend beyond a limit of 12 nautical miles."

During the discussions in the Seabed Committee many of its members have expressed their willingness to accept 12 miles as the breadth of the territorial sea, but some have stated that they are prepared to do so only if other conditions on which they insist are satisfied. The United States, which has long been an advocate of the three miles limit as a customary rule of international law, tabled with the Seabed Committee Draft Articles, the first of which would establish a maximum breadth of 12 miles for the territorial sea.[33] But, in introducing this proposal in Sub-Committee II on August 3, 1971, the United States delegate said that the United States Government was prepared to take into account the views of others and to agree to a treaty fixing the maximum breadth of the territorial sea at 12 nautical miles " if there was adequate agreement concerning international straits."[34] Other States would be prepared to accept a territorial sea of 12 miles if, but only if, their fisheries jurisdiction were adequately safeguarded. Iceland, which claims and is now attempting to enforce fishery limits of 50 miles, has said in the Seabed Committee that if fisheries jurisdiction were adequately safeguarded she would not consider a territorial sea of 12 miles to be an insurmountable obstacle.[35] Many members of the Seabed Committee now couple their willingness to accept a 12 mile territorial sea with their advocacy of an economic zone extending beyond the territorial sea. (See below.) For example, the paragraphs on the territorial sea in the Declaration of Santo Domingo, which have been referred to above, are followed by paragraphs relating to " an area adjacent to the territorial sea called the patrimonial sea," and the paragraph in the Yaoundé Conclusions about the territorial sea is immediately followed by a paragraph relating to " the right to establish beyond the territorial sea an Economic Zone."[36]

A few Latin American States still continue to maintain that " there is no juridical or logical basis for a 12 mile limit "[37] and claim that coastal States have the right " to establish unilaterally the extension of their sovereignty and jurisdiction on the basis of reasonable criteria, having due regard for geographical, geological and biological characteristics and the need for a rational exploitation of resources."[38] This view appears to have been shared by a few African States; for example, Sierra Leone and Guinea have declared, respectively, a 200 mile and a 130 mile territorial sea limit.[39] Support for those few States who advocate an extensive limit for the territorial sea itself has, however, been provided by a new member of the Seabed Committee. China, in a statement made in the United Nations General Assembly on November 15, 1971, said that " The Chinese Government and people resolutely support the struggle initiated by Latin American countries and peoples to defend their rights over the 200 mile territorial sea and to protect the resources of their respective countries." [40] More recently, the representative of China has said in Sub-Committee II of the Seabed Committee that " Every coastal State in the world [has] the right to define the extent of its territorial sea and to exercise its sovereign rights therein." [41]

It is, however, clear from the discussions in the Seabed Committee in recent months that those States which have, in the past, insisted on the control of navigation and over-flight beyond 12 miles are becoming relatively isolated, and that a large number of developing States will not be opposed to a territorial sea of a maximum breadth of 12 miles provided their resource-oriented claims to more extensive jurisdiction for certain purposes can be met.

Measurement of the territorial sea—Archipelagoes

In general, the principles relating to the measurement of the territorial sea which are embodied in the 1958 Geneva Convention on the Territorial Sea and the Contiguous Zone have not been questioned or re-opened in the Seabed Committee. But States, such as Indonesia and Fiji, which consist of islands forming an archipelago, have stressed " the unique geographical conditions of archipelago countries " and have claimed that such States have the right " to regard the waters between and around their islands as one single unit." [42] Representatives of such States have emphasised that the question of archipelagoes was never fully discussed at the 1958 and 1960 Law of the Sea Conferences. They claim that the principles enunciated in 1951 by the International Court of Justice in the *Anglo-Norwegian Fisheries Case*, and reflected in Article 4 of the above-mentioned Convention, can and should be extended to non-coastal archipelagoes.[43] They therefore advocate that in the case of such archipelagoes " base lines should be drawn round the outer extremity at low-water mark " of all islands in a group between which an intrinsic relationship can reasonably be deemed to exist, and that the limits of the territorial sea should be drawn outward of those base lines.[44]

The question of international straits

Closely connected with the question of the breadth of the territorial sea is the question of free transit through straits, particularly, though not exclusively, those connecting one part of the high seas with another. It has already been noted that the United States has made its willingness to accept a 12 mile limit for the territorial sea dependent on free transit through straits used for international navigation, and at the summer session of the Seabed Committee in 1972 the United States delegate re-affirmed that the objectives of the draft Articles tabled by the United States on August 3, 1971 [45] continued to constitute " basic elements of United States oceans policy." [46] At the same time as this re-affirmation was made the United States made further proposals (which are outlined below) designed " to alleviate the legitimate concern of coastal States regarding navigational safety " in international straits.[47]

The right of free transit through international straits is strongly upheld by other maritime States, including the United Kingdom, France and the Soviet Union. The last State has, however, in draft Articles which it has tabled[48] and in a statement made by its representative at the 1972 summer session of the Seabed Committee, drawn a distinction between " two categories of straits, each of which would be subject to a different legal régime." [49] The first category consists of straits lying off the major international routes and used by coastal States only. The status of such straits would be governed by rules relating to territorial waters, including the right of innocent passage. This régime, the Soviet representative stated, would also apply to " straits which connected a part of the high seas to the territorial waters of one or more States." [50] The second category of straits enumerated by the Soviet Union are " straits used by international shipping and of interest to all countries." In the case of such straits " the interests of the international community call for the application of a régime of free passage." [51] Although the Soviet definition of an international strait is narrower than that acceptable to the United States, both of these maritime Powers have rebutted the contentions voiced in the Seabed Committee that a régime of innocent passage would suffice for international straits. The Soviet representative has said that " . . . experience in recent years has shown that the régime of innocent passage [is] sometimes interpreted in different ways " [52]; and in very similar language the United States representative has said that the right of innocent passage provided for in the 1958 Convention is a " standard which could be abused if a coastal State interpreted it subjectively " and that it was therefore " inadequate when applied to international straits." [53]

The majority of developing States have not so far taken a public position on the question of straits. It has, however, been maintained by a few of them that the concept of free transit through straits would serve only the interests of the big maritime Powers. Malaysia and Indonesia have argued that what are sometimes called international straits are, in fact, national waters.[54] Tanzania has also recently expressed a similar opinion, and has stated that a strait is an " integral part of the territorial waters of a coastal State whose sovereignty must be fully safeguarded " and that " various regulations issued by States for their territorial waters . . . should . . . apply to straits." [55] Amongst older States, China has said that " straits lying within the coastal waters of a coastal State . . . are under the national authority of that State, even if they are used for international navigation." [56] Spain has also indicated strong opposition to the concept of free transit through straits, and has said that " Proposals for allowing free passage through straits were justified only by the political, military and strategic interests of a few States " and that " The proposals in question were still more serious with reference to the over-flying of straits by military aircraft." [57]

As already indicated, the United States has very recently sought " to alleviate the legitimate concern of coastal States regarding navigational safety in international straits," and has made proposals for this purpose. Under these proposals, the right of free transit in straits would be guaranteed by treaty, but the treaty would also provide for the mandatory observance by all surface ships of IMCO traffic separation schemes in straits, the observance of ICAO rules by State aircraft exercising free transit rights over straits, and strict liability for accidents caused by deviation from the relevant rules and regulations.[58] Both Spain and Tanzania have already objected to these proposals.[59]

Other States besides the Soviet Union have maintained that all straits cannot be treated alike, and that they should be defined more precisely.[60] Some States have suggested that there should be two different régimes for passage through international straits—one for straits which would be newly overlapped by territorial seas if the breadth of the latter were extended, and one for straits which are at present entirely territorial sea. One State, at least, would base entire freedom of passage on the width of the straits; Italy " would like to see a total lack of restrictions on the right of free passage of straits more than 24 miles wide." [61] Other States consider that straits which are the subjects of special multilateral treaties (*e.g.*, the Montreux Convention) are *sui generis*; and some States advocate that any straits to which special strategic considerations apply should continue to be treated as a special category.[62]

Some States (*e.g.*, Ethiopia) have seen a liberalisation of the principle of innocent passage as a possible alternative to absolute freedom of transit.[63] Without stating specifically that one was alternative to the other, the representative of Canada recently expressed in the Seabed Committee his belief that a consensus was emerging " on the need to modernise the traditional doctrine of innocent passage, both to protect the interests of coastal States and to safeguard the right of access from one area of the high sea to another." [64]

Another possibility that has been suggested in the Seabed Committee is that in straits traditionally used for international navigation coastal States should fix the limits of their territorial sea in such a way as to provide high seas corridors of sufficient width for free navigation.[65] This suggestion has, however, had little support, and the notion of such international corridors appears to some of the newer coastal States as likely to be " detrimental to the sovereignty of a coastal State." [66]

B. The Question of Fisheries

This question has two main aspects: one is exploitation rights, and the other is conservation. Neither of these aspects has, however, been considered separately in the United Nations Seabed Committee, and both have been used as arguments by States claiming more extensive jurisdiction. Furthermore, in recent months many of the developing States have tended to merge discussion of the question of fishery limits in discussion of proposals for the creation of an economic zone or patrimonial sea beyond the limits of the territorial sea. These proposals are considered below under the heading of " Special Jurisdiction," but that they cover living as well as non-living resources was foreshadowed in the summer of 1971 by the representative of Venezuela, who, introducing the concept of the patrimonial sea, said that in this sea " the coastal State would have exclusive fishery rights, as well as the right to explore and exploit the resources of the seabed and its subsoil."[67] Certain developing States have, moreover, made statements to the effect that it is vital to set up a limit of 200 miles for the conservation of fishery resources.[68]

The traditional concept of freedom of fishing on the high seas has been attacked in the Seabed Committee as lacking a rational basis, and conferring more benefit on rich and powerful countries than to poor countries.[69] Even those States which continue to support the concept of freedom of fishing on the high seas have recognised, in the words of the United Kingdom representative, that the problem is one of "striking a fair balance between the claims of individual States to an exclusive right to exploit the waters in the vicinity of their coasts, and the general freedom of all States to fish in the high seas."[70]

At the 1972 summer session of the Seabed Committee proposals designed to strike this fair balance were introduced by the United States representative, who tabled a revised Article on Fisheries.[71] He said that his Government were " more than ever committed to the species approach " and to international and regional fisheries organisations, but " had come round to the opinion that the coastal State should have the right to regulate the fish stocks inhabiting its coastal waters as well as its anadromous resources," *e.g.*, salmon, and " believed that inherent in that right was a preference in favour of the coastal State in the utilisation of such stocks."[72] However, he continued, " only international organisations could regulate highly migratory and truly oceanic stocks," *e.g.*, tuna.[73] A working paper on Management of the Living Resources of the Sea [74] tabled by Canada is based on a similar concept since it provides for different treatment of various fish stocks according to their biological character, including migratory habits.

The Soviet Union has submitted fishery proposals [75] which also envisage certain preferential rights for coastal States, but only if such States are developing countries, and with respect to coastal species only. The object of such preferential rights is stated to be to permit developing States to " make broad use of the high seas which are adjacent to them in the interests of their own countries and their national fishing industry."[76] It is therefore envisaged that developing States should be able, beyond a 12 mile territorial sea, to reserve for themselves such quantity of fish as their fishing vessels are able to catch, taking into account the growth of their fishing fleets.[77] The Soviet proposals are reflected in a Declaration on Principles of Rational Exploitation of the Living Resources of the Seas and Ocean in the Common Inteiests of all Peoples adopted at a Conference of Ministers of Eastern European States held at Moscow on July 6–7, 1972,[78] paragraph 5 of which refers to developing countries being given " certain preferential rights enabling them to develop their national fishing industry and overcome their technological backwardness." The Declaration also states (in paragraph 6) the belief that a solution to the problem of fisheries " can be found on the basis of a reasonable combination, through the international regulation of fishing, of the interests of coastal States and of countries which engage in long-distance fishing " and that such a solution cannot be found " by the adoption of unilateral measures by individual countries."

Japan has accorded some recognition of a greater role for coastal States. Her representative in the Seabed Committee stated that she would be prepared to recognise as a general principle that developing coastal States should be entitled, in the waters adjacent to a 12 mile limit from the coast, to preferential fishing rights.[79] This concept of preferential rights for developing coastal States is now embodied in a working paper tabled by Japan in the Seabed Committee, which also contemplates some very limited preferences for developed States in their coastal fisheries.[80]

As mentioned above, the developing States have not, in general, made separate proposals in respect of fisheries or fishery limits since many of them favour the creation of an economic zone adjacent to the territorial sea in which the coastal State would have, *inter alia*, exclusive fishery rights. But some of the land-locked States or States with a restricted coastline do not view with equanimity the concept of a 200 mile exclusive fishery zone since they would " have to go much further afield to fish " if such exclusive zones were created.[81] To meet this difficulty some of the States which are in favour of the concept of an economic zone have suggested a policy of co-operation for the development of regional fisheries; this is, for instance, one of the suggestions made in the Yaoundé Conclusions.[82]

In a Working Paper tabled in the Seabed Committee [83] Canada recognises the coastal State's " special interest in and responsibility for the conservation of the living resources of the sea adjacent to its coast," and envisages that it " would have the authority required to manage those resources in a manner consistent with its special interest and responsibility, as well as preferential rights in the harvest of such resources." This Working Paper develops ideas outlined by the Canadian representative in Sub-Committee II at an earlier stage when he said that Canada envisaged that " . . . the coastal State would assume responsibility, as custodian for the international community, for the conservation and management of free-swimming fishery resources far beyond the limits of exclusive national jurisdiction " but that " the system would not include the exclusive right to exploit those species, although provision would be made for according preferential rights to the coastal States in recognition of their admitted special interest."[84]

A joint Working Paper tabled by Australia and New Zealand[85] similarly envisages the coastal State having exclusive jurisdiction over the living resources of the sea in an adequately wide zone of the high seas adjacent to its territorial sea, and that it will be the responsibility of the coastal State " to provide proper management and utilisation of the living resources within its zone of exclusive jurisdiction." The Working Paper does not suggest any specific limit to this fishery zone but in a statement in the Seabed Committee relating to the joint Working Paper the representative of New Zealand said that such a zone might form part of a more general economic zone.[86]

The joint Working Paper tabled by Australia and New Zealand indicates (as does the Canadian Working Paper) that the concept of coastal State jurisdiction does not preclude a role for international fishery commissions, which might be either global or regional in nature.

The role of international fishery commissions in any future régime for fisheries has been stressed by the representatives of other States in the Seabed Committee. As already mentioned, the latest United States proposals contemplate international arrangements for highly migratory species, such as tuna. The United Kingdom representative in the Seabed Committee has said that " A regulatory power should be granted to regional commissions on which all States with an interest in the fisheries would be represented."[87] Norway had advocated the strengthening of the scope and power of regional fisheries.[88]

Whilst welcoming the recognition in recent Working Papers that it is the coastal State that has the greatest interest in conserving coastal fish resources, Iceland does not consider that either the United States or Canadian proposals go far enough in their present form to be acceptable. Iceland has stated in the Seabed Committee its belief that there is no reason why the same fishery limits should be applied everywhere. Iceland has reiterated in the Seabed Committee its contention that what it claims to be its geographical continental shelf area—an area to a distance of 50 to 70 miles from the coast—constitutes the national fishery limits of Iceland. Iceland has also recently claimed that many States are " prepared to follow Iceland, Nigeria, Oman and Senegal in the adoption of legislation to extend their fishery limits."[89] The Icelandic view that fishery limits can be unilaterally decided is not, however, supported by many States. Many would agree with the opinion expressed by India that for each State to be conceded the right to decide its own fishery limits " would contain the seeds of future conflict."[90]

C. Special Jurisdiction

A number of proposals have been put forward in the Seabed Committee for special coastal State jurisdiction beyond the limits of the territorial sea. In the context of these proposals there arise two questions which are closely linked: (i) the extent of such jurisdiction; (ii) the content of that jurisdiction.

Before the mandate of the Seabed Committee was enlarged at the end of 1970, the question of special coastal State jurisdiction was considered only in the context of exploitation of the natural resources of the seabed. What was then envisaged was the establishment of a boundary between those areas of the seabed in which coastal States already enjoyed sovereign rights for the purposes of exploration and exploitation of the natural resources of the continental shelf and those areas of the seabed which would be subject to a new international régime. In this context the judgment of the International Court of Justice in the *North Sea Cases* was referred to by Canada and other members of the Seabed Committee as making it clear that the rights of coastal States over the continental shelf arise by virtue of the fact that the shelf is an extension of their land mass.[91]

In the same context the question of amending the open-ended definition of the continental shelf in Article 1 of the 1958 Convention on the Continental Shelf was also discussed.[92] It was felt by some members of the Committee that it would be unnecessary and unwise to amend this definition, since to do so would prejudice the existing rights of coastal States.[93] Suggestions for a new definition of the continental shelf were, however, made. For example, the representative of Uruguay, whilst preferring the maintenance of the existing open-ended definition, said that if there were a new definition of the continental shelf, this should include not only the seabed as far as the 200 metre isobath, but also the continental shelf beyond that isobath, and that the 2,500 metre isobath (corresponding to the base of the continental slope) should be adopted as the outer limit of the continental shelf.[94]

At the present time, there seems to be a general consensus in the Seabed Committee that coastal States should retain existing sovereign rights in respect of the seabed as far as the 200 metre isobath. For the limit of the boundary between areas subject to national jurisdiction and the international seabed area, various possibilities have been suggested,[95] but none of them have met with general acceptance.

When the mandate of the Seabed Committee was enlarged, the question of special coastal State jurisdiction was no longer confined to the resources of the seabed and the subsoil thereof; it also arose, as has already been indicated, in the context of fisheries jurisdiction. A number of States represented in the Committee considered that there should be a zone adjacent to the territorial sea in which the coastal State should have exclusive fisheries jurisdiction, and at an early stage in the discussions a limit of 200 miles was suggested by some members of the Committee as the extent of that zone.

At the 1971 summer session of the Seabed Committee Venezuela introduced a compromise proposal[96] the elements of which were:

(1) a territorial sea under the exclusive sovereignty and jurisdiction of the coastal State " with a reasonable width of, say, 12 miles."
(2) maintenance of the existing rights of coastal States in respect of continental shelves up to the 200 metre isobath;
(3) an economic zone (referred to by Venezuela as " the patrimonial sea ") of not more than 200 miles measured from the base line of the territorial sea, in which there would be freedom of navigation and overflight, but in which the coastal State would have an exclusive right to all resources.

The Venezuelan proposal immediately attracted a good deal of support from African, Latin American and Caribbean States. At the 1972 summer session of the Seabed Committee, Kenya tabled draft Articles on the concept of an exclusive economic zone.[97] The second of these draft Articles provides that coastal States shall " have the right to establish an Economic Zone beyond the territorial sea for the primary benefit of their peoples and their respective economies in which they shall exercise sovereign rights over natural resources for the purposes of exploration and exploitation," and that within this zone " they shall have exclusive jurisdiction for the purpose of control, regulation and exploitation of both living and non-living resources of the Zone and their preservation, and for the purpose of prevention and control of pollution." A later Article provides that " Economic Zone shall not, in any case, exceed 200 nautical miles measured from the base lines used for determining the territorial sea." This latest proposal for the establishment of an economic zone beyond the territorial sea has been supported by India and a number of other States, including Iceland.[98] Mexico has, in particular, welcomed the similarity between Kenya's proposal and the Santo Domingo Declaration.[99] Both contemplate a 12 mile territorial sea with an exclusive resource zone extending to 200 miles, but there are certain differences between them. In particular, the Santo Domingo Declaration appears to contemplate the possibility of extending national jurisdiction to embrace the entire continental margin, with the result that sovereign rights could be claimed beyond 200 miles; Kenya, on the other hand, would limit the coastal State's resource jurisdiction for all purposes to 200 miles, and the draft Articles contemplate some types of preference for other States in the same region. The Yaoundé Conclusions [100] also support the concept of an economic zone within which coastal States would have exclusive jurisdiction for the purpose of control regulation and national exploitation of the living resources of the sea, and for the purposes of the prevention and control of pollution. It is also contemplated that the exploitation of the living resources within the economic zone should be open on a regional basis to " land-locked and near land-locked States."

In general, the proposals for an economic zone seem to contain the seeds of a possible compromise. The discussions in the Seabed Committee have shown that the majority of the developing States represented there would be content with a territorial sea of 12 miles if their economic needs, particularly in relation to fisheries, were safeguarded. But the discussions in the Seabed Committee have also shown a recognition by older and developed States that where extensive jurisdictional claims have been made these have, for the most part, been resource oriented; the proposals for the establishment of an economic zone therefore go some way to meet anxieties older States have expressed over so-called " creeping jurisdiction " by specifically limiting the jurisdiction of the coastal State in the economic zone and by recognising that the establishment of a limit for the territorial sea is a separate issue from the establishment of limits for the exercise by coastal States of other and lesser forms of jurisdiction.

The approach of some of the older States to the concept of an economic zone is still, however, a cautious one even if the concept is given a qualified blessing. At the summer meeting of the Seabed Committee in 1972 the representative of the United States said that his Government could not agree " to any type of economic zone that does not accommodate its basic interests," but that " in order to promote agreement " they would " be prepared to accept the principle that coastal States should have broad jurisdiction over adjacent waters and seabed areas beyond the territorial sea as part of an over-all law of the sea settlement." He added that such jurisdiction should be limited by international standards which would protect the interests of other States and those of the international community.[101]

The Soviet Union sees at least some objections to the concept of an economic zone. Speaking in the context of fisheries the representative of the Soviet Union in the Seabed Committee has said that proposals for establishing such a zone " would give the coastal State the possibility of exploiting the resources of the high seas as it saw fit and at will over vast tracts adjacent to its territorial waters without considering the interests of other countries." [102] On the other hand, the concept of the economic zone was regarded by the representative of Uruguay as too limited, since it is " based solely on economic and conservational grounds and ignores factors of a political and security nature." [103]

During the discussions in the Seabed Committee, extensive limits for the purposes of resource jurisdiction have been opposed by a number of land-locked and near land-locked States. Land-locked States have, on various occasions, affirmed that any extension of the limits of national jurisdiction would have the effect of moving them even further from the sea,[104] and in the context of seabed resources land-locked and near land-locked States have favoured the narrowest possible limits of national jurisdiction so as to give the international régime, from which they would benefit, the largest possible area. In a Working Paper [105] sponsored by Afghanistan, Austria, Belgium, Hungary, Nepal, the Netherlands and Singapore, it was proposed that the seabed and subsoil outside the territorial sea and lying either beyond the 200 metre isobath or beyond a distance of 40 miles measured from the territorial sea, according to the choice made by any particular State, should constitute the international seabed area.

There have, however, been indications that regional arrangements might be made which would accommodate the interests of land-locked and near land-locked States. For example, Venezuela suggested in the Seabed Committee that it might be " appropriate to consider a compensatory system for the land-locked developing States within a regional framework," *e.g.*, part of the resources extracted from the area of the patrimonial sea belonging to other States might be paid into a fund for the development of the land-locked countries in the same continent. As has already been seen, the Yaoundé Conclusions contemplate assistance to land-locked and near land-locked States on a regional basis, and Article VII of the draft Articles tabled by Kenya says that in fixing the limits of the economic zone, up to a maximum of 200 nautical miles, " the rights and interests of developing land-locked, near land-locked, shelf-locked States and States with narrow shelves shall be taken into consideration." [106]

In the context of special jurisdiction the emergence of the concept of the economic zone is of great importance. As has already been noted, it may contain within itself the seeds of a possible compromise. It has attracted support which was denied to proposals for the establishment of an intermediate zone which would have been part of the international area, but in which the coastal State would have acted as agent or trustee for the international community and would have exercised certain powers and enjoyed certain preferential rights; *e.g.*, the proposal in the United States draft convention for the establishment of a trusteeship zone between the 200 metre isobath and the end of the continental margin.[107]

The trend in favour of the concept of an economic zone beyond the territorial sea, and extending to a limit of 200 miles from the base lines from which the territorial sea is measured, is in no way affected by the adoption on December 18, 1972 by the United Nations General Assembly of a Resolution [108] proposed by the land-locked and shelf-locked States which requests the Secretary-General of the United Nations to prepare " a comparative study of the extent and the economic significance, in terms of resources, of the international area that would result from each of the various proposals on limits of national jurisdiction " presented to the Seabed Committee. A large number of member States abstained from voting on this Resolution, and a counter-Resolution, proposed by Peru, requesting the Secretary-General to prepare in connection with the above-mentioned study " a comparative study of the potential economic significance for riparian States, in terms of resources " of the same proposals was carried by a large majority.[109]

D. The International Régime for the Seabed beyond the Limits of National Jurisdiction

As has been made clear in the preceding section of the present paper, no agreement has been reached in the Seabed Committee on what should constitute the limits of national jurisdiction, although many States now favour the establishment of an economic zone with a maximum breadth of 200 miles from the base lines from which the territorial sea is measured. That the nature of the international régime must, at least to some extent, be dependent on the limits of national jurisdiction has been emphasised in the Seabed Committee, and the representative of Poland has recently said in the First Committee of the United Nations General Assembly that a situation might arise " in which all, or almost all, mineral resources that could be exploited in the coming decades would come under the jurisdiction of coastal States " and that in such a situation " the usefulness of establishing an international organisation, with wide powers and responsibilities, could be questionable." [110]

It is therefore not surprising that more progress has been made toward broad general principles governing the seabed and the ocean floor beyond the limits of national jurisdiction than in drawing up detailed provisions on the machinery required for regulating the international régime. As already mentioned at the beginning of the present paper, the General Assembly adopted at its XXVth Session a Declaration of Principles Governing the Seabed and the Ocean Floor and the Subsoil Thereof beyond the Limits of National Jurisdiction [111] and Sub-Committee I of the Seabed Committee has set up a Working Party charged with the task of preparing draft Articles on the " Status, scope and basic provisions of the régime, based on the Declaration of Principles." At present the draft contains a number of alternative provisions [112] and reflects different approaches to the nature of the régime which have been disclosed during the discussions in the Seabed Committee.

It would seem, however, that there is broad agreement on the following:

(a) some area of the seabed, no matter how defined, exists over which no State should claim sovereignty, sovereign rights, or special jurisdiction;
(b) some international agency, whether a licensing authority or an operating agency should be created with at least some power over the seabed beyond the limits of national jurisdiction;
(c) some revenue from the resources of some part of the ocean floor should be shared with, or devoted to the needs of the developing countries.[113]

Beyond these broad areas of agreement, many differences still exist, in particular in regard to the nature, powers and functions of the Authority which would be set up by the treaty instituting the international régime for the purpose of administering it to a greater or less extent.

Nature, powers and functions of the Authority

At one end of the spectrum there are a few States which envisage the Authority as being, ultimately at least, in complete control of the exploration and exploitation of all natural resources of the ocean and its seabed outside the limits of national jurisdiction. This approach is the one indicated in the draft Ocean Space Treaty tabled by Malta.[114] In its most extreme form it has been criticised as likely to be " some kind of super-agency with powers surpassing the combined powers of the Security Council, IMCO, ICAO, WHO, WMO, ITU, GATT and IAEA." [115]

In a rather less extreme form, the concept of an Authority with wide powers has been supported by a number of developing States. It should be set up, it has been said, as " a subject of international law to represent mankind," [116] and to it would be entrusted the exploration, exploitation and marketing of seabed resources. For this purpose, it should be as powerful as possible.[117] Chile, for example, considers that " the international authority should be granted jurisdiction over both the area and its resources " and has said that jurisdiction over the area would signify " that the authority should control the whole economic process—exploration, exploitation and marketing of resources and distribution of profits—and be given power to exploit directly." [118] China would, apparently, also favour an Authority with wide powers, since it contemplates common ownership "by all the peoples of the world" of the seabed area situated beyond the limits of national jurisdiction and its resources.[119]

The concept of an Authority with wide powers is reflected in a Working Paper tabled by a number of Latin American States [120]; this contemplates, *inter alia*, that the Authority would be able to enter into service contracts with other enterprises or itself establish "companies" to exploit the resources of the seabed. Some States (*e.g.*, Brazil) also envisage that the Authority would be empowered to co-ordinate and even to undertake activities relating to scientific research and exploration.[121]

A number of Afro-Asian States have also expressed themselves as being "in favour of a strong machinery with exclusive powers over all activities in the area beyond national jurisdiction." [122] They have, however, shown some flexibility: Sri Lanka, for example, envisages the principal activities of the Authority as "the exploration and exploitation of the seabed . . . on its own or through contractors or appropriately negotiated joint ventures, or a combination of these methods, as well as to regulate, supervise and control such exploration by others through a system of licensing." [123]

Developed States, with experience of the cost of exploration and exploitation have, however, pointed out that an Authority with the wide powers envisaged would entail a great financial burden, which would diminish the resources conceived of as the common heritage of mankind. Such States, for example, as the United Kingdom have stressed the enormous cost of an operational organisation,[124] others, for instance Japan, while endorsing this, have particularly stressed that direct operations would involve a very large staff of technicians, engineers and accountants! [125] Such States, therefore, envisage an Authority with certain regulatory powers, and the power to issue licences to States for exploration and exploitation in accordance with criteria laid down in the treaty instituting the régime. In general, they consider that licences should be issued only to States who might then issue sub-licences to contractors. It has also been suggested that there might possibly be two types of licence—a general non-exclusive exploration licence and an exclusive exploitation and exploration licence.[126]

A number of Latin American States have expressed themselves as against the powers of the Authority being restricted to mere co-ordination and the granting of licences.[127] This, they claim, would enable the same few countries to continue with their old activities and give the common heritage to private interests and the highly developed countries.[128] This view of the matter appears to overlook the actual proposals for licensing made, for instance, in the United Kingdom Working Paper,[129] which envisages a quota system which has been recognised by the representative of a developing State in Asia as intended "to help the developing countries participate in and profit from seabed exploitation."[130] Under this system, it has been suggested by the United Kingdom representative in the Seabed Committee, larger quotas might be given to poorer States.

The importance of some equitable system of licensing is underlined by the fact that there are States which consider that the Authority should ultimately undertake exploration and exploitation activities, either on its own or as joint ventures, but that meanwhile it should be empowered to issue licences for the exploration and exploitation of the seabed directly to States.[131] However, Kuwait, which regards licensing as one of the major functions of the Authority in the initial stages, considers that licences should not be granted to States or to groups of States but to physical and juridical persons.[132]

E. Preservation of the Marine Environment (including the Prevention of Pollution) and Scientific Research

As has already been noted, Sub-Committee III of the Seabed Committee is charged with consideration of these questions and with the preparation of draft treaty articles relating to them.

Progress in this Sub-Committee was slow at the beginning; most of its members appeared to be awaiting the results of the Stockholm Conference on the Human Environment. The Conference produced, *inter alia*, a Declaration containing a number of Principles for the Preservation of the Marine Environment, and under its Action Plan invited States " to co-operate in the appropriate international forums in ensuring that seabed exploration and exploitation activities beyond the limits of national jurisdiction should not result in pollution to the marine environment." This invitation was communicated to Sub-Committee III, and there was general agreement that the basic legal principles concerning marine pollution which could be drawn from the conclusions of the Stockholm Conference could form a basis for general treaty Articles. There was also general agreement with the view expressed by the United States representative that the question of pollution from exploration and exploitation of the seabed " could scarcely be considered separately from the other elements of the seabed régime " and should be considered by Sub-Committee I.[133] At its 23rd meeting on July 28, 1972, the Sub-Committee decided to set up a working group on marine pollution whose function it will be to draft texts leading to the formulation of draft treaty articles on the preservation of the marine environment and the prevention of marine pollution. The Working Group invited members of the Sub-Committee to submit written observations and draft treaty Articles by, at latest, January 15, 1973. In the discussions in the Sub-Committee it has been stressed that it is not the function of the Working Group or the Sub-Committee itself to draft technical provisions, and the importance of co-operation with other organisations concerned with the preservation of the marine environment (*e.g.*, IMCO) has been stressed.

The Sub-Committee has received from some of its members working papers and draft resolutions relating to the prevention and control of marine pollution, *e.g.*, a Working Paper submitted by Canada on the preservation of the marine environment[134] designed, *inter alia*, to focus the work of the working group on marine pollution, and a draft resolution on preliminary measures to prevent and control marine pollution tabled by Australia, Bulgaria, Canada, Greece, Iceland, the Netherlands, Norway, Sweden, the Ukraine and the U.S.S.R.[135]

Sub-Committee III also considered the question of scientific research at its 1972 summer session. Views were divided as to the extent to which there could be freedom of scientific research. Mexico expressed the view that " within the patrimonial sea or exclusive economic area the coastal State must be able if it wishes to control all scientific research."[136] A more balanced view was expressed in a Working Paper on Marine Scientific Research Principles tabled by Canada, and commended by Brazil and Japan.[137] In introducing this paper the Canadian representative said that " the rights of coastal States were emphasised, but it was also stressed that all States, whether coastal or not, had the right to conduct or authorise scientific research in the marine environment."[138]

A joint working paper, relating mainly to research on the high seas, was submitted by the U.S.S.R., the Ukraine and Bulgaria.[139] Although it contemplates assistance in promoting the research capabilities of developing and land-locked countries, it was stigmatised as " reactionary " by the representative of Colombia, who also said that

" an international authority would be the ideal place for the preparation and implementation of a world policy of marine scientific research." [140] The United Kingdom representative said that he did not consider that the functions of the international authority should include research programmes,[141] as appeared to be contemplated in one of the draft articles set out in a Latin American working paper.[142] The United Kingdom representative also suggested that on all questions relating to scientific research the international seabed authority should look to existing institutions (such as the IOC) for advice; this view was concurred in by the representative of Bulgaria.

CONCLUSIONS

Although all of the closely inter-related issues which have been discussed by the Seabed Committee are of great legal significance, the problem of reaching agreed solutions is one of a political nature. As the representative of the United States emphasised in the First Committee of the General Assembly in the autumn of 1972, " hard political decisions " will be necessary " for an overall accommodation of interests on the law of the sea." [143] The process of reaching such decisions has now, perhaps, begun. Discussions at the summer session of the Seabed Committee in 1972 were of a more constructive nature, and the Chairman of the Seabed Committee stated in the First Committee during the autumn session of the General Assembly his belief that " while much preparatory work still remains to be done, a compromise on the basic issues is definitely within reach." He added that " When this compromise has been worked out . . . the process of drafting treaty Articles should not be a matter of insuperable difficulty." [144]

Whether these hopes will materialise will depend on what progress is made at the two further sessions of the Seabed Committee which—under operative paragraph 2 of the Resolution adopted by the General Assembly at the close of its XXVIIth Session [145] —were held in the spring and summer of 1973 with a view to completing the preparatory work for the Law of the Sea Conference. If the progress made in the Seabed Committee in 1973 is not substantial, it would seem that the Conference, or at least its first substantive session which—under operative paragraph 4 of the same Resolution —is to be held at Santiago, Chile in April/May, 1974 may have to be further postponed.

REFERENCES

1. G.A. Res. 2750C (XXV).
2. The words quoted are from a statement by Mr. Amerasinghe, Chairman of the Seabed Committee, at a meeting of the First Committee of the General Assembly—A/C1/PV 1843, p. 16.
3. On Mar. 27, 1972 the Chairman of Sub-Committee I announced the composition of a 33 member working group to study the scope and basic provisions of an international seabed régime—A/AC.138/SC.I/SR.44, p. 1.
4. A/AC.138/SR.66, p. 1.
5. G.A. Res. 2340 (XXII).
6. G.A. Res. 2467 (XXIII).
7. G.A. Res. 2467 (XXIII); 2574 (XXIV).
8. A/AC.138/25.

9. A comparative table (A/AC.138/L.10) prepared by the UN Secretariat and distributed on Jan. 28, 1972 listed 12 such documents and referred to a thirteenth consisting of draft articles on the breadth of the territorial sea, straits and fisheries submitted to Sub-Committee II by the U.S.A. Since that date a number of other documents have been tabled.

10. These texts are reproduced in the Seabed Committee's Report to the General Assembly—A/8721—at pp. 81–108.

11. For the list so adopted, see A/8721, pp. 5–8.

12. A/AC.138/66. Earlier lists were tabled by Bulgaria (A/AC.138/45); Norway (A/AC. 138/52); Latin American States and Spain (A/AC.138/56); Afro-Asian States and Yugoslavia (A/AC.138/58).

13. A/AC.138/SC.III/SR.29, p. 25.

14. A/C1/L.634.

15. G.A. Res. 3029A (XXVII)—A/PV.2114, p. 38.

16. A/AC.138/SC.II/SR.32, p. 10 (Soviet delegate); A/AC.138/SC.I/SR.37, p. 3 (Czechoslovakian delegate).

17. A/AC.138/SR.73, p. 2 (Nicaraguan delegate).

18. A/AC.138/SC.II/SR.19, p. 6 (Maltese delegate).

19. A/AC.138/SR.62, p. 6 and A/AC.138/SR.73, pp. 4–5.

20. At the 1958 Conference 86 States were present, of whom 47 might be classified as developing States (21 Asian States; six African States; and 20 Latin American States).

21. R. Y. Jennings, " A Changing International Law of the Sea," (1972 B) 31 *Cambridge Law Journal* 48.

22. Statement by Maltese delegate—A/AC.138/SR.83, p. 2.

23. A/AC.138/SC.II/SR.12, p. 12.

24. Statement by the delegate of Kenya in the First Committee of the UN—A/C1/PV. 1903, pp. 48–50.

25. On Apr. 14, 1972 the U.K. Government filed with the International Court of Justice an Application instituting proceedings against Iceland. On June 5, 1972 the Government of the Federal Republic of Germany filed a similar Application. On Aug. 17, 1972 the Court issued two Orders indicating interim measures of protection in the *Fisheries Jurisdiction Cases* so instituted. On Feb. 2, 1973 the Court found, in each of these cases, that it had jurisdiction to entertain the Applications and to deal with the merits of the dispute.

26. A/AC.138/50.

27. A/AC.138/SR.80, p. 6—statement by the delegate of Ecuador.

28. This depth was proposed by the Indian delegation in the Fourth Committee of the Conference—A/CONF/13/C4/L29 (Rev. 1)—as part of a definition of the continental shelf designed to substitute a depth criterion alone for the combination of depth and exploitability in the International Law Commission's draft article.

29. A/AC.138/50.

30. Statement by the representative of Mexico—A/AC.138/SC.II/SR.11, p. 7.

31. A/AC.138/80.

32. A/AC.138/79.

33. A/AC.138/SC.II/L.4 and Corr. 1.

34. A/AC.138/SC.II/SR.8, p. 2.

35. A/AC.138/SC.II/SR.9, p. 2.

36. A/AC.138/80, p. 4; A/AC.138/79, p. 1.

37. Statement by the delegate of Ecuador at the 1972 summer session of the Seabed Committee—A/AC.138/SR.80, p. 3.

38. A/AC.138/SC.II/SR.16, p. 8.

39. A/AC.138/50.

40. A/PV.1983, p. 97.

41. A/AC.138/SC.II/SR.36, p. 2.

42. A/C1/PV.1906, p. 16.

43. A/AC.138/SR.62, p. 6.

44. A/AC.138/SR.73, pp. 4–5.

45. A/AC.138/SC.II/L.4 and Corr. 1.

46. A/AC.138/SC.II/SR.37, p. 2.

47. A/AC.138/SC.II/SR.43, p. 10.

48. A/AC.138/SC.II/L.7.

49. A/AC.138/SR.83, p. 26.
50. A/AC.138/SR.83, p. 27. This proposal, if accepted, would exclude from the right of free transit such waters as the Straits of Tiran, and would, in effect, partially abrogate Art. 16 (4) of the 1958 Convention on the Territorial Sea and the Contiguous Zone which provides that " There shall be no suspension of the innocent passage of foreign ships through straits which are used for international navigation between one part of the high seas and another part of the high seas *or the territorial sea of a foreign State*." (Emphasis supplied.)
51. A/AC.138/SR.83, p. 26.
52. A/AC.138/SR.83, p. 28.
53. A/AC.138/SC.II/SR.43, p. 10.
54. A/AC.138/SC.II/SR.11, p. 2 (Malaysia); A/AC.138/SC.II/SR.31, p. 19 (Indonesia).
55. A/AC.138/SC.II/SR.40, pp. 4–5.
56. A/AC.138/SC.II/SR.36, pp. 2 and 4.
57. A/AC.138/SC.II/SR.42, p. 2.
58. A/AC.138/SC.II/SR.37, pp. 2–3.
59. A/AC.138/SC.II/SR.40, p. 5 (Tanzania); A/AC.138/SC.II/SR.42, p. 2 (Spain).
60. This suggestion has, for instance, been made by the Canadian delegate who would also like to see improved the definition of what coastal States are or are not entitled to do in the straits so defined—A/AC.138/SR.63, p. 12.
61. A/AC.138/SC.II/SR.15, p. 9.
62. See, for instance, statement by the Australian delegate—A/AC.138/SC.II/SR.15, pp. 7–8.
63. A/AC.138/SC.II/SR.11, p. 5. Ethiopia at one stage proposed in the Seabed Committee a working party to prepare draft articles to make the conditions of exercise of the right of innocent passage more flexible by revising Art. 14 (4) of the 1958 Convention on the Territorial Sea and the Contiguous Zone.
64. A/AC.138/SR.83, pp. 13–14.
65. A/AC.138/SC.II/SR.11, p. 4.
66. A/AC.138/SC.II/SR.16, p. 13.
67. A/AC.138/SC.II/SR.15, p. 14.
68. See, *e.g.*, statement by the delegate of Mauritania—A/AC.138/SC.II/SR.32, p. 2.
69. See, *e.g.*, of such statements, those made by the delegates of Brazil—A/AC.138/SC.II/SR.4, p. 3—and Chile—A/AC.138/SC.II/SR.31, pp. 29–30.
70. A/AC.138/SC.II/SR.14, p. 3.
71. A/AC.138/SC.II/L.9.
72. A/AC.138/SC.II/SR.40, p. 2.
73. *Ibid.* p. 3.
74. A/AC.138/SC.II/L.8.
75. A/AC.138/SC.II/L.6.
76. A/CI/PV.1911, p. 7.
77. *Ibid.*
78. This Declaration has been tabled in the Seabed Committee and circulated under the reference A/AC.138/85.
79. A/AC.138/SC.II/SR.31, p. 7.
80. A/AC.138/SC.II/L.12.
81. See, *e.g.*, statement by the delegate of Singapore—A/AC.138/SC.II/SR.16, p. 11.
82. A/AC.138/79.
83. A/AC.138/SC.II/L.8.
84. A/AC.138/SR.63, p. 10.
85. A/AC.138/SC.II/L.11.
86. A/AC.138/SC.II/SR.43, p. 10.
87. A/AC.138/SC.II/SR.14, p. 4.
88. A/AC.138/SC.II/SR.40, p. 4.
89. A/AC.138/SR.83, p. 24.
90. A/AC.138/SC.II/SR.16, p. 16.
91. A/AC.138/SR.63, pp. 11–12.
92. The term " continental shelf " is defined as " The seabed and subsoil of the submarine areas adjacent to the coast but outside the area of the territorial sea, to a depth of 200 metres

or, beyond that limit, to where the depth of the superjacent waters admits of the exploitation of the natural resources of the said area."

93. A/AC.138/SC.II/SR.16, p. 2.

94. A/AC.138/SC.II/SR.16, p. 3. Other suggestions of a similar kind were made by the delegates of Argentina (A/AC.138/SC.II/SR.10, pp. 8–9) and Nigeria (A/AC.138/SC.II/SR.7, p. 2).

95. Amongst these are the following: 200 metre isobath; 500 metre isobath; 40 nautical miles; 200 nautical miles; edge of continental margin.

96. A/AC.138/SR.64, p. 3.

97. A/AC.138/SC.II/L.10.

98. A/AC.138/SR.83, p. 25.

99. A/AC.138/SR.II/SR.42, p. 5.

100. A/AC.138/79.

101. A/AC.138/SR.83, p. 16.

102. A/AC.138/SC.II/SR.12, p. 6. See also A/AC.138/SR.85, pp. 15–16.

103. A/AC.138/SC.II/SR.16, pp. 3–4.

104. A/AC.138/SR.64, p. 8.

105. A/AC.138/55.

106. A/AC.138/SC.II/L.10.

107. A/AC.138/25.

108. G.A. Res. 3029B (XXVII). There were 69 votes in favour, 15 against, and 41 abstentions—A/PV.2114, pp. 39–40.

109. G.A. Res. 3029C (XXVII). There were 100 votes in favour, none against, and 28 abstentions—A/PV.2114, p. 41.

110. A/C.1/PV.1905, p. 27.

111. G.A. Res. 2749 (XXV).

112. Texts illustrating areas of agreement and disagreement were issued as document A/AC.138/L.18/Add.3.

113. See Gerard J. Mangone, *The United Nations, International Law and the Bed of the Sea*, p. 43 (Ocean Studies 303).

114. A/AC.138/53.

115. A/AC.138/SR.63, p. 9—statement by Canadian delegate.

116. See statement by Colombian delegate—A/AC.138/SR.64, p. 7.

117. See statement by Bolivian delegate—A/AC.138/SC.I/SR.15, p. 2.

118. A/AC.138/SC.I/SR.43, p. 6; A/AC.138/SR.79, p. 3. See also statement by Venezuelan delegate—A/AC.138/SR.64, p. 5.

119. A/AC.138/SC.I/SR.51, p. 2.

120. A/AC.138/49.

121. A/AC.138/SC.I/SR.47, p. 4.

122. See, *e.g.*, statement by Algerian delegate—A/AC.138/SR.65, pp. 8–9.

123. A/AC.138/SC.I/SR.43, p. 14.

124. A/AC.138/46.

125. A/AC.138/SC.I/SR.46, p. 1.

126. See, for instance, statement by Australian delegate—A/AC.138/SC.I/SR.42, p. 5.

127. See, for instance, statement by Colombian delegate—A/AC.138/SR.64, p. 8.

128. See, for instance, statement by Uruguayan delegate—A/AC.138/SC.I/SR.46, p. 18.

129. A/AC.138/46.

130. A/AC.138/SC.I/SR.43, p. 15—statement by delegate of Sri Lanka.

131. See, for instance, statement by representative of Sweden—A/AC.138/SC.I/SR.43, p. 17; and concept of a " developing organisation " put forward in a Polish Working Paper (A/AC.138/44).

132. A/AC.138/SC.I/SR.43, p. 21.

133. A/AC.138/SC.III/SR.25, p. 2.

134. A/AC.138/SC.III/L.26.

135. A/AC.138/SC.III/L.25.

136. A/AC.138/SC.III/SR.28, p. 2.

137. The Canadian Working Paper appeared as Doc. A/AC.138/SC.III/L.18. For Brazil's comment, see A/AC.138/SC.III/SR.28, p. 3, for Japan's comment, see A/AC.138/SC.III/SR.28, p. 13.

138. A/AC.138/SC.III/SR.27, p. 2.
139. A/AC.138/SC.III/L.23.
140. A/AC.138/SC.III/SR.29, p. 6.
141. A/AC.138/SC.III/SR.28, pp. 17, 19.
142. A/AC.138/49.
143. A/C1/PV.1904, pp. 38–40.
144. A/C1/PV.1903, p. 16.
145. G.A. Res. 3029A (XXVII). This Resolution was adopted unanimously.

CHAPTER 28

The EEC and the Law of the Sea

By D. Vignes *

A FEW years ago the presentation of a study on the law of the sea and the European Communities might well have been taken as a joke since the popular idea of the extent of the Community's authority at that time corresponded to the territory of the member States. Yet as early as 1964, which, although six years after the establishment of the EEC, was six years before the Community actually adopted a common fisheries policy, provision had been made for adopting such a policy. This can be seen from Article 10 of the European Fisheries Convention which states that: " Nothing in the present Convention shall prevent the maintenance or *establishment* of a special régime in matters of fisheries . . . as between States Members . . . of the European Economic Community . . ."[1]†

Even today the contribution being made by the Community [2] to the development of the law of the sea is relatively small when compared with Community activities in many other fields, and also with international activity in the field of conventions and jurisdiction relating to the law of the sea. Even though the main reason for this contribution being so small is that the number of other areas of Community responsibility has forced the institutions to set its priorities elsewhere, it must nevertheless be said that the development of Community activity in respect of the sea will always be handicapped owing to competition from member States themselves, because in the present state of affairs, they are still incontrovertibly sovereign. In respect of the majority of activities carried out at sea, on the other hand, the important role of several of the member States in maritime affairs, the development of their fleets, the extent of their fishing activities and the contributions which fisheries make to their national incomes, and the significance of oil prospecting on the continental shelf, combine to make the sea a matter of fundamental importance for the Community. Luxembourg alone perhaps is not concerned, and yet it is worth mentioning that one interesting aspect of the preparations for the Third Conference on the Law of the Sea is that the subject of non-coastal States is being given great attention. The factors just mentioned caused considerable attention to be paid to fisheries problems in the negotiations for the accession of the United Kingdom, Norway, Denmark and Ireland to the Community.[3] If Norway had also became a member of the Community one could conceivably now look on the North Sea as " *mare nostrum* "[4]

However, in respect of present developments in the law of the sea and the positive contribution the Community can make to these developments, two factors are worthy of attention. One, unfortunately, if not actually negative, is at least limited, namely, the lack of Community powers in this area, whereas the other is developing daily: the Community's contribution to legislation on fisheries.

* Professor, Institut d'Etudes Européennes, Free University of Brussels.
† For references, see p. 345.

I. The lack of Community powers in the field of the law of the sea

There is a standing joke in all the Working Parties and Drafting Committees that meet in Brussels: should one say " the Communities and their member States " or " the member States and their Communities "? The undertones of these two phrases could be enlarged upon *ad infinitum*. As for our topic, the rivalry between the Communities and the member States cannot conceal the fact that the law of the sea forms an integral part of public international law, of which the main authors, and some would say the sole authors, are the States. Whatever illustrious role may appear to be reserved to the Community on the international chessboard, at present the " navy chessboard " belongs mainly to the member States. The lack of Community powers and authority has two aspects, namely substantive authority and territorial authority, the latter also including external relations. We must add, but without giving too much weight to this point, since it does not specifically concern the subject of this chapter, that the lack of Community powers also results from restrictions on the power conferred within the institutional structure, in particular the fact that the Communities have no power of enforcement or constraint; that there is no Community policeman. However, this is of little real importance to the subject before us as the member States must assist the Communities in this respect.

1. *Substantive aspects of the lack of Community powers in relation to the sea*

In reiterating the fact that it is only States which are important in relation to the regulation of the seas,[5] it is also worth pointing out that the Community's powers are functional and mainly economic, that, in general, responsibilities of a public nature are exercised by the States and not by the Communities, and that the activities carried out on the sea are far from being exclusively economic in nature. Activities in the military sphere therefore fall outside the scope of the Community. Fortunately the emphasis at present is on the peaceful uses of the sea and the ocean, but there again it is to be feared that States themselves claim the right to define what is peaceful!

These, however, are not the only limits on Community powers. Turning to shipping, such concepts as " innocent " or " peaceful passage " arise which fall partly within the province of security. On the other hand, the Community does have a potential field of activity by virtue of the powers which it may take in relation to " sea transport " (Article 84 (2)),[6] although it has not yet acted under the provisions of that Article.

Clearly its responsibilities in relation to fisheries are going to be considerable. Curiously, under the Treaty of Rome, fish appear among the agricultural products (Article 38 and Annex II) which explains why the substantial development of Community agriculture has been reflected in fishery activities.

The same has not been true of activities based on the continental shelf. Although these are basically economic, they are also closely bound up with the territorial jurisdiction of the member States, to an even greater extent than fisheries (see below). Products connected with oil come within the sphere politically reserved to the States. The memorandum of the Commission in 1970 on the continental shelf does not seem to have been followed up in any way.[7] It should nevertheless be stated that in the light of recent developments in exploiting the sea's resources, the new prospects which its mineral wealth could open up are of interest to the industrial development of the Community.

Other matters falling within the jurisdiction of the Community, but again perhaps not exclusively, are problems such as marine pollution and scientific research.

Even though it can thus be seen that military, security, and strategic aspects limit the Communities' competence in matters relating to the sea, they still have a wide area of authority over the sea, fisheries and the resources of the seabed. But, as is the case with any power, the territorial aspect is also important.

2. *Territorial aspects of the Community's jurisdiction and its jurisdiction over external relations*

(*a*) *Territorial powers of the Community.* The Community's territorial powers are spelled out by Article 227 (1) of the EEC Treaty, which, adapted as a result of the enlargement of the Community, is the main provision on its competence:

> " This Treaty shall apply to the Kingdom of Belgium, the Kingdom of Denmark, the Federal Republic of Germany, the French Republic, Ireland, the Italian Republic, the Grand Duchy of Luxembourg, the Kingdom of the Netherlands and the United Kingdom of Great Britain and Northern Ireland." [8]

It should be noted that this Article speaks only of the member States and not of *the territories* of the member States.[9] However, it is not the only Article to deal with this matter. A number of articles of the Treaty explicitly limit the Community's competence to the *territories* of the member States. Thus Articles 52 *et seq.* govern the right of establishment " in the territories " of member States [10] and Articles 48 *et seq.* secure freedom of movement for workers " *within* the Community." Similarly, the European Social Fund operates " *within* the Community " (Article 123).

On the other hand, other articles provide for Community competence which, by its very nature, is to be exercised outside the territories of the member States. A case in point is Article 84 of the Treaty, which enables the Community to lay down provisions for sea transport. Moreover, loans by the European Investment Bank may, albeit exceptionally, be invested outside the European territories of member States (Article 18 of the Statute of the EIB).

As there are no Treaty provisions laying down general rules, the territorial powers of the Community have had to be defined in individual cases.[11] For example, with regard to the customs union between the member States, the Council Regulation of June 28, 1968, on the common definition of the concept of the origin of goods [12] considered as obtained in a member State " products taken from the seabed or beneath the seabed outside territorial waters, if that country has, for the purposes of exploitation, exclusive rights to such soil or subsoil " (Article 4 (2) (h)).[13] The same Regulation applies the definition of a product originating in a member State to fish taken from the sea by vessels registered in that country, irrespective of the place where the fishing took place (Article 4 (f)). It is to be noted, as is readily understandable bearing in mind the basic provisions, that a broad extra-territorial definition of the Community's powers was chosen in this Regulation. The Regulation of September 27, 1968, on the definition of the customs territory of the Community was rather more circumspect, inasmuch as it is laid down that it " shall not affect the customs system applicable to the waters and foreshores situated between the coast or shore and the limit of territorial waters (Article 4)." [14]

The problem has also been left open in other texts, *e.g.*, the Council Directive of July 7, 1964,[15] concerning the attainment of freedom of establishment and freedom to provide services in respect of activities of self-employed persons in mining and quarrying, and the Council Directive of March 13, 1969,[16] concerning the attainment of freedom of establishment and freedom to provide services in respect of activities of self-employed persons engaged in exploration (prospecting and drilling). An unambiguous solution would have been most desirable in these cases.[17] Finally, it should be noted that other texts, too, have restricted the Community's authority to the territory of member States. Thus, as regards Community VAT for example, according to the texts as they stand at present, only such operations as are conducted within the territory of member States, including their territorial waters, have to be taken into account.[18]

Such a diversity of solutions leads to the conclusion that the application of the Treaty is not dependent upon the concept of territory, and it is justifiable to suppose that the Community, apart from the indisputable powers exercised over the territory proper of member States, should extend its authority beyond that territory in relation to those questions which the member States themselves rightfully regulate by statute, provided that such questions normally fall within the basic and economic competence of the Community, since the powers of the Community have not been expressly restricted to the territory of member States.[19]

Proceeding from these theoretical considerations to examine various aspects of maritime law, a number of different situations can be foreseen.

As we have observed, territorial waters, and, even more, internal waters, do not appear to present any difficulties so long as the powers of member States are recognised so far as those waters are concerned. The fact that they are " territorial waters " and that those States exercise sovereign jurisdiction over them, enables them, under Community Law, to be considered in the same way as the territory of the member States.

On the other hand, if the nationals of a member State are granted certain rights to fish in the territorial waters of a third State, it cannot be said that a right relating to a territorial question is involved here and that there is reason to claim that the rights of such nationals should be shared by the nationals of other member States. (An example of this would be the rights enjoyed by French fishermen in the territorial waters of Newfoundland.)

With regard to the intermediate space, *i.e.*, the rights to fish exercised by the member States beyond the limits of their territorial waters, the " reserved waters " within the meaning of the 1964 Convention—it would appear that, in so far as a member State claims the power to regulate them, the Community itself is justified in exercising its own jurisdiction over them if it decides to prevent the member State concerned from acting in a manner which is not in conformity with the Treaty, *e.g.*, in a discriminatory manner benefiting its own nationals only. In any event, that is the effect of Article 2 of the Regulation of October 20, 1970, which is the principal Community rule on the subject.

It is necessary to go further and to say that, on the basis of that argument, the exercise by a member State of its statutory powers beyond the external limits of its territorial waters will be a matter of concern to the Community from such time as that member State exercises those powers to the exclusion of every other State. The problem of the continental shelf arises in this context. It is certainly consistent with the logic of Community powers, which we have developed heie, that these should extend to the continental shelf, although it is not altogether certain that the member States are prepared to admit such an extension of Community authority.[20]

(b) *Extra-territorial powers of the Community*. Reference has been made above to certain cases of the exercise of extra-territorial powers of the Community, either those expressly provided for in the Treaty, *e.g.*, maritime transport and the European Investment Bank, or those depending upon the inseparable nature of an activity which is partly extra-territorial and partly internal, particularly as regards customs treatment within the Community of produce harvested outside it. Just as in other cases in which the competence of the Community has been extended, it would still be possible to speak of an extra-territorial application of its policy to agreements, whenever agreements concluded abroad between non-Community firms are in breach of Community rules within the Community.[21] It is precisely under the same reasoning that the competence of the Community can be invoked to extend to *pollution* of the sea, if there is a risk of such pollution causing harm to its coasts and territorial waters. Certain Community regulations based upon such reasoning exist, which, although enforceable in Community territory, nevertheless concern external interests and activities. Thus, as regards fisheries, it is appropriate to cite texts which regulate or co-ordinate the policies of the member States in relation to fishing fleets, including fishing fleets on the high seas (Articles 6–11 of Council Regulation No. 2141/70 of October 20, 1970,[22]) or which relate to the marketing standards for fish or the powers of producers' organisations to ensure the rational conduct of fishing.[23] Although none of these questions is governed by the law of the sea, they nevertheless deserve mention in this context.

Of still greater importance in another connection is the express extension of the Community's powers deriving from Article 102 of the Act of Accession, which concerns conservation policy, and the general terms of which apply not only to territorial and reserved waters but also to the high seas. That Article reads as follows: " From the sixth year after accession at the latest, the Council, acting on a proposal from the Commission, shall determine conditions for fishing with a view to ensuring protection of the fishing grounds and conservation of the biological resources of the sea." [24]

(c) *The Community's competence in external negotiations.* It is not intended here to enlarge upon the power to negotiate external agreements on behalf of the Community. It is a highly controversial subject, the discussion of which would be beyond the scope of the present study. So far as we are concerned, the matter can be briefly summed up as follows: does it rest with the Community to conclude international treaties in matters relating to the law of the sea or is it the concern of the States to do so? It is true that the EEC Treaty contains an article regarding procedure in the matter of international agreements negotiated by the institutions of the Community, *viz.* Article 228; but it applies only " where this Treaty provides for the conclusion of agreements between the Community and. . . ." A minority of commentators interpret this Article as meaning that, apart from those cases in which the Treaty makes express provision for the conclusion of an agreement essentially concerned with tariff agreements (Article 113) and agreements establishing association (Article 238), Article 228 is inapplicable. The Court of Justice did not share that view[25] but decided that by virtue of the " legal personality " conferred upon it under Article 210, the Community was free to negotiate agreements with third countries on all internal matters.

Be that as it may, under the terms of that judgment, where Community matters are concerned, only its institutions can bind the Community and not its member States, even when " acting collectively." Does that mean that the Community will have to sign future conventions on the law of the sea if the Community is to be bound by them? It would appear so. The preliminary question arising here is, namely, whether all the contracting States to future conventions will accept the presence of the Community, something which implies a certain evolution on the part of certain States, particularly in Eastern Europe. In any case, the Community's signing them does not rule out the possibility of the member States signing the conventions too (even if not concurrently with the Community) as regards those matters which come within the

Community's competence, at least in their own name where the conventions contain provisions which are beyond the scope of the Community.[26]

The reason for making this analysis at such length is because it seems necessary to describe the restrictions on the Community's powers, for these present numerous possibilities so far as the Community is concerned. Having to justify certain powers at some length might tend to give rise to the belief that they were doubtful, or were even being questioned, which in most cases is not so. It is in fact only because a set of novel concepts—the participation by an entity which is not a State in forming the law of the sea—is involved that the reader's patience has been thus tried. His indulgence is invoked on the further plea that this exposition has been essential for the understanding of the concrete rules attaching to that participation.

II. Community participation in the development of the law of the sea governing fisheries

The Community's commercial strength is most important in the field of fisheries. Some of the rules relating to customs, fiscal and commercial techniques governing fishery products have already been cited.[27] Furthermore, the Community has established a " common organisation of the market in fishery products " [28] and laid down a " common structural policy for the fishing industry " [29]; or, in other words, it has implemented its common agricultural policy in this sector. The measures adopted on that occasion, however, go considerably beyond the regulations applying to trade in agricultural products, in the sense that they constitute important measures affecting the law of the sea. Might it not be found, however, that such results are inadequate? The fact is that the views of the member States on the subject differ widely and that, as far as the law of the sea is concerned, each of them, on account of conflicting interests and traditional national attitudes, has experienced difficulty in accepting a common attitude. Such divergent interests can be shown by a reference to the Community's increasing awareness of the problems presented by the law of the sea and by examining the few positive legal provisions that have been enacted on the subject. The most important of these is the provision already mentioned which prohibits all discrimination between the nationals of the member States as regards fishing rights in territorial and reserved waters.

1. *The emergence of a Community policy on the sea*

The Community made its first appearance at the negotiations relating to fisheries in London in 1964. While it did not sign the Convention, the possibility of the establishment of special relations between the member States [30] and between the latter and associated States of the Community was left open. Even although the member States signed the Convention, two were not concerned, namely Luxembourg and Italy, and France is the only one of the original member States which has so far put it into force.[31] The United Kingdom, Denmark and Ireland are all concerned and all have signed the Convention.

When a proposal by the Commission on the subject of fishing rights was put before the Council of the European Communities in 1968, it was treated with a certain reserve, especially by France. The idea behind that proposal was, in fact, to put the territorial and reserved waters on a Community (or federalised) basis. That idea runs more or less counter to the opinion prevailing in 1964 that fishing in those waters was reserved to the nationals of each State concerned, which to some extent accounted for French hesitancy on the subject. Finally, in conjunction with other Community measures which were more to France's liking,[32] the Regulations on fishing were adopted under the triple motto, propounded by M. M. Schumann, the French

Minister of Foreign Affairs, of completion (of the common agricultural policy); of enlargement of the Community (to include the United Kingdom); and expansion of the Common Market in other fields. Certain member States pressed more eagerly for the adoption of those Regulations, allegedly because of the secret wish on the part of their nationals to be allowed to fish in Norwegian waters. Whether by mere coincidence or by Machiavellian design, the date on which the Regulation was adopted at the first reading was June 30, 1970, the very day on which the applicant States signified their agreement to the implementation of Common Market policies as a whole, subject to minor adjustments and time limits. That was more than enough to cause Norway to be the first among the States to demand the amendment of Regulation No. 2141/70. All the applicant States rallied behind Norway, each negotiating on its own behalf but benefiting from the gains of the others. The original member States were reticent and, by a curious shifting of position, those who at one time had shown themselves most reticent in regard to this Regulation (particularly France) were the first to urge that it remain unamended, convinced, as they were, of the necessity for yielding nothing that the Community had acquired, whereas the Netherlands and Germany, which had been highly enthusiastic about the proposal in 1970, in the interests of smoothing the path towards enlargement of the Community, proved more tractable.[33] In the end, after Norway had fought a rearguard action, from which a protocol to the Act of Accession, now devoid of purpose, emerged, the 1970 text in all essentials remained unaltered even though the spirit behind it has perhaps changed.

Common ground was sought at the preparatory meetings of the UN Seabed Committee for the Third Conference on the Law of the Sea (New York, March 1972, and Geneva, July–August 1972), which were attended by most of the member States [34] and at which the Community was present in what was a very unofficial capacity.[35] An EEC clause similar to that in the 1964 Fisheries Convention was mentioned in the debate, curiously enough by the delegate from Mexico. Does that imply that the divergences are lessening? The Icelandic fisheries dispute would tend to be evidence to the contrary. Two member States do not recognise the extension by Iceland of her exclusive fishing zone to a limit of 50 miles. The United Kingdom and the Federal Republic of Germany have, moreover, submitted the case to the International Court of Justice. Denmark,[36] on the other hand, at the meeting of the Scandinavian Ministers of Foreign Affairs on September 4, 1972, approved the common view and encouraged Iceland's resistant attitude. Belgium went even further by signing an agreement with Iceland on September 7, 1972, under whose terms special rights within the new limit were accorded to Belgian nationals, thus implying recognition. The confusion would appear to be complete.

The referenda that took place in Norway and Denmark have now settled the question of enlargement of the Community, in the one case in a negative, and in the other case, in a positive way, but there has been no clarification of views as regards the major problem which is associated with the legitimacy of the claim by the developing countries as a whole, and by some other States also, to an exclusive zone varying from 50 to 200 miles and reserved to inshore fishermen.

That constitutes, however, an important question for every member State and for the Community. In fact, as positive Community Law stands at present, a member State which reserves to its nationals beyond its own territorial waters any zone adjacent to such waters must, without exception, allow the nationals of the other member States to benefit from it. If, as is easy to foresee, the tendency on the part of States to increase the width of the zone reserved to their nationals, calculated from the base line, is continued, that zone falling within the domain of the Community will become larger and larger, subject, perhaps, to certain exceptions. This problem will be dealt with again when considering the Community system.

2. *Community rules regarding fisheries*

These rules are essentially concerned with non-discrimination in reserved waters and with the control of conservation; there are other more diffuse rules deriving from the provisions of certain conventions concluded with third States.

(a) *The regulations relating to reserved waters.* It is perhaps somewhat pretentious to give such a title to the existing rules. It might even give rise to the belief that " Community waters " exist. It is true that a process of federalisation and unity did underlie the rules governing reserved waters, but this federalising process is at present restricted to the establishment of a rule of non-discrimination between the reserved waters of the different member States without envisaging a complete and uniform set of rules to apply to such waters. There are nevertheless other rules supplementing the regulations, *e.g.*, power of the Community to adopt measures for the conservation of stocks (Article 5 of EEC Regulation No. 2141/70).[37] Hence the reason for having chosen the broader title.

Article 2 (1) of EEC Regulation No. 2141/70 [37] contains the basic provision relating to non-discrimination in treatment among member States as regards access to and use of fishing grounds by their respective nationals. Member States must therefore ensure equal conditions of access and use of the sea for all fishing vessels flying a flag of a member State and registered in Community territory. That means these waters referred to shall be all such waters as come under the sovereignty or within the jurisdiction of the member States, as are defined by the laws of each State,[38] subject to certain exceptions.

The only phrase in this Article which may require some explanation is that applying to waters " coming under the sovereignty or within the jurisdiction " of a member State. If the phrase " waters coming under the sovereignty " is unquestionably intended to cover the territorial waters—and, what is more, inland waters also—it may well be asked, on the other hand, what is meant by " waters within the jurisdiction " of a member State? Notwithstanding what has already been said about the use of this word " jurisdiction," [39] what the Community had in mind was the waters adjacent to the territorial sea, the access to and the use of which a member State, by virtue either of a Treaty or of a national legislative provision, had reserved to its own nationals. As the law stands at present, the only reserved waters which appear to exist are those outside the territorial waters of the United Kingdom, Denmark and Ireland under the terms of the 1964 Convention where such waters extend from three to 12 miles. The other member States have no reserved waters outside their territorial waters (France: 12 miles; Italy: six miles; Germany, Belgium and the Netherlands: three miles).

That the waters subject to the Community non-discrimination rule are, so to speak, self-chosen may appear surprising. If, say tomorrow, a member State follows Iceland and extends its reserved waters to 50 miles, that measure, designed to reserve the use of the fishing grounds concerned to the member State's own nationals, will benefit all the citizens of the other member States and thus fail somewhat in its purpose.

Is it possible to go still further and argue that it should be the task of the Community to determine the extent of such reserved waters? We think it inconceivable that it could do so as regards territorial waters since they involve jurisdictional limits which are not solely of an economic character. On the other hand, as regards reserved waters, where, moreover, the question of harmonisation of the various laws of the member States arises (Article 100 of the EEC Treaty), in other words adoption of Community standards (more specifically on the basis of Article 235 of the EEC Treaty), we consider it possible for the Community to do so. In fact, however, that is not the real problem.

The real problem connected with reserved waters, as Regulation No. 2141/70 admits, is that there is no uniform solution applicable to it. Claims made by States to create reserved waters are far from new and go as far back as perhaps 80 years, but fresh impetus has arisen because of the development of fishing vessels with enormous catching capacity out of all proportion to the lesser facilities available to local fishermen. In this respect such claims represent a form of protection of local small industry or enterprise against big business interests. More recently, it has been extended further, or rather made a matter of politics, being classed as an aspect of the struggle for development, *i.e.*, the struggle on the part of the fishermen in the developing countries to maintain by means of inshore fishing their supplies of protein and thus their possibilities of development. It should at once be stated that as far as the Community is concerned, it is the aspect of the defence of local industry, rather than that of promoting development which is at issue. It is that aspect which caused the Council, principally at the instance of France, to make provision in its Regulation No. 2141/72, for an exception in favour of " the *local population* of the coastal regions (fishing grounds situated within a limit of three nautical miles only are concerned here) if that population *depends primarily on inshore fishing* " (Article 4, para. 1). This exception is in any event a limited one, applying only within the first three miles calculated from the base lines and even then only for a defined period, *i.e.*, until November 1, 1975. It is for the Council of the Communities, acting on a proposal from the Commission, to specify the fishing areas concerned (Article 4, para. 2). After 1975, it might be possible to conceive of there being adopted within the framework of conservation measures (Article 5), certain restrictions applying within specified areas and in relation to certain fishing measures or fishing gear. Under the terms of this text however, no provision is made to establish any connection between these measures and the problems of the local populations.

It is this reservation in favour of the local population which has been reinforced by the provisions of the Act of Accession.[40] The new provisions specify a derogation from the non-discrimination rule of a limit up to the first six miles, but that derogation applies exclusively to those local fishermen who had traditionally exercised the privilege, and prevails only in the absence of any acquired rights on the part of other nationals of the member States (see Article 100 of the Act of Accession). This exception to the rule can apply within an area of six to 12 miles, but only in certain specifically defined areas of France, the United Kingdom, Denmark and Ireland (Article 101).[41] The same date of expiry is fixed for the two limits, namely December 31, 1982, at the latest, though it is not out of the question that that date could be extended, having regard to " the economic and social development of the coastal areas of the member States and the state of stocks of fish " (Article 103). It is to be noted, moreover, that by 1982 at the latest, the Council " shall examine the provisions which could follow the derogation in force until December 31, 1982," a formula which appears to be deliberately imprecise, but which might indirectly throw some light on Protocol No. 21 on the fisheries régime for Norway. Is there evidence in these provisions of the beginnings of lasting recognition of the rights reserved to the local populations if they essentially depend upon inshore fishing for their subsistence? That is certainly not the only means by which the Community could come to their aid, but aid could be contributed in the form of reorganisation and redevelopment, in addition to such conservation measures as restrictions upon certain fishing practices in their particular sector. In raising these questions, moreover, it will be recalled that assisting the economically weak and protecting the poorer regions constitutes a basic rule of Community action. This means that it is not possible to predict what Community action will be and, what is more, whether that action will further accentuate the policy of non-discrimination in the territorial and reserved waters of the member States.

(b) *Community measures on conservation.* Reference has on various occasions been made to these measures, which vary in kind and have been taken in two phases.

Under the terms of Regulation No. 2141/70, the conservation measures in question refer to territorial and reserved waters in which there is a risk of over-fishing of certain stocks. These measures " may include restrictions relating to the catching of certain species, to areas, to fishing seasons, to methods of fishing and to fishing gear " (Article 5). Furthermore, in both this Regulation and its twin Regulation No. 2142/70, reference is made to the adoption of specific measures for appropriate action and to the co-ordination of structural policies of member States in the matter of conservation policy not only within the 12 mile limit, but also on the high seas.

Within the framework of the Act of Accession, Community conservation measures are widely defined in other terms. Under them the Community may " determine conditions for fishing with a view to ensuring protection of the fishing grounds and conservation of the biological resources of the sea " (Article 102). There is no longer any question here of measures concerned being limited to a 12 mile zone. The Community could thus exercise its powers on the high seas so far as Community nationals are concerned, by virtue of this express extra-territorial extension of jurisdiction. Would it then, subject to what has already been said, still be able to participate in international conventions having reference to these matters? That question remains undecided.

(c) *Conventions to which the Community is party.* These are two in number. The first is the *pactum de contrahendo* resulting from a declaration made by the African States and Malagasy Republic which concluded an Association Agreement with the Community in 1969, under the terms of which they declared themselves prepared to negotiate, without discrimination, bilateral agreements with any member State of the Community on the exercise of fishing rights within the territorial waters under their jurisdiction, in accordance with their local laws.

The second is more curious, if less theoretical. It relates to the insertion in the Agreement between the Community and the Republic of Iceland of July 22, 1972, of a suspensive clause (contained in Article 2 of Protocol No. 6) to the effect that certain parts of that Agreement would not enter into force " if a solution satisfactory to the member States of the Community and to Iceland has not been found for the economic problems arising from the measures adopted by Iceland concerning fishing rights."

III Conclusions

The attitudes and practices of the Community concerning the law of the sea may appear rather sparse. That is due both to the fact that the Community is of fairly recent date and also that it has had little time to devote to this branch of law, in which evolution is particularly slow. Now that a certain competence and authority has been acquired, however, those attitudes and practices should increase.

The Community has been active only in the matter of waters reserved for inshore fishing, without having made any pronouncements regarding either the extent of those waters, or the widespread tendency towards claims over very large areas of reserved waters. What it has mainly done in this field is to enact a rule of non-discrimination between the nationals of the member States of the Community within the reserved waters of these States. It has also been concerned with studying the problem of the waters which are reserved to populations settled along the coasts which are largely dependent upon inshore fishing for a livelihood.

Wide powers over territorial waters and the high seas have been conferred on the Community to enable it to play its part in enforcing conservation.

REFERENCES

1. D. Vignes, " La Conférence européenne sur la pêche et le droit de la mer," in (1964) *Annuaire français de Droit international* (hereinafter referred to as A.F.D.I.) 670–688 at 681. See also the article by Y. Van der Mensbrugghe in (1969) *Revue belge de Droit international*, 87–145; it should be noted that this article does not deal specifically with the law of the sea but is entitled: *La mer et les Communautés européennes.*

2. This article refers variously to the European Communities and the European Economic Community (EEC) as well as the Treaty establishing the latter; obviously marine problems could also affect the European Coal and Steel Community (ECSC) and particularly the European Atomic Energy Community (Euratom), but in view of the slow rate of development of that Community and the limited Community powers in respect of military matters, to which we will return elsewhere, there is little comment to make about these two Communities within the scope of this article.

3. O. Druer, " De Saint Malo à Tromsoe, les droits des pêcheurs riverains dans la négociation," *Revue du Marché Commun* (special issue on Norway) (January 1972) 7 and 8, and P. Lemaitre, in the same *Revue*, Sept. 1971, 146 at 313–316. See also the rather negative legal attitude of the Norwegian delegation in respect of the introduction of Community responsibilities in fishery matters in the study by C. A. Fleischer, " L'accès aux lieux de pêche et le Traité de Rome," (1971) 141 *Revue du Marché Commun* 148.

4. The Norwegians rejected EEC membership in a referendum held on Sept. 25, 1972.

5. " Every State, whether coastal or not, has the right to sail ships under its flag on the high seas," Art. 4 of the 1958 Convention on the High Seas. (See however, Art. 7 on " ships employed on the official service of an inter-governmental organisation flying the flag of the organisation " and a European Parliament report by M. van der Goes van Naters on *Les Problèmes que Posent les Relations des Communautés européennes avec l'Extérieur, en Particulier le Droit de Légation et de Pavillon* (Ass. Parl. doc. 88–1960) and the Resolution adopted by the Parliament on Nov. 19, 1960 (OJ No. 79 of Dec. 16, 1960).

6. In this connection, see Y. van Mensbrugghe, *op. cit.* pp. 87 *et seq.*

7. A. Wenger, " La C.E.E. et le plateau continental " (1971) 143 *Revue du Marché Commun.*

8. The rest of this Article contains provisions which are not relevant in this context, concerning Algeria and the French overseas departments, overseas countries and territories, etc.

9. The solution adopted in Art. 227 is the opposite of that adopted by the ECSC and Euratom Treaties, which apply only to the *territories* of the member States.

10. The same applies to services to be provided *within* the Community (Art. 59).

11. P. Daillier, " Les frontières douanières de la Communauté Economique Européenne " (1968) A.F.D.I. 789.

12. EEC Regulation No. 802/68 in O.J. No. L.148 of June 1968, O.J.E.C. special ed., English ed., 1968 (I), p. 165.

13. However, the effects of this rule are considerably restricted by the fact that Art. 3 of this Regulation states that it does not apply to petroleum products.

14. EEC Regulation No. 1496/68, O.J. No. L.238 of Sept. 28, 1968, p. 1, O.J.E.C. special ed., English ed., 1968 (II), p. 436.

15. Directive 64/428/EEC, O.J. No. 117 of July 23, 1964, O.J.E.C. special ed., English ed., 1963–1964, p. 151.

16. Directive 69/82/EEC, O.J. No. L.68 of Mar. 19, 1969, O.J.E.C. special ed., English ed., 1969 (I), p. 111.

17. See A. Wenger, *op. cit.*, regarding this question.

18. Directive 67/228/EEC of Apr. 11, 1967, O.J. No. 71 of Apr. 14, 1967, p. 1303 *et seq.*, O.J.E.C. special ed., English ed., 1967, p. 16.

19. Our sole concern here is one of terminology (and, indeed, of French terminology alone) and relates to the use of the word " *compétence.*" The Regulation of Oct. 20, 1970 (see below)—like the 1964 Fisheries Convention—tends to use the word " juridiction " rather than " compétence," but we consider that it is a question of an anglicism in this case. The 1964 Convention speaks, moreover, of exclusive jurisdiction within the belt of between three and six miles, but it also speaks of the right to fish and the power to regulate the fisheries within the belt of between six and 12 miles. Similarly, a recent memorandum of the EEC Commission speaks of " l'exercice individuel de pouvoirs souverains de la part d'un Etat membre ayant pour objet ou pour conséquence l'introduction d'une réglementation publique, [qui] touche directement à l'exercice de l'activité économique couverte par le Traité [qui s'exerce dans des] limites territoriales que l'Etat impose lui-même de façon souveraine."

20. A. Wenger, *op. cit.*

21. See Orders of the European Court of Justice of July 14, 1972, in the cases: 48/69 *I.C.I.* v. *EEC Commission*, 49/69 *Badische Anilin-Und Soda-Fabrik AG* v. *EEC Commission*, 51/69 *Farbenfabriken Bayer AG* v. *EEC Commission*, 52/69 *J. R. Geigy AG* v. *EEC Commission*, 53/69 *Sandoz AG* v. *EEC Commission*, 54/69 *S. A. Française des Matières Colorantes* v. *EEC Commission*, 55/69 *Cassella Farbwerke Mainkur AG* v. *EEC Commission*, 56/69 *Farbwerke Hoechst AG* v. *EEC Commission*, 57/69 *Azienda Colori Nazionali—A.C.N.A. S.p.A.* v. *EEC Commission*.

22. O.J. No. L.236/1 of Oct. 27, 1970, O.J.E.C. special ed., English ed., 1970 (III), p. 703.

23. Regulation 2142/70, Arts. 2 *et seq.*, and 5 *et seq.*, also of Oct. 20, 1970, in the same O.J. No. L.236/5, O.J.E.C. special ed., English ed., 1970 (III), p. 707.

24. The jurisdiction concerned will normally be exercised as from Jan. 1, 1978.

25. Regarding the judgment in the matter of Commission *v.* Council of Mar. 31, 1971, reference is primarily made to the (contrary) findings of Avocate-General Dutheillet de Lamothe, Rec., XVII, pp. 263 *et seq.*, and also to W. Ganshof van der Meersch in (1972) *Cahiers de droit européen* 127–158 (approval of the principle, inquiries as to application). J. Rideau (1972) *Dalloz* 453–460 (*idem*); J. V. Louis (1971) *Cahiers de droit européen* 479 (benevolent approval), L. J. Constantinesco (1971) *Revue trimestrielle de droit européen* 796 *et seq.* (absolute approval in an ironical vein); R. Kovar in (1971) A.F.D.I. 386–418 (approval with hints of reserve); J. Raux, in (1972) *Revue générale de droit international public*, pp. 36–68 (approval). Reference might also be made to a violent anonymous criticism contained in the newspaper *Le Monde* of Apr. 27, 1971, and another unsigned criticism appearing in (1971) 144 *Revue du Marché Commun* 212.

26. It seems, moreover, to be established practice that an agreement concluded and ratified by the member States has the effect of tacitly amending the EEC Treaty and thereby committing the Communities, even if the procedure for revision of the Treaty is not employed. It might well be asked whether that does not amount to by-passing the procedure.

27. See nn. 21 and 23 and preceding text.

28. Regulation No. 2142/70 of the Council of the European Communities of Oct. 20, 1970, O.J. No. L.236 of Oct. 27, 1970, p. 5. O.J.E.C. special ed., English ed., 1970 (III), p. 707.

29. Regulation No. 2141/70 of the same date, same O.J., p. 1. O.J.E.C. special ed., English ed., 1970 (III), p. 703.

30. See n. 1 and preceding text.

31. M. Voelckel, " Aperçus sur l'application de la Convention européenne des pêches " (1969) A.F.D.I. 761–763 and also F. Monconduit, " L'extension des zones de pêche réservées aux pêcheurs français " (1967) *idem.* 685–690. With the extension of French territorial waters to 12 miles, however, under the Law of Dec. 24, 1971, such participation is somewhat theoretical.

32. France is interested in the commercial aspect referred to above, n. 23.

33. See particularly O. Druer, *op. cit.*

34. Not by Ireland and Luxembourg. The Federal Republic of Germany was present as an observer only.

35. It is also participating in the work of various Regional Commissions, particularly those of the North-East and Northwest Atlantic.

36. Certain citizens of that country, *i.e.*, the inhabitants of the Faroe Islands, have been given certain rights in the Icelandic 50 mile zone under an Agreement of Aug. 16, 1972.

37. See n. 29 above.

38. Member States shall notify other member States and the Commission of the existing laws and administrative rules and regulations concerning the application of such laws in the field referred to above as well as of all alterations they intend to make therein (Art. 2, para. 2 and 3).

39. See n. 19 above.

40. It would have been reinforced so much more (and might even have been permanent) in the event of Norway's accession (Protocol No. 21 to the Act of Accession).

41. Other provisions of Art. 100 reinforce the restrictive character of the derogation: for example, under para. 1, second sentence, of that Article, the coastal member State which restricts fishing in its waters is prevented from allowing its nationals to fish there under conditions less restrictive than those applying in practice at the time of accession, or, in other words, from exhausting such fishing grounds.

Index